Neuropsychology of Malingering and Non-Credible Presentations

Neuropsychology of Malingering and Non-Credible Presentations: Perspectives on Validity Assessment is a comprehensive guide to understanding and addressing concerns about the accuracy of cognitive performances and symptom reports during neuropsychological evaluations. This updated second edition reflects major advances in the field, offering practical strategies for diagnosing, documenting, and managing validity issues in both clinical and forensic contexts.

This book begins with foundational concepts of validity assessment, including the evolution of key terms and statistical principles. It then moves into detailed case examples across diverse settings – civil and criminal litigation, disability evaluations, and routine clinical practice – illustrating how performance and symptom validity concerns arise and are addressed. Additional chapters explore cultural and linguistic considerations, ethical and professional issues, and the integration of multiple data sources such as interviews, behavioral observations, and psychometric testing. The content emphasizes real-world application while avoiding unnecessary technical jargon.

This book is designed for advanced trainees and experienced professionals in clinical neuropsychology, as well as those working in forensic psychology and related fields. It serves as a practical resource for anyone seeking to improve their ability to detect, interpret, and manage non-credible presentations across a wide range of evaluation contexts.

Joel E. Morgan is double board certified in clinical neuropsychology and pediatric neuropsychology. He is in independent practice of lifetime clinical and forensic neuropsychology in New Jersey, USA.

Jerry J. Sweet is board certified in clinical neuropsychology and clinical psychology. He has taught and supervised young neuropsychologists in Evanston, Illinois, most of whom were about to enter the field.

Kyle B. Boone is board certified in clinical neuropsychology and is in independent practice in forensic neuropsychology in Torrance, California, USA.

Ryan W. Schroeder is a board-certified clinical neuropsychologist. He evaluates clinical patients at the Robert J. Dole VA Medical Center and also performs forensic evaluations in his private practice in Wichita, Kansas, USA.

Neuropsychology of Malingering and Non-Credible Presentations

Perspectives on Validity Assessment

Second Edition

Edited by Joel E. Morgan, Jerry J. Sweet, Kyle B. Boone, and Ryan W. Schroeder

Routledge
Taylor & Francis Group
NEW YORK AND LONDON

Second edition published 2027
by Routledge
605 Third Avenue, New York, NY 10158

and by Routledge
4 Park Square, Milton Park, Abingdon, Oxon, OX14 4RN

Routledge is an imprint of the Taylor & Francis Group, an informa business

First edition published by Psychology Press 2009

ISBN: 9780367436902 (hbk)
ISBN: 9780367436919 (pbk)
ISBN: 9781003005063 (ebk)

DOI: 10.4324/9781003005063

Typeset in Sabon
by codeMantra

To Jerry L. Sweet, Ph.D., ABPP-ABCN

We have had the great gift of being able to work with, and to be mentored by, someone who has had one of the most significant impacts on the practice of clinical neuropsychology, and particularly forensic neuropsychology, namely, our co-editor Jerry Sweet. What is unique about Jerry is that he has always managed to have a clear vision for what the field of clinical neuropsychology needed and the path it should take, as evidenced by his steady hand when guiding the American Academy of Clinical Neuropsychology as its president, to his representation of Clinical Neuropsychology as a trustee of the American Board of Professional Psychology, to his comprehensive surveys documenting clinical neuropsychology practice, to consensus guidelines that educated regarding appropriate use of performance validity tests, and more recently, to his recognition of the urgent need to buttress test security standards in light of escalating attacks on the tools of our profession. He has always understood what was critical and essential for our field long before the rest of us.

A touchstone is defined as someone who serves as a consistent point of reference as a source of wisdom and integrity, and who provides trustworthy guidance and clarity when the path is unclear. Jerry, you are our touchstone, and we view it as an honor to have been your co-editors on this book.

Kyle, Joel, and Ryan
October 2025

To Jerry L. Sweet, Ph.D., ABPP-ABCN

We have had the great gift of being able to work with, and to be mentored by, someone who has had one of the most significant impacts on the practice of clinical neuropsychology, and particularly forensic neuropsychology, namely, our co-editor Jerry Sweet. What is unique about Jerry is that he has always managed to have a clear vision for what the field of clinical neuropsychology needed and the path it should take, as evidenced by his steady hand when guiding the American Academy of Clinical Neuropsychology as its president, to his representation of Clinical Neuropsychology as a trustee of the American Board of Professional Psychology, to his comprehensive surveys documenting clinical neuropsychology practice, to consensus guidelines that educated regarding appropriate use of performance validity tests, and more recently, to his recognition of the urgent need to buttress test security standards in light of escalating attacks on the tools of our profession. He has always understood what was critical and essential for our field long before the rest of us.

A touchstone is defined as someone who serves as a consistent point of reference as a source of wisdom and integrity, and who provides trustworthy guidance and clarity when the path is unclear. Jerry, you are our touchstone, and we view it as an honor to have been your co-editors on this book.

Kyle, Joel, and Ryan
October 2025

Contents

Contributors

Patrick Armistead-Jehle, Ph.D., ABPP-CN
Concussion Clinic, Munson Army Health Center, Fort Leavenworth, KS, USA

William B. Barr, Ph.D., ABPP-CN
NYU Grossman School of Medicine, New York, NY, USA

Michael R. Basso, Ph.D., ABPP-CN
Department of Psychiatry and Psychology, Mayo Clinic-Rochester, Rochester, MN, USA

Yossef S. Ben-Porath, Ph.D., ABPP-CP
Department of Psychological Sciences, Kent State University, Kent, OH, USA

Kevin Bianchini, Ph.D., ABN
Jefferson Neurobehavioral Group, Metairie, LA, USA

Laurence M. Binder, Ph.D., ABPP-CN
Independent Practice, Portland, OR, USA

Kyle B. Boone, Ph.D., ABPP-CN
Independent Practice, Torrance, CA, USA

Kirsty E. Bortnik, Ph.D., ABPP-CN
Pickup Family Neurosciences Institute, Hoag Memorial Hospital Presbyterian, Irvine, CA, USA

Brian L. Brooks, PhD
Brooks Assessment, Vancouver, BC and Calgary, AB, Canada; University of Calgary, Calgary, AB, Canada

Shane S. Bush, Ph.D., ABPP-CN, ABPP-CP, ABPP-RP, ABPP-GP
Long Island Neuropsychology, P.C., Lake Ronkonkoma, NY, USA

Diana Campos, M.A.
The Chicago School of Professional Neuropsychology at Xavier University, New Orleans, LA, USA

Michael Chafetz, Ph.D., ABPP-CN
Algiers Neurobehavioral Resource, LLC, New Orleans, LA, USA

Brechje Dandachi-FitzGerald, PhD
Department of Clinical Psychological Science, Maastricht University, Maastricht, The Netherlands

Jeremy J. Davis, Psy.D., MBA, ABPP-CN
Department of Neurology, UT Health San Antonio, San Antonio, TX, USA

George J. Demakis, Ph.D., ABPP-CN
University of North Carolina Charlotte, Charlotte, NC, USA

Anthony P. De Marco, Psy.D., ABPP-CN
IGEA Braine, Spine, and Orthopedics, Union, NJ, USA

Robert L. Denney, Psy.D., ABPP-CN, ABPP-FP
Missouri Memory Center, Citizens Memorial Hospital, Bolivar, MO, USA

Jacobus Donders, Ph.D., ABPP-CN, ABPP-RP
Mary Free Bed Hospital, Grand Rapids, MI, USA

Dana M. Doucette, MC
Neurobehavioral Associates, Edmonton, AB, Canada

Kristin Fiano, Ph.D., ABPP-CN
The IMA Group, Savannah, GA, USA

Laura Fry, Ph.D.
Department of Rehabilitation Medicine, University of Minnesota, Minneapolis, MN, USA

Roger O. Gervais, Ph.D., ABPP-CP
Neurobehavioral Associates and University of Alberta, Edmonton, AB, Canada

Tannahill Glen, Psy.D., ABPP-CN
Neuropsychology Inc. and MD Anderson Cancer Center/Baptist Medical Center, Jacksonville, FL, USA

Diana S. Goldstein, Ph.D., ABPP-CN
Michigan Avenue Neuropsychologists, Chicago, IL, USA

Christopher J. Graver, Ph.D., ABPP-CN
Madigan Army Medical Center, Tacoma, WA, USA

Kevin W. Greve, Ph.D., ABPP-CN
Jefferson Neurobehavioral Group, Metairie, LA, USA

Thomas Guilmette, Ph.D., ABPP-CN
Providence College, Providence, RI, USA and Alpert Medical Center of Brown University, Providence, RI, USA

Paige Haley, Psy.D.
Algiers Neurobehavioral Resource, LLC, New Orleans, LA, USA

David E. Hartman, Ph.D., MS, ABN, ABPP-CP
Medical and Forensic Neuropsychology, Chicago, IL, USA

Nancy Hebben, Ph.D., ABPP-CN
Department of Psychiatry, Harvard Medical School, Boston, MA, USA and Department of Psychiatry, Cambridge Health Alliance, Cambridge, MA, USA

Mathew J. Holcomb, Ph.D.
Jefferson Neurobehavioral Group, New Orleans, LA, USA

Farzin Irani, Ph.D., ABPP-CN
AAA Neuropsychology, Malvern, PA, USA

Joette James, Ph.D., ABPP-CN
Alina Assessment Services, Washington, DC, USA

Richard F. Kaplan, Ph.D., ABPP-CN
University of Connecticut School of Medicine, Farmington, CT, USA

Paul M. Kaufmann, J.D., Ph.D., ABPP-CN
Wayne State University School of Medicine, Detroit, MI, USA

Kristen M. Klipfel, Ph.D.
Isaac Ray Forensic Group, LLC, Chicago, IL, USA

Glenn J. Larrabee, Ph.D., ABPP-CN
Independent Practice, Sarasota, FL, USA

Julie K. Lynch, Ph.D.
Albany Neuropsychological Associates, Albany, NY, USA

James L. McAbee, Ph.D., HSP
Jefferson Neurobehavioral Group, Metairie, LA, USA

William S. MacAllister, Ph.D., ABPP-CN
Neurosciences Department, Alberta Children's Hospital, University of Calgary – Department of Pediatrics, Calgary, Alberta, Canada

Robert J. McCaffrey, Ph.D., ABN, ABPdN
Department of Psychology (Emeritus), University at Albany, State University of New York, and Albany Neuropsychological Associates, Albany, NY, USA

Stephen N. Macciocchi, Ph.D., ABPP-CN
Atlanta Neuropsychology, LLC, Marble Hill, GA, USA

Bernice A. Marcopulos, Ph.D., ABPP-CN
Department of Graduate Psychology, James Madison University, Harrisonburg, VA, USA and Department of Psychiatry and Neurobehavioral Sciences, University of Virginia School of Medicine, Charlottesville, VA

Phillip K. Martin, Ph.D., ABPP-CN
University of Kansas School of Medicine – Wichita and Robert J. Dole VA Medical Center, Wichita, KS, USA

Thomas Merten, Ph.D.
Department of Neurology, Vivantes Klinikum im Friedrichshain, Berlin, Germany and Psychologische Hochschule Berlin, Berlin, Germany

Melanie L. Middelkoop, MC, R. Psych.
Neurobehavioral Associates, Edmonton, AB, Canada

Scott R Millis, Ph.D., ABPP-CN, ABPP-CP, ABPP-RP, Cstat, PStat®
Department of Physical Medicine & Rehabilitation, Department of Neurology, Wayne State University School of Medicine, Detroit, MI, USA

Joel E. Morgan, Ph.D., ABPP-CN
Independent Practice, Cedar Knolls, NJ, USA

Lorna Myers, Ph.D.
Northeast Regional Epilepsy Group, New York, NY

Nathaniel W. Nelson, Ph.D., ABPP-CN
University of St. Thomas, Minneapolis, MN, USA

Maria K. Nikolova, Ph.D.
Madigan Army Medical Center, Tacoma, WA, USA

Howard Oakes, Psy.D., ABPP-CN
Hartford Hospital, Hartford, CT, USA

Gabriel P. Ovsiew, B.A.
Department of Psychiatry, University of Illinois College of Medicine, Chicago, IL, USA

Zachary J. Resch, Ph.D.
Department of Neurology, New York University Langone Health, New York, NY, USA

Ryan W. Schroeder, Psy.D., ABPP-CN
Robert J. Dole VA Medical Center and Independent Practice, Wichita, KS, USA

James D. Seward, Ph.D., ABPP-CN
Independent Practice, Scottsdale, AZ

Elisabeth M. S. Sherman, Ph.D., R.Psych.
Sherman Consulting and Assessment, Calgary, AB, Canada

Robert D. Shura, Psy.D., ABPP-CN
Research & Academic Affairs Service Line, Salisbury VA Health Care System, Salisbury, NC, USA and VA Mid-Atlantic Mental Illness Research, Education, and Clinical Center, Durham, NC, USA and Department of Neurology, Wake Forest School of Medicine, Winston-Salem, NC, USA

Jason R. Soble, Ph.D., ABPP-CN
Department of Psychiatry and Department of Neurology, University of Illinois College of Medicine, Chicago, IL, USA

Julie A. Suhr, Ph.D.
Department of Psychology, Ohio University, Athens, OH, USA

Jerry J. Sweet, Ph.D., ABPP-CN, ABPP-CP
Department of Psychology & Behavioral Sciences (Emeritus), Endeavor Health, Evanston, IL, USA

Tara L. Victor, Ph.D., ABPP-CN
California State University – Dominguez Hills, Carson, CA, USA

Douglas M. Whiteside, Ph.D., ABPP-CN
Department of Rehabilitation Medicine, University of Minnesota, Minneapolis, MN, USA

Megan R. Whitman, Ph.D.
Central Regional Hospital, Butner, NC, USA

Karim Z. Yamout, Psy.D., ABPP-CN
Private Practice, Bradenton, FL, USA and Bethlehem University, Bethlehem, Palestine

Foreword

Neuropsychology of Malingering and Non-Credible Presentations: Perspectives on Validity Assessment is an updated and expanded second edition of the *Neuropsychology of Malingering Casebook* that was edited by Morgan and Sweet in 2009. The original version provided an extensive review of the literature up to that time, with case examples that demonstrated the use of specific tests and other methods to evaluate the validity of the performances and symptom reports of examinees. Of course, a lot has happened in the field of validity assessment since then. For example, there is a greater appreciation of the difference between performance validity and symptom validity (Larrabee, 2015), the formal criteria for the definition of malingering have been thoroughly revised (Sherman et al., 2020), and the field has more fully embraced the need for inclusion of multiple measures of validity during all neuropsychological evaluations, including those for routine clinical purposes or involving school-age children (Sweet et al., 2021). This updated version builds on that progress to offer the reader a comprehensive yet accessible overview of the current state of the art when it comes to diagnosing, documenting, and managing concerns about validity during neuropsychological evaluations.

This book starts out by discussing foundational elements of validity assessment in neuropsychology (Section 1). This is then followed by many case examples that highlight various topics and diagnostic considerations as they relate to validity assessment and non-credible presentations. These case examples include civil litigation (Section 2), criminal litigation (Section 3), other forensic contexts such as disability and Workers' Compensation (Section 4), and non-forensic clinical settings (Section 5). The book then concludes with chapters on ethics and professional issues (Section 6).

The list of contributing authors pretty much reads like a Who's who? in the area of the literature on validity assessment. However, the authors are consistently careful to avoid getting into the weeds of obscure academic concepts. Instead, they clearly illustrate how findings from medical records review, history and interview, behavioral observations, and quantitative test data can be integrated to evaluate the degree to which cognitive test scores can be assumed to reflect accurately the examinee's abilities, as well as to what extent their subjective symptoms are reported truthfully. The reader will also appreciate that many of the chapters reflect examples of validity failures that can occur outside of the common context of tangible external incentives such as financial gain. There is appropriate appreciation of complicating psychosocial factors and comorbid psychopathology, without getting into either blaming the patient or making excuses for validity failures. Instead, the focus is on the facts, with careful consideration of the need to avoid both false positives as well as iatrogenic effects.

This book will be an excellent resource for persons in their advanced level of training in clinical neuropsychology as well as more seasoned practitioners. The wide range of settings and conditions covered by the various case examples provides a treasure trove of opportunities for practitioners to consider ways to evaluate and deal with validity considerations during neuropsychological evaluations across the spectrum of service delivery.

Jacobus Donders, Ph.D., ABPP
Mary Free Bed Hospital
Grand Rapids, MI

References

Larrabee, G. J. (2015). The multiple validities of neuropsychological assessment. *American Psychologist, 70*(8), 779–788. https://doi.org/10.1037/a0039835

Sherman, E. M. S., Slick, D. J., & Iverson, G. L. (2020). Multidimensional malingering criteria for neuropsychological assessment: A 20-year update of the malingered neuropsychological dysfunction criteria. *Archives of Clinical Neuropsychology, 35*(6), 735–764. https://doi.org/10.1093/arclin/acaa019

Sweet, J. J., Heilbronner, R. L., Morgan, J. E., Larrabee, G. J., Rohling, M. L., Boone, K. B., … Conference Participants. (2021). American Academy of Clinical Neuropsychology (AACN) 2021 consensus statement on validity assessment: Update of the 2009 AACN consensus conference statement on neuropsychological assessment of effort, response bias, and malingering. *The Clinical Neuropsychologist, 35*(6), 1053–1106. https://doi.org/10.1080/13854046.2021.1896036

Section I

Foundations of Validity Assessment in Neuropsychology

Neuropsychologists are experts in brain–behavior relationships, that is, in being able to appreciate the links between brain structure and behavior. In addition to understanding these connections, neuropsychologists are uniquely skilled at utilizing objective tests to evaluate and quantify the degree of any cognitive, behavioral, and/or psychological dysfunction. These tests, while objective, rely on examinee motivation, engagement, and cooperation. If an examinee were to provide suboptimal motivation or engagement, lack cooperation, or inaccurate responses with an intent of deceiving the clinician, the individual's capabilities and functioning would not be accurately captured. In recognizing this, the field of neuropsychology has embraced the concept that we must verify the accuracy of neuropsychological test data in an objective and evidence-based manner, which is accomplished through the application of empirically validated performance and symptom validity tests. The chapters within this section provide fundamental information on validity assessment, detailing the evolution of validity testing, statistical issues underlying validity tests, and methods of examining for false-positive findings, and in applying these tests to all examinees, including culturally and linguistically diverse individuals.

DOI: 10.4324/9781003005063-1

1 Deception, Response Bias, Malingering, Effort, and Invalidity

The Conceptual Evolution of Neuropsychological Validity Testing

Ryan W. Schroeder and Phillip K. Martin

Neuropsychological validity testing, terminology used to describe validity tests and non-credible performance, and conceptual conclusions drawn from validity test results have evolved over time. Some of the changes have been subtle, while others have been more significant. In this chapter, we provide a historical overview and brief discussion of the conceptual evolution of neuropsychological performance validity testing.

Psychologists' investigation of methods to detect deceptive and malingered behavior via cognitive testing can be traced back to the early 1900s (Carone & Bush, 2013). In one of the first identified studies on the topic, Yerkes and Berry (1909) published results of four experiments that used an 'association reaction method' to determine if an examinee's reaction times could differentiate feigning from honest responding. Some of the experiments, for example, made an examinee privy to information that others did not know (e.g., what item was hidden under a box). An examiner then read word lists, which contained words that referred to the information that was known by the examinee (e.g., words that were associated with the item that was hidden under the box). As soon as the examinee heard each word, he was asked to provide another associated word as quickly as possible while also trying to conceal knowledge of the item that had previously been seen. The examinee's reaction time in providing each associated word was recorded, and it was found that the reaction time was noticeably longer with words associated with the concealed items.

Research on the association reaction method continued and, in 1920, Marston published an article titled "Reaction-Time Symptoms of Deception." In this article, he referred to association reaction method tests as "deception tests" (p. 72), and he stated that the ultimate purpose of these tests was to assist with legal testimony. He described that "the future of all deception tests lies in the possibility of their introduction as a basis for expert testimony" (pp. 72–73). He went on to state that "We must, therefore, seek objective, quantitative measurements of the psycho-physiological symptoms of the deceptive consciousness" (p. 73).

Additional research on 'deception tests' ensued, resulting in multiple articles being published in the 1920s, including "Psychophysical Symptoms of Deception" (Langfeld, 1920), "Reaction-Times and the Consciousness of Deception" (Goldstein, 1923), and "Negative Type Reaction-Time Symptoms of Deception" (Marston, 1925). Psychologists' expanding awareness of 'deception tests' in the early 20th century was captured by writings from Langfeld, who noted that the reaction time experiments "are well known to all experimental psychologists" and "the method has in fact become sufficiently standardized to be used in training courses in laboratory technique" (p. 319). With that said, the association reaction method seemed to be less commonly utilized in clinical practice based on Langfeld's statement that "The method has on several occasions been used to detect actual crime, but

DOI: 10.4324/9781003005063-2

for the most part such experiments have been performed under the artificial conditions of the laboratory in order to test the reliability of the results" (p. 319).

Interestingly, a clear shift in psychological validity testing procedures occurred in the late 1930s to early 1940s. By this time, psychological research on the association reaction method had substantially slowed, and psychological researchers essentially stopped using the term 'deception test' in peer-reviewed publications. Around this time, André Rey, began publishing research that notably advanced the neuropsychological validity testing literature (1941). Specifically, he showed that performance curve analyses and more modern-day performance validity tests (PVTs), including the Dot Counting Test and Word Recognition Test, could identify examinees who were feigning cognitive deficits (Frederick, 2003). Rey's validity testing work was largely motivated by concerns from insurance companies that claimants were feigning impairment. Likely related to this concern, Rey utilized his tests with real patients/claimants, and he used the terms 'malingerer' and 'malingering' in publications.

The next major advancement within performance validity testing came in the 1970s and 1980s. In 1975, Pankratz and colleagues published a case study in which they used a new test paradigm called a forced choice test to evaluate "deafness in the hysterical or malingering patient." In 1983, Pankratz adapted the forced choice method to questions pertaining to "feigned memory deficit," and he referred to this type of validity testing as 'symptom validity testing' (Bianchini, Mathias, & Greve, 2001). Pankratz' work ultimately spawned the development of multiple standardized forced choice validity tests, including the Digit Memory Test (Hiscock & Hiscock, 1989), Portland Digit Recognition Test (Binder & Willis, 1991), Computerized Assessment of Response Bias (Conder, Allan, & Cox, 1992), and the Victoria Symptom Validity Test (Slick, Hopp, & Strauss, 1995). As can be seen, new terminology within validity assessment research also started emerging in the 1980s and 1990s, including the terms 'symptom validity testing' (and symptom validity test) and 'response bias' (and response bias test).

In addition to those specific tests noted above, a wave of additional validity tests emerged during the 1980s and, especially, 1990s. While many were based on a forced choice paradigm, some freestanding and embedded validity tests were developed that utilized other methods (e.g., Rey 15 Item Test and Reliable Digit Span). Research on the validity tests was almost exclusively forensic in nature (Suchy, 2019), often investigating the accuracy of validity tests to differentiate between simulated malingerers or forensic claimants suspected of malingering and non-malingering examinees (Bianchini, Mathias, & Greve, 2001). Because the expanding validity testing research heavily focused on forensic activities and malingering, invalid presentations, and noncredible test findings during neuropsychological evaluations essentially became synonymous with malingering. Consequently, neuropsychologists began using the term "malingering test" in the 1990s, and an extremely popular validity test published in the mid-1990s was even named the Test of Memory Malingering (Tombaugh, 1996).

In 1999, Slick, Sherman, and Iverson published the landmark article "Diagnostic Criteria for Malingered Neurocognitive Dysfunction: Proposed Standards for Clinical Practice and Research." Within the publication, the authors wrote about the "widespread and concerted research" (p. 1385) and test development over the previous decade regarding the detection of malingering. More significantly, though, they proposed formal probabilistic criteria for making determinations of malingering of cognitive dysfunction based on validity test performance, behavioral observations, and collateral information, designed for use in both neuropsychological practice and research. The field of neuropsychology quickly embraced

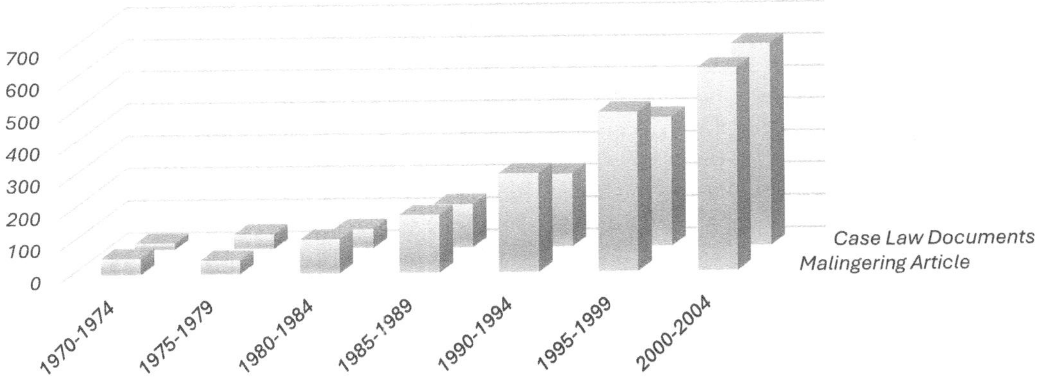

Figure 1.1 Number of articles on "malingering" as identified by an EBSCOhost search and number of case law documents containing "neuropsycho" as identified by a Google Scholar case law search.

the proposed criteria, with many practitioners viewing them as the gold standard for determining malingering in forensic practice.

Through the mid-2000s, the volume of 'malingering' research in neuropsychology continued to expand (Suchy, 2019), which was likely related to neuropsychologists' increasing involvement in forensic activities. Figure 1.1 depicts the results of (1) a formal literature search within psychology databases (i.e., an EBSCOhost search using the databases: APA PsycArticles, APA PsycInfo, and Psychology and Behavioral Sciences Collection) for the term 'malingering' and (2) a Google Scholar case law search for the term 'neuropsycho' to capture case law documents that include the terms neuropsychology, neuropsychologist, and neuropsychological. As can be seen, the increase in 'malingering' research within neuropsychology from 1970 to 2004 closely mirrors the increase in neuropsychologists' involvement in legal cases during the same time span.

In the mid-2000s, a noticeable shift in the validity assessment literature occurred (Suchy, 2019). Although neuropsychologists continued to research 'malingering' detection within forensic settings, a growing amount of research emerged examining PVTs within non-forensic settings. In fact, by 2007, 15%–20% of validity assessment articles addressed non-forensic activities. The literature demonstrated that some individuals within non-forensic contexts also produce invalid data on neuropsychological testing. This resulted in a growing shift away from the conceptualization that malingering was the predominant, if not nearly exclusive, cause of invalid test results to a belief that factors outside of malingering (e.g., level of effort applied toward testing) can cause validity tests failure, especially in clinical settings. Consequently, use of the term 'malingering test' declined, while use of terms such as poor effort, insufficient effort, inadequate effort, and suboptimal effort became more popular. The term 'effort test' eventually became commonplace within the neuropsychological literature. To this point, the 2009 publication of the *American Academy of Clinical Neuropsychology consensus conference statement on the neuropsychological assessment of effort, response bias, and malingering* (Heilbronner et al., 2009) even noted that "Measures used to identify problematic effort are often identified as *effort tests*" (italics were present in the original publication; p. 1096).

In the late 2000s to early 2010s, concerns emerged about broadly using the term 'effort' when referring to invalid test findings. In another landmark paper, Larrabee (2012) argued that using the term 'effort test' can be misleading because the results of PVTs do not necessarily provide data regarding the degree of effort expended on testing. Specifically, he noted that the common definition of effort was providing exertion toward the completion of a task, which can range from full effort to no effort. Larrabee stated that PVTs, however, were not constructed to measure the continuum of effort. Instead, these tests were created to identify atypical patterns of performance as compared with both normal individuals and individuals with genuine neuropsychological conditions. Thus, Larrabee argued that validity test failures do not necessarily detect 'poor effort' but, rather, indicate that an examinee's performance is so atypical that the performance cannot be considered a valid representation of their true ability.

Boone (2013) also discussed that terms such as inadequate effort or poor effort can be misleading. She noted that using such terms suggests that examinees who fail validity tests simply do not provide enough effort to obtain valid results. This, however, is not always the case in practice. In the context of malingering, for example, an examinee effortfully attempts to appear impaired, potentially even going so far as to score at a statistically below chance level on a forced choice performance validity test. Within this context especially, the validity test results do not indicate that there is poor effort. Conversely, they indicate that the examinee effortfully performed in a negative direction in an attempt to appear more disabled than they truly are.

Because the terms 'effort' and 'effort test' were noted as being misleading, and because 'validity test' was seen as being the most accurate description of tests designed to detect noncredible performance, Larrabee (2012) proposed adoption of the term 'validity test.' In differentiating validity tests based on symptom-report (e.g., validity scales within various versions of the Minnesota Multiphasic Personality Inventory) and validity tests based on cognitive test performance (e.g., the Test of Memory Malingering), he recommended the use of the specific terms of 'symptom validity test' and 'performance validity test,' respectively. Survey data published in 2015 indicated that the majority of neuropsychologists quickly adopted Larrabee's suggested terminology (Martin, Schroeder, & Odland, 2025). Specifically, North American neuropsychologists were asked what the preferred term was for a neuropsychological measure utilized to assess for noncredible test performance. It was found that nearly 74% of neuropsychologists preferred the term performance validity test while only about 14% preferred the term effort test, 7% preferred the term symptom validity test, 2.5% preferred the term response bias test, and less than 1% preferred the term malingering test.

In the decade since Larrabee proposed the aforementioned change in terminology, neuropsychologists have continued to publish a significant amount of validity assessment research. A recent EBSCOhost search of psychology databases (i.e., APA PsycArticles, APA PsycInfo, and Psychology and Behavioral Sciences Collection) indicates that neuropsychologists continue to prefer the term 'performance validity test.' Specifically, Figure 1.2 shows the number of articles that contained the terms performance validity test, effort test, response bias test, and malingering test. As can be seen, the number of articles using the term performance validity test has largely continued to grow in proportion to the number of articles using other terms for validity tests.

Another clear trend in the professional literature is the ongoing (and growing) movement of examining validity testing within non-forensic contexts (Suchy, 2019). In fact, since 2016, the number of validity assessment articles being conducted in general clinical settings has essentially matched or exceeded the number of validity assessment articles focusing on malingering and forensic topics. The growth of this literature is not limited to

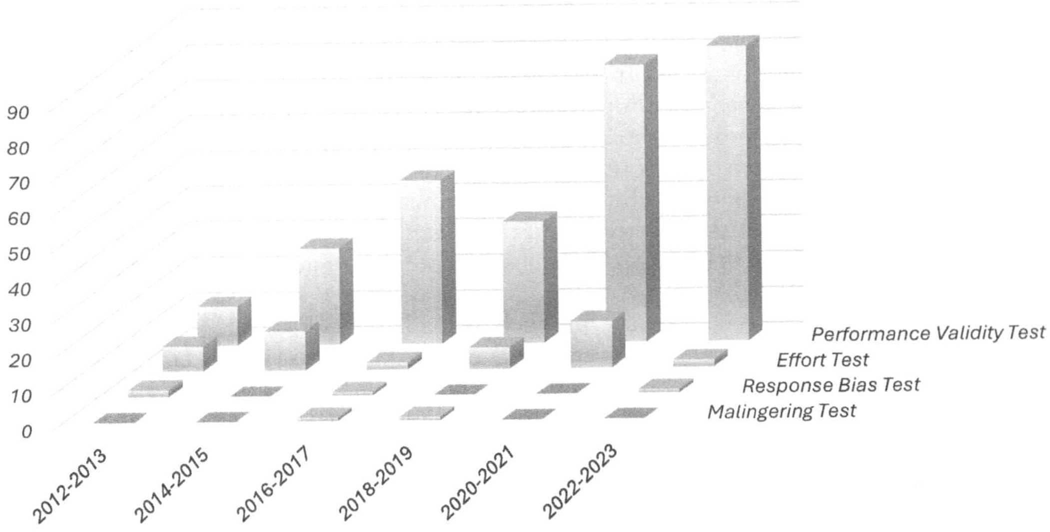

Figure 1.2 An EBSCOhost literature search showing the number of articles containing each term across a 12-year timespan.

articles, as research posters, professional presentations, and even books (e.g., Carone & Bush, 2018; Kirkwood, 2015; Schroeder & Martin, 2022) have begun to focus on validity testing in non-forensic settings. Indeed, even this second edition of the *Neuropsychology of Malingering Casebook* (herein renamed), has a section within it devoted to validity assessment within clinical evaluations.

The ever-expanding validity assessment literature base continues to highlight the fact that invalidity can realistically occur in both forensic and clinical settings (Schroeder & Martin, 2022; Sweet et al., 2021). Additionally, factors that dramatically increase risk for invalidity in clinical settings are external incentives (which can include financial, academic, drug/medication-related, and other incentives) and medically unexplained symptoms (Martin & Schroeder, 2020; Schroeder & Martin, 2022). Furthermore, hidden external incentives exist in some clinical cases, and base rates of invalidity can increase – sometimes to the same rate as that seen in forensic contexts – when hidden external incentives are present (Schroeder, Clark, & Martin, 2022). It is likely for all of these reasons that the American Academy of Clinical Neuropsychology (2021) consensus statement on validity assessment concludes that,

> In order to provide bases for diagnoses and interpretations, the current consensus is that all clinical and forensic evaluations must proactively address the degree to which results of neuropsychological and psychological testing are valid. There is a strong and continually-growing evidence-based literature on which practitioners can confidently base their judgments regarding the selection and interpretation of validity measures.
>
> (Sweet et al., 2021, p. 1053)

In short, validity assessment has become a standard of practice within the field of neuropsychology.

Conclusions

In summary, the professional literature base regarding psychologists' detection of noncredible presentations, as well as neuropsychologists' use of PVTs, has dramatically expanded over time. While validity tests largely emerged from a forensic need to detect deceptive actions and malingering, subsequent research has indicated that factors outside of malingering can sometimes result in validity test failure. This research seems to have caused one of the most significant shifts in the conceptualization and description of validity tests and noncredible responding. At present, validity testing is viewed as being essential in both forensic and general clinical contexts (Martin, Schroeder, & Odland, 2025; Sweet et al., 2021). The term 'validity assessment' is currently the preferred term within neuropsychology when discussing methods to detect noncredible presentations regardless of whether in forensic or clinical settings. The term 'performance validity tests' (or 'performance validity indices') is currently preferred when describing performance-based validity measures, and the term 'symptom validity tests' (or 'symptom validity indices') is currently preferred when describing symptom report-based validity measures. The term 'invalidity' is typically used to refer to invalid findings regardless of the cause of the invalid findings. Finally, while the term malingering is not as broadly used as it once was, it can still be appropriately used at times when it is believed that an individual has intentionally exaggerated or feigned his or her dysfunction in an attempt to obtain an external incentive (Sweet et al., 2021).

References

Bianchini, K. J., Mathias, C. W., & Greve, K. W. (2001). Symptom validity testing: A critical review. *The Clinical Neuropsychologist*, *15*(1), 19–45.

Binder, L. M., & Willis, S. C. (1991). Assessment of motivation after financially compensable minor head trauma. *Psychological Assessment: A Journal of Consulting and Clinical Psychology*, *3*(2), 175.

Boone, K. B. (2013). *Clinical practice of forensic neuropsychology: An evidence-based approach*. Guilford Press.

Carone, D. A., & Bush, S. S. (2013). Introduction: Historical perspectives on mild traumatic brain injury, symptom validity assessment, and malingering. In D. A. Carone & S. S. Bush (Eds.), *Mild traumatic brain injury: Symptom validity assessment and malingering* (pp. 1–29). Springer.

Carone, D. A., & Bush, S. S. (2018). *Validity assessment in rehabilitation psychology and settings*. Oxford.

Conder, R., Allen, L., & Cox, D. (1992). *Computerized Assessment of Response Bias test manual*. Durham, NC: Cognisyst.

Frederick, R. I. (2003). A review of Rey's strategies for detecting malingered neuropsychological impairment. *Journal of Forensic Neuropsychology*, *2*(3–4), 1–25.

Goldstein, E. R. (1923). Reaction times and the consciousness of deception. *The American Journal of Psychology*, 562–581.

Heilbronner, R. L., Sweet, J. J., Morgan, J. E., Larrabee, G. J., Millis, S. R., & Conference Participants 1. (2009). American Academy of Clinical Neuropsychology Consensus Conference Statement on the neuropsychological assessment of effort, response bias, and malingering. *The Clinical Neuropsychologist*, *23*(7), 1093–1129.

Hiscock, M., & Hiscock, C. K. (1989). Refinding the forced-choice method for the detection of malingering. *Journal of Clinical and Experimental Neuropsychology*, *11*, 967–974.

Kirkwood, M. W. (2015). *Validity testing in child and adolescent assessment: Evaluating exaggeration, feigning, and noncredible effort*. Guilford Press.

Langfeld, H. S. (1920). Psychophysical symptoms of deception. *The Journal of Abnormal Psychology*, *15*(5–6), 319.

Larrabee, G. J. (2012). Performance validity and symptom validity in neuropsychological assessment. *Journal of the International Neuropsychological Society*, *18*(4), 625–630.
Marston, W. M. (1920). Reaction-time symptoms of deception. *Journal of Experimental Psychology*, *3*(1), 72.
Marston, W. M. (1925). Negative type reaction-time symptoms of deception. *Psychological Review*, *32*(3), 241.
Martin, P. K., & Schroeder, R. W. (2020). Base rates of invalid test performance across clinical non-forensic contexts and settings. *Archives of Clinical Neuropsychology*, *35*(6), 717–725.
Martin, P. K., Schroeder, R. W., & Odland, A. P. (2015). Neuropsychologists' validity testing beliefs and practices: A survey of North American professionals. *The Clinical Neuropsychologist*, *29*(6), 741–776.
Martin, P. K., Schroeder, R. W., & Odland, A. P. (2025). Neuropsychological validity assessment beliefs and practices: A survey of North American neuropsychologists and validity assessment experts. *Archives of Clinical Neuropsychology*, *40*(2), 201–223.
Pankratz, L. (1983). A new technique for the assessment and modification of feigned memory deficit. *Perceptual and Motor Skills*, *57*(2), 367–372.
Pankratz, L., Fausti, S. A., & Peed, S. (1975). A forced-choice technique to evaluate deafness in the hysterical or malingering patient. *Journal of Consulting and Clinical Psychology*, *43*(3), 421.
Rey, A. (1941). L'examen psychologique dans les cas d'encéphalopathie traumatique.(Les problems.). *Archives de psychologie*.
Schroeder, R. W., Clark, H. A., & Martin, P. K. (2022). Base rates of invalidity when patients undergoing routine clinical evaluations have social security disability as an external incentive. *The Clinical Neuropsychologist*, *36*(7), 1902–1914.
Schroeder, R. W., & Martin, P. K. (2022). *Validity assessment in clinical neuropsychological practice: Evaluating and managing noncredible performance*. Guilford Press.
Slick, D. J., Hoop, G., & Strauss, E. (1995). *The victoria symptom validity test*. Psychological Assessment Resources.
Slick, D. J., Sherman, E. M., & Iverson, G. L. (1999). Diagnostic criteria for malingered neurocognitive dysfunction: Proposed standards for clinical practice and research. *The Clinical Neuropsychologist*, *13*(4), 545–561.
Suchy, Y. (2019). Introduction to special issue: Current trends in empirical examinations of performance and symptom validity. *The Clinical Neuropsychologist*, *33*(8), 1349–1353.
Sweet, J. J., Heilbronner, R. L., Morgan, J. E., Larrabee, G. J., Rohling, M. L., Boone, K. B., … & Conference Participants. (2021). American Academy of Clinical Neuropsychology (AACN) 2021 consensus statement on validity assessment: Update of the 2009 AACN consensus conference statement on neuropsychological assessment of effort, response bias, and malingering. *The Clinical Neuropsychologist*, *35*(6), 1053–1106.
Tombaugh, T. N. (1996). *Test of memory malingering*. Multi-Health Systems, Inc.
Yerkes, R. M., & Berry, C. S. (1909). The association reaction method of mental diagnosis (Tatbestandsdiagnostik). *The American Journal of Psychology*, *20*(1), 22–37.

2 What Clinicians Really Need to Know about Symptom and Performance Validity

Statistical and Measurement Matters

Jeremy J. Davis and Scott R. Millis

Detection is, or ought to be, an exact science, and should be treated in the same cold and unemotional manner. You have attempted to tinge it with romanticism, which produces much the same effect as if you worked a love-story or an elopement into the fifth proposition of Euclid.

Sir Arthur Conan Doyle (1859–1930)
The Sign of Four, 1890

Brief History of Performance and Symptom Validity

Literature on the concept of malingering dates, at least, to the early biblical era with a passage describing David feigning mental illness: "And he changed his behaviour before them, and feigned himself mad in their hands, and scrabbled on the doors of the gate, and let his spittle fall down upon his beard" (1 Samuel 21:13). More recent historical references include widespread malingering during the U.S. Civil War, when detection methods included use of anesthesia among other approaches (Connor, 2006). The development of Workers Compensation systems in the 1800s provided another source of external incentive with terms "compensation neurosis" and "accident neurosis" used to describe symptom exaggeration in the context of compensable injuries (Hall & Hall, 2012). The diagnostic challenges inherent in differentiating malingering from other psychiatric conditions like posttraumatic stress and somatoform disorders were highlighted by the efforts to evaluate and treat soldiers suffering from "shell shock" during World War I (Tatu & Bogousslavsky, 2014). By World War II, shell shock was sometimes referred to as "battle fatigue," but the diagnostic challenges continued with a famous example in which George Patton slapped two hospitalized soldiers whom he thought were claiming battle fatigue as a means to avoid returning to combat (Lovelace, 2019).

In current neuropsychological practice, performance validity refers to the credibility of responses to neurocognitive tasks (that are *performed* by the test taker), while symptom validity refers to the credibility of report of psychiatric, physical, and cognitive complaints (that are *self-reported* by the test taker). Correspondingly, performance validity tests (PVTs) are objective measures validated to document whether test takers are performing to true ability on neurocognitive tasks, while symptom validity tests (SVTs) are objective measures validated to assess for credibility of symptom report. The origins of current psychometric approaches to performance and symptom validity assessment can be traced to the 1940s with the first freestanding PVT reported in Rey's publication describing the Dot Counting Test (1941), and in early simulation studies in the U.S. Hunt

DOI: 10.4324/9781003005063-3

and Older (1943) compared responses on three cognitive measures from participants with apparent borderline intellectual ability and cognitively intact participants instructed to feign impairment. In contrast to the borderline intellectual ability group, simulators showed less consistency in responses with errors on objectively easy items and correct responses to objectively harder items.

Early work addressing validity of symptom report relied on discrepancies in presentation across different aspects of the evaluation (i.e., completing cognitive versus projective tests) in cases "in which there was a very strong suspicion that the patient's subjective physical complaints ... were being deliberately simulated to avoid duty" (Benton, 1945, p. 94). In these cases, an inconsistency was sometimes observed between normal range IQ scores and a pattern of responding to projective measures described as involving a "low total number of responses, complete failure to respond, slow reaction time, and constrained attitude" unexpected in the absence of intellectual disability or active psychosis (Benton, 1945, p. 94). Goldstein (1945) developed what would now be understood as an "embedded" PVT (i.e., embedded within standard neurocognitive tests, then termed a "malingering key") that assigned points for failing easy items and passing harder items on 18 of 50 items on the Visual Classification Test, which was a non-verbal measure of cognitive ability used in candidate selection for military service. The embedded indicator showed remarkable classification accuracy with 96% sensitivity and 86% specificity reported in the development sample. The use of forced-choice methods to examine validity emerged in research in the 1960s and 1970s that initially used the approaches in assessing functional sensory deficits (Grosz & Zimmerman, 1965; Pankratz et al., 1975; Theodor & Mandelcorn, 1973) and were eventually extended to assessment of feigned memory problems (Pankratz, 1983).

Research in performance and symptom validity has been an area of substantial growth in neuropsychology based on content of journals (Martin et al., 2015; Suchy, 2019) and conference presentations (Sweet et al., 2002). Additional evidence of growth can be observed in the space devoted to these matters in widely used reference texts. For example, in Lezak (1983), coverage of performance validity was limited to a two-paragraph section on malingering (p. 236) and four pages describing four specific measures (pp. 618–622), but the most recent edition (Lezak et al., 2012) devotes 32 pages to the topic. Similarly, Spreen and Strauss (1991) did not include content related to performance or symptom validity, Strauss and colleagues (2006) allotted 39 pages to it, and the latest volume (Sherman et al., 2022) includes 146 pages. Edited volumes focused on performance and symptom validity have grown in size: Boone (2013) appears relatively brief at 481 pages compared with the second edition that has 710 pages (Boone, 2021). One potential explanation for this increase has been the expansion of validity considerations from the forensic arena to include clinical contexts (Schroeder & Martin, 2022; Suchy, 2019).

Accompanying this growth in research and related publications has been evolution in terminology used to describe validity issues. Much of the early work focused on malingering and described PVTs as *malingering tests* (Goldstein, 1945; Hunt & Older, 1943). Although malingering remains relevant as a diagnostic consideration in evaluation contexts with secondary gain, the field has moved beyond the formulaic conceptualization that validity test failure equals malingering (Sweet et al., 2021). The forced-choice methods developed to evaluate functional sensory complaints were referred to as *symptom validity testing* (Pankratz, 1979), and the term was initially used to describe the procedure of constructing and administering a test with stimuli specific to the complaints of a given patient (e.g., visual deficits) that was interpreted according to binomial probability (Heubrock & Petermann, 1998).

Over time, a number of standardized tests using a forced-choice, recognition memory format were adapted (e.g., Recognition Memory Test; Millis, 1992) or developed (e.g., Test of Memory Malingering; Tombaugh & Tombaugh, 1996) for use as freestanding validity measures. With increased use of these standardized measures, *symptom validity testing* and *SVTs* came to designate the category of measures and specific measures, respectively, rather than the general method (Bianchini et al., 2001).

In the mid-1990s, the terms *effort* and *effort tests* appeared in the literature (Guilmette et al., 1994; Millis et al., 1995). They were used somewhat interchangeably with symptom validity and SVT, and this usage pattern continued through the early 2000s (Bush et al., 2005; Heilbronner et al., 2009). The effort label captured an important element of the foundational premise of neuropsychological evaluation that interpretation of performance-based tasks assumes the measures have been attempted to the best of the examinee's ability (i.e., with optimal effort). The label fits well with aspects of examinations conducted by other healthcare professionals, including observation during physical examination of give-way (also give-away or collapsing) weakness in which a limb collapses in response to minimal force from the examiner (Stone et al., 2002). Functional capacity evaluations conducted by physical therapists often include considerations related to "sincerity of effort" in motor testing (Bhuanantanondh et al., 2018) in recognition of the importance of ascertaining whether measured strength represents the true ability of the examinee. Limitations of the term became clear, including a contradiction between the label and the nature of the tasks: Freestanding *effort* tests are actually easy to complete, so easy, in fact, that modal scores of healthy individuals are often perfect (Tombaugh, 1996). Also, there is an apparent paradox related to the nature of *effort* measures and their intended purpose: To determine if an examinee is providing optimal effort on challenging cognitive tasks, performance is examined on an objectively easy measure. Finally, although *effort* tests are easy to pass, it remains challenging to underperform in a convincing manner (Martin et al., 1996; Davis & Wall, 2014), and it is likely effortful to elude detection while underperforming. Following a lively session at an international conference (Bigler et al., 2010), Larrabee (2012) proposed use of *performance validity* to refer to the validity of a test of ability and *symptom validity* to refer to the validity of symptoms reported in interview or on self-report measures. These terms have become widely adopted and remain the current terms of choice with consensus support (Sweet et al., 2021).

Judgment under Uncertainty

As noted above, the evolution of terminology used by neuropsychologists to refer to performance and symptom validity likely reflects an underlying conceptual shift from considering validity assessment as primarily a forensic matter to appreciating a broader scope of relevance and understanding the determination of validity to be a necessary component of neuropsychological evaluation across contexts (Bush et al., 2005; Schroeder & Martin, 2022; Sweet et al., 2021). Whether in clinic or in consultation on a medicolegal matter, the neuropsychologist's work in making a decision about performance and symptom validity can be understood as involving two components: data collection and interpretation (Dawes et al., 1989). Data collection methods in validity assessment (i.e., embedded and freestanding PVTs and SVTs) are vast and beyond the scope of this chapter (see Boone, 2021 for a comprehensive review of the current validity armamentarium). Discussing methods of interpretating of data from PVTs and SVTs, however, is one of our goals. This interpretive process is one of decision-making or "judgment under uncertainty" (Tversky & Kahneman, 1974).

For almost 70 years, the merits of two approaches to these decision-making tasks have been scrutinized and debated in the social sciences and medicine: clinical judgment and actuarial methods (Meehl, 1954). The approach based on clinical judgment involves combination and interpretation of data in the mind of the decision-maker, and the actuarial (also called statistical) approach follows an established decision-making process or algorithm using empirical associations among data and outcomes (Dawes et al., 1989). Given a foundation in clinical psychology, it might initially appear likely that the former approach would be the most relevant to the field of neuropsychology and the various decisions, diagnostic and otherwise, that are to be made by neuropsychologists. After all, as highly trained, subspecialized, scientist-practitioners in a helping profession, it seems reasonable that our clinical judgment would be reliable and accurate. Alas, neuropsychologists are people, and "people are poor judges of other people" (Dahlstrom, 1993). As Meehl (1986, p. 372) noted:

> Surely we all know that the human brain is poor at weighting and computing. When you check out at a supermarket, you don't eyeball the heap of purchases and say to the clerk, "Well it looks to me as if it's about $17.00 worth; what do you think?" The clerk adds it up.

Given the complexities involved in "weighting and computing" clinical matters and the human limitations in doing so, the default response of clinicians (and people, in general, as noted by Tversky and Kahnemann, 1974) is to use mental shortcuts or heuristics in decision-making. The resulting decisions are prone to a variety of cognitive biases. Examples of common heuristics and cognitive biases are listed in Table 2.1.

In light of the limitations of clinical judgment, how should the scientifically minded neuropsychologist proceed? An initial step is to appreciate research demonstrating the poor accuracy of clinical judgment (e.g., Grove et al., 2000; Heaton et al., 1978) as an important call to action rather than a "slap" aimed from researcher to clinician (Faust, 1986, p. 426). A related consideration is to recognize that while additional work remains, considerable progress has been made in validity assessment in the past 45 years (Faust et al., 2021) in terms of developing freestanding and embedded PVTs, and in increasing reliance on statistical interpretative approaches with wider adoption of logistic regression and broad recognition of relevant concepts in classification accuracy. It would likely be challenging to replicate the study design of Heaton and colleagues because contemporary neuropsychological experts in validity assessment would not likely rely on clinical judgment alone to determine validity status (Schroeder et al., 2016).

It can also be helpful to consider that there remain situations in which informed professional judgment remains useful:

> Formalized decision rules should not be followed blindly or robotically because situations may arise that attenuate or negate their value. In one instance a child fell asleep during the administration of a memory test but the examiner nevertheless included the memory score when tallying test results. We are not aware of any intelligent advocate of formalized decision procedures who would endorse such a foolish act, but to disapprove of such mindless missteps does not provide logical support for the argument that data should almost always be integrated via subjective or impressionistic judgment.
>
> (Faust et al., 2021, p. 42)

Table 2.1 Cognitive Heuristics and Biases in Clinical Decision-Making

Heuristic/Bias	*Definition*
Affirming the consequent	Incorrectly concluding the converse of a true statement is true (Sethy, 2021). For example, brain injury causes low Trail Making Test-B (TMT-B) scores. Given a low TMT-B score, there must have been a brain injury.
Anchoring and adjustment	Anchoring refers to an initial value attributed to an unknown and adjustment is the subsequent change in the estimate. Final value attributions are higher or lower based on the value of initial estimate (i.e., the anchor; Tversky & Kahneman, 1974).
Availability	Decision-making based on how readily information comes to mind (Tversky & Kahneman, 1974). Subtypes include: • Reliance on salient data: Prevalence of unusual or highly salient conditions are likely overestimated compared with common ones, because the atypical stands out and comes to mind more easily (Wedding & Faust, 1989). • Illusory correlation: Overestimation of the level of association between variables (Chapman & Chapman, 1969).
Configural analysis	Human capacity for weighting and integrating multiple data sources is limited, and efforts to do so typically involve data reduction rather than actual integration of multiple data points (Lichtenstein & Slovic, 1971).
Confirmation bias	Pursuing only information that supports a hypothesis, disregarding information that refutes it, and not considering alternative hypotheses (Wedding & Faust, 1989). • Premature closure: Moving too quickly to a diagnostic impression (Nickerson, 1998).
Conservatism	Evaluating data sequentially without updating a diagnostic hypothesis based on the additional information (Edwards, 1968).
Hindsight bias	Believing a specific outcome would have been readily predicted once the outcome is known (Wedding & Faust, 1989).
Ignoring covariation	Considering a limited number of relationships among a variable or indicator and a diagnosis (i.e., sign present–condition present) rather than the complete set of outcomes between a diagnostic indicator and diagnosis (Wedding & Faust, 1989).
Post hoc fallacy	Inferring causality on the basis of sequential events from the Latin phrase *post hoc, ergo propter hoc* (i.e., after this, therefore because of this; Grouse, 2016).
Representativeness	Decision-making based on the degree to which an individual's presentation fits with an internalized conceptualization of a given diagnostic category (Tversky & Kahneman, 1974).

To consider other illustrations, imagine an examinee who limps around clinic wincing with antalgic gait but is observed walking normally in the parking lot, or another examinee who stutters intermittently with a strange accent during interview but was heard in the waiting room speaking with normal rate, volume, and articulation while talking on a cell phone. As Faust would likely remind us, the true diagnostic value of these observations or "compelling inconsistencies" (Heinly et al., 2005; Sherman et al., 2022) is unknown unless the full associative pattern is established (i.e., the two-by-two contingency table of positive and negative instances on indicator and condition), but there likely remains some utility of the observation while the empirical work is conducted. It may also be fruitful to recall that, although

Heaton et al. (1978) demonstrated the poor overall classification accuracy of clinical judgment, there are instances in which clinical judgment may be accurate:

> One of these four individuals [who were excluded from analysis] had started to fake, but he was so obvious about it that the technician severely reprimanded him and threatened to call the attorney who had supposedly referred him for testing. From that point on, the subject earned above average scores on all tests given.
>
> (p. 893)

There are recommended debiasing strategies that can be followed to reduce errors in clinical judgment (Arkes, 1981; Wedding & Faust, 1989). A valuable foundational step is to study the literature on heuristics, cognitive biases, and clinical judgment in general and to complement this knowledge-base with additional work specifically addressing clinical judgment in neuropsychological evaluation. Classic work on heuristics in decision-making include Tversky and Kahneman (1974) and Plous (1993). Meehl is an interesting source for original discussion of the actuarial versus clinical judgment debate (1954, 1986). Cognitive biases are covered in Faust (1986), Wedding and Faust (1989), and Bowes et al. (2020). Excellent summaries of the many studies of clinical judgment are provided by Faust (1986) and Dawes et al. (1989). Clinical judgment in neuropsychology related to validity considerations is addressed by Heaton et al. (1978), Wedding and Faust (1986), Faust et al. (1988a, 1988b), Garb and Schramke (1996), Trueblood and Binder (1997), and Dandachi-FitzGerald et al. (2017). A recent review and updated critique of validity concerns in neuropsychological evaluation is provided by Faust and colleagues (2021). The benefit of debiasing techniques is understandably an area that warrants empirical demonstration. Limited work to date shows variable/mixed results (Lilienfeld et al., 2009). An additional caveat with attempts to improve clinical judgment is that a thorough understanding of the limits of clinical judgment, while potentially helpful for reducing overconfidence in one's own decision-making, is an insufficient remedy for those limits.

Edified and humbled by knowledge of our limitations, there are several active measures that can be followed to improve decision-making. First, generate alternative diagnostic hypotheses and list disconfirmatory data for preferred hypotheses. It may be helpful to use a form as illustrated in Figure 2.1 that contains space for preferred and alternative hypotheses and for supporting and refuting data for these hypotheses.

A related approach that has been recommended in medical decision-making is implementation of a diagnostic time out in complicated cases to avoid premature closure on the first hypothesis generated (Ely et al., 2011). The neuropsychological decision-making environment is rarely going to be as fast paced in some medical settings (e.g., operating room or trauma bay), but delaying development of a preferred hypothesis and considering alternatives will support optimal decision-making.

A second useful approach to reduce cognitive bias involves reliance on base rates (or prevalence) of conditions of interest in one's setting. In the following section, we will outline a quantitative approach to using base rate information according to Bayes' theorem (Joseph et al., 1995) to refine probability estimates of a condition of interest. It can also be helpful to review several more general considerations about base rates, including atypical presentations, prevalence of specific diagnoses in a given setting, occurrence of low scores, and the nonspecific nature of certain symptoms. Regarding atypical presentations, it has been noted that clinicians tend to focus on atypical aspects of a particular case and to assign more weight to them than more common features leading to overestimates of the prevalence of rare disorders

Hypotheses	*Evidence for*	*Evidence against*
Primary		
Alternative 1		
Alternative 2		

Figure 2.1 Example diagnostic hypothesis worksheet.

and to overdiagnosis (Wedding & Faust, 1989). In medicine, a well-known aphorism captures the advice succinctly: When you hear hoof beats, think horses, not zebras (Dundes, 1999). Turning to condition base rates, it is to be expected that the frequency of certain presenting conditions and diagnoses will vary by clinic setting. For example, the base rate of cases with traumatic brain injury would be expected to be higher in a rehabilitation setting than in a memory disorders clinic. From a validity perspective, base rates also vary with lower estimates of invalidity in many clinical settings (Martin & Schroeder, 2020) compared with forensic settings (Larrabee et al., 2009a). The diagnostic tools used in decision-making should improve over the base rate, or else they are contributing more error to the process (Faust et al., 2021). Awareness of the frequency of low scores among normal populations is a useful safeguard against over-interpreting low scores produced by examinees. Heaton et al. (2004) found the median number of below-cutoff scores (<40 *T*) was 3 out of 25 tests and that only 13.2% of the normative sample produced no scores in that range. Other research has shown similar findings leading to recognition that the presence of below-cutoff scores is to be expected in healthy adult samples (Binder et al., 2009; Palmer et al., 1998; Schretlen et al., 2008). A final consideration related to base rates is that symptoms overlap between conditions ranging from depression to generalized anxiety and posttraumatic stress to what has been labeled post-concussion syndrome. Regarding the latter, the research has identified multiple clinical groups that report post-concussion symptoms including psychiatric and pain disorders, and the symptoms are not uncommon in healthy control groups (Dean et al., 2012; Gouvier et al., 1992; Gunstad & Suhr, 2001; Mittenberg et al., 1992).

A third method of improving decision-making is to use statistical decision rules and multivariable statistical decision methods. The advantage of statistical decision-making over clinical judgment was initially proposed by Meehl (1954), and numerous subsequent studies have confirmed it (Meehl, 1986). Consistent with what statistical method proponents have recommended, simple algorithms to interpret PVTs have demonstrated excellent classification accuracy with freestanding (Martin et al., 2020b) and embedded measures (Schroeder et al., 2012) and have performed much better than the chance-level predictions produced by clinical judgment alone (Heaton et al., 1978). One of the most straightforward and parsimonious approaches is the PVT failure tally model that simply aggregates the number of PVT scores outside of expectation across embedded and freestanding measures and considers two or more scores to be evidence of invalidity. Although used in a wide range of research studies (Bashem et al., 2014; Boone, 2021; Davis et al., 2012a, 2012b; Davis & Millis, 2014a; Miller et al., 2011; Sugarman & Axelrod, 2015; Wolfe et al., 2010), by practicing neuropsychologists (Martin et al., 2015), recommended by experts in performance validity (Schroeder et al., 2016), and supported by the most recent consensus statement on performance and symptom validity (Sweet et al., 2021), questions have arisen about the approach. Recognizing that the number of abnormal scores in a neuropsychological test battery increases with the size of the test battery, it is reasonable to wonder whether the number of PVT failures would also increase in relation to the number of PVTs administered. Several studies have explored this possibility in clinical and forensic samples and, to date, not much support for a strong relationship between the number of PVTs administered and PVTs failed has been found (Davis & Millis, 2014a, 2014b; Larrabee, 2014). Davis (2018) examined observed and predicted PVT failure rates in a sample of older adults and documented significant differences between observed and predicted rates in all sample subsets.

An important consideration when interpreting PVT failure in civil and criminal forensic contexts and in other situations involving external incentive is malingering. Although malingering is referenced in diagnostic classification systems, including the *Diagnostic and Statistical Manual of Mental Disorders* and International Classification of Diseases, the criteria used by many neuropsychologists were first introduced by Slick and colleagues (1999) and recently revised by Sherman and colleagues (2022). The need to update the criteria was noted to reflect several factors, including a substantial increase in validity assessment tools, recognition of the conceptual distinction between symptom and performance validity, and the importance of including consideration of malingered psychiatric and somatic symptoms in addition to cognitive deficits. The revised criteria also included "compelling inconsistencies" as a source of evidence regarding feigning or exaggeration. The phrase was originally proposed by Greve and colleagues to describe "the difference in the way a patient presents when being evaluated compared with when they are not aware of being evaluated is such that it is not reasonable to believe the patient is not purposely controlling the difference" (2005, p. 408). The Sherman et al. revised criteria define malingering as "the volitional feigning or exaggeration of neurocognitive, somatic, or psychiatric symptoms for the purpose of obtaining material gain and services or avoiding formal duty, responsibility, or undesirable outcome" (Sherman et al., 2022, p. 739). Malingering is indicated by four criteria: (a) presence of external incentive; (b) invalid presentation indicative of feigning or exaggeration; (c) marked discrepancies between obtained data and/or symptom report and other sources of evidence (e.g., expectations given the condition of interest, records, or collateral information); and (d) criterion B behaviors are not better accounted for by another condition (e.g., dementia, intellectual disability, or reduced functional independence due to severe cognitive impairment). The types of invalid presentations were categorized as neurocognitive, psychiatric, somatic, or mixed. A flow chart summarizing the revised malingered neuropsychological dysfunction criteria is shown in Figure 2.2.

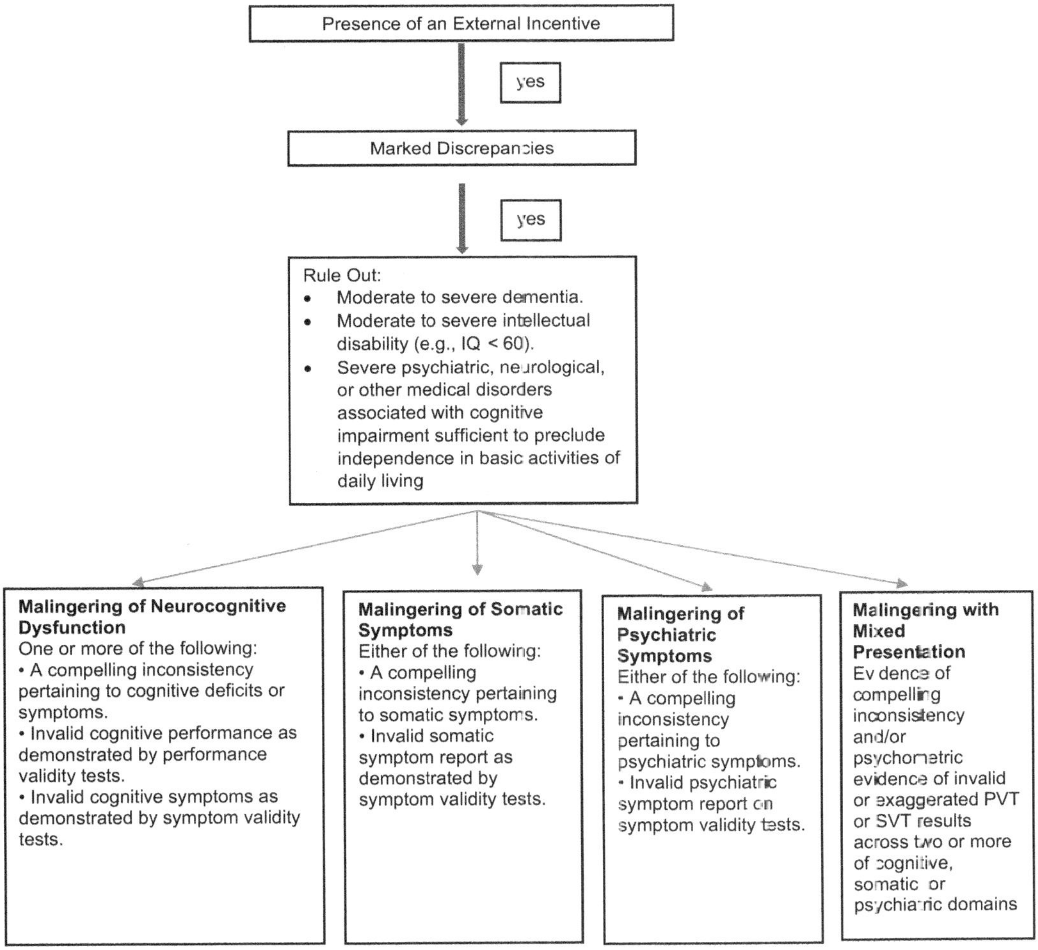

Figure 2.2 Decision-making diagram for diagnosing malingering of neuropsychological conditions according to revised criteria (Sherman et al., 2022).

Refining Diagnostic Hypotheses with Tests

> Testing is used in the process of hypothesis refinement to help formulate a working diagnostic hypothesis, defined previously as one that is sufficiently unambiguous to set the stage for making decisions about further invasive testing, treatment, or judgments about prognosis.
>
> (Kassirer & Kopelman, 1991, p. 17)

Given the limitations of clinical judgment, it should be reassuring that neuropsychologists now have access to a wide range of freestanding and embedded PVTs to use in the decision-making process. There remain several important considerations. First, as in the use of any test, whether of cognitive ability or psychological state, successful deployment of a PVT requires an understanding of the psychometric properties of the measure, evidence of the fit between the measure and the population of interest, and classification accuracy of the measure across different settings and disorders. Some of these characteristics of PVTs might vary or, in certain cases, even be unknown. Regarding freestanding PVTs, foundational psychometric properties like reliability, which is often established through a test–retest approach, can be challenging to demonstrate given the nature of the test.

Using the Test of Memory Malingering (TOMM; Tombaugh, 1996) as an example, cognitively normal adults produced nearly perfect scores on Trial 2 (M = 49.9, SD = 0.4) and Retention (M = 49.9, SD = 0.5), and perfect scores were shown on these trials by 92.9% to 95.8% of the normative sample (p. 11). Given the extent of range restriction observed in TOMM Trial 2 and Retention trial score in the normative sample, it can be expected that attempting to demonstrate reliability by calculating test–retest reliability coefficients would lead to underwhelming results not because of measurement error but due to the restricted range phenomenon. Examining the reliability of freestanding PVTs will likely require use of other methods, including split-half reliability. Split-half reliability has been shown to be useful in situations in which the construct under consideration is not stable and is expected to vary according to the state of the examinee (e.g., State-Trait Anxiety Inventory; Metzger, 1976; Spielberger et al., 1983).

Evidence for the state-like nature of examinee performances on ability measures can be observed anecdotally in response variability across the test battery (Boone, 2009) and can be inferred from underperformance strategies reportedly used by simulators feigning impairment, including targeted feigning on specific tests (Kanser et al., 2017). Additional anecdotal evidence is provided by the aforementioned study of Heaton and colleagues (1978) in which the reprimand of the technician led to normalized test performance in one case. Otherwise, empirical evidence demonstrating the state-like nature of invalid performance is more limited with only two studies directly addressing it, to our knowledge. In the first study, Suchy and colleagues (2012) found that 68% of examinees confronted by the examining neuropsychologist about invalid data performed in the valid range on a PVT that was re-administered following the confrontation. A recent randomized controlled trial, however, did not show any difference between confronted and non-confronted examinees in subsequent PVT and cognitive test performance (Roor et al., 2024). A potentially meaningful difference between studies is that Roor and colleagues used a technician to provide the statement about validity concerns rather than the consulting neuropsychologist. Perhaps future research might investigate the relative weight of the message (i.e., severe reprimand versus corrective statement) and the messenger (i.e., technician versus neuropsychologist).

A second important consideration is that the sensitivity and specificity of a test may vary across disorders. Continuing to focus on the TOMM, a recent meta-analysis found a range of sensitivity and specificity values across samples of different populations (Martin et al., 2020). Using the manual recommended cutoff for Trial 2, for example, showed perfect specificity in multiple simulation studies, weighted mean specificity of 0.97 in neurologic and psychiatric samples, and specificity of 0.70 in dementia samples. It is necessary that neuropsychologists know the operational characteristics of the PVTs and SVTs they routinely employ given examinee characteristics and the conditions commonly seen. Given the importance of minimizing false positive errors with validity measures (Sweet et al., 2021), it is vital to understand the groups and conditions at risk for increased false positive findings, including individuals requiring full-time nursing care (Meyers & Volbrecht, 2003) and persons with dementia (Dean et al., 2009), cognitive compromise that can sometimes appear within the context of severe schizophrenia (Gorissen et al., 2005; Ruiz et al., 2020), and a history of prolonged coma due to severe traumatic brain injury (Larrabee, 2003). Steps to mitigate the risk of increased false positives may include adjusting cutoffs (Dean et al., 2009; Loring et al., 2016) and using measures developed for specific populations (Chafetz, 2011).

Putting a Single Test to Work

As a starting point, we initially focus on employing a single test result, while acknowledging that neuropsychologists typically interpret dozens of test results, which will be addressed in the next section. To contextualize a positive test result adequately, one must consider multiple indices of diagnostic accuracy, including sensitivity, specificity, likelihood ratios, and the area under a receiver operating characteristic (ROC) curve. Let's start by examining the relationship between a diagnostic test introduced in the previous edition of this volume (i.e., the mythical Millis Effort Test; Millis, 2009) now in its second edition (Millis Davis Validity Measure; MD-Val) and a diagnosis (i.e., malingered neuropsychological dysfunction based on Sherman et al., 2022 criteria) using a 2 × 2 contingency table. Results for the 340 individuals in this hypothetical study are shown in Table 2.2.

Table 2.2 Diagnostic Efficiency Statistics for Hypothetical Validity Indicator

		Condition of interest		
		Present	Absent	
Test result	+	200 a (TP)	24 B (FP)	224 a – b
	–	16 c (FN)	100 d (TN)	116 c – d
		a + c 216	b + c 124	a + b + c + d 340
		Sensitivity (SEN)	a/(a + c)	93%
		Specificity (SPE)	d/(d + b)	81%
		Likelihood ratio +	SEN/(1 – SPE)	4.5
		Likelihood ratio –	(1 – SEN)/SPE	0.1

Note. Two-by-two contingency table for hypothetical validity indicator. TP = true positive; FP = false positive; FN = false negative; TN = true negative.

From the contingency table, one can generate measures of accuracy of the MD-Val in detecting malingering:

1 Sensitivity is the proportion of persons with the condition of interest who obtain a positive score on the diagnostic indicator (i.e., fail the test). That calculation goes as follows:
   a/(a + c) = 200/216 = 0.93, or 93%.
2 Specificity is the proportion of persons without the condition of interest who obtain a negative score on the diagnostic indicator (e.g., pass the test). That calculation goes:
   d/(b + d) = 100/124 = 0.81, or 81%.

It should be pointed out that positive predictive value (PPV or posterior probability) and prevalence were not calculated from data in the table because this was a case-control study. That is, "cases" were gathered, namely, patients meeting the Sherman et al. criteria for malingered neuropsychological dysfunction. Controls with unequivocal evidence of traumatic brain injury were then matched to cases. If PPV is to be accurately estimated from a case-control study, the prevalence of the disorder of interest must be a reasonable estimate in the population. In this contrived example, the prevalence of malingering was 64%, which may or may not be an accurate reflection of malingering prevalence in forensic neuropsychology practice, but is likely an overestimate in a clinical setting like an inpatient rehabilitation hospital. For this reason, we strongly encourage reporting a range of PPVs based on different prevalence rate estimates rather than presentation of a single PPV estimate.

An important next consideration in diagnostic accuracy values are likelihood ratios that combine sensitivity and specificity data into a single summary index given a positive or negative test result (Straus et al., 2006). The positive likelihood ratio is the percentage of people with the condition of interest who produce a positive test result (i.e., true positives or cell A in Table 2.2) divided by the percentage of people without the condition of interest who produce a positive test result (i.e., false positives or cell B in Table 2.2). The positive likelihood ratio formula is:

Logistic regression (LR)+ = Sensitivity/(1 − Specificity).

The positive likelihood ratio tells us how many times more likely persons with the condition of interest are to have a positive test result than persons without the condition of interest. The negative likelihood ratio is the percentage of people with the condition of interest who produce a negative test result (i.e., false negatives or cell C in Table 2.2) divided by the percentage of people without the condition of interest who produce a negative test result (i.e., true negatives or cell D in Table 2.2). The negative likelihood ratio tells us how many times less likely persons with the condition of interest are to have a negative test result than persons without the condition of interest. The negative likelihood ratio formula is:

LR− = (1 − Sensitivity)/Specificity.

Positive and negative likelihood ratios are useful because they support the interpretation of test findings using Bayes' theorem. Simply stated, Bayes' theorem indicates that the probability of a condition of interest being present can be determined by combining the initial probability of the condition being present (i.e., the base rate or prevalence in a specific clinical setting) with the findings of a diagnostic test. In terms of likelihood ratios, the pre-test odds (or base rate converted to odds) of the condition of interest are multiplied by the likelihood ratio from the observed test result (i.e., LR+ or LR– for a positive or negative test result, respectively) to obtain the post-test odds. Post-test odds can be converted to a probability to facilitate interpretation of the test result. Formulas important to these calculations include the conversion from odds to probability and the conversion from probability to odds stated, respectively, as:

Probability = Odds/(1 + Odds)
Odds = Probability/(1 – Probability).

To demonstrate, let's suppose that a 30-year-old man presents six months status—post uncomplicated mild traumatic brain injury with an initial Glasgow Coma Scale score of 15 and head CT in the emergency department that was negative for acute intracranial injury. When evaluated in an independent neuropsychological evaluation, the individual was known to be involved in personal injury litigation based on a claim of cognitive deficits subsequent to traumatic brain injury. In this context, it would be prudent to assume a higher probability of invalidity than in a clinical setting (Martin & Schroeder, 2020; Mittenberg et al., 2002). Based on empirical evidence documented in the professional literature (e.g., Larrabee et al., 2009b), the prior probability (or base rate) of an invalid profile would be estimated at 40%. Converting the prior probability to odds, we calculate the following equation: 0.4/(1 – 0.4) = 0.4/0.6 = 2/3 = 0.667. Let us assume that this examinee was administered the MD-Val and produced a positive test result or failed the PVT as such performances are commonly described. Given the hypothetical data shown in Table 2.2, a positive finding on the MD-Val is associated with a LR+ of 4.8. The base rate odds can be multiplied by the odds from the diagnostic test result to produce the post-test odds: 0.667 ×.8 = 3.2. Converting post-test odds to probability: 3.2/(1 + 3.2) = 3.2/4.2 = 0.76. Given the positive result on the MD-Val, the posterior probability of invalidity in this case is 76%; thus, it is clearly more probable than not that data are indeed invalid.

In terms of the effect on post-test probability, likelihood ratios can be considered small (2–5), moderate (5–10), and large (>10; Grimes & Schulz, 2005). Use of a nomogram (Figure 2.3) facilitates clinical use of likelihood ratios by eliminating the need for calculation of post-test probabilities.

A ruler placed on the estimated pre-test probability of the condition of interest (left column) and aligned with the likelihood ratio from the test (middle column) allows the post-test probability (right column) to be read from this line. For example, assuming pre-test probability (or base rate) of the condition of interest of 10% and a positive test result with a likelihood ratio of 10, placing a ruler on the pre-test probability and intercepting the likelihood ratio column at 10 demonstrates post-test probability of about 50%, which is a relatively large shift in diagnostic probability. The ruler approach can be seen to match the following calculations:

1 Convert probability to odds: P/(1 – P) = .1/(1 – 0.1) = 0.1/0.9 = 1/9 = 0.11.
2 Multiply pre-test odds by the likelihood ratio to produce post-test odds: 0.11 × 10 = 1.1.
3 Convert post-test odds to probability: O/(1 + O) = 1.1/(1 + 1.1) = 1.1/2.1 = 0.52, which is about 50% as indicated by the nomogram.

Multiple issues arise when using this approach to weigh diagnostic evidence, though. First, refining clinical judgment with likelihood ratios assumes the availability of reasonably accurate estimates of the prior probability of the condition of interest. Regardless of clinician

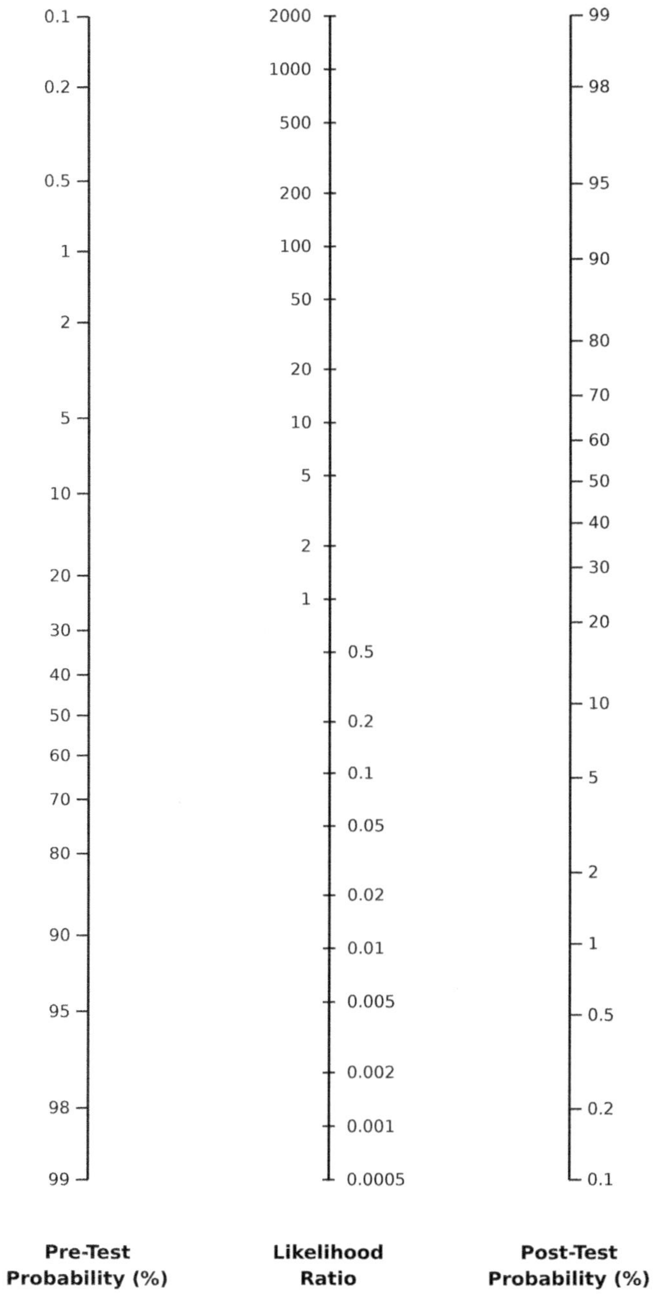

Figure 2.3 Nomogram for combining pre-test probability with likelihood ratio from diagnostic test to show post-test probability.

awareness, any system of diagnosis, whether quantitative or not, uses prevalence rates, and diagnostic accuracy varies according to the estimates or assumptions made about prevalence rates. When consideration is not given to the prior probability of a condition of interest, an implicit assumption is made that the prevalence is 50%, which is often not an accurate estimate. Therefore, the diagnostic value of the test result may be inflated. The quantitative system recommended in this chapter makes explicit the assumptions underlying decision-making processes. Second, the example in this section focused on a single test result for illustrative purposes. Neuropsychologists, however, rarely rely on a single, fixed diagnostic cutoff score for any test, and diagnostic decision-making occurs in different contexts. In a real-world setting, the relative costs of false positive and false negative errors are not constant across situations, which may necessitate adjustment of the cut score. Shifting the cutoff on a diagnostic test alters sensitivity and specificity in an inverse fashion: When sensitivity is increased, specificity decreases. To assist clinicians in diagnostic decision-making, journal editors and test publishers are strongly encouraged to publish the full range of cutoff scores and associated likelihood ratios. Related to the preceding point, diagnosis can be refined by considering that high sensitivity and high specificity serve different diagnostic purposes. Given a test cutoff with very high sensitivity, a negative test result rules out the diagnosis. Conversely, given a test cutoff with very high specificity, a positive test result rules in the diagnosis. A mnemonic for this observation popular in medical literature is SNOUT and SPIN. In other words, a test with high **s**e**n**sitivity, when **n**egative, rules **out** the condition of interest, and a test with high **sp**ecificity, when **p**ositive, rules **in** the condition of interest (Straus et al., 2006).

Although extremely useful in diagnostic decision-making, the likelihood ratio does have limitations as a single indicator of diagnostic accuracy. As its name suggests, it is a ratio of two random variables and, thus, it is difficult to estimate its standard error and sampling distribution (Zhou et al., 2002). This issue limits the utility of likelihood ratios as a means of comparing two or more diagnostic tests statistically to determine whether one test is superior to the other(s). The likelihood ratio remains important in defining the optimal decision thresholds but needs to be supplemented. A useful summary statistic in this regard is the area under the ROC curve, or AUC. The ROC curve is a graph of a test's sensitivity plotted on the *y*-axis versus its false positive rate (i.e., 1 – specificity) plotted on its *x*-axis. Each point on the graph is generated by a different cutoff score on the test. Each point can be connected, a curve can be generated, and the AUC can be estimated parametrically using maximum likelihood estimation or nonparametrically following the trapezoidal rule. Data from Davis and colleagues (2012b) were used to generate an ROC curve to evaluate an LR model to detect invalidity on the basis of Auditory Verbal Learning Test variables and in comparison with an ROC curve based on AVLT Recognition alone (Figure 2.4).

There are multiple ways of interpreting the ROC curve area (Zhou et al., 2002): (1) average sensitivity for all possible values of specificity, (2) average specificity for all possible values of sensitivity, and (3) the probability that a randomly selected examinee with the condition of interest disorder has a positive test result indicating greater suspicion than that of a randomly selected examinee without the condition of interest. AUC values can be statistically compared; Hosmer and Lemeshow (2000) offer guidelines for interpreting the magnitude of AUC:

a AUC = 0.50: No discrimination
b 0.70–0.80: Acceptable discrimination
c 0.80–0.90: Excellent discrimination
d ≥0.90: Outstanding discrimination.

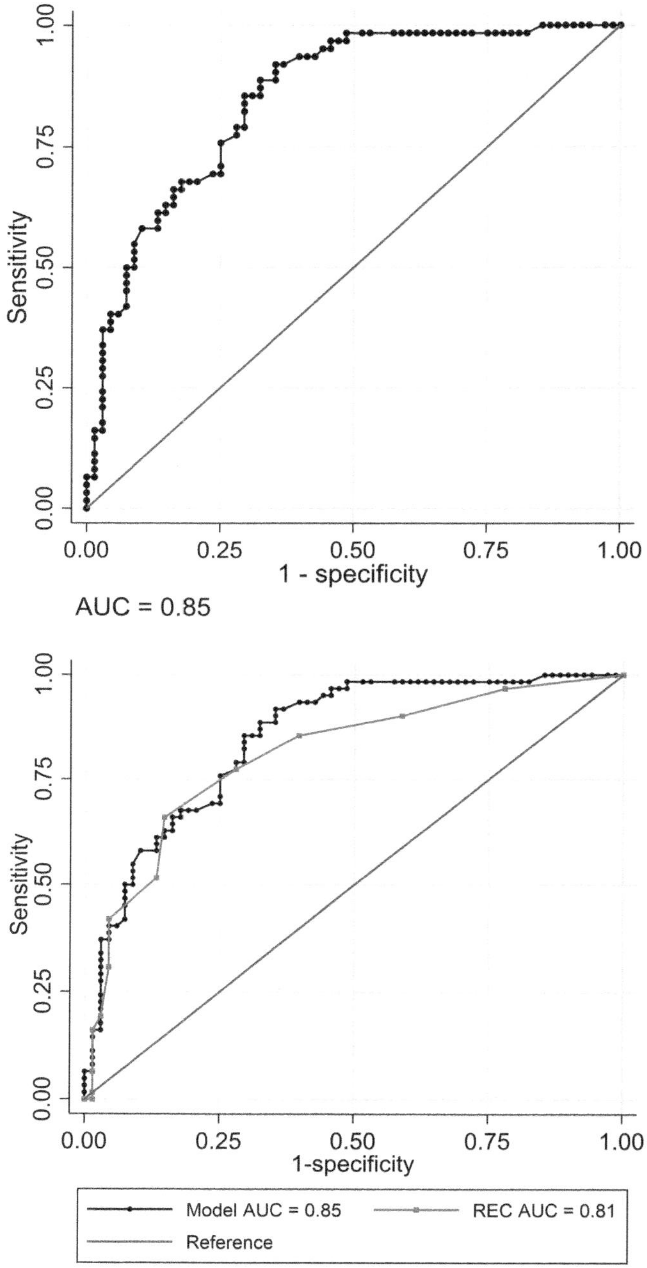

Figure 2.4 Receiver operating characteristic curves for AVLT logistic regression model (top) and for the model and recognition (REC) compared (bottom). AVLT = Auditory Verbal Learning Test.

Putting Multiple Tests to Work

As previously mentioned, neuropsychologists typically examine dozens of scores across a test battery. We now consider the multivariable context of combining the results from multiple validity indicators. Although the statistical and measurement issues are similar in combining cognitive tests and validity tests, the latter considerations introduce additional complications and raise several challenging questions: Are the validity indicators redundant or does each test provide incrementally useful information? Given an evaluation context with known incentive, should the neuropsychological consultant be more confident in diagnosing malingered neuropsychological dysfunction if the examinee fails five validity measures rather than one? Do all validity tests deserve equal weighting or do some scores count more than others?

With knowledge of the limits of clinical judgment and of human capacity for "weighting and computing" (Meehl, 1986, p. 372), it appears prudent to pursue statistical methods of combining information from multiple validity measures. One such approach that was commonly studied in the earlier days of validity research (e.g., Heaton et al., 1978) is discriminant function analysis (DFA). Although popular in more general social science research, DFA has multiple limitations that preclude its widespread use today, including strong statistical assumptions rarely met in clinical settings (e.g., multivariate normality and homogeneous variance–covariance matrices), interpretive challenges, and lack of inferential tests for individual predictors. Another statistical approach to combining information from multiple validity indicators that has been explored is chaining of likelihood ratios with the posterior probability from the first test being used as the prior probability for the next test. This method assumes that the tests are statistically independent. Although some data show limited associations among specific validity indicators (Davis et al., 2012a), as with the inter-correlations observed among other cognitive tests, PVTs are not always uncorrelated and, thus, violate the assumption of independence.

LR remains a promising method of combining multiple validity indicators into a composite that can be used to differentiate two groups. LR does not have the restrictive assumptions of DFA or require independence of predictors as in likelihood chaining. In LR, the relative importance of individual predictor variables can be readily determined, and the LR function can be used to calculate the probability that an individual belongs to one of the groups in the following manner. Analogous to ordinary least squares (OLS) multiple regression for continuous dependent variables, coefficients are derived for each predictor variable (or covariate) in LR. Rather than using OLS to fit the model and derive the coefficients, LR uses the maximum likelihood estimation to fit the model iteratively. Another difference between linear regression and logistic regression is the use of a logit link function to transform the linear model of predictors to a binary outcome. Once a model is derived, the resulting linear composite known as the logit (also known as the logged odds or linear predictor) can be calculated by multiplying the raw scores on each predictor variable by its respective coefficient (e.g., $\beta 1 \times 1 + \beta 2 \times 2$) and adding a constant. The logit is the log odds of group membership, so if it is exponentiated, it produces the odds of group membership. Converting from odds to probability the resulting model output yields the probability that an individual belongs to one of two groups based on raw scores entered into the formula. The link function in LR is the natural logarithm, so the exponentiation to convert from log odds to odds involves raising the base of the natural logarithm, *e*, to the value of the logit. To the sixth decimal place, the value of *e* is 2.718281.

In practice, the steps of exponentiating the logit and converting from odds to probability are often reported in the same step with values that can be entered into spreadsheet software (e.g., Miller et al., 2011; Sugarman & Axelrod, 2015). The formula for this conversion is:

$$\text{Probability} = \frac{e^{\alpha+\beta 1x1+\beta 2x2}}{1+e^{\alpha+\beta 1x1+\beta 2x2}}$$

To illustrate, let us consider an example from a LR model based on the Auditory Verbal Learning Test (AVLT; Lezak, 1983) reported by Davis and colleagues (2012b). The final LR model included AVLT raw scores on Total Learning (TL) and Recognition (REC) and resulted in the following equation for generating the linear combination of covariates:

Linear combination of covariates = 6.611 – (TL *.106) – (REC *.258)

Imagine results from one examinee, Mr. A, who produced a raw score of 50 on TL and a raw score of 14 on REC. Entering those values into the linear combination and the aforementioned equation for converting to probability results in:

$$\text{Probability A invalid} = \frac{e^{6.611-(50\times.106)-(14\times.258)}}{1+e^{6.611-(50\times.106)-(14\times.258)}} = \frac{e^{6.611-(5.3)-(3.612)}}{1+e^{6.611-(5.3)-(3.612)}} = \frac{e^{-2.301}}{1+e^{-2.301}} = \frac{0.100}{1.100} = .09$$

Now, imagine results from a second examinee, Ms. B, who produced a raw score of 15 on TL and a raw score of 8 on REC. Entering those values into the linear combination and the aforementioned equation for converting to probability results in:

$$\text{Probability B invalid} = \frac{e^{6.611-(15\times.106)-(8\times.258)}}{1+e^{6.611-(15\times.106)-(8\times.258)}} = \frac{e^{6.611-(1.59)-(2.064)}}{1+e^{6.611-(1.59)-(2.064)}} = \frac{e^{2.957}}{1+e^{2.597}} = \frac{19.24}{20.24} = .95$$

Given these results, the examiner might conclude a low probability of invalid AVLT performance for Mr. A and a high probability of invalid AVLT performance for Ms. B. As demonstrated in these hypothetical cases, the diagnostic utility of the LR regression model becomes immediately obvious: It helps to distance or even liberate us from rigid "all or nothing" thinking. Rather than yielding dichotomous categories of examinee performance (i.e., invalid or valid), the model produces a range of probabilities. A probability of invalidity of 51% may be quite different from a probability of 91%. In addition, LR models provide the option of raising or lowering the probability threshold given the diagnostic context and the relative costs of false positive versus false negative errors.

Advantages and Disadvantages of Multivariable Models

Multivariable validity composites may be more resistant to coaching, especially when based on standard neuropsychological tests. For example, people can be taught to readily identify digit recognition or computer-administered forced-choice recognition memory PVTs, but they may experience greater difficulty spotting validity-based multivariable indicators derived from memory tests or different cognitive measures in the same domain. Given that complex behavior and variable reasons might contribute to invalidity, multivariable composites will likely measure the behaviors more effectively than single tests. In addition to the capacity to produce probability statements, LR models can assist in determining the tests or variables that produce incremental power in differentiating groups and estimate optimal weights for the tests. One downside to LR is that one needs to have sufficiently large samples to fit the models, generally 10–20 cases per variable. For binary LR, the sample estimate is based on the size of the smaller of the two groups—not the total sample (Harrell, 2001).

In the previous edition of this volume, Millis (2009) observed that neuropsychologists had relatively few cross-validated multivariable composite validity indicators except for those derived from the California Verbal Learning Test (CVLT; Ashendorf, O'Bryant, & McCaffrey, 2003; Coleman et al., 1998; Demakis, 2004; Millis et al., 1995; Slick et al., 2000; Sweet et al., 2000). He noted that the ongoing attention to derive single embedded and freestanding PVTs appeared shortsighted and recommended that additional effort be directed toward derivation and cross-validation of multivariable validity indicators using LR. In the interim, multivariable validity indicators have been developed for additional memory tests, including the second edition of the CVLT (Wolfe et al., 2010; Whiteside et al., 2015a), the AVLT (Davis et al., 2012b), and combinations of variables across different memory measures (Schutte et al., 2011) with preliminary work on the third edition of the CVLT focused on single embedded indicators (Donders & Vos, 2023; Martin et al., 2023). The AVLT model has been cross-validated (Loring et al., 2016; Poreh et al., 2017), but cross-validation remains a need for other multivariable memory indicators. Miller and colleagues (2011) and Bashem and colleagues (2014) examined combinations of freestanding and embedded PVTs. Language measures have also been the focus of efforts to derive multivariable validity indicators (Sugarman & Axelrod, 2015; Whiteside et al., 2015b) but cross-validation of these models has yet to be conducted. Other work has explored the benefits of considering response time in addition to standard scoring on freestanding PVTs (Erdodi et al., 2017; Kanser et al., 2019; Patrick et al., 2021). While the growth in multivariable models is promising, additional work remains to be done in cross-validating the models that have only been studied in one sample. An additional promising area for further development is creation of embedded multivariable models that might be deployed by a large number of providers across different settings. Although variability across test batteries has likely been a limiting factor to such a development, it is reasonable to imagine proposing a model based on the most promising embedded PVTs across several domains. With a sufficiently large sample, the derivation and cross-validation analyses could be conducted using randomized sample subsets.

Addressing Causation

To this point, our focus has been on the role of clinical judgment and test results in diagnostic decision-making. The question of causation closely follows diagnosis. If neuropsychological dysfunction is identified, what is the likely cause? Although test results and classification statistics may be of assistance, alone they are insufficient to answer the question of causation. Sir Austin Bradford Hill proposed a set of criteria (Table 2.3) designed to establish an argument of causation related to toxins, which can be applied to causation more generally (Grimes & Schulz, 2002).

Of the criteria, temporal sequence and experimental evidence provide the strongest support for cause–effect relations, but it is recognized that experimental evidence from randomized controlled trials is rare in the diagnostic arena. On the other hand, data on dose–response relationships, strength of association, and consistency of association are often available and can provide "intermediate" support for causation. For example, a dose–response relationship has been identified in traumatic brain injury with greater cognitive impairment following increased severity of injury (Rohling et al., 2003).

Table 2.3 Hill Criteria for Causation

Criterion	*Question*	*Comment*
Temporal sequence	Did the event, accident, or exposure precede the outcome?	If A is causing B, then A should necessarily occur prior to B. Recall bias may preclude accurate recollection of historical data. Longer intervals make interpretation more difficult. Outcome may be multi-determined
Strength of the association	How strong is the effect?	If A causes B, A and B can be shown to be associated with each other. This is a necessary but not sufficient condition for establishing causation
Coherence with existing knowledge	Is the postulated causal relationship consistent with what is already known about the condition or disorder?	A new discovery will not have a track record. Others could have been consistently wrong
Specificity of association	Does the event, injury, or exposure result in only one outcome?	Multiple disorders produce the same
Dose–response relationship or biological gradient	Does a higher exposure result in more of the outcome? Or is increased injury severity associated with greater impairment?	May be difficult to observe in all disorders
Biological plausibility	Does the association make neuropsychological, biological, and/or physiological sense?	Assumes that our current scientific model is correct and complete
Consistency of association	Is the association consistent with all of the available evidence?	If A causes B, then evidence supporting this relationship will be found consistently
Analogous evidence	Is the association similar to others?	If some condition similar to A causes an outcome similar to B, then this is evidence that A causes B
Experimental evidence	Has a randomized, controlled trial been performed?	It is not always possible to conduct controlled trials

Statistical and Methodological Controversies

Any discussion of PVTs however focused, would be incomplete without mentioning the various controversies that have arisen as the scientific foundation and methods of applying validity instruments in forensic and clinical settings have evolved. It is beyond the scope of this chapter to review the complete history of controversial topics related to PVTs, but consideration of the broader literature reveals at least two categories into which these controversies can be placed. One type of controversy appears to be a necessary by-product of adherence to the scientific method. The process of closely scrutinizing propositions and testing hypotheses is inherently competitive with the winning idea or method determined objectively by accumulating empirical evidence. A second type of controversy, which we label *flash pan* controversy, might initially appear to be as deeply rooted in the scientific method as those in the first category, but over time is found to have a relatively briefer span of relevance with limited evidence of enduring contribution to knowledge development.

To provide an example of the first type of controversy—the healthy debate or vigorous testing of competing hypotheses—we reflect on the possibility that progress in the science of PVTs over the last 40 years or so may have occurred in part in response to criticism aimed at the scientific basis (or lack thereof) of expert (neuro)psychological testimony provided in the 1980s and early 1990s. Faust and Ziskin (1988) bluntly summarized their position on the matter: "We began by asking whether expert witnesses achieve reasonable certainty and aid the trier of fact. The scientific evidence clearly suggests that clinicians fail to satisfy either legal standard for expertise" (1988, p. 34). A response was mustered by Putnam and colleagues (1992) that agreement among independent neuropsychological experts "should provide some reassurance to those concerned persons who purport that neuropsychological assessment and clinical prediction are fatally flawed enterprises having no place in the courts of law" (1992, p. 316). In response, Faust (1994) posed a question: "Suppose I have my palm examined independently by two readers who both agree I will live a long life. Would Putnam et al. object if I were then to claim this should offer some reassurance to those who doubt palm readers?" (p. 3). Without taking a position on the historical debate and with the benefit of retrospection, we consider the subsequent explosion of PVT research literature (Martin et al., 2015; Suchy, 2019) and exponential growth in the use of neuropsychological experts (Kaufman, 2016; Kaufman & Greiffenstein, 2013) as evidence that the field has successfully differentiated itself from palm readers in the forensic arena. The question remains as to whether we would have reached a similar position without the criticism and debate related to forensic consultation. It appears, in this case, that healthy debate led to progress.

Turning to the second category of controversial topics related to PVTs—the flash pan controversies—these matters rapidly garner widespread attention and then fade from relevance without leading to substantive change in the field. They may initially appear threatening either to the practice of forensic neuropsychology or to the scientific basis of PVTs. After a period of intense discussion on organizational email discussion boards, there may be a flurry of activity from conference presentations to publications that, as in the first category of controversies, outline different positions, present evidence, and pose points and counterpoints. The key distinction, however, is that the salience of this class of controversy fades without contributing to substantial improvement in the field. As one example, in the early 2000s, there was a flare-up of controversy about the optimal forensic neuropsychological test battery with published opinion that use of anything other than a fixed battery (e.g., Halstead–Reitan Neuropsychological Test Battery; Reitan & Wolson, 1993) would be deemed inadmissible (Russell, 2007). Although aspects of the controversy lingered to the point of being deemed a myth of forensic neuropsychology (Greiffenstein, 2009), the question of a fixed versus flexible battery dwindled in consequence. Ultimately, the issue was rendered moot, not because of the preponderance of evidence on one side or the other, but simply because neuropsychologists stopped using fixed test batteries. After Sweet and colleagues (2015) documented a 25-year downward trend in the use of a fixed battery, the most recent version of the AACN salary survey no longer contained an item related to test battery (Sweet et al., 2020).

A recent series of publications (Leonhard, 2023a, 2023b, 2023c) is causing a current controversy that, with time, will likely prove to be among the ranks of the flash pan controversies. There is insufficient space to address thoroughly the numerous issues raised in these publications, but other efforts completed (Faust, 2023) and in progress (Kanser et al., 2025) will continue to provide counterpoint on the matter. We highlight several problematic aspects of the arguments Leonhard raised in his first paper (2023a) focused on statistical issues and methodology. A fundamental flaw that undermines many of the propositions forwarded in his commentary is the inaccurate conflation of a positive finding on a PVT with a determination of malingering. Leonhard relies on the 1940s era conceptualization of PVTs with terminology reminiscent of the "malingering key" of Goldstein (1940) and references to the body of PVT publications as the "malingering literature" (Leonhard, 2023a, p. 584). Although findings from one or more PVTs may be data incorporated into a determination of malingering, by definition, that determination cannot be made on the basis of a test score alone, because the test score alone does not reflect the necessary contextual factors. Furthermore, while theoretical and research literature on the topic of malingering is accurately labeled *malingering literature*, it is misleading to refer to the entirety of the performance and symptom validity literature in this manner.

A second fundamental error in the assertions made by Leonhard (2023a) is that PVTs are so strongly associated as to be collinear leading to the conclusion that "all 18 validity tests are slightly different versions the same test" (p. 600). Disregarding questionable psychometric support for his use of tetrachoric correlations (see Islam & Rizwan, 2021; StataCorp, 2023) in the interest of time, this claim can be examined from several simpler perspectives and found wanting. As a starting point, any clinical neuropsychologist who has practiced for more than a couple of years has likely observed the wide range of responses shown by examinees who perform invalidly, which was cogently noted by Boone (2009) to be the rationale for expanding the PVT armamentarium. Invalidly performing examinees do not complete tests in the same manner, and the substantial variability in the measures on which underperformance is shown could not be captured if PVTs were "slightly different versions of the same test" (Leonhard, 2023a, p. 600). Leonhard extends this fallacious line of reasoning stating "suffice it to say that many PVTs, such as the TOMM, RDS, MVST, PDRT, WMT, or Rey 15-Item Test ... are close variants of a prototypical theme where, upon having been serially presented with simple stimuli, examinees are challenged with recognition trials, free recall trials, or both" (2023a, p. 595). Although PVTs that rely on a two-choice, forced alternative recognition memory format are methodologically similar, the claim that such measures (e.g., TOMM, MSVT, WMT, and PDRT) are close variants of RDS belies either gross ignorance or intentional misrepresentation of the nature of the PVTs under question. Later in the same paragraph, Leonhard claims that Finger Tapping "may be redundant with memory tests" (2023a, p. 595). Perplexing statements like these undermine confidence in the commentary as a whole. Would you purchase a map from a cartographer whose sales pitch referenced the flat nature of the earth? Even if we set aside the evident limitations in Leonhard's knowledge of PVTs and his apparent lack of experience in implementing PVTs, a separate problem with his recommendation to reduce the number of PVTs used to eliminate information redundancy is that strong associations among variables are not necessarily evidence of information redundancy. Examining data used in the previously mentioned work of Davis et al. (2012b), we explore the Leonhard redundancy standard with several commonly used neuropsychological measures. Trail Making Test A and B showed a robust relationship ($r = 0.62$, $p < 0.0001$). Even stronger associations were observed between dominant and nondominant hand raw scores on Finger Tapping ($r = 0.87$, $p < 0.0001$) and Grooved Pegboard ($r = 0.83$, $p < 0.0001$). It appears that memory measures are also vulnerable: Auditory Verbal Learning Test TL and Delayed Recall trials were moderately correlated ($r = 0.76$, $p < 0.0001$), and Rey Complex Figure Test Immediate and Delayed Recall trials showed an even stronger association ($r = 0.92$. $p < 0.0001$). Applying Leonhard's logic, should we use either TMT-A or TMT-B, administer Finger Tapping and Grooved Pegboard to only one hand, and forego use of delayed recall trials on memory measures since they are "redundant" with immediate recall trials? The answer is a clear and emphatic, "No!" Should we alter the evidence-based practice of clinical neuropsychology, including use of PVTs in clinical and forensic contexts in response to the most recent flash pan controversy? No. Should we continue to advance the science of clinical neuropsychology by focusing on issues raised in healthy debate while recognizing that flash pan controversies will come and go? Yes.

Epilogue

From Millis (2009):

> [Over three] decades ago, Chuck Matthews (1990) voiced concerns about what he characterized as the "malignant bloom nourished by the head injury industry" and neuropsychology's role in it, which, he predicted, "will end badly" (p. 333). At that time, there was a proliferation of for-profit head injury rehabilitation facilities that employed large numbers of neuropsychologists. Growth seemed unlimited. Whether fueled by naïveté, greed, or both, this was also a time when every head injury, regardless of severity or plausibility, seemed to get the label of permanent brain damage, typically buttressed by neuropsychological "data." But this irrational exuberance could not go on forever Although many rehabilitation facilities provided much-needed treatment for their clients, some of these centers were nothing more than head injury charm schools that were designed to benefit treatment providers, plaintiff attorneys, and, occasionally, the litigating patient. Eventually, Medicare fraud, insurance audits, tort reform, and changes in insurance coverage caused a shakeout in the industry. During this period of change, the pendulum was also beginning to swing in the other direction in terms of how clinicians understood mild head injury and its natural course of recovery. Good experimental design was largely responsible for the conceptual shift, but effort measures alerted neuropsychologists to other diagnostic possibilities. Early in its inception, clinical neuropsychology's seminal contribution to science was the demonstration of the association between brain dysfunction and performance on behavioral tests. When its later development is viewed retrospectively, neuropsychology's finding that "effort matters" is likely to be judged as of equal importance. Some would also argue that this latter development helped to prevent events from ending badly for neuropsychology.

References

Arkes, H. R. (1981). Impediments to accurate clinical judgment and possible ways to minimize their impact. *Journal of Consulting and Clinical Psychology*, *49*(3), 323.

Ashendorf, L., O'Bryant, S. E., & McCaffrey, R. J. (2003). Specificity of malingering detection strategies in older adults using the CVLT and WCST. *The Clinical Neuropsychologist*, *17*(2), 255–262.

Bashem, J. R., Rapport, L. J., Miller, J. B., Hanks, R. A., Axelrod, B. N., & Millis, S. R. (2014). Comparisons of five performance validity indices in bona fide and simulated traumatic brain injury. *The Clinical Neuropsychologist*, *28*(5), 851–875. https://doi.org/10.1080/13854046.2014.927927

Benton, A. L. (1945). Rorschach performances of suspected malingerers. *The Journal of Abnormal and Social Psychology*, *40*(1), 94.

Bhuanantanondh, P., Nanta, P., & Mekhora, K. (2018). Determining sincerity of effort based on grip strength test in three wrist positions. *Safety and Health at Work*, *9*(1), 59–62. https://doi.org/10.1016/j.shaw.2017.06.001

Bianchini, K. J., Mathias, C. W., & Greve, K. W. (2001). Symptom validity testing: A critical review. *The Clinical Neuropsychologist*, *15*(1), 19–45. https://doi.org/10.1076/clin.15.1.19.1907

Bianchini, K. J., Greve, K. W., & Glynn, G. (2005). On the diagnosis of malingered pain-related disability: Lessons from cognitive malingering research. *The Spine Journal*, *5*(4), 404–417.
Bigler, E. D., Kaufmann, P. M., & Larrabee, G. J. (2010, February). Admissibility and appropriate use of symptom validity science in forensic consulting. *Talk presented at the 38th Annual Meeting of the International Neuropsychological Society*, Acapulco, Mexico.
Binder, L. M., Iverson, G. L., & Brooks, B. L. (2009). To err is human: "Abnormal" neuropsychological scores and variability are common in healthy adults. *Archives of Clinical Neuropsychology*, *24*(1), 31–46. https://doi.org/10.1093/arclin/acn001
Boone, K. B. (2006). *Assessment of feigned cognitive impairment: A neuropsychological perspective*. Guilford Press.
Boone, K. B. (2009). The need for continuous and comprehensive sampling of effort/response bias during neuropsychological examinations. *The Clinical Neuropsychologist*, *23*(4), 729–741.
Boone, K. B. (2021). *Assessment of feigned cognitive impairment: A neuropsychological perspective* (2nd ed.). Guilford Press.
Bowes, S. M., Ammirati, R. J., Costello, T. H., Basterfield, C., & Lilienfeld, S. O. (2020). Cognitive biases, heuristics, and logical fallacies in clinical practice: A brief field guide for practicing clinicians and supervisors. *Professional Psychology: Research and Practice*, *51*(5), 435.
Bush, S. S., Ruff, R. M., Troster, A., Barth, J., Koffler, S. P., Pliskin, N. H., & Silver, C. H. (2005). NAN position paper: Symptom validity assessment: Practice issues and medical necessity. *Archives of Clinical Neuropsychology*, *20*(4), 419–426.
Chafetz, M. (2011). Reducing the probability of false positives in malingering detection of social security disability claimants. *The Clinical Neuropsychologist*, *25*(7), 1239–1252.
Chapman, L. J., & Chapman, J. P. (1969). Illusory correlation as an obstacle to the use of valid psychodiagnostic signs. *Journal of Abnormal Psychology, 74, 217–280.*
Coleman, R. D., Rapport, L. J., Millis, S. R., Ricker, J. H., & Farchione, T. J. (1998). Effects of coaching on detection of malingering on the California Verbal Learning Test. *Journal of Clinical and Experimental Neuropsychology*, *20*(2), 201–210.
Connor, H. (2006). The use of anaesthesia to diagnose malingering in the 19th century. *Journal of the Royal Society of Medicine*, *99*(9), 444–447. https://doi.org/10.1177/014107680609900914
Dahlstrom, W. G. (1993). Tests: Small samples, large consequences. *American Psychologist*, *48*(4), 393–399. https://doi.org/10.1037/0003-066X.48.4.393
Dandachi-FitzGerald, B., Merckelbach, H., & Ponds, R. W. (2017). Neuropsychologists' ability to predict distorted symptom presentation. *Journal of Clinical and Experimental Neuropsychology*, *39*(3), 257–264. https://doi.org/10.1080/13803395.2016.1223278
Davis, J. J. (2018). Performance validity in older adults: Observed versus predicted false positive rates in relation to number of tests administered. *Journal of Clinical and Experimental Neuropsychology*, *40*(10), 1013–1021.
Davis, J. J., McHugh, T. S., Axelrod, B. N., & Hanks, R. A. (2012a). Performance validity and neuropsychological outcomes in litigants and disability claimants. *The Clinical Neuropsychologist*, *26*(5), 850–865. https://doi.org/10.1080/13854046.2012.686631
Davis, J. J., & Millis, S. R. (2014a). Reply to commentary by Bilder, Sugar, and Helleman (2014 this issue) on minimizing false positive error with multiple performance validity tests. *The Clinical Neuropsychologist*, *28*(8), 1224–1229.
Davis, J. J., & Millis, S. R. (2014b). Examination of performance validity test failure in relation to number of tests administered. *The Clinical Neuropsychologist*, *28*(2), 199–214.
Davis, J. J., Millis, S. R., & Axelrod, B. N. (2012b). Derivation of an embedded Rey Auditory Verbal Learning Test performance validity indicator. *The Clinical Neuropsychologist*, *26*(8), 1397–1408. https://doi.org/10.1080/13854046.2012.728627
Davis, J. J., & Wall, J. R. (2014). Examining verbal memory on the Word Memory Test and California verbal learning test. *Archives of Clinical Neuropsychology*, *29*(8), 747–753.
Dawes, R. M., Faust, D., & Meehl, P. E. (1989). Clinical versus actuarial judgment. *Science*, *243*(4899), 1668–1674.

Dean, P. J., O'Neill, D., & Sterr, A. (2012). Post-concussion syndrome: Prevalence after mild traumatic brain injury in comparison with a sample without head injury. *Brain Injury*, *26*, 14–26.
Dean, A. C., Victor, T. L., Boone, K. B., Philpott, L. M., & Hess, R. A. (2009). Dementia and effort test performance. *The Clinical Neuropsychologist*, *23*(1), 133–152.
Demakis, G. J. (2004). Application of clinically derived malingering cutoffs on the CVLT and the WAIS-R to an analog malingering study. *Applied Neuropsychology*, *11*, 220–226.
Donders, J., & Vos, M. (2023). Utility of CVLT-3 response bias as a measure of performance validity after traumatic brain injury. *The Clinical Neuropsychologist*, *37*(1), 91–100. https://doi.org/10.1080/13854046.2022.2051152
Dundes, A. (Ed.). (1999). *International folkloristics: Classic contributions by the founders of folklore.* Bloomsbury Publishing PLC.
Edwards, W. (1968). Conservatism in human information processing. In B. Kleinmutz (Ed.), *Formal representation of human judgment* (pp. 17–52). Wiley.
Erdodi, L. A., Tyson, B. T., Shahein, A. G., Lichtenstein, J. D., Abeare, C. A., Pelletier, C. L., Zuccato, B. G., Kucharski, B., & Roth, R. M. (2017). The power of timing: Adding a time-to-completion cutoff to the Word Choice Test and Recognition Memory Test improves classification accuracy. *Journal of Clinical and Experimental Neuropsychology*, *39*(4), 369–383. https://doi.org/10.1080/13803395.2016.1230181
Ely, J. W., Graber, M. L., & Croskerry, P. (2011). Checklists to reduce diagnostic errors. *Academic Medicine*, *86*(3), 307–313. https://doi.org/10.1097/ACM.0b013e31820824cd
Faust, D. (1986). Research on human judgment and its application to clinical practice. *Professional Psychology: Research and Practice*, *17*, 420–430. https://doi.org/10.1037/0735-7028.17.5.420
Faust, D. (1994). Comment on Putnam, Adams, and Schneider, "One-day test-retest reliability of neuropsychological tests in a personal injury case. *Psychological Assessment*, *6*, 3–4.
Faust, D. (2023). Invited Commentary: Advancing but not yet advanced: Assessment of effort/malingering in forensic and clinical settings. *Neuropsychology Review*, *33*(3), 628–642.
Faust, D. F., Gaudet, C. E., Ahern, D. C., & Bridges, A. J. (2021). Assessment of malingering and falsification: Continuing to push the boundaries of knowledge in research and clinical practice. In A. M. Horton & C. R. Reynolds (Eds.), *Detection of malingering during head injury litigation* (pp. 1–156). Springer.
Faust, D., Hart, K., & Guilmette, T. J. (1988a). Pediatric malingering: The capacity of children to fake believable deficits on neuropsychological testing. *Journal of Consulting and Clinical Psychology*, *56*, 578–582. https://doi.org/10.1037/0022-006X.56.4.578
Faust, D., Hart, K., Guilmette, T. J., & Arkes, H. R. (1988b). Neuropsychologists' capacity to detect adolescent malingerers. *Professional Psychology: Research and Practice*, *19*, 508–515. https://doi.org/10.1037/0735-7028.19.5.508
Faust, D., & Ziskin, J. (1988). The expert witness in psychology and psychiatry. *Science*, *241*(4861), 31–35.
Garb, H. N., & Schramke, C. J. (1996). Judgment research and neuropsychological assessment: A narrative review and meta-analyses. *Psychological Bulletin*, *120*, 140–153. https://doi.org/10.1037/0033-2909.120.1.140
Goldstein, H. (1945). A malingering key for mental tests. *Psychological Bulletin*, *42*(2), 104–118. https://doi-org.libproxy.uthscsa.edu/10.1037/h0056446
Goldstein, M. A. (1940). Speech without a tongue. *Journal of Speech Disorders*, *5*(1), 65–69.
Grouse, L. (2016). Post hoc ergo propter hoc. *Journal of Thoracic Disease*, *8*(7), E511–E512. https://doi.org/10.21037/jtd.2016.04.49
Gorissen, M., Sanz, J. C., & Schmand, B. (2005). Effort and cognition in schizophrenia patients. *Schizophrenia Research*, *78*(2–3), 199–208.
Gouvier, W. D., Cubic, B., Jones, G., Brantley, P., & Cutlip, Q. (1992). Postconcussion symptoms and daily stress in normal and head injured college populations. *Archives of Clinical Neuropsychology*, *7*, 193–211.

Greiffenstein, M. F. (2009). Clinical myths of forensic neuropsychology. *The Clinical Neuropsychologist*, *23*(2), 286–296.

Grimes, D. A., & Schulz, K. F. (2002). Bias and causal associations in observational research. *The Lancet*, *359*(9302), 248–252.

Grosz, H. J., & Zimmerman, J. (1965). Experimental analysis of hysterical blindness: A follow-up report and new experimental data. *Archives of General Psychiatry*, *13*(3), 255–260.

Grove, W. M., Zald, D. H., Lebow, B. S., Snitz, B. E., & Nelson, C. (2000). Clinical versus mechanical prediction: A meta-analysis. *Psychological Assessment*, *12*(1), 19.

Guilmette, T. J., Whelihan, W., Sparadeo, F. R., & Buongiorno, G. (1994). Validity of neuropsychological test results in disability evaluations. *Perceptual and Motor Skills*, *78*(3, Pt 2), 1179–1186. https://doi-org.libproxy.uthscsa.edu/10.2466/pms.1994.78.3c.1179

Gunstad, J., & Suhr, J. A. (2001). "Expectation as etiology" versus "the good old days": Postconcussion syndrome symptom reporting in athletes, headache sufferers, and depressed individuals. *Journal of the International Neuropsychological Society*, *7*, 323–333.

Hall, R. C., & Hall, R. C. (2012). Compensation neurosis: A too quickly forgotten concept?. *The Journal of the American Academy of Psychiatry and the Law*, *40*(3), 390–398.

Harrell, F. E. (2001). *Regression modeling strategies: with applications to linear models, logistic regression, and survival analysis* (Vol. 608). Springer.

Heaton, R., Miller, S., Taylor, M., & Grant, I. (2004). *Revised comprehensive norms for an expanded Halstead-Reitan Battery: Demographically adjusted neuropsychological norms for African-American and Caucasian adults*. Psychological Assessment Resources, Inc.

Heaton, R. K., Smith, H. H., Lehman, R. A., & Vogt, A. T. (1978). Prospects for faking believable deficits on neuropsychological testing. *Journal of Consulting and Clinical Psychology*, *46*(5), 892.

Heilbronner, R. L., Sweet, J. J., Morgan, J. E., Larrabee, G. J., Millis, S. R., & Conference Participants 1. (2009). American Academy of Clinical Neuropsychology Consensus Conference Statement on the neuropsychological assessment of effort, response bias, and malingering. *The Clinical Neuropsychologist*, *23*(7), 1093–1129.

Heinly, M. T., Greve, K. W., Bianchini, K. J., Love, J. M., & Brennan, A. (2005). WAIS digit span-based indicators of malingered neurocognitive dysfunction: Classification accuracy in traumatic brain injury. *Assessment*, *12*(4), 429–444.

Heubrock, D., & Petermann, F. (1998). Neuropsychological assessment of suspected malingering: Research results, evaluation techniques, and further directions of research and application. *European Journal of Psychological Assessment*, *14*(3), 211–225.

Hosmer, D. W., & Lemeshow, S. (2000). *Applied logistic regression* (2nd ed.). John Wiley & Sons. DOI:10.1002/0471722146

Hunt, W. A., & Older, H. J. (1943). Detection of malingering through psychometric tests. *United States Naval Medical Bulletin*, *41*, 1318–1323.

Islam, T., & Rizwan, M. (2021). *Comparison of correlation measures for nominal data*. Presented in Communications in Statistics: Simulation and Computation.

Joseph, L., Gyorkos, T. W., & Coupal, L. (1995). Bayesian estimation of disease prevalence and the parameters of diagnostic tests in the absence of a gold standard. *American Journal of Epidemiology*, *141*(3), 263–272.

Kanser, R. J., Rapport, L. J., Bashem, J. R., Billings, N. M., Hanks, R. A., Axelrod, B. N., & Miller, J. B. (2017). Strategies of successful and unsuccessful simulators coached to feign traumatic brain injury. *The Clinical Neuropsychologist*, *31*(3), 644–653. https://doi.org/10.1080/13854046.2016.1278040

Kanser, R. J., Rapport, L. J., Bashem, J. R., & Hanks, R. A. (2019). Detecting malingering in traumatic brain injury: Combining response time with performance validity test accuracy. *The Clinical Neuropsychologist*, *33*(1), 90–107. https://doi.org/10.1080/13854046.2018.1440006

Kanser, R. J., Rohling, M. L., & Davis, J. J. (2025). Determining whether false positive rates increase with performance validity test battery expansion. *The Clinical Neuropsychologist*, *39*(6), 1546–1558.

Kassirer, J., & Koppelman, R. (1991). *Learning clinical reasoning*. Lippincott, Williams, & Wilkins.

Kaufmann, P. (2016). Neuropsychologist experts and civil capacity evaluations: Representative cases, *Archives of Clinical Neuropsychology*, *31*(6), 487–494. https://doi.org/10.1093/arclin/acw053

Kaufmann, P. M., & Greiffenstein, M. F. (2013). Forensic neuropsychology: Training, scope of practice, and quality control. *NAN Bulletin*, *27*(1), 11–15. https://www.nanonline.org/docs/ResearchandPublications/NANBulletin/Spring%202013%20Bulletin.pdf.

Larrabee, G. J. (2003). Detection of malingering using atypical performance patterns on standard neuropsychological tests. The Clinical Neuropsychologist, *17*(3), 410–425.

Larrabee, G. J. (2012). Performance validity and symptom validity in neuropsychological assessment. *Journal of the International Neuropsychological Society*, *18*(4), 625–630.

Larrabee, G. J. (2014). False-positive rates associated with the use of multiple performance and symptom validity tests. *Archives of Clinical Neuropsychology*, *29*(4), 364–373.

Larrabee, G. J., Millis, S. R., & Meyers, J. E. (2009a). 40 plus or minus 10, a new magical number: Reply to Russell. *The Clinical Neuropsychologist*, *5*, 841–849.

Larrabee, G. J., Millis, S. R., & Meyers, J. E. (2009b). 40 plus or minus 10, a new magical number: Reply to Russell. *The Clinical Neuropsychologist*, *23*(5), 841–849.

Leonhard C. (2023a). Review of Statistical and Methodological Issues in the Forensic Prediction of Malingering from Validity Tests: Part I: Statistical Issues. *Neuropsychology Review*, *33*(3), 581–603. https://doi.org/10.1007/s11065-023-09601-7

Leonhard C. (2023b). Review of statistical and methodological issues in the forensic prediction of malingering from validity tests: Part II-Methodological Issues. *Neuropsychology Review*, *33*(3), 604–623. https://doi.org/10.1007/s11065-023-09602-6

Leonhard C. (2023c). Quo vadis forensic neuropsychological malingering determinations? Reply to Drs. Bush, Faust, and Jewsbury. *Neuropsychology Review*, *33*(3), 653–657. https://doi.org/10.1007/s11065-023-09606-2

Lezak, M. D. (1983). *Neuropsychological assessment*. Oxford University Press.

Lezak, M. D., Howieson, D., B., Bigler, E. D., & Tranel, D. (2012). *Neuropsychological assessment*. Oxford University Press.

Lichtenstein, S., & Slovic, P. (1971). Reversals of preference between bids and choices in gambling decisions. *Journal of Experimental Psychology*, *89*(1), 46.

Lilienfeld, S. O., Ammirati, R., & Landfield, K. (2009). Giving debiasing away: Can psychological research on correcting cognitive errors promote human welfare?. *Perspectives on Psychological Science*, *4*(4), 390–398.

Loring, D. W., Goldstein, F. C., Chen, C., Drane, D. L., Lah, J. J., Zhao, L., Larrabee, G. J., & Alzheimer's Disease Neuroimaging Initiative (2016). False-positive error rates for reliable digit span and auditory verbal learning test performance validity measures in amnestic mild cognitive impairment and early Alzheimer Disease. *Archives of Clinical Neuropsychology*, *31*(4), 313–331. https://doi.org/10.1093/arclin/acw014

Lovelace, A. G. (2019). "Slap heard around the world": George Patton and shell shock. *Parameters*, *49*(3), 79–91. https://doi.org/10.55540/0031-1723.2776.

Martin, R. C., Hayes, J. S., & Gouvier, W. D. (1996). Differential vulnerability between postconcussion self-report and objective malingering tests in identifying simulated mild head injury. *Journal of Clinical and Experimental Neuropsychology*, *18*(2), 265–275. https://doi.org/10.1080/01688639608408281

Martin, P. K., & Schroeder, R. W. (2020). Base rates of invalid test performance across clinical non-forensic contexts and settings. *Archives of Clinical Neuropsychology*, *35*(6), 717–725. https://doi.org/10.1093/arclin/acaa017

Martin, P. K., Schroeder, R. W., & Odland, A. P. (2015). Neuropsychologists' validity testing beliefs and practices: A survey of North American professionals. *The Clinical Neuropsychologist*, *29*(6), 741–776.

Martin, P. K., Schroeder, R. W., Olsen, D. H., Maloy, H., Boettcher, A., Ernst, N., & Okut, H. (2020). A systematic review and meta-analysis of the Test of Memory Malingering in adults: Two decades of deception detection. *The Clinical Neuropsychologist*, *34*(1), 88–119. https://doi.org/10.1080/13854046.2019.1637027

Martin, B. J., Sober, J. D., Millis, S. R., Hanks, R. A., Reslan, S., & Waldron-Perrine, B. (2023). CVLT-3 response bias as an indicator of performance validity in a litigating population. *The Clinical Neuropsychologist*, *37*(1), 81–90. https://doi.org/10.1080/13854046.2021.1993347

Matthews, C. (1990). They asked for a speech. *The Clinical Neuropsychologist*, *4*, 327–336.

Meehl, P. E. (1954). *Clinical versus statistical prediction*. University of Minnesota Press.

Meehl, P. E. (1986) Causes and effects of my disturbing little book. *Journal of Personality Assessment*, *50*(3), 370–375. https://doi.org/10.1207/s15327752jpa5003_6

Metzger, R. (1976). A reliability and validity study of the State-Trait Anxiety Inventory. *Journal of Clinical Psychology*, *32*(2), 276–278.

Meyers, J. E., & Volbrecht, M. E. (2003). A validation of multiple malingering detection methods in a large clinical sample. *Archives of Clinical Neuropsychology*, *18*(3), 261–276.

Miller, J. B., Millis, S. R., Rapport, L. J., Bashem, J. R., Hanks, R. A., & Axelrod, B. N. (2011). Detection of insufficient effort using the advanced clinical solutions for the Wechsler Memory Scale, Fourth Edition. *The Clinical Neuropsychologist*, *25*(1), 160–172. https://doi.org/10.1080/13854046.2010.533197

Millis, S. R. (1992). The Recognition Memory Test in the detection of malingered and exaggerated memory deficits. *The Clinical Neuropsychologist*, *6*(4), 406–414.

Millis, S. R. (2009). What clinicians really need to know about symptom exaggeration, insufficient effort, and malingering: Statistical and measurement matters. In J. E. Morgan & J. J. Sweet (Eds.), *Neuropsychology of malingering casebook* (pp. 21–37). Psychology Press.

Millis, S. R., Putnam, S. H., Adams, K. M., & Ricker, J. H. (1995). The California Verbal Learning Test in the detection of incomplete effort in neuropsychological evaluation. *Psychological Assessment*, *7*(4), 463–471. https://doi-org.libproxy.uthscsa.edu/10.1037/1040-3590.7.4.463

Mittenberg, W., DiGiulio, D. V., Perrin, S., & Bass, A. E. (1992). Symptoms following mild head injury: Expectation as aetiology. *Journal of Neurology, Neurosurgery & Psychiatry*, *55*, 200–204.

Mittenberg, W., Patton, C., Canyock, E. M., & Condit, D. C. (2002). Base rates of malingering and symptom exeggeration. *Journal of Clinical and Experimental Neuropsychology*, *24*(8), 1094–1102.

Nickerson, R. S. (1998). Confirmation bias: A ubiquitous phenomenon in many guises. *Review of General Psychology*, *2*(2), 175–220.

Palmer, B. W., Boone, K. B., Lesser, I. M., & Wohl, M. A. (1998). Base rates of "impaired" neuropsychological test performance among healthy older adults. *Archives of Clinical Neuropsychology*, *13*(6), 503–511.

Pankratz, L. (1979). Symptom validity testing and symptom retraining: procedures for the assessment and treatment of functional sensory deficits. *Journal of Consulting and Clinical Psychology*, *47*(2), 409.

Pankratz, L. (1983). A new technique for the assessment and modification of feigned memory deficit. *Perceptual and Motor Skills*, *57*(2), 367–372. https://doi-org.libproxy.uthscsa.edu/10.2466/pms.1983.57.2.367

Pankratz, L., Fausti, S. A., & Peed, S. (1975). A forced-choice technique to evaluate deafness in the hysterical or malingering patient. *Journal of Consulting and Clinical Psychology*, *43*(3), 421.

Patrick, S. D., Rapport, L. J., Kanser, R. J., Hanks, R. A., & Bashem, J. R. (2021). Performance validity assessment using response time on the Warrington Recognition Memory Test. *The Clinical Neuropsychologist*, *35*(6), 1154–1173.

Plous, S. (1993). *The psychology of judgment and decision making*. McGraw-Hill.

Poreh, A., Tolfo, S., Krivenko, A., & Teaford, M. (2017). Base-rate data and norms for the Rey Auditory Verbal Learning embedded performance validity indicator. *Applied Neuropsychology: Adult*, *24*(6), 540–547. https://doi-org.libproxy.uthscsa.edu/10.1080/23279095.2016.1223670

Putnam, S. H., Adams, K. M., & Schneider, A. M. (1992). One-day test-retest reliability of neuropsychological tests in a personal injury case. *Psychological Assessment*, *4*(3), 312.

Reitan, R. M., & Wolfson, D. (1993). *The Halstead–Reitan neuropsychological test battery; theory and clinical interpretation* (2nd ed.). Neuropsychology Press.

Rey, A. (1941). L'examen psychologique dans les cas d'encephalopathie traumatique. *Archives de Psychologie, 28*, 286–340.
Rohling, M. L., Meyers, J. E., & Millis, S. R. (2003). Neuropsychological impairment following traumatic brain injury: A dose-response analysis. *The Clinical Neuropsychologist, 17*(3), 289–302.
Roor, J. J., Dandachi-FitzGerald, B., Peters, M. J. V., & Ponds, R. W. H. M. (2024). Providing a brief corrective statement does not improve test performance in patients invalidating testing: A multisite, single-blind randomized controlled trial. Advanced online publication. *The Clinical Neuropsychologist*. https://doi.org/10.1080/13854046.2024.2382340
Ruiz, I., Raugh, I. M., Bartolomeo, L. A., & Strauss, G. P. (2020). A meta-analysis of neuropsychological effort test performance in psychotic disorders. *Neuropsychology Review, 30*(3), 407–424.
Russell, E. W. (2007). Commentary on "A motion to exclude and the 'fixed' versus 'flexible' battery in 'forensic' neuropsychology". *Archives of Clinical Neuropsychology, 22*, 787–790.
Schretlen, D. J., Testa, S. M., Winicki, J. M., Pearlson, G. D., & Gordon, B. (2008). Frequency and bases of abnormal performance by healthy adults on neuropsychological testing. *Journal of the International Neuropsychological Society, 14*(3), 436–445. https://doi.org/10.1017/S1355617708080387
Schutte, C., Millis, S., Axelrod, B., & VanDyke, S. (2011). [image omitted] Derivation of a composite measure of embedded symptom validity indices. *The Clinical Neuropsychologist, 25*(3), 454–462. https://doi.org/10.1080/13854046.2010.550635
Schroeder, R. W., & Martin, P. K. (Eds.). (2022). *Validity assessment in clinical neuropsychological practice: Evaluating and managing noncredible performance*. Guilford Publications.
Schroeder, R. W., Martin, P. K., & Odland, A. P. (2016). Expert beliefs and practices regarding neuropsychological validity testing. *The Clinical Neuropsychologist, 30*(4), 515–535. https://doi.org/10.1080/13854046.2016.1177118
Schroeder, R. W., Twumasi-Ankrah, P., Baade, L. E., & Marshall, P. S. (2012). Reliable Digit Span: A systematic review and cross-validation study. *Assessment, 19*(1), 21–30. https://doi.org/10.1177/1073191111428764
Sethy, S. S. (2021). *Introduction to logic and logical discourse*. Springer.
Sherman, E. M. S., Tan, J., & Hrabok, M. (2022). *A compendium of neuropsychological tests: Fundamentals of neuropsychological assessment and test reviews for clinical practice*. Oxford University Press.
Slick, D. J., Iverson, G. L., & Green, P. (2000). California Verbal Learning Test indicators of suboptimal performance in a sample of head-injury litigants. *Journal of Clinical and Experimental Neuropsychology, 22*(5), 569–579.
Slick, D. J., Sherman, E. M., & Iverson, G. L. (1999). Diagnostic criteria for malingered neurocognitive dysfunction: Proposed standards for clinical practice and research. *The Clinical Neuropsychologist, 13*(4), 545–561.
Spielberger, C. D., Gorsuch, R. L., Lushene, R., Vagg, P. R., & Jacobs, G. A. (1983). *Manual for the State-Trait Anxiety Inventory*. Consulting Psychologists Press.
Spreen, O., & Strauss, E. (1991). *A compendium of neuropsychological tests: Administration, norms, and commentary*. Oxford University Press.
StataCorp. (2023). *Stata 18. Statistical Software*. StataCorp LLC.
Strauss, E., Sherman, E. M. S., & Spreen, O. (2006). *A compendium of neuropsychological tests: Administration, norms, and commentary* (3rd ed.). Oxford University Press.
Stone, J., Zeman, A., & Sharpe, M. (2002). Functional weakness and sensory disturbance. *Journal of Neurology, Neurosurgery, and Psychiatry, 73*(3), 241–245. https://doi.org/10.1136/jnnp.73.3.241
Suchy, Y. (2019). Introduction to special issue: Current trends in empirical examinations of performance and symptom validity. *The Clinical Neuropsychologist, 33*(8), 1349–1353.
Suchy, Y., Chelune, G., Franchow, E. I., & Thorgusen, S. R. (2012). Confronting patients about insufficient effort: The impact on subsequent symptom validity and memory performance. *The Clinical Neuropsychologist, 26*(8), 1296–1311. https://doi.org/10.1080/13854046.2012.722230

Sugarman, M. A., & Axelrod, B. N. (2015). Embedded measures of performance validity using verbal fluency tests in a clinical sample. *Applied Neuropsychology. Adult*, *22*(2), 141–146. https://doi.org/10.1080/23279095.2013.873439
Sweet, J. J., Benson, L. M., Nelson, N. W., & Moberg, P. J. (2015). The American Academy of Clinical Neuropsychology, National Academy of Neuropsychology, and Society for Clinical Neuropsychology (APA Division 40) 2015 TCN professional practice and 'salary survey': Professional practices, beliefs, and incomes of US neuropsychologists. *The Clinical Neuropsychologist*, *29*(8), 1069–1162.
Sweet, J. J., Heilbronner, R. L., Morgan, J. E., Larrabee, G. J., Rohling, M. L., Boone, K. B., Kirkwood, M. W., Schroeder, R. W., Suhr, J. A., & Conference Participants (2021). American Academy of Clinical Neuropsychology (AACN) 2021 consensus statement on validity assessment: Update of the 2009 AACN consensus conference statement on neuropsychological assessment of effort, response bias, and malingering. *The Clinical Neuropsychologist*, *35*(6), 1053–1106. https://doi.org/10.1080/13854046.2021.1896036
Sweet, J. J., King, J., Malina, A., Bergman, M., & Simmons, A. (2002). Documenting the prominence of forensic neuropsychology at national meetings and in relevant professional journals from 1990 to 2000. *The Clinical Neuropsychologist*, *16*(4), 481–494, https://doi.org/10.1076/clin.16.4.481.13914
Sweet, J. J., Wolfe, P., Sattlberger, E., Numan, B., Rosenfeld, J. P., Clingerman, S., & Nies, K. J. (2000). Further investigation of traumatic brain injury versus insufficient effort with the California Verbal Learning Test. *Archives of Clinical Neuropsychology*, *15*(2), 105–113.
Tatu, L., & Bogousslavsky, J. (2014). World War I psychoneuroses: Hysteria goes to war. *Frontiers of Neurology and Neuroscience*, *35*, 157–168. https://doi.org/10.1159/000360060
Theodor, L. H., & Mandelcorn, M. S. (1973). Hysterical blindness: A case report and study using a modern psychophysical technique. *Journal of Abnormal Psychology*, *82*(3), 552.
Tombaugh, T. N., & Tombaugh, P. W. (1996). *Test of memory malingering (TOMM)*. New York/Toronto: Multi-Health Systems.
Trueblood, W., & Binder, L. M. (1997). Psychologists' accuracy in identifying neuropsychological test protocols of clinical malingerers. *Archives of Clinical Neuropsychology*, *12*, 13–27. https://doi.org/10.1016/S0887-6177(96)00027-3
Tversky, A., & Kahneman, D. (1974). Judgment under uncertainty: Heuristics and biases. *Science*, *185*, 1124–1131.
Wedding, D., & Faust, D. (1989). Clinical judgment and decision making in neuropsychology. *Archives of Clinical Neuropsychology*, *4*(3), 233–265.
Whiteside, D. M., Gaasedelen, O. J., Hahn-Ketter, A. E., Luu, H., Miller, M. L., Persinger, V., Rice, L., & Basso, M. R. (2015a). Derivation of a cross-domain embedded performance validity measure in traumatic brain injury. *The Clinical Neuropsychologist*, *29*(6), 788–803. https://doi.org/10.1080/13854046.2015.1093660
Whiteside, D. M., Kogan, J., Wardin, L., Phillips, D., Franzwa, M. G., Rice, L., Basso, M., & Roper, B. (2015b). Language-based embedded performance validity measures in traumatic brain injury. *Journal of Clinical and Experimental Neuropsychology*, *37*(2), 220–227. https://doi.org/10.1080/13803395.2014.1002758
Wolfe, P. L., Millis, S. R., Hanks, R., Fichtenberg, N., Larrabee, G. J., & Sweet, J. J. (2010). Effort indicators within the California Verbal Learning Test-II (CVLT-II). *The Clinical Neuropsychologist*, *24*(1), 153–168. https://doi.org/10.1080/13854040903107791
Zhou, X. H., Obuchowski, N. A., & McClish, D. K. (2002). Comparing the accuracy of two diagnostic tests. *Statistical Methods in Diagnostic Medicine*, 165–194.

3 Case History and Psychometric Characteristics of False-Positive Cases

Glenn J. Larrabee

Case History Characteristics of False-Positive Cases

The term "false positive" as applied to performance validity tests (PVTs) and symptom validity tests (SVTs) applies to generating the performance and/or symptom complaint as a result of actual clinical disorder rather than representing an attempt to portray impairment that is not present. In other words, a false positive occurs when someone failing a PVT is doing so because they truly are unable to pass the PVT. Slick, Sherman, and Iverson (1999) realized the importance of minimizing false-positive errors in the diagnostic criteria they proposed for malingered neurocognitive dysfunction. In addition to Criterion A for the presence of a substantial external incentive, the Slick et al. rule-out criteria (D) specified that behaviors meeting criteria from Criterion B (evidence from neuropsychological testing) and/or Criterion C (evidence from self-report) are not fully accounted for by psychiatric, neurological, or developmental factors. Note that specification of these D criteria provided a means of assessing and controlling the false-positive rate in the application of the criteria to research on malingering.

The Slick et al. criteria represented a landmark publication in the assessment of malingering and invalid clinical presentation. These criteria allowed the design of "known groups" (criterion groups) research for development of novel PVTs and SVTs. Moreover, the Slick D criteria led to the inclusion of comparison groups of clinical cases with bona fide psychiatric, neurologic, or developmental disorders so that the false-positive rate for a particular procedure or combination of procedures can be determined. Research by Larrabee (2003) and Victor, Boone, Serpa, Buehler, and Ziegler (2009) supported use of cutoff scores with a 10% false-positive rate, which has later been empirically shown to be the optimal false-positive rate in validly performing examinees (Larrabee, Rohling, & Meyers, 2019). A 10% false-positive rate has also been recommended by Sherman, Slick, and Iverson (2020) in a revision of their diagnostic criteria paper, as well as in the AACN revised consensus statement on the evaluation of response bias and malingering (Sweet, Heilbronner, Morgan, Larrabee, Rohling, Boone, & conference participants, 2021).

There is a central role played by the false-positive rate in determining the Positive Predictive Value (PPV) otherwise known as the probability of the condition of interest (COI). PPV = True Positives/True Positives + False Positives. The false-positive rate also is part of the positive likelihood ratio (LR+), defined as Sensitivity/1 – Specificity (Note: Sensitivity or Sn is the percentage of persons with the COI detected by the test; Specificity or Sp is the percent of persons negative for the COI who score negative on the test; the converse of Sp is the false-positive rate, 1 – Sp). Thus, the LR+ represents the likelihood that a positive test score comes from the group having the COI contrasted to persons misidentified by the test

DOI: 10.4324/9781003005063-4

as having the COI. For example, consider that a cut score on the Test of Memory Malingering (TOMM) has a sensitivity of 0.50 and a specificity of 0.90. The LR+ then becomes 0.50/1–0.90 or 5.0. This LR+ indicates that the cut score for the PVT is 5 times more likely to come from the group with the COI than the group that does not have the COI. The interested reader can refer to the updated AACN response bias paper (Sweet et al., 2021) for more information regarding diagnostic statistics, including key references (also see Dandachi-Fitzgerald & Martin, 2022).

Both Larrabee (2003) and Victor et al. (2009) recommended specifying the characteristics of those cases who were identified as false positives, to enhance the use of their data by clinicians making conclusions about PVT and SVT performance case in an individual clinical case. In someone who has failed one or more PVTs, the clinician is advised to conduct a "false-positive" analysis, to see if their case possesses characteristics associated with false-positive errors (Larrabee, 2022). In Larrabee (2003), false positives were associated with moderate and severe traumatic brain injury (TBI). In Victor et al., false positives were associated with learning disability, severe TBI, and English as a second language. Dementia and amnestic mild cognitive impairment (amnestic MCI) have been associated with PVT failure on some PVTs (Loring, Goldstein, Chen, Drane, Lah, Zhao, & Larrabee, 2016), as have subjects with schizophrenia with negative symptoms (Strauss, Morra, Sullivan, & Gold, 2015), and subjects with low IQ (Dean, Victor, Boone, & Arnold, 2008), dementia (Dean, Victor, Boone, Philpott, & Hess, 2009), and in persons who require a 24-hour supervised living setting (Meyers & Volbrecht, 2003).

In Larrabee (2022), I presented a six-step process for analysis of PVT and SVT results:

1 Use multiple PVTs and SVTs that maintain at least 0.90 specificity for your examinee's diagnostic category.
2 Failure of two or more PVTs/SVTs indicates invalidity, although caution is advised when using more than ten validity tests.
3 Conduct a false-positive analysis, ruling out effects of severe neurological, psychiatric, and developmental disorders (e.g. severe TBI, Alzheimer's disease, schizophrenia, and intellectual disability).
4 Be aware that (a) as the number of failed PVTs or SVTs increases, it is increasingly likely that these results represent truly invalid clinical presentation, and (b) this is particularly true for scores falling substantially beyond the cutoff on more than one validity test.
5 Recognize that someone with sufficient native ability to perform a test should not exceed cutoffs on a PVT that simulates or mimics that cognitive ability (e.g. normal performance on the WMS-IV Visual Memory Index suggests sufficient visual memory to perform in the valid range on the TOMM).
6 Understand the impact of external incentives. If present, the odds increase that the positive validity test findings are true hits (true positives). If absent, the odds decrease that the positive validity test finding(s) are true hits, although not to a degree that justifies automatic conclusions of false-positive findings. Be aware, though, that external incentives may exist but be concealed.

The remainder of this chapter will focus on six case studies that were mis-classified as false positive in research I have previously published (Larrabee, 2003, 2009, 2014). Some of these case data have been cited in these prior investigations (Larrabee, 2014, 2022) but is more extensively reviewed in the present chapter. Essentially, the current chapter was designed as a multiple case study review of false-positive PVT and SVT results.

In Larrabee (2003), I identified embedded/derived scores and patterns of performance that discriminated a group of 24 litigating cases, primarily mTBI, who also scored significantly worse-than-chance on the Portland Digit Recognition Test (PDRT; Binder & Kelly, 1996), meeting criteria for definite Malingered Neurocognitive Dysfunction (MND) from a combined group of 12 moderate and 15 severe TBI cases judged to have credible performance. The 5 tests identified as embedded/derived PVTs included Benton Visual Form Discrimination (VFD; Benton, Sivan, Hamsher, Varney, & Spreen, 1994) total points < 26, combined Finger Tapping (FT; Heaton, Grant, & Matthews, 1991) dominant plus non-dominant raw score total <63, Reliable Digit Span (RDS; Greiffenstein, Baker, & Gola, 1994) <8, Wisconsin Card Sorting Test (WCST; Heaton, Chelune, Talley, Kay, & Curtiss, 1993) Failure-to-Maintain Set (FMS) >1, and MMPI-2 (Butcher, Dahlstrom, Graham, Tellegen, & Kaemmer, 1989) Fake Bad Scale (FBS; Lees-Haley, English, & Glenn, 1991) raw score >21. A pass/fail tally of each of the 5 measures showed that 21 of 24 cases (87.5%) with evidence of definite MND were correctly identified and 88.9% of the moderate/severe TBI were correctly identified (11.1% false-positive rate) using a failure criterion of 2 or more. This yielded an LR+ of 87.5/11.1 or 7.88.

These findings were cross-validated in a new group of 17 litigants, most of whom had mTBI, with two clinical groups having neurologic (*n* = 13) and psychiatric (*n* = 14) diagnoses. Neurologic diagnoses included multiple sclerosis (1), seizure disorder (2), stroke (2), ruptured aneurysm/AVM with surgical repair (3), herpes simplex encephalitis (1), surgically resected colloid cyst of the 3rd ventricle with postsurgical memory disorder (1), amnestic MCI that later progressed to Alzheimer's disease (2), and one case with multiple problems (severe TBI, stroke, and alcohol abuse). The psychiatric diagnoses included major depressive disorder (11), adjustment disorder with depressed mood (2), and schizoaffective disorder (1). In this replication, the litigating subjects were identified as manifesting probable MND by (1) failing the PDRT between a zero false-positive cutoff (but above chance) level or 2nd percentile cutoff (2% false-positive rate), and (2) invalid performance on an additional PVT (e.g. TOMM, Tombaugh, 1996; Rey 15 Item Test, Rey, 1964). Replication showed that 15 of 17 (88.2%) of the probable MND cases were correctly identified at a failure criterion of 2 or more PVTs, with 100% of the neurologic and psychiatric cases identified. The LR+ cannot be computed because there were no false positives on cross-validation.

In Larrabee (2009), I developed embedded PVT scales for the Continuous Recognition Memory Test (CRM; a yes/no task of recognizing recurring from non-recurring pictures of common stimuli, such as a fish, developed by Hannay, Levin, & Grossman, 1979), and the Continuous Visual Memory Test (CVMT; a yes/no recognition memory test requiring discrimination of recurring from non-recurring abstract designs; Trahan & Larrabee, 1996). Using the same subjects as reported in Larrabee (2003), I identified those recurring and non-recurring items that were correctly identified by the moderate/severe TBI cases, but misidentified by the cases with definite MND. This resulted in a 33-item scale for the CRM, and a 20-item scale for the CVMT. A CRM cut score of <26 correctly identified 87.5% of definite MND, with only a 7.4% false-positive rate in TBI, for an LR+ of 11.82. A CVMT cut score of <14 correctly identified 83.3% of definite MND, at a false-positive rate of 11.3% in the moderate/severe TBI sample, for an LR+ of 7.5. On cross-validation comparing those litigants with probable MND to the mixed neurologic and psychiatric case group, the CRM cut score of <26 correctly identified 52.9% of probable MND, at a false-positive rate of 3.7%, LR+ of 14.30. A CVMT cut score of <14 identified 35.3% of probable MND with a false-positive rate of 7.4%, for an LR+ of 4.77.

In Larrabee (2014) I combined the embedded/derived PVTs and the one SVT into one set of seven procedures: VFD, FT, RDS, WCST FMS, MMPI-2 FBS, CRM, and CVMT. I also combined the definite and probable MND subjects and moderate/severe TBI, neurologic and psychiatric cases previously reported in Larrabee (2003, 2009). This yielded a probable MND/definite MND sample of 41, and a combined moderate/severe TBI, neurologic and psychiatric sample of 54 cases. This combined data set was employed to address the false-positive rates associated with the use of multiple PVTs and SVTs, compared with results of simulated PVT failure using Monte Carlo simulation (Berthelson, Mulchan, Odland, Miller, & Mittenberg, 2013). It was demonstrated that the Monte Carlo simulations over-estimated the false-positive rate based on actual patient data using the combined Larrabee papers (2003, 2009), and using data published on the WAIS-IV Effort Assessment (Pearson, 2009). This was likely due to skewed data in the clinical data set compared with the normally distributed data in the MND groups (Davis & Millis, 2014; Larrabee et al., 2019). In the combined clinical sample, the average per-test PVT/SVT failure rate for the 6 PVTs and 1 SVT was 9.0%, with a range of 3.7% (VFD, FT) to 18.5% (WCST FMS). The average intercorrelation of all 7 PVTs/SVT was 0.063. In the combined data set, failure of ≥ 2 PVTs/SVT correctly identified 40/41 or 97.6% of MND, and 48/54 clinical cases or 88.9%, yielding an LR+ of 97.6/11.1% or 8.79.

The present chapter provides review of the six false-positive cases in Larrabee (2014) that resulted from using a cutoff of ≥ 2 PVT/SVT failures out of 7 total. Note that the false-positive rate is inversely related to the number of PVTs and SVTs administered in validly performing clinical groups. For example, in Larrabee (2014) 28 out of 54 (52%) failed zero PVTs/SVT, 20 out of 54 (37%) failed 1 PVT/SVT, 4 out of 54 (7%) failed 2 PVTs/SVT, and 2/54 (4%) failed 3 PVT/SVTs. No clinical case failed 4 or more PVTs/SVT.

The goal of the current chapter is to present examples of how one would analyze these data in a manner such as to identify both clinical history that may be predictive of false-positive risk, as well as particular score patterns that may indicate increased risk of false-positive identification. Table 3.1 presents the PVT/SVT data for the six cases, and Table 3.2 presents T scores for key neuropsychological measures, including Controlled Oral Word Association (COWA; Benton, Hamsher, & Sivan, 1994), Grooved Pegboard (Heaton et al., 1991), Wechsler Adult Intelligence Scale (WAIS-R, Wechsler, 1981) Vocabulary, WAIS-R

Table 3.1 Performance and Symptom Validity Scores for False-Positive Cases ((Failing ≥2) PVTs)

Case #	*VFD*[1] <26	*Tapping*[2] <63	*RDS*[3] <8	*FMS*[4] >1	*FBS*[5] >21	*CRM*[6] <26	*CVMT*[7] <14
Case 1 moderate TBI	31	78	8	2*	24*	32	17
Case 2 severe TBI	26	73	8	3*	24*	31	20
Case 3 severe TBI	26	62*	8	0	20	21*	17
Case 4 severe TBI	26	70	7*	2*	14	28	12*
Case 5 severe TBI	25*	78	10	0	13	21*	11*
Case 6 stroke	32	91	14	2*	15	31	9*

[1] Visual Form Discrimination raw score,
[2] Finger Tapping (r + l, raw total),
[3] Reliable Digit Span,
[4] Wisconsin Card Sorting Failure-to-Maintain Set,
[5] MMPI-2 FBS Symptom Validity Scale,
[6] Continuous Recognition Memory Test,
[7] Continuous Visual Memory Test.
* Indicates a failing score on the validity test. See the text for references.

Table 3.2 T Scores (Mean = 50, Standard Deviation = 10) for Select Neuropsychological Tests

Case #[a]	*COWA*[1]	*Voc*[2]	*BD*[3]	*GPB*[4] *D/ND*	*Arith*[5]	*Trails B*[6]	*VSRT CLTR*[7]	*VSRT Delay*[8]	*VR Im*[9]	*VR Del*[10]
1 Mod/TBI	38	57	57	42/53	50	45	36	56	62	61
2 Sev/TBI	39	43	47	31/38	37	27	31	27	46	49
3 Sev/TBI	48	40	43	2/50	37	34	16	0	45	15
4 Sev/TBI	32	40	43	41/16	43	29	1	0	26	19
5 Sev/TBI	52	53	43	18/29	47	42	3	0	23	0
6 Stroke	48	53	60	51/61	53	54	48	56	68	71

[a] Case descriptions are the same as in Table 3.1.
[1] Controlled Oral Word Association,
[2] WAIS-R Vocabulary,
[3] WAIS-R Block Design,
[4] Grooved Pegboard Dominant/Non-Dominant,
[5] WAIS-R Arithmetic,
[6] Trail Making B,
[7] Verbal Selective Reminding Test Consistent Long-Term Retrieval,
[8] Verbal Selective Reminding Test delayed recall,
[9] WMS Visual Reproduction immediate recall,
[10] WMS Visual Reproduction delayed recall. See the text for references.

Block Design, WAIS-R Arithmetic, Trails B (Heaton et al., 1991), Verbal Selective Reminding Test (VSRT, Consistent Long-Term Retrieval, CLTR and 30 minute delayed recall; Larrabee, Trahan, Curtiss, & Levin, 1988), and Wechsler Memory Scale (WMS, Wechsler, 1945; Trahan, Quintana, Willingham, & Goethe, 1988; Immediate and Delayed Recall).

Case Examples

Case 1 was a 60-year-old, right-handed female, who was a high-school graduate, and worked as a realtor. She was referred by plaintiff counsel, three years eight months status post TBI with brief loss of consciousness, Glasgow Coma Scale of 14 at the scene with flaccid right upper extremity. She was amnestic for the accident, with her first memory being in the hospital. Post traumatic amnesia was two to four days. She was hospitalized for five days. CT scan of the head both acutely and two months post trauma showed damage in the left parietal ventricular white matter and left internal capsule/lateral thalamus. The data were consistent with a mild complicated (moderate) TBI. Examination was conducted in 1997.

She was administered the Rey 15 Item Test (scoring 14/15), and she scored 32 on the PDRT Easy, with 9/9 on PDRT Hard. She had bilateral severe microsmia, with a University of Pennsylvania Smell Identification Test score < 5th percentile. She scored in the invalid range on the WCST (FMS = 2) and FBS (raw = 24). She scored within the valid range on the remaining 5 PVTs. Regarding key neuropsychological abilities, she had a T score of 38 on Controlled Oral Word Association, a T of 57 on WAIS-R Vocabulary and on WAIS-R Block Design, T scores (dominant/non-dominant) for Grooved Pegboard were 42/53, WAIS-R Arithmetic was a T of 50, Trails B was T of 45, Verbal Selective Reminding was a T score of 36 for CLTR during the learning trials, with a 30-minute delayed recall a T score of 56. Visual Reproduction Immediate was a T score of 62, and Visual Reproduction Delay was a T score of 61.

The above data show that Case 1 scored just over the cutoff of 1 for WCST FMS. Note that combining the moderate/severe TBI, neurologic and psychiatric cases shifted the false-positive rate on the WCST FMS to 18.5% (cf. Larrabee, 2014), a factor that may have led to a false-positive FMS in Case 1. The MMPI-2 FBS was 2 raw score points over the cutoff of 22 or more. Note that per the Pearson publication on the FBS (Ben-Porath, Graham, & Tellegen, 2009), a raw score of 24 yields a nongendered T score of 77, which is below the T score cutoff of 80 or more that is associated with possible overreporting of symptoms, recommended by Ben-Porath et al. Thus, Case 1 shows several factors related to false-positive identification. First, scores that are just over cutoff in someone with unequivocal neurological insult may sometimes be false positives, particularly on PVTs that have individual false-positive rates equal to or higher than 10%. Second, subsequent research on the MMPI-2 FBS has illustrated adjustments to cutting scores that impact the false-positive rate (Greiffenstein, Fox, & Lees-Haley, 2007).

Case 2 was a 44-year-old right-handed Caucasian female with a high-school degree plus licensed practical nurse (LPN) training, who worked as an LPN, and was examined in 1989. She was not in litigation and was referred by her neurologist for concerns regarding deterioration in memory. She had a history of severe TBI as a child, prior to age 7. CT scan of the head showed a prior craniotomy, with low-density regions in the frontal lobes bilaterally, interpreted as most likely postsurgical areas of encephalomalacia. My evaluation of her was conducted 37 years post injury. PVT and SVT scores exceeding cutoff included 3 on FMS on the WCST and a MMPI-2 FBS of 24. Neuropsychological data in Table 3.2 show that her greatest impairments occurred on the Verbal Selective Reminding Test, Trail Making B, and right-hand Grooved Pegboard.

Case 2 suggests that history of severe TBI with chronic frontal lesions can be seen in association with PVT failure on the WCST FMS. Her MMPI-2 FBS, while elevated based on data at the time of examination (1989), is at a current T score of 77, the same as noted in Case 1. Both fall below a T score of 80 that is suggestive of increased probability of exaggeration.

Case 3 was a 26-year-old right-handed Asian American male, with 12 years of education, referred by defense counsel. He was examined in 1990, over three years following a severe TBI resulting in two weeks of coma and one week of post traumatic amnesia. CT scan on the day of injury showed subarachnoid hemorrhage. He complained of memory problems and right-sided weakness when seen by me. On my examination of him I did not administer any PVTs as he was examined in 1990, prior to widespread use of PVTs and SVTs. His neuropsychological test scores in Table 3.2 were consistent with his history of injury and, clinically, he was considered to be a credible case of severe TBI (see Rohling, Meyers, & Millis, 2003). He had particular difficulty on right-hand Grooved Pegboard (T score of 2, with left hand T score of 50), and on verbal and visual memory (Verbal Selective Reminding CLTR and 30-minute delayed recall T scores of 16 and 0, and WMS Delayed Visual Reproduction T score of 15).

On PVT and SVT scores (extracted for research purposes years after the evaluation), he performed in the invalid range on Finger Tapping, with a combined score of 62, right at the cutoff of <63. Note that his combined Finger Tapping score was entirely due to his right hemiparesis (right-hand FT raw score of 18.0, left hand score of 44.0). Otherwise, his only PVT or SVT failure was on the Continuous Recognition Memory Test, with a score of 21 that falls within the range where false positives can occur (Larrabee, 2009). Clinically, I would not call his data "invalid" as his performance was consistent with his clinical history of severe TBI with two weeks of coma and residual hemiparesis. Thus, in my opinion, he was clearly a "false-positive" case.

Case 4 was in litigation, referred for examination by defense counsel. He was a 25-year-old, left-handed Caucasian male with 13 years of education. Examination was in 1998, 13 months status post severe TBI, followed by one month of coma and two months of posttraumatic amnesia (PTA). He had 4 CT scans during his hospitalization, with the 4th scan (10 days post trauma) showing left basal ganglia hemorrhage with edema. There was compression of the right lateral ventricle, and a tiny hemorrhagic contusion in the posterior left parietal area. At the time of discharge to inpatient rehabilitation, he had right hemiplegia.

He was administered PVTs and scored 12/15 on Rey 15-item Test, 48/50/50 on the TOMM, and had 24/36 on PDRT Easy, as well as on PDRT Hard. T scores were <40 for COWA (32), right-hand GPB (T = 16; note he had right hemiparesis, left hand was T = 41), and Trails B (T = 29). His greatest impairments on standard neuropsychological measures were in verbal and visual memory, with VSRT CLTR a T score of 1, and VSRT delayed recall a T score of 0. Immediate Visual Reproduction was a T of 26 with Delayed Visual Reproduction a T of 19. Although data for IQ is not reported in Table 3.2 for reasons of space limitations, Case 4 had a Verbal IQ of 77 and Performance IQ of 76, consistent with significant decline in intellectual functioning.

On PVT and SVT assessment, he scored in the invalid range on RDS with a score of 7, WCST FMS with a score of 2, and CVMT with a score of 12. Note that two of three PVTs were one point beyond the cutoff (RDS 7, FMS 2). Additionally, the CVMT embedded PVT was two points beyond the cutoff. This case shows that very severe TBI can result in elevated PVT failure, but that such failure is not dramatic; rather, performance is just beyond cutoff, and in the range where false-positive errors occur on individual PVTs.

Case 5 was a 25-year-old right-handed Caucasian male with 14 years of education (associate degree). He was in litigation and seen for examination in 1989, 4 years post injury. History was significant for a severe TBI, characterized by 13 days of coma, and 4 months of PTA. He had residual motor deficits in the right arm and leg (hyperactive reflexes) and residual dysphasia. His primary complaint was poor memory.

I did not administer any PVTs as this man was examined in 1989, prior to the widespread use of PVTs. His test scores did appear to be consistent with his history of severe TBI (see Rohling et al., 2003). On neuropsychological testing, he produced very low scores on the GPB, with a T score of 18 for the right hand and 29 for the left (the right–left difference was consistent with his residual motor deficits). He also showed evidence of very poor verbal and visual learning and memory, with VSRT CLTR a T score of 3 and VSRT delay a T score of 0. WMS Immediate Visual Reproduction was a T score of 23, with WMS Delayed Visual Reproduction was a T score of 0.

On examination of PVT and SVT scores (extracted for research purposes years after the evaluation), he produced a score right at cutoff for Visual Form Discrimination (25; one point higher would have been in the range of valid performance). On the CRM and CVMT, his PVT scores of 21 and 11, respectively, did not fall just below cutoff (<26 for CRM, <14 for CVMT), but both performances were within the range of false-positive scores (extending down to 21 for CRM and down to 10 for the CVMT).

Case 6 is a 61-year-old right-handed Caucasian female with 12 years of education, referred by her neurologist in 1995 for evaluation of consequences of a stroke four months status post event. She complained of memory change and change in her ability to prepare materials at work as an accounting clerk. She had initial paralysis of her right upper and lower extremity, and CT scan of the brain showed an old, small right caudate infarct.

She was administered the Rey 15 Item Test and scored 15/15 (this examination was done in 1995, when the development and use of PVTs was just beginning to emerge in North American clinical practice). Test performances in Table 3.2 were entirely within the range of expectation, based on her educational and occupational history.

On analysis of PVT and SVT scores (examined later on for research), she scored right at the cutoff of >1 on WCST FMS. Her CVMT PVT score of 9 fell well below the cutoff of <14, in the range where false positives were not seen in the derivation sample based on 12 moderate TBI and 15 severe TBI cases. Note that none of the TBI cases in Table 3.1 scored this low.

Conclusions

To summarize the above findings and the data in Tables 3.1 and 3.2, five of six false-positive cases in the Larrabee investigations (2003, 2009, 2014) had abnormal imaging on CT scan of the brain. Also, five of the six had TBI (1 case mild complicated/moderate, 4 cases severe with prolonged coma and PTA). Neuropsychological sequelae were common, most often seen in memory and processing speed (see Table 3.2), and cases with history of unilateral motor impairment performed poorly on the GPB, showing residual motor function impairment. Of all the clinical measures administered, the VSRT was the most sensitive to neuropsychological impairment in the present investigation, largely due to the presence of one case of mild complicated TBI, and four cases of severe TBI (length of coma 2 weeks, 1 month, and 13 days, respectively for cases 3, 4, and 5). For one case, length of coma and PTA were unavailable due to remote history of TBI, but this case had evidence of prior craniotomy, and bilateral encephalomalacia in the frontal lobes on CT scan of the brain. Case 4 had performance consistent with significant decline in intellectual functions, with WAIS-R VIQ of 77 and Performance IQ (PIQ) of 76, following his severe TBI with one month of coma and two months of PTA.

The most common PVT failures occurred on the WCST FMS (4 out of 6 cases), with the second most common failure on the CVMT PVT (3 out of 6 cases). On the WCST, 3 of the 4 false-positive cases with FMS >1 scored just above cutoff. On the CVMT, 1 of the 3 cases scored 2 items beyond cutoff, whereas the other 2 false-positive cases were unequivocally beyond the cutoff score.

Review of other embedded/derived PVTs/SVT showed 5 of 6 false-positive cases passing the VFD (the one case not passing scored right at the cutoff of 25). FT also showed 5 of 6 false-positive cases passing (the one case not passing scored right at the cutoff of 62, and this score was directly the result of residual hemiparesis, causing a residual unilateral motor impairment). Five of 6 false-positive cases scored in the valid performance range of 8 or higher on RDS. Four of 6 cases scored below the MMPI-2 FBS raw score of 22 or more. The two scoring in the range of exaggeration obtained scores of 24, which subsequent research has shown is a valid-range score at a nongendered T score of 77; by contrast, the possibility of exaggeration on FBS is linked to T scores of 80 or greater (Ben-Porath et al., 2009). Four of 6 false-positive cases performed above cutoff (valid range) on the CRM, with 3 of 6 scoring above cutoff (valid range) on the CVMT.

These data show that scores falling just beyond cutoff, but still within the range where false-positive cases can potentially occur, may well be false positives in cases with unequivocal brain injury. This is particularly true of cases with a history of severe TBI. In the present sample, this is seen most clearly in performance on the WCST FMS. When considering subsequent research on WCST FMS (e.g. Greve, Heinly, Bianchini, & Love, 2009), this may not be surprising. Greve and colleagues' research indicates that the FMS cutoff score of >1 can result in false-positive findings, with false-positive rates predictably increasing as severity of injury increases. On the other hand, the VFD, RDS, and FT scores do not commonly appear to fall in the range of invalid performance, at least in this small sample of 6 false positive out of 54 combined cases of moderate/severe TBI, neurological, and psychiatric subjects reported in Larrabee (2014).

Author Note

Glenn J. Larrabee, Ph.D., is a co-author of the Continuous Visual Memory Test and receives royalties from the sale of this test. He also provides forensic services as an expert in clinical neuropsychology.

References

Ben-Porath, Y. S., Graham, J. R., & Tellegen, A. (2009). *The MMPI-2 Minnesota Multiphasic Personality Inventory-2. Symptom Validity (FBS) Scale.* Minneapolis: University of Minnesota Press.

Benton, A. L., Sivan, A. B., & Hamsher, K. de S. (1994). *Multilingual aphasia examination* (3rd Ed.). Lutz, FL: Psychological Assessment Resources.

Benton, A. L., Sivan, A. B., Hamsher, K. de S., Varney, N. R., & Spreen, C. (1994). *Contributions to neuropsychological assessment* (2nd Ed.). New York: Oxford.

Berthelson, L., Mulchan, S. S., Odland, A. P., Miller, L. J., & Mittenberg, W. (2013). False positive diagnosis of malingering due to the use of multiple effort tests. *Brain Injury, 27,* 909–916.

Binder, L. M., & Kelly, M. P. (1996). Portland Digit Recognition Test performance by brain dysfunction patients without financial incentives. *Assessment, 3,* 403–409.

Butcher, J. N., Dahlstrom, W. G., Graham, J. R., Tellegen, A., & Kaemmer, B. (1989). *Manual for the administration and scoring the Minnesota Multiphasic Personality Inventory-2.* Minneapolis: University of Minnesota Press.

Dandachi-Fitzgerald, B., & Martin, P. K. (2022). Clinical judgment and clinically applied statistics. In R. W. Schroeder & P. K. Martin (Eds.), *Validity assessment in clinical neuropsychological practice* (pp. 107–125). New York: Guilford Press.

Davis, J. J., & Millis, S. R. (2014). Examination of performance validity test failure in relation to number of tests administered. *The Clinical Neuropsychologist, 28,* 199–214.

Dean, A. C., Victor, T. L., Boone, K. B., & Arnold, G. (2008). The relationship of IQ to effort test performance. *The Clinical Neuropsychologist, 22,* 705–722.

Dean, A. C., Victor, T. L., Boone, K. B., Philpott, L. M., & Hess, R. A. (2009). Dementia and effort test performance. *The Clinical Neuropsychologist, 23,* 133–152

Greiffenstein, M. F., Baker, W. J., & Gola, T. (1994). Validation of malingered amnesia measures with a large clinical sample. *Psychological Assessment, 6,* 218–224.

Greiffenstein, M. F., Fox, D., & Lees-Haley, P. R. (2007). The MMPI-2 Fake Bad Scale in detection of noncredible brain injury claims. In K. B. Boone (Ed.), *Assessment of feigned cognitive impairment.* New York: Guilford Publications.

Greve, K. W., Heinly, M. T., Bianchini, K. J., & Love, J. M. (2009). Malingering detection with the Wisconsin Card Sorting Test in mild traumatic brain injury. *The Clinical Neuropsychologist, 23,* 343–362.

Hannay, H. J., Levin, H. S., & Grossman, R. G. (1979). Impaired recognition memory after head injury. *Journal of Clinical and Experimental Neuropsychology, 11,* 444–460.

Heaton, R. K., Chelune, G. J., Talley, J. L., Kay, G. G., & Curtiss, G. (1993). *Wisconsin card sorting test manual. Revised and expanded.* Odessa, FL: Psychological Assessment Resources.

Heaton, R. K., Grant, I., & Matthews, C. G. (1991). *Comprehensive norms for an expanded Halstead-Reitan Battery: Demographic corrections, research findings, and clinical applications.* Odessa, FL: Psychological Assessment Resources.

Larrabee, G. J. (2003). Detection of malingering using atypical performance patterns on standard neuropsychological tests. *The Clinical Neuropsychologist, 17,* 410–425.

Larrabee, G. J. (2009). Malingering scales for the continuous recognition memory test and the continuous visual memory test. *The Clinical Neuropsychologist, 23,* 167–180.

Larrabee, G. J. (2014). False-positive rates associated with the use of multiple performance and symptom validity tests. *Archives of Clinical Neuropsychology, 29,* 364–373.

Larrabee, G. J. (2022). Synthesizing data to reach clinical conclusions regarding validity status. In R. W. Schroeder & P. K. Martin (Eds.), *Validity assessment in clinical neuropsychological practice* (pp. 193–210). New York: Guilford Press.

Larrabee, G. J., Rohling, M. L., & Meyers, J. E. (2019). Use of multiple performance and symptom validity test measures: Determining the optimal per-test cutoff for analysis of invalidity, analysis of skew, and inter-test correlations in valid and invalid performance groups. *The Clinical Neuropsychologist, 33,* 1354–1372.

Larrabee, G. J., Trahan, D. E., Curtiss, G., & Levin, H. S. (1988). Normative data for the Verbal Selective Reminding Test. *Neuropsychology, 2,* 173–182.

Lees-Haley, P. R., English, L. T., & Glenn, W. J. (1991). A fake bad scale on the MMPI-2 for personal injury claimants. *Psychological Reports, 68,* 203–210.

Loring, D. W., Goldstein, F. C., Chen, C., Drane, D. L., Lah, J. J., Zhao, L., & Larrabee, G. J. (2016). False-positive error rates for Reliable Digit Span and Auditory Verbal Learning Test performance validity measures in amnestic mild cognitive impairment and early Alzheimer's disease. *Archives of Clinical Neuropsychology, 31,* 313–331.

Meyers, J. E., & Volbrecht, M. E. (2003). A validation of multiple malingering detection methods in a large clinical sample. *Archives of Clinical Neuropsychology, 18,* 261–276.

Pearson (2009). *Advanced clinical solutions for use with WAIS-IV and WMS-IV.* San Antonio: Pearson Education.

Rey, A. (1964). *L'examen psychologique en psychologie.* Paris: Presses Universitaires de France.

Rohling, M. L., Meyers, J. E., & Millis, S. R. (2003). Neuropsychological impairment following traumatic brain injury: A dose-response analysis. *The Clinical Neuropsychologist, 17,* 289–302.

Sherman, E. M. S., Slick, D. J., & Iverson, G. L. (2020). Multidimensional malingering criteria for neuropsychological assessment: A 20-year update of the malingered neuropsychological dysfunction criteria. *Archives of Clinical Neuropsychology, 35,* 735–764.

Slick, D. J., Sherman, E. M. S., & Iverson, G. L. (1999). Diagnostic criteria for malingered Neurocognitive dysfunction: Proposed standards for clinical practice and research. *The Clinical Neuropsychologist, 13,* 545–561.

Strauss, G. P., Morra, L. F., Sullivan, M. S., & Gold, J. M. (2015). The role of low cognitive effort and negative symptoms in neuropsychological impairment in schizophrenia. *Neuropsychology, 29,* 282–291.

Sweet, J. J., Heilbronner, R. L., Morgan, J. E., Larrabee, G. J., Rohling, M. L., Boone, K. B., ...& Conference Participants. (2021). American Academy of Clinical Neuropsychology (AACN) 2021 consensus statement on validity assessment: Update of the 2009 AACN consensus conference statement on neuropsychological assessment of effort, response bias, and malingering. *The Clinical Neuropsychologist, 35,* 1053–1106.

Tombaugh, T. N. (1996). *Test of memory malingering.* North Tonowanda, NY: Multi-Health Systems.

Trahan, D. E., & Larrabee, G. J. (1996). *Continuous visual memory test.* Lutz, FL. Psychological Assessment Resources.

Trahan, D. E., Quintana, J., Willingham, A. C., & Goethe, K. E. (1988). The Visual Reproduction subtest: Standardization and clinical validation of a delayed recall procedure. *Neuropsychology, 2,* 29–39.

Victor, T. L., Boone, K. B., Serpa, J. G., Buehler, J., & Zeigler, E. A. (2009). Interpreting the meaning of multiple symptom validity test failure. *The Clinical Neuropsychologist, 23,* 297–313.

Wechsler, D. (1945). A standardized, memory scale for clinical use. *Journal of Psychology, 19,* 87–95.

Wechsler, D. (1981). *WAIS-R manual.* New York: The Psychological Corporation.

4 Including Symptom Validity Assessment in Forensic Evaluations

Megan R. Whitman and Yossef S. Ben-Porath

Forensic neuropsychological evaluations typically rely on both self-report and performance-based assessment. The self-report component, which is the focus of this chapter, may include broadband tests of personality and psychopathology (e.g., Minnesota Multiphasic Personality Inventory-3 [MMPI-3]; Ben-Porath & Tellegen, 2020a), narrowband instruments (e.g., Beck Depression Inventory-II [BDI-II]; Beck et al., 1961, 1996), and structured and unstructured interviews. For a forensic examiner to obtain valid information, a test-taker must be able and willing to respond accurately to self-report-based measures. Ben-Porath (2013) has described several threats to the validity of self-report-based assessments (described in detail later in this chapter), including non-content and content-based invalid responding. Symptom Validity Tests (SVTs) are used to assess for these threats.

When individuals are evaluated in forensic contexts, they have incentives to portray themselves and their symptoms in a manner that increases the likelihood of receiving a desirable outcome. In civil cases, they may fabricate or exaggerate symptoms to appear more dysfunctional than they genuinely are (i.e., to over-report symptoms) in order to receive worker's compensation, disability or personal injury awards, and in a criminal court, they may be motivated to over-report pathology to avoid or reduce the severity of sentencing. On the other hand, the forensic neuropsychology examinee may also be motivated to exaggerate or fabricate socially desirable personal qualities (i.e., under-report) in order to appear more virtuous than they are and increase sympathy from evaluators or others involved in the legal decision-making process.

Given these incentives, assessing the manner in which a forensic examinee approaches the test-taking process, especially with regard to self-report-based assessment (i.e., self-report measures and interviews), is critical. SVTs are designed to assess for over- or under-reporting, as well as invalid responding that is not based on the content of the self-report test items (i.e., non-content-based invalid responding), including non-responsiveness (i.e., providing non-scorable responses), fixed content-inconsistent responding (i.e., responding in a fixed manner regardless of the content of the test item), and random, or variable, content-inconsistent responding (i.e., responding randomly to test items regardless of their content).

The goal of this chapter is to describe methods of assessing the extent to which examinees engage in non-content-based invalid responding, over-reporting, and under-reporting during forensic neuropsychological evaluations. We will describe similarities and differences of commonly used SVTs with regard to methodology and the content they assess. We chose these two characteristics (methodology and content) because utilizing multiple methodologies is a gold-standard professional practice (Heilbronner et al., 2009), and SVT item content is relevant to the types of symptoms examinees claim in various contexts (Wygant

DOI: 10.4324/9781003005063-5

et al., 2007). Next, we will describe recent research demonstrating the importance and effectiveness of SVTs in neuropsychological evaluations. Last, we identify challenges for using SVTs and recommendations for evidence-based practice.

Approaches to Symptom Validity Assessment: Examples Using MMPI-3

According to an international survey of forensic examiners (Neal & Grisso, 2014), the MMPI family of instruments was the most commonly used tool in several types of forensic evaluations. For example, in disability evaluations, the MMPI was used by 35.8% of respondents in at least one of their two most recent evaluations, followed by other trauma-related symptom measures (27.6%), the Beck Anxiety Inventory (BAI; Beck et al., 1988) and BDI/BDI-II (17.2% each), the Personality Assessment Inventory (PAI; Morey, 2007; 13.8%), and the Structured Inventory of Malingered Symptomatology (SIMS; Smith & Burger, 1997; 13.8%). Several of these tools include embedded SVTs (the MMPI instruments, some trauma-related symptom measures, such as the Detailed Assessment of Posttraumatic Stress-2 [DAPS; Briere, 2001; Petri et al., 2020] and Trauma Symptom Inventory-2 [TSI-2; Briere, 2011], as well as the PAI), whereas the SIMS is a stand-alone SVT, and the BAI and BDI measure only substantive content (although an embedded SVT has recently been developed for the BDI-2; Fuermaier et al., 2023), relying on other tools to provide information on examinees' approaches to the test-taking process.

Because it is commonly used in forensic evaluations (Neal & Grisso, 2014) and because neuropsychologists commonly utilize its embedded SVTs (Martin et al., 2015, 2025), we will demonstrate methods for assessing symptom validity using the most recent version of the MMPI, the MMPI-3 (Ben-Porath & Tellegen, 2020a, 2020b), as well as the predecessor to the MMPI-3, the MMPI-2-Restructured Form (MMPI-2-RF; Ben-Porath & Tellegen, 2008/2011; Tellegen & Ben-Porath, 2008/2011). The MMPI-3 consists of 335 true-false items scored on 10 validity scales and 42 scales measuring transdiagnostic dimensional constructs. We will also briefly describe similarities and differences between SVTs scored on the MMPI-3 and other SVTs with regard to the content of the items and the methodology used to assess for invalid responding.

Research findings on the nine MMPI-2-RF validity scales can be applied to the interpretation of MMPI-3 validity scale scores because they served as the foundation for and are highly correlated with their MMPI-3 counterparts (Ben-Porath & Tellegen, 2020b). Specifically, two over-reporting scales, the Symptom Validity Scale (FBS) and Response Bias Scale (RBS) consist of the same items across the two versions of the test. The remaining validity scales are highly correlated across test version. In the *MMPI-3 Technical Manual* (Ben-Porath & Tellegen, 2020b), the test authors report correlations between the 10 MMPI-3 and 9 MMPI-2-RF validity scales, scored from a booklet that included the items necessary to score each test. The authors used data from 1,492 members of the normative sample whose responses were changed to reflect fixed "True," or fixed "False," responding to evaluate correlations between MMPI-2-RF and MMPI-3 inconsistent responding indicators. They used data from undergraduate students who were instructed to feign psychopathology in the context of a criminal pre-trial evaluation, and students who were asked to feign Attention Deficit Hyperactivity Disorder (ADHD), as well as a sample of forensic disability claimants to evaluate correlations between over-reporting scale scores across test versions. Last, the authors used data from students asked to simulate under-reporting in the context of pre-employment psychological evaluations as well as public safety candidates to evaluate correlations between under-reporting scale scores across test version.

Overall, correlations across test versions were at least 0.88 (median = 0.90) for the content-inconsistent responding scales, 0.84 (median = 0.99) for the over-reporting scales, and 0.87 (median = 0.93) for the under-reporting scales in the respective samples. The extensive literature on MMPI-2-RF validity scales can therefore be applied to interpretations of MMPI-3 validity scale scores (see University of Minnesota Press, 2023, for an updated list of MMPI-2-RF references, organized into categories, including validity scale research, available from the test publisher).

Assessing Non-Content-Based Invalid Responding

Test-takers may engage in non-content-based invalid responding for a number of reasons, including a careless or uncooperative approach to the testing process, but also due to reading or language limitations, difficulty sustaining attention, cognitive impairment, or confusion due to double negatives imbedded in an item. Regardless of the reason, non-content-based invalid responding results in test scores that do not accurately represent an individual's true standing on the constructs intended to be measured. Content-inconsistent responding can also artificially increase SVT scale scores, resulting in apparent, but not actual over- or under-reporting (Burchett et al., 2016). Therefore, it is important to rule out non-content-based invalid responding before concluding that an individual is engaging in an over- or under-reporting response style.

The MMPI-3 includes a Cannot Say (CSN) count in addition to three scales that measure content-inconsistent responding, including Combined Response Inconsistency (CRIN), Variable Response Inconsistency (VRIN), and True Response Inconsistency (TRIN). CNS is a count of non-scorable responses, or the number of items to which a test-taker either did not respond, or to which they responded both "True" and "False." VRIN measures variable content-inconsistent responding, that is, inconsistently responding "True" and "False," to self-report items. TRIN measures fixed content-inconsistent responding, that is, indiscriminately responding "True" or indiscriminately responding "False" to self-report items. When scoring TRIN, the number of indiscriminate "True" and "False" responses is counted separately and then the latter is subtracted from the former (with a constant added to avoid a negative raw score) to obtain an indication of the direction of fixed inconsistent responding ("True" or "False"). The CRIN raw score consists of the sum of VRIN, the number of inconsistent "True" responses, and the number of inconsistent "False" responses, to provide an overall measure of inconsistent, random responding.

VRIN and TRIN were developed by identifying 53 and 33 item pairs, respectively, that include similar (for VRIN) or opposite (for TRIN) content. For example, an individual's responses would be content-inconsistent if they responded "True" to two items with the content, "I enjoy social activities," and "I don't enjoy going to social events," and doing so would indicate fixed, inconsistent "True" responding seemingly regardless of the item content. The MMPI-3 TRIN scale has a T-score with a string that indicates whether the fixed responding was in the True direction ("T") or the False direction ("F"). Conversely, if an individual were to respond "True" to an item with the content "I enjoy social activities," but "False" to an item with the content, "I enjoy going to social events," then this would be an example of variable inconsistent responding as assessed by the VRIN scale.

Other instruments include non-content-based invalid responding scales as well. Most measures include some indication of non-scorable responses, like the MMPI-3 CNS count. For example, standard interpretive guidelines for the Battery for Health Improvement 2 (BHI-2) indicate that substantive scales are invalid and uninterpretable when 25% or more of their items are non-scorable (Bruns & Disorbio, 2003). Some other measures also include scales intended to measure non-content-based invalid responding. For example, the PAI Inconsistency (ICN) scale comprises item pairs for which half should be answered similarly based on item content and empirical identification of similarly answered items during test development, and half of which should be answered oppositely, which is similar to the MMPI-3 CRIN scale. Other scales use a different approach to identifying content-inconsistent responding, such as the BHI-2, which includes four Validity Items that have extreme or "bizarre" content that are rarely endorsed. If three or more of these items are endorsed, the BHI-2 protocol is deemed invalid due to "bizarre responding." Similarly, PAI Infrequency (INF) scale comprises items with very low endorsement frequencies in normative and clinical samples with unusual, albeit not "bizarre," content. Overall, these scales help identify content-inconsistent responding due to intentionally careless approach to test-taking, or other reasons, such as problems with language or reading comprehension or confusion, including possibly from double negatives.

Assessing Over-Reporting

The MMPI-3 includes five scales that measure over-reporting, representing a range of item content and two methodologies for identifying invalid responding: Infrequent and Non-credible responses. Three scales were developed to measure infrequently claimed problems in distinct contexts: Infrequent Responses (F), Infrequent Psychopathology Responses (Fp), and Infrequent Somatic Responses (Fs). Items selected for F were responded to in the keyed direction by no more than 15% of men and women in the MMPI-3 normative sample and are not scored on Fp or Fs. Fp items were responded to in the keyed direction by no more than 20% of individuals in a composite sample of mental health patients from various settings, with item content related to psychopathology. Finally, items on Fs were responded to in the keyed direction by no more than 25% of a medical patient sample with content describing somatic complaints.

Two MMPI-3 over-reporting scales were constructed by identifying noncredible manifestations of pathology. These scales, the Symptom Validity Scale (FBS) and RBS, and were both unchanged from their predecessor MMPI version, the MMPI-2-RF. FBS, previously labeled "Fake Bad Scale," was originally developed by Lees-Haley et al. (1991) to identify noncredible responding by personal injury litigants, who would be expected to over-report medical, somatic, or cognitive "damage" rather than severe psychopathology. RBS was developed by Gervais et al. (2008) to identify noncredible symptom reporting in forensic neuropsychological or disability evaluations; these authors identified 28 items that distinguished individuals who passed Performance Validity Tests (PVTs) from those who failed PVTs in the context of disability evaluations. Burchett and Bagby (2022) review research on the utility of MMPI-2-RF and MMPI-3 over-reporting scales.

Overall, these five scales represent two methodologies, identifying infrequently endorsed items and identifying items that were associated with noncredible symptom reporting or invalid responding on PVTs. They also highlight the importance of considering item content. Individuals assessed for different reasons might be expected to exaggerate or fabricate different types of dysfunction. For example, those evaluated for mild traumatic brain injury (mTBI) may over-report neurocognitive problems, whereas those evaluated for criminal responsibility may over-report psychotic symptoms (see Tylicki et al., 2021, and Sellbom et al., 2022, for information on using the MMPI-3 to assess over-reporting among head injury litigants and in forensic assessments, respectively). Indeed, Wygant et al. (2007)

reported that SVT failure was associated with claimed somatic and cognitive symptoms among civil litigants but global psychopathology among criminal dependents. However, some evidence has indicated that individuals claim similar symptoms particularly when feigning posttraumatic stress disorder (PTSD), mTBI, or comorbid PTSD and mTBI (Morris et al., 2021). Additionally, evidence from some factor analytic research has indicated that PVTs tend to load onto a single factor, whereas SVTs load on multiple factors, depending on the type of content included in their items (Nelson et al., 2007).

Other instruments include over-reporting SVTs that use various methodologies. The PAI Negative Impression (NIM) scale and DAPS-2 Negative Bias (NB) scale each represent a combination of both infrequency and noncredible manifestations methodologies, including statistically unlikely and infrequently endorsed items or items with bizarre or unlikely symptom manifestations. Other SVTs identify over-reporting based on configural patterns of scores (e.g., the PAI Malingering Index [MAL]; Morey, 1996) or weighted patterns of scores (e.g., PAI Rogers Discriminant Function [RDF]; Rogers et al., 1996). Some tools include multiple over-reporting SVTs representing a range of item content (e.g., SIMS), whereas other instruments include over-reporting scales with general content (e.g., DAPS-2 and BHI-2). In general, it is important for practitioners to be familiar with the methodology used to identify over-reporting and the item content that contributes to SVT elevations on any particular scale.

Assessing Under-Reporting

The MMPI-3 includes two under-reporting SVTs: Uncommon Virtues (L) and Adjustment Validity (K). These scales were developed using a composite sample of public safety candidates, who are both generally high-functioning and likely to report possessing relatively uncommon virtues and positive adjustment due to self-selection into the public safety occupations. Moreover, the prior exclusion of applicants who were deemed psychologically unsuitable after applications, panel interviews, and/or background investigations, and demand characteristics of the hiring process also increased the likelihood of these candidates to report possessing uncommon virtues and positive adjustment. Items scored on L were answered in the keyed direction by no more than 40% of the public safety candidate sample, had item content reflecting virtues, and were sufficiently associated with items from the MMPI-2-RF L-r scale. Items selected for the K scale could not have been scored on L, had item content related (as keyed) to positive psychological adjustment, and were sufficiently associated with MMPI-2-RF K-r items among men and women in the public safety candidate sample. Therefore, L and K each reflect differential item content; L represents an infrequency methodology, whereas K represents a noncredible response methodology.

Whereas many self-report tools include over-reporting scales, fewer include under-reporting SVTs. The PAI includes Positive Impression Management (PIM), which indicates denial of minor personal shortcomings that also have low endorsement frequencies in normative and clinical samples, but higher endorsement frequencies in samples that were instructed to engage in positive impression management. The DAPS-2 includes a Positive Bias scale, which consists of the number of "Never" responses a test-taker makes to low-level psychological symptoms most individuals would endorse experiencing to some extent. Like over-reporting SVTs, some under-reporting SVTs utilize configural pattern methodologies (e.g., PAI Defensiveness Index [DEF]; Morey, 1996) and weighted scale scores (e.g., PAI Cashel Discriminant Function; Cashel et al., 1995). Some inventories include SVTs intended to simultaneously measure both over- and under-reporting, such as the BHI-2 Defensiveness scale, which consists of items that differentiated between dissimulators instructed to both "fake good" and "fake bad," such that high scores are interpreted as indicating positive bias, and low scores indicate NB.

Importance of Using SVTs

SVTs that Assess Content-Inconsistent Responding

Including scales to measure content-inconsistent responding is important not only for identifying threats to the validity of substantive scale scores, but also for identifying threats to interpreting other SVTs. For example, content non-responsiveness artificially lowers scores on SVTs and substantive scales. Random responding can artificially increase scores on SVTs given the increased probability of individuals inadvertently endorsing infrequent or unlikely items. Fixed responding, which can also affect measures that rely on graded or Likert-scale responses formats, can artificially increase or decrease scores on other SVTs, depending on the keyed direction of items scored on those scales. For example, L and K mainly comprise items keyed "False." Consequently, fixed "True" responding can artificially reduce L and K scores, whereas fixed False responding can artificially increase scores on those scales.

Handel et al. (2010) conducted a simulation in which their findings supported the utility of MMPI-2-RF VRIN-r and TRIN-r scores for detecting increasing levels (0%–70%) of content-inconsistent responding. They also demonstrated that these response styles artificially increase substantive scale scores, typically only after about 20% or 30% of simulated random responding or 10% simulated fixed "True" responding. Fixed "False" responding resulted in artificially reduced substantive scale scores, especially after at least 20%–30% simulated false responses were inserted. Finally, convergent validity coefficients for the MMPI-2-RF Restructured Clinical scales were reduced when simulated non-content-based invalid responding exceeded 30%, whereas discriminant validity coefficients (i.e., those in which meaningful associations were not hypothesized) were generally similar regardless of invalid responding.

The effects of non-content-based invalid responding on the validity of over- and under-reporting SVT scores has also been documented. Specifically, Burchett et al. (2016) inserted 0%–100% random, fixed true, or fixed false responses into MMPI-2-RF protocols. These authors found that although VRIN-r and TRIN-r were useful in detecting most cases of invalid responses, even after excluding individuals based on VRIN-r and TRIN-r elevations, some test-takers were misclassified as over-reporting by Fp-r and Fs scores. Burchett et al.'s findings highlight the importance of considering non-content-based invalid responding, even in the moderate range, before interpreting over-reporting SVTs, especially when the SVT is brief in length, uses an infrequency methodology, consists of mostly true-keyed items, or requires relatively low scores to reach interpretable cutoffs.

Content-Based SVTs

Associations with Self-Report Validity

SVTs are designed to assess the validity of a test-taker's self-report. Therefore, higher SVT scores should be associated with lower substantive scale score validity coefficients. Following a critique by McGrath et al. (2010) who argued that there was inadequate empirical evidence to conclude that SVTs are needed in practice, new research sought to demonstrate that SVT scores are in fact associated with lower substantive scale validity coefficients. For example, Burchett and Ben-Porath (2010) designed a simulation study in which undergraduate students completed several measures of various forms of psychopathology. They then were administered the MMPI-2-RF with instructions to either (a) follow standard instructions (i.e., SI), (b) feign somatic problems, or (c) feign psychopathology. The authors calculated correlations between MMPI-2-RF substantive scale scores and related criterion measures for each group and compared these validity coefficients across the SI group and each of the feigning groups. Validity coefficients were substantially attenuated for feigning groups relative to the SI group, with greater reductions in validity for the psychopathology group relative to the somatic problems group. Over-reporting on the MMPI-2-RF has also been associated with attenuated validity coefficients for MMPI-2-RF substantive scale scores in samples of forensic disability litigants (Wiggins et al., 2012).

Whitman et al. (2021) extended the Burchett and Ben-Porath (2010) study to investigate the effects of under-reporting (in addition to over-reporting) on substantive scale score validity using a similar design with the MMPI-3. Undergraduate students were administered a variety of measures before they were assigned to one of three instructional groups for completing MMPI-3: (a) respond following standard instructions (i.e., SI), (b) over-report psychopathology in the context of a criminal responsibility evaluation, or (c) under-report in the context of a pre-employment evaluation. Again, correlations between MMPI-3 and criterion measure scores were substantially attenuated in the over- and under-reporting groups relative to the SI group. In this study, the authors also conducted additional analyses in which they compared validity coefficients across groups defined by MMPI-3 SVT scores rather than by simulation group. These analyses more directly demonstrated that clinically significant over- and under-reporting as identified by MMPI-3 F and Fp scores and L and K scores, respectively, are associated with substantially attenuated substantive scale score validity. These authors also reported classification accuracy estimates that supported the utility of MMPI-3 SVT scores at test manual-specified T-score cutoffs.

Similar research has also demonstrated that, in the context of higher over-reporting SVT scores, validity coefficients for substantive scale scores are lower relative to normative elevations on SVT scores. For example, Gardner and Boccaccini (2017) demonstrated that PAI NIM scores moderated the associations between Antisocial Behavior and subscale scores and clinician ratings on a psychopathy measure, such that validity coefficients of a moderate effect size were attenuated to near-zero at higher NIM scores. Similarly, Calhoun et al. (2000) demonstrated that 70% of college student dissimulators who were instructed to feign PTSD-produced PAI profiles that, in the absence of consideration for response style, indicated PTSD as a likely diagnostic consideration.

Associations with Performance

SVT scores can provide supporting evidence of exaggerated cognitive complaints and psychopathology in the context of other SVTs and PVTs. Exceeding SVT cutoff scores has been associated with higher rates of PVT failure, indicating that SVTs are sensitive to non-credible cognitive performance (see, e.g., special issue [Giromini et al., 2022] articles for recent reviews of over-reporting research using various instruments). For example, Tylicki et al. (2020) conducted an early study on the utility of MMPI-3 over-reporting scales. In a sample of forensic disability claimants, these authors utilized several SVTs (DAPS NB, BHI-2 Self-Disclosure, and PAI NIM and MAL scales) and PVTs from the Word Memory Test (WMT; Green, 2005), Non-Verbal Medical Symptom Validity Test (NV-MSVT;

Green, 2008), and California Verbal Learning Test-II (CVLT-II; Delis et al., 2008) to create incentive-only, possible malingered neurocognitive dysfunction (MND), probable MND, and definite MND, per the Slick et al. (1999) criteria. They reported that not only did MMPI-3 over-reporting scale scores discriminate between pass- and fail-groups for single PVTs, but they also differentiated probable/definite MND from incentive-only and possible MND groups with generally very good classification accuracy estimates.

SVTs can also be used alongside PVTs to predict neurocognitive performance. For example, Ord et al. (2021) reported results of multiple regression analyses in which SVT and PVT scores each explained unique variance in symptom reports in a sample of combat veterans, indicating that including both types of validity indicators in test batteries is not redundant. These authors and Van Dyke et al. (2013) each conducted factor analyses of SVT, PVT, symptom report, and cognitive performance measures and results of each study supported three factor models with separate cognitive performance, symptom self-report (including SVT), and PVT factors, further providing evidence of the utility of using both SVTs and PVTs in neuropsychological evaluations.

Recent research has indicated that simultaneous over- and under-reporting on the MMPI-3 predicts higher SVT scores and poorer performance on PVTs beyond over-reporting scores alone. Specifically, Whitman et al. (2023) conducted a study using a sample of forensic disability claimants who completed the MMPI-3 and several other PVTs, SVTs, self-report measures, and neurocognitive performance-based measures. They identified individuals who produced elevations on both the MMPI-3 over-reporting and the under-reporting scales as well as individuals who produced elevations on over-reporting, but not under-reporting scales. Those who engaged in over- and under-reporting consistently failed PVTs at a higher rate and scored higher on over- and under-reporting SVTs and measures of emotional and cognitive complaints, but lower on measures of externalizing problems, especially related to substance use. The authors concluded that individuals who over- and under-report are likely engaging in a selective response style, in which they emphasize their positive qualities and pre-alleged injury adjustment (i.e., under-report) but also their post-alleged injury problems (i.e., over-report). This approach to testing has also been qualitatively described as a "virtuous victim" response style (e.g., Greiffenstein et al., 2007).

Challenges and Recommendations for Symptom Validity Assessment

Practitioners are faced with several challenges to interpreting SVT scores. Some of these are particularly relevant in forensic assessments, such as "coaching" by examinees' legal representatives who themselves may be motivated to aid the examinee in obtaining a favorable outcome in the psychological evaluation (see, Victor & Abeles, 2004, for a review). Others are issues common in most assessment contexts, such as factors other than intentional noncooperation, over-reporting, or under-reporting that contribute to SVT elevations (i.e., confounds) and mild to moderate elevations or inconsistent findings across multiple SVTs. Next, we describe these challenges and provide recommendations for practitioners to address them.

Coaching

Examinees may receive "coaching," or information about how to respond to psychological tests to portray their symptoms in a particular way (i.e., symptom coaching), and/or how to avoid detection of feigning by SVTs (i.e., test coaching), from their legal representatives or even from their own internet searches. Recently, Spengler et al. (2018) surveyed attorneys' attitudes regarding coaching clients on the MMPI-2. Over half (53%) of attorneys indicated that they inform clients about the MMPI-2 Validity Scales, and more than 70% of attorneys reported that they believe they should provide their clients advice and preparation about responding to psychological testing. Although these findings are concerning, forensic practitioners can prepare to use MMPI-3 appropriately in forensic evaluations (see, e.g., Ben-Porath et al., 2022), and some research indicates that SVT scores can discriminate between individuals instructed to respond honestly or to feign, including those who were coached and uncoached, particularly at higher cutoff scores.

For example, Aparcero et al. (2021) conducted a meta-analysis of 99 studies that investigated the impact of coaching on detection of over-reporting using MMPI-2 (Butcher et al., 1989). Overall, they reported evidence that coaching on detection avoidance strategies reduced the effectiveness of MMPI-2 over-reporting scales, but the over-reporting scales were nevertheless able to identify exaggeration or feigning with moderate to very large effect sizes even in the context of coaching. More recent simulations studies have also indicated that MMPI-3 over-reporting scales are able to meaningfully distinguish genuine responders and individuals who were symptom-coached for feigning PTSD and/or mTBI (Morris et al., 2021) or test-coached for avoiding "lie detection" while feigning symptoms for a compensation-seeking claim (Reeves et al., 2022). Research using other tests, such as SIMS (Jelicic et al., 2011; Veltri & Williams, 2013), TOMM (Jelicic et al., 2011), and PAI (Hopwood et al., 2010; Rogers et al., 2012), has also indicated that SVTs are relatively robust to the effects of symptom and test coaching. However, the effect of coaching may be greater when symptoms of particular disorders, such as schizophrenia, are feigned relative to others, such as PTSD or generalized anxiety disorder (e.g., Veltri & Williams, 2013).

To counter the effects of coaching, we recommend that practitioners utilize multiple SVTs and PVTs in their evaluations, particularly ones that rely on various methodologies for identifying invalid responding (Boone, 2009). The greater the variety of validity indicators used in an assessment, the less likely it is that a test-taker can successfully be coached to escape detection of invalid responding.

Confounds

Test-takers can produce elevations on SVTs due to several different factors other than invalid responding, which create confounds that must be considered in their interpretation. First, as already discussed, reading or language limitations, difficulty sustaining attention, cognitive impairment, and confusion related to double negatives imbedded in items can all result in elevations on non-content-based invalid responding scales. Content-inconsistent responding can artificially increase over-reporting and under-reporting scales as well. Other confounds that can contribute to elevations on SVTs include genuine psychopathology or medical conditions, cultural variables (e.g., racial, linguistic, and traditional backgrounds), emotional distress, and genuine good adjustment. These factors should always be assessed and need to be ruled out as sole contributors to elevations prior to concluding that SVT scores are due to noncooperation, malingering, or defensiveness.

Genuine psychopathology or medical conditions can, to some extent, result in elevations on some SVTs. SVTs that are rigorously developed and validated, however, should only indicate mild to moderate elevations in such a circumstance, whereas high scores should not be sensitive to genuine symptoms (Burchett & Ben-Porath, 2019). Interpretive guidelines for the MMPI-3 Validity Scales include consideration of genuine psychopathology or medical conditions for mild to moderate elevations, but as cutoff scores increase, it becomes increasingly unlikely that genuine conditions alone would result in elevations at that level (Ben-Porath & Tellegen, 2020a). For scales that may be more sensitive to genuine psychopathology, it is recommended to utilize higher cutoff scores and to rely on consistency with other SVTs to derive conclusions. Some have indicated that SVTs consisting of items with "quasi-rare" symptoms, or the inclusion of items that are rare in normative populations but not necessarily in patient samples, are particularly sensitive to genuine psychopathology (Sharf et al., 2019). For example, Glassmire et al. (2017) found that MMPI-2-RF Fp-r item demonstrated lower endorsement rates relative to F-r items among forensic psychiatric inpatients adjudicated as not guilty by reason of insanity and who had no known reason to over-report. Therefore, relying not only on consistency across SVTs, but also using SVTs with appropriate methodologies and with relevant item content can help practitioners rule out genuine psychopathology as a confound for SVT elevations. Increasing interpretive cutoffs, as reflected in MMPI-3 interpretive guidelines, can also help increase the specificity of assessment, albeit at a potential cost to sensitivity.

Cultural factors can also contribute to SVT elevations in several ways. Lilienfeld (2013) discussed the potential for ethnicity and cultural variables to impact neuropsychological test performance, with potential drivers of differences, including misunderstandings of test instructions, inappropriate content, differential prior exposure to material, poor rapport between examiner and examinee, and differences in access to education, as well as genuine discrepancies. Dixon et al. (2023) provide an example of the impact of item content on SVTs for interpretation of scores across Black, Latinx, and White students and forensic psychiatric inpatients. For this study, three Black female and three Black male psychologists rated the degree to which items on MMPI-2-RF and MMPI-3 reflect cultural mistrust, which is adaptive among people of color (Whaley, 2001). Of the 335 items on MMPI-3, only 9 were identified as potentially reflecting an adaptive cultural mistrust rather than an over-reporting response style. In a college student sample, Black students endorsed the highest number of these items, followed by Latinx, then White students with small to moderate effect sizes. The same was not true for forensic patients, for whom generally high levels of mistrust were reflected across the board. Of the nine items identified, only three belonged to item pairs scored on CRIN, VRIN, or TRIN, whereas three were scored on F and one was scored on Fp. Thus, cultural mistrust alone is insufficient to contribute meaningfully to elevations on these scales.

An example of a cultural factor that can, to some extent, impact SVT scores is traditional or religious upbringing. For example, among mental health outpatients, individuals who identified as protestant produced a higher average MMPI-2-RF L-r score relative to the MMPI-2-RF normative sample (Bridges & Baum, 2013). This finding is consistent with results from a meta-analytic study by Rosen et al. (2016) who found that samples reflecting strongly held Christian and Judeo faith-based values scored an average of half a standard deviation (five T-score points) higher than the normative sample, although many of the included studies were conducted in contexts where significant demand characteristics could have led to under-reporting as well. Bagby et al. (2020) sampled undergraduate students who identified as Muslim and who did not have demand characteristics for under-reporting but did complete more extensive measurement of their beliefs. Their findings were consistent with previous research suggesting that traditional faith values are associated with L-r scores that are a half standard deviation higher than the test normative sample, as well as a novel finding that increased strength in Muslim faith was associated with increased L-r scores. MMPI-3 interpretive guidelines regarding L scores incorporate these findings (Ben-Porath &

Tellegen, 2020a) by identifying a traditional upbringing as a potential confound to be considered when interpreting scores in this scale. Forensic practitioners should be aware of potential effects of religious beliefs and traditional upbringing on any SVT they administer and interpret, implementing higher cutoff scores for interpretation as appropriate.

Overall, cultural variables, such as linguistic differences, race and ethnicity, gender or sexual identity, age, socioeconomic status, educational level, religious beliefs, and many others, should be considered when selecting SVTs, administering them, and integrating data across sources of information; however, relatively little empirical research has accumulated on related topics. Using the forensic interview to assess cultural, linguistic, and socioeconomic differences can also be helpful (Barber Rioja & Rosenfeld, 2018), as well as reviewing the content of items contributing to scale elevations. As noted by Burchett and Ben-Porath (2019), future research should evaluate SVTs for differential predictive validity on the basis of cultural variables (e.g., Shkalim et al., 2016).

Mixed Findings

Another challenge for practitioners occurs when multiple SVTs yield indeterminate or potentially conflicting results. Mild to moderate elevations are sometimes considered indeterminate because they could be attributed to some of the confounds just described rather than invalid responding. When test-takers produce elevations on SVTs at levels indicating that a protocol is clearly invalid (e.g., T-score 100 or higher on the MMPI-3 F or Fp scales), the classification accuracy of the SVT is superior when compared with mild to moderate elevations. For example, Rogers et al. (2012) demonstrated how removing an "indeterminate group" who scored within five T-score points of PAI validity scale cutoff scores would improve the overall classification accuracy rates for detecting feigned trauma-related disabilities. However, in practice, test-takers may score within the indeterminate range. Using multiple validity scales that were developed with varying methodologies and that consist of different types of content may help clarify an individual's overall approach to testing. Moreover, we recommend against interpreting below threshold validity scale scores as representing "valid responding," especially to counter evidence of over-reporting. Rather, consistent with Chafetz (2022), negative validity indicator results should merely be interpreted as not indicating over-reporting.

Conflicting results occur when some SVTs indicate no problems with symptom validity, whereas others indicate invalid responding, and evaluators are challenged with determining whether and how to interpret scores across other measures. Relatively little guidance on how to integrate scores across multiple SVTs has been provided by empirical research studies (Lilienfeld et al., 2013). Some research has indicated that at least two PVT and SVT failures indicates probable invalid clinical profiles (Larrabee, 2014). However, Odland et al. (2015) reported important base rate information and recommendations for integrating multiple validity indicators, in which the number of validity indicators that was recommended depends on factors such as the overall number of tests administered. It is also worth noting that some forensic neuropsychologists believe failure of only one SVT/PVT may be sufficient for concluding invalidity, depending on the extent of failure.

Summary

Including SVTs to assess test-takers' approaches to self-report testing is critical, particularly when conducting forensic neuropsychological evaluations. Invalid response styles, including non-content-based invalid responding, over-reporting, and under-reporting all threaten the validity of self-report measures. A test-taker may engage these response styles intentionally or unintentionally. Using multiple SVTs to assess each of these three response styles can reduce the risk of inaccurate conclusions about a test-taker's psychological functioning based on psychological test scores. In addition, using SVTs that vary with regard to their methodology and the content of their items is likely to assist practitioners in overcoming challenges to symptom validity assessment, such as coaching, confounds, and mixed findings. In conclusion, we offer several recommendations for practitioners using SVTs in their neuropsychological assessments:

- A test battery should include SVTs intended to measure non-content-based invalid responding, including non-responsiveness, random responding, and fixed true or fixed false responding, as well as over-reporting, and under-reporting.
- SVTs included in test batteries should reflect multiple methodologies to strengthen any conclusion drawn from them. Common methodologies for detecting invalid response styles include identifying infrequent claims and ones associated empirically with noncredible responding. The MMPI-3 F, Fp, and Fs scales are examples of the former, whereas FBS and RBS represent the latter.
- SVTs included in test batteries should be sensitive to the specific types of problems an individual is claiming. For example, if an individual is claiming to have a disability due to posttraumatic stress, then over-reporting SVTs known to be sensitive to over-reporting PTSD symptoms should be included in the assessment.
- Before concluding that an individual is likely engaging in intentional noncooperation, exaggeration, malingering, or defensiveness in the context of an SVT elevation (particularly those in the mild to moderate range), practitioners should consider and rule out confounds that may have contributed to an elevation. Examples of these confounds include language limitations, inattentiveness, cognitive impairment, confusion around double negatives imbedded in items, content-inconsistent responding that artificially increases over- and under-reporting SVT scores, genuine psychopathology or medical conditions, cultural variables (e.g., racial, linguistic, and traditional backgrounds), emotional distress, and genuine good adjustment.
- Practitioners can have increased confidence in conclusions about particular response styles in the context of higher SVT elevations (e.g., T scores of 100 on the MMPI-3 F, Fp, or Fs scales and 90 or higher in FBS or RBS), multiple SVT elevations (including simultaneous over- and under-reporting scale elevations, and particularly across SVT methodologies), and when confounds are ruled out.

Additional Resources

- Advanced MMPI-3 Validity Scales Interpretation On Demand with 3 APA CEs.
- MMPI-2-RF and MMPI-3 Reference Lists from the University of Minnesota Press.
- American Academy of Clinical Neuropsychology (AACN) 2021 consensus statement on validity assessment: Update of the 2009 AACN consensus conference statement on neuropsychological assessment of effort, response bias, and malingering (Sweet et al., 2021).

Author Notes

The statements and opinions in this article are those of the authors. Regarding potential conflicts of interest, Yossef S. Ben-Porath receives research funding from the MMPI-3 test publisher, the University of Minnesota Press and is a paid consultant for the test distributor, Pearson Assessments. As co-author of the MMPI-3, he receives royalties on sales of the test.

References

Aparcero, M., Picard, E. H., Nijdam-Jones, A., & Rosenfeld, B. (2021). The impact of coaching on feigned psychiatric and medical symptoms: A meta-analysis using the MMPI-2. *Psychological Assessment, 33*(8), 729–745. https://doi.org/10.1037/pas0001016

Bagby, R. M., Onno, K. A., Mortezaei, A., & Sellbom, M. (2020). Examining the "traditional background hypothesis" for the MMPI-2–RF L-r scores in a Muslim faith–based sample. *Psychological Assessment, 32*(10), 991–995. https://doi.org/10.1037/pas0000941

Barber Rioja, V., & Rosenfeld, B. (2018). Addressing linguistic and cultural differences in the forensic interview. *International Journal of Forensic Mental Health, 17*(4), 377–386. https://doi.org/10.1080/14999013.2018.1495280

Beck, A. T., Epstein, N., Brown, G., & Steer, R. A. (1988). An inventory for measuring clinical anxiety: Psychometric properties. *Journal of Consulting and Clinical Psychology, 56*(6), 893–897. https://doi.org/10.1037/0022-006X.56.6.893

Beck, A. T., Steer, R. A., & Brown, G. (1996). *Beck Depression Inventory–II (BDI-II)* [Database record]. APA PsycTests. https://doi.org/10.1037/t00742-000

Beck, A. T., Ward, C. H., Mendelson, M., Mock, J., & Erbaugh, J. (1961). An inventory for measuring depression. *Archives of General Psychiatry, 4*(6), 561–571.

Ben-Porath, Y. S. (2013). Assessing personality and psychopathology with self-report inventories. In J. R. Graham & J. A. Naglieri (Eds.), *Handbook of Psychology: Assessment Psychology* (2nd ed., Vol. X, pp. 622–644). John Wiley & Sons.

Ben-Porath, Y. S., Heilbrun, K., & Rizzo, M. (2022). Using the MMPI-3 in legal settings. *Journal of Personality Assessment, 104*(2), 162–178. https://doi.org/10.1080/00223891.2021.2006672

Ben-Porath, Y. S., & Tellegen, A. (2008/2011). *MMPI-2-RF (Minnesota Multiphasic Personality Inventory–2 Restructured Form): Manual for Administration, Scoring, and Interpretation*. University of Minnesota Press.

Ben-Porath, Y. S., & Tellegen, A. (2020a). *MMPI-3 Manual for Administration, Scoring, and Interpretation*. University of Minnesota Press.

Ben-Porath, Y. S., & Tellegen, A. (2020b). *MMPI-3 Technical Manual*. University of Minnesota Press.

Boone, K. B. (2009). The need for continuous and comprehensive sampling of effort/response bias during neuropsychological examinations. *The Clinical Neuropsychologist, 23*(4), 729–741. https://doi.org/10.1080/13854040802427803

Bridges, S. A., & Baum, L. J. (2013). An examination of the MMPI-2-RF L-r scale in an outpatient protestant sample. *Journal of Psychology & Christianity, 32*(2), 115–123.

Briere, J. (2001). *Detailed Assessment of Posttraumatic Stress: DAPS: Professional Manual*. Psychological Assessment Resources.

Briere, J. (2011). *Trauma Symptom Inventory-2nd Edition (TSI-2) Professional Manual*. Psychological Assessment Resources. https://doi.org/10.1002/9780470479216.corpsy1010

Bruns, D., & Disorbio, J. M. (2003). *Battery for Health Improvement 2 Manual*. Pearson.

Burchett, D., & Bagby, R. M. (2022). Assessing negative response bias: A review of the noncredible overreporting scales of the MMPI-2-RF and MMPI-3. *Psychological Injury and Law, 15*, 22–36. https://doi.org/10.1007/s12207-021-09435-9

Burchett, D., & Ben-Porath, Y. S. (2010). The impact of over-reporting on MMPI-2-RF substantive scale score validity. *Assessment, 17*(4), 497–516. https://doi.org/10.1177/1073191110378972

Burchett, D., & Ben-Porath, Y. S. (2019). Methodological considerations for developing and evaluating response bias indicators. *Psychological Assessment, 31*(12), 1497–1511. https://doi.org/10.1037/pas0000680

Burchett, D., Dragon, W. R., Smith Holbert, A. M., Tarescavage, A. M., Mattson, C. A., Handel, R. W., & Ben-Porath, Y. S. (2016). "False feigners": Examining the impact of non-content-based invalid responding on the Minnesota Multiphasic Personality Inventory-2 Restructured Form content-based invalid responding indicators. *Psychological Assessment, 28*(5), 458–470. https://doi.org/10.1037/pas0000205

Butcher, J. N., Dahlstrom, W. G., Graham, J. R., Tellegen, A., & Kaemmer, B. (1989). *MMPI–2: Minnesota Multiphasic Personality Inventory–2: Manual for Administration and Scoring*. University of Minnesota Press.

Calhoun, P. S., Earnst, K. S., Tucker, D. D., Kirby, A. C., & Beckham, J. C. (2000). Feigning combat-related posttraumatic stress disorder on the *Personality Assessment Inventory*. *Journal of Personality Assessment, 75*(2), 338–350. https://doi.org/10.1207/S15327752JPA7502_11

Cashel, M. L., Rogers, R., Sewell, K., & Martin-Cannici, C. (1995). The Personality Assessment Inventory (PAI) and the detection of defensiveness. *Assessment, 2*(4), 333–342. https://doi.org/10.1177/107319119500200400 4

Chafetz, M. D. (2022). Deception is different: Negative validity test findings do not provide "evidence" for "good effort." *The Clinical Neuropsychologist, 36*(6), 1244–1264. https://doi.org/10.1080/13854046.2020.1840633

Delis, D. C., Kaplan, E., Kramer, J. H., & Ober, B. A. (2008). *California Verbal Learning Test-Second Edition (CVLT-II)*. ECPA.

Dixon, J. N., Caddell, T. M., Alexander, A. A., Burchett, D., Anderson, J. L., Marek, R. J., & Glassmire, D. M. (2023). Adapting assessment processes to consider cultural mistrust in forensic practices: An example with the MMPI instruments. *Law and Human Behavior, 47*(1), 292–306. https://doi.org/10.1037/lhb0000504

Fuermaier, A. B., Dandachi-Fitzgerald, B., & Lehrner, J. (2023). Validity assessment of early retirement claimants: Symptom overreporting on the Beck Depression Inventory–II. *Applied Neuropsychology: Adult*. Advance online publication. https://doi.org/10.1080/23279095.2023.2206031

Gardner, B. O., & Boccaccini, M. T. (2017). Does the convergent validity of the PAI Antisocial Features scale depend on offender response style? *Journal of Personality Assessment*, *99*(5), 481–493. https://doi.org/10.1080/00223891.2017.1296846

Gervais, R. O., Ben-Porath, Y. S., Wygant, D. B., & Green, P. (2008). Development and validation of a Response Bias Scale (RBS) for the MMPI-2. *Assessment, 14*(2), 196–208. https://doi.org/10.1177/1073191106295861

Giromini, L., Young, G., & Sellbom, M. (2022). Assessing negative response bias using self-report measures: New articles, new issues. *Psychological Injury and Law, 15*, 1–21. https://doi.org/10.1007/s12207-022-09444-2

Glassmire, D. M., Jhawar, A., Burchett, D., & Tarescavage, A. M. (2017). Evaluating item endorsement rates for the MMPI-2-RF F-r and Fp-r scales across ethnic, gender, and diagnostic groups with a forensic inpatient sample. *Psychological Assessment, 29*(5), 500–508. https://doi.org/10.1037/pas0000366

Green, P. (2005). *Green's Word Memory Test for Microsoft Windows: User's Manual*. Green's Publications.

Green, P. (2008). *Manual for the Nonverbal Medical Symptom Validity Test*. Green's Publishing.

Greiffenstein, M. F., Fox, D., & Lees-Haley, P. R. (2007). The MMPI-2 Fake Bad Scale in detection of noncredible brain injury claims. In K. Boone (Ed.) *Assessment of Feigned Cognitive Impairment: A Neuropsychological Perspective* (pp. 210–235). Guilford Publications.

Handel, R. W., Ben-Porath, Y. S., Tellegen, A., & Archer, R. P. (2010). Psychometric functioning of the MMPI-2-RF VRIN-r and TRIN-r scales with varying degrees of randomness, acquiescence, and counter-acquiescence. *Psychological Assessment, 22*(1), 87–95. https://doi.org/10.1037/a0017061

Heilbronner, R., Sweet, J., Morgan, J., Larrabee, G., & Millis, S., Conference Participants. (2009). American Academy of Clinical Neuropsychology consensus conference statement on the neuropsychological assessment of effort, response bias, and malingering. *The Clinical Neuropsychologist, 23*, 1093–1129. https://doi.org/10.1080/13854040903155063

Hopwood, C. J., Orlando, M. J., & Clark, T. S. (2010). The detection of malingered pain-related disability with the Personality Assessment Inventory. *Rehabilitation Psychology, 55*(3), 307–310. https://doi.org/10.1037/a0020516

Jelicic, M., Ceunen, E., Peters, M. J. V., & Merckelbach, H. (2011). Detecting coached feigning using the test of Memory Malingering (TOMM) and the structured inventory of Malingered Symptomatology (SIMS). *Journal of Clinical Psychology, 67*(9), 850–855. https://doi.org/10.1002/jclp.20805

Larrabee, G. J. (2014). False-positive rates associated with the use of multiple performance and symptom validity tests. *Archives of Clinical Neuropsychology, 29*(4), 364–373. https://doi.org/10.1093/arclin/acu019

Lees-Haley, P. R., English, L. T., & Glenn, W. J. (1991). A Fake Bad scale on the MMPI–2 for personal injury claimants. *Psychological Reports, 68*, 203–210.

Lilienfeld, S. O., Thames, A. D., & Watts, A. L. (2013). Symptom validity testing: Unresolved questions, future directions. *Journal of Experimental Psychopathology, 4*(1), 78–87. https://doi.org/10.5127/jep.028312

Martin, P. K., Schroeder, R. W., & Odland, A. P. (2015). Neuropsychologists' validity testing beliefs and practices: A survey of North American professionals. *The Clinical Neuropsychologist, 29*(6), 741–776. https://doi.org/10.1080/13854046.2015.1087597

Martin, P. K., Schroeder, R. W., & Odland, A. P. (2025). Neuropsychological validity assessment beliefs and practices: A survey of North American neuropsychologists and validity assessment experts. *Archives of Clinical Neuropsychology, 40*(2), 201–223.

McGrath, R. E., Mitchell, M., Kim, B. H., & Hough, L. (2010). Evidence for response bias as a source of error variance in applied assessment. *Psychological Bulletin, 136*(3), 450–470. https://doi.org/10.1037/a0019216

Morey, L. C. (1996). *An Interpretive Guide to the Personality Assessment Inventory (PAI)*. Psychological Assessment Resources.

Morey, L. C. (2007). *Personality Assessment Inventory (PAI): Professional Manual*. Psychological Assessment Resources.

Morris, N. M., Mattera, J., Golden, B., Moses, S., & Ingram, P. (2021). Evaluating the performance of the MMPI-3 over-reporting scales: Sophisticated simulators and the effects of comorbid conditions. *The Clinical Neuropsychologist, 36*(8), 2361–2369. https://doi.org/10.1080/13854046.2021.1968037

Neal, T. M. S., & Grisso, T. (2014). Assessment practices and expert judgment methods in forensic psychology and psychiatry: An international snapshot. *Criminal Justice and Behavior, 41*(12), 1406–1421. https://doi.org/10.1177/0093854814548449

Nelson, N.W., Sweet, J. J., Berry, D. T., Bryant, F. B., & Granacher, R. P. (2007). Response validity in forensic neuropsychology: Exploratory factor analytic evidence of distinct cognitive and psychological constructs. *Journal of the International Neuropsychological Society, 13*(3), 440–449. https://doi.org/10.1017/S1355617707070373

Odland, A. P., Lammy, A. B., Martin, P. K., Grote, C. L., & Mittenberg, W. (2015). Advanced administration and interpretation of multiple validity tests. *Psychological Injury and Law, 8*, 46–63. https://doi.org/10.1007/s12207-015-9216-4.

Ord, A. S., Shura, R. D., Sansone, A. R., Martindale, S. L., Taber, K. H., & Rowland, J. A. (2021). Performance validity and symptom validity tests: Are they measuring different constructs? *Neuropsychology, 35*(3), 241–251. https://doi.org/10.1037/neu0000722

Petri, J. M., Weathers, F. W., Witte, T. K., & Silverstein, M. W. (2020). The Detailed Assessment of Posttraumatic Stress-Second Edition (DAPS-2): Initial psychometric evaluation in an MTurk-recruited, trauma-exposed community sample. *Assessment, 27*(6), 1116–1127. https://doi.org/10.1177/1073191119880963

Reeves, C. K., Brown, T. A., & Sellbom, M. (2022). An examination of the MMPI-3 validity scales in detecting overreporting of psychological problems. *Psychological Assessment, 34*(6), 517–527. https://doi.org/10.1037/pas0001112

Rogers, R., Gillard, N. D., Wooley, C. N., & Ross, C. A. (2012). The detection of feigned disabilities: The effectiveness of the Personality Assessment Inventory in a traumatized inpatient sample. *Assessment, 19*(1), 77–88. https://doi.org/10.1177/1073191111422031

Rogers, R., Sewell, K. W., Morey, L. C., & Ustad, K. L. (1996). Detection of feigned mental disorders on the Personality Assessment Inventory: A discriminant analysis. *Journal of Personality Assessment, 67*(3), 629–640.

Rosen, G. M., Baldwin, S. A., & Smith, R. E. (2016). Reassessing the "traditional background hypothesis" for elevated MMPI and MMPI-2 Lie-scale scores. *Psychological Assessment, 28*(10), 1336–1343. https://doi.org/10.1037/pas0000262

Sellbom, M., Wygant, D. B., Tarescavage, A. M., & Ben-Porath, Y. S. (2022). Using the MMPI-3 in forensic psychological assessments. In C. Garofalo & J. J. Sijtsema (Eds.), *Clinical Forensic Psychology* (pp. 515–537). Palgrave Macmillan. https://doi.org/10.1007/978-3-030-80882-2_26

Sharf, A. J., Rogers, R., Williams, M. M., & Henry, S. A. (2019). The effectiveness of the MMPI-2-RF in detecting feigned mental disorders and cognitive deficits: A meta-analysis. *Journal of Psychopathology and Behavioral Assessment, 39*, 441–455. https://doi.org/10.1007/s10862-017-9590-1

Shkalim, E., Ben-Porath, Y. S., Handel, R. W., Almagor, M., & Tellegen, A. (2016). Psychometric examination, adaptation, and evaluation of the Hebrew translation of the MMPI-2-RF VRIN-r and TRIN-r validity scales. *Journal of Personality Assessment, 98*(6), 608–615. https://doi.org/10.1080/00223891.2016.1174705

Slick, D. J., Sherman, E. M. S., & Iverson, G. L. (1999). Diagnostic criteria for malingered neurocognitive dysfunction: Proposed standards for clinical practice and research. *The Clinical Neuropsychologist, 13*(4), 545–561. https://doi.org/10.1076/1385-4046(199911)13:04;1–Y;FT545

Smith, G. P., & Burger, G. K. (1997). Detection of malingering: Validation of the Structured Inventory of Malingered Symptomatology (SIMS). *The Journal of the American Academy of Psychiatry and the Law, 25*(2), 183–189. https://doi.org/10.1037/t04573-000

Spengler, P. M., Walters, N. T., Bryan, E., & Millspaugh, B. S. (2018). Attorneys' attitudes toward coaching forensic clients on the MMPI-2: Replication and extension of attorney survey by Wetter and Corrigan (1995). *Journal of Personality Assessment, 102*(1), 56–65. https://doi.org/10.1080/00223891.2018.1501568

Sweet, J. J., Heilbronner, R. L., Morgan, J. E., Larrabee, G. J., Rohling, M. L., Boone, K. B., ... & Conference Participants. (2021). American Academy of Clinical Neuropsychology (AACN) 2021 consensus statement on validity assessment: Update of the 2009 AACN consensus conference statement on neuropsychological assessment of effort, response bias, and malingering. *The Clinical Neuropsychologist, 35*(6), 1053–1106.

Tellegen, A., & Ben-Porath, Y. S. (2008/2011). *Minnesota Multiphasic Personality Inventory-2-Restructured Form (MMPI-2-RF): Technical Manual*. University of Minnesota Press.

Tylicki, J. L., Gervais, R. O., & Ben-Porath, Y. S. (2020). Examination of the MMPI-3 over-reporting scales in a forensic disability sample. *The Clinical Neuropsychologist, 36*(7), 1878–1901. https://doi.org/10.1080/13854046.2020.1856414

Tylicki, J. L., Tarescavage, A. M., & Wygant, D. B. (2021). Assessment of malingering among head injury litigants with the MMPI-2, MMPI-2-RF, and MMPI-3. In A. M. Horton, Jr., & C. R. Reynolds (Eds.), *Detection of Malingering during Head Injury Litigation* (3rd ed., pp. 289–307). Springer. https://doi.org/10.1007/978-3-030-54656-4_8

University of Minnesota Press. (2023). *MMPI-3 references*. https://www.upress.umn.edu/test-division/MMPI-3/mmpi-3-refs

Van Dyke, S. A., Millis, S. R., Axelrod, B. N., & Hanks, R. A. (2013). Assessing effort: Differentiating performance and symptom validity. *The Clinical Neuropsychologist, 27*(8), 1234–1246. https://doi.org/10.1080/13854046.2013.835447

Veltri, C. O. C., & Williams, J. E. (2013). Does the disorder matter? Investigating a moderating effect of coached noncredible overreporting using the MMPI-2 and PAI. *Assessment, 20*(2), 199–209. https://doi.org/10.1177/1073191112464619

Victor, T. L., & Abeles, N. (2004). Coaching clients to take psychological and neuropsychological tests: A clash of ethical obligations. *Professional Psychology: Research and Practice, 35*(4), 373–379. https://doi.org/10.1037/0735-7028.35.4.373

Whaley, A. L. (2001). Cultural mistrust and mental health services for African Americans: A review and meta-analysis. *The Counseling Psychologist, 29*(4), 513–531. https://doi.org/10.1177/0011000001294003

Whitman, M. R., Gervais, R. O., & Ben-Porath, Y. S. (2023). Virtuous victims: Disability claimants who over- and under-report. *The Clinical Neuropsychologist, 37*(8), 1584–1607. https://doi.org/10.1080/13854046.2023.2185686

Whitman, M. R., Tylicki, J. L., & Ben-Porath, Y. S. (2021). Utility of the MMPI-3 Validity Scales for detecting over-reporting and under-reporting and their effects on substantive scale validity: A simulation study. *Psychological Assessment, 33*(5), 411–426. https://doi.org/10.1037/pas0000988

Wiggins, C. W., Wygant, D. B., Hoelzle, J. B., & Gervais, R. O. (2012). The more you say the less it means: Overreporting and attenuated criterion validity in a forensic disability sample. *Psychological Injury and Law, 5*, 162–173. https://doi.org/10.1007/s12207-012-9137-4

Wygant, D. B., Sellbom, M., Ben-Porath, Y. S., Stafford, K. P., Freeman, D. B., & Heilbronner, R. L. (2007). The relation between symptom validity testing and MMPI-2 scores as a function of forensic evaluation context. *Archives of Clinical Neuropsychology, 22*(4), 489–499. https://doi.org/10.1016/j.acn.2007.01.027

5 Validity Testing within the Context of Culturally and Linguistically Diverse Examinees

Farzin Irani and Karim Z. Yamout

Introduction

The world and the sociodemographics of those who present for neuropsychological evaluations are changing. While there is recognition of the role of cultural and linguistic diversity factors in neuropsychological evaluations, the specific influences of these variables on validity testing and interpretation are not always well understood. It is not always clear *how* one can understand cultural and linguistic factors to contextualize interpretations of validity test data. This chapter, therefore, aims to contribute to and advance the understanding and application of cultural and linguistic diversity factors in interpreting validity test data. We do not focus on reviewing classification accuracies of specific validity tests and their application to various culturally and linguistically diverse (CLD) groups since that has been covered elsewhere (see Salazar, Lu, & Boone, 2021; Nijdam-Jones & Rosenfeld, 2017; Strutt & Stinson, 2022; Bridges & Ahern, 2016). Instead, our aim in this chapter is to take a practical approach that reviews the existing validity literature as it relates to CLD considerations in neuropsychological/psychological evaluations, and then identify variables that might impact major approaches to validity testing and interpretation of the data for CLD groups.

We begin by reviewing the reasons why it is important to consider cultural and linguistic factors in forensic contexts. This includes a review of organizational statements recognizing the important role of CLD considerations, understanding changes in global and national demographics that necessitate greater attention to these factors, and discussing how cultural competence challenges can emerge in legal contexts. We then specifically review considerations related to admissibility of expert opinion regarding expert witness qualifications as well as admissibility of data when working with CLD examinees. Next, we review the major approaches to validity testing present in the literature, along with cultural considerations for validity measurement and interpretation. Finally, we provide practical suggestions to increase cultural understanding and maximize obtaining valid results for examinees who might disengage for reasons other than malingering.

Guidance from Professional Organizations

The importance of considering the role of cultural and linguistic diversity variables in the administration and interpretation of validity tests has been highlighted by several neuropsychology organizations. For example, the National Academy of Neuropsychology (NAN) in their position paper on validity testing (Bush et al., 2005) noted that "cultural factors may

DOI: 10.4324/9781003005063-6

lead to either exaggeration of symptoms or denial of symptoms without any conscious or unconscious motivation to 'deceive'" (p. 425). This NAN policy paper further asserted that

> neuropsychologists working with culturally diverse populations must ensure that their assessment of response validity includes a thorough examination of the examinee's cultural background. The use of SVTs with culturally diverse populations for whom validation data do not exist must be carefully considered, and practitioners must be able to justify decisions for doing so.
>
> (p. 425)

Similarly, the American Academy of Clinical Neuropsychology (AACN) 2021 consensus statement on validity assessment (Sweet et al., 2021) notes that "(t)he presence of cultural, ethnic, and/or language factors known to affect performance results necessitates that clinicians adjust thresholds for identifying response bias" (p. 1068). The group adds, "(n)europsychological validity assessment research methods in the 2020s should include consideration of generalizability, or limitations, regarding such factors as ethnic/cultural diversity, language, and education." More broadly, these recommendations are consistent with APA Ethical Principles of Psychologists and Code of Conduct and its Specialty Guidelines for Forensic Psychology, which also highlight the importance of individual and group differences as they relate to age, gender, gender identity, race, ethnicity, culture, national origin, religion, sexual orientation, disability, language, socioeconomic status, or other relevant individual and cultural differences (APA 2013, 2017).

Maintaining Relevance

The previously noted organizational statements emphasizing the importance of considering CLD factors are consistent with changes in the demographics of the world and those who present for forensic and clinical neuropsychological evaluations. According to the U.N. World Population Prospects (2022), in the next three decades, the regional distribution of the population in 2050 will significantly differ from that of today. Central and Southern Asia are expected to become the most populous regions in the world by 2037, and between 2022 and 2050, sub-Saharan Africa's population is expected to almost double, and will account for more than half of the growth of the world's population. Europe and Northern America are projected to reach their peak population sizes and experience population declines in the late 2030s due to sustained low levels of fertility and high emigration rates for some countries. In the United States, according to the most recent U.S. Census Bureau population reports, the White population is projected to shrink over coming decades due to falling birth rates and rising deaths with aging (Vespa, Medina & Armstrong, 2020). The population of people who are two or more races is projected to be the fastest-growing racial or ethnic group over the next several decades, followed by Asians and Hispanic/Latinx communities which are predicted to double. The nation's foreign-born population is projected to rise, and, beginning in 2030, net international migration from Asian and Latin American countries is expected to overtake natural increase as the driver of population growth.

An increasing ethnoracially pluralistic society has also changed the languages spoken in U.S. homes. According to a 2019 U.S. Census Bureau report on language use in the United States, while English remains the most common language spoken at home for 78% of the U.S. population, over time, there has been a significant increase in those who speak a language other than English at home (Dietrich & Hernandez, 2022). Spanish is the most-frequent non-English language spoken in U.S. homes, followed by Chinese, Tagalog, Vietnamese, and Arabic, while several Indigenous languages are becoming endangered (Dietrich & Hernandez, 2022, Cranney, 2019).

Thus, it is increasingly likely that forensic and clinical neuropsychologists will interface with CLD examinees. Bridges and Ahern (2016) suggest that since CLD groups tend to be overrepresented in jobs that involve substantial risk for disability or injury and are also disproportionately present in correctional settings, they are likely to be overrepresented in forensic neuropsychology evaluations. Yet, data that further documents sociodemographic characteristics of forensic populations served by neuropsychologists is notably limited. Most recently, LaDuke et al. (2018) conducted a survey of neuropsychologists engaged in forensic assessment practices where they do report some sociodemographic characteristics (e.g., age, gender, ethnicity) of neuropsychologists and the populations to whom they provide services (e.g., client's age, neuropsychological conditions). However, further information about linguistic and cultural backgrounds of the populations served by forensic neuropsychologists was not gathered. This forms an area of future research, especially since there are disparities in gender and ethnic identity among neuropsychologists engaged in forensic practice (LaDuke et al., 2018). Relatedly, ethical and other challenges for fair access to neuropsychological services by CLD groups has been an area of concern and priority for the field and includes expanding the toolkit of measures to better serve CLD groups (American Academy of Clinical Neuropsychology Relevance, 2050).

Cultural Competency and Validity in the Forensic Arena

The validity of an evaluation, such as whether the examiner conducted a competent, valid, and defensible evaluation and interpreted it correctly, can be challenged in any context. In a clinical setting, a neuropsychologist may evaluate a patient and render a clinical opinion, only to have another neuropsychologist disagree with the first neuropsychologist's procedures, methods, or conclusions. In the forensic arena, a neuropsychologist may evaluate a CLD examinee, generate an opinion, and present that opinion in court, only to have that opinion challenged by another expert or by an opposing attorney. The objection to an opinion may be based on any number of factors, including cultural, linguistic, and other diversity considerations, and the merit of the challenge will need to be decided by the trier of fact (e.g., judge, jury). For example, in *State of Washington v. Sisouvanh* (State v. Sisouvanh, 2012; Bergkamp, McIntyre, & Hauser, 2023), the question arose of the defendant's (Sisouvanh) competency to stand trial. Sisouvanh was born in a refugee camp in Thailand and her family was of ethnic lowland Laotian origin. The defendant was evaluated by a psychologist who testified in court that the defendant was malingering and feigning mental illness. The court ruled that the defendant was competent, largely based on the findings of feigning. The defendant was subsequently convicted of aggravated first-degree murder. The defendant appealed the conviction arguing that the evaluating psychologist was not culturally competent and did not consider cultural factors from the defendant's background in reaching the opinion that the defendant was malingering. In this manner, the appeal was based on alleged inadequate consideration of CLD factors in the psychological evaluation. The Washington Supreme Court ultimately sided with the State court's acceptance of the psychologist's findings. However, the Supreme Court also noted that "a trial court could not properly accept the competency evaluation of an expert who refuses to acknowledge the importance of cultural competency and who failed to reasonably account for the need for cultural competency in his or her evaluation" (State of Washington v. Sisouvanh, 2012, pp. 624–625). This case demonstrates that cultural competency and consideration of cultural factors in evaluations, including evaluations of malingering, can be made a relevant matter to challenge an expert's opinion in a legal case.

Admissibility of Expert Opinion

Expert Witness Qualifications

In the forensic arena, neuropsychological evaluation results are used to educate the trier of the fact (e.g., judge, jury) in a court proceeding. Courts rely on neuropsychological evaluation results as evidence to inform their decisions. However, there are criteria to be met for a witness, including a neuropsychologist, to be viewed as an "expert" by the court. While different states may have different rules defining an expert, here we will present how the Federal Rules of Evidence (FRE) define experts for federal courts. FRE criteria apply in federal courts, but their language and criteria are also adopted by several states. According to the FRE 702, "A witness who is qualified as an expert by knowledge, skill, experience, training, or education…" (Fed. R. Evid. 702). According to this rule, then, a neuropsychologist testifying in a legal matter in courts where the criteria for FRE 702 apply may be questioned as to their qualifications to examine a CLD examinee.

The criteria by which the neuropsychologist may be measured, and by which the neuropsychologist may have to "prove" their qualifications as an "expert" (and therefore be allowed to present expert testimony), are whether the neuropsychologist has knowledge, skill, experience, training, or education in evaluating CLD examinees. Neuropsychologists evaluating CLD examinees who intend to testify as to the validity of an examinee's evaluation may want to pursue experiences that further their qualifications as experts in that domain (validity testing of CLD examinees) based on those criteria (knowledge, skill, training, or education). This pursuit of competency by the neuropsychologist would further be consistent with Standard 2.08 of the Specialty Guidelines for Forensic Psychology which requires forensic practitioners to appreciate individual and group differences as they related to age, gender, gender identity, race, ethnicity, culture, national origin, religion, sexual orientation, disability, language, socioeconomic status, or other relevant individual and cultural differences, and to consider boundaries of their expertise, make appropriate referrals, or gain the necessary training, experience, consultation, or supervision to work with these groups (APA, 2017).

Admissibility

Once the neuropsychologist is qualified as an expert, their testimony will be subject to admissibility criteria outlined by FRE 702. In 1993, the Supreme Court, in the case of *Daubert v. Merrell Dow Pharmaceuticals* (1993), held that FRE 702 sets forth the standards for admissibility of scientific evidence (to which neuropsychological evidence belongs). According to the ruling, a witness's (including a neuropsychologist's) testimony must be "based upon sufficient facts or data," must be "the product of reliable principles and methods," and the neuropsychologist witness must have "applied the principles and methods reliably to the facts of the case." Neuropsychologists examining a CLD examinee for the purpose of presenting findings to a court that abides by these criteria may need to be ready to demonstrate that the above criteria apply to their evaluation, including to their assessment of validity.

In presenting concrete factors that can be examined as a way of satisfying the above admissibility criteria, FRE 702 further asserts that "Many considerations will bear on the inquiry, including whether the theory or technique in question" (1) can be or has been tested, (2) whether the technique or theory has been subject to peer review and publication, (3) the known or potential rate of error of the technique or theory when applied, (4) the existence and maintenance of standards and controls, and (5) whether the technique or theory has been generally accepted in the scientific community. Again, the neuropsychologist who plans to testify as to the findings of their evaluation with a CLD examinee, and offer their testimony as evidence to the court, must be ready to show how their evaluation meets these criteria.

While the above discussion focuses on federal rules, State cases set forth their own criteria for admissibility. Most states at this point have adopted the *Daubert* criteria, while some states continue to operate under the less restrictive criteria set forth by *Frye v. United States* (1923). The neuropsychologist planning to take on a role of expert witness for the courts is encouraged to familiarize themselves with their State's criteria for defining witnesses and their State's standards for admissibility.

While criteria such as peer-reviewed publication and error rates are typically available for validity tests among samples that belong to cultural, linguistic majority groups from Western countries, such data may not be available for samples that directly match the CLD examinee's background. Fujii and Wong (2005) noted this issue, outlining that there are situations in which the above five criteria (testable, peer-reviewed, known error rate, existence of standards, and general acceptability) may not all be satisfied when evaluating a CLD examinee. In such cases, Fujii and Wong propose that the examiner can use the Hypothesis Testing Methodology as a method to meet the *Daubert* admissibility criteria of basing the testimony on "sufficient data," relying on "reliable principles and methods," and applying the "principles and the methods reliably to the facts of the case." Fuji and Wong argue that the scientific method does precisely those things. For further details of the Hypothesis Testing method proposed by Fujii and Wong, the reader is referred to the authors' (2005) original work.

The ability to provide a competent validity evaluation for CLD examinees in the clinic presents its own challenges to the validity of the examination itself. However, when that evaluation enters the legal arena, such as to be provided as expert testimony, the same challenges to validity must be addressed, along with additional challenges to admissibility. While we present some of the nuances that need to be considered when examining CLD individuals in the forensic arena, since admissibility is a legal matter, the examiner planning on presenting validity findings to the court is advised to seek additional sources of information, such as legal advice or case laws that apply to their jurisdiction to prepare to address these matters should they come up. Knowledge of the existing literature related to validity testing approaches and its application to CLD examinees is an important component of satisfying admissibility criteria, which we turn to next.

Validity Assessment Approaches

Validity assessment refers broadly to the assessment of whether the data gleaned from an examinee during a neuropsychological examination accurately represents the examinee's current neuropsychological functioning. This is a crucial component of evaluations and is based on a robust peer-reviewed literature (Sweet et al., 2021). This literature has established that performance validity testing allows the measurement of whether an examinee's performance on cognitive tests can be interpreted as an accurate representation of the individual's cognitive functioning, while symptom validity testing refers to measurement of the validity of reported symptom complaints, most often regarding psychological/emotional conditions (Larrabee, 2012; Sweet et al., 2021). Performance validity tests (PVTs) and symptom validity tests (SVTs) are both important to consider in neuropsychological contexts for several reasons. For example, performance invalidity increases financial burden through Social Security Disability claims (Chafetz & Underhill, 2013) and can lead to court decisions that are based on false evidence (e.g., a court adjudicating a defendant incompetent based on the defendant's feigned mental illness; a court awarding a plaintiff damages based on feigned cognitive impairment). Other considerations regarding validity assessment outcomes are covered elsewhere in this book and will not be restated here.

Performance Validity Testing

We present here two validity testing approaches: below-chance performance and cut-off score performance. We discuss each with their relevant cultural considerations.

Below-Chance Performance

Below-chance test performance is one method of performance validity testing. It relies on statistical improbability whereby an examinee is given multiple test items with a set number of possible response options. If the examinee picks the wrong response for many test items, whereby that number of wrong responses is large enough to be deemed statistically improbable, then the conclusion is made that the examinee chose the wrong response purposefully (Sherman, Slick, & Iverson, 2020). A clear argument can be presented that such a finding of statistical improbability of that many wrong answers cannot be explained or reframed as statistically probable based on cultural or linguistic factors. In other words, the argument cannot be made that cultural or language-related influences were primary contributors to the atypically large number of wrong answers at below-chance levels since the examinee would have to intentionally pick the wrong answer to obtain that large number of wrong answers. While independence from diversity-related influences makes this type of validity method attractive for use with CLD populations, this approach is not as sensitive as other approaches due to the high bar that needs to be reached to satisfy the criterion of statistical improbability (i.e., significantly below chance). As such, this approach is highly specific but not very sensitive (Rogers & Bender, 2013). For clarity, sensitivity involves measuring the percentage of non-credible individuals who are detected as non-credible with a PVT (true positive), while specificity measures the percentage of credible individuals who were correctly classified as credible by a PVT, with 90% being a generally accepted practice (Sweet et al., 2021).

Cut-Off Score Performance

Unlike the below-chance PVT method, the cut-off score method relies on examining specific scores below which (or above which, depending on the response type and direction), an examinee's test score is interpreted as being non-credible. For this method, cut-off scores are established, and continuously empirically cross-validated, and at times updated, based on different populations and conditions (Sweet et al., 2021). For example, whereas a score of 5 errors on a hypothetical validity test may be considered as a cut-off score depicting invalid performance for examinees with mild traumatic brain injury, such a score may not be indicative of invalid performance for an individual with an intellectual disability. In a similar vein, an argument can be made that cut-off scores may need to be validated, and potentially adjusted, for CLD populations. This argument is consistent with the AACN 2021 consensus statements asserting that "(t)he presence of cultural, ethnic, and/or language factors known to affect performance results necessitates that clinicians adjust the threshold for identifying response bias" (Sweet et al., 2021, p. 1068) if one considers that a cut-off score can be considered one such "threshold." While a number of studies do exist that establish cut-off scores for some validity measures in some culturally diverse samples (see Salazar, Lu, & Boone, 2021; Nijdam-Jones & Rosenfeld, 2017; Strutt & Stinson, 2022; Bridges & Ahern, 2016 for reviews), there is consensus in the field that more such studies are needed (Sweet et al., 2021). The updated Sherman et al. (2020) malingering criteria (Sherman, Slick, & Iverson, 2020) specifically highlight the need for further research to validate malingering criteria for "linguistically, ethnically, and culturally diverse populations" (p. 758).

An additional consideration with regard to identifying cut-off scores for performance invalidity is the consideration of establishing a criterion group. Two of the common research designs for establishing and validating cut-off scores are the Simulation Design and the Known-Groups Design. In the Simulation Design, research participants are asked to simulate a feigned disorder, and then their responses on a test are typically compared against a group of controls and a group of genuine respondents who have the disorder. In the Known-Groups Design, the researchers must construct a criterion group of respondents who have been identified, with a high degree of confidence via validated PVTs and other methods, to be performing invalidly. The main criticism for the Simulation Design is that it has limited external validity (Rogers & Bender, 2013), and in fact, the Known-Groups Design carries some level of consensus as the favored design (Larrabee, 2007; Nelson & Doane, 2013). However, as Larrabee (2007) and Rogers and Bender (2013) note, and as Schroeder et al. (2018) demonstrate, it is critical to have an appropriately composed criterion group. The relatively limited research, identifying well-validated validity measures for some CLD groups, creates a challenge for researchers trying to independently establish a "known group" or "criterion group" of malingerers or invalid performers in some culturally diverse samples.

Unlikely Symptom Patterns

This method of validity assessment does not utilize formal PVTs; instead, it relies on deviation from clinical expectations that certain diseases have typical impairment patterns that are considered characteristic (e.g., impairments restricted to encoding) or are associated with specific levels of severity (e.g., different severity of encoding impairment in complex mild traumatic brain injury versus Alzheimer's type of dementia). Test performances that fail to conform to such patterns, particularly when the level of deviation is marked, raise the suspicion for the possibility of invalid performance (Rogers, 2008). Since this method relies on the "normative" clinical presentation of syndromes, it may, in some circumstances, be vulnerable to influence by cultural factors regarding how that syndrome manifests (e.g., symptom presentation, validated scores on neuropsychological testing for that CLD sample) in a CLD examinee. We describe some of these culturally relevant influences in subsequent sections.

Symptom Validity Testing

As opposed to PVTs, which are performance based, SVTs can be understood as the examinee's response style when endorsing/reporting psychological, cognitive, and physical symptoms. SVTs include freestanding tests with a single purpose in evaluating symptom report credibility (e.g., Miller Forensic Assessment of Symptoms Test [M-FAST], Structured Inventory of Malingered Symptomatology [SIMS]), and validity scales constructed from items contained within standard personality inventories (e.g., Response Bias Scale from the Minnesota Multiphasic Personality Inventory – 3 [MMPI-3], Cognitive Bias Scale from the Personality Assessment Inventory [PAI]). Validity of self-reported symptoms is often measured through approaches that include symptom endorsements that conform to known invalid patterns, endorsement of unusual or implausible symptoms, and deviation from clinical expectations.

Symptom Endorsements That Conform to Known Invalid Patterns

This method relies on analyzing item endorsement on a psychological test and/or validity scale and identifying patterns of responding that are like patterns produced by invalid respondents. Since this is a norm-based approach, meaning that it relies on normative data produced by other respondents, the argument can be made that it can be influenced by diversity factors and therefore may not produce results that are as accurate for certain diverse examinees as it would for examinees who are culturally more like the normative sample. For example, since many existing mood and personality test measures were initially normed on predominantly White samples, some assessments found statistical differences in scores between norming samples and CLD groups (Weiss & Rosenfeld, 2012). With that said, recent research has suggested that these differences in scores are generally not substantial enough to be the sole cause for clinical scale elevations and thus may be appropriate for use with some diverse populations (Whitman et al., 2018).

Endorsement of Unusual and/or Implausible Symptoms

This method relies on an examinee endorsing non-credible and/or implausible symptoms. Examinees who are naïve to psychological and cognitive impairments may endorse symptoms that are known, by the learned and expert scientific/clinical community (but not the naïve examinee), to be unusual or non-credible. An argument can be made that what may be implausible to the "norm" community may be plausible for some CLD communities. For example, Nijdam-Jones and Rosenfeld (2017) found in their review of the literature that the M-FAST, which partially builds on identifying symptom invalidity based on the examinee endorsing unusual symptoms, had higher rates of false positive identification errors (i.e., respondents endorsing higher numbers of implausible symptoms) among CLD samples than among North American English-speaking samples. At the same time, other validity tests (e.g., SIMS) demonstrated minimal variability across cultures and languages that were studied. Thus, consideration of the tools being used within the context of the examinee's cultural background can inform decision-making about the plausibility of symptoms.

Deviation from Clinical Expectation

While not an SVT itself, this method of validity assessment proposes that certain diseases have typical/expected symptom patterns. Even when the symptoms are not "implausible" or fantastical, symptom reports that nevertheless deviate significantly from that typical/expected pattern should raise the suspicion for invalid responding. However, interpretation of endorsement of such symptoms and patterns should be culturally informed. For example, an examinee who might describe symptoms of a "heavy head" that they attribute to a mild traumatic brain injury that occurred years ago, may not be referring to a headache, but instead using culturally nuanced language to describe ongoing stress. As another example, one of the authors (KZY) was once asked to evaluate a non-native English speaker for competency to proceed. The examinee had been suspected of feigning an implausible allegation that he developed multiple personalities after a mild traumatic head injury. A deeper exploration of his claim revealed that he had developed somatic responses to stressors after the injury (a culturally plausible response to stress) and had explained his somatic symptoms as a personality change due to being possessed by "jinn" (a pre-Islamic concept that is present in Arab and Muslim cultures).

Overall, this validity assessment concept is not very different from the concept of endorsing unusual/implausible symptoms except that, in the case of the deviation from clinical expectation, the symptoms themselves may be plausible (e.g., headaches, somatic symptoms). The verbiage used (e.g., "heavy head" for headaches) or culturally acceptable concepts (e.g., possession by jinn to understand new somatic symptoms) used to describe them may translate into what sounds like non-credible or invalid reports. Since this method relies on clinical judgment of what is normal, it is again potentially vulnerable to influence by diversity factors and/or bias.

Validity Measurement in CLD Populations

Other authors have more critically and comprehensively reviewed the literature on specific PVTs in CLD groups, and they have identified classification accuracies of the tests when used with various CLD examinees (e.g., Salazar, Lu, & Boone, 2021; Nijdam-Jones & Rosenfeld, 2017; Strutt & Stinson, 2022; Bridges & Ahern, 2016). Consequently, these data will not be covered in depth here, but instead, we provide a brief overview and encourage further immersion in this literature when working with an examinee from a specific CLD group. If research data are absent for that group, limitations can be discussed along with decision-making that incorporates multiple sources of information to form reasonable clinical opinions.

When reviewing various validity tests with CLD samples between 2002 and 2015, Nijdam-Jones and Rosenfeld (2017) found that the most-studied SVTs for psychiatric symptom validity were the SIMS, the M-FAST, and versions of the MMPI. The most frequently studied PVTs at the time were the Word Recognition Test, Test of Memory Malingering, and Rey 15-item Test, each with various classification accuracy statistics for CLD groups. The most frequently used method to identify invalidity was the cut-off score method, with comparisons with either known groups or simulator groups. It was stated that

> (t)he results of this review suggest that clinicians should be aware of variability in classification accuracy when using feigning assessment measures with diverse populations. Of particular concern are those studies that found high rates of false positives when using the measures with samples that differed, whether linguistically, ethnically, or culturally, from the samples that were used to develop the instruments (i.e., English-speaking, from Western countries).
>
> (pp. 1331–1332)

The authors recognized that the literature was meager even when widened to include dissertations. For instance, there were only 45 studies and dissertations published between 2002 and 2015 regarding validity testing with CLD groups, without any significant increase over time in the rate of such publications.

More recently, Salazar, Lu, and Boone (2021) summarized additional research on PVTs with Spanish speakers (Mexico, Spain, Central and South America, bilinguals), Chinese-speaking populations, and other ethnic groups. They also presented various adjustments to thresholds for certain tests when needed, while highlighting methodological concerns in some of the literature. For example, critical reviews of the literature highlight the fact that many studies include small sample sizes and tendencies to use general terms like "Spanish speakers" to include people from various countries who are heterogeneous in educational quality and other sociodemographic proxy variables. The absence of participants with no formal education or those who were illiterate in some studies also precludes generalizability to those examinee samples. Additional considerations include the periodic use of healthy community volunteers who are not presenting with neurological or psychiatric conditions, which can result in specificity rates that overestimate performance in patient populations.

When considering the CLD validity assessment literature as a whole, the authors conclude that, although the volume of research addressing the use of PVT with diverse populations is modest, there is converging evidence from United States and international studies that existing instruments retain their utility when applied to non-English monolingual or limited English-proficient Hispanic/Latino and Asian populations. They suggest that some tests require cut-off adjustments to maintain adequate specificity and sensitivity, though, and there needs to be greater recognition of education as a major moderating factor that requires the use of adjusted scores to retain specificity comparable with that of the original normative sample.

Therefore, as recommended by the recent consensus statement on validity assessment, it is important to "maintain familiarity with the latest scientific literature in this area, assigning weight according to the rigor of the studies and the relevance of samples whose demographic and injury/illness severity characteristics most closely match the practitioner's case at hand" (Sweet et al., 2021, p. 1065). This critical analysis along with a comprehensive multi-method approach that is rooted in cultural competence can strengthen hypothesis testing and defensibility of evaluations in the legal arena.

Interpretation of Validity Test Findings

A neuropsychologist with adequate cultural competence, optimally with proficient language skills to directly evaluate the examinee in their preferred language if need be, and who has sufficient familiarity of pertinent research should be able to confidently and competently incorporate existing validity testing into their neuropsychological evaluations. When invalid findings are identified, the neuropsychologist will want to consider reasons for this. Secondary gain (e.g., malingering) and primary gain (e.g., emotional support) should be considered. In addition, there can be other unintentional culturally based influences on test performance. We turn to discussing some of them within the context of CLD groups.

Malingering

According to the *Diagnostic and Statistical Manual of Mental Disorder-5th Edition* (*DSM-5*; APA, 2013, p. 727) malingering is "the intentional production of false or grossly exaggerated physical or psychological symptoms, motivated by external incentives…" and it "should be strongly suspected if any combination of the following is noted":

a Medicolegal context.
b Marked discrepancy between the individual's claimed stress or disability and the objective findings and observations.
c Lack of cooperation during the diagnostic evaluation and in complying with the prescribed treatment regimen.
d The presence of antisocial personality disorder.

These criteria require intentional feigning (and/or exaggeration) of symptoms for the purpose of procuring gain (e.g., disability) or avoiding harm (e.g., incarceration) in the context of a "clearly identifiable and substantial external incentive." However, as indicated in the most recent AACN consensus statement on validity assessment (Sweet et al., 2021), "invalid test findings should not be directly equated to malingering, especially in non-forensic settings, as validity measures can be negatively affected by factors that are not necessarily intentional or motivated by an external incentive" (p. 1061). Simply equating suboptimal validity test performance with malingering is an oversimplification.

A challenge is that relying on clinical judgment alone to determine the extent to which symptom exaggeration is voluntary or intentional can sometimes be problematic given the known limitations of relying exclusively on subjective clinical judgment to detect malingering (e.g., Faust et al., 1988). This is particularly relevant for CLD groups where culturally mediated unintentional reasons for inaccurate symptom presentations might also be influencing test performance (see below). Just as the context of an evaluation needs to be considered in determinations about malingering in clinical versus forensic contexts (Sweet et al., 2021), this is also true for cultural factors.

Cultural contextual considerations extend to the *DSM-5* features described for malingering since cultural influences can impact subjective experience and expression of internal discomfort or pain. As a result, apparent non-credible presentations and test findings may be confounded by unconventional, non-typical manifestations in a CLD examinee. Additionally, there is evidence of racial bias in diagnosing antisocial personality disorder that is influenced by ways that symptoms are expressed (e.g., Black cultural expressions of depression) or environmental influences from poverty and other factors that can lead to lying or stealing behaviors (Garb, 2021; Bridges & Ahern, 2016). Similarly, while the *DSM-5* malingering specifications include lack of cooperation with treatment regimens, it is worth noting that treatment compliance can be influenced by cultural mistrust or systemic barriers for many ethnic groups. As such, it becomes important to consider rates of false positive errors when using *DSM-5* characteristics suggestive of possible malingering, and to carefully explore the role of potential cultural influences on each descriptor.

While not directly related to neuropsychological exams, this point is relevant to diagnosing malingering in general since it has been documented that there are differences in racial demographics of malingering diagnoses noted in hospital inpatient and emergency room settings (e.g., Udoetuk et al., 2020). Base rates of malingering and symptom exaggeration in neuropsychological patient referrals from civil (i.e., personal injury cases) and criminal legal settings have been estimated to be at 10%–40% in those seeking compensation for a range of clinical disorders (Mittenberg et al., 2002; Martin & Schroeder, 2020). However, information about CLD representation in these samples is limited. Similarly, rates of feigning for disability compensation have been reported to range from 45% to 59% of adult cases, with an estimated cost of U.S.$20 billion for adult mental disorder claimants in the United States (Chafetz & Underhill, 2013). However, here again, information on the distribution of CLD groups is often quite limited.

The complex, multi-layered influences on malingering diagnoses for CLD groups need further attention in the professional literature. This may be why Sherman, Slick, and Iverson (2020) clarify that "future research can better inform the next revisions of the criteria… on studying and validating the criteria in linguistically, ethnically, and culturally diverse populations" (p. 758). Therefore, the examiner assigning a determination of malingering to a CLD examinee should carefully consider and rule out alternative hypotheses that might account for the findings and conclusions, and they should be prepared to provide adequate and defensible explanations of why a conclusion of malingering was provided.

Somatic Symptom and Related Disorders

In contrast to malingering, which is associated with deliberate negative response bias that is motivated by external gain, psychological gain present in somatic symptom disorders can also distort symptom report and test performance. The *DSM-5* states that somatic symptom-related disorders involve prominent somatic symptoms associated with significant distress and impairment that are commonly encountered in medical settings and may be influenced by

> genetic and biological vulnerability (e.g., increased sensitivity to pain), early traumatic experiences (e.g., violence, abuse, deprivation), and learning (e.g., attention obtained from illness, lack of reinforcement of non-somatic expressions of distress), as well as cultural/social norms that devalue and stigmatize psychological suffering as compared with physical suffering.
>
> (DSM-5, p. 310)

Somatoform disorders are more common in some diverse populations. For example, Yutaka, Janca, Asai, and Sartorius (2012) present perspectives from different cultures across the world on somatoform manifestations of different mental illnesses. Among the explanations proposed is that when mental illness is a taboo in some cultures, the expression of that mental illness can take the form of other symptoms that are considered culturally more acceptable. In such cases, emotional distress may present as physical and/or cognitive symptoms. Therefore, differentiating somatic symptom/somatoform disorders from external incentive-motivated feigning and other threats to validity can be a critical aspect of validity evaluation.

While cultural and linguistic diversity-related contributions are not exclusive contributors to somatoform disorders, an understanding of these factors and their contributions to somatic and cognitive symptom expression greatly informs impressions regarding neuropsychological test data and validity findings. Somatic symptoms are prominent in various "culture-bound syndromes" and "idioms of distress" that are influenced by various linguistic and cultural factors. In these cases, somatic symptoms may be understood as related variously to "family, work, or environmental stresses; general medical illness; the suppression of feelings of anger and resentment; or certain culture-specific phenomena, such as semen loss" (*DSM-5*, p. 313). Taking the time to understand an examinee's cultural beliefs related to somatic expressions of distress, as well as keeping abreast with the relevant literature, can help support or refute hypotheses about the veracity of symptom complaints.

Other Interpersonal and Cultural Influences on Engagement or Motivation

Beyond motivation for intentional or unintentional gain, there are other factors that might lead to attenuated performance validity scores in a neuropsychological evaluation with a CLD examinee. While these factors may not account for performance that is below chance, significantly below cut-offs, or below appropriately validated thresholds, nor severe deviations from clinical expectations for brain–behavior relationships and cultural norms, they could impact motivation for an examinee to perform at best. Therefore, they are worth being aware of as they could be potential threats that could be mitigated to maximize an examinee's motivation to engage and cooperate with the evaluation.

Attitudes toward Testing

Martin, Schroeder, and Odland (2015) conducted a survey of North American neuropsychologists. Within that survey, it was reported that neuropsychologists believed that an examinee's attitude toward testing (e.g., oppositional, non-compliant, or indifferent attitude) is the second most-frequent cause of invalidity in forensic settings and the third most-frequent cause of invalidity in clinical settings. Martin and Schroeder expanded on this topic in another survey of North American neuropsychologists in 2020. In this latter survey, it was reported that neuropsychologists believe that 37.5% of individuals with oppositional attitudes toward testing invalidate results in non-forensic settings. While the authors did not detail the specific causes of these oppositional attitudes, the finding seems to acknowledge that neuropsychologists believe that examinees' test results may be attenuated, and invalidated, by the examinees' attitudes and potentially their relationships with the testing.

From our work with CLD examinees, in forensic and non-forensic settings, we anecdotally identify attitudes that can impact test performance for CLD examinees. For example, some CLD examinees may enter the testing session, naïve to and unfamiliar with Western testing paradigms and expectations. As Fujii (2018) has outlined, neuropsychological examinations "can be perceived as strange and uncomfortable for a person from a different culture." Test wiseness, or familiarity with the particulars of a testing situation (e.g., working quickly, social facility with a stranger), can influence test performance (Ardila, 2007). In their study of test performance by bilingual Arabic-English speakers, Ali et al. (2022) similarly noted that some tasks "may appear [as] trivial tasks to someone who was socialized outside the Western culture and educational system that emphasizes paper-and-pencil testing and performance metrics from an early age" (pp. 10–11). Such examinees may perceive the tests as childish or irrelevant. In such scenarios, the examinee might dismiss the tests, fail to adequately engage with them, and underperform on them.

Other examples may include CLD examinees who distrust a majority culture examiner or majority culture system (be it the health system or the judicial system) and doubt that they will listen to their complaints. Such an examinee may feel compelled to exaggerate their symptoms to highlight their concerns to the examiner and not let the examiner dismiss their (the examinees') experience. While such situations could invalidate the testing results, the invalidity here may be due to factors other than malingering. Such anecdotal offerings admittedly do not have a place in empirically informed interpretation and case-formulation. The ability to operationalize these matters and subject them to empirical review, however, could advance our understanding of the potential relevance of these cultural and diversity factors on validity testing. Further, attitudes toward testing may be remediable and avoidable; this is also an area of needed future research. The field of neuropsychology would benefit from further investigating the contributions of various attitudes toward testing on test-taking approach and PVTs, particularly in CLD samples.

Rapport

Rapport between examiner and examinee might also influence attitudes toward testing. In both forensic and non-forensic contexts, rapport is important since it is thought that the more at ease an examinee is, the greater the likelihood they will engage and cooperate with the evaluation. Powell and Bartholomew (2003) have argued that development of rapport in a cross-cultural forensic context should not be perceived as a compromise in professionalism, impartiality, or authority, but instead when an examiner shows acceptance of examinees' cultural backgrounds, this can empower examinees to reduce their subjective experience of threat, and increase willingness to cooperate in the interview or assessment. Rioja and Rosenfeld (2018) argue that paying special attention to rapport-building during forensic interviews with CLD examinees from a culturally sensitive lens can allow more accurate interpretations of verbal responses to the examiner's questions and greater attunement to nonverbal behaviors and their significance. This is needed to avoid misunderstandings that could lead to incorrect conclusions about important psycho-legal questions, if not handled with cultural sensitivity.

In addition to supporting accurate data gathering during forensic interviews, rapport can also impact neuropsychological test performance. Barnett et al. (2018) demonstrated effects of rapport by creating "warm and positive" high rapport conditions characterized by enthusiastic greetings, small talk, warmth, eye-contact, smiling, and affirmations. Examinees obtained higher scores on some neuropsychological tests in these high rapport conditions. In contrast, low rapport examiners who were perceived to be "cold and clinical" resulted in lower neuropsychological test scores. Interactions by ethnicity were not specifically investigated in this study nor subsequent neuropsychological investigations in this area. While the impact of rapport on PVT test performance specifically has not been studied yet, this is another investigative area that could be particularly relevant for CLD groups. The challenge in forensic contexts, however, will be to objectively quantify rapport and its presumed impact in a defensible manner.

Stereotype Threat

Stereotype threat is hypothesized to present in the form of an examinee performing on a test in a manner consistent with the stereotype they perceive to apply to them. In their meta-analysis, Nguyen and Ryan (2008) discussed the effects of gender-based (female examinees) and race-based stereotypes on test (math, cognitive abilities) performance. They found that particularly when a negative stereotype (a stereotype that paints the examinee as being somehow deficient in the skill measured by the test) is activated in the exam setting, stereotype threat attenuated the test performance of minority examinees. Integrated models of stereotype threat suggest that this threat disrupts performance and executive resources by (a) eliciting a physiological stress response that directly impacts prefrontal processing, (b) creating a tendency to actively monitor performance, and (c) re-allocating resources to suppress negative thoughts and emotions (Schmader, Johns, & Forbes, 2008). These authors posit that these three mechanisms combine to consume executive resources needed to perform cognitive tasks. Perceived discrimination and stereotype threat have also been shown to negatively impact performance on other neuropsychological tests (Thames et al.,

2013; Whaley, 2021). While there is limited research examining the impact of stereotype threat on PVTs specifically, Suhr and Gunstad (2005) have found that individuals subjected to a diagnosis threat paradigm did not demonstrate differences on the Word Memory Test despite performing somewhat more poorly on cognitive testing. Likewise, Slick and Sherman (2013) posit that the expectancy effects found in research regarding diagnosis threat have been relatively small, and unlikely to account for findings consistent with probable or definite malingering in compensation-seeking cases.

Practical Suggestions

While examinee presentation that is clearly motivated by malingering for external financial gain may not provide much opportunity for remediation, the following practical suggestions are provided to maximize opportunities to demonstrate cultural competence and potentially reduce the impact of unintentional cultural or interpersonal influences on the interpretation of the validity of the evaluation.

Obtain Relevant Cultural Knowledge, Awareness, and Skills

There are many resources, peer-reviewed articles, trainings, and continuing education opportunities that can provide broad and specific cultural knowledge to guide accurate interpretation of evaluation results with CLD examinees. Multiple sociodemographic variables that have been empirically linked to test performance in cultural contexts include education/literacy, culture/acculturation, language, economics, communication style, testing situation, intelligence, and context of immigration, each with cognitive neuroscience underpinnings (Fujii, 2018, 2023, Pedraza, 2019). While it is beyond the scope of this chapter to list all available educational resources, culturally competent neuropsychologists can seek out the relevant cultural knowledge (e.g., Fujii, 2016, 2018), be self-reflective about themselves and their own biases or "spots" (e.g., Sandeen, Moore & Swanda, 2018), consider their impact on others (e.g., Hamilton et al., 2022), commit to strengthening their skills in multicultural competence, including the use of interpreters (e.g., Fujii, Santos, & Della Malva, 2022; Sánchez & Judd, 2022), and understand the impact of various individual, community, and systemic influences on an examinee's presentation (e.g., Diaz-Santos et al., 2022).

This approach toward cultural competence would be consistent with the Specialty Guidelines for Forensic Psychology (2013) which specifically emphasize the need for evaluators to consider "linguistic, and cultural differences that might affect their judgments or reduce the accuracy of their interpretations" (p. 15). Likewise, the APA Ethics Code (2002) Standard 9.02 (b) advises that "Psychologists use assessment instruments whose validity and reliability have been established for use with members of the population tested. When such validity or reliability has not been established, psychologists describe the strengths and limitations of test results and interpretation." A further standard (9.06) counsels that

> When interpreting assessment results, including automated interpretations, psychologists take into account the purpose of the assessment as well as the various test factors, test-taking abilities, and other characteristics of the person being assessed, such as *situational, personal, linguistic, and cultural differences*, that might affect psychologists' judgments or reduce the accuracy of their interpretations. They indicate any significant limitations of their interpretations.

Focus on Building Rapport

Rapport can be increased through the cultural understanding of various surface and deep-level aspects of cultural backgrounds. For example, clinical interviews provide opportunities to gather information about preferred terminology for cultural identification, ethnocultural history, immigration/relocation background, language history, communication style, education quality and quantity, literacy levels, socioeconomic influences, values and customs, gender- and sexuality-based influences, spirituality- and religion-based influences, acculturation and systemic barriers, mental health views, and approaches to neuropsychological assessment (Irani, 2022). While not all these variables may be necessary to answer the referral question in a forensic context, an examiner who is sensitive to relevant cultural variables can help a CLD examinee feel more comfortable with the examiner and evaluation process. Practical strategies that can build rapport in cross-cultural forensic interviews include taking the time to get to know the examinee, using greetings that are culturally appropriate, ensuring a welcoming physical environment, avoiding behaviors or terms considered offensive, being flexible and sensitive to the examinee's needs, listening and reflecting accurately, not assuming the examinee understands the roles and nature of a forensic examination process, and clarifying the formal nature of investigative forensic evaluations (Powell & Bartholomew, 2003).

Ensure Fairness in Testing

The American Education Research Association Standards for Educational and Psychological Testing (AERA, 2014) for fairness in testing include ensuring that test takers feel comfortable with the examiner and the testing situation, tests are free of biases, test takers do not experience disadvantages in processing and responding to test items, and valid interpretations for the intended use of a specific test can be drawn from the test taker's score (Fujii, 2018). To ensure valid interpretations of the test data, examiners need to aware of the neuropsychological literature on the effect of cultural variables on neuropsychological test performance (e.g., Agranovich & Puente, 2007; Ardila, 2005, 2007a; Fujii, 2016, 2018; Loewenstein et al., 1994; Weiss & Saklofske, 2020; Wong, 2000; Irani, 2022). For instance, cultural influences have been shown on test data for speed-accuracy trade-offs, stimulus familiarity on naming, list learning, story memory and other tests, development of executive functioning skills, and performance on nonverbal so-called "culture-free" tests (e.g., Ardila, 2007; Boone et al., 2007; Cho et al., 2021; Rosselli & Ardila, 2003; Sabbagh et al., 2006). Awareness of these influences can help examiners reduce the likelihood of making false positive errors in data interpretation.

In ensuring that test takers do not experience disadvantages in processing and responding to test items, Nguyen and Ryan's (2008) meta-analysis suggested that threat-removal strategies also have the potential to improve test performance. Specific strategies that can mitigate stereotype threat priming in testing include removing threatening environmental cues, presenting tests as insensitive to differences, increasing visibility and representation in testing environments, engaging in reconstruction interventions to reduce perceived threats to engage optimal performance, improving cross-group interactions by creating identity safety, and supporting individual coping strategies such as reappraisal, self-affirmation, and mindfulness (VanLandingham et al., 2022). The specific applicability of these strategies in forensic contexts, however, is currently unknown.

Rely on Validity Tests that have the Most Applicability

Obtaining below-chance scores on a validity test can be considered the most definitive indication of intentional feigning, with little if any room for accounting for such a score using cultural explanations that can over-ride the explanation of intentional feigning (Sherman, Slick, & Iverson, 2020). Below-chance performance is a very high bar to reach, though, compromising the sensitivity of such a design. Further, not all validity tests are structured to allow for the opportunity to obtain a below-chance score. Fortunately, validity test results beyond the below-chance range can still be useful in the context of CLD examinees. For example, studies are already emerging that present sensitivity, specificity, and other validation metrics for various validity tests among CLD examinees (Strutt & Stinson, 2022). To this effect, when choosing a validity test that has been subjected to validation among CLD examinees, we reiterate the AACN 2021 consensus statement on validity testing recommending that it is important to assign "weight according to the rigor of the studies and the relevance of samples whose *demographic* and injury/illness severity characteristics most closely match the practitioner's case at hand" (Sweet et al., 2021, p. 1065, *italics added for emphasis*).

As Strutt and Stinson (2022) also concluded based on their review of the literature of validity test performances among CLD clients, language and very low education have different impacts on different PVTs. They therefore advised that "clinicians should select those PVTs for which research allows for appropriate generalization" (p. 227). The potential and hope is that through this research, validity tests may be identified that are least prone to cultural influence and threshold adjustments, if needed. We would reiterate, however, that in relying on a validity test that has been subjected to validation among CLD examinees, we caution the examiner to weigh the power of the test against the validation method to which it was subjected. For example, the examiner is encouraged to be aware of the pitfalls for each of the simulators and the known-group designs in establishing cut-off scores for validity tests. We further offer that the examiner could rely on validity tests that survey endorsement of implausible or improbable symptoms, particularly when those symptoms deviate markedly from expectation and when cultural factors can be ruled out as an alternative explanation for those symptoms. Finally, and again consistent with the AACN consensus statement, the examiner is advised to rely on multiple validity tests, rather than on a singular validity test or method (Sweet et al., 2021).

Conclusions

Neuropsychologists are increasingly interfacing with CLD groups in clinical and forensic settings. Cultural competency and consideration of cultural factors in evaluations can be made a relevant matter to challenge an expert's opinion in a legal case. Therefore, neuropsychologists need to be prepared to withstand attacks to whether they conducted a competent, valid, and defensible evaluation and interpreted the data correctly. In adversarial forensic settings, challenges can include demonstrating whether the neuropsychologist has the sufficient knowledge, skills, experience, training, or education-based qualifications to qualify as an expert witness for a CLD examinee. Other objections could include whether expert witness testimony will be admissible in the courtroom based on FRE 702 criteria involving testability, peer review, known error rates, existence of standards, and general acceptability. While the forensic neuropsychological research literature with CLD groups and validity testing is still growing, a scientific hypothesis testing method can continue to be used to defend admissibility of opinions. This approach requires maintaining cultural competence and staying current with relevant case law and the scientific literature on cultural or linguistic influences on neuropsychological evaluations.

The literature on validity testing forms an important component of this knowledge base. We posit that while language or cultural factors are unlikely to impact statistically improbable below-chance performance on performance validity tests, there may need to be adjustments to some PVT cut-off scores for identifying invalidity in certain CLD groups, along with greater consideration of the paucity of research for well-validated criterion groups in some CLD samples. Interpretation of PVT or SVT data regarding unlikely symptom patterns or "implausible" symptoms needs to consider how syndromes can manifest within cultural contexts to rule out false positive identification errors regarding decisions about invalidity. This is particularly relevant since the existing literature suggests classification accuracy rates can sometimes vary with certain CLD groups. The limitations of the existing literature highlight the need to maintain familiarity with relevant topics in this area and assign weight according to the rigor of the studies and the relevance of samples whose demographic characteristics match with that of the examinee.

Interpretation of validity test data for CLD groups in forensic contexts can be confidently and competently completed by neuropsychologists who have built adequate foundational cultural competence and gained sufficient familiarity with existing research in this area. Suboptimal performance on validity tests can be influenced by various contributions. Most pertinent to forensic practice, a diagnosis of malingering requires careful consideration of cultural influences on the applicability of each diagnostic criterion for a CLD examinee, recognition of the need to further study and validation of malingering criteria in CLD groups, and readiness to defend the diagnosis after alternative hypotheses have been ruled out.

While cultural factors are unlikely to account for PVT performance that is below-chance, validity test scores that are notably below cut-off or adjusted thresholds, or findings that are severely deviant from clinical and cultural expectations, other interpersonal and cultural influences could impact a CLD examinee's motivation to engage and cooperate with an evaluation. Firstly, attitudes toward testing might attenuate or invalidate tests results, possibly due to unfamiliarity with Western testing paradigms (test wiseness) or cultural mistrust that leads to symptom exaggeration or oppositional attitudes. Secondly, rapport during forensic interviewing increases comfort and might reduce subjective experiences of threat. Poor rapport between examiners and examinees can negatively impact neuropsychological test scores, although the impact on PVTs is yet unknown. Thirdly, CLD groups are particularly vulnerable to stereotype threat, which has been shown to attenuate cognitive test performance, although so far, its impact on PVT performance is thought to be limited. While expectancy effects from these three variables are likely to be small and unlikely to fully account for findings consistent with probable or definite malingering, they could inform alternative hypotheses and minimally help an examiner be attuned to factors that could be influencing a CLD examinee.

Therefore, some practical suggestions to protect against challenges related to examiner qualifications in working with CLD examinees include obtaining relevant cultural knowledge, awareness, and skills; focusing on rapport-building; ensuring fairness in testing by being aware of the effect of cultural variables on test performance; and identifying the best-fitting performance and/or symptom validity tests and methods that can be applied to CLD examinees.

Ultimately, the evaluation of validity with a CLD examinee requires careful consideration of linguistic and cultural influences on the evaluation, justification for validity test selection and potentially adjusted thresholds, and awareness of the strategies that were used to appreciate cultural and linguistic influences on the neuropsychological evaluation. Overall, this approach, rooted in cultural competence, can help support valid and defensible evaluations with CLD examinees.

References

Agranovich, A. V., & Puente, A. E. (2007). Do Russian and American normal adults perform similarly on neuropsychological tests? Preliminary findings on the relationship between culture and test performance. *Archives of Clinical Neuropsychology*, *22*(3), 273–282.

Ali, S., Crisan, I., Abeare, C. A., & Erdodi, L. A. (2022). Cross-cultural performance validity testing: Managing false positives in Examinees with Limited English proficiency. *Developmental Neuropsychology*, *47*(6), 273–294.

American Academy of Clinical Neuropsychology Relevance 2050 Initiative. https://theaacn.org/relevance-2050/relevance-2050-initiative/

American Education Research Association, American Psychological Association, & the National Council on Measurement in Education. (2014). *Standards for educational and psychological testing* (2nd ed.). Washington, DC: American Education Research Association.

American Psychiatric Association. (2013). *Diagnostic and statistical manual of mental disorders: DSM-5* (Vol. 5, No. 5). Washington, DC: American Psychiatric Association.

American Psychological Association. (2013). Specialty guidelines for forensic psychology. *American Psychologist*, *68*(1), 7–19. https://doi.org/10.1037/a0029889

American Psychological Association. (2017). Ethical principles of psychologists and code of conduct. https://www.apa.org/ethics/code/index.html

Ardila, A. (2005). Cultural values underlying psychometric cognitive testing. *Neuropsychology Review*, *15*, 185–195.

Ardila, A. (2007). The impact of culture on neuropsychological test performance. In B. Uzell, M. Ponton, & A. Ardila (Eds). *International handbook of cross-cultural neuropsychology* (pp. 23–44). Mahwah, NJ: Lawrence Erlbaum Associates.

Barnett, M. D., Parsons, T. D., Reynolds, B. L., & Bedford, L. A. (2018). Impact of rapport on neuropsychological test performance. *Applied Neuropsychology: Adult*, *25*(3), 258–265.

Bergkamp, J., McIntyre, K. A., & Hauser, M. (2023). An uncomfortable tension: Reconciling the principles of forensic psychology and cultural competency. *Law and Human Behavior*, *47*(1), 233–248.

Boone, K. B., Victor, T. L., Wen, J., Razani, J., & Ponton, M. (2007). The association between neuropsychological scores and ethnicity, language, and acculturation variables in a large patient population. *Archives of Clinical Neuropsychology*, *22*, 355–365.

Bridges, A. J., & Ahern, D. C. (2016). Assessment of malingering in minority populations. In F. R. Ferraro (Ed). *Minority and cross-cultural aspects of neuropsychological assessment* (pp. 436–458). New York: Psychology Press.

Bush, S. S., Ruff, R. M., Tröster, A. I., Barth, J. T., Koffler, S. P., Pliskin, N. H., ... & Silver, C. H. (2005). Symptom validity assessment: Practice issues and medical necessity NAN policy & planning committee. *Archives of Clinical Neuropsychology*, *20*(4), 419–426.

Chafetz, M., & Underhill, J. (2013). Estimated costs of malingered disability. *Archives of Clinical Neuropsychology*, *28*, 633–639.

Cho, I., Park, J., Song, H. J., & Morton, J. B. (2021). Disentangling language status and country-of-origin explanations of the bilingual advantage in preschoolers. *Journal of Experimental Child Psychology*, *212*, 105235.

Cranney, S. (2019). Which American languages are dying? Quantifying the demographic vulnerability of indigenous languages in the United States. Working Paper Number SESHD-WP2019-08. United States Census. https://www.census.gov/content/dam/Census/library/working-papers/2019/demo/sehsd-wp2019-08.pdf

Daubert v. Merrell Dow Pharm, Inc., 509 U.S. 579 (U.S 1993)
Diaz-Santos, M., Anderson, K., Miranda, M., Wong, C., Yañez, J. J., & Irani, F. (2022). Stepping into action: The role of neuropsychologists in social justice advocacy. In F. Irani (Ed). *Cultural diversity in neuropsychological assessment* (pp. 63–78). New York: Routledge.
Dietrich, S., & Hernandez, E. (2022). Language use in the United States: 2019 American Community Survey Reports. United States Census Bureau. https://www.census.gov/content/dam/Census/library/publications/2022/acs/acs-50.pdf
Faust, D., Hart, K., Guilmette, T. J., & Arkes, H. R. (1988). Neuropsychologists' capacity to detect adolescent malingerers. *Professional Psychology: Research and Practice*, *19*(5), 508–515. https://doi.org/10.1037/0735-7028.19.5.508
Fed. R. Evid 702 (2009).
Frye v. United States, 293 F. 1013 (D.C. Cir. 1923).
Fujii, D. (2016). *Conducting a culturally-informed neuropsychological evaluation.* Washington, DC: American Psychological Association Press.
Fujii, D. (2018). Developing a cultural context for conducting a neuropsychological evaluation with a culturally diverse client: The ECLECTIC framework. *The Clinical Neuropsychologist, 32*, 1356–1392.
Fujii, D. (2023). Incorporating intersectionality in neuropsychology: Moving the discipline forward. *Archives of Clinical Neuropsychology: The Official Journal of the National Academy of Neuropsychologists*, *38*(1), 154–167. https://doi.org/10.1093/arclin/acac075
Fujii, D., Santos, O., & Della Malva, L. (2022). *Interpreter-assisted neuropsychological assessment: Clinical considerations.* (pp. 135–147). New York: Routledge.
Fujii, D., & Wong, T. (2005). Neuropsychological assessment with Asian-American immigrants: Recommendations for meeting *Daubert* standards. *Journal of Forensic Neuropsychology*, *4*(4), 3–25.
Garb, H. N. (2021). Race bias and gender bias in the diagnosis of psychological disorders. *Clinical Psychology Review*, *90*, 102087.
Hamilton, A., Brown, S., Johnson, V., & Lad, S. (2022). *Liberating the narratives of BIPOC neuropsychologists: Unpacking microaggressions through lived experiences*. In F. Irani (Ed.), *Cultural diversity in neuropsychological assessment: Developing understanding through global case studies* (pp. 50–61). Oxfordshire: Routledge.
Irani, F. (2022). *Cultural diversity in neuropsychological assessment: developing understanding through global case studies.* Oxfordshire: Routledge.
LaDuke, C., Barr, W., Brodale, D. L., & Rabin, L. A. (2018). Toward generally accepted forensic assessment practices among clinical neuropsychologists: A survey of professional practice and common test use. *The Clinical Neuropsychologist*, *32*(1), 145–164.
Larrabee, G. J. (Ed.). (2007). *Assessment of malingered neuropsychological deficits.* New York: Oxford University Press.
Larrabee, G. L. (2012). Performance validity and symptoms validity in neuropsychological assessment. *Journal of the International Neuropsychological Society, 18*, 625–630.
Loewenstein, D. A., Argüelles, T., Argüelles, S., & Linn-Fuentes, P. (1994). Potential cultural bias in the neuropsychological assessment of the older adult. *Journal of Clinical and Experimental Neuropsychology*, *16*(4), 623–629. https://doi.org/10.1080/01688639408402673
Martin, P. K., Schroeder, R. W., & Odland, A. P. (2015). Neuropsychologists' validity testing beliefs and practices: A survey of North American professionals. *The Clinical Neuropsychologist*, *29*(6), 741–776.
Martin, P. K. & Schroeder, R. W. (2020). Base rates of invalid test performance across clinical non-forensic contexts and settings. *Archives of Clinical Neuropsychology, 00*, 1–9.
Mittenberg, W, Patton, C, Canyock, EM, et al. (2002). Base rates of malingering and symptom exaggeration. *Journal of Clinical and Experimental Neuropsychology*, *24*, 1094–102.
Nelson, N. W., & Doan, B. M. (2013). Research and symptom validity assessment in mild traumatic brain injury cases. In D. A. Carone & S. S. Bush (Eds.), *Mild traumatic brain injury: Symptom validity assessment and malingering* (pp. 119–144). New York: Springer.

Nguyen, H. H. D., & Ryan, A. M. (2008). Does stereotype threat affect test performance of minorities and women? A meta-analysis of experimental evidence. *Journal of Applied Psychology*, *93*(6), 1314.

Nijdam-Jones, A., & Rosenfeld, B. (2017). Cross-cultural feigning assessment: A systematic review of feigning instruments used with linguistically, ethnically, and culturally diverse samples. *Psychological Assessment*, *29*(11), 1321.

Pedraza, O. (Ed.). (2019). *Clinical cultural neuroscience: An integrative approach to cross-cultural neuropsychology*. New York: Oxford University Press.

Powell, M. B., & Bartholomew, T. (2003). Interviewing and assessing clients from different cultural backgrounds: Guidelines for all forensic professionals. In D. Carson & R. Bull (Eds). *Handbook of psychology in legal contexts* (pp. 625–643). New York: John Wiley & Sons.

Rioja, V., & Rosenfeld, B. (2018). Addressing linguistic and cultural differences in the forensic interview. *International Journal of Forensic Mental Health*, *17*(4), 377–386.

Rogers, R. (Ed.). (2008). *Clinical assessment of malingering and deception* (3rd ed.) New York: Guilford Press.

Rogers, R., & Bender, S. D. (2013). Evaluation of malingering and related response styles. In R. K. Otto & I. R. Weiner (Eds.), *Handbook of psychology volume 11: Forensic psychology* (3rd ed., pp. 517–540). Hoboken, NJ: John Wiley & Sons.

Rosselli, M., & Ardila, A. (2003). The impact of culture and education on non-verbal neuropsychological measurements: A critical review. *Brain and Cognition*, *52*(3), 326–333.

Sabbagh, M. A., Xu, F., Carlson, S. M., Moses, L. J., & Lee, K. (2006). The development of executive functioning and theory of mind. A comparison of Chinese and U.S. preschoolers. *Psychological Science*, *17*(1), 74–81.

Salazar, X. F., Lu, P. H., & Boone, K. B. (2021). The use of performance validity tests in ethnic-minority and non-English-dominant populations. In K. Boone (Ed). *Assessment of Feigned Cognitive Impairment: A Neuropsychological Perspective* (pp. 578–608).

Sánchez, O., & Judd, T. (2022). Multicultural education and training in neuropsychology: Let's talk about skill acquisition! In F. Irani (Ed). *Cultural diversity in neuropsychological assessment* (pp. 18–33). New York: Routledge.

Sandeen, E., Moore, K. M., & Swanda, R. M. (2018). Reflective local practice: A pragmatic framework for improving culturally competent practice in psychology. *Professional Psychology: Research and Practice*, *49*(2), 142.

Schmader, T., Johns, M., & Forbes, C. (2008). An integrated model of stereotype threat effects on performance. *Psychological Review*, *115*, 336–356.

Schroeder, R. W., Martin, P. K., Heinrichs, R. J., & Baade, L. E. (2018). Research methods in performance validity testing studies: Criterion grouping approach impacts study outcomes. *The Clinical Neuropsychologist*, *33*, 466–477.

Sherman, E. M., Slick, D. J., & Iverson, G. L. (2020). Multidimensional malingering criteria for neuropsychological assessment: A 20-year update of the malingered neuropsychological dysfunction criteria. *Archives of Clinical Neuropsychology*, *35*(6), 735–764.

Slick, D. J., & Sherman, E. M. (2013). Differential diagnosis of malingering. In D. A. Carone & S. S. Bush (Eds). *Mild traumatic brain injury: Symptom validity assessment and malingering* (pp. 57–72). New York: Springer.

State of Washington v. Sisouvanh, 175 Wn.2d 607 (Wash. 2012). https://law.justia.com/cases/washington/supreme-court/2012/85422-0.html

Strutt, A. M., & Stinson, J. M. (2022). Performance validity testing with culturally diverse individuals and non-native English speakers. In R. W. Schroeder & P. K. Martin (Eds). *Validity assessment in clinical neuropsychological practice: Evaluating and managing noncredible performance* (pp. 211–232). New York: Guilford Press.

Suhr, J. A., & Gunstad, J. (2005). Further exploration of the effect of "diagnosis threat" on cognitive performance in individuals with mild head injury. *Journal of the International Neuropsychological Society*, *11*(1), 23–29.

Sweet, J. J., Heilbronner, R. L., Morgan, J. E., et al. (2021). American Academy of Clinical Neuropsychology (AACN) 2021 consensus statement on validity assessment: Update of the 2009 AACN consensus conference statement on neuropsychological assessment of effort, response bias, and malingering. *The Clinical Neuropsychologist, 35*(6), 1053–1106.

Thames, A. D., Hinkin, C. H., Byrd, D. A., et al. (2013). Effects of stereotype threat, perceived discrimination, and examiner race on neuropsychological performance: Simple as black and white? *Journal of International Neuropsychological Society, 19*, 583–593.

Udoetuk, S., Dongarwar, D., & Salihu, H. M. (2020). Racial and gender disparities in diagnosis of malingering in clinical settings. *Journal of Racial and Ethnic Health Disparities*, *7*, 1117–1123.

United Nations Department of Economic and Social Affairs, Population Division (2022). World Population Prospects 2022: Summary of Results. UN DESA/POP/2022/TR/NO. https://www.un.org/development/desa/pd/sites/www.un.org.development.desa.pd/files/wpp2022_summary_of_results.pdf

VanLandingham, H., Ellison, R. L., Laique, A., Cladek, A., Khan, H., Gonzalez, C., & Dunn, M. R. (2022). A scoping review of stereotype threat for BIPOC: Cognitive effects and intervention strategies for the field of neuropsychology. *The Clinical Neuropsychologist*, *36*(2), 503–522

Vespa, J., Medina, L., & Armstrong, D.M. (2020). Demographic Turning Points for the United States: Population Projections for 2020 to 2060. *Current Population Reports, P25–1144,* U.S. Census Bureau, Washington, DC.

Weiss, R. A., & Rosenfeld, B. (2012). Navigating cross-cultural issues in forensic assessment: Recommendations for practice. *Professional Psychology: Research and Practice*, *43*(3), 234–240. https://doi.org/10.1037/a0025850

Weiss, L. G., & Saklofske, D. H. (2020). Mediators of IQ test score differences across racial and ethnic groups: The case for environmental and social justice. *Personality and Individual Differences*, *161*, 109962.

Whaley, A. L. (2021). Stereotype threat and neuropsychological test performance in the US African American population. *Archives of Clinical Neuropsychology*, *36*(7), 1361–1366.

Whitman, M., Tarescavage, A. M., Glassmire, D. M., Burchett, D., & Sellbom, M. (2018). Examination of differential validity of MMPI-2-RF scores by gender and ethnicity in a forensic sample. *Psychological Assessment*, *31*(3), 404–409. https://doi.org/10.1037/pas0000677

Wong, T. M. (2000). Neuropsychological assessment and intervention with Asian Americans. In E. Fletcher-Janzen, T. L. Strickland, & C. R. Reynolds (Eds.), *Handbook of cross-cultural neuropsychology* (pp. 43–53). New York: Springer.

Yutaka, O., Janca, A., Asai, M., & Sartorius, N. (Eds.). (2012). *Somatoform disorders: A worldwide perspective* (Vol. 3). New York: Springer Science & Business Media.

6 The Critical Importance of Assessing Validity in Forensic Neuropsychological Evaluations

Tannahill Glen

Validity Assessment Is Historically a Component of Neuropsychological Investigation

Neuropsychologists have offered opinions as experts in the legal arena for at least 50 years (Sweet et al., 2021). Well before the earliest documented expert testimony, though, clinicians and researchers recognized that there should be some means of assessing the credibility of cognitive test scores. Edouard Claparede, the Swiss psychologist who originally developed the word list learning test modified and published by Andres Rey, recognized that non-injury factors could influence test performance. He described consideration of weighing potential incentive to feign amnesia and objective symptoms, rather than merely self-report (Boake, 2000). In 1941, his doctoral student, Rey, created the Word Recognition List to detect feigned amnesia on his test of list learning, followed by the Dot Counting Test, and the 15 Item Test. Rey interpreted failure on the simple tasks as evidence of "doubtful collaboration" of the examinee, while successful performance could be assumed to reflect "collaboration sufficient…for us to push further the investigations" (Rey, 1958, pp. 122–123).

Remarkably, even at that early time, Rey's description of the measures demonstrated his understanding that *in the absence of significant and easily identifiable cognitive impairment*, the examinee should be able to complete the easy task without difficulty. This concept remains influential today: Sherman, Slick, and Iverson, in their update on criteria for Malingered Neurocognitive Dysfunction (2020), opined that the mere presence of cognitive impairment does not preclude intentional exaggeration of deficits, and they defined significant impairment: moderate to severe dementia, moderate to severe intellectual disability, and severe psychiatric, medical, or neurological disorder "with cognitive impairment sufficient to preclude independence in basic activities of daily living" (p. 741). Green, Montijo, and Brockhaus (2011) also described this important distinction when interpreting a well-known stand-alone performance validity test (PVT): a profile of severe memory impairment on the Word Memory Test should be produced by persons with "well documented and clinically evident" signs of severe impairment, at a level that interferes with independence in activities of daily living (Green, 2003).

During the same period that methods to detect feigned *cognitive* performance were being developed, Meehl and Hathaway (1946) described the need to objectively adjust scores for bias in *psychological* response styles, rather than relying on clinical judgment alone. To reduce misinterpretation of results when test-takers exhibited the tendency to be overly self-critical or, conversely, overly guarded in one's responses on the Minnesota Multiphasic Personality Inventory (MMPI; Hathaway & McKinley, 1943), the authors developed three

DOI: 10.4324/9781003005063-7

validity scales (*L*, *F*, and *K*). The L scale was designed to identify persons who presented themselves in an overly positive light, in a pattern rarely reported by test-takers, colloquially referred to as "faking good." The F scale, similarly, identified items rarely endorsed by early samples, and it served as a "red flag" of sorts alerting examiners to a problem with the test taker's understanding of the task (Caldwell, n.d.). The K scale was developed as a subtler correction for a tendency to deny problems (McKinley, Hathaway & Meehl, 1948).

Other MMPI validity scores have been created and published over the years. Gough developed the F–K (F minus K) and Dissimulation (Ds) scales in the 1950s, both of which were designed to identify the more sophisticated malingerer. The MMPI-2 (Butcher, Dahlstrom, Graham, Tellegen & Kaemmer, 1989), contained the Fb (F-back scale), and the VRIN (Variable Response Inconsistency Scale) and TRIN (True Response Inconsistency) scales (Burke, 2007). The Fb scale was designed to confirm F scale response consistency in the latter portion of the test, while VRIN and TRIN scales were designed to detect inconsistent or random responding, which could invalidate results (Cox, Weed & Butcher, 2009). In 1995, the Infrequency-Psychopathology Scale (F[p]) was published, meant to identify persons endorsing items rarely reported even by persons with psychiatric illness (Arbisi & Ben Porath, 1995). Later, the FBS scale was added, originally referred to as the Fake Bad Scale, later termed the Symptom Validity Scale (Lees-Haley, English & Glenn, 1991). The response bias (RBS, assessing over-reporting of cognitive symptoms) scale (Ben Porath & Tellegen, 2020) was added to the MMPI-2-RF. The most recently published version of the test, the MMPI-3, includes the Combined Response Inconsistency (measuring both systematic and random responding).

An important common thread embedded within Rey's memory research and the development of the MMPI is an awareness that test scores may reflect multiple variables, ranging from socioeconomic factors to educational or cultural history, to potential incentives, whether internal or external. For instance, Rey expressed understanding that exaggeration of memory impairment may be "calculated behavior" (malingering) or a behavioral response, like under-engagement (Rey, 1958, p. 121). Similarly, while the MMPI L scale could indeed identify persons who tended to present themselves in a beatific manner, it was also sensitive to variables such as religious affiliation (Rosen, Baldwin & Smith, 2016).

As the previous examples demonstrate, neurocognitive and psychological researchers understood that multiple factors, including motivational factors, can significantly impact test performance, and they wrote extensively about the importance of using clinical information and normative sample comparison to optimize the predictive value of scores (Iverson, Henrichs, Barton & Allen, 2002). This comprehensive and empirically sophisticated approach to validity assessment is what makes neuropsychological evaluation so informative and reliable in the forensic arenas. After all, secondary gain—advantages that can result from having signs of illness or disease, such as avoidance of work duties or incarceration or financial gain)—is present in all cases with forensic involvement.

In 1961, British neurologist Henry Miller published an influential report on the relationship between secondary gain on symptom reporting in 200 forensic cases involving reported head injury. Miller documented an inverse relationship between severity of injury and the presence of what he termed "accident neurosis," characterized by subjective somatic symptoms, atypical onset and/or course of symptoms, and prolonged course of return to normal activities. Miller found that persons with more severe head injury characteristics reported lower levels of occupational disability than those will milder injury characteristics, a finding that has since been replicated (e.g., Greiffenstein & Baker, 2006). Miller diagnosed 47 of those 200 examinees (24%) with accident neurosis, a number close to current, replicated estimates of a base rate of malingering between 30% and 50% in forensic contexts (Larrabee, Millis & Meyers, 2009).

In a follow-up study of 50 of those individuals diagnosed as having accident neurosis, Miller found that in the subsequent two years, 42 of the 50 cases reached settlement, 4 claims were abandoned, and 4 claims were rejected after trial. Nearly all (45/50) examinees evidenced resolution of the claimed symptoms (Miller, 1961). Only two were still unable to work due to their initial symptoms. Miller, in two lectures on which his 1961 article was based, attributed the prolonged symptoms, which resolved after case conclusion, to the presence of secondary gain—external incentives like avoiding work and financial gain (see Ross, 2019 for review).

Interestingly, Miller described post-settlement "disappearance of contractures" in three individuals who had reported hand injuries. This evokes the uncommon but fascinating "clenched fist syndrome," not described in reports until 1980, and defined in current medical literature as a conversion or factitious disorder involving finger flexion contractures (Meiwandi & Papadakis, 2019). Swiergosz, Kasdan, and Wilhelmi (2017) published a case series of 21 patients diagnosed with malingering after presenting with this condition, who had diagnoses of Reflex Sympathetic Dystrophy of the hand (now referred to as Complex Regional Pain Syndrome), and who were seeking financial compensation for injuries. The authors noted that the impact of secondary gain is especially relevant to diagnostic evaluation in cases where litigation and/or other external incentives are present.

Overall, the most consequential effect of Miller's work was to spur statistically grounded investigation by non-neurologists into the post-concussion syndrome in a forensic setting (Ross, 2019), resulting in new emphasis on methodological and statistical rigor (Weighill, 1983). Moreover, a body of inquiry into the accuracy of clinical judgment (versus actuarial judgment) developed, indicating the importance of combining objective evidence with clinical judgment in the detection of malingering or other diagnoses (Faust, Hart, Guilmette & Arkes, 1988; Dawes, Faust & Meehl, 1989). With expertise in the quantitative evaluation of cognitive, somatic, and psychological deficits that are often reported in secondary gain cases, neuropsychologists and other clinical psychologists were well positioned for these examinations.

In the 1990s, two additional factors drove the ensuing growth in research and use of validity assessment. First, quantifying the impact of secondary gain on test scores was necessary as neuropsychologists' involvement in forensic activities increased—especially regarding claims of traumatic brain injury (TBI) (Binder & Rohling, 1996). Second, research on TBI and concussion rapidly expanded as classification accuracy and avoiding misleading interpretation of study results became critical. Over the next two decades, published research on validity assessment increased exponentially, evolving from the common conception that validity failure is synonymous with malingering, to the modern consensus that validity assessment is a means of ensuring test data accuracy (Schroeder & Martin, 2022).

Validity Assessment Is Not Unique to Neuropsychology

Measurement of test data validity is not limited to neuropsychology, as it is also an established practice in other areas of scientific and medical evaluation (Greer, Chambliss & Mackler, 2005). In radiology, for example, motion artifact is common in magnetic resonance imaging (MRI), especially when examining small lesions, and may result in misinterpretation or unreliable analysis of results (Havsteen, Ohlhues, Madsen, Nybing, Christensen & Christensen, 2017). Both human (subjective) and automated (objective) methods of motion artifact detection have been applied in clinical and research practice to increase the validity of imaging findings (Hakky, Pandey, Kwak, Jara & Erbay, 2013; Lorch et al., 2017). Similarly, specimen validity tests in urine screenings for medication adherence or drug testing (Ko, Merritt & Dawson, 2013) are used by all major laboratory corporations to ensure the reliability of interpretation of results that have implications for patient care and public safety.

This is not unlike neuropsychological validity testing, described by Emhoff, Lynch, and McCaffrey (2018) as providing "an objective basis for placing confidence in the test data" as a reliable reflection of the examinee's current status. Clinician judgment is no substitute for validity testing: objective estimation of validity is vital to the evaluation process, given evidence that clinician subjective judgment is not adequate for the detection of invalidity (Dandachi-FitzGerald, Merckelbach & Ponds, 2017; Faust, Hart, Guilmette & Arkes, 1988).

Validity Assessment Is Recommended by Professional Organizations in Neuropsychology

Assessment of validity in neuropsychological evaluations has been strongly endorsed by the two major clinical professional organizations in the field, in part because reliance on clinical judgment without objective data is not sufficiently accurate and increases the risk of false-positive or false-negative errors (Dandachi-Fitzgerald, Marckelbach & Ponds, 2017). The National Academy of Neuropsychology's (NAN) 2005 position article (Bush et al., 2005) on validity testing states that when secondary gain is present and may influence results, clinicians "can, and must...utilize procedures to assist in the determination of the validity of the information and test data obtained" (p. 246). Recognizing the evolution of the empirical evidence for, and increasing sophistication of, validity assessment methods, the American Academy of Clinical Neuropsychology (AACN) consensus statement (Sweet et al., 2021) describes neuropsychologists' "nearly universal acceptance" of the importance of validity assessment regardless of the evaluation context (clinical or forensic). Thus, validity measurement is not only a major aspect of the neuropsychological forensic examination, but it is central to the ethical and competent practice of the neuropsychologist.

Validity Assessment Is Endorsed by Professional Organizations in Medicine and Other Specialties

Assessment of validity has been endorsed by non-neuropsychological professional organizations whose members often rely on neuropsychological evaluations in their own services. As Schroeder and Martin (2022) noted, the American Medical Association (AMA, 2008) described validity testing in cognitive evaluations as "standard practice," (p. 351) and an important part of any objective evaluation of impairment. An AMA Guide publication also notes the importance of assessing validity of patients' presentations, including the use of questionnaires and scales (Patterson et al., 2012). The National Academies' Committee on Psychological Testing, Including Validity Testing, for Social Security Administration Disability Determinations (The National Academies, 2015) reported that validity indicators are recommended, and that all neurocognitive evaluations should include a conclusion regarding validity of the examination (e.g., related to application for Social Security disability).

While extending the support of validity assessment in medical communities, the use of symptom validity tests (SVTs) is described as a core competency for the medicolegal expert in physiatry (Lacerte, 2019). Finally, the American Psychological Association Specialty

Guidelines for Forensic Psychology (2013) recommend that forensic practitioners "identify any substantive limitations that may affect the reliability and validity of the facts or opinions offered, and communicates these to the decision maker" (4.02.02, p. 6), entirely consistent with neuropsychology practice standards for validity assessment and reporting.

Validity Assessment Is Recommended in Clinical Settings

Consideration of external incentives is not limited to forensic contexts, as clinical assessments frequently involve potential incentives such as access to financial supports, medications, or accommodations (Sherman, Slick & Iverson, 2020). In such evaluations, a patient may obtain desired incentives not for optimal performance (such as on tests like the SAT or LSAT) but for lower scores suggestive of impairment or disability. Schroeder, Clark, and Martin (2022) reported invalid performance data in 58.6% of examinees considering application for Social Security benefits, 44.6% of those currently seeking benefits, and 39.3% of those already receiving benefits—compared with only 8.5% of examinees without an identified financial incentive.

Assessment of validity is not restricted to clinical populations with a clear financial incentive, such as potential litigation or disability application; Kemp et al. (2008) found that 11% of non-litigating patients with medically unexplained symptoms failed two or more validity measures. Bush et al. (2005) described validity testing in the clinical realm as "medically necessary" in order to elucidate brain–behavior relationships for referring physicians, and to increase the accuracy of diagnosis and treatment planning. An example of a clinical scenario in which validity testing would be extremely important is a patient with psychogenic non-epileptic seizures—a relatively common condition that has been associated with performance invalidity (Binder, Salinsky, Storzbach & Tadrous-Fernanz, 2021), and in which invalid range test performance may lead to the reconsideration of treatment approach.

Validity testing is not restricted to isolated clinical groups such as persons with concussion or somatic symptomology: assessment of validity is also supported for persons with dementia (McGuire, Crawford & Evans, 2019) and epilepsy (Kim, Torres, Kang & Drane, 2022) and patients with moderate to severe TBI (Uiterwijk, Stargatt & Crowe, 2022), among others. Notably, validity assessment is appropriate for persons with genuine cognitive impairment, as it has been demonstrated that cognitive dysfunction in and of itself typically does not explain multiple PVT failures (Critchfield et al., 2019). It is also appropriate to employ validity testing in child and adolescent assessment (Emhoff, Lynch & McCaffrey, 2018).

When genuine cognitive impairment is suspected based on medical records, historical information, observations, or patterns of performance in testing, research suggests many validity indicators maintain acceptable false-positive classification rates at published cutoffs (Kanser, Logan, Steward, Vanderbleek & Kamper, 2022). Responsible clinicians will be familiar with literature on the selection of appropriate PVTs/SVTs for patients with cognitive impairment and utilize the most accurate measures and appropriate cut offs.

While mood dysfunction may influence subjective and objective cognitive functions—for instance, memory and processing speed deficits associated with Major Depressive Disorder (MDD) (Hu et al., 2023)—psychiatric disturbance does not cause validity test failure (Tart-Zelvin et al., 2023). Nor should test score invalidity be interpreted as a "cry for help," a metaphor that is neither operationally defined nor falsifiable (Dandachi-FitzGerald, Merckelbach & Merten, 2022). Nor does the presence of chronic pain cause validity test failure

(Bianchini et al., 2014). MDD and chronic pain are frequently cited by attorneys as explanations for validity test failure; the effective witness will be able to cite evidence showing that this is not an adequate explanation.

Validity Assessment Is Recommended in Forensic Settings

By definition, the presence of an external incentive characterizes the context of forensic neuropsychological evaluations; for instance, in civil and criminal litigation, there may be claims for lost wages and compensation for damages, or the opportunity to avoid work duties or responsibility for actions (Sherman, Slick & Iverson, 2020). Furthermore, in forensic neuropsychological assessment, internal and external incentives are not mutually exclusive: a factitious disorder such as Clenched Fist Syndrome that can result in special accommodations, such as restricted use or examination of the extremity, may be present in a personal injury case with clear financial gain.

The mere presence of external or internal incentive does not predict invalid responding or exaggerated self-reported symptoms, but rather is a risk factor that raises concern. However, when invalidity or RBS is identified in a forensic setting, the neuropsychologist should consider differential diagnoses (e.g., a significant genuine condition) or designation (such as malingering) for this specific reason:

> When present, such invalid performances preclude the use of those data as a basis for: (1) opinions with regard to attribution to the cause at issue (e.g., accident, injury), (2) the nature and extent of possible deficits and disability, and (3) guiding treatment or evaluating treatment effectiveness.
>
> (Heilbronner et al., 2009, p. 1104)

This does not imply that invalid performance precludes the expert from opining on *any* cause or level of deficits/ability; it simply means that invalid data cannot be used as evidence of cerebral dysfunction or disability. Hence, the neuropsychologist who encounters an invalid performance may well go on to state opinions about incentives, designation of malingered dysfunction or psychiatric diagnoses when evidence is present, level of engagement, inconsistency of a presentation with accepted models of neurologic function, and/or consistency of evidence of optimal functioning (such as the ability to drive long distances without incident in a person claiming severe oculomotor or perceptual impairment).

The distinction is important because it has been argued that invalid test results are unreliable data that cannot be used as a basis for opinion (Lockhart, 2015). However, Federal Rules of Evidence [FRE] 702 (1975) refer to "sufficient facts or data" and "reliable principles and methods." Therefore, a set of invalid test data in addition to evidence from interviews, records, and other sources is certainly "*sufficient* facts or data," and *analysis* of those data can be applied according to *reliable* principles and methods (empirically supported, peer-reviewed, and/or published neuropsychological literature).

Qualitative Validity Assessment Is an Integral Part of the Forensic Neuropsychological Evaluation

According to the most recent AACN consensus statement on validity assessment (AACN, 2021), qualitative information is important, as it provides the opportunity to compare test performance to reported and observed functioning. Indeed, "marked discrepancies" comprise two of the four major criteria for the diagnosis of Neurocognitive, Somatic, and Psychiatric Malingering (Sherman, Slick & Iverson, 2020).

Criterion B (Sherman, Slick & Iverson, 2020, p. 744) includes evidence of "compelling inconsistencies," which can be "evidence of invalid presentation [allowing] malingering to be identified even when there is no test data at all" (p. 744). The authors note that compelling inconsistencies are "stark contradictions" directly observed by the examiner, "not definitive evidence of malingering but rather of feigning or exaggeration" (p. 744). Compelling inconsistencies are also included in the diagnostic criteria for Malingered Pain-Related Disability (Bianchini, Greve & Glynn, 2005). For example, this author evaluated a plaintiff claiming limb paralysis and severe physical and emotional disability due to Complex Regional Pain Syndrome. Testing was limited due to the plaintiff's reported inability to use a pencil due to hypersensitivity to tactile stimuli or lift any object heavier than a piece of paper. During the exam, she was observed to spontaneously lean over and lift her substantial handbag using the affected limb, and then rummage through her purse with the same hand, looking for an item, both in stark contrast to the earlier behaviors.

Sherman, Slick, and Iverson (2020) specifically state that compelling inconsistencies allow for the identification of malingering independent of other criteria (such as invalid cognitive test scores) and even without psychometric data at all (such as when evaluation is limited by various factors to record review and interview).

Criterion C (Sherman, Slick & Iverson, 2020, p. 753) pertains to marked discrepancies between test data (cognitive test performance or symptom reporting in testing) and known course of a condition, records, and/or collateral report. An example would be a claimant who is still successfully employed in a clerical position after sustaining mild concussion with no loss of consciousness, but who performs at the 1st percentile across all measures of memory and learning.

Although inconsistency of symptom reporting and performance has long been associated with invalidity or exaggerated impairment (Bush et al., 2005), a recent study challenged that concept. Boskovic, Zwaan, Baillie, and Merckelbach (2021) compared a group of college students with genuine symptoms with a group asked to convincingly report non-existent symptoms over a series of days so they would appear to belong to the "truth telling" group. The feigning group did not report symptoms less consistently across days, but individuals in the group did report more symptoms and greater symptom intensity than the genuine symptom group. The authors opined that the results suggest that neither consistency nor inconsistency of symptom reporting should be used as the sole discriminator between valid and invalid reporting. Their results are consistent with previous work suggesting feigning strategies can be typically categorized as *amplified* or *unlikely* symptom production (Rogers & Correa, 2008).

Despite the seeming conflict, it should be noted that the strategies of symptom or impairment amplification or atypicality described by Rogers and Correa are very similar to examples of compelling inconsistencies and marked discrepancies described by Sherman, Slick, and Iverson (2020), and can be viewed as the same constructs. Thus, minor inconsistency of qualitative evidence (e.g., an examinee reporting anomia, but speaking fluently in interview) is not prima facie evidence of invalidity of presentation. Instead, qualitative evidence can and should be reviewed for signs of significant discrepancies that can suggest amplification or manufacturing of symptoms or impairment.

Forensic examiners should also bear in mind that it is possible for validity testing to be passed due to coaching or prior exposure to specific details about validity assessment. Gutheil (2003) opined that coaching of litigants by their attorneys is a forensic and ethical problem "as old as the law itself" (p. 2). Gutheil's interesting editorial piece describes examples of clear coaching, but also "possible" or "ambiguous" coaching. In one example, a leaflet provided by an attorney to clients undergoing examination detailed verbal instructions about how *not to respond* to certain investigation such as assessment of disproportionate pain response to light stimulus that is not reproduced later. Indeed, a more recent survey of attorneys practicing in specialties in which psychological testing is common (Spengler, Walters, Bryant & Millspaugh, 1995) found that more than half of attorneys surveyed reported sharing information about MMPI-2 validity scales.

Thus, coaching or advance knowledge of examiner techniques may render validity assessment less informative. When this eventuality is suspected, non-psychometric data may be relied upon to support a diagnosis of Malingering of Neurocognitive Dysfunction or other presentations. Carone (2013) reported strategies for the detection of non-credible presentations after claimed concussion. That chapter is a highly recommended reading exercise for forensic examiners for its compilation of various methods, including qualitative variables (e.g., within-task inconsistency, atypical errors), observable neuromedical indicators (such as the absence of atrophy in an unused limb in Complex Regional Pain Syndrome), and distraction tests.

Failure to Assess Validity Ignores High-Base-Rate Conditions

Neuropsychologists must consider differential diagnosis in selecting tests and interpreting test results. For example, if asked to evaluate an 80-year-old man whose family is concerned about memory decline, the competent neuropsychologist will be careful to choose some measures to assess for memory performance; mild cognitive impairment (MCI) is a high-base-rate condition seen in about one-quarter of those from 80 to 84 years of age (Petersen et al., 2018). Similarly, it would be important to screen for mood disturbance, as nearly a third of older adults have evidence of depression (Zenebe, Akele, Selassie & Necho, 2021). Failure to consider or test for either of those conditions that is quite common among the population being considered would be improper. Likewise, it has consistently been shown that invalidity occurs at high base rates (between 30% and 50%) in groups where external incentives are present (Larrabee, Millis & Meyers, 2009; Schroeder, Clark & Martin, 2022). Thus, failure to use validity assessment in those contexts is akin to failing to assess for MCI or mood dysfunction in an older adult with cognitive decline. Iverson (2006) stated that the clinician who fails to assess validity in a forensic evaluation is not performing a competent evaluation, and, in large part, this is related to the consideration of high-base-rate conditions in the differential diagnosis.

Validity Assessment Is Ethical and Beneficial to Society

There is real societal harm that can result from failure to consider validity or RBS: the economic cost of malingering of mental health conditions has been estimated at US$20 billion annually (Chafetz and Underhill, 2013). Mistaken use of costly and limited medical care may exclude others with genuine medical conditions from obtaining those services (Zwick et al., 2021). Society is more exposed to risk if persons working in professions with public impact (e.g., police officers, pilots, physicians) are able to 'pass' fitness testing without analysis of validity (Boone et al., 2022).

Some have suggested that labeling invalidity and malingering can be harmful to examinees. Lockhart (2015) opined that a forensic psychologist, above all, has an ethical mandate to avoid doing harm, citing the American Psychological Association (APA) ethical guideline of "Beneficence and Nonmaleficence" (APA, 2020): "Psychologists strive to benefit those with whom they work and take care to do no harm" (p. 3). Lockhart warned that harm could occur by assigning the "malingerer" label without adequate evidence, but this position fails to recognize existing recommendations for validity testing. APA Specialty Forensic Guidelines 11.01 (Accuracy, Fairness, and Avoidance of Deception, p. 16) and 11.04 (Comprehensive and Accurate Presentation of Opinions in Reports and Testimony, p. 17) indicate the importance of objectively and accurately reporting results and impressions (APA, 2013). To avoid validity assessment or identification of validity failures out of concern the examinee may experience emotional distress or lose a desired outcome is not an objective position. Furthermore, feigning impairment or illness, if undetected or unreported, can lead to unnecessary invasive procedures or medications, even in cases with forensic involvement, and reluctance to identify invalid presentations may lead to such interventions (Rumschik & Appel, 2019).

Validity Assessment Accounts for Racial, Cultural, Educational, and Socioeconomic Differences

A number of PVTs and SVTs have been shown to have validity in persons from various ethnoracial backgrounds (Soble et al., 2023) and have been adapted for use in different languages in non-English speaking countries (Bajjaleh, Braw & Elkana, 2021). Research has also shown the utility of validity tests in examinees with low educational attainment (Soble et al., 2023). Examiners should exercise appropriate caution in interpreting validity scores for plaintiffs or defendants with low intellectual functioning (Hood et al., 2022) or use of English as a second language (Lippa, 2018).

Although some research has suggested race is not correlated with validity test failure (Zinke, Lam, Harden & Fogg, 2010; Whitman, Tarescavage, Glassmire, Burchett & Sellbom, 2019), some studies have shown that race accounts for a modest degree of variance in performance on validity tests (Denning & Horner, 2024; Braun, Fountain-Zaragoza, Halliday & Horner, 2023). Consistent with the AACN Position Statement on Race Norms (2021), race may be a proxy for variables related to historical disparities in educational opportunities, nutritional resources, and medical care, for example. Regardless, recent research suggests that failure on two or more PVTs is not associated with race (Denning & Horner, 2024) consistent with current recommendations for clinicians to rely on multiple PVT failure as the most reliable indicator of validity (Sherman, Slick & Iverson, 2020).

In practice, this would be manifest by the use of measures with appropriate normative data whenever possible, and knowledge of base rates for scores in the relevant population; for example, this author evaluated an older male of South American descent whose first language was Spanish, but who immigrated to the United States decades earlier, and operated his own business in fluent English, even in written contracts and business communications. In deposition, the use of validity testing was challenged given his cultural background and use of English as a second language, but references were provided to show his PVT performance was atypical even compared with persons using English as a second language (Martin et al., 2020) and to scores for Spanish-speaking older men from Latin America (Rivera et al., 2015).

The testifying expert should also be familiar with studies with findings contrary to those being cited, and be able to explain or cite any studies suggesting the need for lower cutoffs or cultural considerations in special populations (Nijdam-Jones, Rivera, Rosenfeld & Arango-Lasprilla, 2017).

Embedded Validity Indicators Are as Empirically Supported as Stand-Alone Validity Tests

Embedded validity indicators (EVIs) are scores within existing neuropsychological tests that have been studied and shown to classify valid or invalid performance at an acceptable level of accuracy (Erdodi & Giromini, 2023). They have become much more commonly used in recent years for several reasons: they are simple to derive from tests already administered rather than separately administered, cost-effective, and not easily identifiable as measures of RBS.

Opposing counsel may argue against the use of EVIs as rogue efforts to discredit a genuinely impaired performance: "Doctor, looking at this test manual, can you show the jury the section on this score you claim is evidence of invalidity? It's not in there, is it? In fact, isn't it true my client's score on the Digit Span test, at the first percentile, shows he has severe attention impairment?" In fact, despite concerns that EVIs may have unacceptably high false-positive rates, conflating performance suppression with genuine cognitive impairment (Glassmire, Wood, Ta, Kinney & Nitch, 2019), multiple publications have indicated EVIs do not, in fact, misidentify cognitive impairment as non-credible performance (Boone, 2021; Schroeder, Twumasi-Ankrah, Baade & Marshall, 2012). Clinicians can review constantly updated peer-reviewed research on EVIs to determine appropriateness of case application and cutoffs with the most optimal sensitivity and specificity.

Validity Tests Are Tools of the Trade and Must Be Protected from Dissemination to Non-Psychologists

Neuropsychologists are required by test-user contracts and ethical standards to protect test content. Clinicians should familiarize themselves with recommendations for protection of test content in challenging situations, such as a deposition in which opposing counsel seeks to describe validity test content on the record (Glen et al., 2021; Boone et al., 2022).

Maintaining the security of test content is an integral responsibility of practicing neuropsychologists (Boone et al., 2022), made more difficult by ever-increasing demands for release of protected materials, including validity test content, to non-psychologists. The tactic has become so commonplace that it is routinely deployed to intimidate, interfere with, and even eliminate the defense expert (Glen et al., 2021).

Good faith efforts to protect content, such as only releasing raw data (in which test content may appear) to non-psychologists when there is a court order, may not be sufficient to maintain their confidentiality. Releasing test content to non-psychologists not only makes it possible for those materials to be used to confer an unfair advantage in future cases, but it sets a precedent that the expert can release such materials if there is an order from the court. This places the expert in a tenuous position: theoretically a court order protects the psychologist from indemnification, or loss of test-user contracts, but also makes it more likely that future efforts to force release of sensitive materials will be successful.

The expert may consider withdrawing from the case, but in some situations, this could lead to legal action from the retaining party, who risks losing their expert and fees and may not be allowed to retain a replacement to the expert, and may risk inflaming the court, who may view this action as fractious. This author is aware of at least one case in which litigation was threatened by the retaining client against an expert who withdrew from a case in response to adversarial court orders. In another case, this author was released mid-case by a client who, frustrated by the increasingly difficult demands of opposing counsel, attempted to find a more pliable expert; the case ended with no neuropsychological expert, and a six-figure plaintiff's verdict.

Experts may wish to seek *advance* protective orders, signed by a judge, before all forensic or medicolegal evaluations, but even a protective order signed by a judge may not be sufficient to ensure validity tests remain confidential (Lewandowki, Boone, Kaufmann, Peck & Glen, 2023). In one case involving this author, copies of raw data, including validity test protocols with responses and test content, were sent to an opposing expert psychologist upon order of the court. A protective order was signed by the judge in advance, stipulating the release of raw data directly to, and only to, this psychologist. Somehow this material made its way to opposing counsel's office, who produced a copy later in the case. Put simply, the "protective" order failed to protect! This author has also seen protective orders amended at the conclusion of a case, then referenced in future cases in which release of raw data, including validity measures, was demanded. In short, validity tests are particularly sensitive materials in forensic evaluations, as their elimination or inefficacy has potential value to plaintiff counsel's case, and thus must be protected stringently against release and misuse by unqualified persons. For interested clinicians, the AACN has a dedicated Forensic Neuropsychology Special Interest Group (FNSIG), which has released the AACN FNSIG Tool Kit. The FNSIG web page includes a decision tree of options for handling such demands (https://theaacn.org/forensic-neuropsychology-special-interest-group/).

Invalid Performance Can Be Detected Using a Variety of Methods

Designation of a test result or an evaluation result as *invalid* indicates the performance is quantitatively or qualitatively highly unlikely (Walczyk, Sewell & DiBenedetto, 2018). Validity measures can detect magnification of symptoms and/or over-reporting of disability (Sweet et al., 2021), as well as under-reporting of shortcomings or magnifying positive traits (Whitman, Gervais & Ben Porath, 2023). Forensic examiners are advised to use both SVTs and PVTs in forensic evaluations (Sweet et al., 2021).

There is no single method of detecting non-credible scores in forensic examinations, and indeed, a number of strategies for their identification have been described, including the floor effect (involving items that should be easily passed), performance curve (assessment of patterns of performance on items based on difficulty), and response latency (Bender & Rogers, 2004). Validity indicators may be stand-alone such as the Test of Memory Malingering (TOMM), embedded in existing tests (such as Forced-Choice Recognition on the California Verbal Learning Test-3, or Reliable Digit Span on the Wechsler Adult Intelligence Scale-IV), atypical scores within an existing test (e.g., ≤2 categories completed on the Wisconsin Card Sorting Test [Greve et al., 2009]) or even qualitative findings (such as impairment of remote memory after concussion or report of severe pain in the absence of any physiologic signs).

Clinicians should consider—and should be prepared to cite—statistical qualities of the scores used to determine validity, including the following:

- Sensitivity (at what level the score correctly detects those with invalid performance)
- Specificity (at what level the score correctly identifies those who are performing validly)
- Hit rate (true positives + true negatives)
- Positive predictive power (percentage of those identified as performing invalidly who are in fact doing so)
- Negative predictive power (percentage of those identified as performing validly who are actually doing so)

(from Walczyk, Sewell & DiBenedetto, 2018).

Failure on only a single-validity measure may simply reflect transient task disengagement or other factors (Lippa, 2018; Victor, Boone, Serpa, Buehler & Ziegler, 2009). At the same time, it is not necessarily proof of valid overall performance (Schroeder et al., 2019). This is because cutoffs for validity tests are set at a high threshold specifically to reduce the chance of false positives and increase positive predictive value. Specificity should be maintained at 0.90 (Sweet et al, 2021). Thus, positive findings should be given more weight than negative results because the chance of the finding being spurious is low.

On the other hand, failure of a single PVT may in some cases be sufficient evidence of invalidity of an exam (Proto et al., 2014), although not sufficient to determine intent or "malingering" assuming that the test performance was not statistically below chance (Sherman, Slick & Iverson, 2020). Multiple validity failures are more concerning for overall invalidity of the examination results than single failures (again, assuming that the failure is not at a statistically below-chance level). When multiple validity failures are identified, the known relationship between test scores and neurocognitive abilities is no longer reliable (Erdodi & Giromini, 2023).

Passing validity measures does not rule out the possibility of magnification of deficits. A 2017 study by Kanser et al. compared performance patterns of persons asked to simulate TBI-related deficits and found "successful" simulators—those who did not fail validity tests but exhibited "impaired" range scores in testing—used information provided about TBI to focus feigned impairment on selected tests, as opposed to deploying a widespread, lower scores strategy.

Magnitude of validity test failure should also be a consideration: some performances are so low they are statistically improbable and, thus, even one such finding should be carefully considered. In fact, a significantly below-chance score on a forced-choice measure (on which a score should reach 50% by purely guessing) is a criterion for Definite Malingered Neurocognitive Disorder (Sherman, Slick & Iverson, 2020), the "smoking gun of intent" (p. 385) as described by Pankratz and Erickson (1990). That said, there is some evidence that even lower magnitude validity test failure, such as a single error on the CVLT-II Forced-Choice Recognition trial, may be meaningful: Erdodi et al. (2018) found that one Forced-Choice Recognition error predicted failure on other PVTs.

Once a forensic examiner has evidence of invalid scores, a *tally* approach may be used to assess the significance of the number of validity failures (Sweet et al., 2021). For instance, a cutoff of failure on three or more independent PVTs (N.B., not failure on two subtests of the same instrument) with individual false-positive rates of ≤10% yielded the greatest sensitivity and specificity and has been shown to carry a low false-positive rate (Larrabee, Rohling & Meyers, 2019). Sherman, Slick, and Iverson (2020) recommended considering a *ratio* of PVT failures to overall number of PVTs administered; for example, ≥2 PVT failures may indicate overall invalidity of an exam if 7 PVTs are administered. However, with a greater number of overall PVTs administered, the ratio of fails to passes should theoretically remain similar (Sweet et al., 2021).

Clinicians involved in forensic neuropsychological evaluations and consultations should familiarize themselves with published criticisms of various analyses of combinations of PVT failures (Berthelson, Mulchan, Odland, Miller & Mittenberg, 2013; Frederick, 2015), and responses to those claims (Sweet et al., 2021; Larrabee et al., 2019).

Sherman, Slick, and Iverson's (2020) summary of validity assessment is most succinct and entirely applicable to forensic neuropsychological evaluation:

> [Examiners should] (a) select individual tests with specificities of.90 or above, (b) administer at least two or three but ideally multiple PVTs, (c) if only a relatively small number

> of PVTs are administered, use a criterion of at least two or more PVT failures as indicative of invalid performance, and (d) as the number of PVTs administered increases, monitor the ratio of PVT score failures to the number of PVT scores administered (p. 13).

and

> ...use (a) PVTs with an acceptable false-positive rate, (b) PVTs that provide non-redundant information, and (c) PVTs that have cutoffs that have been validated in clinical studies (i.e., known-groups design) (p. 12).

Invalid Performance Indicates Some Data Cannot Be Used to Infer Brain Dysfunction

Failure of validity tests means that some neuropsychological data gathered during the examination are unlikely to be an accurate estimate of current functioning, and test performance is no longer correlated with brain structure and function (Erdodi & Giromini, 2023). Thus, low scores seen in a forensic evaluation, in the presence of invalidity, cannot be used to infer brain damage or cognitive impairment.

It is not uncommon for an examinee to fail validity testing in one realm yet have an entirely *normal* performance in the other—not just on validity tests but on scores in general. For instance, one may see clear invalidity of MMPI-3 responses with a cognitive test performance that is soundly in the average range, or fail a memory-related validity test, but pass those involving attention and concentration. Attorneys may argue that validity test failure only impacts the cognitive realm associated with the failure; for instance, a failed stand-alone memory validity test should not mean that low scores on measures of attention or executive functioning are also invalid. Critically, while SVT failure prompts caution in relying on an examinee's self-report, SVT failure is also associated with invalidity of neurocognitive tests. Some studies have indicated the two constructs are dissociable, and that SVT performance does not predict failure on PVTs (e.g., Boe & Evald, 2022; De Boer et al., 2022). However, Fox (2011), in a review of 220 cases, found that for persons with SVTs in the valid range, neuropsychological test results demonstrated the expected relationship between scores and objective evidence of brain damage; for those whose SVT scores were in the invalid range, the expected relationship between cognitive test scores and brain damage was absent. Other studies have also documented correlation between PVT failure and SVT failure for certain measures, such as the TOMM retention trial (Zakzanis, Gamada & Jeffay, 2012) and the Victoria Symptom Validity Test (Haggerty, Frazier, Busch & Naugle, 2007).

In short, failure of multiple, independent PVTs/SVTs simply indicates that one may not be able to use test data to infer brain dysfunction or as the basis for opinion on level of disability or performance abilities (Proto et al., 2014) or interpret normal scores as accurate indicators of cognitive ability (Martinez et al., 2021). It should be noted, however, that the AACN (Guilmette et al., 2020) guidelines for labeling validity test scores state the position that:

> ...attaining an invalid range score on a PVT does not always or automatically indicate the presence of malingering or "compromised effort" and may or may not invalidate all testing results...it is ultimately the clinician who is responsible for judging, based on the totality of information available, what those scores mean and how they should be interpreted.
>
> (p. 13)

Invalid performance does not mean the examiner cannot offer an opinion. Sometimes attorneys for a plaintiff or defendant may seek to challenge and even exclude expert opinion, arguing that if test scores are invalid, it means the entire examination and any opinions stemming from it must be invalid as well. This represents a distortion of the use of validity assessment, which is not used to prove whether or not brain injury exists, but to detect evidence of test-taking behavior that colors data that may support or contradict claims of impairment. Also, validity testing in a forensic case is only one part of the examination process, so the expert may form an opinion based on other available evidence, such as interviews, videotaped depositions, employment and hospital records, and pre-incident records, and the trier of fact will ultimately determine whether the claimed impairment is genuine. For example, in one case in which this author participated, examination of a defendant appealing a death penalty sentence was attempted but was not completed due to the defendant's highly atypical and uncooperative behavior, especially given this author was retained by his own counsel. However, the exhaustive record review revealed serious childhood TBI, so MRI of the brain was recommended, and significant right frontal encephalomalacia was discovered, which this author testified contributed to a lifelong history of psychosocial challenges.

Validity Test Performance May Be Labeled or Referenced

The AACN (Guilmette et al., 2020) published guidelines for labeling validity test scores. The recommendations suggest using one of the phrases below to describe individual scores on validity tests (p. 13):

- The examinee's score on a stand-alone PVT was within the valid range.
- On an embedded PVT, the examinee attained an indeterminate range score.
- The forced-choice memory PVT score was within the invalid range.

For scientific evidence and testimony to be admissible in a court of law, it must meet either the Frye standard or, as is now law in most states, the Daubert standard. Forensic neuropsychologists should understand that they may be required to cite a reference for a validity measure's cutoff score, error rate, or evidence of peer review and publication, and that the basis for one's opinion (e.g. specific evidence of invalidity) may be noted in the forensic report and queried in deposition and testimony.

Another consideration for referencing and documentation of validity test findings in forensic reports is that any one comprehensive neuropsychological evaluation may generate hundreds of individual scores. The MMPI-3 alone contains 52 scales, and the California Verbal Learning Test-3 (CVLT-3) written protocol contains 30 potential scores, with the computerized scoring system generating 73 scores for the same measure. This does not account for additional scores, such as those from embedded measures.

Opposing counsel may ask, "Dr. Jones, isn't it true that you failed to list the 39 scores on which my client's performance was normal? Why did you fail to mention his normal valid score on the Psychoticism scale of the MMPI-3?" Reporting and commenting on each of those measures is neither necessary nor desirable, and the effective forensic neuropsychologist will have reviewed all those scores and can testify to that issue. Many of those scores are not clinically relevant in the context of the forensic case. For instance, the expert would be unlikely to specifically describe a single score on the Psychoticism scale of the MMPI-3 in a concussion case where a 50-year-old plaintiff with no mental health history presented with minimal psychological complaints. But if asked, the expert may note that it is the cumulative weight of the failed validity scores that increases confidence in diagnosis, not the number of items "passed." Further, those many individual scores are not "validity tests," so the attorney is conflating the concepts of "scores within normal limits" and "valid performance." Finally, it may be helpful to bring to the attention of the opposing counsel that there are many items that do not appear in the report, at the discretion of the clinician—for instance, the phrase, "The plaintiff does not have schizophrenia," does not appear in the report because it is irrelevant to the case at hand.

Validity Assessment Does Not Exist in a Vacuum

Detection of invalidity is different from *diagnosis* of malingering (Sweet et al., 2021). Clinicians should understand the difference and make this distinction clear in reports and testimony. If and when evaluation results support a diagnosis of malingering, it is important to document supporting evidence consistent with invalid test results to avoid the experience of being a "witness in a vacuum" where one is the sole witness testifying about invalidity and its implications. It is an uncomfortable position to be the sole witness in a forensic case testifying that invalid test performance has resulted in an underestimation of the examinee's abilities, at a level suggestive of intentional misrepresentation. In the majority of cases in which invalid scores are documented, additional evidence in records or from interviews supports the idea that the examinee's presentation may not be fully explained by the claimed condition.

For example, this author documented a clearly invalid test performance in a plaintiff claiming severe cognitive impairment and disability after a reported, but unwitnessed, concussion with no evidence of having met any concussion diagnosis criteria. Similar non-credible behaviors were described throughout medical records (e.g., a failed Functional Capacity Evaluation, inability to remember important autobiographical information, and allodynia that limited physical exams). These instances were described in the neuropsychological report and referenced whenever possible in testimony, to show that the invalid exam was not an outlier, and in fact was consistent with others' findings and medical records.

Validity Assessment Is Not Lie Detection

Although common lore imbues mental health and legal professionals with perceptive abilities in detecting falsehoods, non-credible presentations cannot be reliably detected by clinical judgment alone. Studies have shown professionals to perform only at about chance level when asked to detect non-credibility (Ekman & O'Sullivan, 1991; Bond & DePaulo, 2006), which is why objective, empirically based measurement of validity is critical in forensic evaluation.

Some attorneys will attempt to define the expert's use of validity assessment as a sort of "lie detector," in an effort to link extensively researched objective validity measurement with polygraph testing. Fewer than half of states allow polygraph evidence to be admitted in court (Majaski, 2021), and an updated report from the National Academy of Sciences described the scientific evidence for the technique as weak, with an unknown error rate (Iacono & BenShakhar, 2019). Public opinion has been equivocal at best regarding the persuasiveness of polygraph evidence (Myers, Latter & Abdollahi, 2006) and extensive use of the technique in popular media (e.g., television talk shows) has likely contributed to that perception (Guy, Halasz & Picheta, 2019).

Iverson (2006) discussed the ethical considerations in assessment of validity and noted that occasionally inferring intentionality of invalidity (intentional exaggeration or malingering) may be "too provocative and pejorative for the clinician's comfort" (p. 81), with some going so far as to suggest a malingering label may be slanderous (Weiss & VanDell, 2017). In those cases, a forensic neuropsychologist can opine on the invalidity of test data and describe differential diagnoses in detail, and the judgment of malingering will be made, or not, by the trier of fact. When a clinician suspects malingering, it is not automatic that they testify that the examinee is symptom-free: malingering and genuine symptomology (from whatever cause) are not mutually exclusive.

For example, this author once testified in a forensic case involving a claim of severe TBI. The plaintiff had a clearly documented history of antisocial behavior, including deception in prior settings, and he met criteria for Malingering with Mixed Presentation. The rather adversarial team of attorneys for the plaintiff had unsuccessfully spent inordinate time seeking to have neuropsychology opinion excluded from trial, and appeared to be angling for an excoriating cross-examination during which a description of malingering would be semantically tortured and ethically eviscerated. Neuropsychological testimony instead steadfastly declined to "call the plaintiff a malingerer" and focused on detailing every marked discrepancy and statistically improbable score, and allowed those compelling descriptions to hang in the air for the jury to consider in determining the credibility of the plaintiff's claim. The verdict indicated the jury did not agree with the plaintiff's version of events.

Interestingly, one criticism of the polygraph is sometimes—erroneously—applied to neuropsychological validity testing as well: that polygraphs do not detect deception and instead measure physiological markers of fear or stress, from which the possibility of deception is inferred (APA, 2004). Attorneys criticizing the use of validity testing may claim PVTs and SVTs also measure anxiety or stress, given the high stakes involved in litigation-related evaluations: might the plaintiff's anxiety over being publicly deemed a "liar" and having his or her claim rejected be sufficient to induce validity test failure? Experts should take care not to be drawn into debate over such semantics. The term "exaggeration" is often portrayed as pejorative as well, when it simply is a behavioral descriptor. Further, use of the term "lying" applied to over-reporting or suppression of performance is inaccurate. A common opposing counsel's tactic is to, with great affront, accuse the examiner of calling the examinee "a liar," but an effective response for such inaccuracies is to reply that whether or not the examinee is telling the truth is a matter for the trier of fact; the examiner is simply testifying as to whether the testing performances are consistent with records or known models of brain functioning.

In any event, it is worth noting that even frank malingering may not be "lying" in the truest sense of the word. It is this author's opinion that sometimes the act of symptom production or magnification exists somewhere in the gray area between conscious (malingered or factitious) and unconscious (somatoform in nature). In that way, it is reminiscent of "doublethink," described by George Orwell in *Nineteen Eighty-Four* (Orwell, 1949) as a state in which one can:

> ...be conscious of complete truthfulness while telling carefully constructed lies, to hold simultaneously two opinions which cancelled out, knowing them to be contradictory and believing in both of them, to use logic against logic, to repudiate morality while laying claim to it...to forget whatever it was necessary to forget, then to draw it back into memory again at the moment when it was needed, and then promptly to forget it again, and above all, to apply the same process to the process itself—that was the ultimate subtlety: consciously to induce unconsciousness, and then, once again, to become unconscious of the act of hypnosis you had just performed.
>
> (p. 32)

Validity Assessment Meets Standards Set for the Admissibility of Scientific Evidence

The criteria for admissibility of scientific evidence set forth in *Daubert v. Merrell Dow Pharmaceuticals, Inc.*, 509 U.S. 579 (1993) are easily met by validity assessment techniques and measures:

1. whether the expert's technique or theory can be or has been tested—that is, whether the expert's theory can be challenged in some objective sense, or whether it is instead simply a subjective, conclusory approach that cannot reasonably be assessed for reliability;
2. whether the technique or theory has been subject to peer review and publication;
3. the known or potential rate of error of the technique or theory when applied;
4. the existence and maintenance of standards and controls; and
5. whether the technique or theory has been generally accepted in the scientific community.

In fact, one could assert that neuropsychological validity tests are exquisitely sensitive to Daubert criteria, given the extensive body of scientific literature published over decades, with defined cut scores, error rates, peer review, and published standards for use.

These *Daubert* criteria are not exclusive and have been supplemented by other factors in recent years, including one requiring the expert to demonstrate that they have accounted for alternative explanations [*Claar v. Burlington N.R.R.*, 29 F.3d 499 (9th Cir. 1994)]. In the context of neuropsychological assessment, this refers to the differential diagnosis process, which includes not only the consideration of alternative diagnostic explanations but also consideration of influential factors in test performance. Research over recent decades documented that non-neurologic factors may influence performance in neuropsychological testing; such as educational history, acute pain, level of engagement, stress, distractibility, psychiatric disturbance, cultural differences, and medication effects (de Koning, 2009). Hartman (2017) described forensic differential diagnosis as requiring consideration of six domains: the claimed condition (e.g., brain injury), other brain syndromes, medical conditions, psychiatric conditions, motivational evidence, and biopsychosocial factors. Invalid test performance is a major indicator that there may be alternative explanations for reported impairments that require consideration along these six domains. Thus, validity assessment in the forensic setting is not only acceptable, but a crucial component of meeting the *Daubert* standard for admissibility of scientific evidence.

This scientific determination of cause and extent of deficits—as opposed to a legal determination by the trier of fact—is the responsibility of the neuropsychologist. Thus, validity assessment in forensic contexts is essential to the role of the neuropsychology expert in such cases.

Summary

Forensic neuropsychology examiners should endeavor to appreciate the breadth and depth of historical literature on validity assessment as it informs the examiner's interpretation of objective and subjective data. The rich complexity of validity research sets neuropsychological assessment apart from other specialties and makes the forensic neuropsychology expert a valuable and credible witness. The effective neuropsychology expert will:

- Practice in line with recommendations set forth in previous articles on validity assessment to facilitate presentation of evidence and testimony that will meet Daubert or Frye standards of admissibility.

- Maintain familiarity with peer-reviewed published articles on normative data, ethics, validity assessment, racial/cultural/language issues in testing, and practice guidelines.
- Be aware of base rates of invalidity in diagnostic and contextual populations relevant to the examinee (e.g., chronic pain, disability-seeking, litigating).
- Consider and document both external and internal incentives and acknowledge possible explanations for or contributors to invalid scores, which may not be external and may include explanations for school or work failures or avoidance of responsibilities or concern that tests will "miss" impairment.
- Incorporate other types and sources of data consistent with one's findings and opinion, but also include or be prepared to discuss evidence to the contrary, such as a clearly abnormal brain imaging report, or witness' report of a period of unconsciousness.
- Adhere to recommendations for score reporting and be prepared to provide references for scoring and interpretation upon request.
- Include formal assessment of validity; both for self-reported symptoms and cognitive test performance.
- Select measures with published, peer-reviewed data on specificity and sensitivity of the measure in the population(s) closest to the examinee/setting.
- Include a statement on the validity of the evaluation, as valid, indeterminate, or invalid (Guilmette et al., 2020).
- Resist efforts to portray validity conclusions as pejorative. "Malingering" is a technical and empirically defined term used in scientific research and clinical case conceptualization.

In summary, assessment of validity in forensic neuropsychology evaluations is consistent with decades of empirical and clinical observations demonstrating that valid cognitive and self-reported data are necessary components of any investigation of brain–behavior relationships.

References

28 USC App Fed R Evid Rule 702: Testimony by Experts (1975). (Pub. L. 93–595, §1, Jan. 2, 1975, 88 Stat. 1937).

American Academy of Clinical Neuropsychology (2021) Position Statement on Use of Race as a Factor in Neuropsychological Test Norming and Performance Prediction: AACN Relevance 2050 Subcommittee on Use of Race in Neuropsychological Test Norming and Performance Prediction. chrome-extension://efaidnbmnnnibpcajpcglclefindmkaj/https://theaacn.org/wp-content/uploads/2021/11/AACN-Position-Statement-on-Race-Norms.pdf Accessed online August 8, 2023.

American Psychological Association (2004). The truth about lie detectors (aka polygraph tests). Published online August 5, 2004. https://www.apa.org/topics/cognitive-neuroscience/polygraph

American Psychological Association (2010). 2010 Amendments to the 2002 "Ethical principles of psychologists and code of conduct." *American Psychologist*, 65 (5), 493–493. doi: 10.1037/a0020168

American Psychological Association (2013). Specialty guidelines for forensic psychology. *American Psychologist, 68*(1), 7–19. doi: 10.1037/a0029889.

Arbisi, P.A., & Ben-Porath, Y.S. (1995). An MMPI-2 infrequent response scale for use with psychopathological populations: The infrequency-psychopathology scale, F(p). *Psychological Assessment*, 7, 424–431.

Bajjaleh, C., Braw, Y.C., & Elkana, O. (2021). Adaptation and initial validation of the Arabic version of the Word Memory Test (WMTARB). *Applied Neuropsychology: Adult*, 1–10.

Ben-Porath, Y.S., & Tellegen, A. (2020). *Minnesota Multiphasic Personality Inventory-3 (MMPI-3): Manual for administration, scoring, and interpretation*. University of Minnesota Press.

Bender, S.D., & Rogers, R. (2004). Detection of neurocognitive feigning: Development of a multi-strategy assessment. *Archives of Clinical Neuropsychology*, 19(1), 49–60. doi: 10.1016/S0887–6177(02)00165-8.

Berthelson, L., Mulchan, S.S., Odland, A.P., Miller, L.J., & Mittenberg, W. (2013). False positive diagnosis of malingering due to the use of multiple effort tests. *Brain Injury*, 27(7–8), 909–916. doi: 10.3109/02699052.2013.793400.

Bianchini, K., Greve, K., & Glynn, G. (2005). On the diagnosis of malingered pain-related disability: Lessons from cognitive malingering research. *Spine Journal*, 5(4), 404–17. doi: 10.1016/j.spinee.2004.11.016. PMID: 15996610.

Bianchini, K.J., Aguerrevere, L.E, Guise, B.J., Ord, J.S., Etherton, J.L., Meyers, J.E., Soignier, R.D., Greve, K.W., Curtis, K.L., & Bui, J. (2014). Accuracy of the Modified Somatic Perception Questionnaire and Pain Disability Index in the detection of malingered pain-related disability in chronic pain. *The Clinical Neuropsychologist*, 28(8), 1376–1394. doi: 10.1080/13854046.2014.986199.

Binder, L., & Rohling, M. (1996). Money matters: A meta-analytic review of the effects of financial incentives on recovery after closed-head injury. *American Journal of Psychiatry*, 153(1), 7–10. doi: 10.1176/ajp.153.1.7. PMID: 8540596.

Binder, L., Salinsky, M., Storzbach, D., & Tadrous-Furnanz, S. (2021). RBANS Validity Measures and the TOMM in Veterans Undergoing Seizure Monitoring, *Archives of Clinical Neuropsychology*, 36(4) 613–619. doi: 10.1093/arclin/acaa079.

Boake, C. (2000). Historical note: Eduard Claparede and the Auditory Verbal Learning Test. *Journal of Clinical and Experimental Neuropsychology*, 22(20), 286–292.

Boe, E., & Evald, L. (2022). Symptom and performance validity in neuropsychological assessments of outpatients 15–30 years of age. *Brain Injury*, 16, 1–7. doi: 10.1080/02699052.2022.2158222.

Bond, C., & DePaulo, B.M. (2006). Accuracy of deception judgments. *Personality and Social Psychology Review*, 10(3), 214–234. doi: 10.1207/s15327957pspr1003_2.

Boone, K.B. (Ed.) (2021). Assessment of feigned cognitive impairment: A neuropsychological perspective. Second edition. Guilford Press.

Boone, K.B., Sweet, J.J., Byrd, D.A., Denney, R.L., Hanks, R.A., Kaufmann, P.M., Kirkwood, M.W., Larabee, G.J., Marcopoulos, B.A., Morgan, J.E., Paltzer, J.Y., Rivera Mindt, M., Schroeder, R.W., Sim, A.H., & Suhr, J.A., (2022). Official position of the American Academy of Clinical Neuropsychology on test security, *The Clinical Neuropsychologist*, 36(3), 523–545. doi: 10.1080/13854046.2021.2022214.

Boskovic, I., Zwaan, L., Baillie, V., & Merckelbach, H. (2021). Consistency does not aid detection of feigned symptoms, overreporting does: Two explorative studies on symptom stability among truth tellers and feigners, *Applied Neuropsychology: Adult*, doi: 10.1080/23279095.2021.1888728.

Braun, S.E., Fountain-Zaragoza, S., Halliday, C.A., & Horner, M.D. (2023). Demographic differences in performance validity test failure. *Applied Neuropsychology: Adult*, 30(5), 483–491. doi: 10.1080/23279095.2021.1958814.

Burke, T. J. (2007). *Detecting malingering on the MMPI-2: An examination of the utility of combining the validity scales in a non-compensatory model.* https://digitalcommons.wku.edu/cgi/viewcontent.cgi?article=1026&context=theses

Bush, S.S., Ruff, R.M., Tröster, A.I., Barth, J.T., Koffler, S.P., ...& Neil H. Pliskin, Silver, C.H. (2005). Symptom validity assessment: Practice issues and medical necessity NAN Policy & Planning Committee, *Archives of Clinical Neuropsychology*, 20(4), 419–426. doi: 10.1016/j.acn.2005.02.002.

Butcher, J.N., Dahlstrom, W.G., Graham, J.R., Tellegen, A., & Kaemmer, B. (1989). *45 46 Minnesota Multiphasic Personality Inventory-2: Manual for administration and scoring*. University of Minnesota Press.

Caldwell, A. (n.d.). What is the K Scale really about? Caldwell Reports. Accessed online January 24, 2024. https://www.caldwellreports.com/kscale/.

Carone, D. (2013). Strategies for non-neuropsychology clinicians to detect noncredible presentations after mild traumatic brain injury. In Carone, D. & Bush, S. (Eds.), *Mild traumatic brain injury: Symptom validity assessment and malingering* (pp. 203–229). Springer Publishing Company.

Chafetz, M.D., & Underhill, J. (2013). Estimated costs of malingered disability. *Archives of Clinical Neuropsychology*, 28(7), 633–639. doi: 10.1093/arclin/act038.

Claar v. Burlington Northern R. Co., 29 F.3d 499 (9th Cir. 1994).

Committee on Psychological Testing, Including Validity Testing, for Social Security Administration Disability Determinations; Board on the Health of Select Populations; Institute of Medicine. (2015). *Psychological Testing in the Service of Disability Determination*. National Academies Press. Available from: https://www.ncbi.nlm.nih.gov/books/NBK305236/ doi: 10.17226/21704

Cox, A.C., Weed, N.C., & Butcher, J.N. (2009). The MMPI-2: History, interpretation, and clinical Issues. In Butcher, J.N. (Ed.), *Oxford handbook of personality assessment* (pp. 250–276). Oxford University Press. doi: 10.1093/oxfordhb/9780195366877.013.0014.

Critchfield, E., Soble, J.R., Marceaux, J.C., Bain, K.M., Chase Bailey, K., Webber, T.A., Alex Alverson, W., Messerly, J. Andrés González, D., & O'Rourke, J.J.F. (2019). Cognitive impairment does not cause invalid performance: Analyzing performance patterns among cognitively unimpaired, impaired, and noncredible participants across six performance validity tests. *The Clinical Neuropsychologist*, 33(6), 1083–1101. doi: 10.1080/13854046.2018.1508615.

Dandachi-FitzGerald, B., Merckelbach, H., & Ponds, R.W. (2017). Neuropsychologists' ability to predict distorted symptom presentation. *Journal of Clinical and Experimental Neuropsychology*, 39(3), 257–264. doi: 10.1080/13803395.2016.1223278.

Dandachi-FitzGerald, B., Merckelbach, H., & Merten, T. (2022). Cry for help as a root cause of poor symptom validity: A critical note. *Applied Neuropsychology: Adult*, February,1–6. doi: 10.1080/23279095.2022.2040025.

Daubert v. Merrell Dow Pharmaceuticals, Inc., 509 U.S. 579 (1993).

Dawes, R.M., Faust, D., & Meehl, P.E. (1989). Clinical versus actuarial judgment. *Science*, 243, 1668–1674.

De Boer, A.B., Phillips, M.S., Barwegen, K.C., Obolsky, M.A., Rauch, A.A., Pesanti, S.D., Tse, P.K., Ovsiew, G.P., Jennette, K.J., Resch, Z.J., & Soble, J.R. (2022). Comprehensive analysis of MMPI-2-RF symptom validity scales and performance validity test relationships in a diverse mixed neuropsychiatric setting. *Psychological Injury and Law*, (November) 1–12. doi: 10.1007/s12207-022-09467-9.

Denning, J.H., & Horner, M.D. (2024). The impact of race and other demographic factors on the false positive rates of five embedded Performance Validity Tests (PVTs) in a Veteran sample. *Journal of Clinical and Experimental Neuropsychology*, (14), 1–11. doi: 10.1080/13803395.2024.2314737. PMID: 38353039.

de Koning, I. (2009). Neuropsychological assessment: Sense and sensibility. *Stroke*, 40(9), 2949–2950. doi: 10.1161/STROKEAHA.109.556050.

Ekman, P., & O'Sullivan, M. (1991). Who can catch a liar? *American Psychologist*, 46(9), 913–20. doi: 10.1037//0003–066x.46.9.913.

Emhoff, M.A., Lynch, J.K., & McCaffrey, R.J. (2018). Performance and symptom validity testing in pediatric assessment: A review of the literature. *Developmental Neuropsychology*, 43(8), 671–707. doi: 10.1080/87565641.2018.1525612.

Erdodi, L. A., & Giromini, L. (2023). Assessing the credibility of clinical presentations using performance and symptom validity tests: Current trends and future directions [Editorial]. *Psychology & Neuroscience*, 16(2), 97–104.

Erdodi, L.A., Hurtubise, J.L., Charron, C., Dunn, A., Enache, A., McDermott, A., & Hirst, R.B. (2018). The D-KEFS Trails as performance validity tests. *Psychological Assessment*, 30(8), 1082–1095. doi: 10.1037/pas0000561.

Erdodi, L.A., Abeare, C.A., Medoff, B., Seke, K.R., Sagar, S., & Kirsch, N.L. (2018). A single error is one too many: The Forced Choice Recognition Trial of the CVLT-II as a measure of performance validity in adults with TBI, *Archives of Clinical Neuropsychology*, 33(7), 845–860. doi: 10.1093/acn/acx110.

Faust, D., Hart, K., Guilmette, T.J., & Arkes, H.R. (1988). Neuropsychologists' capacity to detect adolescent malingerers. *Professional Psychology: Research and Practice*, 19(5), 508–515. doi: 10.1037/0735-7028.19.5.508.

Fox, D.D. (2011). Symptom validity test failure indicates invalidity of neuropsychological tests. *The Clinical Neuropsychologist,* 25(3), 488–95. doi: 10.1080/13854046.2011.554443. PMID: 21491351.

Frederick, R. (2015, March). *Too much information: Problems with using multiple malingering tests [Invited lecture].* American Psychology-Law Conference, San Diego, CA.

Glassmire, D.M., Wood, M.E., Ta, M.T., Kinney, D.I., & Nitch, S.R. (2019). Examining false-positive rates of Wechsler Adult Intelligence Scale (WAIS-IV) processing speed-based embedded validity indicators among individuals with schizophrenia spectrum disorders. *Psychological Assessment,* 31(1), 120–125. doi: 10.1037/pas0000650.

Glen, T., Barisa, M., Ready, R., Peck, E., & Spencer, T. R. (2021). Update on third party observers in neuropsychological evaluation: An interorganizational position paper. *The Clinical Neuropsychologist, 35*(6), 1107–1116.

Green, P. (2003). Word Memory Test, Accessed online August 8, 2023. https://wordmemorytest.com/

Green, P., Montijo, J., & Brockhaus, R. (2011). High specificity of the Word Memory Test and Medical Symptom Validity Test in groups with severe verbal memory impairment. *Applied Neuropsychology*, 18(2), 86–94. doi: 10.1080/09084282.2010.523389.

Greer, S., Chambliss, L., & Mackler, L. (2005). What physical exam techniques are useful to detect malingering? *Journal of Family Practice*, 54 (7), 719–722.

Greiffenstein, M.F., & Baker, W.J. (2006). Miller was (mostly) right: Head injury severity inversely related to simulation. *Legal and Criminological Psychology, 11*, 131–145.

Greve, K.W., Heinly, M.T., Bianchini, K.J., & Love, J.M. (2009). Malingering detection with the Wisconsin Card Sorting Test in mild traumatic brain injury. *The Clinical Neuropsychologist,* 23(2), 343–362. doi: 10.1080/13854040802054169.

Guilmette, T.J., Sweet, J.J., Hebben, N., Koltai, D., Mahone, E.M., Spiegler, B.J., Stucky, K., Westerveld, M., & conference participants (2020). American Academy of Clinical Neuropsychology consensus conference statement on uniform labeling of performance test scores, *The Clinical Neuropsychologist*, doi: 10.1080/13854046.2020.1722244.

Gutheil, T.G. (2003). Reflections on coaching by attorneys. *Journal of the American Academy of Psychiatry and Law,* 31(1), 6–9.

Guy, J., Halasz, S., & Picheta, R. (2019). Tabloid talk show cancelled after guest's death. Published online May 15, 2019. https://www.mercurynews.com/2019/05/15/tabloid-talk-show-canceled-after-guests-death/

Haggerty, K.A., Frazier, T.W., Busch, R.M., & Naugle, R.I. (2007). Relationships among Victoria symptom validity test indices and personality assessment inventory validity scales in a large clinical sample. *The Clinical Neuropsychologist,* 21(6), 917–928. doi: 10.1080/13854040600899724.

Hartman, D. (2017). Differential diagnosis in neuropsychology. In Morgan, J. & Ricker, J. (Eds.), *Textbook of clinical neuropsychology* (1146). Taylor and Francis.

Hakky, M., Pandey, S., Kwak, E., Jara, H., & Erbay, S.H. (2013). Application of basic physics principles to clinical neuroradiology: Differentiating artifacts from true pathology on MRI. *American Journal of Roentgenology,* 201(2), 369–377. doi: 10.2214/AJR.12.10394.

Hathaway, S.R., & McKinley, J.C. (1943). *The Minnesota Multiphasic Personality Inventory*. University of Minnesota Press.

Havsteen, I., Ohlhues, A., Madsen, K.H., Nybing, J.D., Christensen, H., & Christensen, A. (2017). Are movement artifacts in magnetic resonance imaging a real problem?-A narrative review. *Frontiers in Neurology, 8*, 232. doi: 10.3389/fneur.2017.00232.

Heilbronner, R.L., Sweet, J.J., Morgan, J.E., Larrabee, G.J., Millis, S.R, & conference participants (2009). American Academy of Clinical Neuropsychology Consensus Conference Statement on the neuropsychological assessment of effort, response bias, and malingering. *The Clinical Neuropsychologist*, 23(7), 1093–1129. doi: 10.1080/13854040903155063.

Hood, E.D., Boone, K.B., Miora, D.S., Cottingham, M.E., Victor, T.L., Zeigler, E.A., Zeller, M.A., & Wright, M.J. (2022). Are there differences in performance validity test scores between African American and White American neuropsychology clinic patients? *Journal of Clinical and Experimental Neuropsychology*, 44(1), 31–41. doi: 10.1080/13803395.2022.2069230.

Hu, Y., Li, J., Zhao, Y., Dong, Z., Qiu, P., Yang, S., Xu, H., Kuang, W., & Gong, Q. (2023). Memory and processing speed impairments in first-episode drug-naïve patients with major depressive disorder. *Journal of Affective Disorders*, 32, 99–107. doi: 10.1016/j.jad.2022.10.048.

Iacono, W.G., & Ben-Shakhar, G. (2019). Current status of forensic lie detection with the comparison question technique: An update of the 2003 National Academy of Sciences report on polygraph testing. *Law and Human Behavior*, 43(1), 86–98. doi: 10.1037/lhb0000307.

Iverson, G.L. (2006). Ethical issues associated with the assessment of exaggeration, poor effort, and malingering, *Applied Neuropsychology*, 13(2), 77–90. doi: 10.1207/s15324826an1302_3.

Iverson, G.L., Henrichs, T.F., Barton, E.A., & Allen, S. (2002). Specificity of the MMPI-2 Fake Bad Scale as a marker for personal injury malingering. *Psychological Reports*, 90(1), 131–6. doi: 10.2466/pr0.2002.90.1.131.

Kanser, R.J., Rapport, L.J., Bashem, J.R., Billings, N.M., Hanks, R.A., Axelrod, B.N., & Miller, J.B. (2017). Strategies of successful and unsuccessful simulators coached to feign traumatic brain injury. *The Clinical Neuropsychologist*, 31(3), 644–653. doi: 10.1080/13854046.2016.1278040.

Kanser, R.J., Logan, P.M., Steward, K.A., Vanderbleek, E.N., & Kamper, J.E. (2022). Specificity of embedded performance validity tests in elderly veterans with Mild and Major Neurocognitive Disorder. *Archives of Clinical Neuropsychology*, 38(5), 772–781. doi: 10.1093/arclin/acac106.

Kemp, S., Coughlan, A.K., Rowbottom, C., Wilkinson, K., Teggart, V., & Baker, G. (2008). The base rate of effort test failure in patients with medically unexplained symptoms. *Jounral of Psychosomatic Research*, 65(4), 319–325. doi: 10.1016/j.jpsychores.2008.02.010.

Kim, M.S., Torres, K., Kang, H.J., & Drane, D.L. (2022). Specificity of performance validity tests in patients with confirmed epilepsy. *The Clinical Neuropsychologist*, 11, 1–18. doi: 10.1080/13854046.2022.2127424.

Ko, M., Merritt, P., & Dawson, E. (2013). Specimen validity testing. *Practical Pain Management*, 13(5). https://www.practicalpainmanagement.com/resources/diagnostic-tests/specimen-validity-testing. Accessed online August 18, 2023.

Lacerte, M. (2019). Medicolegal expert core competencies and professionalism. *Physical Medicine and Rehabilitation Clinics of North America*, 30 (3), 637–648. doi: 10.1016/j.pmr.2019.03.010.

Larrabee, G.J., Millis, S.R., & Meyers, J.E. (2009). 40 plus or minus 10, a new magical number: Reply to Russell. *The Clinical Neuropsychologist*, 23(5), 841–849.

Larrabee, G.J., Rohling, M.L., & Meyers, J.E. (2019). Use of multiple performance and symptom validity measures: Determining the optimal per test cutoff for determination of invalidity, analysis of skew, and inter-test correlations in valid and invalid performance groups. *The Clinical Neuropsychologist*, 33(8), 1354–1372. doi: 10.1080/13854046.2019.1614227.

Lees-Haley, P.R., English, L.T., & Glenn, W.J. (1991). A Fake Bad Scale on the MMPI-2 for personal injury claimants. *Psychological Reports*, *68*(1), 203–210. doi: 10.2466/pr0.1991.68.1.203.

Lewandowki, A.G., Boone, K.B., Kaufmann, P.M., Peck, E.A., & Glen, T. (2023, August 3–5). Ethical and professional arguments against third party observation of neuropsychological evaluations. APA Convention, Washington, D.C. United States. https://convention.apa.org/agenda/agenda-at-a-glance

Lippa, S.M. (2018). Performance validity testing in neuropsychology: A clinical guide, critical review, and update on a rapidly evolving literature. *The Clinical Neuropsychologist*, 32(3), 391–421. doi: 10.1080/13854046.2017.1406146.

Lockhart, J. (2015). How should validity testing impact expert's opinion? *Archives of Forensic Psychology*, 1(2), 78–96.

Lorch, B., Vaillant, G., Baumgartner, C., Bai, W., Rueckert, D., & Maier, A. (2017). Automated detection of motion artefacts in MR imaging using decision forests. *Journal of Medical Engineering*, June 11. doi: 10.1155/2017/4501647.

Majaski, C. (2021). Are lie detector tests admisable in court? Published online February 2, 2021. https://www.lawinfo.com/resources/criminal-defense/are-lie-detector-tests-admissible-in-court.html.

Martin, P.K., Schroeder, R.W., Olsen, D.H., Maloy, H., Boettcher, A., Ernst, N., & Okut, H. (2020). A systematic review and meta-analysis of the Test of Memory Malingering in adults: Two decades of deception detection. *The Clinical Neuropsychologist*, 34(1), 88–119. doi: 10.1080/13854046.2019.1637027.

Martinez, K.A., Sayers, C., Hayes, C., Martin, P.K., Clark, C.B., & Schroeder, R.W. (2021). Normal cognitive test scores cannot be interpreted as accurate measures of ability in the context of failed performance validity testing: A symptom- and detection-coached simulation study. *Journal of Clinical and Experimental Neuropsychology,* 43(3), 301–309. doi: 10.1080/13803395.2021.1926435.

McGuire, C., Crawford, S., & Evans, J.J. (2019). Effort testing in dementia sssessment: A systematic review. *Archies of Clinical Neuropsychology,* 34(1), 114–131. doi: 10.1093/arclin/acy012.

McKinley, J.C., Hathaway, S.R., & Meehl, P.E. (1948). The Minnesota Multiphasic Personality Inventory: VI. The K Scale. *Journal of Consulting Psychology,* 12(1), 20–31. doi: 10.1037/h0061377.

Meehl, P.E., & Hathaway, S.R. (1946). The K factor as a suppressor variable in the MMPI. *Journal of Applied Psychology,* 30, 525–564. Reprinted in Dahlstrom, W.G., & Dahlstrom, L.E. (1980). *Basic readings on the MMPI: A new selection on personality measurement.* University of Minnesota Press.

Meiwandi, A., & Papadakis, M. (2019). The clenched fist syndrome: Case report of a clinical rarity of special interest for psychiatrists and hand surgeons. *BMC Psychiatry, 19*(1), 349. doi: 10.1186/s12888-019-2348-4.

Myers, B., Latter, R, & Abdollahi-Arena, M.K. (2006). The court of public opinion: Lay perceptions of polygraph testing. *Law and Human Behavior,* 30(4), 509–23. doi: 10.1007/s10979-006-9041-0.

Miller, H. (1961). Accident neurosis. *British Medical Journal,* 5231, 992–998.

Nijdam-Jones, A., Rivera, D., Rosenfeld, B., & Arango-Lasprilla, J.C. (2017). A cross-cultural analysis of the Test of Memory Malingering among Latin American Spanish-speaking adults. *Law and Human Behavior,* 1(5), 422–428. doi: 10.1037/lhb0000250.

Orwell, G. (1949). *Nineteen Eighty-Four.* Martin, Secker & Warburg Ltd..

Pankratz, L., & Erickson, R.C. (1990). Two views of malingering. *The Clinical Neuropsychologist,* 4(4), 379–389.

Patterson, C.S., Barth, R.J., Brigham, C.R., Talmage, J.B., Leclair, S., & Coupland, M. (2012). Malingering and other considerations: With an emphasis on document review. *AMA Guides Newsletter,* 17(1), 1–12.

Petersen, R.C., Lopez, O., Armstrong, M.J., Getchius, T.S.D., Ganguli, M., Gloss, D., Gronseth, G.S., Marson, D., Pringsheim, T., Day, G.S., Sager, M., Stevens, J., & Rae-Grant, A. (2018). Practice guideline update summary: Mild cognitive impairment: Report of the Guideline Development, Dissemination, and Implementation Subcommittee of the American Academy of Neurology. *Neurology,* 90(3), 126–135. doi: 10.1212/WNL.0000000000004826.

Proto, D.A., Pastorek, N.J., Miller, B.I., Romesser, J.M., Sim, A.H., & Linck, J.F. (2014). The dangers of failing one or more performance validity tests in individuals claiming mild traumatic brain injury-related postconcussive symptoms. *Archives of Clinical Neuropsychology,* 29(7), 614–24. doi: 10.1093/arclin/acu044.

Rey, A. (1958). *L'examen clinique en psychologie.* Paris, France: Presses universitaires de France.

Rivera, D., Perrin, P.B., Weiler, G., Ocampo-Barba, N., Aliaga, A., Rodríguez, W., Rodríguez-Agudelo, Y., Aguayo, A., Longoni, M., Trapp, S, Esenarro, L., & Arango-Lasprilla, J.C. (2015). Test of Memory Malingering (TOMM): Normative data for the Latin American Spanish speaking adult population. *NeuroRehabilitation,* 37(4), 719–35. doi: 10.3233/NRE-151287.

Rogers, R., & Correa, A.A. (2008). Determinations of malingering: Evolution from case-based methods to detection strategies. *Psychiatry Psychology and Law,* 15, 213–23. doi: 10.1080/13218710802014501.

Rosen, G.M., Baldwin, S.A., & Smith, R.F. (2016). Reassessing the "traditional background hypothesis" for elevated MMPI and MMPI-2 Lie-scale scores. *Psychological Assessment,* 28(10), 1336–1343. doi: 10.1037/pas0000262.

Ross, R. (2019). Between Shell Shock and PTSD? 'Accident Neurosis' and its sequelae in post-war Britain. *Social History of Medicine,* 32(3), 565–585. doi: 10.1093/shm/hkx118.

Rumschik, S.M., & Appel, J.M. (2019). Malingering in the Psychiatric Emergency Department: Prevalence, Predictors, and Outcomes. *Psychiatric services, 70 2,* 115–122.

Schroeder, R.W., Clark, H.A., & Martin, P.K. (2022). Base rates of invalidity when patients undergoing routine clinical evaluations have social security disability as an external incentive. *The Clinical Neuropsychologist,* 36(7), 1902 1914. doi: 10.1080/13854046.2021.1895322.

Schroeder, R.W., & Martin, P.K. (2022). Validity assessment in clinical settings: How it differs from forensic settings and why it is important. In Schroeder, R.W. & Martin, P.K. (Eds.), *Validity assessment in clinical neuropsychological practice: Evaluating and managing noncredible performance* (pp. 3–10). The Guilford Press, 33(3), 466–477. doi: 10.1080/13854046.2018.1484517.

Schroeder, R.W., Martin, P.K., Heinrichs, R.J., & Baade, L.E. (2019). Research methods in performance validity testing studies: Criterion grouping approach impacts study outcomes. *The Clinical Neuropsychologist,* 33(3), 466–477. doi: 10.1080/13854046.2018.1484517.

Schroeder, R.W., Twumasi-Ankrah, P., Baade, L.E., & Marshall, P.S. (2012). Reliable digit span: A systematic review and cross-validation study. *Assessment,* 19(1), 21–30. doi: 10.1177/1073191111428764. Epub 2011 Dec 6. PMID: 22156721.

Sherman, E.M.S., Slick, D.J., & Iverson, G.L. (2020). Multidimensional malingering criteria for neuropsychological assessment: A 20-year update of the malingered neuropsychological dysfunction criteria. *Archives of Clinical Neuropsychology,* 35(6), 735–764. doi: 10.1093/arclin/acaa019.

Soble, J.R., Cerny, B.M., Rhoads, T., DeBoer, A.B., Sharp, D.W., Ovsiew, G.P., Phillips, M.S., Pesanti, S.D., Jennette, K.J., & Resch, Z.J. (2023). Do demographic factors influence detection of invalid neuropsychological test performance using common performance validity tests? A multisite investigation. *Neuropsychology,* 37(2), 218–232. doi: 10.1037/neu0000880

Spengler, P.M., Walters, N.T., Bryan, E., & Millspaugh, B.S. (1995). Attorneys' attitudes toward coaching forensic clients on the MMPI-2: Replication and extension of attorney survey by Wetter and Corrigan. *Journal of Personality Assessment,* 102(1), 56–65. doi: 10.1080/00223891.2018.1501568.

Sweet, J.J., Heilbronner, R.L, Morgan, J.E., Larrabee, G.J., Rohling, M.L., Boone, K.B., Kirkwood, M.W., Schroeder, R.W., Suhr, J.A., & Conference Participants (2021). American Academy of Clinical Neuropsychology (AACN) 2021 consensus statement on validity assessment: Update of the 2009 AACN consensus conference statement on neuropsychological assessment of effort, response bias, and malingering, *The Clinical Neuropsychologist,* 35(6), 1053–1106. dOI: 10.1080/13854046.2021.1896036.

Swiergosz, A.M., Kasdan, M.L., & Wilhelmi, B.J. (2017). The Unexpected Hand Patient. *EPlasty,* 17 (e16).

Tart-Zelvin, A., Navis, B.A., Lamping, E.M., Langenecker, S.A., Ryan, K.A., McInnis, M.G., & Marshall, D.F. (2023). Low rate of performance validity failures among individuals with bipolar disorder. *Journal of the International Neuropsychological Society,* 29(3), 298–305. doi: 10.1017/S1355617722000145.

Uiterwijk, D., Stargatt, R., & Crowe, S.F. (2022). Objective cognitive outcomes and subjective emotional sequelae in litigating adults with a traumatic brain injury: The impact of performance and symptom validity measures. *Archives of Clinical Neuropsychology,* 37(8), 662–1687. doi: 10.1093/arclin/acac039.

Victor, T.L., Boone, K.B., Serpa, J.G., Buehler, J., & Ziegler, E.A. (2009). Interpreting the meaning of multiple symptom validity test failure. *The Clinical Neuropsychologist,* 23(2), 297–313. doi: 10.1080/13854040802232682.

Walczyk, J.J., Sewell, N., & DiBenedetto, M.B. (2018). A review of approaches to detecting malingering in forensic contexts and promising cognitive load-inducing lie detection techniques. *Frontiers in Psychiatry,* 9, 700. doi: 10.3389/fpsyt.2018.00700.

Weighill, V.E. (1983). Compensation neurosis': A review of the literature. *Journal of Psychosomatic Research,* 27(2), 97–104. doi: 10.1016/0022–3999(83)90085-5.

Weiss, K.J., & Van Dell, L. (2017). Liability for diagnosing malingering. *Journal of American Academy of Psychiatry and Law,* 45(3), 339–347.

Whitman, M.R., Gervais, R.O., & Ben-Porath, Y.S. (2023). Virtuous victims: Disability claimants who over- and under-report. *The Clinical Neuropsychologist,* 3(8), 1–24. doi: 10.1080/13854046.2023.2185686.

Whitman, M. R., Tarescavage, A. M., Glassmire, D. M., Burchett, D., & Sellbom, M. (2019). Examination of differential validity of MMPI-2-RF scores by gender and ethnicity in predicting future suicidal and violent behaviors in a forensic sample. *Psychological Assessment,* 31(3), 404.

Zakzanis, K.K., Gammada, E., & Jeffay, E. (2012). The predictive utility of neuropsychological symptom validity testing as it relates to psychological presentation. *Applied Neuropsychology*, 19(2), 8–107. doi: 10.1080/09084282.2011.644099.

Zenebe, Y., Akele, B., W/Selassie, M., & Necho, M. (2021). Prevalence and determinants of depression among old age: A systematic review and meta-analysis. *Annals of General Psychiatry*, 20(1), 55. doi: 10.1186/s12991-021-00375-x.

Zinke, J.L., Lam, C.S., Harden, R.N., & Fogg, L. (2010). Examining the cross-cultural validity of the English short-form McGill Pain Questionnaire using the matched moderated regression methodology. *Clinical Journal of Pain*, 26(2), 153–162. doi: 10.1097/AJP.0b013e3181b99f56.

Zwick, T., Sharp, C., Severn, D., & Simpson, S.A. (2021). Malingering in the emergency setting. *Cureus*, 13(6), e15670. doi: 10.7759/cureus.15670.

Section II

Civil Litigation

Much of the forensic work that involves neuropsychologists pertains to civil litigation. Civil litigation typically relates to remedying or redressing "wrongs," including injuries that have been committed by an individual or entity against another individual or group of individuals. To rectify the damage that has occurred, the wrongdoer typically financially compensates the victim(s) to such a degree that it "makes good" for the harm that has been inflicted. While this is easy to understand conceptually, the application of this can be challenging as it involves accurately determining liability and measuring the claimed damages that are to be compensated. Neuropsychologists are often called upon to help measure potential cognitive, behavioral, and/or psychological injuries. Therefore, neuropsychologists must be aware of the law, possible external incentives involved in civil litigation, methods to accurately evaluate neuropsychological losses within an individual, and ways to determine if abnormalities are causally related to claimed damages. The multiple chapters contained within this section provide expert perspectives on issues regarding differential diagnosis in civil litigation, and the techniques and reasoning that neuropsychologists use to improve the likelihood of making accurate conclusions.

DOI: 10.4324/9781003005063-8

7 Moderate-to-Severe Traumatic Brain Injury in a Preschool Child

Untying the Gordian Knot

Robert J. McCaffrey and Julie K. Lynch

A moderate-to-severe traumatic brain injury sustained in childhood can result in long-term deficits in cognitive, academic, emotional, behavioral, and adaptive functioning. Neuropsychological recovery continues for at least a 30-month period (Anderson, Godfrey, Rosenfeld, & Catroppa, 2012) although recovery of executive functions has been documented at five to ten years following a moderate-to-severe traumatic brain injury (Beauchamp, Catroppa, Godfrey, Morse, Rosenfeld, & Anderson, 2011). Some children experience long-term deficits (Anderson et al., 2012; Catroppa, Godfrey, Rosenfeld, Hearps, & Anderson, 2012; Sequin, Cagner, Tuerk, Barrios, MacKay, & Beauchamp (2022), but others show good recovery with minimal to no cognitive or functional deficits (Babikian, Merkley, Savage, Giza, & Levin, 2015; Fay, Yeates, Wade, Drotar, Stancin, & Taylor, 2009).

In a systematic review of this research, Sequin et al. (2022) reported their findings that children who sustained a moderate-to-severe traumatic brain injury before age 6 had lower performance in the areas of intelligence, attention, executive skills, social cognition, achievement, social skills, and adaptive functioning compared with children with a mild traumatic brain injury or orthopedic injuries, as well as typically developing children. A mild traumatic brain injury generally was associated with good neuropsychological outcome although some of the research findings showed long-term social and behavioral issues. Catroppa et al. (2012) examined the functional outcome of children ten years following a traumatic brain injury sustained at age 1–8 years. Their findings indicated persistent deficits in adaptive functioning following a severe traumatic brain injury, and a trend for increased behavioral issues and poorer arithmetic skills following a mild, moderate, or severe traumatic brain injury. A prospective longitudinal study (Anderson et al., 2012) of children ten years following a traumatic brain injury sustained between ages 2 and 7 found significantly lower IQ scores in children with a mild, moderate, or severe traumatic brain injury compared with a control group of typically developing children, with the lowest scores documented in children with a severe traumatic brain injury. It is noteworthy that the IQ scores of the children with moderate and severe traumatic brain injuries were within the low average to average range. Similar findings have been reported for executive functions following a severe traumatic brain injury sustained at age 7 or earlier. At ten years post injury, Beauchamp et al. (2011) found that scores on executive function tests involving goal setting/planning and processing speed were within the low average to average range for children with a severe traumatic brain injury but significantly lower than the scores of a control group comprising typically developing children. Scores on executive function tests involving attentional control and cognitive flexibility were comparable between the two groups. Interestingly, the children with severe traumatic brain injury also had shown a deficit in cognitive flexibility when assessed at five years post injury but this was not evident

DOI: 10.4324/9781003005063-9

at the ten-year reassessment. Beauchamp et al. (2011) described these findings as suggesting the possibility of cognitive recovery five or more years after sustaining a severe traumatic brain injury but with evidence of subtle persisting impairment in components of executive functioning (i.e., goal setting, processing speed) at ten years post injury. The children with mild and moderate traumatic brain injuries did not evidence deficiency in any component of executive functions.

A traumatic brain injury sustained at a younger age typically has a poorer outcome. Children who are age 9 or younger at the time of injury have been found to have a poorer cognitive outcome than children in late childhood at the time of injury. However, some research indicates that children in middle childhood (ages 7–9) at the time of injury have the worst cognitive outcome (Anderson, Spencer-Smith, Leventer, Coleman, Anderson, Williams, Greenham, & Jacobs, 2009; Crowe, Catroppa, Babl, Rosenfeld, & Anderson, 2012). Adolescence may be another age period associated with increased risk for poor cognitive outcome, specifically in executive functioning (Krasny-Pacini, Chevinard, Lancien, Escolano, Laurent-Vannier, De Agostini, & Meyer, 2017). The importance of age at time of injury parallels the maturational process of the brain with more rapid growth (i.e., myelination, synaptogenesis, dendritic arborization) occurring at specific time periods. A traumatic brain injury sustained during these maturational periods may have a greater impact on cognitive development, particularly cognitive skills that are dependent on the maturing brain regions. Brain injuries sustained at or before age 9 occur in the context of rapid brain development as well as the development of foundational cognitive skills, both of which are considered to underlie the increased vulnerability to a poor outcome. Brain injuries sustained during adolescence may interrupt the development of executive functions that are rapidly developing during this age period.

In addition to age and the severity of injury, the child's pre-injury status, family functioning, and sociodemographic factors impact outcome following a traumatic brain injury (Anderson et al., 2012; Babikian et al., 2015; Bolikal, Narad, Raj, Kennelly, & Kurowski, 2021; Crowe et al., 2012; Fay et al., 2009). Children with behavioral, adaptive, and/or academic problems prior to injury are at increased risk for persistent cognitive and/or functional deficits and later decline in functioning following a traumatic brain injury (Anderson et al., 2012; Catroppa et al., 2012, Fay et al., 2009). Lower household income, lower caregiver education, poor parenting skills, and family dysfunction have been associated with an increased risk for persistent deficits and deterioration in functioning over time in traumatic brain injury, possibly related to fewer available rehabilitative/treatment resources, parent/caregiver adeptness in advocating for healthcare and educational services, and increased stress in lower-income families (Fay et al., 2009; Krasny-Pacini et al., 2017; Zonfrillo, Haarbauer-Krupa, Want, Durbin, Jaffe, Temkin, Bell, Tulsky, Bertisch, Yeates, & Rivera, 2021).

Some children appear to recover fully from a more severe traumatic brain injury. Fay et al. (2009) found that children with a severe traumatic brain injury in early to late childhood had an increased risk of deficits (defined as scores < 10th percentile) in neuropsychological, behavioral, adaptive, and academic functioning at four years post injury; however, their findings also indicated that a substantial proportion of these children, 48%–67%, showed minimal or no deficits in neuropsychological, behavioral, adaptive, or academic functioning. Moran, Babikian, Del Piero, Ellis, Kernan, Newman, Giza, Mink, Johnson, Babbitt, and Asarnow (2016) also found a subset of children with a moderate-to-severe traumatic brain injury showed no neuropsychological deficits at 12 months post injury.

An additional consideration is the potential impact of a traumatic brain injury in early childhood on the cognitive skills that typically develop in later childhood and adolescence (e.g., goal setting/planning), indicating a risk for cognitive sequelae emerging years after an early injury (Anderson et al., 2009; Beauchamp et al., 2011; Babikian et al., 2015). Delayed onset of deficits in adaptive, behavioral, emotional, and academic functioning has been reported following moderate and severe traumatic brain injuries (Fay et al., 2009). An increase in attentional symptoms, as rated by parents and teachers at 24 months post injury, has also been reported for some children following mild, moderate, or severe traumatic brain injuries (Bolikal et al., 2021). The potential for persisting cognitive deficits and later emerging deficits underscores the importance of monitoring children, particularly children who have sustained a severe traumatic brain injury, in terms of their neuropsychological status and academic achievement to determine appropriate interventions to improve long-term outcome.

In evaluating the neuropsychological status of children and adolescents, consideration must be given to performance and symptom validity assessment. Validity assessment is an essential part of an every pediatric neuropsychological evaluation as it provides an objective basis for placing confidence in the test data as an accurate assessment of the child's or adolescent's current ability level and behavioral/emotional functioning. The 2021 updated American Academy of Clinical Neuropsychology consensus conference statement (Sweet, Heilbronner, Morgan, Larrabee, Rohling, Boone, Kirkwood, Schroeder, Suhr, & Conference Participants, 2021) includes the recommendation for the routine use of performance validity tests (PVTs) and symptom validity tests (SVTs) in clinical and forensic pediatric neuropsychological evaluations. At the time of an initial AACN consensus statement in 2009, there had been little empirical investigation of validity assessment with children and adolescents and, therefore, insufficient information was available to inform a neuropsychological practice recommendation. Pediatric validity assessment, however, was identified as an important issue that required further study (Heilbronner, Sweet, Morgan, Larrabee, Millis, & Conference Participants, 2009). In the years following the initial consensus statement, research has shown that young children are capable of deceptive behavior (Clegg, Lynch, Mian, & McCaffrey, 2021) and that a percentage of children and adolescents produce invalid neuropsychological test data, with the base rate of performance invalidity approaching 20% in some clinical groups (Green & Flaro, 2003, 2021; Kirkwood & Kirk, 2010; Kirkwood, Peterson, Connery, Baker, & Grubenhoff, 2014) and 60% in forensic groups (Chafetz, Abrahams, & Kohlmaier, 2007; McCaffrey & Lynch, 2020). Moreover, an association between failed performance validity test scores and neuropsychological test scores has been empirically demonstrated. Children failing one or more freestanding PVT have been found to perform significantly lower on neuropsychological measures of intelligence, memory, attention, executive functions, academic achievement, and motor functioning (Green & Flaro, 2021; Kirk, Baker, Kirk, & MacAllister, 2020; Nayar, Ventura, DeDios-Stern, Oh, & Soble, 2022).

The 15 years since the initial AACN consensus statement has seen an increase in validity measures for use with pediatric groups. Two freestanding PVTs have been developed specifically for children and adolescents, the Memory Validity Profile (Sherman & Brooks, 2015) and Pediatric Performance Validity Test Suite (McCaffrey, Lynch, Leark, & Reynolds, 2020). There also has been an increase in research examining the utility of freestanding PVTs that were originally developed for use with adults with pediatric samples. The Test of Memory Malingering (TOMM; Tombaugh, 1996), Word Memory Test (WMT, Green, Allen, & Astner, 1996), and Medical Symptom Validity Test (MVST, Green, 2004) have been empirically validated for use with children as young as age 5 with a variety of clinical diagnoses using standard cutoff scores, with a few exceptions (DeRight & Carone, 2015; Emhoff, Lynch, & McCaffrey, 2018; Kirk et al., 2020; Schneider, Kirk, & Mahone, 2014;

Ventura, DeDios-Stern, Oh, & Soble, 2021). These exceptions include children and adolescents with low intellectual ability (IQ ≤ 70), very severe cognitive impairment, pervasive developmental disorder, or conduct disorder as research has demonstrated these clinical groups to have higher failure rates on the TOMM using the standard cutoff score (Clark, Martin, Okut, & Schroeder, 2020; McAllister, Nakhutina, Bender, Karantzoulis, & Carlson, 2009; Perna & Loughlin, 2014). On the WMT, higher failure rates using the standard cutoff score have been reported among children with severe reading disorders (Larochette & Harrison, 2012). In addition, the WMT and MSVT require a Grade 3 reading level. To date, only one study has examined the use of the Victoria Symptom Validity Test (VSVT, Slick, Hopp, Strauss, & Thompson, 1997) with children and adolescents. The findings suggest that the standard VSVT cutoff scores may be appropriate for use in pediatric neuropsychological evaluations, if supported by additional research (Brooks, 2012). There have been a handful of studies examining the Rey 15-Item Test (Rey, 1964) and the Rey 15-Item Test plus recognition trial (Boone, Salazar, Lu, Warner-Chacon, & Razani, 2002) with pediatric samples. Findings suggest that the Rey 15-Item Test may not be appropriate for children under age 10 given evidence of a higher failure rate in younger children (Constantinou & McCaffrey, 2003). The Rey 15-Item plus recognition trial showed good classification accuracy in a mild traumatic brain injury pediatric sample who were age 9 and older (Green, Connery, Baker, & Kirkwood, 2014) but this test requires further empirical study.

Freestanding PVTs have been examined with children and adolescents with traumatic brain injury, though most of these studies involved mild traumatic brain injuries samples. In our review of the research literature on freestanding PVT use with pediatric samples, we identified seven studies that included children with a moderate-to-severe traumatic brain injury and provided data regarding the PVT failure rate in this clinical group. In the identified studies, the moderate-to-severe traumatic brain injury samples were either part of a larger pediatric traumatic brain injury sample or a subgroup of a mixed clinical sample. These studies are presented in Table 7.1. The TOMM has undergone the most research with this pediatric group, with findings indicating low failure rates using standard cutoff scores.

Table 7.1 Studies Examining Freestanding Performance Validity Tests in Pediatric Samples with Moderate-to-Severe Traumatic Brain Injuries

Source	*PVT*	*Sample*	*Age*	*% Invalid Range*
Brooks et al. (2019)	MVP	Clinically referred TBI sample (severity unspecified)	5–19	4.5
Wilson and Lesica (2021)	MVP	Clinically referred neurological sample (21% with mild-to-severe TBI)	6–16	1.4
Carone (2008)	MSVT	Clinically referred neurological sample (81% with moderate-to-severe TBI)	6–18	5.0
Donders (2005)	TOMM	Clinically referred mixed sample (55% with mild-to-severe TBI)	6–16	3.0
Donders and Gardner (2020)	TOMM Trial 1 TOMMe10	Clinically referred mild-to-severe TBI sample	6–16	7.0 5.5
Loughan and Perna (2014)	TOMM	Clinically referred sample with TBI (severity unspecified)	6–18	21.0
Ploetz et al. (2016)	TOMM	Clinically referred complicated mild-to-severe TBI	5–18	9.0

MVP = Memory Validity Profile; MSVT = Medical Symptom Validity Test; TOMM = Test of Memory Malingering; TOMMe10 = First 10 items on TOMM Trial 1.

The exception is the Loughan and Perna (2014) study, which found a 21% failure rate in children with traumatic brain injury, but the injury severity was not indicated in this study.

Embedded PVTs have been developed for several pediatric neuropsychological tests, including the California Verbal Learning Test – Children's Version (Delis, Kramer, Kaplan, & Ober, 1994) and Child and Adolescent Memory Profile (Sherman & Brooks, 2015), and embedded PVTs developed for adults have been examined for use with children and adolescents (e.g., Reliable Digit Span, Reliable Digit Span-Revised, and Digit Span Age-Corrected Scaled Score from Wechsler Intelligence Scales; Failure to Maintain Set from the Wisconsin Card Sorting Test). The embedded validity tests from the Digit Span subtest have received the most research attention, and findings have been mixed. Many studies have found high failure rates in nonclinical and clinical pediatric samples using adult cutoffs, and the appropriate cutoff scores may vary for different pediatric clinical groups (Emhoff et al., 2018; Kirk et al., 2020; Ventura et al., 2021).

Several pediatric behavioral rating scales and personality measures now incorporate symptom validity scales to determine the accuracy of the child/adolescent's symptom report, as well as the accuracy of the symptom reports provided by parents and teachers. These include the Minnesota Multiphasic Personality Inventory – Adolescent (Butcher, Williams, Graham, Archer, Tellegen, Ben-Porath, & Kraemmer, 1992), Minnesota Multiphasic Personality Inventory – Adolescent – Restructured Form (Archer, Handel, Ben-Porath, & Tellegen, 2016), Personality Assessment Inventory – Adolescent (Morey, 2007), Behavioral Assessment Scale for Children – Third Edition (Reynolds & Kamphaus, 2015), Personality Inventory for Youth (Lachar & Gruber, 1995), and Millon Adolescent Clinical Inventory – II (Millon, Tringone, Grossman, & Millon, 2020).

There are several review papers and chapters regarding performance and SVTs for children and adolescents, which provide guidance in selecting validity tests appropriate for specific clinical groups and age ranges (Clegg et al., 2021; Colbert, Maxwell, & Kirkwood, 2021; DeRight & Carone, 2015; Emhoff et al., 2018; Kirkwood, 2015; Kirk, Baker, Kirk, & MacAllister, 2020).

The Case of Mr. T.J.

Background: T.J. was a ten-year-old Caucasian male who sustained a moderate-to-severe traumatic brain injury at age 4 when he fell several feet. On the day of the injury, a head CT scan showed a comminuted depressed skull fracture of the frontal bone, diffuse bilateral frontoparietal subdural hematomas greater on the right, and mild mass effect on the right cerebral hemisphere with slight shift to the left. He was intubated due to labored breathing and hospitalized for several days with close monitoring by the neurosurgical team. He was started on antiseizure medication prophylactically. Subsequent head CT scans showed a slight decrease in the subdural hematomas. Neurosurgical intervention was not considered necessary. Findings from an Occupational Therapy evaluation prior to discharge indicated that T.J.'s expressive language and gross motor skills were delayed. At the time of a neurosurgical follow-up two weeks after discharge, T.J.'s mother reported that he was experiencing constant headaches, emotional lability, and gait instability. Over the next month, the headaches resolved, and his functioning was described as having "returned to normal" by his mother.

There were no documented concerns expressed by his parents or physicians in the medical records until T.J. entered kindergarten approximately one year post injury. His teacher noted emotional lability, episodes of unresponsiveness, episodes of disorganized speech and behavior, and staring spells during the school day. He was referred for a neurological consultation and an Occupational Therapy evaluation. Electroencephalogram (EEG) findings were reportedly normal. Findings from the Occupational Therapy evaluation were significant for below-average scores on a test of visuomotor integration and motor coordination and he was observed to exhibit awkward motor patterns, and difficulties with balance and graphic skills. Occupational Therapy services were provided at school through Grade 1 with improvement noted in his gross motor skills.

T.J. exhibited behavior issues during the latter part of kindergarten, which continued through Grade 1. Teachers described concerns about inappropriate/disruptive behavior, distractibility, impulsivity, effort toward schoolwork, and homework completion. There were few behavioral concerns documented in the school records in Grades 2 and 3, except for occasional issues with sustained attention and homework completion. Academically, T.J. was generally meeting grade expectations except for reading comprehension issues and poor handwriting legibility that emerged in Grade 3. His scores on the iReady Reading assessment were at grade level, but scores were below grade level on the iReady Math assessment.

In Grade 3, he was referred to the Committee on Special Education by his mother due to T.J.'s history of traumatic brain injury. T.J.'s mother reportedly perceived him as struggling academically and exhibiting inappropriate and disruptive classroom behavior, although his teacher reportedly characterized him as a kind and socially appropriate student who had many friends. The teacher reported that he was meeting grade expectations but had difficulty with reading comprehension and handwriting legibility at times. An Occupational Therapy evaluation, conducted due to concerns about handwriting quality, found that T.J.'s visuomotor and visuoperceptual abilities were within the average to exceptionally high range, and significantly stronger than had been found at the time of Occupational Therapy evaluation at age 5. His handwriting was considered legible. Occupational Therapy services were not recommended. In addition, T.J. underwent a psychoeducational evaluation. The Behavior Assessment Scales for Children-Third Edition (BASC-3) was completed by T.J.'s mother and teacher. Symptom validity indicators were within the valid range on both BASC-3 profiles. His mother and teacher both indicated that T.J. exhibited problems with attention, hyperactivity, conduct, and atypical behaviors. His mother indicated that these issues were more significant (i.e., ratings in the Clinically Significant Range) than the teacher (i.e., ratings in the At-Risk range). In addition, his mother indicated that T.J. exhibited depressive behaviors, social withdrawal, and poor self-control; teacher ratings in these areas were within the normal range. T.J. was deemed eligible for a 504 plan with classroom and testing accommodations, and Academic Intervention Service for math based upon his score on the iReady Math assessment.

In Grade 4, T.J. was meeting grade expectations in all areas except reading comprehension, which was improving. His teacher indicated that he worked very hard in all areas and was respectful to everyone.

Six years following the injury, T.J. was referred by defense counsel for an independent neuropsychological evaluation in the context of litigation. He was in Grade 5.

Interview: T.J.s mother participated in the clinical interview. T.J. resided with his mother and three older siblings. His father was not involved with the family. Both parents reportedly had a high school education. His mother reported that T.J. was a full term infant delivered via C-section with no postpartum complications. She indicated, however, having taken prescription headache medication as needed and smoking one half pack of cigarettes daily across her pregnancy with T.J. He was left-handed, and there was a family history of left-handedness.

In reviewing his current status, his mother reported that he was no longer experiencing headaches. She described him as occasionally sad and preferring to play video games rather than interact with peers. When asked about his school functioning, his mother stated that he needed to re-read information occasionally. She indicated that T.J. had a Section 504 Accommodation Plan at school. She was not able to describe his current grades or academic functioning. He was not prescribed any medication at the time of the evaluation.

Record Review: According to information within the medical records, T.J. was a healthy four-year-old child at the time of the traumatic brain injury. There were no developmental concerns documented in the pre-accident medical records or reported by his mother during the clinical interview. T.J.'s educational records contained an annual review of his Section 504 Accommodation Plan that was completed shortly following this independent neuropsychological evaluation. According to information within the annual review, he was provided academic accommodations that consisted of preferential seating, simplification of directions, use of a word processer, extended test-taking time, and testing location with minimal distractions. He was performing well academically and there were no concerns expressed by his teachers. Behaviorally, he was described as polite and respectful. His grades were within the average range across all areas.

Behavioral Observations: T.J. was somewhat shy and soft spoken but responded to all inquiries and participated with all test procedures. Speech was normal, and he appeared to understand test directions without issue. He did not exhibit any motor restlessness, distractibility, or impulsivity.

Test Results: T.J.'s scores on two freestanding PVTs were within the valid range (TOMM: Trail 1 = 44, Trial 2 = 50, Retention Trial = 49; MSVT: Immediate Recognition = 95.0, Delayed Recognition = 90.0, Consistency = 90.0, Paired Associates = 50.0, Free Recall = 55.0). While the Behavior Rating Scales for Children is a typical component of pediatric evaluations in our practice, this was not administered because of constraints in obtaining ratings from school personnel for comparison with T.J.'s ratings and his mother's ratings, as is standard practice for obtaining a comprehensive assessment of behavioral and emotional functioning.

On the Reynolds Intellectual Assessment Scales – 2 (RIAS-2), T.J.'s intellectual abilities were within the low average range, with comparable performances on the nonverbal and verbal subtests. Processing speed was within the average range. On the memory subtests, there was a statistically significant difference between verbal and nonverbal memory scores although a discrepancy of this size was not uncommon in the normative sample (base rate > 20%). Verbal memory was within the low average range for immediate recall of two narratives, and nonverbal memory was within the average range for immediate recognition of geometric designs.

T.J.'s performance on the Woodcock Johnson IV indicated that his knowledge of words and factual information was within the low average to average range. Reasoning skills were within the average to high average range. Sustained attention and verbal working memory were within the average to high average range. Information processing speed and visuospatial abilities were within the average range.

On the Wide Range Assessment of Memory and Learning – 2 (WRAML-2), T.J.'s score on a test of verbal working memory was within the high average range and within the average range on a test of visual working memory. T.J. performed within the average range on verbal memory tests involving verbal learning and delayed recall of short stories and a word list. On visual memory tests, his immediate reproduction of geometric shapes was within the below-average range. On the delayed recognition trial, his score was within the low average range. His performance was within the low average range on the immediate recall and delayed recognition of the Picture Memory subtest (Table 7.2).

Table 7.2 TJ's Test Scores from the Defense Expert's Neuropsychological Evaluation

Test	*Score*
Reynolds Intellectual Assessment Scales	
INDEX/Subtest	T Score
COMPOSITE INTELLIGENCE	40
VERBAL INTELLIGENCE	43
Guess What	41
Verbal Reasoning	42
NONVERBAL INTELLIGENCE	43
Odd-Item Out	44
What's Missing	43
COMPOSITE MEMORY	44
Verbal Memory	39
Nonverbal Memory	54
SPEEDED PROCESSING	47
Speeded Naming Task	42
Speeded Picture Search	53
Woodcock Johnson IV: Tests of Cognitive Abilities	
CLUSTER/Test	Standard Score
GENERAL INTELLECTUAL ABILITY	94
COMPREHENSION-KNOWLEDGE	88
Oral Vocabulary	85
General Information	94
FLUID REASONING	107
Number Series	93
Concept Formation	117
SHORT-TERM WORKING MEMORY	111
Verbal Attention	101
Numbers Reversed	116
COGNITIVE PROCESSING SPEED	—
Letter-Pattern Matching	94
AUDITORY PROCESSING	—
Phonological Processing	98
LONG-TERM RETRIEVAL	—
Story Recall	97
VISUAL PROCESSING	—
Visualization	101
PERCEPTUAL SPEED	—
Letter-Pattern Matching	94
COGNITIVE EFFICIENCY	104
Verbal Attention	101
Numbers Reversed	116
Wide Range Assessment of Memory and Learning-2	
INDEX/Subtest	T Score
GENERAL MEMORY	44
VERBAL MEMORY	50
Story Memory	49
Verbal Learning	52
VISUAL MEMORY	35
Design Memory	34
Picture Memory	39
ATTENTION/CONCENTRATION	53
Finger Windows	42
Number Letter	62

(*Continued*)

Table 7.2 (Continued)

Test	*Score*
Test of Memory Malingering	
Trial 1	44
Trial 2	50
Retention	49
Medical Symptom Validity Test	
Immediate Recognition	95.0
Delayed Recognition	90.0
Consistency	90.0
Paired Associates	50.0
Free Recall	55.0

The neuropsychological findings were interpreted to be within normal limits. T.J.'s scores across the neuropsychological test battery were within the low average to high average range, except for one low score on one visual memory test (below-average range). The finding of one below-average test score was considered to be consistent with the expected degree of variability found with healthy, neurologically normal children (Donders & Strong, 2016) and not indicative of acquired neuropsychological impairment. Additionally, the absence of neuropsychological impairments corresponded to T.J.'s current functioning at school where teachers denied any significant academic or behavioral concerns.

Subsequent Evaluation: T.J. was seen for an independent neuropsychological evaluation at the request plaintiff's counsel one year later. PVT scores were in the valid range. On the neuropsychological testing, T.J.'s index score on a measure of planning ability was reportedly within the low average range and statistically lower than the mean of his index scores on the cognitive battery (base rate < 20%). Scores on tests of working memory were within the high average range, and scores on tests of attention and visuospatial/verbal reasoning were within the average range. The variability in test scores was interpreted as more likely a consequence of cognitive impairment than normal test score variability considering the nature of the traumatic brain injury, and structural changes documented earlier. The plaintiff's neuropsychological expert concluded that the neuropsychological evaluation findings indicated a diagnosis of Mild Neurocognitive Disorder Due to a Traumatic Brain Injury.

The neuropsychological raw test data from the plaintiff's independent neuropsychological evaluation was requested for review; however, the case was settled.

Discussion: The objective findings from neuropsychological assessments completed by the plaintiff and defense experts were very consistent. In both evaluations, T.J. passed PVTs and his scores on neuropsychological testing were within the low average to high average ranges. The neuropsychological test findings were considered by both experts to be remarkable given that T.J. had sustained a moderate-to-severe traumatic brain injury involving bilateral frontoparietal regions seven years earlier. At issue was the interpretation of test score variability.

The commonality of intra-individual variability and obtaining one (or more) low test scores in a neuropsychological battery has been repeatedly demonstrated with normally developing children and healthy adults (Brooks, 2010, 2011; Brooks, Holdnack, & Iverson, 2011; Brooks Iverson, Sherman, & Holdnack, 2009; Brooks, Sherman, & Iverson,

2010; Cook, Karr, Brooks, Garcia-Barrera, Holdnack, & Inverson, 2019; Putzke, Williams, Glutting, Konold, & Boll, 2001; Schretlen, Munro, Anthony, & Pearlson, 2003). A child's intellectual functioning and parental education level have been found to be negatively associated with the number of low test scores found within a test battery (Brooks, 2010, 2011; Brooks et al., 2009; Brooks et al., 2010). Although the base rates of low test scores and test score variability have been examined for several neuropsychological and intellectual tests, the tests used in evaluating T.J. have not yet undergone such examination. The original WRAML was studied regarding the base rate of test score variability within the standardization sample, with reported findings of substantial subtest and index score variability (Putzke et al., 2001). As examples, 15%–21% of the standardization sample had at least one subtest scaled score of 4 or below. Regarding variability, approximately 25% of the standardization sample had a difference of 9 or more between the highest and lowest subtest age-corrected scaled score, and 80% had a discrepancy of 6 or more. There also was variability across index scores, with 50% of the standardization sample having at least one discrepancy of 20 or more and 15% having a discrepancy of 30 or more. While this study provided additional information regarding the degree of variability exhibited by healthy individuals, T.J. was administered the WRAML-2.

Various clinical populations have been found to exhibit more intra-individual test score variability than healthy individuals, and this variability has been conceptualized to reflect neural integrity or neurodevelopment. Increased intra-individual test score variability has been reported for children with Attention Deficit/Hyperactivity Disorder (Belle, van Hulst, & Durston, 2015; Halliday, Kim, MacDonald, Garcia-Barrera, Hundza, & Macoun, 2021), Autism Spectrum Disorder (Belle et al., 2015), and Fetal Alcohol Spectrum Disorder (Ali, Kerns, Mulligan, Olson, & Astley, 2018). Increased intra-individual test score variability also has been associated with traumatic brain injury in an *adult* sample, with a positive correlation between injury severity and degree of variability (Hill, Rohling, Boettcher, & Meyers, 2013). Intra-individual test score variability with pediatric traumatic brain injury samples has not been studied.

Is it possible to determine if the test score variability exhibited by T.J. was within the range of "normal variability" or reflective of cognitive impairment due to a moderate-to-severe traumatic brain injury (TBI)?

The plaintiff's neuropsychological expert considered that T.J. had exhibited variability across both the defense and plaintiff's experts' neuropsychological evaluation, and that this variability was due to moderate-to-severe TBI. On the plaintiff's neuropsychological evaluation, T.J. had obtained a low average range planning index score, which was statistically significantly lower than the mean index score on the test battery. Reference to the test manual indicated that the base rate of the difference score is 19.4% (Naglieri, Das, & Goldstein, 2014). Is a difference score that was found in the test profiles of 19.4% of the normative sample rare enough to be regarded as diagnostically or clinically meaningful? The defense neuropsychological expert reported that T.J. obtained one below-average score (5th percentile) on a visual memory subtest from the WRAML-2, with the other WRAML-2 scores ranging between low average and high average. As indicated, data on the base rate of low scores in the standardization sample of the WRAML-2 are not available. Referencing the base rate studies of other pediatric memory tests, it seems that this finding may not be unusual. A base rate study of the Children's Memory Scale (Brooks et al., 2009) found that 22.4% of the normative sample had one or more index scores ≤ 5th percentile. As described earlier, a base rate study of the original WRAML found that 15%–21% of the standardization sample had at least one scaled score of 4 or lower.

Disentangling normal test score variability from variability due to neurological injury is challenging, particularly in this case where there is evidence of diffuse bilateral neurological injury. In the context of the research on intra-individual test score variability, T.J.'s neuropsychological test scores were not more variable than found in normally developing children. Further, most of his neuropsychological test scores were within the low average to high average range, and he was functioning well both academically and behaviorally, with grades within the average range in all areas. There was little evidence that T.J. was currently exhibiting neuropsychological impairment consequent to the moderate-to-severe traumatic brain injury sustained seven years earlier. As reported in the literature, some children show full recovery following a moderate-to-severe traumatic brain injury (Fay et al., 2009; Moran et al., 2016).

At the same time, however, there are research findings demonstrating that low average to average range neuropsychological test scores represent a subtle impairment for some children with a history of a moderate-to-severe traumatic brain injury (Anderson et al., 2012; Beauchamp et al., 2011). Could this be the case for T.J.? A child's academic functioning/grades, standardized test scores, and school behavior are good indicators of pre-injury functioning, and can assist with determining if normal range neuropsychological test scores are below expectation for a particular child. In younger children who have not yet entered the school system at the time of injury, as is the current case, medical records may contain information as to whether there were any concerns about the child's development and behavior prior to injury, and if the child's medical and family history is significant for any developmental risk factors. Additionally, information regarding the child's sociodemographic background may assist with estimating expected cognitive ability level. In considering this background information, there were minimal indications that T.J.'s low average to high average neuropsychological test scores represented a decline for him. T.J.'s parents completed high school, and he resided within a fairly stable lower middle-class home. There was no additional information available about his father's developmental, medical, or occupational background. T.J.'s pre-injury medical records were significant only for prenatal tobacco exposure across the pregnancy, which is a developmental risk factor (Joelsson, Chudal, Talati, Suominen, Brown, & Sourander, 2016; Gutvirtz, Wainstock, Landau, & Sheiner, 2019).

A final issue is the possibility that the traumatic brain injury has impacted developing cognitive abilities and, while not currently apparent, cognitive impairment will emerge later (sometimes referred to as "growing into deficit"). The delayed emergence of cognitive impairment, particularly regarding executive skills, has been reported in several studies (Anderson et al., 2009; Beauchamp et al., 2011; Babikian et al., 2015). Based on T.J.'s neuropsychological findings and current functioning, there did not appear to be a high probability for emerging issues although this remained within the realm of possibilities. This raises the question as to whether a forensic evaluation should be postponed until adolescence to monitor for emerging issues with later developing cognitive abilities. This, however, could impact the provision of care and educational services for the injured child.

References

Ali, S., Kerns, K.A., Mulligan, B.P., Olson, H.C., & Astley, S.J. (2018). An investigation of intra-individual variability in children with fetal alcohol spectrum disorder (FASD). *Child Neuropsychology, 24*, 617–637. https://doi.org/10.1080/09297049.2017.1302579

Anderson, V., Godfrey, C., Rosenfeld, J.V., & Catroppa, C. (2012). Predictors of cognitive function and recovery 10 years after traumatic brain injury in young children. *Pediatrics, 129*, e254. https://doi:10.1542/peds.2011-0311

Anderson, V., Spencer-Smith, M., Leventer, R., Coleman, L., Anderson, P., Williams, J., Greenham, M., & Jacobs, R. (2009). Childhood brain insult: can age at insult help us predict outcome? *Brain, 132*, 45–56. https://doi:10/1093/brain/awn29

Archer, R.P., Handel, R.W., Ben-Porath, Y.S., & Tellegen, A. (2016). *Minnesota Multiphasic Personality Inventory-Adolescent-Restructured Form (MMPI-A-RF): Administration, scoring, interpretation, and technical manual.* Minneapolis: University of Minnesota Press.

Babikian, T., Merkley, T., Savage, R.C., Giza, C.C., & Levin, H. (2015). Chronic aspects of pediatric traumatic brain injury: review of the literature. *Journal of Neurotrauma, 32*, 1849–1860. https://doi:10/1089/neu.2015.3971

Beauchamp, M., Catroppa, C., Godfrey, C., Morse, S., Rosenfeld, J.V., & Anderson, V. (2011). Selective changes in executive functioning ten years after severe childhood traumatic brain injury. *Developmental Neuropsychology, 36*, 578–595. https://doi:10.1080/875656641.2001.555572

Bolikal, P.D., Narad, M., Raj, S., Kennelly, M., & Kurowski, B.G. (2021). Biopsychosocial factors associated with attention problems in children after traumatic brain injury. *American Journal of Physical Medicine & Rehabilitation, 100*, 215–228. https://doi:10.1097/PHM0000000000001643

Boone, K.B., Salazar, X., Lu, P., Warner-Chacon, K., & Razani, J. (2002). The Rey 15-Item recognition trial: a technique to enhance sensitivity of the Rey 15-Item Memorization Test. *Journal of Clinical and Experimental Neuropsychology, 24*, 561–573.

Brooks, B.L. (2010). Seeing the forest for the trees: Prevalence of low scores on the Wechsler Intelligence Scale for Children, Fourth Edition (WISC-IV). *Psychological Assessment, 22*, 650–656. https://doi:10.1037/a0019781

Brooks, B.L. (2011). A study of low scores in Canadian children and adolescents on the Wechsler Intelligence Scale for Children, Fourth Edition (WISC-IV). *Child Neuropsychology, 17*, 281–289. https://doi:10.1080/09297049.2010.537255.

Brooks, B.L. (2012). Victoria symptom validity test performance in children and adolescents with neurological disorders. *Archives of Clinical Neuropsychology, 27*, 858–868. https://doi:10.1093/arclin/acs087

Brooks, B.L., Fay-McClymont, T.B., MacAllister, W.S., Vasserman, M., & Sherman, E.M.S. (2019). A new kid on the block: the memory validity profile (MVP) in children with neurological conditions. *Child Neuropsychology, 25*, 561–572. https://doi.org/10.1080/09297049.2018.1477929

Brooks, B.L., Iverson, G.L., Sherman, E.M.S., & Holdnack, J.A. (2009). Healthy children and adolescents obtain some low scores across a battery of memory tests. *Journal of the International Neuropsychological Society, 15*, 613–617. https://doi:10.1017/S1355617709909065

Brooks, B.L., Sherman, E.M.S., & Iverson, G.L. (2010). Healthy children get low scores too: Prevalence of low scores on the NEPSY-II in preschoolers, children, and adolescents. *Archives of Clinical Neuropsychology, 25*, 182–190. https://doi:10.1093/arclin/asq005

Butcher, J.N., Williams, C.L., Graham, J.R., Archer, R.P., Tellegen, A., Ben-Porath, Y.S., & Kaemmer, B. (1992). *MMPI–A: Minnesota Multiphasic Personality Inventory–Adolescent: Manual for administration, scoring, and interpretation.* Minneapolis: University of Minnesota Press.

Carone, D.A. (2008). Children with moderate/severe brain damage/dysfunction outperform adults with mild-to-no brain damage on the medical symptom validity test. *Brain Injury, 22*, 960–971. https://doi.10.1080/02699050802491297

Catroppa, C., Godfrey, C., Rosenfeld, J.V., Hearps, S.S.J.C., & Anderson, V.A. (2012) Functional recovery 10 years after pediatric traumatic brain injury: outcome and predictors. *Journal of Neurotrauma, 29*, 2539–2547. https://doi:10.1089/neu.2012.2403

Chafetz, M. D., Abrahams, J. P., & Kohlmaier, J. (2007). Malingering on the social security disability consultative exam: A new rating scale. *Archives of Clinical Neuropsychology, 22*(1), 1–14. https://doi.org/10.1016/j.acn.2006.10.003

Clark, H.A., Martin, P.K., Okut, H., & Schroeder, R.W. (2020). A systematic review and metaanalysis of the utility of the Test of Memory Malingering in pediatric examinees. *Archives of Clinical Neuropsychology, 35*, 1312–1322.

Clegg, R.A., Lynch, J.K., Mian, M.N., & McCaffrey, R.J. (2021). Performance validity assessment in pediatric evaluations. In C. R. Reynolds and A. M. Horton, Jr. (eds.), *Detection of Malingering during Head Injury Litigation*, 3rd Edition (pp. 309–336). New York: Springer.

Colbert, A.M., Maxwell, E.C., & Kirkwood, M.W (2021). Validity assessment in pediatric populations. In K. B. Boone (ed.), *Assessment of Feigned Cognitive Impairment*, 2nd Edition (pp. 633–655). New York: Guilford Press.

Constantinou, M., & McCaffrey, R.J. (2003). Use of the TOMM for evaluating children's effort to perform optimally on neuropsychological measures. *Child Neuropsychology, 9,* 81–90. https://doi-org.libproxy.albany.edu/10.1076/chin.9.2.81.14505

Cook, N.E., Karr, J.E., Brooks, B.L., Garcia-Barrera, M.A., Holdnack, J.A., & Iverson, G.L. (2019). Multivariate base rates for the assessment of executive functioning among children and adolescents. *Child Neuropsychology, 25,* 836–858. https://doi.org/10.1080.09297049.2018.1543389

Crowe, L.M., Catroppa, C., Babl, F.E., Rosenfeld, J.V., & Anderson, V. (2012). Timing of traumatic brain injury in childhood and intellectual outcome. *Journal of Pediatric Psychology, 37,* 745–754. https://doi:10.1093/jpepsy/jss070

Delis, D.C., Kramer, J.H., Kaplan, E., & Ober, B.A. (1994). *California Verbal Learning Test – Children's Version.* San Antonio, TX: The Psychological Corporation.

DeRight, J., & Carone, D.A. (2015). Assessment of effort in children: A systematic review. *Child Neuropsychology, 21, 1–24.*

Donders, J. (2005). Performance on the test of memory malingering in a mixed pediatric sample. *Child Neuropsychology, 11,* 221–227. https://doi.1080.09297040490917298

Donders, J., & Strong, C. A. H. (2016). Latent structure of the Behavior Rating Inventory of Executive Function—Adult Version (BRIEF–A) after mild traumatic brain injury. *Archives of Clinical Neuropsychology, 31*(1), 29–36.

Donders, J., & Gardner, V. (2020). Utility of abbreviated versions of the test of memory malingering in children with traumatic brain injury. *Applied Neuropsychology - Child, 9,* 355–359. https://doi.org/10.1080/21622965.2020.1750109

Emhoff, S.M., Lynch, J.K., & McCaffrey, R.J. (2018). Performance and symptom validity testing in pediatric assessment: a review of the literature. *Developmental Neuropsychology, 43,* 671–707. https://doi.org/10.1080/87565641.2018.1525612

Fay, T.B., Yeates, K.O., Wade, S.L., Drotar, D., Stancin, T., & Taylor, H. G. (2009). Predicting longitudinal patterns of functional deficits in children with traumatic brain injury. *Neuropsychology, 23,* 271–282. https://doi:10.1037/a0014936

Green, P. (2004). *Green's Medical Symptom Validity Test (MSVT) for Microsoft Windows (user manual).* Edmonton, Canada: Green's Publishing.

Green, P., Allen, L., & Astner, K. (1996). *Manual for Computerised Word Memory Test, U.S. version 1.0.* Durham, NC: Cognisyst.

Green, P., & Flaro, L. (2003). Word memory test performance in children. *Child Neuropsychology, 9,* 189–207. https://doi:10.1076/chin.9.3.189.16460

Green, P., & Flaro, L. (2021). Performance validity test failure predicts suppression of neuropsychological test results in developmentally disabled children. *Applied Neuropsychology – Child, 10,* 65–81. https://doi:10.1080/21622965.2019.1604342

Green, C.M., Kirk, J.W., Connery, A.K., Baker, D.A., & Kirkwood, M.W. (2014). The use of the Rey 15-Item Test and recognition trial to evaluate noncredible effort after pediatric mild traumatic brain injury. *Journal of Clinical and Experimental Neuropsychology, 36,* 261–267. https://doi:10.1080/13803395.2013.879096

Gutvirtz, G., Wainstock, T., Landau, D., & Sheiner, E. (2019). Maternal smoking during pregnancy and long-term neurological morbidity of the offspring. *Addictive Behaviors, 88,* 86–91. https://doi.org/10/1016/j.addbeh.2018.08.013

Halliday, D.W.R., Kim, Y., MacDonald, S.W.S., Garcia-Barrera, M.A., Hundza, S.R., & Macoun, S.J. (2021). Intraindividual variability in executive and motor control tasks in children with attention deficit hyperactivity disorder. *Journal of Clinical and Experimental Neuropsychology, 43,* 568–578. https://doi.org/10.1080/13803395.2021.1965097

Heilbronner, R.L., Sweet, J.J., Morgan, J.E., Larrabee, G.J., Millis, S.R., & Conference Participants (2009). American academy of clinical neuropsychology consensus conference statement on the neuropsychological assessment of effort, response bias, and malingering. *The Clinical Neuropsychologist, 23,* 1093–1129. https://doi:10.1080/13854040903155063

Hill, B.D., Rohling, M.L., Boettcher, A.C., & Meyers, J.E. (2013). Cognitive intra-individual variability has a positive association with traumatic brain injury severity and suboptimal effort. *Archives of Clinical Neuropsychology, 28,* 640–648. https://doi:10.1093/arclin/act045

Joelsson, P., Chudal, R., Talati, A., Suominen, A., Brown, A.S., & Sourander, A. (2016). Prenatal smoking exposure and neuropsychiatric comorbidity of ADHD: a Finnish nationwide population-based cohort study. *BMC Psychiatry, 16.* https://doi:10.1186/s12888-016-1007-2

Kirk, J.W., Baker, D.A., Kirk, J.J., & MacAllister, W.S. (2020). A review of performance and symptom validity testing with pediatric populations. *Applied Neuropsychology: Child, 9,* 292–306. https://doi.org/10.1080/21622965.2020.1750118

Kirkwood, M.W. (2015). Review of pediatric performance and symptom validity tests. In M.W. Kirkwood (ed.), *Validity Testing in Child and Adolescent Assessment: Evaluating Exaggeration, Feigning, and Noncredible Effort* (pp. 79–106). New York: Guilford Press.

Kirkwood, M.W., & Kirk, J.W. (2010). The base rate of suboptimal effort in a pediatric mild TBI sample: Performance on the Medical Symptom Validity Test. *The Clinical Neuropsychologist, 24,* 860–872. https://doi.org/10.1080/13854040903527287

Kirkwood, M.W., Peterson, R.L., Connery, A.K., Baker, D.A., & Grubenhoff, J.A. (2014). Postconcussive symptom exaggeration after pediatric mild traumatic brain injury. *Pediatrics, 133,* 643–650. https://doi.10.1542/peds.2013-3195

Krasny-Pacini, A., Chevignard, M., Lancien, S., Escolano, S., Laurent-Vannier, A., De Agostini, M., & Meyer, P. (2017). Executive function after severe childhood traumatic brain injury- age-at-injury vulnerability periods: the TGE prospective longitudinal study. *Annals of Physical and Rehabilitation Medicine, 60,* 74–82. https://doi.org/10.1016/j.rehab.2016.06.001

Lachar, D., & Gruber, C. P. (1995). *Personality Inventory for Youth (PIY) Manual: Technical Guide.* Los Angeles, CA: Western Psychological Services.

Larochette, A.C., & Harrison, A.G. (2012). Word memory test performance in Canadian Adolescents with learning disabilities: A preliminary study. *Applied Neuropsychology: Child, 1,* 38–47. https://doi.org/10.1080/21622965.2012.665777

Loughan, A.R., & Perna, R. (2014). Performance and specificity rates in the Test of Memory Malingering: An investigation into pediatric clinical populations. *Applied Neuropsychology: Child, 3,* 26–30.

MacAllister, W.S., Nakhutina, L., Bender, H.A., Karantzoulis, S., & Carlson, C. (2009). Assessing effort during neuropsychological evaluation with the TOMM in children and adolescents with epilepsy. *Child Neuropsychology, 15,* 521–531.

McCaffrey, R.J., & Lynch, J.K. (2020). Base rates of performance validity test failure among children and young adult litigants with histories of elevated blood lead levels. *Journal of Pediatric Neuropsychology, 6.* https://doi.org/10.1007/s40817-020-00091-6

McCaffrey, R.J., Lynch, J.K., Leark, R.A., & Reynolds, C.R. (2020). *Pediatric Performance Validity Test Suite.* Toronto, Canada: MHS Assessments.

Millon, T., Tringone, R., Grossman, S., & Millon, C. (2020). *Millon Adolescent Clinical Inventory-II (MACI-II).* Bloomington, MN: Pearson Assessments

Moran, L.M., Babikian, T., Del Piero, L., Ellis, M.U., Kernan, C.L., Newman, N., Giza, C.C., Mink, R., Johnson, J., Babbitt, C., & Asarnow, R. (2016). The UCLA study of predictors of cognitive functioning following moderate/severe pediatric traumatic brain injury. *Journal of the International Neuropsychological Society, 22,* 512–519. https://doi:10.1017/S1355617716000175

Morey, L.C. (2007). *Personality Assessment Inventory–Adolescent professional manual.* Lutz, FL: Psychological Assessment Resources.

Naglieri, J.A., Das, J.P., & Goldstein, S. (2014). *Cognitive Assessment System-Second Edition Interpretive and Technical Manual.* Austin, TX: Pro-Ed.

Nayar, K., Ventura, L.M., DeDios-Stern, S., Oh, A., & Soble, J.R. (2022). The impact of learning and memory on performance validity tests in a mixed clinical pediatric population. *Archives of Clinical Neuropsychology, 37,* 50–62. https://doi.org/10/1093/arclin/acab040

Ploetz, D. M., Mazur-Mosiewicz, A., Kirkwood, M.S., Sherman, E.M.S., & Brooks, B.L. (2016). Performance on the test of memory malingering in children with neurological conditions. Child Neuropsychology, *22*, 133–142. https://doi.org/10/1080/09297049.2014.986446

Putzke, J.D., Williams, M.A., Glutting, J.J., Konold, T.R., & Boll, T.J. (2001). Developmental memory performance: Inter-task consistency and base-rate variability on the WRAML. *Journal of Clinical and Experimental Neuropsychology, 23*, 253–264. https://doi:10.1076/jcen.23.3.253.1189

Rey, A. (1964). *The Clinical Examination in Psychology*. Paris, France: Presses Universitaires de France.

Reynolds, C.R., & Kamphaus, R.W. (2015). *Behavior Assessment System for Children–Third Edition manual*. Bloomington, MN: Pearson.

Schneider, H.E., Kirk, J.W., & Mahone, E.M. (2014). Utility of the Test of Memory Malingering (TOMM) in children ages 4–7 with and without ADHD. *The Clinical Neuropsychologist, 28*, 1133–1145. https://doi.org/10/1080/13854046.2014.960004

Schretlen, D. J., Munro, C. A., Anthony, J. C., & Pearlson, G. D. (2003). Examining the range of normal intraindividual variability in neuropsychological test performance. *Journal of the International Neuropsychological Society*, *9*(6), 864–870.

Sequin, M., Gagner, C., Tuerk, C., Lacombe Barrios, J., MacKay, P., & Beauchamp, M.H. (2022). What about the little ones? Systematic review of cognitive and behavioral outcomes following early TBI. *Neuropsychology Review, 32*, 906–936. https://doi.org/10.1007/s11065-021–09517-0

Sherman, Elisabeth M.S., & Brooks, B.L. (2015). *Memory Validity Profile (MVP)*. Lutz, Florida: Psychological Assessment Resources.

Sherman, Elisabeth M.S., & Brooks, B.L. (2015). *Child and Adolescent Memory Profile (ChAMP)*. Lutz, Florida: Psychological Assessment Resources.

Slick, D.J., Hopp, G., Strauss, E., & Thompson, G.B. (1997). *Victoria Symptom Validity Test*. Odessa, FL: Psychological Assessment Resources.

Sweet, J.J., Heilbronner, R.L., Morgan, J.E., Larrabee, G.J., Rohling, M.L., Boone, K.B., Kirkwood, M.W., Schroeder, R.W., Suhr, J.A., & Conference Participants (2021). American Academy of Clinical Neuropsychology (AACN) 2021 consensus statement on validity assessment: Update of the 2009 AACN consensus conference statement on neuropsychological assessment of effort, response bias, and malingering. *The Clinical Neuropsychologist, 35*, 1053–1106. https://doi:10.1080/13854046.2021.1896036

Tombaugh, T.N. (1996). *TOMM: Test of Memory Malingering*. Toronto, Canada: Multi-Health Systems, Inc.

Van Belle, J., van Hulst, B.M., & Durston, S. (2015). Developmental differences in intra-individual variability in children with ADHD and ASD. *Journal of Child Psychology and Psychiatry, 56*, 1316–1326. https://doi:10.111/jcpp12417

Ventura, L.M., DeDios-Stern, S., Oh, A., & Soble, J.R. (2021). They're not just little adults: the utility of adult performance validity measures in a mixed clinical pediatric sample. *Applied Neuropsychology – Child, 10*, 297–307. https://doi.org/10/1080/21622965.2019.1685522

Wilson, K., & Lesica, S. (2021). Performance on the memory validity profile in a mixed clinic-referred pediatric sample. *Child Neuropsychology, 27*, 516–531. https://doi.org/10.1080/09297049.2020.1870676

Zonfrillo, M.R., Haarbauer-Krupa, J., Wang, J., Durbin, D., Jaffe, K.M., Temkin, N., Bell, M., Tulsky, D.S., Bertisch, H., Yeates, K.O., & Rivara, F.P. (2021). Effect of parental education and household poverty on recovery after traumatic brain injury in school-aged children. *Brain Injury, 35*, 1371–1381. https://doi.org/10.1080/02699052.2021.1972141

8 A Case of Severe Traumatic Brain Injury in a Child

Malingering of Neurocognitive Dysfunction or Malingering by Proxy

Elisabeth M. S. Sherman and Brian L. Brooks

The Case of AA

AA was a 13-year-old male plaintiff referred to the examiner by a defense attorney for an independent neuropsychological examination subsequent to a motor vehicle collision at age 7. In all, AA underwent a total of four neuropsychological examinations, as follows:

- An inpatient clinical screening 15 days after the collision conducted by a hospital-based neuropsychologist
- An outpatient clinical neuropsychological evaluation one year after the collision by the same hospital-based neuropsychologist
- An independent neuropsychological assessment two years after the collision by a neuropsychologist retained by the plaintiff attorney (i.e., plaintiff evaluation)
- An independent neuropsychological assessment five years after the collision by a neuropsychologist retained by the defense attorney (i.e., defense evaluation)

AA's parents and two siblings had also been involved in the same collision and were also engaged in litigation. One 23-year-old female sibling was also seen for independent neuropsychological examination (defense evaluation) by the same examiner who evaluated AA.

Background

Pre-Collision Records

There were no relevant pre-existing conditions. Pre-collision medical records, including well-baby visits and yearly examinations with the family doctor indicated only normal intermittent childhood illnesses, such as flu. School records indicated generally average grades with above-average marks in the year prior to the collision (i.e., B+ to A−).

Collision and Injury Details

Emergency Medical Services and hospital records indicate that AA, a seven-year-old Asian-Canadian boy, was an unbelted passenger ejected after a rollover collision at highway speed. AA's father fell asleep at the wheel while driving with AA, AA's mother, and two of AA's older siblings, causing the vehicle to cross the center line and hit an oncoming truck. AA was found unconscious by bystanders approximately 30 m from the vehicle. An attorney representing the other driver's motor vehicle insurance company had retained the

DOI: 10.4324/9781003005063-10

examiner. The insurance company had, in turn, launched a countersuit alleging negligence by the father in causing the child's injuries; the examiner was not involved in this secondary lawsuit. Because AA was a minor and his parents were involved in the lawsuit, an aunt was serving as the child's litigation representative.

Glasgow Coma Scale (GCS) was 3 initially, increasing to 6 at the scene; AA was noted to have a deviated left pupil, left limb weakness, and to be nonverbal and noncombative. He was taken by ambulance to hospital, where he was intubated and sedated and then transferred to a tertiary-care children's hospital by air ambulance. At admission, he had contusions to the chest wall, frontal scalp bruising, abrasions to the forehead, a C1–C2 fracture, pneumothorax, splenic contusion, left femur fracture, and left hip fracture. His parents and older siblings were hospitalized at a nearby adult hospital.

MRI of the brain on the day of injury indicated multifocal intracranial injuries, including diffuse axonal injury of white matter in the frontal lobes, small bilateral frontal cortical non-hemorrhagic contusions, injury to the splenium of the corpus callosum, and a temporal bone fracture.

During hospitalization, records indicate that AA had flat affect, was speaking minimally, was drowsy, and had no memory of the collision. Headaches, dizziness, and orthopedic pain were also reported, as was anxiety due to fear of pain during mobilization and medical care. There was no mention in the hospital records of any problems with depression, anxiety, or posttraumatic stress disorder (PTSD), but problems with pain control associated with orthopedic injuries were documented.

Inpatient Clinical Neuropsychological Evaluation 15 Days Post Collision

AA was first assessed as an inpatient 15 days after injury by a clinical neuropsychologist at a tertiary-care children's hospital. At that time, AA was ambulating by wheelchair and noted to be cooperative, but fatigued. Only a computerized neurocognitive screening test was administered for the CNS Vital Signs test (CNS VS; Gualtieri & Johnson, 2006). On this test, AA demonstrated deficits in sustained attention, processing speed, and executive functioning (1st percentile; see *Test Results* section of this chapter). AA reported that he had headaches, dizziness, sleep issues, and numbness/tingling, but no self-report scales were completed due to his age and fatigue. The neuropsychologist concluded that it was relatively early in the child's recovery and that additional improvement was expected. Academic support, special education coding, and an Individual Education Plan were recommended.

Discharge and Return to School

AA was discharged four weeks after the collision; at that time, he was mobilizing with a walker, but had ongoing leg pain, dizziness, and headache. The parents were instructed to contact the school and arrange for accommodations and academic coding.

School records indicate that AA returned to school shortly after discharge. Initially, there was a mild decrease in marks that improved to pre-collision levels by end of year (i.e., with B+ to A− marks). Despite being recommended in the discharge report, AA received no accommodations on returning to school.

Outpatient Clinical Neuropsychological Evaluation One Year Post Collision

In the year after the collision, AA attended several different clinics including an outpatient pediatric brain injury clinic, an orthopedic clinic, and a physiatry clinic, and he continued to be seen regularly by his family doctor. The outpatient clinic and family doctor records indicated that he was doing well overall, except for increased irritability at home, but not at school. However, the parents declined psychology involvement because they felt that his irritability was mild and not causing impairment in daily life. There continued to be no mention of depression, anxiety, or PTSD symptoms in any of the records; headaches, dizziness, and orthopedic pain continued to be reported. However, no physical therapies or pain medications were sought out by the parents, despite recommendations.

AA was re-assessed by the hospital neuropsychologist one year post collision. The neuropsychologist concluded that there had been remarkable recovery and that cognition had improved such that AA had broadly average or better scores on all tests, except for problems with sustained attention (see *Test Results* section of this chapter). While AA's primary language was English, his parents' first language was Mandarin. Their English-language fluency was sufficient for conversational speech but not for reliable completion of parent questionnaires. In the interview, the father reported AA experiencing a severe decline in cognition and behavior, including marked changes in anger control as a result of the index collision. Self-report questionnaires were entirely within normal limits, including on scales measuring depression, anxiety, social functioning, and physical symptoms.

AA's presentation was felt to be consistent with a diagnosis of Secondary Attention Deficit Hyperactivity Disorder (S-ADHD) caused by severe traumatic brain injury (Max, Schachar, & Ornstein, 2012). Stimulant medication treatment was suggested, but AA's parents did not pursue this. Due to the parental concerns about anger control, AA was referred to a psychologist, but again the parents did not follow through with treatment.

AA was seen intermittently by his family physician who continued to document report of headaches. No cognitive, behavioral, or mental health complaints were noted in any of these visits or in the school records. AA's school marks after this point continued to be generally consistent with his pre-collision grades with marks ranging from good to excellent in core subjects and with no indications of any persisting academic declines or behavior problems at school.

Plaintiff Independent Neuropsychological Evaluation Two Years Post Collision

Two years post collision, AA was assessed by a neuropsychologist at the request of the plaintiff attorney as part of civil litigation to determine the extent of injuries and disability related to the index collision. At that time, AA was nine years old.

AA was administered four performance validity tests, which he passed; he also scored within normal limits across tests measuring IQ, executive functioning, attention, speeded information processing, motor skills, visual and verbal learning and memory, and most aspects of academic achievement skills (see *Test Results* section of this chapter). Teacher questionnaires were all in the normal range, indicating no psychological or behavioral problems. Parent questionnaires were not available due to language barriers, but in the interview, the father again reported severe declines in cognition and behavior, including marked changes in anger control. AA himself reported struggling harder in school to obtain the same marks as he had pre collision and that he continued having headaches.

The plaintiff neuropsychologist concluded that even though AA had scored in the broadly average range, it was possible, given the severity of his brain injury, that his average scores represented a decline compared with his premorbid functioning. He also noted that AA had continued doing quite well in school despite the collision but was reporting struggling more to keep up than he was before the brain injury. Based on the subjective reports of cognitive decline, academic weaknesses, headaches, and anger issues, the plaintiff neuropsychologist concluded that AA had suffered mild cognitive impairment, emotional lability, and academic difficulties as a result of the collision and that these problems were permanent in nature.

Defense Independent Neuropsychological Evaluation Five Years Post Collision

AA continued obtaining the same marks in school, with no reports of anger issues in either the medical or school records. Medical records continued to indicate headache complaints. Approximately five years after the collision, AA, now age 13, was referred by a defense attorney for an independent neuropsychological assessment.

As already noted, AA's parents and siblings were also engaged in litigation at the time of the defense evaluation, with one adult sister, age 22, also assessed by the examiner two days prior to AA. At that time, the older sister was instructed not to share any information with AA about the testing. Subsequently, the assessment of the older sister was found to be invalid based on multiple failed performance validity tests, including chance performance on a forced-choice Performance Validity Test (PVT) (i.e., Victoria Symptom Validity Test [VSVT]) and marked discrepancies between the test scores and records such that she met criteria for Malingering of Neurocognitive Dysfunction (Sherman, Slick, & Iverson, 2020).

The specifics of AA's defense neuropsychological evaluation are shown below.

Behavioral Observations and Interview

AA presented as a reserved, polite, soft-spoken, cooperative, and interpersonally appropriate young boy. He was attentive to questions, a good historian in terms of his medical and school history, and spoke clearly and thoughtfully. AA reported that his main difficulties were headaches, difficulties focusing, moodiness, anger problems, and pain, but he also stated that he was doing relatively well overall despite these problems.

His father and older sister were also interviewed to obtain collateral information; both reported that there had been dramatic declines in AA's cognition and behavior due to the collision, including severe anger problems, moodiness, and irritability. They also specifically stated that AA was under-estimating the degree to which the collision had affected his cognition and behavior.

During the testing, AA was consistently cooperative but at times appeared tired. His attention was generally good but at times, some instructions had to be repeated and he was slow to respond, especially during PVTs. No pain behaviors were observed, and AA tolerated the two days of testing without complaint or need for additional breaks.

Test Results

PVT Results

PVT results for the neuropsychological evaluations are presented in Table 8.1. These indicated valid PVT results until the defense evaluation five years post collision, with AA passing all PVTs in the two prior evaluations conducted closer in time to the collision (i.e., 0% of PVTs failed) but failing 3 of 4 PVTs (i.e., 75% of PVTs failed) in the defense assessment conducted five years after the collision. Non-redundant PVTs validated in children were used with cut-off scores based on acceptable specificity values of 90% as per recommendations for PVT use in malingering determination (Sherman et al., 2020).

Table 8.1 PVT Results across Clinical, Plaintiff, and Defense Evaluations

	One Year Post (*Outpatient Clinical Assessment*)	*Two Years Post* (*Plaintiff Assessment*)	*Five Years Post* (*Defense Assessment*)	Changes Over Time
ChAMP Validity Indicator (VI-SS)	38 (Valid)	40 (Valid)	21 (*INVALID*)	*Invalid only in defense evaluation*
TOMM Trial 1	47 (Valid)	43 (Valid)	30 (*INVALID*)	*Invalid only in defense evaluation*
VSVT Difficult Items	21 (Valid)	20 (Valid)	10 (*INVALID*)	*Invalid only in defense evaluation*
Reliable Digit Span (RDS)	7 (Valid)	7 (Valid)	8 (Valid)	*Consistently valid*
Failure Rate (% of failed PVTs)	0%	0%	75%	

NOTE. ChAMP, Child and Adolescent Memory Profile; TOMM, Test of Memory Malingering; VI-SS, ChAMP Validity Indicator-SS; VSVT, Victoria Symptom Validity Test. The ChAMP-VI-SS is the sum of scaled scores for Lists Recognition, Instructions Recognition, Objects Delayed, and Places Delayed; scores below a cut-off of ≤32 are deemed invalid based on a pediatric TBI sample failing 2 PVTs (Brooks et al., 2023).

More specifically, AA failed the Validity Indicator-SS (VI-SS), an embedded PVT from the Child and Adolescent Memory Profile, a comprehensive pediatric memory battery (ChAMP, Sherman & Brooks, 2015a, b). The ChAMP VI-SS measures exaggeration on verbal and visual memory tests and has been validated for pediatric traumatic brain injury. The ChAMP-VI-SS is the sum of scaled scores for ChAMP Lists Recognition, Instructions Recognition, Objects Delayed, and Places Delayed; scores below a cut-off of ≤32 are deemed invalid based on a pediatric TBI sample failing 2 PVTs (Brooks, Fay-McClymont, MacAllister, Vasserman, Mish, & Sherman, 2023). AA's score of 21 on the ChAMP VI-SS was well below the cut-off for invalidity for pediatric traumatic brain injury patients (Brooks et al., 2023). Other research also supports the utility of individual ChAMP subtests as empirically validated embedded PVTs (Brooks, MacAllister, Fay-McClymont, Vasserman, & Sherman, 2018).

In addition to the VI-SS, AA failed the Test of Memory Malingering (TOMM) and VSVT based on established pediatric cut-offs (Brooks, 2012; Kirkwood, 2015). On the VSVT, AA's score on Difficult items was at chance level, a score found only in 5% or fewer of children with known neurological conditions and, thus, was an implausibly low score (Brooks, 2012).

Symptom Validity Test (SVT) Results

Multiple self-report rating scales were administered across evaluations except for the inpatient screening two weeks post collision. None were indicative of exaggerated self-report, including validity indicators from the MEMRY (Sherman & Brooks, 2017), BRIEF-2 (Gioia, Isquith, Guy, & Kenworthy, 2015), and BASC-3 (Reynolds & Kamphaus, 2015). In total, over a dozen different SVTs were administered across multiple self-report scales and all were in the valid range. The only questionable validity score was on the Revised Children's Manifest Anxiety Scale, 2nd Edition (RCMAS-2, Reynolds & Richmond, 2008)

Table 8.2 Standard Scores for IQ Scores across Time (Percentiles in Parentheses)

WISC-V	*One Year Post*	*Two Years Post*	*Five Years Post*	Changes Over Time
	(Outpatient Clinical Assessment)	*(Plaintiff Assessment)*	*(Defense Assessment)*	
Full-Scale IQ	105 (63rd)	101 (53rd)	98 (45th)	—
Verbal Comprehension Index	104 (61st)	93 (32nd)	100 (50th)	—
Visual-Spatial Index	107 (68th)	111 (77th)	95 (37th)	—
Working Memory Index	-	88 (21st)	80 (9th)	—
Processing Speed Index	112 (79th)	118 (88th)	92 (30th)	*Late-onset decrease*

NOTE. WISC-V: Wechsler Intelligence Scale for Children—Fifth Edition.

administered one year after the collision by the hospital neuropsychologist. This showed defensiveness/denial but no overreporting of symptoms.

Cognitive Testing Results

Full-scale IQ remained relatively stable over time, including in the defense assessment despite failed PVTs (Table 8.2). There were slight decreases in other scores that were likely within measurement error, including a decrease in the Working Memory Index from the 21st to 9th percentile but which were nevertheless suspicious for exaggeration of deficits especially within the context of failed PVTs.

The most striking finding was on the computerized CNS VS test (Gualtieri & Johnson, 2006), a measure of attention, executive functioning, and motor skills, which had been administered 15 days post collision. The severe sustained attention deficits apparent at this inpatient evaluation subsequently resolved by one year post collision, but then *re-appeared* five years later in the defense assessment, along with new deficits in executive functioning and processing speed, with three previously normal scores declining to the first percentile (Table 8.3).

Moreover, the Processing Speed Index (PSI) declined by 26 points from the time of the plaintiff assessment to the defense assessment indicating unexplained new-onset slowness during the defense evaluation (Table 8.2).

Late-onset deficits appearing only in the defense assessment were also apparent on other tests of attention and processing speed and in other cognitive domains such as verbal memory and visual memory (Table 8.4). However, tests of language, visual-spatial skills, and motor skills appeared more impervious to exaggeration with largely normal scores maintained across assessments.

On achievement tests, there were unexplained decreases, including a decreased score for grammar and mechanics in a writing sample, likely the result of producing a more low-quality writing sample compared with prior evaluations, and decreases/plateauing in spelling and math that did not align with the B+ to A− marks on report cards (Table 8.5).

Overall, scores on multiple neuropsychological tests indicated the emergence of new, late-onset "deficits" at the defense assessment five years post collision that had not been present in earlier evaluations, including in a prior plaintiff evaluation.

Table 8.3 Percentiles for Attention, Executive Functioning, and Motor Speed on the CNS VS (Deficits Shown in Italics)

CNS VS	*Two Weeks Post*	*One Year Post*	*Two Years Post*	*Five Years Post*	Changes Over Time
	(Inpatient Clinical Assessment)	*(Outpatient Clinical Assessment)*	*(Plaintiff Assessment)*	*(Defense Assessment)*	
Symbol Digit Coding Correct	81	94	—	84	—
Symbol Digit Coding Errors	55	55	—	*1*	*Late-onset deficit*
Stroop Test Commission Errors	23	34	—	13	—
Stroop Test Complex RT Correct	37	79	—	1	*Late-onset deficit*
Shifting Attention Correct Responses	37	42	—	45	—
Shifting Attention Correct RT	18	55	—	55	—
Continuous Performance Test Correct	*1*	58	—	*1*	*Re-emergence of deficit*
Continuous Performance Test Choice RT	27	63	—	40	—
Finger Tapping Dominant	42	42	16	68	—
Finger Tapping Non-Dominant	32	42	37	75	—

NOTE. CPT, Continuous Performance Test; FTT, Finger Tapping Test; SAT, Shifting Attention Test; SDC, Symbol Digit Coding; RT, Reaction Time; ST, Stroop Test. Late-onset deficits were defined by a broadly normal score on initial assessment followed by a score falling below the 10th percentile on retest.

Table 8.4 Percentiles for Working Memory, Processing Speed, Executive Functioning, Sustained Attention, Language, Visual-Spatial, Memory, and Motor Testing Results (Deficits Shown in Italics)

	One Year Post	*Two Years Post*	*Five Years Post*	Changes Over Time
	(Outpatient Clinical Assessment)	*(Plaintiff Assessment)*	*(Defense Assessment)*	
WISC-V				
Similarities	50	50	63	—
Vocabulary	63	50	50	—
Block Design	63	95	75	—
Matrix Reasoning	63	75	50	—
Digit Span	37	16	16	—
Picture Span	—	37	16	—
Symbol Search	75	91	*5*	*Late-onset deficit*
Coding	75	75	75	—

(*Continued*)

Table 8.4 (Continued)

	One Year Post *(Outpatient Clinical Assessment)*	*Two Years Post* *(Plaintiff Assessment)*	*Five Years Post* *(Defense Assessment)*	Changes Over Time
T.O.V.A.				
Omission Errors	*<1*	69	*<1*	*Re-emergence of deficit*
Commission Errors	32	51	7	*Late-onset deficit*
Response Time	30	52	14	—
Response Time Variability	10	28	*<1*	*Late-onset deficit*
ChAMP Lists				
Immediate	62	84	75	—
Delayed	50	37	25	—
Recognition	69	75	*<1*	*Late-onset deficit*
ChAMP Instructions				
Immediate	50	84	9	Late-onset deficit
Delayed	37	50	9	Late-onset deficit
Recognition	69	75	16	—
ChAMP Objects				
Immediate	43	52	25	—
Delayed Recognition	50	41	37	—
ChAMP Places				
Immediate	62	50	2	*Late-onset deficit*
Delayed	50	52	1	*Late-onset deficit*
NEPSY-II				
Word Generation Semantic	—	25	75	—
Word Generation Letter	—	50	63	—
Auditory Attention Total Correct	—	84	26–50	—
Response Set Total Correct	—	84	26–50	—
Inhibition - Naming, Combined	84	84	16	*Late-onset decrease*
Inhibition - Inhibition, Combined	37	50	2	*Late-onset deficit*
Inhibition - Switching, Combined	9	9	9	*Stable deficit*
WIAT-III				
Listening Comprehension	—	55	5	*Late-onset deficit*

NOTE. ChAMP, Child and Adolescent Memory Profile; NEPSY-II, A Developmental Neuropsychological Assessment–Second Edition; T.O.V.A., Test of Variables of Attention; WIAT-III, Wechsler Individual Achievement Test–Third Edition; WISC-V, Wechsler Intelligence Scale for Children–Fifth Edition. Late-onset deficits were defined by a broadly normal score on initial assessment followed by a score falling below the 10th percentile on retest.

Self-Reported Symptoms on Rating Scales

Self-ratings one year post collision as part of the outpatient clinical evaluation were entirely within normal limits, indicating no self-reported emotional or behavioral problems (Table 8.6). Teacher ratings were unavailable due to the testing occurring during the summer months. In the plaintiff assessment two years post collision, there were again no problems reported on self-ratings, with teacher ratings indicating no emotional or behavioral problems whatsoever on the same scale.

In the defense assessment five years post collision, there were numerous new elevations across self-ratings indicating multiple new problem areas involving cognitive, psychiatric,

Table 8.5 Percentiles for Achievement Testing across Time (Grade Equivalents in Parentheses)

	Two Years Post (Plaintiff Assessment)	Five Years Post (Defense Assessment)	Changes Over Time
WIAT-III			
Reading Comprehension	32 (3.9)	42 (6.7)	—
Oral Reading Fluency	73 (7.1)	58 (9.2)	—
Grammar and Mechanics	68 (6.7)	*4* (3.8)	*Late-onset deficit*
Spelling	91 (10.4)	50 (8.7)	*Late-onset decrease*
Math Problem Solving	50 (5.1)	*7* (4.5)	*Late-onset deficit*
Numerical Operations	45 (5.1)	55 (9.1)	—

NOTE. WIAT-III: Wechsler Individual Achievement Test–Third Edition. Late-onset deficits were defined by a broadly normal score on initial assessment followed by a score falling below the 10th percentile on retest.

Table 8.6 T Scores for Self-Rated Memory and Executive Functioning across Time (MEMRY; BRIEF-2; Clinically Elevated Scores Shown in Italics)

Test	Two Years Post (Plaintiff Assessment) Results	Five Years Post (Defense Assessment) Results	Changes Over Time
Memry Self-Report			
Learning	53	*91*	*Late worsening*
Daily Memory	42	*80*	*Late worsening*
Executive/Working Memory	40	78	*Late worsening*
Everyday Memory Index	48	*88*	*Late worsening*
BRIEF-2 Self-Report			
Behavior Regulation Index	44	49	—
Emotion Regulation Index	52	*64*	*Late worsening*
Cognitive Regulation Index	56	*75*	*Late worsening*
Global Executive Composite	54	*66*	*Late worsening*

NOTE. Changes described as "Late Worsening" denote changes of 1.5 SDs or more not apparent in prior evaluations. BRIEF-2, Behavior Rating Inventory of Executive Function–Second Edition; MEMRY, Multidimensional Everyday Memory Ratings for Youth.

and somatic concerns. Self-report scales measuring cognitive problems indicated severe executive, memory, and attention problems (BRIEF-2, MEMRY, BASC-3; Tables 8.6 and 8.7). There were also marked problems with school functioning, as well as anxiety, depression, and somatization on self-ratings, none of which had been reported in any prior evaluations (BASC-3; Table 8.7). In the defense evaluation, the plaintiff attorney refused to allow teacher ratings and so these were unavailable. However, school records indicated no behavioral problems and no teacher concerns, in contrast to the self-ratings. There was also no evidence of any emotional or behavioral problems in any of the family physician records.

Overall, there was a marked, late reporting of multiple cognitive, psychiatric, and somatic problems on self-ratings that had not been evident in prior evaluations (Table 8.6) and which had not been reported in family doctor records or school records.

Table 8.7 T Scores for Self-Rated Psychological, Somatic, and Behavioral Problems Over Time (Clinically Elevated Scores Shown in Italics)

One Year Post Collision (Outpatient Clinical Assessment)			*Two Years Post*	*Five Years Post*	Changes Exceeding 1.5 SDs
			(Plaintiff Assessment)	*(Defense Assessment)*	
Test	Results	Test	Results	Results	
CDI-2 RCMAS-2 SEARS Peds-QL	All results entirely within normal limits on these scales measuring depression, anxiety, physical symptoms, and social functioning	BASC-3 SELF-REPORT			
		School Problems	43	62	*Late worsening*
		Internalizing Problems	42	*66*	*Late worsening*
		Inattention/ Hyperactivity	39	*65*	*Late worsening*
		Emotional Symptoms Index	45	*70*	*Late worsening*
		Personal Adjustment*	54	30	*Late worsening*
		Attitude to School	41	*71*	*Late worsening*
		Attitude to Teachers	47	62	*Late worsening*
		Sensation Seeking	50	46	—
		Atypicality	39	48	*Late worsening*
		Locus of Control	42	49	—
		Social Stress	42	51	—
		Anxiety	48	*77*	*Late worsening*
		Depression	40	58	*Late worsening*
		Sense of Inadequacy	49	*68*	*Late worsening*
		Somatization	50	*87*	*Late worsening*
		Attention Problems	41	*77*	*Late worsening*
		Hyperactivity	38	51	—
		Relations with Parents*	51	41	—
		Interpersonal Relations*	59	34	*Late worsening*
		Self-Esteem*	58	34	*Late worsening*
		Self-Reliance*	44	29	*Late worsening*

NOTE. Changes described as "Late Worsening" denote changes of 1.5 SDs or more not apparent in prior evaluations. BASC-2, Behavior Assessment System for Children, Second Edition; CDI-2, Children's Depression Inventory 2; Peds-QL, Pediatric Quality of Life Inventory; RCMAS-2, Revised Children's Manifest Anxiety Scale; SEARS, Social Emotional Assets and Resilience Scales.

* High scores on these scales reflect positive adjustment in contrast to the remainder of the scales where elevations indicate clinically significant problems.

Interpretation of Test Results

There were multiple indications of exaggeration in this case indicative of malingering as per updated multidimensional malingering criteria (Sherman, Slick, & Iverson, 2020).

First, there was failure on 3 of 4 PVTs in the defense evaluation, a 75% PVT failure rate using non-redundant, well-validated PVTs with acceptable specificity rates in children with traumatic brain injury. This amply fulfills Criterion 1B of the malingering criteria (i.e., *Invalid Neurocognitive Presentation based on one or more invalid scores on PVTs*).

Second, results of multiple neuropsychological tests indicated the emergence of new, late-onset "deficits" or performance decreases that had not been present in earlier assessments. The most striking was that related to the computerized CNS VS test, which showed initial cognitive deficits two weeks post collision, which had resolved by one year post collision but which re-emerged in the defense assessment along with previously normal scores decreased to the 1st percentile (Table 8.3). As well, deficits in processing speed are one of the most commonly reported cognitive sequelae of severe brain injury in children, yet this examinee had the opposite pattern on serial testing of the PSI (i.e., no deficits early on followed by worsening over time). This is, of course, inconsistent with the nature of severe traumatic brain injury, which is usually associated with a pattern of early deficits followed by resolution or plateauing.

Late-onset "deficits" were also apparent on additional tests of processing speed, attention, executive functioning, verbal memory, and visual memory. However, tests of language, visual-spatial skills, and motor skills appeared relatively impervious to exaggeration of cognitive deficits, indicating that exaggeration occurred within select domains and not across all cognitive domains. This is a common finding in neuropsychological research on exaggeration and why experts recommend, including multiple PVTs to detect exaggeration (e.g., Boone, 2012).

Notably, there was a persistently low score on a test measuring executive inhibition/switching over time (i.e., NEPSY-II, 9th percentile), one potential indication of persisting collision-related cognitive deficit. However, because healthy children tested with lengthy cognitive batteries obtain a small number of low scores (Brooks, 2011; Brooks, Sherman, & Iverson, 2010), this single low score was not sufficient evidence to conclude that there was persisting executive dysfunction as a result of brain injury, although this remained a possibility.

Overall, the late "deficits" exhibited on cognitive tests across time and across multiple cognitive domains in the absence of plausible alternate explanations are incompatible with the natural course of severe traumatic brain injury. There was also no corroborative evidence of cognitive problems in the medical or school records.

The cognitive testing results thus met the following malingering criteria pertaining to *marked discrepancies* (Criterion C, Sherman et al., 2020):

- C1 (i.e., marked discrepancy between the expected natural history of brain injury and the cognitive test scores with evidence of an implausible late-onset worsening over time)
- C2 (i.e., marked discrepancy between the cognitive testing results and the medical and school records)

With regard to self-reported information, there was no evidence of invalid presentation during the evaluation based on either *compelling inconsistencies involving neurocognitive, somatic, or psychiatric presentation* (Criterion B1a, B2a, or B3a) or *invalid scores on SVTs measuring neurocognitive, somatic, or psychiatric symptoms* (Criterion B1c, B2b, or B3b). However, there was a marked, late emergence of multiple cognitive, psychiatric, and somatic concerns on self-ratings in the defense evaluation that had not been evident in prior evaluations (Tables 8.6 and 8.7), which were not reflected in family doctor records or school records and which did not appear to be the result of alternate causes unrelated to the collision, such as unrelated stressors.

The self-ratings thus did not fulfill Criterion B pertaining to invalidity of SVTs but did fulfill Criterion C because of evidence of *Marked Discrepancies*:

- C1 (i.e., marked discrepancy between the expected natural history of brain injury and psychological injury with normal self-ratings closer in time to the collision followed by late, severe self-reported problems involving persisting cognitive, somatic, and psychiatric complaints)
- C2 (i.e., marked discrepancy between self-ratings and the medical and school records)

Table 8.8 Case AA Evidence Supportive of Malingering of Neurocognitive Dysfunction According to the Multidimensional Malingering Criteria

Criterion		*Evidence*
A	*External incentive*	Personal injury litigation
B	*Invalid presentation on examination indicative of feigning or exaggeration*	Met criteria B1a based on failure on 3 out of 4 PVTs
C	*Marked discrepancies*	Met criteria C1 for marked discrepancies between test results and natural history and pathogenesis of the condition in question (i.e., traumatic brain injury and psychological injury) Met criteria C2 for marked discrepancies between cognitive and psychological test results and the medical and school records Criteria C3 was not relevant because the informants in this case were not deemed to be reliable
D	*Not accounted for by another condition*	There were no other relevant exclusionary diagnoses
	Specifiers	*Malingering of Neurocognitive Dysfunction* Met criteria B1a for feigned cognitive deficits but not for other self-reported symptoms and so did not meet criteria for *Malingering of Somatic Symptoms*, *Malingering of Psychiatric Symptoms*, or *Malingering with Mixed Presentation*, although these were strongly suspected

Note. Based on Sherman et al. (2020).

Overall, Case AA thus met criteria for Malingering of Neurocognitive Dysfunction involving exaggeration of neurocognitive deficits as per Tables 8.7 and 8.8.

Summary and Conclusions

As shown clearly in Tables 8.1–8.7, Case AA demonstrated a pattern of implausible, late-onset "deficits" in cognition on neuropsychological tests combined with late-occurring emergence of severe self-reported cognitive, psychiatric, and somatic problems that were inconsistent with both the natural history of brain injury and psychological injury and inconsistent with the medical and school records.

Although there were implausible and late-occurring cognitive, psychiatric, and somatic symptoms on self-reported scales, self-reported symptoms did not meet criteria for malingering due to the absence of compelling inconsistencies observed during the evaluation (Criterion B2a or B3a) or invalid scores *on SVTs* (Criterion B2b or B3b). Instead, the examinee presented as cooperative and appropriate on examination and there were no failed SVTs. There was thus insufficient evidence to support additional specifiers relating to self-reported symptoms such as Malingering of Psychiatric Symptoms, Malingering of Somatic Symptoms, or Malingering with Mixed Presentation although these were strongly suspected. The examiner nevertheless concluded that the self-ratings were implausible, atypical for the conditions in question, unexplained by alternate factors, and that on the balance, the child's presentation more likely than not indicated exaggeration of psychiatric and somatic symptoms in the context of clear Malingering of Neurocognitive Dysfunction.

As already noted, AA's parents and siblings were also engaged in litigation at the time of the defense evaluation, with one adult sister, age 22, also assessed by the examiner two days prior to AA. At that time, the older sister was instructed not to share any information with AA about the testing and agreed to not discuss the testing with AA. Subsequently, the examination of the older sister was found to be invalid, with the same validity tests failed, including a chance-level performance on the VSVT; the sibling thus also met criteria for Malingering of Neurocognitive Dysfunction. Additionally, both the father and sister were interviewed for the defense examination and both reported that there had been dramatic declines in AA's cognition and behavior, but this was discrepant with the records indicating no cognitive, academic, or behavioral problems.

Overall, it is plausible that family members—possibly providing modeling or instructions on malingering—were important factors in explaining how AA exaggerated cognitive deficits in the defense examination but not in earlier examinations. It is also possible that AA became aware of the external incentives that he had not been aware of at a younger age and that he purposefully exaggerated cognitive and psychological deficits during the defense examination at age 13, but not in earlier evaluations when he was younger. Whether this case represents Malingering of Neurocognitive Disorder in a younger adolescent or Malingering by Proxy is discussed as follows.

Discussion

Malingering in Children and Adolescents

At its most basic level, malingering involves deceiving to obtain material gain or to evade unpleasant duties. But can minors really malinger, or should the label of malingering be reserved for adults? Whether children and adolescents are capable of malingering is a complex question. However, parents and adults who work with children such as educators and coaches know that children are quite capable of dissimulation, exaggeration, and outright fabrication. It is also well documented that deception can be knowingly employed for material gain by children starting in the preschool years (e.g., Peterson & Peterson, 2015). The rate of PVT failure in children is also much higher in settings where there are external incentives to exaggerate deficits. For instance, there is a 5% to 10% PVT failure rate in pediatric medical settings where there are minimal external incentives compared with a rate of 30% or higher in pediatric evaluations where there are clear external incentives (Chafetz, 2015; Kirkwood, 2015).

In the updated Sherman et al. (2020) Multidimensional Malingering criteria, the newest revision of the Slick et al. (1999) criteria, external incentives were specifically broadened to include those relevant to children and adolescents such as avoiding school, avoiding examinations or home responsibilities, avoiding being returned to an abusive situation, obtaining school accommodations to improve marks on standardized examinations (e.g., to gain access to better colleges), and obtaining stimulants for ADHD, drugs that can be sold for profit by adolescents or used for recreational purposes. In some of these cases, parents and other authority figures may be unaware that the young examinee is engaging in deception.

The Sherman et al. (2020) malingering criteria do not exclude malingering based on age but specify that Malingering by Proxy is a designation needing further study. Malingering by Proxy occurs when there are compelling grounds to believe that the examinee acted primarily under the guidance, direction, influence, or control of another individual, such as a parent or other authority figure encouraging, coercing, or training the vulnerable examinee to exaggerate deficits in order to obtain external rewards. The Malingering by Proxy specifier applies to the adult influencing the vulnerable examinee, not to the examinee.

In the medical literature, Malingering by Proxy typically refers to exaggerated reports of physical symptoms, not the exaggeration of cognitive deficits, although this occurs in some conditions (e.g., coercion of a child to fake non-epileptic seizures to receive child disability benefits). Malingering by Proxy during neuropsychological evaluations has been documented in Social Services disability eligibility evaluations and neuropsychological evaluations of child litigants but remains generally understudied (Chafetz, 2008; Chafetz & Dufrene, 2014; Chafetz & Prentkowski, 2011; Lu & Boone, 2002).

Case Studies of Malingering in Pediatric Personal Injury Litigants

Compared with research on adults, there exist very few studies of malingering in pediatric personal injury litigants as defined by established criteria, with most studies involving case reports. Most of these described cases of mild traumatic brain injury and not more severe forms of traumatic brain injury. In these reports, the cases are generally described as instances of Malingering by Proxy whether the child was actively participating by exaggerating deficits or responding validly with the parents actively engaged in exaggerating information.

One of the earliest such case reports is the case described by Lu and Boone (2002; see also Flaro & Boone, 2009) involving a nine-year-old boy struck by a vehicle who was seen for an independent neuropsychological evaluation. The child had a GCS of 11, no loss of consciousness, and brain imaging indicated subarachnoid hemorrhage and right frontal lobe contusion; the child produced a below-chance performance on a PVT, the Warrington Recognition Memory Test, along with implausibly low scores on other cognitive tests. The mother reported that the child had strong pre-collision academics and behavior that was deemed untruthful; in addition, the plaintiff attorney was the boy's stepfather and thus in a position to influence the child but kept this from the opposing counsel. The case was described as a probable case of Malingering by Proxy.

Henry (2005) described an eight-year-old seen in the context of personal injury litigation who had a GCS of 14, loss of consciousness of less than one minute, and brain imaging indicating a skull fracture but no intracranial injury; this child produced below-chance scores on two PVTs (i.e., TOMM and CARB). The father reported severe symptoms that were discrepant with other information, including the child's self-report. Whether this was a case of Malingering and/or of Malingering by Proxy was not explicitly stated in the case report.

McCaffrey and Lynch (2009) describe the case of a 13-year-old girl in a high-speed collision who had a GCS of 13, depressed skull fracture, right temporal contusion, and right frontal epidural hematoma on imaging. This child failed two standalone PVTs and performed implausibly low on memory tests (i.e., <1st percentile despite no memory deficits in daily life); her mother also provided incorrect reporting of premorbid academic and behavioral history. The authors concluded that this was a case of Malingering by Proxy.

Baron (2018) described the case of a ten-year-old child who sustained a moderate traumatic brain injury although no information was provided on length of loss of consciousness, GCS, or brain imaging to verify brain injury severity. In the independent neuropsychological evaluation, the child had multiple behaviors suggestive of noncredible performance and performed below cut-offs on the TOMM, even though he had done well on this PVT in a prior evaluation. When questioned by the examiner, the child confessed to having been instructed by his mother to deliberately make mistakes during the evaluation. The case was described as an example of Malingering by Proxy.

Overall, of these published personal injury cases involving pediatric brain injury, most involved *complicated* mild traumatic brain injuries based on GCS and imaging and not more severe injuries, with one case involving moderate traumatic brain injury but with no GCS or imaging reported. Most cases involved both the child and the parent engaging in exaggeration based on failed PVTs or implausible symptom reporting and were conceptualized as cases of Malingering by Proxy. Almost all cases involved evidence that the parent either failed to disclose pre-existing conditions or provided exaggerated and implausible reports of post-collision cognitive and behavioral deficits discrepant with records, particularly school records, and in one case, evidence that the plaintiff attorney himself was in a parenting role and thus in a position to directly influence the child. In one case, there was definite evidence of parental influence because the child confessed to being told by the parent to malinger; in the other cases, parental influence and coercion was presumably assumed but not confirmed by confession. Outright confession is typically uncommon in most evaluations where malingering occurs.

Severe Traumatic Brain Injury and Pediatric Malingering

The prevalence of malingering in children with severe traumatic brain injuries has not been well studied but is estimated to be very low. For example, in a hospital sample of 110 children with traumatic brain injuries of varying severity, 13% failed two PVTs; of these, 93% were mild traumatic brain injury cases, and only a single child with a traumatic brain injury described as moderate to severe failed two PVTs (Brooks et al., 2023).

Case AA is of interest for several reasons, including that it was a case of malingering co-occurring with verified severe traumatic brain injury, it was an instance of malingering in a minor, and it involved elements of Malingering by Proxy with an adult sibling possibly serving as a model of how to exaggerate on cognitive tests and self-reported tests and with a parent providing incorrect information about the child's symptoms.

This case demonstrates how severe traumatic brain injury itself is not a rule-out for malingering. The Sherman et al. (2020) criteria clearly state that malingering can co-occur with neurological, medical, and psychiatric conditions, with exclusions specifically consisting of moderate to severe intellectual disability (e.g., IQ < 60), moderate to severe dementia, and severe psychiatric, neurological, or other medical disorders with cognitive impairment sufficient to preclude independence in basic activities of daily living. In this case, malingering co-occurred with a severe traumatic brain injury that was not associated with major IQ losses or loss of independence in daily activities, consistent with malingering criteria.

Conclusions and Caveats

This case brings up several issues important to consider in conducting independent neuropsychological evaluations of children and adolescents.

First, differentiating child malingering from Malingering by Proxy involves a careful review of evidence due to the different ways in which deception can manifest in neuropsychological assessment involving children and parents. Three scenarios illustrate the complexity inherent in identifying deception in child evaluations. In the first, the parent originates the plan to deceive and carries the plan out independently, and the child is unaware; the parent deliberately exaggerates by providing a falsified history in the interview and exaggerates symptoms on parent rating scales. If the child is not colluding and provides valid cognitive and self-report data, this represents a clear case of Malingering by Proxy. In such cases, examiners may notice the child withdrawing, appearing surprised, or disputing the parent's assertions of deficits; the parent may also specifically inform the examiner in private that the child's reporting is faulty to support the view that the child is impaired.

A second scenario involves a parent instructing a child to malinger, but with both the child and parent providing a falsified history and invalid SVTs, with the child also failing PVTs or having implausible deficits on testing. In this case, both Malingering by the Child and Malingering by Proxy by the parent could be considered, with the Malingering by Proxy determination likely taking precedence due to the child being a minor and thus in a position of being influenced.

In a third scenario, the child acts alone to obtain an external reward, such as feigning deficits to avoid returning to school after a mild traumatic brain injury, by failing PVTs and exaggerating problems on standardized questionnaires, with the parent unaware of the deceptive behavior. This would represent malingering in a child and not Malingering by Proxy. Although this latter scenario was not directly relevant to Case AA, it is nevertheless important to look carefully for external incentives that matter to children in cases of PVT or SVT failure during neuropsychological evaluation. This may help identify children who are employing malingering behaviors to avoid common child responsibilities such as school, or rarer but much more severe situations involving avoiding abuse which require comprehensive and prompt intervention.

The nomenclature for these different scenarios still needs to be further elucidated, but examiners should be aware that pediatric independent evaluations involve more complexities than does the typical adult evaluation. Whether children and adolescents can fully appreciate the implications of malingering during personal injury litigation is debatable, but in this case, a 13-year-old was likely aware that exaggerating deficits could yield a larger settlement for himself and his family, which he had not been aware of at a younger age. On the balance, this was most likely a case of Malingering by Proxy that also likely involved malingering by the child.

The lack of sensitivity of the pediatric SVTs in this case should also be noted. Although there are very few studies on this question, one study found that among children with traumatic brain injury who failed PVTs, only 6% failed SVTs (Kirk, Hutaff-Lee, Connery, Baker, & Kirkwood, 2014). Unlike SVTs for adults, very few pediatric SVTs have been developed specifically to detect exaggeration in personal injury litigants, which may limit their sensitivity to exaggeration in independent neuropsychological evaluations. It may also be the case that children are less likely to exaggerate on rating scales than are adults, but more work in refining pediatric SVTs and more research in pediatric populations where external incentives may influence self-report and informant reports are needed.

In sum, although rare in practice, pediatric malingering and Malingering by Proxy in children who have sustained bona fide severe traumatic brain injuries do occur and can be identified based on the Sherman et al. (2020) criteria.

Available Online Resources/E-Links

Multidimensional Malingering criteria (Sherman et al., 2020):
https://academic.oup.com/acn/article/35/6/735/5830790?login=false

References

Baron, I. S. (2018). *Neuropsychological Evaluation of the Child* (Second Edition). New York: Oxford University Press.

Boone, K. B. (2012). *Clinical Practice of Forensic Neuropsychology: An Evidence-Based Approach*. New York: Guilford Press.

Brooks, B. L. (2011). A study of low scores in Canadian children and adolescents on the Wechsler Intelligence Scale for Children (WISC-IV). *Child Neuropsychology*, 17(3), 281–289. https://doi.org/10.1080/09297049.2010.537255

Brooks, B. L. (2012). Victoria Symptom Validity Test performance in children and adolescents with neurological disorders. *Archives of Clinical Neuropsychology*, 27(8), 858–868. https://doi.org/10.1093/arclin/acs087

Brooks, B. L., Fay-McClymont, T. B., MacAllister, W. S., Vasserman, M., Mish, S., & Sherman E. M. S. (2023). New Child and Adolescent Memory Profile embedded performance validity test. *Archives of Clinical Neuropsychology*. Jan 6:acac110. https://doi.org/10.1093/arclin/acac110. Online ahead of print.

Brooks, B. L., MacAllister, W. S., Fay-McClymont, T. B., Vasserman, M., & Sherman, E. M. (2018). Derivation of new embedded performance validity indicators for the child and adolescent memory profile (ChAMP) objects subtest in youth with mild traumatic brain injury. *Archives of Clinical Neuropsychology*, *34*(4), 531–538.

Brooks, B. L., MacAllister, W. S., Fay-McClymont, T. B., Vasserman, M., & Sherman, E. M. S. (2019). Derivation of new embedded performance validity indicators for the Child and Adolescent Memory Profile (ChAMP) Objects subtest in youth with traumatic brain injury. *Archives of Clinical Neuropsychology*, 34(4), 531–538.

Brooks, B. L., Sherman, E. M. S., & Iverson, G. L. (2010). Healthy children get low scores too: Prevalence of low scores on the NEPSY-II in preschoolers, children, and adolescents. *Archives of Clinical Neuropsychology*, 25(3), 182–190. https://doi.org/10.1093/arclin/acq005

Chafetz, M. D. (2008). Malingering on the social security disability consultative exam: Predictors and base rates. *The Clinical Neuropsychologist*, 22, 529–546.

Chafetz, M. D. (2015). Disability: Social Security Supplemental Security Income exams for children. In M. Kirkwood (Ed.), *Validity Testing in the Assessment of Children and Adolescents* (pp. 273–290). Guilford: New York.

Chafetz, M., & Dufrene, M. (2014). Malingering-by-proxy: Need for child protection and guidance for reporting. *Child Abuse & Neglect*, 38(11), 1755–1765. https://doi.org/10.1016/j.chiabu.2014.08.015

Chafetz, M., & Prentkowski, E. (2011). A case of malingering by proxy in a Social Security disability psychological consultative examination. *Applied Neuropsychology*, 18(2), 143–149. https://doi.org/10.1080/09084282.2011.570619

Flaro, L., & Boone, K. (2009). Using objective effort measures to detect noncredible cognitive test performance in children and adolescents. In *Neuropsychology of Malingering Casebook* (pp. 387–394). Psychology Press. In J. E. Morgan & J. J. Sweet (Eds.), *Neuropsychology of Malingering Casebook* (pp. 377–385). New York: : Psychology Press.

Gioia, G. A., Isquith, P. K., Guy, S. C., & Kenworthy, L. (2015). *Behavior Rating Inventory of Executive Function* (Second Edition) Lutz, FL: PAR Inc.

Gualtieri, C. T., & Johnson, L. G. (2006). Reliability and validity of a computerized neurocognitive test battery, CNS Vital Signs. *Archives of Clinical Neuropsychology*, 21(7), 623–643.

Henry. G.K. (2005). Childhood malingering: Faking neuropsychological impairment in an 8-year-old. In R. L. Heilbronner (Ed.), *Forensic Neuropsychology Casebook* (pp. 205–217). *Neuropsychology*, 18(2), 143–149. https://doi.org/10.1080/09084282.2011.570619

Kirk, J. W., Hutaff-Lee, C. F., Connery, A. K., Baker, D. A., & Kirkwood, M. W. (2014). The relationship between the self-report BASC-2 validity indicators and performance validity test failure after pediatric mild traumatic brain injury. *Assessment*, 21(5), 562–569. https://doi.org/10.1177/1073191114520626

Kirkwood, M. W. (2015). *Validity Testing in Child and Adolescent Assessment: Evaluating Exaggeration, Feigning, and Noncredible Effort*. New York: Guilford.

Lu, P. H., & Boone, K. B. (2002). Suspect cognitive symptoms in a 9-year-old child: Malingering by proxy? *The Clinical Neuropsychologist*, 16(1), 90–96. https://doi.org/10.1076/clin.16.1.90.8328

Max, J. E., Schachar, R. J., & Ornstein, T. J. (2012). Preinjury and Secondary Attention Deficit/Hyperactivity disorder in pediatric traumatic brain injury forensic cases. In E. M. S. Sherman & B. L. Brooks (Eds.), *Pediatric Forensic Neuropsychology* (pp. 258–274). New York: Oxford University Press.

McCaffrey, R. J., & Lynch, J. K. (2009). Malingering following documented brain injury: Neuropsychological evaluation of children in a forensic setting. In J. E. Morgan & J. J. Sweet (Eds.), *Neuropsychology of Malingering Casebook* (pp. 377–385). New York: Psychology Press.

Peterson, E. R. I. C., & Peterson, R. L. (2015). Understanding deception from a developmental perspective. *Validity testing in child and adolescent assessment*, 42–61.

Reynolds, C. R., & Kamphaus, R. W. (2015). *Behavior Assessment System for Children–Third Edition*. Bloomington, MN: Pearson.

Reynolds, C. R., & Richmond, B. O. (2008). *Revised Children's Manifest Anxiety Scale–Second Ddition*. Los Angeles, CA: Western Psychological Services.

Sherman, E. M. S., & Brooks, B. L. (2015a). *Child and Adolescent Memory Profile*. Lutz, FL: Psychological Assessment Resources, Inc.

Sherman, E. M. S., & Brooks, B. L. (2015b). *Memory Validity Profile*. Lutz, FL: Psychological Assessment Resources, Inc.

Sherman, E. M. S., & Brooks, B. L. (2017). *Multidimensional Everyday Memory Ratings for Youth*. Lutz, FL: Psychological Assessment Resources, Inc.

Sherman, E. M. S., Slick, D. J., & Iverson, G. I. (2020). Multidimensional malingering criteria for neuropsychological assessment: A twenty-year update of the Malingered Neurocognitive Dysfunction criteria. *Archives of Clinical Neuropsychology*, 35(6), 735–764. https://doi.org/10.1093/arclin/acaa019

Slick, D. J., Sherman, E., & Iverson, G. (1999). Diagnostic criteria for malingered neurocognitive dysfunction: Proposed standards for clinical practice and research. *Clinical Neuropsychologist*, 13, 545–561.

9 Sport-Related Concussion and Chronic Traumatic Encephalopathy in Elite Athletes

William B. Barr

Introduction

The topic of sport-related concussion (SRC) has generated much controversy over the past 30 years. This has resulted in the publication of many guidelines and recommended practices for ensuring the care of athletes who are actively engaged in contact sports, including football, ice hockey, and soccer at both amateur and professional levels (Patricios et al., 2023). Much attention has focused on the diagnosis and management of acute concussions in elite athletes and the potential long-term effects of contact sports and the development of chronic traumatic encephalopathy (CTE), a neuropathological condition alleged to develop in retired athletes from chronic exposure to repetitive head injuries (RHIs) sustained over the course of an extended sports career (McKee et al., 2009). As a result, neuropsychologists are now evaluating an increasing number of retired athletes in routine clinical care and in the context of various class-action lawsuits and other legal cases against professional sports leagues and other athletic associations. It is important for neuropsychologists to understand the various medical, psychological, and other factors that can influence neuropsychological test performance in this population. In this chapter, we present the cases of two retired elite American football players who have been involved respectively in litigation against the National Football League (NFL) and the National Collegiate Athletic Association (NCAA).

Case Number One – Clinical History[1]

AW is a 32-year-old right-handed Black, Non-Hispanic male who played linebacker in the NFL for eight years. He completed this neuropsychological evaluation in the context of a long-term disability work-up for an alleged career-ending concussion sustained three years earlier. According to his report, he experienced a brief loss of consciousness (one to two seconds), headache, and confusion in a professional football game after he was knocked down by an opponent blocker on a pass play over the middle and struck his head on the ground. He was taken off the field, evaluated by team medical staff, and did not return to play. The injury occurred in the team's final game of the season. He reported continuing headache, light-sensitivity, and mood changes over the next several days. He underwent arthroscopic surgery on the left knee two weeks later. There were continuing reports of headache, light-sensitivity, and frustration over subsequent weeks while undergoing rehabilitation treatments for the knee. He claimed that the headache and other symptoms disrupted his rehabilitation and preparation for the next season. He was eventually cut from the team and his career ended as his contract was not picked up by any other organization.

DOI: 10.4324/9781003005063-11

At the time of this evaluation, AW was reporting continuing headaches, occurring once or twice weekly. He claimed that he had become frustrated about not being able to perform prior activities. He also described the onset of difficulties with memory and problem solving after the concussion. He stated that he had attempted to work as a financial analyst at a major investment firm one year after he stopped playing football but was laid off from the job due to conflicts with his supervisor and other employees. He stated that he had developed mood swings and worsening cognitive difficulties, which had reportedly prevented him from obtaining other jobs. He was living in a home with his wife of eight years and three children, spending his time working out at gyms, engaging in volunteer coaching activities, and monitoring personal investments. He stated that his wife had recommended that he try to calm down as he had apparently exhibited increasing irritability toward others in the home. He reported that he was not actively engaged in any treatment with a psychiatrist or any other mental health professional. He was not taking any prescription medications. He was unaware of any family history of mental health or neurological conditions.

The claimant was born and raised in the southeastern United States in a home with his mother, two brothers, and a sister. Both parents were born in the United States and English was the only language spoken in the home. He reported that his father passed away when he was young and had worked as a skilled laborer. His mother worked as an office administrator for a local business. Both parents had attained 12 years of formal education. He stated that he was unaware of any complications with his birth or early development. He described a "normal" childhood. He characterized himself as an active kid who excelled in sports from an early age. He indicated that there had been some mild difficulties with attention in school. However, he was considered a "solid" student and there was no formal diagnosis of any learning disability or attention deficit hyperactivity disorder. He graduated from a public high school and completed three years of college, majoring in business administration with a reported 3.1 grade point average. He did not return to complete his undergraduate degree.

He played football, basketball, and ran track while in high school. He started playing tackle football in a youth league at the age of 8. He played tight end and linebacker for his high-school football team and became a starter in his sophomore year. He received attention from college recruiters during his junior year and eventually accepted an athletic scholarship to play at the Division I level for a team in the Southeastern Conference. He played three years of collegiate football as a starting linebacker. He was named to the all-conference team as a junior and was chosen in the third round of the NFL draft. He played in a total of 114 games as a linebacker for three teams over an eight-year professional NFL career. He continues to believe that his career was cut short due to the concussion sustained in the last game of his final season.

In terms of his medical history, AW had reportedly maintained excellent health as a youth in the context of his continuing sports activities. He reported that he drank alcohol and smoked marijuana on occasion but denied any history of excessive substance use. While there were no physical injuries in high school, he had experienced some ongoing discomfort in his left knee in college which never required surgery. He missed two games during his freshman year due to a shoulder separation. He described two "minor" concussions when he was in high school causing him to sit out one game. There was a more significant concussion in college which caused him to miss one game during his sophomore year. He reported three concussions during his tenure in the NFL preceding the fourth "career-ending" concussion. He disclosed that he was entered into the NFL concussion protocol for two of those injuries, missing a total of three games.

The claimant had hired an attorney within months of being laid off from his job as a financial analyst due to concerns about continuing effects of the reported concussion. Claims of disability had been made outside of the NFL Class Action Settlement. He was sent to a neurologist who concluded that he was disabled due to symptoms of post-concussion syndrome causally related to the injury sustained in his final game. He received a series of brain MRI studies. No abnormality was detected on standard T2-FLAIR sequences. DTI results reportedly showed abnormalities considered, "most compatible with the effects of TBI". He had completed neuropsychological testing in another office six-months prior to this evaluation. The report listed deficits in processing speed and memory representing continuing effects of concussion. The test battery did not include any performance validity tests (PVTs). There were observations of some dysphoria attributed to ongoing concussion effects, although there was no formal assessment of symptoms through self-report inventories. He was diagnosed with Mild Neurocognitive Disorder due to cognitive and behavioral effects of RHI obtained through his professional football career and as a result of more specific effects of the most recent concussion.

Case Number Two – Clinical History

GB is a 64-year-old White, Non-Hispanic male who played the position of defensive lineman in the NFL for four years. He was referred for a comprehensive neuropsychological assessment in the context of an active lawsuit against the NCAA. According to his attorneys, he had developed symptoms of dementia approximately ten years earlier, characterized by personality changes and an accelerating pattern of cognitive decline. He had reportedly misfiled papers to become eligible for compensation through the NFL Settlement. He was taking legal action against the NCAA for allegedly failing to warn him of the inherent risks of playing collegiate football and the likelihood of developing neurocognitive disorder as a direct result of repetitive head impacts sustained during his four-year career as a college football player.

At the time of this evaluation, GB's wife reported that her husband had exhibited a rather sudden and unexpected change in behavior approximately ten years ago. At that time, he became uncharacteristically irritable and made some bad business decisions as the owner of some rental properties. She also noted that he had become more careless in his grooming with a tendency to wear dirty clothes and skip showers at times. She described an increasingly frequent tendency for him to forget things when he went to the store. He started to misplace items within the home, such as his keys, wallet, and sunglasses. He had also developed a new tendency to blow up at the smallest inconveniences.

GB reported that he was really unsure why he was undergoing this evaluation. He stated that all he knew was that a lawyer had told him to come to the appointment. He was living with his wife at that time in a private home in Southern California. He had worked in banking for many years after football and had transitioned from that line of work to focus more on maintaining investments and properties over the past 20 years. He continued to drive and monitor the sites of his rental properties. He was able to remain unsupervised and prepare meals for himself when his wife was out of the home.

The plaintiff was born and raised in the Central Valley region of California in a home with his mother, father, and three siblings. Both parents were born in the United States and English was the only language spoken in the home. His father had attained a bachelor's degree and worked as a bank manager. His mother had completed two years of college and worked in the home. GB stated that he had a great childhood and got along well with other kids in the neighborhood. He described himself as an average student with no history of any learning or attention issues. While he played baseball and other sports as a child, he did not play organized football until the 9th Grade when he joined his high school's freshman football team. He had been recruited for the team by coaches due to having grown to a height of 6'3" and weight of 240-lbs. He made the varsity team as a sophomore and was named to the all-state team as a defensive tackle during his senior year. He received a "full-ride" athletic scholarship to attend a Pacific 10 Conference (Pac-10) school and graduated from that institution after four years with a 2.7 grade point average. He was drafted by an NFL team in the 6th round after his senior year. He was on that team's reserve squad for most of his four years in the league, playing in a total of six NFL games. He was cut from the team during training camp in his fifth year, which served as the end of his professional football career.

There was no history of any major medical conditions during childhood. At the time of this evaluation, GB weighed 320-lbs and had over the past 20 years received medical diagnoses of diabetes, hypertension, hypercholesterolemia, and obstructive sleep apnea. He was prescribed medications for treatment of those conditions and was using a CPAP machine "on and off" when he slept. He had sustained an ankle injury during college, which caused him to miss three games during his junior year. He had developed arthritic conditions in other joints which were reported to be actively affecting his gait and balance. He denied any history of concussion from sports or other activities. He stated that there had been many times when he had been "dinged" or saw stars as a college player and in the NFL but was sent back in to play afterward because, as he explained, that is how things were back in those days. He reported that he had never received any form of psychological or psychiatric treatment. There was no reported family history of mental health or neurological conditions, including dementia.

After developing the reported behavioral and cognitive changes, GB saw a local neurologist who diagnosed him as having CTE due to his complaints in the context of the football career and the lack of any family history of Alzheimer's disease. His lawyer sent him to medical specialists who concluded that he was exhibiting symptoms of CTE due to his playing days in college, since that is where he reportedly sustained the greatest number of "untreated" cumulative head impacts. An MRI of the brain reportedly showed increased T2 signal in periventricular and white matter regions, which were interpreted as representing effects of brain trauma, but instead would be consistent with, and expected for, his older age and vascular health issues (diabetes, hypertension, and hypercholesterolemia).

On his lawyer's request, GB completed another neuropsychological evaluation two years prior to this exam. He was reported to have obtained a FSIQ score of 58 on the WAIS-IV at that time with index scores falling within a similarly low range. Comparably low scores were reported on WMS-IV indices and on nearly all other tests that were administered during that exam. Scores on the TOMM and a number of embedded PVTs were reported to have fallen below standard cutoffs. Results of those measures were considered uninterpretable due to the presence of dementia. GB completed the MMPI-2-RF with VRIN and TRIN scores falling below a T-score level of 65. Scores on other scales (F-r, FBS-r, RBS) exceeding T = 65 were considered to represent effects of confusion rather than symptom magnification.

Sport-Related Concussion (SRC) and Chronic Traumatic Encephalopathy (CTE)

When conducting neuropsychological evaluations of head-injury claims in elite athletes, it is important to distinguish between what are alleged to be persisting effects of a discrete

SRC as opposed to longer-term effects allegedly due to cumulative effects of repetitive head impact (RHI) exposure over the course of the athlete's amateur and professional career. Increased public attention to SRC developed in the 1990s after a number of high-profile professional athletes were either withheld from competition or were forced to retire after sustaining a highly visible SRC. After some initial controversy about management of acute effects of SRC, the NFL and other professional sports leagues developed specific protocols for assessment and treatment of SRC (Pieroth & Hanks, 2014). Neuropsychologists have played a significant role in the development of these protocols (Lovell & Barr, 2004).

Similar to concussions sustained in non-athletes, SRC is conceptualized from a scientific perspective as a functional disturbance of the brain caused by a variety of physiological factors (Giza & Hovda, 2014). While there have been recent advances in the development of imaging and blood-based biomarkers, the diagnosis of SRC continues to be made on a clinical basis, incorporating history-taking and evaluation of signs and symptoms (Barr, 2014, 2023). Results from large prospective studies indicate that symptoms of SRC resolve in most athletes within a period of three to four weeks (Broglio et al., 2022). Similar to injuries sustained outside of the sport setting, athletes with complaints extending well beyond that time frame are considered to have persisting symptoms after concussion (PSAC), a term that has been offered as an alternative to the controversial post-concussion syndrome (Broshek et al., 2022).

In contrast to the effects of a single SRC in active players, some retired athletes have been reported to develop CTE, a neuropathologically defined entity characterized by a unique pattern of hyperphosphorylated tau (p-tau) deposition in neurons and astroglia distributed around small blood vessels and in the depths of the cortical sulci (McKee, 2020). CTE is alleged to be a result of long-term exposure to RHI acquired through participation in collision sports and in other contexts. The exact mechanism responsible for the tau deposition and its clinical relevance remain undetermined as are the prevalence and risk factors for CTE and evidence that its clinical symptoms undergo a progressive decline (Barr & Karantzoulis, 2019; Fortington et al., 2025; Iverson et al., 2015; Iverson & Gardner, 2021). Despite a plethora of published studies, advances in CTE research remain limited by the fact that there is no accepted definition for what constitutes a specific "subconcussive" blow to the head or any means of determining how that blow differs from one that causes a discrete TBI (Belanger et al., 2016; Manley et al., 2017). As a result, attempts to quantify RHI have, to date, been limited to gross time estimates of head-injury exposure established retrospectively by summing up the total years of football competition (Stamm et al., 2015).

It is important for clinicians to remember that CTE is a neuropathological diagnosis that can only be made on a post-mortem basis. Traumatic Encephalopathy Syndrome (TES) is the term that has been developed to define the clinical syndrome associated with CTE (Montenigro et al., 2014). Controversies regarding CTE and TES have arisen due to the neuropathological and clinical overlap with many common clinical conditions, including depression, Alzheimer's disease, and other neurodegenerative disorders (Iverson & Gardner, 2021; Schaffert et al., 2021). Active and former athletes undergoing evaluations for cumulative effects of RHI need to be evaluated for the presence of TES while ruling out the presence of other possible conditions causing disturbances in cognition and behavior, including mood disorders and neurovascular effects of chronic medical conditions, including diabetes, hypertension, and high cholesterol (Grashow et al., 2020).

The challenge up until recently has been the lack of established clinical criteria to define TES. Recently developed NINDS Consensus Criteria for TES diagnosis define required RHI exposure levels, core clinical features (e.g., cognitive impairment and neurobehavioral dysregulation), and a progressive course with features that are not fully accounted for by other neurologic, psychiatric, or medical conditions (Katz et al., 2021). However, it is important to remember that these consensus-based criteria have been developed to guide clinical and epidemiologic research and are not intended to be utilized in making a clinical diagnosis.

There are a number of published studies on neuropsychological test performance in active and retired NFL players. Initial studies focused on standardization and use of an abbreviated battery of standard paper–pencil tests which had been administered to active players at preseason baseline and within 24-hours of a concussion (Lovell & Barr, 2004; Solomon et al., 2015). Included in a series of controversial articles published in *Neurosurgery* in the 2000s, there was a report that NFL players showed no test evidence of neurocognitive impairment more than seven days following a concussion (Pellman et al., 2004). Subsequent focus was placed on the use of a computerized neurocognitive battery (ImPACT) for assessment and management of concussion symptoms in NFL players (Solomon & Haase, 2008). Research has shown that the majority of players exhibit a full recovery from concussions sustained in NFL games with a median return time of nine days following injury (Mack et al., 2022). While there is an estimated 20%–30% rate of persisting post-concussion symptoms in general athlete samples (Makdissi et al., 2017), the rate observed in NFL players remains unreported.

A relatively larger number of studies have been published on neuropsychological test performance in retired NFL players. Some have reported mild impairments in verbal memory, confrontation naming, and executive functions in NFL players although the effect sizes have been small and many of the studies have lacked appropriate controls (Schaffert et al., 2020). Reports of a positive relationship between head-injury exposure and neurocognitive impairment have been used as evidence supporting the development of cognitive changes due to CTE (Stamm et al., 2015). However, the majority of studies have not found a relationship between years of exposure and neuropsychological performance in NFL players and other athlete samples (Iverson et al., 2021). Based on the existing evidence, some have suggested that cognitive changes in NFL players resemble mild cognitive impairment as it is seen in non-athlete samples (Randolph et al., 2013). As with non-athlete samples, there is current interest in examining how health and lifestyle factors contribute to neuropsychological performance in retired NFL players independent of any hypothesized relationship to CTE (Grashow et al., 2020; Walton et al., 2025).

Performance Validity and Symptom Validity Testing in Elite Athletes

Much of our scientific knowledge on the development and use of PVTs has been obtained through studies of personal injury litigants alleging effects of mild traumatic brain injury. Based on data converging from various sources, one can expect an estimated 40% PVT failure rate in settings where test takers have the potential to obtain a (financial) secondary gain (Larrabee et al., 2009). Most published studies of PVT use in athletic settings have focused on failure rates in athletes undergoing preseason baseline testing. The term "sandbagging" has been used to describe a phenomenon where athletes underperform on neuropsychological tests with the goal of evading detection of a SRC later in the season (Schatz & Glatts, 2013). Failure rates of PVTs on baseline testing have been estimated as high as 20%–30% in some high-school and collegiate samples (Messa et al., 2022). A much lower rate of 6% has been reported on limited data from NFL players (Solomon & Haase, 2008) even though some high-profile players have admitted to sports journalists the practice of sandbagging on preseason baseline testing (Reilly, 2012).

There is generally less concern about malingered neurocognitive impairment in elite athletes given the social, professional, and financial incentives for them to return to play. The general assumption has been that athletes engaged in impression management with medical professionals are more likely to exhibit "reverse malingering", a term used in the occupational health literature to identify situations where workers attempt to continue working despite physical or mental limitations (Lurati, 2013). With this in mind, neuropsychologists practicing in a sport setting need to be on the alert for athletes attempting to "fake good" on neuropsychological testing. Additionally, studies have shown that approximately 50% of high-school athletes will fail to disclose a head injury or intentionally underreport the severity and extent of post-concussion symptoms on self-report measures (McCrea et al., 2004; Register-Mihalik et al., 2013). There appear to be various educational, intrapersonal, extra-personal, and environmental factors underlying an athlete's decision to not disclose an injury. Comparable rates of nondisclosure are reported in a study of NFL players with 50% reporting in retirement that they had intentionally withheld information from the team's medical staff of the occurrence of at least one concussion over the course of their career (Kerr et al., 2018).

Given factors unique to the athletic setting, far less attention has been paid to identifying over-reporting or attempts at malingering concussion symptoms in athlete samples. However, it is quite reasonable to assume that there are situations when athletes will have an internal or external incentive to deliberately exaggerate symptoms and/or underperform on neurocognitive testing to avoid a return to their sport. For example, a young athlete guided by overzealous parents might attempt to malinger persisting effects of an injury in an effort to leave a sport that they find undesirable. In a limited number of studies from pediatric samples, it has been reported that 17%–28% of youth athletes exhibit invalid test profiles following an SRC (Chase et al., 2020). The factors underlying PVT failure in these athletes remains unknown, although it has been demonstrated that anxiety and fear of repeat injury are common concerns, influencing long-term report of symptoms from concussion in this age group even in individuals who have recovered from concussion (Anderson et al., 2019). While there has been media coverage of high-profile athletes experiencing persisting post-concussion symptoms, the prevalence and clinical features of these cases go unreported. The neuropsychological test battery used for assessment and management of SRC in active NFL players does not include PVTs (Ellenbogen et al., 2018). As a result, there is no information on the rates of PVT failure or attempted malingering in that group during the acute stage of recovery.

Self-report symptom measures play a critical role in the diagnosis and management of SRC (McLeod & Leach, 2012). While there may be a general underreporting of SRC, experience has shown that athletes are rather reliable in reporting symptoms once they are entered into a concussion recovery profile. Studies have shown that self-report symptom measures are more sensitive to acute effects of SRC than are computerized neurocognitive measures (Nelson, LaRoche, et al., 2016). There are also indications that scores from standardized symptom inventories administered at preseason and in the acute stage of recovery are useful in predicting the course of recovery from SRC (Nelson, Tarima, et al., 2016). Studies of SRC employing self-report symptom measures are not known to include embedded or free-standing symptom validity tests or scales (SVTs) such as in the Minnesota Multiphasic Personality Inventory (MMPI-3), Personality Assessment Inventory (PAI), or Structured Inventory for Malingered Symptoms (SIMS). As a result, there have been no published studies examining the prevalence or characteristics of symptom over-reporting in professional athlete samples.

One encounters a totally different situation with the use of PVTs and SVTs in retired professional athletes undergoing the assessment of potential long-term effects of cumulative head-injury exposure. Due to concerns about CTE, many professional athletes are now seeking neuropsychological evaluations to determine whether they are exhibiting documented effects of neurocognitive decline, resulting from their careers in contact sports. Others are receiving evaluations to determine eligibility for compensation through any one of a number of personal or class-action lawsuits against professional and amateur sports leagues. It is thus no surprise that concerns about malingering and symptom exaggeration have arisen due to the potential for financial gain. Neuropsychologists face a challenge in these settings regarding assessment of performance validity in this population given that many examinees are older adults who might be susceptible to developing symptoms of dementia due to a variety of different, unrelated causes. Research has shown that the use of standard PVT cutoff scores can lead to a high false-positive rate, particularly in those cases with advancing forms of dementia (McGuire et al., 2019).

The NFL Settlement, the most publicized of the CTE lawsuits, has incorporated neuropsychological testing into its Baseline Assessment Program (Brody, NFL Concussion Settlement). Neuropsychologists participating in that program use a standardized battery developed for the identification of one of a number of specific forms of dementia (e.g., Alzheimer's, Parkinson's, or Amyotrophic Lateral Sclerosis) or a graded level of Mild Neurocognitive Disorder. The test battery also includes a number of commonly used PVTs and SVTs. There is little information on the rate of PVT or SVT failure in this program or in retired NFL players in general. Based on previous research in settings with potential financial gain, one could expect a 40% failure rate. Examining NFL Settlement data available on the internet, one finds denials in nearly 30% of the claims, many of which can be assumed to be related to identified cases of attempted malingering (Settlement, 2025). This contrasts with a much lower rate of PVT failure (4.7%) reported in NFL players entering a research program designed to examine the clinical characteristics of TES (Alosco et al., 2023). Additional studies are clearly needed to determine the specificity and sensitivity of PVTs and SVTs in patients evaluated for dementia and particularly in the context of CTE litigation.

Case Number One – Clinical Findings

AW arrived on time for the neuropsychological evaluation accompanied by legal counsel. The attorney accompanied his client for the interview but departed at the beginning of the standardized neuropsychological testing. AW was neatly groomed and attired in a light blue warmup suit and sneakers. He ambulated without assistance and did not wear eyeglasses during the evaluation. Communication skills were good although he was a lot less than an enthusiastic personal historian. He exhibited a limited range of affect. There was no bizarre or unusual behavior. He denied any history of auditory hallucinations, delusions, panic attacks, or PTSD symptoms. However, he did describe some occasional sadness, which "comes and goes". There were complaints of headache, light-sensitivity, tinnitus, and frustration. He also reported problems with remembering events and struggles with problem solving. He was able to comprehend and follow test instructions. There was no influence of any apparent sensory or motor limitations. There were no outward signs of physical discomfort. He asked, "how much more" on multiple occasions. He showed no obvious signs of fatigue after more than four hours of testing.

Tests and scores from AW's neuropsychological evaluation are listed in Table 9.1. He performed within the average range on the WAIS-IV consistent with an estimate of his "pre-injury" functioning (TOPF). He exhibited a strength in perceptual reasoning skills with relative weaknesses in processing speed and working memory. Performances on most tests of executive functions and memory were in the range of "low average" to "below average" (Guilmette et al., 2020). The major exception was his relatively intact verbal fluency. He reported mild-to-moderate symptoms of anxiety and depression on brief inventories with

Table 9.1 Neuropsychological Test Battery – Case Number One (AW)

Age: 32 Sex: Male Handedness: Right Race/Ethnicity: Black/Non-Hispanic Education: 15 years		
Wechsler Adult Intelligence Scale	**Scaled Score**	**Standard Score**
Test of Premorbid Functioning		SS = 102
Full Scale IQ		SS = 95
Verbal Comprehension Index (VCI)		SS = 96
• Vocabulary	ss = 11	
• Similarities	ss = 10	
• Information	ss = 8	
Perceptual Reasoning Index (PRI)		SS = 113
• Block Design	ss = 14	
• Matrix Reasoning	ss = 11	
• Visual Puzzles	ss = 12	
Working Memory Index (WMI)		SS = 83
• Digit Span	ss = 7	
• Arithmetic	ss = 7	
Processing Speed Index (PSI)		SS = 84
• Coding	ss = 7	
• Symbol Search	ss = 7	
Executive Functions & Memory	**Raw Score**	**Normed**
Trail Making Test		
• Part A	42 s	z-score = –1.97
• Part B	90 s	z-score = –1.72
Stroop Color Word Test (Golden)		
• Word	75	T-Score = 34
• Color	50	T-Score = 30
• Color Word	42	T-Score = 47
Verbal Fluency		
• FAS	38	z-score = -0.61
• Animals	24	z-score = 0.10
California Verbal Learning Test (CVLT-II)		
• Total – 5 Trials	35	T-Score = 36
• Long Delay Free Recall	7	z-score = –1.5
• Hits/False Positives	13/0	
• Discriminability (d')	2.7	z-score = 0
Wechsler Memory Scale (WMS-IV)		
• Logical Memory I	18	ss = 7
• Logical Memory II	12	ss = 6
• Visual Reproduction I	34	ss = 8
• Visual Reproduction II	14	ss = 6

(*Continued*)

Table 9.1 (Continued)

Performance Validity	Raw Score	
Fifteen Items Test (FIT)		
• Recall	12	Cutoff ≤ 11
• Recognition	13	Cutoff ≤ 11
• Total	25	Cutoff ≤ 22
Dot Counting Test (DCT)		
• Ungrouped – Average In Seconds	13.0	
• Grouped – Average In Seconds	8.5	
• Errors	2	
• E-Score	23.5	Cutoff ≥ 13.8
Test of Memory Malingering		
• Trial 1	36	Cutoff <42
• Trial 2	35	Cutoff < 49
• Retention	31	
Reliable Digit Span	10	Cutoff < 7
CVLT Forced Choice	13	Cutoff < 14
Self-Report (Symptom Validity)	**Raw Score**	
Beck Depression Inventory (BDI-II)	19	Cutoff > 36
Beck Anxiety Inventory (BAI)	9	Cutoff > 36
Sports Concussion Assessment Tool (SCAT-5)		
• Symptom Severity Score	57	
Minnesota Multiphasic Personality Inventory (MMPI-2-RF)		
• VRIN-r	2	T-Score = 43
• TRIN-r	12	T-Score = 57
• F-r	10	T-Score = 88
• Fp-r	7	T-Score = 102
• F-s	4	T-Score = 74
• FBS-r	21	T-Score = 92
• RBS	17	T-Score = 101
• L-r	0	T-Score = 37
• K-r	3	T-Score = 35
• EID	20	T-Score = 64
• THD	10	T-Score = 81
• BXD	14	T-Score = 70
• RCd	15	T-Score = 69
• RC1	9	T-Score = 65
• RC2	2	T-Score = 42
• RC3	10	T-Score = 61
• RC4	10	T-Score = 65
• RC6	6	T-Score = 80
• RC7	15	T-Score = 70
• RC8	12	T-Score = 86
• RC9	22	T-Score = 74

a moderate level of "post-concussion" symptoms on another measure. On the MMPI-2-RF, a profile associated with thought disorder was obtained, which would be unusual in the absence of any reporting of unusual symptoms or behaviors and no family history of mental health conditions.

A variable pattern of scores was observed across various PVTs. Failing scores were obtained on two standalone measures (DCT & TOMM) and on one embedded measure

(CVLT-FC). The scores on the Beck inventories were below the cutoff levels for identifying questionably high scores (Fuermaier et al., 2025; Snodgrass et al., 2024). Greater elevations were observed on several of the validity scales from the MMPI-2-RF. Specifically, large elevations on FBS-r and RBS provided rather strong support for magnified reporting of cognitive and somatic symptoms. A marked elevation on the Fp-r scale indicated that the unexpected thought disorder profile was a likely product of exaggerated symptom reporting of infrequent, rarely reported symptoms.

This evaluation was performed three years after the AW's reported career-ending concussion that serves as the basis of his ongoing lawsuit. This was the last of 7 concussions reported over the course of his entire football career extending from youth leagues to the NFL. Based on the published literature, one would not expect any direct continuing cognitive or psychological effects of the last concussion. Athlete studies including those involving NFL players have failed to demonstrate deficits on neuropsychological tests extending beyond one to two weeks (Broglio et al., 2022; Pellman et al., 2004). Findings from larger-scale meta-analyses indicate that neurocognitive deficits due to concussion would be undetectable on neuropsychological testing three years following an injury (Rohling et al., 2011). Further, a large majority of studies have generally found no effect of sporadic, repeated concussion on cognitive function (Belanger et al., 2010).

Neuropsychological testing showed a number of unusual fluctuations in this case. AW performed notably better on most of the WAIS-IV subtests with a nearly uniform profile of lower scores observed on measures of executive functioning and memory. Most of those test scores were much lower than what would be expected in the acute stage of recovery from an SRC. PVT results indicated that AW was not fully engaged in the testing due to apparent psychological and/or motivational factors. He exhibited a "psychotic" profile on the MMPI-2-RF, which is very atypical following any type of concussion with a validity profile consistent with symptom magnification. Taken together, the test battery provided no valid findings of any continuing neurocognitive or psychological effects of the SRC sustained in AW's final game as an NFL player and no support for the diagnosis of Mild Neurocognitive Disorder as concluded on the basis of a previous evaluation that did not include the use of PVTs.

Case Number Two – Clinical Findings

GB came to the appointment with his wife who provided most of the information about his history and changes in cognition and behavior that she had witnessed over the past ten years. GB was well groomed and neatly attired. He ambulated without assistance and wore eyeglasses for most of the examination. He spoke slowly with a simple vocabulary in an almost childlike manner. He questioned why he was there on more than one occasion. At one point, he asked the examiner if he was there to discuss his investments. He reported that he was unable to remember many details from his life, including the years he played football. He became upset about his inability to remember things and started to cry at one point. He stated that he has been frustrated in recent months and has felt that his life has no purpose. He denied suicidal ideation. He stated that he avoids social situations because he feels that others are talking about him. He denied hallucinations and delusions. He exhibited fluctuations in attention during the testing and required repeated instructions for many tasks. He required refocusing at times, although there was no need to discontinue any of the tests. There were no limitations due to sensory or motor issues. He completed self-report questionnaires rather quickly and efficiently particularly after he was told that those were the last tests in the evaluation. There were no signs of any obvious fatigue after 4.5 hours of testing.

Tests and scores from GB's neuropsychological evaluation are listed in Table 9.2. The score of 12 obtained on the Montreal Cognitive Assessment when taken at face value is consistent with an advanced form of dementia, which is inconsistent with this man's history, outward appearance, behavior during this evaluation, and ability to function independently in activities of daily living. His performance on the WAIS-IV was in the exceptionally low range. The level of performance on that test was actually higher than what was reported in a report from a neuropsychological examination performed two years earlier. A relatively uniform profile of exceptionally low scores was observed on measures of executive functions and memory. Most of the test scores were comparable to those listed in the report from the prior evaluation. As mentioned, GB was able to complete the self-report inventories independently with relative ease. The findings were in ranges with a severe level of depressive affect and a markedly high level of nonspecific "post-concussion" symptoms, in the context of low reported anxiety.

Scores below published cutoff levels were obtained on multiple PVTs. GB obtained low scores on all three standalone measures included in the neuropsychological test battery (FIT, DCT, & TOMM). He also obtained below cutoff scores on two embedded indices, including the RDS and the discrimination score from the HVLT-R. While there could be concern about false-positive cases of PVT "failure" in a 64-year-old evaluated for memory concerns, many of the scores in this case fell below cutoffs adjusted for geriatric or memory-disordered samples. GB was not administered any commonly used SVT such as the MMPI, PAI, or SIMS. However, the score obtained on the BDI-II exceeds published cutoff levels

Table 9.2 Neuropsychological Test Battery – Case Number Two (GB)

Age: 64 Sex: Male Handedness: Right Race/Ethnicity: White/Non-Hispanic Education: 16 years (BA)		
Montreal Cognitive Assessment	Raw Score = 12/30	
Wechsler Adult Intelligence Scale	Scaled Score	Standard Score
Test of Premorbid Functioning		SS = 64
Full Scale IQ		SS = 64
Verbal Comprehension Index (VCI)		SS = 76
• Vocabulary	ss = 7	
• Similarities	ss = 5	
• Information	ss = 5	
Perceptual Reasoning Index (PRI)		SS = 69
• Block Design	ss = 5	
• Matrix Reasoning	ss = 5	
• Visual Puzzles	ss = 4	
Working Memory Index (WMI)		SS = 60
• Digit Span	ss = 5	
• Arithmetic	ss = 4	
Processing Speed Index (PSI)		SS = 71
• Coding	ss = 3	
• Symbol Search	ss = 6	

(*Continued*)

Table 9.2 (Continued)

Executive Functions & Memory	Raw Score	Normed
Trail Making Test		
• Part A	106 s	z-score = −1.97
• Part B	246 s	z-score = −1.72
Stroop Color Word Test (Golden)		
• Word	43	T-Score = 18
• Color	18	T-Score = 9
• Color Word	10	T-Score = 15
Verbal Fluency		
• FAS	14	z-score = −2.45
• Animals	13	z-score = −1.28
Hopkins Verbal Learning Test		
• Total – 3 Trials	15	T-Score = 24
• Delayed Recall	0	T-Score < 20
• Hits/False Positives	9/3	
• Discrimination	6	T-Score < 20
Wechsler Memory Scale (WMS-IV)		
• Logical Memory I	12	ss = 4
• Logical Memory II	4	ss = 2
• Verbal Paired Associates I	5	ss = 3
• Verbal Paired Associates II	3	ss = 4
• Visual Reproduction I	27	ss = 7
• Visual Reproduction II	7	ss = 5
Performance Validity	**Raw Score**	
Fifteen Items Test (FIT)		
• Recall	4	Cutoff ≤ 11
• Recognition	3	Cutoff ≤ 11
• Total	7	Cutoff ≤ 22
Dot Counting Test (DCT)		
• Ungrouped – Average in Seconds	26.9	
• Grouped – Average in Seconds	7.3	
• Errors	4	
• E-Score	38.2	Cutoff > 13.8
Test of Memory Malingering		
• Trial 1	28	Cutoff < 42
• Trial 2	33	Cutoff < 49
• Retention	31	
Reliable Digit Span	4	Cutoff < 7
HVLT-R Discrimination	6	Cutoff < 6
Self-Report (Symptom Validity)	**Raw Score**	
Beck Depression Inventory (BDI-II)	37	Cutoff > 36
Beck Anxiety Inventory (BAI)	8	Cutoff > 36
Sports Concussion Assessment Tool (SCAT-5)		
• Symptom Severity Score	106	

associated with exaggerated symptom reporting, enabling use of this test as an SVT in this case (Fuermaier et al., 2025). The BDI-II score obtained in this case is also higher than what was reported in any of the individual cases reported in a study performed on a series of retired NFL players (Casson et al., 2014). There are currently no cutoff values reported for extreme scores on the SCAT-5.

The range of test scores in this neuropsychological battery was much lower than what has been reported in samples of retired NFL players (Schaffert et al., 2020). While one might entertain the presence of an underlying neurocognitive disorder such as Alzheimer's disease, that condition had been ruled out by a neurologist who had examined GB in the past. The claim made in the lawsuit against the NCAA was that GB was exhibiting cognitive decline due to CTE, which had allegedly developed due to repetitive head impacts obtained specifically during his four years as a collegiate football player. However, in the report from the current neuropsychological evaluation, a reminder was included that CTE is a neuropathological diagnosis that can only be made on the basis of post-mortem analysis. Given the medical history and MRI findings, one might be more concerned about the effects of an underlying neurovascular process. However, the test scores were considered implausibly low given GB's medical history, reported daily functioning, and behavioral observations. The possibility of malingering was raised due to the findings from PVTs and SVTs. The conclusion was that there was no valid test evidence of neurocognitive impairment to support the presence of any conceivable brain effects due to contact football as an NCAA player or any other cause.

Conclusions

Over the past 30 years, head injuries in NFL players and other athletes have spurred controversies and have, more importantly, led to general advances in our understanding and care of SRC (Barr, 2020). Neuropsychology has played a critical role in developing and implementing much of the methodology currently used in assessment and tracking cognitive and psychological symptoms following concussion. Stemming from the controversies, neuropsychologists are also being asked to evaluate an increasing number of athletes involved in litigation associated with their injuries. It is important that neuropsychologists performing those evaluations are well informed about the complex factors affecting an elite athlete's recovery from a reported head injury. They also need to be equipped with the latest assessment techniques, including tests designed to assess performance and symptom validity in these athletes.

While there is much overlap in the effects of head injury in athletes and non-athletes, there are also several important differences. Studies have shown that SRCs generally lead to lower reported symptom levels and more rapid recovery than concussions sustained outside of the sport setting (Roby et al., 2024). When it comes to long-term effects, athletes with extended playing careers are alleged to be more at risk for development of dementia than other individuals due to cumulative exposure to RHI uniquely associated with their profession. However, it is important to note that when performing a neuropsychological assessment of any individual, athlete or non-athlete, there are multiple medical, social, and psychobiological factors that can influence the experience of concussion and its course of recovery. Due to our training and methodology, neuropsychologists are in a unique position to be able to evaluate how those factors come into play when encountering an elite athlete reporting continuing effects of head injury.

Most of the literature on PVT use in athletes has focused on the issue of sandbagging and detecting athletes who might be attempting to conceal a concussion and its symptoms so that they can remain on the field. However, with more widespread head-injury litigation, neuropsychologists are evaluating increasing numbers of athletes reporting chronic long-term effects of head injury with a potential for a secondary financial gain. Without available literature on test cutoffs and rates of malingering in athlete samples, neuropsychologists are commonly forced to rely on their clinical skills and judgment when evaluating long-term effects of concussion in elite athletes. As highlighted in the two cases presented in this chapter, it is important to evaluate whether the history and behavioral presentation in those cases resembles the clinical features reported in published studies of athlete samples. It is also important to determine whether the data obtained through neuropsychological testing provide a valid assessment of the athlete's cognitive and behavioral functioning.

There is no doubt that there will be many groundbreaking advances in our evaluation and treatment of concussion over the next 30 years. We are already seeing important advances in the identification of biological and neuroimaging biomarkers that will revolutionize our identification of concussion in its acute stage (Tabor et al., 2023). In the coming years, we will also undoubtedly obtain the necessary data to determine the source and clinical significance of tau as reported in samples of retired athletes and whether those athletes are at risk for a pattern of cognitive and behavioral decline that can be distinguished from Alzheimer's disease and other common forms of dementia. By adapting to the advancing science, neuropsychology will continue to play an important role in evaluating the effects of head injuries in this population.

Note

1 AW and GB are representations of real cases with fabricated details to protect identity.

References

Alosco, M. L., Barr, W. B., Banks, S. J., Wethe, J. V., Miller, J. B., Pulukuri, S. V., Culhane, J., Tripodis, Y., Adler, C. H., Balcer, L. J., Bernick, C., Mariani, M. L., Cantu, R. C., Dodick, D. W., McClean, M. D., Au, R., Mez, J., Turner, R. W., 2nd, Palmisano, J. N.,...Project, D. C. R. (2023). Neuropsychological Test Performance of Former American Football Players. *Alzheimers Res Ther, 15*(1), 1. https://doi.org/10.1186/s13195-022-01147-9

Anderson, M. N., Womble, M. N., Mohler, S. A., Said, A., Stephenson-Brown, K., Kontos, A. P., & Elbin, R. J. (2019). Preliminary Study of Fear of Re-Injury following Sport-Related Concussion in High School Athletes. *Dev Neuropsychol, 44*(6), 443–451. https://doi.org/10.1080/87565641.2019.1667995

Barr, W. B. (2014). Mild Traumatic Brain Injury. In M. Sherer & A. M. Sander (Eds.), *Handbook on the Neuropsychology of Traumatic Brain Injury*. Springer.

Barr, W. B. (2020). Believers versus Deniers: The Radicalization of Sports Concussion and Chronic Traumatic Encephalopathy (CTE) Science. *Canadian Psychology, 61*, 151–162.

Barr, W. B. (2023). Concussion and Repetitive Head Injury Exposure in Adult Active and Retired Athletes. In Y. Suchy & J. Miller (Eds.), *Neuropsychological Interviewing: Gathering Information in the Adult Clinic*. Guilford Press.

Barr, W. B., & Karantzoulis, S. (2019). Chronic Traumatic Encephalopathy. In L. D. Ravdin & H. L. Katzen (Eds.), *Handbook on the Neuropsychology of Aging and Dementia* (Second Edition ed.). Springer.

Belanger, H. G., Spiegel, E., & Vanderploeg, R. D. (2010). Neuropsychological Performance Following a History of Multiple Self-reported Concussions: A Meta-analysis. *J Int Neuropsychol Soc, 16*(2), 262–267. https://doi.org/10.1017/S1355617709991287

Belanger, H. G., Vanderploeg, R. D., & McAllister, T. (2016). Subconcussive Blows to the Head: A Formative Review of Short-term Clinical Outcomes. *J Head Trauma Rehabil, 31*(3), 159–166. https://doi.org/10.1097/htr.0000000000000138

2014, (NFL Concussion Settlement). https://www.nflconcussionsettlement.com/ViewDoc.aspx?dp=Amended%20Class%20Action.pdf

Broglio, S. P., McAllister, T., Katz, B. P., LaPradd, M., Zhou, W., McCrea, M. A., & Investigators, C. C. (2022). The Natural History of Sport-Related Concussion in Collegiate Athletes: Findings from the NCAA-DoD CARE Consortium. *Sports Med*, *52*(2), 403–415. https://doi.org/10.1007/s40279-021-01541-7

Broshek, D. K., Pardini, J. E., & Herring, S. A. (2022). Persisting Symptoms After Concussion: Time for a Paradigm Shift. *PM R*, *14*(12), 1509–1513. https://doi.org/10.1002/pmrj.12884

Casson, I. R., Viano, D. C., Haacke, E. M., Kou, Z., & LeStrange, D. G. (2014). Is There Chronic Brain Damage in Retired NFL Players? Neuroradiology, Neuropsychology, and Neurology Examinations of 45 Retired Players. *Sports Health*, *6*(5), 384–395. https://doi.org/10.1177/1941738114540270

Chase, D., Slicer, K., & Schatz, P. (2020). Relationship between Standalone Performance Validity Test Failure and Emotionality among Youth/student Athletes Experiencing Prolonged Recovery following Sports-related Concussion. *Dev Neuropsychol*, *45*(7–8), 435–445. https://doi.org/10.1080/87565641.2020.1852239

Ellenbogen, R. G., Batjer, H., Cardenas, J., Berger, M., Bailes, J., Pieroth, E., Heyer, R., Theodore, N., Hsu, W., Nabel, E., Maroon, J., Cantu, R., Barnes, R., Collins, J., Putukian, M., Lonser, R., Solomon, G., & Sills, A. (2018). National Football League Head, Neck and Spine Committee's Concussion Diagnosis and Management Protocol: 2017–18 season. *Br J Sports Med*, *52*(14), 894–902. https://doi.org/10.1136/bjsports-2018-099203

Fortington, L. V., Cassidy, J. D., Castellani, R. J., Gardner, A. J., McIntosh, A. S., Austen, M., Kerr, Z. Y., & Quarrie, K. L. (2025). Epidemiological Principles in Claims of Causality: An Enquiry into Repetitive Head Impacts (RHI) and Chronic Traumatic Encephalopathy (CTE). *Sports Med*, *55*(2), 255–274. https://doi.org/10.1007/s40279-024-02102-4

Fuermaier, A. B. M., Dandachi-Fitzgerald, B., & Lehrner, J. (2025). Validity Assessment of Early Retirement Claimants: Symptom Overreporting on the Beck Depression Inventory - II. *Appl Neuropsychol Adult*, *32*(3), 712–718. https://doi.org/10.1080/23279095.2023.2206031

Giza, C. C., & Hovda, D. A. (2014). The New Neurometabolic Cascade of Concussion. *Neurosurgery*, *75*, S24–S33. https://doi.org/10.1227/neu.0000000000000505

Grashow, R., Weisskopf, M. G., Baggish, A., Speizer, F. E., Whittington, A. J., Nadler, L., Connor, A., Keske, R., Taylor, H., Zafonte, R., & Pascual-Leone, A. (2020). Premortem Chronic Traumatic Encephalopathy Diagnoses in Professional Football. *Ann Neurol*, *88*(1), 106–112. https://doi.org/10.1002/ana.25747

Guilmette, T. J., Sweet, J. J., Hebben, N., Koltai, D., Mahone, E. M., Spiegler, B. J., Stucky, K., Westerveld, M., & Conference, P. (2020). American Academy of Clinical Neuropsychology Consensus Conference Statement on Uniform Labeling of Performance Test Scores. *Clin Neuropsychol*, *34*(3), 437–453. https://doi.org/10.1080/13854046.2020.1722244

Iverson, G. L., Buttner, F., & Caccese, J. B. (2021). Age of First Exposure to Contact and Collision Sports and Later in Life Brain Health: A Narrative Review. *Front Neurol*, *12*, 727089. https://doi.org/10.3389/fneur.2021.727089

Iverson, G. L., Gardner, A., McCrory, P., Zafonte, R., & Castellani, R. J. (2015). A Critical Review of Chronic Traumatic Encephalopathy. *Neurosci Biobehav Rev*, *56*, 276–293. https://doi.org/10.1016/j.neubiorev.2015.05.008

Iverson, G. L., & Gardner, A. J. (2021). Symptoms of Traumatic Encephalopathy Syndrome are Common in the US General Population. *Brain Commun*, *3*(1), fcab001. https://doi.org/10.1093/braincomms/fcab001

Katz, D. I., Bernick, C., Dodick, D. W., Mez, J., Mariani, M. L., Adler, C. H., Alosco, M. L., Balcer, L. J., Banks, S. J., Barr, W. B., Brody, D. L., Cantu, R. C., Dams-O'Connor, K., Geda, Y. E., Jordan, B. D., McAllister, T. W., Peskind, E. R., Petersen, R. C., Wethe, J. V.,...Stern, R. A. (2021). National Institute of Neurological Disorders and Stroke Consensus Diagnostic Criteria for Traumatic Encephalopathy Syndrome. *Neurology*, *96*(18), 848–863. https://doi.org/10.1212/wnl.0000000000011850

Kerr, Z. Y., Register-Mihalik, J. K., Kay, M. C., DeFreese, J. D., Marshall, S. W., & Guskiewicz, K. M. (2018). Concussion Nondisclosure During Professional Career Among a

Cohort of Former National Football League Athletes. *Am J Sports Med*, *46*(1), 22–29. https://doi.org/10.1177/0363546517728264

Larrabee, G. J., Millis, S. R., & Meyers, J. E. (2009). 40 Plus or Minus 10, A New Magical Number: Reply to Russell. *Clin Neuropsychol*, *23*(5), 841–849. https://doi.org/10.1080/13854040902796735

Lovell, M. R., & Barr, W. B. (2004). American Professional Football. In M. R. Lovell, R. J. Echemendia, J. T. Barth, & M. W. Collins (Eds.), *Traumatic Brain Injuyr in Sports: An International Neuropsychological Perspective*. Swets & Zeitlinger.

Lurati, A. R. (2013). Reverse Malingering-staying on the Job at Any Cost. *Workplace Health Saf*, *61*(7), 297–298. https://doi.org/10.1177/216507991306100704

Mack, C. D., Herzog, M. M., Solomon, G., Putukian, M., Lee, R. Y., Matava, M. J., Cardenas, J., Theodore, N., & Sills, A. (2022). Return to Full Participation Following Concussion in the National Football League, 2015 Through 2020. *Clin J Sport Med*, *32*(5), e605–e613. https://doi.org/10.1097/JSM.0000000000001050

Makdissi, M., Schneider, K. J., Feddermann-Demont, N., Guskiewicz, K. M., Hinds, S., Leddy, J. J., McCrea, M., Turner, M., & Johnston, K. M. (2017). Approach to Investigation and Treatment of Persistent Symptoms Following Sport-related Concussion: A Systematic Review. *Br J Sports Med*, *51*(12), 958–968. https://doi.org/10.1136/bjsports-2016-097470

Manley, G., Gardner, A., Schneider, K. J., Guskiewicz, K. M., Bailes, J., Cantu, R. C., Castellani, R. J., Turner, M., Jordan, B. D., Randolph, C., Dvorak, J., Hayden, K. A., Tator, C. H., McCrory, P., & Iverson, G. L. (2017). A Systematic Review of Potential Long-term Effects of Sport-related Concussion. *Br J Sports Med*, *51*(12), 969–977. https://doi.org/10.1136/bjsports-2017-097791

McCrea, M., Hammeke, T., Olsen, G., Leo, P., & Guskiewicz, K. (2004). Unreported Concussion in High School Football Players: Implications for Prevention. *Clin J Sport Med*, *14*(1), 13–17.

McGuire, C., Crawford, S., & Evans, J. J. (2019). Effort Testing in Dementia Assessment: A Systematic Review. *Arch Clin Neuropsychol*, *34*(1), 114–131. https://doi.org/10.1093/arclin/acy012

McKee, A. C. (2020). The Neuropathology of Chronic Traumatic Encephalopathy: The Status of the Literature. *Semin Neurol*, *40*(4), 359–369. https://doi.org/10.1055/s-0040-1713632

McKee, A. C., Cantu, R. C., Nowinski, C. J., Hedley-Whyte, E. T., Gavett, B. E., Budson, A. E., Santini, V. E., Lee, H. S., Kubilus, C. A., & Stern, R. A. (2009). Chronic Traumatic Encephalopathy in Athletes. *Journal of Neuropathology and Experimental Neurology*, *68*(7), 709–735. https://doi.org/10.1097/nen.0b013e3181a9d503

McLeod, T. C., & Leach, C. (2012). Psychometric Properties of Self-report Concussion Scales and Checklists. *J Athl Train*, *47*(2), 221–223. https://doi.org/10.4085/1062-6050-47.2.221

Messa, I., Korcsog, K., & Abeare, C. (2022). An Updated Review of the Prevalence of Invalid Performance on the Immediate Post-Concussion and Cognitive Testing (ImPACT). *Clin Neuropsychol*, *36*(7), 1613–1636. https://doi.org/10.1080/13854046.2020.1866676

Montenigro, P. H., Baugh, C. M., Daneshvar, D. H., Mez, J., Budson, A. E., Au, R., Katz, D. I., Cantu, R. C., & Stern, R. A. (2014). Clinical Subtypes of Chronic Traumatic Encephalopathy: Literature Review and Proposed Research Diagnostic Criteria for Traumatic Encephalopathy Syndrome. *Alzheimers Res Ther*, *6*(5), 68. https://doi.org/10.1186/s13195-014-0068-z

Nelson, L. D., LaRoche, A. A., Pfaller, A. Y., Lerner, E. B., Hammeke, T. A., Randolph, C., Barr, W. B., Guskiewicz, K., & McCrea, M. A. (2016). Prospective, Head-to-Head Study of Three Computerized Neurocognitive Assessment Tools (CNTs): Reliability and Validity for the Assessment of Sport-Related Concussion. *J Int Neuropsychol Soc*, *22*(1), 24–37. https://doi.org/10.1017/S1355617715001101

Nelson, L. D., Tarima, S., LaRoche, A. A., Hammeke, T. A., Barr, W. B., Guskiewicz, K., Randolph, C., & McCrea, M. A. (2016). Preinjury Somatization Symptoms Contribute to Clinical Recovery after Sport-related Concussion. *Neurology*, *86*(20), 1856–1863. https://doi.org/10.1212/WNL.0000000000002679

Patricios, J. S., Schneider, K. J., Dvorak, J., Ahmed, O. H., Blauwet, C., Cantu, R. C., Davis, G. A., Echemendia, R. J., Makdissi, M., McNamee, M., Broglio, S., Emery, C. A., Feddermann-Demont, N., Fuller, G. W., Giza, C. C., Guskiewicz, K. M., Hainline, B., Iverson, G. L., Kutcher, J. S.,… Meeuwisse, W. (2023). Consensus Statement on Concussion in sport: The 6th International

Conference on Concussion in Sport-Amsterdam, October 2022. *Br J Sports Med*, *57*(11), 695–711. https://doi.org/10.1136/bjsports-2023-106898
Pellman, E. J., Lovell, M. R., Viano, D. C., Casson, I. R., & Tucker, A. M. (2004). Concussion in Professional Football: Neuropsychological Testing--Part 6. *Neurosurgery*, *55*(6), 1290–1303; discussion 1303–1295.
Pieroth, E. M., & Hanks, C. (2014). Management of Concussion in the Professional Football Player. *Prog Neurol Surg*, *28*, 171–183. https://doi.org/10.1159/000358778
Randolph, C., Karantzoulis, S., & Guskiewicz, K. (2013). Prevalence and Characterization of mild Cognitive Impairment in Retired National Football League Players. *J Int Neuropsychol Soc*, *19*(8), 873–880. https://doi.org/10.1017/s1355617713000805
Register-Mihalik, J. K., Guskiewicz, K. M., McLeod, T. C., Linnan, L. A., Mueller, F. O., & Marshall, S. W. (2013). Knowledge, Attitude, and Concussion-reporting Behaviors among High School Athletes: A Preliminary Study. *J Athl Train*, *48*(5), 645–653. https://doi.org/10.4085/1062-6050-48.3.20
Reilly, R. (2012). Talking football with Archie, Peyton, Eli. *ESPN*. https://sports.espn.go.com/espn/news/story?id=6430211
Roby, P. R., Mozel, A. E., Arbogast, K. B., Buckley, T., Caccese, J. B., Chrisman, S. P. D., Clugston, J. R., Eckner, J. T., Esopenko, C., Hunt, T., Kelly, L. A., McDevitt, J., Perkins, S. M., Putukian, M., Susmarski, A., Broglio, S. P., Pasquina, P. F., McAllister, T. W., McCrea, M.,...Investigators, C. C. (2024). Postinjury Outcomes After Non-Sport-Related Concussion: A CARE Consortium Study. *J Athl Train*, *59*(3), 289–296. https://doi.org/10.4085/1062-6050-0181.23
Rohling, M. L., Binder, L. M., Demakis, G. J., Larrabee, G. J., Ploetz, D. M., & Langhinrichsen-Rohling, J. (2011). A Meta-analysis of Neuropsychological Outcome after Mild Traumatic Brain Injury: Re-analyses and Reconsiderations of Binder et al. (1997), Frencham et al. (2005), and Pertab et al. (2009). *Clin Neuropsychol*, *25*(4), 608–623. https://doi.org/10.1080/13854046.2011.565076
Schaffert, J., Didehbani, N., LoBue, C., Hart, J., Rossetti, H., Lacritz, L., & Cullum, C. M. (2021). Frequency and Predictors of Traumatic Encephalopathy Syndrome in a Prospective Cohort of Retired Professional Athletes. *Front Neurol*, *12*, 617526. https://doi.org/10.3389/fneur.2021.617526
Schaffert, J., LoBue, C., Fields, L., Wilmoth, K., Didehbani, N., Hart, J., & Cullum, C. M. (2020). Neuropsychological Functioning in Ageing Retired NFL players: A Critical Review. *Int Rev Psychiatry*, *32*(1), 71–88. https://doi.org/10.1080/09540261.2019.1658572
Schatz, P., & Glatts, C. (2013). "Sandbagging" Baseline Test Performance on ImPACT, Without Detection, is More Difficult than it Appears. *Arch Clin Neuropsychol*, *28*(3), 236–244. https://doi.org/10.1093/arclin/act009
Settlement, N. C. (2025). Summary Report. https://www.nflconcussionsettlement.com/ViewDoc.aspx?dp=Guide_ToPublicReports.pdf
Snodgrass, M. A., Bieu, R. K., & Schroeder, R. W. (2024). Development of a Symptom Validity Index for the Beck Anxiety Inventory. *Clin Neuropsychol*, 1–16. https://doi.org/10.1080/13854046.2024.2429162
Solomon, G. S., & Haase, R. F. (2008). Biopsychosocial Characteristics and Neurocognitive Test Performance in National Football League players: An Initial Assessment. *Arch Clin Neuropsychol*, *23*(5), 563–577. https://doi.org/10.1016/j.acn.2008.05.008
Solomon, G. S., Lovell, M. R., Casson, I. R., & Viano, D. C. (2015). Normative Neurocognitive Data for National Football League Players: An Initial Compendium. *Arch Clin Neuropsychol*, *30*(2), 161–173. https://doi.org/10.1093/arclin/acv003
Stamm, J. M., Bourlas, A. P., Baugh, C. M., Fritts, N. G., Daneshvar, D. H., Martin, B. M., McClean, M. D., Tripodis, Y., & Stern, R. A. (2015). Age of First Exposure to Football and Later-life Cognitive Impairment in Former NFL Players. *Neurology*, *84*(11), 1114–1120. https://doi.org/10.1212/wnl.0000000000001358
Tabor, J. B., Brett, B. L., Nelson, L., Meier, T., Penner, L. C., Mayer, A. R., Echemendia, R. J., McAllister, T., Meehan, W. P., 3rd, Patricios, J., Makdissi, M., Bressan, S., Davis, G. A., Premji, Z., Schneider, K. J., Zetterberg, H., & McCrea, M. (2023). Role of Biomarkers and Emerging Technologies in

Defining and Assessing Neurobiological Recovery After Sport-related Concussion: A Systematic Review. *Br J Sports Med*, *57*(12), 789–797. https://doi.org/10.1136/bjsports-2022-106680
Walton, S. R., Carneiro, K. A., Smith-Ryan, A. E., Stoner, L., Kerr, Z. Y., Brett, B. L., Chandran, A., DeFreese, J. D., Mannix, R., Lempke, L. B., Echemendia, R. J., McCrea, M. A., Guskiewicz, K. M., & Meehan, W. P., 3rd. (2025). Health-Promoting Behaviors and Their Associations With Factors Related to Well-Being Among Former National Football League Players: An NFL-LONG Study. *J Athl Train*, *60*(2), 185–197. https://doi.org/10.4085/1062-6050-0537.23

10 Performance Validity Testing in Multiple Symptom and Ability Domains and Testing the Clinical Significance of Below Chance Results with $p \leq 0.20$

Laurence M. Binder

Several well-standardized forced-choice tests (FCTs) are available for assessing the performance validity of memory complaints. These FCTs have cutoff scores for determining whether scores are valid. Most invalid scores on FCTs are above a statistical level of chance performance. Clinicians sometimes incorrectly ignore failing FCT scores that are above chance. It is more difficult for clinicians to overlook FCT scores that are significantly below chance.

The interpretation and importance of significantly below chance results on FCTs is straightforward. Significantly below chance results on FCTs indicate deliberate underperformance (Sherman et al., 2020; Sweet et al., 2021). The level of probability that should be selected for testing of the hypothesis that a particular score is below chance has been discussed. Binder et al. (2014) stated that the probability level of 0.05 that is conventionally used for hypothesis testing of the difference between group means was too conservative for the analysis of FCT results. They provided a rationale and data supporting a probability level of $p \leq 0.20$ with a single tail test.

The rationale for testing with a single tail was that the hypothesis of below chance was unidirectional and there was no need for significance testing if performance was better than chance. The rationale for using $p \leq 0.20$ was that the 0.05 level of probability promulgated by pioneer statistician R.A. Fisher was established to test the hypothesis of experimental group differences. In Fisher's work, the statistical issue often was comparison of agricultural crop yields produced by different farming methods. The level of probability most appropriate for comparisons of group means was not established to test the hypothesis that FCT data from an individual was significantly below chance. Furthermore, expert testimony in court does not require uncertainty to be five percent or less; the usual legal standard for expert testimony is more probable than not (Reynolds & Horton, 2012).

Data in support of using a probability level of 0.20 for determining significance of FCT results came from scores on the Warrington Recognition Memory Test – words of 136 examinees with mild-to-severe TBI with no financial incentives (Binder, Larrabee, & Millis, 2014). No member of the TBI group scored worse than 23 of 50 (46%) correct. Analysis of the probability of significance of a score of 22 of 50 correct, the empirically derived cutoff with zero false positives (100% specificity) for this sample, using the z approximation, yielded $p < 0.21$. The exact binomial calculation was $p < 0.24$. No one scored at the level of $p \leq 0.20$. The probability of $p \leq 0.20$ derived from this sample was supported by data in the literature on the same test and on other FCTs showing that patients without financial incentives performed better than chance (Grote et al., 2000; Macciocchi et al., 2006). Another study supporting the use of $p \leq 0.20$ for forced-choice significance testing found that only 9 of 1,630 cases (0.6%) with no known external incentives for poor performance

DOI: 10.4324/9781003005063-12

scored worse than this probability level on standardized FCTs (Binder & Chafetz, 2018). In a third study with 5,103 participants, neurocognitive performance for each participant was summarized by an Overall Test Battery Mean (OTBM et al., 2001; Rohling et al., 2004). The group with a FCT result worse than chance at $p \leq 0.20$ had an OTBM as low as the group that failed six or more performance validity tests (PVTs) while performing better than chance on all FCTs. Furthermore, the OTBM mean in the group that failed FCTs at the 0.20 level of significance was not significantly different from the OTBM mean of the group that failed at the 0.05 level of significance (Rohling et al., 2023).

The American Academy of Clinical Neuropsychology (AACN) Consensus Statement on performance and validity testing (Sweet et al., 2021) implied an endorsement of the $p \leq 0.20$ level of probability for testing of the hypothesis that the results of FCTs were significantly below chance by citing Binder et al. (2014). The updated criteria for diagnosing malingered neuropsychological dysfunction (Sherman et al., 2020) also cited Binder et al. (2014) in their discussion of the diagnostic importance of below chance results. There do not appear to be any published disagreements with the conclusion reached by Binder et al. (2014), Binder and Chafetz (2018), and Rohling et al. (2023) that a 0.20 level of probability should be used for assessing the hypothesis that a FCT result is significantly worse than chance.

Most FCTs assess memory complaints. Memory is not the only ability domain that can be assessed with PVTs. Complaints of visual processing and vision difficulties occur frequently among forensic cases of mild traumatic brain injury (mTBI), and visual processing PVTs are useful for such cases. Both cases described in this chapter had visual complaints, and the Dot Counting Test, a PVT that assesses visual complaints, was administered to both examinees. Both cases also exhibited extreme slowing on finger-tapping, a test that serves as an embedded measure of performance validity.

Cases of alleged mTBI presented in this chapter will illustrate the use of the 0.20 p level in the evaluation of the results obtained from FCTs. The first case will also illustrate the value of unstandardized measures of coordination to show that sometimes subjective complaints and findings are likely explained by psychological factors such as malingering. Some historical details were changed or left vague to deidentify these cases.

The Case of Ms. A

Background

A woman in her 40s claimed injuries from a rear-end motor vehicle accident (MVA). She stopped working and her lawyer sued for damages resulting from the MVA. A few years later, she was referred by the law firm representing the defendant for independent neuropsychological evaluation.

Records Review

Evaluated medically the same day, she reported striking her head on the headrest without loss of consciousness. Concussion was diagnosed, apparently because she described herself as not feeling right mentally. She did not report any alteration of level of consciousness that defines a concussion (Silverberg et al., 2023; VA/DOD Management and rehabilitation of post-acute-mild TBI work group, 2021). Within a day she reported headache, sensitivity to light and noise, dizziness, and imbalance. Within weeks, she reported double vision. A physical therapy evaluation a few weeks after the MVC found no eye movement abnormalities.

A functional neurologist (chiropractic neurologist) reported that on finger-to-nose testing of coordination, instead of touching the tip of her nose with the tip of her index finger, she touched above her left eyebrow. The functional neurologist later commented on signs that she thought were psychogenic, including falling without making any postural adjustments to avoid the fall or injury.

A neuro-optometrist diagnosed postconcussion syndrome (PCS), exophoria, vertigo, heterophoria, and deficiencies of pursuit eye movements and recommended prism lenses and vision therapy.

A medical neurologist who performed an independent medical examination (IME) a year after her MVA opined that abnormalities of her gait, finger-to-nose testing, and oculomotor examination were of functional origin and pointed out that her visual complaints began well after the MVA and were unrelated to the MVA. In the neurologic IME, she displayed hesitancy and unsteadiness while walking, in contrast to walking normally when she entered the exam room. On finger-to-nose testing with her dominant right hand, she missed her nose altogether and placed the palm of her hand on her cheek. In contrast, she had no abnormality in touching one foot to the heel, shin, and knee of the opposite leg or when performing rapid alternating movements with any of her extremities. The neurologist found no eye movement abnormality. A brain MRI was normal.

Another IME by a different medical neurologist occurred four years after the MVA. On the SLUMS, a brief structured mental status exam, her score of 20/30 was abnormal, and the neurologist thought her effort was incomplete. Testing of the strength of her extremities demonstrated incomplete effort and ratchety movements. Finger-to-nose testing showed similar results in each arm with consistent near misses both in touching the examiner's finger and in touching her nose. The neurologist concluded that the findings were functional with the differential diagnoses including anxiety and malingering.

Interview

She complained of some symptoms that are common in the first few weeks after concussion, including memory and word-finding difficulties, problems comprehending oral and written language, headaches, dizziness, and loss of balance. In addition, she reported symptoms that are not typical of people with recent concussions or with lingering complaints after possible concussions, including stuttering, episodic difficulty with swallowing, and sometimes awakening because she felt as though she was choking. Despite her vision complaint of inability to judge distance, she continued to drive. She drove 15 miles from her residence to my office for the neuropsychological evaluation. She had not returned to work since the MVA.

Remarkably, she also claimed that she sometimes missed her mouth when she was trying to feed herself with a utensil and that she sometimes missed her lips when she was holding a cup of liquid, striking her teeth instead. Prior to the MVA, she had a history of anxiety. She reported earning a high school diploma.

Test Results and Behavioral Observations

Testing was not valid. She failed all the PVTs. On the Test of Memory Malingering (TOMM), across three trials, she was correct on 19, 20, and 10 items. Her total score of 49/150 correct was statistically significantly worse than chance, $p = 0.000013$. The TOMM score signified that she deliberately provided incorrect answers, because it was statistically unlikely that she could have performed that badly if she had been guessing the answer for each item.

She was able to complete the VSVT despite her reported difficulty with computer screens. She demonstrated that she understood the task and that she could manipulate the mouse by making no errors on the 24 easy items. On the difficult items, she was correct on 8/24, a performance worse than chance at the 0.08 level. Considering that she performed worse than chance and the far superior performance on the same test by people with medically uncontrollable epilepsy and moderate–severe TBI that can severely compromise cognitive function (Grote et al., 2000; Macciocchi et al., 2006), there was no doubt that she was deliberately providing wrong answers to the difficult items.

The Green Medical Symptom Validity Test (MSVT) is a FCT that is easier than the Green Word Memory Test. Well-oriented patients in rehabilitation for moderate–severe TBI all obtained passing MSVT scores on immediate and delayed recognition trials (Macciocchi et al., 2017). Impaired children also performed well on the MSVT. For example, according to comparison group data provided by the test software, a group of children averaging

Table 10.1 Test scores for Ms. A and Ms. B

	Ms. A	*Ms. B*
Tomm Trial 1, 2, and Retention and Total	T1 19, T2 20, Retention 10. Total 49/150 correct p = 000013	T1 21, T2 21, Retention 23. Total 65/150 correct $p < 0.07$
VSVT	Easy 24, Difficult 8. p = 08 for Difficult items	Easy 21, Difficult 5. $p < 0.004$ for Difficult items
Green MSVT	IR 75%, DR 60%, CNS 65, PA 60%, FR 45%. Not genuine impairment profile (Hard Mean – Easy Mean = 14.2)	
Dot Counting Test E Score	41.8	89.0
Reliable Digit Span	6	4
D-KEFS Color Word Interference Test Scaled Scores	Conditions 1, 3, and 4 refused or not finished, Condition 2 SS 1	
HVLT-R Recall	Trial 1: 4, Trial 2: 5, Trial 3: 6. Total learning score 15 below first percentile. Delay 3, below first percentile. Recognition: 5 true positive, 2 false positive, Recognition discrimination below first percentile	Trial 1: 2, Trial 2: 3, Trial 3: 1. Total learning score 6 below first percentile. Delay 0, below first percentile. Recognition: 8 true positives, 5 false positive, Recognition discrimination below first percentile
BMVT-R	Trial 1: 0, Trial 2: 1, Trial 3: 0, Total 1, Delayed Recall 1. Recognition 3 true positive, 1 false positive. All scores below first percentile	Trial 1 3, Trial 2: 4, Trial 3: 5, Total 12, Delayed Recall 3. Recognition 3 true positive, 2 false positives. Total learning, delayed recall, and recognition discrimination scores all at or below first percentile
Finger-Tapping	Right (dominant) 8.4, Left 10.0	Right (dominant) 8.4, Left 9.0

(*Continued*)

Table 10.1 (Continued)

	Ms. A	*Ms. B*
	Case 1 continued	Case 2 continued
Phonemic Fluency COWAT FAS	22 words, fifth percentile	11 words, below first percentile
Semantic/Animal Fluency	20 words, 39th percentile	6 words, below first percentile
NAB Naming	No errors, normal	
WAIS-IV Index and Scale Scores		
VCI		72, third percentile
PRI		69, second percentile (prorated)
WMI	71	55, below first percentile
PSI		56, below first percentile
IQ		57, below first percentile (prorated)
Similarities	7	5
Vocabulary		6
Information		4
Block Design	10	5
Matrix Reasoning		
Visual Puzzles		4
Digit Span	3	1
Arithmetic	7	3
Symbol Search	6	1
Coding	Refused	3
Trail Making Part A		
Trail Making Part B	30-s 34th percentile 127-s second percentile	65-s first percentile 259-s below first percentile
Neurobehavioral Symptom Inventory	Completed 2 of 22 items	Validity:10–22
MMPI-2-RF/MMPI-3	MMPI-2-RF Validity Scales unremarkable. Restructured clinical scales (RCS): somatic complaints = 70 (85% of the items in the scale were answered). No other RCS elevations	MMPI-3 RBS 87 (elevated). Other validity scales unremarkable. RCS somatic complaints 72. No other RCS elevations

14 years of age and an IQ of 85 had mean scores that were nearly perfect – the immediate recognition mean was 100% and the delayed recognition mean was 99%. A group of learning disabled children with a mean IQ of 91 all obtained perfect scores on immediate and delayed recognition memory. A third group of children with a mean verbal IQ of only 64 obtained a mean score on immediate recognition of 96% and a mean score on delayed recognition of 94%. In contrast, on the same test, she obtained these failing scores: immediate recognition 75% and delayed recognition 60%. She did not obtain a profile consistent with genuine memory impairment.

She also performed in the invalid ranges on the Brief Visuospatial Memory Test-Revised (BVMT-R), Hopkins Verbal Learning Test-Revised (HVLT-R), Digit Span, and the finger-tapping test. The BVMT-R and HVLT-R embedded measures of validity employ the recognition discrimination index of each test, that is, recognition memory true positives (hits) minus recognition memory false positives. Because the recognition memory trials on these memory tests are easier than the learning and recall trials, the recognition discrimination indexes are valid embedded PVTs (Bailey et al., 2018; Olsen et al., 2019; Sawyer et al., 2017).

Finger-tapping is useful as an embedded PVT because it is not sensitive to the effects of TBI, unless the TBI causes motor deficits in the upper extremities that are evident in a neurological evaluation (Dikmen et al., 1995). Finger-tapping cutoff scores for poor effort have been established. Arnold et al. (2005) found that for males with head injury, a dominant hand score of 35 or less had specificity of 0.94. The comparable cutoff score for females was a dominant hand score of 32 or less. Similar scores were suggested by Axelrod et al. (2014).

On WAIS-IV Similarities, she demonstrated no aphasic disturbance and scored at the 16th percentile. In solving mental arithmetic problems (WAIS-IV Arithmetic), she scored at the 16th percentile.

She performed inconsistently on measures of visual processing speed, and she failed a PVT in this domain. On the Dot Counting Test (DCT), her E score of 41.8 was far into the invalid range. The Color Word Interference Test of the D-KEFS is a Stroop-type test with subsequent validation as an embedded PVT (Eglit et al., 2020). Its use as a PVT is based partly on the fact that the first-two timed conditions (subtests) of naming colors and reading words are easy compared with the last two conditions that require inhibition and a combination of inhibition and switching, respectively. She refused or failed to complete Conditions 1, 3, and 4. Her Condition 2 (word reading) scaled score of 1 and her refusals on the other conditions were consistent with invalid performance.

On Symbol Search, requiring visual processing speed, she scored at the 9th percentile. She refused the Coding task, claiming that it was too visually complex. She performed normally on Part A of Trail Making. When a more cognitively complex component of divided attention was required in Trail Making (Part B), her time of 127 seconds was abnormal at the 2nd percentile. She performed normally on a measure requiring visual perceptual reasoning, Block Design.

Considering her scores on the PVTs described above, it was unsurprising that she performed abnormally on memory testing. On the HVLT-R, presented with a list of 12 words, her total of 15 words recalled during the three learning trials was below the 1st percentile. On delayed recall, her score of three words was below the 1st percentile. Recognition included only 5/12 hits and two false positive errors. Her recognition discrimination index of 3 was in the invalid range (Bailey et al., 2018; Sawyer et al., 2017). On the BVMT-R, requiring visual memory, her total recall across the three learning trials was well below the 1st percentile as was her delayed recall. On recognition memory, she correctly identified 3/6 targets with one false positive error. Her recognition discrimination index of 2 was far below the 1st percentile and in the range of invalid responding (Bailey et al., 2018; Olsen et al., 2019).

On a timed measure of phonemic fluency, (FAS) she scored at the 5th percentile. In contrast, on a timed measure of categorical fluency for animals, she scored at the 39th percentile.

She made no errors in 31 trials on a measure requiring visual confrontation naming from the Neuropsychological Assessment Battery (NAB). However, at times, her performance was bizarre. She called a picture of a common projectile a "fish" and then self-corrected.

Her performances on measures of upper extremity coordination were also bizarre. On finger-tapping with her dominant right hand, her score of 8.4 was below 20% of the normal mean. With her left hand, her time of 10.0 was about 25% of the normal mean. In contrast, people with much more serious TBIs, unless they result in motor deficits easily demonstrated by neurologic exams, typically have normal or very close to normal performance on the same tests. Her severe finger-tapping impairment demonstrated poor effort (Arnold et al., 2005; Axelrod et al., 2014).

It was not consistent with her poor finger-tapping that on the grooved pegboard, a much more difficult measure of manual dexterity, she performed better than she performed on finger-tapping with each hand. Her right hand time was 80 seconds was at the 8th percentile, and her left hand time of 74 seconds was normal at the 30th percentile. On the grooved pegboard, she demonstrated an inconsistent intention tremor with her right hand, occasionally tremulous only when placing the pegs and not when picking them up. Furthermore, the occasional tremor during the grooved pegboard was inconsistent with her performance on finger-to-nose testing, where she demonstrated no tremor. She also demonstrated no tremor on tasks requiring use of a pencil. When she completed the MMPI-2-RF, she filled out the bubble-type answer sheet without strain or marking outside the bubbles. On Trail Making, her lines were not tremulous.

On finger-to-nose testing with a target and her eyes open, she moved her right hand smoothly, showing no evidence of ataxia. She had no problem touching the tip of her finger to the target; however, she did not properly touch her nose on the return. She demonstrated a similar problem with her left hand on finger-to-nose testing with a target. With finger-to-nose testing with her eyes open and no target, her task was to extend her arm fully and then bring her index finger to the tip of her nose. With her right hand and again with her left hand, she brought the tip of her finger to her forehead and complained of dizziness. On finger-to-nose testing with no target and her eyes closed, she brought her finger to her forehead or to the top of the frame of her glasses.

Her finger-to-nose performance was bizarre and not consistent with the neurologic problem of ataxia that the test is designed to assess. Her finger-to-nose performance was not consistent with her lack of difficulty drinking water from a water bottle that she brought to the appointment. She drank repeatedly without difficulty. Furthermore, she had no difficulty operating a computer mouse used for the VSVT and the MSVT.

The Neurobehavioral Symptom Inventory is a paper and pencil questionnaire with an embedded symptom validity test (Lange et al., 2015). She claimed that it was visually too complex for her and refused it.

She completed the paper and pencil version of the MMPI-2-RF, however, opting for this version rather than the computerized version. She did not answer 5 of the 338 items. Four of the five answers that she did not provide are on the restructured clinical scale measuring somatic complaints (RC 1), and she answered only 85% of the items on that scale. Nonetheless, on this scale, she obtained an abnormally elevated score of 70, consistent with a person who has physical complaints that exceed objective medical findings. She did not report any emotional problems on the MMPI-2-RF. She denied symptoms of depression, anxiety, and other emotional concerns.

Interpretation of Test Results

On two FCTs, she performed significantly worse than chance, demonstrating that she deliberately provided wrong answers. She failed the VSVT Difficult Items at the 0.08 level of probability and the TOMM at the 0.000013 *p* level. She failed every designated performance validity test, including the TOMM, VSVT, Green MSVT, and DCT. She also failed embedded measures of performance validity on the BVMT-R, HVLT-R, Digit Span (Reliable Digit Span), finger-tapping, and the Color Word Interference Test. Her upper extremity coordination problems were inconsistent. Her score on the VSVT Difficult Items at the

0.08 level of probability was sufficiently low to establish that she deliberately provided wrong answers, even if the TOMM had not been administered.

Summary and Conclusions

In my medicolegal report, I used unequivocal language to describe her intentionality in providing wrong answers on the VSVT and the TOMM. I explained that the TOMM probability level meant that the probability was 13 out of 1,000,000 that, if she was guessing on each item, that she would have been unlucky enough to guess incorrectly on 101 of the total of 150 items. I also wrote that her lack of coordination on finger-to-nose testing was a psychologically caused abnormality no less exaggerated than someone clownishly putting an ice cream cone onto their forehead instead of into their mouth. I stated that abnormal neurocognitive test results did not provide evidence of cognitive impairment, because the results were invalid. One would not expect residual neuropsychological impairment from such a minor injury (Iverson et al., 2019; Rohling et al., 2011). This legal case was adjudicated in arbitration, and the decision of the arbitrators is unknown.

The Case of Ms. B

Background

Ms. B was a female about age 50 who reported a work-related injury. An object reportedly fell on her head while she worked as the manager of a small store. She was referred by her Workers' Compensation insurer for independent neuropsychological evaluation several months after the reported injury.

Records Review

She reported that everything went black for a moment, a self-report that apparently led to physicians diagnosing concussion. CT and MRI scans showed no brain abnormalities. Over time, she reported worsening symptoms, including headaches, cognitive difficulty, and memory loss.

Interview

She reported more than 12 years of education, better-than-average high school grades, no history of mental health treatment or substance abuse, and work history at jobs that required normal intelligence.

Test Results and Behavioral Observations

She failed PVTs and demonstrated that she deliberately provided wrong answers on FCTs. On the VSVT, she demonstrated that she understood what she was supposed to do by correctly answering 22/24 of the easy items. This score shows suboptimal effort (Silk-Eglit et al., 2016). On the difficult items of the VSVT, she obtained a score of 5/24 correct, $p < 0.004$.

On the TOMM, across three trials she was correct on 21, 21, and 23 items. Her total score of 65/150 correct was significantly worse than chance, $p < 0.07$. After just a few items on trial one, she was crying and said that the oral feedback about whether her answers were correct or not was very upsetting to her. At that point, she was providing more wrong answers than right answers. Therefore, the crying was staged for dramatic effect.

On the DCT, assessing the validity of visual processing speed, she performed much worse than people with well-documented brain injuries and diseases of the brain. Her E score of 89 was far worse than the cut off and one of the worst scores on this test that I have ever obtained.

In summary, she failed all three designated measures of performance validity by wide margins. On the two FCTs, she performed statistically significantly worse than chance, indicating it was highly likely that she deliberately provided wrong answers.

The remainder of the neurocognitive testing also was invalid, including her IQ of 57. When a person with a history of concussion obtains IQ scores much lower than would be predicted from their educational level, it is likely that those extremely low scores are the product of invalid performance (Martin et al., 2017; Moore et al., 2020). It is likely that developmentally, her intelligence was of at least average range (90–109). She reported obtaining a regular high school diploma and having attended some college, and she held a managerial position when injured. Per standardization data for the WAIS-IV, only 25% of the population have IQs below 90. One would not expect that someone with a history of concussion would obtain IQ or index scores as low as hers unless they were exaggerating cognitive difficulties. On subtests of WAIS-IV, she missed extremely easy items that should not be missed by people with mild TBI. Her reliable Digit Span was only 4, consistent with invalid performance.

On the Brief Visuospatial Memory Test-Revised, scores on recall and recognition memory were abnormal. She was below the 1st percentile on recognition discrimination with only three targets correctly identified and two false positive errors. Her abnormally low score on recognition discrimination was also consistent with poor effort (Bailey et al., 2018).

On the Hopkins Verbal Learning Test-Revised, total learning and delayed recall scores were below the 1st percentile. She correctly recognized only 4/12 target words and added five false positive recognition errors. The resulting recognition discrimination index was far below the 1st percentile and indicative of poor effort and invalid performance (Bailey et al., 2018).

On a timed measure of phonemic fluency, she scored well below the 1st percentile. On a timed measure of categorical fluency for animals, she also performed well below the 1st percentile.

On Part A of Trail Making, her time of 65 seconds was about double what would be average and at the 1st percentile. Part A of Trail Making normally is not sensitive to the effects of a TBI such as hers after six months from the date of injury (Dikmen et al., 1995). Part B of Trail Making is more complex than Part A because it requires divided attention. Her time of 259 seconds was about four times slower than the mean time expected.

On finger-tapping, her right hand score was less than 20% of the mean expected score and her left hand score was less than 25% of the expected mean score. Her finger-tapping scores were not consistent with her normal dexterity when manipulating a computer mouse on computerized tests.

The Neurobehavioral Symptom Inventory has a set of validity items, the validity-10 subscale. She obtained a score of 22, consistent with exaggeration of symptoms. A score of 22 has a specificity of 0.94. In a forensic practice setting with a high base rate of exaggeration, the positive predictive value is 0.86 (Lange et al., 2015).

On the MMPI-3, she obtained an elevated score on the Response Bias Scale (RBS) of 87, consistent with exaggerated cognitive symptoms. On the Restructured Clinical Scales, the only elevation was on a measure of somatic complaints with a score of 72, consistent either with genuine physical complaints or exaggerated physical complaints.

Interpretation of Test Results

Ms. B performed worse than chance, $p < 0.004$ for Difficult items on the VSVT and worse than chance, $p < 0.07$, on the total TOMM score, showing that she deliberately provided wrong answers and exaggerated on memory testing. Other failed memory PVTs were embedded measures in Digit Span (Reliable Digit Span) and the recognition discrimination scores of the HVLT-R and the BVMT-R. In the domain of visual processing, her DCT E score of 89 was extraordinarily high, far worse than any cutoff score. Her finger-tapping scores could not be plausibly explained except by exaggeration. There was symptom exaggeration on the MMPI-3 and the Neurobehavioral Symptom Inventory. The outcome of her Workers' Compensation claim is unknown.

Discussion

Ms. A and Ms. B performed invalidly across multiple domains of abilities. Both cases had finger-tapping scores on both hands of 10 and below, compared with the normal mean for females in the 40s. Finger-tapping scores are relatively unaffected by concussion in people with valid performance. Persons whose head injury was serious enough to require hospitalization but who followed commands within an hour of injury were tested a year after injury had median finger-tapping scores of 49 on the dominant hand and 46 on the nondominant hand (Dikmen et al., 1995). In a sample of unilateral stroke patients that was restricted to those who could complete a battery of motor tests, mean tapping scores for dominant and nondominant hands for the affected hand, the hand contralateral to the lesion, were greater than 40 (Haaland & Delaney, 1981). Finger-tapping scores in these two cases were worse than those obtained by most people with Parkinsonism (Matthews & Haaland, 1979): people with Parkinson's Disease motor involvement so severe that they underwent pallidotomy for relief of motor abnormalities averaged 30.9 on their right hands (standard deviation 10.8) and 30.2 with their left hands (standard deviation 10.7; Riordan et al., 1997). Finger-tapping scores as low as Case 1 and Case 2 are invalid (Arnold et al., 2005; Axelrod et al., 2014). Case 1 also demonstrated non-organic dyscoordination on nonstandardized testing, especially on finger-to-nose testing.

Both Ms. A and Ms. B performed significantly worse than chance on FCTs that assessed memory complaints. On the TOMM, Ms. A had a probability worse than chance of 0.000013 and less than 0.08 on the VSVT. On the VSVT Difficult items, Ms. B had a probability worse than chance of less than 0.004 and less than 0.07 on the TOMM. The FCT results on the VSVT of Ms. A and on the TOMM on Ms. B were significantly worse than chance with probability levels well under 0.20 (Binder et al., 2014; Binder & Chafetz, 2018; Rohling et al., 2023).

Visual processing difficulties were exaggerated by both cases. Both cases failed the DCT. Ms. A used vision complaints as an excuse to not complete some of the testing.

Both Ms. A and Ms. B failed other embedded measures of validity discussed above.

Ms. A did not fail any symptom validity tests (SVTs), failing to complete the Neurobehavioral Symptom Inventory and completing the MMPI-2-RF. Ms. B failed SVTs, including the Validity-10 index of the Neurobehavioral Symptom Inventory and the MMPI-3 RBS scale.

These cases illustrate the application of a probability level of 0.20 and below for standardized FCTs when assessing performance validity. They also illustrate the value of standardized and nonstandardized testing of dexterity and motor abilities. Upper extremity motor deficits are not characteristic of people with TBI (Dikmen et al., 1995). Some people claiming prolonged symptoms after alleged concussions exaggerate on measures of upper extremity coordination and dexterity.

In my reports of these evaluations, I stated that these examinees deliberately gave wrong answers and explained that they performed significantly worse than chance on tests with items that had a 0.5 probability of being guessed correctly. I pointed out that in these cases, the abnormally low scores provided no evidence of genuine neuropsychological impairment because the results showed deliberate underperformance. I discussed the lack of objective evidence of cognitive deficits and the conclusion from the neuropsychological outcome literature on mTBI that one would not expect cognitive deficits after the injuries that they allegedly sustained (Iverson et al., 2019; Rohling et al., 2011).

The neuropsychological outcome literature on mTBI was important, in my view, because it demonstrated that it was unlikely that these examinees had permanent cognitive impairment from their alleged injuries and that it could not be reasonably argued that my evaluations showed both exaggerated results and genuine impairment. In Workers Compensation Claims in Oregon (Ms. B), where I practice, a lack of objective evidence of neuropsychological impairment has considerable legal weight, and it is important to point out that lack of objective evidence in neuropsychological reports. In Oregon lawsuits decided by three arbitrators (Ms. A) or by juries, the probative weight of a lack of objective evidence of impairment is determined by the triers of fact. The attorney for the defendant in lawsuits alleging permanent brain injury after possible mTBI can argue that testimony about the lack of objective evidence of impairment and the favorable neuropsychological outcome after mTBI should persuade the trier of fact that damages for permanent brain injury should not be awarded.

Ms. A and Ms. B were malingering. They had financial incentives and their underperformance on testing was intentional.

Malingering was defined as a "volitional exaggeration or fabrication of cognitive dysfunction for the purpose of obtaining substantial material gain, or avoiding or escaping formal duty or responsibility" (Martin et al., 2015, p. 552). Sherman et al. (2020, p. 739) defined malingering as "the volitional feigning or exaggerating of neurocognitive, somatic, or psychiatric symptoms for the purpose of obtaining material gain and services or avoiding formal duty, responsibility, or undesirable outcome." Both definitions are cited in the current AACN position paper on validity assessment (Sweet et al., 2021). Both the AACN position paper (Sweet et al., 2021) and Sherman et al. (2020) stated that results that were significantly below chance on forced-choice testing indicate that wrong answers were given deliberately and were consistent with a diagnosis of malingering when occurring within a context of external incentives for impairment. A diagnosis of malingering was defensible for both cases.

References

Arnold, G., Boone, K. B., Lu, P., Dean, A., Wen, J., Nitch, S., & McPherson, S. (2005). Sensitivity and specificity of finger tapping test scores for the detection of suspect effort. *The Clinical Neuropsychologist*, *19*(1), 105–120. https://doi.org/10.1080/13854040490888567

Axelrod, B. N., Meyers, J. E., & Davis, J. J. (2014). Finger Tapping Test performance as a measure of performance validity. *The Clinical Neuropsychologist*, *28*(5), 876–888. https://doi.org/10.1080/13854046.2014.907583

Bailey, K. C., Soble, J. R., Bain, K. M., & Fullen, C. (2018). Embedded performance validity tests in the Hopkins Verbal Learning Test-Revised and the brief visuospatial memory test-Revised: A replication study. *Archives of Clinical Neuropsychology*, *33*(7), 895–900. https://doi.org/10.1093/arclin/acx111

Binder, L. M., & Chafetz, M. D. (2018). Determination of the smoking gun of intent: Significance testing of forced choice results in social security claimants. *The Clinical Neuropsychologist, 32*(1), 132–144. https://doi.org/10.1080/13854046.2017.1337931

Binder, L. M., Larrabee, G. J., & Millis, S. R. (2014). Intent to fail: Significance testing of forced choice test results. *The Clinical Neuropsychologist, 28*(8), 1366–1375. https://doi.org/10.1080/13854046.2014.978383

Dikmen, S. S., Machamer, J. E., Winn, H. R., & Temkin, N. R. (1995). Neuropsychological outcome at 1-year post head injury. *Neuropsychology, 9*(1), 80–90. https://doi.org/10.1037/0894-4105.9.1.80

Eglit, G. M. L., Jurick, S. M., Delis, D. C., Filoteo, J. V., Bondi, M. W., & Jak, A. J. (2020). Utility of the D-KEFS Color Word Interference Test as an embedded measure of performance validity. *The Clinical neuropsychologist, 34*(2), 332–352. https://doi.org/10.1080/13854046.2019.1643923

Grote, C. L., Kooker, E. K., Garron, D. C., Nyenhuis, D. L., Smith, C. A., & Mattingly, M. L. (2000). Performance of compensation seeking and non-compensation seeking samples on the Victoria symptom validity test: Cross-validation and extension of a standardization study. *Journal of Clinical and Experimental Neuropsychology, 22*(6), 709–719. https://doi.org/10.1076/jcen.22.6.709.958

Haaland, K. Y., & Delaney, H. D. (1981). Motor deficits after left or right hemisphere damage due to stroke or tumor. *Neuropsychologia, 19*(1), 17–27. https://doi.org/10.1016/0028-3932(81)90040-3

Iverson, G. L., Karr, J. E., Gardner, A. J., Silverberg, N. D., & Terry, D. P. (2019). Results of scoping review do not support mild traumatic brain injury being associated with a high incidence of chronic cognitive impairment: Commentary on McInnes et al. 2017. *PloS one, 14*(9), e0218997. https://doi.org/10.1371/journal.pone.0218997

Lange, R. T., Brickell, T. A., Lippa, S. M., & French, L. M. (2015). Clinical utility of the Neurobehavioral Symptom Inventory validity scales to screen for symptom exaggeration following traumatic brain injury. *Journal of Clinical and Experimental Neuropsychology, 37*(8), 853–862. https://doi.org/10.1080/13803395.2015.1064864

Macciocchi, S. N., Seel, R. T., Alderson, A., & Godsall, R. (2006). Victoria Symptom Validity Test performance in acute severe traumatic brain injury: Implications for test interpretation. *Archives of Clinical Neuropsychology, 21*(5), 395–404. https://doi.org/10.1016/j.acn.2006.06.003

Macciocchi, S. N., Seel, R. T., Yi, A., & Small, S. (2017). Medical Symptom Validity Test performance following moderate-severe traumatic brain injury: Expectations based on orientation log classification. *Archives of Clinical Neuropsychology, 32*(3), 339–348. https://doi.org/10.1093/arclin/acw112

Martin, P. K., Hunter, B. P., Rach, A. M., Heinrichs, R. J., & Schroeder, R. W. (2017). Excessive decline from premorbid functioning: Detecting performance invalidity with the WAIS-IV and demographic predictions. *The Clinical Neuropsychologist, 31*(5), 829–843. https://doi.org/10.1080/13854046.2017.1284265

Martin, P. K., Schroeder, R. W., & Odland, A. P. (2015). Neuropsychologists' validity testing beliefs and practices: A survey of North American professionals. *The Clinical Neuropsychologist, 29*(6), 741–776.

Matthews, C. G., & Haaland, K. Y. (1979). The effect of symptom duration on cognitive and motor performance in parkinsonism. *Neurology, 29*(7), 951–956. https://doi.org/10.1212/wnl.29.7.951

Miller, L. S., & Rohling, M. L. (2001). A statistical interpretive method for neuropsychological test data. *Neuropsychology Review, 11*(3), 143–169. https://doi:10.1023/a:1016602708066

Moore, R. A., Lippa, S. M., Brickell, T. A., French, L. M., & Lange, R. T. (2020). Clinical utility of WAIS-IV 'excessive decline from premorbid functioning' scores to detect invalid test performance following traumatic brain injury. *The Clinical Neuropsychologist, 34*(3), 512–528. https://doi.org/10.1080/13854046.2019.1668059

Olsen, D. H., Schroeder, R. W., Heinrichs, R. J., & Martin, P. K. (2019). Examination of optimal embedded PVTs within the BVMT-R in an outpatient clinical sample. *The Clinical Neuropsychologist, 33*(4), 732–742. https://doi.org/10.1080/13854046.2018.1501096

Reynolds, C. R., & Horton, Jr. A. M. (2012). Clinical acumen, common sense, and data-based decision making in the assessment of dissimulation during head injury litigation. In Reynolds, C. R., & Horton, Jr., A. M. (Eds.), *Detection of malingering during head injury litigation* (pp. 351–370). New York: Springer.

Riordan, H. J., Flashman, L. A., & Roberts, D. W. (1997). Neurocognitive and psychosocial correlates of ventroposterolateral pallidotomy surgery in Parkinson's disease. *Neurosurgical Focus*, *2*(3), e7. https://doi.org/10.3171/foc.1997.2.6.8

Rohling, M. L., Binder, L. M., Demakis, G. J., Larrabee, G. J., Ploetz, D. M., & Langhinrichsen-Rohling, J. (2011). A meta-analysis of neuropsychological outcome after mild traumatic brain injury: Re-analyses and reconsiderations of Binder et al. (1997), Frencham et al. (2005), and Pertab et al. (2009). *The Clinical Neuropsychologist*, *25*(4), 608–623. https://doi.org/10.1080/13854046.2011.565076

Rohling, M. L., Binder, L. M., Larrabee, G. J., & Langhinrichsen-Rohling, J. (2023). Forced choice test score of $p \leq .20$ and failures on ≥ six performance validity tests results in similar Overall Test Battery Means. *The Clinical Neuropsychologist*, 1–17. Advance online publication. https://doi.org/10.1080/13854046.2023.2284975

Sawyer, R. J., Testa, S. M., & Dux, M. (2017). Embedded performance validity tests within the Hopkins Verbal Learning Test - Revised and the Brief Visuospatial Memory Test - Revised. *The Clinical Neuropsychologist*, *31*(1), 207–218. https://doi.org/10.1080/13854046.2016.1245787

Sherman, E. M. S., Slick, D. J., & Iverson, G. L. (2020). Multidimensional malingering criteria for neuropsychological assessment: A 20-year update of the malingered neuropsychological dysfunction criteria. *Archives of Clinical Neuropsychology, 35*(6), 735–764. https://doi:10.1093/arclin/acaa019

Silk-Eglit, G. M., Lynch, J. K., & McCaffrey, R. J. (2016). Validation of Victoria symptom validity test cutoff scores among mild traumatic brain injury litigants using a known-groups design. *Archives of clinical neuropsychology*, *31*(3), 231–245. https://doi.org/10.1093/arclin/acv108

Silverberg, N. D., Iverson, G. L., ACRM Brain Injury Special Interest Group Mild TBI Task Force members: Cogan, A., Dams-O-Connor, K., Delmonico, R., Graf, M. J. P., Iaccarino, M. A., Kajankova, M., Kamins, J., McCulloch, K. L., McKinney, G., Nagele, D., Panenka, W. J., Rabinowitz, A. R., Reed, N., Wethe, J. V., Whitehair, V., ACRM Mild TBI Diagnostic Criteria Expert Consensus Group: Anderson, V., ... Zemek, R. (2023). The American Congress of rehabilitation medicine diagnostic criteria for mild traumatic brain injury. *Archives of Physical Medicine and Rehabilitation*, *104*(8), 1343–1355. https://doi.org/10.1016/j.apmr.2023.03.036

Sweet, J. J., Heilbronner, R. L., Morgan, J. E., Larrabee, G. J., Rohling, M. L., Boone, K. B., Kirkwood, M. W., Schroeder, R. W., Suhr, J. A., & Conference Participants. (2021). American Academy of Clinical Neuropsychology (AACN) 2021 consensus statement on validity assessment: Update of the 2009 AACN consensus conference statement on neuropsychological assessment of effort, response bias, and malingering. *The Clinical Neuropsychologist, 35*(6), 1053–1106. https://doi.org/10.1080/13854046.2021.1896036

VA/DOD The Management and Rehabilitation of Post-Acute Mild Traumatic Brain Injury Work Group. (2021). VA/DoD https://www.healthquality.va.gov/guidelines/rehab/mtbi/

11 Neurobehavioral Impairment versus Malingering Following Moderate–Severe Traumatic Brain Injury

Stephen N. Macciocchi

Background

Mr. AH is a 51-year-old white man who sustained a moderate–severe traumatic brain injury (MSTBI) during a motor vehicle accident (MVA) three years prior to the current examination. Prior to sustaining a MSTBI, Mr. AH had a history of cardiovascular disease (CVD), which required a stent and medication, but his cardiac function was stable when he was injured and did not change following his MSTBI. Mr. AH had no history of neurological trauma-disease prior to his MSTBI. He also had no history of diagnosed psychiatric or substance use conditions. Mr. AH was reportedly a productive worker in a local waste management position for several decades prior to his MSTBI. Following his MSTBI, Mr. AH was hospitalized for several weeks in a local trauma center and then for numerous weeks in an inpatient neurorehabilitation program, following which he completed a six-week multidisciplinary outpatient therapy program focused on mitigating his residual neurocognitive and neurobehavioral deficits.

When examined, Mr. AH had retained counsel to litigate his personal injury and Workers' Compensation claims. Mr. AH's attorney and defense counsel were scheduled to mediate his case, but defense counsel expressed concern about the plaintiff neuropsychologist's opinion, which stated Mr. AH was "totally and permanently disabled" and he required "24-hour supervision" in his home and community, possibly for the duration of his life. Consequently, defense counsel requested a second neuropsychological assessment to determine whether Mr. AH was totally and permanently disabled and the extent of daily supervision he required.

Behavioral Observations

Mr. AH ambulated independently, but somewhat slowly with no overt gait or balance problems. Mr. AH did not evidence any significant hearing or vision limitations, but he used glasses to read during his examination. Mr. AH was alert and oriented to time, place, and situation. His speech was fluent with generally normal prosody and no overt evidence of paraphasias or dysnomia, but at times, his narrative and discourse was digressive, and in some instances clearly tangential. His language comprehension was functional for examination purposes and he had no difficulty understanding test instructions. Mr. AH's social pragmatics were generally intact, although he made sexually inappropriate comments directed toward the examining female psychometrist. Mr. AH also appeared frustrated and at times became angry, most often when tests were cognitively challenging. He was impulsive when responding to some test items and he continued to be impulsive despite frequent guidance

DOI: 10.4324/9781003005063-13

regarding the need to follow test instructions. Mr. AH worked slowly, and he reported being fatigued at several points in time, so he was given several breaks during the examination to optimize his performance.

Interview

Before beginning Mr. AH's clinical interview and testing, he and his spouse were educated regarding the nature, purpose, and conditions of the examination, including the importance of optimal engagement and performance during the entire examination. Mr. AH consented verbally and in writing to complete the examination, which was witnessed and assented to by his spouse who was his power of attorney. Mr. AH was initially reticent to discuss his injury and symptoms, but after a brief period, he became more relaxed and discussed his injuries and current functioning in more detail. He denied recall of his MVA and subsequent hospitalizations. He was able to recall some aspects of his outpatient treatment. He also recalled being tested about one year prior by a "doctor", but he could not recall the neuropsychologist's name, what tests were administered, whether a report was generated or whether he received feedback based on his performance.

Even though Mr. AH was aware he sustained injuries during his MVA, he was unable to clearly and coherently describe how his MSTBI had affected his life, other than to say he got tired easily and he had to follow his spouse's wishes, which he described as annoying. Mr. AH initially denied having any significant neurocognitive limitations, but when pressed, he admitted his memory was less proficient following his injury, but "still as good" as his spouse and same-aged peers. Mr. AH also denied experiencing any behavior or psychological problems. However, according to medical records and his family, he had routinely been socially inappropriate in his home, neighborhood, and community as evidenced by him making sporadic, unbecoming sexual comments and his angry comportment in interpersonal interactions, which deviated substantially from his pre-injury demeanor. When queried about work, Mr. AH stated he had not returned to work since his accident, but he stated that if he was given a chance, he could perform his job without significant problems. He also believed he could return to driving, even though his spouse was adamant about not letting him drive.

Mr. AH recalled speaking with an attorney about his MSTBI on one occasion, but he could not recall the attorney's name or content of their discussion other than his attorney was trying to "help him" get his medical bills paid. Mr. AH was not engaged in therapy when examined, although he apparently was prescribed home-based cognitive therapy tasks, which he reported completing only when forced to by his wife. When examined, he was prescribed Lisinopril, aspirin, Aricept, and Sildenafil, which he understood to be blood pressure, memory, and "sex" medications. Mr. AH did not evidence socially inappropriate behavior during his clinical interview. Finally, Mr. AH denied and did not evidence overt neuropsychiatric symptomatology, including hallucinations, delusions, compulsions, apathy, or self-injurious ideation.

Record Review

Mr. AH's records included documents from emergency medical services (EMS), his local trauma center, a regional, inpatient neurorehabilitation program, an associated outpatient neurorehabilitation program and a neuropsychological report written by a consultant retained by his attorney. Based on records, Mr. AH had to be extracted from his vehicle following the MVA. His Glasgow Coma Scale (GCS) score was an eight when initially examined by EMS personnel approximately 30 minutes after his MVA. Due to agitation,

Mr. AH was sedated twice (Versed 5 mg) by EMS staff while being transported to a local trauma center. When examined in the hospital emergency department, he was initially unresponsive, possibly due to sedation. His GCS score returned to an eight approximately 36 hours after admission. Neuroimaging (CT scan) revealed a right frontal-parietal subdural hematoma (SDH) with a minimal midline shift (8 mm) and a Grade 2, left, frontal subarachnoid hemorrhage (SAH). Mr. AH did not evidence neurological deterioration, so he was treated conservatively despite his intracranial lesions. After five days, Mr. AH's GCS score improved to 12, even though repeat neuroimaging revealed no clinically significant change in his SDH or SAH volume. Mr. AH required intermittent sedation for agitated behavior during his acute care admission. Repeat imaging revealed an observable decrease in his SDH volume after ten days, but he remained confused (GCS = 13). Although Mr. AH had a history of cardiovascular disease (CVD), including a stent, he experienced no cardiovascular or other medical complications while hospitalized. At the time of his transfer to inpatient neurorehabilitation, he was reported to be intermittently irritable, agitated, and uncooperative, despite being prescribed Buspar 50 mg.

When admitted to inpatient neurorehabilitation, Mr. AH's Rancho Los Amigos level was 5–6 according to rehabilitation staff. He was generally cooperative, but not fully and consistently oriented. He also was resistant to engaging in therapy, especially occupational therapy. He was treated by multidisciplinary staff for cognitive (attention and memory deficits) and physical problems (balance and unsafe ambulation). Mr. AH was also treated by neuropsychology staff for neurobehavioral problems, including anosognosia for his functional limitations and inappropriate behavior, such as sexually provocative discourse and intermittent anger outbursts. His neurobehavioral problems diminished over the duration of his rehabilitation hospitalization, as did his physical limitations. When discharged from inpatient neurorehabilitation, Mr. AH was temporally and spatial oriented, able to ambulate independently with standby supervision, and able to comport himself more appropriately in social situations. He continued evidence attention and executive and memory deficits based on a brief neurocognitive assessment. Mr. AH was discharged to the care of his family and subsequently completed outpatient neurorehabilitation therapy primarily focused on his neurocognitive and neurobehavioral symptoms, including memory impairment and behavior dyscontrol. After approximately six weeks, Mr. AH was discharged from outpatient therapy and he returned home, despite persisting neurocognitive and neurobehavioral problems. His follow-up care included home health services for approximately one month and physiatry appointments every three months.

Test Results

Mr. AH had numerous low ($T < 40$) neurocognitive test scores. He also had numerous invalid PVT scores (8). Mr. AH's overall test battery mean declined from mildly impaired ($T = 35$) during his initial examination one year earlier to moderately impaired during the current examination ($T = 29$). Mr. AH also evidenced moderate over-reporting on several MMPI-2-RF validity scales (F-s, FBS-r, and RBS), but his over-reporting of cognitive and somatic symptoms on the MMPI-2-RF contrasted with his general denial of cognitive and somatic symptoms when questioned during his interview. He also had modest elevations on 3 MMPI-2-RF clinical and problem scales (RC1, COG, NUC), which were consistent with his injury history. Because Mr. AH's family reported he had limited awareness of cognitive deficits and because he evidenced similar unawareness when examined, the extent to which elevations on MMPI-2RF validity scales reflect symptom exaggeration is not entirely clear (Ben-Porath, 2012). Neurocognitive, performance, and symptom validity scores are reported in Tables 11.1–11.3.

Table 11.1 Neurocognitive Scores

Intellectual Functioning	*Time 1*	*Time 2*	*Comment*
			NC = No comparison
Wechsler Adult Intelligence Test-IV			
Verbal Comprehension Index	90	72	Lower score
Perceptual Reasoning Index	88	69	Lower score
Working Memory Index	66	71	Stable score
Processing Speed Index	76	53	Lower score
Full Scale Iq Score	80	61	Lower score
Estimated General Pre-Morbid Ability			
TOPF Reading Score	82	85	Stable score
TOPF Demographic Score	NA	90	NC
Executive functioning			
Wisconsin Card Sorting Test			
Perseverative Responses	NA	$T = 29$	NC
Perseverative Errors	NA	$T = 27$	NC
Categories Completed (1)	NA	$T < 30$	NC
Failure to Maintain Set (2)	NA	$T < 35$	NC
Category Test	$T = 35$	NA	NC
Delis Kaplan Executive Functioning			
Color-Word Interference			
Color Naming	NA	$T = 25$	NC
Word Reading	NA	$T = 25$	NC
Inhibition	NA	$T = 25$	NC
Inhibition-Switching	NA	$T = 33$	NC
Delis Kaplan Trail Making			
Visual Scanning	NA	$T = 25$	NC
number Sequencing	NA	$T = 25$	NC
Letter Sequencing	NA	$T = 25$	NC
Inhibition-Switching	NA	$T = 25$	NC
Number-Letter Switching	$T = 32$[1]	$T = 31$	NC
Verbal Fluency			
Phonemic Fluency	$T = 35$[2]	$T = 34$	Stable score
Category Fluency	NA	$T = 29$	NC
Category Switching	NA	$T = 29$	NC
Switching Accuracy	NA	$T = 40$	NC
Language Functioning			
Boston Naming Test			
Correct Responses	$T = 34$	$T = 25$	Lower score
Memory functioning			
Wechsler Memory Scale			
WMS-IV Logical Memory I	$T = 36$	$T = 32$	Lower score
WMS-IV Logical Memory II	$T = 32$	$T = 40$	Higher score
WMS-IV Visual Reproduction I	$T = 50$	$T = 46$	Stable score
WMS-IV Visual Reproduction II	$T = 43$	$T = 45$	Stable score

(*Continued*)

Table 11.1 (Continued)

Intellectual Functioning	*Time 1*	*Time 2*	*Comment*
California Verbal Learning Test-II			
CVLT-II Trial 1	NA	$T = 40$	NC
CVLT-II Trial 1–5	NA	$T = 35$	NC
CVLT-II Short Delayed Free Recall	NA	$T = 35$	NC
CVLT-II Short Delayed Cued Recall	NA	$T = 30$	NC
CVLT-II Long Delayed Free Recall	NA	$T = 30$	NC
CVLT-II Long Delayed Cued Recall	NA	$T = 35$	NC
Motor			
Finger Tapping Test: Dominant ($R = 31$)	NA	$T = 21$	NC
Finger Tapping Test: Non-Dominant ($L = 34$)	NA	$T = 30$	NC

Table 11.2 PVT Scores

Performance Validity			*Scores*
Rey-15			
Recall	8	NA	<Expectation (9)
Dot Counting			
E Score	20	NA	<Expectation (17)
Medical Symptom Validity Test			
Immediate Recognition	NA	80%	<Expectation (90%)
Delayed Recognition	NA	70%	<Expectation (90%)
Consistency	NA	70%	<Expectation (90%)
Test Of Memory Malingering			
Trial 1	NA	30/60%	<Expectation (45–49)
Trial 2	NA	33/66%	<Expectation (45–49)
Retention	NA	35/70%	<Expectation (45–49)
Victoria Symptom Validity Test			
E Trial	NA	20	<Expectation (24)
H Trial	NA	12	<Expectation (17)
Total	NA	32	<Expectation (41)
Color-Word Interference Test			
Scaled Score Total	NA	5	<Expectation (17)
CVLT- II Forced Choice			
Number Correct	NA	10	<Expectation (14)
Advanced Clinical Solutions (Acs)			
Reliable Digit Span (6)	NR	<15%	<Expectation (7/>25%)
Logical Memory Recognition (18)	NR	<15%	<Expectation (21/>25%)
Visual Reproduction Recognition (2)	NR	<5%	<Expectation (4/>25%)
ACS Combined Base Rates			
Clinical Sample ($N = 371$)	NR	2%	Highly infrequent
TBI sample ($N = 36$)	NR	0%	Highly infrequent

Table 11.3 SVT Scores

MMPI-2-RF	*Score*	*Interpretation*
Validity Scales		
Variable Response Inconsistency	*T* = 43	No inconsistency
True Response Inconsistency	*T* = 50	No inconsistency
Infrequent Responses	*T* = 78	Over-reporting
Infrequent Psychopathology	*T* = 59	No over-reporting
Infrequent Somatic Symptoms	*T* = 84	Over-reporting
Symptom Validity	*T* = 80	Over-reporting
Response Bias	*T* = 82	Over-reporting
Clinical Scales (T > 70)	Score	Description
Somatic Complaints	*T* = 79	Mildly elevated
Neurologic Complaints	*T* = 80	Moderately elevated
Cognitive Complaints	*T* = 78	Mildly elevated

Interpretation

Based on records, Mr. AH sustained a MSTBI. He also had a history of CVD, but no pre-injury history of neurocognitive impairment or cardiovascular-related changes in brain morphology on MRI. Mr. AH had eight invalid PVT scores, which greatly exceeds the number of invalid PVT scores considered sufficient to meet malingering criteria (Sherman, Slick and Iverson, 2020). He also evidenced mild-moderate symptom over-reporting on the MMPI-2-RF, which did not invalidate his MMPI-2-RF profile, but raised concerns about cognitive and somatic symptom over-reporting. In contrast, he denied experiencing neurocognitive impairment unless repeatedly questioned, so the extent to which symptom validity is a concern was not clear.

Whether simply counting the number of Mr. AH's invalid PVTs or using Naïve Bayes or Likelihood Ratio methodology, the probability Mr. AH's PVT scores are invalid exceeds 97% (Holdnack, Millis, Larrabee et al., 2013; Davis, 2021; Sweet, Heilbronner, Morgan et al., 2021). In addition to pervasively invalid PVT performance, Mr. AH also evidenced a decline in neurocognitive performance on a subset of tests relative to his first examination, despite collateral reports of improved functioning at home and in his community. His decline in test performance was inconsistent with known patterns of brain function following a MSTBI. In addition, he performed more proficiently on genuine memory tests like the WMS-IV and CVLT than on PVTs such as the VSVT, MSVT, and TOMM, which require virtually no memory capacity.

Even though Mr. AH would be expected to have clinically meaningful neurocognitive impairment secondary to his MSTBI, his brain injury alone cannot explain his low PVT scores and decreased performance on neurocognitive tests over time. In such cases, malingering must be considered as a possible, if not probable diagnosis. Nevertheless, factors other than malingering could also explain Mr. AH's deficient PVT and neurocognitive test performance. For instance, he repeatedly denied experiencing neurocognitive impairment and neurobehavioral problems, which were reported by reliable, collateral sources, and were observed during his examination. Not only did Mr. AH evidence anosognosia, which is common following MSTBI (Steward and Kretzmer, 2021), but he was highly oppositional when examined. He also could not appreciate why optimal performance was in his best interest, despite education and encouragement before and during his neuropsychological examination. Anosognosia aside, simply being oppositional when being examined can cause low PVT and neurocognitive scores (Martin and Schroeder, 2020). Therefore, a case can be made that Mr. AH's test data is invalid, but his inability to appreciate his residual neurocognitive and neurobehavioral impairment and his oppositional attitude toward and variable cooperativeness during his examination raised concerns regarding a malingering diagnosis (Sherman, Slick and Iverson, 2020).

Summary and Conclusions

Mr. AH sustained a MSTBI that required extended hospitalization and treatment. When comparing Mr. AH's first and second examinations, he evidenced clinically non-credible decline in neurocognitive test performance consistent with his increased number of invalid PVTs (Davis, McHugh, Axelrod et al., 2012; Proto, Pastorek, Miller et al., 2014; Copeland, Mahoney, Block et al., 2016; Uiterwijk, Stargatt and Crowe, 2022). Mr. AH also displayed general unawareness of his neurocognitive and neurobehavioral impairments, which was accompanied by an oppositional attitude toward being tested. The extent to which his anosognosia and oppositional demeanor negatively impacted his test performance, including his performance on PVTs is not entirely clear, but given clinical observations related to his lack of engagement, oppositional attitude, denial of impairment, and poor judgment argues against concluding he was malingering as would be assumed based solely on PVT scores. Nevertheless, Mr. AH's data is clearly invalid and certainly underestimates his optimal neurocognitive abilities, so specific referral questions related to damages caused by his MSTBI cannot be answered based on his current test data.

Discussion

Mr. AH's case highlights several important considerations when performing examinations of persons with MSTBI. First, extensive research shows persons who sustain a MSTBI will experience residual neuropsychological impairment and functional disability in some form although there is variability in outcomes (Bramlett and Dietrich, 2015; Hammond, Perkins, Corrigan et al., 2021; CDC.gov/TBI; www.tbindsc.org). High rates of morbidity following MSTBI is in large part due to the current lack of efficacious pharmaceuticals targeting the primary component of MSTBI, including axonal, glial, and dendritic damage (Solnick, Maas, Narayan et al., 2014; Maas, Steyerberg, and Citerio, 2021). In other words, the primary component of MSTBI cannot be treated via traditional medical interventions. In any case, Mr. AH would be expected to evidence at least moderate, residual neurocognitive impairment (Dikmen, Machamer, and Winn, 1995; Rohling, Millis, and Meyers, 2003). Second, despite sustaining a MSTBI with known morbidity, obtaining a reliable estimate of Mr. AH's functioning was complicated by his very high number of invalid PVT scores as well as clinically non-credible neurocognitive test performance in some domains, which has previously been reported following MSTBI (Bianchini, Greve, and Love, 2009; Paniak, 2009; Sweet and Giuffre Meyer, 2011). In other words, while Mr. AH meets existing guidelines for malingered neurocognitive dysfunction, there are neurobehavioral factors that complicate a malingering diagnosis (Sherman, Slick, and Iverson, 2020).

Before directly addressing whether Mr. AH was malingering, a brief review of performance validity issues may be helpful. First, some neuropsychologists have expressed concerns about using performance validity metrics when persons have significant neurological injuries (Bigler, 2012), but extensive research reveals persons who are alert, oriented, able to attend when tested, and who have sufficient endurance to complete a neuropsychological assessment perform at or above empirically established expectations on PVTs (Green, Rohling, Lees-Haley and Allen, 2001; Larrabee, 2003; Slick, Tan, Strauss et al., 2003; Macciocchi, Seel, Alderson and Godsall, 2006; Macciocchi, Seel, Yi, and Small, 2013; Jones, 2013; Carone, Green and Drane, 2013; Green and Flaro, 2015; Gates, Metcalf, Sabaz et al., 2023). Despite Mr. AH's MSTBI history, he was alert, oriented, able to engage in testing, and, to a large degree, functional in basic activities of daily living (IADL) at home, so he should not have had difficulty scoring above empirically derived expectations on the PVTs administered.

Second, some researchers also argue that administering multiple PVTs while not considering both positive and negative PVT results may lead to an increase in false positive malingering diagnoses (Berthelson, Mulchan, Odland et al., 2013; Bilder, Sugar and Hellemann, 2014; Frederick, 2015). In contrast, numerous PVT investigators disagree (Davis and Millis, 2014a, 2014b; Larrabee, 2014a, 2014b; Larrabee, Rohling and Meyers, 2019; Davis, 2021; Chafetz, 2022). Despite research showing multiple PVT use does not increase false positive malingering diagnoses, some investigators continue to insist the use of multiple PVTs is diagnostically problematic (Leonhard, 2023), primarily based on complex statistical simulations. The statistical issues involved in mathematically combining positive and negative PVT findings is beyond the scope of this case discussion, but Larrabee, Rohling and Meyers (2019), Davis (2021), and Rohling, Larrabee and Davis (2025) have demonstrated multiple PVTs can be administered without exceeding a 10% false positive rate. In other words, examiners can be confident of administering multiple PVTs, even in cases like Mr. AH's. As an aside, Erdodi (2023) concluded "there is no such thing as too many PVTs, only insufficiently conservative multivariate cutoffs". Fortunately, neuropsychologists have access to resources for determining false positive rates when utilizing multiple PVTs (Davis, 2021; Erdodi, 2023; Rohling, Binder, Larrabee et al., 2024).

Put another way, assuming all test data is valid following MSTBI is at best naïve and at worst potentially harmful to examinees' well-being, as well as society at large (Chafetz and Underhill, 2013; Denning and Shura, 2019). For instance, research has shown even persons being examined in clinical contexts have invalid data rates ranging from 15% to 25%, so validity concerns are not confined to litigation cases (Sherer, Davis, Sander et al., 2013; Marcopulos, Caillouet, Bailey et al., 2014; An, Kaploun, Erdodi et al., 2016; Jennette, Williams, Resch et al., 2022; Martin and Schroeder, 2020; Roor, Peters, Dandachi-FitzGerald et al., 2024). Regardless, critics of administering multiple PVTs in forensic cases seem to ignore or misunderstand that practice guidelines do not only consider PVT scores, but all neuropsychological data, which may reveal anomalous patterns of test performance and behavior (Sweet, Heilbronner, Morgan et al., 2021). In other words, practice guidelines do not stipulate clinicians must rely solely on PVT scores when assessing performance validity, let alone when concluding that malingering is present (Sherman, Slick and Iverson, 2020; Sweet, Heilbronner, Morgan et al., 2021). Simply put, most clinicians are reluctant to address performance validity, let alone malingering, when examinees are neurologically impaired. Nevertheless, sooner or later, clinicians will face similar questions when examining persons with MSTBI or other significant neurological conditions. Not surprisingly, Meehl (1973) addressed this dilemma decades ago when he argued clinicians can and should be "soft hearted", but not "soft headed", so compassion and objectivity are not mutually exclusive.

Setting compassion aside, given Mr. AH's test data, examiners have several reasonable courses of action. The first option is to simply state Mr. AH's test data are invalid and cannot be used to address any referral questions. Many neuropsychologists would choose this option without hesitation. A second option is to conclude Mr. AH's test data are invalid, but he would be expected to evidence moderate impairment based on existing MSTBI outcome research. As an example, decades ago, Dikmen, Machamer, and Winn (1995) showed persons like Mr. AH who were unable to reliably follow commands for 14–28 days had moderate neurocognitive impairment at one year post-injury. Rohling, Meyers, and Millis (2003) also found the duration of unconsciousness (LOC) and post-traumatic amnesia were strongly associated with residual impairment following MSTBI. While investigators have shown various TBI severity metrics are useful when estimating residual impairment following MSTBI, research also shows neuropsychological test data collected early following injury may be an even better predictor of MSTBI deficits at one year post-injury (Hanks, Millis, Ricker et al., 2008). Unfortunately, in Mr. AH's case, there were no available early post-injury neurocognitive test data and his initial neuropsychological examination was more likely than not invalid based on PVT scores, so clinicians taking this approach would have to rely on existing MSTBI outcome research that used similar injury severity surrogates to estimate MSTBI-related residual neurocognitive impairment.

Many clinicians would not consider the second option mentioned, but in some cases, doing so may inform the court and treaters about expected injury consequences and treatment needs following MSTBI. In other words, Mr. AH clearly has a history of a life-altering brain injury. He also has residual impairment based on records and reliable collateral resources. Behavioral observations also document the presence of anosognosia and inappropriate behavior, both of which are common sequelae of MSTBI (Steward and Kretzmer, 2021). Nonetheless, addressing specific referral questions based on existing MSTBI research can be risky. As an example, not all persons who sustain a MSTBI perform similarly due to variable injury characteristics (Rohling, Millis and Meyers, 2003; McCrea, Giacino, Barber et al., 2021). Second, the extent to which existing MSTBI outcome research can be fully trusted is unclear. A case in point is Sherer, Davis, Sander et al. (2013) who found "poor performance validity was common [>25%] in a research sample of persons with medically documented [MSTBI] who were not evaluated in conjunction with litigation, compensation claims, or current report of symptoms". Subsequently, the authors along with other colleagues more closely examined patterns of invalidity in this sample (N = 141) and found different explanations for underperforming on neurocognitive tests (Sherer, Sander, Ponsford et al., 2020). While this decade-old research should have been a warning to all MSTBI investigators, a very recent TRACK-MSTBI outcome publication (McCrea, Giacino, Barber et al., 2021) apparently failed to examine performance validity in their sample even though embedded PVTs were available for analysis (Ashendorf and Sugarman, 2016; Ashendorf,, 2019; Pliskin, DeDios, Stern et al., 2021). Consequently, if clinicians use data from existing research cohorts to estimate expected impairment, attention should be paid to whether the researchers included, analyzed, and reported performance validity data, not to mention excluded MSTBI participants who performed sub-optimally on PVTs.

Overall, most neuropsychologists will be referred persons with MSTBI at some point in their career, even if they are not employed in neurorehabilitation settings (Sweet, Klipfel, Nelson et al., 2021). Mr. AH's examination data and existing research substantiates the need for including multiple PVT measures in all neuropsychological examinations following MSTBI (Bianchini, Greve, and Love, 2009; Paniak, 2009; Sweet and Giuffre Meyer, 2011). Neuropsychologists must consider the sensitivity, specificity, and appropriateness of specific PVTs but there are various empirically validated PVTs that can be utilized when performing assessments following MSTBI (Macciocchi, Seel, Alderson et al., 2006; Macciocchi, Seel, Yiet al., 2013; Silk-Eglit, Lync and McCaffrey, 2016; Critchfield, Soble, Marceaux et al., 2019; Larrabee, Rohling and Meyers, 2019; Martin, Soble, Millis et al., 2023; and Uiterwijk, Stargatt and Crowe, 2022).

When clinicians encounter cases with multiple PVT failures and/or clinically implausible neurocognitive test scores suggesting possible, if not probable, malingering following MSTBI, diagnosing malingering without considering competing explanations for suboptimal test performance such as neurobehavioral dysfunction (anosognosia and/or oppositional behavior) is ill advised. Even when the test data is invalid, neuropsychologists can educate the referral source and ultimately the court about injury characteristics, treatment history, behavioral observations, collateral behavioral reports, and relevant test data. The point here is two things can be true at the same time, but clinicians would be smart to decline providing any specific opinions on Mr. AH's current functioning for either litigation or clinical purposes based solely on existing research.

Finally, when it comes to diagnosing or not diagnosing malingering in Mr. AH's case, there is evidence arguing for and against a malingering diagnosis. For instance, he had pervasively invalid PVTs and clinically non-credible neurocognitive test data, but on the other hand, he evidenced anosognosia, oppositional and inappropriate behavior during his examination, which was also consistently observed at home and in his community. In other words, his motivation to engage fully in testing was compromised by neurobehavioral deficits. Moreover, his behavior alone has been shown to be associated with invalid PVT scores and clinically non-credible neurocognitive test scores (Martin and Schroeder, 2020). Therefore, while clinicians could argue Mr. AH's PVT and neurocognitive test scores were consistent with malingering, his neurobehavioral dysfunction suggests he had "significantly diminished capacity to appreciate laws or mores against malingering or inability to conform behavior to such standards" (Sherman, Iverson, and Slick 2020). In such cases, clinicians must decide how to weigh evidence when determining the basis and cost–benefit of diagnosing malingering. In this case, there is a plausible clinical alternative to malingering when explaining Mr. AH's low PVT and neurocognitive test scores. In other words, Mr. AH simply did not care how he performed despite the importance of documenting his impairment for the court. Put another way, opining he was malingering is less persuasive given his anosognosia, oppositional behavior, and poor judgment when being tested.

References

An, KY, Kaploun, K, Laszlo, A, Erdodi, LA and Abeare, CA (2016) Performance validity in undergraduate research participants: A comparison of failure rates across tests and cutoffs, *The Clinical Neuropsychologist*, 31(1): 193–206.

Ashendorf, L and Sugarman, MA (2016) Evaluation of performance validity using a rey auditory verbal learning test forced choice trial, *The Clinical Neuropsychologist*, 30(4):599–609.

Ashendorf, L (2019) Rey auditory verbal learning test and rey-osterrieth complex figure test performance validity indices in a VA Polytrauma sample, *The Clinical Neuropsychologist*, 33(8):1388–1402.

Berthelson, L, Mulchan, SS, Odland, AP, Miller, LJ and Mittenberg, W (2013) False positive diagnosis of malingering due to the use of multiple effort tests, *Brain Injury*, 27(7–8):909–916.

Bianchini, KJ, Greve, KW and Love, JM (2009) Definite malingered neurocognitive dysfunction in moderate/severe traumatic brain injury, *The Clinical Neuropsychologist*, 17(4):574–580.

Bigler, ED (2012) Symptom validity testing, effort, and neuropsychological assessment, *Journal of the International Neuropsychological Society*, 18(4):632–640.

Bilder, RM., Sugar, CA and Hellemann, GS. (2014) Cumulative false positive rates given multiple performance validity tests: Commentary on Davis and Millis (2014) and Larrabee (2014). *The Clinical Neuropsychologist*, 28: 1212–1223.

Bramlett, HM and Dietrich, WD (2015) Long-term consequences of traumatic brain injury: Current status of potential mechanisms of injury and neurological outcomes, *Journal of Neurotrauma*, 32:1834–1848.
Carone, DA, Green, P and Drane, DL (2013) Word memory test profiles in two cases with surgical removal of the left anterior hippocampus and para-hippocampal gyrus, *Applied Neuropsychology: Adult*, 21(2):155–160.
Centers for Disease Control and Prevention. National Center for Health Statistics: Mortality Data on CDC WONDER. April 2023.
Chafetz, M. D. (2022). Deception is different: Negative validity test findings do not provide "evidence" for "good effort. *The Clinical Neuropsychologist*, *36*(6), 1244–1264.
Chafetz, M and Underhill, J (2013) Estimated costs of malingered disability, *Archives of Clinical Neuropsychology*, 28(7):633–639.
Copeland, CT, Mahoney, JJ, Block, CK, Linck, JF, Pastorek, NJ, Miller, BI, Romesser, JM and Sim, AH (2016) Relative utility of performance and symptom validity tests, *Archives of Clinical Neuropsychology*, 31:18–22.
The CRASH-3 Collaborators. Effects of tranexamic acid on death, disability, vascular occlusive events, and other morbidities in patients with acute traumatic brain injury (CRASH-3): A randomized, placebo-controlled trial. *Lancet* 2019, 394:1713–1723.
Critchfield, E, Soble, JR, Marceaux, JC, Bain, KM, Bailey, KC, Webber, TA, Alverson, WA, Johanna Messerly, J, Gonzalez, DA and O'Rourke, JF (2019) Cognitive impairment does not cause invalid performance: Analyzing performance patterns among cognitively unimpaired, impaired, and noncredible participants across six performance validity tests, *The Clinical Neuropsychologist*, 33(6):1083–1101.
Davis, JJ, McHugh, TS, Axelrod, BN and Hanks, RA (2012) Performance validity and neuropsychological outcomes in litigants and disability claimants, *The Clinical Neuropsychologist*, 26(5):850–865.
Davis, JJ and Millis, SR (2014) Examination of performance validity test failure in relation to number of tests administered, *The Clinical Neuropsychologist*, 28:199–214.
Davis, JJ and Millis, SR (2014) Reply to Commentary by Bilder, Sugar, and Helleman (2014) on Minimizing False Positive Error with Multiple Performance Validity Tests, *The Clinical Neuropsychologist*, 28(8):1224–1229.
Davis, J (2021) Interpretation of data from multiple performance validity tests, In Boone, KB (Ed), *Assessment of feigned cognitive impairment* (pp. 283–306). Guilford, New York.
Denning, JH and Shura, RD. (2019) Cost of malingering mild traumatic brain injury-related cognitive deficits during compensation and pension evaluations in the veteran's benefits administration, Applied Neuropsychology. *Adult*, 26(1):1–16.
Dikmen, SS, Machamer, JE, Winn, HR and Temkin, NR (1995) Neuropsychological outcome at 1-year post head injury, *Neuropsychology*, 9:80–90.
Erdodi, LA (2023) Cutoff elasticity in multivariate models of performance validity assessment as a function of the number of components and aggregation method, *Psychological Injury and Law*, 16(4):1–23.
Frederick, R (2015) Too much information: Problems when using multiple malingering tests. American Psychology Law Society, AAFP Distinguished Contributions Award Address.
Gates, TM, Metcalf, K, Sabaz, M, Young, K, Anandakumar, T and Simpson, GK (2023) What are the predictors of TOMM failure in clinical TBI populations? A retrospective analysis, *Journal of the International Neuropsychological Society*, 29(4):336–345.
Green, PW, Rohling, ML, Lees-Haley, PR and Allen, LM (2001) Effort has a greater effect on test scores than severe brain injury in compensation claimants, *Brain Injury*, 15:1045–1060.
Green, PW and Flaro, L (2015) Results from three performance validity tests (PVTs) in adults with intellectual deficits, *Applied Neuropsychology: Adult*, 22(4):293–303.
Hammond, FM, Perkins, SM, Corrigan, JD, Nakase-Richardson, R, Brown, AW, O'Neil-Pirozzi, TM, Zasler, ND and Greenwald, BD (2021) Functional change from five to fifteen years after traumatic brain injury, *Journal of Neurotrauma*, 38(7):858–869.

Hanks, RA Millis, SR, Ricker, JH, Giacino, JT, Nakese-Richardson, N, Frol, AB, Novack, TA, Kalmar, K, Sherer, M and Gordon, WA (2008) The predictive validity of a brief inpatient neuropsychologic battery for persons with traumatic brain injury, *Archives of Physical Medicine and Rehabilitation*, 89(5):950–957.

Holdnack, JA, Millis, S, Larrabee, GJ and Iverson, GL (2013) Assessing performance validity with the ACS. In J. A. Holdnack, L. W. Drozdick, L. G. Weiss, & G. L. Iverson (Eds.), *WAIS-IV, WMS-IV, and ACS: Advanced clinical interpretation* (pp. 331–365).

Jennette, KJ, Christopher, P, Williams, CP, Resch, ZJ, Ovsiew, GP, Durkin, NM, O'Rourke, JJF, Marceaux, JC, Critchfield, EA and Soble, JR (2022) Assessment of differential neurocognitive performance based on the number of performance validity tests failures: A cross-validation study across multiple mixed clinical samples, *The Clinical Neuropsychologist*, 36(7):1915–1932.

Jones, A (2013) Victoria Symptom Validity Test: Cutoff scores for psychometrically defined malingering groups in a military sample, *The Clinical Neuropsychologist*, 27(8):1373–1394.

Larrabee, GL (2003) Detection of malingering using Atypical performance patterns on standard neuropsychological tests, *The Clinical Neuropsychologist*, 17(3):410–425.

Larrabee, GJ (2014a) False-positive rates associated with the use of multiple performance and symptom validity tests, *Archives of Clinical Neuropsychology*, 29:364–373.

Larrabee, GJ (2014b) Minimizing false positive error with multiple performance validity tests: Response to bilder, sugar, and hellemann (2014 this issue), *The Clinical Neuropsychologist*, 28(8):1230–1242. https://doi.org/10.1080/13854046.2014.988754

Larrabee, GJ, Rohling, ML and Meyers, JE (2019) Use of multiple performance and symptom validity measures: Determining the optimal per test cutoff for determination of invalidity, analysis of skew, and inter-test correlations in valid and invalid performance groups, *The Clinical Neuropsychologist*, 33(8):1354–1372.

Leonhard, C (2023) Review of Statistical and Methodological Issues in the Forensic Prediction of Malingering from Validity Tests: Part I: *Statistical Issues Neuropsychology Review*, 33:581–603. https://doi.org/10.1007/s11065-023-09601-7

Maas, AIR, Steyerberg, EW and Citerio, G (2021) Tranexamic acid in traumatic brain injury: Systematic review and meta-analysis trumps a large clinical trial? *Intensive Care Medicine*, 47:74–76.

Macciocchi, SN, Seel, RT, Alderson, A and Godsall, R (2006) Victoria Symptom Validity Test performance in acute severe traumatic brain injury: Implications for test interpretation, *Archives of Clinical Neuropsychology*, 21:395–404.

Macciocchi, SN, Seel, RT, Yi, A and Small, S (2013) Medical symptom validity test performance following moderate-severe traumatic brain injury: Expectations based on orientation log classification, *Archives of Clinical Neuropsychology*, 32 (2017):339–348.

Marcopulos, BA, Caillouet, BA, Bailey, CM, Tussey, C, Kent, JA, and Frederick, R (2014). Clinical decision making in response to performance validity test failure in a psychiatric setting. *The Clinical Neuropsychologist, 28*(4), 633–652.

Martin, PK and Schroeder, RW (2020) Base rates of invalid test performance across clinical non-forensic contexts and settings, *Archives of Clinical Neuropsychology*, 35:717–725.

Martin, BJ, Sober, JD, Millis, SR, Hanks, RA, Reslan, S and Waldron-Perrine, B (2023) CVLT-3 response bias as an indicator of performance validity in a litigating population, *The Clinical Neuropsychologist*, 37(1):81–90.

McCrea, M, Giacino, JT, Barber, J, Temkin, NR et al. (2021) Functional outcomes over the first year after moderate to severe traumatic brain injury in the prospective, longitudinal TRACK-TBI study, *JAMA Neurology*, 78(8):982–992.

Meehl, PE (1973) *Why I Do Not Attend Case Conferences, In Psychodiagnosis: Selected papers*, 225–302, Minneapolis: University of Minnesota Press.

Paniak, C (2009) Moderate to severe traumatic brain injury: Probable malingering and then not. In J. E. Morgan & J. J. Sweet (Eds.), *Neuropsychology of malingering casebook* (pp. 101–120). Psychology Press.

Pliskin, JI, DeDios Stern, S, Resch, Z.J, Saladino, KF, Ovsiew, GP, Carter, DA, and Soble, JR(2021). Comparing the psychometric properties of eight embedded performance validity tests in the

Rey Auditory Verbal Learning Test, Wechsler Memory Scale Logical Memory, and Brief Visuospatial Memory Test–Revised recognition trials for detecting invalid neuropsychological test performance. *Assessment, 28*(8), 1871–1881.

Proto DA, Pastorek NJ, Miller BI, Romesser JM, Sim AH, and Linck JF (2014) The dangers of failing one or more performance validity tests in individuals claiming mild traumatic brain injury-related post-concussive symptoms, *Archives of Clinical Neuropsychology*, 2014(7):614–624.

Rohling, ML, Meyers, JE and Millis, SR (2003) Neuropsychological impairment following traumatic brain injury: A dose-response analysis, *The Clinical Neuropsychologist*, 17:289–302.

Rohling, ML, Binder, LM, Larrabee, GJ, and Langhinrichsen-Rohling, J. (2024). Forced choice test score of p≤. 20 and failures on≥ six performance validity tests results in similar overall test battery means. *The Clinical Neuropsychologist, 38*(5), 1193–1209.

Rohling, ML, Larrabee, GL and Davis, JJ (2025) Collinearity, tetrachoric correlation, and criterion group assignment of examinees failing only one performance validity test (PVT): Testing Leonhard's (2023) PVT critique, The Clinical Neuropsychologist, DOI: 10.1080/13854046.2025.2508472

Roor, JJ, Peters, MJV, Dandachi-FitzGerald, B and Ponds, RWHM, (2024) Performance validity test failure in the clinical population: A systematic review and meta-analysis of prevalence rates, *Neuropsychology Review*, 34:299–319.

Sherer, M, Davis, LC, Sander, AM, Nick, TG, Luo, C, Pastorek, N and Hanks, R (2013) Factors associated with word memory test performance in persons with medically documented traumatic brain injury, *The Clinical Neuropsychologist*, 2015 29(4):522–541.

Sherer, M, Sander, AM, Ponsford, J, Vos, L, Poritz, JMP, Ngan, J and Novelo, LL (2020) Patterns of cognitive test scores and symptom complaints in persons with TBI who failed performance validity testing, *Journal of the International Neuropsychological Society*, 26(9):932–938.

Sherman, EMS, Slick, DJ and Iverson, GL (2020) Multidimensional malingering criteria for neuropsychological assessment: A 20-Year update of the malingered neuropsychological dysfunction criteria, *Archives of Clinical Neuropsychology*, 35:735–764.

Silk-Eglit, GM, Lync, JK and McCaffrey, RJ (2016) Validation of Victoria Symptom Validity Test cutoff scores among mild traumatic brain injury litigants using a known-groups design, *Archives of Clinical Neuropsychology*, 31:231–245.

Slick, DJ, Tan, JE, Strauss, E, Mateer, CA, Harnadek, M and Sherman, EMS (2003) Victoria symptom validity test scores of patients with profound memory impairment: Non-litigant case studies, *The Clinical Neuropsychologist*, 17(3):390–394.

Solnick, BE, Maas, AI, Narayan, RK et al. (2014) A clinical trial of progesterone for severe traumatic brain injury, *New England Journal of Medicine*, 371:2467–2476.

Stewart, KA and Kretzmer, T (2021) Anosognosia in moderate to severe traumatic brain injury: A review of prevalence, clinical correlates and diversity considerations, *The Clinical Neuropsychologist*, 36(8):2021–2040.

Sweet, J and Giuffre Meyer, D (2011) Well documented, serious brain dysfunction followed by malingering. In J. Morgan, I. S. Baron, & J. Ricker (Eds.)_*Casebook of clinical neuropsychology* (pp. 200–212). New York: Oxford University Press.

Sweet, JJ, Heilbronner, RL, Morgan, JE, Larrabee, GJ et al. (2021) American Academy of Clinical Neuropsychology (AACN) 2021 consensus statement on validity assessment: Update of the 2009 AACN consensus conference statement on neuropsychological assessment of effort, response bias, and malingering, *The Clinical Neuropsychologist*, 35(6):1053–1106.

Sweet, JJ, Klipfel, KM, Nelson, NW and Moberg, PJ (2021) Professional practices, beliefs, and incomes of U.S. neuropsychologists: The AACN, NAN, SCN 2020 practice and "salary survey" *The Clinical Neuropsychologist*, 35(1):7–80.

Uiterwijk, D, Stargatt, R and Crowe, SF (2022) Objective cognitive outcomes and subjective emotional sequelae in litigating adults with a traumatic brain injury: The impact of performance and symptom validity measures, *Archives of Clinical Neuropsychology*, 37:1662–1687.

12 "Malingering by Proxy" in an Elderly Litigant

Tara L. Victor and Kyle B. Boone

In the original publication outlining diagnostic criteria for malingered neurocognitive dysfunction (MND), Slick et al. (1999) suggested that "MND by proxy" should be considered when test takers fail to perform to true ability on neurocognitive testing in response to "directions or pressure from others" (p. 555). Beginning in the early 2000s, case reports began to appear documenting "malingering by proxy" in juveniles, in which parents orchestrated feigning of cognitive dysfunction by their children when undergoing neuropsychological testing in the context of compensation-seeking (Chafetz & Dufrene, 2014; Chafetz & Prentkowski, 2011; Lu & Boone, 2002; see also Amlani et al., 2016; McCaffrey & Lynch, 2009). The category of "Malingering by Proxy" was added to MND criteria in 2013 (Slick & Sherman, 2013), and as Sherman et al. (2020) explain in the 20-year update of MND criteria, the category of "Malingering by Proxy occurs when there are compelling grounds to believe that the examinee acted primarily under the guidance, direction, influence, or control of another individual" (p. 756). Examples are provided that focus on children of parents who perceive external incentives for underperformance in their children.

However, dependent children are not the only population at risk for being coached and otherwise manipulated by caregivers and family members into displaying cognitive abnormalities on neuropsychological testing that in fact do not exist, or to fail to cooperate in the context of neuropsychological examinations. Anyone vulnerable to the influence of others by virtue of their age, disability status, or dependency (physical, financial, or otherwise) are also potentially at risk. In the following de-identified case, we describe a neuropsychological evaluation conducted in the context of personal injury litigation, in which the elderly plaintiff failed numerous performance validity tests (PVTs), and then discontinued the exam claiming physical discomfort, but only after being pressured to do so by her adult daughter. The daughter had also attempted to observe the evaluation and to examine test materials, and she misrepresented the extent of cognitive and physical symptoms in her mother. The case is then briefly discussed in light of its practical implications.

The Case of B.R.

Background

The plaintiff was an 87-year-old widowed female suing in the context of a ground level fall that had occurred slightly more than two years prior to the defense neuropsychological evaluation. In the claimed incident, she had been walking up to the front door of her residence, and uneven pavement caused by tree roots provoked her to fall. In accident records, it was documented that the plaintiff reported that she had been returning from shopping,

DOI: 10.4324/9781003005063-14

and was holding her keys in her right hand, a package in the crook of her left elbow, and her purse over her right shoulder. She relayed that she could not remember if she had locked her car, so she turned to go back and check, at which point she fell.

B.R. struck her left hip and head in the fall; in the emergency room she was evaluated for left hip pain, left hand/wrist pain, and closed head trauma. She was noted to have a scalp laceration and forehead contusion. On exam she was alert and oriented (equivalent to Glasgow Coma Scale of 15), and she was neurologically intact, with the exception that she reported no recall for the event. Noncontrast head CT did not demonstrate trauma-related findings. Left hip x-ray revealed minimally displaced left femoral neck fracture, for which she underwent partial hip replacement on the day of injury under general anesthesia, and total hip replacement six months later. Neurology consultation five days post-injury concluded that there was "no evidence for post-concussion syndrome" and "no evidence for ongoing brain injury."

Claimed symptoms at the time of neuropsychological evaluation were loss of memory, decreased attention and concentration, word-finding problems, difficulty understanding others, headaches, nausea, dizziness and balance problems, neck pain, left hip pain, lower back pain, sleep problems, anger/irritability, and anxiety and depression. B.R.'s daughter indicated on the history form that her mother did not remember anything regarding the day of the injury and therefore "does not know firsthand" what happened to her. When directly asked if she lost consciousness in the fall, B.R. replied "no," but then her daughter, who was present during the interview, corrected her, reporting that her mother was "in and out of consciousness" at the scene. B.R. subsequently stated that she "woke up" in the hospital two days later. The plaintiff stated that her last memory before the fall was "getting out of [her] car" and "walking toward the house," and that her first memory after the fall was "in the hospital the next day." The plaintiff's daughter further stated that her mother was "blacked out" for "a good few months" following the injury. Prior to the fall, the plaintiff was described as independent in all instrumental activities of living, including driving and handling errands (e.g., going to the deli), but after the accident, she was described as having lost the ability to drive secondary to orthopedic injuries, thereby reducing her independence. The plaintiff's daughter also reported that since the fall, her mother became completely dependent for paying bills, managing finances, shopping, and preparing meals. In a questionnaire completed by the plaintiff's daughter, 42 out of a possible 47 cognitive symptoms were endorsed as present in the plaintiff and attributed to the litigated fall.

While B.R. and her daughter were attributing the plaintiff's headaches, loss of balance, anxiety/depression, and cognitive changes to the fall, and denying the presence of these symptoms prior to the accident, B.R.'s medical records one to three years prior to the fall documented all of these conditions as having pre-dated the fall. When asked as to whether she had a history of falling prior to the litigated incident, B.R. stated that she did not remember. According to records, she had in fact sustained previous fractures related to falls. Whereas the plaintiff's claim was that she fell due to tree root damage to sidewalks, medical records regarding the accident indicated that she "took a step backwards and tripped over her own foot." Moreover, she was judged to have chronic gait instability and deconditioning at the time of the fall. The plaintiff's daughter had reported to hospital staff on the day of the fall that her mother experienced chronic chest pain and shortness of breath, and that her mother had undergone cardiac evaluation a week prior to the fall. However, when the neuropsychological examiner asked about the cardiac evaluation referenced in records, the daughter claimed that it was "just a normal routine check-up," but this was contradicted by medical records showing that the mother had been diagnosed with coronary artery disease.

Also of note, the plaintiff was diagnosed with sleep apnea/nocturnal hypoxia two months after the fall for which she used nocturnal oxygen, and she additionally had diagnoses of hyperlipidemia and hypertension. In other words, there was evidence of a pre-existing cardiovascular condition and other risk factors for dizziness/vertigo and falls; specifically, research has shown that dizziness/vertigo and falls are elevated in hypertension (Lopes et al., 2013), high cholesterol (Ogun et al., 2014), hypothyroidism (Ayhan et al., 2019), cardiac disease (Maarsingh et al., 2010), and sleep apnea (Foster & Machala, 2020).

Past medical history was also noteworthy for: aortic aneurysm; degenerative arthritis of the cervical spine, lumber spine, and left knee; fractured toe and rib one year prior to the fall; right hip fracture 15 years earlier; wrist fracture 13 years earlier; osteoporosis; gastroesophageal reflux disease; shingles; and some hearing loss. Surgical history included left knee replacement nine years prior to the fall, right hip replacement approximately 15 years prior to the fall, left wrist fusion after wrist fracture, appendectomy, arthroscopy of left shoulder, aortic valve surgery, and endarterectomy. The plaintiff and her daughter indicated they could not remember the medications she was taking at the time of the neuropsychological evaluation; medical records indicated recent prescription fulfillments of the following: trazadone, gabapentin, hydrocodone (daily), venlafaxine, pantoprazole, omeprazole, atenolol, levothyroxine, simvastatin, and atorvastatin. As mentioned earlier, medical records indicate B.R. was being treated for depression, anxiety, and cognitive changes prior to the claimed injury. Family history of dementia and current or past problems with substance use were denied.

The plaintiff was a retired university administration employee with 14 years of education and no history of neurodevelopmental disorder. She resided with her daughter and daughter's family following the fall. Daily activities at the time of evaluation included watching TV, knitting "all day," reading "mysteries," and helping her daughter wash dishes.

Behavioral Observations

The plaintiff was right-handed and English-speaking. She arrived on time to the evaluation accompanied by her daughter; the daughter had been reported as attending other independent medical evaluations and attempting to observe them. Indeed, her daughter expressed her intent to observe the neuropsychological testing; however, the daughter was not allowed to observe (per state regulations and the need to abide by standardized test administration) and she remained in the office lobby following the clinical interview.

The plaintiff was well groomed and casually dressed. She ambulated with a walker, which she reported that she used at all times, even though medical records following her left hip replacement after the injury indicated that she had graduated to the use of a cane. No vision or hearing difficulties or other motor or behavioral limitations that would impair her ability to comply with test administration requirements were noted. During the interview, the plaintiff was alert, oriented to person, place, time and situation, and cooperative. When asked about her understanding of the purpose of the examination, B.R. indicated that she knew it was in the context of litigation surrounding her fall and that she would be undergoing testing. She had no difficulty understanding test instructions and guidelines. Speech was fluent and normal in pace. There were no cognitive abnormalities noted in spontaneous interactions. Thought processes were generally linear and logical; the plaintiff was a generally adequate, but reluctant, historian, often looking at her daughter before responding. She reported that she had slept well the night before the evaluation.

Social skills were solidly intact. Rapport was established and easily maintained throughout the evaluation, and no obvious psychiatric symptoms were observed; mood was generally euthymic, and affect was broad and appropriate to content of speech. B.R. denied current or past history of suicidal or homicidal ideation, mania, delusions, or hallucinations.

Several breaks were taken, and all but one were initiated by the daughter (who knocked on the door indicating that her mother needed breaks). No pain behaviors or outward signs of visible discomfort were observed during the evaluation. At the conclusion of the cognitive testing and after completion of two-thirds of the personality inventory (MMPI-2-RF), B.R. indicated that she felt "fine" to continue the evaluation but asked to take a bathroom break. When she exited the office, her daughter commented that she was "surprised" her mother had been able to tolerate lengthy testing. Oddly, the daughter walked into the testing room and attempted to peruse the personality test booklet. She then exited the room and followed her mother into the bathroom, and was overheard to whisper, "What did you agree to?" When they left the bathroom, the daughter indicated that they needed to leave despite the fact that personality testing had not been completed. The daughter reported to the examiner that while in the bathroom her mother had been crying and stating that she was experiencing marked pain and "felt sick." However, when the examiner directly asked B.R. (who appeared calm and in no discomfort) regarding these complaints, she did not corroborate them until she was prompted to do so by her daughter (who was mouthing instructions to the plaintiff not quite out of the line of sight of the examiner).

Interpretation and Interpretation of Test Results

As shown in Table 12.1, B.R. failed five of five dedicated measures of neurocognitive test performance validity; specifically, she failed the TOMM (Trial 1 = 33; Trial 2 = 42; retention = 42; Martin et al., 2020), the Dot Counting Test (E-score = 36; McCaul et al., 2018), Rey 15-item plus recognition (18; Poynter et al., 2019), Rey Word Recognition Test (3; Bell-Sprinkel et al., 2013), and the Coin-in-hand Test (7/10 correct, Schroeder et al., 2012).

Table 12.1 Neuropsychological Exam Scores

Domain/Test	*Score*	*Interpretation*
Global Cognitive Function		
MMSE	18	Abnormal
Attention/Working Memory		
WAIS-III Digit Span ACSS	5 (5%)	Borderline
Processing Speed		
Trails A	46 seconds (72%)[a]	Average
Language		
Boston Naming Test	38 (9%)[a]	Low Average
Visual Perceptual/Spatial		
WAIS-III Picture Completion ACSS	5 (5%)	Borderline
Rey Figure copy	14.5 (<1%)[a]	Impaired

(*Continued*)

Table 12.1 (Continued)

Domain/Test	*Score*	*Interpretation*
Verbal Memory		
RAVLT Trial 1	2	
Trial 2	4	
Trial 3	7	
Trial 4	8	
Trial 5	10 (50%)[a]	Average
Distractor List	2	
Short delay	9 (66%)[a]	Average
Long Delay	8	
Recognition	8 (1%)[a]	Impaired
Visual Memory		
Rey Figure 3-Minute Delay	10 (19%)[a]	Low Average
Executive Function		
Trails B	125 seconds (67%)[a]	Average
Motor Function		
Finger Tapping Dominant (Right)	27.3 (1%)[b]	Impaired
Nondominant (Left)	19.3 (1%)[b]	Impaired
Psychiatric Symptom Scales		
Geriatric Depression Scale	22	Severe
Geriatric Anxiety Scale	8	Significant
Performance Validity Testing (PVT)		
TOMM		
Trial 1	33	Fail[c]
Trial 2	42	Fail[c]
Retention	42	Fail[c]
Rey Word Recognition Test Total	3	Fail[d]
Dot Counting Test E-score	36	Fail[e]
Coin in the Hand Test	3 errors	Fail[f]
Rey 15-item		
Recall	9	Fail[g]
Recognition	9	Fail[g]
Combination score	18	Fail[g]
Finger Tapping		
Dominant	27.3	Fail[h]
Digit Span		
Reliable Digit Span	5	Fail[i]
3-digit time	6.5 seconds	Fail[i]
4-digit time	10.0 seconds	Fail[i]
RAVLT		
Effort equation	11	Fail[j]
Recognition	8	Fail[j]
WAIS-III Picture Completion		
Most Discrepant Index	2	Fail[k]
Rey figure		
Copy	14.5	Fail[l]
Effort equation	32.5	Fail[l]

Notes: [a]meta-norms; Mitrushina et al. (2005); [b]Trahan et al. (1987), in Mitrushina et al. (2005); [c]Martin et al. (2018); [d]Bell-Sprinkel et al. (2013); [e]McCaul et al. (2018); [f]Schroeder et al. (2012); [g]Poynter et al. (2018); [h]Arnold et al. (2005); [i]Babikian et al. (2006); [j]Boone et al. (2005); [k]Solomon et al. (2010); [l]Reedy et al. (2013).

Examination of scores on performance validity indices from standard cognitive tests (i.e., embedded measures) also revealed failing scores on six of six measures. Specifically, the plaintiff failed Rey Complex figure variables (copy = 14.5; effort equation = 32.5; Reedy et al., 2013), Digit Span variables (ACSS = 5; RDS = 5; 3-digit time = 6.5"; 4-digit time = 10.0"; Babikian et al., 2006), Picture Completion (Most Discrepant Index = 2; Solomon et al., 2010), RAVLT variables (recognition = 8; effort equation = 11, Boone et al., 2021), finger tapping (dominant [R] = 27.3; nondominant [L] = 19.3; Arnold et al., 2005), and RAVLT and Digit Span interpreted in combination (RAVLT recognition = 8; RDS = 5; Loring et al., 2016).

Results of neurocognitive testing (with interpretations adjusted for age) revealed impaired scores in finger dexterity; impaired to borderline visual perceptual/spatial skills; borderline attention; low average word-retrieval and visual memory; and average processing speed, timed executive skill, and verbal memory (with the exception of recognition). However, the fact that the B.R. failed performance validity measures across 11 out of 11 separate tests indicated that she was not performing to true ability, and that obtained neuropsychological test scores were an underestimate of actual ability level.

It was of concern that the plaintiff was age 87, and PVTs generally are not validated in individuals in this age range. Relatedly, the question arose as to whether B.R. had developed cognitive deterioration to the level of a dementia, and if this accounted for the widespread failures on performance validity indicators on the current exam. Indeed, examinees with dementia fail PVTs at relatively higher rates despite performing to true ability on testing (Bortnik et al., 2013; Dean et al., 2009; Bortnik & Dean, 2021; McGuire et al., 2019). However, the plaintiff still failed PVTs when cut-offs were used that are adequately protective for individuals with actual dementia (and who typically are of advanced age). For example, using cut-offs selected for at least 90% specificity in dementia, B.R. still failed a forward Digit Span time score (cut-off >4.0" for 4-digit string; Dean et al., 2009), Dot Counting E-score (cut-off ≥ 22; Bortnik & Dean, 2021) and mean grouped dot counting time (cut-off >7"; Boone et al., 2002), and Rey Word Recognition Test (cut-off <5 total; Dean et al., 2009), and she failed RAVLT and RDS scores examined in combination as recommended by Loring et al. (2016) when evaluating individuals in the context of amnestic mild cognitive impairment and early Alzheimer's disease (RAVLT recognition ≤9 and RDS ≤6). Additionally, the plaintiff failed a forced choice measure specifically designed to discriminate actual versus feigned dementia (Coin-in-Hand Test = 3 errors; Schroeder et al., 2012).

Also of note, there were inconsistent patterns of performance in her testing. For instance, the plaintiff obtained an MMSE score of 18, which would suggest the presence of a moderate dementia, whereas more elaborate objective memory measures were low average to average, which would be inconsistent with dementia. Also of note, on a neurology consult five days post-injury, B.R. was judged not to have post-concussive syndrome, whereas more than two years post-injury, she performed substantially below expectation on various neuropsychological tasks. Cognitive function does not decline remote from traumatic brain injury, and implausible decline in cognitive performance can be used as evidence of performance invalidity (Heilbronner et al., 2010). Moreover, the *Diagnostic and Statistical Manual for Mental Disorders – 5th edition* (*DSM-5-Text Revision*, 2022) advises that:

> To be attributable to TBI, the NCD (neurocognitive disorder) must manifest either immediately after the brain injury occurs or immediately after the individual recovers consciousness after the injury...
>
> (p. 708)

One year after the accident, the plaintiff's daughter was reporting to treaters that the plaintiff's cognitive problems were worsening, and brain MRI at that time revealed mild atrophy and old microhemorrhage, which suggested that B.R. may have been experiencing progressive brain deterioration related to cerebrovascular disease. Additionally, the plaintiff had numerous medical conditions that have been shown empirically to lead to cognitive decline, such as sleep apnea (Stranks & Crowe, 2016; Wallace & Bucks, 2013), hypertension (Gifford et al., 2013; Qin et al., 2021; Verdelho et al., 2007), high cholesterol (Kivipelto et al., 2001), and coronary artery disease (Zheng et al., 2012), as well as use of medications that impact cognition (e.g., gabapentin; Martin et al., 2001). However, her functionality in daily life activities (spending time reading "mysteries" and knitting), as well as her ability to provide relevant information on interview and obtain normal range scores on memory testing, would be inconsistent with current frank dementia.

Injury characteristics on the day of injury indicate that at most B.R. sustained a concussion/mild traumatic brain injury. She was judged to be alert and oriented in the emergency department (equivalent to Glasgow Coma Scale of 15), and brain imaging did not reveal any trauma-related findings. When asked on neuropsychological exam two years post-injury if she had lost consciousness in the accident, the plaintiff replied "no," which was consistent with her report to the cardiologist who consulted on the day of the accident. B.R. claimed post-traumatic amnesia of two days on neuropsychological interview, but this would not be reflective of anterograde amnesia given that she was recorded to be oriented in the emergency room (ER) after the accident. It is possible that the plaintiff's subsequently reported two-day memory loss post-injury was due to medications for sedation and pain control associated with her hip surgery on the day of injury.

To the extent that the plaintiff experienced a concussion/mild traumatic brain injury as a result of the fall (criteria for concussion are loss of consciousness <30 minutes, Glasgow Coma Scale = 13–15, anterograde amnesia <24 hours, and no trauma-related findings on brain imaging), reviews of the literature on neuropsychological function in mild traumatic brain injury, involving dozens of studies and thousands of patients in the aggregate (see Carroll et al., 120 studies; Dikmen et al., 2009, 33 studies), including six meta-analyses (39 studies, n = 1463, Belanger et al., 2005; 21 studies, n = 790, Belanger & Vanderploeg, 2005; 8 studies, Binder et al., 1997; 17 studies, n = 634, Frencham et al., 2005; 25 studies, n = 2828, Rohling et al., 2011; 16 studies, n = 742, Schretlen & Shapiro, 2003), show that individuals who experience mild brain trauma return to baseline by weeks to months post-injury. Likewise, headaches, dizziness/balance problems, and psychiatric symptoms, such as anxiety and depression, are not found on a long-term basis after concussion (Mickevičiene et al., 2004; Panayiotou et al., 2010). Research additionally shows that, barring injury complications, older individuals exhibit similar relatively rapid recovery from concussion as do younger individuals (Albrecht et al., 2016; Goldstein & Levin, 2001; Goldstein et al., 2001; Mosenthal et al., 2004). Kinsella et al. (2014) reported that cognition was no different in concussed older individuals at three months than that of older adults sustaining non-brain injuries, and Hume et al. (2023) found no significant neurocognitive differences between older adults with head injury and older adults with other (non-head) injuries at three months, a pattern repeatedly evident in studies of younger individuals. Finally, mTBI does not increase the risk for dementia (Godbolt et al., 2014; LoBue et al., 2019) and a history of TBI does not hasten neurocognitive decline in older adults with and without cognitive impairment (Schaffert et al., 2023).

Conclusions and Discussion

While B.R. appeared to be a willing participant in misrepresenting her abilities on neurocognitive exam (i.e., she obtained low scores on empirically validated PVTs, which cannot be explained by her medical-neurological or psychiatric history, and there were inconsistencies in her pattern of performance as well as between her self-reported history/symptoms and medical records), the plaintiff's daughter was actively attempting to control and manipulate the evaluation through seeking to observe the testing and examine test materials, and by coaching her mother to discontinue the exam (i.e., encouraging her to claim discomfort that she was not actually experiencing). Notably, nursing notes from two years earlier during the plaintiff's fall-related hospitalization revealed discrepancies between the daughter's report of "confusion" in her mother versus the nurses' observations of normal cognitive function, which suggests that the daughter's intention to misrepresent her mother's injury dated to shortly after injury.

The fact that the daughter overrode the plaintiff's assertion to the neuropsychological examiner that she felt "fine" to continue the examination indicates that the daughter wielded more decision-making influence over her mother's exam behaviors than did the plaintiff herself. The power differential in the relationship possibly stemmed from the fact that B.R. resided in the daughter's home, and therefore was to some degree dependent on the daughter. In circumstances in which elderly individuals tested in the context of compensation-seeking are pressured by family and/or caretakers to either demonstrate cognitive abnormalities that are not in fact present, and/or to not cooperate in neuropsychological evaluations, we judge that it is appropriate to view the behavior as "malingering by proxy."

Malingering by proxy has implications for clinical guidelines that recommend interviewing family members regarding plaintiff characteristics. That is, in the context of disability-seeking or litigation, family members may misrepresent the level of dysfunction of elderly plaintiffs, either through over-endorsement of symptoms on interview or on symptom questionnaires, and/or through claiming that elderly family members are not able to tolerate the demands of exams (both of which occurred in the present case). This caution is consistent with recent research on the lack of reliability of informant reporting in examinees with evidence of performance invalidity in incentivized contexts (Nelson & Lovett, 2019; Quilty et al., 2018; Webber et al., 2022). Webber et al. (ibid) explain, "These findings call into question the trustworthiness of informant reports of examinee functioning when there is increased suspicion for symptom and (in particular) performance invalidity and suggest that it is important to be cautious when interpreting informant report measures for these examinees" (p. 11). This is why the updated criteria for MND emphasize the presence of inconsistency between test performance and the report of "trustworthy informants," defined as "one who does not have a vested interest in the outcome of the evaluation" (Sherman et al., 2020, p. 19).

References

Albrecht, M. A., Masters, C. L., Ames, D., Foster, J. K., AIBL Research Group. (2016). Impact of mild head injury on neuropsychological performance in healthy older adults: Longitudinal assessment in the AIBL cohort. *Front Aging Neuroscience, 12*(8), 105.

Amlani, D., Grewal, G. S., & Feldman, M. D. (2016). Malingering by proxy: A literature review and current perspectives. *Journal of Forensic Science, 61*(Suppl 1), S171–176.

Arnold, G., Boone, K. B., Lu, P., Dean, A., Wen, J., Nitch, S., & McPherson, S. (2005). Sensitivity and specificity of finger tapping test scores for the detection of suspect effort. *The Clinical Neuropsychologist, 19*(1), 105–120.

Ayhan, K. U. L., Bilen, A., Bilge, N., Sarihan, K., Uzkeser, H., Dayanan, R., & Baygutalp, F. (2019). Balance disorders and hypothyroidism: A rare cause worth remembering. *ENT Updates*, *9*(3), 172–179.

Babikian, T., Boone, K. B., Lu, P., & Arnold, G. (2006). Sensitivity and specificity of various digit span scores in the detection of suspect effort. *The Clinical Neuropsychologist*, *20*(1), 145–159.

Belanger, H. G., Curtiss, G., Demery, J. A., Lebowitz, B. K., & Vanderploeg, R. D. (2005). Factors moderating neuropsychological outcomes following mild traumatic brain injury: A meta-analysis. *Journal of the International Neuropsychological Society*, *11*(3), 215–227.

Belanger, H. G., & Vanderploeg, R. D. (2005). The neuropsychological impact of sports-related concussion: A meta-analysis. *Journal of the International Neuropsychological Society*, *11*(4), 345–357.

Bell-Sprinkel, T. L., Boone, K. B., Miora, D., Cottingham, M., Victor, T., Ziegler, E., ... Wright, M. (2013). Re-examination of the rey word recognition test. *The Clinical Neuropsychologist*, *27*(3), 516–527.

Binder, L. M., Rohling, M. L., & Larrabee, G. J. (1997). A review of mild head trauma. Part I: Meta-analytic review of neuropsychological studies. *Journal of Clinical and Experimental Neuropsychology*, *19*(3), 421–431.

Boone, K. B. (2017). Self-deception in somatoform conditions. In Kyle B. Boone. (Ed)., *Neuropsychological evaluation of somatoform and other functional somatic conditions* (pp. 3–42). New York: Taylor & Francis.

Boone, K. B., Lu, P., Back, C., King, C., Lee, A., Philpott, L., ... Warner-Chacon, K. (2002). Sensitivity and specificity of the Rey Dot Counting Test in patients with suspect effort and various clinical samples. *Archives of Clinical Neuropsychology*, *17*(7), 625–642.

Boone, K. B., Sherman, D., Mishler, J., Daoud, G., Cottingham, M., Victor, T. L., ... & Wright, M. (2022). Cross-validation of RAVLT performance validity indicators and the RAVLT/RO discriminant function in a large known groups sample. The Clinical Neuropsychologist, *36*(8), 2342–2360.

Bortnik, K. E., & Dean, A. C. (2021). Performance validity testing in patients with dementia. In Kyle B. Boone (Ed.), *Assessment of feigned cognitive impairment: A neuropsychological perspective, 2nd edition* (pp. 481–503). New York: The Guilford Press.

Bortnik, K. E., Horner, M. D., & Bachman, D. L. (2013). Performance on standard indexes of effort among patients with dementia. *Applied Neuropsychology: Adult*, *20*(4), 233–242.

Carroll, L., Cassidy, J. D., Peloso, P., Borg, J., Von Holst, H., Holm, L., ... Pépin, M. (2004). Prognosis for mild traumatic brain injury: Results of the WHO Collaborating Centre Task Force on Mild Traumatic Brain Injury. *Journal of Rehabilitation Medicine*, *36*(0), 84–105.

Chafetz, M., & Dufrene, M. (2014). Malingering-by-proxy: Need for child protection and guidance for reporting. *Child Abuse & Neglect*, *38*(11), 1755–1765.

Chafetz, M., & Prentkowski, E. (2011). A case of malingering by proxy in a Social Security disability psychological consultative examination. *Applied Neuropsychology*, *18*(2), 143–149.

Dean, A. C., Victor, T. L., Boone, K. B., Philpott, L. M., & Hess, R. A. (2009). Dementia and effort test performance. *The Clinical Neuropsychologist*, *23*(1), 133–152.

Dikmen, S. S., Corrigan, J. D., Levin, H. S., Machamer, J., Stiers, W., & Weisskopf, M. G. (2009). Cognitive outcome following traumatic brain injury. *The Journal of Head Trauma Rehabilitation*, *24*(6), 430–438.

Foster, C. A., & Machala, M. (2020). The clinical spectrum of dizziness in sleep apnea. *Otology & Neurotology*, *41*(10), 1419–1422.

Frencham, K. A., Fox, A. M., & Maybery, M. T. (2005). Neuropsychological studies of mild traumatic brain injury: A meta-analytic review of research since 1995. *Journal of Clinical and Experimental Neuropsychology*, *27*(3), 334–351.

Gifford, K. A., Badaracco, M., Liu, D., Tripodis, Y., Gentile, A., Lu, Z., ... Jefferson, A. L. (2013). Blood pressure and cognition among older adults: A meta-analysis. *Archives of Clinical Neuropsychology*, *28*(7), 649–664.

Godbolt, A. K., Cancelliere, C., Hincapié, C. A., Marras, C., Boyle, E., Kristman, V. L., Coronado, V. G., Cassidy, J. D. (2014). Systematic review of the risk of dementia and chronic cognitive impairment after mild traumatic brain injury: Results of the International Collaboration on Mild Traumatic Brain Injury Prognosis. *Arch Phys Med Rehabilitation, 95*(3), S245–S256.

Goldstein, F. C., & Levin, H. S. (2001). Cognitive outcome after mild and moderate traumatic brain injury in older adults. *Journal of Clinical and Experimental Neuropsychology, 23*(6), 739–753.

Goldstein, F. C., Levin, H. S., Goldman, W. P., Clark, A. N., & Altonen, T. K. (2001). Cognitive and neurobehavioral functioning after mild versus moderate traumatic brain injury in older adults. *Journal of the International Neuropsychological Society, 7*(3), 373–383.

Heilbronner, R. L., Sweet, J. J., Attix, D. K., Krull, K. R., Henry, G. K., & Hart, R. P. (2010). Official position of the American Academy of Clinical Neuropsychology on serial neuropsychological assessments: The utility and challenges of repeat test administrations in clinical and forensic contexts. *The Clinical Neuropsychologist, 24*(8), 1267–1278.

Hume, C., Mitra, B., Wright, B., & Kinsella, G. J. (2023). Cognitive performance in older people after mild traumatic brain injury: Trauma effects and other risk factors. *Journal of the International Neuropsychological Society, 29*(7), 651–661.

Kinsella, G. J., Olver, J., Ong, B., Gruen, R., & Hammersley, E. (2014). Mild traumatic brain injury in older adults: Early cognitive outcome. *Journal of the International Neuropsychological Society, 20*(6), 663–671.

Kivipelto, M., Helkala, E. L., Hänninen, T., Laakso, M. P., Hallikainen, M., Alhainen, K., ... Nissinen, A. (2001). Midlife vascular risk factors and late-life mild cognitive impairment: A population-based study. *Neurology, 56*(12), 1683–1689.

LoBue, C., Munro, C., Schaffert, J., Didehbani, N., Hart, J., Batjer, H., Cullum, C. M. (2019). Traumatic brain injury and risk of long-term brain changes, accumulation of pathological markers, and developing dementia: A review. *Journal Alzheimers Dis., 70*(3), 629–654.

Lopes, A. R., Moreira, M. D., Trelha, C. S., & de Moraes Marchiori, L. L. (2013). Association between complaints of dizziness and hypertension in non-institutionalized elders. *International Archives of Otorhinolaryngology, 17*(02), 157–162.

Loring, D. W., Goldstein, F. C., Chen, C., Drane, D. L., Lah, J. J., Zhao, L., & Larrabee, G. J. (2016). False-positive error rates for reliable digit span and auditory verbal learning test performance validity measures in amnestic mild cognitive impairment and early Alzheimer disease. *Archives of Clinical Neuropsychology, 31*(4), 313–331.

Lu, P. H., & Boone, K. B. (2002). Suspect cognitive symptoms in a 9-year-old child: Malingering by proxy? *The Clinical Neuropsychologist, 16*(1), 90–96.

Martin, R., Meador, K., Turrentine, L., Faught, E., Sinclair, K., Kuzniecky, R., & Gilliam, F. (2001). Comparative cognitive effects of carbamazepine and gabapentin in healthy senior adults. *Epilepsia, 42*(6), 764–771.

Martin, P. K., Schroeder, R. W., Olsen, D. H., Maloy, H., Boettcher, A., Ernst, N., & Okut, H. (2020). A systematic review and meta-analysis of the Test of Memory Malingering in adults: Two decades of deception detection. *The Clinical Neuropsychologist, 34*(1), 88–119.

Maarsingh, O. R., Dros, J., Schellevis, F. G., van Weert, H. C., Van der Windt, D. A., ter Riet, G., & van der Horst, H. E. (2010). Causes of persistent dizziness in elderly patients in primary care. *The Annals of Family Medicine, 8*(3), 196–205.

McCaffrey, R. J., & Lynch, J. K. (2009). Malingering following documented brain injury: Neuropsychological evaluation of children in a forensic setting. In J. E. Morgan & J. J. Sweet (Eds.), *Neuropsychology of Malingering Casebook* (pp. 377–385). New York: Psychology Press.

McCaul, C., Boone, K. B., Ermshar, A., Cottingham, M., Victor, T. L., Ziegler, E., ... Wright, M. (2018). Cross-validation of the Dot Counting Test in a large sample of credible and non-credible patients referred for neuropsychological testing. *The Clinical Neuropsychologist, 32*(6), 1054–1067.

McGuire, C., Crawford, S., & Evans, J. J. (2019). Effort testing in dementia assessment: A systemic review. *Archives of Clinical Neuropsychology, 34*(1), 114–131.

Mickevičiene, D., Schrader, H., Obelieniene, D., Surkiene, D., Kunickas, R., Stovner, L. J., & Sand, T. (2004). A controlled prospective inception cohort study on the post-concussion syndrome outside the medicolegal context. *European Journal of Neurology*, *11*(6), 411–419.
Mitrushina, M., Boone, K. B., Razani, J., & D'Elia, L. F. (2005). *Handbook of normative data for neuropsychological assessment*. New York: Oxford University Press.
Mosenthal, A. C., Livingston, D. H., Lavery, R. F., Knudson, M. M, Lee, S., Morabito, D., Manley, G. T., Nathens, A., Jurkovich, G., Hoyt, D. B., & Coimbra, R. (2004). The effect of age on functional outcome in mild traumatic brain injury: 6-month report of a prospective multicenter trial. *Journal Trauma*, *56*(5), 1042–1048.
Nelson, J. M., & Lovett, B. J. (2019). Assessing ADHD in college students: Integrating multiple evidence sources with symptom and performance validity data. *Psychological Assessment*, *31*(6), 793–804.
Ogun, O. A., Janky, K. L., Cohn, E. S., Büki, B., & Lundberg, Y. W. (2014). Gender-based comorbidity in benign paroxysmal positional vertigo. *PloS one*, *9*(9), e105546.
Panayiotou, A., Jackson, M., & Crowe, S. F. (2010). A meta-analytic review of the emotional symptoms associated with mild traumatic brain injury. *Journal of Clinical and Experimental Neuropsychology*, *32*(5), 463–473.
Poynter, K., Boone, K. B., Ermshar, A., Miora, D., Cottingham, M., Victor, T. L., ... Wright, M. (2019). Wait, there's a baby in this bath water! Update on quantitative and qualitative cut-offs for Rey 15-Item Recall and Recognition. *Archives of Clinical Neuropsychology*, *34*(8), 1367–1380.
Qin, J., He, Z., Wu, L., Wang, W., Lin, Q., Lin, Y., & Zheng, L. (2021). Prevalence of mild cognitive impairment in patients with hypertension: A systematic review and meta-analysis. *Hypertension Research*, *44*(10), 1251–1260.
Quilty, L. C., Cosentino, N., & Bagby, R. M. (2018). Response bias and the personality inventory for DSM-5: Contrasting self- and informant-report. *Personality Disorders*, *9*(4), 346–353.
Reedy, S. D., Boone, K. B., Cottingham, M. E., Glaser, D. F., Lu, P. H., Victor, T. L., & Wright, M. J. (2013). Cross validation of the Lu and colleagues (2003) Rey-Osterrieth Complex Figure Test effort equation in a large known-group sample. *Archives of Clinical Neuropsychology*, *28*(1), 30–37.
Rohling, M. L., Binder, L. M., Demakis, G. J., Larrabee, G. J., Ploetz, D. M., & Langhinrichsen-Rohling, J. (2011). A meta-analysis of neuropsychological outcome after mild traumatic brain injury: Re-analyses and reconsiderations of binder et al., Frencham et al., and Pertab et al. *The Clinical Neuropsychologist*, *25*(4), 608–623.
Schaffert, J., Chiang, H. -S., Fatima, H., LoBue, C., Hart, J., & Cullum, C. M. (2023). History of traumatic brain injury does not alter course of neurocognitive decline in older adults with and without cognitive impairment. *Neuropsychology*, *37*(8), 923–932.
Schretlen, D. J., & Shapiro, A. M. (2003). A quantitative review of the effects of traumatic brain injury on cognitive functioning. *International Review of Psychiatry*, *15*(4), 341–349.
Schroeder, R. W., Peck, C. P., Buddin Jr, W. H., Heinrichs, R. J., & Baade, L. E. (2012). The coin-in-the-hand test and dementia: More evidence for a screening test for neurocognitive symptom exaggeration. *Cognitive and Behavioral Neurology*, *25*(3), 139–143.
Sherman, E. M. S., Slick, D. J., & Iverson, G. L. (2020). Multidimensional malingering criteria for neuropsychological assessment: A 20-year update of the malingered neuropsychological dysfunction criteria. *Archives of Clinical Neuropsychology*, *35*, 735–764.
Slick, D. J., & Sherman, E. M. S. (2013). Differential diagnosis of malingering. In Kirkwood, M. K. (Ed.), *Mild traumatic brain injury: Symptom assessment validity and malingering* (pp. 57–72). New York: Springer Publishing Company.
Slick, D. J., Sherman, E. M., & Iverson, G. L. (1999). Diagnostic criteria for malingered Neurocognitive dysfunction: Proposed standards for clinical practice and research. *The Clinical Neuropsychologist*, *13*(4), 545–561.
Solomon, R. E., Boone, K. B., Miora, D., Skidmore, S., Cottingham, M., Victor, T., ... Zeller, M. (2010). Use of the WAIS-III picture completion subtest as an embedded measure of response bias. *The Clinical Neuropsychologist*, *24*(7), 1243–1256.

Stranks, E. K., & Crowe, S. F. (2016). The cognitive effects of obstructive sleep apnea: An updated meta-analysis. *Archives of Clinical Neuropsychology, 31*(2), 186–193.

Verdelho, A., Madureira, S., Ferro, J. M., Basile, A. M., Chabriat, H., Erkinjuntti, T., ... Salvadori, E. (2007). Differential impact of cerebral white matter changes, diabetes, hypertension and stroke on cognitive performance among non-disabled elderly. The LADIS study. *Journal of Neurology, Neurosurgery & Psychiatry, 78*(12), 1325–1330.

Wallace, A., & Bucks, R. S. (2013). Memory and obstructive sleep apnea: A meta-analysis. *Sleep, 36*(2), 203–220.

Webber, T. A., Sullivan-Baca, E., Modiano, Y. A., Taiwo, Z., & Grabyan, J. M. (2022). Validity of informant report interpretations: Role of examinee performance and symptom invalidity. *Psychological Assessment, 34*(2), 125–138.

Zheng, L., Mack, W. J., Chui, H. C., Heflin, L., Mungas, D., Reed, B., ... Kramer, J. H. (2012). Coronary artery disease is associated with cognitive decline independent of changes on magnetic resonance imaging in cognitively normal elderly adults. *Journal of the American Geriatrics Society, 60*(3), 499–504.

13 Posttraumatic Stress Disorder and Malingering in Civil Litigation

Nancy Hebben

The case discussed in this chapter was chosen to illustrate the issues that accompany the assessment of possible malingering in a plaintiff presenting with claims of posttraumatic stress disorder (PTSD) and mild traumatic brain injury (mTBI). In order to effectively manage and treat conditions that impact mental or cognitive health, it is critical that these conditions are diagnosed reliably and accurately, using sensitive instruments. Unlike an X-ray or blood test that are directly dependent on physical or biological states that for the most part are not under the control of the person being assessed, the measurement or assessment of psychological conditions are often dependent on test performance or self-report that to a large extent is under the control of the respondent. If the person being examined is not willing to cooperate and do their best at performing a task, or not willing to accurately report their subjective states or level of discomfort, the accuracy of the assessment can be severely compromised. Inaccurate assessment of such psychological conditions can have significant consequences, including the incorrect application of therapies and pharmacological agents, and in some cases, unfair or incorrect adjudication of legal claims. Complex cases, such as the one described here, illustrate the challenges of assuring the validity of the standard techniques used by psychologists to assess cognitive and emotional status.

Referrals for evaluations of PTSD co-occurring with claims of mTBI (concussion) and/or post-concussion syndrome (PCS) after an accident are common in the forensic practices of neuropsychologists. As part of their examination of these claimed conditions, forensic neuropsychologists must assess the accuracy of these diagnoses. According to the Sweet et al. (2021) practice survey, the most common referral question or topic of interest in forensic activities is closed head injury/traumatic brain injury, with PTSD as the third most common, indicating that PTSD and PCS are frequently claimed injuries in compensation cases, often claimed together. Neuropsychologists are uniquely suited for evaluation of these claims because of their education, training, and knowledge and the tools they have available (Sweet et al., 2023). Specifically, neuropsychologists, in addition to tests of cognition and mood, have at their disposal performance validity tests (PVTs), which assess the validity of measures of ability, and symptom validity tests (SVTs), which assess the validity of examinee complaints (Larrabee, 2012). Both are necessary in a neuropsychological evaluation because an examinee may score in the noncredible range on one or the other or on both, invalidating the data obtained as accurately reflecting current status (Kim et al., 2024; see also Chapter 14 in this volume). The first type of validity tests, PVTs, are measures designed to be insensitive to cognitive impairment, but sensitive to task engagement, and while success on these measures does not confirm adequate or good

DOI: 10.4324/9781003005063-15

task engagement, failure on these measures is interpreted as indicative of motivational issues and incomplete compliance with testing. PVTs are necessary because without objective testing an examiner cannot know if an examinee is truly fully engaged with a task and because compliance with testing is important to obtaining test results that can be taken as valid and reliable reflections of current true ability. In some instances, PVTs can signal symptom exaggeration and/or active suppression of effort but that is not their primary purpose. The second type of validity tests, SVTs, are instruments designed to gauge the accuracy of an individual's self-reported symptoms because inconsistent reporting, under-reporting, and over-reporting of symptoms can distort an examinee's self-reported symptoms. SVTs complement PVTs. Just as PVTs are necessary in a test battery to gauge the validity of an individual's performances on cognitive tests, SVTs are necessary to assess the accuracy of an individual's subjective symptom report. Especially in a forensic context, where the stakes are high for both plaintiffs and defense, neuropsychologists cannot presume that an examinee is fully engaged, giving full effort or portraying symptoms accurately during an evaluation.

Whether working for plaintiff's attorney or defense's attorney, any supposition of "full effort" and an accurate report of symptoms should be customarily investigated and, as part of the investigation, the issue of invalid responding and malingering must be explored. This is necessary because high rates of exaggeration and malingering are seen in compensation-seeking samples and the cost of malingering is extraordinarily high. Chafetz (2011), using base rates of failure on validity tests, estimated that in 2008, federal and state disability programs spent an estimated U.S. $180 billion on adult and pediatric patients who were probably malingering and U.S. $42.85 billion to U.S. $55.7 billion on patients who were definitely malingering. Other research focused on estimating the costs of malingered disability has revealed that feigning disability in order to receive disability compensation occurs in 45.8% to 59.7% of Social Security Disability examinations, propelling the estimated cost of malingering in medicolegal cases in 2011 to U.S. $20.02 billion (Chafetz and Underhill, 2013).

Broadly speaking, neither PTSD nor PCS is a difficult disorder to feign as information about PTSD symptoms and symptoms after concussion is widely available. Both PTSD and symptoms attributed to PCS may be feigned in civil and criminal litigation to obtain disability payments, personal injury litigation settlements, or to reduce criminal charges. Although logistically obtaining accurate statistics is difficult, base rates of malingering of PTSD may be as high as 20%–30% in personal injury litigation contexts (Lees-Haley, 1997) and base rates of malingering in mTBI may be as high as 40% (Larrabee, 2003).

Nonetheless, given the prevalence, it becomes clear that an assessment of a person claiming to have PTSD after a motor vehicle accident in which no one was seriously hurt must include measures to assess the veracity of claims and diagnoses. With a person claiming permanent brain injury and cognitive and emotional problems after a putative mTBI sustained in that motor vehicle accident (MVA), it becomes necessary that a comprehensive assessment determine the source of the person's complaints. Is this malingering? Is this iatrogenesis or is this an example of a nocebic effect leading to a more negative outcome? Is this misattribution? Is this a somatic symptom disorder? Is there another disorder that can explain their symptom report and behavior?

Just as mTBI can only be diagnosed when all or some specific neurodiagnostic indicators are present, PTSD can only be diagnosed when the criterion specified in *DSM-5* (2013) and *DSM-5-TR* (2022) are met. *DSM-5* (2013) moved PTSD from the anxiety disorders section to the trauma-related disorders section and specified eight criteria that are needed for a PTSD diagnosis. The first and perhaps most important of these is criterion A, which requires exposure to

> actual or threatened death, serious injury, or sexual violence in one (or more) of the following ways: 1) directly experiencing the traumatic event(s); 2) witnessing, in person, the events(s) as it occurred to others; 3) learning that the traumatic event(s) occurred to a close family member or friend, the events must have been violent or accidental; 4) experiencing repeated or extreme exposure to aversive details of the traumatic event(s) (e.g., first responders collecting human remains; police officers repeatedly exposed to details of child abuse.
>
> (*DSM-5-TR*, p. 301)

Examples of Criterion A traumatic stressors include exposure to combat, physical assault, sexual abuse or assault, natural or man-made disasters, being kidnapped or taken hostage, childhood physical or sexual abuse, torture, severe accidents, rescue work involving exposure to death or mortal injury and/or medical incidents that are catastrophic or sudden (e.g., waking during surgery). PTSD is actually an unusual response to a traumatic incident. According to the National Center for PTSD, even when as many of 70% of individuals having been exposed to at least one Criterion A trauma during their lifetime (Benjet et al., 2016), only about 6% of the U.S. population will have PTSD at some point in their lives and only 5% of the U.S. population will have PTSD in any given year. The *DSM-5* lists similar national lifetime prevalence rates from two U.S. National epidemiological studies that found lifetime prevalence rates ranging from 6.1% to 8.3% with a national 12-month prevalence rate of 4.7%. In addition, the National Center for PTSD and the *DSM-5* indicate that PTSD symptoms following an actual Criterion A event generally remit following exposure to a traumatic stressor, with the steepest remission in the first 12 months after diagnosis. Common misconceptions about PTSD are that any "traumatic" experience is sufficient to cause PTSD, that PTSD is necessarily chronic or that it is a person's perception of the trauma that is all that is necessary for PTSD to develop.

When the context is one of secondary gain and malingering is a possibility, a systematic evaluation must be undertaken even when PTSD is a legitimately expected outcome after a traumatic event, that is, when Criterion A is met. That approach must include record review, collateral information, interview, and the administration of instruments designed to assess for the presence of PTSD and to detect symptom exaggeration or feigning (see, for example, Matto, McNiel, & Binder, 2019). When assessing for PTSD, self-report of posttraumatic symptoms cannot be relied on even if that self-report comes in the form of a symptom checklist (Sweet, 2009). Despite assertions otherwise, there continues to be no best measurement tool for the identification of PTSD (Guriel & Fremouw, 2003). Many instruments designed to diagnose PTSD lack symptom validity scales altogether (e.g., the Clinician-Administered PTSD Scale for *DSM-5* [CAPS-5]; PTSD Checklist for *DSM-5* [PCL-5]) and some instruments designed to diagnose PTSD and assessment of malingering contain relatively insensitive validity measures, such as the Trauma Symptom Inventory-2 (Gray, Elhai & Briere, 2010; Henry & Gornbein, 2022). To offset this deficiency, it is important to include these aforementioned instruments, and instruments such as the MMPI-2-RF or MMPI-3 because they include scales of symptom validity. In fact, the MMPI-2, the predecessor to MMPI-2-RF and the MMPI-3 (i.e., the "MMPI Family"), has been considered to be "arguably the best known and most effective test for detecting malingered PTSD" (Demakis & Elhai, 2011).

The Case OF MS. B.[1]

Ms. B. was a woman in her late fifties who was referred to me by a defense attorney for evaluation of her claim of PTSD and brain injury as a result of a MVA in June of 2015. Ms. B had previously undergone assessment two years after the accident on referral by a nurse practitioner to a psychologist at a local hospital.

Background Information

Ms. B. has a four-year college education and was working as a case manager at the time of the accident. She has been married twice, divorced once, and was considering separating from her second husband at the time of her MVA. She has two adult children from her first marriage, one of whom is in remission from a brain tumor and the other of whom was severely assaulted, suffering multiple orthopedic injuries and requiring surgeries for repair with a reasonable recovery. She also has two children from her second marriage, both of whom were living with her and her husband at the time of the MVA. Family history also includes a brother who died as a result of a car accident.

Medical history was significant for hypercholesterolemia, hypertension, migraine, and insomnia. Medications were Lipitor and lisinopril. Ms. B. denied a history of smoking and reported drinking alcohol 2–3 times a week, although at some points she had been drinking daily.

In terms of mental health history, Ms. B. began seeing a psychiatrist in 2009 because of stress. Therapy records revealed her belief that she has been experiencing discrimination in her workplace for years and has been harassed by a co-worker, who she thinks wants her job. Further, she believes that her company is trying to force her out. In response to this stress, she complained of loss of appetite, crying, insomnia, frequent awakenings, racing thoughts, and decreased concentration. Other stressors she described included raising two teenagers, moving from one town to another and having to leave her friends behind and significant relational problems with her husband. She does not like where she lives and worries that if her husband divorces her, she will lose access to his more plentiful income. Her records included diagnoses of anxiety and depression, treated with lorazepam, Klonopin, and Lexapro.

Review of the Accident

At the time of the MVA, Ms. B was an unrestrained rear seat passenger in a vehicle that swerved off the road into a bush in someone's front yard when the driver had a medical issue. At the time of the accident, she was leaning over to get her phone from her bag and remembers hearing the driver coughing and then her head and body going forward into the back of the passenger seat. She has a full memory of the accident and denied loss of consciousness (LOC). She was already walking at the scene prior to the arrival of emergency medical technicians (EMTs). EMTs described Ms. B. as alert and oriented X 4 with a Glasgow Coma Scale score of 15. She was able to give her past medical history as including high cholesterol, hypertension and her medications as Lipitor, lisinopril and lorazepam. She reported tenderness to her forehead, cervical spine, underneath the right breast to right flank and right ankle. She was noted to have a contusion to the right hand with tenderness below her pinky finger, abrasions to the left knee and shin and bruising to right and left shins. Primary impression of the EMTs was pain.

In the emergency department (ED) at the hospital, Ms. B. was able to provide details regarding the MVA. She complained of left paraspinal cervical muscle tenderness and right hand tenderness and also head and neck pain, reportedly describing her symptoms as mild in severity. On exam, she was found to be alert and oriented, with normal motor and sensory function and no focal deficits. Affect, judgment, and mood were considered normal. Imaging of the right hand, right knee, chest, feet, and abdomen/pelvis showed osteoarthritic changes, but did not reveal any acute traumatic injury. CT scan of the brain was unremarkable for acute intracranial findings or skull fracture and maxillofacial CT did not reveal facial fracture, but showed postsurgical changes in the paranasal sinuses and mild mucosal thickening in the frontal and ethmoid sinuses. CTs of the cervical, lumbar, and thoracic spines were negative for acute injury, but revealed osteopenia and degenerative changes. Workup was considered unremarkable. No acute traumatic process was identified on physical exam or by imaging. Final diagnoses were motor vehicle collision and whiplash injury. There was no diagnosis of concussion.

Three days following discharge from the ED, Ms. B. complained to a nurse practitioner (NP) of headache and neck pain, which she said "was associated with" anxiety, decreased concentration, photophobia, fatigue, dizziness, and nausea. She denied "memory loss, aphasia, facial drooping, weakness, numbness, paresthesia, fever, chills, malaise, change in vision, tinnitus, decreased hearing, phonophobia, shortness of breath, chest pain, palpitations, vomiting, and decreased range of motion of neck and her arms." Based on her symptom report, although in the absence of having established the presence of the neurodiagnostic indicators of concussive brain injury, the NP assessed "concussion-mild" and advised "brain rest" and avoidance of glowing screens.

In the immediate months following the MVA, Ms. B.'s symptom complaints grew in type and degree. She complained of having intermittent and unpredictable symptoms despite some improvement. Her complaints came to include dizziness and nausea and trouble parallel parking because of being unable to coordinate the necessary actions and feeling off balance when dancing. She complained of trouble "multitasking," planning meals, and difficulty when driving if listening to music or talking with a passenger, although she did not report any fear of driving or riding in cars. She complained of fatigue, mild intermittent nausea, frustration, crying, feeling upset, feeling embarrassed, sleeping a lot, and being "emotionally flat," saying she was avoiding activities that previously brought her joy. Because of her complaints she was referred for MRI of the brain, which was interpreted as unremarkable.

Five months after the accident, Ms. B. self-referred to a neurologist, to whom she reported a different story than immediately after the accident, saying she was belted at the time of the accident and also that she had a one-minute period of LOC. She also reported improbable memory problems, such as forgetting how to work her shower after the MVA. She expressed being unable to work mostly because of cognitive issues. Her Modified Somatic Perception Test (MSPQ) score was 14 and on a symptom checklist Ms. B. checked 22 of 26 symptoms for a total symptom score of 109/156. Neurological examination was unremarkable. Five months after the MVA, Ms. B. also presented to her psychiatrist and complained she was "unable to drive" because she feared getting into an accident, although later in deposition Ms. B. testified she never stopped driving for more than a week after the MVA and her records and social media indicated she traveled frequently by car and plane after the MVA. There was no report of other psychological symptoms that could be considered posttraumatic in nature; her psychiatrist diagnosed PTSD.

Nine months after the MVA, Ms. B. returned to her neurologist, who noted she had made "dramatic improvement," such that on the symptom checklist she checked only 4 symptoms for a total symptom score of 4. Ms. B. was considered essentially asymptomatic and completely normal on exam. She complained of what she said were "some very mild occasional issues with memory," but that she was not convinced these were related to her "concussion." Impression was resolved PCS and she was discharged from the neurologist's care.

Then, 17 months after the MVA, and after not having seen her psychiatrist in a year, Ms. B. returned to him and complained of low energy, anhedonia, irritability, and trouble with concentration and memory, which she said had all "continued" and were worsened than in the year before. Her psychiatrist reported he saw what he called "newly emerging PTSD symptoms of occasional nightmares, avoidant behavior (related to cars, including 'inability to drive'), occasional hyperarousal and psycho-emotional reactivity to cues related to cars/accidents [plus] occasional flashbacks." Pertinent negatives on psychiatric review of systems were depressed mood, irritability, and numbness, among other symptoms. There was no mention in this record that Ms. B had moved out of the family home and was now living apart from her second husband after he had begun the process of divorce.

Also, despite full clearance of her post-accident complaints by nine months post-accident, Ms. B. returned to the neurologist's office, where she met with a NP and reported symptoms had "returned" after going back to work following a period of "traveling." She continued to take the lorazepam that she had taken for years and now took prazosin daily "as needed." The NP had Ms. B. complete a symptom checklist on which she checked 21/26 symptoms for a total symptom score of 93/156. The NP then decided Ms. B. needed a rehabilitation program, comprising occupational therapy with a focus on her newly developed "visual dysfunction," and Vasper therapy, a low-intensity 21-minute exercise system that combines liquid cooling, muscle compression, and interval training. The NP also referred Ms. B. for neuropsychological assessment with a psychologist working at the hospital and advised her to stay off of work. She also had her undergo another MRI, which showed no interval change compared with the prior unremarkable MRI.

Deposition

Relevant information in deposition included Ms. B.'s testimony that she usually took vacations separately from her husband and that she takes trips approximately twice a year, but sometimes more. She testified that after the accident she took many trips: taking holidays in Iceland, Belize, Portugal, Mexico, and London after which she drove around the Lakes Region in England. She acknowledged having driven to a spa in Vermont and to visit a friend in New York City. In deposition, Ms. B. testified that with the exception of one week she did drive after the accident, including taking her children to school and to their activities because her husband would not.

In deposition, Ms. B.'s testimony revealed that she could recall what happened before, during, and after the accident, including her thoughts about what was happening at the time and recalling striking the back of the seat in front of her. She testified that she remembered the ambulance arriving and traveling in the ambulance to the hospital. In deposition, Ms. B. testified that after the accident, she did not know how to turn the shower on and she did not know what button to push on the printer, although she knew how to do a Google search to find out how. She testified that after the accident she did not know how to use a house key, but she was able to email and she does not remember having any difficulty using her computer. She testified that at first she did not understand how to turn the steering wheel of her car, and how to activate the turn signal. She testified she "would sit in the car for like an hour or two until I was able to do this."

In deposition, Ms. B. testified that her problems with co-workers at work continued and that she and her second husband were divorcing and she had moved out of the family home into an apartment. She testified that her first marriage ended in divorce because of physical abuse.

She testified that prior to the accident, she had a cleaning woman come into her home once a week, but she no longer has a cleaner and does the work herself. She lives alone now and she cooks all of her own meals, does her own laundry, is responsible for her own medications, and manages her own finances. She drives and likes to travel and work in her garden.

Prior Neuropsychological Evaluation

Background

Two years after the MVA and two years before my evaluation, Ms. B. underwent neuropsychological testing by a psychologist affiliated with the neurologist's practice. According to the psychologist's report, Ms. B. was referred for testing due to continuing cognitive, physical, and emotional symptoms since her "first lifetime concussion" in June 2015. In providing information about the MVA, Ms. B. – in contrast to her report in records contemporaneous with the MVA – said that she does not know if she lost consciousness and that she does not have a clear memory of the accident. She also reported she was told at the ED that she had a concussion and she should follow up with her primary care physician (PCP), but did not do so for several days because she was "terrified to drive." She complained that after the MVA, she had difficulty following conversations, could not answer simple questions, could not multitask, and if faced with a decision, she would become nauseated and vomit. The psychologist reviewed records only from the neurologist's office, and in doing so, acknowledged that Ms. B was considered recovered nine months after the MVA. She said Ms. B. reported a return of symptoms recently after increased responsibilities at her job and at home. Now, Ms. B. was complaining of becoming overwhelmed, experiencing brief periods of having trouble figuring out what to do, difficulties with planning and organizing and getting tasks started, headaches, vision difficulties, and increasing fatigue. She complained that she had been planning to seek a promotion at work but the accident "derailed" her plan. Ms. B. admitted to a lifelong history of anxiety for which she was taking lorazepam and said she was recently divorced. There is no mention of her having been under psychiatric care for years.

Ms. B. arrived at the evaluation unaccompanied and presented as well-groomed and nicely dressed. She was observed to be "generally polite and cooperative" throughout the evaluation process and speech was described as "fluent" with normal volume, rate, and prosody. She was also described as "generally attentive and focused" throughout the evaluation. Ms. B. reportedly complained that she felt the evaluation was long and that she "was getting tired" of being there.

Test Results

Ms. B participated in a fairly comprehensive cognitive evaluation (see Tables 13.1–13.3 and 13.5), including measures of intellectual functioning, memory, language, visuospatial ability, and executive functioning. Assessment of emotional status was done via the Personality Assessment Inventory (PAI) and self-report of complaints was via a symptom checklist before and after the evaluation. No stand-alone measures of performance validity were administered and validity was not mentioned in the report.

Table 13.1 Results from Performance Validity Measures Administered to Ms. B.

PVT Measure	*Two Years Post-Accident*	*Four Years Post-Accident*
Word Memory Test:	Percent	Percent
Immediate Recall		77.5*
Delayed Recall		65.0*
Consistency		72.5*
Multiple Choice		55.0*
Paired Associate		45.0*
TOMM:	Raw Score	Raw Score
Trial 1		45
Trial 2		49
Word Choice Test		41*
Dot Counting Test		16.33*
Reliable Digit Span	9	7
Logical Memory Delayed Recognition	24	23
Visual Reproduction Delayed Recog.		5
CVLT Forced Choice Delay	16	15

* These scores fall in the noncredible range for mTBI/concussion.

Table 13.2 Results from Symptom Validity Measures Administered to Ms. B.

SVT Measure	*Two Years Post-Accident*	*Four Years Post-Accident*
MMPI-2-RF:	T score	T score
VRIN-r		53
TRIN-r		73_{F}*
F-r		111*
Fp-r		68
Fs		91*
FBS-r		96*
RBS		97*
L-r		62
K-r		45
SIMS:	Raw score	Raw score
NI		12*
AF		5*
P		0
LI		4*
AM		7*
Total		28*
PAI:	T score	T score
INC	40	
INF	44	
NIM	47	
PIM	52	

* These scores are elevated.

Table 13.3 Test Score Results from Cognitive Measures Administered to Ms. B.

Measure	*Two Years Post-Accident*	*Four Years Post-Accident*
TOPF	Standard score (%ile)	Standard score (%ile)
Predicted full scale IQ*	107 (68)	108 (70)
WAIS-IV		
Index:	Standard score (%ile)	Standard score (%ile)
VCI	114 (82)	116 (86)
PRI	121 (92)	121 (92)
WMI	111 (77)	105 (63)
PSI	97 (42)	108(70)
FSIQ	115 (84)	117 (87)
Subtest:	Scaled score (%ile)	Scaled score (%ile)
Similarities	14 (91)	13 (84)
Vocabulary	11 (63)	
Information		13 (84)
Block Design	13 (84)	13 (84)
Matrix Reasoning	14 (91)	14 (91)
Digit Span	11 (63)	9 (37)
Digits Forward	9 (37)	8 (25)
Digits Backward	11 (63)	8 (25)
Digit Sequencing	12 (75)	12 (75)
Arithmetic	13 (84)	13 (84)
Symbol Search	11 (63)	13 (84)
Coding	8 (25)	10 (50)
Conners CPT3:	T Score	T Score
Detectability	52	
Omissions	47	
Commissions	52	
Perseverations	46	
Hit Reaction Time (RT)	60	
Hit RT Standard Deviation	44	
Variability	44	
HRT Block Change	45	
HRT ISI Change	49	
WMS-IV:	Scaled score (%ile)	Scaled score (%ile)
Symbol Span	9 (37)	13 (84)
Spatial Addition		12 (75)
Trail making A & B*:	Raw score (%ile)	Raw score (%ile)
A: Number Sequencing	25" (38)	29" (24)
B: Number-Letter Sequencing	63" (38)	86" (12)
DKEFS:		
Verbal Fluency:	Scaled score (%ile)	Scaled score (%ile)
Letter Fluency	15 (95)	12 (75)
Category Switching Total	16 (98)	14 (91)
Category Switching Accuracy	15 (95)	13 (84)
Color-Word Interference Test:		
Color Naming	9 (37)	7 (16)
Word Reading	9 (37)	7 (16)
Inhibition	12 (75)	11 (63)
Inhibition/Switching	13 (84)	13 (84)
Wisconsin Card Sorting Test*	Raw Score (%ile)	Raw Score (%ile)
Categories Completed		6 (>16)
Trials to First Category		13 (>16)
Failure to Maintain Set		1 (>16)

(*Continued*)

Table 13.3 (Continued)

Measure	*Two Years Post-Accident*	*Four Years Post-Accident*
	Standard score (%ile)	Standard score (%ile)
% Total Errors		94 (34)
% Perseverative Resp.		96 (39)
% Perseverative Errors		96 (39)
% Nonperseverative Errors		90 (25)
% Conceptual Level		91 (27)
Tower Test:	Scaled score (%ile)	Scaled score (%ile)
Total Achievement	11 (63)	
Twenty Questions:		
Initial Abstraction	9 (37)	
Total Questions Asked	10 (50)	
Total Weighted Achievement	11 (63)	
DKEFS	Scaled score (%ile)	Percentile
Category Fluency	13 (84)	14 (91)
Naming:	Raw score (%ile)	Raw score (%ile)
Boston Naming Test*	57 (42)	56 (27)
Irregular Word Reading:	Standard score (%ile)	Standard score (%ile)
Test Of Premorbid Functioning	101 (53)	102 (55)
Rey Complex Figure Test	Raw score (%ile)	Raw score (%ile)
Copy	29 (2–5)	35 (>16)
WMS-IV Subtest	Scaled score (%ile)	Scaled score (%ile)
Logical Memory:		
Immediate Recall	13 (84)	11 (63)
Delayed Recall	13 (84)	10 (50)
Visual Reproduction:		
Immediate Recall		9 (37)
Delayed Recall		10 (50)
Word list learning:	CVLT-II	CVLT-3
Trial	Raw score (%ile)	Raw score (%ile)
1	5 (16)	5 (25)
2	9 (50)	8 (37)
3	12 (69)	11 (63)
4	14 (84)	12 (63)
5	15 (84)	14 (75)
Total Learning 1–5	55 (76)	50 (50)
List B	6 (50)	6 (63)
Short Delay Free	14 (84)	12 (75)
Short Delay Cued	15 (84)	13 (63)
Long Delay Free	14 (84)	13 (75)
Long Delay Cued	15 (84)	13 (63)
Delayed Recognition Hits	15 (50)	15 (50)
Rey Complex Figure Test:	Raw score (%ile)	Raw score (%ile)
Immediate Recall	10.5 (5)	6 (<1)
Delayed Recall	10.5 (4)	12 (10)
Delayed Recognition	19 (21)	17 (3)
BVMT-R*:	Raw score (%ile)	Raw score (%ile)
Trial 1	7 (76)	
Trial 2	7 (31)	
Trial 3	10 (66)	
Total Learning Trials 1–3	24 (58)	
Delayed Recall	10 (73)	

* These tests are demographically adjusted.

Conclusions

The psychologist concluded that "overall, [Ms. B.'s] scores across neuropsychological domains were in the average range and above, with some clear areas of relative weakness." The psychologist described Ms. B. as having shown "good scores across measures of intellectual ability, working memory and auditory-verbal memory," but a pattern of "relative weaknesses on measures of visual memory and higher order intellectual functioning," because of a disorganized approach to copying a complex geometric figure and an inability to recall details in her subsequent recall of the figure, difficulties the psychologist related "to the visual issues she has experienced since her injuries." The psychologist also concluded, "Further evidence of disturbance in higher order executive functioning was seen in [Ms. B.'s] performance on the Tower Test," where "[a]lthough she was able to solve each tower, she was mildly inefficient in doing so, especially in comparison to her superior range visuospatial skills." The psychologist went further to state that "difficulty with organization and planning has also been evident in her daily life, as [Ms. B.] reports feeling very overwhelmed and being unable to make decisions or approach more complex tasks." The psychologist decided that "these cognitive inefficiencies do appear to be related, in part, to her mild traumatic brain injury" and suggested that the findings were indicative of "dysregulation in attentional and executive function processes" due to "neuropsychological weakness in frontal-subcortical brain systems" as "inefficiency in such brain systems is often found in traumatic brain injury, as injury to the frontal lobes is common."

Regarding the scores on the symptom checklist, the psychologist reported that Ms. B. checked 19 of 26 symptoms with a symptom total of 63/156 before the evaluation and 21 of 26 symptoms with a symptom total of 87/156 after the evaluation. The psychologist reported the PAI as "valid," but noted that the PAI clinical profile revealed no marked elevations that should be considered to indicate the presence of clinical psychopathology. The psychologist focused only on an elevation on the Traumatic Stress subscale of the Anxiety-Related Disorders clinical scale, which the psychologist believed to be "consistent with PTSD." The psychologist made no mention of the elevation on the Conversion subscale of the Somatization clinical scale or the elevation on the Affective subscale of the Anxiety clinical scale. The psychologist did not indicate that Ms. B.'s report on the PAI was of experiencing a great deal of tension and difficulty relaxing, as well as difficulties consistent with mild or transient depressive symptomatology, nor did the psychologist indicate that Ms. B.'s report on the PAI indicated concerns about physical functioning and health matters in general, problems in sensory and motor dysfunction in particular, symptoms that can be seen in conversion disorders. The previous psychologist did not note that Ms. B.'s report on the PAI did not generate any diagnostic considerations other than rule outs of persistent depressive disorder, conversion disorder, and/or unspecified personality disorder with obsessive-compulsive features. Instead, the psychologist concluded that Ms. B. is "experiencing significant anxiety associated with PTSD" and attributed this to damage in the "dorsomedial and ventromedial prefrontal cortex," areas that the psychologist said are damaged in concussion. The psychologist diagnosed PTSD, PCS, and concussion with LOC of 30 minutes or less. The psychologist made the diagnosis of PTSD without establishing that the MVA was a criterion event and that Ms. B. had the required symptoms and the required number of symptoms necessary for the diagnosis and the psychologist makes the diagnosis of concussion and PCS without corroboration of the details of the accident.

Subsequent Neuropsychological Evaluation

My evaluation of Ms. B. occurred two years after the first one and approximately four years after the accident at the request of the defense attorney. Prior to my evaluation and report, I reviewed pre-accident and post-accident medical records, the accident report, employment records, Ms. B.'s deposition transcripts, and the report and raw data from the psychologist who evaluated her two years after the accident. During interview, Ms. B. complained of high levels of anxiety related to one of her children applying to college and the other joining the armed forces. She also complained of problems with focusing, paying attention, memorizing, and concentrating. She reportedly struggled when learning new things. When driving to Canada, she felt "very disoriented." Specifically, her car was running out of gas, but she did not pull over to get gas because she found it very overwhelming to choose an exit on the highway. Her indecision did not result in actually running out of gas and she was able to reach her destination. She offered no spontaneous complaints that would indicate posttraumatic symptoms.

Behavioral Presentation

Ms. B. arrived at the evaluation on time having driven herself. She was casually dressed and well-groomed, and was alert and oriented to person, place, date, and time, knowing the date without assistance when signing the consent form. She was generally cooperative. Eye contact appeared normal. Vision (corrected for near) and hearing (uncorrected) appeared adequate for participation in the exam. Speech was fluent and Ms. B. was very talkative. No unusual word-finding difficulties were observed. She did not have difficulty comprehending task instructions and did not require repetition of instructions. There were no obvious difficulties deploying, focusing, maintaining, and switching attention across tasks. Ms. B. had no trouble manipulating the computer on her own or finding her way to and from the lobby.

Test Results

Validity Tests

As evident in Tables 13.1 and 13.2, the most striking features of the evaluation were failures on stand-alone PVTs, a mild lowering (and raising) of some scores in Ms. B.'s profile compared with two years before, and elevations on over-reporting scales of the MMPI-2-RF and on the Structured Inventory of Malingered Symptomatology (SIMS). Review of Ms. B.'s scores on measures sensitive to engagement, effort, and motivation revealed that several, including the Word Memory Test, the Dot Counting Test, and Word Choice fell below expected parameters in the noncredible range in the context of Ms. B.'s reported injury. These findings and the lowering of scores on some working memory and memory measures relative to her prior evaluation created problems interpreting the test scores she obtained in terms of whether they were accurate reflections of her current level of cognitive functioning. In the context of failed PVTs, areas of normal or average functioning can be interpreted as intact, though they should also be understood to possibly be higher/stronger had there been consistently optimal performance/engagement.

Ms. B.'s scores on the MMPI-2-RF validity scales raised concern about inconsistent responding, but not to the level that they invalidated her responses. In addition, there were multiple markers of over-reporting of psychological, somatic, and cognitive symptoms, including memory problems. She obtained scores beyond cut-off (i.e., noncredible) for over-reporting on the F-r, Fs, FBS-r, and RBS validity scales. On the MMPI-2-RF, Ms. B. reported a considerably larger than average number of infrequent responses, a much larger than average number of somatic symptoms rarely described by individuals with genuine medical conditions, an unusual combination of responses that is associated with noncredible reporting of somatic and/or cognitive symptoms, and an unusual combination of responses that is associated with noncredible memory complaints. In the context of her history and presenting problems, responses most likely indicated over-reporting and/or exaggeration. As a result, the scores she obtained on the "clinical scales" must be interpreted with caution, especially the scales related to psychopathology, and somatic and cognitive complaints. Problems involving symptom invalidity were also evidenced on the SIMS, where Ms. B.'s total score was significantly elevated above the recommended cut-off score for the identification of likely feigning in a forensic population.

Cognitive Tests

As seen in Table 13.3, the test scores obtained by Ms. B. did not reveal anything out of the ordinary in a neuropsychological test protocol, other than what appeared to be lesser effort on a memory measure now than in the prior evaluation. Among the many relatively independent test scores collected over two evaluations, low scores were seen consistently on only one test (i.e., RCFT). (See Table 13.4 for descriptive labels for the cognitive tests.) Overall, Ms. B. showed a normal range of skills' variability across the battery of tests. She scored in the above-average range on a measure of intellect and none of her index scores was abnormally different from any other. Performances on measures of attention, concentration, and higher-order executive function were normal and at levels expected given intellectual and educational background. Performances on verbal learning and memory tests were consistent

Table 13.4 Descriptive Labels for Cognitive Test Scores (Guilmette et al., 2020)

Label	*Percentile*	*Standard Score*	*Scaled Score*	*T Score*
Normally distributed standard, scaled, T, and percentile scores:				
Exceptionally high score	≥98	≥130	≥16	>70
Above average	91–97	120–129	14–15	64–69
High average	75–90	110–119	12–13	57–63
Average	25–74	90–109	8–11	44–56
Within normal limits	16–84	85–115	7–12	40–60
Low average	9–24	80–89	6–7	37–43
Below average	2–8	70–79	4–5	30–36
Exceptionally low score	≤2	≥130	≤3	≤29
Scores demographically adjusted for age, sex, race, and/or education				
Above expectation	>84			
At expectation	16–84			
Below expectation	<16			
One-tailed tests (non-normally distributed scores)				
Above normal limits	84			
Within normal limits	16–84			
Below normal limits	<16			

with that expected given measured intellect and were not supportive of complaints in memory. Performances on two measures of visual learning and memory were intact; performance on a third was below expectations, but cannot be used in isolation to document reduced visual memory. There were no findings that could be considered as revealing neurocognitive dysfunction secondary to a putative concussion sustained in a MVA four years before.

Self-Report Measures of Personality, Mood, and Posttraumatic Symptoms

As can be seen in Table 13.5, what Ms. B. attempted to highlight in her self-report on the MMPI-2-RF was a diffuse pattern of somatic and vague neurological complaints. Her pattern of report indicated there is likely a psychological component to her complaints, that she is very likely to develop physical symptoms in response to stress and that she is likely to reject psychological interpretations of her complaints and very likely to be preoccupied with poor health. On the MMPI-2-RF, she also attempted to highlight a diffuse pattern of cognitive difficulties, including problems in memory and concentrating, but also intellectual limitations, and confusion. In addition, on the MMPI-2-RF, Ms. B. also attempted to highlight significant emotional distress consisting of anxiety and depression. Ms. B. also reported

Table 13.5 Score Results from Psychological Measures Administered to Ms. B.

Measure	*Two Years Post-Accident*	*Four Years Post-Accident*
MMPI-2-RF	T score	T score
Somatic/Cognitive Dysfunction		
RC1		83
MLS		87
GIC		64
HPC		73
NUC		91
COG		86
Emotional Dysfunction (EID)		69
RCd		64
SUI		91
HLP		52
SFD		52
NFC		54
RC2		76
INTR-r		74
RC7		63
STW		65
AXY		100
ANP		80
BRF		71
MSF		43
NEGE-r		73
Thought Dysfunction (THD)		70
RC6		61
RC8		73
PSYC-r		66
Behavioral Dysfunction (BXD)		63
RC4		68
JCP		70

(*Continued*)

Table 13.5 (Continued)

Measure	*Two Years Post-Accident*	*Four Years Post-Accident*
SUB		50
RC9		56
AGG		67
ACT		53
AGGR-r		47
DISC-r		56
Interpersonal Functioning		
FML		68
RC3		46
IPP		62
SAV		80
SHY		52
DSF		68
PAI	T score	T score
SOM	62	
Conversion	78	
Somatization	46	
Health concerns	59	
ANX	68	
Cognitive	64	
Affective	75	
Physiological	58	
ARD	65	
Obsessive-compulsive	68	
Phobias	37	
Traumatic stress	75	
DEP	63	
MAN	36	
PAR	40	
SCZ	47	
BOR	45	
ANT	43	
AGG	52	
SUI	42	
STR	34	
NON	43	
RXR	55	
DOM	39	
WRM	38	
Beck depression inventory-2		27
Beck anxiety inventory		24

a history of suicidal ideation and/or attempts, although on a straight-forward self-report measure of depression (i.e., the BDI-II) and to me, she denied she had any plans, means or intent of suicide. On the MMPI-2-RF, Ms. B. also reported unusual thought processes that could include somatic delusions. Some of the many diagnostic considerations based on her report on the MMPI-2-RF included malingering of emotional symptoms, somatoform (or somatic symptom) disorder, depression and/or anxiety-related disorder, anger-related disorders, and personality disorders manifesting unusual thoughts and perceptions. On face valid self-report measures of anxiety and depression symptoms, Ms. B. reported moderate

Table 13.6 Results from PCL-5 Administered to Ms. B.

PCL-5 Scoring Summary Sheet	*Four Years After MVA*		
Criterion A: Trauma Event	*Criterion Event:* No		
Symptom criteria	*Total severity*	*# Symptoms*	*Criterion met*
Criterion B: Intrusive	7/20	3	Yes
Criterion C: Avoidance	4/8	2	Yes
Criterion D: Cognitions and mood	3/28	1	No
Criterion E: Arousal and reactivity	7/23	3	Yes
Total severity score	21/80	9/20	No

anxiety symptoms and moderate depressive symptoms. Neither of these scales contain internal validity measures, however, and given the evidence of exaggeration of symptoms on symptom validity measures, these scores cannot be viewed as accurate.

Despite Ms. B.'s MVA not meeting diagnostic Criterion A for PTSD, she was asked to complete the PCL-5, a self-report measure of posttraumatic symptoms that does not have any internal validity measures. As can be seen in Table 13.6, her report on this measure four years after the MVA indicated she did not meet total severity criteria or all the necessary symptom criteria for a diagnosis of PTSD.

Because of evidence of over-reporting on multiple symptom validity measures, the interpretations of the MMPI-2-RF and other self-report measures must be viewed with caution as they very likely – at a minimum – indicate noncredible reporting of somatic and cognitive symptoms and possible over-reporting of general psychological dysfunction, such as anxiety. Responses on the SIMS indicated over-reporting of neurological, affective, and memory symptoms. As noted above, over-reporting on the symptom validity scales means self-report of symptoms cannot be relied upon as showing the existence or degree of psychopathology.

Overall, the cognitive test scores obtained from Ms. B during my evaluation and the previous one did not reveal neurocognitive dysfunction or that, despite obtaining noncredible scores on some performance validity measures, she was manipulating her performances on cognitive tests to appear neurocognitively impaired. In contrast, her report on the MMPI-2-RF and the SIMS indicated significant over-report of emotional, somatic, and cognitive symptoms, which in the context of her history and her lawsuit pertaining to the MVA in June 2015, indicated a very high likelihood that she is malingering her PTSD or – at the very least – misattributing what she reports as posttraumatic symptoms to the MVA in June 2015.

Summary and Conclusions

This case highlights multiple important issues in the neuropsychological evaluation of PTSD malingering: the importance of a thorough review of records; the administration of the appropriate test instruments, including sensitive and specific performance and symptom validity measures, as well as the correct interpretation of the data obtained; the relegation of self-report to its proper place in an evaluation; and the potential nocebic influence of treating clinicians and their diagnoses.

It is my view that in Ms. B.'s case, she was misdiagnosed both with PTSD and with a concussion and PCS by her treaters who did not seek any corroboration of her report of the accident or her symptoms. Without knowledge of whether Ms. B.'s accident was a Criterion

A event and without any systematic assessment of posttraumatic symptoms, but based on her misrepresentation that she was afraid of driving, she was diagnosed with PTSD. In addition, without establishing the presence of the neurodiagnostic indicators of concussive brain injury at the time of injury from sources other than Ms. B., and then based on Ms. B.'s over-report on symptom checklists, she was diagnosed with concussion and PCS. With these diagnoses now in her medical records, Ms. B. was then able to continue in her life as she had before the accident without actually having to change her behavior (i.e., driving and traveling extensively according to her testimony in deposition and her social media) and without having to demonstrate any neurocognitive impairment or psychological pathology when assessed two years after the MVA.

Review of the tests administered by the psychologist two years after the MVA indicated that the evaluation did not meet industry standards (Sweet et al., 2021). No PVTs were administered and no sensitive SVTs were included. Instead, the psychologist administered a personality inventory with insufficient validity markers and a symptom checklist containing no symptom validity measures at all. That evaluation produced no test results that would support that Ms. B. had neurocognitive dysfunction or that she had neurocognitive dysfunction or "inefficiencies" that could be causally related to a putative concussion two years before by means of an explanation completely contrary to the concussion research literature and that ignores the research that documents how much variability there is in neuropsychological profiles of neurologically normal individuals (see, for example, Binder, Iverson & Brooks, 2009). The psychologist also did not systematically assess for the presence of PTSD. The psychologist did not document that a Criterion A event occurred or that Ms. B. met the diagnostic criteria for PTSD, and she did not corroborate Ms. B.'s self-report with a review of records. Instead, she used an elevation on a single subscale of a personality inventory as evidence of PTSD. No matter if a clinical evaluation or a forensic one, neuropsychological test data cannot be interpreted in a vacuum; it must be clearly set within a person's history (Hebben & Milberg, 2009).

Although it cannot be documented with any degree of certainty, it is my view that is likely that when Ms. B. was finally evaluated by me in the context of her lawsuit, she felt it necessary to over-report her "psychological" distress so that her diagnosis of PTSD would be retained. I suspect she did not significantly underperform on the cognitive tests because a significant decrement compared with her prior evaluation would be unexpected. If these suspicions are correct, they clearly portray Ms. B as having a mindset of impression management.

Web Links and Online Materials

American Psychological Association: Posttraumatic Stress Disorder: https://www.apa.org/topics/ptsd/index

Anxiety & Depression Association of America: PTSD Resources: https://adaa.org/understanding-anxiety/posttraumatic-stress-disorder-ptsd/resources

Distinguishing PTSD from 'False PTSD: Tips for Clinicians': https://psychnews.psychiatryonline.org/doi/full/10.1176/appi.pn.2019.8a6

Matto, M., McNiel, D.E., & Binder, R.L. (June 2019). A systematic approach to the detection of false PTSD. *Journal of the American Academy of Psychiatry and the Law Online*. https://jaapl.org/content/early/2019/06/10/JAAPL.003853-19

Mayo Clinic: Post-traumatic stress disorder (PTSD): https://www.mayoclinic.org/diseases-conditions/post-traumatic-stress-disorder/symptoms-causes/syc-20355967

National Institute of Mental Health: https://www.nimh.nih.gov/health/topics/post-traumatic-stress-disorder-ptsd

NIH National Library of Medicine MedlinePlus: Post-Traumatic Stress Disorder: https://medlineplus.gov/posttraumaticstressdisorder.html

Posttraumatic Stress Disorder (PTSD) Alliance: http://www.ptsdalliance.org/

U.S. Department of Veterans Affairs National Center for PTSD: https://www.ptsd.va.gov

Note

1 Certain identifying details, including her initial, have been modified slightly to protect this woman's identity.

References

Benjet, C., Bromet, E., Karam, E.G., Kessler, R.C., Mclaughlin, K.A., Ruscio, A.M., Shahly, V., Stein, D.J., Petukhova, M., Hill, E., Alonso, J., Atwoli, L., Bunting, B., Bruffaerts, R., Caldas-De-Almeida, J.M., De Girolamo, G., Florescu, S., Gureje, O., Huang, Y., Lepine, J.P., Kawakami, N., Kovess-Masfety, V., Medina-Mora, M.E., Navarro-Mateu, F., Piazza, M., Posada-Villa, J., Scott, K.M., Shalev, A., Slade, T., ten Have, M., Torres, Y., Viana, M.C., Zarkov, Z., & Koenen, K.C. (2016). The epidemiology of traumatic event exposure worldwide: Results from the World Mental Health Survey Consortium. *Psychological Medicine. 46*, 327–343.

Binder, L.M., Iverson, G.L., & Brooks, B.L. (2009). To err is human: "Abnormal" neuropsychological scores and variability are common in healthy adults. *Archives of Clinical Neuropsychology, 24*, 31–46.

Chafetz, M. (2011). The psychological consultative examination for Social Security Disability. *Psychological Injury and Law, 4*, 235–244.

Chafetz, M., & Underhill, J. (2013). Estimated costs of malingered disability. *Archives of Clinical Neuropsychology, 28*, 633–639.

Demakis, G.J., & Elhai, J.D. (2011). Neuropsychological and psychological aspects of malingered posttraumatic stress disorder. *Psychological Injury and Law, 4*, 24–31.

Gray, M.J., Elhai, J.D., & Briere, J. (2010). Evaluation of the Atypical Response scale of the Trauma Symptom Inventory-2 in detecting simulated posttraumatic stress disorder. *Journal of Anxiety Disorders, 24*, 447–451.

Guilmette, T.J., Sweet, J.J., Hebben, N., Koltai, D., Mahone, E.M., Spiegler, B.J., Stucky, K., Westerveld, M. & Conference Participants (2020). American Academy of Clinical Neuropsychology consensus conference statement on uniform labeling of performance test scores. *The Clinical Neuropsychologist, 34*, 437–453.

Guriel, J., & Fremouw, W. (2003). Assessing malingered posttraumatic stress disorder: A critical review. *Clinical Psychology Review, 23*, 881–904.

Hebben, N., & Milberg, W. (2009). *Essentials of Neuropsychological Assessment*, 2nd Ed. Hoboken, NJ: John Wiley & Sons, Inc.

Henry, G.K., & Gornbein, J. (2022). Posttraumatic stress disorder and noncredible symptom reporting on the Trauma Symptom Inventory-2. *Applied Neuropsychology, 29*, 100–105.

Kim, S., Currao, A., Brown, E., Milberg, W.P., & Fortier, C.B. (2024). Importance of validity testing in psychiatric assessment: Evidence from a sample of multimorbid post-9/11 veterans. *Journal of the International Neuropsychological Society, 30*(4), 410–419.

Larrabee, G.J. (2003). Detection of malingering using atypical performance patterns on standard neuropsychological tests. *The Clinical Neuropsychologist, 17*, 410–425.

Larrabee, G. J. (2012). Performance validity and symptom validity in neuropsychological assessment. *Journal of the International Neuropsychological Society, 18*(4), 625–630.

Lees-Haley, P.R. (1997). MMPI-2 base rates for 492 personal injury plaintiffs: implications and challenges for forensic assessment. *Journal of Clinical Psychology, 53*, 745–755.

Matto, M., McNiel, D.E., & Binder, R.L. (2019). A systematic approach to the detection of false PTSD. *Journal of the American Academy of Psychiatry and Law*, *47*, 325–334.

Sweet, J.J. (2009). Posttraumatic stress disorder and neuropsychological malingering: A complicated scenario. In J. E. Morgan & J. J. Sweet (Eds.) *Neuropsychology of Malingering Casebook* (pp. 155–169). New York: Psychology Press.

Sweet, J.J., Boone, K.B., Denney, R.L., Hebben, N., Marcopulos, B.A., Morgan, J.E., Nelson, N.W., & Westerveld, M. (2023). Forensic neuropsychology: History and current status. *The Clinical Neuropsychologist*, *37*, 459–474.

Sweet, J.J., Heilbronner, R.L., Morgan, J.E., Larrabee, G.J., Rohling, M.L., Boone, K.B., Kirkwood, M. W., Schroeder, R.W., Suhr, J.A., & Conference Participants (2021) American Academy of Clinical Neuropsychology (AACN) 2021 consensus statement on validity assessment: Update of the 2009 AACN consensus conference statement on neuropsychological assessment of effort, response bias, and malingering. *The Clinical Neuropsychologist*, *35*, 1053–1106.

Sweet, J.J., Klipfel, K.M., Nelson, N.W., & Moberg, P.J. (2021). Professional practices, beliefs, and incomes of U.S. neuropsychologists: The AACN, NAN, SCN 2020 practice and "salary survey". *The Clinical Neuropsychologist*, *35*, 7–80.

14 Noncredible Cognitive and Psychological Presentations in Forensic Neuropsychological Evaluations

Divergence of Performance Validity and Symptom Validity Findings

Nathaniel W. Nelson and Jerry J. Sweet

Introduction

A tenet of neuropsychological case conceptualization is that examinees' test results can be interpreted as accurate reflections of their functioning only after results have first been shown to be credible. While it is always preferable for examinees to perform to the best of their abilities, and report symptoms with transparency, the reality is that examinees present themselves in a less-than-forthright manner with alarming regularity, especially in forensic evaluation settings in which there are powerful external incentives to appear more impaired than may be the case. Base rates of response invalidity in civil and administrative settings (e.g., Workers' Compensation, personal injury litigation), are very high, ranging from 20% to more than 50% in some samples (e.g., see Greve et al., 2009; Martin & Schroeder, 2020; Svete et al., 2025). For good reason, response validity assessment has been recognized as a critical component of the neuropsychological evaluation, as emphasized in position papers that have been published by national neuropsychology organizations, such as the American Academy of Clinical Neuropsychology (AACN; Heilbronner et al., 2009; Sweet et al., 2021) and the National Academy of Neuropsychology (Bush et al., 2005).

While signs of response invalidity certainly bolster the examiner's confidence in assigning a formal designation of 'malingering', it is important to recognize that response invalidity is not, of itself, sufficient to "diagnose" malingering. According to the *DSM-5-TR*, the essence of malingering is the *intentional* production of "false or grossly exaggerated physical or psychological symptoms" that is "motivated by external incentives", such as work avoidance or financial gain. Moreover, the *DSM-5-TR* recommends that malingering should be strongly considered: (1) in medicolegal contexts (e.g., during litigation); (2) when there is a "marked discrepancy between the individual's claimed stress or disability and the objective findings and observations"; (3) when examinees exhibit a "lack of cooperation during the diagnostic evaluation and in complying with the prescribed treatment regimen"; and (4) among those with "antisocial personality disorder". The designation of malingering also entails other essential considerations, such as ruling out the possibility that noncredible presentations may be motivated by factors other than an external incentive (e.g., the assumption of a "sick role" in the case of factitious disorder) or when they are not intentional in their production (e.g., as in the case of functional neurological and other somatic disorders).

While the *DSM-5-TR* provides general factors that can be helpful to consider when contemplating a malingering designation, these considerations are not without limitation. Indeed, the *DSM* malingering considerations have generally remained static for decades,

DOI: 10.4324/9781003005063-16

across previous (e.g., *DSM-IV*, *DSM-IV-TR*, *DSM-5*) and current (*DSM-5-TR*) editions, and have not kept pace with the inordinate response validity and malingering research that has been conducted in recent decades (e.g., see Sweet et al., 2021). In fact, the superficial nature of the *DSM-IV* (APA, 1994) definition of malingering was a primary impetus for the development of the prominent Malingered Neurocognitive Dysfunction (MND) criteria (Slick et al., 1999), which have been implemented widely across clinical, research, and forensic evaluation contexts in ensuing decades. Berry and Nelson (2010) also faulted the *DSM* for its seeming presumption that "malingerers will fake bad on most, if not all of the procedures they undergo" (p. 297). The *DSM* criteria were also criticized for their inadequate capture of heterogeneous physical, psychological, and cognitive presentations that noncredible examinees often displayed on evaluation.

More recently, Sherman et al. (2020) provided an update to the Slick et al. (1999) MND criteria, which provided refined definitions of cognitive response bias, as well as "other forms of malingering pertinent to neuropsychological evaluation such as exaggeration of self-reported somatic and psychiatric symptoms" (p. 735). With continued recognition of the limitations inherent to the *DSM-5* malingering considerations, the latest Sherman et al. criteria allow for greater precision in the classification of malingering, with specifiers that included malingering of neurocognitive dysfunction, somatic symptoms, psychiatric symptoms, or "mixed" presentations. In making such distinctions, the Sherman et al. criteria have provided a greater level of nuance and relevance vis-à-vis the diversity of noncredible symptoms and impairments that examinees may exhibit in forensic neuropsychological evaluations.

Extensive empirical research studies further exemplify the multifaceted nature of the response validity construct. Examinees may present with noncredible cognitive impairments that are most readily detected by *performance validity measures*; over-reported psychological, emotional, physical, cognitive, and/or sensory symptoms that are most readily identified by *symptom validity measures*; or some admixture of *subverted* cognitive performances and over-reported symptoms. This reality highlights the importance of including both forms of response validity measures, performance validity *and* symptom validity tests (SVTs), to inform the differential diagnosis of malingered neuropsychological deficits, particularly in forensic examination contexts (cf., Martin et al., 2015; Sherman et al., 2020; Sweet et al., 2021).

In one early examination of the relationship between performance validity and symptom validity constructs, Nelson et al. (2007) conducted an exploratory factor analysis of multiple performance validity tests (PVTs) and MMPI-2 symptom validity scales in a sample of 122 compensation-seeking claimants, including 96 personal injury litigants (78.7%) and 26 Workers' Compensation claimants (21.3%), most (59.8%) of whom presented in relation to claims of disabling traumatic brain injury. The authors found evidence for four distinct factors: (1) *symptom under-reporting* (MMPI-2 scales L, K, S); (2) *over-reported 'neurotic' symptoms* (FBS, RBS, Md); (3) *over-reported 'psychotic' symptoms* (F, Fp, Dsr2); and (4) *noncredible cognitive performance* (VSVT, TOMM, LMT). While these factors were largely independent, a modest association was noted between factors 2 and 3, suggesting that some proportion of the sample engaged in *over-reporting* of non-specific cognitive and somatic complaints (FBS, RBS, Md) *with* simultaneous *under-performances* on performance validity testing.

Results of more recent studies conducted across diverse samples have also highlighted the complexity of noncredible presentations that examinees may display on evaluation, and the importance of including both forms of response validity measures in neuropsychological evaluations. The distinctiveness of performance validity and SVTs have been demonstrated among personal injury claimants with histories of concussion claims (Zakzanis et al., 2012), military veterans with histories of concussion and/or post-traumatic stress (Aase et al., 2021; Ord et al., 2021), neurorehabilitation outpatients (Boe & Evald, 2023), adults assessed for attention-deficit hyperactivity disorder (Lee et al., 2023; Ovsiew et al., 2023; Wallace et al., 2019; White et al., 2022), electrical injury claimants (Obolsky et al., 2022), seizure disorder patients (Binder et al., 2021), and other diverse clinical groups (Deboer et al., 2023; Holcomb et al., 2023). Overall, Holcomb et al. (2023) concluded that "symptom and performance validity are distinct clinical constructs" (p. 520). Likewise, DeBoer et al. (2023) concluded that performance validity and symptom validity were "dissociable constructs" and recommended that clinicians "include both SVTs and PVTs as part of a comprehensive neuropsychological evaluation as they provide unique information regarding performance and symptom validity" (p. 61). Such an approach is in fact consistent with the consensual advice of subject matter experts (e.g., Sweet et al., 2021).

In sum, recent research studies and organizational consensus statements support the notion that invalid responding and malingering are not 'one size fits all' constructs; non-credible presentations may consist of symptom over-report, subversion of cognitive performance, or both. In civil forensic contexts, malingering is frequently observed among examinees with claims of disabling traumatic brain injury, particularly mild traumatic brain injury/concussion (Sweet et al., 2021). To illustrate the potential divergence of cognitive and psychological malingering that examiners may encounter within the forensic setting, the present chapter juxtaposes two examinees who were referred for independent neuropsychological examinations related to claims of disabling concussion (Mr. X and Ms. Y). While presentations were interpreted as potentially malingered in both cases, these cases illustrate that the quality of cognitive versus psychological symptom exaggerations and invalid response styles was remarkably distinct, despite very similar fact patterns of (mild) injury severity.

(Please note that the background information and findings summarized in the cases below have been modified to maintain anonymity.)

The Case of Mr. X

Background (Mr. X)

Mr. X was a 25-year-old, White, high school educated man with an alleged history of traumatic brain injury sustained at the site of his workplace approximately two years prior to evaluation. He expressed a variety of cognitive concerns that he identified as primary impediments to his ability to resume work. He was referred for an independent neuropsychological evaluation in the context of continuing Workers' Compensation proceedings.

Behavioral Observations (Mr. X)

Mr. X was a right-hand dominant man who arrived on time and unaccompanied for evaluation. He reportedly traveled alone by self-driven automobile from his residence, approximately three hours from the evaluation site. He presented as casually dressed and was well groomed. He made use of corrective lenses. Gait appeared normal; movement in general was quite slowed, particularly during the completion of motor tasks. Mr. X's receptive language capacities were believed to be grossly intact based upon his satisfactory comprehension of interview questions and task instructions. Conversational speech was fluent, prosodic, and articulate. He was generally cooperative when responding to interview questions; he provided an accurate account of his remote and more recent background information, including a detailed summary of events associated with the claimed head injury that was the subject of Workers' Compensation proceedings, as confirmed by available records. He provided an accurate summary of current events during the clinical interview.

Mr. X provided a type-written document that he prepared, which summarized myriad cognitive limitations that he had experienced after the time of claimed injury. While he identified attention and memory limitations as particular areas of concern, he did not exhibit any difficulties focusing on or recalling recent events in response to interview questions. Notwithstanding his significant cognitive complaints, Mr. X presented with euthymic mood and congruent affect. Task approach seemed less than invested in performing to potential, and haphazard at best, during the completion of most presented tasks (e.g., quickly responding he did not know or remember test items, without due consideration).

Interview (Mr. X)

Mr. X described a work incident that resulted in a head injury approximately two years prior to the current neuropsychological evaluation while performing the duties of a security guard for his employer (a retail outlet store). Prior to the incident, Mr. X was preparing to open the store before the start of business that day. As he reached for a set of office keys from a wooden shelf (estimated weight of 30 pounds) that was positioned approximately three feet above his head, the shelf fell from the wall and struck him directly on the top of the scalp. The incident was not witnessed; information pertaining to his acute-stage presentation was restricted to retrospective self-report alone. Mr. X was reportedly stunned by the head injury, but denied having sustained loss of consciousness, disorientation, confusion, or other potential signs of altered mental status. He described a continuous recall for events that immediately preceded (i.e., standing and reaching for the keys moments before) and followed (i.e., seeing the shelf and the keys lying on the floor) the head injury. Mr. X sat down at a nearby desk soon after the head injury to survey his symptoms. At that point, he experienced subtle head pain at the site where he was struck. While he continued to experience head pain for the rest of the day (which he managed with Tylenol), Mr. X managed to complete the remainder of his work shift with usual effectiveness and without incident. Mr. X reported the incident to his supervisor at some point but denied that his supervisor or work peers expressed any concerns about his work performance that day. He declined any need for medical attention on the date of injury itself. Overall, his self-assessment was that he was fine, and on that basis he drove home after completing his work shift, ate dinner, and described an uneventful course of sleep that evening.

Upon awakening the next day, Mr. X experienced physical symptoms (e.g., severe headache, nausea, and light and sound sensitivity) that had worsened overnight. He notified his supervisor that he would not be able to work that day. His supervisor walked him through a formal incident report by phone and then urged Mr. X to consult emergency medical providers for evaluation of his symptoms. Mr. X drove approximately 30 minutes to an emergency department, where he underwent head and neck scans (he was uncertain of study results). He was discharged a couple hours later with diagnoses of whiplash and concussion. Medical providers recommended that he remain off work for one week. However, Mr. X did not resume work in any capacity after the work injury owing to claimed symptoms, some of which had improved with time, and others of which had worsened in severity.

In terms of physical symptoms, as noted, Mr. X experienced headache on the date of claimed injury and developed various other physical symptoms the next day. However, physical symptoms improved rapidly in the first week of claimed injury. In fact, Mr. X denied any experience of headache or any other physical symptoms at approximately three weeks post-injury; he denied any experience of pain, sensory, motor, or other physical symptoms at the time of the current evaluation. Moreover, while Mr. X noted that he may have been somewhat irritable on the date of injury, and in subsequent days, he adamantly denied any experience of recent emotional difficulties that he attributed to the work injury.

By contrast, Mr. X described a delayed onset and progressively worsening course of cognitive limitations that he identified as a primary impediment to his ability to resume work as usual. He identified the onset of his cognitive limitations to the era of two weeks post-injury, when he attempted to resume computer-related tasks at home. He offered that his cognitive symptoms may have been masked by the significant headaches that he experienced in the initial weeks after the incident, and that he was only aware of any cognitive limitations after the physical symptoms had subsided. At the time of evaluation, he described difficulties maintaining focus in conversation, while reading, and viewing television programs. Mr. X identified memory limitations as a primary concern. He struggled to recall what his spouse and others discussed in recent conversations. He struggled to keep scheduled appointments unless they were clearly marked on his calendar. Mr. X described significant word-finding difficulties in conversation. He had discontinued reading due to lack of retention.

Despite his claimed cognitive limitations, Mr. X denied any limitations in performing activities of daily living. He dressed, bathed, and groomed without difficulty. He managed finances independently and with usual effectiveness. He was not working at the time of evaluation but was able to perform 20 hours of volunteer work each week at a local church. Cooking was described as normal. Mr. X continued to drive without limitation.

Remote history indicated that Mr. X grew up as an only child in a rural town with his mother and father. He denied any early history of abuse or adversity. He denied early academic limitations and attention or behavioral difficulties. He graduated high school with average grades. He worked in various temporary positions (e.g., fast food) for a time after high school and eventually completed necessary training for work as a security guard. He had worked in the retail security position for approximately five years, until the time of the claimed head injury. He reportedly enjoyed the work and related well with his supervisor and peers.

Health history was significant for an extended course of occupational and speech therapies through a multidisciplinary rehabilitation center in the months after the work injury, ostensibly for management of post-concussive syndrome. He denied any previous history of neuropsychological evaluation. He may have sustained a concussion during his participation in high-school football but did not seek medical attention at the time and denied any persistent sequela after the incident. Mr. X denied any other history of significant head injury during his lifetime. Health history was otherwise unremarkable. He denied any previous consultation with mental health providers, psychotropic providers, or psychotherapists. He denied any current use of alcohol or other substances.

Record Review (Mr. X)

Records from the date of the work-related head injury itself were not available for review, as Mr. X did not seek medical attention, or file a formal injury report, until the day thereafter. Emergency department notes from the time of initial medical evaluation confirm that he presented for evaluation of headache after a shelf fell on his head the day before. Headache and other symptoms (e.g., blurred vision, nausea) had reportedly worsened overnight. Physical examination of the head revealed no evidence of trauma. Neurological examination revealed that he was fully oriented to person, place, time, and situation. His Glasgow Coma Scale (GCS) status was documented as 15/15. Strength and sensation were normal, without evidence of focal neurological deficit. Results of a head CT were negative for intracranial disturbance. He was discharged with a diagnosis of whiplash and possible concussion. A follow-up brain MRI conducted approximately three months post-injury was also negative for intracranial abnormality. Despite the lack of definitive evidence that Mr. X had, in fact, sustained a brain injury at the time of the work incident, records confirm that he participated in approximately six months of speech and occupational therapies at a 'head injury rehab clinic'. Results of brief cognitive screening were *unusually* diminished at approximately five months post-injury (MoCA = 13/30). Rehabilitation providers apparently interpreted this finding at face value, without consideration of obvious validity or motivational concerns. Based solely upon this diminished test score, and the extent of his cognitive complaints, they advised that he remain off work indefinitely.

Test Results (Mr. X)

Table 14.1 compares response validity test results obtained at the time of Mr. X's examination with those demonstrated by Ms. Y, while Table 14.2 compares performances on cognitive ability tasks and psychological test results for both examinees.

Neuropsychological Test Results (Mr. X)

Mr. X was referred for an independent neuropsychological evaluation to inform his cognitive and psychological status, in the context of continuing Workers' Compensation proceedings (i.e., not in a clinical/treating context).

Results of four stand-alone PVTs were exceptionally low relative to very conservative cut-scores. Multiple performance validity indices derived from and embedded within standard ability measures were also uniformly diminished according to very conservative cut-scores that have been published across a wide array of clinical samples. Taken together, these collective results suggest that the neuropsychological profile could not be interpreted as an accurate reflection of Mr. X's abilities.

At face value, performances across virtually every cognitive domain assessed were diminished, and at times exceedingly so. Overall intellectual functioning was diminished relative to what would be expected on the basis of Mr. X's premorbid background and premorbid estimate. Below average to exceptionally low performances were also noted across the domains of attention/concentration, language, visual-spatial, executive, learning/memory, and motor functioning.

Psychological Test Results (Mr. X)

Two extreme validity-scale elevations demonstrated on extended personality testing reveal a significant denial of minor shortcomings that most healthy individuals endorse, a personal sense of virtuosity, and under-reporting of symptoms. These findings would preclude the interpretation of substantive scales as a fully accurate rendering of Mr. X's psychological and emotional functioning. At face value, higher-order, restructured clinical, and specific problem scales were consistently below a threshold of clinical or diagnostic significance relevance. Mr. X also endorsed minimal symptoms of depression and anxiety on face valid, screening measures of emotional functioning.

Table 14.1 Response Validity Results for Mr. X (Performance Invalidity) and Ms. Y (Symptom Invalidity)

	Mr. X	*Ms. Y*
Performance Validity		
VSVT[a]		
Easy Correct	3*	24
Hard Correct	3*	23
Total Correct	6*	47
TOMM[b]		
Trial 1	28*	50
Trial 2	24*	n/a
Retention	23*	n/a
Rey-15 Item Test[c]		
Recall	7*	15
Recog TP	4*	14
Recog FP	3	0
Combination	8*	29
DCT[d]		
E-Score	51*	11
WAIS-IV Digit Span[e]		
Reliable Digit Span (RDS)	5*	9
ACSS	3*	7
Finger Tapping[f]		
DH (Raw)	9.2*	38.1
NDH (Raw)	10.2*	42.1
Rey CFT[g]		
Combination	32*	59
CVLT-II[h]		
Forced-Choice	8/16*	16/16
Stroop[i]		
Word (T)	<20*	38
Color (T)	<20*	41
Color-Word (T)	<20*	46
Trail Making Test[j]		
A (T)	<20*	45
Symptom Validity		
MMPI-3/MMPI-2-RF	MMPI-3 (T)	MMPI-2-RF (T)
CRIN	37	n/a
VRIN	38	37
TRIN	53	49
F[k]	48	119*
Fp[k]	45	90*
Fs[k]	52	120*
FBS[k]	69	95*
RBS[k]	63	117*
L[l]	87*	55
K[l]	69*	40
PCL[m]		(Raw)
	n/a	66*

Table 14.2 Cognitive and Psychological Profiles of Mr. X. (Invalid Cognitive Performances) and Ms. Y (Invalid Psychological and Emotional Symptoms)

	Mr. X	*Ms. Y*
Achievement		
WRAT-5	*(SS)*	*(SS)*
Word Reading	89	91
Intellectual Functioning		
WAIS-IV	*(SS)*	*(SS)*
FSIQ	72 (Prorated)	91
VCI	77 (Prorated)	103
PRI	84 (Prorated)	90
WMI	72	81
PSI	76	87
Block Design	8	8
Similarities	6	7
Digit Span	5	7
Matrix Reasoning	n/a	8
Vocabulary	n/a	12
Arithmetic	6	8
Symbol Search	6	8
Visual Puzzles	6	8
Information	5	10
Coding	5	6
Executive Functioning		
WCST	n/a	*Raw (%ile)*
Categories	n/a	6 (>16)
FMS	n/a	1 (>16)
Stroop	*Raw (T)*	*Raw (T)*
Word	30 (<20)	80 (40)
Color	33 (<20)	68 (43)
Color-Word	30 (46)	40 (47)
Trail Making Test	*Raw (T)*	*Raw (T)*
A	88 (<20)	30 (45)
B	120 (<40)	90 (40)
Language Functioning		
COWAT	*Raw (T)*	*Raw (T)*
	24 (36)	49 (56)
Animal Naming Fluency	*Raw (T)*	*Raw (T)*
	10 (31)	23 (47)
Visual-Spatial Functioning		
Rey CFT	*Raw (%ile)*	*Raw (%ile)*
Copy Trial	20 (<1)	34 (>16)
Motor Functioning		
Finger Tapping	*Raw (T)*	*Raw (T)*
DH	9.2 (<20)	38.1 (34)
NDH	10.2 (<20)	42.1 (34)
Behavioral Dyscontrol Scale	*(Raw)*	*(Raw)*
Total Score	19/19	19/19

(*Continued*)

Table 14.2 (Continued)

	Mr. X	*Ms. Y*
Verbal Learning/Memory		
WMS-IV		*Raw (SS)*
Logical Memory I	n/a	21 (8)
Logical Memory II	n/a	19 (9)
Logical Memory Recog	n/a	28/30 (C%>75)
CVLT-II	*Raw (T or z)*	*Raw (T or z)*
Trials 1–5	29 (T = 33)	58 (T = 63)
Trial B	4 (z = -1.5)	5 (z =.5)
SF Recall	4 (z = -1.5)	9 (z =.5)
SC Recall	7 (z = -1.5)	12 (z = 0)
LF Recall	7 (z = -1.0)	13 (z =.5)
LC Recall	5 (z = -2.0)	12 (z = 0)
Recog TP/FP	8/0	15/0
Visual Learning/Memory		
WMS-IV	n/a	*Raw (SS)*
VR I	n/a	30 (7)
VR II	n/a	24 (10)
VR Recog	n/a	5/7 (C%>75)
Rey CFT	*Raw (%ile)*	*Raw (%ile)*
Immediate Recall	6 (<1)	25 (49)
Delayed Recall	4 (1)	17 (30)
Total Recognition	14(<1)	21 (37)
Psychological/Emotional		
MMPI-3/RF	MMPI-3 (T)	MMPI-2-RF (T)
EID	34	89
THD	50	85
BXD	35	49
RCd	38	81
RC1	55	89
RC2	44	97
RC3	n/a	72
RC4	37	48
RC6	41	77
RC7	40	93
RC8	47	91
RC9	37	51
PHQ-9	*Raw (Rating)*	*Raw (Rating)*
	1 (Minimal)	19 (severe)
GAD-7	*Raw (Rating)*	*Raw (Rating)*
	3 (Minimal)	20 (severe)
PCL	n/a	*Raw (Rating)*
	n/a	61 (clinical)

Interpretation of Test Results (Mr. X)

Multiple stand-alone and embedded performance validity indicators were strikingly beyond very conservative cut-scores. In fact, one performance validity index was significantly below a chance-level of responding; the likelihood of obtaining such a diminished performance based on random responding alone would be essentially statistically impossible and clearly consistent with purposeful responding (i.e., 6/48, about once out of 12 million). These collective signs of performance invalidity implicated a very strong likelihood of *intentional* endorsement of incorrect items; the neuropsychological profile could not be interpreted as an accurate reflection of Mr. X's cognitive abilities. At face value, Mr. X demonstrated markedly diminished cognitive performances across virtually every cognitive domain assessed that are far below an estimate of his premorbid abilities.

Extended personality testing also revealed clear signs of symptom invalidity in the form of symptom under-report that limited the interpretation of the psychological profile as an accurate rendering of Mr. X's psychological and emotional functioning. At face value, substantive scales were uniformly within a normal range, without any evidence of clinically or diagnostically relevant symptoms.

Summary and Conclusions (Mr. X)

Medical records documenting Mr. X's acute-stage presentation on the date of injury itself were not available for review (he did not seek medical attention until the day after the incident). Based on retrospective self-report alone, Mr. X denied that the head injury resulted in a loss of consciousness (LOC) and there is no evidence of posttraumatic amnesia (PTA) based upon his detailed summary of events that preceded and followed the incident. His GCS status was fully intact (15/15) approximately 24 hours post-injury, and neuroimaging studies conducted the day after the incident, and several months later, were unremarkable for intracranial disturbance. With this, it was determined that the work injury likely resulted in no more than a very mild and uncomplicated traumatic brain injury (uncomplicated concussion) at most. In fact, it was quite possible that there was no brain injury whatsoever. Neuropsychological outcomes associated with any possible concussion sustained at the time of the work injury would be regarded to be very favorable, without any evidence of persisting deficits at the very late recovery stage (i.e., two years post-injury) during which the neuropsychological evaluation was completed (e.g., see *DSM-5-TR*, 2022).

According to criteria developed by Sherman et al. (2020), Mr. X's noncredible presentation was most consistent with malingering of neurocognitive dysfunction. Specifically, the evaluation was conducted in a secondary gain context (Workers' Compensation) in which identifiable and substantial external incentives (e.g., work avoidance, financial gain) were present at the time of the examination (criterion A). He exhibited multiple signs of "compelling inconsistencies pertaining to cognitive deficits" over the course of the evaluation, such as markedly diminished simple auditory attention without difficulty maintaining focused attention on interview (criterion B1a), as well as multiple invalid performances, including but not limited to one significantly below-chance performance validity finding (criterion B1b). Marked discrepancies were also noted between the extent of diminished performances and the natural history of recovery that is associated with uncomplicated concussion (criterion C1), and his reported abilities in everyday functioning, such as his ability to engage in volunteer activities, drive, and perform other instrumental daily activities (criterion C3). Mr. X's presentation and test performances were also inconsistent with known medical, neurological, or psychiatric conditions (criterion D).

The Case of Ms. Y

Ms. Y was a 48-year-old, high school educated, White woman who was involved in a motor vehicle accident that resulted in a claimed traumatic brain injury with associated cognitive deficits, and a coincident claim of psychological injury (chronic post-traumatic stress disorder [PTSD]). She was referred for an independent neuropsychological evaluation of cognitive and psychological status by a defense attorney in the context of personal injury litigation proceedings.

Behavioral Observations (Ms. Y)

Ms. Y was a tall, right-handed woman who arrived on time for evaluation accompanied by her spouse. She presented with casual dress. She was neatly groomed and made use of corrective lenses throughout the evaluation. Ms. Y exhibited a normal gait and no obvious limitations in movement were noted. Conversational speech was fluent and prosodic. Ms. Y responded to most interview questions openly and appropriately. She provided a detailed summary of her remote and more recent background information, including events related to the alleged accident and the course of her subsequent care. However, Ms. Y clearly minimized (and even outright denied) the extent to which she experienced emotional difficulties prior to the motor vehicle accident during the clinical interview. For example, whereas she denied any premorbid history of supportive counseling or psychotherapy for many years prior to the accident, records described an extended course of individual psychotherapy for management of major depressive symptoms in preceding months.

Mood was noted as depressed and anxious. Affect, however, was of broad range, with appropriate expressions of humor at times. Notably, despite her report of significant emotional issues, including severe PTSD, Ms. Y did not exhibit any outward signs of distress at any time during the evaluation, including the portion of the interview that involved the recounting of events surrounding the motor vehicle accident. Moreover, although Ms. Y reported an experience of significant (chronic) headache attributable to the accident-related head injury, no outward signs of pain or other physical discomfort were noted during the evaluation. Task approach was noted to be linear, goal-directed, and quite efficient. Ms. Y took breaks as needed during the evaluation to make use of the restroom. She elected to work through the customary lunch break in the interest of a timely completion to the evaluation. She was not unduly fatigued because of this.

Interview (Ms. Y)

Ms. Y was involved in a motor vehicle accident approximately six years prior to neuropsychological evaluation that reportedly resulted in a head and traumatic brain injury while traveling as an unaccompanied driver during the busy rush hour. Prior to the incident, Ms. Y recalls that she and other drivers were traveling along a freeway through congested traffic. As she brought her vehicle (a two-ton pickup truck) to a halt to avoid colliding with the vehicle in front of hers, another vehicle (compact sedan) approached from behind, failed to stop, and collided directly with the rear bumper of Ms. Y's vehicle at an estimated velocity of five miles per hour. Both vehicles remained operable after the incident. Ms. Y denied that the other driver or any others in the vicinity were injured or that their lives were in danger at any time.

Ms. Y was belted at the time of the accident. She denied that airbags deployed. She was reportedly nudged forward and then backward; she reportedly struck the back of the head against the headrest. Ms. Y stated that she sustained loss of consciousness for perhaps 30 seconds after striking the head based upon her limited recall for events that transpired immediately afterward. While she denied any difficulty recalling events that preceded the incident (her last memory prior to impact was seeing the offending vehicle in her rearview mirror), she reported having limited recall for certain details that ensued shortly thereafter (e.g., she apparently drove her truck to the shoulder of the road to prevent from interrupting traffic, but Ms. Y denied any recollection for this). Her first reported full memory after the accident was sitting in her truck at the side of the road and then exiting the vehicle independently to survey the damage to her truck. She recalls that she took photos of the minor damage that was sustained to her bumper. Ms. Y also recalled interacting with the other driver, who apologized for their inability to prevent the collision. The driver apparently inquired as to whether Ms. Y needed ambulance service or other medical assistance, and she declined. Ms. Y and the other driver drove away from the scene after exchanging insurance information.

Ms. Y denied any experience of physical, cognitive, or emotional symptoms as she drove home the remaining 20 minutes and arrived without incident. However, after arriving home, she experienced various physical (e.g., headache, nausea without emesis, dizziness) and cognitive (e.g., inattention, confusion) symptoms that prompted her to drive to a local emergency department where she underwent initial evaluation of her symptoms. Providers believed that she had sustained a concussion, based upon her subjective report of symptoms. She was advised to avoid driving and refrain from work until her symptoms improved.

At the time of neuropsychological evaluation, Ms. Y described a complex constellation of symptoms that she attributed to the motor vehicle accident six years before. Physical symptoms included constant migraine headaches, neck, back, and shoulder pain that resulted in limited mobility. Sensory symptoms included light and sound sensitivity, dizziness, blurred vision, bilateral tinnitus, and diminished olfaction. She described frequent nausea and gastrointestinal upset. Motor symptoms included gait imbalance and greater tendency to drop items when using her hands.

Cognitively, Ms. Y described primary limitations in attention and memory functioning, which had progressively *worsened* with time and tended to fluctuate coincident with the severity of her migraine headaches. She described inefficiency in completing tasks at home and in the workplace, difficulty multi-tasking, and loss of motivation in initiating daily tasks. Regarding memory, Ms. Y described variable recall for conversations with friends and loved ones, without particular benefit of reminders. She was prone to misplace common items (e.g., keys, purse). She described word-finding difficulties in conversation, though this issue had reportedly improved with speech therapy. Ms. Y described herself as an avid reader; she denied any significant limitations in retaining what she read, though she often avoided reading as it precipitated headaches.

Ms. Y also described an experience of significant emotional difficulties. While she denied any significant distress in the initial days, weeks, and months post-accident, she described that she went on to develop PTSD at approximately one year after the incident. When asked to describe her understanding of which specific symptoms were associated with this condition, Ms. Y described an experience of frequent nightmares (e.g., consisting of the car approaching from behind) and flashbacks associated with the accident. At the same time, Ms. Y denied any symptoms of heightened arousal when discussing the accident or potential signs of avoidance in response to trauma reminders. In fact, she reportedly discussed the accident with friends and family with some regularity and found this to be quite calming for her. She continued to drive by the accident site on her way to work each day and denied any significant symptoms of arousal or distress when doing so.

Ms. Y denied any significant limitations in performing activities of daily living. She continued to manage basic and instrumental activities (e.g., financial management; medication management) with usual effectiveness. She denied any regular volunteer activities but continued to work on a full-time basis and without restriction (in fact, she denied ever having discontinued work at any time after the motor vehicle accident and had attained excellent performance reviews). Ms. Y denied having discontinued driving at any time after the motor vehicle accident. While she felt uneasy at times when driving in unfamiliar territory, she denied any tendency to become lost while driving or safety concerns.

Remote history revealed that Ms. Y grew up in a metropolitan city with her mother and father. She denied any early history of childhood adversity. She denied any early educational concerns, learning disorder, attention deficit, or other early neurodevelopmental history. Ms. Y attained average marks in elementary school and high school. She completed a certificate program in medical technology and worked as a medical technician until the time of the motor vehicle accident. While medical providers recommended that she discontinue work after the motor vehicle accident, Ms. Y did not heed this recommendation as she needed the money. She denied having discontinued work at any time after the accident and continued to work on a full-time basis, without restriction (aside from an accommodation to miss work to keep scheduled medical appointments, as needed). She denied that her supervisor, work peers, or patients had expressed any concerns about her ability to perform her duties as usual. Work performance reviews before and after the accident were reportedly excellent.

Ms. Y's health history was significant for consultation with a physiatrist in the months after the motor vehicle accident, and multidisciplinary rehabilitation (speech, occupational, physical, vision therapies) related to her symptoms. She denied any history of other significant head injury during her lifetime. Ms. Y had a history of hypertension, which was well managed pharmacologically. There was also a remote history of carpal tunnel syndrome. She denied any other significant health history. Ms. Y denied any significant psychiatric history prior to the incident motor vehicle accident (though records confirmed a history of individual psychotherapy and psychotropic management of major depression in the months preceding the accident). As noted, she did not experience any significant emotional difficulties in the initial months post-accident but she reportedly went on to develop trauma-like symptoms at approximately one year post-accident. At that time, she established care with a psychiatrist, and it was this provider who offered a formal diagnosis of PTSD as related to the motor vehicle accident. In addition to psychotropic medication for treatment of her trauma symptoms, Ms. Y participated in weekly eye movement desensitization therapy (EMDR) with a social worker.

Record Review (Ms. Y)

Premorbid psychiatric records documented several months of cognitive-behavioral psychotherapy with a licensed psychologist for treatment of major depressive disorder, which terminated approximately three months prior to the incident motor vehicle accident. Records also reveal a brief (several weeks) trial of psychotropic management with an anti-depressant, which Ms. Y discontinued due to a side effect (nausea).

Emergency medical records from the date of the accident confirmed that Ms. Y presented in relation to a motor vehicle collision that had transpired approximately three hours before. She reported having struck the back of her head against the headrest at the time of the collision. She was uncertain whether she sustained loss of consciousness but did describe an experience of subtle confusion soon afterward. Review of systems included mild headache, nausea, dizziness, and inattention. Physical examination revealed that her head was atraumatic. Neurological examination was unremarkable, without evidence of focal symptoms or signs. Ms. Y was fully oriented to person, place, time, and situation. GCS status was 15/15. Psychiatric status was normal; Ms. Y's mood and affect was unremarkable, without reference to acute stress. Emergent head CT was read as a normal study for her age. Providers offered a diagnosis of concussion with uncertain loss of consciousness.

Follow-up consultation with Ms. Y's primary care physician one week after the accident revealed that her physical and cognitive symptoms had improved, though she did describe slight discomfort (e.g., mild, intermittent headache) and processing concerns (e.g., distractibility when operating computers). Nevertheless, she had resumed work the very day after the accident and did not perceive that she needed work accommodations. She did express interest in future rehabilitation therapies, however, and records show that she initiated speech, occupational, and physical therapies after that time (continuing to the time of the current neuropsychological evaluation). Records confirmed that Ms. Y also expressed significant emotional issues that she attributed to the motor vehicle accident, the onset of which was delayed to more than one year post-accident (only after retaining an attorney around that same time), which a treating psychiatrist diagnosed as PTSD, and warranted continued psychotropic and psychotherapeutic management (including the ongoing trial of EMDR with a social worker).

Test Results (Ms. Y)

Neuropsychological Test Results (Ms. Y)

As shown in Table 14.1, Ms. Y completed four stand-alone PVTs. *Performances on these tasks were uniformly within an expected range.* In addition, multiple embedded performance validity indices were well within expectation. Considering these findings, the neuropsychological profile was interpreted as likely being an accurate reflection of Ms. Y's cognitive abilities.

Performances across cognitive domains were broadly consistent with Ms. Y's demographic and educational background. Overall intellectual ability was within the low average range, with relatively better developed nonverbal relative to verbal abilities, which were generally consistent with a word identification task that may serve as an approximation of premorbid abilities. Performances across the domains of attention/concentration, language, visual-spatial, and executive functioning were also broadly normal, with relative weaknesses noted on select cognitive efficiency tasks. Learning/memory abilities were consistently within a normal and expected range, and at times high average (e.g., acquisition of a word list). Motor performances were variable, with subtly diminished basic finger tapping.

Psychological Test Results (Ms. Y)

Multiple validity scales derived from an extended personality inventory were significantly elevated, and at times to an extreme degree. Two validity-scale elevations suggested a magnitude of symptom endorsement that was highly unusual even among patients with histories of credible, severe psychological, emotional, and medical problems. Another extreme elevation was observed on a scale that has been shown to be strongly predictive of cognitive response bias. The overall symptom validity-scale profile was strongly suggestive of symptom exaggeration, or over-reporting of mood-related symptoms, as well as noncredible endorsement of non-specific somatic and cognitive complaints. These results precluded the interpretation of substantive scales as an accurate reflection of Ms. Y's psychological and emotional functioning, and necessitated consideration of a determination of malingering.

In addition, Ms. Y completed two face valid self-report measures of emotional functioning, which revealed severe endorsement of depression and anxiety. She also endorsed extreme symptoms on a trauma screening instrument.

Interpretation of Test Results (Ms. Y)

Results of neurocognitive testing were broadly intact, without psychometric evidence of impairment that might be attributed to any remote history of concussion (or otherwise), or to support any formal neurocognitive disorder on that basis. Psychological and emotional testing, however, were invalid, strongly indicative of an over-reporting response style, and prompted consideration of malingering.

Summary and Conclusions (Ms. Y)

Based upon information obtained through the clinical interview, and acute-stage emergency medical records, it was unclear that the motor vehicle accident resulted in blunt force head trauma of sufficient force to result in LOC or altered mental status. While Ms. Y reported that the accident resulted in perhaps 30 seconds of LOC during the interview, records showed that it was uncertain that the accident resulted in LOC. Whether her limited recall for events that followed immediately after the accident might reflect a brief period of LOC, PTA, or some other factor (e.g., the element of surprise and brief psychological re-orientation to what had happened) was unclear, any LOC and/or PTA that she may have sustained was likely to have been quite brief in duration based on her recall for events that followed in the minutes and hours that ensued. Records documented her GCS status as 15/15 within hours of the accident, neurological examination was nonfocal, and brain imaging was negative for intracranial disturbance. Based on this acute-stage information, the neuropsychologist determined that the motor vehicle accident likely resulted in no injury to the brain and, at an unlikely extreme, was no more than a mild and uncomplicated traumatic brain injury (uncomplicated concussion).

From a strictly neurocognitive perspective, results of the evaluation did not reveal any objective signs of impairment that might be attributed to any possible concussion sustained two years before. Notwithstanding Ms. Y's subjective report of cognitive limitations, objective performances were consistently intact across cognitive domains. The overall neuropsychological profile was likely consistent with a normal range of intraindividual variability and attested to the high level of functioning that she maintained in everyday life (including but not limited to her ability to maintain the very same work duties that she performed prior to injury, full-time, and without restriction). Performances were interpreted as congruent with a premorbid level of ability, without evidence of impairment attributable to remote concussion (or otherwise).

In addition to producing a normal cognitive profile, the varied and rather extreme physical, cognitive, and emotional complaints that she reported after the accident were highly incongruent with known recovery patterns that follow concussion and were also disproportionate to the nature and severity of any possible concussion that she may have sustained. The absence of acute stress in the hours, days, weeks, and months post-accident (per available medical records), and the delayed onset of trauma symptoms one year thereafter, was also incongruent with a history of motor vehicle accident that resulted in no more than a possible mild concussion. While a treating psychiatrist offered a diagnosis of PTSD approximately one year post-accident, it was not evident that the provider conducted a systematic review of *DSM-5-TR* (APA, 2022) criteria to support such a diagnosis. For instance, a motor vehicle accident that resulted in no more than a very mild concussion at most, and did not involve the loss of life (or threat of death) to Ms. Y or anyone else would not likely constitute a criterion A event as defined by the *DSM-5-TR*. And while Ms. Y described a delayed onset of potential intrusion/re-experiencing symptoms (e.g., flashbacks, nightmares), on interview, she denied other potential trauma symptoms, most notably symptoms of avoidance in response to trauma reminders. In short, the onset, course, and quality of her reported symptoms during the clinical interview were not consistent with what would be typical of chronic PTSD symptoms and would strongly implicate alternate contributing factors.

Applying the Sherman et al. (2020) criteria, Ms. Y's noncredible presentation was most consistent with Malingering with Mixed Presentation. The neuropsychological evaluation was conducted in a secondary gain context (personal injury litigation) in which an identifiable external incentive (e.g., financial gain) was present (criterion A). She exhibited clear and compelling signs of invalid presentation that were indicative of symptom over-report, including psychometric evidence of exaggerated cognitive (criterion B1c), somatic (criterion B2b), and psychiatric symptoms (criterion B3b) that were disproportionate relative to patients not only with histories of mild traumatic brain injury, but other far more severe and debilitating conditions as well. The delayed onset and chronic course of Ms. Y's various symptoms were also discrepant with the natural history of concussion and PTSD (criterion C1) and her level of functioning in everyday life (criterion C3). The extent of symptom over-report was also disproportionate relative to what is typical of various medical, neurological, and psychiatric conditions (criterion D).

General Discussion

Mild traumatic brain injury (concussion) is among the most frequently evaluated conditions in forensic neuropsychological practice (Sweet et al., 2021). Neuropsychological outcomes associated with concussion are characteristically time-limited, with most patients returning to a baseline level of neuropsychological functioning within days, weeks, or months post-injury. Based upon this favorable prognosis, the *DSM-5-TR* (APA, 2022) suggests that chronic symptoms following concussion

> *should trigger consideration of other potential causes of neurocognitive symptoms and functional limitations, including major depressive disorder, posttraumatic stress disorder (PTSD), anxiety disorders, substance use disorders, sleep disturbances, negative injury perceptions and poor expectations for recovery.*
>
> (p. 709)

As the current case reports illustrate, in addition to these factors, clinicians and examiners should also consider (and rule out) malingering, especially in consideration of the high percentage of concussion patients who initiate secondary gain proceedings (e.g., Workers' Compensation; personal injury litigation), and who also exhibit noncredible symptoms and impairments in late recovery stages. Moreover, clinicians and examiners are encouraged to recognize the complex nature of response validity, and that malingering can present quite differently from one examinee to the next. In the current chapter, we have attempted to illustrate the divergent nature of noncredible presentation that two examinees exhibited, despite similar possible injury severity (uncomplicated or no concussion), on formal neuropsychological evaluation. Indeed, the current case studies suggest that malingering was likely the most plausible explanation for the implausible presentations, though their presentations were quite distinct.

Perhaps the most salient feature of Mr. X's presentation was the *extent* of performance invalidity that was observed across multiple stand-alone and embedded tests. Performance validity findings were not only unexpectedly poor relative to what has been published among validly presenting patients and examinees with remote histories of mild traumatic brain injury, but various other far more severe and debilitating conditions as well. One performance was statistically and significantly below chance and was far less than what would be expected based on random guessing alone. This performance was also significantly diminished relative to what has been documented across an array of clinical samples, such as patients with documented histories of seizure disorder (Grote et al., 2000); acute-stage, severe traumatic brain injury (Macciocchi et al., 2006); schizophrenia and psychosis (Strauss et al., 2015); multiple sclerosis, dementia, and other mixed neurological conditions (Loring et al., 2007); and pediatric neurology patients (Brooks, 2012). In fact, this below-chance performance was far lower than those of healthy volunteers who were instructed to feign their deficits associated with hypothetical attention-deficit hyperactivity disorder (Frazier et al., 2008), learning disorder (Frazier et al., 2008), and traumatic brain injury (Slick et al., 1996). These collective signs of performance invalidity were strongly suggestive of *intentional* performance subversion, judged to have been displayed in the interest of secondary gain issues (e.g., securing financial award and/or work avoidance), and consistent with malingering of neurocognitive dysfunction (Sherman et al., 2020).

Another noteworthy feature of Mr. X's presentation was his minimal endorsement of physical, cognitive, psychological, and emotional symptoms on formal self-report measures. In stark contrast to the myriad noncredible performance validity findings that he demonstrated, symptom validity-scale elevations (L, K) were consistent with an overly positive portrayal of psychological adjustment and virtuosity, in other words, an extreme case of symptom *under-report*.

What might explain this seemingly counterintuitive combination of *performance invalidity* and *symptom under-report*? The results of Whitman et al. (2023) might provide some insight. The authors examined the MMPI-3 profiles of a large sample (n = 848) that underwent psychological evaluation in relation to disability claims. Specifically, the authors compared the presentations of those who exclusively over-reported their symptoms (OR-) with those who showed signs of both symptom over-report *and* under-report (OR+). The authors found that the OR+ group demonstrated significantly greater frequencies of performance invalidity (and cognitive 'impairments') relative to the OR– group, differences that could not be explained by age or educational background. As examples, whereas only 2.6% of the OR– participants demonstrated noncredible performance on Reliable Digit Span (RDS), more than 15% of the OR+ group demonstrated noncredible RDS performance; whereas 38.8% of the OR– group underperformed on the CVLT-II FC, 50.0% of the OR+ did so. While Mr. X did not engage in simultaneous symptom over-report and under-report, the combination of symptom under-report and extreme performance invalidity may nonetheless reflect the notion of a "virtuous victim" presentation, whereby claimants attempt "to portray themselves as good people to whom bad things (e.g., work-place accidents) happened in hopes of receiving favorable recommendations from the evaluator" (p. 18). The combination of symptom under-report with extreme performance invalidity could also reflect a process of minimizing the extent to which Mr. X experienced difficulties prior to the work incident (cf., Greiffenstein & Baker, 2001), while maximizing the extent of his 'cognitive impairment' that he attributed to that event.

Ms. Y, on the other hand, exhibited a very different pattern of noncredible presentation and probable malingering on neuropsychological evaluation. Unlike Mr. X, who demonstrated uniformly diminished performance validity findings, results of some of the very same PVTs were consistently within an expected range. This suggested that cognitive performances were likely to represent an accurate reflection of her abilities. Results of a comprehensive neuropsychological evaluation were well within expectations relative to her background. The collective results supported the notion of positive neurocognitive recovery relative to any concussion that she may have sustained at the time of the motor vehicle accident and were very much consistent with the high level of functioning that she maintained in everyday life (e.g., ability to work effectively and without restriction).

However, unlike Mr. X who minimized/under-reported his symptoms, Ms. Y exhibited clear signs of over-reported physical, cognitive, and psychological difficulties that were consistent with Malingering with Mixed Presentation (Sherman et al., 2020). The complex constellation of physical, cognitive, and psychological symptoms that Ms. Y displayed was reminiscent of the work of Greiffenstein and Baker (2008), who proposed an "over-endorsement continuum hypothesis," whereby "the more complex the post-traumatic presentation after mild neurological injury, the stronger the association with response bias" (p. 565). While the severity of Ms. Y's claimed concussion was strikingly consistent with Mr. X's (e.g., minimal if any LOC, PTA, GCS status of 15, negative intracranial findings), the dual claim of disabling concussion *and* PTSD likely contributed to the complexity of noncredible (over-reported) symptoms that she displayed on personality testing.

Specifically, Ms. Y demonstrated disproportionate elevations on symptom validity scales that have been shown to be particularly sensitive to feigned somatic and cognitive complaints. The magnitudes of elevations observed on Fs-r, RBS, and, to a slightly lesser extent, FBS-r, were well above what is typical across various clinical samples, such as moderate–severe traumatic brain injury (Schroeder et al., 2012; Youngjohn et al., 2011); chronic pain samples (Block et al., 2012); seizure and other mixed neurological samples (Schroeder et al., 2012); and other mixed psychiatric samples (Sellbom et al., 2012).

The delayed onset, chronic duration, and extreme magnitude of Ms. Y's claimed trauma symptoms were also disproportionate to what was known of her presentation soon after the motor vehicle accident. For example, records did not reveal any clear signs of an acute stress response on the date of injury (or in subsequent weeks or months), and the delayed onset of her claimed difficulties, more than one year post-accident, arose only after her retention of an attorney related to a personal injury litigation suit. The quality of Ms. Y's symptoms expressed during the clinical interview was also inconsistent with what would be typical of an individual who experienced chronic PTSD symptoms. For example, she denied any experience of intrusive thoughts or emotions in the month prior to evaluation, and there was not any evidence of avoidance of trauma reminders. She continued to drive, for example, denied any particular symptoms of discomfort or distress when discussing the event, and reportedly found it quite soothing to recount the accident with friends and family.

Yet, despite the general absence of trauma symptoms or signs noted during the clinical interview, or in her reported activities, results of formal psychological assessment revealed signs of symptom over-report that are often observed among individuals who embellish or over-report trauma symptoms. The extreme F-r elevation alone precluded the interpretation of substantive scales on the MMPI-3, and the additional elevation on Fp-r suggested a somewhat greater endorsement of symptoms than was typical of varied psychiatric symptoms with serious (credible) psychological and emotional difficulties (Ben-Porath & Tellegen, 2008). Results of a trauma screening measure (PCL-5) were also extreme and revealed endorsement of symptoms that were disproportionate to military personnel with extensive histories of trauma exposure (Shura et al., 2023) and other mixed forensic samples with trauma claims (Schroeder et al., 2025).

Conclusion

Claimants who present for neuropsychological evaluation in forensic contexts often display noncredible symptoms, and/or performances, that may support a classification of malingering. Yet, malingering may present variously, and response validity that provides the foundation for a malingering designation is multifaceted. In the current chapter, we have attempted to illustrate two case studies of claimants who, despite very similar severities of claimed traumatic brain injury, displayed very distinct patterns of noncredible presentations (and probable malingering) at the times of their respective examinations. Cases like these highlight the importance of simultaneous and comprehensive performance validity and symptom validity testing to establish the credibility of demonstrated performances and self-reported symptoms. It should be noted that the current case examples were evaluated in *Worker's Compensation/Administrative (Mr. X) and civil litigation (Ms. Y)* forensic contexts. Malingering can certainly differ in other evaluation settings, such as *criminal* contexts, where the intention could be to present oneself as so impaired and dysfunctional as to be unable to stand trial or not be able to be held responsible for behaviors that could otherwise be considered in clear violation of the law.

We conclude by emphasizing the importance of the differential diagnosis process. The malingering classification is most commonly warranted in secondary gain contexts and when response validity findings are especially egregious (as in the two cases reported here). However, we cannot over-state the importance of considering (and ruling out) other conditions that might better explain noncredible presentations, especially when response validity findings may be modestly abnormal or equivocal, and especially when one considers the stigma that often accompanies the 'malingering' designation. For instance, clinicians and examiners are encouraged to recognize the relatively high prevalence of response invalidity and noncredible presentation that may be observed among patients with functional neurological disorders and other psychiatric conditions (see Giromini & Erdodi, 2023; Edwards et al., 2023; Hallet et al., 2022; Henry et al., 2018), and the reservation of the malingering label only when formal classification criteria, such as the Sherman et al. (2020) MND criteria, have been clearly satisfied. We state the obvious that invalid performance and malingering are not the same.

References

Aase, D. M., Soble, J. R., Shepard, P., Akagi, K., Schroth, C. et al. (2021). Concordance of embedded performance and symptom validity tests and associations with mild traumatic brain injury and posttraumatic stress disorder among post-9/11 veterans. *Archives of Clinical Neuropsychology, 36*, 424–429.

American Psychiatric Association. (1994). *Diagnostic and statistical manual of mental disorders* (4th ed.). Washington, DC: Author.

American Psychiatric Association. (2022). *Diagnostic and statistical manual of mental disorders* (5th ed., text rev.)

Ben-Porath, Y. S., & Tellegen, A. (2008). *Minnesota Multiphasic Personality Inventory – 2-Restructured Form manual for administration, scoring, and interpretation*. Minneapolis, MN: Pearson.
Berry, D. T. R., & Nelson, N. W. (2010). DSM-5 and malingering: A modest proposal. *Psychological Injury & Law, 3*, 295–303.
Binder, L. M., Tadrous-Furnanz, S. K., Storzbach, D., Larrabee, G. J., & Salinsky, M. C. (2021). The rate of psychiatric disorders in veterans undergoing intensive EEG monitoring is associated with symptom and performance invalidity. *The Clinical Neuropsychologist, xx.*
Block, A. R., Ben-Porath, Y. S., & Marek, R. J. (2012). Psychological risk factors for poor outcome of spine surgery and spinal cord stimulator implant: A review of the literature and their assessment with the MMPI-2-RF. *The Clinical Neuropsychologist, 27*, 81–107.
Boe, E. W., & Evald, L. (2023). Symptom and performance validity in neuropsychological assessments of outpatients 15–30 years of age. *Brain Injury, 37*, 230–236.
Brooks, B. L. (2012). Victoria Symptom Validity Test performance in children and adolescents with neurological disorders. *Archives of Clinical Neuropsychology, 27*, 858–868.
Bush, S. S., Ruff, R. M., Troster, A. I., Barth, J. T., Koffler, S. P., et al. (2005). Symptom validity assessment: Practice issues and medical necessity NAN policy & planning committee. *Archives of Clinical Neuropsychology, 20*, 419–426.
DeBoer, A. B., Phillips, M. S., Barwegen, K. C., Obolsky, M. A., Rauch, A. A., et al. (2023). Comprehensive analysis of MMPI-2-RF symptom validity scales and performance validity test relationships in a diverse mixed neuropsychiatric setting. *Psychological Injury and Law, 16*, 61–72.
Edwards, M. J., Yogarajah, M., & Stone, J. (2023). Why functional neurological disorder is not feigning or malingering. *Nature Reviews Neurology, 19*(4), 246–256.
Frazier, T. W., Youngstrom, E. A., Naugle, R. I., Haggerty, K. A., & Busch, R. M. (2008). The latent structure of cognitive symptom exaggeration on the Victoria Symptom Validity Test. *Archives of Clinical Neuropsychology, 22*, 197–211.
Giromini, L., & Erdodi, L. A. (2023). Assessing the credibility of clinical presentations using performance and symptom validity tests: Current trends and future directions – part II. *Psychology & Neuroscience, 3*, 217–224.
Greiffenstein, M. F., & Baker, W. J. (2001). Comparison of premorbid and postinjury MMPI-2 profiles in late postconcussion claimants. *The Clinical Neuropsychologist, 15*, 162–170.
Greiffenstein, M. F., & Baker, W. J. (2008). Validity testing in dually diagnosed post-traumatic stress disorder and mild closed head injury. *The Clinical Neuropsychologist, 22*, 565–582.
Greve, K. W., Curtis, K. L., Bianchini, K. J., & Ord, J. S. (2009). Are the original and second edition California veral learning test equally accurate in detecting malingering? Assessment, *16*, 237–248.
Grote, et al. (2000). Performance of compensation seeking and non-compensation seeking samples on the Victoria Symptom Validity Test: Cross-validation and extension of a standardization study. *Journal of Clinical and Experimental Neuropsychology, 22*, 709–719.
Hallett, M., Aybek, S., Dworetzky, B. A., McWhirter, L., Staab, J. P., & Stone, J. (2022). Functional neurological disorder: new subtypes and shared mechanisms. *Lancet Neurology, 21*(6), 537–550.
Heilbronner, R. L., Sweet, J. J., Morgan, J. E., Larrabee, G. J., Millis, S. R, & Conference Participants (2009). American Academy of Clinical Neuropsychology Consensus Conference Statement on the neuropsychological assessment of effort, response bias, and malingering. *The Clinical Neuropsychologist, 23*, 1093–1129.
Henry, G. K., Heilbronner, R. L., Suhr, J., Gornbein, J., Wagner, E., & Drane, D. L. (2018). Illness perceptions predict cognitive performance validity. *Journal of the International Neuropsychological Society, 24*, 1–11.
Holcomb, M., Pyne, S., Cutler, L., Oikle, D. A., & Erdodi, L. A. (2023). Take their word for it: The inventory of problems provides valuable information on both symptom and performance validity. *Journal of Personality Assessment, 105*, 520–530.
Lee, G. J., Do, C., & Suhr, J. (2023). Noncredible presentations of symptoms and functional impairment in the assessment of adult attention-deficit/hyperactivity disorder. *Psychology & Neuroscience, 16*, 284–301.

Loring, D. W., Larrabee, G. J., Lee, G. P., & Meador, K. M. (2007). Victoria Symptom Validity Test performance in a heterogenous clinical sample. *The Clinical Neuropsychologist, 21*, 522–531.

Macciocchi, S. N., Seel, R. T., Alderson, A., & Goldsall, R. (2006). Victoria Symptom Validity Test performance in acute severe traumatic brain injury: Implications for test interpretation. *Archives of Clinical Neuropsychology, 21*, 395–404.

Martin, P. K., & Schroeder, R. W. (2020). Base rates of invalid test performance across clinical non-forensic contexts and settings. *Archives of Clinical Neuropsychology, 35*(6), 717–725.

Martin, P. K., Schroeder, R. W., & Odland, A. P. (2015). Neuropsychologists' validity testing beleiefs and practices: A survey of North American professionals. *The Clinical Neuropsychologist, 29*, 741–776.

Nelson, N. W., Sweet, J. J., Berry, D. T. R., Bryant, F. B., & Granacher, R. P. (2007). Response validity in forensic neuropsychology: Exploratory factor analytic evidence of distinct cognitive and psychological constructs. *Journal of the International Neuropsychological Society, 13*, 440–449.

Obolsky, M. A., Resch, Z. J., Fellin, T. J., Cerny, B. M., et al. (2022). Concordance of performance and symptom validity tests within an electrical injury sample. *Psychologyical Injury and Law, 16*(1), 73–82.

Ord, A. S., Shura, R. D., Sansone, A. R., Martindale, S. L., Taber, K. H., & Rowland, J. A. (2021). Performance validity and symptom validity tests: Are they measuring different constructs? *Neuropsychology, 35*, 241–251.

Ovsiew, G. P., Cerny, B. M., De Boer, A. B., Petry, L. G., et al. (2023). Performance and symptom validity assessment in attention deficit/hyperactivity disorder: Base rates of invalidity, concordance, and relative impact on cognitive performance. *The Clinical Neuropsychologist, 37*(7), 1498–1515.

Schroeder, R. W., Baade, L. e., Peck, C. P., VonDran, E. J., Brockman, C. J. et al. (2012). Validation of the MMPI-2-RF validity scales in criterion gropu neuropsychological samples. *The Clinical Neuropsychologist, 26*, 129–146.

Schroeder, R. W., Spector, J., Snodgrass, M., & Bieu, R. K. (2025). Validation of PCL-5 symptom validity indices in a cross-cultural forensic sample. *Journal of Clinical and Experimental Neuropsychology, 47*, 117–127.

Sellbom, M., Wygant, D., & Bagby, M. (2012). Utility of the MMPI-2-RF in detecting non-credible somatic complaints. *Psychiatry Research, 197*, 295–301.

Sherman, E. M. S., Slick, D. J., & Iverson, G. L. (2020). Multidimensional malingering criteria for neuropsychological assessment: A 20-year update of the malingered neuropsychological dysfunction criteria. *Archives of Clinical Neuropsychology, 35*, 735–764.

Shura, R. D., Rowland, J. A., Miskey, H. M., Ord, A. S., Magnante, A. T., et al. (2023). Symptom validity indices in the posttrauamtics stress disorder checklist for DSM-5. *Journal of Traumatic Stress, 36*, 919–931.

Slick, D. J., Hopp, G., Strauss, E., & Spellacy, F. J. (1996). Victoria Symptom Validity Test: Efficiency for detecting feigned memory impairments and relationship to neuropsychological tests and MMPI–2 validity scales. *Journal of Clinical and Experimental Neuropsychology, 18*, 911–922.

Slick, D. J., Sherman, E. M. S., & Iverson, G. L. (1999). Diagnostic criteria for malingered neurocognitive dysfunction: Proposed standards for clinical practice and research. *The Clinical Neuropsychologist, 13*, 545–561.

Strauss, G. P., Morra, L. F., Sullivan, S. K., & Gold, J. M. (2015). The role of low cognitive effort and negative symptoms in neuropsychological impairment in schizophrenia. *Neuropsychology, 29*, 282–291.

Svete, L. J., Tindell, W. W., McLouth, C. J., & Allen, T. S. (2025). A retrospective analysis of rates of malingering in a forensic psychiatry practice. *The Journal of the American Academy of Psychiatry and the Law, 53*, 26–34.

Sweet, J. J., Klipfel, K., Nelson, N. W., & Moberg, P. (2021). Professional practices, beliefs, and incomes of U.S. neuropsychologists: The AACN, NAN, SCN 2020 practice and 'salary survey'. *The Clinical Neuropsychologist, 35*, 7–80.

Wallace, E. R., Garcia-Willingham, N. E., Walls, B. D., Bosch, C. M., Balthrop, K. C., & Berry, D. T. R. (2019). A meta-analysis of malingering detection measures for attention-deficit/hyperactivity disorder. *Psychological Assessment, 31*, 264–270.

White, D. J., Ovsiew, G. P., Rhoads, T., Resch, Z. J., Lee, M. et al. (2022). The divergent roles of symptom and performance validity in the assessment of ADHD. *Journal of Attention Disorders, 26*, 101–108.

Whitman, M. R., Gervais, R. O., & Ben-Porath, Y. S. (2023). Virtuous victims: Disability claimants who over- and under-report. *The Clinical Neuropsychologist, 37*(8), 1584–1607.

Youngjohn, J. R., Wershba, R., Stevenson, M., Sturgeon, J., & Thomas, M. L. (2011). Independent validation of the MMPI-2-RF somatic/cognitive and validity scales in TBI litigants tested for effort. *The Clinical Neuropsychologist, 25*, 463–476.

Zakzanis, K. K., Gammada, E., & Jeffay, E. (2012). The predictive utility of neuropsychological symptom validity testing as it relates to psychological presentation. *Applied Neuropsychology, 19*, 98–107.

15 Is It Now Time to Dispense with the Concept of Nonconscious Conversion/Functional Neurological Disorder?

Kyle B. Boone

The purpose of performance validity testing is to ascertain as to whether a test taker is performing to true ability on various neurocognitive measures. Failure on performance validity tests (PVTs) in a forensic context is considered to be primarily due to malingering (Martin et al., 2024). In ***malingering***, the individual deliberately fabricates symptoms for an external goal, such as disability compensation, lawsuit damages, prescription of drugs, test-taking and classroom accommodations, avoiding criminal responsibility, and being excused from military service. Conversely, in ***factitious disorder***, the individual is thought to deliberately feign symptoms, but the goal is psychological and idiosyncratic to the individual, and can encompass desiring attention and care from medical treaters, to "tricking" medical personnel (Bass & Halligan, 2014). Factitious disorder is considered to be the fourth most likely cause of performance invalidity in forensic cases, and the eighth most common cause of invalidity in clinical neuropsychological cases (Martin et al., 2024). The question arises as to whether patients with somatoform disorder also show failures on PVTs. Patients with ***somatoform/somatic symptom disorder*** are preoccupied with physical symptoms, magnify the significance of minor symptoms, and view themselves as more dysfunctional than is actually the case. A subset of patients with somatoform/somatic symptom disorders, namely those judged to have a ***conversion/functional neurologic disorder***, are thought to create nonphysiologic symptoms mimicking central nervous system (CNS) disorders that are "not intentionally produced" (DMS-5-TR, 2022, p. 364), due to psychological factors. Recently, a category of ***functional cognitive disorder*** has been postulated (Kemp, Kapur, Graham, & Reuber, 2022), although this term appears to encompass both minimal to nonexistent cognitive dysfunction attributable to health anxiety, as well as extreme dissociative disorder-related nonplausible cognitive symptoms (e.g., fugue state), and therefore does not appear to add diagnostic clarity.

Performance Validity Testing in Conversion/Functional Neurological Disorder

In a previous review of performance validity testing in somatoform disorders (Boone, 2021), it was found that somatoform patients (who will be subsequently referred to as patients with somatic symptom disorder given the change in terminology in the *DSM-5*) generally do not have an increased rate of PVT failure in the absence of motive to feign, but that patients with conversion disorder tend to have much higher rates of PVT failure. For example, in the conversion disorder known as psychogenic nonepileptic seizures (PNES), some studies have shown elevated rates of failure on the Portland Digit Recognition Test and finger agnosia errors (e.g., 33%–37%; Binder et al., 1994; see also Binder et al., 1998), the Word Memory Test (51%, Drane et al., 2006; 35%, Williamson et al., 2012), and the

DOI: 10.4324/9781003005063-17

Test of Memory Malingering (TOMM) (25.3%; Salinsky et al., 2020), as well as noncredible performance on finger tapping and grip strength (Kalogjera-Sackellares & Sackellares, 1999; Sackellares & Sackellares, 2001). Studies that failed to document differences on PVTs between PNES and epilepsy cases were often confounded by significant percentages of compensation-seekers in the latter group (e.g., Crager et al., 2006). In an early study of PNES and actual epilepsy patients undergoing continuous video/audio-EEG monitoring, PNES patients recognized fewer target words on the California Verbal Learning Test (CVLT) compared with epilepsy patients, and using a "negative response bias index," sensitivity was 61% and specificity was 91% (Bortz et al., 1995). Subsequently, Tyson and colleagues (2018) documented significantly lowered performance on CVLT-II Forced Choice in PNES patients versus patients with actual seizures (14.7+2.4 versus 15.8+0.7); if recommended validity cut-offs of 14 (Schwartz et al., 2016) or 15 (Erdodi et al., 2018) were applied, it is likely that the majority of the PNES patients would have failed this embedded PVT. Roor et al. (2024), in a recent systematic review and meta-analysis of studies PVT failure in clinical populations, reported that the pooled rate of PVT failure was highest for patients with PNES (33%).

Similar findings have been observed in the conversion disorder known as psychogenic movement disorder. Van Beilen and colleagues (2009) documented that 38% of their psychogenic movement disorder patients failed the Amsterdam Short Term Memory Test (ASTM), while Heintz et al. (2013) found a 24% failure rate on the ASTM. Likewise, Criswell et al. (2010) observed lowered finger-tapping performance in psychogenic movement disorder patients as compared with patients with Parkinson's disease, essential tremor, and dystonia, despite the fact that the psychogenic patients were younger; cut-offs associated with a ratio of actual finger-tapping performance to predicted tapping performance resulted in 89% specificity and 77% sensitivity to psychogenic movement disorder.

Of note, validity tests used in conversion disorder patients may be most effective in identifying noncredible presentations when they are customized to the primary nonphysiologic physical symptom. Noncredible performance on forced choice validity techniques tailored to the claimed disability have been observed in cases of nonphysiologic deafness (36% correct; Pankratz, Fausti, & Peed, 1975), as well as "hysterical" blindness (Theodor & Mandelcorn, 1973) and nonphysiologic numbness (Greve et al., 2003). For latter cases, Shaibani and Sabbagh (1998) describe a "yes-no" test in which patients are to close their eyes and are told to answer "yes" if they perceive touch to the affected limb, and "no" if they do not feel a touch; repeated "no" responses when the numb limb is touched is consistent with a pseudosensory syndrome.

The Meaning of Multiple PVT Failures in Conversion/Functional Neurological Disorder

Unfortunately, minimal information is available regarding failure across multiple PVTs in patients with conversion disorder, although survey data reveal that neuropsychologists estimate that 50% patients with somatoform disorder, conversion disorder, or medically unexplained symptoms demonstrate invalid neurocognitive testing (Martin & Schroeder, 2020). Clinical experience with somatic symptom disorder patients indicates that they, as a group, report an excessive number of symptoms, including cognitive symptoms, but neuropsychological testing is often relatively normal, a presentation termed "cognitive hypochondriasis" (Boone, 2009). However, patients with conversion disorder often perform poorly on neuropsychological testing and fail numerous standalone and embedded PVTs (see the case report of conversion disorder presenting with "foreign accent syndrome"; Jones et al. 2011, discussed in Boone, 2021). The few investigations employing multiple PVTs in primarily conversion disorder patients have reported relatively low rates of multiple failures (Di Vico et al., 2023; Kemp et al., 2008), but unfortunately, the tests and/or cut-offs employed had low sensitivity, thereby handicapping attempts to document multiple failures.

While sporadic PVT failures can sometimes be observed in credible test takers (Victor et al., 2009), the empirical literature consistently shows that failure on three or more PVTs is associated with virtually 100% specificity; that is, it is not found in credible test takers except in populations with profound neurocognitive dysfunction (e.g., dementia, Bortnik & Dean, 2021; very low intelligence, Smith et al., 2014; Victor & Boone, 2021). Recent revised diagnostic criteria for malingered neurocognitive dysfunction include failure on two or more out of seven PVTs (Sherman et al., 2020), and failure on two or more PVTs is also the most common approach endorsed by neuropsychologists to document performance invalidity (Martin et al., 2024). Failure on increasing numbers of PVTs can be viewed as evidence of deliberate feigning of cognitive dysfunction given that multiple failures on the types of easy tasks that constitute PVTs likely exceed one's ability to self-deceive regarding one's cognitive function (Boone, 2021). In other words, the multiple failures on simple tasks (e.g., involving counting, letter identification, finger tapping, recognition of information just presented) would be in conflict with repeated observations by the test taker as to their actual intact level of cognitive function. In a similar manner, extreme symptom reports on personality testing, and extreme behavioral symptom presentations (dramatic nonepileptic seizures, and nonphysiologic vocal tics, limb paralysis, etc.), likely exceed one's ability to self-deceive.

Moreover, failure on PVTs occurs when the test taker directs attention to the task. For example, I (and they) will have observed normal movement/use of their fingers throughout the exam until I say to them, "Now I am going to measure how quickly you can move your index fingers." I place the finger tapper in front of them and demonstrate its use (i.e., how quickly one can in fact tap), but inexplicably, discoordinated and slowed performance may then be observed. Similarly, they might exhibit very slowed and inaccurate recitation of digits forward, but when distracted by being told to repeat number strings in reverse order, they may be observed to spontaneously rehearse number strings quickly and accurately in forward order in getting ready to repeat digits backward. Further, if they score significantly below chance on forced choice tests, this requires that they in fact "knew" correct answers but elected to provide incorrect responses. If they are turning attention to the specific task to produce underperformance, how can the behavior then be "nonconscious" or "not intentional"? How can something be "nonconscious" that one is paying attention to?

Arguably, multiple failed PVTs in patients diagnosed with conversion disorder provide evidence that conscious fabrication is present, just as high multiple PVT failure rates have illuminated the substantial prevalence of deliberate neurocognitive performance invalidity in compensation-seeking settings. In other words, we need to "trust our tests" – in the absence of intellectual disability and dementia-level cognitive function, multiple PVT failures signal conscious feigning.

Evidence for Conscious Processes in Conversion/Functional Neurological Disorder

Despite the historical view that conversion disorder symptoms are "nonconscious," research provides evidence for conscious processes during nonphysiologic symptoms in various types of conversion disorder. For example, numerous studies have documented conscious processes during PNES episodes and psychogenic movement behaviors (as listed below and further discussed in Boone, 2021).

Evidence for Conscious Processes in PNES

1 PNES patients report higher levels of awareness/responsiveness, and more vivid recalled experiences during the episodes, than do patients with actual epilepsy (Nani & Cavanna, 2014); three-quarters of PNES patients report being conscious but unable to react "sometimes" to "always" during an event, and over a quarter indicated that they were "always" conscious (Reuber et al., 2011). More than 75% recall memory items introduced during the episode as compared with 10% of partial complex seizure patients (Bell et al., 1998), and in 62% of PNES patients, but in no patients with complex partial seizures, does memory recall for information provided during the seizure exceed >50% (Bell et al., 1998).
2 Ictal social responsiveness is present in PNES; presence of others intensifies or alleviates ictal intensity in 50% of PNES, as compared with no impact in actual seizures (Wardrope et al., 2020); PNES episodes frequently occur in medical social settings "including medical waiting rooms and exam rooms" (Slocum, 2021, p. 98).
3 Nearly half of PNES patients are able to follow simple commands during episodes such as to shake hands (Bell et al., 1998).
4 PNES patients often display purposeful movements during the episodes (such as reaching for persons and objects or moving items away; Reuber & Rawlings, 2016).
5 Episodes rarely result in self-injury.
   a A quarter of actual seizure patients experience lacerations to the mouth as compared with no PNES patients (Oliva et al., 2008).
   b PNES patients do not lose balance and fall if seated in a chair (Ali et al., 2011).
6 PNES episodes rarely include incontinence (Ali et al., 2011), whereas incontinence occurs in approximately a quarter of actual seizure patients (Oliva et al., 2008).
7 PNES patients avoid noxious stimuli during the seizure events (e.g., will not allow touching of the cornea with a cotton swab; Ali et al., 2011).
8 PNES patients may delay PNES until in a place of safety (Stone & Carson, 2013).
9 Episodes are not accompanied by post-ictal confusion (Ali et al., 2011).
10 The number of PNES episodes declines immediately after patients are informed of the diagnosis, whereas this is not observed in actual epilepsy patients (Farias et al., 2003; Gambini et al., 2014; Duncan et al., 2011; Mayor et al., 2012).
11 PNES can be provoked through suggestion, for example, placing a patch with alcohol on the neck of patients in combination with the suggestion that this technique causes seizures (77% sensitivity; 100% specificity; Lancman et al., 1994).

All of these listed characteristics argue for the presence of conscious awareness of symptom production in patients with PNES. Krumholz and Niedemeyer (1983) described PNES as "more often composed of purposeful, asynchronous, ***apparently consciously integrated*** (bold added) motor activity, such as writhing and thrashing" (p. 47). In fact, Stone and Carson (2013) describe a case series of PNES patients who ultimately divulged some conscious control over seizure events. The authors note that "a number of our patients were aware of exerting conscious control over the onset of their blackouts," and they conclude that "in some cases, patients deliberately choose to have an attack in order to escape from the sensation" (e.g., panic);" "the common theme was that the rising somatic and cognitive symptoms were so intolerable that it was preferable to make a conscious choice to pass out rather than to put up with it" (p. 822).

Evidence for Conscious Processes in Psychogenic Movement Disorder

Nonphysiologically disordered movements decrease with distraction, and increase when attention is focused on the symptom:

1 In psychogenic tremor, the tremor in the affected hand decreases when the patient does an activity with the unaffected hand (thereby decreasing attention to the tremor), and reaction time increases in the unaffected hand during tremor in the affected hand (precisely because it is difficult to engage in two different purposeful movements at once), patterns not found in patients with neurologically based movement disorders (Kumru et al., 2004, 2007).
2 In psychogenic Parkinsonism, patients "often demonstrate slow and deliberate movement when asked to perform a particular task, but are able to function normally when distracted or when they do not think they are being observed" (Jankovic, 2011); in addition, inexplicably, speech "often becomes stuttering, 'baby like' or demonstrating a foreign accent" (Jankovic, 2011).
3 Psychogenic tremor patients who kept a five-day diary of tremor activity while wearing an actigraph to track actual tremor activity reported tremor most of the day, and more tremor than patients with physiologically based tremor, "despite having almost no tremor recorded by actigraphy;" tremor activity increased "when attention was turned toward the symptom (around the time they had to fill in the diaries)" (Parees et al., 2012).
4 The more precise and accurate the information given to patients regarding deliberate movements required for a task, the worse the performance; conversely performance is normal when it is difficult to discern what precise movements are needed (Parees et al., 2013). In other words, when patients ***understand*** what movements are required, and therefore can exert cognitive control and decision-making over the movements, performance is poor.

Parees et al. (2013) conclude that in these patients "movement becomes normal when attention is diverted away from the movement or when movement is triggered covertly ....impairments observed in patients with functional symptoms are ***manifest only during periods of explicit attention to movement*** (bold added)." In other words, psychogenic movements are the product of directed attention and disappear when attention is diverted. The fact that abnormal psychogenic movements appear only when the patient is providing attention to the symptom arguably confirms conscious awareness of behavior, i.e., how can one not be conscious of what one is directing attention to? If symptoms are created nonconsciously, they should not be present when the person is focusing attention on them, but return when attention is diverted – which is exactly the opposite pattern as is observed in these patients.

In a final example of conscious control over psychogenic movement disorder symptoms, in a treatment study of this condition, some patients showed a dramatic and rapid improvement in response to a double-bind suggestion, i.e., telling them full recovery constituted proof of an organic etiology and failure to recover constituted conclusive evidence of a nonorganic or psychiatric etiology (Shapiro & Teasell, 2004; Teasell & Shapiro, 1994).

Nicholson, Stone, and Kanaan (2011) conclude that in conversion disorder there is a "spectrum of awareness or conscious control, both between individuals and within an individual over time" (p. 1270). A survey of neurologists in fact revealed that slightly more than half (57%) viewed conversion disorder as "entangled" with feigning (Kanaan, Armstrong, & Wessely, 2011); 44% thought the two conditions overlapped, while 9% viewed feigning as a subset of conversion disorder, and 4% estimated that conversion disorder was a subset of feigning. Similarly, a recent survey of psychiatrists showed that 56% judged conversion disorder and feigning to overlap, with an additional 14% considering feigning to be a subset of conversion disorder, and a further 2% viewing conversion disorder as a subset of feigning (Dent et al., 2020); thus, almost three-quarters of the psychiatric sample (72%) judged conversion disorder and feigning ***not*** to be separate and distinct conditions.

Development of the Concept of Nonconscious Symptom Creation in Conversion/ Functional Neurologic Disorder

The research summarized above provides evidence that conversion disorder symptom production involves conscious processes; if so, where did the concept of nonconscious symptom creation in conversion disorder come from?

It is well understood that psychological conditions and diagnoses are shaped by the societies in which they are created. For example, homosexuality was historically considered to be a psychiatric condition, and was only removed from the *Diagnostic and Statistical Manual (DSM)* in 1973.

When considering the origins of the concept of nonconsciously created conversion disorder symptoms, a diagnosis primarily provided to women, it is relevant to consider the descriptions of "ideal" women in the Victorian age (when hysteria and conversion disorder were first conceptualized). Women were described as "fragile, innocent, modest, polite, obedient, chaste, submissive, delicate flower incapable of deciding anything except menu and her evening attire" (http://byronsmuse.wordpress.com/2013/11/18/women-in-the-victorian-era). Per Virginia Woolf (in Wikipedia, "Women in the Victorian Era"), women were to be

> immensely sympathetic, immensely charming, utterly unselfish...she sacrificed herself daily...In short, she was so constituted that she never had a mind but preferred to sympathize always with the minds and wishes of others. Above all...she was pure. Her purity was supposed to be her chief beauty.

Would such a woman be viewed as able to consciously fabricate symptoms? Not likely. Thus, arguably, an interpretation had to be developed to "explain" how women came to produce nonphysiological symptoms. Hence the creation of a "disorder" involving nonconscious symptom production. Of note, conversion disorder versus malingering diagnoses have varied as a function of socioeconomic status (Kanaan & Wesseley, 2010); lower socioeconomic patients were judged to be malingering, whereas upper-class patients (especially women) were considered to have conversion disorder.

Kanaan and Wessely (2010a) revealed that many of the cases of hysteria described by Charcot (an early pioneer in "hysteria") "were notoriously staged by the patients to accord with his diagnostic formulation and therefore remain in the Salpêtrière." Therefore, the correct diagnosis would have been factitious disorder or malingering, not a nonconsciously produced conversion disorder. In the *DSM-III* description of factitious disorder, it is admitted that previously some conditions now classified as factitious "would have been subsumed within the category of Hysteria." Nicholson et al. (2011) note that the "neat distinction between malingering, factitious disorder, and conversion disorder is relatively new," and that the current system in which each is placed in its own category "was political as much as medical."

Changing Views Regarding Nonconscious Bases of Behavior and the Prevalence of Deliberate Feigning

Two important arcs can be observed in the past decades: (1) society as a whole appears less accepting of the idea that organized behaviors can be executed outside of conscious awareness, and (2) there is growing appreciation within the field of mental health, and particularly with the subspecialty of neuropsychology, that deliberate faking of symptoms is common, particularly in the context of secondary gain.

As discussed in an earlier work by this author (Boone, 2021), starting a hundred or so years ago and continuing into the 1930s, 1940s, and 1950s, movie and TV show plots not uncommonly depicted individuals who, due to head injury or hypnosis, engaged in behaviors supposedly out of conscious awareness; these plot lines have essentially disappeared. Likewise, decades ago, some live entertainment shows utilized hypnosis, in which audience members were purportedly placed in a trance-like state and instructed to engage in silly behaviors that were apparently out of their awareness. However, interestingly, they generally did not follow orders to engage in behaviors they would have been at variance with moral beliefs (see Erickson, 1939), raising clear evidence that they were in control of their behaviors. Such shows have disappeared. This shift in entertainment away from showcasing trance states suggests that society as a whole is less receptive to viewing nonconsciously produced behaviors as plausible.

Concurrently, within the mental health field, there is declining acceptance of the concept of nonconscious behaviors, and increasing recognition of the significant prevalence of deliberately feigned symptoms. Hypnotic interventions, in which patients are hypnotized and given therapeutic "suggestions" supposedly outside of conscious awareness, used to be a common treatment paradigm, but search of requirements for advanced degrees in psychology reveals no hypnosis coursework. The concept of multiple personality disorder/dissociative identity disorder, in which the individual has multiple distinct personalities, some of which engage in behaviors allegedly outside the awareness of the other personalities, was commonly accepted in the 1940s through the 1980s, but subsequent empirical research has effectively questioned its existence (e.g., Lilienfeld et al., 1999; Merskey, 1992; Piper & Merskey, 2004; Spanos, 1996). The iconic multiple personality case of Sybil, which fomented interest in multiple personality disorder, was ultimately shown to be a fraud (see *Sybil Exposed*, Nathan, 2008). Examination of YouTube videos of actual psychiatric interviews from the 1950s of individuals purportedly with multiple personality disorder (e.g., see Multiple personality disorder: The three faces of Eve. Eve White. Eve Black. Jane. https://youtu.be/zhOnrNjCnIY?si=TlSySgnO6aZZHEP4), show what now would be viewed as highly unsophisticated, obviously "manufactured" presentations of differing personalities (some of which are claimed not to be aware of each other), that would not likely be viewed as credible by today's mental health practitioners.

Likewise, a not insubstantial number of patients considered to have dissociative disorder are likely malingering; surveyed neuropsychologists estimated that 11% of compensation-seeking patients with putative diagnoses of dissociative disorder were judged to be malingering

(Mittenberg et al., 2002). Mangiulli et al. (2022), in their review of 128 case studies of dissociative amnesia, concluded that malingering was not appropriately considered as an alternative explanation; for example, the presence of malingering was not entertained when cases involved secondary gain (e.g., claimed loss of memory for a crime), and in cases in which significantly below chance performance on forced choice measures was documented (considered incontrovertible evidence of deliberate underperformance or the "smoking gun of intent," Pankratz & Erickson, 1990). Further, case authors inappropriately argued that malingering could only be identified if a patient "confesses," or that the noncredible data reflected only a "cry for help." Marcopulos and colleagues (2016) describe a patient who was considered to have dissociative amnesia/fugue until neuropsychological testing revealed failed PVT and symptom validity test (SVT) performances (TOMM and Structured Inventory of Malingered Symptomatology); when confronted, the patient admitted to her deception. Marcopulos et al. raised the critical question: "Does the unconscious have a place in modern forensic psychology and neuropsychology?"

Prior to the development and use of PVTs, malingering was considered rare in mental health contexts (Stinnett, 1987). However, Larrabee (2009) has confirmed an approximately 40+10% neurocognitive malingering rate based on failed PVTs in settings with external motive. Just as use of PVTs helped illuminate and educate regarding the high rate of deliberate feigning of neurocognitive symptoms in contexts with external gain, PVT data likewise can shed light on a likely high rate of factitious disorder in patients otherwise diagnosed with conversion disorder.

Why Has Conversion/Functional Neurological Disorder Not Been Viewed as a Factitious Disorder?

Lazzari et al. (2023) have argued that functional neurological disorder overlaps with factitious disorder, and Kanaan and Wessely (2010b) cite several authors who concluded that conversion disorder and factitious disorder are not separate categories but rather "neighbors on a spectrum of simulated disorders" (p. 47).

If conversion disorder is actually a type of factitious disorder, why has it not been viewed as such? Factitious disorders are in fact underdiagnosed, and physicians are more comfortable diagnosing conversion disorder than factitious disorder (Bass & Halligan, 2014). Spence (1999) pointed to the doctor/patient relationship in the emergence and maintenance of conversion disorder symptoms: "both doctor and patients were (consciously or otherwise) invested in the notion of an unconscious psychic mechanism."

There are three likely reasons why conversion disorder has not been viewed as a factitious disorder:

1 The idea of nonconscious feigning of CNS symptoms has been entrenched, and left unquestioned, in training programs, and was mirrored by societal views.
2 Clinicians view it as more "tactful" and face-saving for the patient, and less confrontational and disruptive of the treating relationship, to describe the behaviors as nonconscious; that is, to conclude the person is not aware of what they are doing.
3 The marked drop in quality of life caused by the symptoms is hard to accept as conscious; we ask, who in their "right mind" would consciously create symptoms that are embarrassing (body jerking/drooling, strange vocal tics, etc.), restrict activities including driving, involve use of canes and wheelchairs when they are not truly needed, etc. It does not "make sense" to us, so we conclude that the person must not be aware of what they are doing.

But are there particular psychological goals in combination with specific coping patterns that spawn conscious feigning of extreme symptoms?

What Psychological Processes Would Give Rise to the Need for Conversion/ Functional Neurological Disorder Symptoms?

Overwhelming psychological pressures: Kozlowska and Williams (2009) suggested that "conversion symptoms are associated with strong emotions or situations that threaten the individual's physical or psychological integrity." Research shows that panic symptoms are common in conversion disorder (Hendrickson et al., 2014; Indranada et al., 2018; Rawlings et al., 2017), with PNES posited as an emotion avoidance reaction (Baslet et al., 2017), or "panic attacks without the panic" (Goldstein & Mellers, 2006).

The argument will be made here that the psychological needs and pressures in patients with conversion disorder are experienced as so overriding that extreme behaviors/symptoms are viewed as necessary to achieve the psychological goal. Eisendrath (1996) argued that in factitious disorder, when achieving the psychological goal (primary gain), there are "substantial secondary losses, but these losses are viewed as less than the psychological gain." In other words, the loss to quality of life caused by the symptoms is viewed as acceptable if the psychological gains are achieved. The psychological goals are so imperative that the person is willing to sacrifice quality of life for them; it is as if the person's "psychological life depends on it." The more prepotent the psychological need, the more extreme and continuous will be the displayed symptoms. In contrast, in malingering, which involves fabrication of symptoms for an external goal, the person only dons their symptoms for exams or whenever otherwise observed, and there is no overall loss of quality of life.

What would be the psychological goals that the individual with conversion disorder symptoms desperately pursues? They would stem from a world view that tells the person what the world is like, how others behave, and what the person needs to do to survive in that world. The world view is powerful and organizes the life, much more so than a single, time-limited, external goal found in malingering, and leads to continuous or semi-continuous symptoms, invalid life role, and loss of quality of life. The "goals" are so all-consuming that sabotage to the quality of life is viewed as "worth it."

What constitutes this problematic "world view?" PNES patients are exposed to greater psychopathology within their families (Krawertz et al., 2001), including increased rates of child trauma/abuse and emotional neglect (Bowman, 1993; Ekanayake et al., 2017; Fiszman et al., 2004; Jones & Rickards, 2021; Kaplan et al., 2013; Kletenik et al., 2022; Ludwig et al., 2018; Myers et al., 2013, 2019; Reuber et al., 2007; Yang et al., 2023), especially sexual abuse (Bowman, 1993; Ekanayake et al., 2017; Reuber et al., 2007; Sharpe & Faye, 2006; associated with more severe PNES, Selkirk et al., 2008), including incest (Roelofs et al., 2002), and often involving "unspeakable dilemmas" (Griffith et al., 1998). Trauma in adulthood, including sexual assault, is also common (Bowman, 1993; Reuber et al., 2007).

Morsy et al. (2021) compiled the types of stressors associated with conversion disorder onset from 51 studies, and documented higher rates of family, relationship, and work problems, followed by abuse/violence, particularly sexual and physical abuse, in conversion disorder patients than in psychiatric controls. Further, the events occurred closer in time to symptom onset than in controls, and there were more "events where symptoms might provide a solution to the stressor" (p. 401).

In a particularly innovative study (Nicholson et al., 2016), patients with psychogenic motor symptoms versus patients with depression and normal controls were rated on stressors, and the extent to which impact of a stressor could be reduced by the person being ill with neurological symptoms, such as weakness. Conversion disorder patients had significantly higher rates of both severe life stressors, and stressors which could be "escaped from" by neurologic symptoms, particularly in increasing closeness to symptom onset; over half of the conversion disorder patients had experienced at least one severe life event in the month before symptom onset (versus 21% in patients with depression). Of additional relevance, the conversion disorder patients reported higher rates of sexual abuse (42%), which "in one third of female patients was contextually relevant to life events at symptom onset" (p. 2617), for example, "seeing or hearing about a previous abuser" (p. 2621). The authors note that

> ***key events and/or a psychological formulation were identifiable for almost all conversion disorder patients*** (bold added) (39/43; 91%)...(but) for the majority (38/43; 88.4%) of patients the key event(s) had not been documented in the clinical notes and/or correspondence during clinical care before entering the study (p. 2621).

In this vein, Morsy et al. (2021) caution that assessment of traumas collected through standard clinical history-taking "runs a clear risk of under-reporting, particularly of event types where disclosure to another may be inhibited, such as those considered illegal or immoral" (p. 415). Beghi et al. (2015) note that reported sexual or physical abuse is divulged at higher rates in PNES patients when semi-structured questionnaires and/or rating scales are employed, as compared with standard clinical data gathering.

The conversion disorder symptoms allow the person to escape from powerful emotions (including panic symptoms), and to assert control and protect themselves in relationships. I have evaluated conversion disorder patients who presented with extreme fragility (e.g., whole body shaking while in a wheelchair) in an apparent attempt to present themselves as nonthreatening and to protect themselves against violent family members. Others have used fainting episodes to distract from and stop escalating conflict in family members. In others, conversion disorder symptoms emerged in adulthood when relationships began to recapitulate abuse and abandonment experienced in childhood; symptoms were used to "force" others to care for them (e.g., watchers had to be present 24/7 to ensure that the PNES patient did not fall out of bed and injure himself; teenage sons had to escort a mother up and down stairs in the home due to her "dizziness"). The extent and magnitude of conversion symptoms can often be viewed as a direct "barometer" as to the extent of dysfunction in the family of origin and adult interpersonal relationships.

Underdeveloped coping resources: It can be asked, "*Aren't there better ways of problem-solving and coping with issues and problems than by developing debilitating symptoms that markedly restrict one's life?*"

Beghi et al. (2015) conceptualized PNES as "a panic reaction in the case of immature or reduced regulation of emotions or inadequate social capabilities" (p. 172). Asad, Saeed, and Kausar (2016) also identified higher rates of avoidance-focused coping strategies, in combination with lowered frustration tolerance, in their sample of conversion disorder patients. Reuber and Elger (2003) suggest that PNES in most patients "result from a mismatch of traumatic experience and their ability to cope."

Unfortunately, the coping patterns and methods of problem-solving in patients with conversion disorder when they are faced with intense emotions and interpersonal difficulties, are regressed and "child-like," and they ultimately result in diminished quality of life. When interacting with such patients, it often feels as if a "three-year-old is at the wheel," trying to navigate solutions to intensely problematic situations. These immature methods of coping attempt to address the psychological need and goal, but ultimately sabotage social relationships and other aspects of quality of life because the developmentally arrested manner of problem-solving has reduced ability to anticipate, or be concerned about, collateral consequences. It is not a coincidence that PNES patients have frequently been reported as arriving for evaluation with stuffed animal toys (Cervanka et al., 2013; Hoerth et al., 2008), and in a description of multiple personality disorder patients, the most common "alter" (personality) was a child (in 86% of cases; Ross, Norton, & Wozney, 1989). If conversion disorder is simply "nonconscious," why do conversion disorder patients frequently present as regressed/childlike, and as "Pollyanna-ish" and naïve/gullible on personality testing (elevation on MMPI-2 Hysteria scale; see Boone, 2017; Derry & McLachlan, 1996)?

The next important question to consider is why do conversion disorder patients have such limited coping options and resources? Research reveals that alexithymia (inability to identify, describe, and label emotions in oneself) is commonly reported in conversion disorder (Baslet et al., 2021; Cuoco et al., 2021; Demartini et al., 2014; Ekanayake et al., 2017; Millman et al., 2024; O'Brien et al., 2015; Schonenberg et al., 2015), with both conversion disorder and alexithymia related to problematic attachment in childhood (fearful attachment, Williams, Ospina, et al., 2019; avoidance attachment, Cuoco et al., 2021).

In other words, in conversion disorder, we have an individual who is attempting to problem-solve what is experienced as an extreme threat to their psychological and/or physical, integrity, but they do not have the emotional awareness to adequately talk themselves through the problem-solving process, nor to accurately label their feelings about the situation. Slocum (2020) argues that PNES is in fact a "communication disorder" in which distress is expressed somatically rather than verbally; "the patient's body may seem to enact a communication of its own as the patient cannot or will not communicate directly about an overwhelming and unspeakable subject." (p. 97). In like vein, Wardrope et al. (2020) suggest that the fact that PNES episode intensity is responsive to social context and interaction argues that it is a nonverbal form of communication of distress or a nonverbal representation of a traumatic memory.

Further complicating the situation, conversion disorder, like factitious disorder (Sutherland & Rodin, 1990), is associated with high rates of comorbid personality disorders (Binzer et al., 1997; Lacey et al., 2007; Noyes et al., 2001; Feinstein et al., 2001), especially borderline and histrionic personality disorders (Lacey et el., 2007; Nicholson, Stone, & Kanaan, 2011; Harden et al., 2009; Galimberti et al., 2003; Rady et al., 2021; Turner et al., 2011).

In summary, it can be hypothesized that conversion disorder symptoms are predicted by the "perfect storm" of: (1) the presence of an extreme psychological need that is viewed as imperative to maintain psychological integrity and equilibrium, and likely involves a desperate desire for recognition, support, and/or protection (including escape from intolerable emotions), and (2) the absence of "adult-"type coping mechanisms that rely on intact ability to process emotions, as well as possible presence of a personality disorder. The specific conversion disorder symptom that emerges may be somewhat arbitrary and modeled after symptoms in family members and others; family history of seizures is common in PNES patients (Bowmen, 1993), and two-thirds of PNES patients (versus 11% of actual seizure patients) reported having witnessed a seizure prior to the onset of their seizures (Bautista, Gonzalez-Salazar, & Ochoa, 2008). Likewise, family history of neurological conditions is frequent in psychogenic movement disorder (Perez et al., 2021). Research shows that conversion disorder subtypes are not distinct (Erro et al., 2016; Hopp et al., 2012; Driver-Dunckley et al., 2011) and that patients with PNES and psychogenic motor symptoms exhibit the same psychological profiles (Hopp et al., 2012).

Nature of "Consciousness" in Patients Diagnosed with Conversion/Functional Neurologic Disorder?

As discussed above, symptom production in conversion disorder is likely conscious, although perhaps "conscious" in terms of how a young child deliberates and solves problems; it is immature and not informed by an adequately developed ability to process emotions, i.e., arrested development.

Further, there are likely three separate, dissociable aspects of "consciousness" in conversion disorder: (1) whether symptoms themselves are consciously created, (2) whether patients are consciously aware as to why they are creating symptoms, and (3) whether patients are consciously aware of underperformance on PVTs. It is most probable that conversion disorder patients are consciously aware of #1 and #3, but may not be aware, or fully aware, of #2. That is, while the impetus for the conversion disorder symptoms might not be entirely conscious (i.e., the person cannot fully articulate why they are creating nonphysiologic symptoms), this does not mean the symptom behaviors and PVT performances are nonconsciously produced. And even if we were to accept that specific conversion disorder symptoms are nonconsciously created, this would not explain failure on multiple PVTs. For example, if a patient were to be nonconsciously demonstrating a nonphysiologic tremor during testing, how would this explain an inability to recognize information on the TOMM? Moreover, if the PVT failures inform us that the person is deliberately underperforming on neurocognitive testing, why then should we attribute a nonconscious or nonintentional origin for conversion symptoms? Does it make sense that the person would deliberately feign some symptoms, but nonconsciously create other symptoms?

Regarding why patients with conversion disorder would feign cognitive symptoms unrelated to their conversion disorder symptoms, arguably they are invested in portraying generalized disability. Alluri et al. (2020) and Driver-Dunckley et al. (2011) reported that more than half of a large series of conversion disorder patients reported cognitive complaints. Some studies show that even with remission of PNES, "patients can remain disabled by psychosocial problems and dependent on state benefits although they have stopped having seizures" (Reuber et al., 2005, p. 1789).

Of additional relevance when discussing consciousness of symptom production, the symptom behaviors, while consciously instigated at the onset of the symptoms, may not be experienced as such over time. The connection between triggers and symptoms may become automatically linked, further decreasing the sense of "conscious control" over symptoms. In this vein, prodromal symptoms may decrease over time in PNES patients, with the "seizure" events subsequently occurring as an automatic learned conditioned response (Stone & Carson, 2013). Reuber and Brown (2017) suggested that PNES patients have a "conditioned, reflex-like element that is embellished by learning and experience" (p. 200).

Support for a scenario in which the individual is aware of consciously creating symptoms, but perceives that they can no longer control the behavior, comes from a fascinating analysis of posts to an online factitious disorder support group (Lawlor & Kirakowski, 2018). The members described numerous incentives for their symptom feigning, including: (1) obtaining affection through adopting the "sick role," (2) the attention they received became "insatiable" (the more attention they received, the more they wanted), (3) a reaction to a difficult childhood, including emotional abuse, rejection/abandonment, and physical and sexual abuse, (4) use as a coping mechanism in managing emotions and stressors, (5) sense of achievement (a sense of satisfaction in controlling and "duping" doctors), (6) making sure a genuine disorder is taken seriously, (7) providing an identity, and (8) external gains (avoiding work confrontations, receiving special dispensation, etc., which arguably crosses into the category of malingering). However, the members reported wanting to stop the factitious disorder behaviors but "feeling it is impossible" and "addiction-like," for which they experienced shame, guilt, feelings of hatred toward themselves, and suicidal ideation; they recognized that the symptoms "consumed them at the expense of their quality of life." It is suspected that many, if not all, of these characteristics also apply to conversion disorder patients, a condition that arguably is a version of factitious disorder.

Is It Time to Dispense with the Concept of "Nonconscious" Symptom Production in Diagnosis and Treatment?

As discussed above, the concept of a nonconscious genesis of conversion disorder symptoms was likely a product of societal views 100 years ago and, arguably, is now obsolete. Moreover, practitioners are expected to determine whether symptoms are consciously/nonconsciously (or "not intentionally" per *DSM-5-TR*, p. 364) produced but with no specific guidance as to how to do this (e.g., no instruction is provided in the *DSM-5*). Additionally, with other psychiatric conditions that involve severe compromise to quality of life and which do not appear "rational" to others, there is no recommendation to determine if the symptoms are consciously or nonconsciously produced, for example, in hoarding, severe obsessive compulsive disorder, anorexia, and impulse control disorders. In these latter conditions, as in conversion disorder, the individuals are aware of what they are doing, but they may not accurately comprehend why they are doing the behaviors. However, admittedly, in these conditions, the individual is not creating symptoms to control or communicate to others, and they are not invested in convincing treaters of the reality of their symptoms, whereas in conversion disorder, it is important to the patient that their physical symptoms be perceived as "real" by others (Kanaan et al., 2009). Arguably, this is because their symptoms are used to manage problematic interpersonal situations, and this function would be undercut if others perceived symptoms as deliberately generated.

Proposed Diagnostic framework: As suggested in an earlier work by this author (Boone, 2021), an alternative diagnostic schema could be developed that incorporates: (1) the type of symptoms that are fabricated (physical, psychological, and/or cognitive), (2) type of incentive (external, internal/psychological, or both), (3) developmental level of the coping strategy (e.g., immature, regressed, and "childlike" versus sophisticated, analytical, and "adult"), and relatedly, impact to quality of life caused by the symptoms, and (4) the extent to which personality disorder plays a role in the symptom manifestation, with more extreme and bizarre symptoms accompanied by personality disorder, particularly borderline and histrionic personality disorder.

Malingering would be represented by external incentive and sophisticated/analytical method of feigning, which does not impact quality of life. Factitious (including conversion) disorder would be reflected in internal incentive, and developmentally arrested coping strategies and sabotage to quality of life, along with likely personality disorder. Evaluation techniques would document PVT and/or SVT failures, and incorporate measurement of alexithymia (Bermond et al., 2015) and developmental level of coping abilities (Eschenbeck et al., 2018; Windle et al., 2011), as well as assessment for personality disorder, along with a careful exploration of trauma/abuse history and other stressors coincident with symptom onset.

In this paradigm, determination of the "consciousness" of the symptom presentation would be dispensed with, which some practitioners already regard as irrelevant in terms of their management of patients (Kanaan et al., 2009). Arguably, the above schema provides the necessary information to proceed with patient treatment and management without addressing "consciousness" or "intentionality" of symptom production. In line with recommendations by Martin and Schroeder (2022), invalidity of the PVT results should be conveyed to patients, but with the clinician making an immediate "hard turn" to focus on factors that are driving the behavior.

Treatment Approaches: Treatment commences with building rapport, and conveying respect and recognition that the patient was confronted with very difficult stressors, which the symptoms were in reaction to, but that the patient is paying a high price for the symptoms, and that in a safe psychotherapeutic environment, they can be helped to explore other approaches that would be less destructive to quality of life. Drane et al. (2023) describe an interesting case of a PNES patient who failed multiple PVTs on initial testing, in addition to obtaining implausibly lowered neurocognitive scores, but following treatment that involved "an empathetic, caring psychotherapeutic relationship that equips these patients with the coping skills to deal with stress and trauma in a direct manner..."(p. 1033), retesting documented passed PVTs and marked improvement in cognitive scores, as well as marked reduction in PNES episodes. Arguably, the development of more effective coping strategies meant that the patient no longer needed to rely on PNES symptoms as a coping or communication mechanism. Of note, PNES onset in this patient coincided with the patient becoming the caretaker of a family member who had repeatedly sexually abused her in childhood.

Cognitive behavioral therapy (CBT), a recommended treatment paradigm for conversion disorder (Baslet et al., 2016; Bodde et al., 2009; Goldstein et al., 2004), can intervene by asking the patient, "How is that (i.e., invalid life role, spending inordinate amount of time and money in treatments) working for you?" The therapist guides the patient to rationally confront the loss to quality of life caused by the symptoms, and to make a reasoned decision as to whether they wish to continue with those behaviors. Treatment facilitates the ability to accurately process, identify, and verbalize emotions, and to consider the consequences of their symptoms, and conveys to the patient that they ultimately have control over symptoms, rather than the therapist colluding in the view that the patient is a passive victim of the symptoms (e.g., a body that has gone "haywire"). Slocum (2021) advocates for use of narrative writing (such as journal writing) as an intervention for PNES, in which the patient is invited to "put significant experiences into words and share in a dialogue where unstated concerns can be given voice and new insights can be discovered" (p. 96).

Other treatment techniques, such as physiotherapy for psychogenic movement disorders, have also shown efficacy by distracting patients from the psychogenic movement symptoms (which can only be maintained by directed attention), and substituting ("relearning") new movements/behaviors (Nielsen, Stone, & Edwards, 2013; Nielsen et al., 2015; Saxena et al., 2020). Similarly, physical therapy approaches have been described in which abnormal movement patterns are "ignored," and appropriate movement patterns are reinforced using feedback and praise (Ness, 2007). In contrast, physical treatments focused directly on stopping the conversion symptom per se (e.g., transcranial magnetic simulation for functional upper limb weakness) may either escalate symptoms or show no long-term effectiveness (McWhirter et al., 2016). Regardless of approach, treatment is difficult for several reasons: (1) symptoms often become an identity that the patient is unwilling to discard, (2) symptoms have provided negative reinforcement (escape from negative feelings) and may have become almost reflexive, compulsive, or addictive, (3) what we view as poor quality of life may not be viewed as such by the patient (and without dissatisfaction with quality of life, there is no impetus for change), and (4) there is often a comorbid personality disorder that will need to be addressed.

The Case of Ms. RR

Ms. RR was a 27-year-old White woman who underwent a neuropsychological evaluation at the request of defense counsel; she had brought a personal injury lawsuit related to a motor vehicle accident with a claim of brain injury and associated cognitive and psychological symptoms, as well as headaches and orthopedic pain. She underwent the neuropsychological exam with the defense-retained examiner 2.5 years after the accident.

Interview

Information regarding accident: Ms. RR was a passenger in a vehicle driven by her mother that was involved in an auto collision. Ms. RR denied a loss of consciousness in the accident but then clarified that, while she did not remember if she passed out, she did recall that she "felt very weak" and "confused about what happened." She recalled that witnesses approached the car, and that an ambulance was summoned. In her deposition she indicated that she texted her father approximately ten minutes after the accident. Ms. RR remembered the ambulance arriving and that she felt "like I would pass out" and "throw up." She recollected that she was helped into the ambulance. Ms. RR stated that she was confused, and gave the example that she had just eaten prior to the accident, but that after the accident she recalled wondering "where we would get food." She was transported to a nearby hospital, where she remembered being treated primarily for her heart condition, postural orthostatic tachycardia syndrome (POTS) and low blood pressure, and that the focus was on "making sure I wasn't fainting." Ms. RR stated that the physician in the emergency room (ER) knew her because he had treated her for her heart condition. She indicated that she remained in the hospital for "just a few hours," and that she wanted to return home.

Current claimed symptoms: Ms. RR reported neck pain and headaches, problems in divided attention, and that when she attempted to read her eyes "dart around" and that she had to "cover half the page to focus on the other part." She indicated that a couple of days after the accident, her mother asked her to read a phone number from her cell phone, and that she could "see it but I couldn't say it – I did not know how." She recalled that her "mother freaked out, I was freaking out." Ms. RR reported that she perceived her cognitive symptoms as static (neither improving nor worsening). She received treatment from a speech therapist, which she had stopped a couple of months before the exam. In terms of psychological symptoms, Ms. RR described reduced coping skills, and she further explained that "when things upset me, it is the end of the world; the 'littlest things' trigger me." She reported that she perceived herself as depressed; she endorsed suicidal ideation, and she indicated that she would bite herself one time per week, and that she stabbed herself ten times on one occasion (not corroborated in any medical records). She also endorsed the presence of anxiety, and when asked regarding anxiety in situations similar to the one in which she was injured, she stated that when she was in a car, "I'm on the lookout – I feel like something bad is going to happen." She indicated that she attended a hockey game during which a player was struck in the head, and that she started "shaking and crying uncontrollably – I had to get out of there." She described panic attacks triggered by "too many noises" in restaurants (such as silverware clinking), which led her to feel "like I'm being attacked." When asked about sleep, Ms. RR stated initially after the accident she was not able to fall sleep until 9 am because she was "afraid of everything" and that it felt like "something was going to attack me – I was afraid of my own dogs – I had to sleep in bed with my mother." She indicated that she did not sleep the night prior to the exam because she anticipated talking about the accident; "all I did was cry last night for hours." Ms. RR reported that she gained approximately 20 pounds after the accident due to less activity and "stress eating" and "comfort eating." Psychological treatment post-accident was limited to a consult with a psychiatrist with some subsequent follow-up phone calls.

Medical and Psychiatric History: Ms. RR reported that she had a premorbid cardiac condition (i.e., POTS) associated with high heart rate and low blood pressure, which caused her to faint. She stated that at age 19, she was fainting up to 30 times per day, and, at age 21, she was diagnosed with POTS. She indicated that she had been admitted to a hospital in a different state and was told that "something was wrong" with her heart but that medical staff "didn't know what it was," and they recommended implantation of a pacemaker. Ms. RR did not want a pacemaker so moved to California at age 21 to seek "more satisfactory treatment" for her heart condition. When seen after the motor vehicle accident at age 25, Ms. RR was reporting syncope one time per day. She denied having sleep apnea, but she indicated that she used oxygen at night for a few years related to her heart condition; she had self-discontinued its use. Ms. RR denied any other significant medical conditions. Her only currently prescribed medication was Klonopin for treatment of claimed posttraumatic stress disorder from the motor vehicle accident.

Psychosocial and educational/occupational history, and family history: Ms. RR was an only child who was raised by her biological parents. She spoke only English; she described herself as "half-Russian," but indicated that Russian was not spoken in the home. She was born in a western U.S. state, but raised in a southern state. She described being home-schooled for her entire education, and reportedly graduated from high school at age 15. She denied any history of learning problems or attention deficit disorder, and stated that she had been told that she was "advanced," particularly in reading. She reported that she had intended to become a biologist but was unable to attend college due to fainting up to 30 times per day. She indicated that she researched online training to become a medical tech, but that the program was "too much to handle." She reported that she has never held employment, and had no current educational or occupational plans. She had never been married nor been in a long-term relationship, but indicated that she dated "sometimes."

Ms. RR denied any history of childhood physical, sexual, or emotional/verbal abuse, or other major trauma in childhood. She denied experiencing other major stressors within the past five years aside from the accident, and she also denied a pre-accident history of psychological symptoms. When asked about family psychiatric history, Ms. RR indicated that her paternal grandfather was "very abusive" to her father and that she is not allowed to see this grandfather. She denied having a family history of POTS or syncope. Of note, Ms. RR's mother reportedly had fibromyalgia, and Ms. RR's father had been judged to be 100% disabled related to back surgeries, and he had not worked in two years. The parents divorced when Ms. RR was 18 (the year before the fainting started); when asked what her reaction was to the divorce, she stated that "it sucks" but that it "didn't bother me" because "it's the norm" (with the example given that her best friends' parents were divorced).

When asked as to her relationship with her mother, Ms. RR stated that prior to the motor vehicle accident, the relationship was "fine," but that post-accident, she "does snap" and "yell" at her mother, and that she would become "so angry, I would want to hit" her mother. In her deposition, Ms. RR indicated that she "probably" tells her mother to "shut up." She reported that she spoke to her father almost daily (he lives out of state) and that she visited him in the summer.

Daily Activities: Ms. RR resided with her mother; she stated that she cannot live independently due to the "fainting." When asked what time she arose in a typical day, Ms. RR reported that it "depends," and that she must obtain eight hours of sleep per night due to her heart condition (i.e., if she did not get enough sleep her heart condition "acts up"); with that said, she estimated that she typically arose around 10 a.m. When asked about typical activities during her day, she responded, "Not much, I hate my life, I can't really do anything anymore." When asked if she socialized, she stated, "Not anymore," and that she does not like to go outside due to "noises." She indicated that she was not able to drive due to her heart condition ("passing out"). Ms. RR reported that her mother handled the cooking, household cleaning and laundry, grocery shopping, and managing of finances. Regarding cooking, Ms. RR stated that if she attempted to put something in the oven or reach in cupboards, this "triggers" the heart condition.

Initial Accident Medical Records

In the Traffic Collision Report, it was noted that Ms. RR "did not complain of pain," but that she "suffers from a heart condition," "felt emotional," and "would faint if she stood up." The paramedic emergency medical report documented Glasgow Coma Scale of 15. Records from the hospital ER indicated that Ms. RR presented following a motor vehicle accident with complaints of right abdominal and mild right lower back pain, but no neck or head injury. It was noted that immediately following the accident, she reportedly experienced near syncope or perhaps brief syncope. On exam, Ms. RR was alert and oriented with normal language, and intact motor and sensory function. She was diagnosed with low back strain but not concussion. Brain MRI one month later was normal.

Behavioral Observations

Ms. RR was accompanied to the exam by her mother. She was of normal height and weight, with long blonde hair and long red fingernails on some fingers (she apologized for not having done her nails prior to the exam); she wore clothing that exposed cleavage. Ms. RR ambulated normally, and vision and hearing appeared to be intact; she did not wear glasses. Speech characteristics were generally unremarkable, and cognition was normal in spontaneous activities; she was able to provide a full history on interview. No pain behaviors (e.g., spontaneous comments regarding pain, massaging body areas, repositioning) were observed, and no fatigue was noted either during, or at the conclusion of, the exam. Ms. RR did not faint, or report that she felt like she might faint, across the several-hour exam.

Ms. RR's presentation was noteworthy for histrionic behaviors. She continuously displayed an "intense" facial expression (i.e., with furrowed brow). She wore mascara that repeatedly ran down her face during her frequent tearfulness. The interview was temporarily discontinued (when she was asked about her current symptoms) due to her extreme tearfulness; a large pile of used Kleenexes accumulated on the exam table. Several tests were discontinued due to the plaintiff's report of not being able to cope with them. She stated that circling letters in a booklet was "freaking me out," and that the noise of a tapper on a finger-tapping task was "making me angry." She also interrupted the presentation of a word list, claiming that she could not concentrate. Ms. RR asked for a bathroom break at approximately two hours into the exam, and when she passed by her mother in the waiting area, the mother asked her daughter in a rather plaintive and overly solicitous voice, "Are you OK?"

Test Results

Neurocognitive PVTs: As shown in Table 15.1, Ms. RR failed three of four dedicated PVTs, and obtained failing scores on three of five embedded PVT indicators. All together she failed performance validity indicators from a total of six of nine separate tests, which indicates that she was not performing to true ability, and that test scores were an underestimate of actual skill level. Due to the multiple failures, cognitive testing was discontinued because Ms. RR was not providing reliable and accurate information regarding her neurocognitive function.

Standard Neuropsychological Test Scores: As can be seen from Table 15.1, across neuropsychological tests, Ms. RR scored within the impaired range in processing speed and visual memory; within the impaired to borderline range in visual perceptual/spatial skills; and within the low average range in attention. It is important to emphasize, though, that these test results are invalid and cannot be interpreted as her true capability.

Emotional/Psychological Assessment: As shown in Table 15.1, Ms. RR's MMPI-2-RF protocol revealed marked, nonplausible over-report of psychiatric, physical, and cognitive symptoms, while portraying her character in an overly favorable light, not attributable to random responding or failure to comprehend item content. Given the markedly high elevation on F-r, particularly in the absence of severe trauma, psychosis, or other obvious

Table 15.1 Ms. RR Test Results

PVTs (bold/italicized = failed):		
Rey 15-item plus recognition:	***Combination = 15***	(Poynter et al., 2018)
Warrington Recognition Memory:	***Total = 38***	(Kim et al., 2010)
Rey Word Recognition Test:	***Total = 6***	(Bell-Sprinkel et al., 2013)
Dot Counting Test:	E-score = 10.84	(McCaul et al., 2018)
B Test	***discontinued on page 2***	
Digit Span	***4-digit time = 5"*** (passed = RDS = 8; ACSS = 5)	(Babikian et al., 2006)
Digit Symbol Recognition:	***equation = 48***	(Kim et al., 2010)
Rey Figure:	***equation = 48***	(Reedy et al., 2013)
Picture Completion:	most Discrepant Index = 4	(Solomon et al., 2010)
Finger Agnosia:	errors = 1	(Trueblood & Schmidt, 1993)
Standard Neuropsychological Test scores:		
WAIS-III Digit Span ACSS:	6	Ninth percentile for age
WAIS-III Digit Symbol ACSS:	4	Second percentile for age
WAIS-III Picture Completion ACSS:	5	Fifth percentile for age
Rey Figure copy:	24	Impaired
Rey Figure immediate recall:	6	<First percentile for age
MMPI-2-RF (significant elevations = bolded/italicized):		
VRIN-r:	43T	
TRIN-r:	50T	
F-r:	***111T***	
Fp-r:	59T	
Fs:	66T	
FBS-r:	***92T***	
RBS:	***97T***	
L-r:	***71T***	
K-r:	38T	

marked psychopathology, it is most likely that Ms. RR was engaging in deliberate misrepresentation of emotional symptoms. Similarly, the substantial elevations on physical and cognitive over-report scales indicate that Ms. RR's report of such symptoms is not accurate and should not be relied upon. Due to the evidence of inaccurate and nonreliable symptom report, data from remaining substantive scales were not interpreted.

Case Conceptualization

Noncredible presentation: This case involved a pre-accident conversion disorder (i.e., repetitive fainting) on which was superimposed a claimed, and litigated, mild traumatic brain injury (mTBI). On neuropsychological testing 2.5 years post-accident, Ms. RR produced a clearly noncredible neurocognitive protocol, indicative of deliberate symptom misrepresentation, on both cognitive and psychological validity indicators. Further, numerous nonplausible inconsistencies were observed across tests. For example, Ms. RR was able to independently complete the MMPI-2-RF, a 338-item true/false personality inventory printed in normal size font across multiple pages, within one hour, but had claimed that a pre-school-level task of circling large letters in a 15-page booklet (b Test) was "freaking me out," and the test was discontinued at page 2. If she was able to complete the MMPI-2-RF with no distress, it makes no sense that she could not tolerate the b Test. Additionally, she was slow to repeat four-number strings in forward order (3" to 7"), but when asked to repeat number strings in reverse order, she very quickly recited numbers in forward order in preparation for saying them in reverse order (demonstrating that she in fact can repeat number strings quickly in forward order).

Also of note, Ms. RR was clearly more functional in activities in daily living than she reported. For example, she stated that she had extreme noise sensitivity such that she could not go to movies, and that hearing air-conditioning noise in another room, or a door shutting, caused her to "snap," and during the exam, she could not tolerate hearing the tapper on a finger-tapping apparatus necessitating that administration be discontinued. However, elsewhere in the interview she referred to attending a hockey game and traveling to visit her father via plane flight, both of which would have exposed her to substantial noise (i.e., the roar of crowds in a stadium, and airline engine noises during flights).

No evidence for mTBI: Regarding Ms. RR's claimed cognitive and psychological symptoms from a TBI, she in fact did not meet criteria for mTBI/concussion per diagnostic criteria issued by the American Congress of Rehabilitation Medicine in 2023 (Silverberg et al., 2023). Specifically, she was not observed/witnessed to show any signs of brain dysfunction by first responders at the accident scene nor by hospital staff in the ER, and brain imaging was normal. Even if she had sustained a concussion, she would have had no residuals from that event by 12 months post injury per: (1) the *DSM-5-TR* (2022, p. 709), (2) six meta-analyses on cognitive outcome from mTBI (Belanger et al., 2005; Belanger & Vanderploeg, 2005; Binder et al., 1997; Frencham et al., 2005; Rohling et al., 2011; Schretlen & Shapiro, 2003), and (3) a recent analysis of studies published since 2011 claiming long-term cognitive anomalies from mTBI, which revealed substandard methodology (Boone, Vane, & Victor, 2024).

Premorbid conversion/functional neurological disorder: Prior to the motor vehicle accident, Ms. RR reportedly had been diagnosed with POTS (unexplained fainting episodes), but it is unclear whether any cardiac abnormalities had actually been detected in her. Research has suggested that psychiatric conditions are the cause of up to 26% of all syncopal cases, and are particularly found in females under age 40 with four or more episodes of syncope in the previous year, and presyncopal symptoms (e.g., palpitations, dizziness, vomiting, chest pain; Andrighetto et al., 1999), characteristics which Ms. RR had. Patients with depression, anxiety, and somatic symptom disorders "frequently complain of somatic symptoms resembling POTS" (Lkhagvasuren et al., 2011), and patients with syncope/POTS, especially unexplained syncope, commonly present with depression, anxiety, panic attacks, and somatic symptom disorders (Anderson et al., 2014; D'Antono et al., 2009; Giada et al., 2005; Kouakam et al., 2002; Lee et al., 2013; Linzer et al., 1992; Oh & Kapoor, 1997; Ventura et al., 2001), and "somatic hypervigilance associated with anxiety, depression, and behavioral amplification contribute to symptom chronicity" (Benarroch, 2012). Patients with psychiatric causes for syncope tend to have more frequent episodes of syncope, more symptoms as a part of their prodrome, are younger, and have more disability due to their syncope and presyncope (Linzer et al., 1990), all characteristics exhibited by the patient. Psychogenic (i.e., nonphysiologic) nonsyncopal collapse (PNSC) is predicted by various factors including ≥20 lifetime fainting spells and ≥2 fainting spells in a day (Heyer et al., 2017), again characteristics of Ms. RR's presentation. Methods have in fact been published to help identify the presence of somatic symptom/conversion reactions and malingering in claimed syncope (Grubb et al., 1992).

Of particular note, Ms. RR's and her mother's reactions to the fainting episodes seemed odd and lacking in appropriate concern, as is often observed in conversion disorder presentations. If a child truly had frequent fainting, it would seem unlikely that she would be allowed to travel on an airplane by herself; according to the patient's mother's deposition testimony:

> *There is no time that she is actually by herself, other than if she goes on a trip. Let's say she goes to her dad, I drop her off, she gets a wheelchair, she's taken to the gate, she gets to the plane. When she arrives, there's a wheelchair waiting, someone takes her down to her luggage, her dad picks her up at the luggage, takes her to the car.*

However, what if she fainted on the plane? Could this not cause the plane to be diverted to a different airport; is that not a concern? It was claimed that Ms. RR had to have someone around all the time due to fainting, but in fact the mother left her alone when she went to work, and Ms. RR reported in her deposition that she showered and ate when left alone; what if she fainted in the shower or when preparing food? If she truly had been experiencing frequent fainting (up to 30 times per day at the onset, and reportedly fainted every morning upon awakening), how did she not sustain repeated facial fractures and injury to other parts of her body due to frequent falls? Ms. RR had declined to take medication that might help with the condition, despite the fact that it reportedly had caused major disability (no further education beyond high school, no employment, no driving, and no independent living). In her deposition in the year after the motor vehicle accident, Ms. RR reported that she had not seen her primary care physician for her heart condition for a year, that she had only seen her current cardiologist on one occasion six months earlier, and that in the past five years, she had only seen a heart specialist "a few times"; it seems odd to have minimal treatment for a condition that had had such a major impact on her life.

Symbiotic and deleterious relationship with mother: Ms. RR and her mother had a problematic relationship with poor boundaries. Her mother continuously kept Ms. RR at home with her rather than encouraging Ms. RR to become independent. Ms. RR was home-schooled for her entire education and did not socialize with other students. It is likely that the mother's claimed chronic pain condition served to secure care and attention from her husband, and when the parents divorced, Ms. RR was expected to fill this role. It is of note that Ms. RR's frequent fainting episodes reportedly began in the year following the divorce of the parents (when she was at the age of 18); her reported extreme fainting spells allowed her to remain at home and not abandon her mother like the father had. At the same time, Ms. RR's mother fostered extreme fear in her that the fainting spells could lead to her death, and that as a result she would have to live with her mother because she had to have someone with her at all times to keep her safe. Ms. RR reported that her frequent fainting spells kept her from pursuing additional education and working, and she stated that she had no current educational or occupational plans. According to her deposition testimony, virtually her only social contact was her mother. Ms. RR's relationship with her mother was keeping her in "suspended animation," and not allowing her to proceed with her life.

Ms. RR likely had very mixed feelings regarding her mother's involvement in her life, for example, on the one hand feeling grateful that someone was there to watch over her and keep her safe from her heart condition, but also experiencing anger that she had not been allowed to become a functional adult, and that her mother also needed her to remain at home for her own needs. Ms. RR stated that prior to the motor vehicle accident, her relationship with her mother was "fine," but that post-accident she "does snap" and "yell" at her mother, and that she would become "so angry, I would want to hit her," and in her deposition, Ms. RR indicated that she "probably" tells her mother to "shut up." Ms. RR's claimed personality change due to the accident enabled her to express her anger at her mother without repercussions; in her deposition, Ms. RR's mother commented that the changes in her daughter post-accident were *"making it very difficult for me because she takes it out on me. And you can't yell at somebody who doesn't have control because of the way their brain is functioning ...."*

Diagnostic formulation: In the suggested diagnostic schema presented above, Ms. RR would be viewed as deliberately creating physical, cognitive, and psychological symptoms for both internal and external incentives, in association with a very reduced level of coping skill and which had significantly impacted quality of life, and likely presence of personality disorder (histrionic and dependent, and perhaps borderline).

Final thoughts: While some might argue that this case is not representative of conversion disorder patients in general due to the presence of a personal injury lawsuit, in fact external incentives are often present in these patients. Quigg et al. (2002) reported that, in their PNES sample, the proportion of patients receiving disability benefits rose from 33% at time of first seizure to 60% at 17-month follow-up. Likewise, Reuber, Pukrop et al. (2003) documented that four years after diagnosis, 51% of PNES patients were receiving disability benefits.

This case illustrates important limitations regarding the use of the term "malingering." Arguably, malingering can be a problematic determination because while a test taker might have external incentive to present with symptoms they do not truly have, behavior is often multi-determined and not entirely captured by the concept of external gain. That is, primary and secondary gain factors may co-exist in the same patient. In the current case, Ms. RR stood to be awarded damages in a lawsuit, thereby providing secondary gain. However, she could have calculated that monetary damages would enable her to separate from her mother and live independently. Thus, the motive may not have been the external incentive per se, but rather the independence from her mother the damages could have afforded her, which arguably is more a primary gain incentive. Further, the personality changes claimed in the "brain damage" lawsuit enabled Ms. RR to express anger/rage toward her mother, behaviors she did not allow herself to engage in prior to the motor vehicle accident; primary gain?

References

Ali, S., Jabeen, S., Arain, A., Wassef, T., & Ibrahim, A. (2011). How to use your clinical judgment to screen for and diagnose psychogenic nonepileptic seizures without video electroencephalogram. *Innovations in Clinical Neuroscience*, *8*(1), 36.

Alluri, P. R., Solit, J., Leveroni, C. L., Goldberg, K., Vehar, J. V., Pollak, L. E., ... Perez, D. L. (2020). Cognitive complaints in motor functional neurological (conversion) disorders: A focused review and clinical perspective. *Cognitive and Behavioral Neurology*, *33*(2), 77–89.

Anderson, J. W., Lambert, E. A., Sari, C. I., Dawood, T., Esler, M. D., Vaddadi, G., & Lambert, G. W. (2014). Cognitive function, health-related quality of life, and symptoms of depression and anxiety sensitivity are impaired in patients with the postural orthostatic tachycardia syndrome (POTS). *Frontiers in physiology*, *5*, 230.

Andrighetto, A. G., John, Â. B., Barbisan, J. N., & Taborda, J. G. V. (1999). Medically unexplained syncope and its relationship to psychiatric disorders. *Arquivos Brasileiros de Cardiologia*, *72*(6), 756–760.

Asad, S., Saeed, S., & Kausar, R. (2016). Level of frustration tolerance and coping strategies used by women with conversion disorder vs those with general medical conditions. *JPPS*, *13*(2), 35–38.

Babikian, T., Boone, K. B., Lu, P., & Arnold, G. (2006). Sensitivity and specificity of various digit span scores in the detection of suspect effort. *The Clinical Neuropsychologist*, *20*(1), 145–159.

Baslet, G., Bajestan, S. N., Aybek, S., Modirrousta, M., D. Clin. Psy, J. P., Cavanna, A., ... LaFrance Jr, W. C. (2021). Evidence-based practice for the clinical assessment of psychogenic nonepileptic seizures: A report from the American Neuropsychiatric Association Committee on Research. *The Journal of Neuropsychiatry and Clinical Neurosciences*, *33*(1), 27–42.

Baslet, G., Seshadri, A., Bermeo-Ovalle, A., Willment, K., & Myers, L. (2016). Psychogenic nonepileptic seizures: An updated primer. *Psychosomatics*, *57*(1), 1–17.

Baslet, G., Tolchin, B., & Dworetzky, B. A. (2017). Altered responsiveness in psychogenic nonepileptic seizures and its implication to underlying psychopathology. *Seizure*, *52*, 162–168.

Bass, C., & Halligan, P. (2014). Factitious disorders and malingering: Challenges for clinical assessment and management. *The Lancet*, *383*(9926), 1422–1432.

Bautista, R. E. D., Gonzales-Salazar, W., & Ochoa, J. G. (2008). Expanding the theory of symptom modeling in patents with psychogenic nonepileptic seizures. *Epilepsy & Behavior*, *13*(2), 407–409.

Beghi, M., Cornaggia, I., Magaudda, A., Perin, C., Peroni, F., & Cornaggia, C. M. (2015). Childhood trauma and psychogenic nonepileptic seizures: A review of findings with speculations on the underlying mechanisms. *Epilepsy & Behavior*, *52*, 169–173.

Benarroch, E. E. (2012, December). Postural tachycardia syndrome: a heterogeneous and multifactorial disorder. In *Mayo Clinic Proceedings* (Vol. 87, No. 12, pp. 1214–1225).Elsevier.

Bell, W. L., Park, Y. D., Thompson, E. A., & Radtke, R. A. (1998). Ictal cognitive assessment of partial seizures and pseudoseizures. *Archives of Neurology*, *55*(11), 1456–1459.

Bell-Sprinkel, T. L., Boone, K. B., Miora, D., Cottingham, M., Victor, T., Ziegler, E., ... Wright, M. (2013). Re-examination of the rey word recognition test. *The Clinical Neuropsychologist*, *27*(3), 516–527.

Bermond, B., Oosterveld, P., & Vorst, H. C. (2015). Measures of alexithymia. In Boyle, G. J., Saklofske, D. H., & Matthews, G. (Eds.), *Measures of personality and social psychological constructs* (pp. 227–256). Academic Press.

Bhatia, K. P., & Schneider, S. A. (2007). Psychogenic tremor and related disorders. *Journal of neurology*, *254*(5), 569.

Binder, L. M., Kindermann, S. S., Heaton, R. K., & Salinsky, M. C. (1998). Neuropsychologic impairment in patients with nonepileptic seizures. *Archives of Clinical Neuropsychology*, *13*(6), 513–522.

Binder, L. M., Salinsky, M. C., & Smith, S. P. (1994). Psychological correlates of psychogenic seizures. *Journal of Clinical and Experimental Neuropsychology*, *16*(4), 524–530.

Binzer, M., Andersen, P. M., & Kullgren, G. (1997). Clinical characteristics of patients with motor disability due to conversion disorder: a prospective control group study. *Journal of Neurology, Neurosurgery & Psychiatry*, *63*(1), 83–88.

Bodde, N. M. G., Brooks, J. L., Baker, G. A., Boon, P. A. J. M., Hendriksen, J. G. M., Mulder, O. G., & Aldenkamp, A. P. (2009). Psychogenic non-epileptic seizures—definition, etiology, treatment and prognostic issues: A critical review. *Seizure*, *18*(8), 543–553.

Boone, K. B. (2021). Performance validity in the context of somatoform/conversion disorders, factitious disorder, and malingering: do we need a new diagnostic schema? In Boone, K. B. (Ed.), *Assessment of Feigned Cognitive Impairment: A Neuropsychological Perspective* (2nd Ed., pp. 433–452). New York: Guilford Press.

Boone, K. B., Vane, R. P., & Victor, T. L. (2025). Critical review of recently published studies claiming long-term neurocognitive abnormalities in mild traumatic brain injury. *Archives of Clinical Neuropsychology, 40*(2), 272–288.

Bortz, J. J., Prigatano, G. P., Blum, D., & Fisher, R. S. (1995). Differential response characteristics in nonepileptic and epileptic seizure patients on a test of verbal learning and memory. *Neurology, 45*(11), 2029–2034.

Bowman, E. S. (1993). Etiology and clinical course of pseudoseizures: Relationship to trauma, depression, and dissociation. *Psychosomatics, 34*(4), 333–342.

Cervenka, M. C., Lesser, R., Tran, T. T., Fortuné, T., Muthugovindan, D., & Miglioretti, D. L. (2013). Does the teddy bear sign predict psychogenic nonepileptic seizures?. *Epilepsy & Behavior, 28*(2), 217–220.

Cragar, D. E., Berry, D. T., Fakhoury, T. A., Cibula, J. E., & Schmitt, F. A. (2006). Performance of patients with epilepsy or psychogenic non-epileptic seizures on four measures of effort. *The Clinical Neuropsychologist, 20*(3), 552–566.

Criswell, S., Sterling, C., Swisher, L., Evanoff, B., & Racette, B. A. (2010). Sensitivity and specificity of the finger tapping task for the detection of psychogenic movement disorders. *Parkinsonism & Related Disorders, 16*(3), 197–201.

Cuoco, S., Nisticò, V., Cappiello, A., Scannapieco, S., Gambini, O., Barone, P., ... & Demartini, B. (2021). Attachment styles, identification of feelings and psychiatric symptoms in functional neurological disorders. *Journal of Psychosomatic Research, 147*, 110539.

D'Antono, B., Dupuis, G., St-Jean, K., Lévesque, K., Nadeau, R., Guerra, P., ... & Kus, T. (2009). Prospective evaluation of psychological distress and psychiatric morbidity in recurrent vasovagal and unexplained syncope. *Journal of psychosomatic research, 67*(3), 213–222

Dean, A. C., Victor, T. L., Boone, K. B., & Arnold, G. (2008). The relationship of IQ to effort test performance. *The Clinical Neuropsychologist, 22*(4), 705–722.

Dean, A. C., Victor, T. L., Boone, K. B., Philpott, L. M., & Hess, R. A. (2009). Dementia and effort test performance. *The Clinical Neuropsychologist, 23*(1), 133–152.

De Gucht, V., & Heiser, W. (2003). Alexithymia and somatisation: A quantitative review of the literature. *Journal of Psychosomatic Research, 54*(5), 425–434.

Demartini, B., Petrochilos, P., Ricciardi, L., Price, G., Edwards, M. J., & Joyce, E. (2014). The role of alexithymia in the development of functional motor symptoms (conversion disorder). *Journal of Neurology, Neurosurgery & Psychiatry, 85*(10), 1132–1137.

Dent, B., Stanton, B. R., & Kanaan, R. A. (2020). Psychiatrists' understanding and management of conversion disorder: S bi-national survey and comparison with neurologists. *Neuropsychiatric Disease and Treatment, 16*, 1965–1974.

Derry, P. A., & McLachlan, R. S. (1996). The MMPI-2 as an adjunct to the diagnosis of pseudoseizures. *Seizure, 5*(1), 35–40.

Di Vico, I. A., Stone, J., Mcwhirter, L., Riello, M., Zanolin, M. E., Colombari, M., ... Tinazzi, M. (2023). Performance validity tests in nonlitigant patients with functional motor disorder. *European Journal of Neurology, 30*(4), 806–812.

Drane, D. L., Hewitt, K. C., Price, M. E., Rush, B. K., Blackmon, K., Okada, N., ... Loring, D. W. (2023). Case study of invalid to valid shift in cognitive performance following successful treatment of psychogenic nonepileptic seizure events. *Journal of Clinical and Experimental Neuropsychology, 45*(10), 1024–1038.

Drane, D. L., Williamson, D. J., Stroup, E. S., Holmes, M. D., Jung, M., Koerner, E., ... Miller, J. W. (2006). Cognitive impairment is not equal in patients with epileptic and psychogenic nonepileptic seizures. *Epilepsia, 47*(11), 1879–1886.

Driver-Dunckley, E., Stonnington, C. M., Locke, D. E., & Noe, K. (2011). Comparison of psychogenic movement disorders and psychogenic nonepileptic seizures: Is phenotype clinically important?. *Psychosomatics, 52*(4), 337–345.

Duncan, R., Razvi, S., & Mulhern, S. (2011). Newly presenting psychogenic nonepileptic seizures: incidence, population characteristics, and early outcome from a prospective audit of a first seizure clinic. *Epilepsy & Behavior*, *20*(2), 308–311.

Eisendrath, S. J. (1996). When Munchausen becomes malingering: factitious disorders that penetrate the legal system. *Journal of the American Academy of Psychiatry and the Law Online*, *24*(4), 471–481.

Ekanayake, V., Kranick, S., LaFaver, K., Naz, A., Webb, A. F., LaFrance Jr, W. C., ... Voon, V. (2017). Personality traits in psychogenic nonepileptic seizures (PNES) and psychogenic movement disorder (PMD): Neuroticism and perfectionism. *Journal of Psychosomatic Research*, *97*, 23–29.

Erdodi, L. A., Abeare, C. A., Medoff, B., Seke, K. R., Sagar, S., & Kirsch, N. L. (2018). A single error is one too many: the Forced Choice Recognition Trial of the CVLT-II as a measure of performance validity in adults with TBI. *Archives of Clinical Neuropsychology*, *33*(7), 845–860.

Erickson, M. H. (1939). An experimental investigation of the possible anti-social use of hypnosis. *Psychiatry*, *2*(3), 391–414.

Erro, R., Brigo, F., Trinka, E., Turri, G., Edwards, M. J., & Tinazzi, M. (2016). Psychogenic nonepileptic seizures and movement disorders: A comparative review. *Neurology: Clinical Practice*, *6*(2), 138–149.

Eschenbeck, H., Schmid, S., Schröder, I., Wasserfall, N., & Kohlmann, C. W. (2018). Development of coping strategies from childhood to adolescence. *European Journal of Health Psychology.*

Farias, S. T., Thieman, C., & Alsaadi, T. M. (2003). Psychogenic nonepileptic seizures: Acute change in event frequency after presentation of the diagnosis. *Epilepsy & Behavior*, *4*(4), 424–429.

Feinstein, A. M. D., Stergiopoulos, V. M. D., Fine, J. M. D., & Lang, A. E. M. D. (2001). Psychiatric outcome in patients with a psychogenic movement disorder: a prospective study. *Neuropsychiatry, Neuropsychology & Behavioral Neurology*, *14*(3), 169–176.

Fiszman, A., Alves-Leon, S. V., Nunes, R. G., Isabella, D. A., & Figueira, I. (2004). Traumatic events and posttraumatic stress disorder in patients with psychogenic nonepileptic seizures: A critical review. *Epilepsy & Behavior*, *5*(6), 818–825

Galimberti, C. A., Ratti, M. T., Murelli, R., Marchioni, E., Manni, R., & Tartara, A. (2003). Patients with psychogenic nonepileptic seizures, alone or epilepsy-associated, share a psychological profile distinct from that of epilepsy patients. *Journal of Neurology*, *250*, 338–346.

Gambini, O., Demartini, B., Chiesa, V., Turner, K., Barbieri, V., & Canevini, M. P. (2014). Long-term outcome of psychogenic nonepileptic seizures: The role of induction by suggestion. *Epilepsy & Behavior*, *41*, 140–143.

Giada, F., Silvestri, I., Rossillo, A., Nicotera, P. G., Manzillo, G. F., & Raviele, A. (2005). Psychiatric profile, quality of life and risk of syncopal recurrence in patients with tilt-induced vasovagal syncope. *EP Europace, 7*(5), 465–471.

Goldstein, L. H., Deale, A. C., O'Malley, S. J. M., Toone, B. K., & Mellers, J. D. (2004). An evaluation of cognitive behavioral therapy as a treatment for dissociative seizures: A pilot study. *Cognitive and Behavioral Neurology*, *17*(1), 41–49.

Goldstein, L. H., & Mellers, J. D. C. (2006). Ictal symptoms of anxiety, avoidance behaviour, and dissociation in patients with dissociative seizures. *Journal of Neurology, Neurosurgery & Psychiatry*, *77*(5), 616–621.

Greve, K. W., Bianchini, K. J., & Ameduri, C. J. (2003). Use of a forced-choice test of tactile discrimination in the evaluation of functional sensory loss: A report of 3 cases. *Archives of Physical Medicine and Rehabilitation*, *84*(8), 1233–1236.

Griffith, J. L., Polles, A., & Griffith, M. E. (1998). Pseudoseizures, families, and unspeakable dilemmas. *Psychosomatics*, *39*(2), 144–153.

Grubb, B. P., Gerard, G., Wolfe, D. A., Samoil, D., Davenport, C. W., Homan, R. W., & Temesy-Armos, P. (1992). Syncope and seizures of psychogenic origin: Identification with head-upright tilt table testing. *Clinical cardiology, 15*(11), 839–842.

Harden, C. L., Jovine, L., Burgut, F. T., Carey, B. T., Nikolov, B. G., & Ferrando, S. J. (2009). A comparison of personality disorder characteristics of patients with nonepileptic psychogenic pseudoseizures with those of patients with epilepsy. *Epilepsy & Behavior*, *14*(3), 481–483.

Heintz, C. E., van Tricht, M. J., van der Salm, S. M., Van Rootselaar, A. F., Cath, D., Schmand, B., & Tijssen, M. A. (2013). Neuropsychological profile of psychogenic jerky movement disorders: Importance of evaluating non-credible cognitive performance and psychopathology. *Journal Neurol Neurosurg Psychiatry*, *84*(8), 862–867.

Hendrickson, R., Popescu, A., Dixit, R., Ghearing, G., & Bagic, A. (2014). Panic attack symptoms differentiate patients with epilepsy from those with psychogenic nonepileptic spells (PNES). *Epilepsy & Behavior*, *37*, 210–214.

Heyer, G. L., Harvey, R. A., & Islam, M. P. (2017). Comparison of specific fainting characteristics between youth with tilt-induced psychogenic nonsyncopal collapse versus reflex syncope. *The American Journal of Cardiology*.

Hoerth, M. T., Wellik, K. E., Demaerschalk, B. M., Drazkowski, J. F., Noe, K. H., Sirven, J. I., & Wingerchuk, D. M. (2008). Clinical predictors of psychogenic nonepileptic seizures: A critically appraised topic. *The Neurologist*, *14*(4), 266–270.

Hopp, J. L., Anderson, K. E., Krumholz, A., Gruber-Baldini, A. L., & Shulman, L. M. (2012). Psychogenic seizures and psychogenic movement disorders: Are they the same patients?. *Epilepsy & Behavior*, *25*(4), 666–669.

Huber, A., Suman, A. L., Biasi, G., & Carli, G. (2009). Alexithymia in fibromyalgia syndrome: Associations with ongoing pain, experimental pain sensitivity and illness behavior. *Journal of Psychosomatic Research*, *66*(5), 425–433.

Indranada, A. M., Mullen, S. A., Duncan, R., Berlowitz, D. J., & Kanaan, R. A. (2018). The association of panic and hyperventilation with psychogenic non-epileptic seizures: A systematic review and meta-analysis. *Seizure*, *59*, 108–115.

Jankovic, J. (2011). Diagnosis and treatment of psychogenic parkinsonism. *Journal Neurol Neurosurg Psychiatry*, *82*(12), 1300–1303.

Jones, H. N., Story, T. J., Collins, T. A., DeJoy, D., & Edwards, C. L. (2011). Multidisciplinary assessment and diagnosis of conversion disorder in a patient with foreign accent syndrome. *Behavioural Neurology*, *24*(3), 245–255.

Jones, L. L., & Rickards, H. (2021). History of abuse and psychogenic nonepileptic seizures: A systematic review. *Seizure*, *92*, 200–204.

Kalogjera-Sackellares, D., & Sackellares, J. C. (1999). Intellectual and neuropsychological features of patients with psychogenic pseudoseizures. *Psychiatry Research*, *86*(1), 73–84.

Kanaan, R., Armstrong, D., Barnes, P., & Wessely, S. (2009). In the psychiatrist's chair: How neurologists understand conversion disorder. *Brain*, *132*(10), 2889–2896.

Kanaan, R. A., & Wessely, S. C. (2010a). The origins of factitious disorder. *History of the Human Sciences*, *23*(2), 68–85.

Kanaan, R. A., & Wessely, S. C. (2010b). Factitious disorders in neurology: An analysis of reported cases. *Psychosomatics*, *51*(1), 47–54.

Kaplan, M. J., Dwivedi, A. K., Privitera, M. D., Isaacs, K., Hughes, C., & Bowman, M. (2013). Comparisons of childhood trauma, alexithymia, and defensive styles in patients with psychogenic non-epileptic seizures vs. epilepsy: Implications for the etiology of conversion disorder. *Journal of Psychosomatic Research*, *75*(2), 142–146.

Kemp, S., Coughlan, A. K., Rowbottom, C., Wilkinson, K., Teggart, V., & Baker, G. (2008). The base rate of effort test failure in patients with medically unexplained symptoms. *Journal of Psychosomatic Research*, *65*(4), 319–325.

Kemp, S., Kapur, N., Graham, C. D., & Reuber, M. (2022). Functional cognitive disorder: Differential diagnosis of common clinical presentations. *Archives of Clinical Neuropsychology*, *37*(6), 1158–1176.

Kim, M. S., Boone, K. B., Victor, T., Marion, S. D., Amano, S., Cottingham, M. E., … Zeller, M. A. (2010). The Warrington Recognition Memory Test for Words as a measure of response bias: Total score and response time cutoffs developed on "real world" credible and noncredible subjects. *Archives of Clinical Neuropsychology*, *25*(1), 60–70.

Kim, N., Boone, K. B., Victor, T., Lu, P., Keatinge, C., & Mitchell, C. (2010). Sensitivity and specificity of a digit symbol recognition trial in the identification of response bias. *Archives of Clinical Neuropsychology*, *25*(5), 420–428.

Kletenik, I., Holden, S. K., Sillau, S. H., O'connell, N., MacGillivray, L., Mack, J., ... Stone, J. (2022). Gender disparity and abuse in functional movement disorders: A multi-center case-control study. *Journal of Neurology, 269*(6), 3258–3263.

Kouakam, C., Lacroix, D., Klug, D., Baux, P., Marquié, C., & Kacet, S. (2002). Prevalence and prognostic significance of psychiatric disorders in patients evaluated for recurrent unexplained syncope. *The American journal of cardiology, 89*(5), 530–535.

Kozlowska, K., & Williams, L. M. (2009). Self-protective organization in children with conversion and somatoform disorders. *Journal of Psychosomatic Research, 67*(3), 223–233.

Krawetz, P., Fleisher, W., Pillay, N., Staley, D., Arnett, J., & Maher, J. (2001). Family functioning in subjects with pseudoseizures and epilepsy. *The Journal of Nervous and Mental Disease, 189*(1), 38–43.

Krumholz, A., & Niedermeyer, E. (1983). Psychogenic seizures: A clinical study with follow-up data. *Neurology, 33*(4), 498–498.

Kumru, H., Begeman, M., Tolosa, E., & Valls-Sole, J. (2007). Dual task interference in psychogenic tremor. *Movement Disorders: Official Journal of the Movement Disorder Society, 22*(14), 2077–2082.

Kumru, H., Valls-Solé, J., Valldeoriola, F., Marti, M. J., Sanegre, M. T., & Tolosa, E. (2004). Transient arrest of psychogenic tremor induced by contralateral ballistic movements. *Neuroscience Letters, 370*(2–3), 135–139.

Lacey, C., Cook, M., & Salzberg, M. (2007). The neurologist, psychogenic nonepileptic seizures, and borderline personality disorder. *Epilepsy & Behavior, 11*(4), 492–498.

Lancman, M. E., Asconapé, J. J., Craven, W. J., Howard, G., & Penry, J. K. (1994). Predictive value of induction of psychogenic seizures by suggestion. *Annals of Neurology: Official Journal of the American Neurological Association and the Child Neurology Society, 35*(3), 359–361.

Larrabee, G. J., Millis, S. R., & Meyers, J. E. (2009). 40 plus or minus 10, a new magical number: Reply to Russell. *The Clinical Neuropsychologist, 23*, 841–849.

Lawlor, A., & Kirakowski, J. (2014). When the lie is the truth: Grounded theory analysis of an online support group for factitious disorder. *Psychiatry Research, 218*(1–2), 209–218.

Lazzari, C., Shoka, A., & Rabottini, M. (2023). Factitious disorder comorbid with borderline personality disorder and dysthymia: From medically unexplained physical symptoms to functional neurological disorder. *Rivista di psichiatria, 58*(5), 205–219.

Lee, S. H., Park, S. J., Byeon, K., On, Y. K., Yim, H. R., & Kim, J. S. (2013). Prevalence and clinical factors of anxiety and depression in neurally mediated and unexplained syncope. *Yonsei medical journal, 54*(3), 583–589.

Lilienfeld, S. O., Kirsch, I., Sarbin, T. R., Lynn, S. J., Chaves, J. F., Ganaway, G. K., & Powell, R. A. (1999). Dissociative identity disorder and the sociocognitive model: Recalling the lessons of the past.

Linzer, M., Felder, A., Hackel, A., Perry, A. J., Varia, I., Melville, M. L., & Krishnan, K. R. (1990). Psychiatric syncope: a new look at an old disease. *Psychosomatics, 31*(2), 181–188.

Linzer, M., Varia, I., Pontinen, M., Divine, G. W., Grubb, B. P., & Estes III, N. M. (1992). Medically unexplained syncope: relationship to psychiatric illness. *The American journal of medicine, 92*(1), S18–S25.

Lind, A. B., Delmar, C., & Nielsen, K. (2014). Struggling in an emotional avoidance culture: A qualitative study of stress as a predisposing factor for somatoform disorders. *Journal of Psychosomatic Research, 76*(2), 94–98.

Lkhagvasuren, B., Oka, T., Kawai, K., Takii, M., Kanemitsu, Y., Tokunaga, S., & Kubo, C. (2011). Prevalence of postural orthostatic tachycardia syndrome in patients with psychiatric disorders. *Psychotherapy and psychosomatics, 80*(5), 308.

Ludwig, L., Pasman, J. A., Nicholson, T., Aybek, S., David, A. S., Tuck, S., ... & Stone, J. (2018). Stressful life events and maltreatment in conversion (functional neurological) disorder: systematic review and meta-analysis of case-control studies. *The Lancet Psychiatry, 5*(4), 307–320.

Mangiulli, I., Otgaar, H., Jelicic, M., & Merckelbach, H. (2022). A critical review of case studies on dissociative amnesia. *Clinical Psychological Science, 10*(2), 191–211.

Marcopulos, B. A., Hedjar, L., & Arredondo, B. C. (2016). Dissociative amnesia or malingered amnesia? a case report. *Journal of Forensic Psychology Practice, 16*(2), 106–117.

Martin, P. K., & Schroeder, R. W. (2020). Base rates of invalid test performance across clinical non-forensic contexts and settings. *Archives of Clinical Neuropsychology, 35*(6), 717–725.
Martin, P. K. & Schroeder, R. W. (2022). A framework for providing clinical feedback when patients invalidate testing. In R. W. Schroeder, & P. K. Martin (Eds.), *Validity assessment in clinical neuropsychological practice: Evaluating and managing noncredible performance* (pp. 47–69). Guilford Publications.
Martin, P. K., Schroeder, R. W., & Odland, A. P. (2015). Neuropsychologists' validity testing beliefs and practices: A survey of North American professionals. *The Clinical Neuropsychologist, 29*(6), 741–776.
Martin, P. K., Schroeder, R. W., & Odland, A. P. (2024). Neuropsychological validity assessment beliefs and practices: A survey of north American neuropsychologists and validity assessment experts. *Archives of Clinical Neuropsychology*, acae102.
Mayor, R., Brown, R. J., Cock, H., House, A., Howlett, S., Singhal, S., ... Reuber, M. (2012). Short-term outcome of psychogenic non-epileptic seizures after communication of the diagnosis. *Epilepsy & Behavior, 25*(4), 676–681.
McCaul, C., Boone, K. B., Ermshar, A., Cottingham, M., Victor, T. L., Ziegler, E., ... Wright, M. (2018). Cross-validation of the Dot Counting Test in a large sample of credible and non-credible patients referred for neuropsychological testing. *The Clinical Neuropsychologist, 32*(6), 1054–1067.
McWhirter, L., Ludwig, L., Carson, A., McIntosh, R. D., & Stone, J. (2016). Transcranial magnetic stimulation as a treatment for functional (psychogenic) upper limb weakness. *Journal of Psychosomatic Research, 89*, 102–106.
Meichenbaum, D. (1977). Cognitive behaviour modification. *Cognitive Behaviour Therapy, 6*(4), 185–192.
Merskey, H. (1992). The manufacture of personalities: The production of multiple personality disorder. *The British Journal of Psychiatry, 160*(3), 327–340.
Millman, L. M., Short, E., Ward, E., Stanton, B., Bradley-Westguard, A., Goldstein, L. H., ... Pick, S. (2024). Etiological factors and symptom triggers in functional motor symptoms and functional seizures: A pilot investigation. *The Journal of Neuropsychiatry and Clinical Neurosciences*, appi-neuropsych.
Mittenberg, W., Patton, C. L., Canyocka, E. M., & Condit, D. C. (2002). A national survey of symptom exaggeration and malingering base rates. *Clinical and Experimental Neuropsychology, 24*, 1093–1102.
Monzoni, C., & Reuber, M. (2009). Conversational displays of coping resources in clinical encounters between patients with epilepsy and neurologists: A pilot study. *Epilepsy & Behavior, 16*(4), 652–659.
Morin, A. (1995). Preliminary data on a relation between self-talk and complexity of the self-concept. *Psychological Reports, 76*(1), 267–272.
Morin, A. (2009). Self-awareness deficits following loss of inner speech: Dr. Jill Bolte Taylor's case study. *Consciousness and Cognition, 18*(2), 524–529.
Morsy, S. K., Aybek, S., Carson, A., Nicholson, T. R., Stone, J., Kamal, A. M., ... Kanaan, R. A. (2022). The relationship between types of life events and the onset of functional neurological (conversion) disorder in adults: a systematic review and meta-analysis. *Psychological medicine, 52*(3), 401–418.
Myers, L., Perrine, K., Lancman, M., Fleming, M., & Lancman, M. (2013). Psychological trauma in patients with psychogenic nonepileptic seizures: Trauma characteristics and those who develop PTSD. *Epilepsy & Behavior, 28*(1), 121–126.
Myers, L., Trobliger, R., Bortnik, K., Zeng, R., Saal, E., & Lancman, M. (2019). Psychological trauma, somatization, dissociation, and psychiatric comorbidities in patients with psychogenic nonepileptic seizures compared with those in patients with intractable partial epilepsy. *Epilepsy & Behavior, 92*, 108–113.
Nani, A., & Cavanna, A. E. (2014). The quantitative measurement of consciousness during epileptic seizures. *Epilepsy & Behavior, 30*, 2–5.

Nathan, D. (2008). *Sybil exposed: the extraordinary story behind the famous multiple personality case*. New York: Simon and Schuster.
Ness, D. (2007). Physical therapy management for conversion disorder: Case series. *Journal of Neurologic Physical Therapy*, *31*(1), 30–39.
Nicholson, T. R., Aybek, S., Craig, T., Harris, T., Wojcik, W., David, A. S., & Kanaan, R. A. (2016). Life events and escape in conversion disorder. *Psychological Medicine*, *46*(12), 2617–2626.
Nicholson, T. R., Stone, J., & Kanaan, R. A. (2011). Conversion disorder: A problematic diagnosis. *J Neurol Neurosurg Psychiatry*, *82*(11), 1267–1273.
Nielsen, G., Stone, J., & Edwards, M. J. (2013). Physiotherapy for functional (psychogenic) motor symptoms: A systematic review. *Journal of Psychosomatic Research*, *75*(2), 93–102.
Nielsen, G., Stone, J., Matthews, A., Brown, M., Sparkes, C., Farmer, R., … Edwards, M. (2015). Physiotherapy for functional motor disorders: A consensus recommendation. *Journal of Neurology, Neurosurgery & Psychiatry*, *86*(10), 1113–1119.
Noyes Jr, R., Langbehn, D. R., Happel, R. L., Stout, L. R., Muller, B. A., & Longley, S. L. (2001). Personality dysfunction among somatizing patients. *Psychosomatics*, *42*(4), 320–329.
O'Brien, F. M., Fortune, G. M., Dicker, P., O'Hanlon, E., Cassidy, E., Delanty, N., … Murphy, K. C. (2015). Psychiatric and neuropsychological profiles of people with psychogenic nonepileptic seizures. *Epilepsy & Behavior*, *43*, 39–45.
Oh, J. H., & Kapoor, W. N. (1997). Psychiatric illness and syncope. *Cardiology clinics*, *15*(2), 269–275
Oliva, M., Pattison, C., Carino, J., Roten, A., Matkovic, Z., & O'Brien, T. J. (2008). The diagnostic value of oral lacerations and incontinence during convulsive "seizures". *Epilepsia*, *49*(6), 962–967.
Pankratz, L., & Erickson, R. C. (1990). Two views of malingering. *The Clinical Neuropsychologist*, *4*(4), 379–389.
Pankratz, L., Fausti, S. A., & Peed, S. (1975). A forced-choice technique to evaluate deafness in the hysterical or malingering patient. *Journal of Consulting and Clinical Psychology*, *43*(3), 421.
Pareés, I., Kassavetis, P., Saifee, T. A., Sadnicka, A., Davare, M., Bhatia, K. P., … Edwards, M. J. (2013). Failure of explicit movement control in patients with functional motor symptoms. *Movement Disorders*, *28*(4), 517–523.
Pareés, I., Saifee, T. A., Kassavetis, P., Kojovic, M., Rubio-Agusti, I., Rothwell, J. C., … Edwards, M. J. (2012). Believing is perceiving: Mismatch between self-report and actigraphy in psychogenic tremor. *Brain*, *135*(1), 117–123.
Perez, D. L., Aybek, S., Popkirov, S., Kozlowska, K., Stephen, C. D., Anderson, J.,… American Neuropsychiatric Association Committee for Research. (2021). A review and expert opinion on the neuropsychiatric assessment of motor functional neurological disorders. *The Journal of Neuropsychiatry and Clinical Neurosciences*, *33*(1), 14–26.
Piper, A., & Merskey, H. (2004). The persistence of folly: Critical examination of dissociative identity disorder. Part II. The defence and decline of multiple personality or dissociative identity disorder. *The Canadian Journal of Psychiatry*, *49*(10), 678–683.
Poynter, K., Boone, K. B., Ermshar, A., Miora, D., Cottingham, M., Victor, T. L., … Wright, M. (2019). Wait, there'sa baby in this bath water! Update on quantitative and qualitative cut-offs for Rey 15-item recall and recognition. *Archives of Clinical Neuropsychology*, *34*(8), 1367–1380.
Quigg, M., Armstrong, R. F., Farace, E., & Fountain, N. B. (2002). Quality of life outcome is associated with cessation rather than reduction of psychogenic nonepileptic seizures. *Epilepsy & Behavior, 3*(5), 455–459.
Rady, A., Elfatatry, A., Molokhia, T., & Radwan, A. (2021). Psychiatric comorbidities in patients with psychogenic nonepileptic seizures. *Epilepsy & Behavior*, *118*, 107918.
Rawlings, G. H., Jamnadas-Khoda, J., Broadhurst, M., Grünewald, R. A., Howell, S. J., Koepp, M., … Reuber, M. (2017). Panic symptoms in transient loss of consciousness: Frequency and diagnostic value in psychogenic nonepileptic seizures, epilepsy and syncope. *Seizure*, *48*, 22–27.
Reedy, S. D., Boone, K. B., Cottingham, M. E., Glaser, D. F., Lu, P. H., Victor, T. L., … Wright, M. J. (2013). Cross validation of the Lu and colleagues (2003) Rey-Osterrieth Complex Figure Test effort equation in a large known-group sample. *Archives of Clinical Neuropsychology*, *28*(1), 30–37.

Reich, S. G. (2006, July). Psychogenic movement disorders. In *Seminars in neurology* (Vol. 26, No. 03, pp. 289–296). Copyright© 2006 by Thieme Medical Publishers, Inc., 333 Seventh Avenue, New York 10001.
Reuber, M., & Brown, R. J. (2017). Understanding psychogenic nonepileptic seizures—phenomenology, semiology and the integrative cognitive model. *Seizure*, *44*, 199–205.
Reuber, M., & Elger, C. E. (2003). Psychogenic nonepileptic seizures: Review and update. *Epilepsy & Behavior*, *4*(3), 205–216.
Reuber, M., Howlett, S., Khan, A., & Grünewald, R. A. (2007). Non-epileptic seizures and other functional neurological symptoms: Predisposing, precipitating, and perpetuating factors. *Psychosomatics*, *48*(3), 230–238.
Reuber, M., Jamnadas-Khoda, J., Broadhurst, M., Grunewald, R., Howell, S., Koepp, M., … Walker, M. (2011). Psychogenic nonepileptic seizure manifestations reported by patients and witnesses. *Epilepsia*, *52*(11), 2028–2035.
Reuber, M., Mitchell, A. J., Howlett, S., & Elger, C. E. (2005). Measuring outcome in psychogenic nonepileptic seizures: How relevant is seizure remission?. *Epilepsia*, *46*(11), 1788–1795.
Reuber, M., & Rawlings, G. H. (2016). Nonepileptic seizures–subjective phenomena. *Handbook of Clinical Neurology, 139*, 283–296.
Roelofs, K., Keijsers, G. P., Hoogduin, K. A., Näring, G. W., & Moene, F. C. (2002). Childhood abuse in patients with conversion disorder. *American Journal of Psychiatry*, *159*(11), 1908–1913.
Roor, J. J., Peters, M. J., Dandachi-FitzGerald, B., & Ponds, R. W. (2024). Performance validity test failure in the clinical population: A systematic review and meta-analysis of prevalence rates. *Neuropsychology Review*, *34*(1), 299–319.
Ross, C. A., Norton, G. R., & Wozney, K. (1989). Multiple personality disorder: An analysis of 236 cases. *The Canadian Journal of Psychiatry*, *34*(5), 413–418.
Sackellares, D. K., & Sackellares, J. C. (2001). Impaired motor function in patients with psychogenic pseudoseizures. *Epilepsia*, *42*(12), 1600–1606.
Salinsky, M., Binder, L., Storzbach, D., Parko, K., Rutecki, P., Goy, E., & Tadrous-Furnanz, S. (2020). Validity testing in veterans with epileptic seizures and psychogenic nonepileptic seizures. *Epilepsy & Behavior*, *111*, 107246.
Saxena, A., Godena, E., Maggio, J., & Perez, D. L. (2020). Towards an outpatient model of care for motor functional neurological disorders: A neuropsychiatric perspective. *Neuropsychiatric Disease and Treatment*, 2119–2134.
Schönenberg, M., Jusyte, A., Höhnle, N., Mayer, S. V., Weber, Y., Hautzinger, M., & Schell, C. (2015). Theory of mind abilities in patients with psychogenic nonepileptic seizures. *Epilepsy & Behavior*, *53*, 20–24.
Schwartz, E. S., Erdodi, L., Rodriguez, N., Ghosh, J. J., Curtain, J. R., Flashman, L. A., & Roth, R. M. (2016). CVLT-II forced choice recognition trial as an embedded validity indicator: A systematic review of the evidence. *Journal of the International Neuropsychological Society*, *22*(8), 851–858.
Selkirk, M., Duncan, R., Oto, M., & Pelosi, A. (2008). Clinical differences between patients with nonepileptic seizures who report antecedent sexual abuse and those who do not. *Epilepsia*, *49*(8), 1446–1450.
Shaibani, A., & Sabbagh, M. N. (1998). Pseudoneurologic syndromes: Recognition and diagnosis. *American Family Physician*, *57*(10), 2485–2494.
Shapiro, A. P., & Teasell, R. W. (2004). Behavioural interventions in the rehabilitation of acute v. chronic non-organic (conversion/factitious) motor disorders. *The British Journal of Psychiatry*, *185*(2), 140–146.
Sharpe, D., & Faye, C. (2006). Non-epileptic seizures and child sexual abuse: A critical review of the literature. *Clinical Psychology Review*, *26*(8), 1020–1040.
Siegrist, M. (1995). Inner speech as a cognitive process mediating self-consciousness and inhibiting self-deception. *Psychological Reports*, *76*(1), 259–265.
Silverberg, N. D., Iverson, G. L., Group, A. B. I. S. I., Cogan, A., Dams-O-Connor, K., Delmonico, R., … Zemek, R. (2023). The American Congress of rehabilitation medicine diagnostic criteria for mild traumatic brain injury. *Archives of Physical Medicine and Rehabilitation*, *104*(8), 1343–1355.

Slocum, R. B. (2021). Breaking the spell: Narrative medicine applications for psychogenic nonepileptic seizures (PNES). *Seizure, 86*, 96–101.
Solomon, R. E., Boone, K. B., Miora, D., Skidmore, S., Cottingham, M., Victor, T., ... Zeller, M. (2010). Use of the WAIS-III picture completion subtest as an embedded measure of response bias. *The Clinical Neuropsychologist, 24*(7), 1243–1256.
Spanos, N. P. (1996). *Multiple identities & false memories: a sociocognitive perspective*. Washington, DC: American Psychological Association.
Spence, S. A. (1999). Hysterical paralyses as disorders of action. *Cognitive Neuropsychiatry, 4*(3), 203–226.
Stinnett, J. L. (1987). The functional somatic symptom. *Psychiatric Clinics of North America, 10*(1), 19–33.
Stone, J., & Carson, A. J. (2013). The unbearable lightheadedness of seizing: Willful submission to dissociative (non-epileptic) seizures. *Journal Neurol Neurosurg Psychiatry, 84*(7), 822–824.
Sutherland, A. J., & Rodin, G. M. (1990). Factitious disorders in a general hospital setting: Clinical features and a review of the literature. *Psychosomatics, 31*(4), 392–399.
Teasell, R. W., & Shapiro, A. P. (1994). Strategic-behavioral intervention in the treatment of chronic nonorganic motor disorders. *American Journal of Physical Medicine & Rehabilitation, 73*(1), 44–50.
Theodor, L. H., & Mandelcorn, M. S. (1973). Hysterical blindness: A case report and study using a modern psychophysical technique. *Journal of Abnormal Psychology, 82*(3), 552.
Travin, S., & Protter, B. (1984). Malingering and malingering-like behavior: Some clinical and conceptual issues. *Psychiatric Quarterly, 56*, 189–197.
Trueblood, W., & Schmidt, M. (1993). Malingering and other validity considerations in the neuropsychological evaluation of mild head injury. *Journal of Clinical and Experimental Neuropsychology, 15*(4), 578–590.
Turner, K., Piazzini, A., Chiesa, V., Barbieri, V., Vignoli, A., Gardella, E., ... Gambini, O. (2011). Patients with epilepsy and patients with psychogenic non-epileptic seizures: Video-EEG, clinical and neuropsychological evaluation. *Seizure, 20*(9), 706–710.
Tyson, B. T., Baker, S., Greenacre, M., Kent, K. J., Lichtenstein, J. D., Sabelli, A., & Erdodi, L. A. (2018). Differentiating epilepsy from psychogenic nonepileptic seizures using neuropsychological test data. *Epilepsy & Behavior, 87*, 39–45.
Van Beilen, M., Griffioen, B. T., Gross, A., & Leenders, K. L. (2009). Psychological assessment of malingering in psychogenic neurological disorders and non-psychogenic neurological disorders: Relationship to psychopathology levels. *European Journal of Neurology, 16*(10), 1118–1123.
van Middendorp, H., Lumley, M. A., Jacobs, J. W., van Doornen, L. J., Bijlsma, J. W., & Geenen, R. (2008). Emotions and emotional approach and avoidance strategies in fibromyalgia. *Journal of Psychosomatic Research, 64*(2), 159–167.
Ventura, R., Maas, R., Rüppel, R., Stuhr, U., Schuchert, A., Meinertz, T., & Nienaber, C. A. (2001). Psychiatric conditions in patients with recurrent unexplained syncope. *EP Europace, 3*(4), 311–316.
Waller, E., & Scheidt, C. E. (2004). Somatoform disorders as disorders of affect regulation: A study comparing the TAS-20 with non-self-report measures of alexithymia. *Journal of Psychosomatic Research, 57*(3), 239–247.
Wardrope, A., Wong, S., McLaughlan, J., Wolfe, M., Oto, M., & Reuber, M. (2020). Peri-ictal responsiveness to the social environment is greater in psychogenic nonepileptic than epileptic seizures. *Epilepsia, 61*(4), 758–765.
Williams, B., Ospina, J. P., Jalilianhasanpour, R., Fricchione, G. L., & Perez, D. L. (2019). Fearful attachment linked to childhood abuse, alexithymia, and depression in motor functional neurological disorders. *The Journal of neuropsychiatry and clinical neurosciences, 31*(1), 65–69.
Williamson, D. J., Holsman, M., Chaytor, N., Miller, J. W., & Drane, D. L. (2012). Abuse, not financial incentive, predicts non-credible cognitive performance in patients with psychogenic non-epileptic seizures. *The Clinical Neuropsychologist, 26*(4), 588–598.
Windle, G., Bennett, K. M., & Noyes, J. (2011). A methodological review of resilience measurement scales. *Health and Quality of Life Outcomes, 9*, 1–18.
Yang, T., Roberts, C., Winton-Brown, T., Lloyd, M., Kwan, P., O'Brien, T. J., ... Malpas, C. B. (2023). Childhood trauma in patients with epileptic vs nonepileptic seizures. *Epilepsia, 64*(1), 184–195.

16 Diagnostic Determination, Fungal Fabrication, and Mushrooming Litigation

Neuropsychological Differential Diagnosis in Toxic Mold Claims

David E. Hartman

Toxic mold exposure cases are not the most common source of neuropsychological referrals, but, like many disorders where non-traumatic neurobehavioral impairment is alleged, the neuropsychologist may be called upon as one of the examining specialists. Unlike more dubious belief systems, e.g., demon possession or electrical allergy, the possibility of actual poisoning or allergic response to mushroom spores cannot be rejected out of hand or arbitrarily attributed to psychopathology or litigation enrollment. As will be seen, understanding such cases is not an *either-or* decision, but nuanced, and grounded in a thorough understanding of the examinee's conditions, neuropsychological toxicology, and medical neuropsychology.

Mold exposure is environmentally ubiquitous, and mold allergy is common in the general population. In a survey of over 1.6 million examinees, 22% tested positive for at least one fungal allergen and 13.7% were positive to ≥2 fungal allergens (Kwong et al., 2023). Mold sensitization in asthmatic examinees may be up to 80% (Simon-Nobbeet al., 2007). Certain molds can be directly neurotoxic, including *Arthrinium sacchari*, *A. sacchariocola*, and *A. phaeospermum* from sugarcane, or *Penitrems*, which grow on cream cheese, walnuts, beer, and hamburger buns, and can cause tremor and incoordination (Choudhuri, 2021). Ergot, a rye mold, contains the amide of d-lysergic acid (Davison, 1976, p. 108) and causes *ergotism,* historically a cause of mass psychosis, with sufferers experiencing delirium, burning sensation in the feet or legs ("St. Anthony's Fire") alternating with cold and other symptoms, including encephalopathy, seizure, and coma (Haschek et al., 2002). Entire towns have been affected (Gabbai et al., 1951).

Verified mold toxicity or poisoning is considered rare, and mainly in immunocompromised individuals, including HIV-infected persons, transplant examinees, and examinees whose immune system is suppressed with chemotherapy or corticosteroids, and/or other conditions, e.g., Lupus. Neurosurgical contamination is possible and IV drug use can be a vector. Cryptococcal meningoencephalitis with disseminated mycosis occurs in 67%–84% of examinees (Goralska et al., 2018). Clinical syndromes from fungal infections can include meningitis, brain abscess, stroke, and disseminated presentations. Low weight infants are a known risk group. Clinical manifestations of neurologic deficits in immune-compromised examinees can include headache, optic edema, paresthesias, impaired mental status, and focal effects of stroke.

Some symptoms are quite common and may be mistaken for CNS toxicity; allergic sensitivity symptoms, including headaches and fogginess, are not of neurotoxic causation. Molds are everywhere in the environment and "the vast majority of these mold spores live in harmony with humans, rarely causing disease" (Borchers et al., 2017). There is even

DOI: 10.4324/9781003005063-18

some evidence that chronic exposure to molds and microbes reduces asthma risk and that children exposed to a diverse fungal environment have lower risk of aerosol sensitization to allergens (Barnes, 2019).

This view is disputed by adherents of toxic mold syndromes and associated claims of mold-induced *sick building syndrome* and *chemical sensitivity*. Peer-reviewed articles and books assert a basis for their claims, including that mold toxicity can cause

> symptoms affecting multiple organs, including the lungs, musculoskeletal system, as well as the central and peripheral nervous systems. Furthermore, evidence has recently implicated exposure to mycotoxins in the pathogenesis of autism spectrum disorder.
>
> (Ratnaseelan et al., 2018)

The Internet is also replete with true believers who claim that an "invisible epidemic .... is making many of us very ill" and if "your symptoms include difficulty in memory, focus and concentration, or maybe even experiencing dizziness when standing up....there's a chance you're suffering from chronic fatigue caused by exposure to toxic mold" (Johnson, 2013). Published articles have documented an admittedly "confusing" set of symptoms, one of which noted, without irony, that some examinees attempt to voluntarily control underlying motor abnormalities leading to "misinterpreting the entire process as psychiatric" (Empting, 2009)

Another author (Rea, 1992) proposed a set of *ad hoc, pseudoscientific* theories about environmental exposures that largely involved relabeling normal human experiences as "pollution overload." The author described such a case in which a young college student developed cold symptoms after moving into a dormitory, and reported vacillating energy during her menstrual cycles; she was also treated for cystitis. The author did not investigate the far more reasonable possibilities that (1) dormitories spread student colds, (2) fluctuating energy or emotional vacillations during menstrual cycles have been observed for millennia, and (3) "honeymoon cystitis" would not be unexpected in a young college-age woman who became sexually active while living in a dormitory (Hartman, 1998). Rea (1992) posited that the young woman's body was being assaulted by unknown environmental toxicants. In response, her parents removed the young woman from college and (presumably on the doctor's advice) isolated her in a special 'nontoxic' room.

Toxic mold cases have understandably caught the attention of attorneys seeking to litigate "the next big toxic tort" especially after the success of "the first and most notorious" claim, *Ballard v. Fire Insurance Exchange*, in which homeowners won a multi-million-dollar award for mold exposure (Perry, 2004). No less a toxic crusader than Erin Brockovich sued after claiming her California home contained toxic mold (Lee, 2003).

Perhaps, in consequence, clinical claims of toxic mold impairments are almost always conflated with litigation; one study found almost all (29/31) examinees alleging toxic mold exposure were suing. Dozens of toxic tort sites have popped up on the Internet, devoted to toxic mold effects and touting specialized litigation expertise. Some neuropsychological experts have even become advocates for the syndrome; one such individual, recommended by the advocacy group *National Toxic Encephalopathy Foundation*, blogged his neuropsychological examination of an individual alleging toxic mold effects, in which he described "administration of tests which have established normative bases and which are known to be sensitive to neurotoxicity" (Singer, 2011). He included the *Dot Counting Test* as a performance validity test (PVT), and using "dementia" norms, concluded that the examinee's E-score of 15 was valid (although it would have been positive for exaggeration had he compared the examinee's score to mixed clinical outpatients; McCaul et al., 2018; Rhoads et al., 2021). No appropriate personality testing was administered, such as the Minnesota Multiphasic Personality Inventory-2-Restructured Form (MMPI-2-RF), which could have detected over-reported patterns of physical and cognitive symptoms. Another clinician asserted that SPECT scans were useful in diagnosing "toxic injury," with one SPECT examinee describing that "when my brain swelled from the mold exposure, I was getting almost no blood flow to my prefrontal cortex" (see Cornish, 2017).

Neuropsychologists unfamiliar with either the controversy regarding effects of mold, or the conflation of mold claims with litigation, should approach each case dispassionately and avoid the logical fallacy of *petitio principii*—assuming symptoms must be neurotoxic because the examinee and their cadre of clinicians have diagnosed "toxic mold syndrome." Each individual's history should be carefully reviewed for any and all conditions, which could be etiological in symptoms, as discussed below.

> Any case of illness claimed to be caused by mold or any other environmental agent requires a searching medical and environmental history, complete physical examination, pertinent laboratory and imaging studies, review of environmental mold data, and, if necessary, a review of hospitalizations and the medical records of other treating physicians. These elements of the medical examination are essential in cases of litigation where the question of fault by someone else is relevant. This is true regardless of whether the physician is engaged by the attorney who represents the plaintiff or the attorney who represents the defendant. Litigated cases, either in the Workers' Compensation or the civil litigation arena, are time-consuming. Only when all pertinent data are available and analyzed, including all reasonable alternatives or explanations for these data (i.e., the differential diagnosis), can the physician provide an expert opinion regarding the question of mold-related disease.
>
> (Terr, 2005)

Examinee symptoms may be legitimate but more likely related to alternative causes, which should be reviewed and potentially ruled out, including:

> mixed (allergic and nonallergic) perennial rhinitis, mixed conjunctivitis, chronic rhinosinusitis, allergic fungal rhinosinusitis, chronic headache syndrome, eustachian tube dysfunction (with or without vertigo), chronic pharyngitis with possible immune dysfunction, chronic cough (extrapulmonic and/or intrapulmonic), bronchospasm/bronchial asthma, and hypersensitivity pneumonitis. Other diagnoses include chronic fatigue syndrome, fibromyalgia syndrome, obstructive sleep apnea, endocrinopathies, and neurocognitive/neuropsychological disorders.
>
> (Weiner, 2010)

Further, "any inflammatory process in the body… can induce diffuse myalgias and arthralgias" (Empting, 2009, p. 579).

Claimed symptoms may also be psychiatric in nature. If examinee history contains numerous unverified claimed diagnoses, some form of somatization is likely. There are rare cases in which claims of toxic mold neurotoxicity are the product of a delusion. One such examinee, described by Lewis and Oldham (2015), used 20 mg of lorazepam daily for one year to treat "neurotoxic" effects of a "black mold infection," and who came to the hospital when his supply ran out. He presented as unkempt and agitated, with labile affect, moderate suspiciousness, and obsessional thoughts. Neuroleptics were offered but refused, and the examinee left the hospital against medical advice (AMA) and declined treatment referral.

Many individuals presenting for neuropsychological evaluation will bring test results that supposedly confirm their "toxic mold" diagnosis, but neuropsychologists should be aware that many of these "tests" lack validity as markers of neurotoxic injury. There are numerous "disreputable practices"

> such as testing homes for mold spores, measuring "mycotoxins" in the urine, and testing examinees for IgG to mold. In truth, none of these techniques have been validated, nor do they have any relevance to any clinical disease. All that these tests that are being performed by laboratories of disrepute does is to further propagate misinformation and inflict unnecessary and often exorbitant costs on examinees desperate for a clinical diagnosis, right or wrong, for their constellation of maladies.
>
> (Chang & Gershwin, 2019)

It is critical to understand that even if mold is present in the environment (which it almost certainly is), that fact alone does not indicate mycotoxicosis:

> There is always a little mold everywhere - in the air and on many surfaces. There are very few reports that toxigenic molds found inside homes can cause unique or rare health conditions such as pulmonary hemorrhage or memory loss. These case reports are rare, and a causal link between the presence of the toxigenic mold and these conditions has not been proven.
>
> (CDC, 2022)

The neuropsychologist presented with blood or antibody tests purporting documentation of mold exposure should be aware that there is no agreed-upon link between home or workplace mold exposure and neurologic or neuropsychological impairment, and no dose–response relationship has been identified (Reinhard et al., 2007).

Cases presenting for neuropsychological examination often have complex medical histories, and the neuropsychologist asked to determine diagnosis may be confronted with complex medical and toxicologic differential diagnostic issues. The following case is presented as an example.

The Case of Ms. M

Background

The examinee was in her early 60s at the time she presented for neuropsychological evaluation. She claimed chronic toxic mold-related symptoms related to working in an office. The office was reportedly found to have mold behind the walls, with subsequent abatement conducted, but the examinee continued to claim chronic and worsening problems from this exposure despite having left her employment where the exposure occurred. A mold analysis of her home detected *Penicillium* and *Cladosporium*, neither of which are neurotoxic.

Her pre-claim history, dating back approximately ten years before her litigated claim, was remarkable for rheumatoid arthritis and lupus. However, records did not include formal test results for either disorder. She was not taking lupus medications at the time of her litigation. Records also included a history of non-cardiac chest and knee pain, along with wrist swelling and headache, all attributed to lupus. The examinee's past medical history was positive for hypertension and hypercholesterolemia, and she had been prescribed Losartan and Pravastatin; possible mild obstructive airway disease was suggested. She had a strong family history of cardiovascular disease in both parents and a brother who had a heart attack before age 60. Of note, her son died of T cell lymphoma at age 13. A psychiatrist recorded that the examinee had been treated for depression following the death of her 13-year-old son, and had taken medications for panic attacks on the anniversaries of his death.

Additional pre-mold exposure records revealed that on one occasion, the examinee presented to an emergency room with slurred speech, blurred vision, shortness of breath, and dizziness that were attributed to anxiety. Records showed that on an additional exam, her cerebellar exam and Rhomberg tests were negative except for "astasia/abasia" (unusual and dramatic gait disturbance that is usually of psychological origin).

Approximately four years prior to her current neuropsychological evaluation, the examinee engaged an attorney and consulted with a physician and an industrial hygienist who were retained, per the attorney,

> in order to determine whether or not there is a causal connection between mold in the work environment and her development of disease including of perennial allergic rhinitis, alopecia, irritated eyes, and skin rash as well as symptoms of bi-frontal headache, joint pain, myalgia, malaise, fatigue, dyspnea, poor memory, and loss of focus;

the consultants provided reports linking mold exposure to these symptoms.

The attorney's industrial hygienist concluded that

> ....these manifestations of disease due to mold exposure are well known to be caused by exposure of persons to a mold-contaminated environment (Mold Remediation in Schools and Commercial Buildings. United States Environmental Protection Agency. Office of Air and Radiation. Indoor Environments Division. EPA 402-K-01-001. March 2001). Despite an extensive work-up, there is no alternative explanation other than occupational mold exposure.

This was disputed by an opposing expert industrial hygienist, who noted that the first expert did not provide information of actual mold exposure, or quantitative measurement of mold levels. He pointed out that the only formal mold testing data showed no statistically significant differences between indoor and outdoor airborne mold count. He noted that the first hygienist compared the examinee's symptoms to those experienced by industrial hazard workers, whose exposures were unrelated to the examinee's.

The same year, the examinee consulted with a physician and brought in an evaluation from an "agency" purporting to have measured her mold exposure. She expressed concern that she had a disseminated fungal infection. That physician reviewed the report, which concluded the examinee was "exposed to high levels of Penicillium, Alternaria, and other hyphal elements," however the consulting physician doubted she had an active disseminating fungal infection. He performed new blood tests and found all results were negative except for elevated angiotensin-converting enzyme (ACE). An MRI scan showed a Chiari I malformation with obliteration of the cerebrospinal fluid (CSF) space, and her primary care physician attributed her headaches to this cause. He noted that while she had been seen by multiple doctors, none felt there was a toxic etiology to her symptoms and that there was no neurologic disability from any alleged toxic exposure to mold. The examinee continued to see different physicians; one report suggested Eustachian tube dysfunction and another suggested that bright red bowel movements were likely the result of "an inflammatory response." A physician's assistant hypothesized that some of the examinee's symptoms may be related to hormonal fluctuations.

This did not convince the examinee, and she continued to claim symptoms of mold neurotoxicity. She told another physician that an infectious disease doctor had informed her she had "fungus" in her chest and she was afraid there was something dormant in her chest that would worsen; she stated that she was "afraid of what is dormant in my blood system from these devastating toxins."

A psychiatrist, seen on referral from plaintiff's attorney, found poor concentration with memory at 1/3 at 3 minutes. He diagnosed the examinee with depression due to mold exposure, anxiety due to mold exposure, cognitive disorder not otherwise specified (NOS) due to mold exposure, amnestic disorder due to mold exposure, sleep disorder due to mold exposure, and adjustment disorder with mixed anxiety and depressed mood, and that the examinee had "severe toxicities due to mold exposure, including pulmonary, dermatologic, ocular, fatigue, other symptoms." He opined that

> the association between chronic mold or other toxic exposure and depression, anxiety, and cognitive disturbance is well known and clearly described...Dr. Ritchie Shoemaker of the Virginia Institute of Neuropsychiatry has noted that "Mold Illnesses are caused by exposure to water-damaged buildings containing toxigenic organisms. These organisms can cause ... chronic Inflammatory response syndrome, symptoms (of which) Include but are not limited to: fatigue, weakness, muscle cramps, unusual pain, headache, light sensitivity, red eyes, blurred vision, tearing, sinus problems, cough, shortness of breath, abdominal pain, diarrhea, memory Issues, focal/concentration issues, word recollection issues, decreased learning of new knowledge, confusion, disorientation, skin sensitivity, mood swings, appetite swings, and sweats" http.vaneuropsychiatry.org/mold-exposure. Dr. Shoemaker and others have determined components of the chronic inflammatory response that promote inflammatory spread into the brain thereby correlating with depression, anxiety, cognitive deficits, fatigue, and, not uncommonly, symptoms of post-traumatic stress disorder.[1]

The psychiatrist also concluded that the examinee

> suffers from significant symptoms of depression, anxiety, and cognitive dysfunction including memory loss, diminished concentration and loss of executive functioning. It Is my professional medical opinion to a high degree of medical certainty that these symptoms are the direct result of her exposure to mold in the workplace.

Neuropsychological Evaluation

Interview

My own examination of the examinee was conducted approximately five to seven years after the alleged mold exposure, upon referral by an attorney defending the workplace mold claim. Asked about her current symptoms, the examinee asserted that they were worsening, which she blamed on a lack of effective mold treatment:

> "the last 2–3 years my memory is getting worse." "The doctors say it's my fog and neurological degenerative cognitive deficits. It means that my mind is cognitively regressing. They said it's as a result of a toxicity in my body and from reports that this is evidence of the mold toxins. They can cause neurological deterioration."

The examinee described that she became lost easily if she attempted to drive and that she became panicked if she drove too far from home. She reported having "constant headaches" that

> the clinic is telling me are progressive because of the mycotoxin and it won't go away. The clinic found mycotoxins in my body and I guess that's why I can't get better. If you have been diagnosed and it's positive and no-one seems to care about treating you.

The examinee stated that she was "so angry" that the "very expensive" treatments recommended for mycotoxins had not been approved.

Regarding other medical conditions aside from claimed lupus and rheumatoid arthritis discussed above, the examinee reported that she was being treated for hypertension and that her general practitioner recently doubled her dose of an antihypertensive. I confirmed that the examinee was still exhibiting hypertensive blood pressure readings, by testing her blood pressure in my office with an electronic cuff (144/76, pulse 82). The examinee informed me that her cholesterol levels were "in the 300s" recently, but that she did not wish to take cholesterol-lowering medication and was trying to watch her diet. She also reported a "very high ACE level."[2]

Behavioral Observations

The examinee did not appear to be depressed or anxious, but was fixated on mycotoxins as the cause of her perceived cognitive and emotional deterioration, claiming she had been told this with certainty by her physicians. She refused to leave the office during lunch, stating she would be unable to find her way back. She had no visual or auditory hallucinations or delusions per se, but repeatedly returned to the idea that "mycotoxins" had caused, and continued to cause, her cognitive and emotional deterioration. Her mental status was generally unremarkable, but thought processes were personalized and perseverative.

Test Results

Performance Validity

Exaggerated responses on *PVTs* (tests assessing for accuracy of cognitive test results) and *symptom validity tests* (SVTs; tests assessing for veracity of symptom report) are the "lens" through which the accuracy of the neuropsychological and/or psychological evaluation must be viewed. Skewed results on PVTs and/or SVTs indicate some degree of symptom portrayal distortion and in such a case, the individual's conventional test results and their self-report of symptoms become unreliable as an index of actual impairment.

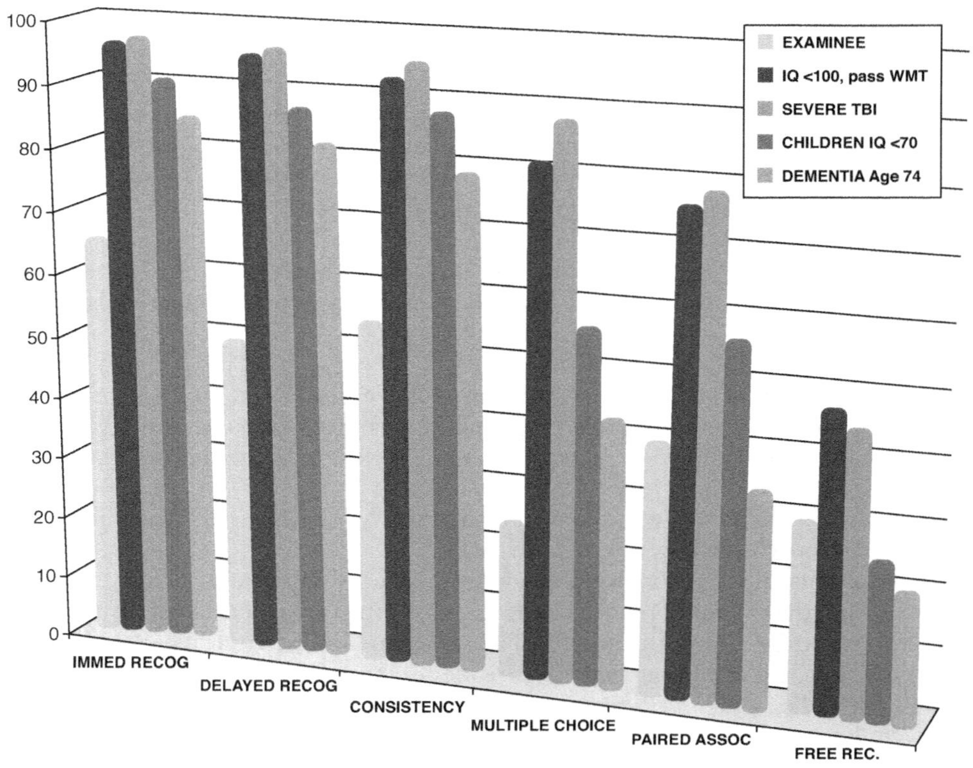

Figure 16.1 Word Memory Test scores compared with clinical reference groups. The examinee's performance falls below that typically observed in severe neurological populations, supporting non-credible cognitive test performance.

In the current evaluation, the examinee produced non-credible scores on PVTs, including the *Word Memory Test* (WMT). As shown in the graph, this examinee performed with lower accuracy on the WMT than do examinees with severe brain injury, or hospitalized examinees with dementia in their 70s, and even lower than intellectually disabled children. Her results are quite unlikely for an ambulatory individual who was able to participate and follow directions during a full-day neuropsychological assessment.

Similar results were displayed on the *Computerized Assessment of Response Bias*, another freestanding PVT. The examinee answered fewer items correctly than do populations recovering from severe traumatic brain injury or who have severe neurologic disease (see graph). Her performance was characterized by the test as being in the range of "very poor effort," and very far below normal controls or persons with frank brain impairment. Qualitatively, scores worsened across three blocks of items, after the examinee was told that the test might become more difficult (although there was no actual or appreciable change in difficulty over test blocks). This suggests that she was attempting to adjust her level of performance in response to what she thought should occur in examinees with brain dysfunction related to mold exposure, and which argues that the change in her test-taking behavior was volitional.

The examinee's Reliable Digit Span score, a measure of attention/working memory plausibility, was 6, a range that most research would classify as nonplausible (Babikian et al., 2006; Schroeder et al., 2012).

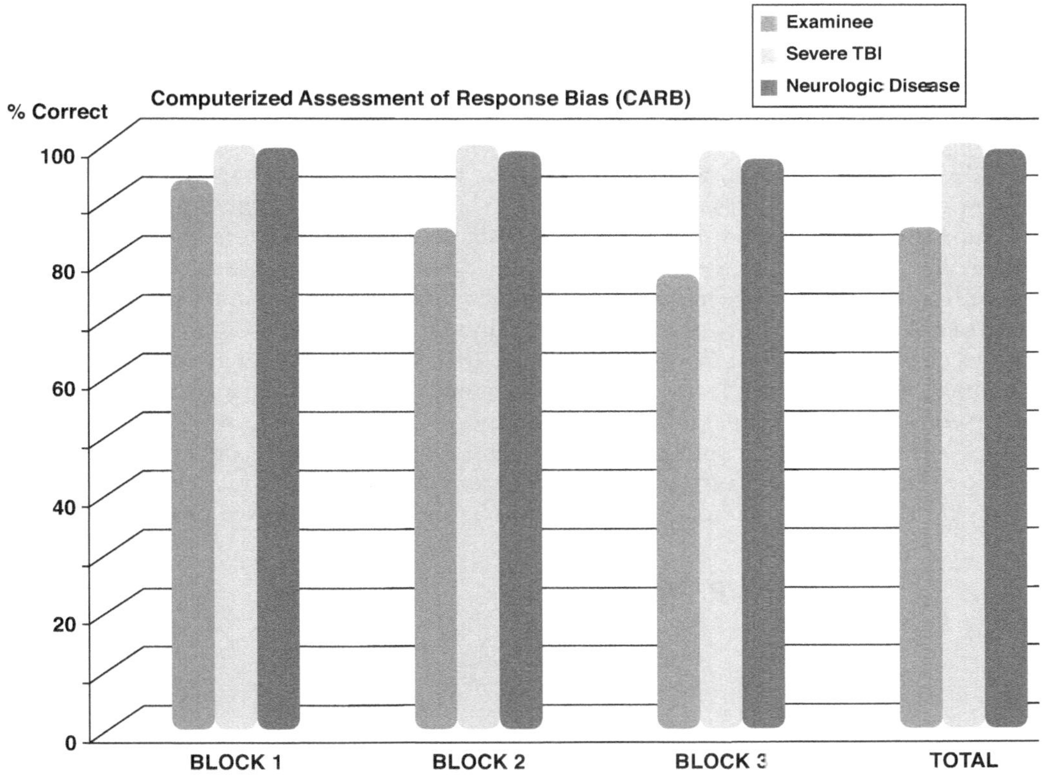

Figure 16.2 The examinee's CARB results compared to severe TBI and neurologic disease group scores.

Symptom Validity

As shown in the graph below, the examinee's MMPI-2RF was remarkable for extreme elevations on several validity scales, indicating likely over-report psychiatric (F-r) and memory/cognitive (RBS) symptoms. Exaggeration was not attributable to random responding or failure to comprehend item content (see TRIN-r and VRIN-r). Likewise, her symptom validity (FBS) score was at the test cut-off for implausible physical and cognitive symptom patterns associated with litigation. The first two diagnostic considerations provided by the test publisher were "Malingering of emotional symptoms" and "Malingering of cognitive/memory symptoms." The examinee's clinical elevations, of doubtful validity considering her elevated F-r, included very high levels of anxiety and depression. She was not observed to be either depressed or anxious during a full-day examination.

Other signs of exaggerated symptom endorsements were found on the *Battery for Health Improvement*-2 (BHI-2), where her overall presentation was unusually pathological. The BHI-2, which examines patterns of biopsychosocial symptom endorsements in examinees with medical conditions, revealed an extreme level of somatic complaints, higher than 99% of credible examinees. She endorsed 23 of the 26 Somatic Complaints items and reported severe peak pain. Her level of complaint would be consistent with extreme preoccupation with physical functioning and hypochondriacal hypervigilance. She endorsed a higher level of problems than would be seen in 87% of clinical examinees and even higher than 72% of examinees *asked to fake bad* on this test.

The examinee's level of "Symptom Dependency" on the BHI-2 was higher than 98% of credible examinees; examinees with scores at this level use symptoms to manipulate environmental support, have entitled expectations, and assert that their condition is of such severity they cannot be expected to cope on their own. She also agreed to a statement regarding whether she is entitled to financial compensation for her injury. The examinee voiced extreme dissatisfaction with her doctors, and animosity toward the medical profession generally. BHI-2 results indicated that she likely blames continuing problems on incompetent treatment and that doctors are collaborating with payors and employers to dismiss her complaints. Scores at this level predict that it is unlikely that she would cooperate with treatment recommendations that conflict with her demands and expectations.

On a self-report inventory of memory complaints Green's Memory Complaints Inventory, endorsement patterns were much more extreme than would be found among women with neurological disease or moderate-to-severe brain injury. She produced an extreme symptom endorsement on items alleging that memory difficulties interfere with work. This was considered self-serving in the context of litigation and a claim of permanent work disability.

The examinee was also administered the *Structured Inventory of Malingered Symptomatology* (SIMS), which contains a mix of realistic and implausible symptoms, and which

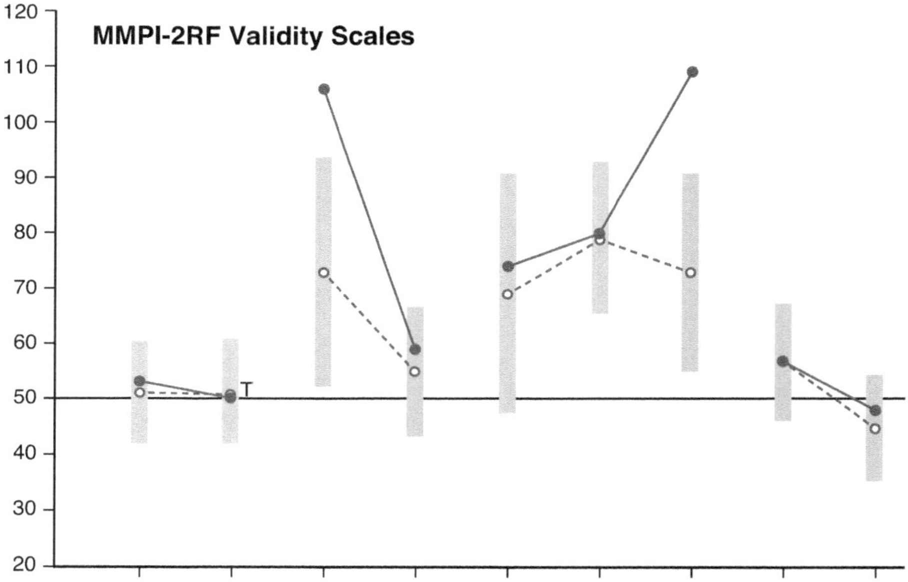

	VRIN	TRIN-r	F-r	Fp-r	Fs	FBS-r	RBS	L-r	K-r
Raw Score	4	11	14	2	4	17	19	4	7
T Score:	53	50	**106**	59	**74**	**80**	**109**	57	48
Comparison Group Data:	Forensic, Disability Claimant (Women), N=480								
Mean Score:	51	51T	73	55	69	79	73	57	45
Standard Dev:	9	10	21	12	22	14	18	11	10
Percent scoring at or below test taker:	71	35	93	79	69	55	97	63	90

Figure 16.3 MMPI-2-RF validity profile. Elevated validity scales indicate substantial over-reporting of symptoms.

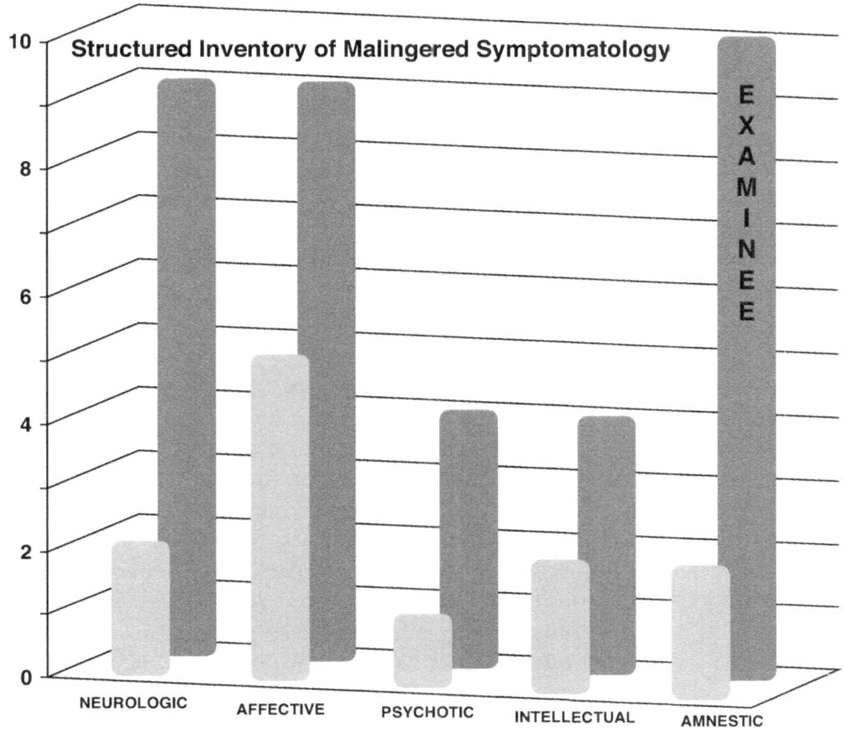

Figure 16.4 SIMS profile with elevated scores across multiple symptom domains.

yields a summary score of general feigning (Total score), and five scales of commonly exaggerated symptom domains: (a) Neurologic, (b) Affective, (c) Psychotic, (c) Low Intelligence, and (e) Amnestic (memory-related). Her SIMS Total Score was several times the test manual exaggeration cut-off and above most subsequent cut-off recommendations, even when considering ongoing medical disorders unrelated to mold exposure. Her highly elevated *Amnestic* (memory-related) subscale, in combination with failed memory-related PVTs, clearly represented exaggerated complaints (see the graph).

Standard Neurocognitive Scores

Because conventional neuropsychological and psychological test results require good cooperation and honest response set to be clinically interpretable, the examinee's repeated PVT failures and non-credible over-report of cognitive/memory symptoms indicate that lowered cognitive scores cannot be accepted as accurate, although normal range scores can be used to document intact skill areas (though in the context of failed PVTs, even normal range scores may underrepresent actual abilities).

On the *Shipley-2*, which estimates general intelligence, the examinee displayed normal vocabulary (94) and visual-spatial manipulation (Block Patterns = 97) but borderline-low average word and number abstraction skills (79). In a 5-part variation of the trail-making tests (*Comprehensive Trail-making Test*), her performance was in the average range for the first three, easier subtests (T53, T55, T45) and low average on the last two, more difficult variations (T44; T43).

On the *Stroop Test (Golden version)*, word reading speed was low average (T42), while speeded color naming was in the mildly impaired range (T36). When instructed to inhibit a reading response, the examinee showed moderately impaired results (T29).

The examinee was also administered the *Wisconsin Card Sorting Test* (WCST), a measure of perseveration and abstract concept formation. She was not unduly perseverative, but made five failures to maintain a correct problem-solving set (FMS); this has been termed "the most common strategy" of malingering for the WCST (i.e., to "avoid too many consecutive correct responses"; Sweet & Nelson, 2007).

Maze completion time on the Neuropsychological Assessment Battery-Screening Module was low average (T44, 27th percentile) while NAB Screening verbal fluency (Word Generation) was in the borderline range (T33, 4th percentile).

Fine motor speed and coordination on a pegboard task (Grooved Pegboard, Heaton norms) were low average bilaterally for the dominant hand (T41) and above average (T61) for the non-dominant hand. Dynamometer hand grip strength was average for the dominant hand (T47) and low average for the non-dominant hand (T41).

Surprisingly, in the context of failed PVTs, recognition memory for abstract designs was normal on the Neuropsychological Assessment Battery-Screening Module's Shape Learning-Delayed Recognition (T48; 42nd percentile) and recall of a brief story paragraph was in the low average range (NAB Screening Module = T43, 24th percentile). Block pattern construction on the NAB Screening Module was low average (Design Construction = T43, 24th percentile) and ability to discriminate small differences among abstract designs was better than average (NAB Screening Module Visual Discrimination T59, 82nd percentile).

Interpretation of Test Results

The examinee exhibited exaggerated and unrealistic test patterns on neuropsychological and psychological tests indicating that her cognitive performance and symptom self-report is not a valid presentation of her condition and should not be relied upon, and that even in the context of what may be a set of legitimately significant chronic medical conditions unrelated to mold exposure, her presentation was considered extreme and non-credible. While repeatedly exaggerated test results do not rule out underlying cognitive or emotional difficulties, her multiple non-credible results obscure and render speculative any difficulties that she may actually have.

Summary and Conclusions

Causes of Cognitive Dysfunction Separate from Claimed Mold Exposure

This case is interesting from a number of standpoints. First, the examinee may have suffered from several medical conditions capable of producing chronic neuropsychological and psychological symptoms of ill-being separate from the question of exposure to mold. Her diagnosis of systemic lupus erythematosus (SLE), if accurate, indicated an autoimmune disorder that can be multisystemic, and produce a wide range of neuropsychological and psychiatric symptoms. Cognitive function

> as measured by formal neurocognitive testing in the clinical domains of attention, memory, processing speed, executive function, motor, and global neurocognitive function in

> SLE examinees is markedly and significantly impaired compared to controls even after simultaneously adjusting for education, pre-morbid intelligence, and depression index.
> (Roldan et al., 2018)

The examinee was also diagnosed with rheumatoid arthritis, which may overlap with her SLE diagnosis, and which has also been documented in research as leading to cognitive decline (e.g., 30% of examinees with rheumatoid arthritis have cognitive impairments; Appenzeller et al., 2004).

The examinee's incidental finding of Chiari Type I Malformation (CM1), a developmental structural brain abnormality, documented displacement of the cerebellar tonsils through the foramen magnum into the spinal canal. CM1 is associated with both cognitive and emotional impairments, including those related to learning, memory, speech fluency, pattern copying, anxiety, and depression (Derevyanko, 2022), and executive function, copy accuracy, visual and verbal memory, naming, processing speed, facial recognition, and theory of mind (Garcia et al., 2018). CM1 causes a range of symptoms that may be mistaken for concussion or other nonspecific brain injuries and physicians are advised to "be aware of CMI as a potential underlying cause of persistent symptoms unresponsive to typical management" (Linsenmeyer et al., 2020).

The examinee additionally has other medical conditions associated with cognitive decline, including hypertension (Carrion-Barbera et al., 2021). Hypertension by itself can contribute to progressive cognitive impairment (Birns et al., 2009; Meyer et al , 2000) with reductions in cerebral blood flow, metabolism, and cognitive function (Fujishima et al., 1995), and is associated with greater cortical atrophy in older adults (Heijer et al., 2003). Hypertension is also frequently associated with depressive disorder, stress-related complaints, and somatoform disorders (Cha & Kim, 2021).

The examinee's reportedly high levels of total cholesterol are also considered a marker for cognitive decline and impairment (Muldoon et al., 2001). Further, the examinee's blood test results were being considered for Sjogren's syndrome, another autoimmune rheumatic disease that produces arthralgia, arthritis, and cardiovascular damage (Lv et al., 2021), and impairments of multiple neuropsychological functions (Indart et al., 2017; Jennings et al., 2010).

The Role of Expert Differential Diagnosis

Every examinee requires expert clinical differential diagnosis (Hartman, 2018); examinees referred for neuropsychological assessment rarely present with a pristine clinical record and a single cause for their symptom presentation. It is always the task of expert neuropsychological assessment to treat the examinee's asserted complaint as a *hypothesis* rather than a proven cause, even when previous clinical opinions support the reported condition. Expert neuropsychologists must carefully review prior diagnoses and their bases, maintaining awareness that other clinicians may have blurred the line between science and *advocacy*. Neuropsychologists must review records to determine if clinical diagnoses were based on objective data or simply examinee insistence that a single event was the primary basis for their symptoms. None of the case example's clinical advocates reported having attempted differential diagnosis of her symptoms, or integrating her pre-claim history of autoimmune disorder and other medical and psychiatric conditions with her current presentation, or checking for performance and symptom validity. Their argument of temporal contiguity between symptoms and mold exposure is also a logical fallacy; that of *post hoc ergo propter hoc*—something that came before must be the cause. The argument is fallacious because contiguity is insufficient to infer medical causality, and logically flawed by failure to consider that the examinee had a variety of conditions capable of individually and collectively contributing to significant clinical ill-being. Objectively, this examinee's clinical records repeatedly demonstrated markers of chronic progressive medical conditions unrelated to her claim of toxic mold exposure, but no internal diagnostic markers of mold toxicity.

Expert neuropsychological assessment must also weigh the value of science behind the diagnosis. In this case, there is good science to support the likelihood this examinee has chronic impairments from multiple vascular, developmental, and autoimmune-related etiologies. In contrast, while mold has been blamed for a constellation of symptoms

> there is no scientific evidence that mold has anything to do with these symptoms. In particular, the concept of toxic mold syndrome has permeated the public consciousness, and mycotoxins have falsely been associated with autoimmune diseases and a variety of other conditions. In fact, there is no evidence that the presence of mycotoxins in the air is enough to cause any disease known to man.
>
> (Chang & Gershwin, 2019)

The Role of Somatization and Iatrogenesis

A separate question revolves around why this examinee is fixated on toxic mold being the cause of her numerous complaints. One possible psychological consideration is Somatoform/Somatic Symptom Disorder, in which individuals magnify the significance of minor physical sensations, are preoccupied with illness despite normal laboratory findings, and view themselves as more dysfunctional than is actually the case. The examinee's endorsement of severe complaint in almost every physical domain measured by Battery for Health Improvement-2 describes someone claiming global impairments that were not validated by objective medical or neuropsychological testing. Somatoform presentations have been described in the context of claimed toxic mold (Stone et al., 2006), as well as some of the other conditions the examinee reported that she has been diagnosed with (e.g., lupus; Barbosa et al., 2010).

Iatrogenesis is another potential explanation for why an examinee would insist on this presentation. On interview, this examinee reported being told by treating physicians that mycotoxins were the cause of her cognitive and emotional deterioration. When examinees are told, incorrectly, that they have particular conditions causing various symptoms, they may adopt this flawed hypothesis as part of their identity; a fixed belief based on their perception that physicians are knowledgeable and reliable diagnosticians. If, however, examinees encounter clinicians who are "true believers" in a syndrome despite weak science, or clinics whose motivation is profit-taking from a vulnerable population, these examinees may be encouraged to believe their subjective misery has a rare and expensive treatable cause.

The malign result is an examinee who believes that the true cause of their problems requires expensive and unnecessary treatment, and that physicians who identify their actual medical conditions are perceived as denying the "toxic mold" care she demands. The secondary pernicious effect of being trapped in a true believer's web is that potentially treatable medical conditions are ignored; the examinee will be unlikely to cooperate with treatment recommendations that conflict with her demands and expectations. Treaters who reinforce her beliefs about toxic mold have iatrogenically caused her to endorse a hypothetical disease for which there is no treatment, and reject treatment for health conditions that could conceivably be managed.

Deliberate Misrepresentation of Symptoms

While this examinee's presentation has strong somatoform and iatrogenic components, her multiple extreme failures on PVTs, and marked nonplausible over-report of psychiatric and cognitive symptoms on objective personality testing, would point to deliberate misrepresentation of function. Research shows that it is rare for examinees with somatoform disorder to fail more than one PVT (Kemp et al., 2008). The examinee appears to be shaping her cognitive test performance to suit her belief system, which is concurrently "validated" by plaintiff experts and her attorney.

Neuropsychologists examining a similar examinee would justifiably conclude that it is difficult to determine extent and severity of actual cognitive or psychological impairments in an examinee with this degree of objective exaggeration and misrepresentation. However, it would be a mistake to toss the examinee out as a malingerer and fail to comment on the likelihood that her medical conditions of record and traumatic psychological experiences (i.e., death of her son) do predict cognitive inefficiencies, depression, anxiety, and poor quality of life. Her over-reported and exaggerated presentation prevents exact measurement of these difficulties, but they are likely present, even if obscured by exaggeration.

It is easier to determine what this examinee does *not* have a "toxic mold" syndrome. Her records contained no evidence of physiological mold toxicity. The examinee's assertion of toxic mold slowing growing inside her chest appears more delusional than rational. With the encouragement of litigation and flawed diagnostic advocates, it seems unlikely that she could be convinced to consider alternative explanations or treatments that would reduce progression of her symptoms. The examinee's concrete, possibly delusional assertions of injury, clinician support, and litigation reinforcement, make for a poor prognosis.

This case illustrates the need for a thorough knowledge of medical neuropsychology, and understanding that a fashionable, litigation-friendly "illness" is not the same as a valid diagnosis. All clinical records related to past diagnoses should be examined for objective adequacy. If studies are cited, those studies should be reviewed for their relationship to the examinee in question and for whether the published conclusions meet *Frye and Daubert* acceptance. Neuropsychologists must always be aware that differential diagnosis of complex cases is nuanced, and attempt, as best they are able, to provide a well-reasoned, scientifically-based assessment of these unusual cases. This case also illustrates the understanding that failure of validity assessment does not rule out the presence of actual cognitive and/or psychological pathology; that PVT/SVT failure obscures, but does not erase, possible underlying symptoms, severity, and origin.

Notes

1 *But see* Philpots, B. H. (2014). Recent Developments: Chesson v. Montgomery Mut. Ins. Co.: Expert Testimony Based on Novel Scientific Methodology Failed to Meet the Frye-Reed Threshold for General Acceptance Because of a Fundamental Divergence of Opinion in the Scientific Community about the Validity of the Methodology and Flaws in the Underlying Analysis. *University of Baltimore Law Forum, 44*, 207–209 where "The court evaluated the expert testimony and scientific literature proffered by both parties and determined that Dr. Shoemaker's methodology was controversial and not generally accepted within the relevant scientific field. Id. at 373–79, 75 A.3d at 947–51. Perhaps most damaging, in light of the fact that the 2014] Chesson v. Montgomery Mut. Ins. Co. 209 causes of action arose in 2002, Dr. Shoemaker acknowledged in a co-authored 2005 paper that his causal theory linking mold exposure to non-respiratory symptoms was controversial and not generally accepted."

2 High ACE (angiotensin converting enzyme) levels can be associated with sarcoidosis, Gaucher disease, leprosy, untreated hyperthyroidism, mycobacterial disease, lymphangiomyomatosis,

diabetes mellitus with severe retinopathy and osteoarthritis, alcoholic cirrhosis, primary biliary cirrhosis, inflammatory bowel disease, coccidioidomycosis, berylliosis, histoplasmosis, silicosis, asbestosis, hyperthyroidism and miliary tuberculosis. journals.lww.com/ lungindia/fulltext/ 2004/21040/ diagnosing_ sarcoidosis___what_is_the_value_of.1.aspx

References

Appenzeller, S., Bertolo, M. B., and Costallat, L. T. (2004). Cognitive impairment in rheumatoid arthritis. *Methods and Findings in Experimental and Clinical Pharmacology, 26*(5), 339–343.

Babikian, T., Boone, K. B., Lu, P., & Arnold, G. (2006). Sensitivity and specificity of various digit span scores in the detection of suspect effort. *The Clinical Neuropsychologist, 20*(1), 145–159.

Barbosa, F., Ferreira, C., Patricio, P., Mota, C., Alcantara, C., and Barbosa, A. (2010). Attachment style in examinees with systemic lupus erythematosus. *Acta Medica Portuguesa, 23*(1), 51–62.

Barnes, C. (2019). Fungi and atopy. *Clinical Reviews in Allergy and Immunology*, https://doi.org/10.1007/ s12016-019-08750-z

Birns, J., Morris, R., Jarosz, J., Markus, H. S., and Karla, L. (2009). Hypertension-related cognitive decline: Is the right time for intervention studies? *Minerva Cardioangiologica, 57*, 813–830.

Borchers, A. T., Chang, C., and Gershwin, M. E. (2017). Mold and human health: A reality check. *Clinical Reviews in Allergy and Immunology, 52*, 305–322.

Carrion-Barbera, I., Salman-Monte, T. C., Vilchez-Oya, F., and Monfort, J. (2021). Neuropsychiatric involvement in systemic lupus erythematous: A review, *Autoimmunity Reviews, 20*, 102780.

Centers for Disease Control and Prevention. (2022). Facts about stachybotrys chartarum. https://www.cdc.gov/mold/stachy.htm

Cha, S., and Kim, S-S. (2021). Comorbidity patterns of mood disorders in adult inexaminees: Applying Association rule mining. *Healthcare, 9*, 1–16.

Chang, C., and Gershwin, M. E. (2019). The myth of mycotoxins and mold injury. *Clinical Reviews in Allergy and Immunology, 57*, 449–455.

Choudhuri, S. (2021). Food toxicology: Fundamental and regulatory Aspects. In Klaassen, C. D., and Watkins, J. B. (Eds.). *Casarett & Doutll's Essentials of Toxicology*, 4th Edition. New York: McGraw Hill, 498–499.

Cornish, E. (Sept. 11 2017 web blog). Toxic mold syndrome: "It was like I lost my personality". https://www.amenclinics.com/blog/toxic-mold-syndrome-it-was-like-i-lost-my-personality/

Davison, K. (1976). Drug induced psychoses and their relationship to schizophrenia. In Kemali, D., Bartholini, G., and Richter, D. (Eds.). *Schizophrenia Today*. Elmsford, New York, Pergamon Press, 105–134.

Derevyanko, K. (2022) Neurocognitive and psycho-emotional disorders in examinees with Chiari Malformation Type I. *Neurology, 98*, 18 supplement 10.1212/WNL.98.18_supplement.2978.

Empting, L. D. (2009). Neurologic and neuropsychiatric syndrome features of mold and mycotoxin exposure. *Toxicology and Industrial Health, 24*, 577–581.

Fujishima, M., Ibayashi, S., Fujii, K., and Mori, S. (1995). Cerebral blood flow and brain function in hypertension. *Hypertension Research, 18*, 111–117.

Gabbai, D. r., Lisbonne, D. r., and Pourquier, D. r. (1951). Ergot poisoning at Pont St. Esprit. *British Medical Journal, 2*(4732), 650–651.

Garcia, M., Lazaro, E., Lopez-Paz, J. F. et al. (2018). Cognitive functioning in Chiari Malformation Type I without posterior fossa surgery. *The Cerebellum, 17*, 564–574.

Goralska, K., Blaszkowska, J., and Dzikowiec, M. (2018). Neuroinfections caused by fungi. *Infection, 46*, 443–459.

Hartman, D. E. (1998). Missed diagnoses and misdiagnoses of environmental toxicant exposure: The psychiatry of toxic exposure and multiple chemical sensitivity. *Psychiatric Clinics of North America, 21*(3), 659–670.

Hartman, D. E. (2018). Differential diagnosis in neuropsychology: A strategic approach. In Morgan, J., and Ricker, J. (Eds.). *Textbook of Clinical Neuropsychology*, 2nd Edition. New York: Routledge, 51–61.

Haschek, W. M., Voss, K. A., and Beasley, V. R. (2002). Selected mycotoxins affecting animal and human health. In Haschek, W. M., Wallig, M. A., and Rousseau, C. G. (Eds.). *Handbook of Toxicologic Pathology*,2nd Edition. New York: Academic Press, 645.

Heijer, T., Skoog, I., Oudkerk, M., de Leeuw, F. E., de Groot, J. C., Hofman, A., and Breteler, M. M. (2003). Association between blood pressure levels over time and brain atrophy in the elderly. *Neurobiology of Aging, 24*, 307–313.

Indart, S., Hugon, J., Guillausseau, P. J., Gilbert, A., Dumurgler, J., Paquet, C., and Sene, D. (2017). Impact of pain on cognitive functions in primary Sjogren syndrome with small fiber neuropathy: 10 cases and a literature review. *Medicine* (Baltimore), *96, e6384*, 1–6.

Jennings, T., Vivino, F., Mandel, S., Goldberg, K., Maitz, E., and Boyer, B. (2010). Neuropsychological impairments in females with primary Sjogren's Syndrome: New Insights. *Practical Neurology, 10*, 15–19.

Johnson, D. (undated blog). Is mold causing your chronic fatigue? *Johnson Center for Health, Integrative and Functional Medicine.* https://www.drbarbarajohnson.com/blog/is-mold-causing-your-chronic-fatigue.

Kemp, S., Coughlan, A. K., Rowbottom, C., Wilkinson, K., Teggart, V., & Baker, G. (2008). The base rate of effort test failure in patients with medically unexplained symptoms. *Journal of Psychosomatic Research, 65*(4), 319–325.

Kwong, K., Robinson, M. Sullivan, A., Letovsky, S., Liu, A. H., and Valcour, A. (2023). Fungal allergen sensitization: Prevalence, risk factors and geographic variation in the United States. *Journal of Allergy and Clinical Immunology*, https://doi.org/10.1016/j.jaci.2023.03.010.

Lee, G. (2003). Activist Erin Brockovich settles suit over mold in Agoura Hills, California Home *Daily News*, (L.A.) September 16 2003, N4.

Lewis, A. S., and Oldham, M. A. (2015). Delusional infestation with black mold presenting to the general hospital. *Primary Care Companion CNS Disorders, 17*, https://doi.org/10.4088/PCC.14l01730.

Linsenmeyer, M., Combs, J., Kegel, N. E., and Franzese, K. (2020). Chiari malformation in the concussion clinic: Diagnosis and management of confounding and overlapping symptoms. *American Journal of Physical Medicine and Rehabilitation, 99*, 1074–1077.

Lv, Jaiqu, Ji, Xiaoxiao, J. Li, Zhen and Hao, H. (2021). The role of the cholinergic anti-inflammatory pathway in autimmune theumatic disease. *Scandinavian Journal of Immunology*, https://doi.org/10.1111 /sji.13092

McCaul, C., Boone, K. B., Ermshar, A., Cottingham, M., Victor, T. L., Ziegler, E., ... & Wright, M. (2018). Cross-validation of the Dot Counting Test in a large sample of credible and non-credible examinees referred for neuropsychological testing. *The Clinical Neuropsychologist*, *32*(6), 1054–1067.

Meyer, J. S., Rauch, G., Rauch, R. A., & Haque, A. (2000). Risk factors for cerebral hypoperfusion, mild cognitive impairment, and dementia. *Neurobiology of Aging, 21*(2), 161–169.

Muldoon, M. F., Flory, J. D., and Ryan, C. M. (2001). Serum cholesterol, the brain and cognition. In Waldstein, S. R., and Elias, M. F. (Eds.). *Neuropsychology of Cardiovascular Disease*. Mahwah, NJ: Erlbaum, 37–59.

NTES (undated) *https://national-toxic-encephalopathy-foundation.org*.

Perry, E. L. (2004). Why fear the fungus? Why toxic mold is and is not the next big toxic tort. https://digitalcommons.law.buffalo.edu/buffalolawreview/vol52/iss1/7 p. 257–299

Philpotts, B. H. (2014). Recent Developments: Chesson v. Montgomery Mut. Ins. Co.: Expert Testimony Based on Novel Scientific Methodology Failed to Meet the Frye-Reed Threshold for General Acceptance Because of a Fundamental Divergence of Opinion in the Scientific Community about the Validity of the Methodology and Flaws in the Underlying Analysis. In *University of Baltimore Law Forum* (Vol. 44, No. 2, p. 7).

Ratnaseelan, A. M., Tsilioni, I., and Theoharides, T. C., (2018). Effects of mycotoxins on neuropsychiatric symptoms and immune processes. *Clinical Therapeutics, 40*, 903–917.

Rea, W. J. (1992). *Chemical Sensitivity*, Vol. 1. Boca Raton, Florida, Lewis Publishers.

Reinhard, M. J., Satz, P., Scaglione, C. A., D'Elia, L. F., Rassovsky, Y., Arita, A. A., Hinkin, C. H., Thrasher, D., and Ordog, G. (2007). Neuropsychological exploration of alleged mold neurotoxicity. *Archives of Clinical Neuropsychology, 22*(4), 533–543.

Rhoads, T., Resche, Z. J., Oysiew, J., White, D. J., Abramson, D. A., and Soble, J. R. (2021). Every second sounds: A comparison of four dot counting test scoring procedures for detecting invalid neuropsychological test performance. *Psychological Assessment,* https://doi.org/10.1037/pas0000970

Roldan, P. C., Jung, R. E., Sibbitt, W. L., Quails, C. R., Flores, R. A., and Roldan, C. A. (2018). Correlation of neurocognitive function and brain lesion load on magnetic resonance imaging in systemic lupus erythematous. *Rheumatology International, 38,* 1539–1546.

Schroeder, R. W., Twumasi-Ankrah, P., Baade, L. E., & Marshall, P. S. (2012). Reliable digit span: A systematic review and cross-validation study. *Assessment, 19*(1), 21–30.

Simon-Nobbe, B., Denk, U., Poll, V., Rid, R., Breitenbach, M. (2007). The spectrum of fungal allergy. *International Archies of Allergy and Immunology, 145,* 58–86.

Singer, R. (March 7 2011, web blog) Chronic neurotoxicity from chronic mold exposure. https://neurotox.blogspot.com/2011/03/chronic-neurotoxicity-from-chronic-mold.html

Stone, D. C., Boone, K. B., Back-Madruga, C., & Lesser, I. M. (2006). Has the rolling uterus finally gathered moss? Somatization and malingering of cognitive deficit in six cases of "toxic mold" exposure. *The Clinical Neuropsychologist, 20*(4), 766–785.

Sweet, J., and Nelson, N. W. (2007). Validity indicators within executive function measures. In Boone, K. (Ed.). *Assessment of Feigned Cognitive Impairment,* New York: The Guilford Press, 152–177.

Terr, A. I. (2005). Toxic mold disease: A diagnosis of litigation. *Annals of Allergy, Asthma & Immunology, 95,* 215–216.

Weiner, H. M. (2010). Forensic approach to medical causation when allergic disease is in the differential diagnosis. *Allergy and Asthma Proceedings, 32,* 1–4.

Section III
Criminal Litigation

Neuropsychologists are increasingly being asked to participate in criminal litigation proceedings.

In contrast to civil litigation, the focus of matters on which neuropsychologists provide expert opinions in criminal proceedings is not damages, but instead on determining competency (e.g., competency to stand trial or to assist in one's defense), whether there should be relief from normal outcomes of conviction (e.g., guilt due to insanity, which might lead to hospitalization instead of prison), and mitigation in post-conviction sentencing (e.g., identifying an intellectual disability to avoid the death penalty). The chapters within this section provide examples of issues that are specific to neuropsychological examinations of criminal defendants. Readers will likely note that there are often different types of examinees in this setting as compared with civil litigation, including low baseline cognitive functioning and severe mental illness, characteristics that have to be carefully disentangled from any symptom misrepresentation related to the unique external incentives in criminal settings.

DOI: 10.4324/9781003005063-19

17 Prescriptions for Profit

The Hippocratic Oath on Trial

Robert L. Denney

Prescriptions for Profit: The Hippocratic Oath on Trial

Prescribing narcotics and anxiolytics can be a lucrative business. So-called "pill mills" or "narcotics mills" have contributed to the narcotic crisis in the United States, although they are far overshadowed by illegal fentanyl importation.[1] I have now been involved in several cases where physicians have ended their careers by the overzealous prescribing of narcotics. In some instances, it reflects the gradual loss of judgment by older physicians, and I have evaluated criminal defendants whose prescriptive behaviors, and/or billing behaviors, fell outside the norm because of poor judgment brought on by a gradual, but progressive, neurodegenerative disease. In some of these instances, the physicians meant well and did not even recognize the inappropriateness of their behavior. I have also examined physicians who appear to prescribe controlled medications in a manner suggestive of strictly financial gain, maybe to catch up from previous poor buying habits or inadequate retirement planning. I have also examined con artists who just happen to be licensed physicians. The case of Dr. Scott (a pseudonym) represents one of those situations listed above; I will let you contemplate which one.

Task at Hand

I was contacted by a U.S. Department of Justice (DOJ) trial lawyer and asked if I would review prior reports and then consider examining a 79-year-old physician who had been charged with four counts of health care fraud and six counts of distribution of controlled substance outside the usual course of professional practice and without legitimate medical purpose (hydrocodone, methadone, alprazolam, and amphetamine/dextroamphetamine). The forensic question included the nature of his cognitive functioning and diagnosis, if there was one, and most importantly, his competence to proceed with criminal adjudication.

U.S. Code, Title 18, Section 4241(a) spells out the statutory standard within the U.S. federal jurisdiction for determining the mental competency of the defendant: The defendant is presently "suffering from a mental disease or defect rendering him mentally incompetent to the extent that he is unable to understand the nature and consequences of the proceedings against him or to assist properly in his defense." This statutory language is very similar across U.S. state jurisdictions as all criminal competency definitions are largely based on the *Dusky* standard (*Dusky v United States*, 1960). That standard "must be whether [the] defendant has sufficient present ability to consult with his lawyer with a reasonable degree of rational understanding and whether he has a rational, as well as factual understanding, of the proceedings against him" (p. 402).

DOI: 10.4324/9781003005063-20

Role Clarification

After clarifying my role as a forensic examiner, outlining the costs of my professional time, and the fact that I would provide my best objective opinion on the issues irrespective of whether the ultimate opinion was favorable to the government's position, I was contracted with the DOJ. Clarifying and understanding our roles is important as will be demonstrated in this case. There is a big difference between a forensic examiner and a treatment expert (Bush et al., 2020; Saks, 1990). Both are experts but have different assumptions, alliances, roles, and oftentimes, methods (Denney & Wynkoop, 2000). Understanding these differences is important for ethical professional work that best gets at the truth of the matter and meets the needs of our client, in this case the attorney hiring the expert (and more broadly, the judicial system). It can also help keep well-meaning professionals from embarrassment (and potential ethical misstep) simply because they do not know any better.

The Case of Dr. Scott

Background

Dr. Scott was a right-handed, male who obtained an MD and PhD (biochemistry) from a reputable university and went on to specialize in internal medicine and developed a successful practice of 48 years. He was healthy throughout his life until, in his early 60s he fell and hit his head on a cupboard and lost consciousness. He awoke quickly, and his wife insisted he be evaluated. He indicated he was evaluated but not hospitalized. He returned to normal life and practice; sometime later, he said, it was found that he had experienced a subdural hematoma which had resolved on its own. He returned to full medical practice with no apparent sequelae. Medical, psychiatric, substance use, and legal histories were otherwise noncontributory. His only medications were atorvastatin 20 mg and 81 mg aspirin daily.

Neuroimaging records related to the brain trauma event became available and demonstrated that Dr. Scott underwent a brain MRI as a result of headache and "transient ischemic attack." The radiologist noted a crescent-shaped collection with hyperintense signal on T1 weighted and iso/hyperintense signal on T2 weighted images in the subdural space on the left side in the temporal and parietal–occipital region, which is suggestive of acute/subacute subdural bleed. There was also another much smaller subdural collection with similar signal characteristics on the right side in the parieto-occipital region. He underwent a head CT scan during the early evening of that same day. The radiologist provided the impression of a moderate amount of subacute subdural hematoma involving the left parietal–occipital and temporal region with minimal amount of subdural collection in the right parietal–occipital region. It was treated conservatively. Fourteen days later, he underwent a computer tomography angiogram which revealed no vascular abnormalities. The CT demonstrated minimal residual left frontoparietal convexity subdural hematoma with slight improvement noted compared with the prior study. Two-month follow-up CT scan revealed the previous left subdural hematoma had essentially resolved with very minimal residual collection measuring approximately 2–3 mm in width. The final impression was that the previous left subdural hematoma had essentially resolved.

Thirteen years after the subdural hematoma, Dr. Scott (now in his mid-70s) became aware that he was under investigation when the state medical board and Drug Enforcement Administration (DEA) investigators interviewed him, shut down his clinic, and sequestered his patient records. Over the course of the prior two years, there had been an undercover

DEA investigation that included patient interviews and a DEA agent acting as a patient (and videotaping the interactions). The investigation demonstrated that Dr. Scott often did not perform physical examinations and did not acquire past medical records, yet he assigned Chronic Pain Syndrome diagnoses based upon the self-reported pain complaints. Further, he would write and sign blank prescriptions for narcotic and anxiolytic medications that were then given to the front desk. His office staff would then fill out the details and hand the prescriptions to patients at the window. Citizens in the area understood this clinic to be the place to go in order to receive narcotic and anxiolytic medications with very little trouble.

Dr. Scott's wife of 25 years noted that she started seeing a change in his behavior the same year that he became aware of being investigated. She noted his memory deteriorated, and this was particularly obvious when they took a trip to Europe after he lost his practice. She said her husband seemed despondent and would get lost easily while they were walking around Europe. She said he had always been full of energy, ideas, and planning, but she began having to plan and make decisions for him.

Post Charges Examinations

I was provided access to defense expert reports, but the court ruled I was not to be provided with the raw data from those examinations. The court had erroneously concluded the only reason I needed that data was on suspicion of malingering rather than verification of proper test administration and scoring, and, consequently, found the "Government seeks extraordinary production of data without substantiating its need for it." Thus, I only had test scores as presented in reports and medical records for most examinations.

Dr. A, Neurologist

The behavioral changes noted by family resulted in Dr. Scott's adult son, who was also a physician, recommending he see a neurologist, Dr. A (after his practice was shut down). Under the cortical functions portion of the initial examination, Dr. Scott was noted to be oriented to person, place, and time. He was attentive. His long-term memory was considered intact. He had good judgment and insight. There was no evidence of constructional apraxia or visuospatial disorientation. His affect was appropriate. His general fund of knowledge was considered excellent. The neurological examination results were listed as normal except for mildly impaired vibration sense in both great toes and the absence of Achilles tendon reflex, bilaterally (findings suggestive of peripheral neuropathy).

Dr. Scott achieved a Montreal Cognitive Assessment (MoCA) score of 23/30. The raw testing was available for review. He missed one point for trail making, one naming item, one abstraction point, 3 of 5 points for words on free recall (recognition was not performed), and one point for date. Of note, missing the date on the MoCA was not consistent with being oriented to person, place, and time as mentioned during the higher cortical functions portion of the neurological examination.

Dr. Scott underwent brain MRI five days later for the purpose of apparent memory loss. The radiologist noted there were no indications of acute ischemic infarction. There was no indication of hemorrhage, mass effect, or midline shift. The expected prominence of ventricles, sulci, and basal cisterns from age-related parenchymal atrophy were apparent. The radiologist noted there were multiple focal areas of increased T2/FLAIR signal in the periventricular and subcortical white matter, compatible with chronic microvascular ischemic changes.

Dr. Scott underwent electroencephalogram the next day. The neurologist provided described a posterior dominant rhythm consisting of "five – seven CPS moderate voltage, semi-rhythmic theta activity," extending anteriorly into the biparietal head regions. Interestingly, he described the presence of varying low amplitude fast beta frequencies apparent in the anterior portion of the brain.

Neurologist, Dr. A, provided the diagnostic impression that this was an abnormal awake and drowsy recording because of diffuse theta slowing of the background rhythm in the bitemporal head regions. He noted it was compatible with a toxic, metabolic, or degenerative process.

The neurologist referred him for neuropsychological consultation under usual clinical reasons. Dr. B completed the examination over two sessions separated by four days. Unbeknownst to Dr. B, Dr. Scott's criminal defense lawyer also requested a cognitive assessment by a board-certified geropsychologist, Dr. C. This examination occurred the day after the first session by Dr. B.

Dr. B, Clinical Psychologist

In reviewing Dr. B's vita, it was noted that there was no formal training in neuropsychology and an educational history in educational and school psychology. Dr. B produced a report indicating she considered herself a neuropsychologist, though. She noted Dr. Scott was referred by his neurologist because of short-term memory issues. She was told by Dr. Scott and his family that they noticed short-term memory problems and cognitive changes in the months "leading up to his retirement." Dr. B provided no indication that she was aware of Dr. Scott being under criminal investigation. Dr. B administered the Rey 15-Item Test on which Dr. Scott obtained 12 out of 15 items correct.

Premorbid intellectual functioning was estimated as being in the superior range based on Dr. Scott's educational history, high average based on the Wechsler Test of Adult Reading score, and very superior range based on Wechsler Adult Intelligence Scale-IV (WAIS-IV) Vocabulary subtest score (Table 17.1).

Table 17.1 Dr. B's Wechsler Adult Intelligence Scale-IV Results for Dr. Scott

Subtest/Index	*Scale Score*	*Percentile*	*Classification*
Similarities	12		
Vocabulary	14		
Information	12		
Comprehension	12		
Verbal Comprehension	114	82	High average
Block Design	11		
Matrix Reasoning	10		
Visual Puzzles	8		
Perceptual Reasoning	98	45	Average
Digit Span	8		
Arithmetic	8		
Working Memory	89	23	Low average
Symbol Search	14		
Coding	13		
Processing Speed	120	91	Superior
Full Scale IQ	106	66	Average

Table 17.2 Dr. B's Wechsler Memory Scale-IV Age-Based Results for Dr. Scott

Index	*Scale Score*	*Percentile*	*Classification*
Auditory Memory	82	12	Low average
Visual Memory	92	30	Average
Immediate Memory	85	16	Low average
Delayed Memory	83	13	Low average

Table 17.3 Dr. B's California Verbal Learning Test-II (CVLT-II) Age and Education Results for Dr. Scott

Scale/Index	*Raw score*	*Classification*
List A Trial 1	3/16	Mild
List A Trial 5	6/16	Mild
Learning Slope		Average
List B	3/16	Low average
Short Delay Free Recall	2/16	Moderate
Long Delay Free Recall	0/16	Significantly impaired

Dr. B also administered the Conner's Continuous Performance Test second edition, Wisconsin Card Sorting Test, Trail Making Test (A & B), Color Trails, and Brief Test of Attention. All results fell within the average or better ranges. He rated himself within normal limits on the Behavior Rating Inventory of Executive Functions, but his wife rated him as having impairments that reached the 99th percentiles on nearly every scale.

Dr. Scott was reported to have performed well on nine subtests of the Delis-Kaplan Executive Function System (D-KEFS). He was administered the Wechsler Memory Scale-IV (WMS-IV) and California Verbal Learning Test-II (CVLT-II) (Tables 17.2 and 17.3), on which he scored lower.

On the CVLT-II, Dr. B noted that category cues did not improve the score, and Dr. Scott had an average number of repetitions and intrusions. Regarding language functioning, she provided this result: "Dr. Scott's expressive language skills are in the low average range (SS 84, 14th %tile) and his receptive language skills are in the average range (SS 105, 63rd %tile)." "Significant word finding difficulties were noted and account for the 21-point difference between scores." Regarding visuospatial functioning, Dr. Scott reportedly obtained a *Koppitz Developmental Scoring System for the Bender Gestalt Test*, second edition, Visual Motor Index scale score of 125 when drawing six Bender cards; however, it took him 30 minutes to complete the task. He scored 27/30 on the visual-organization test. Dr. B concluded he had no impairment in visual-organization skills. Dr. B noted that Dr. Scott performed within normal limits on all emotional rating scales. Overall, Dr. B concluded that Dr. Scott had Mild Cognitive Impairment (MCI), amnestic type and aphasia, anomic type.

Dr. C, Board-Certified Geropsychologist

Dr. C completed an assessment at the request of defense counsel and performed testing the day after Dr. Scott's first day of testing with Dr. B, producing a report titled, Neuropsychological Evaluation. Per that report, Dr. Scott indicated that he abruptly retired after a state official walked in and told him he was taking away his medical license immediately. He said he was also aware that he was facing possible criminal charges. He said it was common for him to see 40–50 patients a day, three times the rate of most physicians, and that he was an expert in treating pain and, therefore, attracted a considerable number of pain patients. Dr. C noted that Dr. Scott was fully independent with all ADL, although his wife historically took care of family finances and cooking. He continued to drive independently, and his interests included walking, detective story reading, and playing classical piano. Dr. Scott reported no changes in his thinking, memory, orientation, or problem-solving. Dr. C administered no performance validity measures and provided this opinion: "He was fully cooperative with testing, and thus results appear to be a valid reflection of his current cognitive functioning." Dr. C's test battery results are listed in Table 17.4.

Dr. C noted that Dr. Scott was aware that he performed far below his expected level on some tests. The defendant "appeared surprised but interested." He performed within normal limits on the Geriatric Depression scale. In summary, Dr. C noted Dr. Scott's "test scores showed clear deficits in verbal memory and deficits on two other tests (semantic fluency and visual-organization skills)." "Across other tests, however, scores were lower than would be expected given his educational and health status." He diagnosed Mild Neurocognitive Disorder with memory deficits being prominent. He recommended Dr. Scott undergo

Table 17.4 Dr. C's Test Battery Results for Dr. Scott

Measure/Scale	*Raw/Standard Scores*
Benton Temporal Orientation Test	1 (WNL)
Animal Naming Test	12 (mild)
MAE Aural Comprehension	17 (WNL)
WRAT IV Reading	66 (StS = 120)
Controlled Oral Word	28 (SS = 8)
Wechsler Adult Short Intelligence Test	
Verbal Iq	113
Performance IQ	106
Full-scale IQ	111
Vocabulary	T = 59
Block Design	T = 59
Similarities	T = 58
Matrix Reasoning	T = 50
RAVLT	
trial 1	3 (SS = 7)
LOT (Learning Over Trials)	9 (SS = 8)
List B	1 (SS = 3)
LTPR (Long-Term Percent Retention)	16% (SS = 5)
STPR (Short-Term percent Retention)	120% (SS = 13)
Logical Memory I	12 (SS = 5)
Logical Memory II	1 (SS = 2)
Boston Naming Test	46 (SS = 8)
Benton Visual form Discrimination	29 (WNL)
Hooper Visual-Organization Test	9 (severely impaired)
Trail Making A	47 (SS = 8)
Trail Making B	182 (SS = 7)
Stroop Word	80 (SS = 8)
Stroop Color	52 (SS = 9)
Stroop Color/Word	22 (SS = 8)

Note. WNL = Within Normal Limits; MAE = Multilingual Aphasia Examination; WRAT = Wide Range Achievement Test; RAVLT = Rey Auditory Verbal Learning Test; SS = Scale Score; T = T-score; StS = Standard Score.

a thorough geriatric medical evaluation at a memory disorders clinic. He opined that it was not possible to know when his memory deficits began, but it was likely the deficits have been present for several months or longer. Dr. C did not examine Dr. Scott's criminal competency nor did he provide an opinion on the issue.

Dr. D, Forensic Psychologist

Dr. D is a clinical psychologist with experience in criminal forensic assessment. He was hired by defense counsel to evaluate the defendant's mental status in terms of his competence to proceed. Dr. D interviewed Dr. Scott over the course of three days, approximately three months after the first two cognitive examinations. He administered the Minnesota Multiphasic Personality Inventory-2 (MMPI-2) and the MacArthur Competency Assessment Tool–Criminal Adjudication (MacCAT-CA).

Dr. D noted that Dr. Scott appeared somewhat disoriented in all spheres, although he presented as an intelligent individual. He was confused and initially not fully aware of the purpose of the evaluation. His speech and thought processes were lucid, but he evidenced confusion at times, needing his wife to correct or clarify his statements or to prompt him to answer. Dr. D noted that the defendant's wife was present during the interview portions of the examination.

Dr. Scott reportedly gave a meaningful history and denied having cognitive difficulties. When confronted by accusations of insurance fraud, Dr. Scott looked puzzled, replying, "That's news to me." He denied knowing the name of his attorney or the possibility that he could be incarcerated; however, he conceded those facts were true after his wife corrected him.

On the MacCAT-CA, Dr. Scott reportedly had significant difficulties in understanding, reasoning, and appreciation of the legal system. All of his scores fell in the clinically significant impairment range, suggesting very little understanding and reasoning of his situation and general criminal legal issues. Dr. D opined that Dr. Scott's ability to factually understand legal proceedings, his rational understanding of the proceedings themselves, and his capacity to assist his counsel were all significantly compromised. Dr. D suggested that difficulties with expressive language skills and word finding would manifest as problems in his ability to "lucidly and coherently" communicate with counsel. He further suggested the deficits in short-term memory and recall of testimony from one day to the next would handicap his ability to make a rational decision about entering a plea. Dr. D opined that Dr. Scott was not competent to factually understand the legal proceedings, rationally understand the proceedings, or assist his counsel in his defense at trial.

Dr. E, Forensic Psychologist

Dr. E is a clinical psychologist with experience in criminal forensic mental health assessment. He was court ordered to perform an independent evaluation of the defendant's competency by the presiding trial judge (Court's expert). He completed this assessment three months after the prior defense requested forensic assessment.

Dr. E performed a clinical interview and administered the Clock Drawing Test, Dementia Rating Scale-2, Validity Indicator Profile, Trail Making Test Parts A and B, Harris Test of Lateral Dominance, and Repeatable Battery for the Assessment of Neuropsychological Status. Dr. Scott reported that he did not understand why he was being evaluated and thought it might be related to defense of his medical practice, but he then added he never killed

Table 17.5 Dr. E's Repeatable Battery for the Assessment of Neuropsychological Status Results for Dr. Scott

Index	*Standard Score*	*Percentile*
Immediate Memory	87	19
Visuospatial/Constructional	78	7
Language	85	16
Attention	91	27
Delayed Memory	76	5
Total Scale Index	76	5

Table 17.6 Dr. E's Dementia Rating Scale-2 Results for Dr. Scott

Index	*Standard Score*	*Percentile*
Attention	35	41–59
Initiation/Perseveration	32	11–18
Construction	4	3–5
Conceptualization	34	19–28
Memory	21	1
Total Score	126	6–10

a patient or had patients suffering as a result of his prescriptions. Later in the interview, however, he did know he had his license taken away because of allegedly writing too many narcotic prescriptions.

Dr. E noted the defendant performed normally on the nonverbal and verbal portions of the VIP. He was right-handed and left eye dominant. Dr. E noted, "a brain with cross dominance of this kind will have difficulty organizing information and learning information visually and auditorily is more difficult--when retrieving information, a cross dominant person becomes anxious and information retrieval is more difficult." His Trail Making Test results fell within the average range for men his age. He also obtained cognitive testing results that fell in the impaired range (Tables 17.5 and 17.6).

Although tasked to evaluate Dr. Scott's competence to proceed, Dr. E did not perform any structured interview or objective testing regarding the issue. Further, he did not even ask him about his understanding of basic criminal procedural issues beyond his understanding of his charges. He said Dr. Scott was oriented to person, place, time, and situation. He also opined that Dr. Scott's thought content was guarded and superficial in that he presented himself as blameless and outraged by the circumstances he was facing. Dr. E wrote that it bordered on delusional ideation. He opined further that the defendant's thought process was disorganized, with circumstantiality and thought blocking, "unspontaneous and faster than normal cadence," and at times louder than normal social volume. Insight and judgment were considered impaired. Dr. E diagnosed Major Neurocognitive Disorder without behavioral disturbances, probable Alzheimer's disease, and he opined that the defendant was not competent to proceed due to cognitive problems.

Court's Order and Commitment

In light of Dr. E's opinion, the government stipulated and all parties agreed that Dr. Scott was not competent to proceed with his criminal case. The court committed him to the U.S.

Attorney General for hospitalization and treatment to restore his competency per statutory requirement. Dr. Scott went into custody and was then transferred to the U.S. Medical Center for Federal Prisoners (MCFP) in Springfield, Missouri, for his period of hospitalization, observation, treatment, and reassessment regarding competence. Approximately five months later, the MCFP forensic examiner provided an additional report.

Dr. F, Forensic Psychologist

Dr. F was a clinical psychologist with significant training/supervision in forensic psychology who worked for the Bureau of Prisons as a forensic examiner for the U.S. district courts. He had the opportunity to observe the defendant for approximately four months in an inpatient setting. The MCFP is a complex of buildings connected by underground tunnels, and criminal defendants are often in open population where they traverse the complex in order to go to the cafeteria, recreation centers, and educational facilities. Dr. F noted that Dr. Scott was fully oriented. His memory and cognition appeared adequate, and he did not seem to have significant impairments in either domain. He functioned well in open population and demonstrated the ability to navigate the somewhat complicated institution with little assistance. He recalled the nature of some of the instruments he was asked to complete during several prior examinations and desired to preemptively finish that part of the current assessment if possible.

Over the course of the three-month hospitalization, he demonstrated the ability to recall information that was provided to him the previous week. He frequently talked about his desire to have the evaluation completed so he could return to his home setting with his wife. He demonstrated the ability to recall the nature of their conversations over days; nonetheless, he would also ask Dr. F about the content of their discussions despite having awareness of what they had talked about. He nonetheless did present with minor memory impairments, such as minor points regarding what he learned in competency restoration groups. His competency was evaluated near the end of his hospitalization.

Dr. Scott was administered the Test of Memory Malingering (TOMM) and obtained 92% correct on Trial 1 and 100% correct on Trial 2. He achieved WAIS-IV results that were in the low average or higher ranges (Table 17.7) but WMS-IV results that were impaired (Table 17.8).

Dr. F concluded that Dr. Scott has demonstrated increasingly poor memory difficulties over several years, but they remained mild based on his ability to function independently. Dr. F noted that past medical records suggested chronic microvascular ischemic changes likely contributed to his neurocognitive decline. He diagnosed Mild Neurocognitive Disorder and vascular disease. Dr. F also noted that it was unclear why Dr. Scott's mental status was so grossly impaired during past competency examinations (e.g., disoriented in all spheres, thought process disorganized by circumstantiality and thought blocking, unspontaneous speech), but his mental status was demonstrably more normal when observed over

Table 17.7 Dr. F's Wechsler Adult Intelligence Scale-IV Results for Dr. Scott

Index	*Standard Score*	*Percentile*
Full-Scale IQ	110	75
Verbal Comprehension	114	82
Perceptual Reasoning	109	73
Working Memory	89	23
Processing Speed	120	91

Table 17.8 Dr. F's Wechsler Memory Scale-IV Age-Based Results for Dr. Scott

Index/Subscale	*Standard Score/Scaled Score*	*Percentile*
Auditory Memory Index	67	1
Logical Memory I	8	25
Logical Memory II	7	16
Verbal Paired Associates I	2	0.4
Verbal Paired Associates II	1	0.1
Visual Memory Index	100	50
Visual Reproduction I	13	84
Visual Reproduction II	7	16
Immediate Memory Index	85	16
Delayed Memory Index	69	2

an extended period of time. He had this insightful conclusion regarding the man's overall functioning:

> Although the decreases in his cognitive functioning and memory have been significant, the fact that he started at a superior higher level of cognitive ability means he has decreased to the approximately average range in most domains. This would be similar to an Olympic runner engaging in a race with a leg injury. The runner's time in a race would be significantly slower for him from a relative standpoint, but compared to the general population their race time may be average. A similar event has happened to Dr. Scott, but the injury is vascular damage to his brain.

Dr. F also noted that the defendant demonstrated the ability to learn and retain information when the data were presented to him in repetitive smaller chunks. He showed the ability to recall the essence of the charges days and weeks after they were initially discussed with him. He demonstrated a basic understanding of what behaviors in which a physician would engage in order to be charged with health care fraud and distribution of controlled substances. He showed the ability to comprehend potential consequences for the alleged offenses, which he described as federal prison. Additionally, Dr. Scott had been attending competency restoration educational groups on a weekly basis and post-training testing scores demonstrated his ability to learn most of the material provided during sessions. Dr. F opined that Dr. Scott was competent to proceed.

Once Dr. Scott returned to his home and was re-examined by his defense experts, defense suggested there was still cause to believe he remained incompetent. The court ordered Dr. E to re-examine the defendant, and Dr. F also had an opportunity to re-examine him on an outpatient basis just prior to a court hearing. Dr. F provided information to the government that the defendant really needed a more thorough assessment by an expert in forensic neuropsychology. The court then granted the government's motion to have him undergo an examination that included cognitive testing and collaboration between disciplines of psychology, neuropsychology, and forensic psychology. Defense experts also had the opportunity to re-examine the defendant so there were updated reports by Drs. B, C, D, and E.

My Assessment

I reviewed available records and the court's order. The EEG results were particularly concerning because they suggested more impairment in global cognitive functioning than suggested by cognitive testing, and they included moderate voltage, semi-rhythmic theta activity, which extended anteriorly into the biparietal head regions as well as varying low amplitude fast beta frequencies. If genuine, these results would suggest a significant encephalopathic condition, which was not consistent with other data. Research demonstrated that diffuse theta slowing along with apparent low amplitude fast beta frequencies was suggestive of sedative drug use, such as benzodiazepine (St. Louis & Frey, 2016). I was concerned that Dr. Scott has self-administered benzodiazepine prior to the EEG, either to reduce anxiety or manipulate the results (the EEG was done the day after the brain MRI, so he likely had ready access to benzodiazepine). Additionally, I wanted another set of neurology eyes to look at the brain MRI results and help gauge the implications from those results. I was able to convince the DOJ to contract with my neurology colleague to perform a record review and opinion report.

I examined the defendant at the U.S. attorney's office in Dr. Scott's home city. I also had the opportunity to meet face to face with his spouse, and she completed the Activities of Daily Living Questionnaire (ADLQ). Test results obtained are presented in Table 17.9.

On the Victoria Symptom Validity Test (VSVT), Dr. Scott achieved these scores: Easy 18/24, $p = 0.9967$, valid; Difficult 12/24, $p = 0.5806$, questionable; and Total 30/48, $p = 0.9703$, valid. The difficult items result was below expectations for a man who might have MCI due to a neurodegenerative disease, and the finding is even rare among those with dementia. For example, Loring and colleagues (2007) administered the VSVT to older medical center patients found to have dementia as part of clinical care ($N = 50$). The mean difficult score was 20.3 (4.0) and only 8% achieved a score as low as Dr. Scott's (i.e., 0.92 specificity). Dr. Scott's score was also well below those of patients with severe traumatic brain injury (Macciocchi et al., 2006) and those with profound memory impairment (Slick et al., 2003). Further, Dr. Scott's results appeared more consistent with the VSVT feigning comparison group than compensation-seeking and non-compensation-seeking examinees (Slick et al., 1997).

Dr. Scott's performance on the Word Memory Test (Figure 17.1) is the dark solid line compared with simulators, neurological patients, and those with mild, moderate, and severe dementia based upon Executive Interview Bedside Assessment (EXIT).

His performance was considered failing but with a possible genuine memory impaired profile. His performance, however, appeared atypical for severely cognitive-impaired patients because his Immediate Recognition score was perfect, yet his free recall score was extremely poor. Dr. Scott's performance during the Nonverbal Medical Symptom Validity Test (NV-MSVT) was atypical as well (Figures 17.2 and 17.3).

The advanced clinical interpretation for the NV-MSVT indicated the performance failed and was more like that of simulators than genuine cognitively compromised individuals. Dr. Scott also produced order violations in that he performed better on more difficult scales yet worse on easier scales. One can see the unusual profile compared with genuine dementia patients as well as the type of profile commonly produced by simulators (Figure 17.3).

The above performance validity findings strongly indicated that Dr. Scott was not putting forth appropriate task engagement during testing, and the patterns suggest exaggeration of deficits. Mrs. Scott completed the ADLQ regarding her husband's current level of instrumental and basic activities of daily living (Table 17.10).

Overall, results suggested no significant compromise in Dr. Scott's daily living skills based on Mrs. Scott's completion of the questionnaire. The employment and total scores in parentheses represent removing his discontinuing work from contributing to an assessment of living skills. I included this change because it was not known if his work discontinuation was due to cognitive compromise or strictly improper behavior. Travel was elevated because he has reportedly gotten lost when driving, and he goes out less often.

Table 17.9 My Obtained Test Results for Dr. Scott

Domain/Test	*Standard Score**	*Percentile Rank**	*AACN Classification*
Attention			
WAIS-IV Digit Span	SS9/T40	16	Low average
Mental Processing Speed			
WAIS-IV Processing Speed	StS105/T49	46	Average
Symbol Search	SS9/T43	24	Average
Coding	SS13/T55	69	Average
Trail A	T39	14	Low average
Language			
NAB Naming	—	<1	Exceptionally low
Letter Fluency	T46	34	Average
Animal Naming	T24	<0.5	Exceptionally low
Motor Functioning			
Grooved Peg Dominant	T54	66	Average
Grooved Peg Nondominant	T53	61	Average
Visuospatial			
WAIS-IV Block Design	10 T43	24	Average
RCFT Copy	34 (raw)	>16	Intact
Learning & Memory			
NAB Memory Module Index	65	1	Exceptionally low
List Learning Immediate	T34	5	Above average
List Learn Short Delay	T31	3	Below average
List Learn Long Delay	T24	<1	Exceptionally low
Shape Learning	T39	14	Low average
Shape Learning Delay	T35	7	Below average
Story Learning Immediate	T27	1	Exceptionally low
Story Learning Delay	T30	2	Below average
Daily Living Immediate	T35	7	Below average
Daily Living Delayed	T28	1	Exceptionally low
Executive Function			
RIAS-2 CIX	75, 95% CI: 72–79	5	Below average
VIX	72	3	Below average
NIX	84	14	Low average
NAB Judgment	T49	46	Average
Trail B	T47	39	Average
WCST Categories	0 of 6	6–10	Below average
WCST Total Errors	T29	2	Below average
WCST Perseverative Errors	T23	<1	Exceptionally low

Note. CI = Confidence Interval; NAB = Neuropsychological Assessment Battery; RIAS = Reynolds Intellectual Assessment Scales-2; NIX = Nonverbal Intellectual Index; RCFT = Rey Complex Figure Test; SS = Age-based Scale Scores; StS = Age-based Standard Scores; VIX = Verbal Intellectual Index; WAIS-IV = Wechsler Adult Intelligence Scale-IV; WCST = Wisconsin Card Sorting Test.

* T-scores and percentiles are based on age and education adjustments, with the exception of RIAS-2 and RCFT, which are age only.

+ Test score classifications are based on Guilmette et al. (2020).

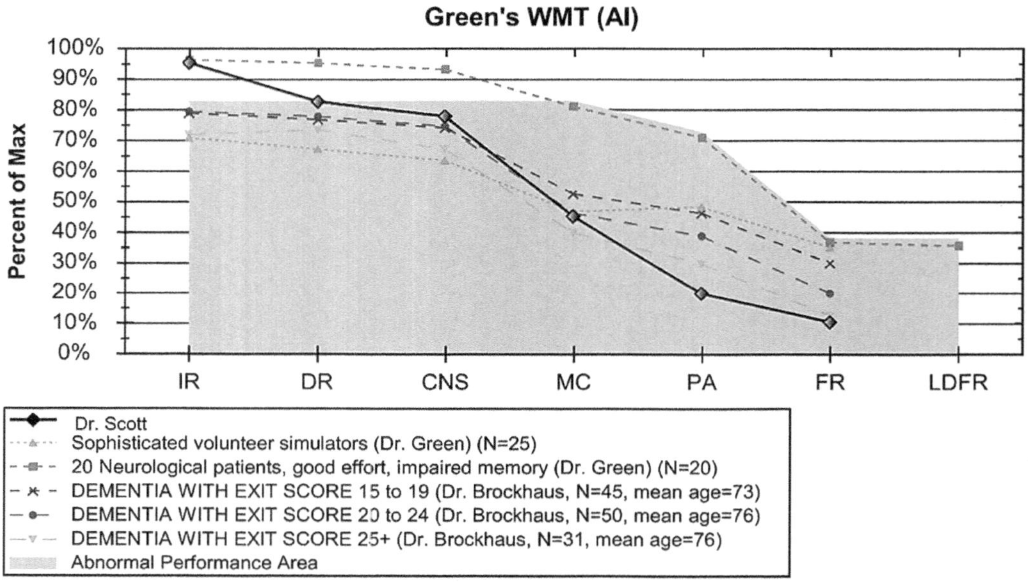

Figure 17.1 My Green's Word Memory Test results for Dr. Scott.

Note. WMT = Word Memory Test; AI = Advanced Interpretation; EXIT = Executive Interview Bedside Assessment (Royal et al., 1992).

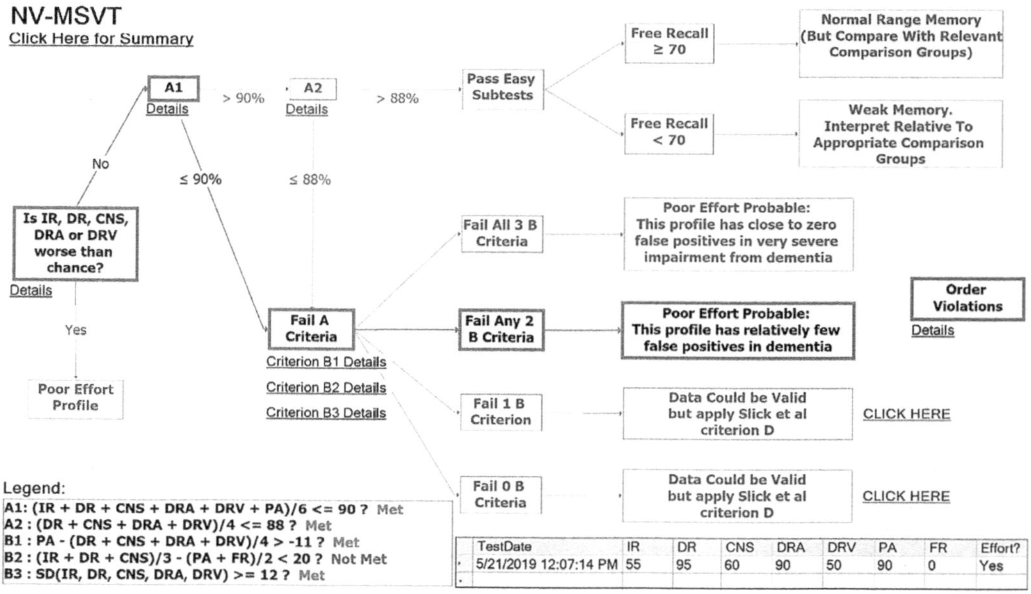

Figure 17.2 Nonverbal Medical Symptom Validity Test Advanced Interpretation Flowchart for Dr. Scott.

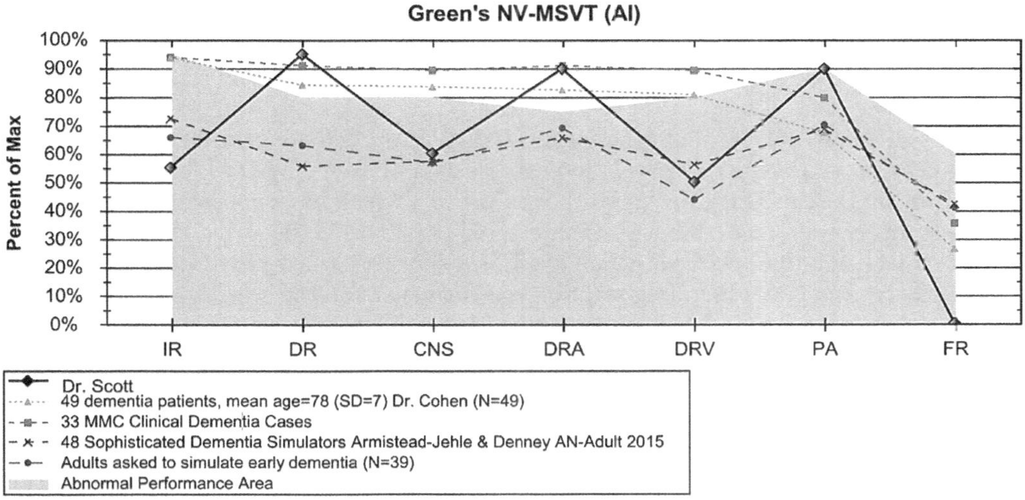

Figure 17.3 Nonverbal Medical Symptom Validity Test Advanced Interpretation Graph (percent correct) for Dr. Scott.

Note. NV-MSVT = Nonverbal Medical Symptom Validity Test; AI = Advanced Interpretation; IR = Immediate Recognition; DR = Delayed Recognition; CNS = Consistency between IR & DR; DRA = Delayed Recognition Architypes; DRV = Delayed Recognition Variations; PA = Paired Associate; FR = Free Recall; MMC = Missouri Memory Center.

Table 17.10 Results of Activities of Daily Living Questionnaire

Domain	*Score (%)*	*Classification*
Self-care activities	22	Minimal decrease
Household care	0	Minimal decrease
Employment/recreation	55 (33)	Mild to moderate decrease
Shopping/money	0	Minimal decrease
Travel	50	Moderate decrease
Communication	22	Minimal decrease
Total	29 (24)	Minimal decrease

Clinical Formulation

I always provide a section in my reports that includes, "clinical formulation," in which I explain my reasoning regarding the diagnostic conclusion. Only afterward do I address the forensic issue. Dr. Scott had experienced a head injury years before during which time he developed two subdural hematomas. Those resolved on their own, and he affirmed no cognitive problems as a result of them. Further, he continued to have a successful medical practice for many years after that event.

The clinical presentation suggested Dr. Scott may have developed mild cognitive difficulties over several years, possibly predating the alleged offense. The following months revealed a seesaw of findings, some suggesting less impairment and others suggesting severe impairment. Through it all, Dr. Scott's MoCA, SLUMS, and MMSE scores remained virtually constant, and at a level suggestive of only MCI. Trail Making Test, Part B, a sensitive measure of brain impairment (Larrabee et al., 2008), remained constantly within the average range as well (even when taking into consideration age and education). Such significant variability of test findings does not make clinical sense in the context of a potential gradually progressive neurodegenerative disease, i.e., many scores would naturally get worse.

Although I was not granted access to raw data from defense examinations, I had the opportunity to review the raw psychological test data obtained by Dr. F because they were created within Bureau of Prisons (a DOJ department), which has a cooperative relationship with U.S. attorneys' offices. He was administered the TOMM; however, the retention trial of the test was not administered, which can lower the test's sensitivity (Greve & Bianchini, 2006). There were no other free-standing performance validity measures administered. Within the WAIS-IV and WMS-IV are embedded validity indicators. Dr. Scott obtained a Reliable Digit Span (RDS) of six, which was lower than expected for a man of superior intellect who demonstrated MoCA and MMSE scores within the normal to mildly impaired ranges and minimal instrumental activities of daily living deficits. Such a finding on its own in this context suggested poor task engagement (McGuire et al., 2019). Further, this score was substantially lower than the RDS of nine he obtained during my examination nearly a year later. Vocabulary-Digit Span is also an embedded validity indicator. Dr. Scott obtained a score of 7, when the cut off for concern for poor task engagement is >3 (Dean et al., 2009). He was administered the recognition portions of Logical Memory (LM), Verbal Paired Associates (VPA), and Visual Reproduction subtests on the WMS-IV. He repeatedly indicated he did not know the words during VPA and demonstrated no learning curve, whatsoever. His performances on VPA Recognition, particularly, but also LM Recognition, were lower than they should have been given his premorbid intellectual level and overall demonstrated level of functioning. Raw test data suggested Dr. Scott was likely not providing appropriate task engagement during the cognitive testing at the U.S. Medical Center irrespective of the TOMM results. The TOMM has demonstrated less than the best sensitivity within the pretrial criminal forensic setting, made worse by not including the retention trial (Fazio et al., 2015; Weinborn et al., 2003).

The overall record of facts suggested that Dr. Scott may have developed mild cognitive deficits, even possibly before his arrest. The undercover videos of his behavior during the examination suggested no significant cognitive deficits, but he did appear to respond to questions in a less than direct manner, and the state medical board investigator's report suggested Dr. Scott might be forgetful. Initial neurologic examination revealed indications of potential mild cognitive difficulty, as he achieved a MoCA score that fell in the potentially mildly impaired range. There was some inconsistency regarding his orientation, however. Additionally, there is still some concern for me in regard to the validity of that finding (and subsequent screening test findings) because this neurology consultation occurred after the state revoked Dr. Scott's license, and he clearly knew he was facing criminal prosecution. Consequently, he had significant motivation, even at this early date, to potentially appear impaired, and those screening measures are easy measures on which to exaggerate as they have no validity scales. He was diagnosed with MCI during the overlapping examinations of Drs. A and B. While these examinations did not use sensitive performance validity measures, at least their results were generally consistent with the neurologic examination and MoCA score.

At this point in the evolution of the case, things became strikingly inconsistent. He underwent brain MRI and EEG. The MRI revealed white matter changes which were deemed to represent small vessel ischemic disease. The radiologist noted the findings were mild. Such findings are not what is typical in a dementia; however, they could correspond to very mild cognitive deficits (Gunning-Dixon et al., 2000). Additionally, the radiologist noted that brain atrophy was age appropriate. Based upon my professional training and experience, these MRI findings are not suggestive of a current dementing condition.

The EEG results give significant pause for concern. At the time of the EEG, Dr. Scott was demonstrating MCI, at most; nevertheless, the EEG was read as indicating moderate voltage, semi-rhythmic theta activity that extended anteriorly into the biparietal head regions as well as varying low amplitude fast beta frequencies. The impression was abnormal recording because of diffuse theta slowing of the background rhythm in the bitemporal head regions. If genuine, this EEG result would suggest a significant encephalopathic condition (i.e., a brain-wide systemic impairment consistent with marked functional abnormalities). The neurologist concluded this result could be compatible with a toxic, metabolic, or degenerative process. While that conclusion may be a stock phrase, it does highlight the issue of a potential toxic process. Research regarding EEG patterns has demonstrated that diffuse theta slowing along with apparent low amplitude fast beta frequencies is suggestive of sedative drug use, such as benzodiazepine (St. Louis & Frey, 2016).

Normally, the neurologist reading the EEG would take such medication under consideration when reviewing the tracings, but in this instance, there was no indication the neurologist knew if Dr. Scott had ingested any such medication. Additionally, I specifically asked Mrs. Scott whether her husband was using any other medications at the time of the EEG, and her recollection was that he may have only been using a cholesterol-related medication (statin). In short, the EEG findings suggested Dr. Scott may have self-medicated using a benzodiazepine or other sedative drug in order to create an abnormal EEG. He certainly would have had access to such medications in his profession but also because the EEG was completed one day after the MRI. It is not uncommon for patients to be prescribed low-dose (and short acting) benzodiazepine to help them get through the MRI experience. While I do not know that Dr. Scott subverted the EEG result, it, nonetheless, raised significant concern in the context of this case and its striking inconsistencies.

Dr. Scott's performance during Dr. D's MacCAT-CA also raised concerns. Given the available cognitive screening tests and results of neuropsychological testing, Dr. Scott's condition was no more severe than MCI or possibly very mild dementia. Long-term memories do not disappear in MCI or mild dementia. Additionally, memory loss with dementia is episodic in nature and always of recent origin unless the dementia has moved from moderate to severe (i.e., recent memories fade first with long-term memories retaining until dementia is severe). It makes no sense, whatsoever, for Dr. Scott to not remember where he went to university, how many siblings he had as a child, or forget that he was a doctor, or the basic roles of courtroom participants.

In addition to the atypical and inconsistent presentation provided by Dr. Scott over the two years prior to my examination, performance validity measures within my examination demonstrated that Dr. Scott was not applying appropriate task engagement. Given the overall record and current clinical findings, it was my professional opinion that Dr. Scott was malingering memory dysfunction and incompetency. The presence of malingering does not eliminate the possibility of some genuine cognitive impairments. If present, however, they were mild. Consequently, I believe it was reasonable to diagnose a rule out of MCI with the caveat that it was impossible to identify it in the presence of exaggeration. MCI, in and of itself, is not severe enough to eliminate a person's competency to proceed.

Forensic Opinion

I administered the Competency Assessment Instrument (revised) to Dr. Scott. This is a structured interview that is flexible and allows for further investigation in all areas. Most of his responses revealed that he had a basic understanding of the key facts regarding his case. Oftentimes, he slipped in statements that were clearly in error or said he did not know, and he did this in a manner that was not consistent with what I would expect for a premorbidly bright man intellectually who potentially had MCI or even mild dementia. His presentation was not consistent regarding his knowledge. Typically, he would have the correct answer some time after he initially denied the knowledge, or he would answer a different question that demonstrated he actually had known the information previously asked. Overall, his performance struck me as fabricated.

An Olympic Runner

Dr. F's analogy of an Olympic runner was on point. Dr. Scott may not have been functioning at his premorbid level, but I believe his overall level of functioning was still within the broadly neurotypical range of the general population, but with a weak memory. It may be fair to suggest he was not competent to practice medicine, but the practice of medicine is a far greater and different type of competency than what is required to proceed through criminal adjudication.

It is important to realize that many of our neuropsychological tests, measuring such things as memory and executive functioning, use norms that are corrected for education level. Consequently, a man with 20 years of education may obtain a score that is moderately impaired, but that same performance for a man with 10 or 12 years of education would not necessarily be impaired. The use of education as a proxy for premorbid intellectual level is standard practice and very helpful in identifying the effects of an illness on that person's overall cognitive functioning. However, that method of normative comparison is not effective when it comes to an across-the-board legal standard such as competency. Irrespective of how much "loss" a person may have demonstrated, all the person needs is enough ability to meet the legal standard. Therefore, the Olympic runner analogy is on point in this case. The MMSE, SLUMS, and MoCA measures demonstrate this fact as they do not have normative corrections for superior levels of education, and in Dr. Scott's record, their total scores have remained stable at the border zone between normal and mildly impaired.

This characteristic of our tests can be demonstrated with the NAB Memory Module for Dr. Scott. Given his age and 20 years of education, his Total Memory standard score was 65 (1st percentile rank), a moderately impaired score. When the years of education were reduced to ten years, then his exact same raw scores equated to a Total Memory standard score of 81 (10th percentile rank), a score falling in the below average to mildly impaired range. I have examined many young criminal defendants with less than 12 years of education and with mild cognitive difficulties of learning and memory in this range who have been found competent to proceed. I used this example simply to inform the court that not all scores are equal as they depend on normative corrections. In my professional opinion, Dr. Scott was malingering lack of memory and lack of knowledge regarding his case. Further, his explanations of basic principles of criminal litigation demonstrated a basic understanding of the process as well as his understanding of the offenses.

The Court Hearing

The court heard testimony from all the above psychologists as well as the defendant's personal neurologist, and my colleague neurologist who had reviewed the images and EEG results. The court put little weight on the testimony of Dr. C, the court's expert, because he was not able to determine a diagnosis beyond "suffering from memory and cognitive deficits" even though he had administered the MacCAT-CA. The court also discounted the testimony of Dr. B because she did not know anything about criminal competency and had not administered any form of competency assessment. I would add there were ethical concerns for a treatment provider to "turn expert witness" after the fact (Bush et al., 2020). In my experience, this latter issue has stung many well-meaning clinicians. She discounted the neurologist testimony in regard to competence because, thankfully, he noted he had no opinion regarding the issue. She discounted the testimony of Dr. C as well because he had not actually assessed Dr. Scott's competence to stand trial. Dr. F indicated that after reviewing my report, his hesitancy about the man's competence was gone, and he agreed the man was competent to proceed. The court discounted Dr. E's testimony because he claimed Dr. Scott had dementia (likely Alzheimer's disease), but the facts of the case did not support the diagnosis based upon criteria set forth in *DSM-5*. Further, Dr. E testified that the past subdural hematomas contributed to the defendant's dementia, and he did not use validity measures as part of his examinations. The court credited the testimony of my neurologist colleague who concluded the imaging findings and objective screening test results supported a mild and stable cognitive difficulty.

The court found Dr. Scott to have MCI, but he was exaggerating cognitive deficits and was competent to stand trial. However, there was more to come, and it is important to note the defendant was present in the courtroom to hear my testimony regarding his performance on validity tests.

Reprise: Another Bite of the Apple

Although the court heard testimony that Dr. Scott's condition had been stable for years and was likely to remain stable in the foreseeable future, the defense motioned the court for another competency hearing because it was believed he had deteriorated and was no longer competent to proceed (and they now had experts from out of state with genuine neuropsychological and criminal forensic credibility). I had the opportunity to reassess Dr. Scott nine months after my first examination. During the intervening time, defense obtained the services of a board-certified neuropsychologist and a board-certified psychiatrist with forensic qualifications in the criminal arena. There was an updated brain MRI that revealed no significant change from the previous study.

The forensic psychiatrist interviewed the defendant and his wife and reviewed records but did no cognitive testing or measures to detect exaggeration or feigning incompetence. He concluded that Dr. Scott was not exaggerating, had significant memory deficits, and was not competent to stand trial due to some form of neurocognitive disorder. In his report, he diagnosed Mild Neurocognitive Disorder and Mild Cognitive Impairment, which he appeared to conflate with dementia. It was unclear if he concluded the defendant's condition was MCI, in the border zone between MCI and mild dementia (or in *DSM-5* terms, Mild Neurocognitive Disorder and Major Neurocognitive Disorder), or mild dementia (also known as Major Neurocognitive Disorder).

The neuropsychologist (Dr. G) administered a thorough neuropsychological test battery that included objective performance validity indicators. He also used more than one competency to stand trial measure. Dr. G agreed that Dr. Scott demonstrated poor task engagement during my examination ten months earlier; however, he "does generally provide reasonable effort" and the results documenting cognitive impairment are "valid" and "results of cognitive function do show some deterioration over time, confirming that there is some progression of his cognitive deterioration, in line with expectation for his condition." He opined Dr. Scott was not competent to proceed.

Now the court allowed me access to defense expert raw data from Dr. G. It was evident that Dr. Scott failed the Word Memory Test but created a profile that was consistent with a genuine memory impairment. He passed the Dot Counting Test and TOMM. Dr. Scott obtained a RDS score of 6, which was borderline but possibly within acceptable limits in the potential context of dementia. Unlike his performance during my examination, Dr. Scott passed the mathematical algorithms of NV-MSVT and, amazingly, produced 100% performances on the easy portions of the test while performing very poorly on the most difficult scale (free recall). The pattern of scores, nonetheless, remained atypical compared with comparison groups of patients with genuine dementia who had such poor free recall scores because his performance was too good on the easier scales.

My Second Examination

Dr. Scott appeared the same as he did ten months earlier. However, his wife rated his functioning as more deteriorated than before based on worse ADLQ scores. He now achieved an RDS of six. Interestingly, the first time, when he correctly answered only 12 of 24 difficult items on the VSVT, he now placed all aspects of the measure in the valid range, obtaining 23 of 24 difficult items correct. He produced a genuine memory impairment profile on the WMT; however, it was consistent with patients who had severe dementia and required convalescent care. He also passed the NV-MSVT (Figure 17.4).

In contrast to his prior performance on the NV-MSVT, his profile now looked genuine (Figure 17.5).

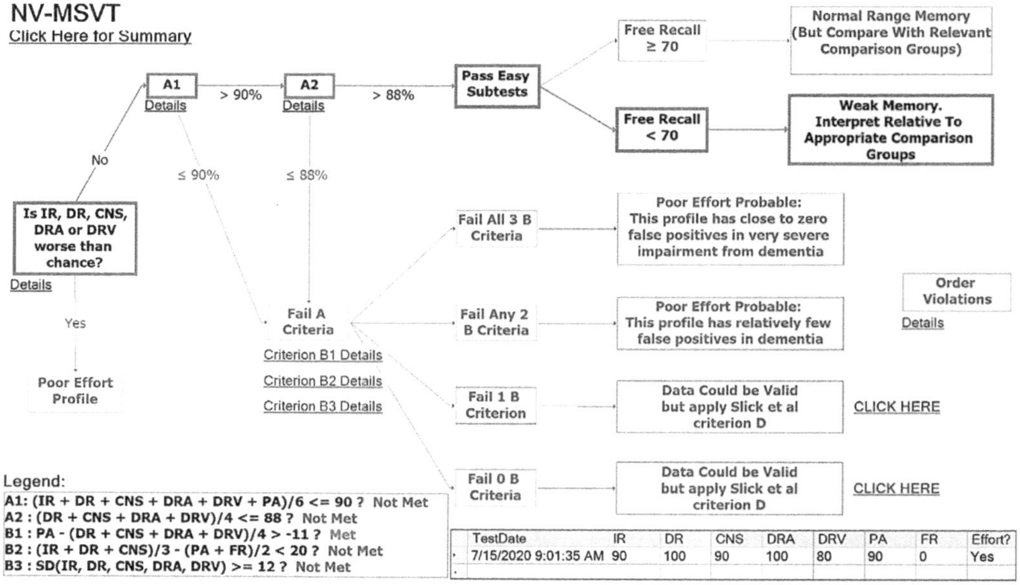

Figure 17.4 Second Nonverbal Medical Symptom Validity Test Result for Dr. Scott (Flowchart).

Note. NV-MSVT = Nonverbal Medical Symptom Validity Test; AI = Advanced Interpretation; IR = Immediate Recognition; DR = Delayed Recognition; CNS = Consistency between IR & DR; DRA = Delayed Recognition Archetypes; DRV = Delayed Recognition Variations; PA = Paired Associate; FR = Free Recall.

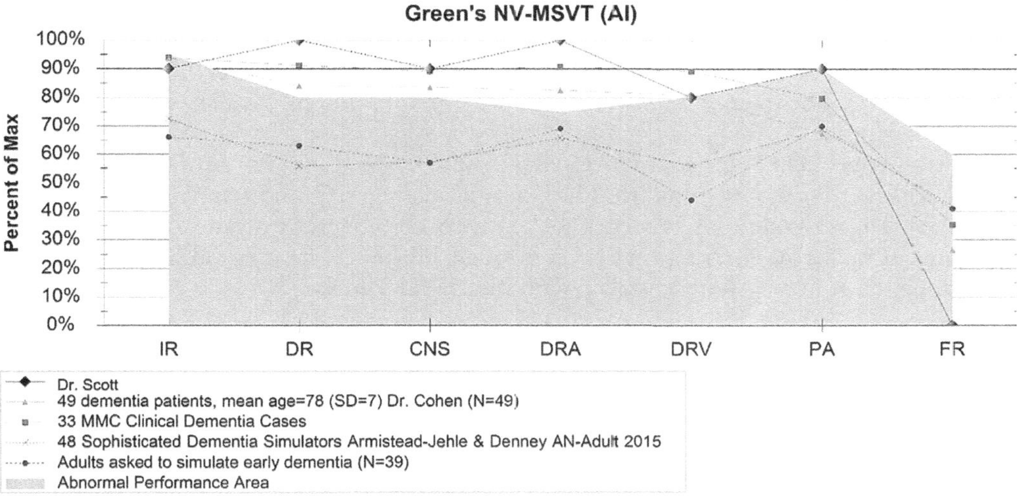

Figure 17.5 Second Nonverbal Medical Symptom Validity Test Result for Dr. Scott (Graph).

Note. NV-MSVT = Nonverbal Medical Symptom Validity Test; AI = Advanced Interpretation; IR = Immediate Recognition; DR = Delayed Recognition; CNS = Consistency between IR & DR; DRA = Delayed Recognition Architypes; DRV = Delayed Recognition Variations; PA = Paired Associate; FR = Free Recall; MMC = Missouri Memory Center.

It was striking that he performed well on all of the easy portions of the test but performed very poorly on free recall, even worse than clinical dementia patients. This was an atypical performance and did not appear credible. He passed the Coin-in-the-Hand Test, but he performed poorly on the Sentence Repetition Test, which has been validated as a validity test among individuals with MCI and dementia (Martin et al., 2020). Given his mixed performance on validity measures, I needed to assess the validity of his claimed ignorance of even basic legal knowledge. It made no logical sense that a premorbidly bright man would lose his understanding of the basic legal system given the proposed neuropathology.

I administered the Denney Competency Related Test (D-CRT) in oral format to Dr. Scott. This 114-item questionnaire was developed as a validity measure to identify individuals feigning incompetence to proceed in criminal adjudication (Denney et al., 2024). Items were developed based upon external expert review and initially analyzed on middle-school children. It was then validated as measuring the construct of competency to proceed in the adult jail setting. It demonstrated criterion validity alongside the MacCAT-CA. It also proved itself as effective at identifying simulators as the WMT. Research demonstrated a sensitivity of 0.90 at the 0.941 specificity level, and an outstanding overall predictive utility (ROC AUC = 0.945, standard error 0.024, $p < 0.0001$, 95% confidence interval: 0.898 to 0.991). It was then shown to have excellent specificity among clinic patients having MCI and mild to moderate dementia (specificity > 0.99). Dr. Scott obtained 69% correct, a score well below the genuine MCI and dementia comparison group [$t(45) = 30.057$, $p < 0.0001$]. The positive predictive power, given Dr. Scott's actual score, was 0.941.

It made no sense that Dr. Scott would not understand (or lose the understanding of) the basic roles of courtroom participants after having lived his entire life in a reasonably affluent setting within the United States. Information about courtroom participants is inundated in our culture, which causes those memories to be more semantic than episodic.

Semantic memories relate to the knowledge of "how things are" rather than specific recollections of discrete events in time. Semantic knowledge does not significantly decline in neurodegenerative diseases until the condition becomes quite profound (Squire & Schacter, 2002). The overall clinical picture presented in this case was not consistent with genuine dementia.

The trial court held another competency hearing, heard testimony from the new defense experts and me. The court found that he was still malingering and remained competent to stand trial. Dr. Scott ultimately struck a deal with the government and pleaded guilty to one count of unlawful distribution of a controlled substance, focused on his prescribing of methadone when he was not registered with the DEA to do so.

Discussion

This case provides an example of several issues that are important for neuropsychologists practicing in criminal forensic settings.

1 **Clinical examiners should not become "forensic" examiners.**
   There have been many papers published that outline the various roles neuropsychologists often have. One of the most classic papers on the issue includes the words, "irreconcilable conflict" in the title (Greenberg & Shuman, 1997). The authors spell out why those conflicts occur and how to avoid them. There are differences between a fact witness, expert treating witness, and forensic expert. No licensed psychologist should enter the criminal forensic arena without understanding the differences and developing a plan for how to navigate professional roles. In that regard, Bush and colleagues (2020), among many other sources, provide good discussions of the issues.
2 **One should have the appropriate training and supervision to complete the task at hand.**
   Dr. B was a well-meaning clinical psychologist with some experience, apparently, in neuropsychology. At least she had enough experience that a neurologist in the community referred patients to her. Her vita did not demonstrate appropriate training or supervision in neuropsychology. It is important that we do not practice outside our areas of competence. I do not know if it was an inadequate vita or an inadequate training history, but one or both issues should be corrected. She certainly did not have training and experience in criminal competency to stand trial, and this became apparent to the judge after seeing how she performed the CST examination and explained her opinions in the courtroom. Practice within the criminal forensic setting is unique and requires proper training in order to not practice outside our areas of expertise (Denney, 2012; Denney & Wynkoop, 2000).
3 **One should understand the referral issue sufficiently to evaluate the required elements.**
   More than one of the experts in this case did not evaluate the core aspects of CST. In order to be not competent to proceed, one must have a mental disease or defect under U.S. Code, Title 18, section 4241(b). The statute also dictates what elements must be covered in the assessment (Section 4247). Those elements must be assessed. The trial judge became noticeably frustrated by experts in her courtroom who did not perform their examinations sufficiently. Some with neuropsychological (rehabilitation psychology and geropsychology) training did not assess competency; those with forensic training did not properly perform a diagnostic assessment. This case exemplified how clinical neuropsychology and forensic psychology combine.

4 **One should apply what is known about a condition's natural course progression to the facts at hand.**

One of the benefits of being involved in a case over time is seeing the way the presumed pathology unfolds. Early examiners do not get this luxury. We know there are specific natural courses for disease entities, including neuropathology. Evaluators cannot check their understanding of pathology at the door when they enter forensic work. This case provided that opportunity to place cognitive testing on the course of that presumed pathology over time, and the pattern of scores did not make clinical sense. Viewing a clinical presentation from the 30,000-foot level is helpful in identifying patterns that make clinical sense. Ultimately, the facts of a forensic neuropsychological case must make clinical sense (Larrabee, 1990).

5 **One should have multiple methods to evaluate performance validity.**

The fact that I needed to re-exam this defendant after ten months and multiple prior examinations made choosing validity tests difficult. I needed to repeat some tests that were used before the hearing, because I suspected this intelligent defendant would learn from hearing the testimony about those tests and possibly pass them upon seeing them again. I have seen this pattern before, and it amazes me that experts do not realize what this means. If the person performed well on the validity test the second time, it demonstrated they were able to perform the test in a passing manner the first time, thus, proving they did not provide appropriate task engagement the first time. Maybe not the "smoking gun" of below random chance performance, but it surely comes close. I also had to come up with novel procedures.

This case also exemplifies the benefit of having validity assessment specific to the ultimate issue, i.e., competency to proceed. This issue is not a concern, say, in personal injury litigation because poor memory, for example, may be the entirety of the problem in civil litigation where memory-based PVTs are used. However, in criminal matters, there is an ultimate legal issue that is most important: in this case, competence to proceed There are several validity measures available pertaining to CST, and examiners should be aware of them (Colwell et al., 2008; Denney et al., 2024; Otto et al., 2010). Having the right tools in one's tool bag is a key to success in the world of forensic neuropsychology.

Note

1 https://www.whitehouse.gov/articles/2025/03/the-staggering-cost-of-the-illicit-opioid-epidemic-in-the-united-states/.

References

Bush, S. S., Connell, M. A., & Denney, R. L. (2020). *Ethical Practice in Forensic Psychology: A Guide for Mental Health Professionals* (2nd edition.) Washington, DC: American Psychological Association.

Colwell, K., Colwell, L. H., Perry, A. T., Wasieleski, D., & Billings, T. (2008). The test of malingered incompetence (TOMI): A forced-choice instrument for assessing cognitive malingering in competence to stand trial evaluations. *American Journal of Forensic Psychology, 26*(3), 17–42. https://www.researchgate.net/publication/234115496_TOMI_Further_Validation_Final_revision_01271

Dean, A. C., Victor, T. L., Boone, K. B., Philpott, L. M., & Hess, R. A. (2009). Dementia and effort test performance. *The Clinical Neuropsychologist, 23*(1), 133–152. https://doi.org/10.1080/13854040701819050

Denney, R. L. (2012). Criminal forensic neuropsychology and assessment of competency. In G. J. Larrabee (Ed.), *Forensic Neuropsychology: A Scientific Approach* (2nd edition.) (pp 438–472). New York: Oxford University Press.

Denney, R. L., Thinda, S., Finn, P. M., Fazio, R. L., Chen, M. J., & Walsh, M. R. (2024). Development of a measure for assessing malingered incompetency in criminal proceedings: Denney competency related test (D-CRT). *Journal of Clinical and Experimental Neuropsychology, 46*(2), 124–140. https://doi.org/10.1080/13803395.2024.2314731

Denney, R. L., & Wynkoop, T. F. (2000). Clinical neuropsychology in the criminal forensic setting. *The Journal of Head Trauma Rehabilitation, 15*(2), 804–828. https://doi.org/10.1097/00001199-200004000-00005

Dusky v. U.S., 362 U.S. 402 (1960).

Fazio, R. L., Sanders, J. F., & Denney, R. L. (2015). Comparison of performance of the test of memory malingering and word memory test in a criminal forensic sample. *Archives of Clinical Neuropsychology, 30*(4), 293–301. https://doi.org/10.1093/arclin/acv024

Greenberg, S. A., & Shuman, D. W. (1997). Irreconcilable conflict between therapeutic and forensic roles. *Professional Psychology: Research and Practice, 28*(1), 50–57. https://doi.org/10.1037/0735-7028.28.1.50

Greve, K. W., & Bianchini, K. J. (2006). Should the Retention trial of the Test of Memory Malingering be optional? *Archives of Clinical Neuropsychology, 21*(1), 117–119. https://doi.org/10.1016/j.acn.2005.06.009

Guilmette, S., Hebben, K., Mahone, S., Stucky, W., & Conference Participants (2020). American Academy of Clinical Neuropsychology consensus conference statement on uniform labeling of performance test scores. *The Clinical Neuropsychologist, 34*, 437–453. https://doi.org/10.1080/13854046.2020.1722244

Gunning-Dixon, F. M., & Raz, N. (2000). The cognitive correlates of white matter abnormalities in normal aging: A quantitative review. *Neuropsychology, 14*(2), 224–232. https://doi.org/10.1037//0894-4105.14.2.224

Larrabee, G. J. (1990). Cautions in the use of neuropsychological evaluation in legal settings. *Neuropsychology, 4*(4), 239–247. https://doi.org/10.1037/0894-4105.4.4.239

Larrabee, G. J., Millis, S. R., & Meyers, J. E. (2008). Sensitivity to brain dysfunction of the Halstead-Reitan vs an ability-focused neuropsychological battery. *The Clinical Neuropsychologist, 22*, 813–825. https://doi.org/10.1080/13854040701625846

Loring, D. W., Larrabee, G. J., Lee, G. P., & Meador, K. M. (2007). Victoria symptom validity test performance in a heterogenous clinical sample. *The Clinical Neuropsychologist, 21*(3), 522–531. https://doi.org/10.1080/13854040600611384

Macciocchi, S. N., Seel, R. T., Alderson, A., & Godsall, R. (2006). Victoria Symptom Validity Test performance in acute severe traumatic brain injury: Implications for test interpretation. *Archives of Clinical Neuropsychology, 21*(5), 395–404. https://doi.org/10.1016/j.acn.2006.06.003

Martin, P. K., Schroeder, R. W., & Olsen, D. H. (2020). Performance validity in the dementia clinic: Specificity of validity tests when used individually and in aggregate across levels of cognitive impairment severity. *The Clinical Neuropsychologist, 36*(1), 165–188. https://doi.org/10.1080/13854046.2020.1778790

McGuire, C., Crawford, S., & Evans, J. J. (2019). Effort testing in dementia assessment: A systematic review. *Archives of Clinical Neuropsychology, 34*(1),114–131. https://doi.org/10.1093/arclin/acy012

Otto, R. K., Musick, J. E., & Sherrod, C. B. (2010). *Inventory of Legal Knowledge: Professional Manual.* Lutz, FL: Psychological Assessment Resources.

Royall, D. R., Mahurin, R. K., & Gray, K. F. (1992). Bedside assessment of executive cognitive impairment: The executive interview. *Journal of the American Geriatrics Society, 40*(12), 1221–1226. https://doi.org/10.1111/j.1532-5415.1992.tb03646.x

Saks, M. J. (1990). Expert witnesses, nonexpert witnesses, and nonwitness experts. *Law and Human Behavior, 14*(4), 291–313. https://doi.org/10.1007/BF01068158

Slick, D. J., Hopp, G., Strauss, E., & Thompson, G. B. (1997). *Manual for the Victoria Symptom Validity Test.* Odessa, FL: Psychological Assessment Resources.
Slick, D. J., Tan, J. E., Strauss, E., Mateer, C. A., Harnadek, M., & Sherman, E. M. (2003). Victoria Symptom Validity Test scores of patients with profound memory impairment: Nonlitigants case studies. *The Clinical Neuropsychologist, 17*(3), 390–394. https://doi.org/10.1076/clin.17.3.390.18090
Squire, L. R., & Schacter, D. L. (Eds) (2002). *Neuropsychology of Memory* (3rd edition.) New York: Guilford Press.
St. Louis, E. K., & Frey, L. C. (Eds) (2016). *Electroencephalography (EEG): An Introductory Text and Atlas of Normal and Abnormal Findings in Adults, Children and Infants.* Chicago, IL: American Epilepsy Society. https://doi.org/10.5698/978-0-9979756-0-4
Weinborn, M., Orr, T., Woods, S. P., Conover, E., & Feix, J. (2003). A validation of the test of memory malingering in a forensic psychiatric setting. *Journal of Clinical and Experimental Neuropsychology, 25*(7), 979–990. https://doi.org/10.1076/jcen.25.7.979.16481

18 Defendants Who Malinger Incompetence

Diana S. Goldstein

In 1989, the American Bar Association's Criminal Justice Mental Health Standards noted that "the issue of present mental incompetency, quantitatively speaking, is the single most important issue in the criminal mental health field" (p. 168). While the number of Competency to Stand Trial (CST) examinations conducted annually in the United States is not known, estimates throughout the years that base numbers on actual CST admissions and/or surveys of public officials calculating annual CST examinations state by state have ranged from 19,000 to 54,000. Other estimates, based on extrapolations related to mental illness within jail populations are over 90,000 (Morris McNiel & Binder, 2021). The gross uncertainty regarding their frequency notwithstanding, CST examinations (also referred to as fitness examinations) are unquestionably the most common type of mental health inquiries asked of and made by psychologists, neuropsychologists, and psychiatrists who have chosen to contribute to the adjudication process in our criminal courts.

The ultimate determination of whether a defendant is competent for trial is of course made by the courts, but mental health experts play a critical role in the process. The process presents an opportunity, valued especially by the clinician who enjoys teaching, to inform the court of recent or current research in our respective fields and to explain the characteristics and potential legal relevance of various mental and neurocognitive disorders. CST is a nonadversarial issue and competency hearings are held for the sole purpose of fact-finding for the court. At least that is the theory of it, if not necessarily the practice.

This chapter presents a case in which a criminal defendant's CST was raised in federal court by his own attorneys. It is one in which a claim of amnesia, by way of dementia, formed the basis for the inquiry. The relevant literature reflects that partial or complete amnesia is a common claim among criminal defendants, comprising some 40% of all criminal cases (Bourget & Whitehurst, 2007; Cima, Merckelbach, Nijman et al., 2002; Cima, Nijman, Merckelbach et al., 2004; Kopelman, 1995; Stout & Farooque, 2008). In the forensic literature, claims of amnesia are generally classified as dissociative or organic amnesia, related to psychosis or posttraumatic stress versus traumatic brain injury, respectively. The theory underlying this dual categorization has been written about extensively and is beyond the scope of this chapter. What can be said is that the frequency of amnesia attributed to organic factors is largely speculative. When asserted, it is typically related to traumatic brain injury, with its effects usually exposed as partial and temporary (amnesia for the offense itself) rather than enduring. Very little is known about forensic amnesia claims as they relate to neurodegenerative disease, let alone the legal relevance of its chronic progressive nature and ultimate path to dementia. The case discussed in this chapter highlights the unique factors and challenges associated with such a claim.

DOI: 10.4324/9781003005063-21

A history of the evolution of the legal concept of CST is provided in the chapter for context, supported by examples of widely recognized cases. Touched on in the process are a number of controversies over the manner in which the field of neuropsychology has addressed dementia in forensic assessments, including employment of the second generation of MND criteria, controversies that became center stage in the course of opposing expert testimony in the case presented. One goal of the chapter is to offer recommendations for resolving such foundational disagreements.

A Case of Claimed Amnesia

You are asked by the U.S. Attorney's Office to review a case involving a 71-year-old widowed male physician whom we shall call Dr. Steadman. He was indicted 12 months earlier on eight counts of Medicaid fraud and eight counts of (associated) wire fraud spanning a 10-year period in his capacity as a consulting pediatric oncologist at multiple hospitals. His license to practice medicine has been temporarily suspended pending litigation. During your initial telephone consult with an Assistant United States Attorney (AUSA), you learn that the defense attorneys motioned for and were granted by the court a CST examination after they raised significant concerns at a status hearing about their client's cognitive capacity to participate in mounting a defense.

Specifically, the defense attorneys claim their client is amnestic for the ten-year period in question, and therefore unable to provide or reconstruct critical details about billing practices and other relevant inner workings of his practice. The defendant, they assert, is able to say he is "in trouble for billing fraud," but at the same time claims he has done nothing wrong and that he maintains his license and continues to practice at several hospitals. He insists he is competent and that no examination is necessary.[1] Dr. Steadman's attorneys believe their client is unable to assist in his defense and note that he has been diagnosed with Alzheimer's dementia of moderate severity and appears to be deteriorating further since they met him 12 months earlier.

The dementia diagnosis was made after the defendant's younger sister had him examined clinically by a neurologist following two episodes in which he was found by neighbors confused and wandering a couple of streets from his home in his bathrobe or pajamas during the afternoon. The first of these episodes occurred approximately three weeks following the indictment and the clinical appointments followed shortly thereafter. The sister noted some irritability on the part of Dr. Steadman when she or Dr. Steadman's son took the car keys away or confronted him about no longer being in practice. She describes this as a personality change. She reported a family history of cardiovascular disease (mother) and pancreatic cancer (father), but denied dementia in her parents who both lived into their mid- to late 80s. She was uncertain of dementia in the extended family.

Medical history establishes a right-handed Caucasian male with a 25-year history of hypercholesterolemia, mild obesity, and clinically well-controlled hypertension. Medications are Lisinopril 15 mg, Amlodipine 10 mg, Lipitor 80 mg, and recently added Namenda 5 mg *bid* by the neurologist. MRI ordered by the neurologist revealed mild atrophy and periventricular white matter changes, both read as normal for age. Electroencephalogram (EEG) was normal. After obtaining a Montreal Cognitive Assessment (MoCA) score of 20/30 during the appointment, the neurologist referred the defendant for a neuropsychological examination, the results of which reflected very poor delayed memory and mild naming difficulties. Based on these findings, the neurologist arrived at a diagnosis of moderate dementia, likely of the Alzheimer's type, with Behavioral Disturbance.

Neither clinical evaluation references Dr. Steadman's legal issues, though other personal stressors are noted (a brother with terminal cancer; family pressure to relinquish medical practice to focus on health; and family plans to permanently take car keys away). The sister had just moved into her brother's home as primary caregiver, largely due to concerns over his wanderings and her wish to help with driving to appointments, etc., though she also stated she wanted to ensure he took his medication properly. More recently, she has reported to the neuropsychologist that she is making plans to move her brother to an assisted living facility and to obtain conservatorship. Dr. Steadman's son states his father frequently asks when he will be returning to the hospital to see patients, at times becoming agitated when he cannot find the car keys the son has taken from him, stating he is needed for academic rounds, scheduled consultations and surgeries, and is going to be late. Both Dr. Steadman's son and sister, as well as the defense attorneys, recognize this as a marked loss of reality and insight.

The motion for a competency examination contains multiple other instances witnessed by the two defense attorneys representing Dr. Steadman, in which the defendant reportedly appeared confused and unable to remember at which hospitals he had privileges, as well as mixing up any number of other personal/historic details. The motion includes that their client recently presented to one of the hospitals thinking he was scheduled for a surgery, only to be turned away by concerned colleagues who told him he was not in fact on the schedule and had no assigned patients currently. This was said to be the second such occurrence in the past three months, and the medical directors suspended his privileges in response. The incident also prompted communication with the medical licensing board, which proceeded to suspend his license pending resolution of the litigation. In addition, the attorneys reported that on one occasion while they accompanied their client to his car in the parking lot following an appointment at their office, Dr. Steadman fell and sustained only minor abrasions on his hands and knees.

The defense attorneys further assert that despite repeated attempts to discuss the case with him, Dr. Steadman appears not to fully appreciate the gravity of the charges against him, vehemently proclaiming his innocence in response to the presentation of the indictment. He reportedly goes on to express concern that as a result of the indictment, he will no longer have access to patient Medicare benefit explanations or otherwise be able to describe and rationalize his particular patient billing practices. As is, he claims he cannot recall with any precision how billing was carried out (who billed from his office, the process by which payments are obtained/transferred to his bank, how he and employees are paid, and the like). He reportedly cannot remember or explain the various billing codes used for various patients in his files, information that is critical to the defense as such coding contributed to the fraud charges. At some point he is said to just become irritated with the whole topic of such conversations and dispenses all of it with the broadside that the government is simply wrong. In addition, his attorneys maintain he often does not recognize them from meeting to meeting or remember their discussions despite taking "notes."

The AUSA would like your opinion on the competency issue, as both the treating neurologist and neuropsychologist offered opinions regarding the competency inquiry at the request of their patient's defense attorneys—a contribution generally acknowledged not to be conflict-free. Both have opined Dr. Steadman is incompetent to proceed to trial based on their diagnosis of probable Alzheimer's disease of moderate severity. Notably, their reports reveal no indications that formal competency inquiries were conducted, a fact from which it can be safely assumed such were not. The AUSA would in addition like to have an opinion on clinical diagnosis, including information on the trajectory of Alzheimer's or any other neurodegenerative disease Dr. Steadman may have, and whether his apparent rapid deterioration and generally negative clinical picture are consistent with the diagnosis.

CST: Historical Antecedents

The notion (or principle) that an individual must be competent to stand trial originated in English common law, dating back to at least the 17th century. As is the case today, a defendant was at the time required to enter a plea to a charge prior to trial. The early articulations of what has become competency doctrine are said by legal scholars to have originated as a reaction by the English courts to defendants who stood mute in the face of the command to enter a plea. In such a circumstance, the court endeavored to determine whether the defendant was "mute of malice" or "mute ex visitation Dei" (by visitation of god)—a practice that continued into the 18th century. If it was determined that the refusal was willful, the court would attempt to force a plea by ordering *peine forte et dure*, a procedure during which increasingly heavier weights were placed upon the individual's chest until he responded appropriately or died. If it was determined the defendant was, as above, "mute ex visitation Dei" (initially a reference to deaf-mute individuals, but eventually expanded to include "lunatics" as well), he would not be subjected to such treatment.

In early cases, the term "insanity" was typically used to indicate present competency status. One still encounters this in the occasional forensic report, but it is a linguistic practice to be strenuously avoided. While both "competency" and "insanity" concern a defendant's mental state, they differ sharply in temporal consideration and legal implications. CST focuses on here-and-now mental state and seeks to measure meaningful participation in current or upcoming proceedings, whereas insanity determinations require a retrospective examination of mental status at the time of an offense and relate to culpability. A recent case puts it in clear perspective when it notes, as the lead opinion did, that the "entry of a plea of not guilty by reason of insanity… presupposes that the defendant is competent to stand trial and to enter a plea" (*Medina v. California*, 1992).

The prohibition against trying an incompetent defendant was well-established in common law by the time the famous commentaries of the 17th-century English jurist Sir Mathew Hale were published (Hale, 1736). Hale observed that:

> If a man in his sound memory commits a capital offense, and before his arraignment he becomes absolutely mad, he ought not by law to be arraigned during such his phrenzy, but be remitted to prison until that incapacity be removed; the reason is, because he cannot advisedly plead to the indictment… And if such person after his plea, and before his trial, become of *non sane memory,* he shall not be tried: for how can he make his defense?

This rule derived from a prohibition against trying a defendant in absentia (i.e., in his physical absence; see *Drope v. Missouri, 420 U.S. 162,* 1975). Notwithstanding its pragmatic origins, requiring a defendant be competent to stand trial also reflected concerns about the fairness and civility of subjecting certain defendants to trial. In the matter of *King v. Frith* (1790), John Frith stood charged with high treason for throwing a stone at King George III's coach as it traveled to the State Opening of Parliament. Frith claimed to be drawing attention to his cause, which he claimed was an illegal deprivation of his livelihood as an Army lieutenant after he was forcibly retired by a superior whom he claimed sent "supernatural agents" to whisper in his ear and "fabricated evidence of insanity against him." He also claimed messianic powers, among other things that led to his hospitalization. Frith was declared unfit to plead by reason of insanity, reflecting the king's treatment of insane persons with forgiveness and forbearance, after the court instructed the jury:

> Gentlemen of the jury, the enquiry which you are now called upon, is not whether the prisoner was in this unfortunate state of mind when the accident happened... but the humanity of the law of England... has prescribed, that no man shall be called upon to make his defence at a time when his mind is in that situation as not to appear capable of so doing; for, however guilty he may be, the enquiring into his guilt must be postponed to that season, when, by collecting together his intellects, and having them entire, he shall be able so to model his defence as to ward off the punishment of the law; it is for you, therefore, to enquire whether the prisoner is now in that state of mind... inasmuch as artful men may put on appearances which are not the reality of the case....

Early American jurisprudence, closely following English common law, also recognized the incompetency concept, initially in case law (e.g., *Commonwealth v. Braley*, 1804, an early case from Massachusetts), but eventually—jurisdiction by jurisdiction, state as well as federal—codified as statutory law. At the end of the century, a federal appeals court in *Youtsey v. United States* (1899) saw fit to elevate the principle that defendants be competent for trial to a fundamental protection guaranteed by the U.S. Constitution:

> It is not due process of law to subject an insane person to trial upon an indictment involving liberty or life.

And in 1966 the U.S. Supreme Court followed suit in *Pate v Robinson*:

> We believe that the evidence introduced on Robinson's behalf entitled him to a hearing on this issue. The court's failure to make such inquiry thus deprived Robinson of his constitutional right to a fair trial... Illinois jealously guards this right. Where the evidence raises a '*bona fide* doubt' as to a defendant's competence to stand trial, the judge, on his own motion, must impanel a jury and conduct a sanity hearing...[2]

Justice Kennedy in his concurring opinion in a later Supreme Court case, *Riggins v. Nevada*, 1992, aptly summarized the procedural stakes involved:

> Competence to stand trial is rudimentary, for upon it depends the main part of those rights deemed essential to a fair trial, including the right to effective assistance of counsel, the rights to summon, to confront, and to cross-examine witnesses, and the right to testify on one's own behalf or to remain silent without penalty for doing so.

Failure to raise competency concerns is today a common ground for appealing a conviction. The matter may not only be raised at any stage of the proceedings (*Pate v. Robinson*, 1966), by either party as well as by the trial judge, but *must* be addressed if there is what the law now calls, per *Robinson v. Pate*, a *bona fide* (i.e., reasonable) doubt as to a defendant's competency to proceed.

The Competency Inquiry in Steadman

In response to defense's motion for a competency hearing in the Steadman matter, the court ordered two separate competency examinations to be submitted simultaneously, as the government and defense could not agree on an expert. This is the court's prerogative; alternatively, the court could have granted an examination to defense by an expert of their choosing with the option of a subsequent rebuttal examination by an expert of the government's choosing. The dual expert approach saves time but means there is no opportunity for opposing experts to review and submit a written rebuttal unless specifically called for by the court. This takes time and, in this case, the court opted against it, possibly in response to the time-sensitive nature of a progressive, neurodegenerative condition being at issue. Therefore, any points of disagreement would have to be elicited through formal direct and cross-examinations or direct court inquiry at the competency hearing. Note that the court is not required to hear from the experts, as the reports are available and will have been reviewed prior to the hearing. However, the author has always been asked to testify unless the sole appointed expert in the matter, and even then, more often than not the court has provided an opportunity for direct "live" inquiry.

Defense raised the competency concern and requested a hearing in the Steadman matter on the basis of federal statute 18 U.S. Code § 4241 (Motion to Determine Competency of Defendant). This statute provides that:

> At any time after the commencement of a prosecution for an offense and prior to the sentencing of the defendant, or at any time after the commencement of probation or supervised release and prior to the completion of the sentence, the defendant or the attorney for the Government may file a motion for a hearing to determine the mental competency of the defendant. The court shall grant the motion, or shall order such a hearing on its own motion...

The Competency Test

So, after all this preliminary hemming, what is the actual test for CST; what are the so-called substantive criteria? Not just whom, but what, do we speak to? What is the legal language we must address when we formulate our findings and conclusions? By the second half of the 20th century, after many attempts by judges in specific cases of lesser or greater renown (Brakel & Brooks, 2001) and much trans-Atlantic as well as intra-Continental borrowing, the law, now statutory in all jurisdictions, had settled on a two-"pronged" articulation of the competency concept, as reflected in the section that completes the federal code cited just above and shared in the statutes of virtually all the states (Brakel, Parry & Weiner, 1985). It states:

> ...if there is reasonable cause to believe that the defendant may *presently be suffering from a mental disease or defect rendering him mentally incompetent to the extent that he is unable to understand the nature and consequences of the proceedings against him or to assist properly in his defense.* [Italics added]

The test, as noted, has two components, or "prongs," cognitive and functional, with a defendant to be found incompetent to stand trial should either fail to be met. Subsequent cases, high-profile and run-of-the mill, have elaborated upon and helped lawyers as well as forensic experts operationalize these two prongs. The *cognitive prong* (sometimes referred to as a factual/intellectual prong) refers to a defendant's basic knowledge of the workings of a court (its nature and purpose), its players, and proceedings. It addresses whether a defendant can appreciate his or her circumstances and the consequences of a conviction. The *functional/assistance prong* addresses the defendant's ability to function within the adjudication process. This requires, *inter alia*, that the defendant possess awareness of his situation and understanding of the substantive issues as applied to him; consideration of settlement options (e.g., to plead guilty and enter into a plea agreement or proceed to trial with basic knowledge and understanding of trial procedures, rights within that process, and respective consequences); the ability to assist counsel in trial preparation (e.g., providing relevant information such as an alibi, circumstances related to self-defense), and in the trial itself (e.g., decision to testify, identifying witnesses and other evidence; identifying issues for the confrontation of witnesses).

Not to be ignored because it is easy to overlook in the context of mental health-related discourse, the statute also requires an assessment of mental disease or defect—and/or in some states, notably Illinois, a physical defect—and whether a defendant's associated impairment significantly impacts his or her competency-related capacities. Of course, a medical diagnosis as such, including amnesia for events surrounding an offense, as in our case, does not necessarily render a defendant incompetent, a feature of the law discussed further, below. When mental illness or cognitive impairment is diagnosed, the manner in which symptoms *presently* impact the accused's functional capacities must be addressed.

Finally, in keeping with the historical roots of competency determinations that distinguished between a defendant remaining mute out of malice versus mute by an act of God, willful, uncooperative, or otherwise disruptive conduct is not grounds for an incompetency determination. A defendant who refuses to speak to his attorney, read his indictment, or otherwise acquire knowledge about his case or the workings of the court despite being capable of doing so is making a willful decision. But hardheadedness, foolishness, or other uncooperative behaviors are not equivalent to incompetency. Related, simple factual ignorance of charges and procedures due to failure to be apprised of the information or refusal to cooperate with attempts at education are not grounds for a conclusion that the defendant is incompetent. Only incapacity is.

The Impact of Dusky v. United States *(1960) on Competency Determinations*

Notwithstanding the fact that, as we saw above, every jurisdiction today has explicit and fairly similarly worded statutory provisions for addressing competency, it is the U.S. Supreme Court's decision in *Dusky v. United States* (1960) that many courts, in particular, the federal courts, rely on today for the operative test, the substantive criteria for assessing CST. Milton Dusky was a 33-year-old man with a history of schizophrenia, including intermittent visual hallucinations, depression, alcoholism, and psychiatric hospitalizations who was arrested and charged with kidnapping and attempted rape of a 15-year-old girl. After his arrest, Dusky was admitted to the U.S. Medical Center for Federal Prisoners in Springfield, Missouri for an evaluation of his competency and sanity. One examiner opined that Dusky was "oriented to time, place, and person" and was denying a "complete memory of the day of the offense." A second examination by psychiatric staff noted Dusky had initially stabilized following admission but had then begun to experience hallucinations with emergent beliefs that he was being framed. This examination concluded that due to schizophrenia, he was unable to properly understand the proceedings against him and to adequately assist counsel in his defense.

The district court (i.e., trial court) went on to find Dusky competent, and he was tried, found guilty, and sentenced. The outcome was appealed and affirmed by the U.S. Court of Appeals for the Eighth Circuit. However, upon review by the Supreme Court of the United States, citing the ambiguity in the expert testimony, questioning the legal sufficiency of the expert evidence and the fact that the examination was more than a year old, the court disagreed with the competency finding:

> Upon consideration of the entire record, we agree with the Solicitor General that the record in this case does not sufficiently support the findings of competency to stand trial, for, to support those findings under 18 U.S.C. § 4241, the district judge would need more information than this record presents.

The court went on to offer what has become the well-known language of Dusky and the minimum standards for determining CST in federal cases:

> We also agree with the suggestion of the Solicitor General that it is not enough for the district judge to find that the defendant [is] oriented to time and place and [has] some recollection of events, but that *the test must be whether he has sufficient present ability to consult with his lawyer with a reasonable degree of rational understanding -- and whether he has a rational as well as factual understanding of the proceedings against him.* [Italics added]

In conducting a competency analysis, clinicians must simply remember that factuality is "not enough"; the inquiry must also address the rationality of the defendant's mind. Most defendants are at least factually competent, even when severe mental illness/psychosis or neurocognitive disorders are active; a defendant's factual knowledge of the law and legal proceedings need not be sophisticated. As to rational ability to consult or assist, a defendant's capacity to consult with counsel "with a reasonable degree of rational understanding" does not of course mean he must possess the level of knowledge of a lawyer or have complete comprehension of case facts. Nor does having a negative or unproductive relationship with one's defense attorney violate the Sixth Amendment, a notion the Supreme Court of Arizona captured well in *Morris v. Slappy* (1983), a case (coincidentally) about an amnesia claim:

> ...limited amnesia does not totally incapacitate the defense and the defendant is free to assist counsel in numerous ways. We believe that a defendant is entitled to a fair trial, but not necessarily to a perfect trial.
>
> (*State v. McClendon*, 1968)

And finally, making an impulsive, emotional decision that poorly reflects risks, benefits, and other consequences does not indicate a defendant's basic abilities are compromised. But should mental illness or neurocognitive disorder impair the thoughts and perceptions about the legal proceedings as such, those in which the defendant is taking part (e.g., a paranoid delusion that the players of the court are conspiring with one another), a finding of incompetence becomes plausible. A defendant's perceptions about the law and legal process must be reality-based if he is to contribute to rational decision-making.

It should be noted that the federal statute 18 U.S. Code § 4241 has not been modified to include the rationality language of Dusky. Nor has it in most states. The case is nonetheless influential and clinicians conducting competency examinations in federal court must address it. It is less clear, owing to doubts that can be raised regarding the constitutional stature of Dusky's gratuitous, unanalyzed, per curiam ruling (a decision by the entire court, or panel, rather than a single judge/justice), whether Dusky carries the same weight in state cases.

Standard of Proof

There is of course no requirement that every defendant be examined for and found competent before a trial. In fact, the law in all jurisdictions presumes a defendant is competent unless (or until) proven otherwise. But by what standard must a defendant be proved competent, and whose burden is it to do so? The English cases that predate our Constitution provided no specific guidance on the appropriate standard of proof in competency determinations, though the court's "whether or not" instruction in *King v. Frith* (1790) and *King v. Pritchard* (1836), among other cases of the era, suggested a "more likely than not"—i.e., preponderance of the evidence—standard for competency determinations at that time.

The vast majority of American jurisdictions followed the English lead and historically applied a "preponderance of proof" standard to competency determinations (e.g., Ohio, *State v. O'Grady*, 1896; Tennessee, *Jordan v. State*, 1911; *Commonwealth v. Simanowicz*, 1913). A notable deviation from that was formally put to the test in *Cooper v. Oklahoma* (1996). In 1989, Byron Keith Cooper was charged with the murder of an 86-year-old man while in the course of committing a burglary. The question of Cooper's competence to stand trial was raised on five separate occasions, both prior to and during his trial. The issue of malingering was additionally raised by Cooper's own attorney during the third request for a competency hearing when he told the court that Cooper's behavior was "odd" and that he refused to communicate with him, stating it could be a serious matter "if he's not faking."

The trial judge applied Oklahoma's standard that a criminal defendant is presumed competent to stand trial unless he proves his incompetence by *clear and convincing evidence*,[3] finding Cooper competent on five separate occasions despite Cooper's persistently bizarre and disruptive behavior and conflicting expert testimony on the issue. Following his conviction, a jury sentenced Cooper to death. In affirming his conviction and death sentence, Oklahoma's Court of Criminal Appeals rejected Cooper's argument that the state's presumption of competence, combined with its clear and convincing evidence standard, violated due process because the burden placed on him was too onerous.

The U.S. Supreme Court reversed, holding that because the Oklahoma's rule risked trying a defendant who may more likely than not be incompetent, it violated Cooper's fundamental right not to stand trial while incompetent. The court noted its previous holding in *Medina v. California*, which established that a state may presume a defendant competent and require him to prove incompetence by a preponderance of the evidence (Medina is primarily about *burden of proof* but also articulated this standard of proof). Such a presumption, the court held, did not undermine a "principle of justice so rooted in the traditions and conscience of our people as to be ranked as fundamental" (the test for a violation of due process articulated in many of the court's precedents). Echoing this analysis, the court also noted Oklahoma's rule requiring a clear and convincing *standard* of proof had no roots in historical practice, as in both early English and American cases, the common-law standard of proof was preponderance of the evidence. As to the contemporary state of the law, the court noted that the preponderance standard was employed by 46 of 50 states[4] and the federal courts at the time of the decision, indicating that the large majority of jurisdictions considered Oklahoma's heightened standard unnecessary to maintain the state's interest in the prompt and orderly disposition of criminal cases.

Finally, relevant to Dr. Steadman's case, the Cooper Court commented on the specific malingering issue raised by the defense attorney:

> Difficulty in ascertaining whether a defendant is incompetent or malingering may make it appropriate to place the burden of proof on him, but it does not justify the additional onus of an especially high standard of proof.

Last, but definitely not least, it must be pointed out with as much clarity as possible that, notwithstanding all the above regarding the standard of proof, its differential measures of certainty, and potential consequences on outcomes, all this pertains only to the legal aspects of any case. For the clinical expert, the standard to which an expert is held in providing testimony remains "reasonable degree of neuropsychological certainty."

Case Findings

Behavioral Observations

Dr. Steadman arrived with his sister to the first day of the two-day examination. Long pauses and slowed speech were noted for approximately an hour, which then normalized and did not return for the remainder of the examination. Conversation built naturally on itself, and on Day 2 of the examination (two days later), at no time did he repeat himself. Dr. Steadman joked that he had tried to recall the long list of words the technician had read him and looked up a word he didn't recognize when asked to read it aloud from the first day of the exam (reference to the CVLT-II and Test of Premorbid Functioning [TOPF]). Gait was slowed but otherwise normal. Affect was mildly restricted for the first hour, then consistently normal in range, mood was euthymic with the exception of one point during the competency examination on Day 2 when the examiner pushed for an explanation of how billing practices had evolved over the years from working for others versus private practice (Dr. Steadman became briefly agitated and maintained he had no memory of how his practice worked other than he was reached by pager in emergencies and that he had privileges at several hospitals, which he accurately named). Thought content reflected no signs of paranoia, grandiosity, magical thinking, delusion, or hostility, and at no time did Dr. Steadman lose his train of thought. Dr. Steadman denied hallucinations of any type and no signs of responding to internal/external stimuli were noted. He worked slowly on testing but did not request instructions be repeated. He tended to give up easily and did not respond to encouragement to guess, occasionally refusing forced-choice options during the mental status and competency examinations, and he came across as oppositional at times during the competency examination. No signs of fatigue or anxiety were observed, and Dr. Steadman denied anxiety and depression on brief psychological measures (Geriatric Depression Scale, Beck Anxiety Inventory, both zero).

Mental Status Exam

MoCA score was 11/30. Dr. Steadman was disoriented to month, date, year (off by three years), day of the week, and season (Fall versus Winter), estimated it was morning hours (correct at approximately 9:30 a.m.), and was able to say he was in a doctor's office. He inaccurately named the president (missing the current and prior administrations) and inaccurately named the immediate president before him. He could not name the governor or longtime mayor (in office more than ten years). He was unable to successfully complete Serial 7s but was able to name the months of the year and days of the week backward, say the alphabet and count backward from 20 to 1 without error.

Dr. Steadman said the United States was currently fighting in Iraq and could spontaneously offer no other current events. He said Donald Trump was a New York real estate/business owner and denied knowledge of him ever having been president (Biden was the current president). In response to multiple-choice current events, he said that Bobby Kennedy was recently assassinated and subsequently refused other multiple-choice presentations. He accurately named the president during the civil war but stated President Lincoln died of natural causes. He was unable to recall five objects he was asked to remember following a short delay, without benefit from cuing or multiple-choice formats. He stated he had just one child, a son (his first-born child is a daughter) and could not recall the names of his son's children though correctly numbered them as three. At no time was Dr. Steadman able to recall the examiner's or testing technician's name. He accurately stated he was under indictment for "billing mistakes" and that the court "wants to see if I'm okay if there's a trial… which there won't be because I didn't do anything wrong… You're evaluating me to see if I can go to trial, if I'm competent, which I am. You work for the prosecutor… you're not my doctor."

Collateral Interview of Sister

Collateral interview with the sister revealed her impression that memory difficulties had begun approximately three years earlier (losing keys, cellphone, once becoming lost while driving, missing some doctor appointments), though she did not witness these difficulties personally until approximately six months earlier (post indictment) and affirmed it was the defendant who offered her the other history. She had personally noticed some word-finding difficulties in the past couple of years. She had reiterated this history to examining clinicians as she was accompanying her brother to all appointments. She denied noticing any other expressive language issues or receptive language difficulties. She denied knowledge of any occupational difficulties prior to her brother's license being suspended. She said she moved into her brother's home to care for him following the first wandering incident "because he can no longer cook for himself, do laundry or clean, and we took his keys, so I do all the shopping now." She said he had always taken his medications on his own and she noticed no difficulties, but her nephew/defendant's son nonetheless arranged to have daily pill packs sent to the home so he would not be responsible for organizing the morning versus evening regimens. He had also taken over all financial matters and removed his father's checkbook and credit cards as a precaution, but the sister denied knowledge of any problematic spending, bounced checks, or tardiness on bills prior to that time. Dr. Steadman had not argued about these things, only about access to the car.

Clinical Interview and Competency Examination

At the start of the clinical interview, Dr. Steadman referred the government's neuropsychologist to available medical records ("I don't remember all of my history, it's all there"). He spontaneously stated only that he had high cholesterol; he denied having hypertension when asked. He said he could not recall his medications and denied knowledge of being prescribed a medication in relation to the memory difficulties he was reporting. He said he had been vaccinated against COVID ("All of the physicians had to, to maintain privileges") and commented it was a challenging time for his patients who could not receive visitors following surgery. He said he stopped drinking alcohol after medical school and denied lifetime drug use.

Dr. Steadman said "I don't think so" when asked if he had previously undergone the type of testing we conducted two days earlier (though he referred to the testing and our technician approximately 30 minutes earlier), similarly denying knowledge of prior examinations by neurology and neuropsychology ("That doesn't sound familiar"). In response to a multiple-choice format, he correctly named two of his three grandchildren but maintained he only had a son (his sister denied any estrangement with his daughter and stated they see one another regularly, approximately twice per month). Dr. Steadman denied memory of the recent fall in the parking lot. He denied having defense attorneys or ever having been in a court of any kind, for any reason (he was previously arraigned and present for a subsequent hearing on the motion for a competency examination).

A formal competency evaluation was conducted two days after testing. Dr. Steadman claimed not to know what he was charged with other than to say, "for how I billed my patients… yes, I'm indicted." After the government neuropsychologist twice explained the reason charges were "Medicaid fraud" due to submitting billing for procedures he had not conducted and "wire fraud" related to submission of such bills over the internet and the transfer of ill-gotten monies from bank to bank, Dr. Steadman nonetheless provided the wrong answer when asked what the charges were, both immediately following explanation as well as at the end of the interview when we returned to those concepts for which education was provided ("It's just for how I billed"). He insisted he had done nothing wrong. He refused to acknowledge or offer a hypothetical that illustrated the numerous ways by which a provider might fraudulently bill insurance for clinical services ("I wouldn't know, I don't do my own billing"). However, he responded affirmatively when given this hypothetical: "If I am a therapist and I see my patient for 30 minutes but submit a billing code for a 60-minute session, is that fraud?"

Dr. Steadman said he didn't understand concepts such as physical versus circumstantial evidence; claimed not to know the various roles of a judge ("Don't they work with the attorneys?"); how indictments are obtained or what a grand jury is ("Never heard of that, I'm not a lawyer"); which constitutional rights a defendant relinquishes by pleading guilty; the concept of a plea bargain and its risks and benefits to both parties; whose option it was to have a bench trial and the potential benefits/risks of opting for one; the burden of proof for a jury trial; what the role of a trial jury is, the number of individuals that comprise it or that unanimity is required for a conviction. He continually stated it was the role of the government to determine guilt. Education on these concepts yielded no change in responses.

Because he refused to acknowledge he had defense attorneys, hypotheticals were required for inquiries regarding working with a defense attorney. Dr. Steadman stated a defendant who did not understand what he is charged with or could not remember what he did could not aid an attorney in a defense, "Because he would be the only one who knew what he did." Related, this meant he could not testify about it or be able to know "if someone is lying" during testimony, as he has no memory of the time period in question. When asked how the hypothetical therapist who billed for longer sessions could defend himself against a fraud claim, Dr. Steadman said bank statements could be used to illustrate the manner in which a practice was paid, by whom, when, and for how much, and this would "trace every step." Similarly, when posed hypothetically, Dr. Steadman said he would not withhold information from an attorney trying to help him as this could "backfire," and he would not have concerns about collusion among attorneys and/or with the court. At that point, he looked at the examiner and stated, "Are you frustrated?"

The competency interview conducted by the defense yielded some similar results, with fewer concepts assessed and without education or hypotheticals employed. However, when asked about plea bargains, Dr. Steadman stated he would accept a plea bargain if he could plead to a lesser charge, one of negligence (in billing practices). "I don't want anyone saying I intentionally stole anything," he explained.

Test Findings

The following table summarizes test findings from the three examinations. Standard scores are based on those for a 71-year-old, right-handed Caucasian male with 20+ years of education. Performance Validity Tests (PVTs) beyond the CVLT-II Forced-Choice trial were not considered by the first examiner but were calculated and reviewed by the experts for purposes of comparison. These scores are bracketed. The government examination (Examination #3) occurred four weeks following the defense's examination, a fact not made available until both exams were completed and the experts were asked to provide one another raw test data and materials.

	Exam 1 (Clinical) 1 month post Indictment	*Exam 2 (Defense) 14 months post Indictment*	*Exam 3 (Gov) 15 months post Indictment*
TOMM Immed, Del, Ret	—	39/50, 44/50, 42/50	39/50, 41/50, 39/50
Dot Counting	—	E-Score: 18.67, 2 errs	E-Score: 14.25, 2 errs
WMT Immed, Del, Consis	—	—	65%, 70%, 47.5%
VSVT Hard Items	—	—	24/24, 15/24, 37/48
WAIS-IV Digit Span AC SS	[10]	10	[7]
Reliable Digit Span	[6]	7	6
CVLT-II Forced Choice	[15/16]	14/16	11/16
WMS-IV Log Mem Recog*	[16/23]	[14/23]	14/23
Booklet Category Test (BCT) Errs T1 & T2	—	[2]	—
JLO	—	—	21
Finger Tapping (Dom H)	[35]	[27.6]	29
MoCA	Neurologist: 20/30	19/30	11/30
TOPF	—	—	Std:101 Predicted FSIQ:102
WRAT-IV Reading	—	Std: 103	—
WAIS-IV FSIQ	110	100	90
VCI	112	98	98
PRI	98	94	84
WMI	120	118	100
PSI	98	88	80
Information	9	9	8
Vocabulary	13	10	9
Similarities	14	10	11
Block Design	10	10	2
Matrix Reasoning	10	9	9

(*Continued*)

	Exam 1 (Clinical) 1 month post Indictment	*Exam 2 (Defense) 14 months post Indictment*	*Exam 3 (Gov) 15 months post Indictment*
Visual Puzzles	9	8	9
Digit Span	10	10	7
Longest DSpan F/B/Seq (raw)	5,5,6	5,5,6	5,4,2
Arithmetic	15	15	13
Symbol Search	10	6	4
Coding	9	10	9
Trails A	—	T: 27, 1:12, 0 err	T: 18, 2:15, 1 err
Trails B	—	T: 36, 2:56, 1 err	T: 31, 4:07, 6 errs
Oral Trails B	—	—	Z: +0.58, 0:22, 0 err
DKEFS Trails VS	ss: 12, 1 err	—	ss: 11, 1 err
Trails NS	ss: 8, 0 err	—	ss: 4, 1 err
Trails LS	ss: 10, 0 err	—	ss: 7, 0 err
Trails NLS	ss: 8, 0 err	—	ss: 3, 4 errs
Trails MS	ss: 7, 0 err	—	ss: 5, 0 err
Stroop Word Reading	—	—	T: 39
Color Naming	—	—	T: 38
Color-Word	—	—	T: 36
Interference Calculation	—	—	T: 45
DKEFS Word	ss: 10, 0 err	ss: 9, 0 err	—
Color	ss: 10, 0 err	ss: 8, 1 err	—
Interference	ss: 5, 1 err	ss: 9, 0 err	—
Interference/Switching	d/c	d/c	—
CVLT Trials 1–5	**CVLT-3** Std: 73 (1,4,5,4,5)	**CVLT-3** Std: 86 (3,6,5,6,6)	**CVLT-2** T: 39 (3,4,6,6,4)
Trial 1	ss: 4 (1)	ss: 8 (3)	Z: –1.0 (3)
List B	ss: 11 (4)	ss: 9 (3)	Z: –1.5 (2)
Short Delay	ss: 3 (0)	ss: 5 (2)	Z: –2.5 (0)
Short Delay Cued	ss: 4 (2)	ss: 5 (4)	Z: –2.0 (3)
Long Delay	ss: 4 (1)	ss: 3 (0)	Z: –2.5 (0)
Long Delay Cued	ss: 7 (6)	ss: 4 (2)	Z: –2.0 (1)
Y/N Recognition	ss: 10 (14/16)	ss: 10 (14/16)	Z: –0.5 (13/16)
Recog False Positives	ss: 4 (16)	ss: 4 (15)	Z: +3.0 (13)
Discriminability	ss: 6	ss: 5	Z: –1.5
Forced Choice	15/16	14/16	11/16
WMS-IV Log Mem* Immed	ss: 7	ss: 8	ss: 5
Logical Memory Delay	ss: 4	ss: 5	ss: 3
Logical Memory Recog	16/23 (25–50%ile)	14/23 (10–16%ile)	14/23 (10–16%ile)
Visual Reproduction Immed	ss: 3	ss: 6	ss: 9
Visual Reproduction Delay	ss: 3 (0)	ss: 3 (0)	ss: 3 (0)
Visual Reproduction Recog	—	—	1/7 (3–9%ile)
JLO	—	—	ss: 9
Visual Reproduction Copy	51–75%ile	9%ile	51–75%ile

(Continued)

	Exam 1 (Clinical) 1 month post Indictment	*Exam 2 (Defense) 14 months post Indictment*	*Exam 3 (Gov) 15 months post Indictment*
Rey Complex Figure Copy	—	2–5%ile	6–10%ile
Letter Fluency	—	—	T: 37
Category Fluency	—	—	T: 37, Z: -0.70
DKEFS Letter Fluency	ss: 10	ss: 9	—
DKEFS Category Fluency	ss: 8	ss: 7	—
BNT-2	MOANS ss: 5	MOANS ss: 6	MOANS ss: 7
WCST % CLR	T: 43	—	T: 37
% Errors	T: 39	—	T: 35
% Perceive Resp	T: 45	—	T: 45
% Perceive Errors	T: 45	—	T: 45
# Categ	2/6 (17–25%ile)	—	1/6 (11–16%ile)
FMS	1 (>16%ile)	—	1 (>16%ile)
DKEFS Proverbs (free)	—	ss: 14	ss: 15
BCT	—	T: 32	—
Finger Tapping	Dom (35) T: 27 Ndom (32) T: 31	Dom (27.6) T: 23 Ndom (24.0) T: 18	Dom (29) T: 23 Ndom (30) T: 27

* Older Adults Version

Testimony at the Competency Hearing

The competency hearing lasted three days, during which expert neurologists and neuropsychologists, treating neurologists and neuropsychologists, and lay witnesses, including family members, neighbors, and hospital colleagues, offered testimony. Opposing sides were respectively aligned from a diagnostic standpoint, with treaters and defense experts offering a probable Alzheimer's diagnosis, and government clinicians arriving at the conclusion that dementia was not supported by evidence. Relevant conclusions and testimony excerpts by opposing neuropsychologists follow.

Performance Validity

The validity of Dr. Steadman's test performances was the most contested aspect of examination findings and the most adversarial issue at the hearing. The different PVT cutoff scores employed by defense and government experts appear in the table following arguments about PVT data below, with references from their respective reports and testimony. Further information related to these measures and the research and its limitations on cutoff scores in dementia cases can be found in recent reviews by Miller and Axelrod (2018), McWhirter, Ritchie, Stone, and Carson (2020), Bortnik and Dean (2021), Merten and Henry (2022), Schroeder and Martin (2022) and Martin, Schroeder, and Olsen (2022).

- **Clinical Opinion**: The first examiner administered no stand-alone PVTs and concluded Dr. Steadman had provided good effort based on the CVLT-II Forced-Choice trial. The report did not mention other potential embedded measures for consideration.

The defense neuropsychologist considered other available embedded PVTs from the clinical examination as passed (WAIS-IV Digit Span scaled score; Reliable Digit Span [RDS]; Finger Tapping), using cutoff scores for mild dementia patients. This normalized otherwise failed RDS and Finger Tapping measures using traditional cutoffs.

The government neuropsychologist considered RDS and Finger Tapping failed and agreed the Digit Span scaled score and CVLT-II Forced-Choice measures were passed, concluding the validity of the test data was compromised due to variable effort; impaired scores could not be considered while unimpaired scores could be interpreted as *the least of* Dr. Steadman's capabilities, with his pattern of relative strengths and weaknesses indeterminable.

Finally, both experts agreed it was considered standard practice to include multiple PVTs in an exam, even in a clinical context, and relying solely on embedded measures was insufficient. However, the defense expert argued the clinical data could be considered valid because the test data between Exams 1 and 2 (his own exam 13 months later, in which a sufficient number of PVTs were administered) were so similar.

- **Defense Expert Opinion**: The defense neuropsychologist employed mild dementia cutoffs for PVTs, the basis for which was the pre-exam consideration of Dr. Steadman's age, medical history, prior diagnosis of dementia, a MoCA score of 20/30 during the recent neurology examination, and collateral information obtained from the sister, which was consistent with the record, all of which "pointed to the realistic likelihood of a dementia process." Such an approach was consistent with the above-mentioned research that has expanded our knowledge of PVT patterns among dementia patients of varying severities and an aspirational goal of the 2020 Malingering of Neurocognitive Dysfunction criteria to avoid false positive malingering determinations (Sherman, Slick & Iverson, 2020).

  The defense expert testified the MRI was not inconsistent with an Alzheimer's diagnosis, citing the lack of 1:1 correlation between structure and function and that a normal EEG similarly was not dispositive given the lack of specificity of such a measurement tool. Considering mild dementia cutoff scores, the only failed PVT from his examination was from the first two trials of the Booklet Category Test (BCT), which he testified had to date not been well studied in dementia groups.

  He further testified traditional PVT cutoffs should not have been used by the government expert given the defendant's history and that when cutoffs for mild dementia patients were appropriately applied to government data, malingering was ruled out because Dr. Steadman's only failures among 11 considered measures were the CVLT-II Forced-Choice trial and Hard Items of the VSVT, "a ratio of failed to passed measures not supported by the MND criteria as indicative of malingering." He further testified these two measures had not been well studied among dementia patients, and therefore without normatively developed cutoff scores should not necessarily be considered failed in any case. He also testified the government expert's WMT findings should be considered unreliable without consideration of the Genuine Memory Impairment Profile (i.e., the full Medical Symptom Validity Test [MSVT], to include the extra memory tests, ought to have been administered).

  Finally, the defense expert testified that the increased performance on a number of measures in the government examination four weeks following his own demonstrated the defendant's good effort (e.g., increased scores on Similarities, Visual Puzzles, VR Immediate Recall, VR Copy, Rey-O Copy, BNT-2, Proverbs, Nondominant Hand Tapping).
- **Government Expert Opinion**: The government neuropsychologist rejected the defense expert's approach of an a priori determination of a dementia diagnosis and employed traditional PVT cutoffs. In her own examination, this yielded failures of the TOMM, DCT, WMT, VSVT (hard items were within chance range), RDS, CVLT-II Forced Choice, and Finger Tapping. Failure of so many independent measures with specificity levels of

at least 0.90 made the likelihood of a false positive determination extremely low; the cognitive data were invalid.

Dr. Steadman's high level of functioning up to the point of indictment, including independence in all instrumental activities of daily living, absence of vocational fitness problems as a surgeon at multiple hospitals, reboarding in pediatric hematology-oncology eight months prior, the acute onset of clinical symptoms and their steep downward trajectory post indictment, noncredible clinical presentation during the examination (i.e., resolving slowed speech, recall of COVID pandemic while claiming amnesia for events during the past decade, similarly, recall of and driving to a hospital to conduct a surgery at which he had privileges for just five years, failure to recall he had a daughter, inaccurate or near-miss recall of famous historical events) and forensic context of the examination with base rates of malingering in criminal matters ranging from 19% to 54% across investigations (Mittenberg, Patton, Canyock & Condit, 2022; Ardolf, Denney & Houston, 2007; Fazio, Denning & Denney, 2015, 2017), supported this conclusion.

The defense expert's determination of cutoff scores by pre-exam "diagnostic considerations" was characterized as a circular and unreliable methodology, and manipulation of the very PVTs used to determine validity of test results pre-indictment level of functioning notwithstanding, reliance on a medical record and collateral data created largely by self-report (and post indictment, no less), the absence of objective dementia-specific imaging, bloodwork or cerebrospinal fluid findings to independently verify the dementia diagnosis, available imaging read as normal for age and failure of other examiners to reconcile pre-indictment levels of functioning and other inconsistencies, supported the unreliability of such a method.

The government expert further testified that data from all three examinations were uninterpretable save a "least as" analysis due to variable to poor effort. That is, while normatively unimpaired performances could be interpreted as *the least of* Dr. Steadman's capabilities, impaired performances could not be interpreted. The inexplicable declines in performance on certain measures from defense to government examinations one month later added credence to this clinical determination (e.g., MoCA, FSIQ, Block Design/PRI, DKEFS Trailmaking, and Logical Memory performances). Modest performance improvements described by the defense expert were rejected as meaningful or evidence of good effort, and attributed instead either to normal measurement error and/or variable effort between examinations. And in those cases where significant improvement was noted (e.g., VR Immediate Recall and VR Copy), she testified this either represented variable effort between examinations or a practice effect that individuals with bona fide cognitive impairment uncommonly demonstrate (Jutten et al., 2020).

The government expert further testified obtaining the GMIP is not required (i.e., the WMT was developed separately and stands on its own), that simulators can produce the GMIP at high rates (Singhal, Green, Ashaye, Shankar & Gill, 2009), that the GMIP does not distinguish well between those with bona fide impairment and poor effort (Axelrod & Schutte, 2010), that significant functional decline in activities of daily living is not reliably associated with those producing the GMIP (Resch, Rhoads, Ovsiew & Soble, 2020), and the GMIP is found among individuals without bona fide cognitive impairment at unacceptably high rates in some investigations where the potential for secondary gain exists (Robinson, Collins, Miller, Pacheco & Wisdom, 2018). She nonetheless agreed research has reliably demonstrated high WMT failure rates among older adults with bona fide and significant cognitive decline, as with all PVTs employed in the examinations.

Finally, the government expert testified the defense neuropsychologist was misinterpreting the MND criteria in ruling out malingering based solely on PVT performance;

a malingering determination could be made when PVT data are unremarkable, or no PVT data are available at all. The criteria pertaining to clinically relevant inconsistencies (exam- and nonexam-related) were easily met in this case. Moreover, nowhere in the MND criteria nor in any position statement by the field was an a priori diagnostic determination required for examinations in which dementia has been raised as a diagnostic possibility. The recent recommendation by Schroeder and Martin (2022) to make such pre-test determinations reflects a benevolent approach to the issue, placing greater weight on avoiding false positive malingering determinations than missing the behavior. This caveat should and will always accompany data interpretation. However, the forensic neuropsychologists will almost always have a far greater amount of collateral information and data available to them than their colleagues in the clinic, making predetermined diagnoses in forensic cases (a "risk assessment," in essence) unnecessary and unsupportable. Malingering in this case could be determined based on such collateral data alone.

	Clinical Exam	*Mild Dementia Cutoffs*	*Defense Exam*	*Traditional Cutoffs*	*Gov Exam*
TOMM Trial 2		< 39[a]	44	< 49[b]	41
DCT		E-Score ≥ 22	18.67	E-Score ≥ 13.8[c]	14.25
WMT Delay Trial	—	N/A	—	≤ 82.5%	70%
VSVT Hard Items	—	Hard Items ≤ 14	—	Hard Items ≤ 17[d]	15
WAIS-IV DSpan AC SS	10	≤ 5	10	≤ 5	7
RDS	6	≤ 5	7	≤ 6	6
CVLT-II FC	15	≤ 13	14	≤ 15[e,f]	11
WMS-IV Log Mem Recog*	16	—	14	< 14/23[g]	14
JLO	—	—	—	≤ 18[h]	21
BCT Errs T1 & T2	—	2	—	> 1 Err T1+T2[i,k]	—
FOT Dom Hand (males)	35	≤ 21	27.6	≤ 35	29

[a] Rudman N., Oyebode J., Jones C., Bentham P. (2011). An investigation into the validity of effort tests in a working age dementia population. *Aging and Mental Health, 15(1)*, 47–57.

[b] Martin P., Schroeder R., Olsen D., Maloy H., Boettcher A., Ernst N., Okut H. (2020). A systematic review and meta-analysis of the Test of Memory Malingering in adults: Two decades of deception detection *The Clinical Neuropsychologist, 34:1*, 88–119.

[c] McCaul C., Boone K., Ermshar A., Cottingham M., Victor T., Ziegler E., Zeller M., Wright M. (2018). Cross-validation of the Dot Counting Test in a large sample of credible and non-credible patients referred for neuropsychological testing, *The Clinical Neuropsychologist, 32:6*, 1054–1067.

[d] Grote C., Kooker E., Garron D., Nyenhuis D., Smith G., Mattingly M. (2000). Performance of compensation seeking and non-compensation seeking samples on the Victoria Symptom Validity Test: Cross-validation and extension of a standardization study. *Journal of Clinical & Experimental Neuropsychology, 22*, 709–719.

[e] Delis D., Kramer J., Kaplan E., Obert B. (2000). *The California Verbal Learning Test* (2nd ed.). San Antonio, TX: Psychological Assessment Resources.

[f] Schwartz E., Erdodi L., Rodriguez N., Ghosh J., Curtain J., Flashman L., Roth er R. (2016). CVLT-II Forced Choice recognition trial as an embedded validity indicator: A systematic review of the evidence. *Journal of the International Neuropsychological Society, 22*, 851–858.

[g] Soble J., Bain K., Bailey C., Kirton J., Marceaux J., Critchfield E., et al. (2019). Evaluating the accuracy of the Wechsler Memory Scale-Fourth Edition (WAIS-IV) logical memory embedded validity index for detecting invalid test performance. *Applied Neuropsychology: Adult, 26*, 311–318.

[h] Whiteside D., Wald D., Busse M. (2011). Classification accuracy of multiple visual spatial measures in the detection of suspect effort. *The Clinical Neuropsychologist. 25*, 287–301.

[i] Tenhula W., Sweet, J. (1996). Double cross-validation of the Booklet Category Test in detecting malingered traumatic brain injury. *The Clinical Neuropsychologist, 10*, 104–116.

[j] DiCarlo M., Gfeller J., Oliveri M. (2000). Effects of coaching on detecting feigned cognitive impairment on the Category Test. *Archives of Clinical Neuropsychology, 15*, 399–413.

[k] Hanson Misialek L., Fazio R., Denney R., Meyers W. (2012). Limited predictive accuracy of the Booklet Category Test in a criminal forensic sample. *Applied Neuropsychology: Adult*, 1–6.

Diagnosis and Competency Determination

- **Clinical Opinion**: The clinical neuropsychologist diagnosed Dr. Steadman with Probable Alzheimer's Disease of Mild Severity, with Behavioral Disturbance (wandering and "confabulation" of continuing to practice medicine). The diagnosis was supported by medical history, collateral information provided by Dr. Steadman's daughter, and test findings.

  Relevant test findings included a significant decline in general intellectual functioning (concluding a Full Scale IQ of 110 was a decline from a likely superior level of intellect given a high average/superior Vocabulary score, considering the MoCA score of 20/30 and level of occupational achievement); a significant VCI-PRI split; diminished processing speed relative to superior working memory on the WAIS-IV; mild to moderately impaired delayed recall for both verbal and visual material; mildly impaired confrontation naming; relatively greater phonemic versus semantic verbal fluency scores; and executive dysfunction (discontinuation of DKEFS Trailmaking inhibition/switching condition, 2/6 categories on the WCST, poor Stroop Interference score, number of CVLT-II false positive responses, and poor CVLT-II List A vs. B discriminability score).

  The clinical neuropsychologist did not conduct a formal competency examination, but offered the opinion that Dr. Steadman was incompetent to stand trial based on the dementia diagnosis. No attempt was made to correlate diagnosis with components of the intellectual or functional prongs of competency, other than to say Dr. Steadman's poor episodic memory rendered him unable to aid in his defense.
- **Defense Expert Opinion**: The defense neuropsychologist diagnosed Dr. Steadman with Probable Alzheimer's Disease of Moderate severity, also with Behavioral Disturbance. This was supported by medical history, family collateral information, and consistency with and further cognitive deterioration from test findings obtained 13 months earlier.

  In addition to citing findings similarly to those of the clinical exam, decline was noted in general intellectual functioning (10-point drop in WAIS-IV FSIQ), information processing speed (10-point drop in WAIS-IV PSI, impaired Trails A), visuoconstruction (VR Copies and impaired Rey-O Copy), and executive dysfunction (impaired Trails B and BCT). The expert interpreted performance improvements to the normal range on Stroop Interference, CVLT-II, and Visual Reproduction Immediate Recall as evidence of good effort, rejecting cross-examination inquiries, suggesting such evidence may belie a true deterioration or reflect variable effort between exams.

  Of the subsequent 10-point drop in FSIQ at the time of the government's exam, the defense expert testified on cross-examination that serial testing can lead to "test fatigue," and he did not find the 10-point drop particularly meaningful, especially since it came largely from the Block Design subtext (ss of 2 at Exam 3). He testified the same was true of the precipitous drop in MoCA score from 19/30 to 11/30. He did concede that such scores indicated the government's data likely underestimated Dr. Steadman's true abilities in some areas, but also pointed out performance stability, even increased test scores on some measures (e.g., Visual Reproduction and Copy; Rey-O Copy; BNT-2; and DKEFS Proverbs). He refused to concede that "good effort" inferred from performance improvements and "test fatigue" inferred from performance declines could alternatively be interpreted as variable effort.

  The defense expert found Dr. Steadman incompetent to proceed, arguing that Dr. Steadman did not understand the full scope of the charges against him, or what led to his being in trouble given he was unable to reconstruct his practice during the time period in question due to memory impairment. It was also argued that Dr. Steadman clearly did not have a rational understanding or appreciate the gravity of the charges against him, or his personal/occupational situation, as despite having his license and privileges suspended, he believed he was still practicing medicine.

As for participating in a trial, Dr. Steadman's impaired attention and concentration was judged to make attending to the protracted nature of the proceedings impossible, and that while his short-term memory may be intact, poor delayed episodic memory made it impossible for him to acquire and hold onto the information that would be presented at a trial. Relatedly, this would directly impede his ability to recognize potential discrepancies in witness testimony, and, along with some word-finding difficulties, to testify reliably on his own behalf. Moreover, given his amnesia for the time period in question, as well as his inability to hold onto new conversations, he was unable to aid his attorneys in any meaningful way in presenting a defense. Finally, the defense expert testified that Dr. Steadman's poor abstract reasoning and problem-solving ability made it impossible for him to make rational decisions regarding the course and nature of his defense, or whether to proceed to trial in the first place.

- **Government Expert Opinion:** The government expert testified a dementia diagnosis was reasonably ruled out in Dr. Steadman's case. Malingering of cognitive impairment was the most parsimonious explanation for Dr. Steadman's inconsistent and nonsensical clinical presentation that began precipitously post indictment.

  The government expert testified that no inferences could be drawn regarding a bona fide profile or decline in cognitive functioning given the test data across exams were invalid. As one example, she pointed out that given Dr. Steadman's medical stability, the significant drop of 10 points in FSIQ over a four-week period between Examinations 2 and 3 could not reasonably be explained other than by variable effort, pointing in particular to the performance drop in Block Design from a scaled score of 10 to 2, and to a lesser extent Digit Span from a scaled score of 10 to 7. This inexplicable decline was also demonstrated by MoCA scores, which remained essentially unchanged over a 13-month period between clinical and defense exams (20/30 in Exam 1; 19/30 in Exam 2) but declined to 11/30 four weeks later during government Exam 3.

  Importantly, the "least as" analysis, ignoring Dr. Steadman's impaired findings and interpreting his normatively unimpaired findings as the least of his capabilities, demonstrated intact functioning in every cognitive domain, with scores ranging from low average to superior. Such was the case in all areas assessed, with the exception of delayed verbal and visual memory. Even here a less effortful recognition memory format demonstrated Dr. Steadman's intact consolidation of contextually based information presented by stories.

  Negative neurodiagnostics, a record comprised largely of Dr. Steadman's self-report, and the lack of scrutiny of inconsistencies in the clinical picture by treating clinicians, who had no access to such information for consideration, was brought out during cross-examination as the defense attorney pointed out the government expert's minority opinion (a common tactic).

  Dr. Steadman was capable of understanding the fraud charges and describing a rational approach to a defense through provision of financial records to an attorney, notwithstanding only when speaking about the illegal billing practices of a hypothetical therapist. The claim of complete amnesia was belied by numerous factors, some among them, including its implausibly circumscribed nature; Dr. Steadman's description of COVID-related events during the same time period; his recall of hospitals at which he held privileges (indeed he successfully drove to one hospital despite only having privileges there for five years, relevant as he claimed amnesia for a ten-year period); the implausibility of misremembering he had a daughter and overlearned historical information such as how President Lincoln died; and the intact tracking ability he demonstrated over many hours of interviewing, reported consistently across examinations. It was concluded that Dr. Steadman had a rational and factual understanding of the charges and proceedings against him and had the capacity to consult meaningfully with his attorneys toward a defense with a reasonable degree of rational understanding, if he opted to; his claim of being unaware of charges against him or having an attorney was willful and deliberate.

Post-Hearing Considerations

Courts and Claims of Amnesia

Is a bona fide amnestic defendant incompetent to stand trial? Defense attorneys frequently argue this is the case because the defendant is unable to recount relevant facts of alleged offense conduct and therefore cannot participate or aid counsel in mounting a defense. However, the courts have typically, if not unanimously, rejected equating amnesia with incompetence. Distrust of such claims appears to underlie such decisions. As one court noted (*Commonwealth ex rel. Cummins v. Price*, 1966), to allow amnesia to preclude trial would "turn over the determination of crime and criminal liability to psychiatrists, whose opinions are usually based in large part upon defendant's self-serving statements, instead of to courts and juries." The same court observed that "for over 100 years, lack of memory in murder cases has been a common and frequent defense."

Courts have nonetheless remained sensitive to the threat amnesia may pose to fair adjudication. Perhaps the most comprehensive attempt to address the issue of proceeding with a prosecution in the context of amnesia is *Wilson v. United States* (1968). In that case, the defendant, charged with assault and robbery, had fractured his skull while being apprehended for the offense; as a result, he claimed (and clinicians verified) that he had no memory of the incidents underlying his charges and was deemed unlikely ever to regain his memory. While finding that his amnesia did not per se bar prosecution, the federal court of appeals issued the following guidelines to assist the trial court in determining whether a fair trial could be held, and via a mandated retrospective review of the proceedings, was in fact held:

1. The extent to which the amnesia affected the defendant's ability to consult with and assist his lawyer.
2. The extent to which the amnesia affected the defendant's ability to testify in his own behalf.
3. The extent to which the evidence could be extrinsically reconstructed in view of the defendant's amnesia. Such evidence would include evidence relating to the crime itself as well as any reasonably possible alibi.
4. The extent to which the government assisted the defendant and his counsel in that reconstruction.

5 The strength of the prosecution's case. Most important here will be whether the government's case is such as to negate all reasonable hypotheses of innocence. If there is any substantial possibility that the accused could, but for his amnesia, establish an alibi or other defense, it should be presumed that he would have been able to do so.
6 Any other facts and circumstances that would indicate whether or not the defendant had a fair trial.

The *Wilson* Court also required the government to assist the defense in preparing its case, including additional cooperation during pretrial discovery. The court in United *States v. Stubblefield* (1971) similarly obliged the U.S. government to assist in reconstructing the events surrounding the alleged offense as well as any possible alibi or other defense.

The Court's Order in Steadman

The court published its 47-page Order Finding Defendant Competent to Stand Trial two months following the hearing. Relevant excerpts follow.

In its review of relevant case law, the court provided several case examples in which courts had found defendants competent despite claims of dementia:

> ...numerous courts have recognized dementia does not prevent a defendant from possessing a rational and factual understanding of the proceedings against him and having the ability to consult with counsel with a reasonable degree of rational understanding. See, e.g., *United States v. Bradley*, No. 05-CR-59-JRH-CLR, ECF 349 (S.D. Ga. filed Jan. 24, 2006) (finding competent a defendant with dementia); *United States v. Vallone*, 698 F.3d 416, 508–511 (7th Cir. 2012) (finding competent a defendant with Alzheimer's dementia); *United States v. Dreyer*, No. 08–41VAP, ECF 279 (C.D. Cal. filed Apr. 19, 2014) (finding competent a defendant with a brain hemorrhage and previous dementia diagnosis).

The court followed with cases involving alleged dementia in which a defendant's malingering was taken into account:

> In light of defendant's malingering, defendant's claimed cognitive impairment carries less significance. See, e.g., *United States v. Kasim*, No. 07-CR-56-PPS-APR, 2010 WL 339084 (D. Ind. Jan. 21, 2010) (finding a likely malingering defendant competent after previously found incompetent with dementia); *United States v. Benson*, No. 12–CR00480–YGR–1, 2015 WL 1869476 (N.D. Cal. Apr. 22, 2015) (defendant with alleged dementia and evidence of malingering found competent); *United States v. Chun*, No. 17-CR204510-VAR-MKM, ECF 87 (E.D. Mich. filed Dec. 6, 2019) (finding a malingering defendant with MCI competent).

And while not citing *Wilson* directly, the court noted:

> The Government may aid in reconstructing bank records for Defense as necessary... we do not find lack of familiarity with billing practices a compelling factor in assisting counsel.

Of understanding charges and aiding in his defense, the court noted:

> When charges against him were framed in the hypothetical, Defendant was able to recall the existence and nature of those charges, identified a rational approach that could be taken in his defense, and he demonstrated knowledge of the manner in which bank records could assist in his defense... and suggested he would plead to lesser charges... The willingness of Defendant to insightfully discuss these details so long as they are presented in the hypothetical dovetails with Defendant's expression during the Government examination that a defendant with amnesia may be incompetent.

Of the disagreement between experts over malingering and whether dementia-specific PVT cutoff scores should have been employed, the court detailed its disagreement with defense's case analysis and emphasized its duty to make a malingering determination:

> The Court finds that the Defendant's expert did not properly consider the evidence related to malingering other than acknowledging in his testimony a motive for malingering existed... he could not reconcile Defendant's pre-indictment level of functioning or discussion of COVID-related hospital protocols during a period for which he claims amnesia... did not address the implausible memory loss of having a daughter or for overlearned historical information... of tracking conversation over many hours of interview...
>
> Defense criticized the PVTs administered by the Government's expert, noting that either the PVTs were not well suited to dementia patients or that different cutoffs for establishing validity should be applied given 'the realistic likelihood of a dementia process.' At its essence, though, the matter before the Court requires it to determine whether Defendant's cognitive symptoms, and most significantly his short-term memory, is legitimate and honestly presented or whether it is feigned or exaggerated in a manner meant to support his claim that he is incompetent to stand trial. As a practical matter, using dementia cutoffs to determine evidence of malingering could have the effect of masking the existence of or extent of such malingering. On the other hand, not using dementia cutoffs could make it unfairly challenging to demonstrate the existence of an actual dementia.
>
> In the end, the Court looks to all the evidence of record to determine the question presented in this case. In this sense, the Court's approach mirrors the 'practical recommendation' set forth in an article offered by the Government (See Gov. Ex. 12, Miller & Axelrod (2018), Performance Validity Assessment: Disentangling Dementia from the Disinterested and the Disingenuous, Forensic Geropsychology: Practice Essentials at 25). This chapter counsels use of 'a process approach including qualitative integration of clinical judgment, strong working knowledge of disease characteristics and comparisons with known clinical groups, behavioral observations and careful scrutiny of the contextual factors surrounding a particular case'...

Finally, the court emphasized the relationship between the malingering determination and its ultimate finding of Dr. Steadman's competency to proceed to trial:

> In the end, the Government's expert concluded that 'Malingering is simply the only reasonable explanation for Dr. Steadman's inconsistent and nonsensical presentation.' After examining an extensive record on the subject, including pre- and post indictment

> medical records and multiple expert reports, the Court concurs with this assessment... the evidence demonstrates many intact areas of cognition, and any actual diminishment of these abilities is not as severe as Defendant presents it and, stripped of the feigning described by the Government's expert and found by the Court herein, Defendant retains the ability to assist properly in his defense... The Court concludes that Defendant meets the relevant legal standard of competency to be tried on the criminal charges set forth in the indictment. Defendant is both able to understand the nature and consequences of the proceedings against him and to assist properly in his defense. 18 U.S.C. § 4241(d).

Commentary

The Steadman case addresses several contemporary issues in forensic neuropsychology and highlights the critical reliance on neuropsychologists by criminal courts in CST cases. The process by which our field makes malingering determinations became the main focus of opposing expert testimony and the court was presented with conflicting approaches to assessing a dementia claim in this regard. The revised MND criteria published in 2020 were discussed at length.

The defense neuropsychologist in this case made an a priori decision that Dr. Steadman's medical history "point[ed] to a realistic likelihood of dementia" and thereby employed PVT cutoff scores obtained from mild dementia patients, arguing the approach was supported by recent research determining optimal PVT cutoff scores among dementia patients of different severities and the MND criteria. He went on to rule out malingering based on a ratio of 2 of 11 failed PVTs. The court rejected the argument, citing failure to reconcile the numerous and significant inconsistencies in Dr. Steadman's clinical presentation and history. The circularity of making a pre-exam diagnosis for purposes of determining PVT cutoff scores was also raised by the court.

The author agrees with the court's case analysis and reiterates the testimony that even without PVT data, the other inconsistencies gleaned from the examination in this case, observational and psychometric, coupled with those from outside of the examination ("compelling inconsistencies" and "marked discrepancies," respectively, to use the MND criteria language), were sufficient for a malingering determination. The MND criteria do not require evidence of PVT failure, or even that all criteria be met. And the conflicting opinions regarding whether the PVT data were failed or not were arguably unproductive and potentially confusing to the court.

An a priori approach to determining which PVT cutoff scores to employ in cases of claimed dementia was recently recommended by Schroeder and Martin (2022), who encouraged "examining for the likelihood of dementia before testing occurs" as part of a multivariable seven-step validity assessment in dementia settings (p. 257, Figure 14.1). This entails relying on demographics, medical history, neuroimaging or genetic testing, reported symptom onset and progression, convergence of reported symptoms to syndrome stereotypes, functioning in activities of daily living per medical records and collateral report, neurologic family history, and behavioral signs of dementia observed during the clinical interview. They note (p. 257):

> ...obtaining this information can help to determine a priori which PVT cutoffs should be utilized given that, as we discuss later, PVT cutoffs vary depending on whether a patient has mild cognitive impairment (MCI), mild dementia, or moderate dementia.

They go on to recommend that clinicians (p. 259):

> look for converging evidence of a most likely impairment severity level, and, when unsure, proceed conservatively by choosing cutoffs associated with the greater level of impairment.

While well intentioned, this pre-test approach to clinical diagnostic decision-making and PVT selection is unlikely to yield reliable results, particularly in forensic cases. Not all of the data points may be available, some are more compelling than others, and those obtained through self-report must always be viewed with skepticism. The neuropsychologist following this approach is likely to have uncertainty due to the lack of complete case information, and the recommendation in that case to "proceed conservatively by choosing cutoffs associated with the greater level of impairment" has no empirical or rational basis and could easily be deemed arbitrary by a court, resulting in disregarded testimony.

Our field's initial malingering criteria (Slick, Sherman & Iverson, 1999) were developed with the perspective that an abundance of caution be used in making malingering determinations, to minimize identifying non-malingering examinees as malingerers as much as possible. Indeed, a "reasonable doubt strategy" was recommended. The revised 2020 MND criteria convey the same aspirational goal of minimizing false positive malingering determinations. This should encourage a thorough case analysis, to be supported and argued well, not taking the benevolent high road to an unreliable end; the pre-test decision-making approach has the potential to corner the forensic neuropsychologist into an untenable position. Even for the neuropsychologist unwilling to ignore compelling case inconsistencies, in the very least, the use of this approach is likely in many cases to result in conflicting data points to contend with and having to argue against one's own PVT data.

There is by now general agreement in the field that our current PVTs do not maintain their specificity when employed in cases of bona fide moderate or severe dementia, resulting in unacceptably high false positive rates. There is nonetheless disagreement as to the utility of dementia-derived PVT cutoff scores as they exist today. Merten and Henry (2022) point out:

> ...the search for a predetermined generalized cutoff for PVTs in dementia patients may not yield reliable results; even the use of stratified cut scores (Martin et al., 2022) may remain unsatisfactory with regard to the large variety of clinical presentations of dementia.
> (p. 297)

Certainly not all dementia *types* are marked by primary memory impairments and should not be expected to produce homogeneous PVT data. Combining dementia cases of different *severity* in "known-groups" designs has likely also contributed to variable sensitivity and specificity rates across investigations and poor predictive power.

Other design and methodological problems have muddied the relatively nascent literature on PVTs in dementia settings (see the aforementioned reviews by Bortnik and Dean [2021], McWhirter, Ritchie, Stone and Carson [2020], and Miller and Axelrod [2018]). Relying on MoCA or MMSE scores or other baseline assessment techniques to designate membership in dementia severity groups is problematic as the legitimacy of such scores must be presumed. Investigations have additionally not always attempted to ensure the purity of their own samples, and very little is known about the base rates of malingering of dementia as dementia patients are typically excluded from PVT research. Context undoubtedly matters, e.g., involvement in criminal or civil adjudication, or application for social security, other disability, or military benefits. However, neuropsychologists do not always know or ask about potential incentives. While early investigations indicated malingering of dementia was likely a low base rate behavior (just 2% of compensation-seeking examinees were claiming dementia in a 2002 survey of neuropsychologists; Mittenberg, Patton, Canyock et al. 2002), more recent investigations indicate noncredible performance in examinees presenting with dementia claims is not as infrequent as once suspected. Martin and Schroeder (2020) found that 7% of individuals 65 and older who presented to a clinic had potential external incentives, and Rienstra et al. (2013) found that 6.5% of individuals with MCI or early dementia involved in an investigation of the relationship between hippocampal volume and memory test performance presented with noncredible symptoms. A 15% rate of test invalidity was found among veterans being seen at a VA medical center in a geriatric memory disorders clinic, which included some below-chance PVT findings (Barker, Horner & Bachman, 2010). To the extent such examinees are included in the dementia samples of PVT investigations, contaminated findings stymie our efforts.

Finally, research design challenges aside, as others (Gaudet, Castelluccio, Gold, et al., 2022), have pointed out, Merten and Henry pointed out the circularity of lowering or developing diagnostic-specific PVT cutoff scores:

> …the condition in question, if authentic, may warrant the application of a lower cut score on a PVT, but this very PVT is used to check the authenticity of the condition in question. This problem has not been solved so far.
>
> (p. 291)

Axelrod and Schutte (2010) similarly characterized as circular the recommendation by Green (2004) "to first identify the probability of a dementia diagnosis before concluding the Dementia Profile should be assessed" in the Medical Symptom Validity Test, "as it would require that the clinician performing the evaluation would have to reach a diagnosis before actually administering the test" (p. 875).

Given these many issues, is pre-test diagnostic decision-making justifiable? As was evident in the Steadman case, available pre-examination information, including demographics, family history, medical records, neuroimaging, self-report, collateral information and a clinical neuropsychological examination, did not ultimately "point to a realistic likelihood of dementia" when such data points could be compared with exam-related evidence (including test data) and a more diligent case analysis was conducted (see Boone, 2016; Bortnik & Dean, 2022, and Schroeder and Martin's other recommended steps for recommended approaches to complement PVT data in malingering determinations). In Steadman, the a priori approach faltered, resulting in "triage error" by the defense neuropsychologist and obscuring a case of malingering. In the author's opinion, this approach is irreconcilably circular and can in some cases become an impediment to reaching conclusions that are supported by compelling evidence, the essence of the job of a forensic neuropsychologist.

Competency determinations are critical to the court's disposition of justice and judges rely strongly on our input. They also rely on our expertise to root out deception because of its relative frequency in criminal matters; the author provides a malingering opinion in every criminal case (even simply to say it has reasonably been ruled out) because of its inherent relevance to such cases. Had Dr. Steadman been found incompetent and unrestorable, barring a finding he was a danger to the community (unlikely), the U.S. Attorney's

Office would ultimately have had no choice but to drop all charges against him. This is not justice. Fortunately, the court conducted the appropriate case analysis, while the defense neuropsychologist did not.

A forensic neuropsychologist is in a unique position to provide cutting edge research findings to the courts. But courts deserve to know and weigh the reliability of the evidence being presented. An evidentiary hearing (a *Daubert* hearing in federal court) on dementia-specific PVT cutoff scores would not have been surprising in this or any other case given the early stage of our empirical literature compiling these cutoff scores, and best practices based on it are likely to change as patient groups employed in research become less heterogeneous and the base rates of malingering among dementia patients in various settings becomes clearer. Our knowledge of the base rate of noncredible performance and malingering in dementia cases will grow if neuropsychologists begin to incorporate inquiries about potential incentives into their examinations and follow AACN guidelines (Sweet et al., 2021) incorporating PVTs into their cognitive exams. It has been this author's experience that the neuropsychologist in a dementia clinic rarely makes such inquiries, or assesses psychometrically for performance validity in adequate ways, as was seen by the first/clinical examination in Steadman, notwithstanding an obvious adjudication context in that case. In the authors' own practice, half of dementia claims in criminal matters were deemed malingered. This base rate is consistent with previous investigations of PVT validation in prison competency restoration samples (49%–54% malingering based on the Slick et al. original 1999 criteria, Ardolf, Denney & Houston, 2007), though is higher than the overall rate of 33% from the author's own criminal felony court clinic (representing a sample of those undergoing initial competency examinations as opposed to those already determined incompetent and sent for restoration) based on the same criteria.[5]

It is clear that the forensic neuropsychologist will address malingered dementia far more often than their counterparts in clinical settings. Going forward, a collective effort to compile data should be made so that direct comparisons between feigning and genuine dementia groups, vetted by consideration of the 2020 MND criteria, can be made. This would go a long way toward advancing our knowledge of the true test performance profiles of malingered cases and if and how they may differ in criminal versus clinical settings. Until such data are gathered, the neuropsychologist practicing in the criminal courts must responsibly offer caveats about dementia-specific PVT scores in their reports and testimony. One of the greatest roles of the forensic neuropsychologist is to teach fact-finders, be they jurors or judges. We must share what we know with the utmost diligence in a fair, nonbiased manner. If new discoveries or areas of research are not ready for prime time, i.e., their reliability has yet to be determined, not only should we make the conscientious decision not to rely on such data in our forensic work but be prepared to address their limitations should the court be presented with the information by a colleague so its evidentiary value can be properly weighed.

Acknowledgment

The author thanks S. Jan Brakel, J.D. for his review of the legal aspects of this chapter.

Notes

1 A defendant or their attorney cannot waive a competency inquiry. However, in certain state courts where trials are held for competency determinations, a trial waiver in lieu of a bench decision is permissible. Federal courts do not hold trials for competency determinations.

2 Note the use of the term "sanity" here refers to competency to stand trial.

3 In *Colorado v. New Mexico*, 467 U.S. 310 (1984), the Supreme Court defined "clear and convincing" as evidence that is highly and substantially more likely to be true than untrue. In other words, the fact finder must be convinced that the contention is highly probable.
4 Statutes from OK (1991), CT, RI and PA (1995) employed the Clear and Convincing standard of proof.
5 The Isaac Ray Forensic Group Database currently consists of 334 consecutively referred felony defendants who underwent adjudication in State and Federal Courts between 2002 and 2018.

References

American Bar Association. (1989). *ABA Criminal Justice Mental Health Standards*. Washington, DC: American Bar Association.

Ardolf B.R., Denney R.L., Houston C.M. (2007). Base rates of negative response bias and malingered neurocognitive dysfunction among criminal defendants referred for neuropsychological evaluation. *The Clinical Neuropsychologist*, *6*, 899–916.

Axelrod B., Schutte C. (2010). Analysis of the dementia profile on the Medical Symptom Validity Test. *The Clinical Neuropsychologist*, *24*(5), 873–881.

Barker M., Horner M., Bachman D. (2010). Embedded indices of effort in the Repeatable Battery for the Assessment of Neuropsychological Status (RBANS). In a geriatric sample. *The Clinical Neuropsychologist*, *24*(6), 1064–1077.

Boone K. (2016). Assessment of neurocognitive performance validity (pp. 39–50). In J. Ricker & J. Morgan (Eds.), *Textbook of Clinical Neuropsychology* (2nd edition). New York: Taylor and Francis.

Bortnik K., Dean A. (2021). Performance validity testing in patients with dementia. In K. Boone (Ed.), *Assessment of Feigned Cognitive Impairment: A Neuropsychological Perspective*. (pp. 481–503). New York: The Guilford Press.

Bourget D., Whitehurst L. (2007). Amnesia and crime. *The Journal of the American Academy Psychiatry and the Law*, *35*, 469–480.

Brakel S., Parry J., Weiner B. (1985). *The Mentally Disabled and the Law* (3rd edition), pp. 694–707, Table 12.1. Chicago, IL: American Bar Foundation.

Cima M., Merckelbach H., Nijman H., Knauer E., Hollnack S. (2002). I can't remember your honor: Offenders who claim amnesia. *German Journal of Psychiatry*, *5*(1), 24–34.

Cima M., Nijman H., Merckelbach H., Kremer K., Hollnack S. (2004): Claims of crime-related amnesia in forensic patients. *International Journal of Law and Psychiatry*, *27*(3), 215–221.

Commonwealth v. Braley, 1 Mass. 102, 103 (1804).

Commonwealth ex rel. Cummins v. Price, 421 Pa. 396, cert denied, 385 U.S. 869 (1966).

Commonwealth v. Simanowicz, 242 Pa. 402 (1913).

Cooper v. Oklahoma, 517 U.S. 348 (1996).

Dusky v. United States, 362 U.S. 402 (1960).

Fazio R., Sanders J., Denney R. (2015). Comparison of performance on the Test of Memory Malingering and Word Memory Test in a criminal forensic sample. *Archives of Clinical Neuropsychology*, *30*(4), 293–301.

Fazio R., Denning J., Denney R. (2017). TOMM Trial 1 as a performance validity indicator in a criminal forensic sample. *The Clinical Neuropsychologist*, *31*(1), 251–267.

Brakel. S.J., Brooks. A.D. (2001). *Law and Psychiatry in the Criminal Justice System*. Littleton, CO: Fred B. Rothman & Co.

Gaudet C., Castelluccio B., Gold D., McLaughlin N., Correia S. (2022). Limitations of performance validity tests in dementia evaluations: The role of base rates. *Psychological Assessment*, *34*(11), 1074–1080.

Green, P. (2004). *Green's Medical Symptom Validity Test (MSVT) for Microsoft Windows User Manual*. Edmonton, Canada: Green's Publishing.

Hale, Sir Matthew. (1971). *Historia Placitorum Coronae. The History of the Pleas of the Crown.* edited by Sollom Emlyn. 2 vols. London, 1736. Reprint. Classical English Law Texts. London: Professional Books, Ltd.

Jordan v. State, 64 Tex. Crim. 187 (1911).
Jutten R., Grandoit E., Foldi N., et al. (2020). Lower practice effects as a marker of cognitive performance and dementia risk: A literature review. *Alzheimers Dement (Amst), 12*(1), e12055. doi: 10.1002/dad2.12055
King v. Frith, 22 How. St. Tr. 307 (1790).
King v. Pritchard, 7 C&P 303 (1936).
Kopelman M. (1995). The assessment of psychogenic amnesia. In A Baddeley, B Wilson & F Watts (Eds.), *Handbook of Memory Disorders* (pp. 427–448). New York: Wiley.
Martin P., Schroeder R. (2020). Base rates of invalid test performance across clinical non-forensic contexts and settings. *Archives of Clinical Neuropsychology, 35,* 717–725.
Martin P., Schroeder R., Olsen D. (2022). Performance validity in the dementia clinic: Specificity of validity tests when used individually and in aggregate across levels of cognition. *The Clinical Neuropsychologist, 36*(1), 165–188.
McWhirter L., Ritchie C., Stone J., Carson A. (2020). Performance Validity tests failure in clinical populations – a systematic review. *Journal of Neurology, Neurosurgery, and Psychiatry, 91*(9), 945–952.
Medina v. California, 505 US 437 (1992).
Merten, T., & Henry, M. (2022). Symptom and performance validity assessment in older adults and patients with dementia and claimed dementia. In *A Handbook of Geriatric Neuropsychology* (pp. 286–303). Philadelphia, PA: Routledge.
Miller J., Axelrod B. (2018). Performance validity assessment: Disentangling dementia from the disinterested and and disingenuous. In S. Bush & L. Heck (Eds.), *Forensic Geropsychology: Practice Essentials* (pp. 25–47). Washington DC: American Psychological Association.
Mittenberg W., Patton C., Canyock E., Condir D. (2002). Base rates of malingering and symptom exaggeration. *Journal of Clinical and Experimental Neuropsychology, 24*(8), 1094–1102.
Morris N., McNiel D., Binder R. (2021). Estimating annual numbers of competency to stand trial evaluations across the United States. *The Journal of the American Academy Psychiatry and the Law, 49*(4), 530–539.
Morris v. Slappy, 461 U.S. 1 (1983).
Pate v. Robinson, 383 U.S. 375, 378 (1966).
Resch Z., Rhoads T., Ovsiew G., Soble J. (2020). A known-groups validation of the Medical Symptom Validity Test and analysis of the Genuine Memory Impairment Profile. *Assessment, 29*(3), 455–466.
Rienstra A., Groot P., Spaan P., Majoie B., Nederveen A., Walstra G., et al. (2013). Symptom validity testing in memory clinics: Hippocampal-memory associations and relevance for diagnosing mild cognitive impairment. *Journal of Clinical and Experimental Neuropsychology, 35*(1), 59–70.
Riggins v. Nevada, 504 U.S. 127 (1992).
Robinson J., Collins R., Miller B., Pacheco V., Wisdom N. (2018). The severe impairment profile: A conceptual shift. *Archives of Clinical Neuropsychology, 33,* 238–246.
Schroeder R., Martin P. (2022). Validity assessment within the memory disorders/dementia clinic. In R. Schroeder & P. Martin (Eds.), *Validity Assessment in Clinical Neuropsychological Practice: Evaluating and Managing Noncredible Performance* (pp. 254–279). New York: The Guilford Press.
Sherman E., Slick D., Iverson G. (2020). Multidimensional malingering criteria for neuropsychological assessment. A 20-year update of the malingered neuropsychological dysfunction criteria. *Archives of Clinical Neuropsychology, 35*(6), 735–764.
Singhal A., Green P., Ashaye K., Shankar K., Gill D. (2009). High specificity of the Medical Symptom Validity Test in patients with very severe memory impairment. *Archives of Clinical Neuropsychology, 24*(8), 721–728.
Slick D., Sherman E., Iverson G. (1999). Diagnostic criteria for malingered neurocognitive dysfunction: Proposed standards for clinical practice and research. *The Clinical Neuropsychologist, 13*(4), 545–561.
State v. McClendon, 103 Ariz. 105 (1968).
State v. O'Grady, 5 Ohio Dec. 654 (1896).

Stout R., Farooque R. (2008). Claims of amnesia for criminal offenses: Psychopathology, substance abuse, and malingering. *Journal of Forensic Science, 53*(12), 18–22.
Sweet J., Heilbronner R., Morgan J., Larrabee G., Rohling M., Boone K., et al. (2021). American Academy of Clinical Neuropsychology (AACN) 2021 consensus statement on validity assessment: Update of the 2009 AACN consensus conference statement on neuropsychological assessment of effort, response bias, and malingering. *The Clinical Neuropsychologist, 35*(6), 1053–1106.
U.S. v Stubblefield, 325 F. Supp, 485 (D. Tenn. 1971).
Wilson v. United States, 391 F.2d 460 (D.C. Cir. 1968).
Youtsey v. United States, 97 F. 937 (6th Cir., 1899).

19 Feigning of Cognitive and Psychotic Disorders in a Criminal Forensic Context

Competency to Stand Trial – Case of Mr. S.

Bernice A. Marcopulos

The U.S. legal system requires that citizens possess basic competency to participate in criminal proceedings (Melton et al., 2018). A trial of a defendant incapable of meaningfully participating denies them their 14th Amendment, the right to receive due process. An incompetent defendant cannot assist counsel and meaningfully participate in the legal process (*Youtsey v. United States*, 1899). Although the requirements vary from state to state, most states follow the Supreme Court decision in Dusky (*Dusky v. United States*, 1960), establishing the basic standard for competency in criminal matters. A defendant should be able to demonstrate a rational and factual understanding of the criminal process they are facing (e.g., roles of the courtroom personnel, such as judge, jury, and prosecutor). The defendant should also be able to consult with their counsel to prepare their defense productively. Most states require that a mental disease or defect must be present that directly impacts the defendant's functioning during the trial as the basis for a legal determination of incompetence.

Defendants are assumed to be competent unless it is demonstrated to the court that they are incompetent to proceed. Concerns regarding trial competency can be raised anytime during legal proceedings (*Drope v. Missouri*, 1975; *Pate v. Robinson*, 1966). Usually, the defense attorney raises the issue, but the prosecutor or the judge can also request a competency to stand trial (CST) evaluation. Approximately one-quarter of defendants undergoing a forensic mental health evaluation for trial competence have been found incompetent to stand trial (Pirelli et al., 2011). Most defendants deemed incompetent to stand trial (IST) have a psychotic disorder (Cochrane et al., 2001; Warren et al., 1991) that can be potentially treated with medication and result in eventual competence. Another cause for trial incompetence can be a cognitive disorder such as intellectual disability, brain damage, or other brain dysfunction.

Incompetent defendants must participate in restoration services until they achieve competence or show that they cannot achieve competency. Defendants can be deemed "unrestorably incompetent" if their neurologic or psychiatric condition does not improve and restoration is ineffective (Gay et al., 2017). For instance, a defendant deemed incompetent due to cognitive impairment from progressive dementia, such as Alzheimer's disease, will decline in functioning over time and is unlikely to benefit from restoration (Heck & Herrick, 2007). On the other hand, a defendant who suffered a traumatic brain injury or stroke may recover sufficiently to achieve trial competency (Mahoney et al., 2018). Cognitive rehabilitation interventions have been suggested to augment traditional competency restoration programs (Schwalbe & Medalia, 2007).

Neuropsychological assessment can delineate the cognitive variables important for CST and postulate whether restoration is likely, depending upon the nature and severity of the

DOI: 10.4324/9781003005063-22

brain disorder and other factors relevant to recovery, such as age and co-morbid health variables (Denney, 2012a; Mallory & Guyton, 2017; Toofanian et al., 2015). Deficits in intelligence, attention, memory, and social intelligence have been associated with incompetence (Nestor et al., 1999). Arredondo et al. (2017) found that 33% of their sample of hospitalized defendants referred to neuropsychology were adjudicated as IST. A higher proportion of defendants diagnosed with a cognitive disorder were adjudicated as IST compared with those diagnosed with a schizophrenia-spectrum, mood, or substance use disorder. The delayed memory subtest of the Repeatable Battery for the Assessment of Neuropsychological Status (RBANS) had the strongest relationship with the determination of competence with standard scores above 85 predicting competence and scores below 50 doubling the chance of IST. Neuropsychological assessment can also suggest practical approaches for restoration and accommodations during court proceedings. However, it is important to note that low test scores and a brain disorder diagnosis do not automatically equal trial incompetence or competence (Tussey et al., 2013). The forensic evaluator must directly assess the specific functional abilities related to comprehending and participating in legal proceedings. They must establish a causal relationship between functional disability and a brain disorder or psychiatric illness.

In addition to evaluating cognitive factors important for CST, neuropsychologists possess an armamentarium of measures and methods for detecting malingered cognitive dysfunction (e.g., Boone, 2021; Sweet et al., 2021). The base rate for malingering in CST evaluations has been found to be high, ranging from 25% to over 50% (Ardolf et al., 2007; Wynkoop & Denney, 1999; Gottfried & Glassmire, 2016). A defendant seeking to delay or avoid trial might malinger either psychiatric symptoms, cognitive deficits, or both (Gottfried & Glassmire, 2016). Defendants may be motivated to feign psychiatric and/or cognitive disorders because they prefer a psychiatric hospital over jail or hope to postpone or even avoid trial. A screening instrument such as the Structured Inventory for Malingered Symptoms can identify several conditions that might be exaggerated or feigned (Lewis et al., 2002). Symptom validity tests, such as those built into the Minnesota Multiphasic Personality Inventory or Personality Assessment Inventory, can detect exaggerated or feigned symptoms (e.g., Hawes & Boccaccini, 2009), while performance validity tests (PVTs, e.g., Test of Memory Malingering) can detect feigned or exaggerated deficits on cognitive tests. The forensic evaluator must determine if the cognitive or psychiatric symptoms are valid and if they directly impact the ability to understand competency-related legal concepts (Tussey et al., 2013). CST is a functional capacity that must be directly assessed (Grisso et al., 2003).

The following case is of a defendant who feigned both psychiatric and cognitive disorders and postponed their trial for nearly a year while forensic evaluators attempted to restore his competency during his psychiatric hospitalization. The defendant received multiple CST evaluations, most concluding that competency could not be determined. The last CST evaluation was performed in the context of a forensic neuropsychological screening evaluation, which provided strong evidence that the defendant was malingering.

The Case of Mr. S.

Background

Mr. S., the defendant, was a 55-year-old man charged with aggravated assault against a minor. The minor was a foster child living in the home with Mr. S. and his wife. After he was arrested and awaiting trial in jail, he reported hearing voices and claimed multiple disabilities due to a recent stroke. He was transferred to the medical unit of a forensic psychiatric hospital for pre-trial treatment and evaluation.

Record Review

The psychiatric intake evaluation soon after hospital admission noted that Mr. S. reportedly suffered two strokes within the last year. Mr. S. could not answer basic questions about his prior residence, education, social, or employment history. He claimed to hear voices telling him to kill himself. Initially, he refused to sign consent forms to allow the hospital to receive medical records or talk to collaterals to obtain additional social and medical history. The forensic hospital psychiatrist diagnosed him with major neurocognitive disorder and schizoaffective disorder. He was prescribed an antipsychotic (Risperdal) for agitation and auditory hallucinations. In addition, he was diagnosed with the following medical conditions: a history of cerebrovascular accident, diabetes mellitus, hypertension, history of obesity, toe amputations, and history of depression.

Mr. S.'s mood and behavior fluctuated throughout his hospitalization. He expressed some threats of self-harm and aggression toward others earlier during his hospitalization. He became frustrated with other residents in the hospital who had invaded his space and gone through items in his room. He claimed he heard voices. He required assistance moving from his wheelchair to his bed and vice versa. He mostly used a wheelchair, although there were notes in the hospital chart stating that he occasionally walked. For example, in one hospital chart note, he came into a treatment room and said, "Watch this doctor." He then parked his wheelchair and walked a few feet to the table. He was referred for physical therapy to improve motor functioning and self-reported right-sided weakness.

Mr. S. was periodically assessed for CST throughout his hospitalization. Mr. S. received an initial competency screening conducted by a forensic psychiatrist in the jail, who concluded that Mr. S. was incompetent. He could not answer basic questions, such as his birthdate or his parent's names. After he was admitted to the hospital, a forensic evaluator on the hospital staff conducted a CST evaluation and also found Mr. S. to be incompetent. He was disoriented and unable to provide even basic details about his life.

Mr. S. was enrolled in CST restoration groups and received individual restoration sessions to help him understand his legal charges and learn about the legal process. A staff psychologist provided weekly individual restoration sessions for Mr. S. The progress notes indicated that Mr. S. appeared confused and had difficulty understanding the material. He demonstrated a long delay in responding to questions. When asked to choose the correct answer between two options, Mr. S. consistently picked the wrong one (e.g., when asked, "Is the person accused of the crime called the defendant or the victim?" Mr. S. said he is the victim). He appeared to deliberately choose the wrong answer when given a choice of potential answers. He would acknowledge the correct answer when educated, but minutes later, he would produce the incorrect answer when re-asked. He expressed extreme confusion about CST concepts. He was inconsistent in demonstrating legal knowledge correctly at one time but not another.

The forensic evaluator at the hospital submitted regular reports to inform the court about Mr. S.'s progress toward CST. He stated that he could not determine Mr. S.'s competence but added: "The limited valid data suggests that he is incompetent." He opined that Mr. S. was incompetent but restorable. In subsequent reports, he noted that Mr. S. had demonstrated improvement in his psychiatric and medical conditions. He showed improved self-regulation and reduced problem behaviors. He had been walking, and his physical therapist noted improvement. Nursing noted he was more independent with activities of daily living (ADLs). However, the report noted his lack of improvement in knowledge and recall of legal concepts after restoration.

The staff psychologist, who had been providing restoration, said forced-choice options showed that Mr. S. intentionally gave wrong answers, and the psychologist questioned Mr. S.'s motivation to learn the material. He did little to answer questions, saying, "I do not know." He answered fewer questions correctly compared with a previous evaluation. Mr. S. reported that he did not know his legal charges and had no court documents because another resident entered his room and "ripped them up." The forensic evaluator stated that he was "unable to determine" his trial competence.

During another CST evaluation, the forensic evaluator administered the Personality Assessment Inventory (PAI; Morey, 2007) and the Inventory of Legal Knowledge (ILK; Musick & Otto, 2010), which was developed to detect feigning of trial incompetence. The ILK is a 61-item true/false questionnaire administered orally to the criminal defendant using knowledge-based statements about the American legal system. The test suggested that Mr. S. was feigning a lack of legal knowledge but also appeared "genuinely confused" about some legal terms. Mr. S.'s PAI was invalid due to over-reporting. Mr. S. reported abuse and abandonment as a child, heroin addiction, depression, and auditory hallucinations. He told the forensic evaluator that he needed help using the phone to call family members. Again, the forensic evaluator equivocated regarding Mr. S's trial competence.

The nursing staff notes in Mr. S.'s hospital chart suggested that he was feigning his deficits. When outside of the restoration classes, he could address staff on the unit by their correct names, use the telephone to call family members independently, and provide personal history and detailed medical information. He was independent in all ADLs (feeding, dressing, bathing, toileting, etc.). Nursing staff described him as intermittently cooperative with finger sticks to test his blood sugar as part of diabetes care. Nursing staff provided medical education regarding his medical conditions, signs, and symptoms. They reported that he understood their instruction, could recall his glucose levels from the previous day, and kept track of the times he must get his finger sticks during the day.

The results of his competency assessments during his hospital stay remained unchanged despite Mr. S. receiving group and individual restoration services. The forensic evaluator conducted another CST evaluation and concluded that Mr. S.'s trial competency could not be determined. He acknowledged the possibility of feigning incompetence but also considered possible cognitive impairment related to a suspected stroke. The forensic evaluator indicated that Mr. S. lacked factual and rational understanding and opined that he was incompetent but restorable.

Mr. S. eventually signed releases to speak with family members and to obtain previous hospital records. The hospital social worker spoke to his ex-wife (his wife at the time of the alleged assault), who corroborated some information Mr. S. shared but refuted other information. She reported that Mr. S. graduated from high school and worked in construction. He had five children with two previous wives. She agreed with Mr. S.'s report of memory loss. Before their divorce, Mr. S. did not seem to remember the incidents prompting his legal charges. His ex-wife was unaware that he had recently had a stroke. She said he had several hospital visits since their divorce but did not know the details. Medical records revealed that several months before his arrest, Mr. S. presented to the E.D. of a local hospital. His glucose was very high, and he admitted not taking insulin or eating well since his wife divorced him and was living alone. He appeared intoxicated. A CT scan of his brain at that time revealed no evidence of a stroke or other intracranial pathology. Hospital records noted, "a personality disorder and conversion disorder may be considered given atypical presentation."

Mr. S. received a neurology consultation in the psychiatric hospital. The neurologist described Mr. S. as "guarded" and responded to most questions with "I do not know. Can you speak more slowly? I cannot remember." The neurologist administered a brief cognitive screening instrument (Montreal Cognitive Assessment, MoCA), and Mr. S. obtained scores of "3." The neurologist commented that Mr. S.'s effort was "...less than ideal" and questioned the validity and reliability of the test. The neurologist was unable to discern whether Mr. S.'s neurological signs and symptoms were due to "genuine" neurological dysfunction or a "psychogenic" cause. He thought that Mr. S's report of a seizure disorder was unreliable. The neurologist also noted that, on a recent electroencephalogram (EEG), Mr. S. appeared to hyperventilate to make his EEG look abnormal deliberately. A recent brain MRI showed no abnormalities. The neurologist recommended neuropsychological testing.

Forensic Neuropsychological Evaluation

Behavioral Observations

Mr. S. presented as a 55-year-old male appearing his stated age, wearing comfortable and clean attire and sitting in a wheelchair. Grooming and hygiene were good. Multiple tattoos were visible on his arms. The room was relatively quiet and semi-private. Other patients and staff could occasionally be seen walking and talking outside the door. Mr. S. was attentive and responsive and did not seem distracted by noise or individuals walking by. His eye contact was direct and focused. He attempted to answer all questions, although there were long pauses, and he frequently shook his head, saying he did not know the answer. He was oriented to person, place, and partially to time (he knew the month and day of the week but misstated the year and missed the date by several days). He seemed to display poor insight into his current situation. He displayed a restricted range of affect. Throughout the interview, he maintained a pleasant, respectful, and passively cooperative attitude. He tolerated the testing and interview well and did not complain of fatigue except in the afternoon when he said he had just awoken from a nap. His thought processes were logical and linear. He was a poor historian. Expressive and receptive language appeared intact. He readily comprehended all interview questions and cognitive test instructions. He described his present mood as "OK." Except for asking to use the bathroom, he sat in his wheelchair for each test session. He did not voice any delusions or appear to respond to internal stimuli. He wore bifocal glasses, which corrected his vision adequately. No hearing issues were noted. He demonstrated long response latencies. He ambulated independently using his wheelchair. He could open the door and move his chair through without assistance. Psychomotor behavior was notable for slowing and awkward pencil grip and manual coordination. He was right-handed and signed the consent form with slow but legible handwriting.

Test Results

Mr. S. was administered cognitive screening measures, including two PVT. On both PVTs, he scored in the range indicating feigned impairment. Mr. S. produced a score on the RBANS Effort Index of 4, which is above Shura et al.'s (2018) conservative cut score of 3. His scores on the TOMM were well below-chance level, indicating that he intentionally chose the incorrect answer and that he intentionally feigned cognitive dysfunction.

Table 19.1 Test Results

Test	*Scores*
Test of Memory Malingering	Raw
Trial 1	14
Trial 2	20
Retention	19
Repeatable Battery for the Assessment of Neuropsychological Status (RBANS)	SS Percentile
Immediate Memory	49 < 0.1
Visuospatial/Construction	56 0.2
Language	40 < 0.1
Attention	53 0.1
Delayed Memory	40 < 0.1
Total	44 < 0.1
Effort Index = 4	
Peabody Picture Vocabulary Test	
Age Equivalent 8.7	59.03

He performed far below normative expectations on a brief neuropsychological test battery (RBANS), with a total index score below the 0.1 percentile (see Table 19.1). Put another way, Mr. S. performed more poorly on this test than 99.9% of the normative population. Individuals with this severe level of cognitive impairment, such as persons in the late stages of Alzheimer's disease, are usually utterly dependent upon others for all daily functions. While he performed in the profoundly impaired range on this test, he nevertheless readily understood test instructions and maintained his focus of attention, behaviors clearly inconsistent with his level of performance.

He also completed a test of basic receptive vocabulary (i.e., Can he understand and recognize simple words?). He scored at the 0.3 percentile, far below normative expectations, and at an early elementary school level (equivalent to an eight-year-old).

Based on his failure on validity tests and his cognitive performances, which were far below expectations on cognitive measures, plus the fact that his daily functioning did not resemble an individual with advanced dementia or profound intellectual disability as these cognitive scores would indicate, the forensic neuropsychologist concluded that he was malingering cognitive dysfunction.

CST Evaluation

In addition to performing neuropsychological testing, the forensic neuropsychologist also directly inquired about Mr. S.'s factual and rational appreciation of his legal situation and his ability to work with his attorney. Mr. S. did not accurately state his legal charges when asked or consistently report the possible sentence he could receive. He said on both occasions, when asked, that he was charged with "three different charges," "arson, assault, and another one," "started a fire in an apartment building." He stated that he thought the assault charges involved "a girl," but he did not know who the girl was or how old she was.

Mr. S. consistently misstated the definitions of a misdemeanor and felony ("a misdemeanor is more serious," "a misdemeanor is bad – you get in trouble for it"). He admitted that he understood that the prosecutor was on the "other team" and was "saying I did it." He indicated that he could not provide the name of his defense attorney, but he said that he knew what he looked like. When told his attorney's name, he indicated that he did not recognize the name. He mixed up the roles of the jury and judge. He stated that the judge in his case was a "girl" but did not know her name. He said that he did not know whether there were witnesses and whether they would testify against him. He expressed a vague idea regarding the concept of plea bargaining ("like buy one, get one free," "you have to put up something to get something"). He was able to state some of the pleas (guilty, not guilty) he can enter and indicate that he understood these concepts. Mr. S. reported that he only met his attorney a few times, and he needs to find out if he is doing a good job. He said he felt comfortable asking questions but did not know how to reach his attorney.

Summary

Despite intensive, lengthy restoration services, Mr. S. did not consistently demonstrate knowledge of his legal charges, courtroom personnel, or procedures to consider him competent to stand trial. Mr. S. showed no improvement in understanding his charges, courtroom personnel, or procedure across all the above CST evaluations. At the same time, the CST evaluators and restoration providers often questioned his effort and the validity of his responses, and there was no clear support for his claim that he suffered strokes. In his most recent CST evaluation, the forensic evaluator opined that Mr. S. was malingering and feigning incompetence.

In summary, all the past medical records obtained by the hospital to identify Mr. S.'s medical history to guide appropriate treatment did not reveal any evidence of a stroke or rehabilitation for any neurological event that could explain his neurocognitive disorder. The neurological evaluation did not confirm that he had a stroke. The neurologist stated that his effort was poor, as also observed during his cognitive assessment. His neurological signs and symptoms were judged as possibly psychiatric as they did not follow the patterns expected for neurological disorders such as stroke. Community hospital records obtained from around the time he claimed he had his strokes made no mention of them. Brain scans and neurological evaluations after his self-reported strokes showed no evidence of stroke. His emergency room visits for routine medical conditions coincided with court dates, suggesting that Mr. S. used these E.D. visits to provide a medical excuse for missing his court dates.

The most recent progress notes from the hospital indicated that Mr. S. had consistently shown an inability (or unwillingness) to learn and recall the competency restoration material presented to him. He claimed he needed help remembering the names of the psychologists providing weekly group or individual restoration sessions despite repeated cues. He consistently misstated his charges and the difference between a misdemeanor and a felony, and he stated that he could not recall his attorney's name.

The question facing the mental health evaluators and the court was whether Mr. S. truly *could not* achieve trial competence or whether he *would not* achieve competence. Several forensic mental health evaluators suspected he was feigning, but they also considered that he may have had "genuine" cognitive deficits. The question arose as to whether any "genuine" deficits, if they did exist, rose to the level that would impair his trial competence and completely prevent him from learning the necessary information to make him competent. The mere presence of cognitive deficits does not automatically render a person IST.

Mr. S.'s purported cognitive impairment and psychiatric symptoms could impact trial competence. However, this impact must be demonstrated in the present and directly demonstrated regarding his current legal charges. During his last CST evaluation, Mr. S. was psychiatrically and medically stable. Mr. S.'s current medical record and the forensic mental health evaluation and cognitive screening revealed no medical, neurological, or psychiatric justification for his continued incompetence. Although Mr. S. did have risk factors for stroke and cognitive impairments (i.e., diabetes and hypertension; Turin et al., 2016; Shou et al., 2015), there was no evidence of a stroke in his medical records.

The neuropsychologist cited hospital staff notes showing that Mr. S. was alert and oriented, called family members independently using phone numbers from memory, and communicated wants and needs to nursing staff using their correct names. The forensic evaluator noted that there had been episodes of non-compliance and aggression, threats to staff, and suicide threats. Mr. S. expressed fear of returning to jail. He occasionally demonstrated knowledge in restoration classes. The forensic evaluator concluded that he was "unable to determine" competency. Mr. S. has presented with persistent, severe cognitive impairment as the basis for incompetence to stand trial due to his self-reported "strokes," which had not been corroborated or documented in any medical records reviewed. He claimed he cannot remember or comprehend the material in restoration classes.

Results of the neuropsychological evaluation indicated that Mr. S. was malingering his cognitive deficits. A neurological evaluation conducted shortly after his admission to the hospital was equivocal regarding the basis for his neurological symptoms, and they suggested a "psychogenic component" to his self-reported symptoms. If he had a stroke, one would expect some recovery of function over time. A "stroke" that allegedly caused issues with ambulation would not invariably also impair learning and memory such that he could not retain information related to his court case. His inability to recall autobiographical details and memories, which are well-established, is also unusual in a stroke. It is often seen in a psychiatric disorder such as psychogenic amnesia or in malingering. No neurological disorder would selectively impair his ability to encode and retain any information related to his legal charges yet allow him to demonstrate intact cognitive functioning regarding other matters, such as keeping track of his diabetes treatment schedule. He claimed selective amnesia for trial competency information. Individuals with severe episodic memory impairment due to a neurological disorder, such as a stroke, typically show impairment in all new learning, not just a particular topic (Cima et al., 2004). They also show profound impairments in everyday functioning, typically requiring extensive assistance and supervision.

Outside of the claimed "strokes," not documented anywhere in Mr. S.'s medical record, no neurological or medical disorder accounted for this selective pattern memory impairment. Mr. S.'s psychiatric hospital record contained documentation from multiple disciplines, including psychology, nursing, neurology, neuropsychology, and forensic psychology, noting discrepancies between his avowed cognitive and physical impairment and his actual observed functioning in the hospital setting. For instance, he told staff he did not know his family members' phone numbers and did not know how to use the phone, but he was observed calling family members independently. He used a wheelchair because of reported lower extremity weakness due to stroke but could ambulate independently using a rolling walker. He claimed inability to use his right, and sometimes his left, arm and hand but was observed to use these upper extremities. He professed an inability to recall information about his legal charges even after being instructed many times in group and individual sessions and frequently reminded by staff members. However, he knew when to get his glucose levels checked for his diabetes and recalled the specific numbers from his previous glucose readings.

These discrepancies could not be accounted for by any medical condition, such as a stroke, but were most parsimoniously explained by malingered cognitive deficits, as indicated by the neuropsychological evaluation. The deficient performance on cognitive measures alone indicated feigning, but the RBANS validity measures and below-chance TOMM scores were self-evident. His PAI also indicated that he was feigning psychosis.

It was not possible to determine whether Mr. S.'s functional memory for personally relevant legal information and court-related events was fully intact because he chose not to demonstrate the knowledge or understanding he may possess to his evaluators. Mr. S. declined to present any knowledge from the intensive restoration efforts he participated in during his hospitalization. Upon direct questioning, he did not demonstrate a factual and rational understanding of his legal situation. He expressed only the vaguest idea of the severe nature of his charges and the possible penalties should he be convicted.

He did not directly or consistently demonstrate his trial competence to his restoration workers, forensic evaluators, or the forensic neuropsychologist. Thus, competency was determined by default. The forensic neuropsychologist opined that Mr. S. had no current psychiatric or cognitive disorder severe enough to prevent him from comprehending the nature and consequences of his legal charges or following the legal proceedings during his trial. There was no evidence that he could not work with his attorney and assist in his defense. The legal standard for competency places the burden on the defendant to prove they are not competent to stand trial. Therefore, since the forensic neuropsychologist found no viable evidence to indicate that Mr. S. was not competent, she opined that Mr. S. was competent to stand trial.

Summary and Conclusions

This case illustrates the advantage of an in-patient stay with a 24-hour observation for data gathering on functioning and the value of neuropsychological assessment to confirm these observations. The case also highlights the importance of seeking and reviewing all medical records and collateral information in suspected malingering. Once the defendant was tested, it was apparent that he was malingering his cognitive deficits. Before testing, forensic evaluators equivocated on whether the defendant was competent. He had risk factors for stroke and exhibited functional impairment. Medical records had not been obtained early in his hospitalization. Neuropsychological assessment helped to determine that Mr. S. was intentionally underperforming when asked to demonstrate his knowledge of his court case and courtroom procedures and personnel to delay his trial and stay at the hospital, where he received intensive medical and psychiatric care and attention.

The defense attorney hired an expert to contest the finding of trial competence. Perhaps surprisingly, the defense expert, a neuropsychiatrist, conceded that Mr. S. was feigning severe cognitive impairment. Nevertheless, he argued that Mr. S.'s multiple medical issues and history of seizures could impair his trial competency. Ultimately, the judge concluded that Mr. S. was competent to stand trial.

Discussion

This defendant postponed his trial by malingering a psychiatric disorder and cognitive impairment from a non-existent neurological disorder. His feigned psychosis was readily identified by constant surveillance as an in-patient and confirmed by an invalid PAI. His feigning of a cognitive disorder was not so readily determined. Before previous medical records were obtained and before neuropsychological testing with validity tests were administered, the hospital staff was hesitant to judge him as feigning cognitive symptoms, even though they suspected malingering. They also were reluctant to state that the defendant was competent to stand trial even though Mr. S. scored below the cut-off on the ILK. The forensic evaluators suspected that Mr. S. may have genuine knowledge deficits. Indeed, the ILK can produce a high false positive rate with psychiatric in-patients and cannot be used alone to determine feigning on a CST evaluation (Gottfried et al., 2017). This case demonstrates the "value-added" of neuropsychological assessment of criminal defendants presenting with cognitive and psychiatric impairment potentially impacting trial competence (see LaDuke et al., 2023). The neuropsychologist was able to integrate the neuromedical information, history, observational data, and neuropsychological testing to confidently declare that Mr. S. was malingering a neuropsychological disorder as a basis for trial incompetence.

Determining whether a defendant is competent to stand trial is essential to preserve their 14th Amendment rights. It is also critical to identify when defendants are malingering cognitive impairment to feign incompetence. A defendant without genuine psychiatric or cognitive impairments who is deemed incompetent may occupy valuable bed space in a public hospital and unnecessarily prolong their judicial process. On the other hand, misidentifying a defendant as malingering has dire consequences that can prejudice them during legal proceedings. The addition of neuropsychological testing can create a more comprehensive picture of the situation for a more accurate determination of CST. This case also importantly illustrates the fact that one can be deemed competent even though competence was not specifically and directly demonstrated. The presence of feigned functional impairment and malingering provides strong enough evidence to presume the presence of competence. This is especially true in cases where significantly below-chance responding is present. Selectively choosing the wrong answer can only be explained by a conscious effort to present oneself as severely impaired, i.e., it has been called "the smoking gun of malingering" (Pankratz & Erickson, 1990).

References

Ardolf, B. R., Denney, R. L., & Houston, C. M. (2007). Base rates of negative response bias and malingered neurocognitive dysfunction among criminal defendants referred for neuropsychological evaluation. *The Clinical Neuropsychologist, 21*(6), 899–916. doi:10.1080/13825580600966391

Arredondo, B. C., Marcopulos, B. A., Brand, J. G., Campbell, K. T., & Kent, J. A. (2017). Cognitive functioning and adjudicative competence. *The Clinical Neuropsychologist, 31*(8), 1432–1448. doi: 10.1080/13854046.2017.1317032

Boone, K. B. (Ed.). (2021). *Assessment of feigned cognitive impairment.* New York: Guilford Publications.

Cima, M., Nijman, H., Merckelbach, H., Kremer, K., & Hollnack, S. (2004). Claims of crime-related amnesia in forensic patients. *International Journal of Law and Psychiatry, 27*(3), 215–221. doi:10.1016/j.ijlp.2004.03.007

Cochrane, R. E., Grisso, T., & Frederick, R. I. (2001). The relationship between criminal charges, diagnoses, and psycholegal opinions among federal pretrial defendants. *Behavioral Sciences and the Law, 19*(4), 565–582.

Denney, R. L. (2012). Criminal forensic neuropsychology and assessment of competency. In G. J., Larrabee (Ed.), *Forensic neuropsychology: A scientific approach* (2nd ed.), New York: Oxford University Press, pp. 438–472.

Drope v. Missouri, 420 U.S. 162 (1975).

Dusky v. United States, 362 U.S. 402 (1960).

Gay, J. G., Vitacco, M. J., & Ragatz, L. (2017). Mental health symptoms predict competency to stand trial and competency restoration success. *Legal and Criminological Psychology, 22*, 288–301. doi:10.1111/lcrp.12100

Gottfried, E., & Glassmire, D. (2016). The relationship between psychiatric and cognitive symptom feigning among forensic inpatients adjudicated incompetent to stand trial. *Assessment, 23*(6), 672–682.

Gottfried, E. D., Hudson, B. L., Vitacco, M. J., & Carbonell, J. L. (2017). Improving the detection of feigned knowledge deficits in defendants adjudicated incompetent to stand trial. *Assessment, 24*(2), 232–243.

Grisso, T., Steinberg, L., Woolard, J., Cauffman, E., Scott, E., Graham, S., ... & Schwartz, R. (2003). Juveniles' competence to stand trial: A comparison of adolescents' and adults' capacities as trial defendants. *Law and Human Behavior*, *27*(4), 333–363.

Hawes, S. W., & Boccaccini, M. T. (2009). Detection of overreporting of psychopathology on the Personality Assessment Inventory: A meta-analytic review. *Psychological Assessment, 21*(1), 112–124. doi:10.1037/a0015036

Heck, A. L., & Herrick, S. M. (2007). Geriatric considerations in restoring competence to stand trial: Two cases of impaired cognition. *Journal of Forensic Psychology Practice, 7*(2), 73–82. doi:10.1300/J158v07n02_06

Laduke, C. L., Tussey, C. M., Marcopulos, B. A., Bender, S. D., & Arredondo, B. C. (2023). Neuropsychological considerations in forensic mental health assessment. In D. DeMatteo & K. C. Scherr (Eds.), *The Oxford handbook of psychology and law.* New York: Oxford University Press.

Lewis, J. L., Simcox, A. M., & Berry, D. T. (2002). Screening for feigned psychiatric symptoms in a forensic sample by using the MMPI-2 and the Structured Inventory of Malingered Symptomatology. *Psychological Assessment, 14*(2), 170.

Mahoney III, J. J., Bender, S. D., Arredondo, B. C., & Marcopulos, B. A. (2018). A forensic case report involving unequivocal severe brain injury and unequivocal response bias. *Journal of Forensic Psychology Research and Practice, 18*(5), 374–387.

Mallory, L. E., & Guyton, M. R. (2017). Competency to stand trial and criminal responsibility in forensic neuropsychology practice. In S. S. Bush, G. J. Demakis, & M. L. Rohling (Eds.), *APA handbook of forensic neuropsychology*. Washington, DC: American Psychological Association, pp. 341–377. doi:10.1037/0000032-015

Melton, G. B., Petrila, J., Poythress, N. G., Slobogin, C., Otto, R. K., Mossman, D., & Condie, L. O. (2018). *Psychological evaluations for the courts: A handbook for mental health professionals and lawyers (4th ed.).* Guilford Press.

Morey, L. C. (2007). *Personality Assessment Inventory professional manual 2nd edition.* Lutz, FL: Psychological Assessment Resources.

Musick, J. E., & Otto, R. K. (2010). *ILK: Inventory of Legal Knowledge.* Lutz, FL: Psychological Assessment Resources.

Nestor, P. G., Daggett, D., Haycock, J., & Price, M. (1999). Competence to stand trial: A neuropsychological inquiry. *Law and Human Behavior, 23*, 397–412.

Pankratz, L., & Erickson, R. C. (1990). Two views of malingering. *The Clinical Neuropsychologist, 4*(4), 379–389.

Pate v. Robinson, 383 U.S. 375 (1966).

Pirelli, G., Gottdiener, W. H., & Zapf, P. A. (2011). A meta-analytic review of comparative competency to stand trial research. *Psychology, Public Policy, and Law, 17*, 1–53. doi:10.1037/a0021713

Schwalbe, E., & Medalia, A. (2007). Cognitive dysfunction and competency restoration: Using cognitive remediation to help restore the unrestorable. *Journal of the American Academy of Psychiatry and Law, 35*, 518–525.

Shou, J., Zhou, L., Zhu, S., & Zhang, X. (2015). Diabetes is an independent risk factor for stroke recurrence in stroke patients: A meta-analysis. *Journal of Stroke and Cerebrovascular Diseases, 24*(9), 1961–1968.

Shura, R. D., Brearly, T. W., Rowland, J. A., Martindale, S. L., Miskey, H. M., & Duff, K. (2018). RBANS validity indices: A systematic review and meta-analysis. *Neuropsychology Review, 28*(3), 269–284.

Sweet, J. J., Heilbronner, R. L., Morgan, J. E., Larrabee, G. J., Rohling, M. L., Boone, K. B., Kirkwood, M. W., Schroeder, R. W., Suhr, J. A., & Conference Participants (2021). American Academy of Clinical Neuropsychology (AACN) 2021 consensus statement on validity assessment: Update of the 2009 AACN consensus conference statement on neuropsychological assessment of effort, response bias, and malingering. *The Clinical Neuropsychologist*. doi:10.1080/13854046.2021.1896036

Toofanian Ross, P., Padula, C. B., Nitch, S. R., & Kinney, D. I. (2015). Cognition and competency restoration: Using the RBANS to predict the length of stay for patients deemed incompetent to stand trial. *The Clinical Neuropsychologist, 29*(1), 150–165.

Turin, T. C., Okamura, T., Afzal, A. R., Rumana, N., Watanabe, M., Higashiyama, A., ... & Miyamoto, Y. (2016). Hypertension and lifetime risk of stroke. *Journal of Hypertension, 34*(1), 116–122.

Tussey, C. M., Marcopulos, B. A., & Caillouet, B. A. (2013). Neuropsychological evaluation of competency in criminal forensic contexts. *Psychological Injury and the Law, 6*, 31–40.

Warren, J. I., Fitch, W. L., Dietz, P. E., & Rosenfeld, B. D. (1991). Criminal offense, psychiatric diagnosis, and psycholegal opinion: An analysis of 894 pretrial referrals. *Journal of the American Academy of Psychiatry and the Law Online, 19*(1), 63–69.

Wynkoop, T. F., & Denney, R. L. (1999). Exaggeration of neuropsychological deficit in competency to stand trial. *Journal of Forensic Neuropsychology, 1*(2), 29–53.

Youtsey v. United States, 97 F. 937, 940 (6th Cir., 1899).

20 Criminal Forensic Evaluation of an Intellectually Disabled Individual

The Importance of Addressing Diversity Issues

Joette James

As the United States becomes an increasingly diverse nation, forensic neuropsychologists have an ethical obligation to become well versed in cross-cultural neuropsychological practices and to consider the impact of sociodemographic variables throughout the evaluation process, including record review, gathering of collateral interview sources, observed behavior during the examination itself, and the interpretation of testing results. The APA Ethics Code (APA, 2017) defines diversity broadly as cultural, individual, and role differences in "age, gender, gender identity, race, ethnicity, culture, national origin, religion, sexual orientation, disability, language, and socioeconomic status," and advises psychologists to be aware of and strive to eliminate the impact of biases based on these factors (General Principle E, Respect for People's Rights and Dignity, APA, 2017). Specific to neuropsychological assessment, research has securely established that diversity in race/ethnicity, culture, language, and education significantly affects neuropsychological test performance, and as such, clinicians should be particularly aware of the potential for misdiagnosis, mischaracterization, and threats to construct validity that these factors pose, especially when conducting evaluations of performance validity, feigned or malingered neurocognitive dysfunction (Peery, Byrd & Strutt, 2017).

Beyond ethical directives, clinicians in the current era have the obligation (and benefit) of adhering to 'best practices,' as defined by scientifically supported practices. Specialty organizations, such as the American Academy of Clinical Neuropsychology (AACN) and the National Academy of Neuropsychology have endorsed consensus conference statements regarding validity assessment and uniform terms for interpretation (Sweet et al., 2021; Guilmette et al., 2020), relevant position papers regarding the necessity of addressing examinee response validity (e.g., Bush et al., 2005), and practice guidelines (Board of Directors, 2007) to guide practitioners who face the fundamental and important challenges of addressing validity of test results and the possibility of malingering when test results are deemed invalid. Indeed, this applies to all examinees regardless of their background.

The existence of racial/ethnic bias in assessment is unfortunately longstanding and can take many forms. While historic definitions of race were based on a biological/genetic conceptualization of perceived shared physical traits and resultant sociocultural status, scholarship has clearly shown that racial classification is a political and social construction with no basis in a coherent biological reality (APA Guidelines on Race and Ethnicity in Psychology, 2019). For example, assertions that the longstanding IQ gap between Black Americans and White Americans is based on race/genetics (e.g., Hernstein & Murray, 1994) have now been thoroughly debunked, and there is a plethora of evidence to show that intelligence as a concept, and specifically as derived from results of intellectual testing, is complex and that

DOI: 10.4324/9781003005063-23

the latter can vary as a function of socioeconomic status and quality of education (Nisbett et al., 2012; Manly et al., 2004).

Nevertheless, bias, both explicit and implicit, continues to pervade neuropsychological assessment, potentially threatening accurate interpretation of test results. Implicit bias, defined as "attitude[s] or stereotype[s] that affect our understanding, actions, and decisions in an unconscious manner," is particularly dangerous, as by definition "these biases, which encompass both favorable and unfavorable assessments, are activated involuntarily and outside one's awareness or intentional control" (Kirwan Institute for the Study of Race and Ethnicity, Ohio State University[1]). Sources of potential implicit bias and threats to construct validity in neuropsychological assessment related to race/ethnicity include measurement bias, test content and response bias, limited representation of Black Americans in normative reference groups, stereotyped threat, and the misuse of demographically corrected norms (Thaler, Thames & Cagigas, 2015; Peery, Byrd & Strutt, 2017). These biases can not only threaten the validity of tests assessing neurocognitive functions, which comprise a standard neuropsychological battery, but they may also affect some performance validity tests (PVTs). Accurate classification of the examinee is critical, as false positives (i.e., classifying an individual's results as invalid/non-credible when they have put forth best effort and their test performance is valid), can have harmful consequences in medico-legal settings.

Individuals with disabilities also face bias, particularly those diagnosed with intellectual disabilities (ID) and severe mental illness. In fact, these two groups are the most socially excluded among the disability population, and they experience significant disparities in healthcare, housing, and employment due to stigma (Ditchman et al., 2013). Societal issues have a significant impact on the lives of individuals with IQs even in the higher end of the ID spectrum (i.e., Full-Scale IQs of 50–55 to 75) and include high rates of classroom segregation, unemployment, obesity, and loneliness, as well as low career success, few specialized legal resources, and vulnerabilities to those who may mislead or harm them (Schalock et al., 2010). In the context of a forensic neuropsychological setting, individuals with ID are at greater risk of being classified incorrectly as performing in a non-credible manner, necessitating that PVT cutoffs be adjusted to maintain adequate specificity in these individuals (Smith et al., 2014). Research suggests that some PVTs are better suited to detect feigned cognitive deficits than others in this population (i.e., measures of visual and verbal recognition; Victor & Boone, 2021). The same authors concluded that the detection of feigned psychiatric symptoms (through symptom validity testing, or SVTs) required considerably more research in order to determine their utility in an ID population (Victor & Boone, 2021).

In the case presented below, in which I was asked to evaluate competency to stand trial of a Black man with ID, I will illustrate the ways in which bias, both in terms of race/ethnicity and disability status, may have negatively affected the State's evaluation of a diverse individual.

The Case of Mr. I.D.

At the time of my evaluation (May 2017), Mr. I.D. was a 32-year-old Black man who had been charged with burglary and grand larceny, as well as subsequently charged with burglary, petty larceny, and looting in a subsequent incident, and with earlier charges of burglary, petty larceny, grand larceny, and peeping Tom. In the burglary and grand larceny counts, it was alleged that two Black males had been seen entering the house of an elderly woman (who was not home at the time) and loading several flat screen televisions onto a truck. The victim and her adult child were notified of the suspicious activity by a neighbor, and the victim and her daughter returned to her home in the late afternoon to find the front door open and a side window broken. Mr. I.D. was identified by fingerprint evidence in the house. Upon arrest, Mr. I.D. was wearing a GPS monitor due to previous charges. He initially denied knowing the victim and his alleged co-defendant. He then admitted to being familiar with the area as his father lived in a duplex near where the crime had taken place, but he was unable to tell the police officer his father's apartment number. When confronted with the fingerprint evidence, and the fact that he had been recently arrested for a burglary on the same street, Mr. I.D. began to sob uncontrollably and told the police officer that he had been coerced into committing the crime by his co-defendant, to whom he owed a substantial amount of money, and who had threatened him with a gun. Mr. I.D. stated that he had feared for his life. The other burglary, petty larceny, and looting charges were related to an incident in which Mr. I.D. allegedly illegally entered a residence (approximately one month after the burglary described above), kicking down the front door, and stealing less than U.S. $2,000 in property, including a television. The looting charge was added as the alleged incident occurred during a state of emergency in the area due to a flood. Law enforcement was notified of the burglary, while it was in progress and apprehended Mr. I.D. after a foot chase. The peeping Tom charge occurred in the context of an incident in which it was alleged that Mr. I.D. entered a ladies' restroom at the community college near his residence for the purposes of watching women use the facilities. A female student reported that upon opening the bathroom stall, she saw the back of Mr. I.D., who then said "Oops, I am sorry I am in the wrong bathroom." Mr. I.D. was identified by the student in a photo array.

The Defendant's History

Background history was obtained from the records reviewed and from the telephone interview with Mr. I.D.'s mother.

Mr. I.D.'s mother did not report any concerns in her pregnancy with Mr. I.D. She reported that he was born full-term and on-time, weighing 7 pounds, 7 ounces. She recalled that he was diagnosed with asthma as a child, as well as a heart murmur, but did not describe any significant medical condition, illnesses, or operations. Mr. I.D.'s mother reported that she was also in special education as a child, and she was considered a "slow learner." She believed that Mr. I.D.'s father was also a "slow learner" and noted that he struggled with spelling. The family history is further significant for a maternal uncle who had an inpatient psychiatric hospitalization. Mr. I.D. is the second of three children born to Mr. I.D.'s mother.

Mr. I.D.'s mother indicated that Mr. I.D. was "slow" from childhood. She recalls that he would eat dog food out of the dog's bowl. He seemed to have difficulty understanding what was said to him and had difficulty carrying out simple tasks, such as taking out the trash. Once Mr. I.D. began school, he struggled to learn and was constantly behind his peers academically.

School records indicate that initial concerns about poor academic progress, inattention, and aggressive behavior with peers were noted in the first grade. In his first psychoeducational evaluation, when he was nearly seven years old, Mr. I.D.'s mother noted that he still wet the bed, wore his clothes backward, and always seemed to get hurt when playing outside. Records indicated that in the second grade, Mr. I.D. qualified for special education services as an Educable Mentally Disabled student. He failed the receptive and expressive language portions of the speech/language screening that was conducted with him in September 1997 and was enrolled in a speech/language program. In January 1998, at the age of 13,

Mr. I.D.'s general intellectual ability was assessed with the Wechsler Intelligence Scale for Children, Third Edition (WISC-III). On this measure, he obtained a Verbal IQ of 52 (<1st percentile), Performance IQ of 48 (<1st percentile), and a Full-Scale IQ of 46 (<1st percentile). Adaptive behavior assessed using the Vineland Adaptive Behavior Scales revealed a Composite Score of 44 (<1st percentile).

Mr. I.D. was on a certificate track for high school, which is typically the case when an individual is unable to complete a diploma. In the school records, he was described as "extremely low functioning" and required a small group setting and individualized attention. An Individualized Education Plan (IEP) from the 9th grade indicated that Mr. I.D. had completed vocational work in Adaptive Horticulture and Small Engine Repair. Educational goals were very rudimentary and included basic social skills such as responding appropriately to adult requests and working cooperatively with others. Vocational goals had included using simple tools, writing correct personal data on an application, and understanding multiple meanings of words. His primary disability code continued to be Educable Mentally Disabled. An assessment with the Woodcock-Johnson Revised Tests of Achievement at age 15 (10/16/2000) revealed reading decoding skills at the 1.5 grade equivalent, reading comprehension at the 1.3 grade equivalent, arithmetic skills at the 4.7 grade equivalent, and mathematical reasoning at the 2.0 grade equivalent. Mr. I.D. did not complete his high-school certificate program.

Mr. I.D. has a history of depressive symptoms and poor attention/focus, for which he has been prescribed Prozac, Depakote, Adderall, and Ritalin at various time periods during his life. Records indicate that, in addition to a diagnosis of mental retardation, Mr. I.D. was given diagnoses of Attention Deficit/Hyperactivity Disorder, Combined Type; Dysthymic Disorder; and Depression – Not Otherwise Specified. His mother reported a history of problems with staying still and disrupting the class. He has a history of outpatient mental health treatment. In the IEP from the 9th grade, Mr. I.D. was described as friendly and as putting forth great effort to adjust to school. However, he also displayed some aggressive behavior, which was predominantly attributed to a "low functioning level." Mr. I.D.'s mother indicated that he had few friends growing up and played mainly with his cousins or sisters.

Records show that Mr. I.D. had been found eligible for services through his state Department of Disabilities and Special Needs Board at the age of 17 and he also qualified for Supplemental Security Income (SSI) disability payments. His eligibility for both was based on his history of mental retardation (now referred to as ID) and "indications of mental illness."

Records described multiple psychosocial stressors during childhood, including parental abandonment (i.e., father in prison), maternal disability (cognitive, as well as physical disability due to an automobile accident), poverty, and homelessness.

Mr. I.D.'s mother reported that her son continues to demonstrate multiple deficits in adaptive functioning. She reported that he has never had a driver's license or a bank account. His common law wife is his payee for his disability checks. She gives him small amounts of money and manages all of the household bills. Mr. I.D.'s mother noted that Mr. I.D. showed a tendency to spend money on trivial items and will lose money if someone does not help him manage it. He was noted to have difficulty regulating his emotions and could become angry easily. She reported that he was able to do some minimal cooking, such as frying an egg, but that she did not feel comfortable with him cooking without supervision. She indicated that Mr. I.D.'s wife helped him with household tasks, such as doing laundry, as he was not able to sort items effectively. At the time of the evaluation, Mr. I.D. had two children (ages two and eleven) with a previous girlfriend. However, they did not live with him and his role in their care was extremely limited.

Previous Evaluations

Mr. I.D.'s competency to stand trial was initially assessed on 12/13/2000. At the time, he was 15 years of age and a patient on the adolescent unit at a local psychiatric facility. The purpose of the hospitalization was to determine his competency to assist in his defense and his criminal responsibility. He was charged with two counts of petty larceny and grand larceny. The report of this evaluation indicated that Mr. I.D. had been previously evaluated by Dr. M., in December 2000 and obtained a Full-Scale IQ of 44. Dr. M diagnosed Mr. I.D. with mental retardation, mild to moderate. Dr. M also indicated that Mr. I.D.'s performance on the Reading Section of the Kaufman Test of Educational Achievement (K-TEA) was equivalent to the 1.4 grade level, which suggested that he was "illiterate." The competency examiner, Dr. C., indicated that Mr. I.D.'s intelligence appeared to be significantly below average. He was unable to spell the word "world" or "tree." When asked the number of days in a week, he said "five." He was unable to give the number of months in a year or name the capital of his state. With regard to competency issues, Dr. C. indicated that Mr. I.D. was unable to read his Miranda warnings and could not spontaneously define the term "plea bargain." She indicated that he voiced an understanding of his Miranda warnings when they were explained "in detail," and that when the term "plea bargain" was explained, he was able to attain "the most rudimentary understanding of it." He was able to name his charges, show understanding of the seriousness of the charges, and the possibility of jail if convicted. He was able to basically define the roles of the judge, the defense attorney, and the prosecutor, as well as concepts related to witnesses and evidence. He reportedly indicated his understanding of the importance of appropriate courtroom behavior. Dr. M concluded that Mr. I.D. was "minimally competent to stand trial."

A subsequent forensic evaluation conducted in December 2000 by Dr. B, at the same psychiatric facility, again concluded that Mr. I.D. was minimally competent to stand trial.

Mr. I.D. underwent another forensic evaluation on behalf of the State in order to determine his competency to stand trial that was conducted jointly by the Department of Disabilities and Special Needs and the Department of Mental Health in June 2016, by psychologist, Dr. H., and psychiatrist, Dr. G. The examiners concluded that Mr. I.D. demonstrated evidence of an ID. However, they concluded that he did not show signs of mental illness and opined that he was competent to stand trial. The examiners also included that Mr. I.D. was malingering both cognitive deficits and psychiatric symptoms. These conclusions were based in part on psychological testing conducted by psychologist, Dr. S., during which Mr. I.D. reportedly endorsed a high level of psychopathology, and extreme and uncommon psychiatric symptoms (Miller Forensic Assessment of Symptoms-M-FAST; Miller, 2001). Additionally, on the M-FAST, Mr. I.D. reportedly presented an overly negative view of himself and displayed symptoms of suggestibility. He also performed *below chance* on a true-false interview measure designed to discriminate between memory-impaired individuals and malingerers and to assign feigned impairment of competency-related information (Inventory of Legal Knowledge, ILK; Musick & Otto, 2006); however, it was not specified whether performance was actually significantly below chance versus still within the range of chance-level scores (e.g., slightly below 50% correct). With regard to competency issues, Mr. I.D. was reportedly unable to state his formal charges or answer basic questions about his case. After significant education in the context of the evaluation about his charges and the criminal justice system, he was able to name his charges, but he could not define them all. He did not seem to believe that his charges were serious. In contrast, he appeared to be familiar with the guilty plea and the consequences of pleading guilty in court. He could not, however, define "not guilty" nor could he indicate the consequences of pleading "not guilty." The examiners opined that Mr. I.D.'s performance on psychological testing stood in contrast with his ability to understand legal proceedings with regard to the prior juvenile case during which competency was assessed (16 years earlier) in 2000, and as such, was consistent with an attempt to feign cognitive deficits.

When Dr. H subsequently testified in Mr. I.D.'s competency hearing, she also cited the following as evidence that he was malingering: on the mental status examination he could not correctly name a past President of the United States or the first President of the United States, he did not know the colors of the American flag, and when asked in what month the fourth of July was celebrated, he stated, "October." She also cited several jail cell telephone calls with his wife, which were indicative of his "street sense" and capacity to have conversations.

Neuropsychological Evaluation of Mr. I.D.

Mr. I.D. presented as a Black American male of average stature. He was alert and oriented to person, place, and time. However, he was unable to tell me his correct age (i.e., stating he was 31 when he was actually 32). Mr. I.D.'s predominant mood was friendly but blunted with a restricted range of affect. Language comprehension was significantly reduced and Mr. I.D. frequently misunderstood task instructions and required constant repetition and simplification of instructions. He was very concrete in his understanding. For example, even with extensive explanation and demonstration, Mr. I.D. was unable to distinguish between an uppercase "L" and its mirror opposite. He also did not understand the concept of repeating digits in a backward sequence. Additionally, Mr. I.D. had severe difficulty expressing himself, especially on open-ended questions and when asked to provide relevant detail when relating events. He had clear difficulty finding the words he needed to express himself and demonstrated long response latencies to questions. It was very difficult to follow and understand his verbal responses, which tended to be fragmented. Sustained attention was good in the individualized setting, and no significant impulsivity was observed. The reader is referred to the Neuropsychological Evaluation Test Summary at the end of this chapter for a summary of test scores.

For the purposes of performance validity testing, Mr. I.D. was administered Green's NVMSVT (a measure that includes an ID normative group) and he passed all five validity indicators. Selection of PVTs is limited for individuals with IQ scores <50, and the decision was made to specifically employ a measure on which there was appropriate comparison data.

Mr. I.D.'s current level of general intellectual functioning was assessed with the WAIS-IV. He earned a Full-Scale IQ (standard score or SS) of 46 (<0.1 percentile), which fell in the Extremely Low range (95% Confidence Interval: 43–51). This score was highly consistent with previous assessments of his intelligence. His verbal reasoning and nonverbal/visual processing skills were measured overall in the Extremely Low range (Verbal Comprehension Index SS = 58, 0.3 percentile; Perceptual Reasoning Index SS = 51, 0.1 percentile), as was working memory, the ability to "hold" and manipulate information "on-line" (Working Memory Index SS = 55, 0.1 percentile), and visual-motor processing speed (Processing Speed Index SS = 50, <0.1 percentile).

Mr. I.D.'s performances were extremely poor on language-based tasks. Picture naming (Picture Vocabulary) on the Woodcock-Johnson was significantly impaired, at the five-year, five-month level. Similarly, Mr. I.D. struggled on tasks of language and listening comprehension. He performed at the 5-year, 0-month level on a measure that required him to listen to orally presented sentences and "fill in" the missing word (Woodcock-Johnson: Oral Comprehension). When asked to listen to longer, orally presented paragraph-length narratives, Mr. I.D. was able to recall only 7 of 50 details immediately (WMS-IV Logical Memory I – <1st percentile). Notably, Mr. I.D.'s recall was very confused on the second story, in that his re-telling of the story was as though he had initially heard a completely different narrative presented. His re-telling of the first story was more accurate, yet quite simplistic, missing many key details. These results showed that Mr. I.D. had significant difficulty capturing information presented in an auditory-verbal manner, with implications for his ability to understand instructions and narratives.

Mr. I.D. additionally demonstrated significant deficits in language-based processing and reasoning, with performance that was far below age-expectations on the verbal tasks of the WAIS-IV, including verbal concept formation (Similarities – <1st percentile), vocabulary knowledge (Vocabulary – 1st percentile), and fact-based knowledge (Information – 2nd percentile). Mr. I.D.'s performance on these measures highlighted his severe impairments in understanding language, reasoning with words (particularly with respect to abstract concepts), and clearly communicating his ideas to others.

Additionally, Mr. I.D.'s single-word reading was assessed using the Word Reading subtest of the WRAT-4. On this measure, he obtained a grade equivalent of 1.4 (0.1 percentile).

Mr. I.D.'s Competency Abilities

The Fitness Interview Test, Revised (FIT-R; Roesch, Zapf & Eaves, 2006) was utilized to assess Mr. I.D.'s competencies. Mr. I.D. could not articulate a basic narrative of the events leading to his arrest. Further, he initially denied having been read his Miranda rights, then later said he was told that he "was gonna have to talk to the police" and "you can speak to a lawyer." He mentioned only two of the charges (i.e., two counts of burglary and peeping Tom, actually a previous charge). He then stated that his lawyer had talked to him about "probation violation." Mr. I.D. demonstrated confusion about the seriousness of the charges. He knew the role of his attorney ("trying to umm...talk to them about what I did or tell the judge I'm not a bad person") and the judge ("last say so"). However, he showed some confusion about the prosecutor/solicitor role, stating "[he/she] is trying to get me...they might go along with the judge and my lawyer...give you probation...tell the judge what I did, not trying to help...trying to help in some kinda way." He initially denied knowing what an oath was, however, when the concept was explained, Mr. I.D. stated: "You're not lying." When asked what could be used as evidence in court, Mr. I.D. said "Uh...that's a good question, it's something that you do, that you did, and the judge tell you what you did." Mr. I.D. did not show an understanding of the concept of pleading not guilty ("that you did it") and stated that when someone pleads "not guilty" they can go home. He seemed to show an indirect understanding of what it means to "plead guilty" in that he talked about possible sentencing options, such as house arrest or jail, but he did not say outright that pleading guilty involved admitting to the offense. He also was unable to discuss how a lawyer might advise someone making one type of plea versus another and did not appear to understand that certain rights were waived with a guilty plea.

Mr. I.D. could not articulate how he would defend himself against the charges initially, but with prompting, indicated possible explanations, such as negative peer influences, stress, and being under the influence of drugs. He did not know how he would plead and did not have a realistic appreciation of what a likely jail sentence would be in his case: "I say, a year." He acknowledged that the court in which he would be tried would have authority over him and that he would need to abide by the court's decision.

Mr. I.D. struggled to provide a coherent narrative with respect to the facts of his case. While he indicated that he liked his attorney and had confidence in her, he could not explain why he did, other than repeating "because she's my lawyer." He initially indicated that he did not know what a plea bargain was but seemed to grasp the basic concept when it was defined. However, while he indicated that he would agree to a plea bargain, he could not think of any questions that he should ask his lawyer if he were considering pleading guilty except "Is everything gonna be okay?" Mr. I.D. indicated that he would say something to the judge if someone told a lie about him in the courtroom. He also understood the importance of appropriate courtroom behavior generally but indicated that "you can speak whenever."

Summary and Conclusions

The case of Mr. I.D. demonstrates examples of inappropriate determination of malingering on the part of the 2016 State competency examiner who failed to consider Mr. I.D.'s cultural experiences and disability. Firstly, all of the examiners were White, and, as such, one must consider the potential impact of stereotypes held by examiners who are of a different ethnic and cultural group than the examinee. Specifically, in Dr. H.'s mental status questions (i.e., the colors of the American flag, the significance of the Fourth of July holiday), her hypothesis about the credibility of Mr. I.D.'s answers was based not on his developmental and academic history, but on her beliefs about what a typical American "should" know and "should" hold to be important. Moreover, the capacity to participate in telephone calls is not outside of the range of capabilities of individuals with ID, particularly when they are about familiar topics. On Dr. S.'s testing, Mr. I.D. reportedly endorsed a high level of psychopathology, and extreme and uncommon psychiatric symptoms (Miller Forensic Assessment of Symptoms-M-FAST; Miller, 2001), but what was not considered was given his poor language comprehension skills, it is unlikely that he understood, or could understand, the questions asked on the M-FAST. Mr. I.D.'s symptoms of suggestibility displayed on the M-FAST are well accounted for by research documenting high levels of suggestibility in individuals with ID (Milne, Clare & Bull, 2002).

Dr. C.'s psychological evaluation demonstrated further bias against individuals with ID. She based her assertions about the credibility of Mr. I.D.'s performance on two measures, the M-FAST and ILK, both of which are extremely problematic in individuals with ID, often resulting in unacceptably high false positive rates (Victor & Boone, 2021; Danzer & Wasser, 2021). Research has suggested that the false positive rate on the M-FAST in individuals with ID is 50% (Graue et al., 2007).

While we wait for the state of the science to evolve, particularly in terms of the representation of Black Americans and individuals with disabilities in normative reference groups, there are still ways to approach validity assessment in a manner that considers diversity and adheres to ethical principles. It is the forensic neuropsychologist's responsibility to be aware of what research exists and assess the appropriateness of the measures they use and the potential need to adjust cutoffs to mitigate bias. Consistent with this, Peery, Byrd, and Strutt (2017) note that plausible alternative explanations for invalid performance may be present in an individual with a diverse background as compared with individuals from the mainstream culture. Finally, these authors recommend a structured decision-making procedure to case conceptualization in individuals with diverse backgrounds, involving systematically gathering and considering information related to developmental, medical and psychiatric history, academic and vocational experiences, cultural practices, lifestyle, and values and expectations (Peery, Byrd & Strutt, 2017).

I ultimately opined that Mr. I.D. was not malingering, and that he was not competent to stand trial, based on his lack of knowledge of key information related to courtroom procedure, legal concepts, and his case, such as the role of the prosecutor, reasonable possible dispositions related to his charges, and the relevance of possible pleas and the plea-bargaining process. I also noted that Mr. I.D.'s significant communication and intellectual deficits would not make it possible for him to adequately assist his attorney. Further, I opined that the longstanding, severe, developmental nature of Mr. I.D.'s deficits would preclude restoration. The judge agreed.

Neuropsychological Evaluation Test Summary

GENERAL INTELLECTUAL FUNCTIONING

Wechsler Adult Intelligence Scale – Fourth Edition (WAIS-IV)

Indices	*Standard Score*	*Percentile*
Verbal Comprehension Index (VCI)	58	0.3
Perceptual Reasoning Index (PRI)	51	0.1
Working Memory Index (WMI)	50	<0.1
Processing Speed Index (PSI)	50	<0.1
Full-Scale IQ	46	<0.1

WAIS-IV Subtests

Subtest	*Scaled Score*	*Percentile*	*Subtest*	*Scaled Score*	*Percentile*
VCI			PRI		
Similarities	2	0.4	Block design	2	0.4
Vocabulary	3	1st	Matrix reasoning	2	0.4
Information	4	2nd	Visual puzzles	1	0.1
WMI			PSI		
Digit span	1	0.1	Symbol search	1	0.1
Arithmetic	1	0.1	Cancellation	1	0.1

LANGUAGE

Woodcock-Johnson IV – Tests of Oral Language

	Age Equivalent
Picture Vocabulary	5–5
Oral Comprehension	5–0

LEARNING/MEMORY

Wechsler Memory Scale – Fourth Edition (WMS-IV)

	Scaled Score	*Percentile*
Logical Memory I	1	0.1

ACADEMIC FUNCTIONING

Wide Range Assessment of Achievement Test, Fourth Edition (WRAT-4)

Subtest	*Standard Score*	*Grade Equivalent*	*Percentile*
Word Reading	55	1.4	0.1

Editor's Addendum

We were deeply saddened at the untimely death of our colleague, Joette James, the author of this chapter. At the time of her passing, two of us (JJS & JEM) had edited her chapter and, as is routine in edited books, had offered comments and recommendations for revision. This occurred immediately prior to her passing. Unfortunately, having invested so much time and energy into her initial submission, Dr. James was unable to complete the chapter. The four editors finalized the chapter, keeping in mind what we viewed as the need for fidelity to Dr. James' overview on the general topic and her appreciation of the subtleties of this particular case.

This chapter by Dr. James helps all of us understand how timely the topics of culture and diversity are in forensic assessment, as well as the importance of analysis of performances by individuals with ID. Reading the chapter with an "editorial eye," also revealed aspects of bias to us that are not always apparent, (i.e., "implicit bias"). Initially, we had questions regarding the interpretation of the data – the examinee's test performances in conjunction with his history and especially the lack of knowledge of our country's history (e.g., the president, 4th of July, colors of the flag) which seemed so basic to us. We wondered just how credible the lack of this basic knowledge was in light of the examinee's IQ (consistently measured across decades) and previous failure of PVTs within a forensic examination. Nagging questions remained, however, regarding the examinee's below-chance performance on a memory questionnaire, unlikely to be completely attributed to ID. While on the fence about that, we nevertheless agreed with Dr. James' conclusions regarding this examinee's incompetence to proceed to trial, and appreciated the nuanced characteristics of decision-making and how a range of opinions could have emerged in this case. The reader is encouraged to speculate about this.

In recent years, there has been a substantial increase in relevant mainstream journal articles that address the importance of applying appropriate normative comparisons for performance tests, as well as cutoffs and variability of effectiveness of PVTs and SVTs, when examining individuals of color and individuals from different cultural backgrounds. Within the growing literature, the detailed textbooks by Fujii (2017) and Irani (2022) are particularly rich resources related to performing culturally informed neuropsychological evaluations. Also, Fujii (2018) has provided a framework for conceptualizing and conducting evaluations with culturally diverse examinees, using the acronym ECLECTIC: Education (level, quality, and literacy), Culture and acculturation, Language spoken and English proficiency, Economics, Communication style, Testing situation (comfort and motivation), Intelligence (conceptualization), and Context of immigration. An example of the application of the ECLECTIC framework can be found in Costello, MacDonald, Papadakis, and Jordan (2024).

Related, the Forensic Neuropsychology Special Interest Group (FNSIG) has created an online listing of articles on "Diversity: Culture, language, education, access, threat to diagnosis" that can be viewed and downloaded at: https://theaacn.org/wp-content/uploads/_pda/2022/05/FNSIG-BIBLIOGRAPHY-Final-May-23-2022.pdf

Readers are also encouraged to explore the major initiative of AACN known as *Relevance 2050*, which highlights the critical need of the specialty of clinical neuropsychology and its specialist members to develop appropriate norms for the increasing diversity of our clinical and forensic examinees.

https://theaacn.org/relevance-2050/relevance-2050-initiative/

Note

1 https://kirwaninstitute.osu.edu/implicit-bias-module-series/module-1-understanding-implicit-bias.

References

American Psychological Association. (2017). *Ethical Principles of Psychologists and Code of Conduct* (2002, Amended June 1, 2010 and January 1, 2017). Retrieved from https://www.apa.org/ethics/code

American Psychological Association, APA Task Force on Race and Ethnicity Guidelines in Psychology. (2019). *Race and Ethnicity Guidelines in Psychology: Promoting Responsiveness and Equity.* Retrieved from https://www.apa.org/about/policy/guidelines-race-ethnicity.pdf

Board of Directors (2007) American Academy of Clinical Neuropsychology (AACN) Practice guidelines for neuropsychological assessment and consultation. *The Clinical Neuropsychologist, 21*(2), 209–231. https://doi.org/10.1080/13825580601025932

Bush, S.B., Ruff, R.M., Troster, A.I., Barth, J.T., Koffler, S.P., Pliskin, N.H., Reynolds, C.R., & Silver, C.H. (2005). Symptom validity assessment: Practice issues and medical necessity. *Archives of Clinical Neuropsychology, 20*, 419–426.

Danzer, G.A., & Wasser, T.C. (2021). A literature analysis of the inventory of legal knowledge. *Journal of the American Academy of Psychiatry and the Law, 49*(1), 1–9.

Ditchman, N., Kosyluk, K., Werner, S., Jones, N., Elg, B., & Corrigan, P.W. (2013). Stigman and intellectual disability: Potential application of mental illness research. *Rehabilitation Psychology, 58*(2), 206–216.

Graue, L.O., Berry, D.T., Clark, J.A., Sollman, M.J., Cardi, M., Hopkins, J., & Werline, D. (2007). Identification of feigned mental retardation using the new generation of malingering detection instruments: Preliminary findings. *The Clinical Neuropsychologist, 21*(6), 929–942.

Guilmette, T.J., Sweet, J.J., Hebben, N., Koltai, D., Mahone, E.M., Spiegler, B., Stucky, K., Westerveld, M., & Conference Participants. (2020). American academy of clinical neuropsychology consensus conference statement on uniform test score labeling of performance tests. *The Clinical Neuropsychologist, 34*, 437–453. https://doi.org/10.1080/13854046.2020.1722244

Hernstein, R.J., & Murray, C. (1994). *The Bell Curve: Intelligence and Class Structure in American Life*. New York: Free Press.

Kirwan Institute for the Study of Race and Ethnicity, Ohio State University. Retrieved from https://kirwaninstitute.osu.edu

Manly, J.J., Byrd, D.A., Touradji, P., & Stern, Y. (2004). Acculturation, reading level, and neuropsychological test performance among African American elders. *Applied Neuropsychology, 11*, 37–46. https://doi.org/10.1207/s15324826an1101_5

Miller, H.A. (2001). *MFAST: Miller Forensic Assessment of Symptoms Test Professional Manual.* Odessa, FL: Psychological Assessment Resources.

Milne, R., Clare, I.C., & Bull, R. (2002). Interrogative suggestibility among witnesses with mild intellectual disabilities: The use of an adaptation of the GSS. *Journal of Applied Research in Intellectual Disabilities, 15*(1), 8–17.

Musick, J., & Otto, R. (2006). *Inventory of Legal Knowledge.* Lutz, Fl: Psychological Assessment Resources.

Nisbett, R.E., Aronson, J., Blair, C., Dickens, W., Flynn, J., Halpern, D.F., & Turkheimer, E. (2012). Intelligence: New findings and theoretical developments. *American Psychologist, 67*(1), 130.

Peery, S., Byrd, D.A., & Strutt, A.M. (2017). Diversity considerations in forensic neuropsychology. In S.S. Bush, G.J. Demakis & M.L. Rohling (Eds.), *APA Handbook of Forensic Neuropsychology* (pp. 379–393). Washington, DC: American Psychological Association.

Roesch, R., Zapf, P. A., & Eaves, D. (2006). *FIT-R: Fitness Interview Test-Revised. A Structured Interview for Assessing Competency to Stand Trial.* Sarasota, FL: Professional Resource Press/Professional Resource Exchange.

Schalock, R.L., Borthwick-Duffy, S.A., Bradley, V.J., Buntinx, W.H.E., Coulter, D.L., Craig, E.M., Gomez, S., Lachapelle, Y., Luckasson, R., Reeve, A., Shogren, K.A., Snell, M.E., Spreat, S., Tassé, M.J., Thompson, J.R., Verdugo Alonso, M.A., Wehmeyer, M.L., & Yeager, M.H. (2010). *Intellectual Disability: Diagnosis, Classification, and Systems of Supports* (11th ed.). Washington, DC: American Association on Intellectual and Developmental Disabilities.

Smith, K., Boone, K., Victor, T., Miora, D., Cottingham, M., Ziegler, E., … & Wright, M. (2014). Comparison of credible patients of very low intelligence and non-credible patients on neurocognitive performance validity indicators. *The Clinical Neuropsychologist*, *28*(6), 1048–1070.

Sweet, J.J., Heilbronner, R.L., Morgan, J.E., Larrabee, G.J., Rohling, M.L., Boone, K.B., Kirkwood, M.W., Schroeder, R.W., Suhr, J.A., & Conference Participants (2021). American Academy of Clinical Neuropsychology (AACN) 2021 consensus statement on validity assessment: Update of the 2009 AACN consensus conference statement on neuropsychological assessment of effort, response bias, and malingering. *The Clinical Neuropsychologist, 35*, 1053–1106. https://doi.org/10.1080/13854046.2021.1896036

Thaler, N.S., Thames, A.D., & Cagigas, X.E. (2015). IQ testing and the African American client. In L.T. Benuto & B.D. Leany (Eds.), *Guide to Psychological Assessment with African Americans* (pp. 63–76). New York: Springer Science + Business Media.

Victor, T.L., & Boone, K.B. (2021). Identification of feigned intellectual disability. In K.B. Boone (Ed.), *Assessment of Feigned Cognitive Impairment: A Neuropsychological Perspective* (pp. 453–480). (2nd ed.). New York: Guilford Press.

Wechsler, D. (2008). *Wechsler Adult Intelligence Scale-IV*. New York: Pearson Assessments.

Additional References

Costello, R., MacDonald, B., Papadakis, J.L., & Jordan, L.L. (2024). Culturally-informed neuropsychological evaluations of patients with spina bifida: Application of the ECLECTIC framework to a complex pediatric medical condition. *The Clinical Neuropsychologist*, 1–27. https://doi.org/10.1080/13854046.2024.2372877

Fujii, D.E.M. (2017). *Conducting a culturally informed neuropsychological evaluation*. Washington, DC: American Psychological Association. https://doi.org/10.1037/15958-000

Fujii, D.E.M. (2018). Developing a cultural context for conducting a neuropsychological evaluation with a culturally diverse client: The ECLECTIC framework. *The Clinical Neuropsychologist, 32*(8), 1356–1392. https://doi.org/10.1080/13854046.2018.1435826

Irani, F. (2022). *Cultural Diversity in Neuropsychological Assessment: Developing Understanding through Global Case Studies*. New York: Routledge.

21 Mild Traumatic Brain Injury in Criminal Litigation

Christopher J. Graver and Maria K. Nikolova

Introduction

Legal matters involving a suspected mild traumatic brain injury (mTBI) are more common in civil litigation than in criminal litigation. Nonetheless, to address whether a mTBI could be a defense in a criminal case, a person accused of a crime can be referred for an evaluation to determine the following: their mental state at the time of the offense, whether that mental state compromised the defendant's cognitive or volitional capacities, and whether they have the capacity to stand trial (Ruff & Jamora, 2008). Can the individual appreciate the legal or moral wrongfulness of the criminal act? Can they refrain from committing the act? Do they have the capacity to understand legal proceedings and assist their counsel? These are the type of questions that benefit from the expertise of mental health and medical professionals. Criminal responsibility presumes that a person has the ability to control their conduct and to choose whether to commit the crime. An insanity defense argues that the defendant is not responsible for their actions due to mental disease or defect at the time of the criminal act, while a diminished responsibility or diminished capacity defense argues that the defendant should not be held fully liable for the crime due to diminished or impaired mental functions at the time of the crime. In this chapter, we will discuss factors to consider in criminal litigation when mTBI is suspected and illustrate these factors using a case.

The idea of severe brain injury having possible ties to violent crime is not new; however, there has been an increase in concussion research and publicity following the 2013 criminal case of NFL player, Aaron Hernandez. Questions were raised about the connection between his history of concussions and violent behavior that eventually led to him being charged with murder. In an opinion piece in Stat News, Bozelko (2017) cites the Hernandez case stating,

> A team of Boston University researchers was asked to examine Hernandez's brain. They reported that he suffered the most severe case of chronic traumatic encephalopathy- a progressive degenerative brain disease often seen in people with a history of repetitive brain trauma- they had ever seen in a person his age.

She goes on to say that such severe injuries would have caused poor judgment and impulse control, two factors that played a role in his incarceration. Of note, studies show little relationship between CTE neuropathology and clinical symptoms in life (Randolph, 2018). There is also significant overlap between signs and symptoms of CTE and common neurodegenerative diseases such as Alzheimer's disease or frontotemporal dementia (Maroon, Winkelman, Bost, Amos Mathyssek, & Miele, 2015) and 90% of older adults have abnormal tau depositions but are not committing violent crimes.

DOI: 10.4324/9781003005063-24

Furthermore, the author fails to mention the inherently aggressive nature of football and the type of personality that may be attracted to the contact sport. The author goes on to argue that traumatic brain injury (severity not specified) should be considered when judging individuals accused of crimes and that the public's biggest objection when it comes to considering a diminished capacity defense is that people can feign their illness and lack of understanding when faced with extreme punishment for their crimes. She posits that head injuries are different from organic mental illness because they can be objectively identified using CT scans instead of relying on the self-report of the accused who may be motivated to malinger. However, neuroimaging may only be supportive, not diagnostic for traumatic brain injury (TBI). Moreover, mental responsibility, diminished capacity, and competency are behaviorally determined, which cannot be seen on a CT scan, and requires neuropsychological evaluation. Therefore, this argument is misleading.

Furthermore, the author uses "TBI" as a global catch phrase for all forms of traumatic brain injury when there are in fact crucial differences in the presentation and long-term implications of mTBI and moderate–severe TBI. A traumatic brain injury can result from a head strike, the brain undergoing an acceleration/deceleration movement without direct contact, and forces generated from a blast or explosion (The American Congress of Rehabilitation Medicine, 2023). Not all head trauma events result in a traumatic brain injury, but in cases where they do, length of time of loss of consciousness (LOC), presence of post-traumatic amnesia (PTA), and the individual's score on the Glasgow Coma Scale (GCS) are taken into account to determine severity. The mild qualifier of TBI is used when there is an alteration in consciousness or LOC less than 30 minutes, PTA less than 24 hours, and a GCS score between 13 and 15. The diagnostic label "concussion" can be used interchangeably with "mild TBI" when neuroimaging is normal. If LOC is greater than 30 minutes, PTA is more than 24 hours, or the GCS scores is less than 13, the TBI is no longer considered to be mild and is classified as either moderate or severe.

Years of research literature illustrates that concussions typically recover in a few days to weeks (McCrea, Iverson, McAllister et al., 2009). Even in the most protractive cases, meta-analyses show that they are fully resolved in 90 days (Gentilini, Nichelli, Schoenhuber et al., 1985; Maddocks & Saling, 1996; Ponsford, Willmott, Rothwell et al., 2000). Beyond this time frame, ongoing symptoms are often not due to the concussion itself. Moreover, delayed onset of symptoms after a mTBI is highly atypical in the absence of secondary and tertiary factors, such as intracranial bleeds; symptom onset of concussions is typically immediate or within moments of impact. Generally, a moderate–severe TBI involves structural neurological changes that might not recover while a mild TBI leads to short-term changes with recovery. By using the catch-all term "TBI," pathologic changes, symptoms, and long-term sequelae of severe TBI are conflated with concussion outcomes, leading to erroneous attributions for individuals with mTBI. As such, we recommend against using the umbrella term of TBI and instead classifying it based on the severity. This chapter will be focusing on mild TBI only.

Misinformation about mTBI and confluence of mTBI and moderate–severe TBI is not limited to the lay public and is a significant problem among professionals as well. For instance, in a study looking at mTBI knowledge in 181 U.S. Army behavioral health professionals, Bradford (2015) found that only 28% of the behavioral health professionals in the sample believed that a majority of people (90%) achieve full recovery after an mTBI. About 66% believed that delayed symptom onset was common and about 28% believed that mTBI causes permanent brain damage and poor functional outcomes. In another study looking at primary care managers (PCM) at various primary care facilities, Seegmiller and colleagues (2018) found that only 55% of PCM's believed that a majority of individuals (85%) who experience an mTBI will achieve full recovery. This number was even less (28%) for behavioral medicine clinicians. These misconceptions are concerning and can lead to misinformation, misdiagnosis, and inappropriate treatment.

For cases where post concussive symptoms continue past 90 days, it is important to look to other factors, including, but not limited to, preinjury medical problems and psychiatric problems (Ponsford, Cameron, Fitzgerald, Grant, Mikocka-Walus, & Schonberger, 2012). In some cases, the identified symptoms may have been present prior to the concussion but were previously dismissed or erroneously attributed to the concussions (Broshek, Marco, & Freeman, 2015). Such misattributions can contribute to a longer recovery. Moreover, studies have also shown that the presence of post concussive like symptoms (i.e., fatigue, poor concentration, forgetfulness, irritability, headache, dizziness) are not unique to mild head injury and are commonly found in healthy individuals (Iverson & Lange, 2003; Wang, Chan, & Deng, 2006). Legal factors may also contribute to post concussive symptoms. In fact, compensation and litigation factors are found to be the most stable predictor of prolonged post concussive symptoms (Carroll, Cassidy, Peloso et al., 2004; Vanderploeg, Belanger, & Kaufmann, 2014).

Another crucial aspect of diagnosing mTBI is ensuring that confounding factors do not fully account for the clinical signs, symptoms, examination, or lab findings that are necessary for the diagnosis of a mTBI (American Congress of Rehabilitation Medicine, 2023). There are times when a concussion is readily diagnosed without consideration for other factors that may be impacting the individual at the time of a head injury such as alcohol or substance intoxication, psychological trauma, acute pain, and preexisting or co-occurring health conditions. For example, studies estimate that as high as 50% of individuals who are treated for any type of traumatic brain injury are intoxicated at the time of their injury (Corrigan, 1995). This number is even higher for those injured in assaults or motor vehicle accidents. Alcohol intoxication at the time of the injury can be a confounding factor in accurately assessing the severity of a head injury not only due to concerns for recall of events but also overlapping symptoms that may impact diagnostic clarity (i.e., altered mental status, GCS, neurological exam).

Moreover, studies have demonstrated a strong link between alcohol use and violence (Mann Zalcman, Smart, Rush, & Suurvali, 2006; Giancola, Levinson, Corman et al., 2009). Alcohol can increase aggression, even in those who are not characteristically predisposed to it (Phil, Lau, & Assaad, 1997). Furthermore, frequent drinkers are more likely to engage in violence than infrequent drinkers (Felson, Teasdale, & Burchfield, 2008). In a study of over 16,000 incarcerated individuals, researchers found that alcohol played a larger role in violent offenses such as physical assault, sexual assault, and homicide compared with offenses such as robberies and burglaries (Felson & Staff, 2010). Concurrently, over 43% of violent incidents involve alcohol use and suspects of violent crimes are almost twice as likely to be intoxicated than suspects of nonviolent crimes (McClelland & Teplin, 2001). In the United States, on average, about 40% of inmates who are incarcerated for violent offenses are under the influence of alcohol (Galbicsek, 2020). The relationship continues to exist even when controlling for past violence and alcohol use (Felson & Staff, 2010). Roughly 40% of convicted murderers were under the influence of alcohol before or during the criminal offense. About 37% of sexual assaults and rapes and 27% of aggravated assaults are committed by perpetrators who were drinking alcohol. Comparatively, only 15% of robberies involve alcohol use. It is important not to dismiss the role that alcohol use plays, especially when considering the presence of both intoxication and a mTBI.

In 2015, the Centers for Disease Control and Prevention (CDC) released information, based on a few studies, stating that there is a history of TBI in about 25%–87% of individuals in jail and prison. These findings are used as an argument for TBI implications in legal matters; however, many of these studies are correlational. Perkes, Schofield, Butler, and Hollis (2011) also found that TBI was more common in a prison group when compared with control. Moreover, they found an association between mTBI, alcohol use, drug use, impulsivity, and dissocial personality traits. However, when factors such as impulsivity and dissocial traits were excluded, a significant relationship between TBI and incarceration was not found. These findings suggest that the preexisting impulsivity, aggression, and risk-taking behaviors that might lead to criminal behavior might also contribute to TBI risk and highlight the importance of examining premorbid behavioral patterns.

Since mTBI recovers fully in less than 90 days, it is unlikely that an mTBI would impact someone's competency in the long term. However, an mTBI may acutely lead to altered mental status and, as a result, are more likely to impact someone's actions in the acute phase than chronically. Beyond the obvious altered mental status and amnesia, behavioral symptoms might appear in the form of automatisms, which are involuntary behaviors of which the individual has no control or awareness (McCrory, 2001). This behavior tends to be inappropriate for the situation and may be out of character. Posttraumatic automatisms typically occur immediately after a head injury during the PTA phase and generally recover within 20–30 minutes. Examples include flailing limbs, refusing to be directed, swinging one's arms if restrained, wandering aimlessly, and exhibiting robotic-like movements. These behaviors are not goal-directed or purposeful, and no premeditation, plaining, or concealment is present.

The following case is a court-ordered evaluation to determine competency to stand trial and criminal responsibility with regard to fleeing the scene of an accident and assaulting first responders after suffering a possible mTBI in a motor vehicle accident. Findings were based on a review of all available legal and medical records, personnel records, collateral information, a clinical interview, behavioral observations, psychological testing, and neuropsychological testing. The defendant and his attorneys claimed that the accused suffered a concussion and that his post-concussion behaviors, such as fleeing and then assaulting law enforcement officers, were out of character, non-volitional, and due to the acute effects of the concussion.

Facts of the Case

Account of the Alleged Offenses

Private Snuffy was a 25-year-old Caucasian male who took a friend out to get a tattoo for his birthday. Upon arrival at the tattoo parlor around 1,700 hours, they discovered that the tattoo parlor had closed. They were able to find another nearby artist, but there was no availability for two hours. In the meantime, they went to a local bar because they had been in training all day and had eaten very little. Private Snuffy had a couple of tacos along with a beer and two shots of tequila over the next two hours, by his report. He then drove back to the tattoo shop around 1,930 hours and was able to get a tattoo. That took approximately 30 minutes, at which time they returned to the bar and he consumed another beer and two shots of tequila. He was unsure how much alcohol he consumed that night, but estimated it could have been as much as eight drinks.

Private Snuffy did not report anything unusual about the day. He went through his usual routine, was not feeling ill, and did not take prescription medications. He recalled the events of the night, including specific conversations that were had until about the last hour at the bar. He recalled discussing with his friend the need to get a ride home due to intoxication before picking up another drink, a Manhattan around 2,300 hours.

Private Snuffy reported that he did not recall consuming the last drink or anything else they discussed while at the bar for the remainder of the evening. He also reported that he did not recall leaving the bar, what time it was, or the events that transpired immediately after. He commented that his next memory was feeling the car hit something hard as he was driving home. After the car came to a stop, he recalled feeling blood on his head and exiting the vehicle. He stated that his memory was patchy for events after that and that "it was like remembering a dream when I look back on it."

According to police reports, Private Snuffy left the bar just before 0000 hours (midnight). He was driving his own vehicle, despite discussing the need to get a ride home, and did not recall why they did not get a ride share or taxi home. At about 0020 hours, he was driving through a residential area with a speed limit of 25 miles per hour. On a slight curve in the road, he struck a utility pole at an estimated speed between 72 and 98 miles per hour. There was evidence of tire marks consistent with critical speed yaw, but no evidence of braking. The car hit the pole on the passenger side front area in an off-set manner, which sheared the metal off the passenger side engine and passenger compartments as it pushed past the utility pole. The driver's side of the vehicle was largely undamaged.

As noted previously, Private Snuffy recalled hitting something and feeling blood on his head. There was no known LOC. Since this was a residential neighborhood, multiple witnesses living in the area called emergency services when they heard the collision. Although there were no direct witnesses to the collision, records show that witnesses were outside immediately afterward and were able to relay details of the accident scene to 911 dispatchers within 30 seconds. According to witnesses, they heard Private Snuffy in the vehicle yelling at the passenger for a short time. He then exited the vehicle, yelled at witnesses to leave him alone when they tried to help, and fled the scene. Witnesses were able to provide an accurate description of his clothing to responding officers and later positively identified him by facial recognition.

Private Snuffy ran down the street and crossed through several yards, jumped multiple fences, and ended up in an apartment complex several streets over. He proceeded to the second floor and was banging on doors trying to get occupants to let him in. According to one occupant, Private Snuffy stated that he killed his friend and needed to escape. When no one opened doors, he proceeded to the third floor landing and witnesses heard him yelling that he was shot and needed aid. One occupant started to open the door and Private Snuffy attempted to force his way into the residence before the occupant was able to get the door closed and locked. Law enforcement was able to set up a containment perimeter approximately eight minutes after the collision. Prior to law enforcement arrival, witnesses observed Private Snuffy alternately hiding and peering over the railing of the landing and "powerfully kicking" various apartment doors in an attempt to gain entry.

Law enforcement approached the site with a K-9 unit and clearly identified themselves as such. Private Snuffy responded by stating that he had been shot and needed assistance. However, he failed to comply with instructions and tried to kick the K-9, at which time the K-9 was released and bit him in the leg. He continued to resist, but officers were able to subdue him and take him into custody. While in the patrol car, Private Snuffy was screaming that he did not consent to being detained, was thrashing about, and attempted to kick out the patrol car's window. A hobble was placed around his feet and he was placed back in the patrol car, but managed to get free of the restraints. Officers used a pressure point to subdue him in order to reapply the restraints. Private Snuffy stated, "I submit! I submit!" and cooperated with officer instructions until the pressure point was released, at which time he struck out at officers, stating "I don't consent!" When interviewed for the forensic assessment, he stated that he was frustrated at being trapped and did everything he could to get away or make it as difficult as possible to detain him.

Law enforcement noted a laceration on Private Snuffy's head while in the patrol car, as well as the bite wound from the K-9. They removed him to get medical attention with Emergency Medical Services (EMS), but he was trying to spit on them and was uncooperative with the examination. A spit sock was placed and officers held him down. His clothes were removed and no trauma was visualized other than a "V"-shaped laceration in the occipital area with minor bleeding and the K-9 bite wound. He was oriented to self, but he was refusing to answer questions. He repeatedly tried to kick officers and it was deemed unsafe to check his back without risking assault, so he was chemically sedated and transported to the hospital for further evaluation. Given signs of intoxication and the odor of alcohol coming from Private Snuffy, a warrant was obtained for a blood draw. His blood alcohol level was 0.16 g/100 mL four hours after the collision (high). The drug screen was negative.

Private Snuffy was hospitalized for approximately 12 hours for observation and to allow the alcohol to metabolize and sedation to wear off. Emergency Department (ED) records show normal chest CT and no thoracic injury, as well as normal abdominal CT. The neurologic exam was normal, as was the CT of his head and neck. The only injuries noted were the scalp laceration, bruising from the seatbelt, and skin abrasions on his arm. There were no notations of altered mental status and no diagnoses related to brain injury, but he was diagnosed with acute intoxication. He was cooperative with hospital staff and there were no further behavioral outbursts during his stay. He was transferred to jail after discharge. The following day, a medical exam revealed that he was fully oriented, physical and neurologic exams were unremarkable, and no new symptoms had emerged. The medical note stated, "No issues noted to balance, gait is strong, purposeful and regular. Pt. responds quickly and purposefully to verbal commands. No complications noted."

Private Snuffy reported that he recalled details of his hospital stay, as well as his time in jail. Jail phone records from the day of booking showed that he called his mother and accurately described being in jail, that had been involved in a motor vehicle collision, accurately described the vehicle he was driving, that he was intoxicated while driving, and that the passenger had died. In contrast, he reported to the receiving medical evaluator the next day that he had been hit by a car and suffered a serious brain injury, but he denied a history of alcohol and drug use. At the time of the forensic assessment, which was approximately five months after the collision, Private Snuffy endorsed ongoing cognitive difficulties, including recent and remote memory loss, and poor concentration that he attributed to a brain injury sustained in the accident.

Personal History

Private Snuffy reported being raised by his mother and denied any history of abuse or developmental disabilities. He reported being an average student with marginal peer relationships due to being bullied through middle school. In high school, he reported getting into trouble for fighting, skipping school, and vandalism. He described a disinterest in school and missing the majority of school days during his senior year, but still was able to graduate on time. He was unmarried and had no children. He joined the U.S. Army at age 18 and was assigned to the infantry.

Medical History

Private Snuffy reported a head injury at age 7 after being hit by a hammer, but denied the need for treatment or any persisting symptoms. He also reported having a hard landing in a parachute jump that caused his neck to snap back and his helmet to come off. He estimated 45 seconds LOC and reported needing help to disengage his parachute, but he stated he was able to continue with the training event without difficulty. He did not seek medical treatment or report any persisting symptoms.

Substance Abuse History

Private Snuffy first tried alcohol at age 12. He initially consumed 6–8 alcohol drinks every weekend, and then progressed to 12–15 beers/night with an intent to get drunk and pass out. Starting in his mid-teens, he acknowledged, "I'd get too drunk and do something stupid." He offered some examples such as "being a dick to people who work at an establishment" or "being drunk on the porch, shirtless with vomit on my shoes." In addition to alcohol, he also reported using mushrooms, ketamine, MDMA, LSD, Molly, cocaine, amphetamine, THC, opioids, trenbolone, Halo HD, and a five-month period of 800 mg of dextromethorphan daily. He continued using alcohol and recreational substances in the military. He was diverted to a multiple substance abuse programs, but did not complete them. At the time of the alleged offense, he was facing administrative discharge from the military due to instances of misconduct and failed substance abuse rehabilitation.

Psychiatric History

Private Snuffy had a history of depression dating to adolescence, but no treatment at that time. He sought behavioral health treatment in the military and the medical chart documented sadness, anhedonia, insomnia, low energy, loss of interest in activities, hopelessness, and rumination. There was one suicide attempt via overdose seven months prior to the incident offense. He was prescribed escitalopram and trazodone that were beneficial to partial remission of depressive symptoms. His symptoms were described as reactionary to situational stressors and disappointments. One provider stated, "Functional impairment appears to be due to immaturity and lack of concern about consequences rather than impairment due to emotional distress." Another provider stated, "Characterological component is strongly considered." The provider went on to describe "a rather pervasive pattern of disregard for and violation of the rights of others since early adolescence" that reflected conduct disorder.

Legal History

Private Snuffy reported being detained after driving a golf cart while intoxicated, but stated that the charges were dropped. He also had been detained for urinating in public while intoxicated, but stated he was never charged. He was arrested for under-age drinking and destroying property during his military service. He was found painting male genitalia on the walls of a government building, as well as kicking out doors and windows "like I was doing a breaching exercise." He was punished with expulsion from his military unit and a reduction in rank. He also made a comment that he had thought about attempting to escape jail, but was waiting to see what happened with his sentencing in the current case.

Behavioral Observations

Private Snuffy arrived on time for the evaluation. There were no behavioral indications of responding to or being distracted by internal stimuli, psychomotor agitation or retardation, hypervigilance, exaggerated startle response, or panic attacks. Posture was normal. During the first interview, he was wearing leg restraints, which restricted his gait. He was not wearing leg restraints during his second interview and gait was unremarkable. He showed mild evidence of restlessness in bouncing his knees. Eye contact was socially appropriate. He was alert and well oriented in all spheres. He was able to focus on the interview and sustain attention throughout. Affect appeared dysphoric, but congruent with speech content and situation. Speech was of a normal rate, volume, and prosody. Thought processes were goal-directed and reality-based. He denied any current suicidal or homicidal ideation, plan, or intent.

Test Results

Private Snuffy scored above the established cutoff for non-credible symptom reporting on the Structured Interview of Reported Symptoms (SIMS) total score. Specifically, he endorsed unusual psychotic symptoms that are not typically present in actual psychiatric patients, atypical symptoms of depression and anxiety, symptoms of memory impairment that are inconsistent with patterns of impairment seen in brain dysfunction or injury, and illogical or highly atypical neurological symptoms. In addition, his subjective memory symptoms on the Memory Complaints Inventory were compared with individuals with a history of mTBI. His scores were approximately 1.3–1.5 standard deviations higher than the comparison group in terms of verbal memory problems, impairment in remote memory, and amnesia for complex behavior. Even more notable was his report of amnesia for antisocial behavior, which was 3.6 standard deviations higher than individuals with a history of mTBI. Thus, self-reported symptoms were inconsistent with those typically reported by individuals with documented mTBI and likely to be exaggerated with particular efforts to claim a lack of memory for potentially criminal behaviors that carry negative consequences. Table 21.1 provides summary of his validity test data.

Private Snuffy's performance validity testing was below established cutoffs on two stand-alone measures and one embedded measure. Scores on the Word Memory Test were as much as 4.8 standard deviations below a comparison group of individuals with mTBI on the easiest subtests (IR and DR). In addition, performance was worse for the easiest subtests as compared with those that require actual memory abilities (FR), which was 0.6 standard deviations *above* the mTBI group. FR was also 0.4 standard deviations above a large sample of healthy individuals with normal memory, indicating objectively intact memory abilities. This non-neurologic pattern was exhibited on other tests. For example, not only was his score on the so-called "hard" portion of the Victoria Symptom Validity Test below the cutoff of 17 shown by Jones (2013) to be associated with 1.0 specificity in a mixed neurologic sample, but there was a clear difference in performance between portions of the task that seemed easy versus those that seemed hard (24/24 versus 14/24) even though objectively they are very similar in difficulty. These results were indicative of invalid data that is artificially lowered compared with his actual abilities. Taken together, the high subjective memory complaints, especially his non-credible claims of amnesia for antisocial behavior, and non-credible memory performance indicated a likely attempt to use memory deficits to deflect criminal responsibility. Nevertheless, strong performance in non-memory domains resulted in an overall test battery mean ($T = 49$) that was comparable to his premorbid estimate ($T = 53$). Table 21.2 provides a summary of his cognitive data.

Table 21.1 Validity Data for Case Vignette 1

Performance Validity	*Raw*	*Symptom Validity*	T-*score*
WMT Immediate Recall	87.5	MCI GMP	55
WMT Delayed Recall	82.5	MCI NIP	56
WMT Consistency	80.0	MCI VSMP	59
WMT Multiple Choice	75.0	MCI VMP	63
WMT Paired Associates	70.0	MCI PIM	39
WMT Free Recall	62.5	MCI MIW	58
VSVT Easy	24	MCI IRM	64
VSVT Hard	14	MCI ACB	65
SIMS		MCI AAB	86
Neurologic Impairment	9		*Raw*
Affective	7	IVA-FAQ+FRCQ	149
Psychosis	4	IVA-ARC+AAQ	107
Low Intelligence	2	CVLT-2 Forced Choice	16
Amnesia	4	Reliable Digit Span	12
Total	26	WCST Regression	0.68

Note. WMT, Word Memory Test; SIMS, Structured Interview for Malingered Symptoms; MCI, Memory Complaints Inventory; GMP, General Memory Problems; NIP, Numeric Information Problems; VSMP, Visuospatial Memory Problems; VMP, Verbal Memory Problems; PIM, Pain Interferes with Memory; MIW, Memory Interferes with Work; IRM, Impairment of Remote Memory; ACB, Amnesia for Complex Behavior; AAB, Amnesia for Antisocial Behavior; *T-scores are relative to individuals with a history of mild traumatic brain injury.

Table 21.2 Cognitive Data for Case Vignette 1

Premorbid Estimate	T-*Score*	*Overall Test Battery Mean*	T-*score*
WTAR	53	OTBM	49
Intellectual	*T*-Score	*Memory*	
WASI-2 FSIQ	57	CVLT-II Immediate Recall	53
WASI-2 VCI	51	CVLT-II SDFR	40
WASI-2 PRI	55	CVLT-II SDCR	35
Attention		CVLT-II LDFR	35
WAIS-III Digit Span	57	CVLT-II LDCR	45
Trail Making Test, Part B	45	CVLT-II Discrimination	55
Trail Making Test, B:A Ratio	56	BVMT-R Immediate Recall	29
IVA-FAQ	31	BVMT-R Delayed Recall	24
IVA FRCQ	35	BVMT-R Retention	37
Executive		BVMT-R Recognition	37
WCST Total Errors	53	*Visuospatial*	
WCST Perseverative Errors	57	WASI-2 Block Design	50
WCST Categories	6 (raw)	BVMT-R Copy	>40
WASI-2 Similarities	56	*Motor and Processing Speed*	
WASI-2 Matrix Reasoning	52	Trail Making Test, Part A	34

(*Continued*)

(*Continued*)

Premorbid Estimate	T-*Score*	*Overall Test Battery Mean*	T-*score*
Language		IVA Auditory Sensory/Motor	65
WASI-2 Vocabulary	57	IVA Visual Sensory/Motor	46
COWAT	51	IVA Auditory Speed	65
Animal Fluency	50	IVA Visual Speed	56

Note. WTAR, Wechsler Test of Adult Reading; WASI-2, Wechsler Abbreviated Test of Intelligence, 2nd Edition; WAIS-III, Wechsler Adult Intelligence Test, 3rd Edition; IVA, Integrated Auditory and Visual Continuous Performance Test; FAQ, Full Attention Quotient; FRCQ, Full Response Control Quotient; COWAT, Controlled Oral Word Association Test; CVLT-II, California Verbal Learning Test, 2nd Edition; BVMT-R, Brief Visuospatial Memory Test, Revised.

Table 21.3 Psychological Data for Case Vignette 1

MMPI-2-RF	*T-score*	*MCMI-III*	*T-score*
Cannot Say	0 (raw)	Disclosure (X)	100
VRIN-r	48	Desirability (Y)	25
TRIN-r	65T	Debasement (Z)	92
F-r	120		
Fp-r	111		
Fs	66		
FBS-r	80		
RBS	76		
L	47		

Note. MMPI-2-RF = Minnesota Multiphasic Personality Inventory-2-Restructured Scale; VRIN, Variable Response Inconsistency; TRIN, True Response Inconsistency; F-r, Infrequent Responses; Fp-r, Infrequent Psychopathology Responses; Fs, Infrequent Somatic Responses; FBS-r, Symptom Validity; RBS, Response Bias Scale; L-r, Uncommon Virtues; K-r, Adjustment Validity; MCMI-III, Million Clinical Multiaxial Inventory, 3rd Edition.

From a psychological perspective, Private Snuffy was administered two objective personality and psychopathology measures. Validity indicators related to content-responding showed that Private Snuffy responded consistently throughout these measures, indicating he was able attend to and comprehend item content. However, review of the other validity scales showed significant overreporting, which was indicated by an excessive number of infrequent responses and assertion of a much larger than average number of symptoms rarely described by individuals with genuine, severe psychopathology. This pattern of overreporting psychiatric symptoms was seen on both measures and thus the substantive scales were not interpreted. Research shows that such invalid reporting is associated with non-credible reporting on symptom questionnaires without included response bias scales (Forbey & Lee, 2011; Forbey, Lee, Ben-Porath, Arbisi, & Gartland, 2013). As such, his test results brought the accuracy of his symptom report into question as well (Table 21.3).

Discussion

Private Snuffy underwent a court-ordered evaluation to determine competency to stand trial and criminal responsibility as it related to his post-collision behavior in the context of possible mTBI. Defense argued that his post-collision behavior was a result of altered mental status associated with mTBI and thus not within the bounds of criminal responsibility.

Diagnosis

As discussed earlier, the altered mental status associated with mTBI can result in combativeness, but this is typically in the form of automatisms and the behavior is not goal-directed or pre-meditated. The accident investigation revealed that there was likely sufficient force in the collision to meet the threshold for an mTBI and he had a laceration on his scalp, indicating something hit his head. The actual accident was not witnessed, but witnesses were present within 30 seconds to verify that he was conscious and talking. Normal neuroimaging also supported nothing more severe than mTBI, if present, but it is noteworthy that no TBI diagnosis was made during his hospitalization immediately following the accident. We did not provide a TBI diagnosis as a result of this examination either as there was no compelling evidence of altered mental status that could be specifically attributed to brain trauma. His report of patchy memory and feeling it was a dream was plausibly connected to the effects of alcohol on the central nervous system.

Based on the available information, Private Snuffy met criteria for an Alcohol Use Disorder, in a Controlled Environment and Adjustment Disorder (related to his legal situation). We considered the possibility that Private Snuffy might suffer from a stress-induced or trauma-related disorder, including Posttraumatic Stress Disorder (PTSD). However, he did not manifest the corresponding criteria (persistent re-experiencing, avoidance, negative alterations in cognitions and mood, and increased arousal) required to make a diagnosis of PTSD. In addition, we assessed for a possible mood disorder, but he did not manifest the criteria (history of major depressive, manic, or hypomanic episode) required for such a diagnosis. Furthermore, we assessed for a psychotic disorder, which can be manifested with hallucinations, delusional beliefs, disorganization to thoughts and behavior, and negative symptoms. Private Snuffy also did not manifest any of the hallmark symptoms of these disorders nor did he show any credible evidence of such symptoms on psychological testing.

Competency to Stand Trial

It was our opinion that Private Snuffy had a factual and rational understanding of the proceedings against him, as evidenced by his ability to describe the actual charges against him (e.g., vehicular manslaughter, fleeing the scene, hit and run, obstruction of justice, communicating a threat, and assault), his understanding of the nature and severity of those charges, his understanding of the roles of key courtroom participants (e.g., defense counsel's role is "to help me, make sure I'm legally represented"), his understanding of basic courtroom proceedings, his understanding of plea options and probable consequences, and his understanding of the possible consequences if convicted (e.g., confinement). In addition, he was able to give examples of what could be used as evidence at trial, such as statements by the first responders and photographs of the scene.

It was also our opinion that Private Snuffy had the ability to work with counsel and conduct or participate in the defense, as evidenced by observation that his thinking is organized and rational enough to work with his assigned counsel in his defense. He expressed that he felt comfortable discussing his case and legal strategy with both his civilian and military defense counsel. He said that if he did disagree with defense's legal strategy, then he would express his opinion and bring it up for discussion. He reported having confidence in defense counsel's ability to represent him and believing defense counsel would try to do a good job for him. Additionally, his thought processes were reality-based, he was not responding to or distracted by internal stimuli, he was able to focus on relevant matters, and he was not exhibiting mania or behavioral problems that would impair his ability to focus on relevant matters or to conduct himself appropriately during proceedings. He reported motivation to participate in his defense in order to obtain the most positive outcome in this case. Consistent with recovery expectation from mTBI, he did not evidence any credible cognitive impairments to impair with his ability to stand trial five months post-collision.

Criminal Responsibility

RCM 916 (k) (1) provides for an affirmative defense to a crime when the accused suffers from a "mental disease or defect" that was so severe at the time of the alleged criminal conduct that he was unable to appreciate the nature and quality or the wrongfulness of his acts. RCM 706 (c) (2) (A) does not define the term "severe mental disease or defect," but it does exclude "an abnormality manifested only by repeated criminal or otherwise antisocial conduct, or minor disorders such as nonpsychotic behavior disorders and personality defects." Additionally, RCM 916 (1) (2) states that voluntary intoxication, whether caused by alcohol or drugs, is not a defense.

Whereas this examination did not diagnose TBI, nor could we definitely rule it out at the time of Private Snuffy's motor vehicle collision, there were no symptoms or signs readily documented or observed that were exclusive to brain injury and unable to be explained by his alcohol intoxication. Individuals who suffer a concussion can have altered mental status that includes feeling confused. Such confusion may result in being dazed, forgetful, aimless wandering, or stimulus-bound automatisms, but outright aggression and goal-directed behaviors to the extent seen in this case are atypical. Instead of sitting in the car dazed or wandering aimlessly around, he almost immediately tried to communicate with his passenger and then self-extricated. After being offered help by witnesses, he fled the scene by a surreptitious route through backyards and over fences, heading for an apartment complex in which to hide, rather than on the sidewalk or even wandering into the street in an illogical manner. He also made statements indicating awareness that his friend might be dead and that he was making efforts to get away, providing evidence of purposeful and thoughtful behavior, if not the most well-reasoned decisions. He also acted in ways that indicated understanding of the situation and how to achieve a goal, such as when a pressure point restraint was used and he stated, "I submit! I submit!" and cooperated. As soon as the pressure point was released, he became combative again, stating, "I don't consent!" Finally, his behavior that night demonstrated consistency with previous aggressive and antisocial behavior while intoxicated, and there was nothing to indicate a unique contribution of mental disease or defect. The use of multiple symptom and performance validity tests was crucial to highlighting Private Snuffy's attempt to present as cognitively and psychiatrically compromised through exaggeration of subjective symptoms, especially non-credible claims of amnesia for complex and antisocial behavior, along with attempts to exaggerate memory impairment on objective tasks in the context of reducing or avoiding the criminal consequences of his post-accident behavior.

Disclaimer

The views expressed are those of the authors and do not reflect the official policy of the Defense Health Agency, the Department of Defense, or the U.S. government.

References

Ben-Porath, Y. S., & Tellegen, A. (2008). *Minnesota multiphasic personality inventory-2 restructured form*. University of Minnesota Press.

Bozelko, C. (2017, December 7). Traumatic brain injury should be a factor when judging individuals accused of crimes [First Opinion]. *STAT News*. https://www.statnews.com/2017/12/07/traumatic-brain-injury-crime/

Bradford, L. S. (2015). Misconceptions about traumatic brain injury among U.S. Army behavioral health professionals. *Rehabilitation Psychology*, *60*(4), 344–352. https://doi.org/10.1037/rep0000057

Broshek, D. K., De Marco, A. P., & Freeman, J. R. (2015). A review of post-concussion syndrome and psychological factors associated with concussion. *Brain Injury*, *29*(2), 228–237. https://doi.org/10.3109/02699052.2014.974674

Carroll, L. J., Cassidy, J. D., Peloso, P. M., Borg, J., von Holst, H., Holm, L., Paniak, C., Pépin, M., & WHO Collaborating Centre Task Force on Mild Traumatic Brain Injury (2004). Prognosis for mild traumatic brain injury: Results of the WHO Collaborating Centre Task Force on mild traumatic brain injury. *Journal of Rehabilitation Medicine*, (43 Suppl), 84–105. https://doi.org/10.1080/16501960410023859

Centers for Disease Control. Traumatic Brain Injuries in Prisons and Jails: An Unrecognized Problem. Available at: https://www.cdc.gov/traumaticbraininjury/pdf/prisoner_tbi_prof-a.pdf. (last visited Sept. 15, 2023).

Corrigan, J. D. (1995). Substance abuse as a mediating factor in outcome from traumatic brain injury. *Archives of Physical Medicine and Rehabilitation*, *76*(4), 302–309. https://doi.org/10.1016/s0003-9993(95)80654-7

Felson, R. B., & Staff, J. (2010). The effects of alcohol intoxication on violent versus other offending. *Criminal Justice and Behavior*, *37*(12), 1343–1360.

Felson, R. B., Teasdale, B., & Burchfield, K. B. (2008). The influence of being under the influence: Alcohol effects on adolescent violence. *Journal of Research in Crime and Delinquency*, *45*(2), 119–141.

Forbey, J. D., & Lee, T. T. (2011). An exploration of the impact of invalid MMPI-2 protocols on collateral self-report measure scores. *Journal of Personality Assessment*, *93*(6), 556–565. https://doi.org/10.1080/00223891.2011.608757

Forbey, J. D., Lee, T. T., Ben-Porath, Y. S., Arbisi, P. A., & Gartland, D. (2013). Associations between MMPI-2-RF validity scale scores and extra-test measures of personality and psychopathology. *Assessment*, *20*(4), 448–461. https://doi.org/10.1177/1073191113478154

Galbicsek, C. (2020). Alcohol-Related Crimes. Available online at: https://www.alcoholrehabguide.org/alcohol/crimes/.

Gentilini, M., Nichelli, P., Schoenhuber, R., Bortolotti, P., Tonelli, L., Falasca, A., & Merli, G. A. (1985). Neuropsychological evaluation of mild head injury. *Journal of Neurology, Neurosurgery, and Psychiatry*, *48*(2), 137–140. https://doi.org/10.1136/jnnp.48.2.137

Giancola, P. R., Levinson, C. A., Corman, M. D., Godlaski, A. J., Morris, D. H., Phillips, J. P., & Holt, J. C. (2009). Men and women, alcohol and aggression. *Experimental and Clinical Psychopharmacology*, *17*(3), 154–164.

Green, P. W. (2003). *Green's word memory test for windows: User's manual*. Green's Publishing. Green, P. (2015). *Green's memory complaints inventory for windows: User's manual*. Green's Publishing.

Iverson, G. L., & Lange, R. T. (2003). Examination of "postconcussion-like" symptoms in a healthysample. *Applied Neuropsychology*, *10*(3), 137–144. https://doi.org/10.1207/S15324826AN1003_02

Jones, A. (2013). Victoria Symptom Validity Test: Cutoff scores for psychometrically defined malingering groups in a military sample. *The Clinical Neuropsychologist*, *27*(8), 1373–1394. https://doi.org/10.1080/13854046.2013.851740

Maddocks, D., & Saling, M. (1996). Neuropsychological deficits following concussion. *Brain Injury*, *10*(2), 99–103. https://doi.org/10.1080/026990596124584

Maroon, J. C., Winkelman, R., Bost, J., Amos, A., Mathyssek, C., & Miele, V. (2015). Chronic traumatic encephalopathy in contact sports: A systematic review of all reported pathological cases. *PloS One, 10*(2), e0117338. https://doi.org/10.1371/journal.pone.0117338

Mann, R. E., Zalcman, R. F., Smart, R. G., Rush, B. R., & Suurvali, H. (2006). Alcohol consumption, alcoholics anonymous membership, and homicide mortality rates in Ontario 1968 to 1991. *Alcoholism, Clinical and Experimental Research, 30*(10), 1743–1751. https://doi.org/10.1111/j.1530-0277.2006.00216.x

McClelland, G. M., & Teplin, L. A. (2001). Alcohol introxication and violent crime: Implications for public health policy. *The American Journal on Addictions, 10*(s1), s70–s85. https://doi.org/10.1080/10550490150504155

McCrea, M., Iverson, G. L., McAllister, T. W., Hammeke, T. A., Powell, M. R., Barr, W. B., & Kelly, J. P. (2009). An integrated review of recovery after mild traumatic brain injury (MTBI): Implications for clinical management. *The Clinical Neuropsychologist, 23*(8), 1368–1390. https://doi.org/10.1080/13854040903074652

McCrory, P. (2001). The medicolegal aspects of automatism in mild head injury. *British Journal of Sports Medicine, 35*(5), 288–290. https://doi.org/10.1136/bjsm.35.5.288

Perkes, I., Schofield, P. W., Butler, T., & Hollis, S. J. (2011). Traumatic brain injury rates and sequelae: A comparison of prisoners with a matched community sample in Australia. *Brain Injury, 25*(2), 131–141. https://doi.org/10.3109/02699052.2010.536193

Pihl, R. O., Lau, M. L.,& Assaad J.-M. 1997. Aggressive Disposition, Alcohol, and Aggression. *Aggressive Behavior, 23*(1), 11–18.

Ponsford, J., Cameron, P., Fitzgerald, M., Grant, M., Mikocka-Walus, A., & Schönberger, M. (2012). Predictors of postconcussive symptoms 3 months after mild traumatic brain injury. *Neuropsychology, 26*(3), 304–313. https://doi.org/10.1037/a0027888.

Ponsford, J., Willmott, C., Rothwell, A., Cameron, P., Kelly, A. M., Nelms, R., Curran, C., & Ng, K. (2000). Factors influencing outcome following mild traumatic brain injury in adults. *Journal of the International Neuropsychological Society: JINS, 6*(5), 568–579. https://doi.org/10.1017/s1355617700655066

Randolph, C. (2018). Chronic traumatic encephalopathy is not a real disease. *Archives of Clinical Neuropsychology, 33*(5), 644–648. https://doi.org/10.1093/arclin/acy063

Ruff, R. M., & Jamora, C. W. (2008). Forensic neuropsychology and mild traumatic brain injury. *Psychological Injury and Law, 1*(2), 122–137. https://doi.org/10.1007/s12207-008-9010-7

Seegmiller, R.A. (2018, June 20–23). Challenges in assessing and assisting military members with mild traumatic brain injuries and persistent post-concussion syndromes [Conference session]. *AACN 2018 Conference*, San Diego, CA, United States. TBI (nanonline.org)

Silverberg, N. D., & Iverson, G. L. (2023). The American Congress of Rehabilitation Medicine diagnostic criteria for mild traumatic brain injury. *Archives of Physical Medicine and Rehabilitation, 104*(8), 1343–1355. https://doi.org/10.1016/j.apmr.2023.03.036

Vanderploeg, R. D., Belanger, H. G., & Kaufmann, P. M. (2014). Nocebo effects and mild traumatic brain injury: Legal implications. *Psychological Injury and Law, 7*(3), 245–254. https://doi.org/10.1007/s12207-014-9201-3

Wang, Y., Chan, R. C., & Deng, Y. (2006). Examination of postconcussion-like symptoms in healthy university students: Relationships to subjective and objective neuropsychological function performance. *Archives of Clinical Neuropsychology, 21*(4), 339–347. https://doi.org/10.1016/j.acn.2006.03.006

Section IV

Administrative Law, Disability, and Other Forensic Evaluations

Forensic neuropsychologists should focus upon providing clear and accurate evidence in the cases in which they are retained, to help relevant stakeholders make reasoned decisions regarding the matter at hand. In civil and criminal litigation, the ultimate decision makers are typically a judge and jury, who are collectively referred to as the triers-of-fact. In other proceedings, such as administrative, disability, and educational accommodation determinations, decision makers are more likely to be case managers, arbitrators, or mediators. Attorneys may also be involved, but they often focus on presenting and framing the expert findings for the decision makers. In this section, experts discuss cases demonstrating the impact and value that neuropsychological evaluations can have in these non-litigation types of settings. Chapters focus on disability cases, Workers' Compensation claims, civil competency examinations, military disability pursuit, and cases related to need for educational interventions.

DOI: 10.4324/9781003005063-25

22 An Integrated Approach to Validity Assessment

Kristin Fiano

In my role as the senior director of clinical and quality assurance oversight for a national IME company, I have the opportunity to review thousands of reports from a range of specialties. The product types include pre-employment evaluations (PEPE), disability-related independent medical evaluations (IME), fitness-for-duty evaluations (FFDE), Worker's Compensation (WC) exams, and file reviews (FR). All of these evaluations either involve potential secondary gain (such as in IME, WC, FR) or are related to the examinee's job status (FFD, PEPE). On the one hand, there is a greater tendency to emphasize problems and on the other, an interest in minimizing problems. Thus, validity is a central concern in all cases. For the most part, examinees undergoing FFDEs and PEPE are motivated to do well, as their careers are at stake. But even in this group, there are the occasional candidates/employees who bring hidden motives to the exam.

The providers conducting these services include forensic psychologists, neuropsychologists, psychiatrists, and a host of physical medicine doctors from various specialties (e.g., neurology, orthopedics, physical medicine and rehabilitation, or occupational medicine). In reviewing these different types of exams from providers with vastly different training, I have been struck by the wide range of skills and methods in how they approach validity and credibility of symptom report. While each provider approaches the issue from a slightly different lens, there is a common thread that ties the best evaluators together, which is the level of integration of all available information. The degree to which this occurs and the types of information used varies depending on provider types and individual differences.

Differences between provider types: The primary difference I have observed between doctor specialties is related to the reliance on subjective clinical impression versus objective data. This is obviously grounded in training, as some professions (psychology and neuropsychology) heavily emphasize objective testing and the need for ways to determine if the results are valid or not. Other professions train more from the perspective of observation/interaction (psychiatry). That is not to say that they are siloed and employ only one method, only that each source of information tends to be weighed a bit differently than others. The degree to which a provider relies on impression versus objective data is on a continuum, ranging from zero reliance on objective data to heavy (and sometimes exclusive) use of that type of data.

Differences within provider types: There is variability (or a bell curve, if you will) within specific provider types as well. This is true whether the expert has a background in medicine/physical health or in behavioral health. Some providers—regardless of profession—are simply better able to weigh various sources of evidence in a comprehensive manner, whereas others tend to be black and white thinkers who may overly rely on

DOI: 10.4324/9781003005063-26

one source of information, such as cut-scores or immediate impressions, to make their decisions. The tendency toward one type of thinking versus another can certainly be influenced by training and experience. This characteristic is also on a continuum, ranging from the more concrete or black-and-white thinker to the more complex thinker.

The following discussion describes the concepts that will be explored further in the case studies presented in this chapter.

Black-and-White Thinking versus Integrated Thinking (*the INTEGRATION Y Axis*):

Black-and-white thinking tends to focus on a single source of information, such as observation, impression, or test data. Integrated thinking requires a more careful analysis and a weighing of ALL available sources of evidence. Not only is this good practice, it is required in certain disability evaluations under Employee Retirement Income Security Act (ERISA) law. The ERISA of 1974 is a "federal law that sets minimum standards for most voluntarily established retirement and health plans in private industry to provide protection for individuals in these plans" (Source: Department of Labor). The law has been updated over time, and while not all policies fall under the governance of ERISA, many of them do. One result of this regulation is that it is incumbent on the doctor performing an IME on behalf of an insurer to conduct that evaluation in an independent, unbiased, impartial, and thorough manner. In following this guideline, providers should consider all sources of data available when rendering opinions.

For the IME doctor, this means carefully considering every medical record provided for review: the claimant's self-report; collateral interview or report from treating providers, employers, friends, and relatives; behavioral observations; and objective evidence such as test data. Again, this is good practice in any situation, but it is not often done well. For instance, among the reports I review, it is common for a neuropsychologist to conclude that

Figure 22.1 The Y-axis reflects the level of integration from low to high, the X-axis reflects the level of test data used from low to high.

test data are invalid (and imply malingering even if not expressly stated) and use this as a stopping point for all other decisions. This is often phrased as such:

"Due to invalid data, I do not find support for any cognitive impairment."

"Due to invalid data, I do not find support for limitations or restrictions."

"The data are invalid and thus no conclusions can be drawn/no opinions can be given."

While it is certainly appropriate to note that the data are invalid and thus cannot be relied upon to support impairment or restrictions, it is not sufficient in and of itself to render an opinion on impairment. If it were, there would be no point in reviewing the records, conducting collateral interviews, or documenting observations. Limiting analysis only to test data shortchanges the process significantly. Note that in the above examples, the first two phrases are similar and might be accurate. However, they reflect black-and-white thinking if this is the only statement. The third statement is problematic and one that I routinely comment on in reports. It is not accurate to say that no opinions can be made when the first part of the sentence *is* an opinion. It is also not helpful to the referral source to abdicate the responsibility of providing an expert opinion based on all the available evidence. Rather than reading the IME question as, "Do your data allow for an opinion on impairment?" the question should be, "Is there reliable/credible evidence to support impairment and any related limitations/restrictions?" In the case of invalid test data, the answer to the question might be "No," and this is indeed an opinion. However, the answer might be "Yes," depending on whether other compelling evidence exists outside of the invalid test data. Sorting through that evidence and rendering a clear, well-founded opinion is the hallmark of the integrated thinker.

The first two sentences in the earlier examples present another problem, if presented in isolation. Oftentimes, an IME report will be reviewed by the claimant's treating provider who might then offer a written rebuttal of the opinions in that report. I recall a recent letter from a treating provider (a neurologist) after he had read a neuropsychological IME report that indicated the data obtained were invalid, using much the same language as the examples given earlier. The neurologist's written response was in effect, "You said your exam is invalid so it is worthless and should not be considered." If read from the perspective of a lay reader (always a good idea), one can see how the phrase "The data from my evaluation are invalid" might be construed as implying a problem with the evaluation itself. A more integrated IME report would have made it clear that the invalid data documented that the claimant's self-report and presentation could not be relied upon in any instance, including self-reported symptoms to the treating providers and for mental status exams that were obtained in those settings. It would have pointed out the inconsistencies between the claimed impairments and other data documenting functionality. Note in this case that the IME neuropsychologist did not state that the claimant was malingering (although there was evidence of such), but instead repeated the phrase "invalid data" multiple times, which the treating neurologist assumed meant a problem with the IME doctor rather than meaning the claimant was likely to be feigning.

However, in some cases, invalid data become the proverbial baby that is thrown out with the bathwater. A claimant can fail performance validity tests (PVTs) and yield an invalid data set, but this might be to some extent moderated by other data. For instance, an extensive record of intensive psychotherapy (both inpatient and outpatient) for years, with multiple treating providers who have been able to observe the individual over time and in different settings, documenting chronic and compelling evidence of impairment in daily life due to the mental health condition, as well as direct observations of significant psychopathology during the IME, might be sufficient in terms of concluding that at least some impairment exists in a claimant and thereby supporting limitations, even in the face of failed PVTs and SVTs (symptom validity tests). Of course, "might be" is not the standard in these cases; instead, the standard is "more likely than not." Reaching this threshold would allow for a conclusion of supported impairments (i.e., information from non-test data is judged to be compelling) or malingering (i.e., there is clear evidence of an exaggeration or feigning of impairment to obtain secondary gain, such as disability benefits).

Impression versus Objective Data (*the DATA-DRIVEN X-Axis*)

Another continuum involves the reliance on testing versus impression (or objective versus subjective data) to make decisions. Both are important. One provider can be an excellent integrated thinker without using objective data. Another provider can use industry standard objective methods and fail to integrate the data with other sources. Keep in mind, however, that *objective* is not necessarily limited to test measures. Video surveillance of a claimant dancing at a nightclub would arguably be considered objective evidence that contradicts the self-report of being unable to be around crowds of people. MRI imaging is also objective evidence. However, for the purposes of this chapter, the use of the term *objective data* generally refers to specific test instruments/results.

These two continuums, Impressionism versus Data Driven on the *X*-axis and Black-and-White Thinking versus Integrated Thinking on the *Y*-axis, provide a framework for the various approaches professionals take in determining whether or not findings are valid and also whether the cause of invalid data is due to malingering. While the *X*-axis is significantly impacted by the type of provider and training background, the *Y*-axis is much less so.

These continuums can be visualized graphically (see Figure 22.1). Where a provider falls on this graph will reflect how integrated their thinking is and how much they rely (or don't rely) on objective data (Figure 22.2).

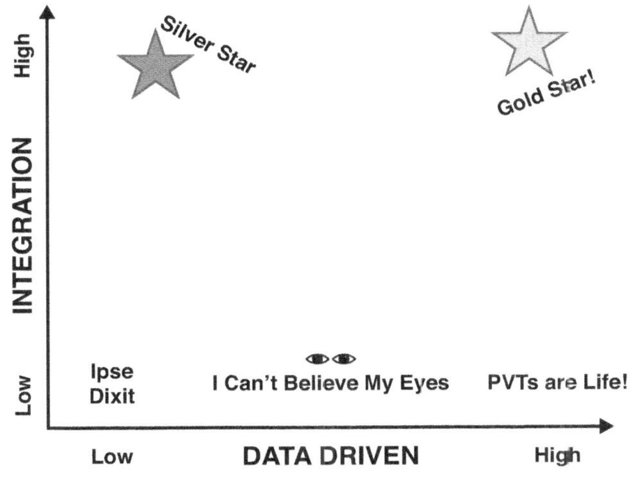

Figure 22.2 Ipse dixit cases are at the lower left quadrant; Silver Star in the upper left; Gold Star in the upper right; PVTs Are Life in the lower right; emerging thinker in the center; and I can't believe my eyes at bottom center.

To illustrate these different approaches, I will present case examples[1] from a variety of provider types. In the extreme lower left quadrant of the graph is a provider who relies heavily on impression, does not integrate data, and does not value objective data. This is similar to the "Ipse Dixit" stance, which is Latin for "He said it himself," sometimes referred to as "Because I said so." This is an assertion without proof. I have encountered this type of argument—if one can call it such—from a variety of providers. While it can occur in psychologists' opinions, it is more common for non-psychologists who do not use objective data. Take for instance the following case example:

Ipse Dixit (ID)

Case Example ID1: A WC case involved a 35-year-old woman who had worked as a bus driver and was involved in a low-speed collision. She reported back pain and was evaluated by an orthopedist. This provider commented on what he felt was an overly emotional reaction to any pain. In his two-page report, he called the presentation "absurd" and concluded that the claimant was malingering due to a lack of objective injury and the level of distress with which the woman presented. He employed very little data integration and relied quite heavily on his impression that the woman was feigning, essentially *because he said so*—ID. It is possible that his conclusions might have been accurate, but it is difficult to know, given the lack of integrated reasoning. He did not reference any features of malingering, other than what he perceived as an exaggerated pain display. Pain can be a very subjective experience that is hard to quantify, and basing opinions on malingering due to what an evaluator perceives as "absurd" behavior also risks injecting significant bias into the exam, including gender or ethnic bias.

What are the signs physical medicine doctors look for to determine if someone is malingering? There are a number of these, such as Waddell's signs. These involve a collection of behaviors first described in 1980 to help identify a nonorganic or psychological basis for physical problems such as back pain. Some physicians also use these to identify malingering behaviors. These five signs include diffuse tenderness and/or non-anatomical tenderness; simulation tests (which include eliciting lumbar pain with downward pressure on the top of the head or with passive external rotation of the shoulder and pelvis together in the same plane); distraction tests (the behavior remits when the patient is distracted with something else); regional weakness or sensory changes that do not align with functional neuroanatomy; and overreaction. This last sign is particularly subjective, as noted in the previous paragraph, and involves a change in demeanor that seems to be out of proportion to the stimulation. Exhibiting any three or more of these five signs typically is judged to be significant for noncredible symptom reporting and/or malingering, or at least a psychological overlay. However, the subjective nature of these signs has the potential for observer bias, as well as failing to account for cultural differences. Professor Waddell himself has argued that these signs are not de facto evidence for malingering. As would be the case with any validity measure used, the findings have to be integrated with other case information. Of course, physicians routinely use other objective sources of information, such as radiological imaging, and these data can be integrated for a better conceptualization of a particular case (Figure 22.3).

Case Example ID2: In this second example, a 40-year-old man who required a professional interpreter was seen in the context of a WC claim for orthopedic injuries. He claimed that he developed lower back and hip pain after performing manual labor involving shoveling large mounds of soil. Although he claimed he felt pain during this activity,

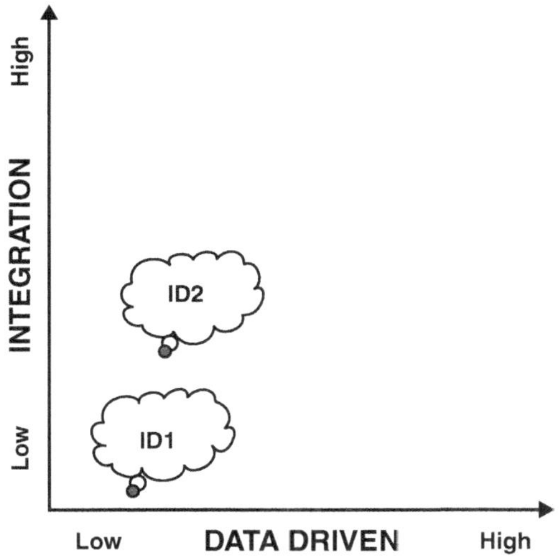

Figure 22.3 Ipse dixit (ID) cases are on the left of the graph because of absence of objective data. ID2 is slightly higher on the integration axis than ID1.

he continued to work for another four days until he was terminated from the job. The day after termination, he began seeking medical care for ill-defined low back pain. Imaging (MRI, X-ray) was unremarkable. The neurological exam was also unremarkable apart from a slow, wobbling gait during toe and heel walking. There were multiple patchy areas of tenderness. The evaluating physician integrated various sources of information, including normal objective findings, discrepant accounts of why the examinee did not report the injury on the day it was reported to have occurred (the examinee reported no one spoke his language, but in fact a supervisor was fluent in this language), and a subjective observation by the physician of symptom embellishment. This physician did rely on several sources of information and integrated them appropriately. Waddell's signs present were used as a data point but not in isolation. Thus, there were several objective sources of information (MRI, X-ray, sensory testing) as well as a subjective sense of symptom magnification that led the physician to conclude this examinee's reported injuries were not supported by the evidence and thus any complaints were not felt to be caused by the work-related event.

This example is not quite ID because there is integration and reference to some objective findings. Thus, I would place this physician's conceptualization further up the *Y*-axis and a bit to the right on the *X*-axis.

PVTs Are Life (PVTL)

At the extreme right lower quadrant of the graph is the provider who is heavily data driven, but with binary rather than integrated thinking. These are almost always neuropsychologists who utilize performance validity measures (which of course is appropriate), but without the type of integrated thinking required to ensure that the results are properly interpreted. I am reminded of a character from the Apple TV series *Ted Lasso* by the name of Dani Rojas, who utters the memorable line, "Football (or Fútbol) is life." For him, there is nothing outside of football (soccer); it is a singular focus, and it means everything.

In the same way, for some neuropsychologists, performance and symptom validity test (PVT/SVT) measures are life. The scores are used with precision and unyielding cutoffs to determine whether or not an examinee is malingering (or scores are invalid), but at the same time, the evaluator ignores other critical information that should be integrated with those scores. Potential reasons for this include a lack of integrated thinking abilities or inherent bias due to being retained by defense counsel or an IME company. In most cases, binary or black-and-white thinking is just easier.

In this section are three case examples, focusing on how PVTs were emphasized, sometimes to the exclusion of other data. In all three cases, there was evidence of failed or marginal validity measures, but the conclusions could have been different had the evaluators adopted an integrated method of analysis (Figure 22.4).

Case Example PVTL1: A middle-aged woman underwent a neuropsychological IME for the purposes of a disability claim. She had a combination of a medical condition (she had been treated for cancer with chemotherapy and radiation) and a notable history of psychological symptoms dating back to childhood. She endorsed significant memory problems in addition to physical symptoms of fatigue and pain. She had been out of work for more than two years by the time of her exam.

The claimant completed the 11th grade and then her General Educational Development (GED), but she reported being a good student prior to that. She was able to earn an associate degree and was trained in medical billing, in which she was employed until voluntarily discontinuing her job due to her perception that she could not perform her duties anymore because of stress and confusion.

During interview, the claimant endorsed having anxiety and depression, and she was taking an antidepressant at the time of the exam. She noted her mood symptoms were severe and described herself as being in crisis all the time. However, the record reviewed reflected only intermittent counseling sessions with the notes being routine and showing essentially normal mental status exams. Her treating provider listed conditions of major depressive disorder and posttraumatic stress disorder (PTSD), which was related to childhood traumas. The record also referenced ongoing fatigue.

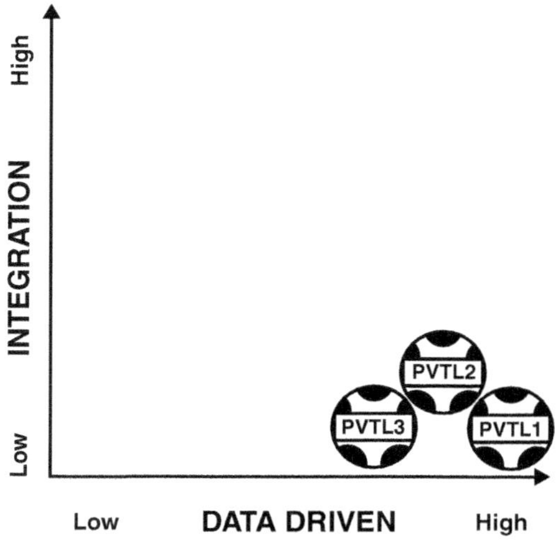

Figure 22.4 PVTs Are Life cases fall in the lower right quadrant of the graph because they rely heavily on PVTs but fail to integrate other sources of data.

The claimant presented a detailed history during interview, remained focused throughout the interview, needed few breaks, and maintained emotional composure throughout. She was socially appropriate, well groomed, and had no difficulties navigating the assessment process (e.g., completing paperwork, finding her way to the office). Although she reported problems in activities of daily living (ADLs) due to low motivation, poor concentration, and fatigue, she also reported being solely responsible for transporting her children to their various events and managing other household responsibilities independently.

The neuropsychologist used an appropriate battery of tests, including four standalone PVTs (TOMM,[2] MSVT,[3] DCT,[4] Rey-15) and two embedded PVTs plus the MMPI-2-RF.[5] The claimant failed multiple PVTs (see Table 22.1). In addition, there was evidence of significant over-reporting on the MMPI-2-RF to the point that the profile was deemed invalid. Despite failing PVTs, the claimant produced an average performance on a list learning task (though with somewhat low recognition, another validity flag) and low average story recall. The only scores that were at or below the 2nd percentile included Trails A, Coding, Semantic Fluency, and the Rey Complex Figure (copy and recall trials). Note that while these scores might suggest some difficulty with speech and general slowing, behavioral observations described the claimant as speaking quickly and confidently during interview. Also, despite the MMPI-2-RF reflecting extreme symptom endorsement, her affect was described as euthymic and upbeat throughout the exam (Table 22.1).

The neuropsychologist concluded that the results "were invalid and thus no opinions can be rendered regarding impairment or limitations/restrictions." On the surface, this was a reasonable conclusion given the test findings. However, the singular focus on the PVT/SVT findings significantly limited the useful information that could be gleaned from this evaluation. A better integration of all available data would have noted that the claimant reported having concentration problems, yet she was able to provide a coherent narrative for more than 90 minutes of interview, her test scores assessing attention were generally in the normal range, and she was driving her children to various activities.

Table 22.1 PVT and MMPI Data for Case PVTL1

PVT	*Score(s)*
TOMM1/2	35/40
MSVT	95/85/80/60/45
DCT	27
Rey-15	12
CVLT-FC	15
RDS	7
MMPI-2-RF	
VRIN-r/TRIN-r	65T/60T
F-r	120T
Fp-r	95T
RBS	112T
Fs	76T
FBS-r	79T
L-r/K-r	68T/40T

Note: TOMM (Test of Memory Malingering); MSVT (Medical Symptom Validity Test); DCT (Dot Counting Test); CVLT-FC (Forced Choice subtest from the California Verbal Learning Test); RDS (Reliable Digit Span); MMPI-2-RF (Minnesota Multiphasic Personality Inventory-2-Restructured Form).

While she reported being "in crisis 24 hours a day," treatment records indicated a low level of therapy intensity (once per month), no psychotropic medications, and no reference in the therapy notes of suicidality or a need for a higher level of care. Her claim of being in crisis on a continuous basis was also contradicted by her ability to maintain emotional composure throughout the lengthy exam. All of this information, based on observation and the record, was quite compelling in establishing that this claimant was far more functional than she reported during the interview. The evaluator could have highlighted other inconsistencies—such as failing memory-based PVTs yet performing normally on some memory tasks—to convey a far more integrated picture of this individual's functionality. In disability evaluations, it is rarely sufficient to conclude "invalid data" and leave it there, because there is typically so much more of the story to tell.

You might have picked up on the fact that the neuropsychologist said no opinions could be rendered regarding diagnosis, impairment, or limitations. As discussed earlier, this is inaccurate. In fact, there was ample evidence that painted a compelling picture of an individual who retained considerable capacity despite her claimed impairments, documented by observation, some test results (even in the context of failed PVTs, normal range memory scores do document normal memory), and no clear need for a higher level of psychiatric treatment. The neuropsychologist could have described all of this and given a clear opinion that the evidence documented functional capacity rather than impairment.

Case Example PVTL2: In a similar case, another neuropsychologist performed an evaluation on a woman who had claimed disability due to a combination of psychiatric symptoms (depression, anxiety) and cognitive symptoms (memory and concentration deficits, presumably secondary to her mood conditions).

However, unlike the previous example, this case was replete with data documenting a decade of very serious mental health problems. The claimant had been in treatment for many years, often supplemented with intensive outpatient programs and occasionally residential programs. She stopped her work as a data analyst to participate in a higher level of psychiatric care, with some declining performance reviews noted in the file prior to her leaving work. Treatment notes consistently described a woman with a fragile emotional state who presented in sessions much as she did during the evaluation. She was taking several psychotropic medications (mood stabilizers, an antidepressant, an anxiolytic).

Behavioral observations during the IME were notable for flat affect at times but tearfulness at other times. Speech was impoverished and she appeared disheveled with poor hygiene. She had a family member living with her (a sister) who managed most of the daily household tasks and who brought her to the evaluation. Her sister described the claimant as having difficulty focusing on even simple tasks at home. The claimant required periodic repetition of instructions during testing (Table 22.2).

The evaluator conducted a reasonable battery of tests, although with just a few PVTs and the MMPI-2-RF. As was the case in the previous example, the claimant failed PVTs—in this instance, both standalone measures Nonverbal Medical Symptom Validity Test (NV-MSVT) and DCT, and one embedded measure (RDS). As an aside, there were fewer PVTs utilized in this case than would be considered industry standard (see Martin et al., 2025), but given that they were failed, further commentary on this is less relevant for this specific case example. The MMPI was deemed invalid due to the high elevations on validity scales, although none of them were at maximal levels. There was also evidence for inconsistent responding that did not rise to a level that would invalidate the profile, but the potential impact of this was not discussed. The neuropsychologist concluded that because the data were invalid, no

Table 22.2 PVT and MMPI Data for Case PVTL2

PVT	*Score(s)*
NV-MSVT	98/78/78/67/71/91/43
DCT	21
RDS	6
MMPI-2-RF	
VRIN-r/TRIN-r	68T/61T
F-r	95T
Fp	69T
FBS-r	88T
RBS	90T
Fs	72T
L-r/K-r	55T/46T

diagnosis or impairment could be supported. Responses to questions were frequently one sentence long (e.g., "There are no valid data to support impairment in this case.").

There was no question that there were validity issues documented in this case and that as a result, the remaining data were likely to underestimate this individual's true abilities. With that said, the report would have been much improved had the neuropsychologist incorporated all of the other substantial data to describe an individual who clearly had impairments based on her psychological condition, even if neurocognitive data could not be used to support specific impairments otherwise. Even in the absence of valid objective test data, the neuropsychologist might have supported impairments in concentration based on observations that were consistent and compelling throughout the day, with the elevated VRIN-r score noted on the MMPI, and which were quite consistent with the medical record and collateral report.

Here is an example of what could have replaced the one sentence response to a question asking about impairments and any limitations:

> The data obtained in this case were deemed invalid due to the validity test failures described in detail earlier in the report. However, there is a compelling consistency across other sources of information that document impairment due to her psychiatric conditions. Specifically, her numerous behavioral health treatment notes described the claimant in ways that were very similar to how she presented in this evaluation. She had trouble tracking information during the interview, did not maintain eye contact, could not modulate her emotions appropriately, and needed frequent repetition of questions or follow up to obtain any detail regarding her history. Her sister, who brought her to the exam, painted a very similar picture of what the claimant is like at home. She very often does not tend to her hygiene, does not participate in any social activities inside or outside the home, and spends much of her day in her bedroom. There is, more likely than not, some level of impact on cognitive abilities such as concentration, although due to invalid data I cannot quantify this. What is clear is that she would be quite limited in her ability to be goal-directed, meet deadlines, interact with co-workers and supervisors, maintain a professional demeanor, and sustain concentration over the course of a workday. The limitations at this level of severity are likely temporary assuming optimized treatment is undertaken, although prognosis for full, sustained resolution of impairment is guarded given that she has previously undergone intensive treatment with only temporary improvement.

Case Example PVTL3: This final example initially seems to fit cleanly into the "PVTs are life" category, but there are other elements to be on the lookout for. While the first two examples resulted in statements of "invalid data" with little additional detail, this neuropsychologist used PVTs to draw a firm conclusion of malingering. The previous examples highlighted situations where other case data were not utilized to complement the validity data. In this case, the PVTs were used almost exclusively while controverting other data.

This claimant underwent an IME for long-term disability benefits. She was similar to the other two examples in terms of demographics (a middle-aged woman), though she had a history of mild (uncomplicated) traumatic brain injury (TBI) related to a fall. At the time of the fall, she had no immediate medical attention but sought services through the emergency department later that day secondary to headache and other physical symptoms. Neuroimaging was consistently unremarkable throughout the life of this claim. The claimant did not report having memory or other cognitive symptoms in the first weeks after her injury. However, at the time of this evaluation two years post injury, she reported memory problems, persisting headaches, dizziness, and word-finding problems.

The record noted a previous cognitive evaluation about two years earlier. That exam did not include validity measures, but the previous provider concluded that the claimant had a mild neurocognitive disorder due to TBI, citing a low average IQ that was below premorbid estimates, as well as scores in the impaired range for attention.

The IME evaluation was appropriately comprehensive. Nine PVTs were considered, although only two of these were standalone measures. Out of these nine, only one was judged to be a failure (TOMM), based on updated norms discussed in the professional literature (see Martin et al., 2020). Additionally, the MMPI was deemed a failure due to the FBS-r and RBS scores. The rest of the test battery reflected scores generally within the average range with a couple of outliers. Based on these findings, the evaluator concluded that the remaining data were invalid. However, in this case, the evaluator further concluded that the examinee was malingering. Neither of the providers in the previous two examples rendered this opinion but instead emphasized invalid data. Drawing a conclusion of malingering in the IME reports I review is uncommon, although there is nothing inherently wrong with it assuming the conclusion is well supported and integrates all available information (Table 22.3).

Table 22.3 Standalone PVT and MMPI Data for Case PVTL3

PVT	*Score(s)*
TOMM	46/48/49
VSVT E/D	23/16
MMPI-2-RF	
VRIN-r/TRIN-r	39T/52T
F-r	74T
Fp-r	59T
Fs	83T
FBS-r	88T
RBS	97T
L-r/K-r	58T/48T

Note: TOMM (Test of Memory Malingering); VSVT E/D (Victoria Symptom Validity Test easy/hard); MMPI-2-RF (Minnesota Multiphasic Personality Inventory-2-Restructured Form).

In my view of the data in this case, the conclusion of malingering was not on solid ground. With respect to integrative thinking, it is noteworthy that the emphasis on PVTs (with only a single "fail") came at the expense of other available data. Most obvious was the fact that the other test data were largely within normal functioning limits. While it is not unheard of to fail PVTs and produce a normal cognitive profile, it is less common in cases of clear malingering.

Also noteworthy was the reliance on the MMPI-2-RF as a PVT rather than an SVT, with specific reference to the MMPI as a measure of "effort." Without the MMPI-2-RF scores, the data revealed only one of nine PVT scores that were failed. Regardless, the neuropsychologist engaged in black-and-white thinking, hinging all answers to IME questions on the PVT and SVT scores, with statements such as, "There are no documented impairments because of malingering." For this neuropsychologist, PVTs Are Life and, apparently, the only source of data needed to draw conclusions. The MMPI did indeed provide evidence for symptom magnification, especially in terms of cognitive symptom report, though it should not have been counted as a PVT failure.

An integrated analysis in this case would have included a discussion of psychological factors on this examinee's presentation and claims of functional impairment. What drove the emergence of symptoms so long after the actual injury? Several possibilities exist, including iatrogenesis, secondary gain and need for benefits, or somatoform reaction. In fact, this claimant may have arguably showed some signs of somatoform reaction based on her MMPI (all six somatic/cognitive dysfunction scales were elevated). However, the neuropsychologist discounted this option because the claimant did not appear bothered by her symptoms. The focus remained on malingering, which in isolation is not very helpful to the reader's understanding of the claimant.

An integrated approach might have included this statement:

> The validity data in this case contain marginally failed scores, which would have the impact of suppressing the rest of the cognitive profile. However, the remaining scores were almost entirely within the normal range and can be used to support the opinion that she has intact abilities in the areas assessed. The previous testing did not assess validity and thus those scores cannot be relied upon. Additionally, the report of emerging memory problems well beyond the acute period of a mild head injury is inconsistent with what the literature describes in a typical recovery trajectory. There is no compelling evidence to support impairment and, indeed, the claimant is living independently and managing basic and instrumental activities of daily living. From a psychiatric standpoint, she does endorse mild depression and anxiety, although this is not at a level that is considered functionally impairing. She was able to interact well during the course of this evaluation, modulated her emotions well, demonstrated good grooming and hygiene, and remained engaged with only the usual number of breaks. In sum, there is nothing in the obtained data to suggest impairment that would impact functionality.

I Can't Believe My Eyes (ICBME)

In some cases, a provider with a less integrative approach might reject findings, such as the MMPI results, because they do not fit with their conceptualization. If this rejection of data is total and is not properly explained by weighing other evidence, this provider would be at the bottom center of the graph (a combination of an ID mindset while also rejecting the data available to them). Faced with an extreme and invalid MMPI profile, the evaluator concludes that this has been caused by genuine psychiatric impairment or ignores it entirely as not relevant and not as valuable as their observations (although in many cases, even the observations do not fit with such extreme symptom endorsement) (Figure 22.5).

Case Example ICBME1: A 52-year-old man presented for a psychiatric IME for the purposes of disability benefits. The psychiatrist conducted his usual aspect of the exam, which involved a clinical interview and review of records, as well as a standard mental status examination. The claimant reported being unable to return to work because of what he described as overwhelming anxiety and depression. These symptoms had been ongoing for many years but escalated in response to some work stressors. The claimant felt that returning to the job would be intolerable. He was being treated primarily by his general practitioner with a low dose of Paxil and had undergone a few counseling sessions. However, at the time of the IME, he had not seen a therapist in several months. He contended that his symptoms were so great that he was unable to do much around the house. However, he did reveal that he worked out at a gym and periodically met with friends for game nights. He arrived at the appointment alone and on time. Grooming and hygiene were good. He had no difficulty completing paperwork or responding to interview questions. The psychiatrist noted most aspects of the mental status exam were "intact" or "good," including focus and attention. The claimant endorsed most symptoms of generalized anxiety disorder and major depressive disorder and reported feeling fatigued and lacking in motivation (Table 22.4).

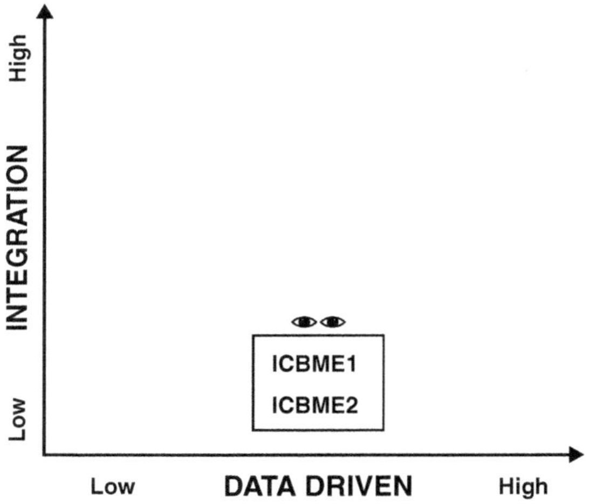

Figure 22.5 ICBME case examples are low on integration and do not use data well.

Table 22.4 MMPI Validity Scales for Case ICBME1

MMPI-2-RF	*Score(s)*
VRIN-r/TRIN-r	37T/62T
F-r	120T
FBS	96T
Fs	72T
RBS	92T
L-r/K-r	72T/38T

As part of this IME, the psychiatrist was also asked to administer an MMPI-2-RF per standardized instructions. This was then sent to an independent psychologist with expertise in the MMPI-2-RF who provided a report to the psychiatrist regarding the findings. The report noted that the claimant responded in a highly consistent fashion. However, the F-r scale was at 120 and other validity scales were close to the ceiling. The interpreting psychologist concluded that due to extreme over-reporting, the clinical profile was invalid for interpretation. Despite the psychiatrist quoting this in the report, he went on to render a diagnosis of severe major depressive disorder and severe generalized anxiety disorder. He further concluded that the claimant was unable to work in any capacity, but he did not provide specific examples of tasks the claimant could not do. The psychiatrist was asked to address the invalid MMPI-2-RF and integrate other sources of data (such as the normal mental status exam and lack of the type of treatment that would be expected for this severity of psychiatric illness) to better support the opinions given. The psychiatrist essentially stated that the extreme MMPI-2-RF findings did not negate the claimant's self-reported impairments, which were taken at face value.

This is an example of being faced with multiple sources of evidence that contradict what the claimant is reporting, yet ignoring it, because the criteria needed for diagnosis were presumably met. However, the psychiatrist did not explain why the claimant's self-report was deemed credible in the face of rather glaring evidence to the contrary. To be clear, self-reported information should certainly be considered, but the reliability of such information must also be clarified.

There are neuropsychologists who fall in this line of thinking too. Faced with markedly poor performance on PVTs, they still find ways to negate what the PVTs are telling them, making exceptions for unknown reasons. In some cases, this might be due to a fear of litigation, i.e., not wanting to name what they are seeing for fear that a licensing board complaint or civil suit will come their way. At other times, it is clear that the evaluating neuropsychologist genuinely likes or feels sorry for the claimant and perhaps cannot reconcile their positive impression with evidence of malingering. In still other instances, the neuropsychologist is not up to speed on the literature and cites various excuses for the PVT failures, such as pain, fatigue, or genuine memory impairment (despite no compelling evidence from other sources of data). There are hints of this in the wording used to describe PVT failures, such as "The examinee was unable to pass…" or "the claimant scored in the impaired range on the TOMM," which implies a genuine deficit rather than a failure to put forth appropriate effort. Still others emphasize the PVTs that were passed with phrases such as "The examinee passed almost half of the administered PVTs" as if this reflects strong effort. Finally, bias due to being retained by the plaintiff's attorney can also impact the evaluator's willingness to call failed PVTs evidence of malingering.

Case Example ICBME2: Sometimes evaluators not only fail to believe their eyes, they seem to have one eye shut. This can result from not administering enough PVTs of sufficient sensitivity to detect suboptimal effort, and then discounting a single failure as falling below the threshold of reflecting invalid test findings.

In this case, the neuropsychologist saw a 32-year-old woman for a long-term disability evaluation. The claimant had no significant neurological event but reported cognitive symptoms secondary to migraines and depression/anxiety. She had a master's degree in nursing and left her job three years earlier due to her headaches and mood symptoms. She commented that her job became much more challenging during the COVID-19 pandemic, given the stress of dealing with extra job duties, longer shifts, the high number of patient deaths, and what she described as a "tough supervisor." Since leaving her job, she spent her days at home gardening and cooking.

Table 22.5 PVT and MMPI Data for Case ICBME2

PVT	*Score(s)*
DCT	30
TOMM1	45
CVLT-FC	15
RDS	8
MMPI-3	
VRIN-r/TRIN-r	33T/68T
F-r	85T
Fp-r	53T
Fs	92T
FBS-r	99T
RBS	88T
L-r/K-r	68T/34T

Records included a previous neuropsychological evaluation performed two years earlier, with the psychologist concluding that the claimant showed evidence of a major neurocognitive disorder. No PVTs or SVTs were included, however. There was a remote motor vehicle accident with no indication of brain injury, but which was judged to have an impact on the claimant's functioning (though she continued working for 15 years without incident).

For the IME evaluation, the claimant arrived to the appointment alone, although she was ten minutes late. She was described as cooperative and had good grooming and hygiene. Speech was intact during interview, although she became tearful on several occasions (Table 22.5).

For validity measures, the neuropsychologist included the first trial of the TOMM, the Dot Counting Test, and two embedded measures. The TOMM first trial was interpreted as a pass whereas the DCT was deemed a failure. The two embedded measures (RDS and CVLT- FC) were judged to be passed. However, given that this examinee had no significant neurological event, such as severe TBI, the CVLT-FC score might have been considered marginal, especially when integrated with the rest of the CVLT findings, which were generally in the low average range. It can be argued that it is necessary to administer a larger complement of PVT measures in a forensic exam than the four used in this evaluation; survey data collected by Martin et al. (2025) indicated that the average number of PVTs given in a forensic exam by neuropsychologists was seven (three standalone and four embedded); use of only four PVTs hindered the current examiner in fully documenting veracity of cognitive test performance. Still, a failure on the DCT and a marginal CVLT-FC score should have raised concerns regarding intentionally poor performance, particularly given that the claimant's E-score on the Dot Counting Test was markedly higher than that of credible patients observed by McCaul et al. (2018), and even substantially higher than the mean score of the noncredible group (10.91+/−5.93 versus 20.07+/−11.70); an E-score of 30 occurs in less than 2% of credible patients drawn from an outpatient hospital neuropsychology clinic with a range of neurological and psychiatric diagnoses. When a test taker achieves a score at which there are virtually no false positives, particularly in a claimant with a rather unremarkable medical/psychiatric history, it would be reasonable to conclude that invalid cognitive test performance has occurred; in other words, not all PVT failures are "equal." Slick and Sherman (2013) argued that PVT scores equivalent to a positive predictive value of

≥95% should be considered equivalent to a significantly below chance pattern on a forced choice PVT. Thus, while the industry generally provides a guideline of failure on two PVTs out of several to determine invalidity (Sherman et al., 2020; Martin et al., 2025), a single failed PVT score associated with such high specificity in a claimant with an unremarkable medical history arguably is sufficient to document invalidity, or at the least to indicate that the claimant was not consistently performing to true ability.

Most striking to me in this particular case was the fact that the examinee's educational background included a master's degree, yet her Full Scale IQ (WAIS-IV) was at the 2nd percentile (70). On the surface, this made no sense at all. It was clear that she was previously functioning at a much higher level than what would be expected based on her measured cognitive abilities. This should raise a large red flag and it would be important to look at functioning in other settings. The claimant reported being highly forgetful at home yet drove herself to the evaluation alone and navigated the intake process relatively easily. She communicated adequately and was described as attentive to tasks. However, her performance on attention-related tasks was quite low (<1%–2%). Processing speed scores were at the 4th percentile overall. However, on the MMPI-2-RF, she responded in a highly consistent manner (VRIN-r = 33T), which argues for intact attention, and completed the test in a faster-than-average time frame, consistent with average or better processing speed. This evidence argued against true impairments in attention and processing speed, but this was not addressed by the evaluator. Additionally, there was evidence of exaggerated reports of cognitive and somatic symptoms on the MMPI-2-RF, but this finding was explained away by the claimant's medical history and subjective report; research has in fact demonstrated that medical patients do not obtain elevated Fs, FBS-r, and RBS scores (see Sellbom et al., 2012, data for medical patients: Fs = 59.29+/–18.70; FBS-r = 53.07+/–12.82; RBS = 55.91+/–15.37). The evaluator weighted self-report heavily despite evidence of contradictory information in terms of test scores versus functionality and despite evidence that self-reported symptoms were likely overstated.

The neuropsychologist concluded that the data obtained were valid and that there was evidence to support severe cognitive symptoms at a level that would impact her ability to function in a workplace. This conclusion was given despite multiple other data points yielding a much different conclusion. Like the psychiatrist in the first example, this neuropsychologist overrode that information by downplaying the PVT/SVT findings.

Case ICBME3: This is not a single case but a quick example of how validity data can work in the opposite direction. In multiple FFDE reports I have reviewed, the examinee produces an MMPI profile that is markedly defensive. This is not surprising given the fact that the individual's job might be at stake. The examinee is attempting to make a positive impression and get back to work. Frequently, the examining psychologist or psychiatrist will conclude the individual is fit for duty almost entirely based on self-report, which often goes something like, "I'm fine; all that stuff they think I said was taken out of context." However, the MMPI is ignored as evidence that self-report might not be reliable. Sometimes canned explanations are included in the report, such as that the MMPI L scale might reflect a traditional upbringing. If this is in fact the case, then it should be discussed and integrated into the interpretation. The interviewing psychiatrist/psychologist should know whether the examinee comes from such a background or not and thus determine if the interpretation is valid for this specific individual. Regardless, it is imperative to integrate other information, such as collateral calls with supervisors or treating providers, to support (or refute) the examinee's self-report.

Silver Star (SS)

The upper left quadrant of the graph reflects a provider who does not use objective data but who does an excellent job of considering various sources of data and integrating all information properly. I know several psychiatrists who fall into this quadrant, and it is always a pleasure to read their reports because of their skillful approach. While they understand what PVTs can do, these tests are not part of their training. They do, however, expertly weigh various sources of evidence in arriving at a conclusion regarding the credibility of the claimant (in an IME or WC case) and use those same skills in providing a rich description of the individual's impairments (if present) in a manner that is helpful to the client (Figure 22.6).

Case SS1 is from one of those psychiatrists I mentioned. He performs many FRs for us, which require a somewhat different perspective than one that includes face-to-face time with the claimant such as in an IME. FRs are exactly what they sound like. The expert reviewer is given the claim file for review, which includes medical records as well as functional impairment statements from treating providers, any daily activity questionnaires from the claimant, internal notes from the insurer, and additional correspondence such as from the claimant's attorney who might include articles and affidavits from family members.

For this case, the psychiatrist reviewed the file of a 32-year-old male claimant who reported severe symptoms of depression and anxiety. He reported having panic attacks on a daily basis and felt unsafe to drive to work because of this. Other symptoms included reduced motivation, irritability, and insomnia. He declined psychotropic medications when seen by his primary care physician. During the exam, judgment was normal and there was no discussion of behaviors that were out of the ordinary. The absence of such information is frequently a problem in these cases, because primary care doctors tend to check boxes (or the nurse does) without providing a rich behavioral narrative of the claimant's presentation. The claimant also saw a psychologist around the same time and reported severe mood symptoms on self-report questionnaires (without validity scales). However, exam findings documented normal speech, concentration, insight, and judgment. The following week, the

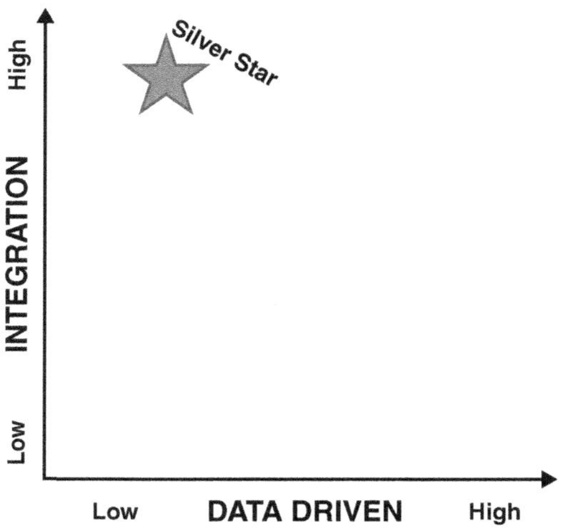

Figure 22.6 Silver start cases are at the upper left quadrant of the graph because of good integration despite lack of objective test data.

claimant reported some improvement, but continued to endorse severe mood symptoms. Over the next year, records documented treatment with the psychologist taking place once or twice per month, with variable reports of increasing and decreasing symptoms. Notably, four months after going on leave from work, his family medicine doctor said she would no longer support keeping him out of work. Shortly after, he sought care with a psychiatric nurse practitioner and reported having anxiety and PTSD, complaining about his primary care doctor's decision to stop certifying his time off work. The psychiatric nurse practitioner (NP) documented good grooming and hygiene, intact speech, stable mood, and normal memory, attention, and concentration. The claimant also returned to his psychologist after a four-month hiatus. By nine months after the time he left work, he was seeing a new provider (social worker), was on medication, and reported improvement with sleep, but continued to report worry and agitation.

In some FRs, the expert is asked to reach out to the treating provider for a peer-to-peer discussion. These can be helpful in eliciting more detail about functionality than is apparent in the record, particularly when notes are comprised mostly of checkboxes. The focus on functionality is critical, because self-reported symptoms alone are not sufficient to adjudicate a claim. Symptoms do not equate to functional impairment. Plenty of individuals with depression and anxiety continue to work. What is important to demonstrate is that symptoms translate to an inability to perform tasks. Self-report is important, but not sufficient. If it was, then no evaluations or reviews would be necessary; one would only have to ask the claimant if they were/were not able to perform work tasks. Given the presence of secondary gain issues, establishing the credibility of self-reported symptoms is critical. This is typically established by integrating all of the various sources of information in the record. As part of the goal of considering all sources of information, in this case, the reviewer reached out to the two most recent treating providers, making several attempts, but these were not successful.

FRs such as this involve a fair amount of detective work, looking for any reference to functional behaviors that would help support or refute the claimed condition. This psychiatrist produced an extensive, detailed analysis of the case file. He acknowledged that the claimant reported severe mood symptoms but contrasted this report with numerous exams in the record documenting entirely normal findings. He noted that despite claims of severe impairment, treatment frequency was quite low, actually lower than routine, with large gaps in treatment and initial refusal of psychotropic medication.

The psychiatrist also pointed out other inconsistencies between the claimant's reported abilities and evidence to the contrary. For instance, while the claimant said he could not drive to work due to his anxiety, the record reflected his self-reported ability to run errands and drive his children to various activities. The psychiatrist further noted the fact that the claimant was rather disgruntled with his work situation, which likely led to the initial request for leave. Being upset with a job is not the same as being functionally impaired, and the psychiatrist expertly laid out the evidence showing that, in fact, this individual retained considerable functionality as documented in his daily activities, normal exams, and low treatment intensity. None of the treatment notes included any observations of anxiety or panic being evident during sessions, and instead his providers consistently described intact speech, memory, and concentration.

This reviewer showed not only an absence of information documenting impairment but also the presence of information documenting intact abilities. This narrative clearly showed that the claimant's self-reported levels of impairment were not credible.

This level of analysis and integration is central to a psychiatric FR, but should also be part of IMEs. Oftentimes a neuropsychologist performing an IME becomes too narrowly focused on PVTs without incorporating a thorough, integrated review of all other available information (see the PVTs Are Life Cases section).

Related to the previous example is a provider who does not use PVTs/SVTs directly but who does appropriately consider this information in their case formulation. This is because they recognize PVTs as yet another meaningful source of data that should be integrated into their conceptualization of the case. This might move them to the top center of the graph. For some of our IMEs where the preferred provider type is a psychiatrist, we offer the service of an expert psychologist to interpret a personality measure with validity scales (typically the MMPI). The best psychiatrists expertly incorporate this information into their report. Others seem to actively ignore such vital information.

Gold Star (GS)

Finally, the upper right quadrant of the graph is the provider who properly utilizes PVTs and properly integrates this and all other sources of data. This quadrant is almost exclusively inhabited by neuropsychologists, given their access to PVTs/SVTs, knowledge of the literature, and (for some) excellent conceptualization skills (Figure 22.7).

Case GS1: This was a disability IME involving a woman 37 years of age who experienced a right posterior cerebral artery (PCA) stroke, with subsequent cognitive and emotional problems. Although she had problems finding the office and was a few minutes late, she had driven herself to the appointment and had no difficulties navigating the intake process. She was slightly impulsive during testing and also admitted to not paying attention to some instructions. She requested clarification on some tasks. Mini Mental status exam was 25/30 due to errors on serial subtraction, her drawings, and a multi-step oral command. Her history was notable for a severe motor vehicle accident (MVA) at age 5 that impacted schooling and required extra help early on, but she graduated on time. She reported a history of childhood abuse.

At the time of her stroke, three years before the exam, she had been working two jobs (managing the schedule in a physical therapy office, checking patients in at a medical office)

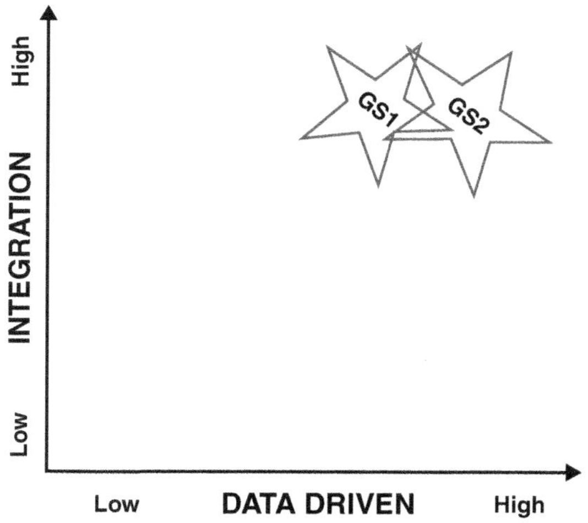

Figure 22.7 Both Gold Star case examples fall in the upper right quadrant, because they use a high level of integration and properly utilize objective data.

and felt "burned out" by the demands. She made no attempts to return to work after the stroke and claimed she had been "diagnosed" as not being able to work anymore. Specifically, she said she was slower and would not be able to organize paperwork. She also acknowledged emotional symptoms of anxiety, PTSD predating the stroke, and insomnia, and she felt that work-related stress would be too much for her to bear. Her ADLs were noted to be intact, and she managed her finances independently. She continued to enjoy some hobbies (art), spent time with friends, and was dating again. She had taken some trips for pleasure.

The claimant had undergone speech therapy and records documented poor test performance during evaluation. In this context, she was administered the Repeatable Battery for the Assessment of Neuropsychological Status (RBANS), the results of which were described as borderline to average. Formal neuropsychological testing was conducted by a clinical provider about two years before the current IME, and the report indicated that she passed validity measures. However, the IME neuropsychologist noted that the data sheet did not reflect any PVTs. Other scores were below average to average. The prior neuropsychologist concluded that she had major neurocognitive disorder, depression, anxiety, and PTSD (Table 22.6).

In the IME neuropsychological evaluation, two standalone and five embedded measures were completed. The neuropsychologist concluded that the TOMM was failed, and the Word Choice score was marginal. Further, the evaluator analyzed the Advanced Clinical Solutions (ACS) measures and determined that two scores fell at the 15% cutoff. Further discussion referenced the frequency that this occurs in the general clinical population (7%), in those with temporal lobectomies (4%) and in those with the same education level (two years of college) as the claimant (1%). This additional context helped support the conclusion of invalid data. Three other ACS scores were below the 25% cutoff and he similarly provided context, ultimately noting that 94%–96% of the population with similar

Table 22.6 PVT and SVT Data for Case GS1

PVT	*Score(s)*
TOMM1/2/3	35/40/48
Albany Consistency Index	13
Word Choice	44
WMS IV LM Recognition	17
WMS IV VPA Recognition	37
WMS IV VR Recognition	4
RDS	9
SVT	
MMPI-2-RF	
VRIN-r/TRIN-r	45/56
F-r	92
RBS	88
Fs	72
FBS-r	80
L-r/K-r	60/38
SIMS Total	12

Note: TOMM (Test of Memory Malingering); WMS IV (Wechsler Memory Scale 4th edition); RDS (Reliable Digit Span); MMPI-2-RF (Minnesota Multiphasic Personality Inventory-2-Restructured Form); SIMS (Structured Inventory of Malingered Symptoms).

conditions performed better than the claimant did. This was a helpful analysis given some marginal scores. The remaining battery was notable for some very low scores for selective attention speed (Ruff 2&7; <1st percentile); Logical Memory I and II (scaled score of 3 and 4, respectively); a Full Scale IQ of 75; and Stroop Scores (Word T = 20, Color T = 29, but Interference T = 46). Arguably some of these latter scores could have counted as failed embedded PVTs given research showing that such low scores fall below validity cutoffs (e.g., Logical Memory, Henry, 2023; Stroop, see Erdodi & Lichtenstein, 2021).

Symptom validity was assessed with the MMPI-2-RF and the SIMS, the latter of which did not reach a level to suggest over-reporting. On the MMPI-2-RF, while there were elevations reflecting emotional dysfunction, depression, anxiety, and somatic symptoms, there was also consistent evidence of over-reporting of psychiatric and cognitive symptoms. The IME neuropsychologist questioned the validity of the profile for clinical interpretation, particularly, as is discussed below, because the claimant did not seek treatment for her claimed symptoms, and they did not impact her ADLs.

The IME neuropsychologist concluded that both the cognitive data and the personality/emotional data were noncredible. They integrated self-reported information (such as the claimant's ability to drive, manage finances, and take care of other ADLs), noting that these abilities were inconsistent with her scores. The IME neuropsychologist explained that the current scores were inconsistent with previous testing (some areas improved, some declined) in a way that was inconsistent with expectations for her recovery trajectory. From a mental health standpoint, the neuropsychologist noted that despite high levels of reported emotional difficulties, the claimant was not under the care of a mental health professional. In fact, she had discontinued services despite her reported symptoms. The previous treater opined that she had a neurocognitive disorder (unspecified) and asserted that she would have problems with concentration. However, this was all based on the claimant's self-report and the treatment records did not describe such difficulties during sessions. The IME neuropsychologist thus integrated information from the record, previous testing, behavioral observation, self-report, and their own battery of tests. They identified inconsistencies among these multiple sources of data and laid out the reasoning clearly and in a way a lay reader could easily understand.

Case GS2: The first GS case concluded invalid data and lack of support for impairment. In this second case, the evaluator took an extra step and concluded malingering. I will note that the majority of reports I read do not include this opinion outright, although it is often implied with phrases such as "implausible" and "completely contradictory" or similar. Most clients do not specifically ask if a claimant is/is not malingering, but there is no prohibition against stating so if that is the conclusion. In an earlier case, I presented what I felt was a heavy-handed approach to concluding malingering, largely because of a failure to fully integrate all of the data.

In this case, the claimant was a married man in his early 50s who experienced a transient ischemic attack six years before this disability IME. He reported that he started experiencing cognitive problems immediately, characterized by not being able to think and having no control over his emotions. Although his symptoms improved, he never felt he was back to baseline. At the time of the evaluation, he still reported significant problems with short-term memory that had never improved. Additionally, he reported some gaps in his long-term memory, with some events (even for long periods) being "blank" for him. He endorsed some unusual somatic symptoms such as pain in his fingernails. He also asserted that neuroimaging had shown "significant shifts in his brain" (the neuropsychologist noted that there was no reference to any positive radiological findings in the available record).

Childhood history was notable for an episode of anaphylactic shock that required hospitalization. Other medical conditions included migraines and sleep apnea. He drank alcohol heavily in his 20s but was not drinking at all at the time of the IME.

Regarding ADLs, he reported being able to do simple projects around the house and yard, prepare simple meals, and garden. However, he described being dizzy and fatigued, which he said limited some tasks. He reported that he was able to drive, but only if someone was in the car with him (the need for this was not clear).

After the transient ischemic attack (TIA), the claimant returned to work but said he was struggling (forgetting how to perform familiar tasks) and had received negative feedback from his supervisors. He lashed out and yelled at them, and he had not returned to work since.

Medical records documented the TIA and indicated that symptoms resolved within six to eight days. Imaging at the time showed only mild microvascular disease consistent with age. The record also noted that the claimant had reported two prior episodes of amnesia lasting several hours almost two decades earlier. Continuous electroencephalogram (EEG) was performed and was normal. The record documented ongoing and significant complaints of memory loss, syncope, and forgetting how to perform math. Positive emission tomography (PET) scan showed mild hypometabolism in the temporal lobes, right greater than left. There were multiple references in the record of the claimant's wife reporting changes in his memory and that he was exhibiting increased anxiety. The claimant himself reported in questionnaires that he was forgetful and had dementia. Within the year prior to the IME, he was reporting hallucinations, and this was assumed to reflect dementia.

Behavioral observations were important in this case (as they are in all cases). Despite the records showing reports of cognitive decline, vertigo, and hallucinations, the claimant showed no difficulties interacting, and he was able to provide a coherent story of his life, detailing his daily routines, his numerous symptoms, and the chronology of events. Apart from brief moments of irritability, his affect was quite normal. His speech was fluent, and there were no motor abnormalities and no indication of vertigo or balance issues. In fact, he was adept at using his cell phone to retrieve important information and he nimbly opened a package of snacks and resealed it easily. Fine and gross motor movements were thus observed to be intact (Table 22.7).

Validity testing included the TOMM, on which the claimant scored quite poorly, with one score at chance levels. The neuropsychologist compared the performance with those with dementia and the scores on Trials 1 and 2 were worse than 98% of that sample. Additional metrics from the TOMM showed that the claimant's performance was worse than those with documented brain damage. On another measure (VSVT),[6] the claimant scored at chance level on the hard trial, which was noted to be very uncommon even in those with severe TBI. Embedded measures also showed evidence of invalidity. Given these findings, the neuropsychologist concluded that the resulting profile was not an accurate reflection of the claimant's true abilities.

Unsurprisingly, the rest of the profile was notable for highly variable performance, with much lower than expected overall cognitive abilities (4th percentile on the WAIS-IV) compared with premorbid estimates at the upper end of average. Noteworthy too was average performance on a story memory task but with list learning and design learning falling at or below the 10th percentile. The neuropsychologist identified atypical patterns in the data, including recognition being worse than recall, and a strong decline between the 30- and 60-minute delay periods. The remaining tests hovered around the 7th to 10th percentile,

Table 22.7 PVT and MMPI Data for Case GS2

PVT	*Score(s)*
TOMM Trial 1, 2, & Retention	22/32/42
IFFI	12
TOMM10	6
VSVT E/D	24/14
RDS	6
RAVLT-X	4
Finger Tapping	71
MMPI-2-RF	
VRIN-r/TRIN-r	44T/57T
F-r	97T
Fp-r	62T
Fs	83T
FBS-r	76T
RBS	92T
L-r/K-r	62T/31T

Note: IFFI: Invalid Forgetting Frequency Index (Buddin et al., 2014).

with poor performance on a measure of speeded dexterity (Grooved Pegboard, <5th percentile) and finger tapping was also remarkably low.

Personality testing (MMPI-2-RF) was notable for multiple elevations on scales reflecting likely over-reporting of various symptoms, including cognitive complaints, even when compared with individuals with known neurological conditions. The clinical profile was thus deemed uninterpretable.

What did this neuropsychologist conclude? By this point, it should be obvious that they found the entire battery to be unreliable due to numerous instances of failed PVTs and evidence of exaggeration of symptoms. Again, this is not an uncommon place to stop for many neuropsychologists, but this neuropsychologist then presented a very clearly thought-out process for explaining their reasoning, integrating multiple sources of information along the way. They referenced, for instance, the poor performance on motor testing and contrasted this with the ease with which the claimant used his fingers for a variety of tasks when not being tested for motor skills. Poor fluency on testing was contrasted with the ease the claimant showed in conversing and relaying his story, often in excellent detail and with accurate chronology. This was contrasted with the variable and poor performance on memory testing, which was entirely inconsistent with behavioral observations. Importantly, the neuropsychologist addressed the numerous instances in the record where various symptoms were reported, at times with providers concluding that the claimant had dementia. The behaviors as described in the record were at odds with the presentation during the neuropsychological IME, and the neuropsychologist pointed out that the few mental status exams in the record were brief and contained no check on validity. Coupled with the clear signs of symptom over-reporting on personality testing, the evaluator further concluded that the claimant's self-report, and that of his wife, could not be relied upon as there was ample evidence that nonorganic factors (i.e., dissimulation) were heavily coloring the presentations across settings.

This neuropsychologist did an excellent job of integrating many sources of evidence and clearly explaining conclusions. However, they also went a step further and discussed the rationale for why the claimant not only provided unreliable data, but was (more likely than not) malingering. This is not a conclusion that most neuropsychologists tend to make in these reports, for a variety of reasons (e.g., concerns about labeling intent, legal challenges). However, if it is expressed, it is imperative that the reasoning for this is crystal clear, evidence-based, and evenhanded. Compare this approach to the earlier case (PVTL3), where the conclusion of malingering seemed to be tossed out on the shakiest of grounds.

In the current case, the neuropsychologist employed the Slick et al. (1999) and Sherman et al. (2020) criteria, carefully outlining all elements in this case that were consistent with a conclusion of malingering:

A There clearly was external incentive (long-term disability benefits) and a likely desire to avoid returning to the grueling nature of his pre-injury work.
B For criterion B, the neuropsychologist detailed how the claimant clearly produced an invalid neurocognitive presentation, citing inconsistencies on memory tests (internal inconsistency) and the behavioral observations (inconsistency across behaviors); invalid scores on PVTs, again highlighting the comparison with known neurologic groups and using an error rate of <5%, and an error rate of below 1% with three PVTs failed; and evidence of exaggerated symptoms on the MMPI-2-RF.
C Discrepancies between the test data/symptom report and other sources of evidence were identified, including the lack of a neurological event that would explain such severe deficits. Here, the neuropsychologist carefully stepped through the record and the multiple potential causes of the claimant's difficulties, in each case explaining why those conditions were either not corroborated by the available evidence or why those conditions would not lead to the widespread deficits presumed in this case. He went on to mention a few highly improbable symptoms that made no biological sense or that were implausible (gaps of remote memory for years). He took the time to compare the claimant's report of when symptoms began (immediately post TIA) with the medical record that clearly contradicted the emergence of such symptoms until much later in the process or highlighted inconsistency with contemporaneous records (collateral report and self-report denying memory issues earlier but reporting them in this IME).
D In this case, given the unusual and numerous symptoms reported, it was rather simple to demonstrate that there were no medical or psychiatric conditions that would explain this combination of symptoms, including dementia. The GS neuropsychologist discussed the potential for a somatoform disorder, but ruled this out, given the numerous inconsistencies and blatantly implausible symptoms.

After providing such a rich narrative and leading the reader through the complex array of information in a clear and understandable manner, the remaining responses to questions were appropriately succinct: No, there is not valid evidence of a neurological condition. Cognitive deficits are not supported. There is no credible support for limitations or restrictions. The most likely conclusion is that the claimant was malingering.

It is truly a pleasure to run across a report such as this, as it demonstrates the incredible skill of some providers. There was no speculation, just a clear presentation of the facts, supported by the literature, and a beautiful integration of a vast amount of information. The client in this case explicitly asked the provider to discuss validity and, if testing was invalid, to provide an explanation of this result. This provider opted to discuss the reason in the context of malingering. This report could have been just as effective without the discussion of malingering, and other providers might have just stated that the claimant did not perform to their best abilities for unknown reasons. However, because the provider opted to include the term malingering, a careful weighing of the evidence to support such a conclusion was imperative.

Final Thoughts

While some providers stubbornly anchor themselves in one extreme quadrant or another, most providers are a bit more fluid than this. Some learn over time and thus become stronger in their integration skills, shifting upward on the graph's *Y*-axis. Some will vacillate in one direction or the other for no apparent reason. It is not clear to me why this happens, although in a few instances, it appears to be related to "thought fatigue." These providers provide conscientious conceptualizations early on, but then increasingly appear to rely on simplistic formulas and cede analysis to a computer program or other short-cuts.

I hope one takeaway from this chapter is how important integrative thinking is when assessing validity. A thoughtful approach is dependent not just on the objective data available, but how that information is integrated across all available sources. It is incumbent on IME providers to consider all data sources (subjective and objective) and help the reader understand how final conclusions were made. This should lead to clearer and more defensible reports.

Notes

1 The cases have been altered significantly to protect privacy. In most cases, information drawn from multiple evaluations has been combined, and, in some cases, the information has been completely fabricated.
2 Test of Memory Malingering.
3 Medical Symptom Validity Test.
4 Dot Counting Test.
5 Minnesota Multiphasic Personality Inventory-2-Restructured Form.
6 Victoria Symptom Validity Test.

References

Buddin Jr, W. H., Schroeder, R. W., Hargrave, D. D., Von Dran, E. J., Campbell, E. B., Brockman, C. J., ... & Baade, L. E. (2014). An examination of the frequency of invalid forgetting on the Test of Memory Malingering. *The Clinical Neuropsychologist*, *28*(3), 525–542.

Erdodi, L. A., & Lichtenstein, J. D. (2021). Information processing speed tests as performance validity tests. In Boone, K. B. (Ed.), *Assessment of feigned cognitive impairment*. New York: Guilford Publications.

Henry, G. K. (2023). Detection of noncredible cognitive performance with Wechsler Memory Scale-IV measures in mild traumatic brain injury litigants. *Applied Neuropsychology: Adult*, *32*(5), 1–8.

Martin, P. K., Schroeder, R. W., & Odland, A. P. (2025). Neuropsychological validity assessment beliefs and practices: A survey of North American neuropsychologists and validity assessment experts. *Archives of Clinical Neuropsychology*, *40*(2), 201–223.

Martin, P. K., Schroeder, R. W., Olsen, D. H., Maloy, H., Boettcher, A., Ernst, N., & Okut, H. (2020). A systematic review and meta-analysis of the Test of Memory Malingering in adults: Two decades of deception detection. *The Clinical Neuropsychologist*, *34*(1), 88–119.

McCaul, C., Boone, K. B., Ermshar, A., Cottingham, M., Victor, T. L., Ziegler, E., ... & Wright, M. (2018). Cross-validation of the Dot Counting Test in a large sample of credible and non-credible patients referred for neuropsychological testing. *The Clinical Neuropsychologist*, *32*(6), 1054–1067.

Sellbom, M., Wygant, D., & Bagby, M. (2012). Utility of the MMPI-2-RF in detecting non-credible somatic complaints. *Psychiatry Research*, *197*(3), 295–301.
Sherman, E. M., Slick, D. J., & Iverson, G. L. (2020). Multidimensional malingering criteria for neuropsychological assessment: A 20-year update of the malingered neuropsychological dysfunction criteria. *Archives of Clinical Neuropsychology*, *35*(6), 735–764.
Slick, D. J., & Sherman, E. M. (2013). Differential diagnosis of malingering. In D. A. Carone & S. S. Bush (Eds). *Mild Traumatic Brain Injury: Symptom Validity Assessment and Malingering* (pp. 57–72). New York: Springer.
Slick, D. J., Sherman, E. M., & Iverson, G. L. (1999). Diagnostic criteria for malingered neurocognitive dysfunction: Proposed standards for clinical practice and research. *The Clinical Neuropsychologist*, *13*(4), 545–561.

23 Performance and Symptom Validity Assessment in Clinical and Forensic Patients with Depression

Thomas Merten and Brechje Dandachi-FitzGerald

Depression and Cognitive Impairment

Depressive disorders, most commonly major depression and dysthymia, are among the most prevalent mental-health problems worldwide (Hasin et al., 2018; Kessing, 2020). Their causes, symptoms, and time courses are as diverse as are the various recommended therapeutic approaches. With the shift of the *Diagnostic and Statistical Manual of Mental Disorders* (*DSM-III*; American Psychiatric Association, 1980) to a predominantly syndromatic approach, the earlier triadic system (organic or symptomatic vs. endogenous vs. reactive or psychoneurotic) was discarded. Consequently, patients with clinically diagnosed depression will present in highly heterogeneous forms with regard to symptomatology, the underlying cause of the illness, its time course, and differential response to antidepressant medication or psychotherapy. Within a number of symptom domains, clinical manifestations may even vary from serious functional deficits to excessive hyperfunction (e.g., sleep, body weight, appetite, motor behavior, sexual drive), or be widely unaffected in some patients.

Cognitive complaints, such as memory and concentration deficits, and slowed thinking speed, are commonly reported by patients and belong to the spectrum of depressive symptoms. However, numerous studies of self-reported cognitive problems have failed to find an association of these complaints to measured cognitive performances, leading some to declare that relying on self-report to establish a psychiatric diagnosis is insufficient, and requires "unbiased objective measures of mental state…" (Pavlova & Uher, 2020).

Test-taking engagement may play a role in neurocognitive performance. In this vein, a central issue regarding cognition in depression relates to "effortful processing" and "motivation on tasks involving effortful processing" (e.g., Hartlage et al., 1993; Porter et al., 2007). When determining the validity of individual test profiles, an important question is whether the patient in question was *willing to perform to the best of their ability* at the time and under the circumstances of the examination. In a sample of 45 patients with unipolar depression and 60 controls, Moritz et al. (2017) found that only one fourth of the patients obtained scores of at least one standard deviation below healthy control means. A pre- and post-assessment motivation check revealed that patients with depression displayed more fear of test outcomes, complained more about negative momentary influences on test performance, and were less motivated when completing tasks. Group differences were largely reduced when these factors were used as covariates in the analyses.

In fact, several studies have shown that patients with diagnosed major depressive disorder (MDD) or other types of depression may present with only minimal or no cognitive dysfunction on neuropsychological assessment (Beblo et al., 2011; Boone et al., 1995; Egeland, Rund et al., 2003; Egeland, Sundet et al., 2003; Rohling et al., 2002); however, other

DOI: 10.4324/9781003005063-27

studies have reported unsystematic group differences in a variety of cognitive domains. Higher-quality studies of effects of depression on cognition limit inclusion of participants to those with diagnosed MDD, excluding other forms of depressive disorder and specifically not relying simply on self-report depression inventories. Relevant meta-analyses report cognitive decline mostly in the areas of executive functions, processing speed, attention, and memory (e.g., Lee et al., 2012). Cognitive difficulties can also be present during remission from a depressive episode (e.g., Rock et al., 2014). Semkovska et al. (2019) reported a systematic review and meta-analysis of 252 studies of cognitive function following a major depressive episode, finding small to large effect sizes in five cognitive domains. However, as has often been the case with depression studies, there was no examination of performance validity. Effect sizes, like Cohen's *d*s, in such studies are often in the small to medium range, but when translated into clinical criteria for categorizing empirical data as recommended by Rogers et al. (2025), the effect sizes are mostly in the range of what these authors call *insubstantial* ($d < 0.75$), *in terms of clinical relevance*. The same is true for the association between depression severity and cognitive functioning, with correlations varying from $r = -0.11$ (for semantic memory) to $r = -0.32$ (for executive functions) in one meta-analysis (McDermott & Ebmeier, 2009). Effect sizes in that study were small and did not exceed 10% of explained variance. These authors also found considerable heterogeneity among studies, which is a common finding of all meta-analyses studying the association between depression and cognitive functioning.

Another relevant fact for many patient groups and study contexts is that there is no substantial association between the degree of self-reported cognitive symptoms and performance on neuropsychological tests. In a nonlitigating sample of 226 patients with memory complaints, Gass and Patten (2020) reported a correlation of $r = 0.42$ between cognitive complaints and level of depression, but neither cognitive complaints nor depression severity were associated with most memory measures employed in the study. An early study by Rohling et al. (2002) employed PVT results to eliminate all cases with noncredible or questionable test profiles from a large sample of compensation-seeking forensic neuropsychology patients. This procedure resulted in a sample of 420 patients with presumably credible test data, 19% of which presented with depression as the leading referral diagnosis. Severity of depressive symptoms was measured by Beck Depression Inventory scores (BDI; Beck & Steer, 1993). While higher BDI scores were associated with higher memory complaints, depressive symptom report had no impact on neuropsychological test results. Similar results were reported by Benitez et al. (2011) for veterans examined in a memory clinic. Several other studies confirmed closer links between subjective cognitive symptoms and depression or psychological distress, but minimal or no associations with cognitive test performance (e.g., French et al., 2014; Moritz et al., 2004).

Among the complicating factors when the relationship between depressive disorders and cognitive impairment is discussed are high rates of comorbidity with other mental disorders and, possibly even more so, with substance abuse, including alcohol use disorder (e.g., Hasin, et al., 2018). Depressive symptomatology is also more likely to develop in the context of significant physical illness, among them numerous diagnoses with potential direct or indirect impact on cognitive integrity. These include diabetes (Roy & Lloyd, 2012), Parkinson's disease (Aarsland et al., 2012), multiple sclerosis (Boeschoten et al., 2017), epilepsy (Fiest et al., 2013), moderate-to-severe traumatic brain injury (Ryttersgaard et al., 2020), cerebral tumor (Huang et al., 2017), stroke (Medeiros et al., 2020), early stages of dementia (Kuring et al., 2018), etc. (see also Egede, 2007; Gold et al., 2020).

Validity Assessment in Patients with Depression

When evaluating patients with depression, a key issue involves the *validity* of psychological test data, that is, how far both: (1) neuropsychological test profiles can be trusted to reflect the true cognitive ability of the patient at the time of the assessment, and (2) the self-reported symptomatology is accurate, or is flawed due to irrelevant responding, over-reporting, or other forms of significant response bias. Formal methods have been developed to assess the credibility of individual test data (and, by inference, the trustworthiness of symptom claims). These include performance validity tests (PVTs; tests validated to verify performance on cognitive tests) and symptom validity tests (SVTs; measures to verify accuracy of symptom report).

Performance Validity Testing

In non-compensation-seeking patients with depression, PVT failure rates are low. In a recent review by Goldberg and Birath (2021), 21 studies were identified that examined performance of depressed patients on numerous performance validity measures, including Digit Span variables, Warrington Recognition Memory Test, Dot Counting Test, Digit Memory Test/Hiscock Forced-Choice Memory Test, Test of Memory Malingering, Rey Fifteen Item Test, Finger Tapping Test, b Test, Letter Memory Test, 21-Item Test, and Victoria Symptom Validity Test. The authors concluded that "Patients with depression (without psychotic symptoms) did not have difficulty with published cut-offs on PVTs…." (p. 426). Similar conclusions were reported in an earlier review (Goldberg et al., 2007) and in Boone (2022).

Most recently, Legemaat et al. (2023) published a systematic review on PVT results in patients with MDD. Their narrow selection criteria led to the inclusion of only seven studies with mostly small sample sizes and a large variety of PVTs, which hampers the comparison of results across the studies. Failure rates between zero (Beblo et al., 2020; Egeland, Sundet et al., 2003; Rees et al., 2001) and 40% (Rowland et al., 2017) were reported, with a mean rate of patients passing PVTs of 94% (aggregated data across N = 229). This is the expected rate for credible populations given that PVT cut-offs are set to allow 10% false positives (Boone, 2012). The normal overall specificity rate is all the more striking given that Legemaat et al. (2023) did not require that studies specifically exclude subjects with motives to feign (e.g., see Rowland et al., 2017; Yanez et al., 2006). Further, the Rowland et al. (2017) and Yanez et al. (2006) studies involved U.S. veterans; elevated PVT failure rates are often found in studies of veterans due to the confound that the Veterans Administration provides clinical care but also disability/compensation determinations (see Boone et al., 2021). When the two military sample studies are removed from the Legemaat et al. (2023) analysis, the remaining studies show negligible PVT failures in depressed populations, consistent with the summary of PVT research in depression by Goldberg and Birath (2021), and the results of individual studies (Ashendorf et al., 2004; Beblo et al., 2020; Considine et al., 2011; Egeland, Sundet et al., 2003b; Rees et al., 2001). Similarly, in a large sample of 736 patients with bipolar disorder engaged in a longitudinal study, Tart-Zelvin et al. (2023) found a very low failure rate on both the Test of Memory Malingering and the Forced-Choice subtest of the California Verbal Learning Test.

In medicolegal psychiatric assessment of compensation-seeking patients, claimed MDD is not rare, thus necessitating verification of accuracy of cognitive test scores and psychological symptom report. Survey data show that depression belongs to the symptom domains perceived as most frequently targeted by patients who feign health problems (Puente-López et al., 2023; Santamaría et al., 2013). It is important to objectively assess the validity of cognitive test results, given that symptoms of major depression include claims of difficulties in concentration and slowed thinking. Stevens et al. (2018) described results of a consecutive sample of 127 compensation-seeking patients with claimed MDD; these authors found a rate of 33% failing on the Word Memory Test (Green, 2003) and 13% failing the Dot Counting Test (DCT; Boone et al., 2002); 52% were judged to meet Slick et al. (1999) criteria for possible malingering, and 33% met criteria for probable malingering. A survey of neuropsychologists conducted by Mittenberg et al. (2002) indicated a likely rate of 15% malingering in compensation-seeking patients with depression.

Symptom Validity Testing

Regarding symptom validity assessment, several scales and instruments were developed to specifically detect noncredible claims of depressive symptoms (see Boone, 2022, for additional review). Mogge and LePage (2004) and Mogge et al. (2008) published the Assessment of Depression Inventory (ADI) composed of 19 genuine *Depression* items (Dep), 16 *Feigning* items (Fg), and six items tapping random responding (*Random*, Rd). Among the most prominent freestanding SVTs, the Structured Inventory of Malingered Symptomatology (SIMS; Widows & Smith, 2005) contains a *Depression* subscale composed of 15 items. Contrary to the other four SIMS subscales describing bizarre, uncommon or extreme symptom claims, the *Depression* scale detects overreport of actual depressive symptoms. Steffan et al. (2003) developed a Malingering Depression (Md) scale for the Minnesota Multiphasic Personality Inventory-2 (MMPI-2; Butcher et al., 1989). Using a logistic regression-derived approach, the Inventory of Problems–29 (IOP-29; Viglione & Giromini, 2020) was created to discriminate between genuine and feigned presentation of mental and cognitive symptoms.

Various of these SVTs have been employed in a number of experimental analog studies to test their classification accuracy in identifying feigned depression (e.g., MMPI-2, Bagby et al., 2000; SIMS and ADI, Clegg et al., 2009; SIMS, Diederich, 2009; Grant et al., 2022; IOP-29, Ilgunaite et al., 2022; MMPI-2 and Personality Assessment Inventory, Lange et al., 2010). In studies which included clinical groups for comparison, analog malingerers scored higher than genuine clinical patients with depression (e.g., MMPI-2, Bagby et al., 2005; MMPI-2-Restructured Form, Marion et al., 2013). Validation studies have also included actual forensic samples; for example, using a cut score of > 5 endorsed pseudosymptoms (85% sensitivity, 88% specificity) on the Self-Report Symptom Inventory (SRSI; Merten et al., 2016), Stevens et al. (2018) reported a 40% failure rate in a sample of 127 forensic cases with claimed MDD.

Highly elevated BDI or BDI-II scores have been proposed as an indicator of noncredible symptom endorsement (Groth-Marnat, 1990; Lees-Haley, 1989). In an initial corroboration of this assertion, Merten et al. (2020) found a significant relationship between BDI-II scores and scores on the SIMS and SRSI. In an unselected sample of 658 patients at a German psychosomatic rehabilitation center (29.0% of whom had a primary diagnosis of depressive disorder), Merten and colleagues documented that 34.5% scored above the SIMS cut score of > 16, and 18.8% scored above the standard cut score on the SRSI (pseudo symptom endorsement > 9). Scores on these two SVTs significantly correlated with BDI-II scores (0.71 and 0.64, respectively). On the BDI-II, 50 patients (7.4%) scored above 40, with 84% of these patients positive on the SIMS or the SRSI or both. In a more recent study, Fuermaier et al. (2023) analyzed a sample of 217 Austrian early retirement claimants and proposed a BDI-II screening cut score of > 37 (58% sensitivity, 90% specificity) and a standard cut score of > 39 (51% sensitivity, 95% specificity) for identifying noncredible symptom endorsement. A number of subsequent studies with different samples followed this line of research (Boucher et al., 2024; Merten, 2024; Shura et al., 2024) and showed that BDI-II scores can be used as an embedded indicator of symptom validity.

Conclusions

The above literature can be summarized as follows:

1 Clinical patients with primary depressive disorders are expected to present with no or small impairment upon neuropsychological testing. Self-report of cognitive complaints reflects subjectively perceived limited resources and is generally discrepant to objective test profiles. Validity assessment generally yields results in the valid range; validity test failure, when it occurs, may reflect true positives, especially where open or hidden secondary gain expectations are present. This explains the higher prevalence of validity test failure in special contexts, such as in U.S. Veterans Administration health centers or in rehabilitation clinics in Germany, where healthcare provision is frequently connected with medicolegal determinations (e.g., Göbber et al., 2012; Merten et al., 2020; Rowland et al., 2017). True depression is not a condition that is expected to *fully account for* apparently invalid presentations indicative of feigning or exaggeration (criterion D of the Sherman et al., 2020, criteria for malingered symptom presentations). Thus, care should be taken not to "explain away" PVT and/or SVT failures by concluding that depression was *causal* to noncredible cognitive test profiles and/or noncredibly elevated or bizarre symptom report. In these cases, the psychologist will have to meet the challenge of providing accurate feedback to the patient that does not sabotage a treating relationship (e.g., Martin & Schroeder, 2021). Overlooking or ignoring feigned symptomatology in clinical patients may have detrimental effects both on society (e.g., through increased healthcare utilization; Horner et al., 2014) and on patients, be it medical, financial, or social (Thomson et al., 2018; van der Heide et al., 2020).

   When depression co-occurs with neurological and medical conditions with known cognitive sequelae, such as moderate or severe traumatic brain injury, measured cognitive deficits will primarily be attributable to these underlying conditions. A comorbid depressive disorder can be anticipated to have a negative impact on patients' wellbeing, their subjective experience of cognitive functioning, and their recovery. On neuropsychological exam, validity indexes will be in the valid range, except when neurological/medical conditions involve severe functional disability, such as dementia and very low intelligence. In these situations, care is necessary to utilize validity cut-offs necessary for maintaining adequate specificity in major neurocognitive disorder (Bortnik & Dean, 2021).

2 A substantial proportion of individuals with claimed depression undergoing forensic evaluations will present with validity test results in the invalid range. In this situation, the assessor will frequently not be able to make valid diagnostic determinations as to the presence or absence of genuine depressive symptomatology and/or true symptom severity. What can be communicated to the trier of fact is that the examinee did not present in a credible manner information that is critical for their deliberations and decisions.

3 A small minority of patients will temporarily present with very severe depression, with reliably verifiable serious consequences on their basic activities of daily living. These are patients suffering from conditions like melancholic depression with excessive somatic

symptomatology or rare occurrences of catatonic depression. Patients with very severe depression may need hospitalization, which may be involuntary, and they may qualify for treatment options such as electroconvulsion. Very severe symptomatology will be obvious in their clinical presentation for any qualified clinician (e.g., severe functional impairment in ADLs). These patients, if capable of undergoing neuropsychological assessment, may present with more notable cognitive dysfunction (e.g., Zaninotto et al., 2016). As far as we are aware, there is no relevant research addressing the question of validity assessment in bona-fide patients with very severe depression. However, particular care should be taken not to misdiagnose cases of severe depression as noncredible responders purely on the basis of failed PVTs that can be affected by a genuine lack of engagement in testing.

Case Vignette: The Case of Mr. L

Background

This is the case description of a young lawyer who specialized in medicolegal work with clients who claimed disability because of mental conditions, such as anxiety, depression, posttraumatic stress, chronic fatigue, and "burn-out." The referral source was a private insurance company that engaged a psychiatrist to conduct a follow-up assessment. The referral question was to determine if the claimant continued to suffer from a severe depression impeding him from working as a lawyer, which if so, would entitle him to a monthly financial compensation equivalent of about U.S.$1,400.

The first author received a phone call by the psychiatric expert, Dr. B., who provided the following account on the case. The patient was of German nationality and had obtained his degree at a German university. He had started to work as a lawyer in Germany, first as employee, and later with his own law firm. Five years ago, he moved to neighboring Austria and continued his legal work there as an employee of a law firm. He reported that he had been highly successful in supporting his clients to win early-pension claims due to mental conditions.

Two years prior to the current evaluation, Mr. L had reportedly suffered a severe depressive episode from which he had never recovered. His treating psychiatrist had certified him to be unfit for work. He participated in behavioral therapy for four months, without success. While his sick leave continued, he had moved back to Germany where his family was living, but he kept an apartment in Austria. One year prior, the independent psychiatric examiner, Dr. B., judged the claimant to display seemingly genuine depressive symptomatology in conjunction with a positive family history (both his father and mother were on early pension, as well as his 26-year-old brother and his 30-year-old sister, with diagnoses of depression). The claimant's symptom report was detailed and comprised an almost complete list of generally acknowledged depressive symptoms. But there had been some peculiarities to the case; for example, Mr. L had arrived to the examination wearing shabby and dirty clothes, most notably, an old brown leather coat full of unappetizing stains. In contrast, the claimant's hair cut was stylish and his fingernails well-groomed. The claimant indicated that he had to excuse himself from the physical examination which was a part of the evaluation because when he had dressed that morning, he had forgotten to put on underwear and was completely naked under his pants. Another peculiarity of the case was that the claimant held seven or eight different contracts for early-pension and sick pay compensations, from a variety of private insurance companies, and from state-sponsored and publicly regulated pension funds, in both Germany and Austria. He proudly reported to the examiner that his claims had been approved by most of the agencies. In fact, he was receiving annual payments exceeding the maximum he had ever earned throughout his professional career.

Although those issues had raised doubts in the examiner, Dr. B. recommended that the depressive disorder be considered genuine and substantial, but, at the same time, his advice was to restrict pension payments to nine months and then to reexamine the claimant. In the meantime, under appropriate treatment, Dr. B. expected the depression to subside.

A year later, the claimant underwent the second independent psychiatric evaluation. In the meantime, the insurance company had obtained information collected by private investigators, who had observed the claimant driving an expensive car and being elegantly dressed when he visited an exclusive golf club in the countryside. He was also observed visiting an expensive restaurant with a woman; both he and the woman were both well dressed and in apparent good mood. None of the behavioral observations of the investigators fit what even laypeople would expect from a severely depressed person. When he showed up for the second evaluation, he was wearing the same shabby old leather coat, and when it came to the physical examination, he stammered: *Oh, sorry doctor, I am so desolate. I woke up too late this morning and was so much in a hurry that I forgot to put on my underwear.* With this, the psychiatrist was convinced that he had made an error of judgment in conclusions in his first forensic report and had fallen prey to a bizarre feigning strategy. After contacting the referring insurance company, he asked the first author of this article to perform an independent neuropsychological evaluation with special emphasis on symptom and performance validity.

Medicolegal Practice in Germany

Due to differences in legal systems, the role of medical and neuropsychological experts in forensic cases in Germany and some neighboring European countries differs significantly from that in the United States (*cf.* Chafetz et al., 2025). The large majority of early-pension and disability claims are settled out of court. Forensic experts are usually hired by private insurance companies who cover all costs for expert opinions, independent of their results. The primary legal and ethical obligation of the expert is to present their determinations independently and impartially regardless of referral source.

In cases where out-of-court settlement cannot be reached, the claimant can file a legal complaint. In those cases, new medical and/or neuropsychological experts are appointed by the judge, not the opposing parties. The legally prescribed role of the expert is to assist the court and give advice to the trier of fact, not to the opposing parties. Specifically, the expert is expected to educate the judge or jury with regard to how to understand and place in perspective the medical and psychological facts relevant to the case in question (data collection, interpretation and explanatory models, relevant factors, knowledge base, causality, etc.).

Neuropsychological Evaluation: History, Symptom Report, and Clinical Presentation

Mr. L did not show up for the first appointment, without having canceled it. After a four-month legal debate between the insurance company and himself, Mr. L finally agreed to undergo the assessment.

Physical appearance: Mr. L appeared wearing the same dirty and worn-out coat that had been described twice by the psychiatric expert; other clothes were also old, shabby, stained, and with holes. Mr. L was unshaven, but his hair cut was elegant, and his fingernails were clean and carefully groomed.

History and activities of daily living: At the time of the assessment, the claimant was 36 years old. He had formal schooling of 13 years; his final examinations at university entrance level showed a rather modest academic performance. He had first studied medicine at a university, but dropped out after two years. After another six years, he completed a university course in law and passed all exams.

Mr. L gave a detailed account of the course of his (claimed) depressive disorder, with exact dates and naming of his doctors and therapists, in chronological order. The details were in full accordance with what was known from the records review. After the first psychiatric evaluation by Dr. B., Mr. L reported having continued antidepressant medication (Quetiapine, an atypical neuroleptic) and had restarted psychotherapy. He was living independently and did his own driving, and did not need support in financial or legal matters, or in activities of daily living. His activities were described as follows: Given that it was winter, he was spending considerable time sleeping. He regularly walked his dog, visited doctors, was active on the Internet, attended cinema and concert performances, and at least once a week he trained at a fitness center. He was a member of both a tennis and a golf club. At least once a month he traveled to Vienna, where he maintained a second apartment and spent a couple of days engaging in mostly cultural and social activities. He had a romantic relationship with a 30-year-old woman who had been on sick leave for a year or so due to a "chronic burn-out" symptomatology. They were planning to marry in six months.

Symptom report: Mr. L reported only few depressive symptoms, in contrast to his detailed report of symptoms on exam a year earlier; on current exam he was reporting sadness, lack of motivation, and affective numbing. Attention and concentration capacities were described as limited. He reported a weight gain of about 10 pounds within the last six months.

Cognitive symptoms: Mr. L spontaneously remarked that he was "not at all stupid," but that he had "forgotten quite a lot." He stated that if he was forced to restart work, he would have to "freshen up" his knowledge base, but at the same time, he considered his memory to be good. He denied difficulties in the domains of speech, language, written language, reasoning, visual perception, and orientation.

Mental status / behavioral observations: During the examination, Mr. L showed remarkable motor slowness, which was not present when he was distracted or when he did not realize he was being observed (for instance, when his mobile phone rang, he was very quick to reach out for it and to answer the call). His speech was slowed during most of the history taking, but not monotonic (vocal pitch and volume were normal). He inconsistently and unconvincingly presented with a number of memory gaps and exaggerated attentional lapses. He repeatedly wrote down notes for test instructions, as if to assist in his recall of tasks, which is very uncommon in credible patients. With regard to objective depressive signs, there was a notable absence of poverty of facial and gestural expression. There were no signs of depressive restlessness or agitation. There were no observable signs of emotional numbing, tiredness, or anxiety.

Neuropsychological Test Results

The neuropsychological test profile is presented in Table 23.1. Despite his educational and social background, Mr. L performed below average in a number of tests. For some domains,

Table 23.1 Cognitive Test Results. Labeling of the Test Scores According to Guilmette et al. (2020)

Domain/Test	*Raw Score/Percentile*	*Score Label*
Screening for Dementia		
Mini-Mental State Examination	30	Within normal expectations
Short-Term Memory/Working Memory		
Wechsler Memory Scale–Revised (WMS-R)		
Digit Span Forward	2nd percentile	Below average
Spatial Span Forward	3rd percentile	Below average
Digit Span Backward	30th percentile	Average
Spatial Span Backward	40th percentile	Average
Memory		
Rey Auditory Verbal Learning Test (RAVLT)		
First Trial (supraspan)	25th percentile	Average
Total First to Fifth Trial	10th percentile	Low average
Fifth Trial	20th percentile	Low average
Interference Trial (List B)	55th percentile	Average
Delayed Recall (30 min)	5th percentile	Below average
Recognition, Total Correct	10th percentile	Low average
Rey Complex Figure Test and Recognition Trial (RCFT)		
Immediate Recall (3 min)	16th percentile	Low average
Delayed Recall (30 min)	2th percentile	Below average
Recognition	31st percentile	Average
Semantic Memory		
Boston Naming Test, German 30-Item Version	28 correct	Normal range
Semantic Word Fluency (Animals, Food, Professions)	29th to 62th percentile	Average
Attention/Processing Speed		
Test Battery for Aattentional Performance		
Motor Reaction Time (Alertness), no Warning Sound	2nd percentile	Below average
Motor Reaction Time, with Warning Sound	2nd percentile	Below average
Selective Attention (Go/Nogo), reaction time	2nd percentile	Below average
Trail Making Test, Part A,Time To Complete		
d2 Test of Attention	20th percentile	Low average
Total Raw Score	7th percentile	Below average
Corrected Total Score	12th percentile	Low average
Visual-Spatial Functions		
Block Design (WAIS-III)	Scaled score = 7	Low average
Visual Organization Test, Short Version	13 correct	Within normal expectations
RCFT Copy Trial, Raw Score	<1st percentile	Exceptionally low
RCFT Copy Time to Complete	>16th percentile	Average

(*Continued*)

Table 23.1 (Continued)

Domain/Test	*Raw Score/Percentile*	*Score Label*
Language		
Aachen Aphasia Test, Screen for Writing and Reading	20 points	Full score (perfect)
Vocabulary Test (Wortschatztest)	verbal IQ = 114	High average score
Executive Functions		
Wisconsin Card Sorting Test (WCST)		
Total Errors	58th percentile	Average
Perseverative Responses	45th percentile	Average
Perseverative Errors	40th percentile	Average
Categories Completed	>16th percentile	Average
Trail Making Test, Part B, Time to Complete		
Letter Fluency	60th percentile	Average
Scores on Three Different Letters (1 min each)	23th to 59th percentile	Low average to Average
Figural Fluency – Five Point Test Corrected Total Score	10th percentile	Low average

significant inconsistencies were remarkable. For example, a severely limited Digit Span and a below-average visual-spatial span performance contrasted with normal Digit Span backward and visual-spatial span backward. Severe spatial distortions on the Copy trial of the Rey Complex Figure Test and Recognition Trial (< 1st percentile) contrasted with a low-average performance on Block Design and a normal performance on the Visual Organization Test. Also, significant motor retardation on a simple reaction time task (Alertness) contrasted with his self-reported activities outside the examination (such as playing tennis and driving long distances).

Performance validity test results (Table 23.2) showed failure on the TOMM and the Medical Symptom Validity Test (MSVT). The latter test results were classified as a Dementia Profile, compatible with the performance of a person with a genuine dementing condition or a neurocognitive disorder of equivalent severity. However, with no evidence of a true dementing condition, either from his behavioral presentation in the examination or his reported activities of daily living, the results were classified as noncredible or invalid. On embedded performance validity indexes, forward Digit Span (maximum span forward = 4) was markedly low and below PVT cutoff. Reliable Digit Span and most other embedded PVTs (derived from RCFT, RAVLT, TMT, and WCST) were in the valid range. RCFT Copy raw score was low (24.5) and the Effort Equation (Lu et al., 2003) yielded a score of 48.5; depending on the cut scores used for these two scores, they were classified either as valid or invalid.

On the Beck Depression Inventory–Second Edition, Mr. L scored 21, which indicated a reported moderate depressive symptomatology. The test profile of the Minnesota Multiphasic Personality Inventory–2 was not interpreted because a number of symptom validity scales

Table 23.2 Performance Validity Test Results

Performance Validity Test	*Raw Score*	*Score Label*
Test of Memory Malingering		
TOMM Trial 1	36 correct	Invalid range
TOMM Trial 2	41 correct	Invalid range
TOMM Trial 3	45 correct	Invalid range
Medical Symptom Validity Test		
Primary validity indicators (IR, DR, Cons)	90/90/80	Invalid range
MSVT profile	90/90/80/50/50	Dementia profile
Embedded Validity Indicators		
Reliable Digit Span	8	Valid range
Digit Span: Maximum Span Forward (MSF)	4	Invalid range
RCFT: Memory error profile	Retrieval	Valid range
RCFT: Atypical errors	ARE: 0; RFE: 0	Valid range
RCFT: Copy trial	24.5	Borderline (depending on cut score used)
RCFT: Effort equation Lu et al. (2003)	48.5	Borderline (depending on cut score used)
TMT B : TMT A	1.55	Valid range
RAVLT: Discrimination (Total hits – False positives)	10	Valid range
WCST: Unique responses, failures to maintain set, perfect mismatches	0 each	Valid range

Table 23.3 Symptom Validity Test Results. Valid Results Were Labeled Based on T Scores

MMPI-2 Validity Indicators	*Raw Scores*	*T Scores*	*Score Label*
Lie scale *L*	1	32	Below average
Infrequency scale *F*	14	62	Average
Defensiveness *K*	10	36	Below average
True Response Inconsistency *TRIN*	10	56	Average
Variable Response Inconsistency *VRIN*	7	52	Average
Infrequency Back Scale F_B	11	70	Above average
Malingered PTSD F_{PTSD}	4	62	Average
Infrequent Response Scale F_P	3	63	Average
Response Bias Scale RBS	12	80	Exceptionally high
Fake Bad Scale FBS	24	—	Invalid
Henry–Heilbronner Index HHI	12	—	Invalid
Malingered Depression *Md*	16	—	Invalid
Malingered Mood Disorder Scale *MMDS*	10	—	Invalid
Gough Dissimulation Scale–Revised *Ds-R*	20	90	Invalid
Obvious-subtle scale	—	175	Invalid

were in the invalid range and signaled significant negative response distortions (Table 23.3). Specifically, numerous scales assessing for veracity of report of depressive symptoms were elevated, and the high score on Response Bias Scale (RBS) and Symptom Validity Scale (FBS) indicated that the claimant's report of memory/cognitive and physical complaints was not likely credible.

Conclusions and Discussion

On the basis of the overall test results, and the marked inconsistencies between different sources of information, the claimant's depression presentation was judged to be noncredible and the test profile invalid. When the revised criteria for malingered neurocognitive dysfunction published by Sherman et al. (2020) were applied, the case would classify as *Invalid mixed symptom presentation* (neurocognitive and psychiatric). In the absence of an objective and reliable evidence for the presence and severity of the underlying genuineness, it was impossible to determine if the symptom claims of Mr. L were grossly exaggerated or completely invented. However, given that the claimant did not produce credible test results, he did not meet the obligation and responsibility to provide an objective evidence of a disabling psychiatric condition.

This was one of the most bizarre cases in the first author's forensic career. Claimants who are medical doctors, neuropsychologists, psychotherapists, and lawyers confront the experts who evaluate them with special challenges when conducting psychiatric and neuropsychological exams because these claimants might have experience and knowledge regarding how to present with credible psychiatric conditions, and/or access to test information that might enable them to manipulate test results when feigning psychiatric conditions. In the case of Mr. L, a number of earlier psychiatric experts had fallen prey to his knowledge of depressive symptom presentations gleaned from his work with litigating mental-health patients (and family members/friends); however, he still displayed marked and bizarre discrepancies not found in actual depression. Professional guidelines for forensic determinations in Germany recommend a thorough validity assessment in all cases of claimed mental-health conditions (Arbeitsgemeinschaft der Wissenschaftlichen Medizinischen Fachgesellschaften, 2019), but this is often neglected and the special role of test-based validity assessment continues to be aggressively contested by some psychiatrists (Schmidt et al., 2011). Subjective symptom report appears to be the predominant information relied upon by many experts in the field of mental disorders, in disregard of a thorough analysis of consistency and plausibility and the inspection of more objective signs, as described by Gupta (2009) for depressive disorders. Mr. L's peculiar attire and hygiene appears to have constituted a special instrument in his toolbox, which other examiners found convincing.

After completion of the neuropsychological expert report, the psychiatrist, Dr. B., recommended that the insurance company not acknowledge the claims of Mr. L as genuine. The insurance company stopped paying the monthly allowances and Mr. L did not file a legal complaint against their decision. No information is available regarding the claimant's other ongoing early-pension and sick-leave benefits. However, a recent Internet search, conducted two years after the evaluation, revealed that he had started working as an independent lawyer in Austria, once again specializing in medicolegal issues!

Author Note

Correspondence concerning this chapter should be addressed to: Thomas Merten, PhD, Vivantes Klinikum im Friedrichshain, Department of Neurology, Landsberger Allee 49, D-10249 Berlin, Germany. Email: thomas.merten@vivantes.de

Brechje Dandachi-FitzGerald, PhD, Department of Clinical Psychological Science, Faculty of Psychology and Neuroscience, Maastricht University, Maastricht, The Netherlands. Email: b.fitzgerald@maastrichtuniversity.nl

References

Aarsland, D., Påhlhagen, S., Ballard, C. G., Ehrt, U., & Svenningsson, P. (2012). Depression in Parkinson disease: Epidemiology, mechanisms and management. *Nature Reviews Neurology, 8*(1), 35–47. https://doi.org/10.1038/nrneurol.2011.189

American Psychiatric Association (1980). *Diagnostic and statistical manual of mental disorders* (3rd ed.). American Psychiatric Association.

Arbeitsgemeinschaft der Wissenschaftlichen Medizinischen Fachgesellschaften (Ed.). (2019). Gutachtliche Untersuchung bei psychischen und psychosomatischen Störungen [Forensic examinations in patients with mental and psychosomatic disorders]. Retrieved January 02, 2024, from https://register.awmf.org/de/leitlinien/detail/051-029

Ashendorf, L., Constantinou, M., & McCaffrey, R. J. (2004). The effect of depression and anxiety on the TOMM in community-dwelling older adults. *Archives of Clinical Neuropsychology, 19*(1), 125–130. https://doi.org/10.1093/arclin/19.1.125

Bagby, R. M., Marshall, M. B., & Bacchiochi, J. R. (2005). The validity and clinical utility of the MMPI-2 Malingering Depression scale. *Journal of Personality Assessment, 85*(3), 304–311. https://doi.org/10.1207/s15327752jpa8503_06

Bagby, M., Nicholson, R., Buis, T., & Bacchiochi. (2000). Can the MMPI-2 validity scales detect depression feigned by experts? *Assessment, 7*(1), 55–62. https://doi.org/10.1177/107319110000700104

Beblo, T., Driessen, M., & Dehn, L. (2020). Memory deficits in patients with major depression: Yes, they are trying hard enough! *Expert Review of Neurotherapeutics, 20*(5), 517–522. https://doi.org/10.1080/14737175.2020.1754799

Beblo, T., Sinnamon, G., & Baune, B. T. (2011). Specifying the neuropsychology of affective disorders: Clinical, demographic and neurobiological factors. *Neuropsychology Review, 21*(4), 337–359. https://doi.org/10.1007/s11065-011-9171-0

Beck, A. T., & Steer, R. A. (1993). *Beck depression inventory*. Manual. The Psychological Corporation.

Benitez, A., Horner, M. D., & Bachmann, D. (2011). Intact cognition in depressed elderly veterans providing adequate effort. *Archives of Clinical Neuropsychology, 26*(3), 184–193. https://doi.org/10.1093/arclin/acr001

Boeschoten, R. E., Braamse, A. M., Beekman, A. T., Cuijpers, P., Van Oppen, P., Dekker, J., & Uitdehaag, B. M. (2017). Prevalence of depression and anxiety in multiple sclerosis: A systematic review and meta-analysis. *Journal of the Neurological Sciences*, *372*, 331–341. https://doi.org/10.1016/j.jns.2016.11.067

Boone, K. B. (2012). *Clinical practice of forensic neuropsychology: An evidence-based approach*. Guilford Press.

Boone, K. B. (2022). Assessment of actual versus feigned depression with symptom and performance validity tests. In S. M. McClintock & J. Choi (Eds.), *Handbook of neurocognitive function in depression* (pp. 193–219). Guilford Press.

Boone, K. B., Lesser, I. M., Miller, B. L., Wohl, M., Berman, N., Lee, A., Palmer, B., & Back, C. (1995). Cognitive functioning in older depressed outpatients: Relationship of presence and severity of depression to neuropsychological test scores. *Neuropsychology, 9*(3), 390–398. https://doi.org/10.1037/0894-4105.9.3.390

Boone, K. B., Litvin, P., & Victor, T. L. (2021). Base rates of feigned mild traumatic brain injury. In K. B. Boone (Ed.), *Assessment of feigned cognitive impairment* (2nd ed., pp. 341–355). Guilford Press.

Boone, K. B., Lu, P., & Herzberg, D. (2002). *The dot counting test*. Western Psychological Services.

Bortnik, K. E., & Dean, A. C. (2021). Performance validity testing in patients with dementia. In K. B. Boone (Ed.), *Assessment of feigned cognitive impairment* (2nd ed., pp. 481–503). Guilford Press.

Boucher, C. M., Giromini, L., Roth, R. M., & Erdodi (2024). The Beck Depression Inventory–Second Edition as a symptom validity test: Importing European cutoffs to the USA. *Psychological Injury and Law, 17*(2), 187–198. https://doi.org/10.1007/s12207-024-09505-8

Butcher, J. N., Graham, J. R., Ben-Porath, Y. S., Tellegen, A., & Dahlstrom, W. G. (1989). *MMPI-2: Minnesota Multiphasic Personality Inventory-2*. University of Minnesota Press.

Chafetz, M. D., Sweet, J. J., Boone, K. B., Cox, D., Hall, V., Kirkwood, M. W., ... & Oldenburg, C. (2025). Neuropsychological review of records in forensic cases: An AACN best practices paper with international perspectives. *The Clinical Neuropsychologist*, *39*(4), 839–869.

Clegg, C., Fremouw, W., & Mogge, N. (2009). Utility of the Structured Inventory of Malingered Symptomatology (SIMS) and the Assessment of Depression Inventory (ADI) in screening for malingering among outpatients seeking to claim disability. *Journal of Forensic Psychiatry & Psychology*, *20*(2), 239–254. https://doi.org/10.1080/14789940802267760

Considine, C. M., Weisenbach, S. L., Walker, S. J., McFadden, E. M., Franti, L. M., Bieliauskas, L. A., & Langenecker, S. A. (2011). Auditory memory decrements, without dissimulation, among patients with major depressive disorder. *Archives of Clinical Neuropsychology*, *26*(5), 445–453. https://doi.org/10.1093/arclin/acr041

Diederich, C. (2009). Der Einsatz von Selbstbeurteilungsverfahren in der Beschwerdenvalidierung [Use of self-report instruments in symptom validity assessment]. Unpublished diploma thesis. Humboldt University Berlin.

Egede, L. E. (2007). Major depression in individuals with chronic medical disorders: Prevalence, correlates and association with health resource utilization, lost productivity and functional disability. *General Hospital Psychiatry*, *29*(5), 409–416. https://doi.org/10.1016/j.genhosppsych.2007.06.002

Egeland, J., Rund, B. R., Sundet, K., Landrø, N. I., Asbjørnsen, A., Lund, A., …, Hugdahl, K. (2003). Attention profile in schizophrenia compared with depression: Differential effects of processing speed, selective attention and vigilance. *Acta Psychiatrica Scandinavica*, *108*(4), 276–284. https://doi.org/10.1034/j.1600-0447.2003.00146.x

Egeland, J., Sundet, K., Rund, B. R., Asbjørnsen, A., Hugdahl, K., Landrø, N. I., …, Stordal, K. I. (2003). Sensitivity and specificity of memory dysfunction in schizophrenia: A comparison with major depression. *Archives of Clinical Neuropsychology*, *25*(3), 79–93. https://doi.org/10.1076/jcen.25.1.79.13630

Fiest, K. M., Dykeman, J., Patten, S. B., Wiebe, S., Kaplan, G. G., Maxwell, C. J., …, Jette, N. (2013). Depression in epilepsy: A systematic review and meta-analysis. *Neurology*, *80*(6), 590–599. https://doi.org/10.1212/WNL.0b013e31827b1ae0

French, L. M., Lange, R. T., & Brickell, T. (2014). Subjective cognitive complaints and neuropsychological test performance following military-related traumatic brain injury. *Journal of Rehabilitation Research & Development*, *51*(6), 933–950. https://doi.org/10.1682/JRRD.2013.10.0226

Fuermaier, A. B. M., Dandachi-FitzGerald, B., & Lehrner, J. (2023). Validity assessment of early retirement claimants: Symptom overreporting on the Beck Depression Inventory–II. Applied Neuropsychology*: Adult*. Advance online publication. https://doi.org/10.1080/23279095.2023.2206031

Gass, C. S., & Patten, S. B. (2020). Depressive symptoms, memory complaints, and memory test performance. *Journal of Clinical and Experimental Neuropsychology*, *42*(6), 602–610. https://doi.org/10.1080/13803395.2020.1782848

Göbber, J., Petermann, F., Piegza, M., & Kobelt, A. (2012). Beschwerdevalidierung bei Rehabilitanden mit Migrationshintergrund in der Psychosomatik [Symptom validation in patients with migration background in psychosomatic medicine]. *Rehabilitation*, *51*(5), 356–364. https://doi.org/10.1055/s-0032-1323669

Gold, S. M., Köhler-Forsberg, O., Moss-Moritz, R., Mehnert, A., Miranda, J. J., Bullinger, M., Steptoe, A., Whooley, M. A., & Otte, C. (2020). Comorbid depression in medical diseases. *Nature Reviews Disease Primers*, *6*, 69. https://doi.org/10.1038/s41572-020-0200-2

Goldberg, H. E., & Birath, J. B. (2021). The impact of psychotic, depressive, bipolar, obsessive-compulsive, and anxiety disorders on performance validity test results. In K. B. Boone (Ed.), *Assessment of feigned cognitive impairment* (2nd ed., pp. 387–432). Guilford Press.

Goldberg, H. E., Madruga, C., & Boone, K. B. (2007). The impact of psychiatric disorders on cognitive symptom validity test scores. In K. B. Boone (Ed.), *Assessment of feigned cognitive impairment: A neuropsychological perspective* (2nd ed., pp. 281–309). Guilford Press.

Grant, A. F., Lace, J. W., Teague, C. L., Lowell, K. T., Ruppert, P. D., Garner, A. A., & Gfeller, J. D. (2022). Detecting feigned symptoms of depression, anxiety, and ADHD, in college students with the Structured Inventory of Malingered Symptomatology. Applied Neuropsychology*: Adult, 29*(4), 443–451. https://doi.org/10.1080/23279095.2020.1769097

Green, P. (2003). *Green's word memory test.* User's Manual. Green's Publishing.

Groth-Marnat, G. (1990). *The handbook of psychological assessment* (2nd ed.). John Wiley & Sons.

Guilmette, T. J., Sweet, J. J., Hebben, N., Koltai, D., Mahone, E. M., Spiegler, B. J., Stucky, K., Westerveld, M., & Conference Participants (2020). American Academy of Clinical Neuropsychology consensus conference on uniform labeling of performance test scores. *The Clinical Neuropsychologist, 34*(3), 437–453. https://doi.org/10.1080/13854046.2020.1722244

Gupta, R. K. (2009). Major depression: An illness with objective physical signs. *The World Journal of Biological Psychiatry, 10*(3), 196–201. https://doi.org/10.1080/15622970902812072

Hartlage, S., Alloy, L. B., Vázquez, C., & Dykman, B. (1993). Automatic and effortful processing in depression. *Psychological Bulletin, 113*(2), 247–278. https://doi.org/10.1037/0033-2909.113.2.247

Hasin, D. S., Sarvet, A. L., Meyers, J. L., Saha, T. D., Ruan, J., Stohl, M., & Grant, B. F. (2018). Epidemiology of adult DSM-5 major depressive disorder and its specifiers in the United States. *JAMA Psychiatry, 75*(4), 336–346. https://doi.org/10.1001/jamapsychiatry.2017.4602

Horner, M. D., van Kirk K. K., Dismuke, C. E., Turner, T. H., & Muzzy, W. (2014). Inadequate effort on neuropsychological evaluation is associated with increased healthcare utilization. *The Clinical Neuropsychologist, 28*(5), 703–713. https://doi.org/10.1080/13854046.2014.925143

Huang, J., Zeng, C., Xiao, J., Zhao, D., Tang, H., Wu, H., & Chen, J. (2017). Association between depression and brain tumor: A systematic review and meta-analysis. *Oncotarget, 8*(55), 94932–94943. https://doi.org/10.18632/oncotarget.19843.

Ilgunaite, G., Giromini, L., Bosi, J., Viglione, D. J., & Zennaro, A. (2022) A clinical comparison simulation study using the Inventory of Problems–29 (IOP-29) with the Center of Epidemiologic Studies Depression Scale (CES-D) in Lithuania. Applied Neuropsychology*: Adult, 29*(2), 155–162. https://doi.org/10.1080/23279095.2020.1725518

Kessing, V. (2020) Epidemiology of mood disorders. In J. R. Geddes, N. C. Andreasen, & G. M. Goodwin (Eds.), *The new oxford textbook of psychiatry* (3rd ed., pp. 691–699). Oxford University Press.

Kuring, J. K., Mathias, J. L., & Ward, L. (2018). Prevalence of depression, anxiety and PTSD in people with dementia: A systematic review and meta-analysis. *Neuropsychology Review*, *28*(4), 393–416. https://doi.org/ 10.1007/s11065-018-9396-2.

Lange, R. T., Sullivan, K. A., & Scott, C. (2010). Comparison of MMPI-2 and PAI validity indicators to detect feigned depression and PTSD symptom reporting. *Psychiatry Research, 176*(2–3), 229–235. https://doi.org/10.1016/j.psychres.2009.03.004

Lee, R. S. C., Hermens, D. F., Porter, M. A., & Redoblado-Hodge, M. A. (2012). A meta-analysis of cognitive deficits in first-episode major depressive disorder. *Journal of Affective Disorders, 140*(2), 113–124. https://doi.org/10.1016/j.jad.2011.10.023

Lees-Haley, P. R. (1989). Malingering traumatic mental disorder on the Beck Depression Inventory: Cancerphobia and toxic exposure. *Psychological Reports, 65*(2), 623–626. https://doi.org/10.2466/pr0.1989.65.2.623.

Legemaat, A. M., Haagedoorn, M. A. S., Burger, H., Denys, D., Bockting, C. L., & Geurtsen, G. J. (2023). Is suboptimal effort an issue? A systematic review on neuropsychological performance validity in major depressive disorder. *Journal of Affective Disorders, 323,* 731–740. https://doi.org/10.1016/j.jad.2022.12.043

Lu, P. H., Boone, K. B., Cozolino, L., & Mitchell, C. (2003). Effectiveness of the Rey-Osterrieth complex figure test and the Meyers and Meyers recognition trial in the detection of suspect effort. *The Clinical Neuropsychologist,* 17(3), 426–440. https://doi.org/10.1076/clin.17.3.426.18083

Marion, B. E., Sellbom, M., Salekin, R. T., Toomey, J. A., Kucharski, L. T., & Duncan, S. (2013). An examination of the association between psychopathy and dissimulation using the MMPI-2-RF validity scales. *Law and Human Behavior, 37*(4), 219–230. https://doi.org/10.1037/lhb0000008

Martin, P. K., & Schroeder, R. W. (2021). Feedback with patients who produce invalid testing: Professional values and reported practices. *The Clinical Neuropsychologist, 35*(6), 1134–1153. https://doi.org/10.1080/13854046.2020.1722243

McDermott, L. M., & Ebmeier, K. P. (2009). A meta-analysis of depression severity and cognitive function. *Journal of Affective Disorders, 119*(1–3), 1–8. https://doi.org/10.1016/j.jad.2009.04.022

Medeiros, G. C., Roy, D., Kontos, N., & Beach, S. R. (2020). Post-stroke depression: A 2020 updated review. *General Hospital Psychiatry, 66*, 70–80. https://doi.org/10.1016/j.genhosppsych.2020.06.011

Merten, T. (2024). Highly elevated scores on the Beck Depression Inventory–Second Edition as an indicator of noncredible symptom report. *Assessment.* Advance online publication. https://doi.org/10.1177/10731911241304214

Merten, T., Kaminski, A., & Pfeiffer, W. (2020). Prevalence of overreporting on symptom validity tests in a large sample of psychosomatic rehabilitation inpatients. *The Clinical Neuropsychologist, 34*(5), 1004–1024. https://doi.org/10.1080/13854046.2019.1694073

Merten, T., Merckelbach, H., Giger, P., & Stevens, A. (2016). The Self-Report Symptom Inventory (SRSI): A new instrument for the assessment of distorted symptom endorsement. *Psychological Injury and Law, 9*(2), 102–111. https://doi.org/10.1007/s12207-016-9257-3

Mittenberg, W., Patton, C., Canyock, E. M., & Condit, D. C. (2002). Base rates of malingering and symptom exaggeration. *Journal of Clinical and Experimental Neuropsychology, 24*(8), 1094–1102. https://doi.org/10.1076/jcen.24.8.1094.8379

Mogge, N. L., & LePage, J. P. (2004). The Assessment of Depression Inventory (ADI): A new instrument used to measure depression and to detect honesty of response. *Depression and Anxiety, 20*(3), 107–113. https://doi.org/10.1002/da.20033

Mogge, N. L., Steinberg, J. S., Fremouw, W., & Messer, J. (2008). The Assessment of Depression Inventory (ADI): An appraisal of validity in an outpatient sample. *Depression and Anxiety, 25*(1), 64–68. https://doi.org/10.1002/da.20247

Moritz, S., Ferahli, S., & Naber, D. (2004). Memory and attention performance in psychiatric patients: Lack of correspondence between clinician-rated and patient-rated functioning with neuropsychological test results. *Journal of the International Neuropsychological Society, 10*(4), 623–233. https://doi.org/10.1017/S1355617704104153

Moritz, S., Stöckert, K., Hauschildt, M., Lill, H., Jelinek, L., Beblo, T., Dietrich, S., & Arlt, S. (2017). Are we exaggerating neuropsychological impairment in depression? Reopening a closed chapter. *Expert Review of Neurotherapeutics, 17*(8), 839–846. https://doi.org/10.1080/14737175.2017.1347040

Pavlova, B., & Uher, R. (2020). Assessment of psychopathology: Is asking questions good enough? *JAMA Psychiatry, 77*(6), 557–558. https://doi.org/10.1001/jamapsychiatry.2020.0108

Porter, R. J., Bourke, C., & Gallagher, P. (2007). Neuropsychological impairment in major depression: Its nature, origin and clinical significance. *Australian and New Zealand Journal of Psychiatry, 41*(2), 115–128. https://doi.org/10.1080/00048670601109881

Puente-López, E., Pina, D., López-López, R., González Ordi, H., Boskovic, I., & Merten, T. (2023). Prevalence estimates of symptom feigning and malingering in Spain. *Psychological Injury and Law, 16*(1), 1–17. https://doi.org/10.1007/s12207-022-09458-w

Rees, L. M., Tombaugh, T. N., & Boulay, L. (2001). Depression and the test of memory malingering. *Archives of Clinical Neuropsychology, 16*(5), 501–506. https://doi.org/10.1016/S0887-6177(00)00064-0

Rock, P. L., Roiser, J. P., Riedel, W. J., & Blackwell, A. D. (2014). Cognitive impairment in depression: A systematic review and meta-analysis. *Psychological Medicine, 44*(10), 2029–2040. https://doi.org/10.1017/S0033291713002535

Rogers, R., Bender, S. D., & Tazi, K. Y. (2025, in press). Forensics: Methodological challenges and empirical evidence. In G. Young, T. Bailey, L. Giromini, J. R. Soble, R. Rogers, & B. Levitt (Eds.), *Handbook of psychological injury and law* (pp. 47–74). Springer Nature.

Rohling, M. L., Green, P., Allen, L., & Iverson, G. L. (2002). Depressive symptoms and neurocognitive test scores in patients passing symptom validity tests. *Archives of Clinical Neuropsychology, 17*(3), 205–222. https://doi.org/10.1016/S0887-6177(01)00109-3

Rowland, J. A., Miskey, H. M., Brearly, T. W., Martindale, S. L., & Shura, R. D. (2017). Word Memory Test performance across cognitive domains, psychiatric presentations, and mild traumatic brain injury. *Archives of Clinical Neuropsychology, 32*(1), 306–315. https://doi.org/10.1093/arclin/acw107

Roy, T., & Lloyd, C. E. (2012). Epidemiology of depression and diabetes: A systematic review. *Journal of Affective Disorders, 142*, S8–S21. https://doi.org/10.1016/S0165-0327(12)70004-6.

Ryttersgaard, T. O., Johnsen, S. P., Riis, J. Ø., Mogensen, P. H., & Bjarkam, C. R. (2020). Prevalence of depression after moderate to severe traumatic brain injury among adolescents and young adults: A systematic review. *Scandinavian Journal of Psychology, 61*(2), 297–306. https://doi.org/10.1111/sjop.12587.

Santamaría, P., Capilla Ramírez, P., & González Ordi, H. (2013). Prevalencia de simulación en incapacidad temporal: Percepción de los profesionales de la salud [Health professionals' perceptions of prevalence of malingering of temporary disability in Spain]. *Clínica y Salud, 24*(3), 139–151. https://doi.org/10.1016/S1130-5274(13)70015-X

Schmidt, T., Lanquillon, S., & Ullmann, U. (2011). Kontroverse zu Beschwerdenvalidierungsverfahren bei der Begutachtung psychischer Störung [Controversy of symptom validity assessment in forensic evaluation of mental disorders]. *Forensische Psychiatrie, Psychologie, Kriminologie, 5*(3), 177–183. https://doi.org/10.1007/s11757-011-0113-8

Semkovska, M., Quinlivan, L., O'Grady, T., Johnson, R., Collins, A., O'Connor, J., Knittle, H., Ahern, E., & Gload, T. (2019). Cognitive function following a major depressive episode: A systematic review and meta-analysis. *Lancet Psychiatry, 6*(10), 851–861. https://doi.org/10.1016/S2215-0366(19)30291-3

Sherman, E. M. S., Slick, D. J., & Iverson, G. L. (2020). Multidimensional malingering criteria for neuropsychological assessment: A 20-year update of the malingered neuropsychological dysfunction criteria. *Archives of Clinical Neuropsychology, 35*(6), 735–764. https://doi.org/10.1093/arclin/acaa019

Shura, R., Schroeder, R. W., Ord, A. S., Bieu, R. K., O'Connor, V. L., Magnante, A. T., Snodgrass, M., Miskey, H. M., Martindale, S. L., & Rowland, J. A. (2024). Symptom validity indices for the Beck Depression Inventory–II: Development and cross-validation in research and clinical samples. *The Clinical Neuropsychologist*. Advance online publication. https://doi.org/10.1080/13854046.2024.2432058

Slick, D. J., Sherman, E. M., & Iverson, G. L. (1999). Diagnostic criteria for malingered neurocognitive dysfunction: Proposed standards for clinical practice and research. *The Clinical Neuropsychologist, 13*(4), 545–561. https://doi.org/10.1076/1385-4046 (199911)13:04;1–Y;FT545.

Steffan, J., Clopton, J., & Morgan, R. (2003). An MMPI-2 scale to detect malingered depression (Md Scale). *Assessment, 10*(4), 382–392. https://doi.org/10.1177/1073191103259548

Stevens, A., Schmidt, D., & Hautzinger, M. (2018). Major depression – a study on the validity of clinicians' diagnoses in medicolegal assessment. *Journal of Forensic Psychiatry & Psychology, 29*(5), 794–809. https://doi.org/10.1080/14789949.2018.1477974

Tart-Zelvin, A., Navis, B. A., Lamping, E. M., Langenecker, S. A., Ryan, K. A., McInnis, M. G., & Marshall, D. F. (2023). Low rate of performance validity failures among individuals with bipolar disorder. *Journal of the International Neuropsychological Society, 23*(3), 298–305. https://doi.org/10.1017/S1355617722000145

Thomson, C. M., Lin, H., & Parsloe, S. (2018). Misrepresenting health conditions through fabrication and exaggeration: An adaptation and replication of the false alarm effect. *Health Communication, 33*(5), 562–575. https://doi.org/10.1080/10410236.2017.1283563

van der Heide, D., Boskovic, I., van Harten, P., & Merckelbach, H. (2020). Overlooking feigning behavior may result in potential harmful treatment interventions: Two cases of undetected malingering. *Journal of Forensic Sciences, 65*(4), 1371–1375. https://doi.org/10.1111/1556-4029.14320

Viglione, D. J., & Giromini, L. (2020). *Inventory of Problems–29*. Professional Manual. IOP-Test, LLC.

Widows, M. R., & Smith, G. P. (2005). *SIMS. Structured Inventory of Malingered Symptomatology. Professional manual*. Psychological Assessment Resources.

Yanez, T. Y., Fremouw, W., Tennant, J., Strunk, J., & Coker, K. (2006). Effects of severe depression on TOMM performance among disability-seeking outpatients. *Archives of Clinical Neuropsychology, 16*(2), 161–165. https://doi.org/10.1016/j.acn.2005.07.009

Zaninotto, L., Solmi, M., Veronese, N., Guglielmo, R., Ioime, L., Camardese, G., & Serretti, A. (2016). A meta-analysis of cognitive performance in melancholic versus non-melancholic unipolar depression. *Journal of Affective Disorders, 201*, 15–24. https://doi.org/10.1016/j.jad.2016.04.039

24 The Feigned Trifecta

Malingered Psychopathology, Cognitive Disorder, and Somatic Disorders

Anthony P. De Marco and Joel E. Morgan

The ultimate goal of the forensic neuropsychologist practicing within a medicolegal context is to provide an independent, unbiased opinion on an examinee's presenting symptomatology based on empirically supported methods and neuropsychological knowledge. Ethical decision-making requires the forensic neuropsychologist to intricately weave together data gathered from record review, interview of the examinee, behavioral observations, and psychometric testing, while incorporating existing neuropsychological, medical, neurologic, and psychiatric literature when rendering an accurate and unbiased expert opinion. Within a typical referral question, regardless of the referral source, is the claim that the examinee's symptoms, whether developed or acquired, have reached some degree of disability that has adversely impacted his or her functioning. As can be seen from other chapters in this collection, many of those questions involve singular symptom presentations with specific deficits claimed due to a specific referral incident, such as the case of an individual claiming cognitive impairment due to a traumatic brain injury or posttraumatic symptomology/emotional distress in response to an identified stressor. Other referral questions are more complex and involve a conflated symptom presentation that is more diffuse and vague in nature, potentially involving multiple biological and psychiatric systems. These questions may include, but not be limited to, conditions such as "post-concussion syndrome," chronic pain, chronic fatigue, fibromyalgia or other somatosensory disorders, or, more recently, the syndrome of "Long-COVID," all of which present with a host of nonspecific cognitive, somatic, neurological, and/or emotional symptoms. These ambiguous presentations are often without well-identified or generally accepted etiological mechanisms or pathways, or a clear timeline of symptom progression or exacerbation. As a result, these referral questions are more complex, and it is up to the forensic neuropsychologist to opine as to whether the examinee's symptom presentation and observed psychometric data are diagnostically consistent with the claimed disorder(s).

An integral part of the forensic neuropsychological decision-making process involves determining whether there is symptom magnification or exaggeration through the administration of performance and symptom validity measures, consistent with current practice guidelines (Sweet et al., 2021), as well as examining the diagnostic consistency between an examinee's presentation and claimed diagnosis(es). Enter the question of malingering. In 2020, Sherman and colleagues (Sherman et al., 2020) provided updated criteria for malingered neuropsychological dysfunction based on the original criteria proposed by Slick, Sherman, and Iverson in 1999 (Slick et al., 1999). The updated criteria, which are multidimensional in nature, not only incorporate an additional two decades of empirically based literature on malingered neuropsychological conditions but also improve diagnostic accuracy by incorporating symptom/presentation discrepancies and employing performance and

DOI: 10.4324/9781003005063-28

symptom validity measures in supporting the diagnosis of malingered cognitive, somatic, and psychiatric conditions.

Along these lines, neuropsychologists are often asked to assess examinees as part of long-term disability insurance reviews. It is not always clear on what basis the initial disability determinations were made, but in many cases, symptom magnification/exaggeration or malingering is not considered. For instance, the Social Security Administration (SSA) defines disability as when an individual is

> not be able to engage in any substantial gainful activity (SGA) because of a medically determinable physical or mental disability(ies) that is either: Expected to result in death or Has lasted or is expected to last for a continuous period of at least 12 months.
>
> (SSA, August 2023)

In performing disability evaluations, the SSA discourages the use of empirically supported performance and symptom validity measures, which they refer to as "malingering tests." More specifically, in the SSA's Program Operations Manual System (POMS), DI 22510.005, the recommendation is:

> Do not purchase an SVT or other metrics designed to address inconsistent symptoms or behavior as part of a CE [consultative examination]. There is no test that, when passed or failed, conclusively determines the claimant's motivation. Malingering requires a deliberate attempt to deceive.
>
> (SSA, 2013)

Of relevant note, it has been documented that malingering occurs in up to 60% adults who are subjected to SSA examinations, which have significant fiscal and societal implications and expense (Chafetz & Underhill, 2013). As such, it has been recommended by the American Academy of Clinical Neuropsychology (AACN) in a 2015 position paper that the SSA's longstanding policy dissuading the use of performance/symptom validity measures be reversed by supporting the use of such measures during consultative examinations. In fact, validity testing is a well-established consideration when claimants are referred for independent medical examinations (IMEs) in the context of private disability claims (see Fiano, in this book).

Along with complex symptom presentations and questionable policy regarding disability determinations, the forensic neuropsychologist's role in the context of long-term benefit re-evaluations is further complicated by potential iatrogenesis of prior practitioners and entrenched self-beliefs of the examinee. By the time of the independent evaluation, not only have claimants been determined to be disabled through an arguably incomplete evaluation process and been receiving disability benefits for an extended period of time, but they also likely have been participating in some form of ongoing treatment of the claimed illness or disability, despite the possibility of unidentified malingered symptomatology. At that point, the belief of disability may have become entrenched in the claimant's self-view and is often perpetuated and maintained by ongoing treatment efforts by often well-intended clinicians, who consider the symptoms to be permanent, disabling, and refractory to treatment. The debate regarding the accuracy of clinical judgment alone in psychology, that is in the absence of psychometric data, has been longstanding (Meehl, 1954), and it is accepted that clinical judgment in isolation certainly can increase a provider's susceptibility to inaccurate conclusions. Occasionally, a claimant presents with a palpable sense of pride in having a presentation that has "never been seen before" by his/her practitioners, or the presentation being so severe or unique that it is "difficult to treat." The chronification of a condition or subjective symptoms (e.g., somatic, cognitive, and/or emotional/behavioral), no matter how bizarre or blatantly feigned, is a manifestation of iatrogenesis to which no practitioner, medical or behavioral, is immune. This highlights the importance of multidimensional assessment, including symptom/performance validity, not only during a neuropsychological/ psychological evaluation, but also as part of treatment. Addressing symptom inconsistencies or invalidity with the individual, as unidentified functional neurological disorder, somatic symptom disorder, and/or malingering is essential as such a presentation will undoubtedly be associated with negative treatment outcomes and may lead to iatrogenic harm. To assist clinicians with this, Martin and Schroeder (2022) developed a collaborative-therapeutic framework for providing feedback to patients in the context of invalid neuropsychological testing that likely can be successfully adapted and applied in other psychological and medical settings. For instance, models of therapeutically conveying diagnosis, optimizing treatment outcome, and reducing iatrogenic harm have been well studied in functional neurological disorders (Mcloughlin et al., 2025; Pierce & Albert, 2022).

In this chapter, we present the case of a woman whose complex presentation involved somatic, cognitive, and psychological symptoms. She displayed an entrenched self-view that she is disabled, a view that was perpetuated by her well-intended, but ultimately misinformed, treating psychologist. This case exemplifies the importance and utility of a multidimensional, forensic neuropsychological evaluation, integrating data from various sources and rendering empirically supported expert opinions in the context of existing literature.

The Case of Mrs. J

Case Synopsis. Mrs. J is a 45-year-old, married female, who at the time of the evaluation, had been out of work and on private disability for approximately three years, initially due to a foot injury, but then due to symptoms associated with a diagnosis of posttraumatic stress disorder (PTSD). In addition to emotional symptoms, Mrs. J endorsed physical and cognitive symptoms, all of which reportedly interfered with her ability to function day to day; she stated, "Every day is very hard." Inconsistencies were readily noted, as the claimant stated that "waking up is a challenge" but also noted that to "stay asleep is also a challenge." She endorsed nightmares and "difficulty talking about things," and she firmly believed that she was unable to "get better." An independent neuropsychological evaluation was requested by her private disability insurance carrier to objectively characterize the claimant's neurocognitive and emotional functioning to gain a better understanding of her level of disability, if at all present.

Social History. Mrs. J completed 16 years of formal education, along with some graduate studies; a history of learning difficulty or attention-based disorder was not reported. The claimant worked as a high school teacher, although she had not worked in three years. When asked about the duration of her last teaching position, she responded that she did not know. She also did not know the location of her previous teaching assignment, or the duration of that tenure either. Mrs. J began receiving disability benefits approximately two and a half years ago, which recently were terminated, as updated records/information did not substantiate her claim. As previously mentioned, the claimant characterized her daily functioning as "very hard," and a family member provided assistance with household chores and activities of daily living. She continues to drive, including driving herself to the current evaluation.

Medical History. Medical history was unremarkable, although Mrs. J initially stopped working due to a foot injury. She reported being prescribed medications for panic attacks at the current time, but she was unable to provide the name of the medications or prescribing physician.

History of Presenting Situation: Mrs. J initially stopped working approximately three years prior to the current evaluation initially due to a foot injury, but she remained out of work due to reported PTSD symptoms. Mrs. J reported that she was the victim of sexual and emotional abuse as a pre-teen. She then noted that, while working as a teacher, she was "verbally abused" by another teacher and felt unsupported by school administrators. These events then reportedly resulted in severe psychiatric symptoms, including PTSD symptoms related to her childhood trauma, which her treating psychologist opined was "delayed onset PTSD." Prior to her leave of absence, despite her reported history, Mrs. J was able to successfully complete her undergraduate studies, maintain gainful employment, and manage her household responsibilities.

Records from her treating psychologist, Dr. L, stated that the claimant experienced severe psychological distress with intense anxiety, depression, intrusive trauma-related thoughts, and dissociative flashbacks associated with trauma experienced in childhood, all subjectively reported. Symptoms reported by the claimant included hypervigilance, disturbed sleep, depressed mood, fear and anxiety, gastrointestinal symptoms, heightened startle response, detachment and depersonalization, and derealization. Several of these symptoms, including the dissociative flashbacks, derealization, and depersonalization, were new and more severe symptoms that were never experienced in the past. Again, these symptoms were self-reported by Mrs. J in the absence of corroboration either through behavioral observations or objective psychometric measures. There were variable claims of cognitive symptoms by the examinee in existing records, with some describing reports of poor concentration, while others contained observations of normal cognition. Mrs. J was deemed by Dr. L to be "disabled" and "not functional." Dr. L's records did not discuss or describe the nature of the claimed functional impairments (such as the manner, behaviors, functions, or activities that are adversely impacted) other than general statements, such as Mrs. J being unable to function or unable to work. The claimant's response to treatment was very slow and her prognosis was considered to be guarded.

Mental Status and Behavioral Observations. Mrs. J presented neatly dressed and with normal hygiene. She appeared younger than her stated age. Speech was productive and prosodic, but sparse and of limited content. She did not fully answer questions, making the clinical interview challenging. Thought processes were logical, with no indication of a thought disorder or departure from normal reality testing. Mood was dysphoric, and her affect was labile but, at times, constricted. There were no signs of depersonalization or other severe psychiatric features. While superficially cooperative, she did not complete the standardized questionnaire used for intake purposes. During testing, of note, there was an observed episode of emesis, which appeared intentionally produced. The examinee coughed and coughed and vomited a tiny amount of water she had been drinking in the wastepaper basket.

Test Results

Performance Validity: Results of performance validity tests (PVTs) are shown in Table 24.1. The claimant performed markedly below established cut-offs on all PVTs. On the first trial of the Test of Memory Malingering (TOMM; Tombaugh, 1997), Mrs. J's score of 23

Table 24.1 Performance Validity Test Results

Test	*Raw*	*Classification*
TOMM		
Trial 1	23	Fail; Invalid responding
GMSVT		
Immediate Recall	35	Fail; Invalid responding
Delayed Recall	40	Fail; Invalid responding
Consistency	65	Fail; Invalid responding
VSVT		
Easy Items	3	Fail; Below chance
Difficult Items	4	Fail; Below chance
Total Items	7	Fail; Below chance
RDS	0	Fail; Invalid responding
CVLT-3		
Forced-Choice Recogn.	2/16	Fail; Below chance

revealed invalid responding (i.e., chance level performance). On Green's Medical Symptom Validity Test (GMSVT; Green, 2004), her immediate and delayed recall scores of 35% and 40%, respectively, strongly indicated invalid responding. The Victoria Symptom Validity Test (VSVT; Slick et al., 1997) also showed below chance responding, as easy items correct was 3/24 and difficult items correct was 4/24. The overall score of total items correct 7/48 was determined to be below chance performance, as a score this low can only be obtained by chance one time out of 10,000. The claimant obtained a reliable digit scale score (RDS) of 0 on the Wechsler Adult Intelligence Scale-Fourth Edition (WAIS-IV; Wechsler, 2008), as she was unable to recite any digits forward or in reverse. Similarly, the forced-choice recognition score on the California Verbal Learning Test-Third Edition was 2 out 16, which is a below chance performance (CVLT-3; Delis et al., 2017).

Symptom Validity: Symptom validity test (SVT) scores are presented in Table 24.2. On the Structured Inventory of Malingered Symptomatology (SIMS; Smith & Burger, 1997), Mrs. J's score of 39 was above the recommended cutoff score of 23 used to identify invalid responding. Four validity scales on the Minnesota Multiphasic Personality Inventory-Second Edition-Restructured Form (MMPI-2-RF; Ben-Porath & Tellegen, 2008/2011) were remarkably elevated with T scores of 119 and 120: Infrequent Response (F-r T-score: 120), Infrequent Psychopathology Responses (Fp-r T-score: 119), Infrequent Somatic Responses (Fs T-score: 120), and Response Bias Scale (RBS T-score: 120). Of note, The Symptom Validity Scale (FBS-r) T-score was also substantially elevated at 111T. The Atypical Response Scale on the Trauma Symptom Inventory-Second Edition (TSI-2; Briere, 2011), was elevated to the 99th percentile. On the Inventory of Problems-29 (IOP-29; Viglione & Giromini, 2020), her false disorder probability score was 0.96.

Impressions based on PVTs and SVTs: As can be seen, scores across many of the administered PVTs, both formal and embedded, were deemed to be below chance level of responding; therefore, the only reasonable explanation was that Mrs. J purposefully and with a conscious effort chose the wrong responses. Conversely, by doing so, she must have known what the correct response would be. This level and style of responding is only seen in individuals feigning cognitive impairment, as such scores are not observed even in

Table 24.2 Symptom Validity Test Results

SIMS	*Raw*		
Neurologic Imp.	11		
Affective Disorders	11		
Psychosis	5		
Low Intelligence	8		
Amnestic Disorders	15		
Total	39		Invalid responding
MMPI-2-RF			
Scale	Raw	T-Score	Classification
F-r	24	120	Invalid responding
$F_{P\text{-}r}$	9	119	Invalid responding
Fs	11	120	Invalid responding
FBS-r	27	111	Invalid responding
RBS	22	120	Invalid responding
VRIN-r	1	39	Normal
TRIN-r	9	65F	Normal
TSI-2	Raw	T-Score	Classification
Response Level	2	56	Normal
Atypical Response	23	>100	Invalid responding
IOP-29	Raw		Classification
FDS	0.96		Noncredible Presentation

Table 24.3 Cognitive Test Results

CVLT-3	*Raw*	*Standard/Scaled Score*	*Classification*
List A Total Trials 1–5	6	45	Extremely low
List A Short Delayed Recall	0	1	Extremely low
List A Long Delayed Recall	0	1	Extremely low

neurodegenerative disease processes. Additionally, SVTs revealed scores that clearly indicated noncredible report of psychopathology, cognitive concerns, and somatic complaints, and were highly atypical even among various clinical samples.

Cognitive Test Results: Due to the blatant response bias revealed by PVTs and SVTs, only Digit Span and the CVLT-3 were administered; the results of the CVLT-3 are presented in Table 24.3. As illustrated, Mrs. J's overall learning was at the <0.1 percentile, as were her short and long delay recall scores (0/16; 0.1 percentile).

Concluding Remarks

This independent evaluation was one that is not uncommon to the forensic neuropsychologist, as it was requested by an individual's insurance carrier to determine the nature and extent of neuropsychological disability. The claimant was seen after being deemed disabled by her treating psychologist and having received disability benefits for approximately two and a half years. While the primary reason for disability was a diagnosis of PTSD, Mrs. J presented with diffuse neuropsychological and somatic complaints, all of which purportedly interfered with her ability to function daily in a meaningful and gainful manner. Her constellation of symptoms was claimed to be associated with significant functional impact, yet she was able to drive to the current evaluation and interact normally with the examiner; if her cognitive test scores had been judged to be valid, she arguably would have needed to be reported to the DMV for consideration of removal of her license due to cognitive dysfunction. Also of note, on interview, she claimed inability to recall older, overlearned information (e.g., the location of a previous teaching position, the durations of teaching positions, the name of her current prescribing physician), which is an unlikely pattern of memory loss. Of additional relevance, her markedly impaired cognitive scores (Digit Span, CVLT-3) are not found in patients with credible PTSD; PTSD patients who pass PVTs and SVTs do not differ from controls in cognitive function (Wisdom et al., 2014). Finally, her claimed episode of "emesis" during the evaluation is a highly unusual and overly dramatic expression of emotional distress.

The examinee's entire claim, up until the current independent evaluation, was based on self-report and the opinion of her well-intended, yet misguided, psychologist, who opined that Mrs. J was "disabled" and "not functional." Functional impairments or deficits were never properly documented, nor were objective psychometric measures of performance or symptom validity used when the treating psychologist formulated their diagnostic impressions.

Returning to the Sherman, Slick, and Iverson revised multidimensional criteria for identifying neurocognitive, somatic, and psychiatric malingering, Mrs. J fulfilled (A) the presence of an external incentive; (B) invalid presentation on examination, indicative of feigning or exaggeration, which requires psychometric evidence (as determined by PVTs or SVTs); and (C) compelling inconsistencies pertaining to the cognitive, somatic, and/or psychiatric symptoms and observed level of functioning. Other conditions that may contribute to the examinee's presentation (e.g., developmental, medical, or psychiatric conditions; Criterion (D), were not corroborated by record review. Her exceptionally low scores across multiple PVTs (including below chance scores), and significantly elevated scores on multiple SVTs made the possibility of a false-positive finding essentially zero.

This case clearly illustrates several vital points that are well-known to and accepted by the forensic neuropsychologist. First, the use of PVTs and SVTs is essential not only during assessments, but also during treatment as misdiagnosis has significant financial, societal, and clinical implications.

Second, this case is an example that well-intended, yet misguided, treating providers may complicate matters through the failure to assess for invalidity, as these providers are implicitly reinforcing and perpetuating such behaviors and the entrenched self-view that one is, in fact, "disabled" and that their symptoms are resistant to treatment. Yet, in this particular case, it is likely that the claimant's self-view is really not one of being *actually* disabled: Her blatant below chance performance on a PVT and grossly over-reported emotional symptoms are more fitting with overt malingering (within the context of her pursuit of maintaining an external incentive) than being a "true believer."

Third, this case illustrates the importance of delving deeply into an examinee's file. In this case, the claimant ostensibly was traumatized earlier in life, sexually and emotionally abused as a pre-teen. Despite this, she went on to accomplish normal, substantial life achievements, i.e., completing her education and maintaining gainful employment. If she was symptomatic, she was well defended and coped. This history would suggest the claimant to be a resourceful, resilient person with considerable fortitude, who despite early emotional and physical trauma, lived an apparently normal life. With this background, then, why would a seemingly less traumatic work-related event be so devastating as to disable her? Here the examiner must take note of the apparent inconsistency in the claimant's overall presentation.

Finally, our case of the blatantly feigned trifecta exemplifies the inherent flaws and implications of the SSA's longstanding policy dissuading the use of "malingering tests" (as they refer to them). This case supports the position statement by the AACN supporting the use of PVTs and SVTs during SSA consultative examinations in order to provide the most accurate and empirically supported diagnostic impressions.

References

Ben-Porath, Y. S., & Tellegen, A. (2008/2011). *MMPI-2-RF (Minnesota Multiphasic Personality Inventory-2 Restructured Form): Manual for Administration, Scoring, and Interpretation*. Minneapolis: University of Minnesota Press.

Briere, J. (2011). *Trauma Symptom Inventory-2 Professional Manual*. Odessa, FL: Psychological Assessment Resources.

Chafetz, M., & Underhill, J. (2013). Estimated costs of malingered disability. *Archives of Clinical Neuropsychology*, Nov, *28*(7), 633–639. https://doi.org/10.1093/arclin/act038. Epub 2013 Jun 25. PMID: 23800432.

Chafetz, M. D., Williams, M. A., Ben-Porath, Y. S., Bianchini, K. J., Boone, K. B., Kirkwood, M. W., ... Ord, J. S. (2015). Official position of the American academy of clinical neuropsychology social security administration policy on validity testing: Guidance and recommendations for change. *The Clinical Neuropsychologist*, *29*(6), 723–740.

Delis, D. C., Kramer, J. H., Kaplan, E., & Ober, B. A. (2017). *California Verbal Learning Test, Third Edition (CVLT-3)*. San Antonio, TX: Pearson.

Green, P. (2004). *Green's Medical Symptom Validity Test (MSVT) for Microsoft Windows:User's Manual*. Edmonton, Canada: Green's Publishing.

Martin, P. K., & Schroeder, R. W. (2022). A framework for providing clinical feedback when patients invalidate testing. In R. W. Schroeder & P. K. Martin (Eds.), *Validity Assessment in Clinical Neuropsychological Practice: Evaluating and Managing Noncredible Performance* (pp. 47–69). The Guilford Press.

Mcloughlin, C., Lee, W. H., Carson, A., & Stone, J. (2025). Iatrogenic harm in functional neurological disorder, *Brain*, *148*(1), 27–38.

Meehl, P. E. (1954). *Clinical versus Statistical Prediction*. Minneapolis: University of Minnesota Press.

Pierce, M. E., & Albert, D. V. F. (2022). Delivering the diagnosis: A practical approach to a patient with a functional neurological disorder. *Seminars in Pediatric Neurology*, *41*, 100948. https://doi.org/10.1016/j.spen.2021.100948. Epub 2021 Dec 2. PMID:35450673.

Sherman, E. M. S., Slick, D. J., & Iverson, G. L. (2020). Multidimensional malingering criteria for neuropsychological assessment: A 20-year update of the malingered neuropsychological dysfunction criteria. *Archives of Clinical Neuropsychology*, Aug 28, *35*(6), 735–764.

Slick, D., Hopp, G., Strauss, E., & Thompson, G. B. (1997). *VSVT: Victoria Symptom Validity Test (Version 1.0)*. Odessa, FL: Psychological Assessment Resources.

Slick, D. J., Sherman, E. M., & Iverson, G. L. (1999). Diagnostic criteria for malingered neurocognitive dysfunction: proposed standards for clinical practice and research. *The Clinical Neuropsychologist*, Nov, *13*(4), 545–561.

Smith, G. P., & Burger, G. K. (1997). Detection of malingering: Validation of the Structured Inventory of Malingered Symptomatology (SIMS). *Journal of the American Academy on Psychiatry and Law*, *25*, 180–183.

Social Security Administration (Effective Dates: 04/08/2013-Present). DI 22510.005- When to Purchase a Consultative Examination (CE). https://policy.ssa.gov/poms.nsf/lnx/0422510005.

Social Security Administration Publication No. 64-030, (Red Book), August 2023, ICN 436900. https://www.ssa.gov/redbook/index.html.

Sweet, J. J., Heilbronner, R. L., Morgan, J. E., Larrabee, G. J., Rohling, M. L., ... Boone, K. B. (2021). American Academy of Clinical Neuropsychology (AACN) 2021 consensus statement on validity assessment: Update of the 2009 AACN consensus conference statement on neuropsychological assessment of effort, response bias, and malingering. *The Clinical Neuropsychologist*, *35*(6), 1053–1106. https://doi.org/10.1080/13854046.2021.1896036

Tombaugh, T. N. (1997). The Test of Memory Malingering (TOMM): Normative data from cognitively intact and cognitively impaired individuals. *Psychological Assessment*, *9*(3), 260–268. https://doi.org/10.1037/1040-3590.9.3.260

Viglione, D. J., & Giromini, L. (2020). *Inventory of Problems–29: Professional Manual.* IOP-Test, LLC.

Wechsler, D. (2008). *WAIS-IV administration and scoring manual.* San Antonio, TX: Psychological Corporation.

Wisdom, N. M., Pastorek, N. J., Miller, B. I., Booth, J. E., Romesser, J. M., Linck, J. F., & Sim, A. H. (2014). PTSD and cognitive functioning: Importance of including performance validity testing. *The Clinical Neuropsychologist*, *28*(1), 128–145.

25 The Workers' Compensation System in the United States

The Case of Mr. S

Howard Oakes

The Workers' Compensation system in the United States is a cornerstone of employee rights and workplace safety, as well as providing financial protection for workers who suffer from job-related injuries or illnesses. Its inception can be traced back to the late 19th century, a time when industrialization was transforming the nation's workforce and workplaces. In the late 19th and early 20th centuries, industrialization brought about significant changes in the American labor force. Workers faced new and sometimes hazardous conditions in factories and mines; workplace injuries were rampant. At the time, employees had limited recourse to seek compensation for work-related injuries.

The first state to enact a comprehensive Workers' Compensation law was Wisconsin in 1911. This groundbreaking legislation provided a no-fault system, ensuring that workers received compensation for job-related injuries regardless of fault. Over the following decades, other states followed suit, creating a patchwork of laws and regulations. Although Worker' Compensation is primarily a state-level program, the federal government has played a role in shaping the system. The 1970 Occupational Safety and Health Act established federal safety standards to protect workers, complementing the Workers' Compensation system's goals.

Key Functions of Workers' Compensation

One of the fundamental principles of Workers' Compensation is the no-fault system. This means that employees do not need to prove employer negligence to receive benefits. Instead, they only need to demonstrate that their injury or illness occurred in the course of employment. This can also include cumulative injuries, rather than a specific work-related event.

Benefits

Workers' Compensation provides coverage for medical expenses associated with a work-related injury or illness that can include doctor's visits, hospital stays, surgery, rehabilitation, and medication. The system also offers wage replacement benefits to compensate for lost income due to a work-related injury or illness. Typically, this benefit amounts to a percentage of the worker's average weekly wage. When a worker cannot return to their previous job due to their injury, Workers' Compensation may also cover vocational rehabilitation to help them acquire new skills and find alternative employment.

DOI: 10.4324/9781003005063-29

Challenges and Reforms

Over the years, the cost of Workers' Compensation insurance has increased, leading to concerns among employers. These rising costs have prompted states to implement reforms aimed at reducing expenses while maintaining adequate benefits for injured workers. Disputes over Workers' Compensation claims can be contentious, with some cases ending up in litigation. Balancing the interests of employers and workers in a fair and efficient manner remains a challenge. The system's decentralized nature has resulted in varying regulations and benefits from one state to another. While this allows states to tailor their systems to local needs, it can also create disparities in worker protections. It also poses a challenge to health care providers who need to be familiar with the specific rules and regulations in which they are providing services, rather than overall national standards.

In conclusion, the Workers' Compensation system in the United States has evolved significantly since its formal inception in the early 20th century. It serves as a vital safety net for workers, providing medical benefits and wage replacement for those injured or who became ill due to their jobs. Although challenges persist, the system remains a crucial element of the American labor landscape, continuously adapting to meet the needs of workers and employers alike.

The Role of Neuropsychology

Neuropsychologists may find themselves involved in the Workers' Compensation system in multiple ways. This can be in the role of an acute care provider within a medical setting, performing clinical evaluations as part of ongoing care, providing ongoing treatment, or in the role of an independent evaluator.

The independent evaluation process in Workers' Compensation claims is a critical step in determining the validity of a claim and the extent of benefits or compensation that an injured worker is entitled to receive. This process is designed to ensure fairness and objectivity in assessing the injuries, disabilities, and related medical issues associated with a workplace injury or illness. The specific details of the independent evaluation process may vary depending on the jurisdiction and the insurance provider, but the general steps involved in a Workers' Compensation claim are as follows:

1 *Injury or Illness Report*: The process typically begins when an employee reports a workplace injury or illness to their employer. It is of critical importance for an employee to report such incidents promptly to ensure timely evaluation, demonstrate the role of the workplace in the injury or illness, and to initiate compensation.
2 *Initial Medical Treatment*: After reporting the injury or illness, the injured worker may receive initial medical treatment from a healthcare provider. This treatment may include first aid, emergency care, or referral to a specialist, depending on the nature and severity of the condition.
3 *Filing a Claim*: To initiate the Workers' Compensation process, the injured worker or their representative must file a Workers' Compensation claim with the relevant state Workers' Compensation board or agency. This claim includes details about the injury or illness, medical records, and any relevant supporting documentation.
4 *Insurance Company Review*: The insurance company that provides Worker's Compensation coverage for the employer will review the claim. They will assess whether the injury or illness is covered under Workers' Compensation and determine the initial benefits to be provided.

5 *Independent Medical Examination (IME)*: In many cases, the insurance company may request an IME, which can also be referred to as a Respondent's Medical Examination (RME). An IME or RME involves an evaluation by a medical professional who is independent of both the employer and the injured worker. This examination aims to provide an unbiased assessment of the worker's condition, including the cause, extent of injury or illness, treatment needed, and any work-related limitations.
6 *IME Report*: The independent medical examiner will generate a detailed report summarizing their findings. This report may be crucial in determining the validity of the claim and the extent of benefits the injured worker is entitled to receive.
7 *Claim Decision*: Based on the information gathered from the injured worker, healthcare providers, and the IME, the insurance company will make a decision regarding the Workers' Compensation claim. This decision may include approving or denying the claim, as well as specifying the type and amount of benefits, if approved.
8 *Appeals Process*: If the injured worker disagrees with the insurance company's decision, they generally have the right to appeal. The appeals process can involve hearings, legal representation, and additional medical assessments to resolve disputes.
9 *Benefit Payments*: If the claim is approved, the injured worker will start receiving Workers' Compensation benefits, which may include compensation for medical expenses, lost wages, vocational rehabilitation, and disability benefits, depending on the severity of the injury or illness.

In summary, it is important to note that the specific procedures and requirements for Workers' Compensation claims can vary by jurisdiction and it is critical for both injured workers and healthcare providers involved in their care to familiarize themselves with the rules and regulations in their area. Additionally, consulting with an attorney experienced in Workers' Compensation can be beneficial for navigating the process, especially if disputes or appeals become necessary.

The Independent Neuropsychological Evaluation

A quality neuropsychological IME can play a crucial role in the evaluation of a Workers' Compensation claim by providing objective, valid, and detailed findings to assist both with the evaluation of the claim by the insurer as well as to ensure the claimant receives the care appropriate to their condition (Lovejoy & Oakes, 2012). To be effective and trustworthy, IME providers should possess several key qualities and characteristics:

1 *Impartiality*: The most critical quality for an IME is its impartiality. Providers not only must be neutral and objective, without any bias toward the party requesting the examination, but also perceived as such by both parties. An unbiased assessment is essential in maintaining the credibility of the IME findings. IME providers should disclose any potential conflicts of interest or relationships that could compromise their impartiality. Transparency in this regard is essential.
2 *Neuropsychological expertise*: IME providers should be highly qualified and experienced within the field of neuropsychology. They should have demonstrable expertise in the specific condition(s) relevant to the case. Ethical practice includes deferring an evaluation referral that includes elements outside of the provider's scope of expertise. Credentials, certifications, and continuing education should be up to date.

3 *Thoroughness*: A good IME provider conducts a comprehensive and thorough evaluation of the patient's medical history, records, and impairing condition prior to conducting an evaluation. They should be cognizant of any information gaps in the records received and seek additional records and/or information as appropriate.
4 *Communication skills*: Effective communication is crucial for an IME provider to explain complex medical concepts and findings clearly and concisely to non-medical stakeholders, such as attorneys, judges, and insurance companies, as well as to other medical providers.
5 *Objectivity*: IMEs should base their assessments on objective medical evidence and scientific principles rather than personal opinions or conjecture. One must avoid making speculative statements without solid foundation.
6 *Integrity and ethics*: Maintaining a high level of professional ethics and integrity is paramount for IME providers. Adherence to ethical guidelines and practice standards established by professional associations and organizations is a basic requirement. IME providers should also conduct themselves professionally and maintain a respectful and compassionate attitude toward the individuals they are evaluating. Lack of sensitivity to the claimant's condition and concerns is not only inappropriate but likely will interfere with establishing the appropriate rapport needed to complete a thorough and reliable examination.
7 *Impartial documentation*: IME providers should document their findings accurately and impartially in their reports. Avoidance of overly technical language and jargon, providing test results in a consistent and comprehensible manner (i.e., Guilmette et al., 2020) as well as a clear and well-structured report is most likely to generate a useful examination report.
8 *Timeliness*: Timely reporting is crucial in such cases. IME providers should strive to complete their assessments promptly and deliver their reports within the agreed-upon time frame. Providers should be emphatic to the demands of both parties (the carrier and the claimant) to an expeditious administration of the claim.
9 *Availability for testimony*: IME providers may be required to testify in proceedings regarding their findings. This is more likely if there are markedly differing opinions regarding the presence of impairment, permanency, or return to work issues. If an IME provider is uncomfortable with the idea of testimony (including cross examination), they should take efforts to increase their skill and expertise in such or opt to defer engaging in independent examinations.
10 *Respect for confidentiality*: IME providers must respect claimant confidentiality and adhere to all relevant privacy regulations when handling medical records and information.
11 *Feedback responsiveness*: IME providers should be open to feedback and willing to address any concerns or questions from the parties involved in the case. This may include providing addendums to answer specific additional questions or to incorporate additionally obtained data (i.e., treatment records, surveillance).

Overall, a good IME provider serves as an unbiased and expert third-party evaluator, contributing to the fair and just resolution of Workers' Compensation claims.

The Case of Mr. S

Given the focus of this book, the following case is an example of an IME in which symptom and performance validity testing (as well as case history) raised concerns about the legitimacy of injuries associated with a Workers' Compensation claim. Consistent with maintaining the confidentiality and anonymity of the actual claimant, names as well as specific identifying details (including dates) have been altered but not the actual test findings or conclusions.

Background

Mr. S is a 59-year-old right-handed Caucasian male who was employed as a plumber when he was reportedly injured in a work-related accident on 6/19/19. His past medical and psychiatric history is largely unremarkable, with the exception of medically managed hyperlipidemia and hypertension. He completed a high school education as well as training and certification as a plumber. He has been married for 32 years and has two grown children who are fully independent. He has been employed by Better Plumbing for the past 16 years.

Employee's Complaint

In a narrative dated 2/2/21 from Mr. S's attorney, Mr. S has asserted sustaining "injuries of a severe and permanent nature" following an accident on 6/19/19 after his vehicle was hit from behind while he was waiting at a bus crossing. He has asserted injuries to his head, neck, back, and both knees. It was also asserted that he has and will continue to experience "pain, discomfort, emotional upset, limitation of motion and restriction of activity". He also reported having been confined to home or his bed from 6/19/19 to 7/1/19.

Record Review: Injury-Related Information

A Connecticut Uniform Police Crash Report indicates that Mr. S was at the intersection of Main Avenue and the town Busway at approximately 2:30 pm on 6/19/19. Mr. S was noted to have been the stopped and belted driver of a work panel van hit from behind by Mr. Orange. There was no reported airbag deployment and minor injuries were reported. Mr. S complained of head and neck pain and was transported to a local hospital. There was no reported loss of consciousness or reported confusion at the scene. Mr. S's vehicle was noted to be drivable, but to have a damaged rear bumper. Mr. Orange was cited for failure to drive a reasonable distance apart resulting in an automobile collision.

An ambulance report of 6/19/19 indicates that emergency medical services had been summoned to evaluate Mr. S by the local Police Department. By the time of the ambulance arrival, a cervical collar had been placed on Mr. S by a police medic. A Glasgow Coma Scale score of 15 was reported. Mr. S was noted to have been able to get out of his vehicle on his own, as well as able to walk to an awaiting stretcher. He was noted to have "minor neck and back pain". He complained of a headache, nausea, and thigh pain while en route to the hospital. Upon arrival at the hospital, he was transferred to their care.

Records from the hospital indicate that Mr. S reported a past history of hyperlipidemia and hypertension. He reported complaints of nausea and headache, and he was now also reporting bilateral knee pain that he thought resulted from his bracing for impact. He also reported having hit his head on the back of the seat. Loss of consciousness was again denied, as was any neurological change. There was no documentation of any trauma to his head, including bruising and/or sensitivity to touch. A cervical x-ray was completed without evidence of fracture. The conclusion was of the presence of a cervical strain and a strain of his knees. He was prescribed Naprosyn and discharged home after about four total hours at the hospital. He was advised to seek care if his symptoms worsened.

Record Review: Post-Injury History

Mr. S was seen for follow-up of his injuries five days later on 6/24/19 by Dr. Sienna at an occupational health clinic. Mr. S now reported that he had struck his head on the protective metal screen behind the driver's seat. He complained of a frontal headache, difficulty concentrating/processing, photophobia, and nausea. He also complained of bilateral knee discomfort. Previously reported left elbow discomfort had resolved. His physical examination did not reveal *any* trauma to the head. His neurological examination was notable for slowed responding and poor finger to nose ability. Dr. Sienna rendered diagnoses of concussion without loss of consciousness, muscle strain, and bilateral knee contusions. He was to rest for two to three days and then return before being cleared to resume working. A referral to physical therapy was made, but the records noted that it was not yet clear that such treatment was needed. Mr. S was advised to defer initiating physical therapy until seen for follow-up.

He returned on 6/27/19 to occupational medicine, and was seen by a different physician, Dr. Brown. Mr. S complained of headache, photophobia, and confusion. He also now reported mild dizziness. He reported that his symptoms had worsened after his visit on 6/24/19, but then again improved. Mr. S now asserted that he had suffered a loss of consciousness at the time of the accident. His neck and back strains were noted as improving. Based on Mr. S's new assertion of a loss of consciousness, Dr. Brown indicated a plan to obtain a head CT to rule-out an intracranial bleed. He was to be referred to a "concussion clinic" to start physical therapy the following week and then follow-up with occupational medicine on 7/1/19.

He returned on 7/1/19 and was seen by a third provider, an advanced practice registered nurse, Mr. Lavender. At this point, he had completed physical therapy (but was doing home exercises) and reported overall improvement. He reported that his remaining difficulties were limited to his feeling "slightly slow with his concentration and a vague airiness continues". He had not obtained the previously ordered head CT, so a new head CT was ordered. He was cleared to return to work the following day with restricted duty to seated work only and limited driving. No rationale was provided for a need to be seated nor were any other physical restrictions asserted.

Mr. S was seen by a physical therapist (Mr. Pink) on 7/1/19 and now reported that he was unable to clearly recall the day of the injury, was unsure of a loss of consciousness, and reported that he could not remember the accident fully. A plan of treatment was made with a goal of a return to full work duties by 7/16/19.

Mr. S was seen by Mr. Lavender again on 7/3/19. He reported feeling well and was informed the head CT from 7/1/19 was negative. Mr. S was to continue on restricted duty, again without any explanation for a seated work only restriction. He was to return after another physical therapy session in one week.

He was seen by Mr. Pink for another physical therapy session on 7/3/19 and complained of difficulty turning his neck and cervical pain. Additional sessions on 7/5/19, 7/8/19, and 7/10/19 were documented, with the exact same "Subjective" description.

Another medical evaluation was completed on 7/11/19 by Dr. Sienna. At this point, Mr. S reported that he was experiencing daily headaches, photophobia, and difficulties with memory, attention, and concentration. He reported being worried about his driving and reported being unable to follow multistep procedures. He also reported that his symptoms were worsened by "screen time". It was not documented when these symptoms had started, as they had been previously denied. Based on his self-report, he was to cease working pending a neurological follow-up at another hospital.

Mr. Pink noted another session of physical therapy on 7/11/19 and Mr. S was discharged with reported resolution of his neck pain. Mr. S was noted to not yet have had made a neurology appointment.

Mr. S was seen by Mr. Lavender again on 7/16/19. He again complained of marked cognitive difficulties. He was to remain out of work pending his neurological consultation.

Mr. S was seen by a neurology physician's assistant (PA), Mr. Purple, on 7/23/19. Mr. S now reported that he was unsure if he had hit his head in the accident. His reporting of symptoms was opined to be consistent with a Postconcussive Syndrome. There was discussion of further follow-up with neurology regarding his headache as well as obtaining neuropsychological testing. Mr. S was to follow-up with his Workers' Compensation provider for authorization of treatment.

Mr. S was next seen on 10/30/19 by a new neurologist, Dr. Lemon, *at the request of his attorney* (per the provided note). This visit was approximately four and a half months post accident; no rationale was provided for the approximately three-month gap in treatment. Mr. S had also reportedly been referred by Mr. Lavender to Dr. Lemon but no documentation of this referral was provided. Mr. S complained of neck pain, worsening headaches, and decreased concentration and reported losing his temper more easily. He now reported having no recall for "the event" and asserted that "his van was totaled". (Mr. S noted in his hearing testimony that he had actually driven the same vehicle after returning to work the following week.) He was noted to have returned to work the week after his injury on a limited basis. Mental status testing was normal. Mr. S agreed to cervical area epidural steroid injections. Dr. Lemon opined that if Mr. S's cervical strain improved, his headaches would decrease and his postconcussive symptoms also would.

Mr. S returned to see Dr. Lemon on 11/6/19 and reported a "20%" improvement. More steroid injections were completed, and he was to follow-up in two weeks.

Mr. S was seen for an initial visit at an orthopedic practice on 11/13/19. Multiple subsequent visits are documented in which it is not entirely clear whether he was seen by a PA, Mr. Neon, or by the orthopedist, Dr. Mango. At the visit on 11/13/19, Mr. S reported having suffered a loss of consciousness in the accident. He denied any headache. It was opined that he suffered from arthritis of both knees and that this had become exacerbated by the 6/19/19 accident. He was to again start physical therapy and take meloxicam.

He began a course of physical therapy on 11/20/19, which was completed on 12/10/19 with reported resolution of his neck issues.

He returned to see Dr. Lemon on 11/21/19 and reported that his neck pain had resolved and that his headaches were now 50% improved. Mr. S was also reporting cognitive dysfunction. Another steroid injection was completed.

He was cleared to return to work without orthopedic restrictions by Dr. Mango on 12/11/19 after reporting doing much better. However, he returned on 12/12/19 to see Dr. Lemon and again complained of cognitive difficulties. His neck was better. Dr. Lemon suggested another month off of work.

Mr. S returned on 1/9/20 to see Dr. Lemon and now reported only being able to look at the TV or his iPad for 20 minutes. He was prescribed nortriptyline 10 mg and again advised to follow-up in a month.

He was seen by occupational medicine on 1/10/20 and was noted as doing well and to be back to all normal activities, but he still had not returned to work.

Mr. S was seen by Dr. Lemon again on 2/5/20 and was now complaining of becoming easily tired. Dr. Lemon suggested a return to work to which Mr. S's response was that he would "think about it".

Provided information indicates that Mr. S went on a trip to Switzerland in March 2020 to visit his son and grandson. He traveled alone to and from Switzerland. He served on jury duty for a day and reported being positive for COVID-19 around 3/14 or 3/15/2020. He was noted to have had symptoms for approximately four days and then full resolution.

In a phone call to Dr. Lemon on 4/7/20, Mr. S requested two more months off from work. He complained of lights bothering his eyes at night. Dr. Lemon agreed to another two months off from work.

Mr. S was seen for an independent neurological examination on 5/12/20 by a Dr. Currant. Dr. Currant noted the *marked* discrepancy in Mr. S's reporting of the details of the accident over time with no head injury reported at the actual time of injury and only being reported later with increasing severity of injury being reported by Mr. S over time. Mr. S's performance on the Montreal Cognitive Assessment (MoCA) test was 27/30 with points lost solely on word recall. Dr. Currant concluded that Mr. S's reporting of details of the accident was not credible, that his clinical course did not makes sense (i.e., his reporting of resolved symptoms and then the symptoms returning months later), that no ongoing disability was attributable to the 6/19/19 accident, and that while he was at maximum medical improvement, the date at which maximum medical improvement had been attained was unclear.

Mr. S was next seen by Dr. Lemon on 12/16/20 and was again complaining of cognitive dysfunction. Another steroid injection was done.

Mr. S complained of neck stiffness to Dr. Lemon on 1/26/21 and another injection was done.

Mr. S reported on 3/3/21 to Dr. Lemon that he continued to feel unable to return to work.

After an eight-month absence, Mr. S returned to Dr. Lemon on 10/13/21 and complained of episodic headaches and memory problems. His mental status examination was again noted as normal. Dr. Lemon recommended screening laboratory tests to screen for dementia. He returned on 11/11/21 and his labs were normal. The first documented formal cognitive testing by Dr. Lemon was completed and was normal (MoCA=29/30). Mr. S was to follow-up in three months.

Mr. S returned to Dr. Lemon on 2/8/22 and again complained of cognitive dysfunction. He was referred for clinical neuropsychological evaluation, which never occurred.

Referral for the Current Evaluation

Mr. S was referred to me by a nurse case manager for the Workers' Compensation carrier by phone regarding the case. She was already familiar with my work and provided an overview of the case, which I felt was within my scope of expertise. We then reviewed the key players in the case to establish that I did not have an obvious conflict of interest. Next, we discussed my fees, an estimated turn around, and arranged for Ms. S's records to be provided to me in advance of a scheduled evaluation date. A deposit was requested and a copy of both my current Curriculum Vitae and billing policy were forwarded on to her.

Currently Reported Symptoms

Mr. S reported that his neck pain and headaches had resolved since his injury, but he was unable to identify any specific point in time in which this occurred. He described headaches as occurring a "couple of times" per week but that they are very short-lived and did not interfere with his activities. His primary complaint was of poor cognitive functioning, including poor attention and memory. Issues with smell and taste, vision, and/or hearing were denied.

He is independent in his basic activities of daily living, but he noted that tasks often take longer to complete. He noted some frustration with his Workers' Compensation carrier as well as employer. He indicated having long-standing conflict with his manager whom he felt had a lack of respect for his years of employment.

Test Results and Interpretation

Mr. S's test findings are presented in Tables 25.1 and 25.2. Performance on two stand-alone measures of performance validity and one of two embedded validity indicators were beyond

Table 25.1 Neuropsychological Test Data.

Test & Cognitive Domain	*Converted Score*	Percentile	*Score Range Label*
PVT			
MSVT Immediate Recognition	-	81%	Below cutoff
MSVT Delayed Recognition	-	88%	WNL
MSVT Consistency	-	73%	Below cutoff
MSVT Paired Associates	-	90%	-
MSVT Free Recall	-	50%	-
TOMM Trial 1, Trial 2	-	32, 41	Below cutoff
TOMM Retention	-	40	Below cutoff
RDS	-	10 raw	WNL
CVLT-3 Forced Choice	-	14/16 raw	Base rate <2.0
Neurocognitive Status / Intellectual Functioning			
TOPF Reading	SS = 107	68	Average
WAIS-IV Full Scale IQ (FSIQ); *prorated*	SS = 98	45	Average
WAIS-IV General Abilities Index; *prorated*	SS = 101	53	Average
Verbal Comprehension Index; *prorated*	SS = 114	82	High average
Perceptual Reasoning Index; *prorated*	SS = 88	21	Low average
Working Memory Index (WMI)	SS = 92	30	Average
Processing Speed Index (PSI)	SS = 97	42	Average
Language Functioning			
WAIS-IV Similarities	SS = 13	84	High average
WAIS-IV Vocabulary	SS = 11	63	Average
WAIS-IV Information	SS = 13	84	High average
BNT-2	T = 43	25	Average
FAS Fluency	T = 62	88	High average
Animal Fluency	T = 48	45	Average
Visual Perceptual Motor Processing			
WAIS-IV Block Design	SS = 9	37	Average
WAIS-IV Matrix Reasoning	SS = 8	25	Average
WAIS-IV Visual Puzzles	SS = 7	16	Low average
RCFT Copy	-	50	Average

(*Continued*)

Table 25.1 (Continued)

Test & Cognitive Domain	*Converted Score*	Percentile	*Score Range Label*
Motor Functioning			
Grooved Pegboard, Right (Drops = 0)	T = 52	55	Average
Grooved Pegboard, Left (Drops = 1)	T = 47	37	Average
Attention & Working Memory			
CVLT-3 Trial 1	SS = 80	9	Low average
CVLT-3 List B	SS = 90	25	Average
WAIS-IV Digit Span	SS = 8	25	Average
WAIS-IV Arithmetic	SS = 9	37	Average
Processing Speed			
WAIS-IV Symbol Search (Errors = 1)	SS = 10	50	Average
WAIS-IV Coding (Errors = 1)	SS = 9	37	Average
Trail Making Test A (Errors = 1)	T = 48	45	Average
Executive Functioning			
Trail Making Test B (Errors = 2)	T = 47	37	Average
WCST Categories Complete	2/6	11–16	Low average Note: 5 "other" responses
WCST Trials to Complete 1st Category	34	6–10	Low average
WCST Failure to Maintain Set	3		
WCST % Conceptual Level Responses	T = 47	37	Average
WCST % Perseverative Errors	T = 40	16	Low average
Learning and Memory			
CVLT-3 Trial 1	SS = 80	9	Low average
CVLT-3 Trials 1–5	SS = 7	16	Low average
CVLT-3 Delayed Recall	SS = 77	6	Below average
CVLT-3 Short-Delay Free Recall	SS = 8	25	Average
CVLT-3 Short-Delay Cued Recall	SS = 7	16	Low average
CVLT-3 Long-Delay Free Recall	SS = 6	9	Low average
CVLT-3 Long-Delay Cued Recall	SS = 4	2	Belo average
WMS-IV Logical Memory I	SS = 10	50	Average
WMS-IV Logical Memory II	SS = 6	9	Low average
WMS-IV Visual Reproduction I	SS = 9	37	Average
WMS-IV Visual Reproduction II	SS = 4	2	Below average
Visual Learning and Memory			
RCFT Immediate Recall	T = 43	25	Average
RCFT Delayed Recall	T = 33	5	Below average
RCFT Recognition Memory	T = 32	4	Below average

Note: Age-matched normative samples were used unless otherwise specified. Score descriptor labels are adapted from the AACN Consensus Conference Statement on Uniform Performance Test Score Labeling (Guilmette et al., 2020). Percentile indicates the percentage of people who obtained the same or lower scores on a given measure.

Table 25.2 Neuropsychological Test Data: MMPI-3.

MMPI-3 Validity Scales	*Standard Score*	*Percentile*	*Descriptor*
CRIN	T = 63	90	Not elevated
VRIN	T = 64	92	Not elevated
TRIN	T = 54F	66	Not elevated
F	T = 72	99	Elevated
Fp	T = 50	50	Not elevated
Fs	T = 58	79	Not elevated
FBS	T = 78	>99	Elevated
RBS	T = 87	>99	Elevated
L	T = 48	42	Not elevated
K	T = 56	73	Not elevated
MMPI-3 Clinical Scales			
EID	T = 48	42	Not elevated
THD	T = 44	27	Not elevated
BXD	T = 39	14	Not elevated
RCd	T = 51	54	Not elevated
RC1	T = 72	99	Elevated
RC2	T = 47	38	Not elevated
RC4	T = 40	16	Not elevated
RC6	T = 40	16	Not elevated
RC7	T = 41	18	Not elevated
RC8	T = 49	46	Not elevated
RC9	T = 42	21	Not elevated

standard cut-offs, raising concern for an invalid test approach that would be expected to result in artificially lowered cognitive scores.

General intellectual abilities fell in the average range, consistent with expected premorbid expectations based on an average performance on a word reading task that is typically resistant to change. Verbal abilities were high average and slightly better than his low average nonverbal skills.

Expressive word knowledge was average. His ability to synthesize different ideas on an abstract verbal reasoning task was high average. His fund of general knowledge was in the above average, representing a relative strength. Phonemic verbal fluency was above average and semantic verbal fluency was average. Performance on a visual confrontation naming task was average.

Simple auditory attention was average. Working memory on a more complex mental computation task was also average. These scores combined to produce an average Working Memory Index. Sustained visual attention on a number cancellation task was average for speed with average accuracy.

Performance was average on a block construction task involving visuospatial problem-solving and visuo-constructional ability, as was performance on a task requiring knowledge of part–whole relationships, simultaneous processing, and perceptual organization. Visual pattern analysis was low average, representing a relative weakness. His copy of a complex geometric figure was within normal limits.

Visuomotor speed on a digit-symbol transcription task was average as was speed on a different measure of visual discrimination. Prompting was required to remind him to work as quickly as possible. Processing speed on a visual scanning and sequencing task was average. With the added demand of mental set-shifting, his performance was similarly average.

On an untimed card-sorting task examining concept formation, novel problem-solving, and mental flexibility, he made a low average number of perseverative responses and lost set three times, which lowered his efficiency and resulted in completion of 2/6 categories. He produced a number of "other" responses that are extremely uncommon in normative samples.

Overall learning on a 16-item verbal list-learning task was low average with an average learning curve across trials (4, 6, 8, 9, 9). He freely recalled 5 items after a delay, which is below average, and did not improve with cues. He appeared to give up easily on tasks with any obvious memory element. He produced a number of intrusion and repetition errors across recall attempts. Recognition memory was also below average. Performance on an embedded validity indicator was below expectations on this task, and there were other unusual response patterns (e.g., producing words on free recall but failing to identify those words on recognition testing). Immediate and delayed recall of short stories were average with 81% retention and intact recognition. Delayed free recall of a complex geometric figure was average. He selected the incorrect figure from an array of similar designs.

Mr. S was administered the MMPI-3 to provide an assessment of mood and personality. He appeared to respond in a consistent manner with no indication of under reporting; however, over-reporting of symptoms was indicated by an unusually high number of infrequent responses associated with non-credible reporting of somatic and cognitive symptoms, including atypical memory complaints. This is suggestive of symptom magnification, which raises the likelihood of artificially elevated scales and a wide range of possible symptomatology. He endorsed diffuse somatic symptoms at a level that is uncommonly reported even by individuals with significant medical or psychiatric conditions. Individuals with similar patterns tend to present with vague neurological complaints, are prone to developing physical symptoms in response to stress, and have difficulty acknowledging the role that emotional factors may play in their difficulties. In addition to somatic and cognitive complaints, his responses resulted in significant elevations on scales associated with reduced positive emotions, low interest and motivation, unhappiness, and general malaise. He is likely to report excessive worry and preoccupation with stress and perceived disappointments. There is no indication of suicidal ideation or psychotic thought processes.

Summary and Conclusions

In the neuropsychological report, I wrote that this evaluation was limited by variable and suboptimal performance identified by measures of performance validity, as well as atypical symptom validity test patterns which indicate that the current results cannot be viewed as a valid representation of Mr. Smith's neuropsychological status. Therefore, scores below levels of expectancy cannot be construed as accurate indicators of his actual ability level. That said, only a few scores on ability testing fell below normal expectations, including performances in complex verbal memory and a task of novel problem-solving, accompanied by minor variability in aspects of attention and speed. Intellectual function was estimated in the average range with stronger verbal abilities relative to nonverbal skills. Given that the majority of scores fell within normal limits compared with peers of similar age and education despite incomplete task engagement, it can be assumed that his true abilities in these areas are at least average or better. Overall, the current findings do not support the presence of cognitive impairment. Mr. S's report of cognitive problems is greater than would be expected based on these results as well as the clinical history that has been obtained.

Formal psychological testing was also limited by elevations on multiple symptom validity scales, indicative of symptom magnification and non-credible symptom endorsement, particularly of cognitive and somatic symptoms. In conclusion, it was my opinion that to a reasonable degree of neuropsychological probability Mr. S's complaints were related to a combination of symptom exaggeration, stress, work dissatisfaction, and normal age-related cognitive changes.

In addition to writing a narrative report, I was also asked to respond to specific referral questions. The questions and my responses to them are provided below.

1 *Please clarify if the reported diagnosis of Postconcussive Syndrome is casually related to the 6/19/19 injury.*

 The clinical history does not support a valid diagnosis of Postconcussive Syndrome. First, the information provided from the scene of injury is not indicative of any neurological alteration nor was there any clear suspicion (and/or documentation) that Mr. S suffered an actual head injury, which would be the basis for developing a Postconcussive Syndrome (PCS). Moreover, a delayed onset of "PCS" symptoms is atypical and symptoms would have reasonably been expected to have been maximal proximal to his injury and not develop months after.

2 *Do the results of your evaluation support the presence of valid cognitive and/or psychiatric impairments? If so, please describe including any appropriate workplace restrictions or limitations?*

 Performance on two stand-alone performance validity tests (PVTs) and one of two embedded validity indicators were beyond standard thresholds. In addition, there were other subtle features of his performances that are uncommon in normative samples and atypical for individuals with bona fide cognitive impairment. Furthermore, multiple symptom validity tests (SVTs) were significantly elevated, indicative of non-credible endorsement of emotional, cognitive, and somatic symptoms. Thus, the possibility of symptom exaggeration and/or feigning must be considered. In the presence of an external incentive (e.g., disability claim), psychometric evidence of exaggerated PVT or SVT results across two or more domains in the absence of another explanatory medical or psychiatric condition, and inconsistencies in symptom reporting (including unsupported, inconsistent referencing of a brain injury and cognitive impairment), it is my opinion that there is sufficient evidence to conclude that assessment results and the claimant's presentation are indicative of non-credible neuropsychological dysfunction.

 The available information indicates that non-clinical factors, namely work dissatisfaction and compensation seeking, likely play a role in the claimant's presentation. The presence of occupational dissatisfaction is documented in the records and precedes any mention of issues related to fatigue, mood, or cognition. Furthermore, Mr. S reported to me that he did not like his manager and felt that he was given the worst assignments when he had been working. He was also displeased with the overall management of the company but given his tenure there had been reluctance to seek work elsewhere. He also indicated that he was unsure if he would again return to work with his employer even if he was able.

3 *In your opinion, has the claimant reached maximal medical benefit? If not, what further treatment is indicated?*

 Given the above, the available information is consistent with the claimant having achieved maximal medical improvement.

Discussion

Kirk Heilbrun describes four broad stages of approaching forensic assessment in his seminal work "Principles of Forensic Mental Health Assessment" (2001). While some of the specifics of his approach are focused on mental health issues, the overall schema has been a useful model for me in forensic neuropsychological assessment as well. The four broad stages address preparation, data collection, data interpretation, and communication. Below is a discussion of my approach to the case above using this model.

Preparation

After receiving a call from a vendor hired by Mr. S's Workers' Compensation carrier to inquire as to my ability and willingness to accept a referral for an independent neuropsychological evaluation, there were several considerations to be made. First, even prior to accepting a forensic referral, I needed to consider the following:

1. Do I have a sufficient understanding of the Workers' Compensation system as a whole and specifically the local rules and regulations in order to accept a referral in this context?
2. Can I identify the relevant forensic issues in this case as well as my role in the process?
3. Is the underlying diagnosis one for which I am familiar and have sufficient expertise to address? Do I have any inherent biases with respect to the diagnosis?
4. Are the financial arrangements clear? Am I limited in the scope of the evaluation I plan to complete by time limits?
5. Are there are any conflicts of interest (either real or potentially perceived) that I need to be aware of?

The importance of the preparation stage cannot be overstated, as problems at this stage will likely lead to significant troubles as the evaluation proceeds. I have made my own mistakes in this regard over the course of my career. As I considered the above questions in this referral, it was important for me to attempt to be as objective as I could regarding my expertise and competence to appropriately complete this evaluation. Based on having both performed many Workers' Compensation evaluations in my state as well as having published work in this area (e.g., Oakes & Peck, 2022), I determined that I did have sufficient expertise to accept a referral within the context of a Workers' Compensation claim. The asserted diagnosis of mild traumatic brain injury was also one for which I am quite familiar and have maintained my competence over time through both continued clinical work as well as continuing education (Raskin, Lovejoy, Stevens, Zamroziewicz, & Oakes, 2014). With respect to bias regarding diagnosis, I needed to consider any preconceived notions I may have irrespective of the specifics of this case. I recognized that I lean toward skepticism of chronic and impairing cognitive impairment following a mild traumatic brain injury as whole. This "bias" is based on my own clinical experience as well as from the available empirical literature. However, I am also keenly aware that some individuals do experience chronic difficulties from what may be considered a very mild traumatic brain injury such that I in no way had an a priori conclusion that impairment cannot or should not be present.

The agreement for my services was based on my hourly billing rate and not on any fixed amount (or hours) for the evaluation, which I avoid. This resolves concerns regarding any disincentive to complete a comprehensive and thorough evaluation. As part of the referral process, I was provided with both the employee's name as well as the names of the providers that have been involved in his care. Having practiced in my state for nearly 30 years, it is not uncommon for me to at least be aware of some of the providers identified. In this case, I noted that I have been engaged in other forensic work that has involved Dr. Lemon. Further, it has been my impression that the quality of the work and opinions of Dr. Lemon have been poor. The follow-up to that impression is the question of whether I can still remain objective regarding the case if I am inclined to be highly skeptical of the opinions offered by Dr. Lemon. Upon reflection, I determined that I could be, as I had previously been. The employee had essentially no say in where he was referred for treatment nor any practical basis to determine the adequacy of Dr. Lemon's evaluation or treatment. Further, the employee had been seen by multiple providers over time such that there were multiple sources of clinical information.

Data Collection

1 Has the referring party provided up to date and complete medical records for review? Are there additional sources of information being provided (i.e., legal documents, surveillance, disability forms) that need to be integrated in the assessment process?
2 In what form shall I obtain informed consent and what should the scope of informed consent be for this kind of evaluation?
3 What information should I seek during the clinical interview?
4 What test battery should be employed?
5 Have I ensured that the evaluation environment is optimal?

Based on my past experience, it is my practice to review the records and other information provided by the referral source at least a week before the scheduled evaluation. This allows for time to identify any missing information that may be needed in time for the referring party to obtain this additional information. In this case, I had not initially been provided with the report from the independent neurological evaluation by Dr. Currant, but I had seen it referenced in other documents. Upon receiving the actual report, the summary of the conclusions that had been reported by Dr. Lemon were not consistent with the actual report by Dr. Currant.

The review of records also provides the opportunity to begin to conceptualize the case and possibly to identify the source of disagreement between the employee and his providers with the insurer, such that this is fully addressed in the evaluation process. It was clear from the record review that the insurer had long believed that Mr. S had recovered and that there was little justification for his having remained out of work for nearly three years. This in turn informed both the scope of the clinical interview, as well as the specific test battery to be administered.

As the goal of the assessment process is to obtain a comprehensive and reliable examination, the establishment of rapport is the first crucial step. This begins with a suitable office environment, a friendly and reassuring attitude, and thorough review of the evaluation process. To this end, I immediately greeted Mr. S upon arrival to my office, offered access to a restroom and a beverage to increase his comfort.

Providing clarification to Mr. S regarding my role in the Workers' Compensation process was critical in the obtaining of informed consent. For most individuals, they have not been engaged in an evaluation process with a healthcare provider that does not include a doctor–patient relationship and this distinction is of utmost importance. Mr. S appeared to not fully realize that Dr. Currant's evaluation had been an independent evaluation, so more prolonged discussion of my role was needed. In addition to standard disclosures regarding threats to confidentiality (i.e., self-harm, child abuse, etc.), an explanation of the potential impact of the findings on his claim of disability needed to be explicitly discussed. It is also my practice to inform an examinee that their full effort and honesty regarding their symptoms was needed and expected throughout the evaluation process and that this was also being assessed as part of the examination process. Further, I attempt to provide reassurance that the tests that are being given are sensitive to their complaints/deficits and will show the difficulties they are reporting, if present. I also inform an examinee that they should immediately let me know if there are any barriers to providing their full effort.

With regard to the clinical interview, I generally complete an outline to work from ahead of time for use while completing the interview with particular attention to noting any conflicts of information that have been found in the record and collateral documentation review process. Errors in medical records are not uncommon and allowing Mr. S to explain or fill in information allowed for greater accuracy.

In deciding on a test battery, the record review gave me some indication of at least a general level of potential impairment as well the demographic background so that appropriate tests were ready to be administered. Based on the records (and subsequent interview), it appeared that if Mr. S did have impairments, they were most likely to be more on the mild spectrum and there was a need to have sufficient sensitivity in the test battery. I also generally employ both embedded as well as stand-alone validity measures that are mixed into the test battery, and have found it useful to obtain a sense of performance validity as early as possible in the evaluation process, so that poor effort or exaggeration can be addressed. As such, I was prepared on the day of the evaluation for the scope of the examination I planned to complete and then was able to verify the sufficiency of my selections based on the interview. By establishing the test battery ahead of time, I was confident of the availability of appropriate demographically matched normative data for this case.

Data Interpretation

1 Have either symptom and performance validity issues been identified?
2 Have valid deficits been identified?
3 Have I given proper weight to the various sources of information obtained?

The first step in the data interpretative process is establishing the reliability and validity of the data obtained. First, during the course of the evaluation, there were no disruptions or complaints of physical discomfort felt to impact on Mr. S's engagement. Second, a review of the validity data reflected clear concerns in this regard given his performance across multiple validity indicators. It was my opinion that his performance on validity measures reflected a pattern of poor effort, rather than an isolated lapse of effort. Third, by continuing to reinforce the need for full engagement and reassurances from Mr. S that he was providing his best effort, the validity results were in my opinion a clearer reflection of effort having been withheld.

His clinical history and the medical records also raised concerns regarding the validity of Mr. S's complaints. Red flags included multiple variations of his recounting salient details of the accident to different providers (e.g., whether he experienced loss of consciousness – first denied and much later endorsed), long delays between follow-up appointments, reporting worsening of cognitive difficulties over time, behaviors inconsistent with his reported deficits (i.e., international solo travel), and a clear reluctance to return to work. Fundamentally, the accident scenario did not appear to have involved *any* injury to the brain, and it should not have resulted in long-standing disability.

A "diagnosis" of Malingering using the *Diagnostic and Statistical Manual of Mental Disorders* (currently *DSM-V*, 2013) in the context of independent neuropsychological evaluations has been problematic over the multiple editions that it has been included. While a full discussion of this issue goes beyond this chapter, the assessment of "intentionality" and lack of any operational definition of lack of cooperation during a diagnostic evaluation are two of the more salient issues. The Slick, Sherman, and Iverson (1999) criteria for Malingered Neurocognitive Dysfunction was a groundbreaking new schema to provide a way to communicate issues of effort and symptom exaggeration. This was subsequently revised and updated in 2020 with the Multidimensional Malingering Criteria for Neuropsychological Assessment (Sherman, Slick, & Iverson, 2020). Using this new model, Mr. S's clinical history and testing results were clearly consistent with "Malingering with Mix Presentation".

Communication

1 Have I provided proper attribution in the record review process and generated a comprehensive and accurate history?
2 Have the report and conclusions been written using plain language, avoided jargon, and actually provided a response to the specific referral questions?

As the conclusions from this evaluation will likely have a significant impact on the claims adjudication process, I attempted to document the record review in detail so that the sources of various information were explicit and did not omit information that was either supportive or unsupportive of his asserted deficits. Moreover, as the report would likely be reviewed by a variety of individuals, I attempted to minimize the use of jargon, provide an explicit explanation of the data, and state my conclusions in plain language.

References

American Psychiatric Association. (2013). *Diagnostic and Statistical Manual of Mental Disorders* (5th ed.) Washington, DC: Author.

Guilmette, T.J., Sweet, J.J., Hebben, N., Koltai, D., Mahone, E.M., ... Spiegler, B.J. (2020). American Academy of Clinical Neuropsychology consensus conference statement on uniform labeling of performance test scores. *The Clinical Neuropsychologist*, 34(3), 437–453.

Heilbrun, K. (2001). *Principles of Forensic Mental Health Assessment Springer*. New York: Springer.

Lovejoy, D.W. & Oakes, H. (2012) The Behavioral Health Provider as a Participant in the Disability Determination Process: Evaluations, Terminology, and Systems. In S. Bush & G. Iverson (Eds.) *Neuropsychological Assessment of Work-Related Injuries* (pp. 321–343). New York: Guilford Press.

Oakes, H.J. & Peck, C.P. (2022). Validity Assessment for Clinical Patients with Workers' Compensation Claims. In J.W. Schroeder & P.K. Martin (Eds.) *Validity Assessment in Clinical Neuropshchological Practice* (pp. 400–417). New York: Guilford.

Raskin, S.A., Lovejoy, D., Stevens, M.C., Zamroziewicz, M., & Oakes, H.J. (2014). Mild Traumatic Brain Injury. In H. Levin, D. Shum & R. Chan (Eds.) *Understanding Traumatic Brain Injury* (pp. 370–412). New York: Elsevier.

Sherman, M.S., Slick, D.J., & Iverson, G.L. (2020). Multidimensional Malingering Criteria for Neuropsychological Assessment: A 20-year update of the malingered neuropsychlogical dysfunction criteria. *Archives of Clinical Neuropsychology, 35*, 735–764.

Slick, D.J., Sherman, E.M., & Iverson, G.L. (1999). Diagnostic criteria for malingered neurocognitive dysfunction: Proposed standards for clinical practice and research. *The Clinical Neuropsychologist, 13(4)*, 545–561.

26 Detecting Malingered Pain-Related Disability in the Context of a Presurgical Psychological Evaluation

James L. McAbee, Kevin Bianchini, Kevin W. Greve, and Matthew J. Holcomb

Pain is a common source of physical disability associated with work-related injuries. Low back pain, in general, is a very common condition. Pain is a subjective experience. The best approach to conceptualizing pain is multimodal, with methodologies to assess and measure pain (Wideman et al., 2019). Approximately 84% of people will suffer from low back pain, 23% will experience chronic low back pain, and 11%–12% of the global population is estimated to be disabled from back pain (Balagué et al., 2012). In addition to low back pain, neck pain has also been identified as a significant source of pain with a reported prevalence rate of 27 per 1,000 people in 2019 (Kazeminasab et al., 2022). The financial cost of neck pain includes the costs of treatment, as well as the costs to the labor force due to reduced productivity (Kazeminasab et al., 2022). An estimate in 2016 reported that low back and neck pain had the highest health care spending in the United States with an estimated U.S.$134.5 billion spent (Dieleman et al., 2020).

The typical course of treatment for chronic pain associated with spinal disorders (i.e., back and neck pain) includes more conservative methods before consideration of surgical intervention. These conservative modalities usually include medication, supportive braces, physical therapy, and therapeutic injections, such as nerve root blocks or epidural blocks (Alentado et al., 2014). For patients who do not experience significant improvement of their pain following conservative treatments, surgery then becomes an option to relieve them of their pain. However, a significant number of patients do not experience good outcomes from surgery. Specifically, following a lumbar surgery to address low back pain, 10%–40% of patients experience worsened or new pain post-operatively, also known as Failed Back Surgery Syndrome (Stanton et al., 2022). Similarly, rates of failed cervical surgery are seen in 2%–30% of patients (Verla et al., 2021).

The medical community has concerned itself with identifying which patients are at elevated risk for poor outcome from spine surgery given the rates of failed outcomes. The causes of failed spine surgery have been reported as complex and multifactorial, consisting of patient-related risk factors, medical factors, and psychological factors. Block and colleagues (2001) developed a presurgical psychological screening (PPS) algorithm based on a semi-structured interview, psychometric tests, review of medical records, and medical risk factors to predict which patients are at elevated risk for poor surgical outcome. This PPS algorithm by Block and colleagues (2001) resulted in 82% accuracy predicting overall outcome from spine surgery. Medical and psychological risk levels were significantly associated with outcome, demonstrating patients with high psychological and medical risk factors experienced the poorest results, and they also determined that psychological testing could predict 78.4% of patient outcomes (Block et al., 2001; Marek et al., 2019). As a result of their study, Block and colleagues have recommended that PPS become a routine

DOI: 10.4324/9781003005063-30

part of the evaluation of chronic pain patients being considered for spine surgery. The U.S. Preventative Services Task Force has also recommended presurgical psychological screening prior to spine surgery, as well as by the North American Spine Society guidelines; however, Young and colleagues (2014) found that a minority of surgeons reported using PPS prior to surgery. Given the statistics of failed spine surgeries and the known implications of psychological factors on spine surgery outcomes, it is important in the context of spine surgery that patients are properly screened with an empirically supported, well-validated PPS prior to the proposed surgical interventions.

Pain, External Incentives, and Malingering

Neck and back pain are seen in the context of compensable events, such as work-related injuries or in incidents where another party is potentially liable. Pain is also a commonly reported complaint in patients involved in disability claims who also claim to have sustained brain injuries (Bianchini & Greve, 2009). Chronic intractable pain has also been associated with prolonged disability and secondary gain concerns (Greve et al., 2009). The presence and magnitude of compensation have been related to heightened reports of pain and reduced treatment efficacy (Harris et al., 2005; Voorhies et al., 2007; Rohling et al., 1995).

Malingering is "the intentional production of false or grossly exaggerated physical or psychological symptoms, motivated by external incentives such as avoiding military duty, avoiding work, obtaining financial compensation, evading criminal prosecution, or obtaining drugs" (*DSM-5*, pp. 726–727). Mittenberg et al. (2002), surveying board-certified neuropsychologists, reported a prevalence of malingering being 31%–33% in cases seen for psychological evaluation because of chronic pain. Using actual clinical data, Greve et al. (2009) demonstrated the prevalence of malingering in chronic pain patients with financial incentive was between 20% and 50%, depending on the specific diagnostic system used and the statistical model's underlying assumptions. Some factors associated with the medico-legal context such as the jurisdiction of a Workers' Compensation claim or attorney representation were associated with slightly higher malingering rates (Bianchini et al., 2006).

Formal, structured, and objective criteria for the diagnosis of *cognitive* malingering were first published by Slick, Sherman, and Iverson in 1999. Since then, these criteria have served as the foundation for the study of malingering and have been subject to repeated review and comment. In 2005, Bianchini, Greve, and Glynn modified the Slick et al. criteria to specifically address malingered pain-related disability (MPRD). Larrabee et al. (2007) reviewed malingering diagnostic systems, their empirical support, and offered integration of the Slick and Bianchini systems. In their published statement, the AACN Consensus Conference Statement on the Neuropsychological Assessment of Effort, Response Bias, and Malingering (Heilbronner et al., 2009) recognized these various systems for diagnosing malingering, concluding that there are evidence-based methods for detecting and diagnosing malingering, and the update to the AACN Consensus Statement recently reaffirmed this position (Sweet et al., 2021). In 2013, Slick and Sherman revised their original system and included aspects of Bianchini et al.'s MPRD diagnostic system as suggested by Larrabee et al. (2007).

One of the contributions of the 2005 Bianchini et al. criteria for MPRD is the idea of "compelling inconsistency," which

> occurs when the difference in the way a patient presents when being evaluated compared to when they are not aware of being evaluated is such that it is not reasonable to believe the patient is not purposely controlling the difference.
>
> (p. 408)

According to the AACN Consensus Conference Statement,

> there is consensus regarding the meaning of significantly below-chance findings and what has been referred to as 'compelling inconsistency' (Bianchini et al., 2005), and both are viewed as individually reflecting a deliberate attempt to misrepresent one's abilities for which there are no alternative explanations.
>
> (p. 1103)

Slick and Sherman (2013) included the "compelling inconsistency" in their updated malingering criteria stating that the finding of compelling inconsistency "should be considered prima facie evidence of definite malingering" (p. 62). Sherman et al. (2020) modified their criteria to that of a multidimensional model that included criteria for malingering of neurocognitive dysfunction, malingering of somatic symptoms, malingering of psychiatric symptoms, and malingering of mixed presentations; however, there is not consensus support for this full model (Sweet et al., 2021). One potentially fatal flaw of the Sherman system for diagnosing malingering in patients whose primary complaints are pain is eliminating the use of PVTs to identify malingering despite the sizable literature demonstrating the efficacy of PVTs for this purpose (Bianchini et al., 2005; Greve et al., 2008; Greve et al., 2013). Thus, because the case we are presenting had pain as a prominent feature, we will use the Bianchini et al. (2005) paper as the integrating conceptual foundation.

The Case of Mr. S

In this chapter, we present a patient who was involved in a work-related injury, and who was formally diagnosed with malingering based on results obtained from a presurgical (spine surgery) psychological evaluation. The patient had previously completed a neuropsychological evaluation related to the same work-related injury; however, there were marked differences in his performances between the two evaluations. At the time of the presurgical evaluation referral, the patient was being considered for an anterior cervical fusion and discectomy (ACDF). The patient's identifying information has been blinded for the purposes of this case study, and he will be referred to as "Mr. Spine (Mr. S)." This case demonstrates the process of diagnosing malingering in a pain patient and the interplay of psychological and social factors that may culminate in intentional exaggeration of pain-related disability. The following text will present the background of the case, describe the findings of the neuropsychological evaluation and the presurgical psychological evaluation, and will describe the findings in the context of existing scientific literature.

Background

Mr. S, a 44-year-old right-handed, Caucasian male, with 11 years of education, was involved in a work-related, unwitnessed slip and fall accident. This fall was associated with loss of consciousness from a blow to the head, as well as other claimed physical and emotional injuries. Mr. S retained an attorney, and he was seeking a financial settlement from his Workers' Compensation carrier around his injury claim with the employer. In addition to medical evaluations, Mr. S also underwent two psychological evaluations. The first evaluation was a neuropsychological evaluation (Exam 1) performed at the request of his case manager and his neurologist to determine the nature and severity of his claimed neurocognitive and/or emotional deficits, if noted, as well as the significance of any functional deficits, and to establish the likelihood/probability of any deficits being related to the injury. The second evaluation was a psychological presurgical evaluation (Exam 2) performed at the request of his case manager and orthopedic surgeon to identify any psychological and/or behavioral factors present in his case, which would elevate the risk for poor outcome from spine surgery. Table 26.1 provides a chronology of important events in this case.

On the day of the accident, Mr. S was a 42-year-old employee who slipped over a railing while working in a car wash, striking the left side of his body on a car as he fell to the ground. The ambulance report documented loss of consciousness and recorded the initial Glasgow Coma Scale (GCS) of 14. When EMS arrived, Mr. S reported he did not remember

Table 26.1 Chronology of Case Events

Months Post-Injury	*Event*
—	Accident
—	Normal computed tomography scan of brain & cervical spine
—	Normal X-ray of left scapula
—	Normal X-ray of thoracic spine
—	Normal X-ray of lumbar spine
—	Normal X-ray left forearm
—	Normal X-ray of pelvis
—	Normal X-ray of left hip
—	Normal X-ray of chest
1	Referred to Orthopedic Surgeon by attorney
3	Referred to physical therapy (PT)
4	Mr. S claimed he was unable to begin PT but Orthopedic Surgeon's office could not obtain from him the reason why he was unable to begin PT
5	MRI of the cervical spine w/o contrast revealed multilevel cervical degenerative disc disease and associated spinal stenosis. Cord contact at several levels with slight displacement of cord at C3–C4 but no significant cord compression. Foraminal stenosis at multiple levels. No focal disc herniations
	Normal MRI of lumbar spine w/o contrast
	Left shoulder MRI w/o contrast revealed AC joint osteoarthritis with mild impingement of underlying rotator cuff. No rotator cuff tear. Mild supraspinatus tendinitis. Minimal accumulation of fluid within subdeltoid bursa said to perhaps be mild bursitis
6	Mr. S complained of memory loss and migraine headaches. Referred to Neurology
9	Mr. S reported word-finding difficulties. Referrals made for Neuropsychological Evaluation and updated MRI of Brain
11	Normal MRI of brain
12	Normal EMG/NCS of left leg & lumbar paraspinal muscles
	EMG/NCS revealed Left C4 radiculopathy with both acute & chronic features
14	Recommendation for cervical epidural steroid injection
15	Mr. S began the neuropsychological evaluation (required four months to complete evaluation)
16	Surgical recommendation for anterior cervical fusion and discectomy (ACDF) at C3–C4.
20	Surgery denied by Workers' Compensation due to Mr. S's failure to undergo the CESI as recommended, as well as lack of psychological evaluation for clearance
21	Presurgical Psychological Evaluation prior to spine surgery (required three months to complete evaluation)

the fall but remembered waking in a pool of water. He reported pain in his neck, back, left leg, and head. By the time he was examined at the emergency room (ER), the GCS was restored to 15. He complained of headache, left neck pain, left scapula pain, left hip pain, and left forearm pain with numbness and tingling. The impression in the ER was of blunt head injury, back strain, cervical strain, contusion to left hip, and contusion to left forearm. Following evaluation, Mr. S was released from the hospital the same day, and he was *not* given a concussion diagnosis at the time.

Afterward, Mr. S continued to report pain complaints in the left shoulder, left neck, both shoulder blades, left hip, left forearm, left elbow, numbness and tingling in the left fingers, and numbness and tingling in both legs. He later claimed additional neurological changes of blurry vision, sensitivity to light, and migraine headaches, as well as cognitive changes, including memory issues, decreased processing speed, poor concentration, and word-finding difficulties. He also claimed emotional changes of depression and suicidal ideation. Mr. S' account of his LOC during the accident also changed over time. Initially, he reported he lost consciousness for up to ten minutes, and, at later evaluations, he reported estimated LOC at five minutes, and later, only up to two minutes. New complaints were endorsed at the presurgical psychological evaluation of difficulty fully voiding his bladder, endorsed sexual dysfunction, and endorsed decreased processing speed since the accident. It is noteworthy that these complaints were never documented in the medical records. A list of his detailed subjectively reported symptoms during Exam 2 is provided in Table 26.2.

Imaging studies were performed on the day of the accident in the ER. The computed tomography scan of the Head w/o Contrast revealed no evidence of acute traumatic injury in the brain or cervical spine. X-rays of the left scapula, thoracic spine, lumbar spine, left forearm, pelvis, left hip, and chest were all normal. Five months post-injury, additional imaging was performed. The updated MRI of cervical spine revealed multilevel degenerative disc disease and associated spinal stenosis without significant cord compression; foraminal stenosis was seen at multiple levels, but no focal disc herniations were evidenced. MRI of the lumbar spine was normal. Left shoulder MRI revealed AC joint osteoarthritis with mild

Table 26.2 Symptoms *Spontaneously Reported* by Mr. S during the Interview for the Second Evaluation

1	Pain in the left shoulder
2	Pain in the neck
3	Pain in both shoulder blades
4	Pain in the left hip
5	Pain in the left forearm
6	Pain in the left elbow
7	Numbness and tingling in the left fingers
8	Numbness and tingling in both legs
9	Blurry vision
10	Sensitivity to light
11	He reported his pains are constant. When asked to rate his pain on a rating scale of 0–10 with a "10" being the most severe amount of pain, he rated his pain as "8"
12	Depressed mood every day
13	Anxiety ever since the accident
14	Irritable ever since the accident
15	Suicidal ideation occurring since the accident without method, plan, or intent
16	Sleep difficulties. He reported difficulty falling asleep due to his pain, as well as achieving only four-hours of sleep per night due to pain

impingement of underlying rotator cuff without rotator cuff tear; mild supraspinatus tendinitis, and minimal fluid accumulation within subdeltoid bursa said to be possible mild bursitis. Eleven months post-injury, Mr. S had a repeat MRI of the brain performed due to new cognitive complaints. The results of the MRI remained normal. At one year post-injury, Mr. S underwent electromyography/nerve conduction studies (EMG/NCS), which revealed normal studies of the left leg and lumbar paraspinal muscles, but did reveal a single finding for left C4 radiculopathy with both acute and chronic features.

Neuropsychological Evaluation

Mr. S was referred for a neuropsychological evaluation by the neurologist due to his cognitive complaints. The evaluation was started 15 months post-injury; however, it took four months for Mr. S to complete the evaluation due to missed and canceled appointments on his part. Mr. S reported to the examiner that he lost consciousness for up to ten minutes and acknowledged his fall was unwitnessed. Mr. S also reported that he was diagnosed with a "small head concussion" during his ER visit on the day of the accident; however, medical records did not reflect any evidence of a concussion diagnosis. Mr. S claimed memory loss and reported misplacing items, difficulty recalling phone numbers, addresses, and appointments. He reported difficulty recalling his children's birthdays and his anniversary. He also reported losing historical information such as remembering his wedding day and attending funerals.

Examination of performance and symptom validity were conducted during the neuropsychological evaluation. His performance validity results were reported as being within normal limits. His general intellectual abilities were observed within the average range. His visual perceptual and constructional functions were globally intact with the exception of spatial/directional skill, which was mildly impaired. Results from the Conner's Continuous Performance Test-2nd Edition revealed a profile consistent with an individual with ADHD (93.1% likelihood). His fine motor speed and dexterity were mildly impaired bilaterally. Language function was reported as "mixed but generally intact with the exception of auditory comprehension and simple calculation." His academic skills were reported as "commensurate with educational attainment with a relative strength in spelling and weakness in mathematical computation." His overall memory and new learning were within normal limits with the exception of visual span of attention and initial encoding of auditory information. Mr. S' executive functions were reported as globally intact.

As can be seen, Mr. S generally performed well on cognitive testing, but the testing did reveal some impairment of attention that the neuropsychologist reported as "his scores in sustained attention most closely match a normative group with Attention-Deficit Hyperactivity Disorder." The neuropsychologist also pointed out there was no evidence of acute injury on neuroimaging and his GCS was 15 at the emergency department. The neuropsychologist opined that Mr. S' perception of cognitive impairment was likely due to environmental stressors such as financial issues, pain, and depression, as well as the empirical evidence of litigation on prolonged symptom recovery.

Regarding physical/somatic and emotional functioning, no overt pain behaviors were observed during the evaluation. Mr. S made jokes throughout testing with the examiner and asked personal questions of the examiner. Despite this, he reported chronic headaches rated 9/10 pain level, he reported sometimes the back of his head swells, and he reported sensitivity to light. He reported tingling in the left fingers and sometimes tingling in the elbow. He reported left hip pain and described the pain as if his bones were rubbing together, causing a pinching sensation. He reported pain in his middle back that he described as "scoliosis" and throbbing "like someone stepped on [his] back." He reported burning pain and stiffness in his left calf and foot. He reported neck and right shoulder pain. Regarding emotional changes/symptoms, Mr. S described waking in the middle of the night crying, suicidal ideation, and loss of appetite.

Results of the Minnesota Multiphasic Personality Inventory-2nd Edition (MMPI-2) suggested intentional symptom overreporting and exaggerated disability. The neuropsychologist documented,

> In a peer review study of clinical pain patients, only 2% of those who were not malingering endorsed the degree of symptoms Mr. S did. In other words, 98% of pain patients with financial incentive presenting this number of problems were known to be exaggerating.

During the neuropsychological evaluation, Mr. S' profile also revealed an "extremely elevated" Modified Somatic Perception Questionnaire (MSPQ) score, and his Pain Disability Index (PDI) score was "higher than 93% of patients suggesting a tendency to view himself as functionally and globally disabled by his pain." The Sullivan Pain Catastrophizing Scale (PCS) score (T = 86) was reported as "severe pain catastrophizing." On the Battery for Health Improvement 2 (BHI-2), Mr. S' profile revealed heightened negative presentation, reported to be higher than 89% of patients asked to fake bad. His endorsement of somatic complaints was higher than 99% of patients. He endorsed anxiety and depression higher than 96% and 92% of patients, respectively, and demonstrated symptom dependency greater than 99% of patients. His job dissatisfaction score was higher than 88% of patients.

Overall, the evaluation revealed six markers of exaggerated symptom reporting; however, the neuropsychologist opined that Mr. S did not meet criteria for malingering, but noted "the pattern of abnormal psychological symptom validity findings cannot be explained by any combination of conditions surrounding the claim and would be best explained as an attempt to magnify physical and emotional problems."

Presurgical Psychological Evaluation

Mr. S was referred for a psychological evaluation for surgical clearance prior to the proposed ACDF by his orthopedic surgeon. During the clinical interview he was observed with euthymic affect. Mr. S recalled the accident, stating that he suffered a slip and fall injury while washing a vehicle at work, striking the left side of his body on the car as he fell to the ground. He discussed losing consciousness for two minutes to the examiner, which was discrepant from his subjective reports to his physicians and to the neuropsychologist (i.e., up to five to ten minutes). He reported on the day of the accident that he was "barely able to move." He noted exacerbating factors of his pain as sitting, lifting, and bending. He reported diffuse pains throughout the left side of his body, headaches, sleep difficulties, emotional changes, and cognitive issues. Mr. S rated all of his pains as "8" at the time of the clinical interview, and he noted a best pain rating of "7" and worst pain rating as "9." His spontaneously reported symptoms are listed in Table 26.2. He was then asked about specific symptoms, which are listed in Table 26.3. When asked about his perception of his ability to return to work in the future, Mr. S expressed beliefs that he was psychologically and physically disabled.

Mr. S reported that he was unaware of any surgical procedures being considered when he was informed of the purpose of the evaluation; however, discussions around the ACDF were documented in the medical records. He also acknowledged that he had never participated in the injections that were recommended by his physician prior to the surgical option, and that he did not participate in physical therapy.

Table 26.3 Symptoms *Endorsed* by Mr. S during the Interview for the Second Evaluation

1	Daily migraine headaches with light sensitivity requiring him to wear sunglasses frequently
2	Pain in the upper back
3	Pain in the midback
4	Issues with constipation
5	Issues with genitourinary system. Inability to fully void his bladder. Sexual dysfunction which he attributed to pain
6	Cognitive issues. Short-term memory loss, poor concentration, decreased processing speed

Regarding his pre-injury history, Mr. S denied any history of abuse or neglect or pre-existing psychological conditions. He denied pre-existing head injuries and denied pre-existing history of seizures. He denied a history of any underlying medical conditions. He reported previously smoking tobacco, using marijuana (ten years), and alcohol; however, he denied active use of any substances at the time of the evaluation.

Mr. S reported that he completed 11 years of education. He reported that he repeated 6th grade but denied specific academic difficulties and denied participation in special education or receiving academic accommodations. Mr. S reported that he later attended a technical college for welding. Occupationally, Mr. S reported that he had worked approximately ten jobs since leaving school, and that he primarily worked in manual labor industries (oil field, construction, etc.).

No overt pain behaviors were observed throughout the three testing appointments; however, Mr. S refused to begin the psychological testing at his initial visit, claiming that his pain was too severe. Several attempts were made to reach Mr. S to reschedule his testing appointment, as he would not reschedule while in the office at the initial visit. He returned to the clinic two months later to begin the testing but informed the examiner upon his arrival that he would not be able to stay for the duration of testing. He later canceled the second scheduled testing appointment 90 minutes before the appointment was to begin. Mr. S then returned to the office one month later to complete his testing. He was observed to have discouraged and distant affect throughout testing.

Test Results

Validity

On the Test of Memory Malingering (TOMM), Mr. S correctly recognized 37 of 50 items on Trial 1, 37 of 50 items on Trial 2, and 45 of 50 on the Retention Trial. Trials 2 and Retention were given despite the low score seen on Trial 1, which represented invalidity, to have additional data points for comparison with known group samples of MPRD. The observed scores were very rarely seen in chronic pain patients who were not malingering (Greve et al., 2006), and they are also below meta-analysis indicated scores for invalidity (Martin et al., 2020). On the Word Memory Test (WMT), Mr. S correctly recognized 65% of items on the Immediate Recognition Trial, 42.5% on the Delayed Recognition Trial, and 42.5% on Consistency. These scores are within a range that identifies membership in a group of malingering pain patients (Greve et al., 2008). These scores are also well below the standard cutoffs (Green et al., 1996).

Mr. S performed poorly on the Reliable Digit Span test with a score of 5, which is 100% specific for malingering (Heinly et al., 2005; Schroeder et al., 2011) when studied with pain patients. He performed within normal limits on forced choice recognition of the CVLT-II, with a total recognition hit score of 10 with a linear shrinkage model of –0.37 (Greve et al., 2008).

Mr. S' response pattern on the MMPI-2 produced an elevation on the MMPI Symptom Validity Scale (FBS) (30 raw score; T = 98). There were also elevations observed on scales F (T = 89) and FB (T = 116). There were significant elevations observed on the clinical scales Hs (T = 97) and Hy (T = 91). These scores are within a range that identifies membership into a group of malingering pain patients. Further, the calculated Myers Index (MI) of the profile was 6, which reflects definite overreporting (Meyers et al., 2002), as well as the calculated Response Bias Scale (RBS) with a score of 18, which reflected overreporting of cognitive and somatic complaints (Gervais et al., 2007).

Review of somatic-related questionnaires revealed elevations associated with intentional exaggeration. Specifically, Mr. S obtained a T-score of 96 on the Sullivan PCS, as well as a score of 62 on the PDI. Both scores are within a range that identifies membership into a group of malingering pain patients. The score observed on the Sullivan PCS is 100% specific (Curtis et al., 2019), and the PDI score observed in this case was seen in only 3% of non-malingering chronic pain patients (Bianchini et al., 2014).

The MSPQ has also revealed high accuracy in detection of MPRD (Bianchini et al., 2014). Mr. S produced a score of 23 during the neuropsychological exam (Exam 1), which is highly specific to malingering. However, during the presurgical evaluation (Exam 2), Mr. S' score on the MSPQ was not clearly significant for malingering of somatic complaints.

A detailed summary of these findings with false-positive error rates and appropriate literature citations are located in Table 26.4.[1]

Table 26.4 Positive Psychometric Tests and Indicators of Malingering with Associated False-Positive Error Rates

Test Indicators	*#1*	*FP%*	*#2*	*FP%*	*Source of FP Data*
TOMM 1	44	NS	37	1	Greve, Bianchini, & Doane, 2006
TOMM 2	50	NS	37	0	
TOMM Ret	50	NS	45	2	
WMT IR	95	NS	65	<2	Greve et al., 2008
WMT DR	97.5	NS	42.5	<2	
WMT Con	92.5	NS	42.5	<2	
RDS Raw	9	NS	5	0	Heinly et al., 2005
CVLT-II Total Hits	—	—	10	NS	Greve, Curtis, Bianchini, & Ord, 2008
CVLT-II Linear Shrinkage Model	—	—	−0.37	NS	
MMPI F	61	NS	89	0	Bianchini et al., 2008; Greve et al., 2013
MMPI Fb	75	8	116	0	
MMPI Fp	48	NS	70	2	
MMPI FBS *Raw*	29	1	30	2	
Scale Hs	94	<7	97	<2	
Scale Hy	96	4	91	<7	
MSPQ Raw	23	0	13	NS	Bianchini et al., 2014
Sullivan PCS	86	0	96	0	Curtis et al., 2019
PDI	60	7	62	3	Bianchini et al., 2014

TOMM = Test of Memory Malingering; WMT = Word Memory Test; RDS = Reliable Digit Span; CVLT-II = California Verbal Learning Test; MMPI = Minnesota Multiphasic Personality Inventory-2; F = Infrequency Scale; Fb = Infrequency (back) Scale; FBS = Faking Bad Scale; Scale Hs = Hypochondriasis; Scale Hy = Hysteria MSPQ = Modified Somatic Perception Questionnaire; Sullivan PCS = Sullivan Pain Catastrophizing Scale; PDI = Pain and Disability Index; FP% = False-positive error rate and is based on performance of non-malingering mild TBI patients/chronic pain patients; NS = Not Significant.

Cognitive Testing

In the context of a presurgical psychological evaluation, Mr. S' cognitive abilities were briefly measured to examine his ability to comprehend the risks associated with the planned surgery and to follow post-operative directives. Mr. S was administered the Wechsler Abbreviated Scale of Intelligence 2nd Edition (WASI-II) during the presurgical evaluation. His performance on Verbal Comprehension yielded a standard score of 83, low average, and his performance on Perceptual Reasoning yielded a standard score of 92, average. Mr. S was also administered the NAB Digit Span, which yielded a scaled score of 4, which fell in an impaired range. However, as previously noted, there were positive indications of negative response bias/suboptimal effort observed on freestanding and embedded cognitive performance validity measures. Thus, the observed performances were likely an underestimate of his true cognitive abilities.

Mr. S was also administered the Wide Range Achievement Test-4th Edition (WRAT-4): Reading during the presurgical evaluation. His performances on Word Reading and Sentence Comprehension yielded standard scores of 94 and 81, which reflected average and low average abilities, respectively. It is notable that his performance on the WMT was significantly below his observed literacy level, which reflects that literacy was not a factor in his low performance on the WMT.

Given that the context of the presurgical evaluation was work-related, the California Verbal Learning Test 2nd Edition (CVLT-II) was administered to assess Mr. S' verbal memory and new learning abilities. He demonstrated benefit from the repeated trials and performed within the average range; however, he did not recall consistently across the trials.

Personality Testing

The Minnesota Multiphasic Personality Inventory-2nd Edition (MMPI-2) was administered to Mr. S given the medico-legal context of the presurgical psychological evaluation, as well as to be used in the empirically supported psychological screening algorithm prior to spine surgery suggested by Block and colleagues. As previously noted, significant elevations were observed on the embedded symptom validity scales F, FB, and FBS. The clinical profile of the MMPI-2 revealed elevations on 8 of 10 scales with scales D, Sc, Pt, Pa, Hs, and Hy being the most elevated. The elevations observed on scales Hs, D, and Hy are known psychological contraindications for spine surgery (Block, Gatchell et al., 2003; Block et al., 2001; Epker & Block, 2001).

The BHI-2 was also administered in the presurgical psychological evaluation. This measure assists in developing a biopsychosocial understanding of patients with chronic pain (Bruns & Disorbio, 2014). Mr. S refused to respond to questions about job-related issues on the measure. His scores, however, reflected a strong negative bias, which was higher than that seen in 86% of patients, and even higher than 70% of the normative sample of patients who were asked to fake bad. His somatic complaints, muscular bracing, and functional complaints were higher than that of 98% of patients. His pattern of endorsement also reflected depression and anxiety symptoms that were higher than that of 99% and 98% of patients, respectively.

Pain-Related Measures

Somatic and pain-related questionnaires were administered in the context of the pain-related presurgical psychological evaluation. Mr. S produced a score on the PDI of 62, which was extremely elevated, and the observed score was also to a level that empirical evidence identifies as belonging to a group of malingering pain patients (Bianchini et al., 2014).

Mr. S was also administered the MSPQ. The measure examines psychological complication through surveying unusual physical symptoms. Mr. S' endorsement on this measure produced a score of 13, which reflected somatization and/or malingering may be present but cannot be reliably differentiated at lower score ranges. A score within this range suggests psychological factors may interfere with physical interventions. However, as previously noted, during the neuropsychological evaluation, he produced a score that was 100% specific to malingering of pain/somatic complaints (Bianchini et al., 2014).

The Sullivan PCS was also administered, as literature has indicated a set of patients demonstrate pain catastrophizing as a specific style of dealing with pain. Mr. S' endorsement yielded a raw score of 50, which equates to a T-Score of 96, which was greater than 99.9% of the normative sample, and the score was also to a level that identifies membership into a group of malingering pain patients (Curtis et al., 2019).

Interpretation of Findings

Mr. S continuously presented to medical providers symptomatically with complaints of chronic pain, chronic headaches, emotional changes, and memory complaints. Due to his ongoing complaints of headaches and cognitive issues, he was referred to Neurology for further evaluation, who then referred him for a neuropsychological evaluation (Exam 1). Shortly thereafter, Mr. S was referred for a presurgical evaluation (Exam 2) prior to a planned ACDF procedure. Here, the conclusions of the two evaluations are briefly described.

Neuropsychological Exam

The following is an excerpt from the neuropsychologists' conclusions:

> Overall results of testing revealed average intellectual abilities commensurate with expectation. There is a possibility of prior history of attentional deficits since his scores in sustained attention most closely match a normative group with Attention-Deficit Hyperactivity Disorder. There is also impairment noted in divided attention; spatial/directional skill; visual span of attention; auditory comprehension; and bilateral fine motor functioning. These deficits are not believed to be secondary to a head injury. It is currently well understood that the most important information needed for determining whether or not a person sustained a brain injury and the severity of the injury, if one was sustained, is determined by the acute neurological characteristics of the injury. According to self-report, if LOC was sustained, it was in short duration. There was no evidence of injury on neuroimaging and his GCS was 15. Scientific literature provides a clear framework for assessing recovery and subsequent problems after a concussion or mild traumatic brain injury. This literature demonstrates that lasting symptoms and physical problems are not anticipated after a concussion or mild traumatic brain injury. The more parsimonious explanation is that Mr. S is perceiving cognitive impairment probably because of other environmental stressors such as financial issues; pain, and depression. Certainly, being involved in litigation is also a factor that has been empirically shown to impact the experience of prolonged symptom recovery.
>
> With regard to emotional functioning and report of pain symptoms, there are six findings of exaggerated symptom reporting on the current assessment. While he does not

meet criteria for malingering, the pattern of abnormal psychological symptom validity findings cannot be explained by any combination of conditions surrounding the claim and would be best explained as an attempt to magnify physical and emotional problems. These findings suggest that Mr. S self-report of symptoms should not be utilized as the primary source of information regarding his pain or emotional well-being. Rather, objective measures are needed to corroborate his symptom reporting.

It is difficult to determine the severity of Mr. S' psychological dysfunction given the blatant overreporting. However, I do not find him to be psychologically or neurocognitively disabled from working. In fact, return to work could provide him with symptom reduction and reduce financial distress.

Presurgical Evaluation

The following is an excerpt from the clinical psychologists' conclusions:

Mr. S was referred for a presurgical psychological screening prior to a planned spine surgery (ACDF C3-C4) to examine relevant psychological and/or behavioral factors in his case which might impact the outcome of surgery. The evaluation consisted of a clinical interview with Mr. S, review of medical records made available to the examiner, and the administration of psychometric assessment measures.

During my interview with Mr. S, he complained of diffuse pains throughout the left side of his body, headaches, sleep difficulties, emotional changes, and continued to present with claims of cognitive issues. His left sided bodily complaints were not, however, corroborated with imaging except for multilevel cervical degenerative changes and associated spinal stenosis without significant cord compression and without evidence of focal disc herniations. Similarly, there were no clear findings from imaging nor the neuropsychological evaluation to explain his subjectively reported cognitive complaints. Mr. S' presentation in the current evaluation and neuropsychological evaluation is unusual in that he did not demonstrate any overt pain behaviors typically seen in pain patients such as sighing, grunting, voicing complaints, shifting in seat, adjusting posture, or standing throughout the duration of testing.

Mr. S attempted to present himself as overly symptomatic on cognitive measures of performance validity in the current evaluation; however, he did not present himself in such a manner during the neuropsychological evaluation when he was being assessed for his ongoing cognitive complaints. A total of 7 cognitive performance validity scales were observed within range of known malingering pain patients. These observations of invalid performance reflected an attempt on Mr. S' part to present himself as overly symptomatic with cognitive issues. This is a rather unusual pattern of behavior for a surgical candidate.

Mr. S' cognitive abilities were briefly measured to assess his ability to comprehend the risks of surgery and his ability to comply with post-operative recommendations. Despite the invalid performances seen on cognitive performance validity measures, his cognitive abilities were intact and were mostly similar to his performances seen in the neuropsychological evaluation. There was no evidence of significant cognitive impairment which would result in cognitive disability.

There are significant concerns about the validity of Mr. S' subjective complaints. Results from the MMPI-2 revealed overreporting on symptom validity scales (F, FB,

FBS) and calculated indices of overreporting (MI, RBS). These scores reflect intentional exaggeration of somatic and cognitive complaints. Similarly, results from pain-related measures (PDI & Sullivan PCS) were positive for overreporting of symptoms. More concerning, these scores were elevated to a level that identifies membership into a group of malingering pain patients with high specificity. Results from the MSPQ revealed a score of 13, which reflected significant psychological complication; however, his MSPQ score at the neuropsychological evaluation was 23, which surpassed the score needed to belong to a group of malingering pain patients.

Additionally, significant elevations were observed on scales Hs, D, Hy, of the MMPI-2 which are known to be associated with poor surgical outcomes. Moreover, the score seen on scale FBS in combination with the elevations observed on scales Hs and Hy are to a level that empirical evidence identifies membership into a group of malingering pain patients (Bianchini et al., 2008). Results from the BHI-2 also revealed a strong negative bias that was higher than that seen in 86% of patients, somatic complaints higher than those seen in 98% of patients, depression and anxiety higher than 99% and 98% of patients, respectively, and symptom dependency higher than 99% of patients. The findings from the BHI-2 are associated with poor outcomes from a rehabilitation stand-point.

There are concerns about Mr. S' motivation for treatment. It is rather unusual for a patient to delay completion of a presurgical evaluation if their motivation is to resolve their pain. In this case, it took 3-months for Mr. S to complete the necessary testing to determine his risk status for spine surgery. Also, Mr. S has not participated in conservative treatments prior to surgical consideration other than the use of pain medications. Specifically, he refused/evaded the cervical epidural steroid injections and physical therapy recommended to him by his treating physician. Mr. S also stated that he has not participated in any psychological treatment to date, despite the recommendation for brief cognitive behavioral counseling for an unspecified depressive disorder and suicidal ideation that was recommended to him by the previous neuropsychologist.

Peer reviewed literature has found that psychological and psychosocial risk factors can have a significant and sometimes dominant influence on symptomatic and functional outcomes from procedures and surgeries offered for pain relief in some patients. Pain-complicating factors can be represented by historical factors, contextual factors, or psychological mechanisms/comorbidities, most of which are unintentional. However, a non-trivial proportion of patients with external incentive for symptoms and disability will present with intentionally exaggerated symptoms (i.e., factitious disorder, malingering). In the case of Mr. S., there are clear indications of intentional exaggeration of cognitive and somatic complaints, as well as incentive (i.e., financial compensation, avoiding return to work).

Based on the use of an empirically supported presurgical psychological screening algorithm prior to spine surgery (Block et al., 2001), Mr. S is at elevated risk for poor surgical outcome. Notably, findings from psychometric testing are to a level associated with poor prognosis from spine surgery. There are also adverse clinical features present in this case including inconsistencies in the patient's subjective reports, medical imaging, and psychometric testing; intentional exaggeration of cognitive and somatic complaints; involvement in a compensable injury; and noncompliance with conservative treatment recommendations. Moreover, Mr. S meets the published diagnostic criteria for Malingered Pain-Related Disability.

Summary and Conclusions

The final conclusion of the examiner for the presurgical psychological evaluation was that Mr. S met published criteria for a diagnosis of MPRD, and that he was at elevated risk for poor outcome from spine surgery. The following section summarizes the findings consistent with the criteria of Bianchini et al. (2005) for MPRD, as well as the use of an empirically supported, well-validated psychological presurgical screening algorithm. These criteria reflect a systemic and comprehensive framework for organizing information gathered from the clinical interview, testing, and records.

The Bianchini et al. criteria are divided into five domains: the first addresses the presence of incentive (Criterion A); the second relates to evidence from physical evaluation that physical abilities, capacities, and/or limitations are consistent with exaggeration of feigning of physical disability (Criterion B); the third relates to evidence from neuropsychological testing that a patient's capacities are consistent with exaggeration or feigning of cognitive disability (Criterion C); the fourth relates to evidence from self-report that symptoms, complaints, or limitations are consistent with exaggeration or feigning of physical, cognitive, or emotional/psychological disability (Criterion D); the fifth describes conditions under which a diagnosis of malingering would be ruled out even if the other criteria are met (Criterion E). See Table 26.5 for a summary of the criteria, and Table 26.6 for specifiers for MPRD.

Table 26.5 Summary of the Bianchini et al. (2005) Criteria for Malingered Pain-Related Disability

A Presence of significant external incentive
B Evidence from physical evaluation
  1 Probable effort bias. One or more well-validated measures of physical capacity is consistent with exaggeration of diminished capacity
  2 Discrepancy between subjective report of pain and physiological reactivity
  3 Nonorganic findings. The presence on physical examination or functional capacity evaluation of signs or symptoms not consistent with known physiological mechanisms. Reported symptoms/complaints are substantially different than would be expected given the medical findings
  4 Discrepancy between the patient's physical presentation during formal evaluation and their physical capacities documented when they are not aware of being observed
A Evidence from cognitive/perceptual (neuropsychological testing)
  1 Definite negative response bias. Below-chance performance ($p < 0.05$) on one or more forced choice measures of cognitive or perceptual function
  2 Probable response bias. Performance on one or more well-validated tests designed to measure exaggeration or fabrication of cognitive or perceptual symptoms is consistent with exaggeration of diminished cognitive capacity
  3 Discrepancy between cognitive/neuropsychological test data and known patterns of brain functioning
  4 Discrepancy between test data and observed behavior
A Evidence from self-report
  1 Compelling inconsistencies
  2 Self-reported history is discrepant with documented history
  3 Self-reported symptoms are discrepant with known patterns of physiological or neurological functioning
  4 Self-reported symptoms are discrepant with observations of behavior
  5 Evidence from formal psychological evaluation that the person has significantly misrepresented their current status in a manner that emphasizes the injury for which compensation is sought
A Behaviors meeting necessary criteria from B, C, D are not fully accounted for by psychiatric, neurologic, or developmental factors

Table 26.6 Diagnostic Categories for the Diagnosis of Malingered Pain-Related Disability

Malingering Specifiers:	
Definite MPRD	Presence of substantial external incentive (Criterion A) "Definitive" evidence of intent (Criterion C1 or D1) Behaviors meeting the criteria for "definitive" intent are not fully accounted for by psychiatric, neurologic, or developmental factors
Probable MPRD	Evidence of significant external incentive (Criterion A) Two or more types of "probable" evidence of intent from Criterion B, Criterion C, and/or Criterion D. This evidence must be well-validated and have a known error rate
Possible MPRD	Evidence of significant external incentive (Criterion A) Evidence does not rise to the level sufficient for a diagnosis of Probable MPRD < Only one type of quantitative "probable" evidence of intent from Criterion B, Criterion C, and/or Criterion D OR < One or more forms of qualitative evidence of intent from Criterion B, Criterion C, and/or Criterion D OR < Evidence sufficient for a diagnosis of MPRD is present BUT Criterion E is not met

Criterion A: Evidence of External Incentive

The Bianchini et al. (2005) criteria require at least one "clearly identifiable and substantial external incentive for exaggeration or fabrication of symptoms" be present at the time of the evaluation for a diagnosis of MPRD to be made. In Mr. S' case, he was an injured worker who was receiving compensation benefits, he was also represented by an attorney, and he was seeking a financial settlement from Workers' Compensation. Thus, the presence of possible financial gain in disability payments and settlements were evidenced, as well as incentive to not to return to work. Thus, *Criterion A* was met in this case.

Criterion B: Evidence from Physical Evaluation

Mr. S reported symptoms/complaints that were substantially different than would be expected given the medical findings. During the neuropsychological evaluation, he reported cognitive complaints of memory loss, misplacing items, difficulty recalling phone numbers, addresses, appointments, losing historical information (i.e., wedding day), and the medical record also noted word-finding difficulties. He also reported that he sustained a concussion on the day of the injury. Medical records, however, did not document any such diagnoses, and imaging of the brain during two imaging studies were normal. He also reported significant headaches and light sensitivity, as well as claiming that the back of his head would swell at times. Additionally, Mr. S' cognitive complaints were not reported until six months post-injury. His subjective claims and delayed onset of symptoms, as well as the unusual symptom report of posterior head swelling are significant discrepancies from the accepted scientific literature on head injuries. Thus, *Criterion B3* was met during exam 1.

Similarly, during the presurgical evaluation, Mr. S continued to complain of cognitive issues despite the objective evidence of normal brain imaging and globally intact neurocognitive function revealed in the neuropsychological exam. Moreover, he endorsed pain in the upper back and midback, issues with constipation, inability to fully void his bladder, and sexual dysfunction attributable to pain. However, none of these physical complaints were ever documented in the medical record by his physicians, and further, the latter symptoms would be indicative of Cauda Equina Syndrome, and there were no documented medical records indicating low back pathology. In fact, the lumbar imaging performed on the day of the injury was normal. Mr. S also reported significant subjective pain ratings at both evaluations of 8–9 out of 10; however, imaging did not reveal evidence of disc bulges nor herniated nucleus pulposus, which would be known to cause substantial pain ratings. Rather, his imaging showed multilevel cervical DDD and associated spinal stenosis without significant cord compression. Thus, Mr. S also met *Criterion B3* in the presurgical evaluation.

Criterion C: Evidence from Cognitive/Perceptual (Neuropsychological) Testing

It was notable that during the neuropsychological evaluation, Mr. S' performance on explicit cognitive performance validity measures were within normal limits; however, during the presurgical psychological evaluation, Mr. S demonstrated invalid performances on several validity tests. He also produced an immediate recognition score below accepted cutoffs. A force-choice test result less than 50% "is not a random or chance occurrence but represents a purposive distortion by the examinee" (Reynolds, 1998, p. 272).

On the TOMM, his performance on Trial 1, Trial 2, and Retention were below published norms for even persons with objectively defined moderate–severe traumatic brain injury who gave good effort (Greve et al., 2006; Martin et al., 2020; Tombaugh, 1996). Additionally, Mr. S demonstrated a positive finding on Reliable Digit Span (Heinly et al., 2005). These findings meet *Criterion C2*, evidence of response bias on one or more well-validated tests designed to measure exaggeration or fabrication of cognitive diminished capacity.

There was clear evidence of exaggerated somatic symptoms on the SVTs of PDI and Sullivan PCS during the presurgical psychological evaluation, as well as scales of the MMPI-2. During the neuropsychological evaluation, Mr. S also demonstrated clear evidence of intentional exaggeration of somatic complaints on the MSPQ and Sullivan PCS. These all meet *Criterion C2*.

Mr. S additionally demonstrated evidence from exaggerated or fabricated psychological dysfunction, which also met *Criterion C2*. During both the neuropsychological evaluation and the presurgical psychological evaluation, Mr. S demonstrated significant elevations on the family of F scales of the MMPI-2, along with scales Hs and Hy, that were in the range of known malingering pain patients. Additionally, the calculated MI of the profile was 6, which reflects definite overreporting, as well as the calculated RBS with a score of 18, which reflected overreporting of cognitive and somatic complaints. Similar results were obtained from validity scales on the MMPI-2 administered during the neuropsychological evaluation.

Criterion D: Evidence from Self-Report

Mr. S' account of the accident and his sustained injuries were inconsistent with the documented history. Specifically, Mr. S continued to claim that he sustained a concussion from the slip and fall accident during the presurgical psychological evaluation; however, the medical records reflected no diagnosis of concussion, and results from the neuropsychological evaluation was not the profile of a brain-injured patient. All imaging performed on the day of the work-related accident were entirely normal, as well as a repeat MRI of the brain 11 months post-injury. Mr. S also changed his estimate of LOC throughout the medical records. At times, he reported that he lost consciousness for up to ten minutes, other times, he reported up to five minutes, and other times, he reported up to two minutes His GCS was noted as 14 in the EMS records and this had been restored to 15 by the time he was evaluated in the ER. Mr. S claimed that he had memory loss following the accident, but results from the neuropsychological exam found his cognitive function to be globally intact, and the examiner opined that scientific literature provides a clear framework for assessing recovery and subsequent problems after a concussion or mild traumatic brain injury. This literature demonstrates that lasting symptoms and physical problems are not anticipated after a concussion or mild traumatic brain injury (Sweet et al., 2013). Thus, there was no neuropsychological basis for his claims of cognitive issues post-injury. As previously noted, his significantly elevated pain ratings and report of symptoms were not supported by objective medical imaging. Thus, *Criterion D2*, "self-reported history is discrepant with documented history" was met. Additionally, Mr. S also denied any knowledge of a planned surgical procedure, ACDF C3–C4, despite the medical records documenting discussions with Mr. S about surgical intervention due to his lack of follow through with more conservative methods of treatment.

In Mr. S' case there was also *Criterion D4* "self-reported symptoms are discrepant with observations of behavior." In both evaluations, Mr. S reported significant pain, rating his pain as 8–9 of 10, and reported light sensitivity. However, during each evaluation, Mr. S did not demonstrate any overt pain behaviors that are typically seen in chronic pain patients. Specifically, he did not grimace, sigh, voice pain complaints, shift in his seat, adjust his posture, nor stand during testing. Rather, he presented throughout each testing session with euthymic affect and was very chatty with the psychometrists throughout testing, often requiring redirection to the test stimuli. Similarly, despite his claims of chronic headaches and light sensitivity, Mr. S did not demonstrate any sensitivities to light throughout either evaluation. Further, his physician recommended physical therapy, which Mr. S did not participate in, and his physician could not obtain a clear reason for why he had not attended physical therapy per the medical record. Additionally, Mr. S did not participate in the recommended cervical epidural steroid injections which were also recommended by his physician. These behaviors related to treatment noncompliance are rather inconsistent with pain patients who are truly seeking to remedy their pain condition.

In both evaluations, there was also clear evidence of *Criterion D5* "evidence from formal psychological evaluation that the person significantly misrepresented their current status in a manner that emphasizes the injury for which compensation is sought." As can be seen from the data gathered through formal psychological assessment, there were clear indications of intentional exaggeration present on the family of F scales form the MMPI-2, RBS, as well as scales Hs and Hy, reflecting exaggeration of somatic, cognitive, and psychological complaints. Moreover, there was evidence of intentional exaggeration on the PDI and the Sullivan PCS during the presurgical evaluation, as well as evidence of exaggeration on the MSPQ and the Sullivan PCS during the previous neuropsychological evaluation.

Criterion E: Behavior Meeting Necessary Criteria from Groups B, C, and D Are Not Fully Accounted for by Psychiatric, Neurologic, or Developmental Factors

Criterion E provides a framework under which findings that are sufficient for a malingering diagnosis would not be classified as malingering. Behaviors that meet necessary criteria that can be *fully* accounted for by genuine psychiatric, neurological, or developmental disorders should not be labeled as malingering. The criterion elucidates that malingering cannot be ruled out unless it can be reasonably demonstrated that positive *Criterion B, C, and D* are not fully accounted for by developmental, medical, or psychiatric conditions. In the case of Mr. S, there were no factors present that would fully account for his observed performances on testing.

Table 26.7 summarizes each of the Bianchini et al. criteria and whether or not each was met in the two evaluations. As can be seen, Mr. S met criteria for malingering in the presurgical psychological evaluation. Specifically, he met criteria for Definite MPRD. He did not, however, meet full criteria for malingering during the first neuropsychological evaluation, but there was evidence of intentional exaggeration to levels only seen in pain patients with incentive to present themselves as overly symptomatic.

Table 26.7 Summary of the Bianchini et al. (2005) Criteria for Malingered Pain-Related Disability and Whether the Criteria Were Met in Each Exam

	Exam 1	*Exam 2*
A Presence of significant external incentive	Yes	Yes
B Evidence from physical evaluation		
1 Probable effort bias on one or more well-validated measures of physical capacity is consistent with exaggeration of diminished capacity	No Data	No Data
2 Discrepancy between subjective report of pain and physiological reactivity	No Data	No Data
3 Nonorganic findings. The presence on physical examination or functional capacity evaluation of signs or symptoms not consistent with known physiological mechanisms. Reported symptoms/complaints are substantially different than would be expected given the medical findings	Yes	Yes
4 Discrepancy between the patient's physical presentation during formal evaluation and their physical capacities documented when they are not aware of being observed	No	No
A Evidence from cognitive/perceptual (neuropsychological testing)		
1 Definite negative response bias. Below-chance performance ($p < 0.05$) on one or more forced choice measures of cognitive or perceptual function	No	Yes
2 Probable response bias. Performance on one or more well-validated tests designed to measure exaggeration or fabrication of cognitive or perceptual symptoms is consistent with exaggeration of diminished capacity	Yes	Yes
3 Discrepancy between cognitive/neuropsychological test data and known patterns of brain functioning	No	No
4 Evidence from self-report		
5 Compelling inconsistencies	No	No
6 Self-reported history is discrepant with documented history	No	Yes
7 Self-reported symptoms are discrepant with known patterns of physiological or neurological functioning	Yes	Yes
A Self-reported symptoms are discrepant with observations of behavior	Yes	Yes
1 Evidence from formal psychological evaluation that the person has significantly misrepresented their current status in a manner that emphasizes the injury for which compensation is sought	Yes	Yes
2 Behaviors meeting necessary from criteria B, C, D are not fully accounted for by psychiatric, neurologic, or developmental factors	Yes	Yes

Presurgical Psychological Screening (PPS)

Mr. S' test findings in the neuropsychological evaluation were not interpreted as indicating malingering, but they did clearly provide evidence of significant exaggeration of symptoms. This obscured and precluded any mental health diagnosis and raised significant concerns about the reliability of his subjective symptoms, including his claims of pain-related functional limitations and disability. The findings from the presurgical evaluation clearly meet published criteria for malingering. The findings of exaggeration and malingering have important implications in the management of patients complaining of persisting/chronic pain in general. The findings mean that subjectively reported symptoms and behaviors under the patient's voluntary control are an unreliable basis for clinical decision-making, including decisions regarding the severity of physical pain, the need for medical treatment, the efficacy of treatment administered, and the degree of pain-related disability. Such patients are at risk of continuing to present themselves symptomatically to medical providers, seeking prescription medications, reporting poor response to medical interventions and procedures, excess utilization of the health care system, undergoing unnecessary surgeries, avoiding a return to work, as well as financial implications regarding patient care and disability. There are also important implications of these findings that are specific to the PPS algorithm published by Block et al.

As previously noted, the Block et al. (2001) PPS algorithm has been demonstrated to be a well-validated model for accurately predicting surgical outcomes from spine surgery in 82% of patients. The original model was based on the use of the MMPI-2, and has been revised for use of the MMPI-2-RF. Notably, the MMPI-family (MMPI, MMPI-2; MMPI-2RF; MMPI-3) remains the most-studied broad-based measures of psychopathology, and are commonly used in medico-legal contexts given the wealth of research behind the measures (Butcher & Ben-Porath, 2004; Butcher & Miller, 2006; Selbom, 2019). As such, in the medico-legal context of a work-related, compensatory injury presented in this chapter, the MMPI-2 was used in the PPS to determine risk status for poor outcome.

The PPS model of Block and colleagues (2001) classifies information obtained through the evaluation process into four domains–interview risk factors, testing risk factors, medical risk factors, and adverse clinical features—each with a set of factors known to increase risk for poor outcome. In the case of Mr. S, several factors were identified during the presurgical psychological evaluation.

During the clinical interview, it was known that Mr. S was involved in a Workers' Compensation claim for his work-related injury, and he also acknowledged that he was represented by an attorney and that he was seeking a financial settlement from the Workers' Compensation carrier around his injuries. When asked about current and past substance use, Mr. S acknowledged a remote history of cannabis use. These factors are known risk factors in the Block et al. (2001) PPS model. He also reported that he had not returned to work since the accident, which far exceeded the PPS model's risk factor of not working greater than two months.

Testing risk factors were reported by Block and colleagues to account for 78.4% of patient outcomes (Block et al., 2001). The MMPI-2 profile administered in this case revealed substantial elevations on 8 of 10 scales with scales D, Sc, Pt, Pa, Hs, and Hy being the most elevated. The elevations observed on scales Hs, D, and Hy are known psychological contraindications for spine surgery (Block et al., 2003; Block et al., 2001; Epker & Block, 2001). Results from the PDI revealed a significant elevation for his perception of pain-related disability, and the Sullivan PCS also revealed a substantial elevation for pain catastrophizing. Moreover, the multiple indications of intentional exaggeration observed on well-validated psychometric measures had significant implications, indicating motivation to present himself in an unfavorable manner. Based only on test data, several significant factors were present that are associated with poor outcome from spine surgery.

Regarding medical factors associated with poor outcome, Mr. S' complaints of pain had surpassed 12 months, which is a known factor in Block's PPS model. Additionally, he was being considered for a highly destructive surgery, also a known factor, and it was striking that surgery was being considered given that he had not fully participated in conservative modalities of treatment. The rationale for the surgery was based largely on a single EMG/NCS study. The previous MRI of the cervical spine did not reveal significant cord compression, bulging discs, nor herniated nucleus pulposus, which would substantiate the need for cervical surgery. There were also no physical findings from imaging studies to account for his other diffuse, left-sided, midback, and lower extremity pain complaints, reflecting nonorganic signs.

Lastly, the Block PPS Model focuses on the presence of adverse clinical features that should be considered. Throughout this chapter, the authors have presented psychometric evidence of intentional exaggeration present in this case, a diagnosis of MPRD, as well as the inconsistencies and noncompliance documented throughout the medical records. These findings reflected the presence of adverse clinical features noted in the Block PPS Model.

Based on the use of Block et al.'s empirically supported PPS model, Mr. S was deemed to be at elevated risk for poor outcome from spine surgery. The model provides a weighted point system for identified psychosocial risk factors and a flow chart diagram for the clinician's use. In this case, when the model is applied to data obtained from *both* evaluations, a score of six was obtained from interview risk factors (i.e., job dissatisfaction, involvement in Workers' Compensation, and remote history of substance abuse). Several risk factors were identified related to testing; however, the model stipulates a maximum point assignment of 4 from the MMPI-2 data. Thus, a maximum score of six was obtained from testing risk factors (i.e., pain sensitivity [Hs, Hy], reactive depression [D], depressed pathological profile [characterized by four or more scale elevations], pain catastrophizing). The score based on medical risk factors was 6 (pain greater than 12 months, highly destructive surgery [ACDF], nonorganic signs).

The total for psychosocial risk factors in this case was 12 and medical risk factors totaled 6. These scores combined placed him in the "poor prognosis" category. If no adverse clinical features were present, the recommendation would be for "noninvasive treatment." However, in this case, adverse clinical factors (intentional exaggeration, inconsistencies, noncompliance, diagnosis of MPRD) were present. Applying this data to Block et al.'s PPS model, the patient remained in the poor prognosis category, but due to the presence of these adverse clinical factors, the recommendation became "discharge the patient" (Block et al., 2001, p. 108).

Discussion

The case presented in this chapter demonstrates a process of detecting MPRD within the context of a presurgical psychological evaluation. This case demonstrates the importance of examining performance and symptom validity and malingering indications whenever there is financial incentive. Within the context of a presurgical evaluation, it is important for examiners to assess for indications of intentional exaggeration, particularly in medico-legal, work-related, and/or disability-related examinations because these are secondary gain contexts.

The patient described in this chapter continued to present to medical providers with substantial subjective pain ratings of the neck despite there being no evidence of bulging discs or herniated nucleus pulposus evidenced on imaging, as well diffuse left-sided pain in the face of normal imaging studies, which reflects improbable physical symptoms given the characteristics of the spine studies. The only positive imaging found was of multilevel cervical DDD with associated spinal stenosis, and later, an EMG/NCS that found left C4 radiculopathy with both acute and chronic features, which his physician used as a basis for surgery. However, there were no positive imaging studies to account for his complaints of other diffuse left-sided pains. It is also notable that, other than the use of medications, the patient did not actively participate in conservative modalities of treatment (i.e., physical therapy, cervical epidural steroid injections) recommended to him by his treating physician, and he seemed to have actively avoided these interventions. Due to his lack of participation in conservative modalities of treatment, his physician recommended cervical spine surgery. The patient in this case also claimed to have no knowledge of a proposed cervical surgery despite this recommendation and discussion about the surgery with the patient being documented in the medical records. It is also rather unusual for a patient with significant, credible pain complaints to delay the presurgical evaluation for several months as the patient did in this case, which raises questions about possible motives to delay surgery or to delay detection of intentional exaggeration.

The patient in this case also claimed to have sustained a concussion with residual cognitive symptoms despite no evidence of such a diagnosis reflected in the medical records, normal repeat brain imaging, and he was found to be cognitively globally intact by the examining neuropsychologist. It is noteworthy that there was no evidence in the records that the patient reported any cognitive complaints until six months after the injury.

The most compelling information that the discrepancies between the patient's subjective complaints and objective findings were a result of malingering was observed in the cognitive performance validity measures and the multiple indications of malingering of somatic complaints. It was also interesting that there was a marked change in the patient's performance on cognitive validity measures between the neuropsychological evaluation and the presurgical evaluation. As noted, he performed within normal limits on cognitive PVTs during the neuropsychological evaluation when he was examined for possible cognitive deficits and received feedback that there was no evidence of cognitive deficits attributable to a head injury. However, the patient demonstrated negative response bias on cognitive PVTs during the presurgical evaluation. This reflected a discernible change in his approach to testing, and the scores observed demonstrated intent to underperform.

This case highlights the unique role psychologists play in the presurgical work-up process, ultimately helping the medical team and the patient avoid a potentially unnecessary surgery. One might question, "*Why would anyone subject themselves to an unnecessary surgery?*" Such behavior seems illogical and potentially self-injurious. Eisendrath (1996) asserted that malingering individuals will avoid *secondary loss* (in this case self-injury) if it is greater than the potential for *secondary gain*. Eisendrath has also argued for a continuum with factitious disorder and malingering both on the continuum. He acknowledges that in some patients there can be both emotional/interpersonal (i.e., "primary" gain) and external/financial sources (secondary gain) present. Fishbain (2003) adopted a different opinion regarding malingering in medical contexts. He posited that malingering cannot account for behaviors of individuals submitting themselves to potentially harmful invasive medical procedures. While it is uncommon for patients to seek unnecessary surgery, this behavior has been documented. Interested readers should review the case of a young woman who also actively pursued medically unnecessary surgery who demonstrated definitive evidence of intentional symptom production and a diagnosis of malingering (Bianchini et al., 2004).

The opinion of Bianchini et al. was that these assertions made by Eisendrath and Fishbain were an oversimplification of a complex psychosocial process and asserted that "malingering is a complex psychosocial phenomenon that should not be ruled in or out on the basis of simplistic clinical rules of thumb" (Bianchini et al., 2004, p. 719). Eisendrath's position is that malingering is intentional, meaning a conscious choice is made to pursue an external goal. Therefore, this decision involves a rational calculation (i.e., secondary loss versus secondary gain). However, patients who malinger respond to external gain such as financial motives (i.e., secondary gain), but this is not necessarily the exclusive source of motivation. They are also subject to interpersonal/emotional needs and conflicts (i.e., seen in factitious disorder) that are not necessarily rational. That is, in *some cases*, such as the case of Mr. S presented in this chapter and by Bianchini et al. (2004), when a patient is malingering, logic/reason may play less of a role in their decision-making about how to present the intentionally exaggerated symptoms. For some malingering patients, unnecessary surgery may be a means to an end of intentional exaggeration, although arguably not a rational decision. Surgery potentially increases the value of the claim. Stated differently, because the behavior is seemingly irrational (getting an unnecessary surgery as part of malingering) does not mean we can assume that it will never happen, even if it occurs rarely in patients who are malingering. Neither the case described in this chapter nor the case described by Bianchini et al. (2004) support Fishbain's contention that illogical choices rule out malingering. In addition, individuals with factitious tendencies are no less subject to influences of secondary gain than they are their own emotional/interpersonal needs characteristic of factitious disorder. The *Diagnostic and Statistical Manual of Mental Disorders* (*DSM-5-TR*) seems to also recognize this concept, as the updated manual states "factitious disorder and malingering are not mutually exclusive. The motives in any single case might be multiple and shifting depending on the circumstances and reactions of others" (APA, 2022, p. 369).

The case described in this chapter and the case described by Bianchini et al. (2004) raise questions about the secondary loss versus secondary gain calculation described by Eisendrath, as there was evidence in both cases of patients who were known to be malingering and seeking unnecessary surgery. The case study presented in this chapter does not say anything about the prevalence of a willingness to engage in potentially self-injurious behavior in malingering patients, but it does support the notion that it can and does occur. The case described in this chapter also demonstrates the importance of using well-validated measures with known error rates to identify patients malingering pain-related disability. In cases such as this, in which secondary gain is identifiable (i.e., financial incentive, avoidance of return to work), it is imperative for psychologists to assess the validity of patient's reported symptoms and cognitive performance.

Note

1 The basis for determining invalid performances were derived from the published criteria of scores with a false-positive error rate of 10% or less consistent with the AACN Consensus Statement (Sweet et al., 2021).

References

Alentado, V. J., Lubelski, D., Steinmetz, M. P., Benzel, E. C., & Mroz, T. E. (2014). Optimal duration of conservative management prior to surgery for cervical and lumbar radiculopathy: A literature review. *Global Spine Journal*, *4*(4), 279–286.

American Psychiatric Association (2022). Somatic symptom and related disorders. In *Diagnostic and Statistical Manual of Mental Disorders* (5th ed., text rev.). Washington, DC: American Psychiatric Association. doi: 10.1176/appi.books.9780890425787.x09_Somatic_Symptom_and_Related_Disorders

Balagué, F., Mannion, A., Pellisé, F., & Cedraschi, C. (2012). Non-specific low back pain. *Lancet, 4*(379), 482–491. doi: 10.1016/S0140–6736(11)60610-7.

Bianchini, K. J., Aguerrevere, L. E., Guise, B. J., Ord, J. S., Etherton, J. L., Meyers, J. E., Soignier, R. D., Greve, K. W., Curtis, K. L., & Bui, J. (2014). Accuracy of the modified somatic perception questionnaire and pain disability index in the detection of malingered pain-related disability in chronic pain. *The Clinical Neuropsychologist, 28*(8), 1376–1394. doi: 10.1080/13854046.2014.986199

Bianchini, K. J., Curtis, K. L., & Greve, K. W. (2006). Compensation and malingering in traumatic brain injury: A dose-response relationship? *Clinical Neuropsychology, 20*(4), 831–47. doi: 10.1080/13854040600875203.

Bianchini, K. J., Etherton, J. L., Greve, K. W., Heinly, M. T., & Meyers, J. E. (2008). Classification accuracy of MMPI-2 validity scales in the detection of pain-related malingering: A known groups study. *Assessment, 15*, 435–449. doi: 10.1177/1073191108317341

Bianchini, K. J., & Greve, K. W. (2009). Chronic pain as a context for malingering. In J. E. Morgan & J. J. Sweet (Eds.), *Neuropsychology of Malingering Casebook* (pp. 307–332). New York: Psychology Press.

Bianchini, K. J., Greve, K. W., & Glynn, G. (2005). On the diagnosis of malingered pain-related disability: Lessons from cognitive malingering research. *The Spine Journal, 5*(4), 404–417. doi: 10.1016/j.spinee.2004.11.016

Bianchini, K. J., Heinly, M. T., & Greve, K. W. (2004). Unnecessary cervical disc surgery for a malingering patient. *Spine Journal, 4*(6), 718–719. doi: 10.1016/j.spinee.2004.06.007

Block, A. R., Gatchel, R. J., Deardoff, W. W., & Guyer, R. D. (2003). *The Psychology of Spine Surgery*. Washington, DC: American Psychiatric Association.

Block, A. R., Ohnmeiss, D. D., Guyer, R. D., Rashbaum, R. F., & Hochschuler, S. H. (2001). The use of presurgical psychological screening to predict the outcome of spine surgery. *The Spine Journal, 1*(4), 274–282.

Bruns, D., & Disorbio, J. M. (2014). The psychological evaluation of patients with chronic pain: A review of BHI 2 clinical and forensic interpretive considerations. *Psychological Injury and Law, 7*(4), 335–361. doi: 10.1007/s12207-014-9206-y.

Butcher, J. N., & Ben-Porath, Y. S. (2004). Use of the MMPI-2 in medico-legal evaluations: An alternative interpretation for the Senior and Douglas (2001) critique. *Australian Psychologist, 39*(1), 44–50. doi: 10.1080/00050060410001660335

Butcher, J. N., & Miller, K. B. (2006). *Personality assessment in personal injury litigation*. In I. B. Weiner & A. K. Hess (Eds.), *The handbook of forensic psychology* (pp 140–166). Hoboken, NJ: John Wiley & Sons Inc.

Curtis, K. L., Aguerrevere, L. E., Bianchini, K. J., Greve, K. W., & Nicks, R. C. (2019). Detecting malingered pain-related disability with the pain catastrophizing scale: A criterion groups validation study. *The Clinical Neuropsychologist, 33*(8), 1485–1500. doi: 10.1080/13854046.2019.1575470

Dieleman, J. L., Cao, J., Chapin, A., Chen, C., Li, Z., Liu, A., Horst, C., Kaldjian, A., Matyasz, T., & Scott, K. W. (2020). US health care spending by payer and health condition, 1996–2016. *JAMA, 323*(9), 863–884. doi: 10.1001/jama.2020.0734

Eisendrath, S. J. (1996). When Munchausen becomes malingering: Factitious disorders that penetrate the legal system. *Bull Am Acad Psychiatry Law, 24*(4), 471–481. Retrieved from https://pubmed.ncbi.nlm.nih.gov/9001745/

Epker, J., & Block, A. R. (2001). Presurgical psychological screening in back pain patients: A review. *Clinical Journal of Pain, 17*(3), 200–205.

Fishbain, D. A. (2003). Re: Secondary loss and pain-associated disability: Theoretical overview and treatment implication. *J Occup Rehabil, 13*, 197–198. doi: 10.1023/a:1024957319161

Gervais, R. O., Ben-Porath, Y. S., Wygant, D. B., & Green, P. (2007). Development and validation of a Response Bias Scale (RBS) for the MMPI-2. *Assessment, 14*(2), 196–208. doi: 10.1177/1073191106295861.

Green, P., Allen, L. M., & Astner, K. (1996). *The Word Memory Test: A User's Guide to the Oral and Computer-administered Forms, US Version 1.1.* Durham, NC: CogniSyst.

Greve, K. W., Bianchini, K. J., Black, F. W., Heinly, M. T., Love, J. M., Swift, D. A., & Ciota, M. (2006). The prevalence of cognitive malingering in persons reporting exposure to occupational and environmental substances. *NeuroToxicology, 27*, 940–950.

Greve, K. W., Bianchini, K. J., & Brewer, S. T. (2013). The assessment of performance and self-report validity in persons claiming pain-related disability. *The Clinical Neuropsychologist, 27*(1), 108–137. doi: 10.1080/13854046.2012.739646

Greve, K. W., Bianchini, K. J., & Doane, B. M. (2006). Classification accuracy of the test of memory malingering in traumatic brain injury: Results of a known-groups analysis. *Journal of Clinical and Experimental Neuropsychology, 28*(7), 1176–1190. doi: 10.1080/13803390500263550

Greve, K. W., Curtis, K. L., Bianchini, K. J., & Ord, J. (2008). Are the original and second edition of the California Verbal Learning Test equally accurate in detecting malingering? *Assessment, 16*(3), 237–248. doi: 10.1177/1073191108326227

Greve, K. W., Ord, J., Curtis, K. L., Bianchini, K. J., & Brennan, A. (2008). Detecting malingering in traumatic brain injury and chronic pain: A comparison of three forced-choice symptom validity tests. *The Clinical Neuropsychologist, 22*, 896–918. doi: 10.1080/13854040701565208

Greve, K. W., Ord, J. S., Bianchini, K. J., & Curtis, K. L. (2009). The prevalence of malingering in chronic pain patients referred for psychological evaluation in a medico-legal context. *Archives of Physical Medicine & Rehabilitation, 90*, 1117–1126. doi: 10.1016/j.apmr.2009.01.018

Harris, I., Mulford, J., Solomon, M., van Gelder, J. M., & Young, J. (2005). Association between compensation status and outcome after surgery: A meta-analysis. *JAMA, 293*, 1644–1652. doi: 10.1001/jama.293.13.1644

Heilbronner, R. L., Sweet, J. J., Morgan, J., Larrabee, G. J., Millis, S. R., & Conference Participants (2009). American Academy of Clinical Neuropsychology Consensus Conference Statement on the Neuropsychological Assessment of Effort, Response Bias, and Malingering. *The Clinical Neuropsychologist, 23*, 1093–1129.

Heinly, M. T., Greve, K. W., Bianchini, K. J., Love, J. L., & Brennan, A. (2005). WAIS digit span-based indicators of malingered neurocognitive dysfunction: Classification accuracy in traumatic brain injury. *Assessment, 12*, 429–444. doi: 10.1177/1073191105281099

Kazeminasab, S., Nejadghaderi, S. A., Amiri, P., Pourfathi, H., Araj-Khodaei, M., Sullman, M. J., Kolahi, A., & Safiri, S. (2022). Neck pain: Global epidemiology, trends and risk factors. *BMC Musculoskeletal Disorders, 23*(26). doi: 10.1186/s12891-021-04957-4

Larrabee, G. J., Greiffenstein, M. F., Greve, K. W., & Bianchini, K. J. (2007). Refining diagnostic criteria for malingering. In G. J. Larrabee (Ed.), *Assessment of Malingered Neuropsychological Deficits* (pp. 334–371). New York: Oxford University Press.

Marek, R. J., Block, A. R., & Ben-Porath, Y. S. (2019). Validation of a psychological screening algorithm for predicting spine surgery outcomes. *Assessment, 26*(5), 915–928. doi: 10.1177/1073191117719512

Martin, P. K., Schroeder, R. W., Olsen, D. H., Maloy, H., Boettcher, A., Ernst, N., & Okut, H. (2020). A systematic review and meta-analysis of the Test of Memory Malingering in adults: Two decades of deception detection. *The Clinical Neuropsychologist, 34*(1), 88–119.

Meyers, J. E., Millis, S. R., & Volkert, K. (2002). A validity index for the MMPI-2. *Archives of Clinical Neuropsychology, 17*(2), 157–169. doi: 10.1093/arclin/17.2.157

Mittenberg, W., Patton, C., Canyock, E. M., & Condit, D. C. (2002). Base rates of malingering and symptom exaggeration. *Journal of Clinical and Experimental Neuropsychology, 24*, 1094–1102. doi: 10.1076/jcen.24.8.1094.8379

Reynolds, C. R. (1998). Common sense, clinicians, and actuarialism. In C. R. Reynolds (Ed.), *Detection of Malingering during Head injury Litigation* (pp. 261–286). New York: Plenum.

Rohling, M. L., Binder, L. M., & Langhinrichsen-Rohling, J. (1995). Money matters: A meta-analytic review of the association between financial compensation and the experience and treatment of chronic pain. *Health Psychology, 14*, 537–547. doi: 10.1037//0278–6133.14.6.537.
Schroeder, R., Twumasi-Ankrah, P., Baade, L., & Marshall, P. (2011). Reliable digit span: A systematic review and cross-validation study. *Assessment, 19*, 21–30. doi: 10.1177/1073191111428764.
Selbom, M. (2019). The MMPI-2-Restructed Form (MMPI-2-RF): Assessment of personality and psychopathology in the twenty-first century. *Annual Review of Clinical Psychology, 15*, 149–155. doi: 10.1146/annurev-clinpsy-050718–095701.
Sherman, E. M. S., Slick, D. J., & Iverson, G. L. (2020). Multidimensional malingering criteria for neuropsychological assessment: A 20-year update of malingered neuropsychological dysfunction criteria. *Archives of Clinical Neuropsychology, 35*, 735–764. doi: 10.1093/arclin/acaa019
Slick, D. J., & Sherman, E. M. S. (2013). Differential diagnosis of malingering. In D. A. Carone & S. S. Bush (Eds.), *Mild Ttraumatic Brain Injury: Symptom Validity Testing and Malingering* (pp. 57–72). New York: Springer Publishing Company.
Slick, D. J., Sherman, E. M. S., & Iverson, G. L. (1999) Diagnostic criteria for malingering cognitive dysfunction: Proposed standards for clinical practice and research. *Clinical Neuropsychology, 13*(4), 545–561. doi: 10.1076/1385–4046(199911)13:04;1–Y;FT545
Stanton, E. W., Chang, K., Formanek, B., Buser, Z., & Wang, J. (2022) The incidence of failed back surgery syndrome varies between clinical setting and procedure type. *Journal of Clinical Neuroscience, 103*, 56–61. doi: 10.1016/j.jocn.2022.06.027
Sweet, J. J., Goldman, D. J., & Guidotti Breting, L. M. (2013). Traumatic brain injury: Guidance in a forensic context from outcome, dose-response, and response bias research. *Behavior Science and the Law, 31*(6), 756–78. doi: 10.1002/bsl.2088.
Sweet, J. J., Heilbronner, R. L., Morgan, J. E., Larrabee, G. J., Rohling, M. L., Boone, K. B., Kirkwood, M. W., Schroeder, R. W., Suhr, J. A., & Conference Participants (2021). American Academy of Clinical Neuropsychology 2021 consensus statement on validity assessment: Update of the 2009 AACN consensus conference statement on neuropsychological assessment of effort, response bias, and malingering. *The Clinical Neuropsychologist, 35*(6), 1053–1106. doi: 10.1080/13854046.2021.1896036
Tombaugh, T. (1996). *Test of Memory Malingering Manual*. New York: MultiHealth System.
Verla, T., Xu, D. S., Davis, M. J., Reece, E. M., Kelly, M., Nunez, M., Winocour, S. J., & Ropper, A. E. (2021) Failure in cervical spinal fusion and current management modalities. *Seminars in Plastic Surgery, 35*(1), 10–13. doi: 10.1055/s-0041–1722853
Voorhies, R. M., Jiang, X., & Thomas, N. (2007). Predicting outcome in the surgical treatment of lumbar radiculopathy using the Pain Drawing Score, McGill Short Form Pain Questionnaire, and risk factors including psychosocial issues and axial joint pain. *The Spine Journal, 7*(5), 516–524. doi: 10.1016/j.spinee.2006.10.013
Wideman, T. H., Edwards, R. E., Walton, D. M., Martel, M. O., Hudon, A., & Seminowicz, D. A. (2019). The multimodal assessment model of pain. *The Clinical Journal of Pain, 35*(3), 212–221. doi: 10.1097/AJP.0000000000000670
Young, A. K., Young, B. K., Riley, L. H., & Skolasky, R. L. (2014). Assessment of presurgical psychological screening in patients undergoing spine surgery: Use and clinical impact. *Journal of Spinal Disorders and Techniques, 27*(2), 76–79. doi: 10.1097/BSD.0b013e31827d7a92

27 Invalidity in Two Civil Competency Examinations

George J. Demakis

The purpose of this chapter is to describe two civil incompetency cases in which the examinee produced invalid test results, a rare occurrence. Most individuals do not want to be adjudicated incompetent, as such a ruling deprives people of essentially all their rights as citizens, including possibly the right to drive. In addition, someone else is assigned to make decisions for them, and the nature of this assistance is overseen by the court. Years ago, one elderly patient I was evaluating said that she would rather be diagnosed with dementia than be viewed as incompetent! In any event, despite the reality that most individuals resist an incompetency adjudication and tend to fight against it, there was a clear motivation for the examinees described here to perform in an invalid manner.

In North Carolina, the Multidisciplinary Evaluation (MDE) is a competency evaluation that, at least in theory, includes psychology, social work, and medicine. Realistically, the vast majority of these evaluations in my practice include only the psychological component, which includes a clinical interview, behavioral observations, psychological testing, record review, and, usually, collateral interviews. The purpose is to assist the court in deciding competency and, if the individual is found incompetent[1], to provide recommendations for guardianship, including who should serve in the role and the nature of the guardianship. The MDE may be completed privately or may be ordered and paid for by a government entity. Where I practice—Mecklenburg County—this is done via the Forensic Evaluations Unit (FEU), which is a local governmental unit and part of the broader Criminal Justice Services. The two cases I present in this chapter were both court-ordered MDE referrals through the FEU.[2]

Subsequent to a referral from the FEU, the evaluation is completed, and the written report is distributed to both the judge or hearing officer overseeing the case and the Guardian ad Litem attorney. The latter is tasked with representing the "best interests" of the individual alleged to be incompetent (i.e., the respondent in legal terms). When the MDE has been completed and other data gathered, the hearing officer subsequently makes the ultimate decision on competency. If the respondent is deemed incompetent—the standard for this is "clear, cogent, and convincing"—a guardian is assigned to make decisions for that person and to manage their affairs. This individual is now known as the ward. The written MDE report is usually sufficient for the hearing officer to make a decision but the evaluator may need to testify.

Case #1: Mr. M

Background: Mr. M was a 32-year-old White man who was brought to the evaluation by his petitioner mother. She stated that her son has lived with her much of his adult life and needs significant assistance with activities of daily living including laundry, as well as medication and financial management. He does not drive and needs assistance with public transportation. By

DOI: 10.4324/9781003005063-31

his description, he spends his days watching television and movies; he does not like to be left alone as he is worried that "something might happen." Mr. M acknowledged multiple mental health symptoms, such as suicidal ideation, anxiety, depression, and auditory hallucinations for which he was hospitalized. He reported hearing voices his entire life but had only recently told his mother about them. His mother has not seen obvious evidence of auditory hallucinations in her son, such as responding to internal stimuli. Nonetheless, he was prescribed Abilify and Prozac two or three months ago. Mr. M acknowledged prior marijuana and alcohol use but denied current use. Mr. M was in special education while in school and does not currently work. He worked in a warehouse for two months, where he had a job coach. Medically, he stated that he has an "overactive thyroid," but does not take medication for this. He denied brain injury, stroke, or seizure. He has never been married and does not have any children.

Legal Situation: Mr. M was facing felony charges of Assault with a Deadly Weapon with Intent to Kill or Inflict Serious Injury eight months before this examination. This alleged offense occurred about two years before my examination and occurred in the context of a fight he had with another patron at a local establishment. According to a witness, Mr. M hit another man with a metal rod and continued striking him about the head even after he had fallen and lost consciousness. The victim suffered a broken jaw, broken orbital bones, and lacerations on the top of his head. This was his first criminal charge.

Medical Records: Mr. M had one psychiatric hospitalization about eight months before the current examination. On discharge, he was diagnosed with Unspecified Mood Disorder, Cannabis Use Disorder, Alcohol Use Disorder, and a rule out diagnosis of Malingering. The latter was noted, in part, because he presented in non-credible ways such as claiming suicidality without evidence of "poor self-care", self-report of hallucinations without evidence of responding to internal stimuli, and a history of untreated depression since he was 12 years old. He could not explain why his depression had recently increased.

Academic Records: Mr. M had an Individualized Education Plan in high school for Mild Intellectual Disability and completed an occupational course of studies. Consistent with this, early testing for developmental disability indicated that his cognitive and functional skills were below the 5th percentile. He also had "speech deficits."

Behavioral Observations: Mr. M presented as alert, but variably attentive and cooperative. During the clinical interview, he readily answered all questions, except one about his legal charges, as his attorney was not there. During testing, however, he appeared variously disengaged and, at times, overwhelmed with even the most basic cognitive tasks. He needed substantial re-direction and assistance to complete some of these. Mood and affect were initially quite anxious, though he became increasingly less anxious as the exam progressed. Speech, language (comprehension), thought content, and thought processes were all intact. There was no overt evidence of psychosis.

Test Results: Mr. M failed two performance validity tests (PVTs), Reliable Digit Span of the WAIS-III (Greiffenstein et al., 1994), and the Coin-in-the-Hand Test (Schroeder et al., 2012). Because of this and his disengaged presentation, limited cognitive testing was completed (see Table 27.1).

Test results were viewed as not accurate representation of cognitive functioning. Performance on these tests was below the 1st percentile and in the exceptionally low range. Notable aspects of performance include:

- On the Mini-Mental State Examination (MMSE), he did not know the season, month, day, date, year, city, or state. He was one year off on the year, but he thought it was January even though the exam was in April.

Table 27.1 Performance Validity Tests and Cognitive Tests for Mr. M

Performance Validity Tests	*Raw Score*	*Classification*
Coin-in-the-Hand Test	6/10	Invalid
Digit Span of WAIS-III RDS	4	Invalid
Cognitive Tests	*Scaled/Raw/ Standard Score*	*Percentile*
WAIS_III Digit Span subtest	3	<1st percentile
Trail Making Test Part A	123 seconds	<1st percentile
Mini-Mental State Examination	5	<1st percentile
Word Reading of WRAT-5	55	<1st percentile

Note: WAIS-III = Wechsler Adult Intelligence Scale. RDS = Reliable Digit Span. WRAT-5 = Wide Range Achievement Test-5.

- On the MMSE, when asked to draw interlocking geometric figures, he drew two interlocking circles.
- On the MMSE, when asked to write a sentence, he wrote "i kant lyfe."
- On the Wide Range Achievement Test-5 Word Reading, he was unable to read even the simplest words such as "how" and "even."
- On the Managing Money subtest of the Independent Living Scales, he counted out 55 cents when asked to count out $1.39.
- On the Health and Safety subtests of the Independent Living Scales, he dialed 811 on an inoperable cell phone when asked how to contact the police.

Case formulation: While academic records confirm that Mr. M had intellectual limitations, the current cognitive testing and presentation were not valid. First, he appeared disengaged during testing and needed substantial encouragement and assistance to complete even simple tasks. At the most basic level, he did not appear to be even trying. Second, he failed two PVTs, even when using cutoffs for individuals with intellectual disabilities or other cognitive impairments (Dean et al., 2008). Such failure raises questions about the accuracy of the other cognitive tests, which were all in the exceptionally low range. Related to this, his performances were excessively and non-credibly impaired even for someone with intellectual limitations as he was, for instance, five months off on the month of the year, he could not write even a simple sentence or read even simple words. Dialing 811 vs. 911 for calling the police was, in my view, a Ganser-like response. These responses are approximate answers to simple or familiar questions, and are of unknown etiology, but may signal malingering. Third, multiple aspects of his history were simply not consistent with a long history of a psychiatric disorder, such as claiming that he has heard voices his whole life, even though having told his mother about these only recently. His presentation more broadly, both on my exam and when psychiatrically hospitalized, was inconsistent with his serious psychiatric complaints. Finally, this presentation was in the context of, at least on the surface, an appealing external incentive (i.e., being adjudicated incompetent). Mr. M may have thought that an incompetency adjudication would help his criminal case; he likely did not know that criminal and civil competency are separate issues. In the end, I described that his invalid presentation precluded diagnosis of either cognitive or psychological issues and did not allow for an accurate recommendation about competency. I subsequently provided the GAL attorney and court with several recommendations regarding how they could obtain such information.

Legal Outcome: Within about a month after submitting my report, the incompetency petition was dismissed, so he was not adjudicated incompetent. A little over one year after my examination, his criminal charge was still pending.

Case #2: Ms. L

Background: Ms. L was a 52-year-old Latina whose adult son filed the incompetency petition. He alleged that she needed assistance managing her finances and business affairs, as well as working with her attorney. In his view, she is "not logical," does not understand email or phone conversations, and does not keep her house clean. In contrast, he stated that she is "okay" in daily life as she lives alone safely. Her bills are paid via automatic pay. She does not take her medications as prescribed because she is distrustful of healthcare providers. Her son attributed these difficulties to the multiple car accidents her mother has had—she has never been held overnight when taken to the Emergency Department and CT scans of her head have been negative. By her account, Ms. L did not think that she was incompetent but acknowledged making bad decisions and having difficulty preparing for her upcoming legal case. She described word-finding difficulty, disorganization, and that she spends a lot of time in bed because she is afraid of what others would think about her or about being perceived as a "fake." Like her son, she attributed her difficulties to three concussions sustained in car accidents several years ago. She denied loss of consciousness or posttraumatic amnesia. In addition to the above symptoms, she described a variety of other symptoms due to the concussions including personality change, head, neck, shoulder, and chest pain, photophobia, burping, difficulty breathing, and throwing up because noise "bothered her." She denied other traumatic brain injuries, stroke, or seizure. The only other medical problem was knee pain due to a tendon injury.

Ms. L is currently seeing a psychiatrist and psychologist for treatment; she stated that she was "doing good." Both providers provided the information below. She denied any prior mental health treatment or mental health difficulties. She does not use drugs but occasionally drinks alcohol.

Ms. L has been divorced for about 12 years—she and her ex-husband have two adult children, neither of whom live with her. She immigrated to the United States as an adult. She earned an MBA degree at a local college. She was a good student throughout school and was never diagnosed with a learning disability or Attention-Deficit/Hyperactivity Disorder.

Legal Situation: According to her son, Ms. L was in a contract dispute with the landlord of her small business in another state. She was being sued for "hundreds of thousands" of dollars because she broke a long-term lease. Ms. L was also pursuing a disability claim at this time (apparently Social Security, but this was unclear), but her first application was rejected.

Medical Records: Ms. L was previously evaluated by two mental health professionals. In an exam by a psychologist about six months before this one, diagnoses given were Mild Neurocognitive Disorder due to traumatic brain injury (TBI), Postconcussive Syndrome, Major Depressive Disorder, and Somatization. The psychologist opined that Ms. L had "markedly declined" due to multiple concussions with associated spine and chronic pain. Even so, he raised multiple questions about the validity of the cognitive and psychological testing as she performed "below normal expectations on three internal performance validity measures" and tests of symptom validity suggested "symptom endorsement and over-exaggeration." A psychiatric exam conducted about one and half years prior to my examination, resulted in diagnoses of Major Depressive Disorder with somatization, psychogenic belching, and cognitive impairment, as well as Postconcussive Syndrome with chronic headaches and neck spasms. The psychiatrist concluded that computerized cognitive testing was "invalid" across a range of domains including memory, attention, and motor speed. On a "Neuropsyc questionnaire", she endorsed significant levels of fatigue, pain, mania, depression, and cognitive issues. On presentation, she was "wildly disorganized and rambling" with air swallowing and belching. He prescribed Valium and Risperdal, but she was not taking these at a follow-up about one month after this exam. In the end, the psychiatrist described that she had somatoform/conversion disorder elements "driven more by social and emotional factors than endogenous injury."

Behavioral Observations: Ms. L drove herself to and from the examination. Though alert and attentive, she appeared variably cooperative, as she was excessively slow on some of the cognitive tests. Hygiene and grooming were poor—she smelled faintly of body odor—and she was sloppily dressed. Ms. L appeared to be in significant pain in various body parts including her shoulder, hand, eye, knees, and tailbone. Her gait was slow, seemingly due to knee pain. She also complained that the overhead indoor lighting was bothering her, and we eventually moved to a room with more natural lighting. Possibly related to this, she complained that she had difficulty seeing objects and test stimuli and would bring them close to her eyes to see them better. This did not appear to affect performance. Throughout the exam, she belched loudly, sometimes multiple times in a row—these did not appear to be related to the content of the conversation nor did they affect testing. Speech was heavily accented, but her language expression and comprehension were good. Thought content was marked by a preoccupation with a prior concussion and her legal case. Thought processes were rambling, tangential, and excessively detailed at times. As such, she tended to be a poor historian. There was no overt evidence of psychosis.

Test Results: Mr. L failed two PVTs, a freestanding test (TOMM; Tombaugh, 1997) and an embedded test (Reliable Digit Span of the WAIS-III). The validity of the cognitive testing is thus questionable and likely an underestimate of true abilities. To that end, as can be seen in Table 27.2, performance was in the exceptionally low or below-average range on most cognitive tests.

Exceptions included performance on Trails B and free clock drawing (CLOX). On psychological testing (Table 27.3), MMPI-2-RF responses were significantly elevated on all five of the overreporting scales (F-r, FP-r, Fs, FBS-r, and RBS), indicating exaggeration of emotional, somatic, and cognitive symptoms. The resulting clinical profile was thus not valid and clinical scales were not interpreted. Similarly, the Beck Depression Inventory-2 (BDI-II) and the Beck Anxiety Inventory (BAI) were both in the severe range and likely exaggerated as well.

Case Formulation: Ms. L's presentation of both cognitive and psychological complaints was not valid. First, her presentation was marked by variable cooperation on cognitive testing and an exaggerated and "over the top" symptom presentation that speaks more to validity and mental health issues than the multiple apparent mild concussions she suffered. Both she and her son attributed her difficulties to the latter. Second, she failed both PVTs, a freestanding one and an embedded one. Some of her cognitive performances were also excessively impaired given her education and history. In a similar vein, multiple MMPI-2-RF validity scales were highly elevated, indicating that she exaggerated psychological symptoms both on this test and the other self-report measures as well. Third, and related to the point above, Ms. L's attribution of her cognitive and psychological difficulties to what appeared to be simple, uncomplicated concussions is not consistent with the long-term outcome of such injuries (these occurred three to four years ago). Of course, this is even if she had suffered such injuries—I did not have access to the medical records,

Table 27.2 Performance Validity Tests and Cognitive Tests for Ms. L

Performance Validity Tests	*Raw Score*	*Classification*
TOMM Trial 1	28	Invalid
TOMM Trial 2	41	Invalid
Digit Span of WAIS-III RDS	6	Invalid
Cognitive Tests	*Raw/Standard Score*	*Percentile*
Wechsler Test of Adult Reading	84	14th
Mini-Mental State Examination	24	<1st percentile
CLOX Free	13	67th
CLOX Copy	12	<1st percentile
Trail Making Test Part A	62 seconds	2nd percentile
Trail Making Test Part B	103 seconds	19th percentile
Controlled Oral Word Association Test	24	2nd percentile
Animal Fluency	11	2nd percentile
WMS-IV Logical Memory I	9	<1st percentile
WMS-IV Logical Memory II	7	2nd percentile
Rey Complex Figure Copy	24.5	≤1st percentile
Rey Complex Figure IR	12	7th percentile
Rey Complex Figure DR	5	<1st percentile
ILS Managing Money Subtest	21	4th percentile
ILS Health & Safety Subtest	23	<1st percentile

Note: TOMM = Test of Memory Malingering; WAIS-III = Wechsler Adult Intelligence Scale; RDS = Reliable Digit Span; CLOX = Executive Clock Drawing Task; WMS = Wechsler Memory Scale; IR = Immediate Recall; DR = Delayed Recall; ILS = Independent Living Scales.

Table 27.3 Screening Tests and Minnesota Multiphasic Personality Inventory-2-Restructured Form Validity Scales for Ms. L

Test	*Raw or T Score*	*Range*
Beck Anxiety Inventory	45	Severe
Beck Depression Inventory-II	52	Severe
MMPI-2-RF Validity Scales		
Variable Response Inconsistency (VRIN-r)	63	Consistent
True Response Inconsistency (TRIN-r)	57-T	Consistent
Infrequent Responses (F-r)	120	Invalid
Infrequent Psychopathology Responses (FP-r)	94	Invalid
Infrequent Somatic Responses (Fs)	91	Invalid
Symptom Validity (FBS-r)	92	Invalid
Response Bias Scale (RBS)	114	Invalid
Uncommon Virtues (L-r)	66	Valid
Adjustment Validity (K-r)	38	Valid

so I could not confirm these. This is not to say that such injuries could not exacerbate prior psychopathology or personality disturbance. Finally, I evaluated Ms. L in the context of apparent secondary gain—appearing incompetent for her upcoming civil legal case. This likely motivated her son to file the incompetency petition, though her involvement and understanding of this were not clear. In the end, even despite the invalidity detailed above, I opined that she did not meet incompetency criteria as she lived alone, drove herself to and from my office without difficulty, and managed at least some of her activities of daily living without difficulty such as cooking, cleaning, and shopping. If she had performed validity on cognitive testing, she should have performed better on these ability tests. As such, Ms. L did not meet the "clear, cogent, and convincing" standard necessary for an incompetency adjudication. Even so, I diagnosed Major Depressive Disorder (with anxious distress) and Somatic Symptom Disorder as psychiatric involvement was obvious, though exaggerated.

Legal Outcome: Shortly after I submitted my report, Ms. L was not adjudicated incompetent.

Take Home Points about Validity Issues in Civil Competency Examinations

I have been conducting MDEs for 20 years and have conducted, in total, almost 300. Most of these have been court-ordered and in the county where I work and practice, but I am occasionally privately retained, both in my home county and in adjacent counties. Overall, validity issues are rare in such cases and these two cases are outliers. I would estimate that validity issues are present in only about 1–2% of cases, a number that is similar to Mittenberg et al.'s (2002) 2% estimation of the rate of malingering in dementia cases, based on a survey of clinical neuropsychologists. I believe that my number is so low because respondents are aware that more can be lost from being adjudicated incompetent vs. gained. I view the two respondents described above as fundamentally mistaken about what can be gained from an incompetency adjudication. While an incompetency adjudication may be perceived as attractive for individuals in certain legal situations, the reality is that such an adjudication does not necessarily affect other legal decisions. One can, for instance, be adjudicated incompetent civilly, yet still be adjudicated competent to proceed to trial on a criminal charge. These are separate legal issues.

With that in mind, I would like to highlight my main approach for competency evaluations, which is no different than the approach I use in other types of cases in which invalidity—and possibly frank malingering—is more common, such as personal injury or disability cases. My approach is similar to the Slick criteria (Sherman et al., 2020), an integrative and multidimensional approach to detect invalidity. This includes consideration of the examination context, performance on PVTs and SVTs, consistency of examination's presentation with history, records, and reliable collateral reports, and ruling out other developmental, neuropsychological, and psychiatric issues. Such an approach is particularly well-suited to more complex cases like Ms. L In the end, I opined on Ms. L's civil competency as I had at least some credible information on her current functioning, but I did not do so for Mr. M In that case, I did not have sufficient valid information to address the referral question about competency, both in the history and test data.

Notes

1 In North Carolina, the relevant statute reads: Incompetent adult means an adult or emancipated minor who lacks sufficient capacity to manage the adult's own affairs or to make or communicate important decisions concerning the adult's person, family, or property whether the lack of capacity is due to mental illness, mental retardation, epilepsy, cerebral palsy, autism, inebriety, senility, disease, injury, or similar cause or condition. N. C. General Statutes § 35A-1101 (7).

2 Several details about each case have been changed to protect confidentiality.

References

Dean, A. C., Victor, T. L., Boone, K. B., & Arnold, G. (2008). The relationship of IQ to effort test performance. *The Clinical Neuropsychologist, 22*(4), 705–722.

Greiffenstein, M. F., Baker, W. J., & Gola, T. (1994). Validation of malingered amnesia measures with a large clinical sample. *Psychological Assessment, 6*(3), 218–224.
Mittenberg, W., Patton, C., Canyock, E. M., & Condit, D. C. (2002). Base rates of malingering and symptom exaggeration. *Journal of Clinical and Experimental Neuropsychology, 24*(8), 1094–1102.
North Carolina General Statutes 35A 1101–7.
Schroeder, R. W, Peck, C. P, Buddin, W. H., Heinrichs, R. J., & Baade, L. E. (2012). The Coin-in-the-Hand Test and dementia: More evidence for a screening test for neurocognitive symptom exaggeration. *Cognitive and Behavioral Neurology, 25*(3), 139–143.
Sherman, E., Slick, D., & Iverson, G. (2020). Multidimensional malingering criteria for neuropsychological assessment: A 20-year update of the malingered neuropsychological dysfunction criteria. *Archives of Clinical Neuropsychology, 35*(6), 735–764.
Tombaugh, T. N. (1997). The Test of Memory Malingering (TOMM): Normative data from cognitively intact and cognitively impaired individuals. *Psychological Assessment, 9*(3), 260–268.

28 Post-Treatment Lyme Disease

Iatrogenic Somatic Symptom Disorder in Combination with Secondary Gain Influences

Richard F. Kaplan

In the book *Cure Unknown*, the author describes chronic Lyme disease as a "contested disease," and "Lyme wars" as a conflict between patients suffering from Lyme disease due to inadequate diagnosis and treatment, and a medical establishment that views Lyme disease as another curable infection (Weintraub, 2008). This ongoing controversy is the background for this case, which involves a disability claim in which the insured reports he is no longer able to work due to ongoing post-treatment Lyme disease (PTLD) symptoms. This case of Mr. CC was selected because of the role of the neuropsychological examination in documenting the absence of brain dysfunction. The claimant reported disabling cognitive symptoms, which were contradicted by neuropsychological findings. The claimant did not appear to be engaging in the fabrication of symptoms found in malingering (as confirmed by his valid and normal test results), but rather was most likely perceiving dysfunction that did not exist, consistent with a somatoform orientation and comorbid depression and anxiety. While malingering per se was not present, pursuit of external gain likely played a role in consolidating the claimant's intractable view of himself as disabled, thereby placing the claimant on a continuum with both somatoform and secondary gain influences.

To put this case in perspective, a brief history of Lyme disease, Lyme neuroborrelioses, efficacy of Center for Disease Control (CDC) recommended treatments for Lyme disease, and prognosis following treatment are provided.

Background

Although the first description of a *Borrelia* infection, now known as Lyme disease, appeared in the literature almost 100 years ago, its etiology and transmission were only recognized in the mid-1970s following an outbreak of arthritis near Lyme, Connecticut. Lyme disease is a tick-borne infection caused by the spirochete *Borrelia burgdorferi* (Steere et al., 1983). A rash (erythema migrans), which starts as a small red spot at the site of the tick bite and expands over time, is an early sign of localized infection. When left untreated, a *Borrelia* infection can disseminate throughout the body, affecting the skin, joints, heart, eyes, and nervous system.

Lyme Neuroborreliosis

The nervous system is involved in approximately 15% of untreated Lyme patients (Pachner & Steere, 1985). The classic neurological symptoms of Lyme disease include either meningitis or multifocal inflammatory changes in the peripheral nervous system, both of which are evident in the neurologic examination (Halperin, 2022). There have been case

DOI: 10.4324/9781003005063-32

reports of more serious neurological involvement related to Lyme disease, although documented cases are rare (Rosendahl et al., 2023). Traditional brain neurophysiological and neuroimaging techniques have not been shown to be highly sensitive to the pathophysiology of neuroborreliosis. The routine EEG is typically normal, and although MRI abnormalities have been described in Lyme patients, these are nonspecific and relatively infrequent (Finkel & Halperin, 1992). Even in patients with confirmed central nervous system involvement, MRI evidence of tissue damage is rare (Agosta et al., 2006). When observed, the MRI abnormalities described in neuroborreliosis suggest an inflammatory process that usually involves the subcortical white matter (Krupp et al., 1991). Single photon emission computed tomography (SPECT), a functional imaging technique that measures regional cerebral blood flow to specific brain regions, once showed promise in localizing the neuroanatomic basis for cognitive symptoms in Lyme disease. Using a quantitative SPECT, some seropositive patients show patterns of multifocal hypoperfusion, most notably in frontal subcortical areas and white matter of the cerebral hemispheres (Logigian et al., 1997). This has led some clinicians to advocate using SPECT in making a definitive diagnosis of Lyme-related brain impairment. However, while sensitive to brain abnormalities, SPECT hypoperfusion is not specific to Lyme disease and can be found in other conditions such as depression (Ito et al., 1996) and chronic fatigue syndrome (Schwartz et al., 1994). Therefore, it cannot be used to reliably make a diagnosis of Lyme-related brain disease.

Diagnosis and Treatment

For people in endemic areas with a tick bite and an erythema migrans rash, the CDC recommends a two-step testing procedure. The first step typically consists of a screening enzyme immunoassay (EIA) or enzyme-linked immunosorbent assay. If results are positive or equivocal, a Western immunoblot test is performed to confirm the results using CDC-recommended guidelines (Halperin, 2022).

Prerequisites to diagnose Lyme neuroborreliosis require evidence of confirmed Lyme disease, nervous system disease, and a causal relationship between the two. Assessment of cerebral spinal fluid (CSF) plays an important role in diagnosing neuroborreliosis (Halperin et al., 2022) and the diagnosis requires clear evidence of intrathecal antibody production to *Borrelia burgdorferi*, by culture, or polymerase chain reaction (Stanek et al., 2014).

Ten days of oral doxycycline, a tetracycline antibiotic, provides an optimal recovery rate. Most patients respond well to this recommended antibiotic regimen if treated in early disease (Lantos et al., 2010). Extending treatment with doxycycline from 10 to 20 days, or adding one dose of ceftriaxone to the beginning of a 10-day course of doxycycline, does not enhance therapeutic efficacy in patients with erythema migrans. Regardless of regimen, objective evidence of treatment failure is extremely rare (Wormser et al., 2006).

Neuropsychology of Lyme Disease

The first neuropsychological studies of Lyme disease appeared in the late 1980s and early 1990s in patients who were initially untreated and developed disseminated disease. In an early neuropsychological study of patients with at least a three-month history of infection and evidence of neurological disease, memory impairment was the most salient deficit with little impairment in other cognitive domains (Logigian et al., 1990). In a study comparing Lyme patients with neuroborreliosis to patients with fibromyalgia or depression with similar memory complaints, the Lyme patients showed greater memory deficits (Kaplan et al., 1992).

Lyme patients with CSF abnormalities had significantly lower memory scores than those without CSF abnormalities (Kaplan & Jones-Woodward, 1997). After standard antibiotic therapy, most patients show significant improvements in their cognitive functioning (Halperin et al., 1988; Logigian et al., 1990) and better cerebral perfusion (Logigian et al., 1997). Krupp et al. (1991) reported that some PTLD patients continue to have lower scores on list learning and word fluency tests compared with normal controls, suggesting the possibility of residual deficits. However, others have shown that PTLD patients perform similarly to other non-neurological patient groups, such as osteomyelitis, when compared with healthy controls (Ravdin et al., 1996). A community study of 168 people with prior Lyme disease found the treated people reported more symptoms of Lyme disease than community controls but there were no differences on objective testing (Shadick et al., 1999). This was recently confirmed in a laboratory study of 106 confirmed Lyme disease patients six months post-treatment (Bechtold et al., 2017). Overall, most PTLD patients with cognitive complaints show little evidence of cognitive dysfunction on objective testing (Kaplan, et al., 2003).

Post-Treatment Lyme Encephalopathy

The etiology of PTLD-related encephalopathy remains controversial (Feder et al., 2007). After the resolution of the objective manifestations of Lyme disease with antibiotic treatment, a minority of patients report diffuse and nonspecific symptoms, including memory loss, naming problems, difficulty concentrating, reduced efficiency, somnolence, fatigue, and musculoskeletal pain. Of 128 patients with confirmed Lyme who were followed for ten years, 10% had one or more PTLD symptoms at one point during the follow-up, less than 5% had a symptom at ten years, and none had functional impairment (Weitzner et al., 2015a, 2015b). PTLD is rarely associated with evidence of a current *Borrelia* infection or CSF abnormalities. Unfortunately, cognitive impairment remains a construct of PTLD and is often misconstrued as evidence of a chronic brain infection. When cognitive symptoms occur with abnormal CSF (either intrathecal production of antibody to *Borrelia*, increased CSF protein, or both), there is a likely neurological basis to the illness. However, nonspecific cognitive symptoms without abnormal CSF are compelling evidence that PTLD is not the basis for a neurologic disorder (Halperin, 2016). Borrowing from treatment studies of fibromyalgia, multidisciplinary approaches that combine medications with nonpharmacologic therapies (such as cognitive behavioral therapy) are usually the best treatments for PTLD (Steere & Arvikar, 2015).

The Case of Mr. CC

Mr. CC was a 60-year-old gentleman who underwent a neuropsychological evaluation in 2018 at the request of his insurer to assess his functional abilities and limitations regarding a claim for disability benefits. The following information was gleaned from an interview with Mr. CC, his medical records, and records from the insurer's consultants.

Interview

Mr. CC was born and raised in Connecticut. When he was in the 11th grade his family moved to Spain for a year. This resulted in falling behind in school and when he returned, having to repeat his senior year. However, he reported no other learning difficulties. He described himself as an "alright" student until his junior and senior years of college when he began filmmaking and excelled. He graduated from a prominent university in 1980 with a bachelor's degree in communications. Mr. CC is self-employed making films for advertising agencies. He has worked in this field since 1978 with different production companies. His work includes pitching ideas to potential clients, and when hired, putting together a crew and producing the film. He noted that this is a very competitive industry, and that procuring work requires "selling himself" to potential clients, although he also receives some work based on his reputation. Once work is secured, the process requires organizing a team of approximately 50 people and directing the film. His work hours vary between 0 and 50+ per week depending on the phase of a project. Tasks include preparing for job calls and self-promotion, writing treatments, casting, directing television commercials, and editing. When between jobs, he may not work at all.

Mr. CC lives with his wife of 37 years, and their 29-year-old son. They have two other adult daughters who reside outside the home. Mr. CC denied ever having smoked cigarettes and reported that he only occasionally drinks alcohol. He also denied past or present problems with alcohol or illicit drug use, adding that he does not like taking medications. At the time of the evaluation, he was not taking any prescription medications. He exercises by walking approximately three miles a day.

Mr. CC reported that he was first diagnosed with Lyme disease in 1989–1990, after having identified the tick bite, developing a "bulls-eye" rash, and testing positive for Lyme disease. He was successfully treated with two months of oral antibiotics and reported no other Lyme-related symptoms until 2004. In 2004, he began to experience some cognitive difficulties, most notably memory loss and difficulty concentrating. He also started stuttering. Other symptoms included headaches, moderate fatigue, and problems with sleep. As discussed in the review of medical records below, Mr. CC was again diagnosed with active Lyme disease in 2008 and 2011, and continued to report fluctuating cognitive and somatic symptoms. A 2016 Lyme test revealed that his Lyme titers were lower and 2017 test showed he no longer met the criteria for active Lyme disease.

With regard to current work-related activities, Ms. CC stated that his inability to communicate effectively was a major problem because interacting with potential clients was the way he obtained work. He described continued difficulty with word finding, particularly with names, and short-term memory loss. For example, during a conference call, he might lose his train of thought and sometimes "blank out." Moreover, as the ability to "think on his feet" and pitch ideas spontaneously was vital to successfully recruiting new business, his cognitive decline was negatively impacting his job success, as well as his ability to perform when he obtained work. He attributed his problems with sleep to restless leg syndrome, a disorder he has had all his life.

When questioned about depression, Mr. CC stated he was "up and down," with symptoms, including loss of interest in things he previously enjoyed and thoughts of harming himself. He reported increased irritability and mood swings, being easily agitated, and having a lower frustration threshold. Mr. CC stated that he "loved" his work, performed his job well, and did not want to stop working. When questioned about changes in the industry that may have affected his work, he responded that such changes were subtle and did not affect his job performance.

Medical Records

In July of 2005, Mr. CC consulted Dr. K, a board-certified neurologist, complaining of a three- to four-month history of aches and pains, and malaise. Mr. CC reported he had removed a tick the preceding May (2005). Mr. CC also described a recurrent upper respiratory infection, periodic limb movements in sleep, and increased irritability. However, he described his sleep as "not bad." Dr. K diagnosed Lyme disease without additional testing and prescribed two months of the antibiotic Biaxin. This resulted in less malaise and decreased fatigue, and Dr. K stopped treatment and put a previous request for a brain MRI on hold. Mr. CC remained relatively symptom free until 2008. He again consulted Dr. K in May 2008, now complaining that his symptoms had returned and included short-term memory loss and some bicep weakness. There was no report of fatigue, joint pain, or night sweats, and his sleep quality was fine. Laboratory testing indicated Mr. CC did have Lyme disease based on CDC criteria. He was prescribed a month of doxycycline, which resulted in overall improvement, including cognition.

In 2011, Mr. CC again consulted Dr. K with complaints of a six- to eight-month history of word finding problems and stuttering, but no other Lyme symptoms. Laboratory testing again showed Mr. CC met the CDC criteria for active Lyme disease. Dr. K prescribed a two-month course of doxycycline, and Mr. CC's symptoms again improved.

In 2012, Mr. CC additionally consulted Dr. K, complaining of a three-month history of cognitive difficulties which Mr. CC described as fluctuating, with some days worse than others. Again, Dr. K diagnosed "protracted Lyme disease" although there was no additional laboratory testing. Mr. CC initially improved after a month of doxycycline therapy but then declined following cessation of treatment.

In 2015, Mr. CC again presented to Dr. K with fatigue, stiffness in his hand, and cognitive decline, most notably memory loss. His sleep was now disturbed by restless leg syndrome two to three times a week. In late 2016 and early 2017, Mr. CC reported fluctuating symptoms as above, but no new symptoms. His Lyme serology was now normal. Nevertheless Dr. K still believed Mr. CC was suffering from PTLD in addition to a complex pain syndrome and restless leg syndrome. Mr. CC was also noted to have low B12 and folic acid. Dr. K recommended B12 and folic acid supplements in addition to another course of antibiotics.

On February 22, 2017, Mr. CC applied for disability benefits based on Dr. K's diagnosis of PTLD, with symptoms that included fatigue, memory loss, and cognitive impairment. In his application Mr. CC reported these symptoms began in 2013, and had resulted in his taking longer to respond to clients, a reduced workload, and a need to depend on others to assist him. Taken together, these ailments were reported as impacting the volume and quality of his work.

Following his application for disability, the insurer had Mr. CC evaluated by a vocational specialist, a board-certified internist, a clinical psychologist, and an infectious disease specialist. The vocational rehabilitation specialist noted Mr. CC's work hours had not changed pre- and post-disability. However, Mr. CC reported that what had changed was the number of projects per year, from 8 to 10 pre-disability to 2–3 post-disability. Mr. CC claimed that he was not as fast, nor as responsive, as he used to be. While he was able to perform all his job duties during the post-2013 period, they were becoming more and more difficult. He also no longer "loved working with ad agencies" and indicated "some personality changes within himself." Prior to 2016, he worked with a partner and thereafter worked alone.

Dr. M, a board-certified internist, and consultant to the insurer, reviewed Mr. CC's disability claim. Although Mr. CC had two positive Lyme IgM antibody titers, in 2008 and 2011, it was her opinion that he received adequate treatment and there was no recent evidence of infection on subsequent Lyme tests. She also opined that there was no objective support for physical restrictions or limitations, but withheld her opinion concerning cognitive impairment until a neuropsychological evaluation was completed.

Dr. K subsequently had Mr. CC screened for cognitive impairment, using NeuroTrax™, a computerized battery of tests that assess memory, executive function, visual spatial perception, verbal function, attention, information processing speed, and motor skills. A brain MRI was also ordered. The NeuroTrax™ results showed above average performances on all measures except speed of processing, with an above average overall score. Although below average, processing speed was within one standard deviation of the age-adjusted normative value. The results of the brain MRI revealed a few nonspecific scattered foci of white matter hyperintensities in both hemispheres on the FLAIR T2 image and were otherwise normal.

Dr. D, a clinical psychologist who reviewed the NeuroTrax report, opined that the results "did not constitute compelling documentation of Mr. CC's occupational functioning capacity due to cognitive deficits." Dr. M, the internist, reviewed Dr. D's behavioral health review together with the MRI report, concluding this additional information did not change her original opinion that impairment of a physical restriction or limitation was not supported. She added that the NeuroTrax™ data could not be taken as evidence of impairment.

Mr. CC was also examined and evaluated by Dr. R, an independent infectious disease specialist. In his opinion, Mr. CC did not have active Lyme disease, but likely had early Lyme disease in the past, and possibly now had PTLD. Dr. R also opined that Dr. K's repeated serological testing for active Lyme disease and extended regimens of antibiotic treatments were not supported by scientific evidence. Dr. R pointed out that there was no evidence for significant cognitive impairment, nor were tests done to assess for CSF evidence of Lyme neuroborreliosis. He believed that Dr. K's diagnosis of Mr. CC was based solely on nonspecific serological and MRI findings, concluding that the facts of the case only weakly supported Dr. K's formulation. Based on the reports of the psychologist and the infectious disease specialist, Dr. M restated her earlier opinion that there was still no evidence restricting or limiting Mr. CC's ability to work due to physical deficits. However, she requested a neuropsychological evaluation to further assess the possibility of cognitive decline.

Behavioral Observations

Mr. CC drove himself to the appointment, arrived on time, and was appropriately groomed and neatly dressed. He was fully alert, friendly, and generally made good eye contact. There was no evidence of formal thought disorder or psychotic/delusional tendencies. Mr. CC was fully aware of the purpose of the evaluation and appeared to be a good historian as his self-report was consistent with medical records. However, he became visibly emotional and almost tearful when discussing the decline in his work. His vision and hearing appeared intact. His speech was coherent, goal-directed, and normal in tone, prosody, rate, and volume; no stuttering or word-retrieval difficulties were observed. He was able to fully understand all directions. During the testing, he reported some neck and back pain, which he attributed to arthritis and rated as a 4–5 on a 1–10 pain scale. Testing was completed in approximately nine hours over two days with several short breaks as needed, and a break for lunch on day 1. On day 1, Mr. CC took Tylenol for a headache. On day 2, he reported that he experienced fatigue from day 1, noting "yesterday was tough."

Table 28.1 Summary of Test Results Day 1

WAIS-IV Subtests	*Raw Score*	*Percentile*	*Description*
Block Design	13	84%	High average
Similarities	11	63%	Average
Digit Span	11	63%	Average
Matrix Reasoning	15	95%	Superior
Vocabulary	14	91%	High average
Arithmetic	8	25%	Average
Symbol Search	10	50%	Average
Visual Puzzles	16	98%	Superior
Information	13	84%	High average
Coding	7	16%	Low average
Block Design	13	84%	High average
WAIS-IV Indices	*Index*	*Percentile*	*Description*
Verbal Comprehension	114	82	High average
Perceptional Reasoning	127	96	Superior
Working Memory	97	42	Average
Processing Speed	92	30	Average
Full-Scale IQ	112	79	High average
WMS Indexes	*Index*	*Percentile*	*Description*
Immediate Memory	93	32	Average
Delayed Memory	88	21	Low average
Auditory Memory	86	18	Low average
Visual Memory	100	50	Average
California Verbal Learning Test II	*Raw Score*	*Percentile*	*Description*
Learning Trials	50	88	High average
Short Delay Free Recall	9	50	Average
Long Delay Free Recall	7	31	Average
Recognition (D')	14	50	Average
FCR	16		Normal
Processing Speed/Executive Functioning	*Raw Score*	*Percentile*	*Description*
Trail Making Test A	29	72	Average
Trail Making Test B	62	69	Average
Controlled Oral Word Association	40	64	Average
Stroop Color Word Reading	65	4	Mildly impaired
Rey Complex Figure Drawing	33	>16	WNL
CalCAP Simple RT	401	26	Average
CalCAP Choice RT	694	1	Extremely low
CalCAP Sequential RT	736	13	Low average

Test Results

Neurocognitive Performance Validity Testing: Validity of performance on cognitive measures was assessed with four independent measures: the Test of Memory Malingering (TOMM), the Dot Counting test, CVLT-2 Forced Choice Recognition, and WAIS-IV Reliable Digit Span. All measures were passed, indicating that Mr. CC was likely performing to true ability, and that obtained scores were an accurate reflection of actual skill level.

Table 28.2 Summary of Test Results Day 2

WAIS-IV Digit Span	*Raw Score*	*SS*	*Description*
Forward	15	15	Superior
Forward	8	10	Average
California Verbal Learning Test II	*Raw Score*	*Percentile*	*Description*
Learning Trials	48	82	High average
Short Delay Free Recall	9	50	Average
Long Delay Free Recall	7	31	Low average
Recognition (D')	13	50	Low average
FCR	16		Normal
Brief Memory Test -Revised	*Raw Score*	*Percentile*	*Description*
Learning Trials	17	16	Low average
Delayed Recall	8	90	High average
Discrimination Index	6	38	Average
Executive Functioning	*Raw Score*	*Percentile*	*Description*
Wisconsin Card Sorting Test Categories	6	<16th	Average
Wisconsin Card Sorting Test Perseverative Errors	9	55	Average
Language	*Raw Score*	*Percentile*	*Description*
Boston Naming Test	60	86	High average
Western Aphasia Repetition	98		WNL
Western Aphasia Sequential Commands	80		WNL
Western Aphasia Reading	40		WNL
Fine Motor Skills	*Raw Score*	*Percentile*	*Description*
Grooved Pegboard Right (Dominant)	84	28	Average
Grooved Pegboard Left	78	63	Average
Performance Validity Testing	*Raw Score*		*Description*
TOMM Trial 1	50		Normal
Dot Counting	11		Normal
Reliable Digits	10		Normal
CVLT-FC	16		Normal
Psychological/Emotional	*Raw Score*		*Description*
Beck Depression Inventory	17		Mild
Beck Anxiety Inventory	7		Minimal
Brief Pain Inventory	0–8		Moderate
Fatigue Severity Scale	37		Moderate

Intelligence Testing: Mr. CC's WAIS-IV full-scale IQ was in the high average range. An analysis of individual subtest performances revealed vocabulary and nonverbal reasoning as relative strengths with arithmetic and processing speed as relative weaknesses. Mr. CC's performance on the Wechsler Test of Adult Reading (WTAR) indicated his current high average Full Scale IQ (FSIQ) is consistent with premorbid functioning estimated by reading level.

Attention/Processing Speed: Performances on digits forward and digits backward were in the high average range. Reaction time (RT) was measured using the California

Computerized Assessment Package (CalCAP) (Raul et al., 2003). Mr. CC performed in the average range on a simple RT measure, but impaired on one of two of the more difficult RT measures. Such fluctuations in processing speed within a test session are more characteristic of depression than neurological disease (McWhirter et al., 2020). Digits forward and digits backward were re-administered on Day 2 to assess possible fatigue on attention. Digits forward improved from high average to superior, while digits backward declined from high average to average. Although there was a slight decline in digits backward on day 2, both sets of scores were well within the normal range.

Visuospatial Skills: Mr. CC's copy of the Rey Complex Figure was in the average range, and he employed a good organizational strategy of drawing the outline of the major figure and then filling in the details.

Memory: Mr. CC was administered a battery of memory tests including measures of verbal memory and visual memory. Performances varied from low average to high average. On memory for information provided in short stories (WMS-IV Logical Memory), Mr. CC earned a score in the low average range in contrast to his memory score for graphic designs (Visual Reproduction), which was in the average range. Mr. CC's ability to learn a list of 16 words on the California Verbal Learning Test (CVLT-2) was in the high average range, with free recall memory after a short and long delay in the average range.

Memory for another list of 16 words (CVLT-2, Alternate Version) was administered on Day 2. Mr. CC's ability to learn the list of 16 words was again in the high average range, with free recall memory after a short delay in the average range. However, delayed free recall declined on day 2 to the low average range. A visual memory test not administered on Day 1 was given on Day 2 (BVMT-R). Scores varied between the three learning trials, but delayed recall was in the high average range.

Executive Functioning: On a measure requiring tracking and sequencing of alternating numbers and letters (Trail Making Test), word generation from letters (Controlled Oral Word Association Test), and a nonverbal problem-solving test in which the task is to change strategies to changing task demands (Wisconsin Card Sorting Test), all scores were solidly in the average range. However, on a test requiring word reading, color naming, and suppression of a dominant response (Stroop Color Word Test), performances were mildly impaired.

Language: Mr. CC's performances in naming, word generation, repetition, following sequential commands, and basic reading comprehension were all well within normal limits.

Emotional/Psychological Assessment: Mr. CC endorsed symptoms on the Beck Depression Inventory that were indicative of mild depression, including feeling discouraged, lack of enjoyment, crying, a loss of interest in others, less energy, irritability, and loss of interest in sex. On the Beck Anxiety Inventory, Mr. CC denied most symptoms associated with anxiety. On the Fatigue Severity Scale given on day 2, he reported a global level of fatigue of 5 on a 1–10 scale. He indicated that within the previous week, fatigue affected his motivation, physical functioning, responsibilities, and work. On the Brief Pain Inventory, Mr. CC reported neck and back pain, which was exacerbated by stress, and leg pain associated with restless leg syndrome. On average, his pain level was 4–5 on 1–10 severity scale, and ranged between 0 and 8; he noted that pain affected his mood and interfered with sleep.

Mr. CC produced a valid MMPI-2-RF profile. Scores on the substantive scales indicated vague neurological and somatic complaints, a diffuse pattern of cognitive difficulties, and emotional and interpersonal dysfunction. He reported multiple somatic complaints, including neck pain, sleep disturbance, and fatigue. Moreover, the profile indicated that he is likely prone to developing physical symptoms in response to stress, and likely to have low tolerance for frustration. There was no indication of a thought disorder or maladaptive behaviors.

Interpretation of the Test Results

Results of neurocognitive testing can be easily understood as being within normal limits. Tabulation of scores from Day 1 showed one impaired score, one borderline score, four low average scores, 15 average scores, four high average scores, and two superior scores, a pattern well within normal limits; lowered scores were obtained on reaction time/processing speed, and some memory tasks. Tabulation of scores from Day 2 showed two low average scores (on memory tasks), nine average scores, three high average scores, and one superior score. In normal healthy controls, the expectation is that the majority of scores will be average range with a scattering of scores above and below average; research has shown that in normal controls with high average intelligence, three-fourths obtain at least one borderline to impaired score across a battery of cognitive tests (Palmer et al., 1998). It is noteworthy that one of Mr. CC's better performances was on the CVLT Long Delay on Day 1, in that verbal list learning has been shown to be the most sensitive to Lyme-related memory loss (Westervelt & McCaffrey, 2002). The fact that his CVLT long delay free recall slipped on day 2 may have been related to his increased fatigue (Ravdin et al., 1996). Overall, the pattern of test scores does not appear to represent a pattern consistent with brain dysfunction. As discussed below, psychological measures highlighted depression and fatigue, and it is possible that Mr. CC's scattered lowered scores are related to either or both of these conditions; major depression is associated with mild declines in processing speed and memory (Boone et al., 1995), while fatigue impacts memory scores in both PTLD and other non-neurological clinical populations, including sleep disorders (Ravdin et al., 1996).

Mr. CC's personality test results were remarkable for evidence of somatoform/somatic symptom disorder as well as depression and interpersonal dysfunction. Of note, his profile indicated a tendency to developing physical symptoms in response to stress.

Discussion and Conclusions

Although Mr. CC had a history of Lyme disease, and his treating physician, Dr. K, continued to ascribe his condition to chronic Lyme disease, there was no medical evidence to substantiate a current Lyme infection based on current medical standards (Lantos et al., 2021). Moreover, for Lyme disease to result in the brain disorder neuroborreliosis, two criteria must be met. There must be objective evidence of an active *Borrelia* infection and a neurological disease. When medical records provide the results of standard laboratory tests and antimicrobial treatment, a record review may be all that is needed to differentiate symptoms related to brain disease versus those occurring with collateral conditions.

Differentiating neuropsychological dysfunction due to brain disease from that related to non-neurological cognitive symptoms, such as those occurring with depression or fatigue, is what neuropsychologists do. Results of neurocognitive testing in Mr. CC revealed an essentially normal cognitive profile, with scattered lowered scores either reflective of normal variability or related to depression and/or fatigue. Despite the presence of secondary gain, malingering appeared unlikely as reflected by Mr. CC's passing performances on several validity measures and generally intact cognitive scores. In contrast, personality measures well-documented the presence of a somatoform orientation and depression.

Of relevance to the current case, available research points to concerns regarding somatoform and other psychiatric underpinnings of claimed long-term symptoms from Lyme disease. Csallner et al. (2013) observed that in the 30% of patients with no organic findings of disease in the context of claimed chronic Lyme symptoms, twice as many bodily symptoms were reported as compared with patients with organic evidence of disease, and patients with "organically unexplained" symptoms were found to have more "excessive health worry," "more illness consequences," were "more convinced of having a serious illness," and "more dissatisfied with medical care." They also elevated on a somatoform screening scale (PHQ-15) and endorsed more depressive symptoms. Itani et al. (2021) reported that in a small subset of claimed Lyme patients who had received more than 180 days of antimicrobial treatment, serology testing was negative and 60% were determined to have a psychiatric rather than physiological condition, primarily involving somatic symptom disorder. Haddad et al. (2019) noted that in a large sample of presumed Lyme disease, confirmation of disease was present in only 10% of cases, over 80% of the sample failed antibiotic treatment, and 31% were provided with a psychiatric diagnosis (e.g., depression, PTSD, "burn out") rather than a medical diagnosis; the authors concluded that "Overdiagnosis and overtreatment of LB (Lyme borreliosis) are real concerns and are increasing. Too many patients are being treated with useless antibiotics for lengthy durations. This carries a risk for the patient and the community. The reasons why this phenomenon is increasing despite knowledge of the problem needs to be investigated."

Reid et al. (1998) observed that 60% of their sample of presumed Lyme disease had no evidence of current or past disease, and 19% had evidence of past but not current Lyme disease. Of note, both groups (previous infection, no infection) reported frequent drug side effects (53% and 55%; common in somatoform disorder, Keeley et al., 2000) and had "high rates of depression (38% and 42%) and stress (52% and 45%)." The authors conclude that "Overdiagnosis and overtreatment of Lyme disease are associated with inappropriate use of health services, avoidable treatment-related illness, and substantial disability and distress." Most recently, in a large sample (>1,000) of patients referred for Lyme disease (Kobayashi et al., 2022), 21% were instead diagnosed with anxiety/depression, and the authors caution, "Most patients with long-term symptoms have either new or pre-existing disorders accounting for their symptoms other than Lyme disease, suggesting overdiagnosis in this population." As early as 2002, Sigal and Hassett warned that "Chronic Lyme disease is the most recent in a continuing series of 'medically unexplained symptoms' syndromes. These syndromes, such as fibromyalgia, chronic fatigue syndrome, and multiple chemical sensitivity, meet the need for a societally and morally acceptable explanation for ill-defined symptoms in the absence of objective physical and laboratory findings." Sigal (1990), in fact, reported that a quarter of his chronic Lyme disease sample were also judged to have fibromyalgia.

Complicating the picture in the current case is the potential impact of compensation-seeking in Mr. CC's somatoform presentation. Interestingly, no research could be identified which directly compared symptom report in somatoform patients with and without financial incentives; however, there is a literature linking financial compensation to poorer outcome. Sharpe et al. (2010) reported that financial benefits at initial assessment of patients with "symptoms unexplained by disease" doubled the odds of a poor outcome at one year, while Reuber et al. (2007) observed that patients with functional neurologic syndromes who were "economically inactive" (with the majority receiving disability benefits or pensions) showed poorer outcome to treatment as compared with patients who were "economically active"; Sharpe et al. (2010) concluded that "it is possible that payment consequent on having symptoms and disability acts to perpetuate them" (p. 696).

In spite of position papers by both the American Academy of Neurology (Halperin et al., 2007) and the Infectious Disease Society of America (IDSA) (Lantos et al., 2010), which provide both evidence-based diagnostic procedures and efficacious treatment protocols for Lyme disease, many misconceptions persist (Auwaerter et al., 2011). There remains a public perception that Lyme disease is a novel condition that is largely untreatable and capable of causing a myriad of health problems (Halperin et al., 2022). There are websites (e.g., LymeDisease.org) and books that proselytize that Lyme disease is under-diagnosed, available blood tests are unreliable, and that extended antibiotic treatment is often necessary. Among advocates arguing for extended treatment are groups of "Lyme literate" physicians whose positions contradict the overwhelming evidence of established science (Halperin, 2008). These physicians and patient advocates continue to promote the idea that a *Borrelia* infection remains difficult to diagnose, and is often incurable, and can only be treated by antibiotics for months and years (Auwaerter et al., 2011).

These advocacy groups also have political clout. In November 2006, the Connecticut Attorney General initiated an antitrust investigation to determine whether the IDSA Lyme disease guidelines violated antitrust laws. Why? If the IDSA guidelines were followed, insurance carriers were no longer liable to pay for the extended treatment deemed necessary by these "Lyme" physicians, hence the call for an investigation. The investigation was stopped in 2008 after a panel of infectious disease experts, who reviewed over 1,000 peer-reviewed articles, concluded the guidelines were appropriate without change based on current medical practices (Lantos et al., 2010). However, the fact that a State Attorney General sought an investigation of the IDSA guidelines (Auwaerter et al., 2011) attests to the political power of these advocacy groups.

Mr. CC's treatment provider, Dr. K, suggested the possibility of a diagnosis of PTLD in Mr. CC. PTLD is a CDC-recognized disorder, although not as the result of an ongoing Borrelia infection (Lantos et al., 2021). The majority of PTLD patients report memory decline as a primary symptom, but do not show evidence of memory impairment on objective testing nor do they benefit from further antimicrobial treatment (Kaplan et al., 2003). Yet, there is a small community of doctors and patient advocates who continue to promote the idea that PTLD is caused by a *Borrelia* infection that is difficult to diagnose, and often incurable (Halperin et al., 2022). Based on Dr. K's repeated use of antibiotics in the absence of infection, it appears Dr. K is a strong advocate of this position, which Mr. CC appreciated; he praised Dr. K in differing from other doctors in the understanding of his disorder.

Information that physicians convey to patients can inadvertently amplify their symptoms and become the source of heightened somatic distress (Barsky, 2017), and it is apparent this was part of the dynamic between Dr. K and Mr. CC, and is reflective of "iatrogenesis" (e.g., symptoms caused/exacerbated/maintained by treaters; see Bender & Matusewicz, 2013).

Advocacy for misinformation is ubiquitous and an increasingly important part of an antiscience movement (Auwaerter et al., 2011). Neuropsychologists can play a unique role in identifying non-credible causes of brain disease in order to be advocates for science-based practice.

References

Agosta, F., Rocca, M. A., Benedetti, B., Capra, R., Cordioli, C., & Filippi, M. (2006) MR imaging assessment of brain and cervical cord damage in patients with neuroborreliosis. *American Journal of Neuroradiology, 27*(4), 892–894. Retrieved from https://www.ajnr.org/cgi/content/abstract/27/4/892

Auwaerter, P. G., Dr, Bakken, Johan, S., MD, Ph D, Dattwyler, R. J., Prof, Dumler, J. S., Prof, Halperin, J. J., Prof, McSweegan, E., Ph D, ... Wormser, G. P., Prof. (2011). Antiscience and ethical concerns associated with advocacy of Lyme disease. *The Lancet Infectious Diseases, 11*(9), 713–719. doi:10.1016/S1473-3099(11)70034-2

Barsky, A. J. (2017). The iatrogenic potential of the physician's words. *JAMA: The Journal of the American Medical Association, 318*(24), 2425–2426. doi:10.1001/jama.2017.16216

Bechtold, K. T., Rebman, A. W., Crowder, L. A., Johnson-Greene, D., & Aucott, J. N. (2017). Standardized symptom measurement of individuals with early Lyme disease over time. *Archives of Clinical Neuropsychology, 32*(2), 129–141. doi:10.1093/arclin/acw098

Bender, S. D., & Matusewicz, M. (2013). PCS, iatrogenic symptoms, and malingering following concussion. *Psychological Injury and Law, 6*, 113–121.

Boone, K. B., Lesser, I. M., Miller, B. L., Wohl, M., Berman, N., Lee, A., ... & Back, C. (1995). Cognitive functioning in older depressed outpatients: Relationship of presence and severity of depression to neuropsychological test scores. *Neuropsychology, 9*(3), 390.

Csallner, G., Hofmann, H., & Hausteiner-Wiehle, C. (2013). Patients with "organically unexplained symptoms" presenting to a borreliosis clinic: Clinical and psychobehavioral characteristics and quality of life. *Psychosomatics, 54*(4), 359–366.

Feder, H. M., Jr, Johnson, B. J. B., McConnell, S., Shapiro, E. D., Steere, A. C., Wormser, G. P., & Ad Hoc International Lyme Disease Group. (2007). A critical appraisal of chronic Lyme disease. *The New England Journal of Medicine, 357*(14), 1422–1430. doi:10.1056/NEJMra072023

Finkel, M. J., & Halperin, J. J. (1992). Nervous system Lyme Borreliosis—Revisited. *Archives of Neurology (Chicago), 49*(1), 102–107. doi:10.1001/archneur.1992.00530250106024

Haddad, E., Chabane, K., Jaureguiberry, S., Monsel, G., Pourcher, V., & Caumes, E. (2019). Holistic approach in patients with presumed Lyme borreliosis leads to less than 10% of confirmation and more than 80% of antibiotic failures. *Clinical Infectious Diseases, 68*(12), 2060–2066.

Halperin, J. J. (2016). EDITORIAL COMMENTARY: Neuroborreliosis: What is it, what isn't it? *Clinical Infectious Diseases, 63*(3), 354–355. doi:10.1093/cid/ciw303

Halperin, J. J. (2022). Nervous system Lyme Disease–Facts and fallacies. *Infectious Disease Clinics of North America, 36*(3), 579–592. doi:10.1016/j.idc.2022.02.007

Halperin, J. J., MD. (2008). Nervous system Lyme disease. *Infectious Disease Clinics of North America, 22*(2), 261–274. doi:10.1016/j.idc.2007.12.009

Halperin, J. J., Eikeland, R., Branda, J. A., & Dersch, R. (2022). Lyme neuroborreliosis: Known knowns, known unknowns. *Brain (London, England: 1878), 145*(8), 2635–2647. doi:10.1093/brain/awac206

Halperin, J. J., Pass, H. L., Anand, A. K., Luft, B. J., Volkman, D. J., & Dattwyler, R. J. (1988). Nervous system abnormalities in Lyme disease. *Annals of the New York Academy of Sciences, 539*(1), 24–34.

Halperin, J. J., Shapiro, E. D., Logigian, E., Belman, A. L., Dotevall, L., Wormser, G. P., ... Bever, C. T. (2007). Practice parameter: Treatment of nervous system Lyme disease (an evidence-based review): Report of the quality standards subcommittee of the American academy of neurology. *Neurology, 69*(1), 91–102. doi:10.1212/01.wnl.0000265517.66976.28

Itani, O., Haddad, E., Pitron, V., Pichon, F., & Caumes, E. (2021). Focus on patients receiving long-term antimicrobial treatments for lyme borreliosis: No lyme but mostly mental disorders. *Infectious Diseases Now, 51*(3), 300–303.

Ito, H., Kawashima, R., Awata, S., Ono, S., Sato, K., Goto, R., ... Fukuda, H. (1996). Hypoperfusion in the limbic system and prefrontal cortex in depression: SPECT with anatomic standardization technique. *The Journal of Nuclear Medicine (1978), 37*(3), 410–414. Retrieved from https://jnm.snmjournals.org/cgi/content/abstract/37/3/410

Kaplan, R. F., & Jones-Woodward, L. (1997). Lyme encephalopathy: A neuropsychological perspective. *Seminars in Neurology, 17*(1), 31–37. doi:10.1055/s-2008-1040910

Kaplan, R. F., Meadows, M. -., Vincent, L. C., Logigian, E. L., & Steere, A. C. (1992). Memory impairment and depression in patients with Lyme encephalopathy: Comparison with fibromyalgia and nonpsychotically depressed patients. *Neurology, 42*(7), 1263–1267. doi:10.1212/wnl.42.7.1263

Kaplan, R. F., Trevino, R. P., Johnson, G. M., Levy, L., Dornbush, R., Hu, L. T., ... Klempner, M. S. (2003). Cognitive function in post-treatment Lyme disease do additional antibiotics help? *Neurology, 60*(12), 1916–1922. doi:10.1212/01.WNL.0000068030.26992.25

Keeley, R., Smith, M., & Miller, J. (2000). Somatoform symptoms and treatment nonadherence in depressed family medicine outpatients. *Archives of Family Medicine*, *9*(1), 46.

Kobayashi, T., Higgins, Y., Melia, M. T., & Auwaerter, P. G. (2022). Mistaken identity: Many diagnoses are frequently misattributed to Lyme disease. *The American Journal of Medicine*, *135*(4), 503–511.

Krupp, L. B., Masur, D., Schwartz, J., Coyle, P. K., Langenbach, L. J., Fernquist, S. K., … Halperin, J. J. (1991). Cognitive functioning in late Lyme borreliosis. *Archives of Neurology (Chicago)*, *48*(11), 1125–1129. doi:10.1001/archneur.1991.00530230033017

Lantos, P. M., Charini, W. A., Medoff, G., Moro, M. H., Mushatt, D. M., Parsonnet, J., … Baker, C. J. (2010). Final report of the Lyme disease review panel of the Infectious Diseases Society of America. *Clinical Infectious Diseases*, *51*(1), 1–5. doi:10.1086/654809

Lantos, P. M., Rumbaugh, J., Bockenstedt, L. K., Falck-Ytter, Y. T., Aguero-Rosenfeld, M. E., Auwaerter, P. G., … Zemel, L. S. (2021). Clinical practice guidelines by the Infectious Diseases Society of America (IDSA), American Academy of Neurology (AAN), and American College of Rheumatology (ACR): 2020 guidelines for the prevention, diagnosis and treatment of Lyme disease. *Clinical Infectious Diseases*, *72*(1), e1–e48. doi:10.1093/cid/ciaa1215

Logigian, E. L., Kaplan, R. F., & Steere, A. C. (1990). Chronic neurologic manifestations of Lyme disease. *The New England Journal of Medicine*, *323*(21), 1438–1444. doi:10.1056/NEJM199011223232102

Logigian, E. L., Johnson, K. A., Kijewski, M. F., Kaplan, R. F., Becjer, J. A., Jones, K. J., … Steere, A. C. (1997). Reversible cerebral hypoperfusion in Lyme encephalopathy. *Neurology*, *49*(6), 1661–1670. doi:10.1212/WNL.49.6.1661

McWhirter, L., Ritchie, C. W., Stone, J., & Carson, A. (2020). Performance validity test failure in clinical populations—a systematic review. *Journal of Neurology, Neurosurgery and Psychiatry*, *91*(9), 945–952. doi:10.1136/jnnp-2020-323776

Pachner, A. R., & Steere, A. C. (1985). The triad of neurologic manifestations of Lyme disease: Meningitis, cranial neuritis, and radiculoneuritis. *Neurology*, *35*(1), 47–63. doi:10.1212/WNL.35.1.47

Palmer, B. W., Boone, K. B., Lesser, I. M., & Wohl, M. A. (1998). Base rates of "impaired" neuropsychological test performance among healthy older adults. *Archives of Clinical Neuropsychology*, *13*(6), 503–511.

Raul, G., Robert, K. H., David J. M., Scott, L., Ronald J. E., Tanya, W., … Igor, G. (2003). Computerized reaction time battery versus a traditional neuropsychological battery: Detecting HIV-related impairments. *Journal of the International Neuropsychological Society*, *9*(1), 64–71. doi:10.1017/S1355617703910071

Ravdin, L. D., Hilton, E., Primeau, M., Clements, C., & Barr, W. B. (1996). Memory functioning in Lyme borreliosis. *The Journal of Clinical Psychiatry*, *57*(7), 282–286. Retrieved from https://www.ncbi.nlm.nih.gov/pubmed/8666568

Reid, M. C., Schoen, R. T., Evans, J., Rosenberg, J. C., & Horwitz, R. I. (1998). The consequences of overdiagnosis and overtreatment of Lyme disease: An observational study. *Annals of Internal Medicine*, *128*(5), 354–362.

Reuber, M., Burness, C., Howlett, S., Brazier, J., & Grünewald, R. (2007). Tailored psychotherapy for patients with functional neurological symptoms: A pilot study. *Journal of Psychosomatic Research*, *63*(6), 625–632.

Rosendahl, S. B., Ravn, P., Lebech, A. M., & Stenør, C. P. M. (2023). Lyme neuroborreliosis with encephalitis: A rare case. *IDCases*, *31*, e01704.

Schwartz, R. B., Garada, B. M., Komaroff, A. L., Tice, H. M., Gleit, M., Jolesz, F. A., & Holman, B. L. (1994). Detection of intracranial abnormalities in patients with chronic fatigue syndrome: Comparison of MR imaging and SPECT. *American Journal of Roentgenology (1976)*, *162*(4), 935–941. doi:10.2214/ajr.162.4.8141020

Shadick, N. A., Phillips, C. B., Sangha, O., Logigian, E. L., Kaplan, R. F., Wright, E. A., … & Liang, M. H. (1999). Musculoskeletal and neurologic outcomes in patients with previously treated Lyme disease. *Annals of Internal Medicine*, *131*(12), 919–926.

Sharpe, M., Stone, J., Hibberd, C., Warlow, C., Duncan, R., Coleman, R., ... & Carson, A. (2010). Neurology out-patients with symptoms unexplained by disease: Illness beliefs and financial benefits predict 1-year outcome. *Psychological Medicine, 40*(4), 689–698.

Sigal, L. H. (1990). Summary of the first 100 patients seen at a Lyme disease referral center. *The American Journal of Medicine, 88*(6), 577–581.

Sigal, L. H., & Hassett, A. L. (2002). Contributions of societal and geographical environments to" chronic Lyme disease": The psychopathogenesis and aporology of a new" medically unexplained symptoms" syndrome. *Environmental Health Perspectives, 110*(suppl 4), 607–611.

Stanek, G., Lusa, L., Ogrinc, K., Markowicz, M., & Strle, F. (2014). Intrathecally produced IgG and IgM antibodies to recombinant VlsE, VlsE peptide, recombinant OspC and whole cell extracts in the diagnosis of Lyme neuroborreliosis. *Medical Microbiology and Immunology, 203*(2), 125–132. doi:10.1007/s00430-013-0322-1

Steere, A. C., & Arvikar, S. L. (2015). EDITORIAL COMMENTARY: What constitutes appropriate treatment of post-Lyme disease symptoms and other pain and fatigue syndromes? *Clinical Infectious Diseases, 60*(12), 1783–1785. doi:10.1093/cid/civ187

Steere, A. C., Grodzicki, R. L., Kornblatt, A. N., Craft, J. E., & Barbour, A. G. (1983). Spirochetal etiology of Lyme disease. *The New England Journal of Medicine, 308*(13), 733–740. doi:10.1056/NEJM198303313081301

Weintraub, P. (2008). *Cure unknown* (1. ed. ed.). New York, NY: St. Martin's Press. Retrieved from https://www.loc.gov/catdir/enhancements/fy0812/2008007816-b.html

Weitzner, E., McKenna, D., Nowakowski, J., Scavarda, C., Dornbush, R., Bittker, S., ... Wormser, G. P. (2015a). Long-term assessment of post-treatment symptoms in patients with culture-confirmed early Lyme disease. *Clinical Infectious Diseases, 61*(12), 1800–1806. doi:10.1093/cid/civ735

Weitzner, E., McKenna, D., Nowakowski, J., Scavarda, C., Dornbush, R., Bittker, S., ... Wormser, G. P. (2015b). Long-term assessment of post-treatment symptoms in patients with culture-confirmed early Lyme disease. *Clinical Infectious Diseases, 61*(12), 1800–1806. doi:10.1093/cid/civ735

Westervelt, H. J., & McCaffrey, R. J. (2002). Neuropsychological functioning in chronic Lyme disease. *Neuropsychology Review, 12*(3), 153–177. doi:10.1023/A:1020381913563

Wormser, G. P., Dattwyler, R. J., Shapiro, E. D., Halperin, J. J., Steere, A. C., Klempner, M. S., ... Nadelman, R. B. (2006). The clinical assessment, treatment, and prevention of Lyme disease, human granulocytic anaplasmosis, and babesiosis: Clinical practice guidelines by the Infectious Diseases Society of America. *Clinical Infectious Diseases, 43*(9), 1089–1134. doi:10.1086/508667

29 Claimed Disability due to Fibromyalgia, PTSD, Depression, Anxiety, and Cognitive Impairment Following Minor Motor Vehicle Collision

Roger O. Gervais, Dana M. Doucette, and Melanie L. Middelkoop

Introduction

Fibromyalgia is a disorder characterized by chronic, widespread pain of unknown etiology, accompanied by symptoms of fatigue, sleep problems, and stiffness, as well as depression and anxiety (Albrecht & Rice, 2016; Bell et al., 2018; Walitt et al., 2015). The prevalence of this disorder ranges from 2.0% to 5.0% of the population, affecting predominantly women (Albrecht & Rice, 2016; Bell et al., 2018; Walitt et al., 2015). Cognitive symptoms are reported in 50% to 90% of patients (Teodoro et al., 2018). The disorder has been associated with adverse life experiences, such as trauma, sexual abuse, and victimization (Albrecht & Rice, 2016; Galvez-Sánchez et al., 2019; Gündüz et al., 2019; Häuser et al., 2011; Imbierowicz & Engle, 2003).

There has been some debate as to whether fibromyalgia can be classified as a somatoform disorder or somatic symptom disorder (SSD; Häuser et al., 2011; Klaus et al., 2017; LoBrutto et al., 2024; Wolfe et al., 2014). Klaus et al. (2017) have found that 82% of individuals with fibromyalgia fulfilled the *DSM-5* criteria for SSD. Other research has found partial overlap between the *DSM-5* criteria for SSD and symptoms reported by individuals with fibromyalgia (LoBrutto et al., 2024; Wolfe et al., 2014). Teodoro et al. (2018) provide a detailed review of cognitive abnormalities in fibromyalgia and chronic fatigue syndrome from the perspective of functional neurological disorders.

While cognitive symptoms are commonly reported in fibromyalgia patients, only a few studies have incorporated formal cognitive performance validity tests (PVTs) when evaluating cognitive functioning in this population. Gervais et al. (2001) observed a PVT failure rate of 35% in a clinical sample of fibromyalgia patients who were receiving or claiming disability, compared with only 4% of patients who were not involved in disability claims. Johnson-Greene et al. (2013), in a study of the relationship between PVT, disability status, and somatic complaints in sample of patients with fibromyalgia, found that 37% of the overall sample failed one or both of the PVT measures. Of those already receiving disability benefits, 25% failed one PVT and 53% failed two PVTs. In a study of neuropsychological impairment in fibromyalgia, Suhr (2003) reported that 18% of fibromyalgia patients failed a PVT measure derived from the Auditory Verbal Learning Test (Barrash et al., 2004). Brooks et al. (2012) examined neuropsychological symptom validity testing in a sample of English-speaking and Spanish-speaking fibromyalgia patients and found that 31.6% of English speakers failed the Word Memory Test (WMT), whereas 56.3% of the Spanish speakers failed the WMT or the TOMM. Potential secondary gains, including litigation, disability incentives, and pursuit of citizenship test accommodations were identified in 57.5% of the sample.

DOI: 10.4324/9781003005063-33

Given the elevated PVT failure rate in fibromyalgia patients described in the above studies, it would be important to incorporate formal performance validity and symptom validity measures in any assessment of fibromyalgia patients where disability incentives are present. The following case study presents the case of a disability claimant presenting with fibromyalgia, depression, anxiety, trauma-related symptoms, and cognitive problems, allegedly following a motor vehicle accident. The details of the case will be reviewed, followed by presentation and interpretation of the test data.

The Case of Ms. H

Background

Ms. H, a 55-year-old postal worker, was referred for an independent psychological assessment by a defense attorney in the context of litigation concerning a motor vehicle collision eight years earlier. She had not returned to work since the collision due to reported chronic pain, posttraumatic stress disorder (PTSD), anxiety, depression, and cognitive difficulties, which she attributed to the subject collision. She was receiving a permanent disability pension for claimed accident-related symptoms. An opinion was sought regarding psychological diagnosis and its relationship to the collision, validity considerations, including potential secondary gains, and prognosis.

Ms. H is married, with no biological children. However, she and her husband have shared custody of his son and daughter from a prior relationship, both in their mid-teens. She described a stable and supportive marital relationship. Her husband has secure full-time employment in a technical occupation. She completed grade 12 with reportedly average grades, followed by one year of college studies. She then worked in a range of foodservice and cleaning jobs before securing her position as a postal worker six years before the motor vehicle collision.

Medical history included fibromyalgia predating the subject collision, as noted in the medical records but not disclosed by Ms. H at the time of assessment. She reported preaccident challenges with PTSD related to a sexual assault in her youth and other significant life stressors but denied any history of depression or anxiety prior to the subject collision. On further questioning, she admitted that she had experienced "difficulties with anxiety and depression" earlier in life but had never been formally treated. There were several medical and psychological treatment notes from the year prior to the subject motor vehicle collision referring to anxiety and depression, but no specific formal diagnosis. Medical summaries subsequent to the vehicle collision referred to pre-existing PTSD, generalized anxiety disorder, and long-standing depression, which were exacerbated by the collision. There was no history of suicidal ideation, self-harm behaviors, alcohol/substance abuse, learning disabilities, or head injuries. She denied any prior motor vehicle collisions, Workers' Compensation claims, or other disability claims. There was no reported mental health history in her family of origin.

At the time of the subject collision, Ms. H was the seatbelted driver and sole occupant of a full-size SUV, which was struck from behind by a small car while stopped in traffic. While she stated that she remembered the collision "like it was yesterday," she could not recall if she had struck her head/body inside the vehicle or whether she had sustained a loss of consciousness. Airbags did not deploy. She stated that there was no secondary impact with other vehicles or objects. She could not recall whether she exited the vehicle, but she specified that there was damage to the rear bumper (<U.S.$800 total, as per repair estimate). Police or Emergency Medical Services (EMS) did not attend the collision.

Ms. H's symptoms immediately following the collision included headaches, neck pain, and other diffuse pain symptoms, including low back pain and elbow pain, which persisted and expanded over time. She also reported anxiety and fear of driving and said she became extremely depressed following the collision. She could not recall if she attempted to return to work following the collision but stated that she was placed on short-term disability three months later, followed by long-term disability.

Ms. H reported that her physical, psychological, and cognitive symptoms have persisted since the collision and have followed a fluctuating course, depending on her level of depression. She reported that she had seen several medical specialists regarding her pain symptoms, and had attended physical therapy, massage therapy, and chiropractic, with minimal benefit. She had started psychological counseling approximately six months prior to the motor vehicle collision, to address trauma related to a sexual assault in her youth. She continued attending weekly to monthly psychological counseling for approximately six years following the collision. Medications included Effexor and Ativan, which she reported had been prescribed prior to the collision.

Behavioral Observations

Ms. H drove herself independently to my office in a small compact car. She presented for her psychological assessment as a casually dressed, appropriately groomed Caucasian woman of 55 years. Her mood appeared depressed, and she reported persistent fatigue and low energy, with some tearfulness. Testing proceeded at an exceedingly slow pace, which led to the assessment being extended over three days. She became tearful during a memory test and commented on her memory problems and how she felt ashamed of her performance. At interview, she was cooperative but frequently tearful and appeared visibly anxious. She shifted occasionally in her chair, with verbal and non-verbal pain behaviors (e.g., moving slowly and stiffly, groaning while bending to pick up a pill bottle she had dropped on the floor). Her receptive and expressive verbal language skills were well developed, but she tended to ramble off topic, and it was challenging to obtain clear answers to the questions.

Interview

Ms. H reported numerous physical, emotional, and cognitive symptoms, and other psychosocial concerns on her intake questionnaire, as listed in Table 29.1.

At interview, she reported physical symptoms, including low back pain, neck pain/stiffness, headaches, and bilateral hand/leg pain, exacerbated by stress and anxiety. She described challenges with memory, concentration, and forgetfulness. She reported variable mood and feelings of worthlessness since the motor vehicle collision. She described anxiety and associated shortness of breath, numbness in the hands and legs, and panic attacks. She stated that she thought about the motor vehicle collision every day and that the memory of the event was still vivid and fear-provoking. She reported no unpleasant dreams or other intrusive symptoms related to the collision. However, she became tearful when describing her substantial weight gain since the collision (size 7–8 to 24+). She denied any suicidal ideation. Medications included Ativan 0.5 mg and mirtazapine 30 mg, occasional regular strength Tylenol, and topical analgesic creams.

Table 29.1 Ms. H's Symptoms on Intake Form

• Headaches	• Bowel problems	• Loneliness
• Back pain	• Mood changes	• Temper
• Tingling sensation	• Anxiety	• Inferiority problems
• Leg/arm pain	• Depression	• Fears
• Balance	• Concentration	• Stress
• Clumsiness	• Self-control	• Work
• Numbness	• Shyness	• Marriage
• Sexual dysfunction	• Unhappiness	• Death in family
• Fibromyalgia	• Organizing/planning	• Being a parent
• Poor appetite	• Making decisions	

Record Review

Preaccident medical records dating back three years prior to the collision indicated diagnoses of fibromyalgia, chronic back pain, depression, anxiety, an apparent conversion disorder (related to episodes of dyspnea), and a previous motor vehicle collision.

Post-collision medical chart notes from Ms. H's physician noted a long-standing pre-collision history of anxiety disorder, depression, and PTSD. There was a history of sexual abuse and assault in her youth. The subject motor vehicle collision was described as minor with no loss of consciousness or significant physical injury. Physical therapy was discontinued after Ms. H experienced a PTSD flashback to the sexual assault many years earlier, during a physical therapy procedure.

Medical chart notes over the following years documented ongoing PTSD symptoms related to the sexual assault, anxiety, depression, and expanding physical pain symptoms. A psychiatric assessment six years post-collision noted Ms. H's history of sexual assault, PTSD, depression, anxiety, chronic pain related to fibromyalgia, and dependent/avoidant personality traits. There was no reference to the subject motor vehicle collision.

Pre- and post-collision counseling notes from Ms. H's psychologist focused on PTSD related to the sexual assault years earlier, as well as on anxiety and physical symptoms attributed to the motor vehicle collision, with associated feelings of having been victimized. Ms. H was angry that an acquaintance had been financially compensated for a collision that was much less severe than hers.

Test Results

Results of the cognitive PVTs are presented in Table 29.2.

Ms. H provided invalid performance on the WMT (Green, 2003), Medical Symptom Validity Test (MSVT; Green, 2004a), and the Non-Verbal Medical Symptom Validity Test NV-MSVT (Green, 2008), with scores that ranged from chance level to below cutoff responding. The "best fit" comparison group for her WMT profile was with a sample of patients asked to fake cognitive impairment. The Test of Memory Malingering (TOMM; Tombaugh, 1996) was failed on all three trials (e.g., Martin et al., 2020). Reliable Digit Span (RDS; Greiffenstein et al., 1994) was below cutoff at 6. California Verbal Learning Test-Second Edition (CVLT-II; Delis et al., 2008) Recognition Hits was below chance at 3/16, and Forced-Choice Recognition accuracy was in the chance range at 9/16 (56%) (Table 29.3).

The MMPI-2-RF was invalidated due to overreporting (F – r = 120T; Fp – r = 111T). Elevated scores were also noted on the other overreporting validity scales (Fs = 91T;

Table 29.2 Performance Validity Test (PVT) Results for Ms. H

Word Memory Test (WMT)	
Immediate Recognition	47.5%
Delayed Recognition	45.0%
Consistency	52.5%
Multiple Choice	35.0%
Paired Associates	20.0%
Free Recall	15.0%
Long-Delay Free Recall	10.0%
Test of Memory Malingering	
Trial 1	38/50
Trial 2	48/50
Retention Trial	44/50
Medical Symptom Validity Test (MSVT)	
Immediate Recognition	55.0%
Delayed Recognition	60.0%
Consistency	65.0%
Paired Associates	50.0%
Free Recall	20.0%
Non-Verbal MSVT (NV-MSVT)	
Immediate Recognition	90.0%
Delayed Recognition	70.0%
Consistency	80.0%
Delayed Recognition Archetype	60.0%
Delayed Recognition Variation	30.0%
Paired Associates	80.0%
Free Recall	35.0%
Reliable Digit Span	6

FBS – r = 89T; and RBS = 120T), denoting the presence of marked overreporting across multiple symptom dimensions. While the substantive scales were not interpretable, they were consistent with the overreporting on the MMPI-2-RF validity scales, which also predicted overreporting on other self-report inventories or tests (Crighton, Tarescavage, Gervais, & Ben-Porath, 2017).

The Personality Assessment Inventory (PAI) validity scales indicated elevated scores on NIM (99T) and RDS (62T), as well as on the supplemental Negative Distortion Scale (95T), Hong Malingering Index (83T), and Multiscale Feigning Index (86T), associated with distortion of the clinical picture and possible malingering. Her score of 25 on the Cognitive Bias Scale (CBS; Gaasedelen et al., 2019; Tylicki et al., 2021) was well above the cutoff associated with noncredible responding. Consistent with the indications of overreporting, the clinical scales contained multiple extreme elevations. The coefficients of fit with profiles of known clinical groups were strongest for motor vehicle accident claimants (0.917), NIM predicted profile (0.864), fake bad (0.699), and chronic pain patients (0.650).

The BHI 2 self-disclosure (66T) and defensiveness (27T) scores suggested symptom overreporting/exaggeration and a potentially invalid protocol. The test report noted a high level of psychological and life problems, which was higher than that seen in 94% of patients and higher than the levels reported by 80% of patients who were asked to fake bad. She

Table 29.3 Personality and Other Self-Report Tests and Inventories

Minnesota Multiphasic Personality Inventory-2-Restructured Form (MMPI-2-RF) T scores

VRIN-r	48	EID	86	MLS	87
TRIN-r	50	THD	100	GIC	88
F-r	120	BXD	40	HPC	78
F_{P-r}	111	RCd	77	NUC	91
Fs	91	RC1	97	COG	86
FBS-r	89	RC2	92	SUI	79
RBS	120	RC3	65	HLP	88
L-r	66	RC4	43	SFD	65
K-r	28	RC6	98	NFC	75
		RC7	86	STW	57
		RC8	90	AXY	100
		RC9	36	ANP	73
				BRF	100
				MSF	59

Personality Assessment Inventory (PAI) T scores

ICN	52	SOM	90	ALC	41
INF	59	ANX	91	DRG	42
NIM	99	ARD	93	AGG	51
PIM	36	DEP	107	SUI	68
Malingering Index	71	MAN	58	STR	73
Rogers Discriminant Function	62	PAR	62	NON	64
Negative Distortion Scale	95	SCZ	100	RXR	23
Hong Malingering Index	83	BOR	75	DOM	36
Multiscale feigning index	86	ANT	44	WRM	30
Cognitive bias scale (raw)	25				

Battery for Health Improvement 2 (BHI 2)		T Scores
	Self-disclosure	66
	Defensiveness	27
	Somatic complaints	77
	Pain complaints	65
	Functional complaints	68
	Muscular bracing	66
	Depression	76
	Anxiety	76
	Hostility	52
	Borderline	58
	Symptom dependency	76
	Chronic maladjustment	52
	Substance abuse	46
	Perseverance	38
	Family dysfunction	38
	Survivor of violence	48
	Doctor dissatisfaction	39
	Job dissatisfaction	35
Beck Depression Inventory – II (BDI-II) – Total		54
Beck Anxiety Inventory (BAI) – Total		51
Modified Somatic Perception Questionnaire (MSPQ) – Total		17

(*Continued*)

Table 29.3 (Continued)

Memory Complaints Inventory (MCI)		% of Max
	General memory problems	82
	Numeric information problems	54
	Visuospatial memory problems	65
	Verbal memory problems	90
	Pain interferes with memory	100
	Memory interferes with work	100
	Impairment of remote memory	33
	Amnesia for complex behavior	67
	Amnesia for antisocial behavior	21
	MCI mean score	68
Detailed Assessment of Posttraumatic Stress		T Scores
	Positive bias	57
	Negative bias	71
	Relative trauma exposure (3 raw)	49
	Peritraumatic distress	60
	Peritraumatic dissociation	63
	Reexperiencing	107
	Avoidance	102
	Hyperarousal	94
	Posttraumatic stress – Total	106
	Posttraumatic impairment	94
	Trauma-specific dissociation	129
	Substance abuse	47
	Suicidality	60

obtained extremely high scores on somatic complaints, depression, anxiety, and symptom dependency, exceeding 99% of the normative patient sample.

The Memory Complaints Inventory revealed extreme scores throughout the profile with an overall mean score of 68%. Her mean score of 40.3% on the implausible memory complaints scales (impairment of remote memory, amnesia for complex behavior, and amnesia for antisocial behavior) was 3.0 standard deviations above the mean of a group of patients with severe brain injury who passed the WMT, consistent with exaggerated memory complaints.

The negative bias and positive bias scales of the Detailed Assessment of Posttraumatic Stress (DAPS) were within the valid range (although anecdotal reports have been critical of the effectiveness of these validity scales and have raised concerns regarding how the scales were validated; see Boone, 2012, pp. 159–160; Chafetz, 2022). The resulting DAPS clinical profile contained extreme elevations on 6 of the 11 scales (reexperiencing, avoidance, hyperarousal, posttraumatic stress total score, posttraumatic impairment, and trauma-specific dissociation), which is consistent with overreporting, as would be predicted by the MMPI-2-RF results (Crighton, et al., 2017). Ms. H specified the subject motor vehicle collision as the index trauma. The DAPS decision rules suggested a diagnosis of severe PTSD. Her score of 17 on the Modified Somatic Perception Questionnaire (MSPQ; Main, 1983) was in the range associated with exaggerated pain reports and malingered pain-related disability/overreporting (Bianchini et al., 2014; Larrabee, 2003), but below the cutoff of 18 recommended by Balasanyan et al. (2018).

In keeping with the PVT results, Ms. H's cognitive test results were arguably lower than would have been expected based on her educational and demographic background. For example, her WAIS-III Verbal, Performance, and Full Scale IQs of 73, 81, and 74, respectively, were inconsistent with her reported grade 12 education with average grades. The Digit Span scaled score of 4 was consistent with noncredible performance (Messerly et al., 2021; Babikian et al., 2006). Her impaired level of performance on the CVLT-II (1–5 total = 29T) was also deemed noncredible based on the recognition hits and FC recognition scores and independent PVT data. Similar conclusions were applicable to WAIS-III Picture Completion (Solomon et al., 2010), Category Test (DeFilippis, & PAR Staff, 2002), Story Recall Test (Green & Allen, 1995), and Emotional Perception Test (Green et al., 2008; Green & Severson, 1986) errors. Cognitive test results are presented in Table 29.4.

Interpretation of Test Results

Multiple PVTs completed by Ms. H in this assessment produced results associated with noncredible performance and invalid cognitive test results, which were predominately below normative expectations based on her demographic and educational background. PVT failure/invalid responding in fibromyalgia has been well documented (Bar-On Kalfon et al., 2016; Johnson-Greene et al., 2013), although PVT failure may be specific to compensation-seeking patients (Gervais et al., 2001; Iverson et al., 2007). There was evidence of substantial negative response bias associated with symptom overreporting on the personality and other self-report symptom inventories. The MMPI-2-RF was invalidated due to overreporting of psychological dysfunction and indicated substantial overreporting of somatic and cognitive complaints. Similarly, there was evidence of overreporting of psychological, somatic, and cognitive symptoms on the PAI, BHI 2, and Memory Complaints Inventory (MCI). While the DAPS validity indicators were technically within the valid range, there were extreme elevations on 6 of the 11 scales consistent with overreporting predicted by the MMPI-2-RF. Furthermore, her claim of PTSD arising from the subject motor vehicle collision was noncredible, as the details of the collision did not support the level of severity required for a *DSM-IV* or *DSM-5* Criterion A trauma event, the gatekeeper to the diagnosis. Further, the patient had returned to driving, which would be inconsistent with the presence of disabling PTSD from a motor vehicle accident, given that a major feature of PTSD is avoidance of reminders of the trauma situation.

Given positive findings on multiple performance and symptom validity indicators, it was my opinion that Ms. H's clinical presentation and self-reports were unreliable and could not be interpreted as valid indications of her true psychological status. Any reported cognitive, emotional, and psychological symptoms attributed to the motor vehicle collision were unreliable and were likely to be grossly exaggerated. Her overall clinical presentation and test results, occurring within the context of litigation, pursuit of compensation, and an active disability claim, met the criteria for at least probable if not definite Malingered Neurocognitive Dysfunction (MND; Slick et al., 1999), as well as the current updated criteria for Malingered Neuropsychological Dysfunction (Sherman et al., 2020).

Summary and Conclusions

The above conclusions were not intended to discount Ms. H's documented pre-collision mental health history, including pre-existing PTSD, generalized anxiety disorder, and depression, and apparent conversion disorder. As noted in the pre-collision medical reporting, the PTSD, generalized anxiety disorder, and depression were related to a sexual assault

Table 29.4 Cognitive Test Results for Ms. H

Wechsler Adult Intelligence Scale – III (WAIS-III)	Std./Scale Score
VIQ	73
PIQ	81
FSIQ	74
Information	7
Digit Span	4
Vocabulary	3
Similarities	5
Arithmetic	8
Comprehension	5
Letter-Number Sequencing	5
Picture Completion	3
Picture Arrangement	6
Block Design	10
Matrix Reasoning	10
Digit Symbol	7
Symbol Search	10
Wide Range Achievement Test – 4 (WRAT4)	Std. Score
Reading	94
Spelling	83
Math Computation	89
Wisconsin Card Sorting Test (WCST)-64	Std. Score
Total Number of Errors (Standard Score)	92
Perseverative Responses	102
Perseverative Errors	101
Nonperseverative Errors	81
Category Test (CT)	30T
Trail Making	Scaled Score
Part A	9
Part B	9
California Verbal Learning Test – Second Edition (CVLT-II)	Raw Score
List A Trials 1–5 Total (Raw, T = 28)	29
List A Trial 1	4
List A Trial 5	7
List B	4
Short-Delay Free Recall	4
Short-Delay Cued Recall	4
Long-Delay Free Recall	2
Long-Delay Cued Recall	2
Recognition Hits	3
Forced-Choice Recognition Accuracy	56%
Story Recall Test	
Immediate Recall (–3.0 SD)	29/80
Delayed Recall (–3.3 SD)	7/80
Emotional Perception Test (EPT) errors (2.8 SD)	29/45
Alberta Smell Test (AST)	
Right nostril	5/10
Left nostril	4/10

in her youth. These conditions frequently co-occur with fibromyalgia, which has also been associated with adverse life experiences, trauma, sexual abuse, and victimization (Albrecht & Rice, 2016; Galvez-Sánchez et al., 2019; Gündüz et al., 2019; Häuser et al., 2011; Imbierowicz & Engle, 2003). She had sought psychological counseling to deal with these concerns prior to the subject collision. Chart notes from her treating psychologist indicated that she had been experiencing increasing emotional distress and decompensation in the months prior to the collision. Post-collision reporting from her physician referred to the collision as minor but felt that it may have aggravated her pre-existing conditions. Psychological records referred to an exacerbation of Ms. H's feelings of being victimized and out-of-control, following the collision.

It was my perspective that Ms. H clearly had substantial pre-existing vulnerabilities to chronic pain, depression, anxiety, and traumatic stress, which might have been temporarily exacerbated by the collision. There was no head injury and no alteration of consciousness in the collision, which might be potentially associated with her reported subjective cognitive symptoms, which in addition to anxiety and depression are commonly reported by fibromyalgia patients (Bell et al., 2018), although research has shown no objective cognitive decline as compared with pain and healthy control groups once the effects of fatigue, pain, and depression are controlled (Suhr, 2003). Furthermore, after eight years, any acute symptoms or exacerbation of pre-existing conditions would have long since resolved. I viewed her attempt to link her ongoing and current problems to the motor vehicle collision as a means of attributing all her problems, distress, life disappointments, physical and emotional health issues, and other psychosocial stressors to an external cause (motor vehicle collision) over which she had no control. In contrast to this apparent belief held by the litigant, the medical records confirmed that she was experiencing virtually the same problems prior to the collision. Her overall condition at the time of the assessment was arguably not substantially different from her pre-collision baseline.

While lingering psychological sequelae would not be expected many years after an essentially trivial collision, Ms. H's presentation more likely than not reflected long-standing pre-existing somatization whereby emotional factors, including depression, anxiety, and traumatic stress were communicated and expressed through the onset, maintenance, or exacerbation of the fibromyalgia and other chronic pain symptoms. However, given the incontrovertible PVT and symptom validity test (SVT) results obtained in this assessment, it was reasonable to conclude that there was substantial volitional symptom overreporting and exaggeration, which could only reasonably be attributed to the pursuit of compensation and disability incentives. Ms. H's test results and general clinical presentation supported a determination of malingered neurocognitive dysfunction, which I described in the report. However, I emphasized that any final determination in this regard was the prerogative of the court.

Discussion

The case of Ms. H exemplifies the importance of establishing the validity of the claimant's overall clinical presentation, including reported psychological, cognitive, somatic, and behavioral symptoms and limitations in a forensic evaluation context where external incentives are invariably present. In keeping with the guidance provided in the American Academy of Clinical Neuropsychology (AACN) 2009 consensus conference statement (Heilbronner et al., 2009) and its update (Sweet et al., 2021), this assessment incorporated multiple freestanding and embedded PVTs and symptom validity measures, which indicated invalid, noncredible performance on cognitive tests and overreported, exaggerated psychological, cognitive, and somatic complaints that could not be attributed to a trivial motor vehicle collision eight years earlier. Rather, as established by review of the pre-collision medical reporting, Ms. H was experiencing largely the same psychological and physical problems, including anxiety, depression, PTSD, and fibromyalgia prior to the subject motor vehicle collision.

As noted by Sweet et al. (2021), examinees may be motivated to attribute their pre-existing symptoms or other dysfunction to more recent or current events, particularly when there is an external incentive to enhance the claimed effects of the injury. It was evident from Ms. H's presentation that she was attempting to attribute most, if not all, of her pre-existing, ongoing, and current problems and disability to the collision. However, health survey results show that 55.8% of people with fibromyalgia under age 65 reported being unable to work due to their health, compared with 5.8% of those without fibromyalgia (Walitt et al., 2015), which suggests that Ms. H would have been at high risk of disability-seeking regardless of the collision.

Apart from obvious external incentives underlying Ms. H's clinical presentation, Ferrari and Russell (2014) discuss the concept of perceived injustice in fibromyalgia, noting that fibromyalgia patients report a higher level of perceived injustice as compared with rheumatoid arthritis patients, which may be associated with higher pain levels, depression, and anxiety. "The data tells us something that we have otherwise long known: fibromyalgia patients have 'more of everything': more pain, more fatigue, more depression, more disability and now, more perceived injustice" (p. 1505). Ms. H's claim of persisting symptoms attributed to the subject collision could be interpreted as a means of assigning responsibility for her multiple long-standing physical and mental health problems to an external cause over which she had no control, and for which she could finally pursue justice and compensation. In this regard, as discussed earlier, Ms. H was angry that an acquaintance had been financially compensated for a collision that was much less severe than hers, no doubt adding to the patient's sense of "injustice."

References

Albrecht, P. J., & Rice, F. L. (2016). Fibromyalgia syndrome pathology and environmental influences on afflictions with medically unexplained symptoms. *Reviews on Environmental Health*, *31*(2), 281–294. https://doi.org/10.1515/reveh-2015-0040

Babikian, T., Boone, K. B., Lu, P., & Arnold, G. (2006). Sensitivity and specificity of various digit span scores in the detection of suspect effort. *The Clinical Neuropsychologist*, *20*(1), 145–159.

Balasanyan, M., Boone, K. B., Ermshar, A., Miora, D., Cottingham, M., Victor, T. L., Ziegler, E., Zeller, M. A., & Wright, M. (2018). Examination of the Modified Somatic Perception Questionnaire (MSPQ) in a large sample of credible and noncredible patients referred for neuropsychological testing. *The Clinical Neuropsychologist*, *32*(1), 165–182. https://doi.org/10.1080/13854046.2017.1330421

Barrash, J., Suhr, J., & Manzel, K. (2004). Detecting poor effort and malingering with an expanded version of the Auditory Verbal Learning Test (AVLTX): Validation with clinical samples. *Journal of Clinical and Experimental Neuropsychology*, *26*(1), 125–140. https://doi.org/10.1076/jcen.26.1.125.23928

Bar-On Kalfon, T., Gal, G., Shorer, R., & Ablin, J. N. (2016). Cognitive functioning in fibromyalgia: The central role of effort. *Journal of Psychosomatic Research*, *87*, 30–36. https://doi.org/10.1016/j.jpsychores.2016.06.004

Bell, T., Trost, Z., Buelow, M. T., Clay, O., Younger, J., Moore, D., & Crowe, M. (2018). Meta-analysis of cognitive performance in fibromyalgia. *Journal of Clinical and Experimental Neuropsychology*, *40*(7), 698–714. https://doi.org/10.1080/13803395.2017.1422699

Bianchini, K. J., Aguerrevere, L. E., Guise, B. J., Ord, J. S., Etherton, J. L., Meyers, J. E., … Bui, J. (2014). Accuracy of the modified somatic perception questionnaire and pain disability index in the detection of malingered pain-related disability in chronic pain. *The Clinical Neuropsychologist*, *28*(8) 1376–1394. https://doi.org/10.1080/13854046.2014.986199

Boone, K. B. (2012). *Clinical practice of forensic neuropsychology: An evidence-based approach*. Guilford Press.

Briere, J. (2001). *Detailed Assessment of Posttraumatic Stress (DAPS): Professional manual*. Psychological Assessment Resources.

Bruns, D., & Disorbio, J. M. (2003). *Battery for Health Improvement-2 manual*. Pearson.

Brooks, L., Johnson-Greene, D., Lattie, E., & Ference, T. (2012). The relationship between performances on neuropsychological symptom validity testing and the MCMI-III in patients with fibromyalgia. *The Clinical Neuropsychologist*, *26*(5), 816–831. https://doi.org/10.1080/13854046.2012.662999

Chafetz, M. D. (2022). Deception is different: Negative validity test findings do not provide "evidence" for "good effort". *The Clinical Neuropsychologist*, *36*(6), 1244–1264.

Crighton, A. H., Tarescavage, A. M., Gervais, R. O., & Ben-Porath, Y. S. (2017). The generalizability of overreporting across self-report measures: An investigation with the Minnesota Multiphasic Personality Inventory–2–Restructured Form and the Personality Assessment Inventory in a civil disability sample. *Assessment*, *24*(5), 555–574. https://doi.org/10.1177/1073191115621791

DeFilippis, N. A. & PAR Staff (2002). *Category Test: Computer Version, Research Edition*. Psychological Assessment Resources.

Delis, D. C., Kaplan, E., Kramer, J. H., & Ober, B. A. (2008). *California verbal learning test-second edition (CVLT-II)*. ECPA.

Ferrari, R., & Russell, A. S. (2014). Perceived injustice in fibromyalgia and rheumatoid arthritis. *Clinical Rheumatology*, *33*(10), 1501–1507. https://doi.org/10.1007/s10067-014-2552-z

Gaasedelen, O. J., Whiteside, D. M., Altmaier, E., Welch, C., & Basso, M. R. (2019). The construction and the initial validation of the cognitive bias scale for the personality assessment inventory. *The Clinical Neuropsychologist*, *33*, 1467–1484. https://doi.org/10.1080/13854046.2019.1612947

Galvez-Sánchez, C. M., Duschek, S., & Reyes Del Paso, G. A. (2019). Psychological impact of fibromyalgia: Current perspectives. *Psychology Research and Behavior Management*, *12*, 117–127. https://doi.org/10.2147/PRBM.S178240

Gervais, R. O., Russell, A. S., Green, P., Allen, L. M., 3rd, Ferrari, R., & Pieschl, S. D. (2001). Effort testing in patients with fibromyalgia and disability incentives. *The Journal of Rheumatology*, *28*(8), 1892–1899.

Green, P. (2003). *Green's Word Memory Test for Windows: User's manual*. Green's Publishing.

Green, P. (2004a). *Green's Medical Symptom Validity Test (MSVT): User's manual*. Green's Publishing.

Green, P. (2004b). *Memory complaints inventory*. Green's Publishing.

Green, P. (2008). *Manual for the nonverbal medical symptom validity test*. Green's Publishing.

Green, P., & Allen, L. M. (1995). *CogniSyst Story Recall Test*. CogniSyst.

Green, P., Flaro, L., & Gervais, R. O. (2008). *Green's Emotional Perception Test (EPT) user's manual for Microsoft Windows*. Green's Publishing.

Green, P., & Severson, G. (1986). *Emotional perception test*. Green's Publishing.

Greiffenstein, M. F., Baker, W. J., & Gola, T. (1994). Validation of malingered amnesia measures with a large clinical sample. *Psychological Assessment*, *6*(3), 218–224. https://doi.org/10.1037/1040-3590.6.3.218

Gündüz, N., Erzincan, E., & Polat, A. (2019). The relationship of intimate partner violence with psychiatric disorders and severity of pain among female patients with fibromyalgia. *Archives of Rheumatology*, *34*(3), 245–252. https://doi.org/10.5606/ArchRheumatol.2019.7090

Häuser, W., Kosseva, M., Üceyler, N., Klose, P., & Sommer, C. (2011). Emotional, physical, and sexual abuse in fibromyalgia syndrome: A systematic review with meta-analysis. *Arthritis Care & Research*, *63*(6), 808–820. https://doi.org/10.1002/acr.20328

Heilbronner, R. L., Sweet, J. J., Morgan, J. E., Larrabee, G. J., Millis, S. R., & Conference Participants (2009). American Academy of clinical neuropsychology consensus conference statement on the neuropsychological assessment of effort, response bias, and malingering. *The Clinical Neuropsychologist*, *23*(7), 1093–1129. https://doi.org/10.1080/13854040903155063

Imbierowicz, K., & Egle, U. T. (2003). Childhood adversities in patients with fibromyalgia and somatoform pain disorder. *European Journal of Pain*, 7(2), 113–119.

Iverson, G. L., Page, J. L., Koehler, B. E., Shojania, K., & Badii, M. (2007). Test of Memory Malingering (TOMM) scores are not affected by chronic pain or depression in patients with fibromyalgia. *The Clinical Neuropsychologist*, *21*(3), 532–546.

Johnson-Greene, D., Brooks, L., & Ference, T. (2013). Relationship between performance validity testing, disability status, and somatic complaints in patients with fibromyalgia. *The Clinical Neuropsychologist*, *27*(1), 148–158. https://doi.org/10.1080/13854046.2012.733732

Klaus, K., Fischer, S., Doerr, J. M., Nater, U. M., Mewes, R. (2017). Classifying fibromyalgia syndrome as a mental disorder?—An ambulatory assessment study. *International Journal of Behavioral Medicine, 24*(1), 230–238. https://doi.org/10.1007/s12529-016-9603-6

Larrabee, G. (2003). Exaggerated pain report in litigants with malingered neurocognitive dysfunction. *The Clinical Neuropsychologist, 17*, 395–401.

LoBrutto, L. R., Keeley, J. W., Dautovich, N. D. (2024). Applying the somatic symptom disorder diagnosis to individuals with fibromyalgia: Strengths and limitations. *Journal of Clinical Psychology in Medical Settings, 2024.* https://doi.org/10.1007/s10880-024-10005-9

Main, C. J. (1983). The Modified Somatic Perception Questionnaire (MSPQ). *Journal of Psychosomatic Research, 27*, 503–514.

Martin, P. K., Schroeder, R. W., Olsen, D. H., Maloy, H., Boettcher, A., Ernst, N., & Okut, H. (2020). A systematic review and meta-analysis of the Test of Memory Malingering in adults: Two decades of deception detection. *The Clinical Neuropsychologist*, *34*(1), 88–119.

Messerly, J., Soble, J. R., Webber, T. A., Alverson, W. A., Fullen, C., Kraemer, L. D., & Marceaux, J. C. (2021). Evaluation of the classification accuracy of multiple performance validity tests in a mixed clinical sample. *Applied Neuropsychology. Adult*, *28*(6), 727–736. https://doi.org/10.1080/23279095.2019.1698581

Morey, L. C. (2007). *Personality Assessment Inventory (PAI): Professional manual.* Psychological Assessment Resources.

Sherman, E. M. S., Slick, D. J., & Iverson, G. L. (2020). Multidimensional malingering criteria for neuropsychological assessment: A 20-year update of the Malingered Neuropsychological Dysfunction criteria. *Archives of Clinical Neuropsychology: The Official Journal of the National Academy of Neuropsychologists*, *35*(6), 735–764. https://doi.org/10.1093/arclin/acaa019

Slick, D. J., Sherman, E. M., & Iverson, G. L. (1999). Diagnostic criteria for malingered neurocognitive dysfunction: Proposed standards for clinical practice and research. *The Clinical Neuropsychologist*, *13*(4), 545–561. https://doi.org/10.1076/1385-4046(199911)13:04;1–Y;FT545

Solomon, R. E., Boone, K. B., Miora, D., Skidmore, S., Cottingham, M., Victor, T., … & Zeller, M. (2010). Use of the WAIS-III picture completion subtest as an embedded measure of response bias. *The Clinical Neuropsychologist*, *24*(7), 1243–1256.

Suhr, J. A. (2003). Neuropsychological impairment in fibromyalgia: Relation to depression, fatigue, and pain. *Journal of Psychosomatic Research*, *55*(4), 321–329. https://doi.org/10.1016/s0022-3999(02)00628-1

Sweet, J. J., Heilbronner, R. L., Morgan, J. E., Larrabee, G. J., Rohling, M. L., Boone, K. B., Kirkwood, M. W., Schroeder, R. W., Suhr, J. A., & Conference Participants (2021). American Academy of Clinical Neuropsychology (AACN) 2021 consensus statement on validity assessment: Update of the 2009 AACN consensus conference statement on neuropsychological assessment of effort, response bias, and malingering. *The Clinical Neuropsychologist*, *35*(6), 1053–1106. https://doi.org/10.1080/13854046.2021.1896036

Teodoro, T., Edwards, M. J., & Isaacs, J. D. (2018). A unifying theory for cognitive abnormalities in functional neurological disorders, fibromyalgia and chronic fatigue syndrome: Systematic review.

Journal of Neurology, Neurosurgery, and Psychiatry, *89*(12), 1308–1319. https://doi.org/10.1136/jnnp-2017-317823

Tombaugh, T. N. (1996). *The test of memory malingering*. Western Psychological Services.

Tylicki, J. L., Rai, J. K., Arends, P., Gervais, R. O., & Ben-Porath, Y. S. (2021). A comparison of the MMPI-2-RF and PAI overreporting indicators in a civil forensic sample with emphasis on the Response Bias Scale (RBS) and the Cognitive Bias Scale (CBS). *Psychological Assessment, 33*(1), 71–83. https://doi.org/10.1037/pas0000968

Walitt, B., Nahin, R. L., Katz, R. S., Bergman, M. J., & Wolfe, F. (2015). The prevalence and characteristics of fibromyalgia in the 2012 National Health Interview Survey. *PloS One*, *10*(9), e0138024. https://doi.org/10.1371/journal.pone.0138024

Wolfe, F., Walitt, B. T., Katz, R. S., & Häuser, W. (2014). Symptoms, the nature of fibromyalgia, and diagnostic and statistical manual 5 (DSM-5) defined mental illness in patients with rheumatoid arthritis and fibromyalgia. *PloS One*, *9*(2), e88740. https://doi.org/10.1371/journal.pone.0088740

30 External Incentive and Performance Validity in Claimed Long COVID

Douglas M. Whiteside, Michael R. Basso, and Laura Fry

The impact of COVID-19 on society cannot be overstated. Major societal changes have occurred since the start of the pandemic in 2020, and the long-term implications of COVID-19 infection are not clear. One of the major challenges is that the science remains unsettled about the impact of COVID-19 on cognitive functioning due to contradictory findings concerning the prevalence and severity of cognitive deficits associated with the disease (Behnood, 2022; Zimmerman, 2021; Ceban et al., 2022). Although the pandemic appears to be waning at the time of this writing, the virus continues to circulate and there are lingering effects that continue to be impactful. Specifically, a heterogeneous condition often termed "Long COVID" has been associated with long-term residual symptoms from COVID-19 infection. However, much remains unclear about Long COVID, even the definition and diagnostic criteria, let alone any sort of phenotypic cognitive profile (Alonso-Canovas et al., 2023). As Alonso-Canovas and colleagues (2023) noted, there are over 200 different potential symptoms of Long COVID across multiple bodily systems, including cognitive complaints, such as concentration problems, memory difficulties, confusion, decreased alertness, and word-finding difficulties (Hastie et al., 2022; Ceban et al., 2022). Further, Alonso-Canovas et al. (2023) asserted that this lack of diagnostic clarity, in association with ongoing stressors and extensive media attention, has likely contributed to the phenomenon of functional neurological disorders (FND) being present in at least some COVID-19 patients. Recently, the National Academies of Science, Engineering, and Medicine published a definition of Long COVID for research and clinical purposes (National Academies of Science, Engineering and Medicine, 2024). Unfortunately, the definition is quite broad and does not require documentation of a positive laboratory test for COVID-19 and there are no inclusionary or exclusionary symptoms.

In response to the pandemic, many institutions established Long COVID clinics to address the heterogeneous symptoms and complaints associated with Long COVID. The institution of the first author has one such center, managed by the Department of Rehabilitation Medicine, of which neuropsychology is one division. As such, neuropsychology has been an integrated component of the Adult Post-COVID clinic since it opened in December 2020. The clinic refers all patients to neuropsychology who present to the clinic with cognitive complaints, such as "brain fog," memory concerns, and attentional issues. Interestingly, while the virus differentially impacted communities of color, such as immigrant communities, particularly early in the pandemic, most of the individuals who present to Long COVID clinics are white, middle to upper class, with mild initial disease, and are not representative of individuals and communities most impacted during the early stages of the pandemic (Price-Haywood et al., 2020). Price-Haywood et al. (2020) and others (Berchick et al., 2019) postulated that several factors, particularly systemic racism, social

DOI: 10.4324/9781003005063-34

determinants of health such as access to care, and mistrust of the healthcare system by communities of color have contributed to this phenomenon. Unfortunately, there is currently insufficient empirical evidence to explain this phenomenon.

Neuropsychological Assessment of Long COVID Patients Although the need to understand cognitive functioning in Long COVID is considerable, surprisingly few methodologically sound and well-controlled studies have been published examining this question. For example, many studies (e.g., Kay, 2022; Becker et al., 2021; Valdes et al., 2022) have not employed performance validity tests (PVTs), which leads to questions about the validity and generalizability of the findings. Even very recent publications in neuropsychology journals have not utilized PVTs when evaluating cognition in COVID-19 (Cavaco et al., 2023).

One article by our group addressed short-term cognitive outcome (Whiteside et al., 2021) following severe COVID-19 infection, requiring hospitalization, while two others investigated long-term cognitive and psychological outcomes in COVID-19 (Whiteside et al., 2022a, 2022b). These articles were the first we are aware of to utilize PVTs, and they remain in a small minority of papers on cognitive functioning in Long COVID. Specifically, Whiteside et al. (2022a) found that 4 of the 53 participants failed at least two PVTs and none of these participants claimed external incentive during the clinical interview. However, later chart review revealed that two of these four patients submitted paperwork for disability shortly after the neuropsychological evaluation, which indicated that they were likely withholding information on their compensation-seeking status, a phenomenon not uncommon in clinical populations (Martin & Schroeder, 2022; Van Egmond et al., 2005). Further, previous research has provided evidence that external incentives are associated with a much higher rate of PVT failures in clinical populations (Bianchini et al., 2006).

Given the initial sample of 53, this is approximately an 8% PVT failure rate. This frequency was replicated recently in Whiteside et al. (2024), which found an approximately 9% PVT failure rate using the standard criteria of 2 or more PVTs failed, with another 8% of the large sample ($N = 247$) failing one PVT. Further, this study found that external incentives were significantly higher in PVT-failing patients (54.5%) compared with those who passed all PVTs (22.1%). Another study by Krishnan et al. (2022) observed very similar results when employing PVTs, suggesting a failure rate in Long COVID clinical referrals similar to other clinical contexts (Mittenberg, 2002). A recent study by Ashton Rennison et al. (2023), which used PVTs, replicated the cognitive findings of Whiteside et al. (2022a) and Krishnan et al. (2022), but they did not report the number of participants excluded due to PVT failure. In a follow-up personal communication (L. Ashton Rennison, personal communication July 19, 2023), the lead author noted that 10/69 participants failed the Test of Memory Malingering (TOMM; Tombaugh, 1997) Trial 1. Those with a raw score <42 and were excluded, for an approximately 14% PVT failure rate. Further, the lead author reported that 4/10 (40%) of those who failed the TOMM were applying for Workers' Compensation or disability benefits. Because the methodology of employing PVTs to screen Long COVID participants is not widely used in the existing research on cognitive functioning in Long COVID, it is not possible to ascertain the impact of non-credible performance in Long COVID studies. Nonetheless, there is legitimate concern that individuals with Long COVID who fail PVTs will bias results in both research and clinical work, and individuals who fail PVTs often have external incentive.

To address this shortcoming in the literature and to emphasize the clinical need for PVTs, recent practice guidance for Long COVID (Koterba et al., 2024) includes recommendations to use PVTs in Long COVID cases, regardless of whether they are clinical or forensic/medicolegal in nature. This is consistent with other practice guidelines and recommendations (Board of Directors, 2007; Bush et al., 2005; Sweet et al., 2021; Schroeder & Martin,

2022a), which indicated that the use of PVTs is appropriate in neuropsychological evaluations regardless of clinical context or referral.

The few studies on Long COVID utilizing PVTs that have been published (Krishnan et al., 2022; Whiteside et al., 2022a, 2024; Ashton Rennison et al., 2023) focused on clinical referrals from Long COVID clinics. However, neuropsychologists often evaluate individuals seen for medicolegal reasons, including lawsuits and disability claims. No Long COVID specific research with medicolegal referrals was found, but Whiteside et al. (2024) and research with other syndromes such as compensation-seeking post-concussion syndrome (PCS; Bianchini et al., 2006; Larrabee et al., 2009) emphasizes the need for PVTs across all evaluation settings. Recent research (Fry et al., 2024) has demonstrated that Long COVID and PCS patients share strikingly similar personality profiles, thereby further strengthening the argument for including PVTs in evaluations of Long COVID cases.

Measurement procedures in Long COVID. Research on cognitive functioning in Long COVID is in the early stages, and current results have not demonstrated consistent findings (Ceban et al., 2022). As noted above, this is likely due to methodological limitations in many of the studies, particularly the lack of PVTs. Regardless of the state of the empirical literature, neuropsychologists are being called upon to conduct evaluations with Long COVID patients. Existing neuropsychological literature is likely to offer some helpful guidance.

The practice guidance (Koterba et al., 2024) cited above emphasizes the need to include PVTs in neuropsychological batteries with Long COVID patients, regardless of referral context. The recommendations emphasize the critical need for PVTs to distinguish patients with possible cognitive impairment versus those who are exhibiting non-credible performance, making the test battery uninterpretable.

Importantly, the Long COVID recommendations are based on general guidelines for PVT use in neuropsychological assessment, such as the American Academy of Clinical Neuropsychology consensus statement on validity assessment (Sweet et al., 2021) and the National Academy of Neuropsychology guidelines (Bush et al, 2005), which noted that non-credible performance may occur in any context, including clinical and medicolegal/forensic. Indeed, research supports the idea that PVTs are failed in clinical contexts at a not insignificant rate, ranging from about 5%, for patients in contexts with rare external incentives, to 40% in contexts where external incentive is always present (Martin & Schroeder, 2020). With regard to Long COVID, the approximately 8%–9% failure rate reported (Krishnan et al., 2022; Whiteside et al., 2022a, 2024) occurred in a context where very few patients openly endorsed having an external incentive. However, having an external incentive is certainly possible and individual patients may not acknowledge this. Likely, the most frequent external incentive for Long COVID cases moving forward will be disability and Workers' Compensation claims, although other incentives such as litigation are certainly possible.

The case described later in this chapter illustrates the issues discussed above which are associated with the need for PVTs in Long COVID cases. This case demonstrates that it is important to use PVTs even when external incentives, such as disability payments, are not typical for the clinical setting or acknowledged by the patient.

Patient variables. Since much remains unknown about cognitive functioning in Long COVID, definitive etiological statements are not possible. In fact, some research (Whiteside et al., 2022a, Krishnan et al. 2022) suggests that cognitive deficits are rare and very mild in patients presenting to Long COVID clinics. However, there are a variety of factors that may impact performance on cognitive tasks. Consistent with the empirical literature (Shou et al., 2021), it is the experience of the authors (Whiteside et al., 2022a, 2022b) that psychological issues, particularly depression, anxiety, and somatization disorders are frequent in this population, with many having premorbid psychiatric histories ranging from mild to severe (e.g., bipolar disorder, PTSD). Further, often these variables have the strongest association with outcome in Long COVID patients (Kachaner et al., 2022; Gouraud et al., 2023).

Specifically, some investigators have hypothesized that Long COVID is a type of somatization disorder (Kachaner et al., 2022; Gouraud et al., 2023) or alternatively a functional neurological disorder (FND) (Joffe & Elliott, 2023; Teodoro et al., 2023). Joffe and Elliott explained that Long COVID has many similarities with somatic symptom disorders, including predisposing factors such as a history of mental illness (Greißel et al., 2024; Hartung et al., 2022), perpetuating factors such as low physical and social activities (Selvakumar et al., 2023), and the absence of evidence for neurological damage. They added that as the societal stress associated with the pandemic continued, Long COVID may have emerged as a mass functional illness due to the expectancy of negative outcomes (e.g., long-term disability and death). This is a continuing area of research and debate as others have expressed contrary opinions (specifically about movement and balance issues; van der Feltz-Cornelis, 2026). Nonetheless, the emerging evidence suggests that psychological issues, including somatization and depression (Mazza et al., 2022; Whiteside et al., 2022a, 2022b) are important in understanding neuropsychological functioning in Long COVID.

Complaints of fatigue are a second, almost ubiquitous, factor in this population (Davis et al., 2023). Many of the patients report ongoing fatigue since their COVID-19 infection, and the mechanisms for this are not clear. Nonetheless, this is a potential factor to consider. Obstructive sleep apnea (OSA) may be one contributing factor to both fatigue and cognitive symptoms reported in Long COVID given that both are associated with untreated or poorly managed OSA (Bucks et al., 2013; Yue et al., 2009). Of note, sleep apnea seems to be a risk factor for developing Long COVID (Mandel et al., 2023). This disorder is also frequent in our Adult Post-COVID clinic and many of the patients report poor or no management of OSA. Thus, the subset presenting for neuropsychological evaluation have some frequent commonalities such as depression/anxiety, fatigue, and OSA symptoms. Interestingly, even with these common issues, the large majority of Long COVID patients pass the PVTs in the neuropsychological assessment battery. This is consistent with existing literature that does not support factors such as mood/anxiety or fatigue as causes of PVT failure (Schroeder & Martin, 2022).

Finally, it is remarkable that Long COVID shares characteristics of other conditions with a strong psychological component, including chronic Lyme disease (Hassett et al., 2008) and post-concussion syndrome (PCS; Larrabee et al., 2014). Initial research (Fry et al., 2024) by our group provides evidence that the PAI profiles of PCS and Long COVID patients are overall remarkably similar, with implications for both treatment and assessment (Hadanny & Efrati, 2016). While this similarity suggests that research adapting interventions for PCS may possess efficacy with Long COVID, it also raises concerns about the potential for elevated PVT failure rates in Long COVID patients. Per Boone et al. (2021), PVT failure rates are at least 40% within the compensation-seeking PCS population. The similarity in psychological profiles between PCS and Long COVID suggests the need for ongoing research on PVT failure rates in Long COVID patients both with and without external motive for underperformance.

Neuropsychological Evaluation Context

Media Influence on Patients' Perception of Long COVID

In many ways, the neuropsychological evaluation context for Long COVID patients is unique or unusual due to media attention related to COVID-19, which has been intense and unprecedented. Other conditions, such as concussion or Lyme disease, do receive media attention, but media focus given to COVID-19 surpasses these other disorders. Unfortunately, much media attention tends to favor sensationalist and/or catastrophic consequences unsupported by the scientific literature. For example, an NBC News headline from March 7, 2022, exclaimed "Even Mild COVID Associated with Brain Damage" based on one unreplicated imaging study out of Great Britain.

Given the large number of studies of cognition in Long COVID that do not examine PVTs (Whiteside et al., 2024) and/or use small samples, perhaps it is not surprising that these provocative studies are most frequently cited by the popular media. It is in this cultural climate that neuropsychologists, including in our Adult Post-COVID clinic, must work, and the potentially iatrogenic effects of popular media depictions are considerable. Since its establishment in the first year of the pandemic, in December 2020, the clinic has seen over 400 patients complaining of Long COVID. The neuropsychological practice associated with the Long COVID clinic has evaluated over 300 separate individuals for neuropsychological evaluation. Prior to the initial papers (Whiteside et al., 2022a, 2022b), an extended battery was utilized. However, after the initial research, it became clear that such a lengthy battery was unnecessary and not more informative than a shorter battery that was reported in Whiteside et al. (2024). The following case is an example of the types of patients typically seen in the clinic who evidenced problematic PVT performance, which based on more recent research is typically about 9% of cases (Whiteside et al., 2024).

The Case of Dr. A

Background

Dr. A is a 51-year-old woman with a Doctor of Osteopathic Medicine (DO) degree who works as an internist. She was referred for a neuropsychological evaluation from the Adult Post-COVID clinic due to cognitive complaints in the context of a history of COVID-19 infection. She reported that she was a good student in school and had no history of individual education plans or academic accommodations. She has been married for 17 years and lives at home with her husband and three children. She relayed that her 16-year-old son carries a diagnosis of autism spectrum disorder, while the other two children have no reported neurologic or psychiatric health history. The patient reported that prior to the COVID-19 pandemic, she was feeling overwhelmed and "burned out" at work, and the pandemic-related issues only increased these feelings.

The patient developed COVID-19 symptoms in January 2021, and polymerase chain reaction testing was positive at that time. She believed she contracted COVID-19 through her work as an internist. She reported no COVID-19 related hospitalization, but she developed a fever that lasted approximately three to four days. She said the reason she was not hospitalized at that time was because the hospitals were very full, but she said she was quite ill and had oxygen saturation levels as low at 84%. She stated that since her COVID-19 diagnosis, she has had multiple episodes in which she has lost consciousness and fallen, although as noted below, she had a premorbid history of syncope, but this was not an active problem at the time of the evaluation.

In terms of other medical history, the patient struck her head and sustained a brief loss of consciousness while playing soccer 15 years ago, but she was not hospitalized and denied durable sequelae of this injury. The patient noted that seven years before the evaluation she often had menstrual-related pain. However, at that time she had a uterine fibroid that ruptured, which subsequently required removal of her uterus and ovaries. She noted that this was a six-month process, but after she healed from her surgeries, she did not experience further pain. The patient denied having any history of medical or neurological diagnoses such as multiple sclerosis, stroke, seizures, Parkinson's disease, hypothyroidism, diabetes, heart disease, cancer, hypertension, liver disease, or kidney disease. She noted that her blood pressure is lower than optimal per her physician, and she has mildly elevated HDL but not LDL levels. She also reported a previous diagnosis of OSA about eight years prior, and she regularly uses a continuous positive airway pressure (CPAP) machine. She wears eyeglasses but denied any eye diseases or hearing problems, but reported loss of sense of taste and anosmia since COVID-19 infection. She also noted having an evaluation for seizures about 12 years ago due to the syncopal episodes, but the results were negative.

At the time of her neuropsychological examination, eight months had passed since acute COVID-19 infection. She complained of significant fatigue since her initial COVID-19 illness. She reported that she attempted to return to work when she initially felt better, but she experienced severe fatigue after working for only one day. She has been unable to work since that time. In addition to fatigue, she reported that she has had difficulty with short-term memory, requiring that she write lists and take pictures to remember information. She also noted having word-finding difficulties, including incorrect word substitutions and occasionally "losing a word." She said these difficulties are worse when fatigued. Further, she will "flip things around" if she does not pay attention. For example, when managing the household finances, number "flipping" and calculation errors have resulted in extended time to complete this task. She said that she worked for a month on her taxes, and she had to have other people double-check the returns. She reported that she becomes distracted easily and cannot multi-task, and that if she tries to work on two things at once, she cannot complete either task. She had been able to organize information efficiently in her head previously, but she can no longer do so.

In addition to reportedly being unable to work, other activities of daily living have also been affected. Dr. A stopped driving because she was concerned that she might cause an accident due to fatigue and inattention. In terms of medication management, she stated that she requires assistance because she has mixed up medications when placing them in a pill-minder box. She indicated that she is unable to do many chores because of fatigue. She relies upon her family to complete household chores such as cooking, cleaning, and grocery shopping.

In terms of psychiatric history, the patient denied current or past depression, as well as family history of depression. She reported that she spends considerable time sleeping and meditating, and that she is attempting to "accept [her] current reality." Despite such efforts, she experiences repeated panic episodes punctuated by fears that "I am going to die." These panic episodes began after her COVID-19 infection, appear randomly for no discernable reason, and have not noticeably changed in frequency or severity over time. She sleeps approximately eight to nine hours nightly but has difficulty falling and staying asleep. She often naps for three hours in the afternoon. Her appetite is "as good as it can be," despite diminished olfaction and gustation. She denied significant changes in her weight. The patient receives treatment from a psychologist that aims to enhance her ability to cope with loss of functioning. She denied suicidal or homicidal ideation or any history of suicide attempts. She also denied hallucinations or delusions or excessive use of alcohol or substances.

During the video interview via a video link to her home, she reclined in her bed and had her eyes closed for most of the interaction. She also had a slow rate of speech and tended to speak in a halting manner. Despite that, she appeared to be a reliable historian with a self-report consistent with the medical records in spite of her memory complaints. Her affect was mildly constricted. There were no indications of disorganization or other symptoms of thought disorder. She was fully oriented to personal information, place, and time, and she was able to name the most recent six presidents of the United States.

Test Results

Formal neuropsychological testing was conducted in person in the clinic with a professional psychometrician. In the Adult Post-COVID clinic, a standard battery of tests is typically administered to individuals for both clinical and research purposes. This fixed battery includes performance validity measures as well as tests of estimated premorbid functioning, attention/working memory, processing speed, memory, language, visual spatial functioning, executive abilities, motor skills, and emotional/personality functioning (specifically, the PAI). However, when patients significantly fail PVTs, it is clinic policy to curtail the testing battery so the remaining tests are not "spoiled" since there is a strong likelihood that additional useful information would not be obtained. Measures that were not administered when performance invalidity was observed included tasks such as the Wisconsin Card Sorting Test, Stroop Test, the Neuropsychological Assessment Battery Naming Test, several subtests from the Wechsler Adult Intelligence Scale-IV (Similarities, Matrix Reasoning, Vocabulary), Hopkins Verbal Learning Test-Revised, and the Clock Drawing Test (many of these measures do not have alternate forms and are susceptible to practice effects). The completed measures and their results are noted in Table 30.1 (the PAI was also administered). Most measures in the table were administered prior to documentation that multiple performance validity tests were failed, but a few were given following the PVT failures in order to "mask" which tests were the PVTs.

Interpretation of Test Results

On the PAI, Dr. A's symptom validity tests (SVTs) did not indicate that she was invalidly reporting psychiatric symptom. Furthermore, she did not endorse significant psychopathology; her highest clinical scale elevation was a T score of 67 on a measure of somatic pre-occupation (SOM scale). Conversely, the results of the partial cognitive battery in Table 30.1 indicate that cognitive testing was invalid with multiple PVT failures, including chance-level performances on some force choice tests (e.g., TOMM Trial 1 and Logical Memory Recognition). Additionally, her cognitive test performances were poor, and they were much worse than would be expected of a physician. If one were to examine the cognitive measures without consideration of her PVT performance and behavioral observations, the results would suggest a patient with severe cognitive impairment. However, even without the invalidating PVT data, there are several points that raise suspicions about the accuracy of the data. Most notably, her presentation and accuracy in reporting her history during the interview suggest intact episodic memory, which is inconsistent with the test data. Additionally, she provided detailed examples of how memory problems adversely affected her life, and she specified factors that exacerbated her memory complaints. Each of these characteristics would be unexpected for someone with memory as impaired to suggested by her neuropsychological scores.

Table 30.1 Neuropsychological Assessment Data Table

Neuropsychological Measure	*Raw Score*	*Standard Score*	*Percentile*	*Interpretation*
Test of Memory Malingering (TOMM)				
Trial 1	29			**Fail**
Trial 2	35			**Fail**
Dot Counting Test (DCT)	15			**Fail**
Wechsler Adult Intelligence Scale – 4th Edition (WAIS-IV)				
Digit Span: Reliable Digit Span	7			Pass
Digit Span	27	ss = 10		Average
Vocabulary	34	ss = 9		Average
Wide Range Achievement Test – 4th Edition (WRAT-4)				
Word Reading		Std =131	98	>12.9 Grade equivalent
Wechsler Memory Scale–4th Edition (WMS-IV)				
Logical Memory I	17	ss = 6		**Low average**
Logical Memory II	7	ss = 4		**Below average**
Logical Memory Recognition	15		<2	**Exceptionally low**
Rey-Osterrieth Complex Figure (RCFT)				
Time to Copy	282 s		>16	Within normal limits
Copy	29		<1	**Exceptionally low**
Short Delay Recall	10.5	$T = 28$	1	**Exceptionally low**
Long Delay Recall	7.5	$T < 20$	<1	**Exceptionally low**
Recognition	16	$T = 21$	<1	**Exceptionally low**
Neuropsychological Assessment Battery (NAB)				
Naming	23	$T = 19$		**Exceptionally low**
Controlled Oral Word Association Test (COWAT)	41	$T = 41$		**Low average**
Animal Fluency Test	17	$T = 36$		**Below average**
Boston Diagnostic Aphasia Examination (BDAE)				
Complex Ideational Material	8	$T = 7$		**Exceptionally low**
Beck Depression Inventory – 2nd Edition (BDI-2)	18			Mild
Beck Anxiety Inventory (BAI)	21			Moderate

Note: ss = scaled score, T = T score, Std = Standard Score, **Bold** = Likely non-credible performance.

Conclusions

In terms of why Dr. A failed PVTs, during the feedback meeting, she did not acknowledge problematic task engagement or non-credible performance. She insisted that she was "trying her best" even when presented with the objective evidence to the contrary. Thus, it is impossible to make conclusive statements about underlying motivational factors. Some of her comments about her employment during the interview provide clues to motivation, however. For example, she did not endorse applying for disability during the interview, but a subsequent review of the electronic medical records revealed she had requested that her primary care provider submit paperwork for long-term disability. Further, she mentioned that she was feeling "burned out" and overwhelmed at work prior to the pandemic, a reasonably common situation among physicians (Amanullah et al., 2020). She elaborated that these feelings exacerbated during the first year of the pandemic, and they commenced before she contracted COVID-19. Finally, she mentioned that she did not plan on returning to work unless she got significantly better, and she anticipated being unable to work indefinitely. Thus, a reasonable hypothesis for the PVT failure was to support her claim of disability.

Some writers have speculated that serious emotional distress (major depressive disorder, anxiety) contribute to PVT failure, although much research in this area does not support this hypothesis (Goldberg & Birath, 2021; Marshall & Schroeder, 2022; Schroeder & Martin, 2022b). Further, in this case, while the patient acknowledged participating in psychotherapy with a clinical psychologist, she did not endorse significant psychopathology consistent with clinical psychological conditions (such as depression or anxiety) on the PAI. Nevertheless, she displayed a slight elevation (T = 67) on a measure of somatic preoccupation (SOM scale). In all, it is reasonable to conclude that emotional or psychiatric issues did not contribute to her PVT failure.

Because this evaluation occurred in the context of a clinical referral from a medical provider (in the Adult Post-COVID clinic), it was not a medicolegal referral for disability. This raises the question of what can or should be done to assist the patient despite the PVT failures. Several recommendations are routinely provided to Long COVID patients, regardless of neuropsychological assessment results, because many present with the same issues. For example, the Long COVID clinic providers emphasize a gradual return to activity and exercise, often in consultation with physical therapy. The physiatrists in the Long COVID clinic have reported good results with this intervention, because many patients have been inactive for months or even years. Using behavioral activation strategies such as this is consistent with emerging empirical literature (Teo & Goodwill, 2022). Second, the patient endorsed problematic sleep and OSA. While she stated that she used her CPAP regularly, this could not be independently verified. Thus, the neuropsychological consultation report included sleep and sleep apnea-focused recommendations. She was also encouraged to continue psychotherapy with attention on her feelings of burnout at work.

Could fatigue impact PVT failures? Fatigue has been reported very frequently in Long COVID, with one study noting a frequency of fatigue in 64% of cases (Joli et al., 2022), but Johnson-Greene et al. (2013) found no association between fatigue and PVT performance. Likewise, Schroeder and Martin (2022b) note that fatigue is not a credible explanation of PVT failure. Furthermore, anecdotally, almost none of the Long COVID patients who presented to the Adult Post-COVID clinic with fatigue complaints failed PVTs (Whiteside et al., 2022a). It is only in the extreme cases where fatigue would be expected to cause PVT failure. For example, the first author of this chapter recently evaluated a different (non-COVID) patient with a sleep disorder who actually fell asleep repeatedly during the

TOMM and other measures. Needless to say, TOMM was invalid, and testing was discontinued shortly thereafter. Excepting these extreme and obvious presentations, fatigue is not an empirically supported cause of PVT failure.

Regardless as to why Dr. A engaged in performance invalidity, the fact that she did render the remainder of test results uninterpretable. This case highlights the importance of utilizing PVTs in clinical cases and not just forensic/medicolegal referrals. As noted earlier in the chapter, research has shown an approximately 8% PVT failure rate in general clinical populations (Mittenberg et al., 2002; Larrabee, 2014; Drane et al., 2006), which is comparable to COVID-19 focused studies such as ours (Whiteside et al., 2022a, 2024). Although several causal explanations for PVT failure discussed above are unlikely (e.g., depression, anxiety, fatigue), our research (Whiteside et al., 2024) and that of others (Denning & Shura, 2019; Leppma et al., 2018) found significantly higher PVT failure rates if an external incentive was present. Thus, if PVTs are not included in a test battery for Long COVID patients, the neuropsychologist might erroneously conclude that abnormal neuropsychological test performance reflects authentic impairment due to COVID-19, opening the door for possible inappropriate eligibility for disability benefits and further iatrogenic effects.

Discussion

The patient presented in this chapter is an excellent example of why it is critical to utilize PVTs with Long COVID patients, even when they do not acknowledge an external incentive such as disability-seeking or litigation involvement. Other recent guidance supports the use of PVTs in Long COVID clinical work and research (Koterba et al., 2024), just as in other clinical populations generally (Sweet et al., 2021; Schroeder & Martin, 2022). This case also highlights the critical need for further research examining PVTs and SVTs in Long COVID, using both clinical and medicolegal samples. It is a reasonable hypothesis that the base rates and types of PVT failures will be similar to other clinical and medicolegal populations, but empirical support is necessary to support this practice.

Related questions for future neuropsychological research incorporating PVTs include addressing the nature and extent of any cognitive deficits in COVID-19. While initial studies supported some cognitive difficulties associated with COVID-19 infection (Whiteside et al., 2021), longer-term studies have shown mixed findings (Whiteside et al., 2022a). The lack of PVTs as one significant methodological limitation with most Long COVID studies may account for the discrepancy in results; research in which PVTs are routinely used should help to clarify this important question. Further research on psychological functioning in Long COVID is critical as well, given that, as discussed above, preliminary investigations have shown that psychological functioning variables can potentially impact the development and maintenance of Long COVID complaints.

If high-quality, methodically sound research provides evidence for cognitive deficits associated with Long COVID, then further questions arise. For example, what is the base rate of these deficits in Long COVID populations? Are there non-COVID factors that better account for cognitive abnormalities, such as concurrent sleep apnea and/or psychiatric conditions? As discussed above, numerous studies now link complaints/evidence of cognitive dysfunction in Long COVID to psychiatric factors such as depression, anxiety, and somatic pre-occupation (e.g., Whiteside et al., 2022b; Fry et al., 2024), which indicates that psychological factors need to be considered before attributing cognitive dysfunction to Long COVID.

In addition to base rates of cognitive dysfunction, what are the severity and permanence of any possible cognitive deficits? Do these patients eventually recover? Are there interventions, such as cognitive rehabilitation, that may benefit this subset?

In summary, the emerging research with PVTs supports the idea that that few patients presenting to Long COVID clinics manifest cognitive deficits, and any objective anomalies have to be interpreted in the context of PVT performance and psychiatric factors. However, these studies do not exclude the possibility that some Long COVID patients may manifest authentic neurocognitive impairment related directly to the infection. The only way to address these issues is to conduct research with appropriate PVTs.

References

Alonso-Canovas, A., Kurtis, M. M., Gomez-Mayordomo, V., Macías-García, D., Gutiérrez Viedma, Á., Mondragón Rezola, E., ... & Pareés, I. (2023). Functional neurological disorders after COVID-19 and SARS-CoV-2 vaccines: a national multicentre observational study. *Journal of Neurology, Neurosurgery & Psychiatry*, *94*(9), 776–777.

Amanullah, S., & Ramesh Shankar, R. (2020). The impact of COVID-19 on physician burnout globally: A review. *Healthcare, 8*(4), 421. https://doi.org/10.3390/healthcare8040421

Ashton Rennison, V. L., Chovaz, C. J., & Zirul, S. (2023). Cognition and psychological well-being in adults with post COVID-19 condition and analyses of symptom sequelae. *The Clinical Neuropsychologist.* Published online on June 23, 2023. https://doi.org/10.1080/13854046.2023.2227407

Becker, J. H., Lin, J. J., Doemberg, M., Stone, K., Navis, A., Festa, J. R., & Wisnivesky, J. P. (2021). Assessment of cognitive function in patients after COVID-19 infection. *JAMA Network Open, 4*(10), e2130645. https://doi.org/10.1001/jamanetworkopen.2021.30645

Behnood, S. A., Shafran, R., Bennett, S. D., Zhang, A. X. D., O'Mahoney, L. L., Stephenson, T. J., Ladhani, S. N., De Stavola, B. L., Viner, R. M., & Swann, O. V. (2022). Persistent symptoms following SARS-CoV-2 infection amongst children and young people: A meta-analysis of controlled and uncontrolled studies. *Journal of Infection, 84*(2), 158–170. https://doi.org/10.1016/j.jinf.2021.11.011

Berchick, E. R., Barnett, J. C., & Rachel, D. (2019). Upton Current Population Reports, P60–267(RV). *Health Insurance Coverage in the United States: 2018,* U.S. Government Printing Office, Washington, DC.

Bianchini, K. J., Curtis, K. L., & Greve, K. W. (2006). Compensation and malingering in traumatic brain injury: A dose-response relationship? *The Clinical Neuropsychologist, 20*(4), 831–847. https://doi.org/10.1080/13854040600875203

Board of Directors. (2007). American Academy of Clinical Neuropsychology (AACN) practice guidelines for neuropsychological assessment and consultation. *The Clinical Neuropsychologist, 21*(2), 209–231.

Boone, K. B., Litvin, P., & Victor, T. L. (2021). Base rates of feigned mild traumatic brain injury. In Boone, K. B. (Ed.), *Assessment of Feigned Cognitive Impairment* (pp. 341–355). New York: Guilford Press.

Bucks, R. S., Olaithe, M., & Eastwood, P. (2013). Neurocognitive function in obstructive sleep apnoea: A meta-review. *Respirology, 18*(1), 61–70.

Bush, S. S., Ruff, R. M., Tröster, A. I., Barth, J. T., Koffler, S. P., Pliskin, N. H., Reynolds, C. R., & Silver, C. H. (2005). Symptom validity assessment: Practice issues and medical necessity NAN policy & planning committee. *Archives of Clinical Neuropsychology, 20*(4), 419–426.

Cavaco, S., Sousa, G., Gonçalves, A., Dias, A., Andrade, C., Pereira, D., Aires, E. A., Moura, J., Silva, L., Varela, R., Malheiro, S., Oliveira, V., Teixeira-Pinto, A., Maia, L. F., & Correia, M. (2023). Predictors of cognitive dysfunction one-year post COVID-19. *Neuropsychology, 37*(5), 557–567. https://doi.org/10.1037/neu0000876

Ceban, F., Ling, S., Lui, L., Lee, Y., Gill, H., Teopiz, K., Rodrigues, Nelson B., Subramaniapillai, M., Di Vincenzo, J., Cao, B., Lin, K., Mansur, R., Ho, R., Rosenblat, J., Miskowiak, K., Vinberg, M., Maletic, V., & McIntyre, R. (2022). Fatigue and cognitive impairment in Post-COVID-19 Syndrome: A systematic review and meta-analysis. *Brain, Behavior, and Immunity, 101*, 93–135.

Davis, H. E., McCorkell, L., Vogel, J. M., & Topol, E. J. (2023). Long COVID: Major findings, mechanisms and recommendations. *Nature Reviews. Microbiology*, *21*(3), 133–146. https://doi.org/10.1038/s41579-022-00846-2

Denning, J. H., & Shura, R. D. (2019). Cost of malingering mild traumatic brain injury-related cognitive deficits during compensation and pension evaluations in the veterans benefits administration. *Applied Neuropsychology: Adult, 26*(1), 1–16.

Drane, D. L., Williamson, D. J., Stroup, E. S., et al. (2006). Cognitive impairment is not equal in patients with epileptic and psychogenic nonepileptic seizures. *Epilepsia, 47*(11),1879–1886. https://doi.org/10.1111/j.1528-1167.2006.00611.x

Fry, L., Logemann, A., Waldron, E., Holker, E., Porter, J., Eskridge, C., Naini, S., Basso, M. R., Taylor, S. E., Melnik, T., & Whiteside, D. M. (2024). Emotional functioning in long COVID: Comparison to post-concussion syndrome using the personality assessment inventory. *The Clinical Neuropsychologist, 38*(4), 963–983.

Goldberg, H. E., & Birath, J. B. (2021). The impact of psychotic, depressive, bipolar, obsessive-compulsive, and anxiety disorders on performance validity test results. In Boone, K. B. (Ed.), *Assessment of feigned cognitive impairment* (pp. 387–432). New York: Guilford Publications.

Gouraud, C., Thoreux, P., Ouazana-Vedrines, C., Pitron, V., Betouche, S., Bolloch, K., Caumes, E., Guemouni, S., Xiang, K., Lemogne, C., Ranque, B., & CASPer-COVID Study Group. (2023). Patients with persistent symptoms after COVID-19 attending a multidisciplinary evaluation: Characteristics, medical conclusions, and satisfaction. *Journal of psychosomatic research, 174*, 111475. https://doi.org/10.1016/j.jpsychores.2023.111475

Greißel, A., Schneider, A., Donnachie, E., Gerlach, R., Tauscher, M., & Hapfelmeier, A. (2024). Impact of pre-existing mental health diagnoses on development of post-COVID and related symptoms: A claims data-based cohort study. *Scientific reports, 14*(1), 2408. https://doi.org/10.1038/s41598-024-52656-6

Hadanny, A., & Efrati, S. (2016). Treatment of persistent post-concussion syndrome due to mild traumatic brain injury: Current status and future directions. *Expert review of neurotherapeutics, 16*(8), 875–887. https://doi.org/10.1080/14737175.2016.1205487

Hartung, T. J., Neumann, C., Bahmer, T., Chaplinskaya-Sobol, I., Endres, M., Geritz, J., ... & Finke, C. (2022). Fatigue and cognitive impairment after COVID-19: A prospective multicentre study. *EClinicalMedicine, 53*.

Hassett, A. L., Radvanski, D. C., Buyske, S., Savage, S. V., Gara, M., Escobar, J. I., & Sigal, L. H. (2008). Role of psychiatric comorbidity in chronic Lyme disease. *Arthritis Care & Research, 59*(12), 1742–1749.

Hastie, C. E., Lowe, D. J., McAuley, A. et al. (2022). Outcomes among confirmed cases and a matched comparison group in the Long-COVID in Scotland study. *Nature Communications, 13*, 5663. https://doi.org/10.1038/s41467-022-33415-5

Joffe, A. R., & Elliott, A. (2023). Long COVID as a functional somatic symptom disorder caused by abnormally precise prior expectations during Bayesian perceptual processing: A new hypothesis and implications for pandemic response. *SAGE Open Medicine, 11*, 20503121231194400.

Johnson-Greene, D., Brooks, L., & Ference, T. (2013). Relationship between performance validity testing, disability status, and somatic complaints in patients with fibromyalgia. *The Clinical Neuropsychologist, 27*(1), 148–158. https://doi.org/10.1080/13854046.2012.733732

Joli, J., Buck, P., Zipfel, S., & Stengel, A. (2022). Post-COVID-19 fatigue: A systematic review. *Frontiers in Psychiatry, 13*, 947973. https://doi.org/10.3389/fpsyt.2022.947973

Kachaner, A., Lemogne, C., Dave, J., Ranque, B., de Broucker, T., & Meppiel, E. (2022). Somatic symptom disorder in patients with post-COVID-19 neurological symptoms: A preliminary report from the somatic study (Somatic Symptom Disorder Triggered by COVID-19). *Journal of Neurology, Neurosurgery, and Psychiatry, 93*(11), 1174–1180. https://doi.org/10.1136/jnnp-2021-327899

Kay, C. D., Costa, A. S., Vannorsdall, T. D., Aduen, P., Vila-Castelar, C., Burstein, S. M., ... Quiroz, Y. T. (2022). Neuropsychological outcomes of COVID-19: A multicenter, cross-cultural study of patients referred for outpatient assessment. *COVID, 2*(9), 1253–1264.

Koterba, C. H., Considine, C. M., Becker, J. H., Hoskinson, K. R., Ng, R., Vargas, G., ... Whiteside, D. M. (2024). Neuropsychology practice guidance for the neuropsychiatric aspects of long COVID. *The Clinical Neuropsychologist, 39*(4), 870–898. https://doi.org/10.1080/13854046.2024.2392943

Krishnan, K., Miller, A., Reiter, K., & Bonner-Jackson, A. (2022). Neurocognitive profiles in patients with persisting cognitive symptoms associated with COVID-19. *Archives of Clinical Neuropsychology, 37*(4), 729–737.

Larrabee, G. J., Binder, L., Rohling, M., & Ploetz, D. (2014). Meta-analytic methods and the importance of non-TBI factors related to outcome in mild traumatic brain injury: Response to Bigler et al. (2013). *The Clinical Neuropsychologist, 27*(2), 215–237.

Larrabee, G. J., Millis, S. R., & Meyers, J. E. (2009). 40 plus or minus 10, a new magical number: Reply to Russell. *The Clinical Neuropsychologist, 23*(5), 841–849. https://doi.org/10.1080/13854040902796735

Leppma, M., Long, D., Smith, M., & Lassiter, C. (2018). Detecting symptom exaggeration in college students seeking ADHD treatment: Performance validity assessment using the NV-MSVT and IVA-Plus. *Applied Neuropsychology: Adult, 25*(3), 210–218.

Mandel, H. L., Colleen, G., Abedian, S., Ammar, N., Charles Bailey, L., Bennett, T. D., Daniel Brannock, M., Brosnahan, S. B., Chen, Y., Chute, C. G., Divers, J., Evans, M. D., Haendel, M., Hall, M. A., Hirabayashi, K., Hornig, M., Katz, S. D., Krieger, A. C., Loomba, J., ... the RECOVER Consortium. (2023). Risk of post-acute sequelae of SARS-CoV-2 infection associated with precoronavirus disease obstructive sleep apnea diagnoses: An electronic health record-based analysis from the RECOVER initiative. *Sleep, 46*(9), 1–8. https://doi.org/10.1093/sleep/zsad126

Marshall, P. S., & Schroeder, R. W. (2022). Validity assessment in patients with psychiatric disorder. In Schroeder, R. W., & Martin, P. K. (Eds.), *Validity assessment in clinical neuropsychological practice* (pp. 319–337). New York: Guilford Press.

Martin, P. K., & Schroeder, R. W. (2020). Base rates of invalid test performance across clinical non-forensic contexts and settings. *Archives of Clinical Neuropsychology, 35*(6), 717–725.

Martin, P. K., & Schroeder, R. W. (2022). Malingering: Maintaining a perspective of clinical care when patients feign. In Schroeder, R. W., & Martin, P. K. (Eds.), *Validity assessment in clinical neuropsychological practice* (pp. 31–46). New York: Guilford Press.

Mazza, M. G., Palladini, M., Villa, G., De Lorenzo, R., Rovere Querini, P., & Benedetti, F. (2022). Prevalence, trajectory over time, and risk factor of post-COVID-19 fatigue. *Journal of Psychiatric Research, 155*, 112–119. https://doi.org/10.1016/j.jpsychires.2022.08.008

Mittenberg, W., Patton, C., Canyock, E. M., & Condit, D. C. (2002). Base rates of malingering and symptom exaggeration. *Journal of Clinical and Experimental Neuropsychology, 24*, 1094–1102.

National Academies of Science, Engineering, and Medicine. (2024). *A long COVID definition: A chronic, systemic disease state with profound consequences*. Washington, DC: The National Academies Press. https://doi.org/10.17226/27768

NBC News. (2022). March 7, 2022. *Even Mild COVID Associated with Brain Damage*. Downloaded June 3, 2023.

Price-Haywood, E. G., Burton, J., Fort, D., & Seoane, L. (2020). Hospitalization and mortality among black patients and white patients with Covid-19. *New England Journal of Medicine, 382*, 2534–2543.

Schroeder, R. W., & Martin, P. K. (2022a). Validity assessment in clinical settings: How it differs from forensic settings and why it is important. In Schroeder, R. W., & Martin, P. K. (Eds.), *Validity assessment in clinical neuropsychological practice* (pp. 3–10). New York: Guilford Press.

Schroeder, R. W., & Martin, P. K. (2022b). Explanations of performance validity test failure in clinical settings. In Schroeder, R. W., & Martin, P. K. (Eds.), *Validity assessment in clinical neuropsychological practice* (pp. 11–30). New York: Guilford Press.

Selvakumar, J., Havdal, L. B., Drevvatne, M., Brodwall, E. M., Lund Berven, L., Stiansen-Sonerud, T., Einvik, G., Leegaard, T. M., Tjade, T., Michelsen, A. E., Mollnes, T. E., Lund-Johansen, F., Holmøy, T., Zetterberg, H., Blennow, K., Sandler, C. X., Cvejic, E., Lloyd, A. R., & Wyller, V. B. B. (2023). Prevalence and characteristics associated with post-COVID-19 condition among nonhospitalized adolescents and young adults. *JAMA Network Open*, *6*(3), e235763. https://doi.org/10.1001/jamanetworkopen.2023.5763

Shou, T., Joca, S., Wegener, G., & Bay-Richter, C. (2021). Psychiatric and neuropsychiatric sequelae of COVID-19 – A systematic review. *Brain, Behavior, and Immunity, 97*, 328–348.

Sweet, J. J., Heilbronner, R. L., Morgan, J. E., Larrabee, G. J., Rohling, M. L., Boone, K. B., ... Conference Participants. (2021). American Academy of Clinical Neuropsychology (AACN) 2021 consensus statement on validity assessment: Update of the 2009 AACN consensus conference statement on neuropsychological assessment of effort, response bias, and malingering. *The Clinical Neuropsychologist*, *35*(6), 1053–1106.

Teo, W. P., & Goodwill, A. M. (2022). Can exercise attenuate the negative effects of long COVID syndrome on brain health? *Frontiers of Immunology*, published online September 16; *13*, 986950. https://doi.org/10.3389/fimmu.2022.986950

Teodoro, T., Chen, J., Gelauff, J., & Edwards, M. J. (2023). Functional neurological disorder in people with long COVID: A systematic review. *European Journal of Neurology*, *30*(5), 1505–1514.

Tombaugh, T. N. (1997). The Test of Memory Malingering (TOMM): Normative data from cognitively intact and cognitively impaired individuals. *Psychological Assessment*, *9*(3), 260–268. https://doi.org/10.1037/1040-3590.9.3.260

Valdes, E., Fuchs, B., Morrison, C., Charvet, L., Lewis, A., Thawani, S., Balcer, L., Galetta, S. L., Wisniewski, T., & Frontera, J. A. (2022). Demographic and social determinants of cognitive dysfunction following hospitalization for COVID-19. *Journal of the Neurological Sciences*, *438*, 1–7. https://doi.org/10.1016/j.jns.2022.120146

van der Feltz-Cornelis, C. M. (2026). Cognition and Long COVID: a Review. *Current Neurology and Neuroscience Reports*, *26*(1), 15.

Van Egmond, J., Kummeling, I., & Balkom, T. A. (2005). Secondary gain as hidden motive for getting psychiatric treatment. *European Psychiatry*, *20*(5–6), 416–421. https://doi.org/10.1016/j.eurpsy.2004.11.012

Whiteside, D. M., Basso, M. R., Niani, S. M., Waldron, E., Holker, E., Porter, J., Melnik, T., Niskanen, N., & Taylor, S. (2022a). Outcomes in post-acute sequelae of COVID-19 (PASC) at 6 months post-infection part 1: Cognitive functioning. *The Clinical Neuropsychologist*, *36*(4), 806–828.

Whiteside, D. M., Basso, M. R., Shen, C., Fry, L., Naini, S., Waldron, E. J., Holker, E., Porter, J., Eskridge, C., Logemann, A., & Minor, G. N. (2024). The relationship between performance validity testing, external incentives, and cognitive functioning in long COVID. *Journal of Clinical and Experimental Neuropsychology*, *46*(1), 6–15.

Whiteside, D. M., Niani, S. M., Basso, M. R., Waldron, E., Holker, E., Porter, J., Niskanen, N., Melnik, T., & Taylor, S. (2022b). Outcomes in post-acute sequelae of COVID-19 (PASC) at 6 months post-infection part 2: Psychological functioning. *The Clinical Neuropsychologist*, *36*(4), 829–847.

Whiteside, D. M., Oleynick, V., Holker, E., Waldron, E., Porter, J., & Kasprzak, M. (2021). Neurocognitive deficits in severe COVID-19 infection: Case series and proposed model. *The Clinical Neuropsychologist*, *35*(4), 799–818.

Whiteside, D. M., Basso, M. R., Shen, C., Fry, L., Naini, S., Waldron, E. J., ... & Minor, G. N. (2024). The relationship between performance validity testing, external incentives, and cognitive functioning in long COVID. *Journal of Clinical and Experimental Neuropsychology*, *46*(1), 6–15.

Yue, H. J., Bardwell, W., Ancoli-Israel, S., Loredo, J. S., & Dimsdale, J. E. (2009). Arousal frequency is associated with increased fatigue in obstructive sleep apnea. *Sleep and Breathing*, *13*, 331–339.

Zimmerman, K., Akinboyo, I., Brookhart, M., Boutzoukas, A., McGann, K., Smith, M., Panayotti, M., Maradiaga, G., Armstrong, S., Bristow, H., Parker, D., Zadrozny, S., Weber, D., & Benjamin, D. (2021). Incidence and secondary transmission of SARS-CoV-2 infections in schools. *Pediatrics (Evanston)*, *147*(4), 1.

31 Evaluations of Active-Duty Service Members in the Context of External Incentives

Patrick Armistead-Jehle

To begin, it is my personal belief that the majority of active-duty service members (ADSMs) are motivated to join and remain in the military by a sense of patriotism and duty to country. A military life, whether it lasts for just a few years or over 30, holds many physical, psychological, spiritual, and social challenges; not only for the ADSM, but also for his or her family. For both those who currently serve and for those who are retired or separated from service, Americans owe (at the very least) a debt of gratitude. With this said, external incentives within the military environment are pervasive and can theoretically influence behavior. The goal of this chapter is not to offer conjecture on the motivation behind test performances within invalid military neuropsychological evaluations, but rather to review these external incentives, provide a case study, and highlight the importance of such incentives in clinical and disability evaluations.

Contexts of External Incentives and the Integrated Disability Evaluation System (IDES) System

There are a several conceivable targets of secondary gain within the active-duty environment; while some of these are similar to civilian settings, others are specific to the military. Regarding the former, symptom exaggeration to seek select types of medication can be a factor. Clearly this can occur with clinical conditions treated with narcotics and opioids, but likely more specific to neuropsychology, one may exaggerate mental health conditions in an effort to be prescribed controlled psychotropic medications, such as benzodiazepines to treat anxiety or stimulant medications to treat attention-deficit/hyperactivity disorder (ADHD). Both classes of medications can be used recreationally; however stimulant medications can also assist with appetite suppression and, in turn, weight loss. Conceivably, these could then be sought to help service members (SMs) who struggle to maintain height and weight standards. Neuropsychological evaluation for differential diagnosis in ADHD is not mandated, but the inclusion of validity testing can help identify those who may not meet criteria for the condition (Shura and Armistead-Jehle, in press).

More specific to the military environment, one could fabricate or exaggerate symptoms in an effort to avoid select duties with an assignment or to avoid duty assignments altogether. This would include working in specific settings within the Garrison environment, as well as combat deployments. Next, noncredible test results can occur in the context of medical separation from the military. In short, when a SM is deemed unable to meet medical retention standards and is unlikely within the next year to reach a point of recovery where medical standards will be met, he/she is referred into the IDES. This process not only determines medical fitness, but it also includes Veteran's Affairs evaluations to determine any degree

DOI: 10.4324/9781003005063-35

of service connection (SC) for medical conditions. The outcome of this evaluation will be a determination of whether the SM can continue with military service and, if not, what percentage of SC the SM will be awarded for his/her various medical conditions. Increasing percentages of SC (0%–100%) correspond to increasing monetary compensation, which is based on the severity of symptoms and purported level of functional impairment.

As the Medical Evaluation Board (MEB) process essentially becomes a disability evaluation, secondary gain and associated symptom exaggeration can be a factor in select examinees. Previous research has demonstrated that SMs engaged in this process have significantly higher rates of performance and symptom validity test failure than those seen in the context of clinical care. More specifically, in a sample of 335 ADSMs engaged in IDES evaluations, Armistead-Jehle and Buican (2012) reported a performance validity test (PVT) failure rate of 54%. This was significantly higher than the 35% in the non-IDES/clinical group. This finding was replicated by Grills and Armistead-Jehle (2016) in a sample of 589 ADSMs. Here the IDES group failed the Word Memory Test (WMT; Green, 2003) at a rate of 52%, compared to the non-IDES/clinical group's failure rate of 37%. A third study by Armistead-Jehle et al. (2018) found similar PVT failure rates (IDES = 57%, non-IDES = 31%) in a sample of 231 SMs. This study also evaluated Minnesota Multiphasic Personality Inventory-2-Restructured Form (MMPI-2-RF) symptom validity testing, finding a 57% failure rate in the IDES group and a 22% failure rate in the non-IDES/clinical group. It is of further note that when an ADSM is referred into the IDES system, all previous medical records (those produced within the military system and those produced by network providers outside of military treatment facilities) are considered in decision making related to medical retention. To this end, varying degrees of secondary gain must be considered ubiquitous in this population.

The Case of Staff Sergeant S[1]

Background

Staff Sergeant (SSG) S was referred by mental health for a neuropsychological evaluation in the context of his history of concussion and current cognitive and psychological concerns. Prior to neuropsychological testing, a thorough records review was completed, and a clinical interview was conducted with SSG S and his wife.

Social/Occupational/Educational History

At the time of evaluation, SSG S was a 40-year-old, right hand dominant Hispanic male with 13 years of education. He was raised largely in New York City. Previous notes indicated a denial of childhood abuse. At the time of the evaluation, the SM had been married for approximately 20 years and described this relationship in generally positive terms. He has one stepchild and three biological children with his wife (one of whom still resides in the home). The patient indicated limited social support outside of his wife. SSG S graduated high school with reportedly average grades. He denied any history of learning disability or other developmental disorders and had not received any type of remedial education. Subsequent to high school, he enlisted in the Army and has had continuous service since. For the past few years, the SM has worked in a largely administrative position. He reported very limited work time in the last five months secondary to medical appointments. Early in his military career, he had a rapid assentation in rank with outstanding initial performance reviews. However, in the past several years, performance ratings have dropped, in part, secondary to "forgetting tasks." SSG S can retire with 20 years of service, but there was question about his medical fitness for duty and he was reportedly being considered for a medical evaluation board. SSG S stated that he was a few classes short of his associate's degree. He had not taken classes in the last half year, but prior to this was achieving adequate marks.

Medical History

According to his medical record, SSG S had a history positive for bilateral tinnitus, posttraumatic stress disorder (PTSD), sensorineural hearing loss, major depressive disorder (MDD), insomnia, foot pain, and shoulder pain. At the time of neuropsychological testing, SSG S was taking temazepam, Ativan, losartan, fluticasone propionate, Seroquel, prazosin, Cymbalta, and meloxicam. There were no recent lab values potentially related to metabolic or central nervous system (CNS) functioning in his electronic medical record (EMR). SSG S was prescribed and wore hearing aids. He denied having any history of seizures, cerebrovascular accidents, CNS related infectious diseases, or developmental conditions. He had a history of multiple concussive injuries, largely during his 2006–2007 deployment. He stated that during this deployment, his vehicle was hit by improvised explosive devices (IEDs) about seven times, with one of these resulting in a period of loss of consciousness for five to ten seconds. The other six blasts reportedly resulted in brief periods of altered consciousness. He reported cursory medical evaluations after some of these events, but he immediately returned to duty. With his 2007–2008 deployment, he also reported numerous other blast exposures within 100 m. SSG S was also deployed in 2003–2004 and 2012. Although he reported multiple firefights and blast exposures from rocket-propelled grenades (RPGs) and rockets, he denied any associated periods of alteration of consciousness, loss of consciousness, or posttraumatic amnesia. Unfortunately, there was no documentation of any such injuries in his medical record. Outside of deployments, he noted several possible concussions via combatives training prior to each deployment. He noted that, given his smaller stature, he was frequently grabbed by the neck and hit in the head by larger soldiers. With this training, SSG S reported several instances of alteration of consciousness, but he denied receiving any related medical care or definite identification of temporally related symptoms. The SM reported having engagement in a variety of rehab services outside of the military medical system; however, many of these notes were not in his military record and thus could not be reviewed in totality for the current evaluation. About six months prior to the neuropsychological evaluation, SSG S was assessed by an ear, nose, and throat (ENT) specialist for a one month history of vertigo. Vestibular Rehabilitation Therapy seemed to improve symptoms, and the SM was discharged secondary to a pending upper extremity surgery that would preclude continued care in the near term. With the current evaluation, the SM stated that he recently re-engaged vestibular therapy. Regarding mental health, the SM presented for care about two years prior to the current evaluation with posttraumatic stress (PTS) and depressive symptoms. He was followed in outpatient psychotherapy and eventually referred to psychiatry as symptoms persisted. Ultimately, a higher echelon of care was needed and the SM underwent a mix of partial hospitalization and intensive outpatient care for about three months. He denied use of tobacco and alcohol. He endorsed infrequent use of caffeine.

History of the Present Illness

During the clinical interview, the SM reported having issues related to PTS, mood, sleep, cognition, chronic pain, vertigo, and headaches. The patient had a well-documented history of PTSD and MDD treatment, with continued report of related symptoms. He reported some degree of mood fluctuation, but criteria for mania or hypomania were not met. The SM stated that he sleeps about four hours per night, with early and middle insomnia. His wife noted that he snores and that she has witnessed apnea events. He endorsed daytime fatigue. The SM stated that he had two sleeps studies in the past year, one was reportedly borderline positive and the other negative. The patient reported having chronic pain across various cites to include his feet and left shoulder. He rated that pain as a fairly constant seven out of ten. The SM also reported chronic headaches, experiencing two to three times per week. He described these as a throbbing pain in the bilateral temporal region. He endorsed associated photophobia, phonophobia, and nausea. He reportedly takes either over the counter Tylenol or Motrin with some relief. He stated that headaches can become disabling and indicated that he presented to the emergency department (ED) a few days ago for related pain. The SM reported the onset of chronic headaches after his 2007 deployment with notable worsening in the recent past. Outside of his recent ED care, he denied having any history of treatment for headaches. The SM also reported having episodes of vertigo that can last up to a week with varying severity. As noted above, he is under the care of a vestibular therapist. Vertigo onset was reported after his 2007 deployment, although treatment was not sought until 2022. Next, the patient reported bilateral tinnitus and hearing loss. He was prescribed hearing aids. Finally, the SM reported having notable memory difficulties for both short and long term information. Regarding the former, he stated that he routinely forgets things like elements of conversations and appointments. Regarding the latter, he noted forgetting important dates (e.g., anniversaries, birthdays), as well as mixing up his children's names and an inability to recall select aspects of previous military experiences (e.g., parts of deployments, past duty stations, etc.). He noted the onset of memory issues after his 2007 deployment. Since then, memory problems have been "off and on," but in general worsening over time. His wife corroborated his report, describing him as "all over the place." However, she noted that, until more recently, his cognitive functioning has been largely adequate. She reported that, as he has become less busy with work and family related activities (as their children are leaving the home), his mood and cognitive difficulties have increased.

Test Results

Performance Validity Testing

Table 31.1 lists the results of the administered PVTs. On the Medical Symptom Validity Test (Green, 2004) he scored well below the cut scores detailed in the test manual, with Immediate Recall and Consistency subtests of 60% and Delayed Recall at 50%. The average of his easy versus hard subtests difference was 19.17. This is below the cut score of 20 suggestive of a genuine memory impairment profile and, thus, akin to those simulating memory impairment. On the Non-Verbal Medical Symptom Validity Test (Green, 2008a), the SM again fell below all manualized cut scores for the easy subtests. Across the various criterion to evaluate a genuine memory impairment profile, he failed criteria B1 and B3, with order violations (e.g., performing better on more difficult subtests). Per Green's Advanced Interpretation Program (Green, 2008b), this is labeled as "Poor Effort Probable." With regard to embedded PVTs, the Repeatable Battery for the Assessment of Neuropsychological Status (RBANS) Effort Index (Silverberg et al., 2007) equaled 2, which is also suggestive of invalid test data. To this end, two well validated stand-alone PVTs and one embedded PVT were failed and as such cognitive test data are deemed an unreliable estimate of the SM's actual abilities.

Table 31.1 Performance Validity Test Results

Test	*Raw*	*Classification*
MSVT		Fail
IR	60%	Fail
DR	50%	Fail
CNS	60%	Fail
PA	40%	
FR	35%	
NV-MSVT		Fail
IR	100%	
DR	80%	
CNS	80%	
DRA	55%	
FRV	90%	
PA	100%	
FR	5%	
Criterion A1	84.2	Fail
Criterion A2	76.3	Fail
Criterion B1	23.75	Fail
Criterion B2	34.17	Passed
Criterion B3	16.73	Fail
Order Violations	Yes	Fail
RBANS		
Effort Index	2	Fail

Symptom Validity Testing

Table 31.2 outlines the symptom validity testing, acquired via the Personality Assessment Inventory (PAI; Morey, 1991) and the Memory Complaints Inventory (MCI; Green, 2019). With the PAI, the Negative Impression Management (NIM) scale had a T-score of 84, which is considered at least moderately elevated. Consequently, PAI clinical scales are likely to be at least somewhat distorted in the direction of over-reporting. The PAI Cognitive Bias Scale raw score of 19 is also considered elevated relative to both civilian and military samples (Gaasedelen et al., 2019; Armistead-Jehle et al., 2020). With the MCI, all plausible subtests were elevated at or above 60%, with an overall mean of 69.5%. Two of the three implausible subtests were also elevated above 40%, with an average of 35.3%. The mean of all subtests was 58.1%. Per interpretation guidelines in Armistead-Jehle and Shura (2021), the overall mean, plausible subtest mean, and implausible subtest mean were all suggestive of over-reported memory complaints. Given these results, the SM is very likely over-reporting cognitive symptoms.

Cognitive Test Results

As expected in the context of failed PVTs, cognitive test data demonstrated low scores across many of the administered measures (Table 31.3). Performances on tasks related to verbal fluency (Animal Naming, FAS, RBANS Semantic Fluency), set shifting (Trails B) and verbal learning and memory (RBANS List and Story Recall) were in the below average or

Table 31.2 Symptom Validity Test Results

PAI	*Raw*	*T-Score*	*Classification*
Negative Impression Management	11	84	Likely Exaggeration
Malingering Index	2	71	Normal
Roger's Discriminant Function	-1.2	48	Normal
Cognitive Bias Scale	19	--	Exaggeration
Inconsistency	6	52	Normal
Infrequency	4	55	Normal
Positive Impression Management	4	25	Normal
MCI			
GMP	68%		Exaggeration
NIP	79%		Exaggeration
VSMP	70%		Exaggeration
VMP	65%		Exaggeration
PIM	75%		Exaggeration
MIW	60%		Exaggeration
IRM	47%		Exaggeration
ACB	42%		Exaggeration
AAB	17%		Normal
Plausible Subscale Mean	69.5%		Exaggeration
Implausible Subscale Mean	35.3%		Exaggeration
Overall Mean	58.1%		Exaggeration

Table 31.3 Cognitive Test Results

Test	*T-Score*	*Range*
Trail Making A	40	Low Average
Trail Making B	32	Average
Digit Vigilance Time	40	Average
Digit Vigilance Errors	40	Average
Letter Fluency (FAS)	32	Average
Category Fluency (Animals)	23	Low Average
RBANS	SS	Range
Total Score	59	Exceptionally Low
Immediate Memory	49	Exceptionally Low
Visuospatial/Constructional	105	Average
Language	57	Exceptionally Low
Attention	72	Below Average
Delayed Memory	56	Exceptionally Low
RBANS Subtests	Z-Score	Range
List Learning	-3.32	Exceptionally Low
Story Memory	-3.41	Exceptionally Low
Figure Copy	-0.21	Average
Line Orientation	0.87	High Average
Picture Naming	-1.27	Low Average
Semantic Fluency	-2.36	Exceptionally Low
Digit Span	-0.73	Low Average
Coding	-3.06	Exceptionally Low
List Recall	-3.32	Exceptionally Low
List Recognition	-6.17	Exceptionally Low
Story Recall	-3.28	Exceptionally Low
Figure Recall	0.15	Average

extremely low ranges. Low average or average scores were mustered on select measures of processing speed (Trails A), confrontational naming (RBANS Picture Naming), sustained attention (Digit Vigilance Test), visual construction and orientation (RBANS Figure Copy and Line Orientation), and visual memory (RBANS Figure Recall). However, (as noted above), given the three failed PVTs, cognitive test data are thought to be entirely invalid.

Psychological Test Results

Unlike the invalid PVTs and symptom validity tests (SVTs) related to cognitive symptoms, symptom validity testing related to psychological functioning was somewhat more nuanced. While the PAI Malingering Index and Roger's Discriminant Functioning were within normal limits, the most robust PAI measure of over-reporting (NIM) was elevated and suggestive of at least some degree of exaggeration. In the current case, the PAI clinical scales (Table 31.4) are likely to over-represent pathology to at least some degree and should be interpreted with caution. With this caveat in mind, the SM's profile was similar to others who report a noncredible amount of psychological distress, marked by somatization, anxiety, and depression. The traumatic stress scale was also elevated (ARD-T T-score = 99), as were scales related to psychotic symptoms. Regarding the latter, as there was no indication of psychosis during interview or in his extended mental health history, this elevation is likely due to over-reporting.

Summary and Conclusions

As outlined above, elevated base rates of failed validity testing within military neuropsychological evaluations (particularly in the context of certain or possible medical boards) have been repeatedly demonstrated. As such, the outlined case is not atypical. For SSG S, cognitive test results and his subjective cognitive concerns are clearly invalid and cannot be used to form an accurate impression of related functional abilities. Based on SVTs specific to psychological functioning (e.g., PAI NIM), there is likely some degree of exaggeration. However, this is not to the extent that would entirely invalidate PAI clinical scales, which indicate distress marked largely by PTS, depressive, and anxious symptoms. An elevated level of psychological distress would also be consistent with his clinical history. To this end, his historical diagnosis of PTSD and MDD could be argued. Though admittedly the strength of this conclusion is weakened and, owing to over-reporting, occupational difficulties related to these diagnoses are more challenging to describe.

It is of note that (at the time of the current writing) the diagnosis of malingering in the military holds special criteria. In 2014, US ARMY OTSG/MEDCOM Policy Memorandum 12–035 was issued and provides direction on how to handle the diagnosis and treatment of PTSD. Embedded within this memorandum is language on the diagnosis of malingering. It concedes the influence of secondary gain in the military context, but states that "the diagnosis of malingering should not be made unless there is substantial and definitive evidence from collateral or objective sources that there are false or grossly exaggerated symptoms that are consciously produced for external incentives (pg. 7)." The memorandum goes onto state that "Poor effort on psychological/neuropsychological tests do not equate to malingering, which requires proof of intent...In addition, this diagnosis requires the signatures of two credentialed care providers, including a supervisor, Department Chief, or Deputy Commander for Clinical Services (pg. 7)." A diagnosis of malingering is a violation of military law and can result in legal action under the Uniform Code of Military Justice to include a

Table 31.4 Psychological Test Results

PAI	*Raw*	*T-Score*
SOM	61	100
ANX	60	91
ARD	49	85
DEP	59	97
MAN	26	53
PAR	36	70
SCZ	45	90
BOR	48	80
ANT	15	52
ALC	3	47
DRG	9	60
AGG	30	68
SUI	12	68
STR	12	64
Subscales		
SOM-C	21	105
SOM-S	24	102
SOM-H	16	78
ANX-C	23	89
ANX-A	20	86
ANX-P	17	86
ARD-O	13	60
ARD-P	12	65
ARD-T	24	99
DEP-C	16	84
DEP-A	20	94
DEP-P	23	91
MAN-A	7	51
MAN-G	6	45
MAN-I	13	62
PAR-H	13	66
PAR-P	6	57
PAR-R	17	78
SCZ-P	10	70
SCZ-S	17	79
SCZ-T	18	90
BOR-A	15	81
BOR-I	13	74
BOR-N	15	81
BOR-S	5	57
ANT-A	6	52
ANT-E	3	49
ANT-S	6	53
AGG-A	11	64
AGG-V	8	54
AGG-P	11	79

potential court martial of the malingering individual and dishonorable discharge from the military. As such, care needs to be exercised in making such a diagnosis. To my knowledge, there have been no empirical studies on how this policy impacts providers' use of the malingering diagnosis within the military setting. In my experience, I have still seen it employed, but for logistic (e.g., having to get a second provider to agree and co-sign) and pragmatic (e.g., the possible legal consequences for the SM) reasons, it is likely applied less often than might be justified.

Having been published in 2014, this US ARMY OTSG/MEDCOM Policy is admittedly antiquated and may undergo revision now that the Defense Health Agency is the commanding authority over the majority of military medicine. Moreover, practically speaking, I have personally seen very limited use of the memorandum and (to my knowledge) there is no analog instruction in the Air Force or Navy. Still, any provider working with the active-duty population should be aware of the potential consequences of a malingering diagnosis.

Discussion

Owing to the potential for any military medical evaluation to ultimately be employed in the medical retention decision making process, secondary gain is essentially omnipresent within all such evaluations to include neuropsychological assessments. Validity testing is, thus, paramount to assure reliability of data. With the current case there was a mild degree of discrepancy between symptom and performance validity measures. That is, multiple PVTs were failed, as were several cognitively based SVTs. His psychological based SVTs also indicated exaggeration, but not to the point of complete invalidity. However, as a number of studies have demonstrated that performance and symptom validity are unique constructs (Nelson, Sweet, Berry, Bryant, & Granacher, 2007; Ord Shura, Sansone, Martindale, Taber, & Rowland, 2021 Van Dyke, Millis, Axlerod, & Hanks, 2013), this is not an unexpected finding. With SSG S, clinical history was helpful in determining his likely diagnoses. Finally, the diagnosis of malingering can carry legal penalties within the military system. This should not necessarily prohibit such a diagnosis, but the clinician should have awareness of potential consequences.

Author Note

Patrick Armistead-Jehle, PhD, ABPP-CN, Concussion Clinic, Munson Army Health Center, 550 Pope Avenue, Fort Leavenworth, KS 66027.

The views, opinions, and/or findings contained in this chapter are those of the author and should not be construed as an official Defense Health Agency, Department of Defense, or U.S. Government position, policy or decision unless so designated by other official documentation.

Correspondence concerning this manuscript should be addressed to Dr. Patrick Armistead-Jehle, Concussion Clinic, Munson Army Health Center, 550 Pope Ave. Fort Leavenworth KS 66027. E-mail: patrick.j.armistead-jehle.civ@health.mil, Phone (913) 684–6771.

Note

1 Select and non-essential details of the patient's history were modified in order to assure anonymity.

References

Armistead-Jehle, P., & Buican, B. (2012). Evaluation context and symptom validity test Performance in a U.S. Military Sample. *Archives of Clinical Neuropsychology, 27*, 828–839.

Armistead-Jehle, P., Cole, W.R., & Stegman, R.L. (2018). Performance and symptom validity testing as a function of medical board evaluation in U.S. military service members with a history of mild TBI. *Archives of Clinical Neuropsychology, 33*, 120–124.

Armistead-Jehle, P., Ingram, P. B., & Morris, C. S. (2020). Personality assessment inventory cognitive bias scale: Validation in a military sample. *Archives of Clinical Neuropsychology, 35*(7), 1154–1161.

Gaasedelen, O.J., Whiteside, D.M., Altmaier, E., Welch, C., & Basso, M.R. (2019). The construction and initial validation of the Cognitive Bias Scale for the Personality Assessment Inventory. *The Clinical Neuropsychologist.*

Green, P. (2003). *Green's Word Memory Test for Windows: User's Manual.* Edmonton, Alberta, Canada: Green's Publishing.

Green, P. (2004). *Green's Medical Symptom Validity Test (MSVT) for Microsoft Windows: User's manual.* Edmonton, Canada: Green's Publishing.

Green, P. (2008a). *Manual for the Nonverbal Medical Symptom Validity Test.* Edmonton, Canada: Green's Publishing.

Green, P. (2008b). *Advanced Interpretation Program.* Edmonton, AB, Canada: Green's Publishing.

Green, P. (2019). *Memory Complaints Inventory.* Edmonton, Canada: Green's Publishing.

Grills, C.E., & Armistead-Jehle, P. (2016). Performance validity test and Neuropsychological Assessment Battery Screening module performances in an active duty sample with a history of concussion. *Applied Neuropsychology: Adult, 23*, 295–301.

Morey, L.C. (1991). *Personality Assessment Inventory.* Odessa, FL: Psychological Assessment Resources, Inc.

Nelson, N.W., Sweet, J.J., Berry, D.T., Bryant, F.B., & Granacher, R.P. (2007). Response validity in forensic neuropsychology: Exploratory factor analytic evidence of distinct cognitive and psychological constructs. *Journal of the International Neuropsychological Society, 13*(3), 440–449.

Ord, A.S., Shura, R.D., Sansone, A.R., Martindale, S.L., Taber, K.H., & Rowland, J.A. (2021). Performance validity and symptom validity tests: Are they measuring different constructs? *Neuropsychology, 35*(3), 241–251.

Silverberg, N.D., Wertheimer, J.C., & Fichtenberg, N.L. (2007). An effort index for the Repeatable Battery for the Assessment of Neuropsychological Status (RBANS). *The Clinical Neuropsychologist, 21*, 841–854.

Shura, R. D., & Armistead-Jehle, P. (2024). Base rates of performance and symptom validity test failures in active duty and veteran samples referred for attention-deficit/hyperactivity disorder evaluation. *Archives of Clinical Neuropsychology, 39*(4), 523–527.

Van Dyke, S.A., Millis, S.R., Axelrod, B.N., & Hanks, R.A. (2013). Assessing effort: Differentiating performance and symptom validity. *The Clinical Neuropsychologist, 27*(8), 1234–1246.

Online Resources Related to Military Specific Neuropsychological Evaluations

The Traumatic Brain Injury Center of Excellence is a thorough and exhaustive resource for current Defense Health Agency policy and clinical practice guidelines on TBI.

https://health.mil/Military-Health-Topics/Centers-of-Excellence/Traumatic-Brain-Injury-Center-of-Excellence

The VA and DoD also have a website dedicated to clinical practice guidelines for a range of conditions relevant to the neuropsychologist, which include mTBI and various psychological diagnoses to include depression, suicide, and PTSD. https://www.healthquality.va.gov/

32 Feigned/Invalid Attention-Deficit Hyperactivity Disorder in Educational Settings

Jason R. Soble, Gabriel P. Ovsiew, and Zachary J. Resch

Attention-Deficit/Hyperactivity Disorder (ADHD) is a neurodevelopmental disorder characterized by persisting, functionally impairing symptoms of inattention, impulsivity, and/or hyperactivity that remain clinically active in approximately 4.4% of adults and is associated with chronic neurocognitive sequalae (Kessler et al., 2006; Pievsky & McGrath, 2018). Although formal *Diagnostic and Statistical Manual of Mental Disorders-Fifth Edition-Text Revision* (*DSM-5 TR*; American Psychiatric Association [APA], 2022) diagnostic criteria require that symptoms arise prior to age 12 and be present across a variety of settings, it is not uncommon that adults with complaints of chronic attention problems, but no formal ADHD diagnosis rendered in childhood/adolescence, are referred for neuropsychological evaluation to assist with diagnostic clarification and treatment planning. In fact, differential diagnosis related to adult ADHD is one of the most common referral reasons for neuropsychological evaluation (Rabin, Paolillo, & Barr, 2016). Evaluating adults for ADHD often presents several challenges across adult clinical settings, but poses several additional unique and multifactorial considerations in adult educational settings (e.g., undergraduate, graduate/professional, and trade/vocational school). As such, careful, evidence-based use of performance (PVT) and symptom (SVT) validity tests is essential for detecting invalid and/or feigned ADHD symptomatology among adults undergoing neuropsychological evaluation in educational settings.

This chapter will outline the many unique challenges associated with objective assessment of invalid/feigned ADHD symptoms in educational settings, with particular emphasis on the constraints posed by the presence of anticipated (and potentially unknown/unanticipated) external incentives, the shortcomings of the extant literature that both limit accurate detection of invalid symptom reporting and test performance and obscure the true base rate(s) of invalidity, the limitations of retrospective symptom reporting (often without the benefit of collateral report), the nonspecific nature of attention difficulties, and the higher incidence of other psychopathologies among individuals with ADHD. Finally, a series of case examples will be presented to highlight different performance and symptom invalidity phenotypes that clinicians may encounter when conducting adult ADHD evaluations in various educational contexts.

Validity Considerations in ADHD Assessment

There are several factors that may influence performance and symptom validity during a neuropsychological evaluation in which ADHD is a diagnostic consideration. Although all of these factors are relevant to ADHD evaluations and should be considered regardless of clinical context, some are particularly salient in educational settings.

DOI: 10.4324/9781003005063-36

External Incentives

As a general rule, clinicians must be wary of external incentives in all neuropsychological evaluations, particularly considering that any clinical neuropsychological evaluation may later be used for forensic purposes. That being said, in many clinical cases, there may be no direct or known incentive for the examinee to manipulate their results, or such an incentive may not be immediately transparent to either the clinician or the examinee at the time of the evaluation. When evaluating for ADHD, however, particularly in an educational setting, there exist distinct external incentives the examiner may readily assume.

Most notably, an ADHD diagnosis very often provides licit access to controlled stimulants (e.g., amphetamines, methylphenidate). Although it is unclear whether these substances actually enhance cognition in neurotypical individuals (Bowman et al., 2023), their common perception as nootropics and their unequivocal recreational potential have served to popularize their abuse in educational settings (Advokat et al., 2008; Teter et al., 2005). That said, inappropriate access to medications due to inaccurate ADHD diagnosis also can result in iatrogenesis and contribute to rising overall healthcare costs (Lakhan & Kirchgessner, 2012). Likewise, under the Americans with Disabilities Act (ADA), a diagnosis of ADHD confers the right to accommodations both at work and at school (Lovett & Harrison, 2021; Suhr & Berry, 2017). Although the ADA does not mandate specific accommodations, accommodations for ADHD in educational settings often include additional time to complete tests and flexible assignment deadlines. Such permissions provide noteworthy benefits even to those without cognitive disorders, and therefore pose substantial incentive to obtain an ADHD diagnosis in academic settings regardless of subjective complaints or impairment. In a similar vein, an ADHD diagnosis also can confer the right to non-standard test administration accommodations (e.g., extended time, extra breaks during testing) in high-stakes standardized testing situations, such as graduate/professional school admission tests and licensure/credentialing examinations. Although these accommodations may not be actively sought in every evaluation, the examiner must nonetheless be aware of their inherent threat to validity when assessing for ADHD.

Symptom Subjectivity

Evaluating ADHD symptoms in adulthood can be challenging, especially in the context of an initial assessment where the diagnosis has not previously been rendered in childhood or adolescence. A diagnosis of ADHD requires the presence of specific symptoms in childhood and at the time of evaluation, but these can be difficult to assess for two reasons.

First, ADHD is a neurodevelopmental disorder in which symptoms must first emerge in childhood as the specific criteria require the presence of symptoms before 12 years of age (APA, 2022). Adult assessment of ADHD therefore requires retrospective consideration of childhood symptoms. Ideally, this is achieved by reviewing formal, contemporaneous reports from collaterals such as teachers, parents, and clinicians, especially considering that adult recall of childhood symptoms may be unreliable (von Wirth et al., 2021). When available, such evidence can establish a more objective timeline of symptom onset and development as well as extent of functional impairment. It can also assist in characterizing the disorder's course over time in order to provide tailored recommendations for treatment. Unfortunately, such documentation regularly either does not exist or is not available to the examiner at the time of the evaluation (Breda et al., 2016). When corroborating evidence is unavailable, it becomes necessary to rely exclusively on the examinee's present subjective report of their symptoms in childhood, which among even the most earnest informants may be skewed. This leads to the other general consideration when evaluating ADHD symptomatology.

Second, symptom reporting is inherently subjective. Although some common deficit patterns may emerge on cognitive testing, the deficits associated with ADHD are heterogeneous (e.g., Pievsky & McGrath, 2018). This means that no pathognomonic neuropsychological profile of ADHD exists, and diagnosis cannot be based solely on cognitive test performance or ability. Rather, diagnosis depends on reported symptoms. This heightens the examiner's reliance on observations primarily provided by the examinee as informant report is considerably harder to obtain in adulthood than in childhood. In the absence of impartial collateral evidence or other objective symptom validation, there is an increased risk of misdiagnosis due to exaggeration or minimization of symptoms, whether volitional or not. Distinguishing feigned from genuine symptoms is made more challenging by the accessibility of diagnostic information on the internet and social media platforms, which can serve to coach examinees seeking to influence their diagnosis. Even in the context of honest responding, ADHD symptoms may be produced or compounded by several other conditions, which can also lead to symptom distortion. For these reasons, the examiner must always carefully consider the credibility of demonstrated or reported symptoms when evaluating for ADHD.

Non-specificity and Co-occurrence

Given that many of the core symptoms of ADHD are shared with other psychiatric conditions, ADHD evaluations will typically entail some degree of differential diagnosis. The challenges posed by this prospect can be represented with two general considerations: symptoms of ADHD are largely nonspecific, and co-occurring psychiatric dysfunction is observed more frequently in those with the disorder (Choi et al., 2022; Kessler et al., 2006). Notably, the chief symptom complaints that commonly raise concern for ADHD (e.g., inattention, distractibility, impulsiveness, lack of initiation, compulsiveness) can also arise in common, non-neurodevelopmental conditions, such as mood and anxiety spectrum disorders, and are often included in the formal diagnostic criteria for these psychiatric disorders (APA, 2022). This can make it difficult to confidently ascribe individual symptoms to ADHD, rather than alternative sources, further highlighting the importance of the developmental onset as a key distinguishing feature. Moreover, the presence of concurrent psychiatric dysfunction, which is often observed in those with ADHD, may obfuscate or exacerbate symptoms of the disorder (Wilens et al., 2002).

Ultimately, non-ADHD psychopathology can result in valid endorsement of ADHD symptoms, so alternative etiologies must be excluded before a diagnosis can be confidently rendered. Credible expression of criterion symptoms on its own is insufficient in a context in which the symptoms may be better explained by a different condition.

Assessment and Detection of Feigned ADHD: Current State of the Literature

Neuropsychological research on adult ADHD generally lags behind the pediatric literature. Moreover, several limitations exist within the current adult ADHD literature that potentially undermine an accurate, objective assessment and confound efforts to establish a reliable base rate of invalidity in this population. These limitations are detailed below to help guide clinical decision-making related to detecting invalid symptom endorsement and neurocognitive test performance among adults referred for ADHD assessment in both educational and non-educational settings.

Variability in Study Methodology and Clinical Groups

Three primary methodological limitations exist in the current adult ADHD literature that make it difficult to determine a reliable base rate of invalidity among individuals undergoing ADHD evaluation in educational settings.

First, there has been extensive reliance on simulator studies to validate and cross-validate PVTs and SVTs among adult ADHD samples, which most commonly compare individuals with documented ADHD to healthy individuals instructed to feign ADHD symptoms (e.g., Frazier et al., 2008; Potts et al., 2022; Young & Gross, 2011). Although simulator studies may be practical when initially validating a measure, they are accompanied by notable limitations. Chiefly, simulator studies do not allow researchers to determine the actual base rate of invalidity in a given clinical population because the "invalid" group consists of participants assigned to feign symptoms a priori. Moreover, the use of healthy controls instead of clinical participants with genuine impairment often inflates classification accuracy (Resch et al., 2021). Since ADHD is associated with both domain-specific (e.g., Keezer et al., 2021; Leib et al., 2021; Phillips et al., 2023) and generalized (Pievsky & McGrath, 2018) cognitive dysfunction in adults, caution should be exercised when referencing pre-existing validity indices that have not been cross-validated at adequate specificity (i.e., ≥90%; Boone, 2013) within this particular clinical population. Fortunately, a growing number of recent studies have identified applicable cut-scores (or lack thereof) by examining validity indices among adult, ADHD-specific clinical populations (e.g., Bing-Canar et al., 2022; Phillips et al., 2023; Robinson et al., 2023; Scimeca et al., 2021). Such indices derived from population-specific cross-validation minimize false positive classification errors, and can readily be employed in ADHD evaluations.

Second, some studies (e.g., Ashendorf et al., 2021, 2022; Ord et al., 2021; Shura et al., 2017) have examined and attempted to cross-validate PVTs and/or SVTs among mixed referral, post-deployment military samples, which include active-duty service members and veterans referred for ADHD evaluation, as well as examinees with other clinical conditions/comorbidities that are more commonly encountered in military samples than among civilian samples, such as mild traumatic brain injury (TBI). It has been established that many unique factors are present in active-duty and veteran populations, including, but not limited to, increased prevalence of internalizing psychopathology, particularly PTSD and mild TBI with chronic post-concussion symptom complaints (Soble et al., 2014), as well as higher rates of potential external incentive associated with cognitive impairment (e.g., disability benefits; see Armistead-Jehle et al., 2017 for a review). Predictably, the base rate of performance invalidity is often higher in veteran populations than among their civilian counterparts, particularly when a history of mild TBI is present (Armistead-Jehle et al., 2021; Young et al., 2016). Further, unlike ADHD, which is associated with heterogeneous cognitive difficulties (Pievsky & McGrath, 2018), meta-analytic studies have shown that mild TBI is not associated with chronic objective neurocognitive deficits as most cognitive symptoms resolve within days to weeks following the injury (Rohling et al., 2011). Thus, some PVT failure cutoffs derived from mild TBI samples may not be appropriate for ADHD examinees. Considering these unique features of veteran samples, findings regarding PVT/SVT cut-scores, invalidity base rates, and invalid ADHD clinical presentations may not necessarily generalize to civilian educational settings.

Third, a portion of the literature that has reported higher median base rates of invalidity (e.g., 20%) in adult ADHD populations is based solely on clinician survey data (Martin & Schroeder, 2020). Although practitioner estimates can provide useful anecdotal insight, they are not as reliable as base rates derived from consecutive case series and objective criterion measures of invalidity among adults undergoing ADHD evaluation. Thus, survey-estimated base rates may not replicate in actual educational settings.

Inconsistent PVTs and Invalidity Criteria

Over the past decade, adult ADHD studies have increasingly attempted to address the above limitations by using clinical samples and objective assessment of performance validity. However, the quantities and types of PVTs used to identify invalid/feigned neurocognitive test performance are inconsistent across studies. This methodological inconsistency contributes to the significant variability in invalidity base rates among adult ADHD studies and for classification accuracy statistics, such as the sensitivity values for PVTs that studies that have attempted to cross-validate in this population. These methodological concerns include the use of freestanding and embedded PVTs that have not been cross-validated in ADHD-specific populations and multiple issues related to the quantity and psychometric quality of PVTs employed in research studies. Most notably, invalidity rates were much higher among samples that classified performance invalidity based on ≥1 PVT failure (e.g., 15%–50%; Harrison et al., 2023; Suhr et al., 2008; Sullivan et al., 2007) than they were among those requiring ≥2 PVT failures (e.g., 10%–26%; Abramson et al., 2023; Ausloos-Lozano et al., 2022; Khan et al., 2022; Marshall et al., 2016; Robinson et al., 2023; Sharland et al., 2018), with several studies employing the latter criterion grouping method reporting an invalidity base rate of roughly 15%–21% among student-predominant clinical samples. Considering that a single PVT failure is not uncommon among valid examinees (Victor et al., 2009), and that the current standard of clinical neuropsychological practice for determining invalidity therefore requires two or more PVT failures (Jennette et al., 2022; Sweet et al., 2021), 15%–20% may more reliably approximate the true base rate of invalidity in educational settings.

Conflation of PVTs and SVTs

Past studies commonly used PVTs and SVTs interchangeably to designate validity status in studies examining invalidity among adult ADHD populations (e.g., Marshall et al., 2010; Nelson & Lovett, 2019; Suhr et al., 2011). However, it is now understood among neuropsychologists that PVTs and SVTs assess unique, non-redundant constructs, with PVTs assessing the credibility of cognitive test performance and SVTs assessing the veracity of self-reported symptoms (Larrabee, 2012). Notably, PVT and SVT results have also been found to be dissociable in ADHD evaluations specifically, such that failing PVTs has minimal impact on ADHD symptom endorsement, and failing SVTs has little appreciable impact on neurocognitive test performance (Ovsiew et al., 2023). Put another way, a large proportion of examinees will fail SVTs, suggesting unreliable ADHD symptom endorsement, but pass PVTs, suggesting credible performance, and vice versa (Harrison et al., 2023; Hirsch et al., 2022; Ovsiew et al., 2023; Shura et al., 2017; White et al., 2022). Considering this observation, rates of performance and symptom validity have been similar but slightly distinct when evaluating both in the context of ADHD evaluations (16% and 22%, respectively; Ovsiew et al., 2023). Therefore, equating and then interpreting PVT and SVT failures as a homogeneous construct may inflate invalidity base rates in clinical research and misinform validity determinations in clinical evaluations. Taken together, cognitive performance validity and symptom endorsement validity must both be assessed and interpreted separately, and clinical neuropsychologists evaluating this population are cautioned against conflating the two.

The PVT/SVT dissociation observed among adult ADHD measures is further complicated by the relative paucity of ADHD-specific SVTs. Although a plethora of freestanding and embedded PVTs exist (see Soble et al., 2021 for a review), many of which have been cross-validated in adult ADHD populations, very few symptom-oriented counterparts are available. In fact, with the exception of a select few ADHD symptom measures such as the Clinical Assessment of Attention Deficit-Adult (CAT-A; Bracken & Boatwright, 2005) and the more recently developed Multidimensional ADHD Rating Scale (MARS; Potts et al., 2021), no well-validated clinical measures contain ADHD-specific SVTs developed and validated a priori to assess overreporting and underreporting. Although some ADHD self-report measures, such as the Conners' Adult ADHD Rating Scale (CAARS; Conners et al., 1999), contain rudimentary SVTs designed to detect inconsistent reporting, ADHD self-report measures generally have demonstrated poor discriminability between genuine and feigned ADHD symptoms when inconsistent reporting or extreme symptom endorsement are used as the criterion for invalidity (Harrison et al., 2007; Musso & Gouvier, 2014; Quinn, 2003; Sollman et al., 2010). Some have attempted to creatively address this lack of ADHD-specific SVTs by developing various indices derived from existing ADHD self-report measures (e.g., CAARS Infrequency Index; Suhr et al., 2011; CAARS Exaggeration Index; Harrison & Armstrong, 2016). These embedded indices have shown some promise, but also remain limited by the fact that they are extracted from the existing items on their respective measures, which were originally designed and validated to assess bona fide ADHD symptoms, not to detect invalid/feigned symptom reporting. As such, further cross-validation of similar embedded SVTs is needed to replicate their accuracy for distinguishing invalid from valid symptom endorsement to enhance their clinical utility in educational settings.

Due to this relative lack of existing ADHD-specific SVTs, another approach for assessing symptom invalidity among adults undergoing ADHD evaluation (e.g., Harp et al., 2011; Harrison et al., 2023; Morris et al., 2023; Robinson & Rogers, 2018; Shura et al., 2017) has been to use validity scales originally developed to detect patterns of general symptom over-endorsement on well-validated, broadband psychopathology measures, such as the Minnesota Multiphasic Personality Inventory-2-Restrucuted Form (MMPI-2-RF; Ben-Porath & Tellegan, 2008) and the MMPI-3 (Tylicki, Gervais, & Ben-Porath, 2022). However, findings from some studies have been lackluster. Although some reported modest utility for detecting feigned ADHD using MMPI-2-RF validity scales that assess for general infrequent responding or infrequent psychiatric symptom endorsement, overall results generally indicated that the MMPI-2-RF validity scales are not particularly robust for detecting feigned ADHD symptom reporting or differentiating noncredible ADHD-specific symptoms from general symptom magnification. Further, a recent study examining the concordance between overreporting on the MMPI-2-RF validity scales and ADHD-specific symptoms on the CAT-A found that nearly 50% of adults undergoing ADHD evaluation had discordant MMPI-2-RF and CAT-A results, with 41% producing MMPI-2-RF validity scale elevations suggesting at least questionable overreporting and normal CAT-A SVT results compared with 9% who produced CAT-A SVT elevations without MMPI-2-RF validity scale elevations (Leib et al., 2022). Additionally, neither group with discordant results predicted PVT failures. Part of this discrepancy, as well as the relative insensitivity of the MMPI-2-RF validity scales for detecting feigned ADHD, may stem from the fact that the MMPI-2-RF validity scales were designed to detect general overreporting of psychopathology, rather than ADHD-specific symptomology. Given that comorbid psychopathology is common among adults with ADHD, with overall odds ratios of 1.5–7.9 for mood, anxiety, substance use, and impulse control disorders, and an approximately 25%–80% prevalence of comorbid depression and anxiety disorders reported in this clinical population (Anastopoulos et al., 2018; Choi et al., 2022; Kessler et al., 2006), elevations on the MMPI-2-RF validity scales may detect emotional distress and more global symptom overreporting rather than circumscribed invalid/feigned ADHD symptoms. A recent study by Keezer and colleagues (2023) lends some support to this hypothesis as patients with only ADHD had a significantly lower base rate of MMPI-2-RF validity scale elevations, as well as lower mean scores across the five overreporting validity scales when compared with those with ADHD and a comorbid psychological disorder (i.e., mood, anxiety, or traumatic stress disorder) and compared with a psychopathology control group.

Key Points in Assessing Validity of ADHD

As highlighted throughout this chapter, differential diagnosis of ADHD can be quite complicated, particularly considering the non-specificity and heterogeneity of symptom presentation, heavy reliance on self-report, and high likelihood of overlapping symptom presentation and frequent co-occurrence of other psychiatric conditions. Not to mention that all of these considerations occur in a context rife with motive for feigning due desire to access accommodations, stimulant medications, and other incentives resulting from an ADHD diagnosis. However, clinicians tasked with meeting these challenges now have a growing arsenal of tools at their disposal, including PVTs validated among examinees being evaluated for ADHD and ADHD-specific and broadband SVTs. Taking into account the literature on the dissociation of SVT/PVT results in this context and modest base rates of performance invalidity and invalid symptom reporting, we strongly recommended that psychoeducational and neuropsychological evaluations of ADHD routinely include both SVTs and PVTs. Comprehensive assessment of performance validity when characterizing cognitive strengths and weaknesses and of symptom validity to evaluate the credibility of supporting symptoms will best aid in accurately diagnosing ADHD. Moving forward, the crucial step in improving assessment in this context will be new inventory development designed and validated specifically for identifying feigned ADHD, while concurrently providing further cross-validation of our existing tools, such as ADHD-specific SVTs like the CAARS Infrequency Index and CAARS Exaggeration Index. It is also worth noting that much of the work on validity assessment in ADHD has been conducted with adult populations and it, therefore, remains unclear the extent to which these concerns regarding assessment of feigned ADHD translate to pediatric populations. This may be a particular fruitful area for future study, especially in light of the fact that pediatric evaluations benefit from the ability to collect and compare collateral reporting of symptoms from parents and teachers, which could assist in the development and validation of more precise ADHD-specific SVTs. With these key assessment considerations in mind, the following case examples are offered as representations of some of the diagnostic challenges frequently seen in psychoeducational and neuropsychological evaluations of ADHD.

Case Examples

Here we present three cases, which were clinically referred for ADHD differential diagnosis and/or treatment planning and were administered a uniform neuropsychological test battery, which included multiple PVTs and SVTs, to highlight some of the diverse patterns of invalid cognitive test performance and/or symptom reporting, which neuropsychologists performing ADHD evaluations in educational settings may encounter.

Patient 1

Patient 1 was a female medical student in her mid-20s with 17 years of formal education referred for neuropsychological evaluation by her psychiatrist to assist with diagnostic clarification of possible ADHD. On clinical interview, the patient complained of current problems with inattention, distractibility, concentration, initiating and completing tasks, and procrastination, which were reportedly affecting her current academic and psychosocial functioning. Patient's report of symptom onset/course was somewhat vague; she described these cognitive problems as lifelong, but had difficulty providing specific details/examples when queried. She otherwise denied physical complaints, sleep problems, psychological disturbance, or substance misuse. Medical/psychiatric history was unremarkable outside of a prior uncomplicated SARS-CoV-2 infection without persisting/long haul symptoms. Her recent psychiatric diagnostic exam, which generated her current referral for neuropsychological evaluation, was negative for any active psychological disorders outside of a rule-out of possible ADHD. Psychosocially, birth and early developmental milestones were unremarkable. She reported that her teachers would sometimes remark that she was "a daydreamer" or "in her own world" in elementary school, but otherwise denied history of learning problems, special education, or grade retention. She also denied ever receiving any formal accommodations in school or on standardized testing, and stated that she generally performed well academically. She completed a bachelor's degree and entered medical school the following semester. She reported being in academic good standing in medical school.

See Table 32.1 for a summary of Patient 1's test results.

In brief, she performed below failure cutoffs on 4/6 PVTs administered throughout, indicating invalid cognitive test performance. Related, her scores on neurocognitive tests generally fell in the extremely low range across most measures, except for working memory and visual learning/memory. An ADHD symptom revealed broadly elevated ADHD symptoms in childhood and currently with scores on embedded SVTs indicating likely symptom overreporting. By contrast, Minnesota Multiphasic Personality Inventory-2-Restrucutred Form (MMPI-2-RF) validity scales revealed possible endorsement of unusual memory complaints, but were otherwise negative for symptom overreporting. Rather, validity scales indicate likely minimization/symptom underreporting, such that the protocol may underestimate psychological difficulties. Her MMPI-2-RF profile was remarkable for a single elevation on the Cognitive Complaints specific problem scale.

Unfortunately, due to objective evidence of ubiquitous performance and symptom invalidity, the evaluation was unable to establish or rule-out a diagnosis of ADHD or any other psychological disorder, nor meaningfully characterize her current neurocognitive status.

Patient 2

Patient 2 was female graduate student in her late 30s with 16 years of formal education referred for ADHD by her family medicine provider due to persisting attention problems that were significantly impeding her academic progress. On clinical interview, the patient endorsed broad complaints with attention/concentration, memory, becoming easily overwhelmed when having to consider multiple pieces of information simultaneously, planning/organization, procrastination, tracking and completing tasks, particularly school

Table 32.1 Case Study Neuropsychological Test Data

	Case #1	*Case #2*	*Case #3*
PVTs-			
Dot Counting Test	Fail	Pass	Fail
RFIT/Recognition	Fail	Pass	Pass
RAVLT Effort Score	Fail	Pass	Fail
BVMT Recognition Discrimination	Pass	Pass	Fail
WAIS-IV Reliable Digit Span	Pass	Pass	Fail
Stroop Word T-score	Fail	Pass	Fail
Neurocognitive Tests-			
RAVLT Total Learning	Abnormal	WNL	Abnormal
RAVLT Delayed Recall	Abnormal	WNL	Abnormal
BVMT-R Total Learning	WNL	WNL	Abnormal
BVMT-R Delayed Recall	WNL	WNL	Abnormal
WAIS-IV WMI	WNL	WNL	WNL
WAIS-IV PSI	Abnormal	WNL	Abnormal
TMT-A	Abnormal	Abnormal	Abnormal
TMT-B	Abnormal	WNL	WNL
Stroop Color-Word	Abnormal	WNL	Abnormal
CPT-3	Abnormal	WNL	Abnormal
SVTs/Psychological Measures-			
CAT-A-			
Infrequency	Elevated	Elevated	WNL
Negative Impression	Elevated	Elevated	WNL
Positive Impression	WNL	WNL	WNL
Childhood Clinical Index	Elevated	Elevated	WNL
Adult Clinical Index	Elevated	Elevated	WNL
Overall Clinical Index	Elevated	Elevated	WNL
MMPI-2-RF			
VRIN-r	WNL	WNL	WNL
TRIN-r	WNL	WNL	WNL
F-r	WNL	Elevated (111T)	WNL
Fp-r	WNL	Elevated (107T)	WNL
Fs	WNL	WNL	WNL
FBS-R	WNL	WNL	WNL
RBS	Elevated (80T)	Elevated (80T)	WNL
L-r	Elevated (81T)	WNL	WNL
K-r	WNL	WNL	WNL
RCd	WNL	Elevated (83T)	WNL
RC1	WNL	WNL	WNL
RC2	WNL	Elevated (76T)	WNL
RC3	WNL	WNL	WNL
RC4	WNL	Elevated (76T)	Elevated (68T)
RC6	WNL	Elevated (66T)	WNL
RC7	WNL	Elevated (86T)	WNL
RC8	WNL	Elevated (70T)	WNL
RC9	WNL	Elevated (69T)	WNL

Note. PVT: performance validity test; RFIT: Rey 15-Item Test; RAVLT: Rey Auditory Verbal Learning Test; BVMT-R: Brief Visuospatial Memory Test-Revised; WAIS-IV; Wechsler Adult Intelligence Scale-Fourth Edition; WMI: Working Memory Index; PSI: Processing Speed Index; TMT: Trail Making Test; CPT-3: Continuous Performance Test-Third Edition; WNL: within normal limits; SVT: symptom validity test; CAT-A: Clinical Assessment of Attention Deficit-Adult; MMPI-2-RF: Minnesota Multiphasic Personality Inventory-2-Restrucutred Form.

assignment and various household tasks, and inefficient problem-solving. She was unable to identify exactly the onset of cognitive problems, but noted their presence to some degree for "a very long time," with fluctuation in intensity based on transient factors (e.g., stress, adverse life circumstances, mood changes). Emotionally, she has struggled with chronic mood and anxiety symptoms since at least adolescence, which have appreciably worsened over the past two years in the context of a divorce and leaving her employment to complete a graduate degree. Regarding substance use, she reported consuming 1–2 glasses of wine per evening to "wind down," but denied problems associated with alcohol misuse, as well as tobacco or drug use. Functionally, she independently manages her instrumental activities of daily living. She reported increased stress associated with living alone for the first time in her adult life and being responsible for various household tasks (e.g., paying bills; meal preparation), which her ex-husband previously managed. Medical/psychiatric history was remarkable for hypothyroidism (stable/controlled with medication), headaches, depression, and anxiety. The patient acknowledged that she likely has had persisting, low-grade mood/anxiety symptoms since at least early adolescence, but only received formal mental health treatment (psychotherapy) once in college when mood symptoms acutely worsened after her then-boyfriend unexpectedly ended their relationship. Psychosocially, she described being reared by parents that she described as "cold and aloof." She also was bullied throughout school for being overweight, which resulted in social anxiety that made it difficult to pay attention in school. Academically, she struggled with math and received tutoring, but denied being diagnosed with learning disorder, special education, or grade retention. She completed a bachelor's degree in marketing. She had worked in advertising for over ten years, but decided to enroll in an educational master's program with the goal of pursuing a different profession in the education field after her divorce.

As included in Table 1, Patient 2 passed 6/6 PVTs, indicating valid cognitive test performance, and demonstrated objectively normal neurocognitive test performance. By contrast, SVTs revealed clear evidence of ADHD and general psychological symptom overreporting on both the CAT-A and MMPI-2-RF, indicating exaggerated symptoms that were invalid for clinical interpretation. Following this evaluation, the patient was referred for evidence-based psychotherapy and psychiatric evaluation for pharmacological treatment.

Patient 3

Patient 3 was a male undergraduate with 15 years of education and an established history of ADHD, referred for evaluation by his treating psychiatrist for updated testing to support his request for accommodations (i.e., extra time allowance and extended breaks) on standardized testing required for professional school admission. On interview, the patient reported lifelong problems with inattention, impulsivity, and hyperactivity. He was first evaluated for and diagnosed with ADHD in elementary school, and pharmacological treatment was initiated, which provided considerable symptom relief. He underwent neuropsychological reevaluation prior to entering high school. Results of this evaluation (which were available for review) reconfirmed his earlier ADHD diagnosis and revealed ongoing deficits in sustained attention, as well as variable working memory and processing speed when he was tested without his medication. The patient denied receiving other academic accommodations and generally earned As and Bs throughout high school and college, which he attributed to his being able to self-impose various compensatory strategies. He denied physical complaints, psychological symptoms, or substance misuse. Medical/psychiatric and developmental history were unremarkable. Other than ADHD, he denied other learning problems or grade retention. At the time of evaluation, he was beginning the final year of his undergraduate degree and preparing to apply for admission for an advanced professional degree.

Neurocognitive test administration occurred while the patient was actively taking his prescribed ADHD medication to determine if any cognitive deficits persisted despite ongoing nootropic treatment. As outlined in Table 1, he failed 5/6 PVTs and produced a globally depressed neuropsychological profile with extremely low scores across most tests, except for the Working Memory Index and Trail Making Test-Part B. By contrast, CAT-A and MMPI-2-RF SVTs were all within normal limits and negative for symptom over-or under-reporting. His CAT-A scores revealed lifelong ADHD symptoms, whereas his MMPI-2-RF was negative for clinically active psychopathology with his single RC4 elevation being driven by juvenile conduct problems. Based on these invalid neurocognitive test tests, it was not possible to identify any potential ongoing cognitive deficits to support recommending academic accommodations.

Summary

These three patient cases highlight the diversity of invalid presentations that neuropsychologists may encounter when assessing ADHD in educational settings and emphasize several key points reviewed above. First, although it could be argued that external incentive is omnipresent in ADHD evaluations given that access to controlled, psychostimulant medications often accompanies a diagnosis, additional unique incentives also need be considered in educational contexts, particularly academic and standardized testing accommodations. Patient 3 exemplifies this point well considering he already had an established ADHD diagnosis for which he was receiving active pharmacological treatment. Nonetheless, there was clear external incentive to perform poorly on neurocognitive testing (i.e., extended time and extra break accommodations for standardized testing), thus reemphasizing the need for comprehensive validity assessment even if an ADHD diagnosis has been well-established previously. By contrast, Patients 1 and 2 demonstrated evidence of at least one type of invalidity, despite not presenting with any known external incentives at the time of evaluation (although it certainly is possible that undisclosed external incentives existed for both of these patients). As such, the presence of known external incentive cannot be the factor that establishes the need for performance and symptom validity assessment in ADHD evaluations. This must be done routinely.

Second, these three clinical cases demonstrate how PVTs and SVTs can be dissociable in ADHD evaluations and must be assessed separately. Specifically, the extant literature shows that examinees undergoing ADHD evaluation commonly do not exhibit both performance and symptom invalidity, and evidence of one type of invalidity cannot be used to infer invalidity in the other domain. These patients exemplify this empirical finding well. For instance, Patient 2 displayed convincing objective evidence of invalid symptom overreporting on SVTs, but normal PVT scores, which provided her evaluating neuropsychologist objective evidence that her cognitive test scores were valid and could be used to formulate conclusions regarding her neurocognitive function. By contrast, Patient 3's normal SVT scores allowed his evaluator to draw conclusions regarding his valid ADHD symptom reporting and psychological status despite being unable to characterize his neurocognitive status due to invalid PVT scores. Unfortunately, some patients, such as Patient 1, will produce both invalid PVT and SVT scores on evaluation, which greatly limits the evaluating neuropsychologist's ability to draw firm diagnostic conclusions.

References

Abramson, D. A., White, D. J., Rhoads, T., Carter, D. A., Hansen, N. D., Resch, Z. J., Jennette, K. J., Ovsiew, G. P., & Soble, J. R. (2023). Cross-validating the Dot Counting Test among an adult ADHD clinical sample and analyzing the effect of ADHD subtype and comorbid psychopathology. *Assessment, 30*(2), 264–273.

Advokat, C. D., Guidry, D., & Martino, L. (2008). Licit and illicit use of medications for attention-deficit hyperactivity disorder in undergraduate college students. *Journal of American College Health, 56*(6), 601–606.

American Psychiatric Association. (2022). *Diagnostic and Statistical Manual of Mental Disorders-Fifth Edition-Text Revision. (DSM-5-TR).* American Psychiatric Association Press.

Anastopoulos, A. D., DuPaul, G. J., Weyandt, L. L., Morrissey-Kane, E., Sommer, J. L., Rhoads, L. H., … & Gudmundsdottir, B. G. (2018). Rates and patterns of comorbidity among first-year college students with ADHD. *Journal of Clinical Child & Adolescent Psychology, 47*(2), 236–247.

Armistead-Jehle, P., Cooper, D. B., Belanger, H. G., Soble, J. R., & Nelson, N. W. (2021). Performance/symptom validity test use with active duty service members and veterans. In K. B. Boone (Ed.), *Assessment of feigned cognitive impairment: A neuropsychological perspective* (2nd ed., pp. 609–632). Guilford.

Armistead-Jehle, P., Soble, J. R., Cooper, D. B., & Belanger, H. G. (2017). Unique Aspects of Traumatic Brain Injury in Military and Veteran Populations. *Physical medicine and rehabilitation clinics of North America*, 28(2), 323–337.

Ashendorf, L., Clark, E. L., & Humphreys, C. T. (2021). The Rey 15-Item Memory Test in US veterans. *Journal of Clinical and Experimental Neuropsychology, 43*(3), 324–331.

Ashendorf, L., Withrow, S., Ward, S. H., Sullivan, S. K., & Sugarman, M. A. (2022). Decision rules for an abbreviated administration of the Test of Memory Malingering. *Applied Neuropsychology. Adult.*

Ausloos-Lozano, J. E., Bing-Canar, H., Khan, H., Singh, P. G., Wisinger, A. M., Rauch, A. A., Ogram Buckley, C. M., Petry, L. G., Jennette, K. J., Soble, J. R., & Resch, Z. J. (2022). Assessing performance validity during attention-deficit/hyperactivity disorder evaluations: Cross-validation of select non-memory embedded validity indicators. *Developmental Neuropsychology, 47*(5), 247–257.

Ben-Porath, Y. S., & Tellegen, A. (2008). *MMPI-2-RF: Manual for administration, scoring, and interpretation.* University of Minnesota Press.

Bing-Canar, H., Phillips, M. S., Shields, A. N., Ogram Buckley, C. M., Chang, F., Khan, H., Skymba, H. V., Ovsiew, G. P., Resch, Z. J., Jennette, K. J., & Soble, J. R. (2022). Cross-validation of multiple WAIS-IV Digit Span embedded performance validity indices among a large sample of adult Attention Deficit/Hyperactivity Disorder clinical referrals. *Journal of Psychoeducational Assessment, 40*(5), 678–688.

Boone, K. B. (2013). *Clinical practice of forensic neuropsychology: An evidence-based approach.* Guilford Press.

Bowman, E., Coghill, D., Murawski, C., & Bossaerts, P. (2023). Not so smart? "Smart" drugs increase the level but decrease the quality of cognitive effort. *Science Advances*, *9*(24), eadd4165.

Bracken, B. A., & Boatwright, B. S. (2005). *Examiner's manual: Clinical assessment of attention deficit – child and adult.* Psychological Assessment Resources.

Breda, V., Rovaris, D. L., Vitola, E. S., Mota, N. R., Blaya-Rocha, P., Salgado, C. A., Victor, M. M., Picon, F. A., Karam, R. G., Silva, K. L., Rohde, L. A., Bau, C. H., & Grevet, E. H. (2016). Does collateral retrospective information about childhood attention- deficit/hyperactivity disorder symptoms assist in the diagnosis of attention-deficit/hyperactivity disorder in adults? Findings from a large clinical sample. *The Australian & New Zealand Journal of Psychiatry, 50*(6), 557–565.

Choi, W. S., Woo, Y. S., Wang, S. M., Lim, H. K., & Bahk, W. M. (2022). The prevalence of psychiatric comorbidities in adult ADHD compared with non-ADHD populations: A systematic literature review. *Plos One, 17*(11), e0277175.

Conners, C. K., Erhardt, D., Epstein, J. N., Parker, J. D. A., Sitarenios, G., & Sparrow, E. (1999). Self-ratings of ADHD symptoms in adults I: Factor structure and normative data. *Journal of Attention Disorders*, *3*(3), 141–151.

Frazier, T. W., Frazier, A. R., Busch, R. M., Kerwood, M. A., & Demaree, H. A. (2008). Detection of simulated ADHD and reading disorder using symptom validity measures. *Archives of Clinical Neuropsychology, 23*, 501–509.

Harp, J. P., Jasinski, L. J., Shandera-Ochsner, A. L., Mason, L. H., & Berry, D. T. R. (2011). Detection of malingered ADHD using the MMPI-2-RF. *Psychological Injury and Law, 4*(1), 32–43.

Harrison, A. G., & Armstrong, I. T. (2016). Development of a symptom validity index to assist in identifying ADHD symptom exaggeration or feigning. *The Clinical Neuropsychologist*, *30*(2), 265–283.

Harrison, A. G., Beal, A. L., & Armstrong, I. T. (2023). Predictive value of performance validity testing and symptom validity testing in psychoeducational assessment. *Applied Neuropsychology. Adult, 30*(3), 315–329.

Harrison, A. G., Edwards, M. J., & Parker, K. C. (2007). Identifying students faking ADHD: Preliminary findings and strategies for detection. *Archives of Clinical Neuropsychology, 22*(5), 577–588.

Hirsch, O., Fuermaier, A. B. M., Tucha, O., Albrecht, B., Chavanon, M.-L., & Christiansen, H. (2022). Symptom and performance validity in samples of adults at clinical evaluation of ADHD: A replication study using machine learning algorithms. *Journal of Clinical and Experimental Neuropsychology, 44*(3), 171–184.

Jennette, K. J., Williams, C. P., Resch, Z. J., Ovsiew, G. P., Durkin, N. M., O'Rourke, J. J. F., Marceaux, J. C., Critchfield, E. C., & Soble, J. R. (2022). Assessment of differential neurocognitive performance based on the number of performance validity tests failures: A cross-validation study across multiple mixed clinical samples. *The Clinical Neuropsychologist, 36*(7), 1915–1932.

Keezer, R. D., Kamm, J. M., Cerny, B. M., Ovsiew, G. P., Resch, Z. J., Jennette, K. J., & Soble, J. R. (2023). Minnesota Multiphasic Personality Inventory-2-Restructured Form (MMPI-2-RF) profiles among adults with attention-deficit/hyperactivity disorder (ADHD): Examining the effect of comorbid psychopathology and ADHD presentation. *Archives of Clinical Neuropsychology*.

Keezer, R. D., Leib, S. I., Scimeca, L. M., Smith, J. T., Holbrook, L., Sharp, D. W., Jennette, K. J., Ovsiew, G. P., Resch, Z. J., & Soble, J. R. (2021). Masking effect of high IQ on the Rey Auditory Verbal Learning Test in an adult sample with Attention-Deficit/Hyperactivity Disorder. *Applied Neuropsychology: Adult.*

Kessler, R. C., Adler, L., Barkley, R., Biederman, J., Conners, C. K., Demler, O., Faraone, S. V., Greenhill, L. L., Howes, M. J., Secnik, K., Spencer, T., Ustun, T. B., Walters, E. E., & Zaslavsky, A. M. (2006). The prevalence and correlates of adult ADHD in the United States: Results from the National Comorbidity Survey Replication. *The American Journal of Psychiatry, 163*(4), 716–723.

Khan, H., Rauch, A. A., Obolsky, M. A., Skymba, H., Barwegen, K. C., Wisinger, A. M., Ovsiew, G. P., Jennette, K. J., Soble, J. R., & Resch, Z. J. (2022). A comparison of embedded validity indicators from the Stroop Color and Word Test among adults referred for clinical evaluation of suspected or confirmed Attention-Deficit/Hyperactivity Disorder. *Psychological Assessment, 34*(7), 697–703.

Lakhan, S. E., & Kirchgessner, A. (2012). Prescription stimulants in individuals with and without attention deficit hyperactivity disorder: Misuse, cognitive impact, and adverse effects. *Brain and Behavior, 2*(5), 661–677.

Larrabee, G. J. (2012). Performance validity and symptom validity in neuropsychological assessment. *Journal of the International Neuropsychological Society, 18*(4), 625–630.

Leib, S. I., Keezer, R. D., Cerny, B. M., Holbrook, L. R., Gallagher, V. T., Jennette, K. J., Ovsiew, G. P., & Soble, J. R. (2021). Distinct latent profiles of working memory and processing speed in adults with ADHD. *Developmental Neuropsychology, 46*(8), 574–587.

Leib, S. I., Schieszler-Ockrassa, C. White, D. J., Gallagher, V. T., Carter, D. A., Basurto, K. S., Ovsiew, G. P., Resch, Z. J., Jennette, K. J., & Soble, J. R. (2022). Concordance between the Minnesota Multiphasic Personality Inventory-2-Restructured Form (MMPI-2-RF) and Clinical Assessment of

Attention Deficit-Adult (CAT-A) over-reporting validity scales for detecting invalid ADHD symptom reporting. *Applied Neuropsychology: Adult, 29*(6), 1522–1529.

Lovett, B. J., & Harrison, A. G. (2021). Assessing adult ADHD: New research and perspectives. *Journal of Clinical and Experimental Neuropsychology, 43*(4), 333–339.

Marshall, P. S., Hoelzle, J. B., Heyerdahl, D., & Nelson, N. W. (2016). The impact of failing to identify suspect effort in patients undergoing adult attention-deficit/hyperactivity disorder (ADHD) assessment. *Psychological Assessment, 28*(10), 1290–1302.

Marshall, P., Schroeder, R., O'Brien, J., Fischer, R., Ries, A., Blesi, B., & Barker, J. (2010). Effectiveness of symptom validity measures in identifying cognitive and behavioral symptom exaggeration in adult attention deficit hyperactivity disorder. *The Clinical Neuropsychologist, 24*(7), 1204–1237.

Martin, P. K., & Schroeder, R. W. (2020). Base rates of invalid test performance across clinical non-forensic contexts and settings. *Archives of Clinical Neuropsychology, 35*(6), 717–725.

Morris, N. M., Lee, T. T. C., Demakis, G. J., & Park, S. (2023). Detecting feigned ADHD in college students using the Minnesota Multiphasic Personality Inventory-2-Restructured Form (MMPI-2-RF). *The Clinical Neuropsychologist, 37*(6), 1154–1172.

Musso, M. W., & Gouvier, W. D. (2014). "Why is this so hard?" A review of detection of malingered ADHD in college students. *Journal of Attention Disorders, 18*(3), 186–201.

Nelson, J. M., & Lovett, B. J. (2019). Assessing ADHD in college students: Integrating multiple evidence sources with symptom and performance validity data. *Psychological Assessment, 31*(6), 793–804.

Ord, A. S., Miskey, H. M., Lad, S., Richter, B., Nagy, K., & Shura, R. D. (2021). Examining embedded validity indicators in Conners Continuous Performance Test-3 (CPT-3). *The Clinical Neuropsychologist, 35*(8), 1426–1441.

Ovsiew, G. P., DeBoer, A. B., Cerny, B. M., Petry, L G., Resch, Z. J., Durkin, N. M., & Soble, J. R. (2023). Performance and symptom validity assessment in attention deficit/hyperactivity disorder: base rates of invalidity, concordance, and relative impact on cognitive performance. *The Clinical Neuropsychologist.*

Phillips, M. S., Bing-Canar, H., Shields, A. N., Cerny, B., Chang, F., Wisinger, A. M., Leib, S. I., Ovsiew, G. P., Resch, Z. J., Jennette, K. J., & Soble, J. R. (2023). Assessment of learning and memory impairments in adults with predominately inattentive versus combined presentation attention-deficit/hyperactivity disorder. *Applied Neuropsychology: Adult.* Advance online publication. https://doi.org/10.1080/23279095.2023.2169887

Phillips, M.S., Wisinger, A. M., Lapitan, F., Ausloos-Lozano, J. E., Bing-Canar, H., Durkin, N. M., Ovsiew, G. P., Resch, Z. J., Jennette, K. J., & Soble, J. R. (2023). Cross-validation of multiple embedded validity indices in the Rey Auditory Verbal Learning Test and Brief Visuospatial Memory Test-Revised in an adult attention-deficit/hyperactivity disorder clinical sample. *Psychological Injury and Law, 16*, 27–35.

Pievsky, M. A., & McGrath, R. E. (2018). The neurocognitive profile of Attention-Deficit/Hyperactivity Disorder: A review of meta-analyses. *Archives of Clinical Neuropsychology, 33*(2), 143–157.

Potts, H. E., Lewandowski, L. J., & Lovett, B. J. (2021). The Multidimensional ADHD Rating Scale: A measure of symptoms, impairment, and symptom validity. *Journal of Clinical and Experimental Neuropsychology, 43*(4), 426–436.

Potts, H. E., Lewandowski, L. J., & Lovett, B. J. (2022). Identifying feigned ADHD in college students: Comparing the Multidimensional ADHD Rating Scale to established validity measures. *Journal of Attention Disorders, 26*(12), 1622–1630.

Quinn, C. A. (2003). Detection of malingering in assessment of adult ADHD. *Archives of Clinical Neuropsychology, 18*(4), 379–395.

Rabin, L. A., Paolillo, E., & Barr, W. B. (2016). Stability in test-usage practices of clinical neuropsychologists in the United States and Canada over a 10-year period: A follow-up survey of INS and NAN members. *Archives of Clinical Neuropsychology, 31*(3), 206–230.

Resch, Z. J., Webber, T. A., Bernstein, M. T., Rhoads, T., Ovsiew, G. P., & Soble, J. R. (2021). Victoria Symptom Validity Test: A systematic review and cross-validation study. *Neuropsychology Review, 31*(2), 331–348.

Robinson, A., Reed, C., Davis, K., Divers, R., Miller, L., Erdodi, L. A., & Calamia, M. (2023). Settling the score: Can CPT-3 embedded validity indicators distinguish between credible and non-credible responders referred for ADHD and/or SLD?. *Journal of Attention Disorders, 27*(1), 80–88.

Robinson, E. V., & Rogers, R. (2018). Detection of feigned ADHD across two domains: The MMPI-2-RF and CAARS for faked symptoms and TOVA for simulated attention deficits. *Journal of Psychopathology and Behavioral Assessment, 40*(3), 376–385.

Rohling, M. L., Binder, L. M., Demakis, G. J., Larrabee, G. J., Ploetz, D. M., & Langhinrichsen-Rohling, J. (2011). A meta-analysis of neuropsychological outcome after mild traumatic brain injury: re-analyses and reconsiderations of Binder et al. (1997), Frencham et al. (2005), and Pertab et al. (2009). *The Clinical Neuropsychologist, 25*(4), 608–623.

Scimeca, L. M., Holbrook, L., Rhoads, T., Cerny, B. M., Jennette, K. J., Resch, Z. J., Obolsky, M. A., Ovsiew, G. P., & Soble, J. R. (2021). Examining Conners Continuous Performance Test-3 (CPT-3) embedded performance validity indicators in an adult clinical sample referred for ADHD evaluation. *Developmental Neuropsychology, 46*(5), 347–359.

Sharland, M. J., Waring, S. C., Johnson, B. P., Taran, A. M., Rusin, T. A., Pattock, A. M., & Palcher, J. A. (2018). Further examination of embedded performance validity indicators for the Conners' Continuous Performance Test and Brief Test of Attention in a large outpatient clinical sample. *The Clinical Neuropsychologist, 32*(1), 98–108.

Shura, R. D., Denning, J. H., Miskey, H. M., & Rowland, J. A. (2017). Symptom and performance validity with veterans assessed for attention-deficit/hyperactivity disorder (ADHD). *Psychological Assessment, 29*(12), 1458–1465.

Soble, J. R., Silva, M. A., Vanderploeg, R. D., Curtiss, G., Belanger, H. G., Donnell, A. J., & Scott, S. G. (2014). Normative data for the Neurobehavioral Symptom Inventory (NSI) and postconcussion symptom profiles among TBI, PTSD, and nonclinical samples. *The Clinical Neuropsychologist, 28(*4), 614–632.

Soble, J. R., Webber, T. A., & Bailey, K. C. (2021). An overview of common stand-alone and embedded PVTs for the practicing clinician: Cutoffs, classification accuracy, and administration times. In R. W. Schroeder & P. K. Martin (Eds.), *Validity assessment in clinical neuropsychological practice: Evaluating and managing noncredible performance* (pp. 126–149). Guilford.

Sollman, M. J., Ranseen, J. D., & Berry, D. T. (2010). Detection of feigned ADHD in college students. *Psychological Assessment, 22*(2), 325–335.

Suhr, J. A., & Berry, D. T. R. (2017). The importance of assessing for validity of symptom report and performance in attention deficit/hyperactivity disorder (ADHD): Introduction to the special section on noncredible presentation in ADHD. *Psychological Assessment, 29*(12), 1427–1428.

Suhr, J. A., Buelow, M., & Riddle, T. (2011). Development of an infrequency index for the CAARS. *Journal of Psychoeducational Assessment, 29*(2), 160–170.

Suhr, J., Hammers, D., Dobbins-Buckland, K., Zimak, E., & Hughes, C. (2008). The relationship of malingering test failure to self-reported symptoms and neuropsychological findings in adults referred for ADHD evaluation. *Archives of Clinical Neuropsychology, 23*, 521–530.

Sullivan, B. K., May, K., & Galbally, L. (2007). Symptom exaggeration by college adults in attention-deficit hyperactivity disorder and learning disorder assessments. *Applied Neuropsychology, 14*, 189–207.

Sweet, J. J., Heilbronner, R. L., Morgan, J. E., Larrabee, G. J., Rohling, M. L., Boone, K. B., and Suhr, J. A., & Conference Participants. (2021). American Academy of Clinical Neuropsychology (AACN) 2021 consensus statement on validity assessment: Update of the 2009 AACN consensus conference statement on neuropsychological assessment of effort, response bias, and malingering. *The Clinical Neuropsychologist, 35*, 1053–1106.

Teter, C. J., McCabe, S. E., Cranford, J. A., Boyd, C. J., & Guthrie, S. K. (2005). Prevalence and motives for illicit use of prescription stimulants in an undergraduate student sample. *Journal of American College Health, 53*(6), 253–262.

Tylicki, J. L., Gervais, R. O., & Ben-Porath, Y. S. (2022). Examination of the MMPI-3 over-reporting scales in a forensic disability sample. *The Clinical Neuropsychologist, 36*(7), 1878–1901.

Victor, T. L., Boone, K. B., Serpa, J. G., Buehler, J., & Ziegler, E. A. (2009). Interpreting the meaning of multiple symptom validity test failure. *The Clinical Neuropsychologist, 23*(2), 297–313.

von Wirth, E., Mandler, J., Breuer, D., & Döpfner, M. (2021). The accuracy of retrospective recall of childhood ADHD: Results from a longitudinal study. *Journal of Psychopathology and Behavioral Assessment, 43*(2), 413–426.

White, D. J., Ovsiew, G. P., Rhoads, T., Resch, Z. J., Lee, M., Oh, A. J., & Soble, J. R. (2022). The divergent roles of symptom and performance validity in the assessment of ADHD. *Journal of Attention Disorders, 26*(1), 101–108.

Wilens, T. E., Biederman, J., & Spencer, T. J. (2002). Attention deficit/hyperactivity disorder across the lifespan. *Annual Review of Medicine, 53*, 113–131.

Young, C. J., & Gross, A. M. (2011). Detection of response bias and noncredible performance in adult attention-deficit/hyperactivity disorder. *Archives of Clinical Neuropsychology, 26*, 165–172.

Young, J. C., Roper, B. L., & Arentsen, T. J. (2016). Validity testing and neuropsychology practice in the VA healthcare system: Results from recent practitioner survey. *The Clinical Neuropsychologist, 30*(4), 497–514.

33 Feigned Learning Disability

Julie A. Suhr

About 5%–15% of children (dependent on the subtype) and 4% of adults have a specific learning disorder (SLD; American Psychological Association, 2013). Children with SLD are less likely to obtain postsecondary education because of their academic difficulties (Newman et al., 2011). However, an increasing number of college students request academic and test accommodations for SLD and attention-deficit/hyperactivity disorder (ADHD), the most common disorders for which academic and high-stakes testing accommodations are sought in postsecondary education (Harrison & Wolforth, 2012). In this chapter, we present two cases, one adolescent and one adult, who presented for SLD evaluation in the context of requesting academic and test accommodations.

Case 1: KC

KC is a 12-year, 10-month-old left-handed boy in 7th grade referred by his mother for concerns that he has a SLD in reading. She felt that, despite spending hours with him every day to complete his homework and hiring tutors for him, he was not achieving his potential. She ascribed KC's math challenges to disinterest rather than lack of capacity. She reported prior but not current concerns with his concentration and attention.

KC lives with his mother and two older sisters; his parents are currently separated. English is spoken at home. His mother has a college education and works in retail. His father has a college education and receives long-term disability due to military-related posttraumatic stress disorder. Both of his sisters have medical conditions for which they receive accommodations and supports at school as well as disability benefits.

No significant issues were described related to KC's gestation or birth. He did not experience significant childhood illnesses or ear infections. He reportedly met developmental milestones appropriately except for being late to talk. His mother reported that KC received speech therapy around the age of four or five but has no ongoing issues with speech. KC has no notable acute or chronic health issues and does not regularly take medication. He has no known hearing issues. He wears glasses. His parents reported no concerns about his sleep quantity or quality.

KC's mother indicated that he is not typically down or depressed; she reported some nervousness when report cards are sent home, but that his self-confidence and self-worth were improving. KC described himself as typically being happy and denied feeling frequently anxious. In contrast, his teacher indicated that he seems sad and depressed, does not initiate play with peers, and is withdrawn and isolated. He reportedly articulated passive suicidal ideation once, around nine years of age, due to feeling overwhelmed with changes in his life (e.g., parents had just separated; adjustment to a new school). He attended one session with a mental health counselor.

DOI: 10.4324/9781003005063-37

KC has attended four different schools due to frequent family moves. Of note, he started school a bit younger than most children. School records show that from kindergarten to second grade, he met expectations in reading, writing, and math, with grades in the A–B range, although he was described as somewhat immature, with self-regulation difficulties. His first school move was in third grade, and his final third year grades were B–Cs. Self-regulation continued to be noted as an area in need of improvement. He moved again in fourth grade following his parents' separation; his final fourth year grades were Cs across the board. At this point, he received a psychoeducational evaluation (described below). His report card at the end of fifth grade noted good improvement, with A's in reading and writing and B+ in math, although it was noted that pandemic lockdowns affected end-of-year evaluations. His family moved again midyear in his sixth grade year, which was also online; he performed generally in the B range across subjects.

KC was seen for a school-based psychoeducational assessment at age 9. At that time, his mother expressed concerns that he had ADHD. Unfortunately, only a narrative summary of the evaluation was available; detailed scores were not available for review. He was described as putting forth good effort on tests, but some scores were also described as potentially underestimates of his ability due to inattention and impulsiveness. Of note, no symptom validity or performance validity tests were given. His performance within indices on the Wechsler Intelligence Scale for Children-IV (WISC-IV) reportedly showed significant variability, although only index scores were reported: Verbal Comprehension Index 84th percentile, Visual Spatial Index 60th percentile, Fluid Reasoning Index 78th percentile, Working Memory Index 33rd percentile, and Processing Speed Index 50th percentile. Thus, all scores fell in the average to high average range. Performance on the Beery Visual-Motor Integration 6th edition fell at the 19th percentile. Performance on a memory battery was described as potentially an underestimate of his ability due to variable attention and engagement. With regard to reading, his scores generally fell in the average range for his age (32nd to 51st percentile). Math performance fell in the low average to average range (19th to 39th percentile). His handwriting was described as generally legible, and his performance across writing subtests fell in the low average to average range (21st to 58th percentile). Scores on listening comprehension and oral expression tasks were described as intact. Responses on collateral report measures suggested parents observed more executive functioning weaknesses than did his teacher, while his teacher observed more emotional distress than his parents. The assessor did not see sufficient support for an ADHD diagnosis. She did not diagnose him with SLD but recommended interventions to help with writing skills and math foundations.

At the time of the more recent evaluation, KC was back in face-to-face school and was receiving some educational supports and assistance, on the basis of his mother's report of weaknesses in receptive language skills, phonological processing skills, expressive language, auditory memory, fine motor skills, and self-regulation. He was receiving a variety of academic and testing accommodations, including but not limited to allowing completion of fewer items for tasks, receiving extra time on tests, permission to use calculator/multiplication charts, and audiotaping and verbatim scripting of his responses or using speech to text software to minimize writing. However, for him to continue to receive these accommodations, a formal evaluation was needed.

Case 2: AC

AC is a 39-year-old man of East Indian heritage referred by the disability services office at his university for an updated assessment of his cognitive and psychological profile. By his report, he was first evaluated and diagnosed with nonverbal learning disability at age 25. He also reported a diagnosis of chronic depression, for which he takes medication. He currently receives academic accommodations for both diagnoses. Of note, although his first language is not English, he completed his high school education in English and did not appear to have English language fluency issues during the evaluation.

AC was a vague historian, and objective documentation of his background was not available, as he did not grow up in North America. His relationship with his parents is reportedly negative (he reported having restraining orders against them) and thus no collateral information was available. He was also not able to provide the results of his prior evaluation; he reported the evaluation was lost when his parents moved many years ago. He indicated that he received his current university accommodation services on the basis of his self-reported concerns and verification of his depression by his family physician.

By his report, there were no concerns about his gestation, birth, or meeting any developmental milestones. He reported that he had trouble with reading, writing, and math from the moment he began school and that his parents hired private tutors to assist him in elementary school. He also reported that he developed memory difficulties after age of 4, when he was seriously burned by cooking oil. He reported that his grades were low in all subjects all the way through to the end of high school; school records were not available to corroborate this report.

He reported being physically abused by both parents from ages 4–18 and growing up isolated because he was not allowed to play with his peers. He also reported having malaria, jaundice, and pneumonia while in third grade, necessitating bed rest for three months. He reported no long-term effects from these illnesses. There is no other medical history of note.

He was inconsistent in the reporting of his depression history, indicating at one point that he had been depressed for the past ten years, but at another point saying it had only been three years. He currently takes Desipramine and Effexor, the latter for his chronic insomnia by his report.

He reported that he moved to North America at 21 to enroll in college, studying business administration, but was asked to leave college due to poor grades. He then sought a diagnosis of ADHD from his family physician, who prescribed him stimulant medication. Due to adverse reaction to the medication, it was discontinued. He then enrolled at another university to study computer science but reportedly left due to poor grades. He received an assessment at age 25 where, by his report, he was diagnosed as having a nonverbal learning disability. He then attended a third university, where he successfully completed an undergraduate degree with a major in economics, receiving accommodations such as double time, a quiet setting for tests, and tutoring support. He reported receiving A–B grades at his third university. At present, he is pursuing a second major in pre-law and aspires to be a lawyer. He sought the present evaluation as he is planning to re-take the Law School Admission Test (LSAT) and needed an updated evaluation to request accommodations. Of note, his prior LSAT scores, which were taken without accommodations, were not available for review.

Background

Children with SLD may qualify for academic accommodations under the Individuals with Disabilities Education Improvement Act (IDEA, 2004), while adults may qualify under the Americans with Disabilities Act Amendments Act (ADA, 2008). Potential receipt of academic or testing accommodations is a strong incentive to malinger academic impairment or disability. Extended time is a particularly popular accommodation request. Thus, it is notable that extended time provides advantages to all students; in fact, students without

SLD/ADHD benefit more from extended time than those with these disorders (Cahan et al., 2016; Lewandowski et al., 2013; Miller et al., 2019). Thus, exaggerating or deliberately feigning SLD could result in significant external gain. In fact, rates of failure on performance validity tests (PVTs) in adults presenting for SLD evaluation range from 9% to 24% (see Harrison et al., 2021 and Suhr et al., 2021, for detailed reviews of base rates).

Unfortunately, these high base rates have not impacted formal assessment, as research shows few neuropsychological and psychoeducational evaluations for accommodation requests include PVTs or symptom validity tests (SVTs) (Harrison et al., 2013; Joy et al., 2010, Nelson & Lovett, 2019). Whether assessors work with adults or children, they often believe they can rely on direct observation to determine whether someone is feigning academic impairment (Flamand, 2015). However, simulator and known groups studies show that individuals feigning reading disorder have test profiles indistinguishable from individuals with reading disorders (see Harrison et al., 2021; Suhr et al., 2021 for detailed reviews of the simulator literature and Harrison et al., 2023 for a recent known groups study). For example, strategies reported by college students asked to simulate reading disorder are similar to what clinicians observe in individuals who do have reading disorder: reading slowly, doing poorly on reading comprehension, forgetting words or information that was read, confusing similar looking words, substituting or omitting words, guessing at unfamiliar words, and losing one's place when reading (Harrison & Davin, in press; Weis & Droder, 2019). Thus, consistent with consensus statements (Sweet et al., 2021), decision-making regarding accommodation receipt should include SVTs and PVTs.

SVTs in SLD

There is no convergence in the types of symptoms that might be self-reported by individuals seeking accommodations by feigning SLD. In fact, SLD is typically diagnosed on the basis of performance (school performance, academic testing; American Psychiatric Association, 2013). However, having a diagnosis does not indicate someone has a disability (American Psychiatric Association, 2013); justification for academic or workplace accommodations requires demonstration that the individual has a condition that substantially limits their ability to perform a major life activity compared with most people in the general population (ADA, 2008). Unfortunately, a lot of weight is put upon self-report of academic impairment (Association on Higher Education and Disability, 2012) rather than objective evidence of difficulty.

Research shows that self-reported academic impairments are very common in people with no history of SLD or ADHD (Jansen et al., 2017; Johnson & Suhr, 2021; Lewandowski et al., 2008; Suhr & Johnson, 2022; Weis & Waters, 2023). Further, a large number of college students without any history of ADHD or SLD score clinically high on formal self-report impairment scales (Bryant et al., 2018; Johnson & Suhr, 2021; Weis & Waters, 2023). Several studies have also documented that self-report impairment scales are vulnerable to malingering (Bryant et al., 2018; Fuermaier et al., 2018; Johnson & Suhr, 2021; Suhr et al., 2017; Suhr et al., 2020). However, as yet, there are no studies identifying SVTs for self-reported academic impairment.

PVTs in SLD

There are far fewer studies of PVT use in SLD relative to ADHD (for reviews of ADHD literature, refer to the two chapters in this volume), and the vast majority are of reading disorder or mixed SLD. To our knowledge, there is only one study of math disorder (Sanders,

2011) and none with writing disorder. However, studies suggest that some freestanding PVTs that are already well-validated – Word Memory Test (WMT), the Medical Symptom Validity Test, the Non-Verbal Medical Symptom Validity Test, the Test of Memory Malingering (TOMM); the Victoria Symptom Validity Test (VSVT), and Word Choice – for use in ADHD and other contexts also are adequately sensitive to and specific to detecting malingered SLD in both children and adults, using standard cutoffs (for reviews see Kirkwood, 2015; Harrison et al., 2021; Suhr et al., 2021). Of particular note, some of these PVTs use nonverbal stimuli, an important consideration for individuals with reading concerns. Even freestanding PVTs with verbal stimuli have reading levels that do not raise concerns except for individuals with severe dyslexia and have low false-positive rates even in children and adolescents with well-documented severe reading disorders (Larochette & Harrison, 2012). Other freestanding PVTs have lower sensitivity to feigned SLD, though they do show adequate specificity (Dot Counting, Rey 15-item Test, Rey Word Recognition Test) or have poor specificity, particularly to SLD (e.g., Automatized Sequences; Kirkwood et al., 2013). See Kirkwood (2015), Harrison et al. (2021) and Suhr et al. (2021) for detailed reviews of cutoffs and accuracy statistics across this literature.

With regard to embedded PVTS, even fewer studies have examined their accuracy for detecting feigned SLD. The Advanced Clinical Solutions for the WAIS and Wechsler Memory Scale provides some cutoffs for both reading and math disorder for Reliable Digit Span (RDS; Greiffenstein et al., 1994) and delayed recognition trials of the Wechsler Memory Scale memory tests. Of note, Harrison et al. (2010) found high false-positive rates in adolescents with SLD using Digit Span Scaled Score cutoffs.

There is also a small but promising literature on PVTs developed specifically for detecting invalid performance in adult-aged reading disorder. Harrison et al. (2008) developed the Dyslexia Assessment of Simulation and Honesty (DASH), a reading test that seems difficult but is actually easy even for those with severe reading problems. Initial studies yielded 100% positive predictive power and 65% negative predictive power. Weis and Droder (2019) developed the College Assessment of Reading Effort (CARE), a test based on the methods used to develop the DASH. The CARE differentiated simulators from honest examinees, with sensitivity, specificity, and predictive power found to be at least 90% in the initial norming studies. Osmon and colleagues (2006) developed the Word Reading Test (WRT), which instructs individuals to select a target word when presented with a similar, but incorrect nontarget word (i.e., words that contain errors attributed to learning problems, such as mirror letters and addition/deletion of letters). The WRT achieved high sensitivity (90%) and specificity (100%) when comparing coached RD simulators with speed simulators and healthy controls (Osmon et al., 2006), though it yielded strong specificity (92%) but moderate sensitivity (68%) when comparing uncoached RD simulators with genuine RD patients (Lindstrom et al., 2009). Finally, the b-test (Boone et al., 2000) evaluates speed of automatic recognition of overlearned symbols. In initial studies, these authors found that both commission errors and omission errors had moderate sensitivity (76.5% and 58.8%, respectively) and specificity in the mid-80s. While these reading-specific PVTs appear to be promising measures for the detection of noncredible reading problems, future studies are necessary to establish the validity and reliability of these measures in multiple clinical settings.

Test Data: KC

KC was dressed appropriately for his age. His mood appeared euthymic and he sometimes smiled at humorous remarks. He was attentive and calm during testing, sometimes being slow to respond. He was apologetic when he took a long time on tasks, saying that thinking is hard for him; sometimes he gave up and said he didn't know. When encouraged, he sometimes guessed correctly on difficult items, but more often he gave up if he felt he was doing poorly. He was observed to read with significant difficulty. He often asked if the examiner could read the words out loud or scribe his answers for him. His handwriting was legible. Of note, although testing was administered as close to standardization as possible, due to pandemic precautions both KC and examiners wore masks and were separated by a clear, plexiglass shield whenever possible.

KC's test scores appear in Table 33.1.

KC fell below cutoffs on three different PVTs. Of note, on memory testing, his scores were in the average range, so his poor performance across PVTs could not be explained by poor memory. In addition, given the nonverbal stimuli for the PVTs he was administered, his performance cannot be explained by reading impairment.

WISC-IV and Woodcock-Johnson-IV (WJ-IV) Tests of Cognitive Ability scores were generally in the average range; while the Processing Speed Index was low average, this was due to an isolated low score on Coding. In contrast, his WJ-IV Tests of Achievement scores fell at or below the first percentile on all clusters and most subtests, with some exceptions (applied problems, word attack, spelling of sounds). His performance on the Comprehensive Test of Phonological Processing-2 was in the average range, as were scores on both the verbal fluency and Color-Word Interference subtests of the Delis-Kaplan Executive Function System (D-KEFS). Of note, on the Comprehensive Behaviour Rating Scale, his parents rated him as showing no difficulties in any domain, while teacher ratings were high on various internalizing and somatic symptoms.

Overall, it is difficult to interpret KC's performance as an accurate indicator of his academic strengths/weaknesses. He is at least of average intellect, although these scores may be underestimates of his overall cognitive abilities. His achievement test scores fall below what would be expected of a child who is doing grade seven work and below what was reported at age 9, although it is notable that tests of phonological decoding were strengths. Overall, the test results cannot be used to support continued academic accommodations.

Test Data: AC

AC arrived for the evaluation carrying LSAT accommodations forms, handed them to the examiner, and asked when the examiner could finish filling them out. He seemed taken aback when it was explained that the forms could not be completed until the entire assessment was complete and an opinion rendered. He spent considerable time explaining LSAT policies for accommodations and how to fill out the forms and send them in, even after the examiner indicated their familiarity with the procedures. His awareness and knowledge regarding the LSAT administration and accommodation process was in sharp contrast to his behavior during testing. He often looked at questions and immediately replied "I can't do that." He refused to try higher-order mental arithmetic questions if he wasn't allowed a calculator. He could not be encouraged to try once he had given up. He immediately pointed out every error that he made, noting them as examples of the problems he has all the time. He worked slowly but did not have difficulty understanding test directions.

Test results are presented in Table 33.2.

He failed multiple PVTs, including the WMT and VSVT, although he passed the TOMM. In addition, his scores on several embedded measures fell below cutoffs, including attention tasks (RDS), memory tasks (Rey Auditory-Verbal Learning Test recognition), and speeded

Table 33.1 Assessment Data for KC

Wechsler Intelligence Scale for Children-5th Edition					
Composite Scores	*SS*	*%*	*Subtest*	*SS*	*%*
			Matrix Reasoning	11	63
Verbal Comprehension	103	58	Similarities	11	63
Visual Spatial	95	37	Block Design	8	25
Fluid Reasoning	103	58	Digit Span	8	25
Working Memory	93	32	Coding	5	5
Processing Speed	80	9	Figure Weights	10	50
Full-Scale IQ	91	27	Vocabulary	11	63
			Visual Puzzles	11	63
			Picture Span	10	50
			Symbol Search	8	25
Woodcock-Johnson 4th edition Tests of Cognition Composite and Subtest Scores					
Composite Scores			**Subtest Scores**		
General Intellectual Ability	81	10	Oral Vocabulary	108	70
Gf-Gc comp	97	41	Number Series	92	30
Comp Knowledge	99	46	Verbal Attention	84	14
Fluid Reasoning	96	39	Letter Pattern Matching	83	12
Short-Term Working Memory	82	12	Phonological Processing	96	40
Cognitive Processing Speed	82	12	Story Recall	90	26
Auditory Processing	93	32	Visualization	92	30
Long-term Retrieval	89	24	General Information	92	30
Visual Processing	96	39	Concept Formation	101	54
Cognitive Efficiency	81	11	Numbers reversed		
			Nonword repetition	93	32
			Visual-Auditory Learning	92	29
			Picture Recognition	100	49
			Pair Cancellation	88	20
Test of Word Reading Efficiency-2					
Sight Word Efficiency	59	<1			
Phonemic Decoding Efficiency	82	12			
Total	69	1			

(*Continued*)

Table 33.1 (Continued)

Wechsler Intelligence Scale for Children-5th Edition					
Composite Scores	*SS*	*%*	*Subtest*	*SS*	*%*
Woodcock-Johnson 4th edition Tests of Achievement Composite and Subtest Scores					
Composite Scores	**SS**	**%**	**Subtest Scores**	**SS**	**%**
Broad Reading	60	0.5	Letter/Word identification	54	0.1
Broad Mathematics	61	0.5	Applied Problems	91	28
Broad Written Language	70	1	Spelling	77	6
Written Expression	69	1	Passage Comprehension	74	4
Academic Skills	52	<0.1	Calculation	65	1
Academic Fluency	54	0.1	Writing Samples	65	1
Phoneme-Grapheme Know	65	0.5	Word Attack	92	29
Brief Achievement	61	0.5	Oral Reading	84	14
			Sentence Reading Fluency	61	0.5
			Math Facts Fluency	50	<0.1
			Sentence Writing Fluency	74	4
			Spelling of Sounds	98	45
Comprehensive Test of Phonological Processing-2					
Elision	9	37			
Rapid Digit Naming	10	50			
Rapid Letter Naming	10	50			
Rapid Symbolic Naming	101	53			
D-KEFS Color-Word Interference			**D-KEFS Verbal Fluency**		
	SS			**SS**	
Color Naming	10		Letter Fluency	9	
Word Reading	10		Category Fluency	9	
Inhibition	8		Category Switching Tot C	8	
Inhibition/Switching	8		Category Switching Acc	9	
Combined Naming & Reading	10				
Child and Adolescent Memory Profile					
Verbal Subtest	**SS**		**Visual Subtests**	**SS**	
Lists	8		Objects	11	
Lists Delayed	11		Objects Delayed	13	
Lists Recognition	13		Places	10	
Instructions	12		Places Delayed	11	

Wechsler Intelligence Scale for Children-5th Edition

Composite Scores	*SS*	*%*	*Subtest*	*SS*	*%*
Instructions Delayed	9				
			Index Scores		
Instructions Recognition	10		Verbal Memory	100	
			Visual Memory	107	
			Immediate Memory	102	
			Delayed Memory	106	
			Total Memory	104	
			Screening Index	97	
			Conners' Comprehensive Behavior Rating Scale		
Validity Tests				*Parent*	*Teacher*
MSVT	**Score**	**Classification**	**Content Scales**	**T**	**T**
Immediate Recall	80	Fail	Emotional Distress	42	90
Delayed Recall	80	Fail	Upsetting Thoughts	47	90
Consistency	75	Fail	Worrying	43	
Paired Associates	65		Social Problems	48	82
Free Recall	55		Defiant/Aggressive	43	44
			Academic Difficulties	55	58
VSVT			Language	57	58
Easy	20/24	Valid	Math	50	55
Hard	12/24	Questionable	Hyperactive/Impulsive	43	58
Total	32		Separation Fears	45	46
Memory Validity Profile			Perfectionistic/Compulsive	43	66
Visual	16	Valid	Violence Potential	44	51
Verbal	10	Invalid	Physical Symptoms	41	74
Total	26	Valid	***Symptom Scales***		
			ADHD Inattentive	41	59
			ADHD Hyperactive	43	56
			Conduct Disorder	44	45
			ODD	41	58
			Major Depressive Episode	42	70
			Manic Episode	41	60
			GAD	46	83
			SAD	45	47
			Social Anxiety Disorder	39	68
			O-C Disorder	46	76
			Autism Spectrum Disorder	41	50

Note: D-KEFS Delis Kaplan Executive Function System; MSVT – Medical Symptom Validity Test; VSVT – Victoria Symptom Validity Test; Tot C = Total Correct; Acc = Accuracy; ODD = Oppositional Defiant Disorder; GAD = Generalized Anxiety Disorder; SAD = Social Anxiety Disorder; O-C Disorder = Obsessive Compulsive Disorder.

Table 33.2 Assessment Data for AC

Wechsler Adult Intelligence Scale 4th edition					
Composite Scores	*SS*	*%*	*Subtest*	*SS*	*%*
			Similarities	10	50
Verbal Comprehension	98	45	Vocabulary	9	37
Perceptual Reasoning	86	18	Information	10	50
Working Memory	83	13	Block Design	5	5
Processing Speed	71	3	Matrix R	10	50
Full-Scale IQ	71	3	Visual Puzzles	8	25
			Digit Span	6	9
			Arithmetic	8	25
			Symbol Search	5	5
			Coding	4	2
Woodcock-Johnson 4th Edition Tests of Achievement Composite and Subtest Scores					
Composite Scores	***SS***	***%***	***Subtest Scores***	***SS***	***%***
Broad Reading	70	2	Sentence Reading Fluency	73	4
Broad Math	86	17	Letter-Word Identification	99	48
Broad Written Language	85	16	Passage Comp	80	9
Broad Achievement	78	2	Word Attack	84	15
Academic Fluency	52	<0.1	Oral reading	90	26
Reading Fluency	61	0.5	Reading Comp	78	7
			Reading Recall	77	7
Woodcock-Johnson 4th Edition Tests of Cognitive Ability			Word Reading Fluency	<40	<0.1
			Calculation	85	16
Visual-Auditory Learning	100	50	Math Facts Fluency	60	0.4
Perceptual Speed	40	<1st	Applied Problems	107	67
			Spelling	95	36
Kaufman Tests of Educational Achievement 3rd Edition			Sentence Writing Fluency	73	4
Written Expression	85	16	Writing Samples	91	27
			Spelling of Sounds	73	3

(*Continued*)

Table 33.2 (Continued)

Rey Auditory-Verbal Learning Test			*Rey Complex Figure Test*		
	Raw	%		*Raw*	%
Trial A1	2	<1	Copy	29	<1
Trial A2	3	<1	3 Min Recall	25	normal
Trial A3	6	<1	30 Min Recall	10	<1
Trial A4	7	<1			
Trial A5	8	<1			
Total 1–5	26	<1			
Retention	4	<1			
Distractor List B	3	<1			
Recognition	4	<1			
Personality Assessment Inventory					
Scale	*T*		*Scale*	*T*	
ICN	61		ANT	54	
INF	44		AGG	54	
NIM	99		ALC	63	
PIM	30		DRG	70	
SOM	85		SUI	68	
ANX	51		STR	77	
ARD	67		NON	61	
DEP	105		RXR	51	
MAN	37		DOM	42	
PAR	72		WRM	26	
SCZ	53				
BOR	63				

(*Continued*)

Table 33.2 (Continued)

Learning and Study Strategies Inventory			*NDRT-G*	*Raw*	*SS*	*%*
Subtest	Classification		Reading Rate	106	166	1
Anxiety	Below Average		Comprehension			
Attention	Average		# attempted	17		
Concentration	Below Average		# correct	4	144	<1
Info Processing	Below Average					
Motivation	Very High					
Selecting Main Ideas	Below Average					
Time Management	Average					
Validity Tests						
WMT	*Score*	*Classification*	*DASH*	*Score*	*Classification*	
Immediate Recall	80	Fail	Feigning Index	5	Fail	
Delayed Recall	80	Fail				
Consistency	75	Fail	*WAIS-IV*			
Paired Associates	65		RDS	6	Fail	
Free Recall	55					
TOMM			*VSVT*			
Trial 1	35	Fail	Easy	20/24	marginal	
Trial 2	41	Fail	Hard	6/24	fail	
Retention	34	Fail	Total	26/48	fail	

Note: DASH – Dyslexia Assessment of Simulation and Honesty; Matrix R = Matrix Reasoning; Comp = Comprehension; NDRT-G = Nelson Denny Reading Test Form G; WMT = Word Memory Test; DASH = Dyslexia Assessment of Simulation or Honesty; TOMM = Test of Memory Malingering; VSVT = Victoria Symptom Validity Test; WAIS-IV = Wechsler Adult Intelligence Scale-IV.

tasks (Wechsler Adult Intelligence Scale 4th ed Symbol Search and Coding scaled scores). He also failed the DASH-R (described above). Symptom validity testing (Negative Impression Management score on the Personality Assessment Inventory; PAI) also showed a marked tendency to exaggerate symptoms.

Although the combination of PVT and SVT failures makes his test performance uninterpretable, it is also notable to compare the pattern of his academic performance to his behavioral presentation and academic history. On tests of academic achievement, his scores are not commensurate with completing a college degree successfully, especially on academic fluency tasks; his scores fall well below the first percentile for reading and math and at the fourth percentile for writing. His performance on the Nelson Denny Reading Test was also notable for slow reading speed, although it should be noted that reading speed on this test is simply examinee's report of how far they got in reading the first item after a few minutes. His reading comprehension was at the first percentile at the standard time limits and remained so with extended time. Of note, he only answered 4 of 17 attempted items correctly within the standard 20 minutes, while in the additional 12 minutes of extended time, he answered 13 more questions and got 10 correct. It is also notable that it took him 42 minutes to complete the PAI, which, according to the manual, has a 4th grade reading level and takes on average 45 minutes to complete. Given that he did not score high on the inconsistency scales, it appears he was able to read and comprehend the PAI in a normal amount of time, in direct contrast to his performance on other reading speed tasks.

Recommendations

Self-reported academic impairment is common and can be easily malingered. Clinicians should not rely on subjective reports of "failure" in prior classes or administrations of high-stakes exams. Sometimes this report may reflect inaccurate personal standards or comparison with a high-performing subgroup of individuals; for example, students who view not getting all As at highly competitive colleges with policies that only 1/3 of students can receive As, or scoring at the 60th percentile on the Medical College Admission Test (MCAT) (relative to a highly elite comparison group, not a normative group) as evidence that they "failed." Whether this is deliberate misreport or inaccurate standards, clinicians should obtain actual grades and high-stakes testing results from academic records to compare with self-report. For example, the prior LSAT scores would have been useful in AC's case. As of yet, there are no validated SVTs specifically for inaccurate reporting of academic impairment, although, as noted in AC's case, the PAI was still potentially useful in determining the validity of his report of depressive symptoms (for which he was also receiving academic and testing accommodations).

It is also important to note that collateral report of impairment may also be invalid. In KC's case, his family has a history of experiencing the benefits of disability diagnoses, which may have led to overreporting his academic impairments. Unfortunately, a focus on getting an SLD diagnosis may have led them to underreport his psychological symptoms, thus risking that a real contributor to his academic struggles would be left untreated. More research is needed on validity scales in collateral report of academic functioning.

It is also easy for children and adults to malinger academic impairment on psychoeducational and neuropsychological tests. As noted above, many existing standalone and embedded PVTs may be useful, although the documented reading level of the examinee should be considered when interpreting their results. Further, not all PVTs are equally effective in SLD evaluation; clinicians should utilize those with good specificity but also with adequate sensitivity. Unfortunately, there are few PVTs focused specifically on invalid academic performance, although some measures such as DASH and CARE have shown promise in reading disorder.

It is also valuable for clinicians to compare test results to real-world functioning, as is illustrated in both cases above, where the scores obtained during testing were not consistent with actual school performance (or, in the case of AC, with his ability to function in everyday life activities). As noted for AC, it can also be valuable for clinicians to consider inconsistencies within testing (reading speed on face valid reading tasks versus personality tests, for example).

It is also important to note that failure on PVTs and SVTs may render results of tests uninterpretable, but that does not negate the possibility that someone is experiencing academic or other struggles. In both cases, there were some signs of potential psychological or cognitive/academic factors that might be contributing to their academic concerns. It is the goal of assessment to integrate together current test results with a full history (that is not limited to self-report) in order to make a final diagnostic determination, with the goal of accurately identifying concerns and recommending appropriate treatment or accommodations.

References

American Psychiatric Association. (2013). *Diagnostic and statistical manual of mental disorders* (5th ed.). https://doi.org/10.1176/appi.books.9780890425596

Americans with Disabilities Act Amendments Act of 2008, 42 U.S.C. § 1201 et seq. (2008). https://www.ada.gov/pubs/adastatute08.pdf

Association on Higher Education and Disability (2012). *Supporting accommodation requests: Guidance on documentation practices.* Retrieved from https://ahead.org/resources/documentation-guidance.

Boone, K. B., Lu, P., Sherman, D., Palmer, B., Back, C., Shamieh, E., … Berman, N. G. (2000). Validation of a new technique to detect malingering of cognitive symptoms: The b Test. *Archives of Clinical Neuropsychology, 15*(3), 227–241. https://doi.org/10.1093/arclin/15.3.227

Bryant, A. M., Lee, E., Howell, A., Morgan, B., Cook, C. M., Patel, K., … Suhr, J. A. (2018). The vulnerability of self-reported disability measures to malingering: A simulated ADHD study. *The Clinical Neuropsychologist, 32*, 109–118. https://doi.org/10.1080/13854046.2017.1346145

Cahan, S., Nirel, R., & Alkoby, M. (2016). The extra-examination time granting policy: A reconceptualization. *Journal of Psychoeducational Assessment, 34*, 461–472. https://doi.org/10.1177%2F0734282915616537

Flamand, H. (2015). Effort-testing in children undergoing psycho-educational assessment using the Medical Symptom Validity Test. *Literacy Informatics and Computer Education Journal, 6*(2), 1896–1903.

Fuermaier, A. B. M., Tucha, O., Koerts, J., Butzbach, M., Weisbrod, M., Aschenbrenner, S., & Tucha, I. (2018). Susceptibility of functional impairment scales to noncredible responses in the clinical evaluation of adult ADHD. *The Clinical Neuropsychologist, 32*, 671–680. https://doi.org/10.1080/13854046.2017.1406143

Greiffenstein, M. F., Baker, W. J., & Gola, T. (1994). Validation of malingered amnesia measures with a large clinical sample. *Psychological Assessment, 6*(3), 218–224. https://doi.org/10.1037/1040-3590.6.3.218

Harrison, A. G., Rosenblum, Y., & Currie, S. (2010). Examining unusual digit span performance in a population of postsecondary students assessed for academic difficulties. *Assessment, 17*, 283–293.

Harrison, A. G., & Davin, N. (in press). Detecting noncredible performance during virtual testing. *Psychological Injury and Law.* https://doi.org/10.1007/s12207-023-09480-6

Harrison, A. G., Beal, A. L., & Armstrong, I. T. (2023). Predictive value of performance validity testing and symptom validity testing in psychoeducational assessment. *Applied Neuropsychology: Adult*, *30*(3), 315–329.

Harrison, A. G., Edwards, M. J., & Parker, K. C. H. (2008). Identifying students feigning dyslexia: Preliminary findings and strategies for detection. *Dyslexia*, *14*(3), 228–244.

Harrison, A. G., Lee, G., & Suhr, J. (2021). Use of performance validity tests and symptom validity tests in assessment of specific learning disorders and attention deficit hyperactivity disorder. In K. B. Boone (Ed.), *Assessment of feigned cognitive impairment* (2nd ed., pp. 525–558). New York: Guilford Press.

Harrison, A. G., Lovett, B. J., & Gordon, M. (2013). Documenting disabilities in postsecondary settings: Diagnosticians' understanding of legal regulations and diagnostic standards. *Canadian Journal of School Psychology*, *28*, 303–322. https://doi.org/10.1177%2F0829573513508527

Harrison, A. G. & Wolforth, J. (2012). Findings from a Pan-Canadian survey of Disability Services Providers in Postsecondary Education. *International Journal of Disability, Community and Rehabilitation*, *11*(1), 1–15.

Individuals with Disabilities Education Improvement Act of 2004, 20 U.S.C. § 1400 (2004). https://www.govinfo.gov/content/pkg/USCODE-2011-title20/pdf/USCODE-2011-title20-chap33.pdf

Jansen, D., Petry, K., Ceulemans, E., Van der Oord, S., Noens, I., & Baeyens, D. (2017). Functioning and participation problems of students with ADHD in higher education. *European Journal of Special Needs Education*, *32*, 35–53.

Johnson, E. E. H., & Suhr, J. (2021). Self-reported functional impairment in college students: Relationship to noncredible reporting, ADHD, psychological disorders, and other psychological factors. *Journal of Clinical and Experimental Neuropsychology*, *43*, 399–411. https://doi.org/10.1080/13803395.2021.1935490

Joy, J. A., Julius, R. J., Akter, R., & Baron, D. A. (2010). Assessment of ADHD documentation from candidates requesting Americans with Disabilities Act (ADA) accommodations for the national board of osteopathic medical examiners COMLEX exam. *Journal of Attention Disorders*, *14*(2), 104–108. https://doi.org/10.1177%2F1087054710365056

Kirkwood, M. (2015). Review of pediatric performance and symptom validity tests. In M. W. Kirkwood (Ed.), *Validity Testing in Child and Adolescent Assessment: Evaluating Exaggeration, Feigning, and Noncredible Effort* (pp. 79–106). New York: Guilford Press.

Kirkwood, M. W., Connery, A. K., Kirk, J. W., & Baker, D. A. (2013). Detecting performance invalidity in children: Not quite as easy as A, B, C, 1, 2, 3 but automatized sequences appears promising. *Child Neuropsychology*, *20*(2), 245–52.

Larochette, A. C., & Harrison, A. G. (2012). Word Memory Test performance in Canadian adolescents with learning disabilities: A preliminary study. *Applied Neuropsychology: Child*, *1*(1), 38–47

Lewandowski, L., Cohen, J., & Lovett, B. J. (2013). Effects of extended time allotments on reading comprehension performance of college students with and without learning disabilities. *Journal of Psychoeducational Assessment*, *31*, 326–336. https://doi.org/10.1177%2F0734282912462693

Lewandowski, L. L., Lovett, B. J., Coding, R. S., & Gordon, M. (2008). Symptoms of ADHD and academic concerns in college students with and without ADHD diagnoses. *Journal of Attention Disorders*, *12*, 156–161. https://doi.org/10.1177%2F1087054707310882

Lindstrom, W.A., Lindstrom, J. H., Coleman, C., Nelson, J., & Gregg, N. (2009). The diagnostic accuracy of symptom validity tests when used with postsecondary students with learning disabilities: A preliminary investigation. *Archives of Clinical Neuropsychology*, *24*, 659–669. https://doi.org/10.1093/arclin/acp071

Miller, S., Zayac, R., Paulk, A., & Lee, S. (2019). Disability accommodation requests: Prevalence and preference of review processes at postsecondary institutions in the United States. *Journal of Postsecondary Education and Disability*, *32*, 217–226.

Nelson, J. M., & Lovett, B. J. (2019). Assessing ADHD in college students: Integrating multiple evidence sources with symptom and performance validity data. *Psychological Assessment*, *31*, 793–804. https://doi.org/10.1037/pas0000702

Newman, L., Wagner, M., Knokey, A. M., Marder, C., Nagle, K., Shaver, D., Wei, X., & SRI International. (2011). *The post-high school outcomes of young adults with disabilities up to 8 years after high school. A report from the National Longitudinal Transition Study-2*. Menlo Park, CA: SRI International.

Osmon, D. C., Plambeck, E. A., Klein, L. & Mano, Q. (2006). The Word Reading Test in adult learning disability: A simulation study. *The Clinical Neuropsychologist, 20*, 315–324. https://doi.org/10.1080/13854040590947434

Sanders, A. L. (2011). *Malingering by college students on evaluations for mathematics learning disabilities* (Doctoral dissertation). Retrieved from *Theses and Dissertations*, Paper 42.

Suhr, J. A., & Johnson, E. E. (2022). First do no harm: Ethical issues in pathologizing normal variations in behavior and functioning. *Psychological Injury and Law, 15*, 253–267.

Suhr, J. A., Cook, C., & Morgan, B. (2017). Assessing functional impairment in ADHD: Concerns for validity of self-report. *Psychological Injury and Law, 10*, 151–160. https://doi.org/10.1007/s12207-017-9292-8

Suhr, J. A., Lee, G. J., & Angers, K. (2021). Validity assessment in academic evaluations. In R. W. Schroeder & P. K. Martin (Eds.), *Validity assessment in clinical neuropsychological practice* (pp. 300–318). Guilford.

Suhr, J. A., Lee, G. L., & Harrison, A. H. (2020). Susceptibility of functional impairment ratings to noncredible reporting in postsecondary students undergoing screening for ADHD. *The Clinical Neuropsychologist*, 1–13. https://doi.org/10.1080/13854046.2020.1817564

Sweet, J. J., Heilbronner, R. L., Morgan, J. E., Larrabee, G. J., Rohling, M. L., Boone, K. B., Kirkwood, M. W., Schroeder, R. W., & Suhr, J. A. (2021). American Academy of Clinical Neuropsychology (AACN) 2021 consensus statement on validity assessment: Update of the 2009 AACN consensus conference statement on neuropsychological assessment of effort, response bias, and malingering. *The Clinical Neuropsychologist, 35*, 1053–1106. https://doi.org/10.1080/13854046.2021.1896036

Weis, R., & Waters, E. A. (2023). Evidence-based accommodations for postsecondary students with disabilities: Beware the base rate fallacy. *Psychological Injury and Law, 16*, 213–226.

Weis, R., & Droder, S. A. (2019). Development and initial validation of a reading-specific performance validity test: The College Assessment of Reading Effort (CARE). *Psychological Injury and Law, 12*, 29–41.

Section V

Clinical Evaluations

Most neuropsychologists engage in some degree of clinical non-forensic work. While it was previously thought that invalid data were rare in clinical settings, relatively recent research has documented that noncredible presentations can occur in clinical cases, with base rates at times approaching those observed in forensic settings. Invalidity is thought to most likely appear in clinical settings when patients are pursuing external incentives (e.g., disability benefits, medications of abuse, or various accommodations), when they report medically unexplained complaints, when they demonstrate oppositional attitudes toward testing, and when they present with predominant psychiatric/mental health issues. Even when none of these factors are known to exist, examinees can still invalidate testing due to having hidden external incentives or other non-external incentive factors. The cases discussed throughout this section highlight these issues, and illustrate that validity test failure in clinical settings should not be ignored or simply "explained away" as false-positive findings.

DOI: 10.4324/9781003005063-38

34 Hidden External Incentives in Clinical Evaluations

A Case Example

Ryan W. Schroeder and Phillip K. Martin

Until recently, it was assumed that the rate of symptom exaggeration and malingering in clinical nonforensic settings was quite low (Mittenberg et al., 2002). This belief was likely shaped by the assumption that external incentives in clinical settings were uncommon and that the vast majority of clinical patients simply pursued evaluations to understand and treat their health concerns. More recent research, however, has documented that a sizable minority of clinical patients have external incentives, and their presenting health complaints are often linked to those incentives (Martin & Schroeder, 2020; Schroeder, Clark, & Martin, 2022).

In one of the earlier studies on the topic, van Egmond and Kummeling (2002) conducted surveys of psychiatric outpatients and their clinicians. The authors found that 42% of therapy patients reported expecting a secondary gain but only 6% of the patients expressed this expectation to their clinicians. Furthermore, it was found that there was an inverse relationship between expectations for secondary gain and treatment outcome, which resulted in the study authors concluding that "secondary gain appeared to be a 'veiled motive' for getting therapy" for some patients (p. 46).

Within neuropsychological research, Chafetz and colleagues (2011) examined base rates of performance validity test (PVT) failure within examinee samples with various external incentives. Unsurprisingly, in a sample of examinees who had external incentives to perform poorly (i.e., Social Security disability claimants), it was seen that 46% of individuals failed validity testing. Comparatively, in a sample of examinees who had strong external incentives to perform well (i.e., individuals looking to reunite with their children), it was found that 0% of examinees failed validity testing. The surprising finding of the study was that of individuals in a vocational rehabilitation program, 7% failed validity testing. The study authors wondered why these individuals, who were seemingly motivated to return to work, failed validity testing. In exploring this, they found that all of the invalidly performing individuals in the vocational rehabilitation program were seeking or had obtained Social Security disability, which suggested that these individuals were covertly malingering to obtain an external incentive that was seemingly inconsistent with the goals of the program in which they were participating.

Schroeder and colleagues (2022) published research that even more directly addressed the issue of hidden external incentives in clinical neuropsychological evaluations. This study was comprised of a consecutive sample of working age, nonforensic patients who underwent routine clinically referred neuropsychological evaluations. Individuals were excluded if they had any identified external incentive other than Social Security disability. Then, individuals were grouped according to whether they reported that they were (1) not pursuing Social Security disability, (2) already receiving Social Security disability, (3) actively

DOI: 10.4324/9781003005063-39

pursuing Social Security disability, or (4) non-committal about Social Security disability. This latter, non-committal, group of patients indicated that they were not pursuing disability and had no definitive plans to pursue disability in the future, but they would consider pursuing disability if it were to be needed.

Consistent with other research (e.g., Chafetz et al., 2011), Schroeder and colleagues (2022) found that >40% of individuals either pursuing or already receiving Social Security disability failed validity testing. Those individuals who were pursuing disability clearly had an external incentive that they were pursuing. Those who were already on disability likely also had an external incentive as Disability Determination Services periodically reviews records to ensure that individuals continue to have a qualifying disability (Social Security Administration, 2017). When full medical reviews are needed, the patient is alerted to this, and Disability Determination Services requests medical reports from the patient's doctors. If healthcare notes show that the patient's medical condition has improved to the point where the patient can regularly work, disability benefits could stop.

Somewhat surprisingly, 39% of individuals in the Schroeder et al. (2022) study who reported being non-committal regarding pursuing disability failed validity testing. This suggested that some of these individuals were likely considering pursuing disability even though they reported being non-committal during the evaluation. Furthermore, 8.5% of individuals who reported that they had no external incentive and were not at all entertaining the thought of disability failed validity testing. This potentially suggested that some of these individuals might have had fully hidden external incentives that impacted their test performances.

The following case is of Ms. Z. She is one of the individuals from the Schroeder et al. (2022) study who reported having no current or future plans to pursue an external incentive, including disability. Despite reporting this, she failed multiple validity tests, and information obtained after the evaluation indicated that she was not fully truthful, and she was likely hiding that she was pursuing disability at the time of the neuropsychological evaluation.

The Case of Ms. Z

Background

The patient was a 51-year-old, right-handed, biracial, female who was divorced and had no children. She was born and raised in the midwestern part of the United States by middle-class parents. No developmental issues, childhood abuse, or childhood neglect were reported. In school, the patient obtained As and Bs in essentially all classes except for math-related classes. She stated that she struggled with math, but she was not diagnosed with a learning disability, she did not receive any special education services, she did not receive any tutoring, and her grades in math were still in the B to C range. She graduated from high school and worked in call center and receptionist settings throughout her career. Indeed, she was working as a receptionist at a busy office before being laid off just one month prior to the neuropsychological evaluation.

The patient reported that she was in her usual, fairly good, state of cognitive and physical health until about 2.5 years prior to the neuropsychological evaluation. Her only diagnoses were gastroesophageal reflux disease and history of mild atrial fibrillation. However, approximately 2.5 years prior to the evaluation, the patient started experiencing problems with short-term memory, attention, verbal expression (word-finding issues and periodic paraphasic errors), comprehension of complex tasks, and mood swings. Around that same time, she also began experiencing a chronic headache. A few months later, she developed blurry vision with periodic double vision. Consequently, she visited her primary care physician, who referred her to a neurologist.

After meeting the neurologist, the patient underwent a magnetic resonance imaging (MRI) study of the brain. Based on this study, it was found that she had a Chiari I malformation. Her cerebellar tonsils were 7 mm below the level of the foramen magnum, and there was associated crowding of the foramen magnum. The patient underwent decompression surgery three weeks later (about 1.5 years before the neuropsychological evaluation). After the surgery, the patient felt that her cognition improved some, to a point where she described that she was only experiencing mild cognitive issues. Approximately six months later, however, her cognition worsened, she experienced episodes of 'zoning out,' she began having low energy, and she developed increased irritability with angry outbursts.

Because of the worsening symptoms, she saw her neurologist again, which was about three months before the neuropsychological evaluation. The patient's neurologist performed a neurologic exam, which included administering the Mini-Mental State Examination (MMSE). The patient scored 28/30 on the MMSE, and the remainder of her neurologic exam was normal. Because of the worsened symptoms with instances of zoning out, though, the neurologist ordered a follow-up MRI, an electroencephalogram (EEG), and a neuropsychological evaluation. The MRI and EEG were completed before the neuropsychological evaluation. The MRI showed expected postoperative changes and minor non-specific subcortical microvascular changes. The EEG, however, was read as showing intermittent slow dysrhythmic discharges in the left temporal region, suggestive of a seizure disorder. Based on this, the patient was prescribed an antiepileptic medication, but she did not take the medication due to concerns that she had about side effects. The only prescription medication that she was taking at the time of the neuropsychological evaluation was omeprazole for her gastroesophageal reflux disease. In addition, she was taking the following over-the-counter medications/supplements: a multivitamin, Claritin, and fish oil.

Neuropsychological Clinical Interview

The patient was clinically referred for the neuropsychological evaluation by her neurologist, with a specific request to examine the patient's cognitive functioning and mood within the context of the history provided above. On the day of the neuropsychological evaluation, the patient arrived at the clinic alone (dropped off by a friend) and on time. During the clinical interview, she reported that she had been significantly struggling with her memory. She stated that this affected her so much that she needed to write information down or she would forget it. She then pulled out a notebook and began reading the clinician a list of symptoms that she had previously written, which revolved around short-term memory difficulties, word-finding problems, and attention issues. When the clinician asked her if she had experienced other cognitive symptoms (e.g., difficulties making decisions), she looked through her notebook to see if the symptoms were written down before responding. Oddly, though, when the clinician asked her about recent historical information (what her neurologist told her about her EEG results, what medication she was recently prescribed, etc.), she was able to freely recall that information without difficulty.

In addition to cognitive symptoms, the patient reported experiencing low energy, increased sleep, episodes of crying, feelings of depression and hopelessness, feelings of and symptoms related to panic (e.g., intense fear, heart racing, and rapid breathing), stress, and suicidal ideation. When asked about stress, the patient stated that she experienced stress related to her health and income. She explained that she was recently laid off from her job because she was missing too much work due to attending medical appointments. She also noted that it was hard for her to arrive at work on time due to relying on others for transportation since she couldn't drive herself anymore due to a state law preventing her from driving secondary to having seizures. Finally, she also acknowledged that there were a few days that she didn't show up for work due to lacking energy and motivation and struggling to get out of bed in the morning.

The patient was asked about her plans for the future. She stated that she was attending all medical appointments and hoping that her health would eventually improve. She stated that, if her health were to improve, she would look for employment. When asked if she was currently looking for employment, she stated that she was not because (1) she felt as though she could not currently work due to her cognition and (2) she was focusing all of her energy on attending medical appointments. When asked if she was looking at pursuing disability, she reported that she was not, as she was hopeful that she would be able to return to work in the coming months.

When asked about other instrumental activities of daily living, the patient stated that she was managing her four medications/supplements without issue. She reported that she was struggling financially, but this was because she was without an income. She denied having difficulty cognitively managing her finances (e.g., organizing and remembering to pay bills). She was cooking without issue, although she was not cooking as much as she used to due to having a low appetite. She was attending all scheduled medical appointments without missing any. Finally, she noted that she was not keeping up with housework, but this was because of low energy and motivation rather than being cognitively unable to do so.

Behavioral Observations

As previously noted, the patient arrived at the clinic alone and on time. She was casually dressed, well groomed, and appeared her stated age. Her posture, gait, and balance appeared unremarkable. She rose from a seated position without difficulty. No resting or action tremor were observed. Eye contact was periodically avoided. The patient's speech was somewhat soft in volume but normal in rate, prosody, and articulation. She spoke in complete and grammatical sentences; no paraphasic errors were noted. She was attentive, and she easily tracked conversation. She was able to comprehend interview questions and test instructions without difficulty. During the clinical interview, she frequently referred to notes that she had written about her symptoms. Outside of this, no noticeable memory problems or lapses occurred. Thought processes were logical and coherent. There was no evidence of delusions or hallucinations. No episodes of zoning out or seizure-like activity were observed or reported. Affect appeared depressed, with periodic tearfulness occurring during the clinical interview when discussing her recent life circumstance. During testing, it was noted that the patient often performed well on easier test items, but she abruptly met discontinuation rules as test items became more challenging. That is, she would miss a subtest item as the material became more difficult, and she would then fail every subsequent item after this point rather than showing a more typical pattern of getting some items periodically wrong until ultimately meeting the discontinuation rule.

Test Results

The patient's PVT results are presented in Table 34.1. She failed four of the eight PVTs that were administered to her. Specifically, she failed the Test of Memory Malingering (TOMM), Dot Counting Test, Medical Symptom Validity Test (MSVT; and there was not a genuine memory impairment profile), and Logical Memory recognition embedded PVT.

For ease of reporting, the most pertinent neurocognitive test results are presented in Table 34.2. The patient's premorbid intellectual ability was assessed with the Test of Premorbid Functioning. There was a significant difference between the patient's demographic estimate and word reading estimate. The demographic estimate (standard score = 90) suggested that the patient's functioning was near the average range, while her word reading estimate (standard score = 76) suggested that she was functioning within a below average or borderline intellectual functioning range. The word reading estimate seemed atypically low given the patient's background and current presentation, and it also underestimated many of her current cognitive performances. Research has also indicated that a number of individuals who fail validity testing underperform on word reading tests designed to predict premorbid functioning (Martin et al., 2018). For all of these reasons, the patient's demographic estimate was considered to be a more likely accurate estimate of her premorbid functioning than her reading estimate.

When compared with the patient's demographically predicted premorbid estimate, she scored slightly lower than expected on the Wechsler Adult Intelligence Scale – 4th Edition (WAIS-IV) Verbal Comprehension Index, with all subtests scores comprising this index being within two scaled score points of each other. Likewise, she scored slightly lower than expected on the WAIS-IV Working Memory Index, but this was due to her Arithmetic subtest performance (scaled score = 5 versus Digit Span subtest scaled score = 8). In addition, the patient scored much lower than expected on all verbal memory tests, the Letter Fluency (but not Category Fluency) test, and the Color-Word test. All other cognitive test scores were within normal and expected limits.

The patient was administered the Minnesota Multiphasic Personality Inventory – 2nd Edition Restructured Form (MMPI-2-RF) to assess her psychological functioning and symptom report. Scores from the validity and restructured clinical scales are presented in Table 34.3. The patient left no question on the MMPI-2-RF unanswered, and her scores on the VRIN-r and TRIN-r scales did not indicate issues with content inconsistent responding. Her over-reporting validity scales, however, indicated concern for over-reporting of symptoms, especially cognitive/neuropsychological symptoms. Finally, she produced clinically elevated scores on the majority of the restructured clinical scales, with her highest

Table 34.1 Performance Validity Test Results

Test	*Scores*
Test of Memory Malingering	Trial 1 = 38, Trial 2 = 44, Retention = 46, IFFI = 42
Dot Counting Test	E-score = 18
Medical Symptom Validity Test	IR = 65%, DR = 80%, CNS = 65%, PA = 80%, FR = 55%
Reliable Digit Span	RDS score = 8
Logical Memory Recognition	Raw score = 16
Visual Reproduction Recognition	Raw score = 6
HVLT-R Recognition Discrimination	Raw score = 8
BVMT-R Recognition Hit	Raw score = 6

Note: IFFI = Invalid Forgetting Frequency Index, IR = Immediate Recognition, DR = Delayed Recognition, CNS = Consistency, PA = Paired Associates, FR = Free Recall, RDS = Reliable Digit Span, HVMT-R = Hopkins Verbal Learning Test - Revised, BVMT-R = Brief Visuospatial Memory Test – Revised.

Table 34.2 Neurocognitive Test Results

Cognitive Domain/Test	*Scores*
Intelligence/WAIS-IV	
Test of Premorbid Functioning	Demographic FSIQ Estimate = 90
WAIS-IV Full Scale IQ	Index Score = 85
WAIS-IV Verbal Comprehension Index	Index Score = 81
WAIS-IV Perceptual Reasoning Index	Index Score = 94
WAIS-IV Working Memory Index	Index Score = 80
WAIS-IV Processing Speed Index	Index Score = 97
Attention	
Digit Vigilance Test Time	T-score = 49
Digit Vigilance Test Errors	T-score = 46
Verbal Memory	
WMS-IV Logical Memory I	Scaled Score = 1
WMS-IV Logical Memory II	Scaled Score = 3
WMS-IV Logical Memory Recognition	Cumulative % ≤2%
HVLT-R Total Recall	T-score = 24
HVLT-R Delayed Recall	T-score = 28
HVLT-R Recognition Discrimination	T-score = 30
Visual Memory	
WMS-IV Visual Reproduction I	Scaled Score = 8
WMS-IV Visual Reproduction II	Scaled Score = 9
WMS-IV Visual Reproduction Recognition	Cumulative % = 51–75%
BVMT-R Total Recall	T-score = 38
BVMT-R Delayed Recall	T-score = 38
BVMT-R Recognition Discrimination	Cumulative % ≥ 16%
Executive Functioning/D-KEFS	
Trail Making: Condition 4	Scaled Score = 7
Verbal Fluency: Letter Fluency	Scaled Score = 3
Verbal Fluency: Category Fluency	Scaled Score = 9
Verbal Fluency: Category Switching	Scaled Score = 10
Color Word: Inhibition Time	Scaled Score = 5
Color Word: Inhibition Errors	Scaled Score = 2
Color Word: Inhibition-Switching Time	Scaled Score = 2
Color Word: Inhibition-Switching Errors	Scaled Score = 4
Tower: Total Achievement	Scaled Score = 9

Note: WAIS-IV = Wechsler Adult Intelligence Scale – 4th Edition, FSIQ = Full Scale IQ, WMS-IV = Wechsler Memory Scale – 4th Edition, HVLT-R – Hopkins Verbal Learning Test – Revised, BVMT-R = Brief Visuospatial Memory Test – Revised, D-KEFS = Delis-Kaplan Executive Function System.

scores reflecting issues related to somatic symptoms, demoralization, and low positive emotions.

Interpretation of Test Results

The patient failed four PVTs, which rendered her cognitive testing invalid. Given that this patient (1) was a clinically referred patient, (2) had legitimate neurologic conditions that could cause cognitive dysfunction, (3) appeared clearly distressed by her current health situation, and (4) denied having any external incentives, the clinician believed that it was

Table 34.3 Minnesota Multiphasic Personality Inventory-2-Restructured Format Results

MMPI-2-RF Scale	*Scores*
VRIN-r	T-score = 48
TRIN-r	T-score = 50
F-r	T-score = 79
Fp-r	T-score = 51
Fs	T-score = 91
FBS-r	T-score = 89
RBS	T-score = 118
L-r	T-score = 62
K-r	T-score = 24
RCd	T-score = 85
RC1	T-score = 95
RC2	T-score = 88
RC3	T-score = 74
RC4	T-score = 46
RC6	T-score = 70
RC7	T-score = 78
RC8	T-score = 76
RC9	T-score = 38

Note: MMPI-2-RF = Minnesota Multiphasic Personality Inventory-2-Restructured Format.

extremely important to ensure that the validity test failures were not false-positive findings. In this regard, it was thought that the pattern of cognitive testing needed to be closely examined for consistencies/inconsistencies with the patient's known neurologic conditions and the validity test findings needed to be heavily scrutinized by comparing them to multiple pertinent empirical research findings.

In examining the pattern of cognitive test results, it was noted that the patient produced a slightly lower than expected score on the WAIS-IV Verbal Comprehension Index, which was almost one standard deviation lower than her Perceptual Reasoning Index score (i.e., scores of 81 versus 94, respectively). While her WAIS-IV Working Memory Index score was also slightly lower than expected, this was accounted for by her Arithmetic performance (Arithmetic scaled score = 5, Digit Span scaled score = 8), and it was kept in mind that the patient reported having a lifelong weakness in math. The patient produced some of her lowest scores on verbal memory tests, scoring in the below average to exceptionally low ranges. Conversely, she scored within the low average to average ranges on all visual memory tests. Finally, she scored within the below average to exceptionally low ranges on most executive functioning tests that included heavy verbal elements (i.e., Letter Fluency and Color Word) while scoring within the low average to average ranges on visually based executive functioning tests (i.e., Trail Making and Tower). It was thought that this pattern of cognitive test results could be seen as potentially lining up with her EEG findings showing left temporal region discharges. Could, then, the validity test findings be false-positive errors that are due to a seizure disorder?

The patient's validity test results were analyzed in comparison with empirical research findings. First, the patient's TOMM performances were compared with results of a meta-analytic research study (Martin et al., 2020). The patient's scores across all three of the trials were associated with specificity rates above 90% even when compared with individuals with neurologic and/or psychiatric conditions (Trial 1 specificity = >93%, Trial 2 specificity = 96%, Retention specificity = 97%). Second, the clinician reviewed the literature on how individuals with epilepsy perform on the TOMM. This research indicated that 90+% of adults, adolescents, and even children with epilepsy pass the TOMM at conventional cutoffs (Cragar et al., 2006; Grant & Werner, 2020; MacAllister et al., 2009; Ploetz et al., 2016). Third, a TOMM consistency score was calculated (i.e., Invalid Forgetting Frequency Index), and it was determined that the patient made 8 inconsistent memory errors. This number of inconsistent memory errors was beyond the empirically established cutoff of 3 (Buddin et al., 2014; Olsen et al., 2021), which indicated invalidity due to inconsistent memory errors in addition to the poor performances on individual subtest trials. Finally, in thinking critically about the patient's performances, it did not make sense that she failed the visually based TOMM due to false-positive errors when all of her visual memory scores on cognitive testing were within normal limits (Larrabee, 2022).

Given that the patient produced very poor scores on verbal memory tests, it could conceptually make sense that her verbally based MSVT failure might be due to a false-positive error. With that said, a review of the professional literature indicated that the MSVT's easy validity indices are rarely failed due to epilepsy. MacAllister and colleagues (2020), for example, documented that even children and adolescents with epilepsy can pass the easy MSVT validity indices about 97% of the time as long as they possess a second-grade or higher reading level. The professional literature also indicated that a false-positive finding on the MSVT easy subtests should be identified by the MSVT's Genuine Memory Impairment Profile. Specifically, research indicated that a genuine memory impairment that accounts for the easy subtest failure, should be identified by the Genuine Memory Impairment Profile 95%–100% of the time (Howe et al., 2007; Green et al., 2011; see Schroeder & Martin, 2021 for review). Interestingly, though, the patient did not produce the Genuine Memory Impairment Profile, which further suggested that genuine memory impairment was not the cause of the MSVT failure.

On the Dot Counting Test, the patient produced an E-score of 18. The literature indicated that this score is consistently associated with specificity rates beyond 90% when applied to individuals without a major neurocognitive disorder (Boone et al., 2002; Martin et al., 2022; McCaul et al., 2018; Soble et al., 2018). While the current patient did produce test scores 2+ standard deviations below the normative mean on some tests (therefore potentially suggesting a major neurocognitive disorder), her daily functioning indicated that she did not have a major neurocognitive disorder (i.e., she did not demonstrate impairment in basic or instrumental activities of daily living due to cognitive dysfunction). In addition to scoring beyond empirically established cutoff scores, it did not make sense that the Dot Counting Test failure would be a false-positive error given that the patient scored within normal limits on attention tests (e.g., Digit Span and Digit Vigilance Test), mental processing speed tests (e.g., WAIS-IV Processing Speed Index), and a visual scanning test (Delis-Kaplan Executive Function System Trail Making Condition 1 scaled score = 9).

The last PVT that the patient failed was the embedded validity index within the Wechsler Memory Scale-4th Edition Logical Memory recognition subtest. It could conceptually make sense that the patient's performance on this validity test might be a false-positive error given that she had EEG findings of left temporal lobe discharges. With that said, the test manual (Pearson, 2009) indicates that there is a 90% specificity rate associated with a cutoff score of 16 (which was the patient's score) in a sample of examinees comprising individuals with a history of temporal lobe epilepsy who subsequently had temporal lobectomies. Thus, this empirical data suggested that the patient's validity test performance was not likely a false-positive error, which converged with the other PVT findings.

After looking at the PVT results individually, the findings were examined as an aggregated group outcome. Specifically, it was noted that the patient failed 4 of the 8 PVTs that were administered to her. When comparing this outcome with the professional literature, research findings further indicated that the patient's validity test results were not false-positive errors. Specifically, Larrabee (2014) has demonstrated that 4+ PVT failures (when 7 are administered) result in a 100% specificity rate. In another article, Larrabee (2019) showed that the failure of 4+ PVTs (when 10 are administered) results in a 96% specificity rate. Outside of Larrabee's research, Martin et al. (2022) observed that the failure of 4+ PVTs (when 7 are administered) results in a 100% specificity rate in individuals with mild neurocognitive disorders and a 99% specificity rate in individuals with mild dementia.

After reviewing the PVTs and cognitive test data, the examiner reviewed the patient's MMPI-2-RF results. Given that PVTs were failed, the examiner first looked at over-reporting validity scales assessing cognitive and neuropsychological dysfunction (i.e., FBS-r and RBS). Per the MMPI-2-RF manual, the patient's FBS-r score raised concern about "possible" over-reporting of somatic and/or cognitive symptoms (p. 29, Ben-Porath & Tellegen, 2008). Given the inconclusive finding of "possible" over-reporting, the examiner compared the patient's scores to data published by Schroeder and colleagues (2012). Schroeder et al. previously published MMPI-2-RF cutoff scores across multiple clinical samples, including a malingering sample, an epilepsy sample, and a psychiatric sample. When the current patient's FBS-r score was compared with these samples, it was seen that her score was the same as the mean score obtained by the malingering group, and the patient's score was also associated with a 93% specificity rate in the psychiatric sample and a 98% specificity rate in the epilepsy sample.

The patient's RBS score also indicated invalid cognitive complaints (Ben-Porath & Tellegen, 2011). Specifically, the MMPI-2-RF RBS supplemental manual indicated that "over-reporting is indicated by a very unusual combination of responses that is strongly associated with non-credible memory complaints" (p. 4). Furthermore, when compared with the data published by Schroeder and colleagues (2012), it was seen that the patient scored higher than 100% of both epilepsy patients and examinees with clear psychiatric symptomatology, and interestingly, she also scored higher than 95% of individuals in the malingering group. These empirical research findings indicated that neither the patient's seizure disorder nor her psychiatric presentation (i.e., presenting with symptoms of depression and anxiety) could account for her invalid endorsement of symptoms, which converged with her PVT failures.

Next, the examiner looked at validity scales assessing over-reporting of psychological symptoms. Per the MMPI-2-RF manual, the patient's F-r scale score could be due to genuine psychological issues or over-reporting of symptoms (particularly if there is no history or current evidence of psychological dysfunction). Because the patient presented with a history of recent psychological disturbance and a notably depressed affect, it was important to examine her Fp-r score as this score "can be particularly helpful when a test taker produces a substantially elevated score on F-r and the interpreter needs to determine whether this reflects over-reporting of genuine dysfunction" (p. 27, Ben-Porath & Tellegen, 2008). The patient's score on Fp-r was well below the clinical cutoff, indicating that there was no evidence of over-reporting on this scale. Likewise, the patient's scores on F-r and Fp-r failed to meet a 90% specificity threshold when compared with the mixed psychiatric group of patients reported in Schroeder et al. (2012). Consequently, it was concluded that there was not strong enough data to assume that the patient's psychological complaints were feigned. Given this, her restructured clinical scale scores, and her presenting psychiatric complaints, it was believed that the patient had significant distress, depression, and anxiety.

Finally, the examiner looked at the patient's Fs scale score to better understand the validity of the patient's somatic complaints. Per the MMPI-2-RF manual, the patient's score raised concern about "possible" over-reporting of somatic symptoms. As with the other validity scale scores, this score was also compared with the Schroeder et al. (2012) data. The patient's score was ten points higher than the mean of the malingering group, it was associated with 90% specificity in the epilepsy group, and it was associated with 86% specificity in the psychiatric group. Given this data, the patient's somatic complaints were considered borderline valid/questionable.

Summary and Conclusions

Regarding psychiatric status, it was concluded that the patient was likely experiencing clinically significant depression and anxiety. Regarding cognitive status, the test findings, if taken at face value, would have potentially suggested left-sided frontal-temporal dysfunction, which would have largely matched expectations from EEG findings. For multiple reasons, though, it was believed that there was an exaggeration of cognitive dysfunction causing testing to be invalid. First, the individual PVT findings of invalidity could not be accounted for by the patient's medical history (as previously discussed in this chapter). Second, as an aggregated whole, failure of four PVTs has been found to be associated with an almost 100% specificity rate (i.e., essentially no false-positive errors). Third, MMPI-2-RF symptom validity indices that have been found to predict PVT failures (i.e., FBS-r and RBS), and which could not be accounted for by the patient's medical or psychiatric history, converged with the PVT findings and indicate that cognitive symptoms were invalid. Fourth, there were compelling qualitative features of the patient's presentation that suggested exaggeration or feigning of symptoms, including responding to cognitive test items atypically and demonstrating an oddly inconsistent ability to recall information during the clinical interview.

In drawing final conclusions about this case, it was believed that the patient had depression and anxiety, and she might have also had some degree of cognitive dysfunction, but she was clearly exaggerating any cognitive dysfunction that might have been present. The reason for her cognitive exaggeration was not completely known but, given her financial hardships and lack of employment, it was wondered if she might have been pursuing disability despite her statement that she was not. One week after testing, the neuropsychologist met with the patient to provide her with feedback on the test results. The neuropsychologist used the feedback model discussed in Martin and Schroeder (2022), and the patient received the information well and never questioned the invalid data. It was recommended that the patient take her prescribed antiepileptic medication, that she engage in psychotherapy related to struggles with her mental health and need for coping with stressors, and that she talk to her prescribing physician about possibly starting a psychotropic medication for her mood.

On her way out of the office after the feedback session, the patient stopped at the receptionist desk and signed a release of information to send the report to a well-known disability attorney. Furthermore, in talking with the patient's neurologist after the neuropsychological evaluation, he indicated that, just before the patient's neuropsychological appointment, she called the neurology office to schedule another follow-up appointment. She stated that she quit her job (not that she was let go as she described during the neuropsychological evaluation), and she was wanting to ensure that her care would not be disrupted until she figured out another way to obtain insurance or direct payment for services. Based on this additional post-evaluation information, it appears very likely that the patient lied about having no intent to seek disability (possibly to keep the neuropsychologist's guard down), and that her validity test failures and exaggeration of symptoms were an intentional action to try to ensure that she would be awarded disability benefits.

Discussion

The presented literature and current case highlight the fact that external incentives can be present within clinical nonforensic evaluations, and they may be hidden from the examiner. Furthermore, even when genuine neurologic and/or psychiatric conditions are present, an exaggeration of symptoms can occur. This latter point was also noted in the first edition of this book (i.e., *Neuropsychology of Malingering Casebook*) where Bergman and Sweet (2009) discussed a case of a woman who was clinically evaluated at an urban public hospital. This woman had a genetically confirmed case of Machado-Joseph disease, she was seeking treatment, and there were no known external incentives present. Despite this, the woman failed validity testing with below chance scores on the TOMM (Trial 1 = 15, Trial 2 = 11, Retention = 7), which indicated that she intentionally exaggerated or feigned cognitive impairment. Because there were no known external incentives, a conclusion of malingering was (appropriately) not made, but it was pointed out that other conditions such as factitious disorder and somatic symptom disorders did not fit the clinical picture well.

In conclusion, because any patient – especially those who are of working age – might have external incentives present even when denied; because the presence of genuine medical, neurologic, and/or psychiatric conditions does not preclude the possibility of invalidity; and because invalidity can potentially occur for reasons outside of malingering; it is imperative that validity testing be included in *all* neuropsychological evaluations whether clinical or forensic. Not identifying invalidity in clinical evaluations can result in erroneous conclusions about a patient's functioning, inaccurate diagnoses, and unnecessary treatment plans, which could cause harm to the patient and other stakeholders (e.g., patient family members, social assistance institutions, and the field of neuropsychology; Martin et al., 2022). When invalidity is identified in clinical cases, it does not have to be labeled as malingering (Sweet et al., 2021), and, in a number of instances, it will likely be beneficial to withhold applying the term even if malingering is suspected. The invalidity, however, should not be overlooked, and it should be addressed in appropriate ways. For more comprehensive published methods and resources for addressing invalidity in clinical cases, we refer the reader to Schroeder and Martin (2022).

References

Ben-Porath, Y. S., & Tellegen, A. (2008). *Minnesota Multiphasic Personality Inventory-2 Restructured Form: Manual for Administration, Scoring, and Interpretation*. University of Minnesota Press.

Ben-Porath, Y. S., & Tellegen, A. (2011). *Minnesota Multiphasic Personality Inventory-2 Restructured Form: Manual for Administration, Scoring, and Interpretation. Response Bias Scale (RBS) Supplement*. University of Minnesota Press.

Bergman, M. A., & Sweet, J. J. (2009). Complexities of the differential diagnosis of malingering: Arguments for the use of effort tests with patients. In J. E. Morgan & J. J. Sweet (Eds.), *Neuropsychology of Malingering Casebook* (pp. 543–556). Taylor & Francis.

Boone, K. B., Lu, P., Back, C., King, C., Lee, A., Philpott, L., ... & Warner-Chacon, K. (2002). Sensitivity and specificity of the Rey Dot Counting Test in patients with suspect effort and various clinical samples. *Archives of Clinical Neuropsychology*, *17*(7), 625–642.

Buddin Jr, W. H., Schroeder, R. W., Hargrave, D. D., Von Dran, E. J., Campbell, E. B., Brockman, C. J., ... & Baade, L. E. (2014). An examination of the frequency of invalid forgetting on the Test of Memory Malingering. *The Clinical Neuropsychologist*, *28*(3), 525–542

Chafetz, M. D., Prentkowski, E., & Rao, A. (2011). To work or not to work: Motivation (not low IQ) determines symptom validity test findings. *Archives of Clinical Neuropsychology*, *26*(4). 306–313.

Cragar, D. E., Berry, D. T., Fakhoury, T. A., Cibula, J. E., & Schmitt, F. A. (2006). Performance of patients with epilepsy or psychogenic non-epileptic seizures on four measures of effort. *The Clinical Neuropsychologist*, *20*(3), 552–566.

Grant, A. F., & Werner, N. J. (2020). Retrospective analysis of the Test of Memory Malingering in a low intellectual quotient intractable epilepsy sample. *Archives of Clinical Neuropsychology*, *35*(6), 726–734.

Green, P. (2011). Comparison between the Test of Memory Malingering (TOMM) and the Nonverbal Medical Symptom Validity Test (NV-MSVT) in adults with disability claims. *Applied Neuropsychology*, *18*(1), 18–26.

Howe, L. L., Anderson, A. M., Kaufman, D. A., Sachs, B. C., & Loring, D. W. (2007). Characterization of the Medical Symptom Validity Test in evaluation of clinically referred memory disorders clinic patients. *Archives of Clinical Neuropsychology*, *22*(6), 753–761.

Larrabee, G. J. (2014). False-positive rates associated with the use of multiple performance and symptom validity tests. *Archives of Clinical Neuropsychology*, *29*(4), 364–373.

Larrabee, G. J. (2022). Synthesizing data to reach clinical conclusions regarding validity status. In R. W. Schroeder & P. K. Martin (Eds.), *Validity Assessment in Clinical Neuropsychological Practice: Evaluating and Managing Noncredible Performance* (pp. 193–210). Guilford Publications.

Larrabee, G. J., Rohling, M. L., & Meyers, J. E. (2019). Use of multiple performance and symptom validity measures: Determining the optimal per test cutoff for determination of invalidity, analysis of skew, and inter-test correlations in valid and invalid performance groups. *The Clinical Neuropsychologist*, *33*(8), 1354–1372.

MacAllister, W. S., Désiré, N., Vasserman, M., Dalrymple, J., Salinas, L., & Brooks, B. L. (2020). The use of the MSVT in children and adolescents with epilepsy. *Applied Neuropsychology: Child*, *9*(4), 323–328.

MacAllister, W. S., Nakhutina, L., Bender, H. A., Karantzoulis, S., & Carlson, C. (2009). Assessing effort during neuropsychological evaluation with the TOMM in children and adolescents with epilepsy. *Child Neuropsychology*, *15*(6), 521–531.

Martin, P. K., & Schroeder, R. W. (2020). Base rates of invalid test performance across clinical non-forensic contexts and settings. *Archives of Clinical Neuropsychology*, *35*(6), 717–725.

Martin, P. K., & Schroeder, R. W. (2022). A framework for providing clinical feedback when patients invalid testing. In R. W. Schroeder & P. K. Martin (Eds.), *Validity Assessment in Clinical Neuropsychological Practice: Evaluating and Managing Noncredible Performance* (pp. 47–69). Guilford Publications.

Martin, P. K., Schroeder, R. W., Boone, K. B., & Bush, S. S. (2022). Ethical considerations associated with validity assessment in clinical evaluations. In R. W. Schroeder & P. K. Martin (Eds.), *Validity Assessment in Clinical Neuropsychological Practice: Evaluating and Managing Noncredible Performance* (pp. 86–103). Guilford Publications.

Martin, P. K., Schroeder, R. W., & Olsen, D. H. (2022). Performance validity in the dementia clinic: Specificity of validity tests when used individually and in aggregate across levels of cognitive impairment severity. *The Clinical Neuropsychologist*, *36*(1), 165–188.

Martin, P. K., Schroeder, R. W., Olsen, D. H., Maloy, H., Boettcher, A., Ernst, N., & Okut, H. (2020). A systematic review and meta-analysis of the Test of Memory Malingering in adults: Two decades of deception detection. *The Clinical Neuropsychologist*, *34*(1), 88–119.

Martin, P. K., Schroeder, R. W., Wyman-Chick, K. A., Hunter, B. P., Heinrichs, R. J., & Baade, L. E. (2018). Rates of abnormally low TOPF word reading scores in individuals failing versus passing performance validity testing. *Assessment*, *25*(5), 640–652.

McCaul, C., Boone, K. B., Ermshar, A., Cottingham, M., Victor, T. L., Ziegler, E., ... & Wright, M. (2018). Cross-validation of the Dot Counting Test in a large sample of credible and non-credible patients referred for neuropsychological testing. *The Clinical Neuropsychologist*, *32*(6), 1054–1067.

Mittenberg, W., Patton, C., Canyock, E. M., & Condit, D. C. (2002). Base rates of malingering and symptom exeggeration. *Journal of Clinical and Experimental Neuropsychology*, *24*(8), 1094–1102.

Olsen, D. H., Schroeder, R. W., & Martin, P. K. (2021). Cross-validation of the Invalid Forgetting Frequency Index (IFFI) from the test of memory malingering. *Archives of Clinical Neuropsychology*, *36*(3), 437–441.

Pearson. (2009). *Advanced Clinical Solutions for the WAIS-IV and WMS-IV: Clinical and Interpretive Manual*. Pearson.

Ploetz, D. M., Mazur-Mosiewicz, A., Kirkwood, M. W., Sherman, E. M., & Brooks, B. L. (2016). Performance on the Test of Memory Malingering in children with neurological conditions. *Child Neuropsychology*, *22*(2), 133–142.

Schroeder, R. W., Baade, L. E., Peck, C. P., VonDran, E. J., Brockman, C. J., Webster, B. K., & Heinrichs, R. J. (2012). Validation of MMPI-2-RF validity scales in criterion group neuropsychological samples. *The Clinical Neuropsychologist*, *26*(1), 129–146.

Schroeder, R. W., Clark, H. A., & Martin, P. K. (2022). Base rates of invalidity when patients undergoing routine clinical evaluations have social security disability as an external incentive. *The Clinical Neuropsychologist*, *36*(7), 1902–1914.

Schroeder, R. W., & Martin, P. K. (2021). Forced-choice performance validity tests. In K. B. Boone (Ed.), *Assessment of Feigned Cognitive Impairment: A Neuropsychological Perspective* (pp. 34–63). Guilford Publications.

Schroeder, R. W., & Martin, P. K. (2022). *Validity Assessment in Clinical Neuropsychological Practice: Evaluating and Managing Noncredible Performance*. Guilford Publications.

Soble, J. R., Santos, O. A., Bain, K. M., Kirton, J. W., Bailey, K. C., Critchfield, E. A., ... & González, D. A. (2018). The Dot Counting Test adds up: Validation and response pattern analysis in a mixed clinical veteran sample. *Journal of Clinical and Experimental Neuropsychology*, *40*(4), 317–325.

Social Security Administration (2017). Reviewing your disability. Ssa.gov/pubs/EN-05–10068.pdf

Sweet, J. J., Heilbronner, R. L., Morgan, J. E., Larrabee, G. J., Rohling, M. L., Boone, K. B., ... & Conference Participants. (2021). American Academy of Clinical Neuropsychology (AACN) 2021 consensus statement on validity assessment: Update of the 2009 AACN consensus conference statement on neuropsychological assessment of effort, response bias, and malingering. *The Clinical Neuropsychologist*, *35*(6), 1053–1106.

Van Egmond, J., & Kummeling, I. (2002). A blind spot for secondary gain affecting therapy outcomes. *European Psychiatry*, *17*(1), 46–54.

35 Navigating Unforeseen Waters

When a Case Initially Involving Clinical Care Later Returns in a Forensic Context

Kristen M. Klipfel and Jerry J. Sweet

As neuropsychologists, many of us spend our workdays assessing patients in a clinical setting to determine whether there is an underlying cognitive or psychological process that might explain certain behaviors with which the patient is presenting. The word "forensic" may seem ubiquitous in our specialty these days, but there are early career and even more experienced clinicians whose practices are entirely based on routine clinical referrals funded by healthcare insurance or public assistance programs. For such clinicians, the term is not thought of often, if at all, and it may spark unnecessary anxiety to answer a call from an attorney, respond to a subpoena requesting the timely release of documents, and/or appear for a deposition related to a past patient who had been assessed in a routine clinical context, not a forensic context. While some neuropsychologists appreciate and enjoy conducting forensic evaluations, as well as the, at times, challenging aspects of these cases, others find it unnerving to be caught off guard, suddenly thrown into a practice area in which they may have little or no prior experience. Other chapters in this book have addressed how to navigate a wide range of forensic issues as they come up, from incorporating performance and symptom validity tests as a basis for identifying credible presentations; to navigating the complexities of civil cases; to assessing various neurological and psychiatric conditions in the forensic realm; to working strictly with criminal defendants; to conducting administrative/quasi legal assessments, such as disability and Workers' Compensation evaluations; to understanding the ethical and professional issues surrounding forensic work.

The case selected for this chapter is one in which an individual was initially seen strictly for the purpose of providing brief psychoeducation related to postconcussive syndrome, following a mild head injury. Although treatment services were being paid for by a Workers' Compensation claim, her care was still being managed by the insurance carrier; lawyers were not involved, and there was no pending litigation. This is a treatment scenario, funded and managed by the Workers' Compensation insurance carrier nurse representative, with no attorney involvement. Given what is known about persistent postconcussive symptoms and the average duration needed to recover from a mild head injury, some of what the patient reported was highly suspicious. As a result, a determination was made to alert the nurse case manager to these observations and recommend the patient undergo an independent medical examination with another provider. The nurse case manager agreed; the individual was seen by a local neuropsychologist. Subsequent to that neuropsychologist's evaluation, now more officially as a Workers' Compensation claimant, the individual was referred back for a second opinion in the form of a second independent neuropsychological evaluation.

DOI: 10.4324/9781003005063-40

"The Case of Ms. S."

Background/Referral Question

Ms. S. is a 35-year-old right-handed single African American female with 12 years of special education. She had been employed as an unskilled laborer cleaning trailers for less than one week, prior to sustaining a work-related injury after hitting her head on a trailer door. Specifically, in September 2020, she sustained a scalp laceration without loss of consciousness and was transported by ambulance to the nearest emergency department. Ms. S. subsequently returned to work on at least five occasions, always unsuccessful in performing work duties for more than a few days at a time, due to reported exacerbation of physical and cognitive symptoms.

At the time of the evaluation in November 2021, almost 15 months after the injury at issue, Ms. S. had been followed by emergency medicine, occupational health, neurology, optometry, physical therapy, audiology, and psychology. She had undergone diagnostic testing, which included three head CTs all carried out within one week of the injury (noted only extracranial scalp edema and incidental mild sphenoid sinus disease; brain findings were normal), a brain MRI two months post injury (noted resolution of the scalp edema and showed incidental cysts/polyps in the sphenoid sinuses), and three CTs of the cervical spine (all normal). Ms. S.'s treating optometrist diagnosed Ms. S. with myopia in both eyes, severe, which he believed was causing blurry vision, one of Ms. S.'s physical complaints that she attributed to the September 2020 work accident. Her physical therapist opined that Ms. S.'s rehabilitation potential was excellent and that she had been making improvements during their sessions. An audiologist noted mild sensorineural hearing loss, unrelated to the work injury and for which she was recommended a hearing aid. Ms. S. was initially seen by the first author for three psychotherapy sessions in March 2021 to provide psychoeducation regarding postconcussion syndrome. Given the lack of symptom improvement approximately six months post injury, and the fact that symptoms varied from one session to the next, it was recommended that Ms. S. undergo an independent medical (neuropsychological) examination (more commonly termed to be an IME) to determine whether additional cognitive and/or psychiatric therapy was warranted.

In July 2021, Ms. S. underwent a Workers' Compensation IME by a local neuropsychologist. The neuropsychologist noted that Ms. S. had passed one stand-alone performance validity measure, as well as one embedded measure, and she had obtained a score that was only one point greater than the cut-off recommended for those with learning difficulties, which was attributed to poor math abilities and impaired cognitive processing. Overall, the neuropsychologist believed Ms. S. had completed testing validly. Objective psychological measures containing embedded symptom validity scales were not administered, given Ms. S.'s low reading level. Ms. S. was diagnosed with a Specific Learning Disability with impairment in reading comprehension (i.e., illiteracy); Posttraumatic Stress Disorder (PTSD); and Major Depressive Disorder (MDD), recurrent, severe, with psychotic features. The neuropsychologist opined that from a psychological standpoint, Ms. S. could return to work on a "limited basis" and with accommodations in place to allow for "mental health breaks and avoidance of PTSD triggers." The neuropsychologist also opined that it was unlikely Ms. S. could return to the position in which she was working prior to the injury; that Ms. S. would benefit from referrals to a psychiatrist for psychotropic medication management and a psychologist for psychotherapeutic management of behaviors and mood symptoms; and that Ms. S. would benefit from a highly structured psychological treatment, such as a partial hospitalization program or an intensive outpatient program, given the severity of her psychiatric symptoms, including auditory hallucinations.

In November 2021, approximately 14 months post work injury, Ms. S.'s treating neurologist discharged Ms. S. from his care, noting that she was at maximum medical improvement, despite a self-report of ongoing and worsening symptoms. Notably, she had failed all medication trials and had been unresponsive to typical headache management. It was the neurologist's opinion that the reported head pain was unrelated to the September 2020 work accident. Readers should also note that the injury was 'self-inflicted' (i.e., not intentionally, but in this instance meaning not due to an act of omission or commission by another worker), and it would not plausibly be expected to have caused any of the diagnosed conditions.

The Workers' Compensation insurance carrier nurse representative subsequently referred Ms. S. for a second opinion independent neuropsychological evaluation with the first author in order to address whether she required additional psychological/psychiatric treatment, including both inpatient and outpatient services, as she had only had three sessions of psychoeducation to date. Psychological/emotional symptom complaints included depression, anxiety, anger, paranoia/auditory hallucinations, and dissociating ("spacing out"). In addition, Ms. S. continued to complain of physical symptoms related to headache, tinnitus, and dizziness, and she expressed cognitive concerns related to poor memory. Over the course of three days in November 2021, a psychological and neurocognitive evaluation was conducted for the purpose of assessing Ms. S.'s current level of emotional and cognitive functioning, and to provide diagnostic impressions and treatment recommendations, if relevant, in order to facilitate care and administrative decisions regarding her return to work.

Behavioral Observations

Ms. S. arrived at the office on time for in-person testing, unaccompanied. Due to COVID-19 protocol, the interview and psychological testing took place remotely and were conducted on two separate days; she logged into these two additional Zoom meetings on time. She was casually dressed and well-groomed on all days, wore a mask as requested when in the office, and appeared her stated age. Eye contact was normal. Gait and posture were normal, and no gross or fine motor abnormalities were noted. She ambulated without difficulty. Ms. S. was always polite, and rapport was adequate. She was fully alert and oriented to person, place, and situation; with regard to time, she was off by one day of the week.

Speech was normal in rate, rhythm, prosody, and volume, and intensity increased as expected at points in conversation during which Ms. S. spoke of the September 2020 work accident and the cognitive, physical, and emotional impact the accident had on her. Ms. S.'s grammar was generally poor, with use of slang, and she used incomplete sentences at times, leaving out functor words. There were no paraphasic or neologistic errors noted in conversational speech or during testing. No signs of significant circumstantiality were observed. Tangentiality was present and particularly notable when discussing current symptom complaints, the frustration she felt toward various medical providers, how tired she was with the Workers' Compensation process, and her perception that people were not looking out for her best interests in general. Thought processes were generally linear and goal-directed, tightly and coherently linked. Speech content reflected no signs of magical or delusional thinking, and at no time did Ms. S. appear paranoid. No signs of thought blocking were noted during speech, and at no time did Ms. S. appear to be responding to internal or external stimuli, despite claiming that she had been experiencing auditory hallucinations since the work accident (see below under "Interview" for details regarding the quality of these hallucinations). Ms. S. denied current suicidal ideation, plan, or intent; suicidality was previously experienced as a child/adolescent.

Ms. S.'s ability to sustain attention was variable throughout the evaluation, requiring the examiner to either repeat a question or repeat the instructions of a test; when statements/task instructions were repeated, she evidenced no comprehension difficulties. Conversation built naturally on itself over the course of the interview, with proper reference to topics already discussed. She claimed her memory for personal history and its chronology was poor, which impacted the quality of information gathered during the interview (e.g., some questions were not answered, but other times she simply guessed the answers to questions). Ms. S.'s affect was generally irritable with congruent mood.

There were instances of distractibility noted during testing and the interview. Some signs of impulsivity were noted during testing (e.g., she needed to be reminded repeatedly to slow down on one task in which feedback was required before she could proceed). Her frustration tolerance on testing was generally poor (e.g., she raised her voice to the examiner when she was provided instructions to one test in particular). She talked aloud to herself during cognitive tasks, particularly during forced choice formats (e.g., she repeated the two options back and forth aloud several times before selecting an answer). She appeared to purposefully provide incorrect responses at times. For example, on a task during which she was required to match various cards to one of four stimulus cards, with the goal of correctly completing six categories with ten correctly placed cards in each, Ms. S. successfully completed five categories. On the sixth category, after correctly placing eight cards, she set the ninth card down too quickly for the examiner to see. When asked to point to the stack on which she had placed the last card, she received verbal feedback that she had placed it correctly. On the next/tenth card, she paused, and then placed it incorrectly in the wrong pile.

Finally, Ms. S. often complained about pain. She rated headache pain as an 8/10 at the start of the remote interview; approximately half-way through the interview she rated it as a 4/10.

Interview

In terms of developmental history, Ms. S. said she was placed in foster care from a young age, and thought her aunt adopted her as an adolescent. She described being emotionally/verbally abused, the victim of bullying, and a loner. Ms. S. thought she may have been struck and physically abused with a metal pipe as a child. She denied experiencing any sexual abuse.

Academically, she did not perform well in school and thought she had been placed in an alternative school from a young age, receiving special education for "everything." Ms. S. noted having a reading disorder, though she was uncertain whether this was ever formally diagnosed. She denied being held back in any grades, stating, "They just gave me my diploma."

With regard to significant behavioral or emotional difficulties as a child or adolescent, Ms. S. said she was arrested three times before the age of 18, stating,

> I got into fights, over 100. I broke someone's arm...I went to jail for breaking that boy's arm. I was maybe 13. I was placed on probation for maybe one year...I was part of a gang fight at school when I was maybe 16. I went to jail overnight and had to do

> 120 hours of community service. I was unsuccessfully discharged because I didn't do it, so then I had to do community service with inmates…I fought with my younger brothers and their friends. I broke someone's nose; it was an accident. I had to do 200 hours of community service and attend anger management class.

In addition to being arrested three times, Ms. S. said she was involved in numerous physical fights, ran away from foster homes on occasion, and stole money and other items from relatives and strangers.

Socially, Ms. S. denied ever being married, but she indicated that she was previously in a long-term partnership with a man for over a decade. After Ms. S. signed her house over to him, as she thought she was going to receive a long prison sentence, he broke up with her. She described a strained relationship with her mother and noted that her father was deceased. Ms. S. has a 14-year-old daughter who primarily resides with her father due to Ms. S.'s current legal status. She said she was currently spending most of her time with siblings and extended family members.

Medical history was significant for two head injuries as an adolescent/young adult. Ms. S. said she ran into a tree and "busted my head open" when she was 14. She denied a loss of consciousness or cognitive sequelae following this incident, and she thought she received 10–15 stitches. Ms. S. said she was hit in the head with a bat during a fight when she was 18, for which she received stitches; she denied having a concussion or experiencing a loss of consciousness following this event. Finally, she indicated that she was shot seven times when she was 25; most bullets were "in and out," one bullet "came out a couple of years ago," and another is still inside of her leg. Ms. S. was unaware of any underlying medical conditions and denied receiving adequate primary care. She was uncertain of the names of medications she was prescribed, though she noted one was a steroid, two were for headaches, and one was for "ringing" in her ears. By description, it appeared that medications were not being taken consistently, as prescribed.

Psychiatric history was significant for childhood onset depression, related to the strained relationship with her mother. As a child, Ms. S. said she engaged in self-injurious behavior, for which she was provided with mental health treatment, including both psychotherapy and psychopharmacological intervention. Ms. S. vaguely described having received disability benefits previously as a result of depression; she said she could not recall when this might have occurred. She also endorsed experiencing anxiety related to the work-related accident. Ms. S. denied receiving mental health treatment as an adult.

Family medical history was significant for high blood pressure (aunt), high cholesterol (uncle), and cancer and diabetes (throughout the family). She was unaware of any family psychiatric history. Additionally, she was unaware of a family history of developmental or learning disabilities.

Substance use consisted of daily tobacco use, approximately one pack of cigarettes per day. Ms. S. also reported using marijuana "every now and then," which helped with pain management. She denied using any other illicit drugs in her lifetime, though a review of records indicated she tested positive in the emergency department for methamphetamine and cocaine. When questioned about the records, Ms. S. alleged that she had been "roofied" (i.e., her drink was spiked with drugs), though she discovered what had happened before she was sexually assaulted. Records also indicated that Ms. S. had been arrested on at least four occasions as an adult, all drug-related offenses for possession and manufacturing of a controlled substance, and all resulting in years of incarceration, half-way houses, and/or probation.

Additional antisocial behavior constituted getting into frequent fights, including fights with the police and others while incarcerated, contributing to a loss of "good time" ("I knocked a couple people out. If I get too mad, I can't stop. If I stomped anyone out, I don't remember. I've got more than rage…"). She also admitted to gang involvement as an adolescent and associate status at the time of the interview ("I don't have to act no more"). Related to her most recent drug charge, she reported having been on probation since the beginning of 2021.

Financially, Ms. S. had been residing with extended family members due to being currently on probation for a state drug charge. She said she had stopped receiving Workers' Compensation benefits, as the insurance company "blew me off." She also denied currently receiving state or federal public assistance (e.g., food stamps, cash assistance).

Ms. S. described a vocational history of temporary and inconsistent work as an unskilled laborer. At the time of the interview, she was not working. Most of her income over the years appeared to have been from involvement in criminal activities.

Symptom complaints were numerous and varied. In terms of cognition, Ms. S. complained of *memory difficulties* since the September 2020 work injury ("I used to be able to memorize. I can't do that no more. You need to show me two or three times…Now that this has happened, I barely remember things I used to. I'm not sure I can remember what they show me [at work]"). Emotional complaints consisted of *depression* ("It has become worse since I had the accident. I have been staying in the house more, not socializing, being embarrassed"); *anxiety* ("It skyrocketed after the injury…I'm not talking to people, going on dates. I have to make up a cool lie because of my scar. I'm always worried about how I look. I worry about what's going to happen to me down the line"); symptoms of *posttraumatic stress* following the work injury ("Anything constantly over my head is nerve-wracking. Anything that can come down or move…I have dreams…I don't remember what happened. I don't know the content. It's like déjà vu. I'm talking in my sleep. I can't describe a dream or nightmare. I'm talking in my sleep, but don't remember. I have been woken up because of screaming"); *anger* ("The accident causes anger…Why did this have to happen to me? What the fuck? Everyone is trying to use me"); *dissociating/"spacing out"* ("I space out a lot. I don't know when I started spacing out, not sure if before or after my accident. It happens sometimes in the middle of conversations"); and *paranoia/auditory hallucinations* ("My paranoia has been up there for no reason…I feel like somebody trying to hurt me. I feel like somebody telling me I need to hurt someone…I hear voices when I'm mad or upset or feel threatened. The voice telling me 'He trying to use you.' The voice has caused me to almost get into a fight"). When asked if the voice was speaking to her in that exact moment, Ms. S. said, "It keeps saying, 'We.' It hasn't said anything about you…I think it's a demon. If I feel fine, it doesn't come up").

With regard to physical complaints, Ms. S. noted frequent *headaches* ("After the accident, I got them every day. Most last an hour or two, some 30 minutes…I've been taking meds more frequently than I should because my head hurt…It was seven months where I was getting headaches daily. I can be comfortable one minute—I can be sitting here with a minor headache—and then want to cry. It will go from a three to a ten. There are days when I don't have headaches"). When asked to clarify whether there are days she is headache-free, she noted, "I always have a headache, but some are more mild than others… There is never a time when I don't have them." She also reported having other *pain* ("I'm having top to lower back pain since the injury…I can walk maybe a half block without pain, and then I have to sit. I never had back pain before [the injury]. My back pain goes from a two to a nine…When it starts hurting, I have back pain that just shuts me down");

dizziness ("Sometimes, it's related to headaches and ears ringing. The room be spinning sometimes. If I have a headache that is an eight or a nine, I get dizzy, and the room spins, and I feel like I want to sit down"); and *tinnitus* ("I never had ringing in my ears before the accident. I be talking to somebody, and their voice fades away, and the ringing gets louder and louder. I get to the point where I can't hear people talking to me. Then it goes down and there's a little ringing. Since the accident happened, there has been constant ringing. It's always there").

Record Review

According to emergency medicine records, Ms. S. arrived at the hospital via ambulance after she hit her head on a trailer door, causing a 15-cm laceration to the top of her head. She denied having lost consciousness, and the Glasgow Coma Scale (GCS) score was a 15/15. Head and cervical spine CTs were both unremarkable. With the exception of the scalp laceration, the physical examination and review of systems were otherwise normal. The laceration was treated with 35 staples and a pressure dressing. She was discharged the same day in a stable condition and provided with a prescription for an antibiotic. Two days later, she presented to the emergency department via ambulance with complaints of increased dizziness, lightheadedness, neck pain, and headache. Neurologically, there were no changes, and CTs of the head and cervical spine remained unremarkable. The clinical impression was dehydration, and she was discharged the same day in a stable condition. Four days later, she again reported to the emergency department with complaints of pain in her eyes, face, and neck, along with experiencing dizzy spells. Again, repeat CTs of the head and cervical spine were unremarkable. Ms. S. was diagnosed with postconcussion syndrome and removed from work for one week. She was prescribed a medication for pain management. Two days later, she was brought to the emergency department via ambulance after falling. Complaints included vision loss/blurry vision, photophobia, nausea, vomiting, headache, dizziness, and stress. The GCS score was a 15/15. Ms. S. was again instructed to remain off work for one week, followed by returning to work full time, if tolerated. She was prescribed a different medication for pain management.

Approximately two weeks after the incident, Ms. S. met with occupational health and alleged that she "passed out" for less than 30 seconds on the day of the accident. She reported changes in vision, nausea and vomiting, muscle weakness in the right leg, dizziness, frequent and severe headaches, and depression. She was diagnosed with a concussion with loss of consciousness, postconcussive syndrome, unspecified nystagmus, and unspecified headache. Ms. S. was referred to neurology and permitted to only perform clerical work in the interim. One week later, she again presented to occupational health, but this time reporting an improvement in duration and frequency of headaches, as well as resolution of dizziness. She was permitted to return to full duty with restrictions (i.e., no work or driving where dizziness would compromise safety, and no climbing stairs or ladders).

Approximately two months post injury, Ms. S. presented to the emergency department with complaints of chronic headaches and photophobia. Brain MRI was unremarkable and showed complete resolution of the scalp hematoma. She was diagnosed with other headache syndrome, discharged the same day in a stable condition, and instructed to take Tylenol and Ibuprofen, as needed, for pain management. She was permitted to return to work the following day, without restrictions. Two weeks later, she presented to the emergency department again with complaints of ongoing headache and tinnitus. She was diagnosed with chronic headache, unspecified and bilateral tinnitus.

In addition to being followed clinically by emergency medicine and occupational health, Ms. S. had been followed by neurology, beginning one month post injury. During the first encounter, she complained of daily headaches, nausea, vomiting, dizziness, photophobia, and phonophobia. Reviews of systems and the physical examination were both normal. Based on ongoing complaints, the neurologist diagnosed her with postconcussive syndrome; prescribed medication, as needed, for headaches; referred her to psychology and optometry; and instructed her to remain off work for four weeks until the next appointment. At the one-month follow-up appointment, Ms. S. reported an improvement in symptoms. She was released to full duty, without restrictions, and instructed to follow-up in two-to-three months. Approximately two weeks later, Ms. S. returned to neurology, complaining of symptom exacerbation. She was prescribed a new medication for headaches and was instructed to remain off work. Two weeks later, Ms. S. was again seen by neurology, and reported the same symptoms, in addition to ringing in her ears and double vision. A new trial of medication was initiated. She was referred to an outpatient cognitive rehabilitation program, as well as an ear, nose, and throat specialist, and she was instructed to remain off work. One month later, Ms. S. followed-up with neurology, and despite reporting an improvement in headaches, she said she continued to experience them daily. She noted an improvement in double vision, and said cognitive rehabilitation was helpful. She was again instructed to take all medications as prescribed and remain off work until the conclusion of cognitive rehabilitation and an evaluation from psychiatry.

Approximately four months passed before Ms. S. met with a new neurologist. During the first encounter, Ms. S. alleged she did not lose consciousness on the day of the accident, though she lost consciousness the following day. Cognitive and physical complaints included headaches, head pain, tinnitus, and lower back pain. The neurologist prescribed a new medication, as needed, for headaches; decreased the other medications she had been prescribed previously; and recommended physical therapy. During the three-month follow-up, the neurologist noted Ms. S. continued to experience headaches and tinnitus and had failed numerous medication trials. Medications were adjusted accordingly, and she was released to full duty status. Two months later, Ms. S. reported an improvement in symptoms, though she admitted she had been noncompliant with medications and had not yet returned to work. The neurologist adjusted Ms. S.'s medications and continued to opine that she remained cleared for full duty. One month later—during Ms. S.'s final office visit—she alleged no improvement in headaches. She was subsequently discharged from the neurologist's care, as she had been unresponsive to typical headache management, and it was the neurologist's opinion that the reported head pain was not the result of the work injury; Ms. S. was at maximum medical improvement.

Neuropsychological Test Results

Date of Exam	*July 2021*	*November 2021*
Performance Validity Tests		
TOMM[1] Trial 1	45/50	29/50
TOMM Trial 2	48/50	34/50
TOMM Retention	—	30/50
VSVT[2] Easy Items	—	10/24
VSVT Hard Items	—	8/24

(*Continued*)

Date of Exam	*July 2021*	*November 2021*
Word Choice Test	—	30/50 (£2%ile)
Rey 15-Item Test	—	9 items, 3 rows
CVLT-II[3] Forced Choice	—	10/16 ([illegible]%ile)
RDS/RDS-R[4]	7/12	5/7
Cognitive Screeners/Orientation		
Montreal Cognitive Assessment	—	17/30
RBANS[5]	—	
Immediate Memory		SS = 57
Visuospatial/Constructional		SS = 60
Language		SS = 47
Attention		SS = 64
Delayed Memory		SS = 40
Total Score		SS = 48
WMS-III[6]	—	
Information and Orientation		3rd%ile
Mental Control	—	SS = 4
Premorbid Functioning		
Test of Premorbid Functioning	—	SS = 47
Intellectual Functioning		
WAIS-IV[7]		
Full Scale IQ	SS = 65	SS = 59
General Ability Index	SS = 69	SS = 64
Verbal Comprehension Index	SS = 72	SS = 63
Vocabulary	SS = 5	SS = 5
Similarities	SS = 5	SS = 1
Information	SS = 5	SS = 5
Perceptual Reasoning Index	SS = 71	SS = 71
Block Design	SS = 4	SS = 4
Matrix Reasoning	SS = 4	SS = 5
Visual Puzzles	SS = 7	SS = 6
Working Memory Index	SS = 83	SS = 63
Digit Span	SS = 7	SS = 2[8]
Digit Span Forward	SS = 6	SS = 7
Digit Span Backward	SS = 7	SS = 2
Digit Span Sequencing	SS = 9	SS = 3
Arithmetic	SS = 4	SS = 5
Letter-Number Sequencing	SS = 7	SS = 6
Processing Speed Index	SS = 56	SS = 59
Coding	SS = 1	SS = 2, 3 errors
Symbol Search	SS = 3	SS = 3, 5 errors
Academic Achievement		
WRAT-4[9] Word Reading	Grade Equivalent: 1.7	Grade Equivalent: 1.8
Learning and Memory	**WMS-IV[10]**	**RBANS**

(*Continued*)

Date of Exam	*July 2021*	*November 2021*
Stories	Logical Memory I: SS = 3	Story Memory: SS = 1
	Logical Memory II: SS = 3	Story Recall: SS = 1
	LM Recognition: 19 ($3–9^{\text{cum}\%}$)	—
Designs	Visual Reproduction I: SS = 3	—
	Visual Reproduction II: SS = 7	Figure Recall: SS = 2
	VR Recognition: 2 ($<2^{\text{cum}\%}$)	—
	VR Copy: 39 ($3–9^{\text{cum}\%}$)	Figure Copy: SS = 1
List Learning	**HVLT-R[11]**	**CVLT-II**
Total Recall	Trials 1–3: Raw = 19, T = 27	Trials 1–5: Raw = 28, T = 28
Long Delay Free Recall	Raw: 4/12, T = <20	Raw: 4/16, z = -2.5
Long Delay Cued Recall	—	Raw: 4/16, z = -2.5
Total Recognition Hits	9/12	Raw: 11/16, z = -3.0
Total Recognition False Positives	3/12	Raw: 10/16, z = 2.5
Total Recognition Discrimination	Raw = 6, T = <20	Raw = 1, z = -2.5
Confrontation Naming	**Boston Naming Test**	**RBANS Picture Naming**
	T = 32	£2%ile
Verbal Fluency	**DKEFS[12] Verbal Fluency**	**COWAT[13]**
Phonemic Fluency	SS = 5	Letters CFL: z = -1.1
Semantic Fluency	SS = 8	Vegetables: z = -1.0; RBANS: SS = 1
<u>Attention/Concentration</u>		
Stroop Color-Word Test		
Stroop Word	—	T = 23
Stroop Color	—	T < 20
Stroop Color-Word	—	T = 26
Stroop Interference	—	T = 51
<u>Executive Functioning</u>		
Trailmaking Test		
Part A	T = 41	T = 43, 0 errors
Part B	T = 46	T = 52, 1 error
WCST[14]		
Categories Completed	3/6 (2–5%ile)	5/6 (11–16%ile)
Total Errors	T = 33	T = 39
Perseverative Responses	T = 51	T = 39
Perseverative Errors	T = 50	T = 41
Nonperseverative Errors	T = 25	T = 37
% Conceptual Level Response	T = 32	T = 41
Trials to 1st Category	Raw = 16 (6–10%ile)	Raw = 14 (6–10%ile)
Failure to Maintain Set	Raw = 1 (>16%ile)	Raw = 2 (11–16%ile)
Learning to Learn	Raw = -14.58 (2–5%ile)	Raw = 1.43 (>16%ile)
<u>Motor Functioning</u>		
Grooved Pegboard		
Dominant hand	T = 21	T = 25, 2 drops
Nondominant hand	T = 30	T = 34, 2 drops

[1] TOMM = Test of Memory Malingering;[2] VSVT = Victoria Symptom Validity Test;[3] CVLT-II = California Verbal Learning Test, second edition;[4] RDS/RDS-R = Reliable Digit Span/Revised Reliable Digit Span;[5] RBANS = Repeatable Battery for the Assessment of Neuropsychological Status;[6] WMS-III = Wechsler Memory Scale, 3rd edition;[7] WAIS-IV = Wechsler Adult Intelligence Scale, 4th edition;[8] On the Digit Span subtest from the RBANS, Ms. S. achieved a scaled score of 8;[9] WRAT-4 = Wide Range Achievement Test, 4th edition;[10] WMS-IV = Wechsler Memory Scale-Fourth Edition (WMS-IV);[11] HVLT-R = Hopkins Verbal Learning Test-Revised;[12] DKEFS = Delis-Kaplan Executive Function System;[13] COWAT = Controlled Oral Word Association Test;[14] WCST = Wisconsin Card Sorting Test.

Summary and Interpretation of Neuropsychological Test Results

Given the noncredible findings during the November 2021 evaluation, including failed performance validity tests (PVTs), chance-range PVT performances, and qualitatively atypical performances, and the absence of a history of neurologic insult (or other factors such as a medication regimen that would explain such poor performances), all cognitive test data were considered invalid. A conservative "least as" approach of interpretation is warranted when suboptimal effort/invalid findings exist; that is, while impaired performances cannot be validly interpreted, *unimpaired* performances can reasonably be interpreted as *the least of* Ms. S.'s capabilities in that respective cognitive domain. From that standpoint, she produced some normal/unimpaired scores in the cognitive domains of attention/concentration, language, visuospatial/visuoconstructional functioning, and executive functioning.

Psychological Test Results

Objective Psychological Inventories[1] *(administered November 2021)*		*Self-Report Questionnaires*
MMPI-2[2]	**PAI**[3]	**DASS**[4] (administered July 2021)
		Depression (severe)
Validity Scales	**Validity Scales**	Anxiety (extremely severe)
VRIN: raw = 2, T = 38	ICN: T = 49	Stress (extremely severe)
F, F_B, F_P: Ts = 120	INF: T = 55	
FBS: raw = 24, T = 82	PIM: T = 36	
L: T = 43	NIM: T = 92	
K and S: Ts = 30	Malingering Index: T = 71	
		BDI-II[5]**/BAI**[6]
		(both administered November 2021)
		BDI-II: raw = 47, severe
		BAI: raw = 49, severe

[1] No objective psychological inventories were administered in July 2021;[2] MMPI-2 = Minnesota Multiphasic Personality Inventory, second edition;[3] PAI = Personality Assessment Inventory;[4] DASS = Depression Anxiety Stress Scale;[5] BDI-II = Beck Depression Inventory, second edition;[6] BAI = Beck Anxiety Inventory.

Summary and Interpretation of Psychological Test Results

Ms. S. was administered the MMPI-2 and PAI on audiotape in order to reduce the reading comprehension requirement. Validity scales indicated that she responded consistently to items on both, but with significant exaggeration or fabrication of psychiatric symptomatology (MMPI-2 F: T = 120, F_B: T = 120, Fp: T = 120; PAI NIM: T = 92, PAI Malingering Index: T = 71). She elevated every clinical scale on the MMPI-2 except Masculinity-Femininity, with T-scores ranging from 67 to 112, the majority in the 80–90s range, and two over 100. On the PAI, she elevated 7 of the 11 clinical scales, with T-scores ranging from 78 to 94. Clinical scales on both the MMPI-2 and PAI were invalid for interpretation as a result of the validity findings. Given that the MMPI-2 and PAI were invalid for interpretation due to extreme over-reporting/exaggeration of psychiatric symptomatology, the BDI-II and BAI were also highly unlikely to be accurate reflections of Ms. S.'s level of depression and anxiety. In fact, recent research has examined whether the BDI-II may serve as an embedded validity indicator in forensic neuropsychological evaluations. Researchers demonstrated that individuals who invalidate self-report symptom validity tests obtained significantly higher BDI-II scores compared with those who were able to pass these same tests. They also found that a cut score of 38 on the BDI-II reached a specificity level of 0.90 and a sensitivity level of 0.58 (Fuermaier et al., 2025).

Summary and Conclusions

Malingering of cognitive and psychological impairment was reasonably concluded as the explanation for Ms. S.'s cognitive and psychological test results, cognitive and emotional complaints, and clinical presentation. In Ms. S.'s case, her motivation (i.e., the external incentive) to perform poorly appeared driven by the possibility that should she be found to have cognitive deficits and/or psychological impairment stemming from the work injury, she would likely receive financial compensation. She failed numerous PVTs during the cognitive examination, and she obtained scores falling substantially below those of individuals with bona fide severe traumatic brain injuries and dementia, among numerous other neurocognitive disorders, but consistent with those involved in litigation, seeking compensable benefits, or feigning cognitive impairment. During the July 2021 IME, the neuropsychologist noted that Ms. S. performed validly on two PVTs, though on a third—the Dot Counting Test—obtained a score of "one point greater than the cut-off recommended for those with learning difficulties," which the neuropsychologist opined was a passing performance.

Additional support for a diagnosis of malingering included numerous test performances being quantitatively and qualitatively atypical, and failing to converge in normal and expected ways for any neurocognitive disorder, developmental or acquired. These included inconsistent performances across tasks measuring the same skill (e.g., average performance on RBANS digit span forward vs. mildly impaired performance on WAIS-IV digit span forward; low average performance on COWAT semantic verbal fluency vs. severely impaired performance on RBANS semantic verbal fluency) and performing worse on a recognition vs. declarative memory trial. Ms. S. also failed/performed poorly on tests that she was previously able to pass/perform adequately during the July 2021 IME. For example, on the TOMM, she obtained passing scores of 45 and 48 on Trials 1 and 2, respectively, though she failed both trials during the November 2021 IME (29 and 34, respectively, the former falls in the chance-range). She also performed adequately on an embedded PVT—the RDS/RDS-R—during the July 2021 examination (scores of 7 and 12, respectively, both of which are passing), though failed both during the November 2021 evaluation (scores of 5 and 7, respectively). It was not considered credible that Ms. S. was able to pass both PVTs during the July 2021 examination, but could not do so again in November 2021. She performed in the low average range on the Working Memory Index of the WAIS-IV in July 2021, but her score fell in the extremely low range during the November 2021 evaluation. Finally, on a nonverbal memory test administered in July 2021, she obtained a low average score, though obtained a moderate/severely impaired score on a similar task during the November 2021 evaluation.

In addition to failing numerous PVTs and performing inconsistently on testing over time, Ms. S.'s symptom complaints across time, including cognitive, physical, and emotional, were inconsistent and highly atypical of an individual recovering from a mild traumatic brain injury (mTBI). For example, on the day of the injury, she reported no loss of consciousness, her GCS score was a 15, and her neurological exam was normal in the emergency department. Two days later, Ms. S. began endorsing new symptoms that were not present on the day of the injury. She continued to follow-up with emergency medicine and neurology in the weeks and months to come, providing inconsistent reports across time (e.g., that she did in fact lose consciousness on the day of the injury; headaches were improving one visit and then worsening the next) and never seemed to improve, despite numerous medical interventions. Her last treating neurologist discharged her from care, opining that she had failed numerous medication trials, head pain symptoms were not the result of the September 2020 injury, and she was at maximum medical improvement.

Importantly, the literature has consistently documented that most individuals who have sustained an mTBI typically experience complete or near complete recovery by several days to no more than three months post injury (Schretlen & Shapiro, 2003; Rohling et al., 2011). In contrast, a portion of individuals with mTBI who present to clinics in the chronic phase for medical or neuropsychological evaluation, or who are in litigation (i.e., individuals reporting ongoing symptoms and problems) perform more poorly on neuropsychological measures—without any specific pattern—and perform worse on neuropsychological testing across time (Belanger et al., 2005). Finally, while some individuals with mTBI report symptoms months and even years following a concussion, the literature suggests that symptoms are less likely to be related to the mTBI as time passes (Meares et al., 2011; Ponsford et al., 2012). As suggested by Silver and Kay (2013), if symptoms persist for more than a few months, increase over time, spread into multiple domains, or are associated with global cognitive impairment, postconcussion syndrome can be ruled out, and other factors are likely to account for the dysfunction. Similarly, Levy et al. (2024) found that at approximately eight weeks post mTBI, subjective cognitive symptoms were likely attributed to outside factors not related to objective cognition.

Notwithstanding evidence of malingering during cognitive testing, Ms. S. demonstrated some normal range scores in four cognitive domains, including attention/concentration, language, visuospatial/visuoconstructional, and executive functioning abilities. Given the invalid findings, these results were likely still an underestimate of optimal capacities, perhaps significantly so (Martinez et al., 2021).

Despite Ms. S.'s ongoing complaints of significant memory difficulties, as well as her profoundly impaired score on the Montreal Cognitive Assessment, no signs of such difficulties were noted during the clinical interview or interactions with the examiner while undergoing testing. Conversation built naturally on itself, no signs of forgetfulness were noted at any point, and Ms. S. had no difficulty understanding or following test instructions, despite asking them to be repeated on occasion. While it is possible that Ms. S. may have met criteria for an intellectual disability, given her approach to the examination (e.g., being an unreliable historian, feigning cognitive and psychological symptom complaints, being evasive in answering historical questions during the interview), a diagnosis could not be made, as cognitive test data were invalid. The history that she provided regarding adaptive functioning skills was not indicative of an individual who required help performing tasks in her daily life (e.g., she could grocery shop and prepare basic meals, she was able to navigate public transportation in a major metropolitan city, she was able to navigate setting up financial benefits like public assistance).

With regard to emotional complaints, Ms. S. complained of persistent anxiety, depression, anger, paranoia/auditory hallucinations, dissociating at times (e.g., "spacing out"), and she described those experiences as being specifically related to the September 2020 work accident. Based on a comprehensive clinical interview, a review of records, and psychological test findings, no psychiatric diagnoses were rendered, as Ms. S. proved to be an unreliable historian (e.g., providing inconsistent descriptions of symptom complaints across providers, providing some inconsistent responses regarding her history), and demonstrated significant exaggeration/fabrication on objective psychological testing. Given the various validity issues described above, it did not seem reasonable to agree with the conclusions drawn by the neuropsychologist who conducted the July 2021 examination, which included diagnoses of PTSD and MDD, recurrent, severe, with psychotic features (notably, no objective psychological inventories were administered during that evaluation). Because Ms. S.'s report was unreliable, it was impossible to say what the nature, breadth, and severity of her psychiatric symptoms were at the time of the November 2021 evaluation, should they be present.

Moreover, the degree of symptomatology, especially psychotic features and PTSD, seemed completely unexpected after a superficial head injury that did not involve altered consciousness. Ms. S.'s history was absent regarding symptoms of psychosis, and her description of auditory hallucinations was highly questionable, related primarily to hearing a voice telling her to hurt others, which was consistent with numerous instances of antisocial behavior in the past. She also said the voice would talk to her when she was mad, upset, or felt threatened, and she described it as a "demon," an atypical description of genuine auditory hallucinations. With regard to the onset of PTSD, it seemed suspect that she would develop PTSD from such a minor head injury—and arguably, she would not even meet Criterion A of PTSD—when her background was significant for numerous events that appeared more aligned with the development of a trauma- and stressor-related disorder. Had genuine psychological symptoms existed, including symptoms of posttraumatic stress and/or psychotic symptoms, given her history, these likely would have pre-dated the September 2020 work injury, and could have been related to a chaotic childhood (e.g., unstable early life care, physical and emotional abuse) inconsistent employment, chronic substance use, and/or living a life of crime (e.g., gang involvement, frequent incarcerations, frequent fights).

In conclusion, Ms. S. met criteria for malingering, according to those outlined by Slick et al. (1999) for malingered neurocognitive dysfunction. There was a clear identifiable external incentive, including a potential financial settlement; an invalid neurocognitive presentation, including inconsistencies pertaining to cognitive deficits, numerous invalid scores on performance validity testing, and psychometric evidence of exaggerated cognitive symptoms; an invalid psychiatric presentation, including inconsistencies pertaining to psychological symptoms and psychometric evidence of exaggerated psychological symptoms on symptom validity tests; marked discrepancies between obtained test data/symptom reports and the natural history/pathogenesis of mTBI and information contained in the record; and behaviors/symptoms that could not fully be accounted for by another developmental (e.g., intellectual disability), medical, or psychiatric condition.

Research Outcomes Related to External Incentives, Low IQ, Cognitive Impairment, and Failed PVTs

As documented in the literature—and has been demonstrated with this case—there is an increased risk of failure on PVTs when external incentives are present (Critchfield et al., 2019). Chafetz et al. (2011) showed that motivation (or lack thereof) can impact whether individuals fail PVTs at disproportional rates, depending on the incentive. For example, they found that low IQ claimants seeking compensation for an inability to work, failed PVTs at higher rates compared with low IQ individuals seeking employment or those seeking reunification with their children.

Related specifically to low IQ, Martin et al. (2018) provided evidence to support the notion that the Test of Premorbid Functioning (TOPF) word reading based estimates of premorbid functioning should not be interpreted when individuals invalidate cognitive testing.

As confidence for performance invalidity increases, underperformance on TOPF word reading decreases, regardless of the effects of education. Other researchers have found that in addition to education, other demographic factors, including age, sex, ethnoracial identity, and premorbid IQ, accounted for little variance in individual PVT performance, and these variables did not significantly predict validity classification (Soble et al., 2022). Green and Flaro (2015) found that a low IQ, defined as ≤ 70, cannot sufficiently explain failure on PVTs.

Related to cognitive impairment more generally, whether developmental or acquired, numerous researchers have provided support that PVTs can be administered to those with cognitive impairment. Essentially, the conclusion has been that a high ratio of failure is likely related to noncredible performance rather than genuine cognitive impairment (Critchfield et al., 2019; Davis & Millis, 2014; Larrabee, 2014, 2003; Meyers et al., 2011; Meyers & Volbrecht, 2003). All of these findings suggest that PVT failure raises serious validity issues within the cognitive profile more generally, such that interpretation of the profile is not warranted, or in the very least should be done so with caution. When validity issues do arise, it may be best to discuss an individual's intact performances, highlighting the fact that those performances are likely an underestimation of genuine abilities.

With regard to symptom complaints, research has demonstrated that those feigning symptoms report significantly higher symptom intensities than individuals with genuine symptom complaints. Examinees deemed to be feigning also endorse more symptoms overall, including both genuine and implausible symptoms, particularly those related to pain (Boskovic et al., 2021). Henry et al. (2018) examined the relationship of psychological variables on the Minnesota Multiphasic Personality Inventory-2 Restructured Format (MMPI-2-RF) to cognitive PVT results. They found that cogniphobia, the perception that cognitive effort will exacerbate neurological symptoms, was related to PVT failure, and occurred more frequently at elevated levels in a forensic sample. They also found that symptom identity, the psychological construct that the perception of current symptoms is the result of illness or injury, was a significant predictor of PVT failure.

Final Thoughts

As noted in the introduction to this chapter, neuropsychologists may find that after a routine clinical interaction, a case may evolve into a forensic matter, which most often occurs well after the event at issue is in litigation. Neuropsychologists are encouraged to learn about the numerous perspectives of this change from clinical to forensic context, for which there are available resources (see Sweet & Klipfel, 2021). The National Academy of Neuropsychology and American Academy of Clinical Neuropsychology published policy papers encouraging clinicians to be mindful of how effort and exaggeration can influence neuropsychological test data, particularly in forensic settings where symptom fabrication is higher than in clinical settings (Bush et al., 2005; Sweet et al., 2021). Importantly, performance/symptom validity testing should not be the only criterion used to determine whether an individual is malingering (Iverson, 2006). Rather, multiple sources of information must be considered, including utilizing more than one performance/symptom validity test, qualitative data points regarding an examinee's performance, and incongruities between impairments and expected performance (Bush et al., 2005; Larrabee, 2005). As has been demonstrated and discussed in the case of Ms. S., she failed all performance and symptom validity tests; qualitatively, her subjective symptom complaints were not aligned with observations made about her current level of functioning; and the pervasive deficits noted on cognitive testing simply contradicted what is known about the typical recovery from an uncomplicated mild head injury.

Available online resources/e-links/relevant publication resources

Anxiety & Depression Association of America, resources on Posttraumatic Stress Disorder: https://adaa.org/understanding-anxiety/posttraumatic-stress-disorder-ptsd/resources

Bush, S. S., Ruff, R. M., Tröster, A. I., Barth, J. T., Koffler, S. P., Pliskin, N. H., Reynolds, C. R., & Silver, C. H. (2005). Symptom validity assessment: Practice issues and medical necessity NAN policy & planning committee. *Archives of Clinical Neuropsychology*, *20*(4), 419–426.

Concussion Legacy Foundation, resources on Post-Concussion Syndrome: https://concussionfoundation.org/PCS-resources/support

Schroeder, R. W., & Martin, P. K. (Eds.). (2021). *Validity assessment in clinical neuropsychological practice: Evaluating and managing noncredible performance*. Guilford Publications.

Sweet, J. J., Heilbronner, R. L., Morgan, J. E., Larrabee, G. J., Rohling, M. L., Boone, K. B., Kirkwood, M. W., Schroeder, R. W., Suhr, J. A., & Conference Participants. (2021). American Academy of Clinical Neuropsychology (AACN) 2021 consensus statement on validity assessment: Update of the 2009 AACN consensus conference statement on neuropsychological assessment of effort, response bias, and malingering. *The Clinical Neuropsychologist*, *35*(6), 1053–1106.

References

Belanger, H. G., Curtiss, G., Demery, J. A., Lebowitz, B. K., & Vanderploeg, R. D. (2005). Factors moderating neuropsychological outcomes following mild traumatic brain injury: A meta-analysis. *Journal of the International Neuropsychological Society*, *11*(3), 215–227.

Boskovic, I., Zwaan, L., Baillie, V., & Merckelbach, H. (2021). Consistency does not aid detection of feigned symptoms, overreporting does: Two explorative studies on symptom stability among truth tellers and feigners. *Applied Neuropsychology: Adult*, *29*(6), 1458–1466.

Bush, S. S., Ruff, R. M., Tröster, A. I., Barth, J. T., Koffler, S. P., Pliskin, N. H., Reynolds, C. R., & Silver, C. H. (2005). Symptom validity assessment: Practice issues and medical necessity NAN policy & planning committee. *Archives of Clinical Neuropsychology*, *20*(4), 419–426.

Chafetz, M. D., Prentkowski, E., & Rao, A. (2011). To work or not to work: Motivation (not low IQ) determines symptom validity test findings. *Archives of Clinical Neuropsychology*, *26*(4), 306–313.

Critchfield, E., Soble, J. R., Marceaux, J. C., Bain, K. M., Chase Bailey, K., Webber, T. A., Alverson, A., Messerly, J., Andrés González, D., & O'Rourke, J. J. (2019). Cognitive impairment does not cause invalid performance: Analyzing performance patterns among cognitively unimpaired, impaired, and noncredible participants across six performance validity tests. *The Clinical Neuropsychologist*, *33*(6), 1083–1101.

Davis, J. J., & Millis, S. R. (2014). Examination of performance validity test failure in relation to number of tests administered. *The Clinical Neuropsychologist*, *28*(2), 199–214.

Fuermaier, A. B., Dandachi-Fitzgerald, B., & Lehrner, J. (2025). Validity assessment of early retirement claimants: Symptom overreporting on the Beck Depression Inventory–II. *Applied Neuropsychology: Adult*, *32*(3), 712–718.

Green, P., & Flaro, L. (2015). Results from three performance validity tests (PVTs) in adults with intellectual deficits. *Applied Neuropsychology: Adult*, *22*(4), 293–303.

Henry, G. K., Heilbronner, R. L., Suhr, J., Gornbein, J., Wagner, E., & Drane, D. L. (2018). Illness perceptions predict cognitive performance validity. *Journal of the International Neuropsychological Society*, *24*(7), 735–745.

Larrabee, G. J. (2003). Detection of malingering using atypical performance patterns on standard neuropsychological tests. *The Clinical Neuropsychologist*, *17*(3), 410–425.

Iverson, G. (2006). Ethical issues associated with the assessment of exaggeration, poor effort, and malingering. *Applied Neuropsychology*, *13*, 77–90.

Larrabee, G. (2005). Mild traumatic brain injury. In G. Larrabee (Ed.) *Forensic neuropsychology: A scientific approach* (pp. 209–236). New York: Oxford University Press.

Larrabee, G. J. (2003). Detection of malingering using atypical performance patterns on standard neuropsychological tests. *The Clinical Neuropsychologist*, *17*(3), 410–425.

Larrabee, G. J. (2014). False-positive rates associated with the use of multiple performance and symptom validity tests. *Archives of Clinical Neuropsychology*, *29*(4), 364–373.

Levy, A. M., Saling, M. M., & Anderson, J. F. (2024). Cognitive symptoms are not associated with cognitive performance in post-acute mTBI. *Archives of Clinical Neuropsychology*, acae060.

Martin, P. K., Schroeder, R. W., Wyman-Chick, K. A., Hunter, B. P., Heinrichs, R. J., & Baade, L. E. (2018). Rates of abnormally low TOPF word reading scores in individuals failing versus passing performance validity testing. *Assessment*, *25*(5), 640–652.

Martinez, K. A., Sayers, C., Hayes, C., Martin, P. K., Clark, C. B., & Schroeder, R. W. (2021). Normal cognitive test scores cannot be interpreted as accurate measures of ability in the context of failed performance validity testing: A symptom-and detection-coached simulation study. *Journal of Clinical and Experimental Neuropsychology*, *43*(3), 301–309.

Meares, S., Shores, E. A., Taylor, A. J., Batchelor, J., Bryant, R. A., Baguley, I. J., Chapman, J., Gurka, J., & Marosszeky, J. E. (2011). The prospective course of postconcussion syndrome: the role of mild traumatic brain injury. *Neuropsychology*, *25*(4), 454–465.

Meyers, J. E., & Volbrecht, M. E. (2003). A validation of multiple malingering detection methods in a large clinical sample. *Archives of Clinical Neuropsychology*, *18*(3), 261–276.

Meyers, J. E., Volbrecht, M., Axelrod, B. N., & Reinsch-Boothby, L. (2011). Embedded symptom validity tests and overall neuropsychological test performance. *Archives of Clinical Neuropsychology*, *26*(1), 8–15.

Ponsford, J. L., Ziino, C., Parcell, D. L., Shekleton, J. A., Roper, M., Redman, J. R., Phipps-Nelson, J., & Rajaratnam, S. M. (2012). Fatigue and sleep disturbance following traumatic brain injury—their nature, causes, and potential treatments. *The Journal of Head Trauma Rehabilitation*, *27*(3), 224–233.

Rohling, M. L., Binder, L. M., Demakis, G. J., Larrabee, G. J., Ploetz, D. M., & Langhinrichsen-Rohling, J. (2011). A meta-analysis of neuropsychological outcome after mild traumatic brain injury: Re-analyses and reconsiderations of Binder et al., Frencham et al., and Pertab et al. *The Clinical Neuropsychologist*, *25*(4), 608–623.

Schretlen, D. J., & Shapiro, A. M. (2003). A quantitative review of the effects of traumatic brain injury on cognitive functioning. *International Review of Psychiatry*, *15*(4), 341–349.

Silver, J. M., & Kay, T. (2013). Persistent symptoms after a concussion. In N. D. Zasler, D. B. Arciniegas, R. D. Vanderploeg, & M. S. Jaffee (Eds.), *Management of Adults with Traumatic Brain* (pp. 475–500). Washington, DC: American Psychiatric Publishing.

Slick, D. J., Sherman, E. M., & Iverson, G. L. (1999). Diagnostic criteria for malingered neurocognitive dysfunction: Proposed standards for clinical practice and research. *The Clinical Neuropsychologist*, *13*(4), 545–561.

Soble, J. R., Cerny, B. M., Rhoads, T., DeBoer, A. B., Sharp, D. W., Ovsiew, G. P., Phillips, M. S., Pesanti, S. D., Jennette, K. J., & Resch, Z. J. (2022). Do demographic factors influence detection of invalid neuropsychological test performance using common performance validity tests? A multisite investigation. *Neuropsychology*, *37*(2), 218–232.

Sweet, J. J., Heilbronner, R. L., Morgan, J. E., Larrabee, G. J., Rohling, M. L., Boone, K. B., Kirkwood, M. W., Schroeder, R. W., Suhr, J. A., & Conference Participants. (2021). American Academy of Clinical Neuropsychology (AACN) 2021 consensus statement on validity assessment: Update of the 2009 AACN consensus conference statement on neuropsychological assessment of effort, response bias, and malingering. *The Clinical Neuropsychologist*, *35*(6), 1053–1106.

Sweet, J. J., & Klipfel, K. M. (2021). Forensic primer for the non-forensic neuropsychologist: When clinicians participate in forensic proceedings. In R. Schroeder & P. Martin (Eds.), *Validity assessment in clinical neuropsychological practice: Evaluating and managing noncredible performance* (pp. 439–459). New York, NY: Guilford.

36 Even Young Children with Epilepsy Pass Freestanding PVTs

William S. MacAllister

Pediatric neuropsychologists working within medical centers are certainly familiar with epilepsy. A diverse condition with an estimated occurrence of about 1% in the population, epilepsy has known cognitive consequences. For example, childhood onset seizure disorders have known effects on overall intellectual function (MacAllister et al., 2019; Sherman et al., 2012), memory (Engle & Smith, 2010; Menlove & Reilly, 2015; Salinas et al., 2018), attention (Dunn et al., 2003; Hermann et al., 2007; MacAllister et al., 2014), motor skills (David & MacAllister, 2022), etc. In this population, cognitive functioning has correlated with epilepsy severity factors such as age of seizure onset, medication polypharmacy, and frequency of seizures.

Validity testing in pediatric neuropsychology was slower to develop in comparison with adult neuropsychology, though publications on the topic now date back over two decades (Constantinou & McCaffrey, 2003; Courtney et al., 2003). In the last 15 years, there has been an explosion of research regarding the utility of performance validity tests (PVTs) in children, with some recent publications specifically examining both embedded and freestanding measures in children with epilepsy (MacAllister et al., 2009, 2020; Welsh et al., 2012). While high false positive rates at previously suggested established cutoffs were seen for reliable digit span, an embedded PVT (Welsh et al., 2012), freestanding measures such as the Test of Memory Malingering (TOMM) and Medical Symptom Validity Test (MSVT) are far more promising, even in those with substantial impairment (though it should be noted that the MSVT requires some basic reading skill).

Again, pediatric clinicians were somewhat "late to the party" as it pertains to validity testing. While most would concede that true 'malingering' may be less common in the pediatric world than in adults involved in litigation, there are certainly instances where feigning (or exaggeration) of deficits may be seem advantageous; for example, teens seeking academic accommodations at school or on "high stakes" college admissions tests such as the Scholastic Aptitude Test or American College Testing. While children with epilepsy certainly may also be motivated to exaggerate deficits in pursuit of accommodations, our experience is that non-credible performances in children with epilepsy are more likely to occur in those with significant psychiatric concerns. Regardless, the vast majority of children and adolescents with seizures pass freestanding validity tests with little difficulty. The following case is one that I had the opportunity to evaluate at the Alberta Children's Hospital.

This six-year-old right-handed girl represents a typical referral in a tertiary care surgical epilepsy center such as ours. The child was born in South Asia but immigrated to North America at age 3. As such, her first language was a relatively uncommon South Asian dialect; she first began learning English as she entered preschool. Though she resides in

DOI: 10.4324/9781003005063-41

a bilingual household, given her full-time English schooling, English was considered her dominant language by the time evaluation was sought.

Regarding her developmental history, she was born full-term weighing 5 lbs. 9 oz. following an unremarkable pregnancy. Early developmental milestones were achieved according to a normal timeline (e.g., walking by her first birthday, first words in her native language prior to her first birthday). However, slower skill development was seen thereafter. More specifically, despite walking on time, she was described as clumsy in daily life. Further, higher order language acquisition (in both her native language and English) was slower to emerge.

Her first seizures were seen at 28 months of age, characterized by left facial twitching, jerking of the left arm and leg, and loss of consciousness. Electroencephalogram (EEG) documented right frontal sharp waves, while magnetic resonance imaging (MRI) of the brain showed gliosis in the right medial occipital lobe. Per the neuroradiology notes, this lesion most likely represented sequela secondary to a perinatal insult/stroke (Figure 36.1).

She trialed numerous epilepsy medications, including valproic acid, clobazam, oxcarbazepine, eslicarbazepine, sultiame, and levetiracetam. Unfortunately, seizures remained uncontrolled and, in fact, grew more severe over time; she experienced multiple episodes of status epilepticus. She was then referred for neuropsychological evaluation as part of a comprehensive surgical workup.

Unfortunately, however, video EEG monitoring just days prior to neuropsychological evaluation documented multifocal and generalized activity. More specifically, discharges were seen independently over the left/midline parietal-central region, left parietal-occipital region, right parietal-central region, and right parietal-occipital region, as well as left frontal regions. There was further EEG activation in sleep, escalating to a spike-wave index

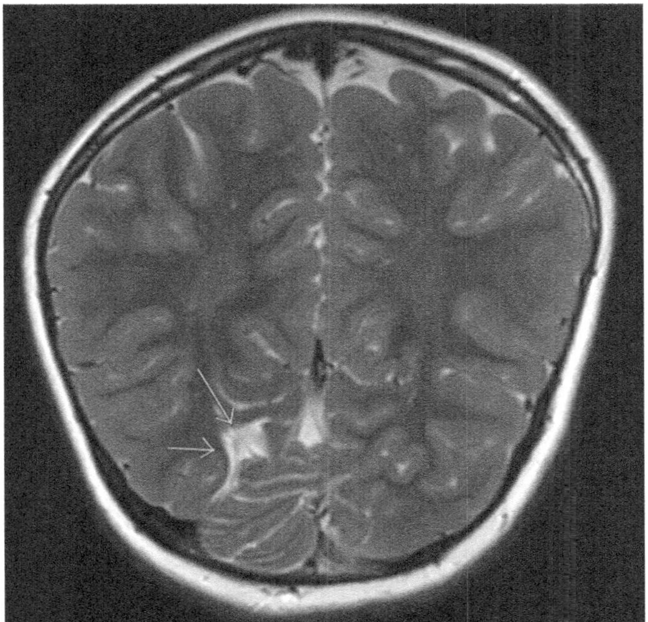

Figure 36.1 Coronal T2 image showing right medial occipital lobe gliosis.

between 80% and 100% over the night, a clinical syndrome known as Developmental Epileptic Encephalopathy with Spike Wave Activation in Sleep (DEE-SWAS, previously known as Electrical Status Epilepticus of Sleep [ESES]). Given the discordance between EEG and MRI, she was deemed a poor surgical candidate, but medical management continued.

On the day of the neuropsychological evaluation, she remained on three anti-seizure medications (ASMs); eslicarbazepine, sultiame, and levetiracetam. On interview, her parents did not report any skill loss (which can be seen in DEE-SWAS), but did report that her younger sister, two years her junior, was outpacing her in terms of language and academic skill development. Attention was also a clear concern. She had just completed kindergarten prior to testing, where she received support with a classification for a severe language delay.

Unsurprisingly given her epilepsy characteristics, overall intellectual function was in the range associated with a mild intellectual disability, though it is interesting to note that, despite the fact that English was her second language and she resides in a bilingual home, the Verbal Comprehension Index was her strongest Wechsler Intelligence Scale for Children – 5th Edition (WISC-V) composite, albeit still in the 'Very low' range (Table 36.1).

Despite the relative strength on the WISC-V Verbal Comprehension Index, she demonstrated language impairment, both qualitatively, and on objective testing. For example, a speech and language evaluation just months prior to neuropsychological assessment documented "severe receptive and expressive language deficits" on the Clinical Evaluation of Language Fundamental – 5th Edition (CELF-5). Challenges with sentence structure were readily observable during the neuropsychological evaluation; for example, at one point, she commented, "Mine kindergarten school is done!" (she was telling the examiner that she had graduated kindergarten and was to enter first grade in the fall). Moreover, there were objective receptive and expressive language deficits on testing (e.g., NEPSY-2 comprehension of instructions 2nd percentile, word generation 1st percentile). She was unable to recite the alphabet in its entirety or recognize all letters in print.

Attention deficits were also prominent; jointly, parents and teachers reported 9 of 9 inattentive presentation attention deficit hyperactivity disorder (ADHD) criteria and 9 of 9 hyperactive/impulsive criteria, in keeping with behavioral observations during testing. Likewise, prominent attention deficits (e.g., Digit Span Forward scaled score = 4, Conners' Kiddie Continuous Performance Test – 2nd Edition [K-CPT-2] commissions T score = 67, perseverations T score = 90), working memory deficits (Digit Span Backward raw score = 0), and processing speed deficits were seen on testing (WISC-V Coding scaled score = 5, Symbol Search scaled score = 3). Interestingly, despite MRI lesion and seizure semiology suggesting right hemisphere seizure onset, verbal memory was more impaired than visual (Child and Adolescent Memory Profile Verbal Memory Index = 52, Visual Memory Index = 82). Fine motor skills were also impaired bilaterally (Purdue Pegboard <1st %ile, bilaterally).

Table 36.1 Wechsler Intelligence Scale for Children – 5th Edition Index Scores

Full Scale IQ	62
Verbal Comprehension Index	75
Visual Spatial Index	70
Fluid Reasoning Index	64
Working Memory Index	64
Processing Speed Index	63

Child and Adolescent Memory Profile Verbal Memory Index (ChAMP) Scores

Subtest	*Subtest-Scaled Score/Composite Standard Score*
Lists	1
Lists Delayed	1
Lists Recognition	1
Instructions	5
Instructions Delayed	1
Instructions Recognition	1
Verbal Memory Index	**52**
Objects	5
Objects Delayed	9
Places	6
Places Delayed	7
Visual Memory Index	**82**

In summary, this young child demonstrated widespread impairments, secondary to presumed in-utero stroke, seizures, and epileptic encephalopathy (i.e., DEE-SWAS). Intellectual functioning was in the "extremely low range" and early academics skills were far behind. Further, attention, language, and memory skills were impaired. While she was formally diagnosed with a Major Neurocognitive Disorder at the time, it is anticipated that she will meet criteria for an intellectual disability in the near future, as adaptive skills will likely develop slowly in the years to come. Despite her young age and widespread and severe deficits, her performances on *freestanding* performance validity testing were entirely within normal limits.

Freestanding PVTs

The TOMM, no doubt familiar to the readers of this book as it is one of the most common PVTs employed by neuropsychologists (Slick et al., 2004), was administered as part of this evaluation. While initially developed as an adult measure, studies validating its use in pediatric populations now date back over 20 years (Constantinou & McCaffrey, 2003), and it has since become the most widely used PVT in pediatric evaluations as well, despite its adult origins (Emhoff et al., 2018; Kirk et al., 2020). Administered early in the course of the evaluation (which was conducted over a single day), the child received a raw score 47 on Trial 1; that is, she passed Trial 1 with a score that exceeds the standard cutoff traditionally applied to the TOMM Trial 2 in adult or pediatric cases. Given this strong Trial 1 performance, Trial 2 and Retention were not administered, a common practice, given research demonstrating that children with adequate scores on Trial 1 go on to pass subsequent trials (Brooks et al., 2012).

Testing resumed following lunch. In the afternoon session, The Memory Validity Profile (MVP) was administered. The MVP was the first freestanding PVT designed, a priori, for use in children and adolescents, though norms span through young adulthood (i.e., age 5–21). The manual reports data on 1,200 youths, malingering simulators, and a large mixed clinical sample that includes children with neurological and neurodevelopmental disorders. Worth highlighting is the fact that the MVP was also the first PVT to include age-adjusted cutoffs, designed to maintain appropriate specificity across the age range.

As can be seen, this child passed all scales of the MVP with little difficulty. In fact, she received a perfect score on the Visual scale. While her score was not perfect on the verbal scale, her performance, even at the young age of 6, exceeded standard manual cutoffs for even the oldest children and young adults in the standardization sample.

Memory Validity Profile Scores

Scale	*Score*	*Interpretation*
MVP Visual	16	Valid (perfect score)
MVP Verbal	14	Valid
MVP Total	30	Valid

Embedded PVTs

As is common in neurodevelopmental cases, particularly those with significant cognitive impact, embedded PVTs fared less well in this case, yielding clear false positives. The ChAMP includes several performance validity indicators, two of which will be briefly described here. Notably, the first was derived at the time of initial standardization, while subsequent ChAMP embedded validity indices were derived post-hoc, in hopes of addressing the limitations of the primary validity index included on the test score printout.

As described in the ChAMP manual, the measure includes a 'Validity Indicator' (VI) score, automatically included on the printout when scoring software is used. The score, which is derived via raw score summaries of all delayed ChAMP subtests that employ a recognition or 3-item forced-choice response paradigm, is a crude index. More specifically, the cutoffs were set to minimize false positives in impaired individuals, flagging only scores that fall *below the level of chance*. The child's score of 40 was interpreted to reflect a "valid profile."

Given the known insensitivity of this original variable, efforts were made to improve upon it. This work ultimately yielded the ChAMP VI-SS. This updated index employs the same subtests, but uses subtest-scaled scores rather than raw scores as, across the age range of the test, expected raw scores differ considerably from the youngest children to the teens and young adults. The index was validated on a head injury sample, with severity ranging from mild traumatic brain injury (mTBI) to severe. The VI-SS yielded far superior classification accuracy than the original ChAMP VI, against a criterion of two failed PVTs on established measures (Brooks et al., 2023). However, the child at hand, with a VI-SS score of 18, fell far below cutoffs. It is worth highlighting here that the sample on which this new measure was validated differs in many ways from the case at hand. First off, the sample included only children and adolescents with TBI, not epilepsy. Further, this validation sample did not include children this young (lowest age limit was 8) and, on average, this sample had less memory impairment.

Perhaps the oldest of "embedded" PVTs, reliable digit span (RDS), could also be calculated in this case. This embedded index is derived from the Digit Span subtest of the Wechsler intelligence tests and prior research on this index has shown promise in pediatric mTBI samples when applying a slightly lower cutoff as compared with adult samples (Kirkwood et al., 2011). Unfortunately, this index has proven to be of limited utility in children with epilepsy. Even at the lower threshold suggested by Kirkwood et al. (2011), a 35% failure rate was seen in children with seizures, in comparison with the 10% failure rate seen on the TOMM (Welsh et al., 2012). The child at hand, with an RDS score of just 2, fell well-below threshold, but certainly presented similarly to many in the Welsh et al. (2012) study, which represents a very similar patient population (i.e., surgical epilepsy).

Patient Follow-Up

Unfortunately, following this evaluation and failed surgical candidacy, her medical status did not improve. She continued to have seizures roughly every four to six weeks, all requiring rescue medication (Midazolam) to abort. Tellingly, seizure semiology evolved and now can involve either side. Again, at onset (age 2), seizures were associated with left side facial twitching, leg, and arm jerking. Now, at age 8, right hand clenching, and right arm and leg tonic movements are seen with some events; that is, she is now believed to have bilateral independent seizure foci. She has recently begun the ketogenic diet; however, at the time of this writing, her EEG characteristics remain similar in terms of DEE-SWAS status, with an 86% spike-wave index in sleep. While her parents are noting some cognitive progress (e.g., she is beginning to read), she remains far behind her younger sibling and the gap continues to widen. She is classified in school as a child with a severe medical and cognitive disorder and receives numerous supports and accommodations in keeping with her needs, including speech/language therapy, occupational therapy, a modified curriculum, access to an educational assistant/aide, etc.

Discussion

The astute reader will note that this chapter seems somewhat out of place in a book on validity and malingering. After all, this is a case of a young girl, with no external incentives, severe/medically refractory epilepsy, passing all freestanding PVTs. Certainly, there is no evidence of malingering, or even intentional underperformance for other reasons. Why would this case be included? The answer is simple: this case illustrates several important points relevant to validity assessment and its relevance to human behavior across the lifespan.

First, this case clearly demonstrates that even young children can pass freestanding PVTs, even those initially designed for use exclusively in adult populations. Again, this six-year-old child, just days out of kindergarten and with severe cognitive deficits, passed the TOMM at standard adult cutoffs applied to Trial 2, on Trial 1. This is a common finding in our center; though less so in the youngest age ranges, the majority of children seen at our hospital never receive TOMM T2 or Retention, as their Trial 1 performances clearly bespeaks their appropriate engagement in testing. I'll add that, in a center like ours, we routinely see very behaviorally complex kids. Even in these cases, TOMM failures are the exception, not the rule, despite variable engagement in testing across the day. I seldom find myself documenting insufficient task engagement as evidenced by failure on the TOMM. More commonly, I find myself documenting something to the effect of "despite passing the TOMM, task engagement was poor (or variable) over the day," then noting that test results are believed to underestimate the child's true abilities. In short, after 15 years of administering the TOMM to very medically involved children and teens, I've come realize that the task is best detecting "intentional underperformance," even at standard adult cutoffs; the TOMM is not particularly sensitive to "phoning it in" and giving bare-minimum effort as I see more false negatives than false positives on this test in behaviorally involved children.

It is also worth highlighting that, though the TOMM was used in this particular case, we have found similar findings on other "adult" PVTs. For example, children with epilepsy (even severe epilepsy similar to that seen here, or status-post epilepsy surgery) perform at or above standard adult cutoffs on the MSVT, provided that they read well enough to take it. Per the manual, the MSVT requires a third grade reading level. However, in our sample of children and adolescents with epilepsy, 96.6% of those with grade 2 or higher reading levels passed the MSVT (MacAllister et al., 2020). Of the three failures seen in this sample, two were unequivocal 'true positives.' One MSVT failure had clear severe psychiatric concerns and also presented with chance-level performances on the TOMM (with lower scores on Trial 2 than on 1 [Trial 1 = 24, Trial 2 = 20]). A second MSVT failure, also with psychiatric factors at play, admitted intentional underperformance in follow-up interview after testing was terminated. The final MSVT failure was secondary to extreme somnolence; the child was observed to nod off during a continuous performance test, prompting discontinuation. Given the young age of the case at hand (six years) coupled with learning challenges (she is unable to recite the alphabet), the MSVT was not an appropriate option here.

In short, PVTs developed for adults seem to work well for the majority of young examinees. Of course, this begs the question "If freestanding adult PVTs work well in children, is there a need to develop child-specific PVTs at all?" While this remains an empirical question, it bears mentioning that independent studies of the MVP have suggested that cutoffs published in the manual are insensitive when compared with better established measures, suggesting this task may be "too easy" (Dodd et al., 2020; Morrison-Steele et al., 2024; Tewolde et al., 2021). Another pediatric-specific PVT, the Pediatric Performance Validity Suite has been developed, but heretofore lacks independent validation in comparison with well-validated PVTs. However, conversations with clinicians who have used this measure in populations with high PVT failure rates (i.e., mTBI) have shared that this task may also be insensitive in comparison with better established (adult) measures.

In addition to illustrating that freestanding PVTs can be passed by young children, even those with severe neurological conditions (in this case, refractory epilepsy and DEE-SWAS), the current case also suggests that culture/language factors may be lesser concern when choosing validity tests, as may have been feared.

Again, this child's family had immigrated from South Asia when she was three years old. Further, while English was now considered her dominant language, she only enjoyed a few years of English exposure (and clearly showed language impairments across both languages). Regardless, she passed freestanding PVTs in both the visual and verbal domains with no difficulty, despite the additional presence of significant cognitive dysfunction (i.e., low IQ, severe attention deficits, and memory deficits). Cultural and language factors in pediatric validity testing are largely unstudied. Of the limited data available, these test results are consistent with recent pediatric TOMM investigations suggesting that pass rates among Whites and People of Color do not significantly differ (Desire et al., 2023).

As seen, the embedded validity indices fared less well in this case, and this is certainly consistent with the available data on embedded indices in children with significant medical/neurological conditions. While the ChAMP VI (original raw score version) suggested valid results, both the ChAMP VI-SS and RDS seemed to indicate underperformance/poor performance validity. However, these results clearly reflect false positives. This warrants a broader discussion on the nature of validity and the populations on which they are most useful.

Generally speaking, effective PVTs have face-validity as cognitive tests, but do not operate as such. Stated another way, these tasks should "look like" bona fide neurocognitive tasks, such that the examinee believes they are measuring cognition. However, they should operate very differently. That is, they should be largely insensitive to true cognitive impairments, correlate poorly with 'real' neuropsychological tests, and share little relation with known disease severity variables (in epilepsy, these include factors such as age of seizure onset, number of ASMs, seizure frequency, episodes of status epilepticus, or DEE-SWAS).

This is very clearly the nature of 'freestanding' PVTs, built from the ground up to satisfy these criteria. Unfortunately, all 'embedded' validity tests are at an extreme disadvantage.

In effect, we are asking these tests to pull "double-duty." That is, on the one hand, we demand tasks such as Digit Span be sensitive to auditory attention and working memory deficits, near universal in neurologic conditions, yet still hope they will function well as PVTs. This is an impossible expectation across the range of pathologies assessed by clinical neuropsychologists. What can be said, however, is that embedded PVTs seem to work well in populations for which little dysfunction (or full recovery) is expected (e.g., mTBI/Concussion) (Kirkwood et al., 2011) but yield high rates of false positive errors in conditions for which non-trivial deficits are expected, such as epilepsy (Welsh et al., 2012). In choosing embedded PVTs to consider in an evaluation, we encourage clinicians to consider the options available to them, then survey the available literature to ensure that the child at hand is well-represented in the literature of that embedded index. Stated another way, it is not enough to ask "has this embedded PVT been studied *in this age range*?" Rather, one must ask, "has this embedded PVT been studied in this age range, *for this specific clinical condition*?" As seen for the ChAMP VI-SS, the only publication matched on neither clinical condition, nor age range.

It is unclear why pediatric clinicians have been slower to adopt validity testing. Many may simply be unaware of the existence of such measures. That said, as training standards have been better codified over the years, I hope this has grown less common over time. Other clinicians, whose income has been dependent on obtaining testing accommodations for students, may be financially incentivized to *not* detect non-credible performances.

However, my inclination is to suspect that many not using PVTs do so because they "fear the false positive." That is, those historically reluctant to employ PVTs may not feel comfortable interpreting results or may be inclined to dismiss all but the most egregious underperformance (i.e., chance or below-chance-level scores) as a false positive. I hope that this case sheds some necessary light on this issue given the cultural/linguistic factors at play, the severe neurological condition, and the unequivocal cognitive impairment; the majority of children pass freestanding measures with no difficulty. I encourage all neuropsychologists to give PVTs to every examinee. Not only is this consistent with current guidelines in the field (Sweet et al., 2021), but familiarity with these measures will inevitably lead to comfort in their interpretation; one mantra I drill into my trainees *ad nauseum* is the following: "Once you see who can pass PVTs, you'll stop questioning the failures."

Of course, this inevitably begs the question "Do false positives occur in children?" Unfortunately, the answer to this question is "yes," albeit at a lower rate than many likely fear. Further, failures are generally "clinically obvious." Generally, those failing freestanding PVTs due to genuine inability to perform them are easily identifiable to well-trained clinicians. These children tend to have obvious (and severe) cognitive deficits in casual observation. On testing, many receive raw score of zero on many Wechsler Scale subtests, as these tasks are simply above their ability level. Most importantly, these children, almost without exception (except in cases of acute decline) have already been identified as children with severe cognitive dysfunction at school, are likely classified for intellectual disabilities, and are likely educated in intensive settings with a low student-to-teacher ratio. In short, those failing PVTs due to genuine cognitive impairment are not easily confused with less impaired children, and there is usually supporting evidence of the level of impairment in both medical and educational records.

In summary, the preceding case example is that of a very young kindergartener, for whom English is a second language, with refractory epilepsy, epileptic encephalopathy, and emerging intellectual disability including low IQ, academic delays, attention impairment, and memory impairment. Despite these substantial deficits, performances on freestanding

PVTs, including those initially developed for adults (i.e., TOMM), as well as pediatric measures (i.e., MVP), were entirely within normal limits. Those working with adults or children in which malingering may be in the differential diagnosis should take note of how impervious these measures are to genuine cognitive dysfunction.

References

Brooks, B. L., Fay-McClymont, T. B., MacAllister, W. S., Vasserman, M., Mish, S., & Sherman, E. M. S. (2023). New child and adolescent memory profile embedded performance validity test. *Archives of Clinical Neuropsychology*, *38*(5), 782–792. https://doi.org/10.1093/arclin/acac110

Brooks, B. L., Sherman, E. M. S., & Krol, A. L. (2012). Utility of TOMM trial 1 as an indicator of effort in children and adolescents. *Archives of Clinical Neuropsychology*, *27*(1), 23–29. https://doi.org/10.1093/arclin/acr086

Constantinou, M., & McCaffrey, R. J. (2003). Using the TOMM for Evaluating Children's Effort to Perform Optimally on Neuropsychological Measures. *Child Neuropsychology*, *9*(2), 81–90. https://doi.org/10.1076/CHIN.9.2.81.14505

Courtney, J. C., Dinkins, J. P., Allen, L. M., & Kuroski, K. (2003). Age related effects in children taking the computerized assessment of response bias and word memory test. *9*(2), 109–116. https://doi.org/10.1076/CHIN.9.2.109.14507

David, C. V., & MacAllister, W. S. (2022). Fine motor impairment in children with epilepsy: Relations with seizure severity and lateralizing value. *Epilepsy and Behavior*, *127*. https://doi.org/10.1016/j.yebeh.2021.108518

Desire, N., Brooks, B. B., & MacAllister, W. S. (2023). Investigating racial, ethnic, and linguistic differences in test of memory malingering failure rates: A preliminary study in a large clinical pediatric and young adult sample. Poster presented at the *Annual Meeting of the American Academy of Clinical Neuropsychology*, Washington, DC.

Dodd, J. N., Murphy, S., & Bosworth, C. (2020). Sensitivity of the memory validity profile (MVP): Raising the bar. *Child Neuropsychology*, *26*(1), 137–144. https://doi.org/10.1080/09297049.2019.1620714

Dunn, D. W., Austin, J. K., Harezlak, J., & Ambrosius, W. T. (2003). ADHD and epilepsy in childhood. *Developmental Medicine and Child Neurology*, *45*(1), 50–54. https://doi.org/10.1017/S0012162203000094

Emhoff, S. M., Lynch, J. K., & McCaffrey, R. J. (2018). Performance and symptom validity testing in pediatric assessment: A review of the literature. *Developmental Neuropsychology*, *43*(8), 671–707. https://doi.org/10.1080/87565641.2018.1525612

Engle, J. A., & Smith, M. Lou. (2010). Attention and material-specific memory in children with lateralized epilepsy. *Neuropsychologia*, *48*(1). https://doi.org/10.1016/j.neuropsychologia.2009.08.005

Hermann, B., Jones, J., Dabbs, K., Allen, C. A., Sheth, R., Fine, J., McMillan, A., & Seidenberg, M. (2007). The frequency, complications and aetiology of ADHD in new onset paediatric epilepsy. *Brain*, *130*(12), 3135–3148. https://doi.org/10.1093/BRAIN/AWM227

Kirk, J. W., Baker, D. A., Kirk, J. J., & MacAllister, W. S. (2020). A review of performance and symptom validity testing with pediatric populations. *Applied Neuropsychology: Child*, *9*(4), 292–306. https://doi.org/10.1080/21622965.2020.1750118

Kirkwood, M. W., Hargrave, D. D., & Kirk, J. W. (2011). The value of the WISC-IV digit span subtest in detecting noncredible erformance during pediatric neuropsychological examinations. *Archives of Clinical Neuropsychology*, *26*(5), 377–384. https://doi.org/10.1093/arclin/acr040

MacAllister, W. S., Désiré, N., Vasserman, M., Dalrymple, J., Salinas, L., & Brooks, B. L. (2020). The use of the MSVT in children and adolescents with epilepsy. *Applied Neuropsychology: Child*, *9*(4). https://doi.org/10.1080/21622965.2020.1750127

MacAllister, W. S., Maiman, M., Vasserman, M., Fay-Mcclymont, T., Brooks, B. L., & Sherman, E. M. S. (2019). The WISC-V in children and adolescents with epilepsy. *Child Neuropsychology*, *25*(7). https://doi.org/10.1080/09297049.2019.1571181

MacAllister, W. S., Nakhutina, L., Bender, H. A., Karantzoulis, S., & Carlson, C. (2009). Assessing effort during neuropsychological evaluation with the TOMM in children and adolescents with epilepsy. *Child Neuropsychology*, *15*(6). https://doi.org/10.1080/09297040902748226

MacAllister, W. S., Vasserman, M., Rosenthal, J., & Sherman, E. (2014). Attention and executive functions in children with epilepsy: What, why, and what to do. In *Applied Neuropsychology: Child*. https://doi.org/10.1080/21622965.2013.839605

Menlove, L., & Reilly, C. (2015). Memory in children with epilepsy: A systematic review. *Seizure*, *25*, 126–135. https://doi.org/10.1016/J.SEIZURE.2014.10.002

Morrison-Steele, M., Crepeau-Hobson, M. F., Kirk, J. J., McLaughlin, S., & Kirk, J. W. (2024). A comparison of MVP and MSVT performance among a diverse clinical pediatric sample. *Applied Neuropsychology: Child*, *13*(1), 45–51. https://doi.org/10.1080/21622965.2022.2121653

Salinas, L., Dalrymple, J., & MacAllister, W. S. (2018). Memory in children with epilepsy: Utility of the WRAML-2 in generalized and focal epilepsy syndromes. *Epilepsy and Behavior*, *89*. https://doi.org/10.1016/j.yebeh.2018.10.002

Sherman, E. M. S., Brooks, B. L., Fay-Mcclymont, T. B., & MacAllister, W. S. (2012). Detecting epilepsy-related cognitive problems in clinically referred children with epilepsy: Is the WISC-IV a useful tool? *Epilepsia*, *53*(6). https://doi.org/10.1111/j.1528-1167.2012.03493.x

Slick, D. J., Tan, J. E., Strauss, E. H., & Hultsch, D. F. (2004). Detecting malingering: A survey of experts' practices. *Archives of Clinical Neuropsychology*, *19*(4), 465–473. https://doi.org/10.1016/J.ACN.2003.04.001

Sweet, J. J., Heilbronner, R. L., Morgan, J. E., Larrabee, G. J., Rohling, M. L., Boone, K. B., Kirkwood, M. W., Schroeder, R. W., & Suhr, J. A. (2021). Academy of Clinical Neuropsychology (AACN) 2021 consensus statement on validity assessment: Update of the 2009 AACN consensus conference statement on .... *Taylor & Francis*, *35*(6), 1053–1106. https://doi.org/10.1080/13854046.2021.1896036

Tewolde, F., Svingos, A., Norheim, N., Turner, E., Jones, L., & Heaton, S. (2021). New cut-score to improve performance of the Memory Validity Profile (MVP) in heterogeneous clinical populations. *Child Neuropsychology*, *27*(5), 601–612. https://doi.org/10.1080/09297049.2021.1876013

Welsh, A. J., Bender, H. A., Whitman, L. A., Vasserman, M., & MacAllister, W. S. (2012). Clinical utility of Reliable Digit Span in assessing effort in children and adolescents with epilepsy. *Archives of Clinical Neuropsychology*, *27*(7). https://doi.org/10.1093/arclin/acs063

37 Credibility Concerns in Psychogenic Non-Epileptic Seizures (PNES)

Kirsty E. Bortnik and Lorna Myers

Psychogenic non-epileptic seizures (PNES) are paroxysmal events consisting of sudden episodes of any combination of altered movement, sensation, or awareness. They resemble epileptic seizures (ES), but they are not accompanied by epileptiform electrical discharges, and they are presumed to be associated with a psychological origin. PNES are categorized as functional neurological disorders (FND)/conversion disorders within the *Diagnostic and Statistical Manual of Mental Disorders*, Fifth Edition (*DSM-5*; American Psychiatric Association, 2013). Prevalence is around 2–33 individuals per 100,000 population (O'Mahony et al., 2023), is approximately three times higher in females (Dworetzky & Baslet, 2017), and accounts for 20%–50% of epilepsy monitoring unit diagnoses at discharge (Smith, 2014). Significant life adversities and psychological trauma are often present in the histories of individuals with PNES. Many adults diagnosed with PNES have a history of childhood sexual, physical, and/or psychological abuse (Myers et al., 2013; Sharpe & Faye, 2006). There is no single psychological profile associated with PNES; psychiatric comorbidities are frequently observed, with high prevalence of depressive disorders (21%–60%), anxiety/panic disorders (11%–50%), posttraumatic stress disorder (35%–49%; Fiszman et al., 2004; Myers et al., 2013), somatic symptom and pain syndromes (22%–84%), dissociative disorders (22%–91%) and personality disorders (10%–86%) (Reuber, 2008). Also, patients with PNES typically have higher anxiety and depression than those with ES (D'Alessio et al., 2006; Green et al., 2017).

The gold standard for diagnosis of PNES includes video-electroencephalography (v-EEG); however, inpatient or ambulatory v-EEG monitoring is not accessible in many parts of the world. Furthermore, some individuals tend to present with very infrequent events, which are difficult to capture during monitoring. Diagnosis of PNES is often delayed, with patients receiving numerous work-ups by medical providers across different specialties (e.g., neurology, psychiatry, cardiology) and unnecessary prescription of antiepileptic medication, which can result in significant complications (e.g., patients with PNES thought to be in status epilepticus are often administered high doses of antiepileptic medication, which can result in impaired consciousness or respiratory failure, and in a few extreme cases, unneeded endotracheal intubation; Dobbertin et al., 2012; Leis et al., 1992). There are also substantial economic and healthcare costs associated with delayed diagnosis; for instance, the annual healthcare cost for patients with undiagnosed PNES in Ireland was €20,995.30 per patient (approximately $22,706 in U.S. dollars) and C$22,939.10 per patient in Canada (approximately $17,055 U.S. dollars) prior to psychotherapeutic intervention (Magee et al., 2014; Russell et al., 2016). Moreover, even after diagnosis, if PNES persists unidentified, a significant number of patients (about 30%) become unemployed (Duncan et al., 2014; Walther et al., 2020) and over half may eventually seek disability status or social security

DOI: 10.4324/9781003005063-42

benefits (Duncan et al., 2014; Reuber et al., 2003). In fact, some studies have found that patients with FND report greater distress, are more likely to not be working for health reasons and receive more disability-related financial benefits than patients with symptoms explained by a neurological disease (Carson et al., 2011).

Given the factors above, many individuals with PNES are frequently referred for neuropsychological evaluation, either as part of clinical treatment planning or within a forensic context (e.g., for disability-related claims). Several studies have examined neuropsychological functioning in patients with PNES and ES to differentiate PNES and ES based on psychometric testing. Findings have been inconsistent; for the most part, individuals with PNES and ES perform comparably, and, when differences are found, those with PNES tend to outperform those with ES; however, differences are small and not specific to a particular cognitive domain, which limits diagnostic utility (Dodrill, 2010; Van Patten et al., 2024). Although there is no PNES-specific cognitive profile that would reliably differentiate PNES from ES, in general, patients with PNES tend to *overestimate* their cognitive impairment. For instance, one study found that despite endorsing greater levels of word-finding difficulty compared with patients with ES, PNES patients in fact performed better on a naming test (Prigatano & Kirlin, 2009). Recent research has examined the utility of multivariate analysis of psychometric testing to differentiate PNES from ES, with the strongest psychometric evidence for PNES being the consistent lack of impairment on tests sensitive to diffuse neurocognitive deficits such as processing speed, working memory, and verbal fluency (Tyson et al., 2018). Moreover, in this study, patients with PNES performed significantly better than those with ES on select measures of verbal learning/memory and language functioning (Tyson et al., 2018). A large systematic review and meta-analysis that examined cognitive performance of 4,193 participants with PNES (from 84 studies) found that those with PNES outperformed those with ES in global cognition and language, with language functioning best discriminating between PNES and ES groups (Van Patten et al., 2024).

There have also been efforts to differentiate PNES from ES via self-report mood/personality measures, given the higher rates of psychological distress in individuals with PNES. For instance, one study administered the Minnesota Multiphasic Personality Inventory-2 Restructured Form (MMPI-2RF: Ben-Porath & Tellegen, 2008) and the Trauma Symptom Inventory – Second Edition (TSI-2; Briere, 2011) and examined psychological trauma and psychiatric comorbidities in PNES and ES. Patients with PNES differed from those with ES on a Somatization scale on the TSI-2 and exhibited significantly higher rates of sexual and "other" trauma (Myers et al., 2019). No statistically significant differences were found between groups on the two MMPI-2-RF subscales that were examined in this study (RCd [demoralization] and RC3 [cynicism]); however, patients with PNES showed a trend toward higher scores on a measure of demoralization compared with those with ES. In another study, the somatic complaints scale of the MMPI-2-RF (RC1) was found to have particular utility in differentiating PNES from ES (hit rate of 68%) and explained unique variance in diagnosis beyond demographic or medical history risk factors (Locke et al., 2010). Sex-based differences in psychiatric presentations have also been reported; compared with females with ES, females with PNES had higher scores on affective scales of the MMPI-2-RF (particularly RC1, RC7, HPC, NUC, and SUI), whereas males with PNES were 5–10 times more likely than males with ES to endorse clinically elevated MMPI-2-R-F cognitive/somatic symptoms (particularly on FBS-r, RC1, and HPC subscales, Del Bene et al., 2017). A recent study examining sex differences in a sample of male veterans found that higher endorsement on RC1 and SUI subscales of the MMPI-2-RF was predictive of a PNES diagnosis whereas higher endorsement on the GIC (gastrointestinal symptoms) was more predictive of ES (Modiano et al., 2021).

Although the MMPI-2/MMPI-2-RF are the most frequently utilized measures in examining psychological characteristics of PNES, several studies have assessed the utility of the Personality Assessment Inventory (PAI; Morey, 1991) in differentiating PNES from ES. A "Nonepileptic Seizure Indicator" (NES) was derived from scores on the PAI Somatization subscales and initially found to have 84% sensitivity and 73% specificity (Wagner et al., 2005). However, subsequent analyses failed to replicate the initial findings, with specificity of the NES around chance levels (56.4%–58.8% per Gale & Hill, 2012 and Testa et al., 2011). Classification accuracy seems to improve when using a combination of scores either from multiple self-report inventories (e.g., Gale & Hill, 2012) or from a combination of scores with other clinical data (Hill & Gale, 2011). In this latter study, a combination of the PAI Conversion subscale score (SOM-C), years since first seizure, and length of seizures ≥ 3 minutes resulted in classification accuracy of 84%.

Assessment of Performance and Symptom Validity in PNES Contexts

Prior chapters within this book have underscored the importance of considering the evaluation context when interpreting performance validity tests (PVTs) and symptom validity tests (SVTs) scores. Multiple PVTs/SVTs are routinely administered, especially in forensic settings, given the higher base rates of malingering in these contexts (Martin, Schroeder, & Odland, 2015). Although malingering base rates tend to be lower within clinical settings (e.g., Mittenberg et al., 2002; Wodushek & Domen, 2018), it would be inaccurate to presume that examinees in this setting are always trying their best when approaching neuropsychological tasks (Schroeder & Martin, 2022). For example, a recent meta-analysis found that the pooled prevalence of PVT failure in the context of routine clinical care was 16%, and further analyses examining failure rates by clinical diagnoses was *highest* for patients with PNES (33%; Roor et al., 2023). These findings converge with those obtained when surveyed neuropsychologists were asked to estimate the base rate of invalid testing in various clinical contexts (Martin & Schroeder, 2020). When compared with those with ES, individuals with PNES fail PVTs at notably higher rates (e.g., Binder et al., 2021; Tyson et al., 2018). Moreover, examination of qualitative response characteristics has shown promise in differentiating PNES from ES: for instance, Bortz and colleagues (1995) found that a negative response bias on the CVLT-II recognition trial demonstrated 61% sensitivity and 91% specificity with overall accuracy of 78%. Impressively, the calculated Odds Ratio suggested that an examinee in this sample who demonstrated a negative response bias was 16.5 times more likely to be diagnosed with PNES. McNally and colleagues (2009) used signal detection theory analysis methods to examine differences in patients with PNES and ES on the Word List Test of the Wechsler Memory Scale, Third Edition (WMS-III; Wechsler, 1997b) and found a similar negative response bias. These data underscore the necessity of routinely including PVTs within a neuropsychological battery when evaluating individuals with PNES.

Separate assessment methods should also be used in determining validity of self-reported psychological symptoms (Sherman, Slick, & Iverson, 2020). The association between exaggeration of cognitive deficits and exaggeration of psychological symptoms is inconsistent (e.g., Jones et al., 2012; Nelson & Sweet, 2008). Examinees may selectively feign or exaggerate cognitive deficits and/or psychological symptoms. Given prior research demonstrating that individuals with PNES tend to overestimate their cognitive deficits, and that levels of psychological distress are higher in individuals with PNES than ES or other neurological conditions, it is essential that the neuropsychologist assess the validity of both cognitive and psychological complaints.

When scores on PVTs/SVTs exceed established cutoffs, considerations should include the possibility of deliberate symptom exaggeration or fabrication when an external incentive is present. In the absence of an external incentive, factors other than malingering that may cause credibility concerns should also be considered.

In the following section, we present two PNES cases: a clinical case (Ms. P) with no apparent motive to feign who appeared to be deliberately misrepresenting both cognitive and psychological function, and a second case (Ms. N), which illustrates a noncredible cognitive and psychiatric presentation in the context of external incentive, thereby meeting criteria for malingering.

The Case of Ms. P

Background

This is a 25-year-old, single woman with 14 years of education who was referred for a neuropsychological evaluation as part of a diagnostic workup for suspected PNES. She initially presented to the neurologist's office with episodes of time loss and dissociation, and one- to two-minute events of full body twitching with her eyes rolled back that began one year before. These events occurred approximately one to two times per week. Ms. P described an aura of feeling detached and confused that lasted several minutes and was also accompanied at times by tics, fast breathing, sporadic head twitching, and crossed eyes just before the full-blown event. Of note, the auras were sufficiently long enough to allow her to pull over if she was driving, or if she was in public, she was able to sit down safely before the onset of the episode to avoid injury. Ms. P never had an episode while at work. She identified emotional stress as a trigger.

Behavioral Observations

Ms. P drove herself to the assessment and arrived independently and on time She was oriented in all spheres and provided details consistent with available medical records. She ambulated independently and there were no observed difficulties in gross motor functions. Speech was within normal limits for rate, rhythm, volume, and prosody. Command and use of language was fluent and intelligible, consistent with her level of education, and there were no obvious word-finding difficulties during casual conversation. Thought process was logical and goal directed. Thought content was appropriate and there was no evidence of suicidal or homicidal ideation or paranoid/delusional thought content. Mood was described as "a little anxious." The assessment was conducted over the course of one testing session, with one break. Ms. P attended well to instructions and recalled prior interactions without difficulty. There were no signs of inattention or impulsivity. Her frustration tolerance was generally good, although during administration of the Test of Memory Malingering (TOMM), she made comments suggesting that the examiner might be "fooling" her as to whether she had seen an item before or not. No PNES episodes were observed during the evaluation.

Interview

At the time of the evaluation, Ms. P reported cognitive difficulties primarily with attention, word-finding, and memory of approximately one-year duration. She was continuing to work part-time in office administration and denied any reductions in her ability to complete work-related tasks. She was fully independent in basic activities of daily living (ADLs) and in higher-level, instrumental activities of daily living (IADLs). Current physical complaints included fatigue, diffuse gastric symptoms, decreased appetite, insomnia, chronic headaches, and intermittent numbness and tingling. Psychiatric history was notable for depression and posttraumatic stress disorder (PTSD) in the setting of documented physical, emotional, and sexual abuse, which occurred throughout her childhood years. There was also an incident of sexual assault in college. At the time of the evaluation (approximately one week after the initial neurology consult), she was taking an anti-depressant (Prozac), prescribed by her psychiatrist. She was not prescribed any antiepileptic medication. Ms. P participated in individual, outpatient psychotherapy intermittently over the years, but had discontinued therapy one month prior to the neuropsychological evaluation. Substance use was notable for prior, significant alcohol consumption in her teen years and the use of stimulants (not prescribed) in college. She denied current use of alcohol or other substances. Developmental history was completely unremarkable (i.e., gestation and delivery normal, met developmental milestones on time). She graduated from high school and obtained an associate degree in communications. She was in a six-month relationship and described her partner as "very supportive" and understanding of these recurrent events, and that when he witnessed the episodes, he was able to offer her comfort and support. There were no noted external gains at the time of the assessment; Ms. P denied applying for disability or having any involvement in litigation proceedings following direct inquiry by the examiner during the clinical interview.

Record Review

Results from neuroimaging one year before the evaluation were unremarkable. Shortly after the neuropsychological evaluation, Ms. P was admitted for several-day v-EEG monitoring. Several of her typical events were captured that were not associated with any EEG changes; the events occurred immediately after Ms. P reported anxiety symptoms.

Test Results and Interpretation

See Table 37.1 for a full summary of test results. Ms. P's performances on stand-alone and embedded PVTs are notable for the following: scores of 36 and 39 on TOMM Trial 1 and Trial 2 respectively, which are below the established cutoffs (Martin et al., 2020; Tombaugh, 1996). She performed below the cutoff on an embedded PVT derived from a combination of scores from the WMS-III Logical Memory test (Bortnik et al., 2010). She also scored below the cutoff on a forced choice embedded PVT derived from a verbal list-learning task (CVLT-II Forced Choice Recognition; Delis et al., 2000; Erdodi et al., 2018). Ms. P obtained scores below cutoffs on a combination of embedded indices derived from the DKEFS Trail-Making Test (Delis et al., 2001), which have been found to have improved sensitivity and specificity compared which cutoffs on any of the individual trail-making trials (Erdodi et al., 2018). In contrast, scores on embedded PVTs derived from the WAIS-IV Digit Span subtest were above established cutoffs. In sum,

Ms. P failed 4 of 5 (80%) PVTs, which is above the ≥ 2 criterion of failure that has been found to best discriminate between credible and noncredible performance (e.g., Larrabee, 2014; Victor et al., 2009). Therefore, results of the neuropsychological evaluation were deemed as invalid, and an unreliable representation of her current cognitive functioning.

Further examination of Ms. P's performances across administered cognitive measures revealed striking inconsistencies that further support the determination of invalid test results. Integrating findings from formal measures of performance validity with other patterns of test performance and qualitative clinical observations is consistent with recommended practice (e.g., Sweet et al., & Conference Participants, 2021). To that end, review of her responses on the TOMM demonstrated inconsistent responding (i.e., several items correctly identified on Trial 1 were not recognized on Trial 2). Ms. P's performances on timed number-sequencing and letter-sequencing tasks (DKEFS Trails 2 and 3) were extremely slow (<2%ile), despite the absence of any pre-existing learning disability and in contrast to her robust scores on a word reading test (WTAR= 81%ile) and expressive vocabulary (WASI Vocabulary = 92%ile). Similarly, Ms. P did not exhibit any evidence of psychomotor slowing during the clinical interview (i.e., walked at a normal pace, rate of speech within normal limits, completed intake paperwork in a reasonable time), yet, contrary to these spontaneously (intact) skills, her score on a timed task of psychomotor speed was exceptionally slowed (DKEFS Trails 5 = 123 seconds; <1%ile). This impaired performance on what might arguably be the easiest trial of the task was also in sharp contrast to and wholly inconsistent with her fully accurate, average range performance on the most difficult trial of the task (DKEFS Trails 4 = 90 s). Finally, although Ms. P scored beyond the cutoffs on embedded PVTs on memory testing, thus rendering the scores invalid, it is worth noting that her dementia-level memory scores (2–5%ile) were inconsistent with her "real world" functioning (i.e., accurate historian of her medical history, able to maintain employment, continued to drive, fully independent in IADLs, was able to return to testing session on time following a break).

As part of the evaluation, Ms. P completed several self-report measures assessing her psychological functioning. Of those administered, only one inventory, the TSI-2 (Briere, 2011) contains two embedded symptom validity scales (SVTs): "Response Level" assesses underreporting or denial of symptoms while the "Atypical Response Scale" (ATR) monitors for exaggeration or fabrication of trauma-related symptoms. Recommended cutoffs for the ATR are raw score ≥8 in general/non-clinical settings and a raw score ≥15 in clinical/forensic setting. A recent study within a forensic setting observed that individuals with claimed PTSD who failed PVTs were also more likely to over-report/exaggerate PTSD symptoms on the TSI-2 compared with those who passed PVTs (Henry & Gornbein, 2022). The authors demonstrated that 90% specificity could be maintained using an adjusted ATR raw score of ≥7 and a raw score on the TRAUMA factor of ≥75. In Ms. P's case, her high scores on the ATR (raw = 10) and TRAUMA factor (raw = 79) were strongly suggestive of PTSD symptom exaggeration.

Summary and Conclusions

Ms. P's failures on PVTs precluded conclusions regarding the presence and extent of any reductions in her cognitive functioning; however, in the context of normal functionality in daily life activities, any actual cognitive inefficiency that might potentially exist would be very mild. Reasons for her failed PVTs are unclear; while the findings indicated a conscious or deliberate exaggeration of cognitive impairment, the lack of an identifiable external incentive meant that Ms. P did not meet the criteria for malingering outlined by Sherman et al. (2020). Nonetheless, her performances on PVTs and compelling inconsistencies during testing rendered the cognitive test results invalid. While she might be experiencing emotional distress, as others have noted, there is no empirical evidence to suggest that psychological distress, which minimally interferes with functional capabilities would account for performances on PVTs similar to those observed in individuals with advanced dementia or notable cognitive impairment (Merten & Merckelbach, 2013; Goldberg & Birath, 2021). Moreover, despite the prevailing assumption that functional neurological symptoms in conversion disorders/FNDs are produced unconsciously, this does not explain the failure on multiple PVTs (see for instance, Boone, 2021); that is, the failure on multiple PVTs would be most consistent with deliberate misrepresentation of function (Boone, 2021). To that end, several patterns of Ms. P's performances on cognitive testing (described above) suggest conscious or deliberate exaggeration of cognitive dysfunction on her part, presumably motivated by an internal gain or incentive (e.g., possibly to maintain a "sick role" thereby continuing to receive support from her significant other). Of further concern, Ms. P's pattern of responses on a measure of PTSD was most consistent with that found in individuals who fail PVTs and who concurrently obtain elevated trauma scores, raising questions regarding the accuracy of her psychological symptom report. That is, although she may be experiencing psychological distress, the inconsistencies between her daily (intact) functioning and significantly elevated (invalid) scores on the TSI-2 preclude accurate determination of the extent of her psychological distress.

Table 37.1 Ms. P Data Summary

Performance Validity			
TOMM			
Trial 1	36/50	—	Invalid
Trial 2	39/50	—	Invalid
WAIS-IV Digit Span			
Age-corrected SS	8	—	Valid
Reliable Digit Span	9	—	Valid
WMS-III Logical Memory Combined Effort Index	42	—	Invalid
CVLT-2 Forced Choice	14/16	—	Invalid
DKEFS			
Trails 4/2 raw ratio	1.7	—	Invalid
SUM (1-3) Age-corrected SS	6	—	Invalid
Estimated Premorbid Intellectual Functioning			
WTAR	41	SS = 113	81%ile
Attention & Concentration			
WAIS-IV Digit Span Total	14	SS = 8	25%ile
Longest Digits Forward	5	Z = −1.4	8%ile
Longest Digits Backward	5	Z = −0.1	47%ile

(*Continued*)

Table 37.1 (Continued)

Psychomotor/Motor Skills			
DKEFS			
Trails 1	41"	SS = 1	<1%ile
Trails 2	52"	SS = 4	2%ile
Trails 3	70"	SS = 1	<1%ile
Trails 5	123"	SS = 1	<1%ile
Visuospatial Functioning			
WASI Matrix Reasoning	26	T = 51	50%ile
Language Functioning			
WASI Vocabulary	67	T = 64	92%ile
DKEFS Letter Fluency	73	SS = 10	50%ile
DKEFS Category Fluency	29	SS = 6	9%ile
Verbal Memory			
CVLT-2			
Trial 1	5	SS = 8	25%ile
Total Trial 1–5	32	T = 32	4%ile
Short Delay Free	9	SS = 8	25%ile
Short Delay Cued	8	SS = 7	16%ile
Long Delay Free	4	SS = 4	2%ile
Long Delay Cued	5	SS = 4	2%ile
WMS-III			
Logical Memory I	50	SS = 12	75%ile
Logical Memory II	12	SS = 5	5%ile
Delayed Recognition	20	—	5–10%ile
Executive Functioning			
DKEFS Trails 4 (0 errors)	90"	SS = 8	25%ile
DKEFS Category Switching Total Correct	12	SS = 8	25%ile
DKEFS Category Switching Total Accuracy	11	SS = 9	37%ile
Psychological Functioning			
QOLIE-31	—	—	—
Total	—	T40	Within normal limits
Seizure Worry	—	T45	Within normal limits
QOL	—	T43	Within normal limits
Emotional well-being	—	T26	Reduced
Energy/Fatigue	—	T33	Reduced
Cognitive	—	T44	Within normal limits
Medication	—	T57	Within normal limits
Social	—	T50	Within normal limits
CES-D	29	—	Severe
TSI-2			
Response Level	0	T45	—
Atypical Response	10	T87	Invalid

(*Continued*)

Table 37.1 (Continued)

Psychological Functioning			
Anx. Arousal	23	T67	—
– Anxiety	10	T62	—
– Hyperarousal	13	T72	—
Depression	18	T57	—
Anger	9	T50	—
Intrusive Experiences	20	T68	—
Defensive Avoidance	20	T63	—
Dissociation	16	T70	—
Somatic Preoccupation	16	T61	—
– Pain	8	T60	—
– General	8	T61	—
Sexual Disturbance	11	T63	—
– Sexual concerns	7	T61	—
– Dysfunctional sexual beh.	4	T60	—
Suicidality	6	T58	—
– Ideation	6	T62	—
– Behavior	0	T47	—
Insecure Attachment	18	T58	—
– Relational Avoidance	7	T53	—
– Reject. Sensitivity	11	T62	—
Impaired Self-Reference	20	T69	—
– Reduced Self-Awareness	10	T65	—
– Other Directedness	10	T71	—
Tension Reduction Behavior	11	T64	—
SELF Factor	56	T62	—
TRAUMA Factor	79	T69	Invalid
EXT Factor	37	T49	—
SOMA Factor	16	T61	—
PDS-5	48	—	Probable PTSD Diagnosis
TAS-20	66	—	Alexithymia

Note. TOMM = Test of Memory Malingering; WAIS-IV = Wechsler Adult Intelligence Scale, 4th Edition; WMS-III = Wechsler Memory Scale, 3rd Edition; CVLT-II = California Verbal Learning Test, 2nd Edition; DKEFS = Delis Kaplan Executive Function System; WASI = Wechsler Abbreviated Scale of Intelligence; QOLIE = Quality of Life in Epilepsy; QOL = Quality of Life; CES-D = Center for Epidemiologic Studies Depression Scale; TSI-2 = Trauma Symptom Inventory-2; SELF = Self-Disturbance; TRAUMA = Posttraumatic Stress; EXT = Externalization; SOMA = Somatization; PDS-5 = Posttraumatic Diagnostic Scale-5; TAS-20 = Toronto Alexithymia Scale-20.

The Case of Ms. N

Background

Ms. N was a 71-year-old, right-handed, woman, with 18 years of education. She was seen at the epilepsy center three years following a motor vehicle accident (MVA), after developing recurrent episodes of full body jerking, which had begun a few weeks after the MVA. She also endorsed a host of other symptoms shortly after the MVA, including headaches, nausea, dizziness, light sensitivity, tinnitus, sleep difficulties, fatigue, and changes in cognitive functioning. Initially, she was referred to a concussion specialist and underwent a course of vestibular therapy. She was referred for an initial clinical neuropsychological evaluation two years after the MVA to assess reports of diffuse cognitive difficulties. Ms. N's recurrent episodes and other symptoms persisted. Ms. N was referred for additional clinical neuropsychological assessment one year after the initial neuropsychological assessment (three years post MVA) once her frustrated concussion specialist suggested her symptoms might be

PNES and encouraged her to be evaluated at an epilepsy center. Ms. N's episodes occurred several times a week, were typically 15–30 seconds in duration, and were associated with feeling confused, and difficulty speaking (with stuttering). Episodes were not associated with any related injury, falls, tongue biting, urinary incontinence, or loss of consciousness. Identified triggers included loud or unexpected noises (e.g., doorbell, dog barking) and stress. She had been employed as a special education teacher working with children with severe emotional disturbance but had initiated a leave of absence at work because she felt she was putting herself and her charges at risk with her episodes (despite never having an episode while in the workplace). Before the accident, she described herself as a very socially active individual but reported that at the time of the second evaluation, she rarely left her home, had stopped working, and was unable to engage in physical exercise. Of note, at the time of the second neuropsychological assessment, Ms. N was in the midst of a lawsuit related to her MVA; her legal case had started shortly after the initial neuropsychological assessment had been conducted.

Behavioral Observations

Ms. N was evaluated at the epilepsy center at the beginning of the COVID-19 global pandemic, and the neuropsychological evaluation was conducted via telehealth where she completed the assessment from her home. She was oriented in all spheres and was an accurate historian of her medical/personal history. Speech was within normal limits for rate, rhythm, volume, and prosody. Language was fluent and intelligible, and there were no obvious word-finding difficulties during casual conversation. Thought process was logical and goal directed. Thought content was appropriate and there was no evidence of suicidal or homicidal ideation or paranoid/delusional thought content. Affect was euthymic. There were no noted signs of inattention, restlessness, or impulsivity. No PNES episodes were observed during the evaluation.

Interview

Ms. N reported a notable decline in her cognition of approximately six months duration; the timeline coincided with a significant intensification of her legal case also six months prior. Ms. N described increasingly frequent confusion and lapses in her memory that reportedly impacted her IADLs (e.g., forgetting to take her medications), and, likely most relevant to the lawsuit, her work performance within the education field (despite never having had an episode at work, she had initiated a leave of absence from work since the onset of these episodes, citing concerns about her safety and potential of these episodes to disrupt the classroom). Current and prior substance use was completely unremarkable. Developmental history was unremarkable for any learning disorders or attention/behavioral difficulties; she was an excellent student and obtained a post-graduate degree in teaching. Apart from a self-initiated leave of absence from work, Ms. N. was otherwise fully independent in basic ADLs and the majority of IADLs. She had been divorced for about 30 years and was living on her own. Her two adult children lived out of state but relied on her to financially assist them with several of their household expenses. Other than the PNES, she was in relatively good physical health (blood pressure and cholesterol were well managed with medication).

Record Review

Review of medical records revealed the following: Ms. N was a restrained driver in a stationary vehicle when she was rear-ended by another vehicle. The airbags did not deploy.

Ms. N reported hitting the back of her head on the headrest and did not lose consciousness. Given reported pain in the back of her head and neck, she was taken by ambulance to the nearest emergency department (ED). ED medical records indicate that her Glasgow Coma Scale was 15/15, spine x-rays were normal, and she was discharged home later the same day. Review of other medical records were notable for brain MRI that was conducted four days after the MVA and compared with an MRI that was obtained three years prior. There were no acute abnormalities; findings were notable for stable, nonspecific, scattered, mild T2 hyperintensities in the cerebral white matter. Ms. N saw a concussion specialist to address her reports of headaches, nausea, dizziness, body jerking, light sensitivity, tinnitus, sleep difficulties, fatigue, and a host of cognitive difficulties (i.e., trouble with word-finding, slowed thinking, attention/concentration deficits, and memory loss) associated with the MVA. The latter resulted in a referral for the first clinical neuropsychological assessment, to determine the extent and severity of persisting symptoms following concussion. Ms. N's medical history is also significant for chronic childhood trauma (years of neglect and physical and sexual abuse by guardian). As part of her workup for PNES at the epilepsy center, Ms. N underwent clinical neuropsychological re-evaluation and v-EEG monitoring. Several of her typical events were captured during monitoring, and these were consistent with PNES.

*Test Results Two Years Post MVA (*Before *Litigation Started)*

See Table 37.2 for test scores. The most relevant points from the initial clinical neuropsychological evaluation are briefly included here for review: Based on a score from one embedded PVT (CVLT-II FCR), the neuropsychologist deemed that Ms. N put forth "adequate effort and motivation" during the assessment. *Of note, Ms. N had not yet started litigation proceedings at the time of the initial clinical neuropsychological evaluation.* As can be seen, overall intellectual functioning was above average, consistent with her demographic background. Almost all scores were within normal limits or higher, suggesting intact cognitive functioning. Self-report questionnaires were suggestive of significant anxiety, but no significant depression symptoms. The neuropsychologist concluded that it was likely that Ms. N's perceived cognitive difficulties were part of the normal aging process and it was recommended that Ms. N seek treatment for significant anxiety symptoms.

*Test Results Three Years Post MVA (*After *Litigation Began)*

Given the constraints of telehealth, particularly at the outset of the COVID-19 pandemic, an abbreviated test battery was administered that did not include any stand-alone PVTs (e.g., TOMM) and thus performance validity was empirically assessed with embedded PVTs only. Although the psychometric properties of stand-alone PVTs are generally better than embedded PVTs (e.g., Miele et al., 2012) several embedded PVTs have been found to have acceptable classification accuracy, particularly when examining scores from multiple embedded PVTs across a neuropsychological battery or using a combination of scores (e.g., Victor et al., 2009; see also Davis, 2021). In examining failure rates on embedded PVTs, using a criterion of ≥2 has consistently demonstrated good sensitivity (83%–87.5%) and specificity (88.9%–100%) across several studies (e.g., Larrabee, 2003a; Meyers & Volbrecht, 2003; Victor et al., 2009).

As can be seen in Table 2, Ms. N performed beyond cutoffs across all (100%) embedded PVTs that were calculated from administered neuropsychological measures. These included embedded measures derived from the WAIS Digit Span subtest (i.e., Reliable Digit Span [RDS]; Greiffenstein et al., 1994; and Age-corrected scaled score [ACSS]; Babikian et al.,

2006), the combined effort indicator from WMS-III Logical Memory test (Bortnik et al., 2010), the CVLT-II Forced Choice Recognition trial (Erdodi, Abeare, et al., 2018), and measures of verbal fluency (Curtis et al., 2008).

Ms. N completed several self-report inventories of psychological functioning. Most of the scores were significantly elevated, particularly when compared with scores from her initial assessment (e.g., minimal depression symptoms previously versus severe depression symptoms currently). Severe PTSD symptoms were endorsed on both inventories assessing trauma-related symptomatology; however, Ms. N's raw score of 15 on the TSI-2 ATR validity scale and very high score on the TRAUMA factor were well beyond cutoffs (Henry & Gornbein, 2022), consistent with over-reporting of psychological symptoms.

Interpretation of Test Scores

Ms. N's cognitive test performances were deemed invalid due to the failure on 4 of 4 PVTs, as well as a marked decline in cognitive scores on subsequent neuropsychological exams remote from injury. Specifically, on original testing two years after the reported injury, her Digit Span ACSS was in the superior range, but one year later was in the impaired range, in the absence of any intervening neurologic event. Such declines in scores remote from injury can be used as evidence of noncredible performance (Sweet et al., 2021). There was also evidence for exaggeration of symptoms on SVTs, based on scoring beyond the cutoff on validity indexes (TSI-2 ATR raw = 15 and TRAUMA factor score of 113 per manual and Henry & Gornbein, 2022). It is worth noting that her raw TRAUMA score was: (1) higher than the range of scores obtained by the initial clinical validity sample (Briere, 2011), and (2) higher than the range of scores obtained by the noncredible group in the Henry and Gorbein (2022) study. Additionally, despite lack of validity indices within other administered symptom measures, comparison of Ms. N's scores with those from credible, clinical samples supported the likelihood of symptom over-endorsement: scores on a second scale assessing posttraumatic symptoms (PDS-5; Foa et al., 2016) were near ceiling levels and significantly higher than those obtained by veterans diagnosed with PTSD due to combat exposure (e.g., Schnurr et al., 2022). Her score of 51/60 on a depression scale (CES-D; Radloff, 1977) was also near ceiling level and about 13 points higher than the mean scores of "acutely depressed" psychiatric patients (Weissman et al., 1977).

Summary and Conclusions

Due to Ms. N's failures on validated PVTs, no firm conclusions could be drawn regarding her cognitive functioning at the time of the evaluation. In considering Ms. N's invalid performances, additional factors that might have accounted for these failures were considered, consistent with current clinical consensus criteria (e.g., Sherman et al., 2020). For instance, given her age, might the PVT failures be due to an incipiently developing neurodegenerative process? Base rates of dementia in individuals aged 71 and older is 13.9%, with prevalence increasing in age (~5% in those aged 71–79 years, to 37.4% in those 90 years and older; Plassman et al., 2007). However, even when using adjusted cut-scores, Ms. N's PVT performances were at or below that shown to be typical of individuals with dementia (Bortnik & Dean, 2021). Additionally, behavioral observations during the assessment and her "real world functioning" were at odds with a dementia process (e.g., fully oriented during assessment, did not require repetition or clarification of test instructions, provided thorough account of medical history, lived independently, handled her finances, managed appointments, and was very conscientious about COVID-19 safety measures).

A review of Ms. N's current test performances with those from the evaluation one year before also revealed striking inconsistencies that defied any plausible explanation/bona fide neurological condition: At the initial assessment, Ms. N's cognitive functioning was well within expected limits two years following the MVA, with no signs of lingering sequelae. The self-reported rapid decline in her cognitive functioning over a six-month period is inconsistent with her known medical history, which was unremarkable for any infection, metabolic derangement, or additional brain insult that may have explained the acute onset and course of cognitive difficulties she was reporting. The only noticeable antecedent was the significant intensification of the lawsuit six months prior, which took place around the same time when Ms. N. reported a significant decline in her cognitive difficulties. Finally, and most importantly, there was a clearly identifiable external incentive (current litigation proceedings with the potential for a substantial financial payout) at the time of the second examination.

Consideration of all the data were strongly suggestive of deliberate exaggeration of both cognitive and psychological symptoms (i.e., Malingering with a Mixed Presentation, per Sherman et al., 2020 criteria). Of note, although Ms. N appeared to be experiencing psychological distress (as suggested by onset of PNES shortly after the MVA that were ultimately confirmed during v-EEG monitoring three years later), the full extent of her psychological difficulties could not be determined given over-reporting of symptoms; we were only able to conclude generally that there was an exaggeration of psychiatric symptoms overlaying her existing psychological distress.

It may interest the reader to know that Ms. N was subsequently referred for psychotherapeutic treatment for PNES, but prognosis/therapeutic success was guarded in light of the neuropsychological findings that suggested deliberate exaggeration of cognitive and psychological symptoms and concerns that Ms. N might potentially lack motivation to improve due to her ongoing legal case. Her therapist noted that Ms. N was engaged during the therapeutic sessions, followed the discussions and content closely, and remembered to complete assigned homework each week (at odds with her reported memory deficits). Ms. N reported a slight reduction in frequency of PNES episodes but had not returned to work or resumed driving at the conclusion of psychotherapy treatment. The outcome regarding her litigation proceedings is unknown; however, no requests or subpoenas for her neuropsychological report or testimony from the treating neuropsychologist were received, presumably because the findings would have hindered rather than helped her case.

Table 37.2 Ms. N Data Summary

	2 yrs post MVA (before litigation)	*2 yrs post MVA (before litigation)*	*Author eval, (3 yrs post MVA, in litigation)*	*Author eval, (3 yrs post MVA, in litigation)*
Premorbid Functioning				
WTAR			SS = 116	86%ile
Performance Validity				
WAIS-IV Digit Span				
ACSS	SS=14	Valid	SS = 4	Invalid
RDS	No raw in original report	—	5	Invalid

(*Continued*)

Table 37.2 (Continued)

	2 yrs post MVA (before litigation)	*2 yrs post MVA (before litigation)*	*Author eval, (3 yrs post MVA, in litigation)*	*Author eval, (3 yrs post MVA, in litigation)*
CVLT-II Forced Choice	16/16	Valid	14/16	Invalid
WMS-III LM Combined Effort Indicator	NA	NA	40.5	Invalid
FAS	—	—	T31	Invalid
Intellectual Functioning				
FSIQ (WAIS-IV)	121	92%ile	—	—
FSIQ (WASI)	—	—	105	63%ile
Attention/Concentration				
Digit Span	SS = 14	91%ile	SS = 4	2%ile
Longest Digits Forward	7	70%ile	3	<1%ile
Longest Digits Backward	4	45%ile	3	16%ile
Visuospatial Functioning				
Matrix Reasoning	SS = 13	84%ile	T = 56	73%ile
Language Functioning				
Vocabulary	SS = 13	84%ile	T = 50	50%ile
BNT-2 Correct	56/60	–	56/60	—
With phonemic cues	+2 (58)	—	+2 (58)	—
DKEFS				
Letter Fluency	SS = 15	95%ile	SS = 6	9%ile
Category Fluency	SS = 12	75%ile	SS = 6	9%ile
Verbal Memory				
CVLT-2				
Trial 1	5	32%ile	4	16%ile
Total 1-5	T = 44	27%ile	T = 28	<1%ile
Short Delay Free	10	z = 0.5	4	z = −1.5
Short Delay Cued	11	z = 0.0	5	z =−2.0
Long Delay Free	10	z = 0.0	3	z = −2.0
Long Delay Cued	11	z = 0.0	4	z = −2.0
Recognition Hits	—	z = −2.5	6	z= −5.0
Recognition False Positives	—	z = 0.0	1	z= −0.5
Logical Memory	(WMS-IV)		(WMS-III)	
Logical Memory I	SS = 11	63%ile	SS = 4	2%ile
Logical Memory II	SS = 11	63%ile	SS = 4	2%ile
Recognition	—	>cum75%ile	—	>50cum%ile
Executive Functioning				
DKEFS Number-Letter	SS = 13	84%ile	—	—
DKEFS Category Switching Total Correct	SS = 16	98%ile	SS = 11	63%ile
DKEFS Switching Total Accuracy	—	—	SS = 11	63%ile

(*Continued*)

Table 37.2 (Continued)

Psychological Functioning		
2 yrs post MVA (before litigation)		
BDI-II	7	Minimal depression
BAI	24	Moderate anxiety
Author eval (3yrs post MVA, in litigation)		
QOLIE-31		
Total	T18	—
Seizure worry	T27	—
QOL	T56	—
Emotional well-being	T15	—
Energy/Fatigue	T26	—
Cognitive	T25	—
Medication	T54	—
Social	T32	—
CES-D	51	Severe depression
TSI-2		
Response Level	T = 43	—
Atypical Response	Raw = 15	Invalid/over-reporting
Anx. Arousal	T81	—
-Anxiety	T76	—
-Hyperarousal	T82	—
Depression	T84	—
Anger	T86	—
Intrusive Experiences	T > 100	—
Defensive Avoidance	T81	—
Dissociation	T > 100	—
Somatic Preoccupation	T69	—
-Pain	T67	—
-General	T68	—
Sexual Disturbance	T52	—
-Sexual Concerns	T53	—
-Dysfunctional Sexual Behavior	T47	—
Suicidality	T86	—
-Ideation	T83	—
-Behavior	T84	—
Insecure Attachment	T83	—
-Relational Avoidance	T77	—
-Reject. Sensitivity	T81	—
Impaired Self-Reference	T94	—
-Reduced Self-Awareness	T95	—
-Other-Directedness	T86	—
Tension Reduction Behavior	T78	—
SELF Factor	Raw = 83 (T90)	—
TRAUMA Factor	Raw = 113 (T98)	Invalid
EXT Factor	Raw = 42 (T84)	—
SOMA Factor	Raw = 22 (T69)	—
PDS-5	73	—
TAS-20	67	—

Note: WTAR = Wechsler Test of Adult Reading; WAIS-IV = Wechsler Adult Intelligence Scale, 4th Edition; ACSS = Age-corrected scaled score; RDS = Reliable digit span; WMS-III = Wechsler Memory Scale, 3rd Edition; CVLT-II = California Verbal Learning Test, 2nd Edition; FSIQ = Full scale IQ; DKEFS = Delis Kaplan Executive Function System; WASI = Wechsler Abbreviated Scale of Intelligence; BNT-2 = Boston Naming Test, 2nd Edition; BDI-II = Beck Depression Inventory; BAI = Beck Anxiety Inventory; QOLIE = Quality of Life in Epilepsy; QOL = Quality of Life; CES-D = Center for Epidemiologic Studies Depression Scale; TSI-2 = Trauma Symptom Inventory-2; SELF = Self-Disturbance; TRAUMA = Posttraumatic Stress; EXT = Externalization; SOMA = Somatization; PDS-5 = Posttraumatic Diagnostic Scale-5; TAS-20 = Toronto Alexithymia Scale-20.

Discussion

Because individuals with PNES present with symptoms that can mimic a neurological disorder along with numerous psychiatric comorbidities and cognitive complaints, they are often referred for neuropsychological assessment for clinical treatment planning and/or forensic evaluations. The two cases highlight ways in which credibility concerns may present in individuals with PNES: In the first case (Ms. P), no identifiable external incentive was present at the time of the assessment and thus per Sherman et al. (2020), Criterion A for MND was not met. Nonetheless, Ms. P's failures on validated PVTs and discrepancies in performances on neuropsychological assessment as well as inconsistencies between her reports of cognitive deficits and "real world" functioning resulted in an invalid neurocognitive profile and suggested conscious fabrication of cognitive deficits, possibly motivated by an internal incentive. She also showed non-plausible over-reporting of PTSD symptoms, with her response pattern comparable to that found in individuals who are noncredible on cognitive testing.

In the second case (Ms. N), there was strong psychometric evidence of cognitive and psychological exaggeration in the setting of a clear and documented external incentive to exaggerate symptoms. This was further supported by marked discrepancies between test data as demonstrated by substantial declines in cognitive test scores when comparing performances across repeated assessment. These discrepancies were inconsistent with her known medical history and certainly implausible as stemming from the MVA. Compelling inconsistencies were also identified during the assessment, which provided further evidence of malingering.

Web Links and Online Information

The following websites contain up-to-date content on PNES for clinicians. The first includes lists of publications organized by topic, book recommendations, and handouts.

The last two websites are for clinicians who wish to further their education on PNES and FND.

www.nonepilepticseizures.com (information on PNES, PNES publications repository, book recommendations, etc.).

www.nonepilepticseizureseducation.com (recorded courses for clinicians on diverse topics, including treatment modalities and working with special populations).

https://www.fndsociety.org/fnd-education/virtual-education-course (FND Society webpage that includes virtual courses and conferences)

References

American Psychiatric Association. (2013). *Diagnostic and Statistical Manual of Mental Disorders* (5th ed.). Washington, DC: Author.

Babikian, T., Boone, K. B. B, Lu, P., & Arnold, G. (2006). Sensitivity and Specificity of Various Digit Span Scores in the Detection of Suspect Effort. *The Clinical Neuropsychologist, 20*, 145–59.

Ben-Porath, Y. S., & Tellegen, A. (2008). *Minnesota Multiphasic Personality Inventory-2 Restructured Form:* manual for administration, scoring, and interpretation. Minneapolis: University of Minnesota Press.

Binder, L., Salinsky, M. C., Storzbach, D., & Tadrous-Furanz, S. K. (2021). RBANS Validity Measures and the TOMM in Veterans Undergoing Seizure Monitoring, *Archives of Clinical Neuropsychology, 36*, 613–619.

Boone, K. B. (2021). Performance validity in somatoform/conversion disorders, factitious disorder, and malingering. Do we need a new diagnostic schema?. In Boone, K. B., editor. *Assessment of Feigned Cognitive Impairment, A Neuropsychological Perspective. Second Edition* (pp. 433–452). Guilford Press: New York.

Bortnik, K. E., Boone, K. B., Marion, S. D., Amano, S., Ziegler, E., Victor, T. L., & Zeller, M. A. (2010). Examination of Various WMS-III Logical Memory Scores in the Assessment of Response Bias, *The Clinical Neuropsychologist*, *24*, 344–357.

Bortnik, K. E., & Dean, A. C. (2021). Performance Validity Testing in Patients with Dementia. In K. B. Boone (Ed.), *Assessment of Feigned Cognitive Impairment: A Neuropsychological Perspective* (pp. 481–503). The Guilford Press.

Bortz, J. J., Prigatano, G. P., Blum, D., & Fisher, R. S. (1995). Differential Response Characteristics in Nonepileptic and Epileptic Seizure Patients on a Test of Verbal Learning and Memory, *Neurology*, *45*, 2029–2034.

Briere, J. (2011). *Trauma Symptom Inventory-2* (TSI-2). Odessa, Florida: Psychological Assessment Resources.

Carson, A., Stone, J., Hibberd, C., et al., (2011). Disability, distress and unemployment in neurology outpatients with symptoms 'unexplained by organic disease'. *Journal of Neurology, Neurosurgery & Psychiatry, 82,* 810–813.

Curtis, K.L., Thompson, L.K., Greve, K.W., Bianchini, K.J. (2008). Verbal fluency indicators of malingering in traumatic brain injury: Classification accuracy in known groups. *The Clinical Neuropsychologist*, *22*, 930–945.

D'Alessio, L., Giagante, B., Oddo, S., Silva, W. W., Solis, P., Consalvo, D., & Kochen, S. (2006). Psychiatric disorders in patients with psychogenic non-epileptic seizures, with and without comorbid epilepsy. *Seizure, 15*, 333–339.

Davis, J. J. (2021). Interpretation of data from multiple performance validity tests. In Boone, K. B., editor. *Assessment of Feigned Cognitive Impairment, A Neuropsychological Perspective. Second Edition* (pp. 283–306). New York: Guilford Press.

Del Bene, V.A., Arce Rentería, M., Maiman, M., Slugh, M., Gazzola, D.M., Nadkarni, S.S, et al. (2017). Increased odds and predictive rates of MMPI-2-RF scale elevations in patients with psychogenic non-epileptic seizures and observed sex differences. *Epilepsy and Behavior, 72,* 43–50.

Delis, D. C., Kramer, J. H., Kaplan, E., & Ober, B. A. (2000). *California Verbal Learning Test – Second Edition* (CVLT-II). London: Pearson.

Delis, D. C., Kaplan, E. F., & Kramer, J. H. (2001). *Delis-Kaplan executive function system.* San Antonio, TX: Psychological Corporation.

Dobbertin, M. D., Wigington, G., Sharma, A., & Bestha, D. (2012). Intubation in a case of psychogenic, non-epileptic status epilepticus. *Journal of Neuropsychiatry and Clinical Neurosciences*, *24*(1), E8. https://doi.org/10.1176/appi.neuropsych.11010022

Dodrill, C. B. (2010). Use of neuropsychological and personality testing to identify adults with psychogenic nonepileptic seizures. In Schacter, S. C., LaFrance, W. C., editors. *Gates and Rowan's nonepileptic seizures.* 3rd ed (pp. 136–141). Cambridge: Cambridge University Press.

Duncan, R, Graham, C. D., & Oto, M. (2014). Outcome at 5–10 years in psychogenic nonepileptic seizures: What patients report vs. what family doctors report. *Epilepsy & Behavior, 37*, 71–74.

Dworetzky, B. A, & Baslet, G. (2017). Psychogenic Nonepileptic Seizures in Women. *Seminars in Neurology,* 37(6):624–631.

Erdodi, L. A., Abeare, C. A., Medoff, B., Seke, K. R., Sagar, S., & Kirsch, N. L. (2018). A single error is one too many: The forced choice recognition trial of the CVLT-II as a measure of performance validity in adults with TBI. *Archives of Clinical Neuropsychology, 33*, 845–860.

Erdodi, L. A., Hurtubise, J., Charron, C., Dunn, A., Enache, A., McDermott, A., & Hirst, R. (2018). The D-KEFS Trails as performance validity tests. *Psychological Assessment, 30,* 1082–1095.

Fiszman, A., Alves-Leon, S. V., Nunes, R. G., D'Andrea, I, & Figueira, I. (2004). Traumatic events and posttraumatic stress disorder in patients with psychogenic nonepileptic seizures: A critical review. *Epilepsy and Behavior, 5*, 818–825.

Foa, E. B., McLean, C. P., Zang, Y., Zhong, J., Powers, M. B., Kauffman, B. Y., Rauch, S., Porter, K., & Knowles, K. (2016). Psychometric properties of the Posttraumatic Diagnostic Scale for DSM-5 (PDS-5). *Psychological Assessment*, *28*, 1166–1171.

Gale, S. D., & Hill, S. W. (2012). Concurrent administration of the MMPI-2 and PAI in a sample of patients with epileptic or non-epileptic seizures: Implications for an inpatient epilepsy monitoring unit, *Epilepsy & Behavior,25,* 181–184.

Goldberg, H. E., & Birath, J. B. (2021). The impact of psychotic, depressive, bipolar, obsessive-compulsive, and anxiety disorders on performance validity test results.
Green, B., Norman, P., & Reuber, M. (2017). Attachment style, relationship quality, and psychological distress in patients with psychogenic non-epileptic seizures versus epilepsy. *Epilepsy and Behavior, 66*, 120–126.
Greiffenstein, M., Baker, W., & Gola, T. (1994). Validation of malingered amnesia measures with a large clinical sample. *Psychological Assessment, 6*, 218–224.
Henry, G. K., & Gornbein, J. (2022). Posttraumatic stress disorder and noncredible symptom reporting on the Trauma Symptom Inventory-2, *Applied Neuropsychology: Adult, 29*, 100–105.
Hill, S. W., & Gale, S. D. (2011). Predicting psychogenic nonepileptic seizures with the personality assessment inventory and seizure variables. *Epilepsy & Behavior. 22*, 505–510.
Jones, A., Ingram, M. V., & Ben-Porath, Y. S. (2012). Scores on the MMPI-2-RF scales as a function of increasing levels of failure on cognitive symptom validity tests in a military sample. *The Clinical Neuropsychologist,26*, 790–815.
Larrabee, G. J. (2003). Detection of malingering using atypical performance patterns of standard neuropsychological tests. *The Clinical Neuropsychologist, 17*, 410–425.
Larrabee, G. J. (2014). False-positive rates associated with the use of multiple performance and symptom validity tests. *Archives of Clinical Neuropsychology, 29*, 364–373.
Leis, A. A., Ross, M. A., & Summers, A. K. (1992). Psychogenic seizures: ictal characteristics and diagnostic pitfalls. *Neurology, 42*, 95–99.
Locke, D. E., Kirlin, K. A., Thomas, M. L., Osborne, D, Hurst, D. F., Drazkowski, J. F., Sirven, J. I., & Noe, K. H. (2010). The Minnesota Multiphasic Personality Inventory-2-Restructured Form in the epilepsy monitoring unit. *Epilepsy & Behavior, 17*, 252–258.
Magee, J. A., Burke, T., Delanty, N., Pender, N., & Fortune, G. M. (2014). The economic cost of nonepileptic attack disorder in Ireland. *Epilepsy and Behavior, 33*, 45–48.
Martin, P. K., & Schroeder, R. W. (2020). Base rates of invalid test performance across clinical non-forensic contexts and settings. *Archives of Clinical Neuropsychology, 35*(6), 717–725.
Martin, P. K., Schroeder, R. W., & Odland, A. P. (2015). Neuropsychologists' validity testing beliefs and practices: A survey of North American professionals. *The Clinical Neuropsychologist, 29*(6), 741–776.
Martin, P. K., Schroeder, R. W., Olsen, D. H., Maloy, H., Boettcher, A., Ernst, N., & Okut, H. (2020). A systematic review and meta-analysis of the Test of Memory Malingering in adults: Two decades of deception detection. *The Clinical Neuropsychologist, 34*(1), 88–119.
McNally, K. A., Schefft, B. K., Szaflarski, J. P., Howe, S. R., Yeh, H.-S., & Privitera, M. D. (2009). Application of signal detection theory to verbal memory testing to distinguish patients with psychogenic nonepileptic seizures from patients with epileptic seizures, *Epilepsy & Behavior,14*, 597–603.
Merten, T., & Merckelbach, H. (2013). Symptom validity testing in somatoform and dissociative disorders: A critical review. *Psychological Injury and Law, 6*, 122–137.
Meyers, J. E., & Volbrecht, M. E. (2003). A validation of multiple malingering detection methods in a large clinical sample. *Archives of Clinical Neuropsychology, 18*, 261–276.
Miele, A. S., Gunner, J. H., Lynch, J. K., & McCaffrey, R. J. (2012). Are embedded validity indices equivalent to free-standing symptom validity tests? *Archives of Clinical Neuropsychology, 27*, 10–22.
Mittenberg, W., Patton, C., Canyock, E. M., & Condit, D. C. (2002). Base rates of malingering and symptom exaggeration. *Journal of Clinical and Experimental Neuropsychology*, 24, 1094–1102.
Modiano, Y. A., Webber, T., Cerbone, B., Haneef, Z., & Pastorek, N. J. (2021). Predictive utility of the Minnesota Multiphasic Personality Inventory-2-RF (MMPI-2-RF) in differentiating psychogenic nonepileptic seizures and epileptic seizures in male veterans. *Epilepsy and Behavior, 116*, Mar;116:107731.
Morey, L. (1991). *The Personality Assessment Inventory professional manual*. Odessa, Florida: Psychological Assessment Resources.
Myers, L., Korman, G., Sarudiansky, M., & Baslet, G. (2021). Using evidence-based psychotherapy to tailor treatment for patients with Functional Neurological Disorders, *Epilepsy & Behavior Reports.16*, 2–7.

Myers, L., Perrine, K., Lancman, M., Fleming, M., & Lancman, M. (2013). Psychological trauma in patients with psychogenic nonepileptic seizures: trauma characteristics and those who develop PTSD. *Epilepsy and Behavior, 28*, 121–126.

Myers, L., Trobliger, R., Bortnik, K., Zeng, R., Saal, E., & Lancman, M. (2019). Psychological trauma, somatization, dissociation, and psychiatric comorbidities in patients with psychogenic nonepileptic seizures compared with those in patients with intractable partial epilepsy. *Epilepsy and Behavior*,92, 108–113.

Nelson, N. W., & Sweet, J. J. (2008). Malingering of psychiatric disorders in neuropsychological evaluations: Divergence of cognitive effort measures and psychological test validity indicators. In Morgan J. E., & Sweet J. J. editors. *Neuropsychology of malingering casebook* (pp. 213–231). New York: Psychology Press.

O'Mahony, B., Nielsen, G., Baxendale, S., Edwards, M. J., & Yogarajah, M. (2023). Economic Cost of Functional Neurologic Disorders, A Systematic Review, *Neurology*, 101 (2) e202–e214.

Plassman, B. L., Langa, K. M., Fisher, G. G., Heeringa, S. G., Weir, D. R., Ofstedal, M. B., Burke, J. R., Hurd, M. D., Potter, G. G., Rodgers, W. L., Steffens, D. C., Willis, R. J., & Wallace, R. B. (2007). Prevalence of Dementia in the United States: The Aging, Demographics, and Memory Study. *Neuroepidemiology, 29,* 125–132.

Prigatano, G. P., & Kirlin, K. A. (2009). Self-appraisal and objective assessment of cognitive and affective functioning in persons with epileptic and nonepileptic seizures. *Epilepsy & Behavior, 14,* 387–392.

Radloff, L. S. (1977). The CES-D scale: A self-report depression scale for research in the general population. *Applied Psychological Measurements, 1,* 385–401.

Reuber, M. (2008). Psychogenic nonepileptic seizures: answers and questions. *Epilepsy and Behavior, 12,* 622–635.

Reuber, M., Pukrop, R., Bauer, J., Helmstaedter, C., Tessendorf, N., & Elger, C. E. (2003). Outcome of psychogenic nonepileptic seizures: 1 to 10 year follow up in 164 patients. *Annals of Neurology, 53*, 305–311.

Roor, J. J., Peters, M. J. V., Dandachi-FitzGerald, B., & Ponds, R. W. H. M. (2023). Performance Validity Test Failure in the Clinical Population: A Systematic Review and Meta- Analysis of Prevalence Rates. *Neuropsychological Review,* Mar 6. doi: 10.1007/s11065- 023–09582-7. Epub ahead of print. PMID: 36872398.

Russell, L. A., Abbass, A. A., Allder, S. J., Kisely, S., Pohlmann-Eden, B., & Town, J. M. (2016). A pilot study of reduction in healthcare costs following the application of intensive short-term dynamic psychotherapy for psychogenic nonepileptic seizures. *Epilepsy &* Behavior, 63, 17–19.

Schnurr, P. P., Chard, K. M., Ruzek, J. I., et al. (2022). Comparison of Prolonged Exposure vs Cognitive Processing Therapy for Treatment of Posttraumatic Stress Disorder Among US Veterans: A Randomized Clinical Trial. *JAMA Network Open,* 5(1):e2136921.

Schroeder, R. W., & Martin, P. K. (Eds.). (2022). *Validity assessment in clinical neuropsychological practice: Evaluating and managing noncredible performance.* New York: Guilford Publications.

Sharpe, D., & Faye, C. (2006). Non-epileptic seizures and child sexual abuse: A critical review of the literature. *Clinical Psychological Review, 26*, 1020–1040.

Sherman, E. M. S., Slick, D. J., & Iverson, G. L. (2020). Multidimensional malingering criteria for neuropsychological assessment: A 20-year update of the malingered neuropsychological dysfunction criteria. *Archives of Clinical Neuropsychology: The Official Journal of the National Academy of Neuropsychologists, 35*, 735–764.

Smith, B. J. (2014). Closing the major gap in PNES research: Finding a home for a borderland disorder. *Epilepsy Currents, 2,* 63–67.

Sweet, J. J., Heilbronner, R. L., Morgan, J. E., Larrabee, G. J., Rohling, M. L., Boone, K. B., Kirkwood, M. W., Schroeder, R. W., Suhr, J. A., & Conference Participants (2021). American Academy of Clinical Neuropsychology (AACN) 2021 consensus statement on validity assessment: Update of the 2009 AACN consensus conference statement on neuropsychological assessment of effort, response bias, and malingering, *The Clinical Neuropsychologist, 35*, 1053–1106.

Testa, S. M., Lesser, R. P., Krauss, G. L., & Brandt, J (2011). Personality Assessment Inventory among patients with psychogenic seizures and those with epilepsy. *Epilepsia*, *52*, e84–88.

Tombaugh, T. N. (1996). *The Test of Memory Malingering*. Toronto: Multi-Health Systems.

Tyson, B. T., Baker, S., Greenacre, M, Kent, K. J., Lichtenstein, J. D., Sabelli, A., & Erdodi, L. A. (2018). Differentiating epilepsy from psychogenic nonepileptic seizures using neuropsychological test data. *Epilepsy & Behavior, 87*, 39–45.

Van Patten, R., Austin, T. A., Cotton, E., Chan, L., Bellone, J. A., Mordecai, K., Altalib, H., Correia, S., Twamley, E. W., Jones, R. N., Sawyer, K., & LaFrance, W. C., Jr (2024). Cognitive performance in functional seizures compared with epilepsy and healthy controls: A systematic review and meta-analysis. *The lancet. Psychiatry*, *11*(7), 516–525.

Victor, T. L., Boone, K. B., Serpa, J. G., Buehler, J., & Ziegler, E. A. (2009) Interpreting the meaning of multiple symptom validity test failure. *The Clinical Neuropsychologist*, *23*, 297–313.

Wagner, M. T., Wymer, J. H., Topping, K. B., & Pritchard, P. B. (2005). Use of the Personality Assessment Inventory as an efficacious and cost-effective diagnostic tool for nonepileptic seizures. *Epilepsy & Behavior;7*, 301–304.

Walther, K., Volbers, B., Erdmann, L., Kurzbuch, K., Lang, J. D., Mueller, T. M, Reindl, C., Schwarz, M., Schwab, S., & Hamer, H. M. (2020). Psychosocial long-term outcome in patients with psychogenic non-epileptic seizures. *Seizure, 83*, 187–192.

Wechsler, D. (1997). *Wechsler memory scale—third edition technical manual*. San Antonio, TX: The Psychological Corporation.

Weissman, M. M., Sholomskas, D., Pottenger, M., Prusoff, B. A., & Locke, B. Z. (1977) Assessing depressive symptoms in five psychiatric populations: A validation study. *American Journal of Epidemiology*, *106*, 203–214.

Wodushek, T. R., & Domen, C. H. (2018). Comparing two models of performance validity assessment in patients with Parkinson's disease who are candidates for deep brain stimulation surgery. *Applied Neuropsychology Adult, 27*, 1–13.

38 Evaluating Veterans

External Incentives in Clinical Settings

Robert D. Shura

Only about 6% of the U.S. population has served in the military (U.S. Department of Veterans Affairs, 2019a), yet the Veterans Health Administration (VHA) is the largest health care system in the United States (U.S. Department of Veterans Affairs, 2019b). A veteran is anyone who has previously served in the U.S. military; however, not all U.S. veterans qualify for VHA healthcare, and many who do qualify chose to not receive care through the VHA. For those who do utilize VHA for health care needs, the Veterans Affairs (VA) offers comprehensive care, including mental health services. Neuropsychological evaluation services are highly utilized within this VA health care system, with common referrals including evaluation of Iraq and Afghanistan veterans who putatively sustained traumatic brain injury (TBI), assessment of attention-deficit/hyperactivity disorder, evaluation of dementia in the aging veteran population, assessment of decision-making capacities, and other clinical evaluations.

Disability and Incentives in VA

Whereas clinical care in the VA resides under the VHA, the Veterans Benefits Administration (VBA) oversees numerous non-healthcare-related benefits programs, such as the GI Bill, VA home loans, and vocational rehabilitation. Part of VBA is the service-connected (SC) disability program, which is the program of monetary disability payments for medical conditions "incurred or aggravated during active military service" (U.S. Department of Veterans Affairs, 2019c, para. 1). A common aspect to the disability process is the Compensation and Pension exam (C&P), which is a forensic evaluation using special templates to determine diagnosis and related impairment. These exams have historically been completed by VA clinicians or devoted C&P examiners within the VA, though more recently there has been a move to using non-VA, contract examiners. Importantly, C&P examiners have access to all VA clinical records for consideration, including neuropsychological and psychological evaluations that were not meant for forensic purpose. Each separate condition is rated at a percentage based on resulting impairment and additionally, a total percentage is determined (which is not just the sum of individual percentages) to reflect overall impairment given all conditions present. The higher the percentage, the more monetary entitlement. Moreover, other rating statuses are available, including Unemployability when being compensated at the 100% rate despite having a lower rating (e.g., while completing inpatient or residential treatment), Permanent and Total Disability for conditions unlikely to improve, and Aid and Attendance for those in need of medical care in the home. Additional benefits programs also exist that can magnify entitlements received. For example, the Caregiver Support Program will reimburse a spouse of a disabled veteran in lieu of paying an outside caregiver to help

DOI: 10.4324/9781003005063-43

with in home care. In short, financial incentive via SC disability and other programs is omnipresent in the VA, even outside of formal C&P examinations. The SC system contrasts with private disability policies in that appeals may be submitted an indefinite number of times, and many who receive disability, even when 100% and at the total and permanent level, retain the capacity to work and continue to do so.

Given the disability incentives present in the VA system, performance and symptom validity assessment is highlighted, as any report may at some time in the future be used to support SC disability. Base rates of invalidity among veterans using the VA vary by type and context. On the performance validity side, Denning and Shura (Denning & Shura, 2019) summarized 50 studies with veterans and active-duty service members to calculate a weighted mean invalid rate on free-standing performance validity tests (PVTs). The resulting mean was 30%. Three years later, using additional studies published, Shura and colleagues (2022) re-calculated the mean of invalid performance, but also broke this down by context: the invalid rates were 16% in research settings, 32% in clinical studies, and 50% in disability samples. Of particular interest is that nearly a third who completed neuropsychological evaluations as part of clinical care produced invalid data using free-standing PVTs.

In contrast to PVTs (that assess performance on cognitive tests), symptom validity tests measure response bias of psychiatric symptoms based on self-report, whether through questionnaires or interviews. The most commonly used symptom validity test (SVT), based on a survey of neuropsychologists, was the Minnesota Multiphasic Personality Inventory-2-Restructured Form (MMPI-2-RF) validity scales, which was used by 36% of respondents (Martin et al., 2015). Within the VA system, large databases are available to pull national data from the electronic record system. One group of authors pulled VA data of over 17,000 veterans who were administered the MMPI-2-RF in order to inform base rates of elevations on embedded symptom validity scales (Ingram et al., 2020). Results indicated that both non-content-based responding and underreporting were relatively rare (< 5% invalid protocols across scales); however, overreporting rates at invalid score ranges were 12%–23% for psychological symptoms (F-r, Fp-r), 20% for somatic symptoms (Fs), 27% for cognitive symptoms (RBS), and 5% for symptoms encountered in civil litigation contexts (FBS-r; Ingram et al., 2020). Of note, the 27% of invalid protocols due to cognitive overreporting rate approaches the 30% rate of underperformance on PVTs noted by Denning and Shura (2019).

One hypothesis for this high rate of invalidity in clinical patients is that many veterans may have had a hidden agenda with plans to use the exam to support their service connection claim. The idea that clinical patients have hidden agendas is not new nor unique to VA. A Dutch study (Van Egmond et al., 2005) surveyed psychiatric outpatients (N = 99) and found that 41% indicated that they expected non-treatment gains from therapy, most notably related to work and social security. Moreover, of the 41 who indicated this, 32 (78%) stated that their therapist was unaware of this expectation. More recently, Schroeder and colleagues (Schroeder et al., 2022) looked at invalidity rates in their clinical sample of outpatient neuropsychology referrals within an academic medical center (N = 232). As part of the interview, all patients were asked if they are receiving, have pending, or intend to apply for social security disability benefits. Of those involved with claims, 46% produced invalid scores on testing (which included multiple PVTs), compared with only 9% of those without disability involvement. Horner and colleagues (2023) conducted a similar study with a clinical, VA veteran sample (N = 1,438). Results indicated that veterans were 1.6 to 1.8 times more likely to invalidate PVTs if they were already receiving SC disability compared with those who were not, and that those seeking disability were 1.8 to 1.9 times more likely to invalidate PVTs compared with those who were not seeking disability. Like Schroeder and colleagues' study, the Horner et al. study used a clinical sample; they excluded veterans evaluated specifically for C&P exams. Finally, and more generally, Dandachi-FitzGerald and colleagues (Dandachi-FitzGerald et al., 2020) surveyed a group of Europeans in the community (N = 401) and asked participants directly if they know someone who feigned or if they themselves have ever feigned. Of the total sample, 59% indicated that they knew someone who had feigned, and 45% admitted to feigning themselves. Given the high rates of feigning both generally and in clinical contexts, the presence of hidden agendas in clinical settings, the relationship of invalidity when disability is involved even obliquely, and the omnipresent VA disability system on top of these processes, one could argue to treat all clinical neuropsychological evaluations within the VA as if they were forensic.

Validity Considerations

There are two interpretive dimensions that might be considered regarding the validity of a given exam. First is the spectrum between what Rogers refers to as the *taint hypothesis*, which posits that any evidence of response bias is, at some level, an indication of a broader, inaccurate presentation (Rogers, 2018). In other words, an examinee's entire presentation becomes suspect with any indication that there is invalid data. In contrast, the *beyond-reasonable-doubt* standard requires conclusive evidence of response bias (Rogers, 2018). From a practical standpoint, this spectrum comes into play when one is determining how many PVTs (though, also applicable to SVTs) to administer, and how many need to be invalid before considering testing inaccurate: if one sways toward the taint hypothesis side conceptually, then a single invalid score on a PVT may be enough to render testing as invalid more generally. The more invalid scores one requires, the more in line with the reasonable-doubt side of the spectrum one aligns.

The second interpretive dimension involves how much of the data will be considered invalid based on validity test scores. At one extreme, one may determine that none of the cognitive data are valid, or that nothing related to self-report is valid (including data obtained during interview) in the case of SVTs. However, moving less extreme, one could only not interpret data of a particular domain (e.g., memory scores), a specific test (e.g., the Rey Auditory Verbal Learning Test), or just one or more specific scores (e.g., recognition score). These two conceptual dimensions intersect at the issue of severity of invalidity. For example, interpretation of a single below chance score on a forced-choice PVT may be interpreted differently than a single, minimally invalid score on an embedded validity index because there is little doubt about the meaning of significantly below chance responding. Likewise, hitting the scale ceilings for all 5 F family scores on the MMPI-3 may have different implications than a minimal elevation on F alone. Given these interpretive nuances, more often than not, one's approach to invalid test scores is more complex than dichotomous classification decisions, as most examinees do not frequently invalidate all validity indicators.

Two Cases from a Polytrauma Clinic

The Polytrauma System of Care is a network within the VA healthcare system that specifically evaluates and treats veterans of the recent conflicts in Iraq and Afghanistan and who have either screened positive for possible TBI with current symptoms, or who had significant injuries requiring extensive rehabilitation (Belanger et al., 2009). The Polytrauma System is both a top-down and bottom-up network of rehabilitation services. From the top-down side, service members who sustain significant trauma while serving in the wars might be stabilized at overseas and/or military hospitals before being transferred to a Polytrauma Rehabilitation Center for comprehensive, acute care. Following, the various Polytrauma Network Sites address post-acute rehabilitation needs. In contrast, from the bottom-up perspective, all Iraq and Afghanistan veterans undergo a four-item screen of possible history of TBI and current postconcussive complaints. There have been concerns raised related to this approach of population-based screening (Belanger et al., 2009), but veterans who screen positive are referred for a comprehensive TBI exam (CTBIE, or second-level TBI evaluation) that is a several-hour exam by a physician or physician's assistant. These exams involve extensive history and chart review, a complete physical exam, and administration of the Neurobehavioral Symptom Inventory. Following the exam, veterans are referred to appropriate specialty services for care needs, either within the Polytrauma Support Clinic Team, or with other service lines in the hospital system. Finally, for VA sites without these more intensive programs and teams, a Polytrauma Point of Contact is available to manage coordination of care as needed.

The following two cases are examples of veterans who were established in the Polytrauma System via the bottom-up route, and both had previously completed the CTBIE before being referred to the Polytrauma neuropsychologist for cognitive evaluations. Of note, both cases were evaluated in the context of clinical care, which was reviewed as part of the verbal consent process at the start of the exams (i.e., it was made clear that the evaluations were not for disability benefits). These two cases were chosen as they represent different aspects of the interpretive continua described previously and across decisions regarding how much data was interpretable, but also for the different facets of the hidden agenda aspect. All cognitive scores for both cases are presented using AACN consensus labels (Guilmette et al., 2020).

The Case of Mr. B

Background

Mr. "B" was a 35-year-old White Marine veteran referred for evaluation of memory and concentration complaints by his treating VA psychiatrist. Because he had previously completed a second-level TBI exam, he was scheduled in the Polytrauma Neuropsychology clinic. On interview, the veteran reported that inattention had been a more long-term issue but stable since discharging 18 years prior, but that memory problems began about a year prior, with a worsening course over the previous four to five months. Memory changes were gradual and without any precipitating factors, were noticed by his girlfriend of three years, continued despite compensatory strategies (lists and reminders), and led to functional issues (missing appointments, problems with relationships for forgetting to do things, etc.). Other cognitive complaints included slowed processing, at times speaking too fast, which turned into mumbling, and variable remote memory. He denied falls and tremors.

Medical history was notable for (per problem list): alcohol abuse, anxiety, dementia due to blast exposure, various pain conditions, insomnia, history of TBI, recurrent and severe major depressive disorder, alcoholic fatty liver, dream anxiety disorder, headache, low testosterone, hyperlipidemia, posttraumatic stress disorder (PTSD), obstructive sleep apnea (OSA), nicotine dependence, and having a spinal cord stimulator implanted two years prior (with noted benefit). Recent labs included normal thyroid stimulating hormone (TSH), vitamin B-12, folate, vitamin D, CBC, A1C, and urine drug screen (UDS). Brain MRI from ten years prior was interpreted to be normal. Polysomnography from four years prior resulted in an apnea hypopnea index of 44 and diagnosis of severe OSA; recent continuous positive airway pressure (CPAP) machine recording indicated compliance on 82% of nights. TBI history included several hard hits with brief alteration of consciousness (AOC) while playing football in high school and five possible blast-related concussions without loss of consciousness but with brief AOC during deployment to Iraq 18 years prior.

Psychiatrically, the veteran has a history of completing various psychotherapies and groups, but no psychiatric hospitalizations. Active psychiatric medications at the time of the exam included risperidone 4 mg, trazodone HCl 150 mg, venlafaxine HCl 150 mg, and zolpidem 10 mg. During the clinical interview on the day of the exam, the veteran described symptoms consistent with: recurrent major depressive disorder starting 14 years prior with most recent episode ending two months prior; panic disorder; and PTSD related to combat. Both acute and chronic suicide risks were determined to be low. He denied a history of illicit substance use and reported that he was consuming alcohol within Centers for Disease Control and Prevention (CDC) limits, but he noted prior heavy use after discharge from the military. He also smoked one pack of cigarettes per day ongoing.

Social history was notable for low grades in school due to being "lazy" until high school; he was able to improve his grades and graduate, though he did not pursue further education. The veteran served in the Marine Corps for two years in the early 2000s as a machine gunner. Highest paygrade was E-3 and he deployed to Iraq one time at the start of the conflict. He had not worked since he was fired from tree work 15 years prior to the exam, which he said was due to aggression at his job. The veteran was SC at 100% and rated permanent and totally disabled. Connected conditions included PTSD (100%), back strain (10%), traumatic brain disease (10%), sciatic neuralgia (10%), and migraine (30%). He denied other pending disability claims, benefits applications, or litigation.

Test Results and Interpretation

Neurobehavioral status examination revealed some restricted affect, but it was grossly normal otherwise; there was no evidence of significant cognitive nor psychiatric impairment. Behavioral observations by the psychometrist were notable for inconsistent psychomotor response, with stiff and slow movements at some times (e.g., tapping the space bar for the Conners Continuous Performance Test-3 [CPT-3]), and fluid, quick movements at others (e.g., leaving to take a break, picking up a pencil that dropped from the table). He was also described as defensive when items were queried, and at times quick to respond and not interested in further consideration of items.

Results from testing are presented in Table 38.1.

Of immediate relevance was that the veteran consistently produced invalid scores across three free-standing PVTs and four embedded validity indicators. Of particular note is that the two forced-choice measures (Medical SVT and Word Choice Test) were right at chance level; although not significantly below chance; if these scores were true reflections of impairment, they would indicate zero memory. On examining cognitive scores, nearly all scores are abnormal (below average or exceptionally low using AACN consensus labels), including very easy tests such as Neuropsychological Assessment Battery Naming subtest. The only average score was reaction time (Hit Reaction Time [HRT]). There was one score on the CPT-3 that was actually well above expectations; however, this was the HRT Block Change score, which compares performance at the end of the test to the beginning of the test: this excellent score does not reflect excellent sustained attention, but it rather shows that he did exceptionally poorly,

Table 38.1 Test Scores from Mr. B

Domain	*Test*	*Score*			*Descriptor*
		Name	*Type*	*Value*	
Performance Validity	MSVT	IR	Raw	40	Invalid score
		DR	Raw	35	Invalid score
		CNS	Raw	45	Invalid score
		PA	Raw	20	
		FR	Raw	15	
	DCT	E-Score	Raw	15	Invalid score
	WCT	Total	Raw	26	Invalid score
	RAVLT	Equation	Raw	3	Invalid score
	WAIS-IV	ERDS	Raw	7	Invalid score
	TMT	A + B	Raw	336	Invalid score
	WCST	FMS	Raw	6	Invalid score
Processing Speed	TMT	Part A	Demo T	39	Low average
	WAIS-IV	Coding	Demo T	41	Low average
	CPT-3	HRT	Inverted T	54	Average
Attention	WAIS-IV	DS Forward	ACSS	2	Exceptionally low
		DS Backward	ACSS	6	Low average
		DS Sequencing	ACSS	4	Below average
	CPT-3	d'	Inverted T	79	Exceptionally low
		Omissions	Inverted T	89	Exceptionally low
		HRT SD	Inverted T	90	Exceptionally low
		Variability	Inverted T	90	Exceptionally low
		Block Change	Inverted T	29	Exceptionally high
		ISI Change	Inverted T	90	Exceptionally low
Language	NAB	Naming	Demo T	35	Below average
Memory	RAVLT	Trial 1	Meta T	32	Below average
		Trial 5	Meta T	25	Exceptionally low
		Trial 6	Meta T	20	Exceptionally low
		Delayed Recall	Demo T	18	Exceptionally low
		1–5 Total	Meta T	16	Exceptionally low
		Recognition	Meta T	< 10	Exceptionally low
Visual-Spatial	NAB	VIS	Demo T	22	Exceptionally low
Executive	TMT	Part B	Demo T	6	Exceptionally low
	FAS	Total	Demo T	33	Below average
	Animals	Total	Demo T	24	Exceptionally low
	CPT-3	Commissions	Inverted T	75	Exceptionally low
		Perseverations	Inverted T	90	Exceptionally low
	WCST	CC	Raw/%ile	2/2–5%ile	Below average
		PE	Demo T	25	Exceptionally low
Psychological	MMPI-3	SVTs	T		Elevated
		F	119		Elevated
		Fp	93		Elevated
		Fs	103		Elevated
		FBS	81		Elevated
		RBS	102		Elevated
		Other Scales	N (%)	30 (71%)	Elevated

Note. Scores in shading are at least intact. MSVT = Medical Symptom Validity Test, IR = Immediate Recognition; DR = Delayed Recognition; CNS = Consistency; PA = Paired Associates; FR = Free Recall; DCT = Dot Counting Test; WCT = Word Choice Test; RAVLT = Rey Auditory Verbal Learning Test; WAIS = Wechsler Adult Intelligence Test; ERDS = Enhanced Reliable Digit Span; TMT = Trail Making Test; WCST = Wisconsin Card Sorting Test; FMS = Failure to Maintain Set; CPT = Conners Continuous Performance Test; HRT = Hit Reaction Time; DS = Digit Span; SD = Standard Deviation; ISI = Inter-Stimulus Interval; NAB = Neuropsychological Assessment Battery; VIS = Visual Discrimination; CC = Categories Completed; PE = Perseverative Errors; MMPI = Minnesota Multiphasic Personality Inventory.

consistently across the 14-minute test. Given this profile, none of the scores were reported or interpreted in the written neuropsychological report. It was noted that the blast exposures would have possibly met threshold for mild TBI, at most, and would not have been expected to cause ongoing problems after a few months. Diagnosis was deferred.

Conclusions

This case is an example of global response bias. The veteran produced invalid scores on both free-standing and embedded performance validity indicators, and across domains of memory, attention, and executive functions. This reflects non-discriminant, global underperformance. Similarly, on the MMPI-3, the veteran elevated all five overreport scales (in the context of no evidence on non-content biased response), indicating negative response bias of self-report across psychological, somatic, and cognitive complaints. Although the clinical profile cannot be interpreted in a meaningful way, it can sometimes be informative to look at the rest of the protocol to see what kinds of symptoms are being overreported. In this veteran's case, in additional to elevating the majority of clinical scales more generally, he also produced a psychotic profile: the highest Higher-Order elevation was on Thought Dysfunction (T = 88), and both RC6 and RC8 were elevated over T 80. This psychotic profile was not consistent with his mental status during the elevation, his medical history, or his report during the clinical interview.

This case is straight forward regarding interpretation (i.e., neither performance nor self-report data were reliable and cognitive scores underestimate the veteran's capabilities) but, despite all of the potential incentives in the VA system, none could be identified with this veteran. He was already 100% SC and rated as permanently and totally disabled, meaning it is unlikely that his disability will be reviewed and reduced in the future. He denied other pending, non-VA disability claims, and there was no application for other benefits such as the Caregiver Support Program. Although malingering was certainly considered given the vastness of invalidity, no secondary gains could be identified. The veteran would thus meet all criteria for the updated malingering criteria (Sherman et al., 2020), *except* the required identification of an external incentive. It was considered that this global invalidity might have been related to uncooperativeness.

Perhaps one of the most interesting aspects of this case is that the veteran was actually evaluated by neuropsychology about 15 years prior. The prior examiner did not administer PVTs nor interpreted embedded indicators, but diagnosed a dementia due to head trauma, with behavioral disturbance. This diagnosis was inappropriate, given the veteran was three years past the blast exposures at that time, and mild TBI would be expected to have well resolved by then given the known course. In the time since the exam, he has continued routing follow-up with primary care and psychiatry, and with monthly psychotherapy. There was no evidence of application to other incentive programs. Attempts to contact the veteran for feedback were unsuccessful, thus there was no opportunity to explore the hypothesis of uncooperativeness accounting for the invalid profile.

The Case of Mr. S

Background

Mr. "S" is a 25-year-old White/Hispanic male who was referred for a neuropsychological evaluation by primary care. He had completed a CTBIE five years prior that determined there was no combat-related TBI; however, he was in a motor vehicle accident (MVA) while stationed in Germany, which occurred five years prior to this exam. For that event, he was sleeping in the back seat and was unrestrained; when the wreck occurred, the car flipped three times before stopping. The veteran reported coming in and out of consciousness, but he needed to be resuscitated in the ambulance on the way to the hospital. He was released two days later and noted frequently spacing out in the weeks following. He reported new onset of short-term memory issues two years after that MVA. At the time of memory decline onset, he was transitioning out of the military, had been kicked out of his mother's home due to relationship stress, and was transitioning to living with his girlfriend. Other cognitive complaints included occasional distractibility and word-finding issues.

Medically, the veteran's problem list only included a diagnosis of low back pain. Recent labs were normal other than a high TSH, which was being evaluated and ultimately led to a new prescription of levothyroxine. Head CT two years prior to the exam was normal, as was a recent polysomnography. Psychiatrically, the veteran experienced a remote bout of depression when going through a divorce, with related increased alcohol use and a suicide attempt by overdose. At the time of the exam, he reported that he was "always in a good mood," though he described recent mild anxiety attacks related to stress. He reported sleeping an average of five to six hours per night, and he described middle insomnia. A sleep study completed a week prior to the neuropsychological exam resulted in an Apnea-Hypopnea Index (AHI) of 4.1, which was not consistent with sleep apnea.

Instrumental activities of daily living (I/ADLs) were reportedly intact. The veteran had been married to his second wife for nearly two years, with a son due a few months after the exam date. He reported good grades in school, and one year of community college, leading to a cyber-security certificate. He was currently working as a veteran liaison officer managing disability claims; he denied performance problems at work. Relatedly, at the time of the examination, he was 90% SC, including a 30% rating for PTSD; he reported that he had a claim pending for "memory and hearing loss." Of note, during the interview and after disclosing this pending claim, it was reiterated that the purpose of the exam was to inform clinical care, not for disability purposes.

Test Results and Interpretation

Neurobehavioral exam was unremarkable and without overt signs of psychiatric or cognitive impairment; he was able to provide a detailed history of both recent and remote events. In contrast to the first case described in this chapter, Mr. S produced a more subtle profile of invalid scores that were specific to verbal memory (Word Memory Test and Rey Auditory Verbal Learning Test [RAVLT] equation). On examining the cognitive profile (see Table 38.2), there were a few scattered below average scores, interpreted as probably reflecting normal variability, but a stark pattern of abnormal scores on the RAVLT and Wechsler Memory Scale-IV (WMS-IV) Logical Memory.

Additionally, when comparing WMS-IV Flexible Battery index scores, there was not a significant difference between the Immediate Memory Index (StS = 69) and the Delayed Memory Index (StS = 76). In contrast, the Auditory Memory Index was exceptionally low (StS = 57) and significantly lower than the Visual Memory Index (StS = 89), which was low average. Base rate of difference was 3.7% and considered uncommon. The Auditory Memory Index was also significantly lower than the WAIS-IV GAI (StS = 81) and at a low base rate of 7.1%. Given the seemingly targeted abnormal performance, verbal memory scores were considered the primarily scores that were invalid and, thus, not reported/interpreted.

Table 38.2 Test Scores from Mr. S

Domain	*Test*	*Score*			*Descriptor*
		Name	*Type*	*Value*	
Performance Validity	WMT	IR	Raw	**67.5**	**Invalid score**
		DR	Raw	**82.5**	**Invalid score**
		CNS	Raw	**70.0**	**Invalid score**
		MC	Raw	55.0	
		PA	Raw	55.0	
		FR	Raw	37.5	
		LDFR	Raw	40.0	
	DCT	E-Score	Raw	11	Valid score
	RWRT	Total	Raw	8	Valid score
	TOMM	Trial 1	Raw	42	Valid score
	RFIT	With recognition	Raw	28	Valid score
	RAVLT	Equation	Raw	11	Invalid score
	WAIS-IV	ERDS	Raw	13	Valid score
	TMT	A + B	Raw	81	Valid score
	WCST	FMS	Raw	0	Valid score
Processing Speed	TMT	Part A	Demo T	55	Average
	WAIS-IV	Coding	Demo T	57	High average
		Symbol search	Demo T	58	High average
	CPT-3	HRT	Inverted T	44	Average
Attention	WAIS-IV	DS Forward	ACSS	8	Average
		DS Backward	ACSS	4	Below average
		DS Sequencing	ACSS	11	Average
		Arithmetic	Demo T	43	Average
	CPT-3	d'	Inverted T	56	Average
		Omissions	Inverted T	48	Average
		HRT SD	Inverted T	40	High average
		Variability	Inverted T	44	Average
		Block change	Inverted T	67	Below average
		ISI Change	Inverted T	46	Average
Language verbal	NAB	Naming	Demo T	43	Average
	WAIS-IV	Vocabulary	Demo T	45	Average
		Information	Demo T	**27**	**Exceptionally low**
Memory	RAVLT	Trial 1	Meta T	32	Below average
		Trial 5	Meta T	**25**	**Exceptionally low**
		Trial 6	Meta T	33	Below average
		Delayed recall	Demo T	**25**	**Exceptionally low**
		1–5 Total	Meta T	**25**	**Exceptionally low**
		Recognition	Meta T	44	Average
	WMS-IV	Logical memory I	Demo T	**25**	**Exceptionally low**
		Logical memory II	Demo T	**29**	**Exceptionally low**
		LM Recognition	Cum. %	3%–9%	Below average
		Visual reproduction I	Demo T	40	Low average
		Visual reproduction II	Demo T	46	Average

(*Continued*)

Table 38.2 (Continued)

Domain	*Test*	*Score*			*Descriptor*
		Name	*Type*	*Value*	
		VR Recognition	Cum. %	3%–9%	Below average
Visual-spatial	NAB	Visual discrimination	Demo T	52	Average
	WAIS-IV	Block design	Demo T	42	Low average
		Visual Puzzles	Demo T	38	Low average
Executive	TMT	Part B	Demo T	46	Average
	FAS	Total	Demo T	34	Below average
	Animals	Total	Demo T	41	Low average
	CPT-3	Commissions	Inverted T	57	Low average
		Perseverations	Inverted T	52	Average
	WCST	Categories complete	Raw/%ile	6/> 16%	WNL
		Perseverative errors	Demo T	60	High average
	WAIS-IV	Similarities	Demo T	33	Low average
		Matrix reasoning	Demo T	51	Average

Note. Scores in shading are invalid embedded validity measures or below average for cognitive measures. Scores with **shading and bold** are invalid free-standing validity measures or exceptionally low scores on cognitive measures. WMT = Word Memory Test; IR = Immediate Recognition; DR = Delayed Recognition; CNS = Consistency; MC = Multiple Choice; PA = Paired Associates; FR = Free Recall; LDFR = Long Delay Free Recall; DCT = Dot Counting Test; RWRT = Rey Word Recognition Test; TOMM = Test of Memory Malingering; RFIT = Rey Fifteen Item Test; RAVLT = Rey Auditory Verbal Learning Test; WAIS = Wechsler Adult Intelligence Test; ERDS = Enhanced Reliable Digit Span; TMT = Trail Making Test; WCST = Wisconsin Card Sorting Test; FMS = Failure to Maintain Set; CPT = Conners Continuous Performance Test; HRT = Hit Reaction Time; DS = Digit Span; SD = Standard Deviation; ISI = Inter-Stimulus Interval; NAB = Neuropsychological Assessment Battery; WMS = Wechsler Memory Scale; LM = Logical Memory; VR = Visual Reproduction;

Table 38.3 Test of Premorbid Functioning Scores for Mr. S

Score	*Actual StS*	*Predicted StS*	*Different?*	*BR (%)*
FSIQ	86	93	Yes	24.1
VCI	78	93	Yes	5.0
PRI	90	96	No	32.7
WMI	86	92	No	30.2
PSI	108	95	Yes	16.6

Note. StS = standard score; FSIQ = Full Scale Intelligence Quotient; VCI = Verbal Comprehension Index; PRI = Perceptual Reasoning Index; WMI = Working Memory Index; PSI = Processing Speed Index.

In contrast, the majority of the remaining scores were thought to likely be valid, and they were interpreted as showing a generally normal profile with normal strengths and weaknesses but without signs of cerebral dysfunction. Nevertheless, the presence of invalid PVTs provides suspicion the examinee may have done even better (see as follows).

Scores from the Test of Premorbid Functioning (TOPF) and Wechsler Adult Intelligence Scale-IV (WAIS-IV) are presented in Table 38.3.

Of note, the Verbal Comprehension Index score was significantly below the TOPF-predicted score, which was primarily driven by performance on the Information subtest. It was hypothesized that this exceptionally low score reflected a *portrayal of remote verbal memory deficit*.

Symptom validity testing was variable. All embedded MMPI-3 overreporting scales were well within normal limits, including RBS (T = 61). The clinical scales on the MMPI-3 reflected a history of problematic externalizing behaviors (BXD, RC4, FML, JCP, RC9, IMP, ACT, CYN) and some anxiety symptoms and irritability (ARX, ANP). In contrast, scores on the Memory Complaints Inventory (MCI) were abnormal with a Total Mean score of 49.4%. Plausible Mean was elevated (≥ 50.0%) at 54.3%, which is 4.4 standard deviations above healthy adults. Specific scale scores were: General Memory Problems = 60.7%, Numeric Information Problems = 58.3%, Visuospatial Memory Problems = 65.0%, Verbal Memory Problems = 60.0%, Pain Interferes with Memory = 41.7% (not elevated), and Memory Interferes with Work = 40.0% (not elevated). The Implausible Mean was also elevated (≥ 30.0%) at 39.6% and 7.1 standard deviations above the mean of healthy adults. Scale scores were: Impairment of Remote Memory = 25.0% (not elevated), Amnesia for Complex Behavior = 64.6%, and Amnesia for Antisocial Behavior = 29.2% (not elevated). Although the MMPI-3 was valid, the MCI showed clear exaggeration of memory complaints, beyond just verbal memory. Given such, memory complaints from the interview were also considered unreliable. Diagnoses were unspecified anxiety disorder, insomnia disorder, and personal history of TBI (likely mild, but possibly moderate severity).

Conclusions

This second case presented a far more nuanced version of invalidity than the first case, via selective focus on "impaired" memory in both self-report and performance. The patient openly disclosed that he had a pending disability claim to increase his service connection rating, including for "memory." During feedback, which was conducted over the phone, a variety of cognitive rehab services available at the facility were discussed, including group, individual, and telehealth formats. He declined all of these programs. At the end of the call, he inquired about when the report would be available in My HealtheVet, the online portal veterans can use to access all of their medical records, as he was intending to submit the report for his disability claim. Of note, he requested this despite the discussion about having invalid memory results, and that otherwise his cognitive functioning was quite intact. It should also be noted that he did not meet criteria for PTSD during this evaluation, despite already being SC for the condition.

One could argue that this veteran met the update criteria for malingering neuropsychological dysfunction (Sherman et al., 2020). First, there was the disclosed presence of external incentive (criterion A) related to an intention to apply for increased disability benefits; intent was also established linking performance to the application of those benefits, as the veteran specifically indicated he was going to submit the report with the claim package. Second, there was invalid presentation on memory tests related to both performance and symptom validity indicators (criterion B). There were also marked discrepancies in that despite the memory complaints, he was functioning quite well at his job and with all I/ADLs, and related to the natural history of the claimed conditions (the memory decline starting two years after the TBI). Finally, the noted feigning and discrepancies could not be accounted for by other conditions (criterion D): he was generally healthy and psychiatrically he only had mild anxiety responses to stress, which were intermittent. Also, he did not meet criteria for PTSD during the evaluation, as he denied avoidance and most other symptoms of PTSD during the neuropsychological exam. Although he would have arguably met criteria for malingering of neurocognitive dysfunction, malingering was not diagnosed. This is because, in clinical settings, malingering as a label in the records could possibly lead to biased treatment later on when treatment is warranted for actual issues (Rubenzer, 2020). Further, it has been argued that what matters more than why somebody is invalid is the interpretive consequence of invalidity, that invalid data and other like data are not usable (Rubenzer, 2020); thus, memory complaints were dismissed for the purpose of this exam, and scores on objective memory tests not reported.

Eight months after this exam, the veteran completed an updated mental disorders C&P. During that exam, his self-report was far different than that presented during the Polytrauma exam: he reported significant panic attacks, strong physical reactions, anhedonia, feeling cutoff from others, anger, hyperalertness, concentration difficulties, memory issues, and insomnia. The C&P examiner did not consider the neuropsychological report, which would have been available for review. Diagnoses were PTSD and alcohol used disorder in full remission. As a result, his PTSD rating was increased from 30% to 70%, his total rating increased from 90% to 100%, and he was determined to be permanent and totally disabled. Again, he did not meet criteria for PTSD based on the neuropsychological exam. In retrospect, one could argue that the neuropsychological report was to be directly used in a forensic fashion, and that a malingering diagnosis, given this knowledge, could have been justified. It is underscored that this C&P exam was based entirely on subjective reports of the veteran, while there was no objective evidence of impairment.

Discussion

These two cases highlight varying degrees of invalid presentations, validity interpretation, and issues related to external incentives. The VA health care system does indeed include significant incentives to be sick, which has been highlighted by others (McNally & Frueh, 2012, 2013). With respect to incentive, the first case was globally invalid, including chance-level performances on forced-choice PVTs, yet SC disability was maxed out, he denied other pending claims, and there was no evidence of involvement with other disability or incentive programs after the evaluation. In contrast, the second case had a planned application for an increase in disability, and he freely volunteered during feedback that he was planning to use the report to support his updated claim related to hearing loss and memory, even after the discussion about invalid memory performance. Despite this, and the fact that he did not meet criteria for PTSD, he was still granted an increase in disability rating specifically for PTSD. He was also rated as 100% and permanent and totally disabled and continues to work full time, ironically, as a liaison officer for the VBA. For neuropsychologists working in VA settings, these cases highlight the need for a thorough evaluation and documentation of both symptom and performance validity, as recommended by the American Academy of Clinical Neuropsychology Consensus Conference (Sweet et al., 2021).

The other contrast across the two cases was the choice to throw out all test scores for the globally invalid case and not report them in the written report versus primarily only throwing out verbal memory scores. For this second case, this left a slew of other scores to work with, ultimately leading to the conclusion that there was no evidence of brain dysfunction. Of note, the decision to not report actual scores/labels of invalid data comes from an attempt to avoid others seeing those scores and misinterpreting them, which does sometimes happen despite clear warning that testing is invalid (Schroeder & Martin, 2022). Finally, the second case reflects the fact that, despite best efforts to accurately diagnose and report findings in clinical documentation, administrative decisions related to disability may contrast a neuropsychologist's conclusions. Subjective and objective evidence is not always given appropriate weight in this regard. Nonetheless, precision in language and explicit justification behind diagnoses is always warranted to minimize potential effects of external incentives.

Disclaimer

The views, opinions, and/or findings contained in this chapter are those of the author and should not be construed as an official Veterans Affairs position, policy, or decision, unless so designated by other official documentation.

Acknowledgment

This work was supported by the Salisbury VA Health Care System and the VA Mid-Atlantic (VISN 6) Mental Illness Research, Education, and Clinical Center. The author declares no conflicts of interest, financial or otherwise.

References

Belanger, H. G., Uomoto, J. M., & Vanderploeg, R. D. (2009). The Veterans Health Administration system of care for mild traumatic brain injury: Costs, benefits, and controversies. *The Journal of Head Trauma Rehabilitation*, *24*(1), 4–13. https://doi.org/10.1097/HTR.0b013e3181957032

Dandachi-FitzGerald, B., Merckelbach, H., Bošković, I., & Jelicic, M. (2020). Do you know people who feign? Proxy respondents about feigned symptoms. *Psychological Injury and Law*, *13*(3), 225–234. https://doi.org/10.1007/s12207-020-09387-6

Denning, J. H., & Shura, R. D. (2019). Cost of malingering mild traumatic brain injury-related cognitive deficits during compensation and pension evaluations in the veterans benefits administration. *Applied Neuropsychology: Adult*, *26*(1), 1–16.

Guilmette, T. J., Sweet, J. J., Hebben, N., Koltai, D., Mahone, E. M., Spiegler, B. J., Stucky, K., & Westerveld, M. (2020). American Academy of Clinical Neuropsychology consensus conference statement on uniform labeling of performance test scores. *The Clinical Neuropsychologist*, *34*(3), 437–453. https://doi.org/10.1080/13854046.2020.1722244

Horner, M. D., Denning, J. H., & Cool, D. L. (2023). Self-reported disability-seeking predicts PVT failure in veterans undergoing clinical neuropsychological evaluation: The Clinical Neuropsychologist. *The Clinical Neuropsychologist*, *37*(2), 387–401. https://doi.org/10.1080/13854046.2022.2056923

Ingram, P. B., Tarescavage, A. M., Ben-Porath, Y. S., & Oehlert, M. E. (2020). Patterns of MMPI-2-Restructured Form (MMPI-2-RF) validity scale scores observed across Veteran Affairs settings. *Psychological Services*, *17*(3), 355–362. https://doi.org/10.1037/ser0000339

Martin, P. K., Schroeder, R. W., & Odland, A. P. (2015). Neuropsychologists' validity testing beliefs and practices: A survey of North American professionals. *The Clinical Neuropsychologist*, *29*(6), 741–776. https://doi.org/10.1080/13854046.2015.1087597

McNally, R. J., & Frueh, B. C. (2012). Why we should worry about malingering in the VA system: Comment on Jackson et al. (2011). *Journal of Traumatic Stress*, *25*(4), 454–456. https://doi.org/10.1002/jts.21713

McNally, R. J., & Frueh, B. C. (2013). Why are Iraq and Afghanistan War veterans seeking PTSD disability compensation at unprecedented rates? *Journal of Anxiety Disorders*, *27*(5), 520–526. https://doi.org/10.1016/j.janxdis.2013.07.002

Rogers, R. (2018). An introduction to response styles. In R. Rogers & S. D. Bender (Eds.), *Clinical assessment of malingering and deception.*, 4th ed. (2018-11350-001; pp. 3–17). The Guilford Press; APA PsycInfo. https://search.ebscohost.com/login.aspx?direct=true&db=psyh&AN=2018-11350-001&site=ehost-live

Rubenzer, S. (2020). The case for assessing for negative response bias, not malingering. *Journal of Forensic Psychology Research and Practice*, *20*(4), 323–340. https://doi.org/10.1080/24732850.2020.1732767

Schroeder, R. W., Clark, H. A., & Martin, P. K. (2022). Base rates of invalidity when patients undergoing routine clinical evaluations have social security disability as an external incentive. *The Clinical Neuropsychologist*, *36*(7), 1902–1914. https://doi.org/10.1080/13854046.2021.1895322

Schroeder, R. W., & Martin, P. K. (2022). Incorporation of validity assessment and validity findings when writing clinical reports. In R. W. Schroeder & P. K. Martin (Eds.), *Validity assessment in clinical neuropsychological practice: Evaluating and managing noncredible performance* (pp. 70–85). Guilford.

Sherman, E. M. S., Slick, D. J., & Iverson, G. L. (2020). Multidimensional malingering criteria for neuropsychological assessment: A 20-year update of the malingered neuropsychological dysfunction criteria. *Archives of Clinical Neuropsychology*, *35*(6), 735–764. https://doi.org/10.1093/arclin/acaa019

Shura, R. D., Denning, J. H., Armistead-Jehle, P., & Axelrod, B. N. (2022). Validity assessment within veterans affairs and active duty settings. In R. W. Schroeder & P. K. Martin (Eds.), *Validity assessment in clinical neuropsychological practice: Evaluating and managing noncredible performance.* (2021–84988-013; pp. 235–253). The Guilford Press; APA PsycInfo. https://search.ebscohost.com/login.aspx?direct=true&db=psyh&AN=2021-84988-013&site=ehost-live

Sweet, J. J., Heilbronner, R. L., Morgan, J. E., Larrabee, G. J., Rohling, M. L., Boone, K. B., Kirkwood, M. W., Schroeder, R. W., & Suhr, J. A. (2021). American Academy of Clinical Neuropsychology (AACN) 2021 consensus statement on validity assessment: Update of the 2009 AACN consensus conference statement on neuropsychological assessment of effort, response bias, and malingering. *The Clinical Neuropsychologist*, *35*(6), 1053–1106. https://doi.org/10.1080/13854046.2021.1896036

U.S. Department of Veterans Affairs. (2019a, November 8). National Center for Veterans Analysis and Statistics: Veteran Population. Retrieved from *ww.va.gov/vetdata/veteran_ population.asp.*

U.S. Department of Veterans Affairs. (2019b, September 25). Veterans Health Administration. Retrieved from *www.va.gov/health.*

U.S. Department of Veterans Affairs. (2019c, June 21). About VA. Retrieved from *www. va.gov/about_va/index.asp.*

Van Egmond, J., Kummeling, I., & Balkom, T. aan. (2005). Secondary gain as hidden motive for getting psychiatric treatment. *European Psychiatry*, *20*(5–6), 416–421. https://doi.org/10.1016/j.eurpsy.2004.11.012

39 A Dementia Evaluation That Uncovered Feigning by a Patient Ultimately Diagnosed with Factitious Disorder Superimposed on Borderline Personality Disorder

Phillip K. Martin and Ryan W. Schroeder

Experts in validity assessment believe malingering to be the most common cause of invalid presentations in both forensic and clinical neuropsychological evaluations (Martin, Schroeder, & Odland, 2025). In making a determination of malingering, a clinician must infer that cognitive underperformance and/or symptom fabrication are both *intentional* and *motivated by an external incentive* (APA, 2025; Sherman et al., 2020). Intentionality can be decisively proven in the presence of below chance performance on standardized forced choice tests, which is colloquially referred to as "the smoking gun of intent" (Pankratz & Erickson, 1990). Even in the absence of below chance performance, though, intentionality can be strongly suspected when other extreme indications of deception occur, such as observing compelling inconsistencies indicative of deliberate exaggeration or feigning (Sherman et al., 2020). Additionally, when multiple improbable findings co-occur, and when there are no other viable explanations to account for the invalidity, intentionally can typically be inferred (Larrabee, 2022).

In cases in which there is not clear evidence of both intentionality and an external incentive, other causes of invalidity, such as somatization and factitious disorder, should be considered. Boone (2007, 2011) has noted that malingering can be distinguished from somatoform disorder and factitious disorder by considering the constructs of self – versus other – deception and pursuit of an external (i.e., secondary gain) versus internal (i.e., primary/psychological gain) incentive. In somatoform disorders, the individual is engaged in an act of deception, but the individual is not aware of the deception because the subject of the deception is oneself. Additionally, the motivation of the deception is internal and psychological. In malingering, the individual is aware of their subterfuge, which is invoked intentionally and for the purpose of deceiving others, and the motivation of the deception is not to meet a psychological (internal) need but to pursue a secondary gain (e.g., financial compensation, release from obligation). In factitious disorder, the individual is aware that they are being deceptive (even if unaware of the reason they are being deceptive), although the motivation for the deception is not the pursuit of an external incentive but to meet their own psychological needs.

In this chapter, we discuss the case of a non-forensic clinical patient who presented in a non-credible manner but did not meet diagnostic criteria for malingering. The patient clearly invalidated testing with a performance on a forced choice measure indicating that her underperformance was intentional. Her motivation for underperformance did not appear to be secondary to the pursuit of an external incentive, though; instead, it appeared related to interpersonal goals secondary to borderline personality disorder (BPD) and factitious disorder.

DOI: 10.4324/9781003005063-44

The Case of Ms. M

Background

The patient was a 58-year-old, widowed, right-handed, White female who attended the evaluation with her youngest daughter. The patient was referred by her primary care physician (PCP) for a dementia workup. Per the patient's PCP records, the patient and her daughter first expressed concerns about the patient's memory approximately 12 months prior to her neuropsychological evaluation. Shortly after that, the patient underwent a magnetic resonance imaging (MRI) study of the brain, which was interpreted as showing "mild atrophy, perhaps slightly more advanced than expected given the patient's age." She was also administered the Montreal Cognitive Assessment (MoCA) by her physician and scored 21/30. A follow-up MoCA was administered approximately six months later, though, and the patient's score *improved* to 27/30. It was also stated in her referral note that the patient reported a significant family history of dementia as her mother, grandmother, and maternal aunt and uncle were all diagnosed in their 60s or 70s. Although not stated in her available medical notes, the patient and her daughter relayed that she was told by her PCP, "your brain is shrinking, and I think you might have Alzheimer's disease." Given the radiologist's much more conservative interpretation, a question of iatrogenesis could be raised, if the PCP quote was accurate.

During the neuropsychological clinical interview, the patient and her youngest daughter (Daughter 1) reported noticing that the patient was having cognitive difficulties, particularly regarding memory, which seemed to have started about two years prior. When asked to describe her memory difficulties, the patient reported that she "forget(s) everything," describing difficulties remembering recent events and conversations as well as significant events from her children's upbringing or her own childhood. She also noted that she often loses track of what she intends to say in conversation and feels mentally "foggy." Upon query, the patient believed that her memory difficulties had worsened over time, although she acknowledged that she continued to have days and weeks in which her cognitive difficulties were largely *absent*.

Daughter 1 reported observing variable problems with the patient's memory, thinking speed, and problem solving. Although concerned about her mother's memory, she noted that "it can be very surprising, and maybe a little convenient, what she remembers versus not." She elaborated that her older sister (Daughter 2) caught the patient, on multiple instances, going through Daughter 2's mail and text messages. However, when the patient was confronted after these occurrences, she claimed that she "couldn't remember" doing that or she would state that she "was probably just confused." Both of the patient's daughters found this to be odd given that "most of the time" they observed that the patient's memory is fairly good. Daughter 1, who accompanied the patient to the evaluation, also noted that the patient and Daughter 2 have "a very co-dependent relationship." She added that Daughter 2, who has lived in the patient's home for about the last two years, has been wanting to move out for some time but has felt compelled to stay because of the patient's memory issues.

In addition to cognitive symptoms, the patient reported significant issues with depression and anxiety, which she indicated to be lifelong. History of sexual abuse by a family member as a child and a much later diagnosis of post-traumatic stress disorder as an adult was also reported. The patient described a history of suicidal ideation with periodic attempts, and other self-harm behaviors (e.g., cutting herself), beginning in childhood, which persisted throughout most of her adulthood. She indicated that she had been psychiatrically hospitalized five or six times as an adult, with the last hospitalization being approximately eight years prior to the current evaluation. She reported a history of diagnoses of BPD, post-traumatic stress disorder, and major depressive disorder (confirmed by her medical records). While she spontaneously described having been diagnosed with BPD, she denied ever receiving any mental health treatment specific to BPD, and she did not demonstrate a clear understanding as to what the diagnosis entailed. Upon further inquiry, the patient endorsed having a long history of impulsivity, unstable sense of self, volatile interpersonal relationships, fears of abandonment, strong fluctuations and instability in mood, and feelings of emptiness, in addition to self-harm.

The patient and her daughter reported that they continue to observe many of the aforementioned BPD characteristics. They agreed that the patient's loneliness and fears of losing relationships increased after her husband passed away four years prior to the evaluation. Since, the patient has become more reliant on her daughters for emotional support, which was one of the primary factors that prompted Daughter 2 to move in with the patient. The patient noted that she often feels lonely and depressed when not with others, and she fears she "won't be able to survive" if Daughter 2 moves out of her home. The patient acknowledged several instances in which she communicated to her daughters an intent to harm herself within the last year, but she denied actually engaging in any acts of self-harm for several years. She reported passive suicidal ideation but denied plan or intent at the time of the evaluation.

Regarding personality changes, Daughter 1 had not observed socially inappropriate or uncharacteristically disinhibited behavior, but she noted that the patient has always been somewhat impulsive. She also denied noticing any increased compulsivity. She did not find the patient to be less empathic and, instead, noted that the patient continued to be very sensitive to others' emotions.

Regarding instrumental activities of daily living (ADLs), Daughter 1 reported that the patient normally manages her instrumental ADLs without difficulty. She noted, however, that the patient "guilt trips" Daughter 2 whenever her daughter wants to do social activities outside of the home or does not include her mother in activities. In such instances, she reportedly tells Daughter 2 that she does not feel safe alone because she can't remember how to prepare simple meals or where to find the bathroom. Daughter 1 reported that the patient is typically independent and has no difficulty managing medications and finances. However, there are times when the patient's mood appears lower, at which point she asks her daughters for help, citing her poor memory. Similarly, Daughter 1 reported that the patient generally drives without difficulty, but she sometimes asks her daughter for assistance, citing that she is unable to remember how to drive or navigate to familiar places.

Regarding psychosocial history, the patient was born and raised in the midwestern part of the United States. Academically, the patient reported that she struggled mildly in math and science, but she never received academic accommodations or had a learning disorder diagnosis. Overall, grades were "average." She graduated from high school and later took a few college courses. She was married 27 years before being widowed four years prior to the evaluation. She has two daughters, both in their 20s.

Occupationally, the patient worked primarily as a receptionist until she was awarded Social Security disability related to psychiatric conditions about 25 years prior to the evaluation. She stopped working at that time, although she re-entered the workforce on a part-time basis about two years prior to the evaluation. Her first such employment was as a part-time cashier at a store at which Daughter 1 also worked. She was doing well initially, but then apparently began having difficulty understanding how to use the cash register to the point that others in the store would express concern to the patient's daughter. Daughter 1 noted that she found these difficulties to be surprising, which is what initially caused her to become concerned about the patient's cognition. The patient then began working part-time as a restaurant host and waitress, employment that persisted to the time of the neuropsychological evaluation. She denied having problems at this workplace and reported that she was well liked by her bosses. The patient further stated that she consistently enjoys going to work because "it is like therapy," elaborating that she enjoys being around others and that her job gives her purpose and "makes me feel like I'm not completely worthless." Her daughter agreed that the patient appears to be enjoying and doing well with this job. She added that when visiting her mother while working and when talking with the restaurant owners, there did not seem to be any indication or concerns of issues with work performance.

Regarding medical history, the patient denied having early childhood medical issues and stated that she met developmental milestones on time. At the time of the evaluation, her only non-psychiatric medical illnesses were hypertension and hyperlipidemia for which she was prescribed lisinopril and atorvastatin, respectively. Changes in movement, balance, and physical functioning were denied. Psychiatric care was managed by a psychiatrist, and she was prescribed escitalopram, paliperidone, and clonazepam. The patient reported that she attended psychotherapy with a social worker briefly in the past related to family stressors (not for treatment of BPD), but she had not seen a therapist for several years.

Behavioral Observations

The patient was casually dressed, adequately groomed, and appeared her stated age. No abnormalities in balance, gait, or posture were observed. Speech was normal for volume, rate, and tone although somewhat flat and lacking in inflection, which appeared congruent with her depressed affect. She understood clinical interview questions and test instructions without difficulty. Thought process were logical and goal oriented. Affect was depressed and constricted. Insight into her psychiatric symptoms appeared limited. During testing, the patient's effort appeared to vary, and the psychometrist who conducted the testing noted that the patient periodically took an abnormally long time to respond, even on simple tasks of basic attention, on which she appeared to be filtering her responses.

Test Results and Interpretation

In planning the test battery, the clinician included several performance validity tests (PVTs) validated for use in dementia (i.e., Dot Counting Test, Reliable Digit Span, Coin-in-the-Hand Test), given the PCP's concern for Alzheimer's disease and the patient's strong family history of dementia. With that said, several presenting factors suggested against the patient having dementia (i.e., relatively younger age, inconsistent presence of cognitive symptoms, good functioning in ADLs the majority of the time). Given this, the test battery also included standard PVTs that are more likely to yield false positive findings in those with dementia but also have higher sensitivity rates than some of the other validity tests (e.g., Test of Memory Malingering [TOMM] and Brief Visuospatial Memory Test – Revised Recognition Hits [BVMT-R RH]).

As seen in Table 39.1, the patient failed four of five PVTs (i.e., TOMM, Dot Counting Test, Coin-in-the-Hand Test, Reliable Digit Span) at standard cutoffs. To demonstrate

Table 39.1 Performance Validity Test Results

Test	*Scores*
Test of Memory Malingering	Trial 1 = 30, Trial 2 = 41, Retention = 40
Dot Counting Test	E-score = 35
Coin in the Hand	Raw score = 3/10
Reliable Digit Span	RDS score = 5
BVMT-R Recognition Hits	Raw score = 6

Note: BVMT-R = Brief Visuospatial Memory Test – Revised.

that the PVT failures were not false positive findings due to dementia, the patient's PVT performances were compared with samples of examinees with dementia. The TOMM was excluded from this consideration given that research has consistently demonstrated that standard TOMM cutoffs fail to maintain adequate thresholds of specificity (i.e., ≥90%) when applied to dementia patients, and there are no uniformly agreed-upon alternate cutoffs for applying the test to dementia samples (Martin et al., 2020). The BVMT-R RH was also excluded from this consideration given that low performance on memory recognition tests is common in dementia, particularly Alzheimer's dementia. In looking at the patient's other PVT failures, all three fell below that of credibly performing individuals with dementia. Specifically, when comparing the patient's performance to published dementia-based cutoffs (Martin et al., 2022), the patient's Dot Counting Test score of 35 would be a failure in mild dementia (97% specificity), her Coin-in-the-Hand Test score of 3/10 would be a failure in both mild and moderate dementia (100% specificity), and her reliable digit span score would be a failure in mild dementia (92% specificity).

It was concluded that the patient's performance on three PVTs at a level considered non-credible even in individuals with mild dementia provided exceedingly strong evidence of invalid performance, particularly given the low suspicion of dementia based on the patient's observed daily functioning, including good work performance. The most striking evidence of invalidity, however, was in her Coin-in-the-Hand Test score, a forced choice test where one would be expected to score around 5/10 simply by guessing at random. The patient, however, scored 3/10, which is statistically below chance (p = 0.17) when considering a p value threshold of 0.20 (see Binder & Chafetz, 2018; Binder et al., 2014). This finding, in particular, was interpreted as evidence of intentional underperformance on cognitive testing.

Given that the cognitive test data were determined invalid, low cognitive scores were deemed uninterpretable. Nonetheless, it is our practice to still examine cognitive data in cases of invalidity given that even individuals producing invalid data might still produce scores within or near the average range at times (Martinez et al., 2021). In such cases, these data can sometimes be used to help exclude significant impairment in the associated domains. As seen by examining the patient's cognitive test scores (Table 39.2), many performances fell well below the average range. That said, delayed recall was either low average or average across three of four memory tests (i.e., Repeatable Battery for the Assessment of Neuropsychological Status Story Memory and Figure Recall; Brief Visuospatial Memory Test – Revised Delayed Recall), which is inconsistent with patient complaints of impaired memory, her primary concern. Additionally, the patient performed in the average range on both Trail Making Test Part B and Delis–Kaplan Executive Function System Tower, which was interpreted as suggesting against significant impairment in executive functioning. Average Trail Making Test scores also argued against significant processing speed deficits.

Table 39.2 Neurocognitive Test Results

Cognitive Test	*Scores*
Test of Premorbid Functioning (TOPF)	
TOPF Demographic FSIQ Estimate	Index score = 98
TOPF Word Reading FSIQ Estimate	Index score = 82
WAIS-IV	
Vocabulary	SS = 6
Matrix Reasoning	SS = 5
Working Memory Index	Index score = 63
Digit Span	SS = 4
Arithmetic	SS = 3
Processing Speed Index	Index score = 76
Symbol Search	SS = 5
Coding	SS = 6
RBANS	
List Learning	SS = 4
List Recall	Cumulative % = < 2nd %ile
List Recognition (11/20)	Cumulative % = < 2nd %ile
Story Memory	SS = 6
Story Recall	SS = 7
Figure Copy	SS = 11
Figure Recall	SS = 8
Line Orientation	Cumulative % = 3rd–9th %ile
Naming	Cumulative % = 17th–15th %ile
Immediate Memory	Index score = 73
Delayed Memory	Index score = 60
Visuospatial	Index score = 89
BVMT-R	
Total Recall	T Score = 28
Delayed Recall	T Score = 37
% Retained = 100%	Cumulative % = >16th %ile
Recognition Discrimination	Cumulative % = >16th %ile
Trail Making Test	
Trails A	T Score = 48
Trails B	T Score = 50
Executive Functioning/D-KEFS	
Verbal Fluency: Letter Fluency	Scaled score = 7
Verbal Fluency: Category Fluency	Scaled score = 5
Verbal Fluency: Category Switching	Scaled score = 5
Color-Word: Inhibition Time	Scaled score = 4
Color-Word: Inhibition Errors	Scaled score = 12
Color-Word: Inhibition-Switching time	Scaled score = 8
Color-Word: Inhibition-Switching errors	Scaled score = 2
Tower: Total achievement	Scaled score = 9

Note: WAIS-IV = Wechsler Adult Intelligence Scale – 4th Edition, FSIQ = BVMT-R = Brief Visuospatial Memory Test – Revised, D-KEFS = Delis–Kaplan Executive Function System.

Table 39.3 Minnesota Multiphasic Personality Inventory-2-Restructured Format Results

MMPI-2-RF Scale	*Scores*
VRIN-r	T score = 63
TRIN-r	T score = 50
F-r	T score = 106
Fp-r	T score = 119
Fs	T score = 66
FBS-r	T score = 61
RBS	T score = 118
L-r	T score = 52
K-r	T score = 28
RCd	T score = 81
RC1	T score = 59
RC2	T score = 61
RC3	T score = 79
RC4	T score = 62
RC6	T score = 89
RC7	T score = 78
RC8	T score = 96
RC9	T score = 56

Note: MMPI-2-RF = Minnesota Multiphasic Personality Inventory-2-Restructured Format.

Table 39.3 provides the patient's Minnesota Multiphasic Personality Inventory-2 Restructured Form (MMPI-2-RF) validity indices and restructured clinical scale scores. There was no evidence of content inconsistent responding on VRIN-r or TRIN-r. The patient's F-r T score was elevated at 106. While scores in this range can be indicative of overreporting of psychological symptoms, they can also be seen when individuals with severe psychopathology validly report symptoms (Ben-Porath & Tellegen, 2008). Because the patient has a significant and well documented psychiatric history, it is important to examine the Fp-r scale. Fp-r provides a clear indication of psychiatric symptom exaggeration given that the scale is comprised of items not typically endorsed even in individuals of severe psychopathology. The MMPI-2-RF manual indicates that T-scores over 100 should be considered invalid; the patient scored 119T, which provides strong evidence of invalid psychological symptom responding. In addition to overreporting psychiatric symptoms, the patient's RBS T score of 118 suggests a feigning of cognitive symptoms. Conversely, there were no indications that the patient was exaggerating physical symptoms given that Fs and FBS-r were within normal limits. Overall, the patient's MMPI-2-RF profile was determined to be largely invalid and uninterpretable.

Summary and Conclusions

Although the patient's cognitive and personality test results were determined to be invalid, it was the clinician's opinion that certain points of data could be relied on to formulate conclusions regarding the patient's cognitive and emotional functioning. First, given her below chance performance on a forced choice PVT and exceedingly elevated scores on two-symptom validity indices of the MMPI-2-RF, the clinician believed that the patient intentionally underperformed on cognitive testing and exaggerated her self-reported cognitive and psychiatric symptoms. Second, although a hidden external incentive could not be completely ruled out, there were no known, reported, or suspected external incentives and there appeared to be a more likely explanation for her symptom exaggeration, so a determination of malingering was not made. Third, given Daughter 1's report of patient's behavior in daily life, it seemed more likely that the patient's reported memory symptoms functioned as a means for manipulating her family into providing support and care. Fourth, given the patient's relatively unimpaired retention on most memory tests, which still likely underrepresented her true ability given strong indications of underperformance, the clinician did not suspect that she had an amnestic dementia, such as Alzheimer's dementia. Fifth, although behavioral variant frontotemporal disease (bvFTD) deserved some degree of consideration given the patient's relatively younger age and her behavioral issues, bvFTD was also believed to be unlikely given that the patient and her family denied core symptoms of bvFTD (e.g., loss of empathy, disinhibition, compulsivity, hyperorality) and because the patient performed in the average range on two tests of executive functioning. Sixth, the patient's cognitive concerns were also unlikely due to cerebrovascular disease given that her MRI findings did not demonstrate cerebrovascular changes. Seventh, given the patient's report of longstanding psychiatric disturbances, history of self-harm, and multiple psychiatric hospitalizations, which were corroborated by her PCP notes, it was apparent that the patient had a longstanding history of persistent and severe psychiatric illness. Eighth, and more specifically, given her trauma history, previous BPD diagnosis, and her daughter's corroboration of her persistent behavioral patterns, the clinician suspected that the patient did indeed have BPD.

Given the above conclusions, it was ultimately determined that the patient's reported cognitive symptoms were unlikely due to a dementia process, which was the referring question, and, instead, were likely being fabricated to manipulate her daughters in satisfying psychological needs related to her personality disorder. The patient's intentionally non-credible presentation in the neuropsychological evaluation was likely viewed by her as necessary to demonstrate that her memory problems were 'real' and to 'prove' that she would continue to require care, nurturance, and support from her daughters. Given (1) the patient's falsification of symptoms to appear ill, (2) her presentation to others as being ill, (3) the absence of a known external incentive, and (4) the fact that her fabricated behaviors are not better explained by another psychiatric disorder, she met *DSM-5* criteria for factitious disorder. Related to the fourth point, it should be noted that BPD, in and of itself, was not the proximal cause of the feigned behavior and invalid testing in that many patients with BPD do not invalidate PVTs. The proximal cause of the invalidity was, instead, the patient's decision to intentionally falsify her symptoms, both to her family and her medical providers, presumably for the purpose of fulfilling psychological and interpersonal needs. Therefore, although characteristics associated with BPD perhaps created the impetus for the patient to falsify symptoms of a cognitive disorder, the intentional falsification of symptoms and flagrant PVT failure was deemed as not directly attributable to her BPD, warranting the additional diagnosis of factitious disorder.

At the same time, it should be recognized that factitious disorder and personality disorders typically go hand in hand. The presence of personality disorders, especially BPD, is almost invariable in factitious disorder (Feldman et al., 1997). While not all patients with BPD exhibit factitious presentations, BPD is a constant presence (Lazzari et al., 2023) in factitious disorder (see also Bass & Wade, 2019; Caselli et al., 2018; Goldstein, 1998; Gordon & Sansone, 2013; Sharma et al., 2021). Therefore, when a clinician determines that a patient's presentation is factitious, concurrent presence of BPD should be carefully considered.

Patient Feedback Session/Follow-Up

Feedback on the test results was provided to the patient and Daughter 1 using the Firm-Beneficent approach detailed by Martin and Schroeder (2022). In brief, when using this model, the clinician begins the feedback session by summarizing the patient history as expressed earlier in the evaluation. Next, the clinician conveys the invalid findings to the patient and family but then makes a 'hard turn' to focus on factors that may be driving the behavior and/or are pertinent for treatment.

In line with Firm-Beneficent approach, a summary of the patient's report and available records was provided, then it was explained that neuropsychological test findings were invalid, which rendered her low cognitive scores uninterpretable. The clinician provided no discussion or inquiry regarding the reason for invalidity. Consistent with the clinician's experience using this method, the patient and her daughter accepted that the test data were invalid and did not have any follow-up questions. It was then noted that, given some of the patient's higher cognitive scores as well as the course and nature of her symptoms, the clinician did not suspect that the patient had Alzheimer's disease or other neurologic conditions that could lead to dementia. The patient's daughter, especially, appeared relieved by this information. It was then noted that the patient's memory complaints likely related to her feelings and beliefs about herself and her feelings of insecurity and fears of abandonment in her relationships with others, particularly her daughters. We discussed common features and symptoms of BPD and how psychotherapy, especially Dialectic Behavioral Therapy (DBT), can be helpful in addressing these issues. After discussing components of DBT, the patient was agreeable to the clinician making a referral for therapy. The patient's daughter added that these findings helped her to understand her mother's challenges regulating emotions and managing relationships with family members; she was appreciative of the discussion.

Discussion

The preceding case demonstrates the necessity of assessing performance and symptom validity even in clinical patients referred for dementia evaluation who do not present with an obvious external incentive. Had the patient's neuropsychological test results and reported symptoms simply been taken at face value, the patient might have been diagnosed with mild cognitive impairment, or possibly mild dementia. By assessing validity, the clinician became aware of the functional nature of the patient's reported symptoms as well as the fact that the patient was intentionally exaggerating her symptoms. This allowed for a more accurate diagnosis and conceptualization of the patient's cognitive complaints, which, in turn, led to a productive discussion with the patient and her family about symptoms and targeted treatments for BPD. As described above, although BPD appeared to be the distal impetus for the patient's manipulative behaviors, the proximal cause of the invalidity was factitious disorder. In addition to meeting *DSM-5* criteria for factitious disorder, the patient appeared to meet the newly proposed Chafetz et al. (2020) criteria for factitious disorder. This case demonstrates how failure of PVTs can be integrated into the Chafetz et al. criteria as psychometric evidence for factitious disorder in cases where non-credible presentations appear intentional but are not motivated by an external incentive. In summary, although factitious disorder is generally thought to be a relative infrequent cause of invalidity (Martin, Schroeder, & Odland, 2025), it does occasionally occur in clinical settings and should be considered as a possibility when malingering is ruled out.

References

American Psychiatric Association. (2013). *American Psychiatric Association: Diagnostic and statistical manual of mental disorders* (5th ed.). Arlington, VA: Author.

Bass, C., & Wade, D. T. (2019). Malingering and factitious disorder. *Practical Neurology*, *19*(2), 96–105.

Ben-Porath, Y. S., & Tellegen, A. (2008). *Minnesota multiphasic personality inventory-2 restructured form: Manual for administration, scoring, and interpretation*. Minneapolis, MN: University of Minnesota Press.

Binder, L. M., & Chafetz, M. D. (2018). Determination of the smoking gun of intent: Significance testing of forced choice results in social security claimants. *The Clinical Neuropsychologist*, *32*(1), 132–144.

Binder, L. M., Larrabee, G. J., & Millis, S. R. (2014). Intent to fail: Significance testing of forced choice test results. *The Clinical Neuropsychologist*, *28*(8), 1366–1375.

Boone, K. (2007). A reconsideration of the Slick et al. (1999). criteria for malingered neurocognitive dysfunction. In K. Boone (Ed.), *Assessment of feigned cognitive impairment* (pp. 29–49). New York: The Guilford Press.

Boone, K. (2011). Somatoform disorders, factitious disorder, and malingering. In M. R. Schoenberg & J. G. Scott (Eds.), *The little black book of neuropsychology: A syndrome-based approach* (pp. 551–566). New York, NY: Springer Publishing.

Caselli, I., Poloni, N., Ceccon, F., Ielmini, M., Merlo, B., & Callegari, C. (2018). A systematic review on factitious disorders: psychopathology and diagnostic classification. *Neuropsychiatry*, *8*(1), 281–292.

Chafetz, M. D., Bauer, R. M., & Haley, P. S. (2020). The other face of illness-deception: Diagnostic criteria for factitious disorder with proposed standards for clinical practice and research. *The Clinical Neuropsychologist*, *34*(3), 454–476.

Feldman, M. D., Rosenquist, P. B., & Bond, J. P. (1997). Concurrent factitious disorder and factitious disorder by proxy: Double jeopardy. *General Hospital Psychiatry*, *19*(1), 24–28.

Goldstein, A. B. (1998). Identification and classification of factitious disorders: An analysis of cases reported during a ten year period. *The International Journal of Psychiatry in Medicine*, *28*(2), 221–241.

Gordon, D. K., & Sansone, R. A. (2013). A relationship between factitious disorder and borderline personality disorder. *Innovations in Clinical Neuroscience*, *10*(11–12), 11.

Larrabee, G. J. (2022). Synthesizing data to reach clinical conclusions regarding validity status. In R. W. Schroeder & P. K. Martin (Eds.), *Validity assessment in clinical neuropsychological practice: Evaluating and managing noncredible performance* (pp. 193–210). New York: Guilford Publications.

Lazzari, C., Shoka, A., & Rabottini, M. (2023). Factitious disorder comorbid with borderline personality disorder and dysthymia: from medically unexplained physical symptoms to functional neurological disorder. *Rivista di psichiatria*, *58*(5), 205–219.

Martin, P. K., & Schroeder, R. W. (2022). A framework for providing clinical feedback when patients invalid testing. In R. W. Schroeder & P. K. Martin (Eds.), *Validity assessment in clinical neuropsychological practice: Evaluating and managing noncredible performance* (pp. 47–69). New York: Guilford Publications.

Martin, P. K., Schroeder, R. W., & Olsen, D. H. (2022). Performance validity in the dementia clinic: Specificity of validity tests when used individually and in aggregate across levels of cognitive impairment severity. *The Clinical Neuropsychologist*, *36*(1), 165–188.

Martin, P. K., Schroeder, R. W., Olsen, D. H., Maloy, H., Boettcher, A., Ernst, N., & Okut, H. (2020). A systematic review and meta-analysis of the Test of Memory Malingering in adults: Two decades of deception detection. *The Clinical Neuropsychologist*, *34*(1), 88–119.

Martin, P. K., Schroeder, R. W., & Odland, A. P. (2025). Neuropsychological validity assessment beliefs and practices: A survey of North American neuropsychologists and validity assessment experts. Archives of Clinical Neuropsychology, *40*(2), 201–223.

Martinez, K. A., Sayers, C., Hayes, C., Martin, P. K., Clark, C. B., & Schroeder, R. W. (2021). Normal cognitive test scores cannot be interpreted as accurate measures of ability in the context of failed performance validity testing: A symptom-and detection-coached simulation study. *Journal of Clinical and Experimental Neuropsychology*, *43*(3), 301–309.

Pankratz, L., & Erickson, R. (1990). Two views of malingering. *The Clinical Neuropsychologist*, *4*(4), 379–389.

Sharma, V., Singh Bhandari, S., Singh, V., & Chandra, A. (2021). A case of factitious disorder: Red herring of psychiatry. *Psychiatria Danubina*, *33*(br 3), 371–372.

Sherman, E. M., Slick, D. J., & Iverson, G. L. (2020). Multidimensional malingering criteria for neuropsychological assessment: A 20-year update of the malingered neuropsychological dysfunction criteria. *Archives of Clinical Neuropsychology*, *35*(6), 735–764.

Section VI

Ethics and Professional Issues

Various ethical and professional issues arise when conducting neuropsychological exams, which include providing feedback to clinical patients who produce invalid neurocognitive results, the interpretation and reporting of neuropsychological findings to key stakeholders in forensic evaluations, and use of the term malingering and admissibility of expert opinions regarding neuropsychological evidence of malingering. Patients might feel unheard, frustrated, or upset. Forensic participants might perceive unfair treatment, increasing the likelihood of concerns and objections. Examiners may not appreciate and guard against influences and pressures that could lead them to provide inaccurate conclusions. The chapters within this section address how to navigate these concerns, with reference to guidance from the American Psychological Association Code of Ethics.

DOI: 10.4324/9781003005063-45

40 Ethical and Professional Issues in Assessing Malingering in a Neuropsychological Examinee

James D. Seward and Thomas Guilmette

Prologue

This chapter explores the ethical and professional issues involved in assigning a diagnosis of malingering, relying heavily on the guidance offered by the *Ethical Principles of Psychologists and Code of Conduct* (hereinafter referred to as the *Ethics Code*) (American Psychological Association, 2017) and the *Specialty Guidelines for Forensic Psychologists* (hereinafter referred to as the *Guidelines*) (American Psychological Association, 2013).[1,2] We discuss how these documents, in conjunction with recent research and policy statements, provide guidance regarding the assessment of malingering in a neuropsychological examinee with respect to the American Psychological Association (APA) general principles of beneficence and non-malfeasance, fidelity and responsibility, integrity, justice, and respect for people's rights and dignity (American Psychological Association, 2017).

Introduction

Distinct from many other diagnostic procedures in the healthcare field (e.g., x-rays or laboratory studies), neuropsychological evaluations depend on the active participation of the examinee, including expending effort to do well. A valid interpretation of the resulting scores assumes that the examinee was a willing partner in the process and put forth his or her best effort. However, a significant percentage of examinees fail to meet this criterion. Of those, a portion of people deliberately perform poorly in a conscious, goal-directed attempt to influence the results to obtain some external benefit.

This deliberate distortion of physical and psychological symptoms for gain is termed malingering. The American Psychiatric Association's *Diagnostic and Statistical Manual of Mental Disorders-Fifth Edition-Text Revision* (*DSM-5-TR*) (2022) categorizes malingering not as a mental disorder, but as a condition "that may be a focus of clinical attention" (p. 821). The formal description of malingering according to *DSM-5-TR* is as follows:

> The essential feature of malingering is the intentional production of false or grossly exaggerated physical or psychological symptoms, motivated by external incentives such as avoiding military duty, avoiding work, obtaining financial compensation, evading criminal prosecution, or obtaining drugs.
>
> (p. 835)

This is as opposed to conditions where an invalid presentation is due to internal incentives, such as in factitious disorder where the aim is to assume a sick role, although factitious

DOI: 10.4324/9781003005063-46

disorder and malingering are not necessarily mutually exclusive as "the motives in any single case might be multiple and shifting" (American Psychiatric Association, 2022, p. 369). Yet, both factitious disorder and malingering share a crucial aspect: deception of illness (Chafetz, Bauer, & Haley, 2020). A critical feature of malingering is *deliberate* deception. While both malingering and factitious disorder involve intentional deception of symptoms, somatic symptom disorder and functional neurological disorder/conversion disorder are thought not to, and thus would be excluded from a malingering classification.

It is critical to consider the validity of a patient's (in a clinical setting) or an examinee's (in a forensic setting) presentation as the first step in the diagnostic process (First, 2024). This is consistent with the ethical principle of fidelity and responsibility in which psycholcgists "are aware of their professional and scientific responsibilities to society and to the specific communities in which they work" (APA, 2017, p. 3), as well as the principle of integrity in which psychologists "promote accuracy, honesty, and truthfulness" in the practice of psychology (APA, 2017, p. 3). This critical first step is essential, regardless of the cause of invalidity.

As written, this *DSM-5-TR* definition is directly applicable to cases of somatic and psychiatric malingering. However, it does not specifically mention cognitive malingering (Sherman, Slick, & Iverson, 2020), although it can easily be inferred that this falls under the rubric of "psychological problems."

Sherman and her colleagues formulated the Multidimensional Criteria for Neurocognitive, Somatic, and Psychiatric Malingering to allow for the consideration of a variety of malingering presentations, including of cognitive impairment. They thus proffered the following definition of malingering:

> Malingering is the volitional feigning or exaggeration of neurocognitive, somatic, or psychiatric symptoms for the purpose of obtaining material gain and services or avoiding formal duty, responsibility, or undesirable outcome.
>
> (Sherman et al., 2020, p. 739)

Malingering, according to Sherman and colleagues (2020), is based on four criteria, which must be "clear and compelling:"

A Presence of an external incentive;
B Invalid presentation on examination indicative of feigning or exaggeration;
C Marked discrepancies between test data and/or symptom report and other kinds of evidence; and
D Behaviors meeting criterion B are not fully accounted for by another condition.

Based on a review of the literature, Sherman et al. (2020) reported that "the percentage of examinees who feign, exaggerate, or fabricate cognitive deficits during neuropsychological examinations" ranges from less than 10% in medical populations with no external incentives to up to 60% in Social Security applicants (p. 736). Larrabee, Millis, and Meyers (2009) maintained that the data across different settings have been sufficiently consistent to propose "a new 'magic number' in neuropsychology: 40 ± 10, representing the average base rate or prevalence of invalid data/probable malingering in settings with external incentives" (p. 843).

In 2021, the American Academy of Clinical Neuropsychology (AACN) issued a consensus statement on validity assessment (Sweet, Heilbronner et al., 2021) asserting that although malingering is more likely to be encountered in forensic contexts given the universal presence of external incentives, malingering should also be considered when invalid responding is suspected in clinical contexts. Consistent with the AACN advisory, Martin and Schroeder (2020) reported from their survey of adult-focused neuropsychologists that in non-forensic contexts, a base rate of invalidity reached 15%, which increased significantly depending on specific clinical contexts, such as examining patients with medically unexplained symptoms (50% estimated invalidity) and with oppositional attitudes toward testing (37.5% estimated invalidity).

The determination of malingering relies significantly on the use of performance and symptom validity tests (Bush et al., 2005; Sherman et al., 2020; Sweet, Heilbronner et al., 2021). Performance validity tests (PVTs) are designed to detect whether an examinee is responding in a valid manner (i.e., responding at actual level of capability) on ability measures. Symptom validity tests (SVTs) are designed to detect whether examinees are being forthright in their self-report of symptoms of psychiatric disturbance, including cognitive complaints. PVTs and SVTs can either be freestanding (stand-alone) or embedded into standard measures.

Validity assessment within both a clinical and forensic context is clearly now the norm in neuropsychological evaluations. For example, Martin, Schroeder, and Odland (2015) reported that in a survey of 419 neuropsychologists, 95% often or always administer embedded validity tests and 87.3% often or always administer freestanding validity tests. In forensic evaluations, respondents administer a total mean of 6.3 validity tests (median = 6). In a different sample of 772 survey respondents who conduct forensic examinations, 74.2% use multiple stand-alone PVTs, 83.6% use multiple embedded PVTs, and 75.5% use SVTs in their forensic evaluations (Sweet, Klipfel, Nelson, & Moberg, 2021). Notably, within the sample of forensic practitioners, only 1.2% indicated that they did not use PVTs or SVTs in their practice.

The administration of psychometric measures of effort and validity in forensic assessments is based not just on research and clinical standards, but also on ethical foundations and principles. These principles guide forensic examiners in their selection and interpretation of validity assessment measures. Bush, Heilbronner, and Ruff (2014) summarized the integration of clinical practice and the APA ethical principles in their conceptualization that "ethical psychologists are guided by a personal commitment to" the following:

> (1) provide beneficial services to examinees, retaining parties, the trier of fact or of the decision-maker, and society at large; (2) minimize the potential for harm to examinees, other involved parties, the legal or administrative system, and the profession of psychology which could arise from unprofessional practices; (3) inspire trust from others that the requested psychological services will be performed as accurately and objectively as possible; (4) promote accuracy, honesty, and truthfulness in all aspects of the services provided, including considering and minimizing their own biases; (5) strive to ensure fairness and equality in access to services, the process and procedures employed, and the services provided; and (6) demonstrate respect for the rights and dignity of those with whom they work providing services that are consistent with best practices.
>
> (p. 202)

The Impact of Malingering

The classification of whether a person is malingering can have significant implications for both the examinee and society. The principle of *primam non nocere* is enshrined in the

Ethical Code Beneficence and Nonmaleficence that states in part, "Psychologists strive to benefit those with whom they work and take care to do no harm" (p. 3). However, that principle "does not imply that psychological conclusions or legal outcomes must be favorable to the examinee or retaining party" (Bush et al., 2014, p. 199). Rather, this principle requires that the psychologist respect the rights and welfare of those with whom they interact professionally and they "are alert to and guard against personal, financial, social, organizational, or political factors that might lead to misuse of their influence" (APA, 2017, p. 3).

As in all clinical endeavors and with all diagnoses, errors in the classification of an examinee as malingering can occur. A false positive determination of malingering can have profound consequences for the examinee. In civil cases, an inaccurate determination of malingering can deny a plaintiff funding for needed therapies. Clinically, a false positive could deny a patient needed medical care. Weiss and Van Dell (2017) wrote that people found to be malingering in medical settings can be charged with "theft of service" (p. 342). In criminal forensic settings, a finding of malingering can lead to a lengthier sentence (Knoll & Resnick, 1999), and in capital cases, a finding of malingering can literally mean the difference between life and death for the defendant. A person determined to be malingering in the military is subject to court-martial (Weiss & Van Dell, 2017).

Sherman et al. (2020) wrote, "Marked discrepancies between sources of evidence are a critical aspect of malingering and, when present, reduce the chances of false positives" (p. 753). A potential source of such discrepancies is the examinee's presentation and report during an interview and information garnered from collateral sources, such as interviews with friends and family, employment, school, and medical records. Social media postings and sources of internet-based data may be informative (Batastini & Vitacco, 2020; Bazzell, 2023). Relevant to criminal cases, correctional facilities often intercept inmate's communications with the outside world (see below). Additional sources of information for incarcerated individuals includes books and media ordered, classes completed, recreational activities, and work assignments (in a prison setting, the latter can include sophisticated tasks such as operating construction equipment and wildland firefighting).

In acknowledgment of the seriousness of the issue, the cut-off scores for PVTs are calculated to emphasize specificity at the expense of sensitivity given that a false positive error (e.g., 1 – specificity) is generally considered more deleterious than a false negative error (e.g., 1 – sensitivity). An acceptable specificity is commonly set at 90% (Sweet, Heilbronner et al., 2021), which would limit the potential false positive error rate to 10%. Neuropsychologists are ethically bound by APA Standard 9.02 (Use of Assessments) to administer PVTs with empirically derived cut-off scores that reflect the considerations noted above regarding false positive and negative errors and to use these procedures "in a manner and for purposes that are appropriate in light of the research on or evidence of the usefulness and proper application of the techniques" (APA, 2017, p. 13). Standard 9.02 also asserts that psychologists "use assessment instruments whose validity and reliability have been established for use with members of the population tested" (APA, 2017, p. 13), which would include validity assessment techniques.

False negative determinations can have consequences for the individual. People who malinger psychiatric conditions may be treated with unnecessary and potentially harmful, costly treatments. False negative determinations can also adversely impact society, which is an ethical consideration noted in Principle B: Fidelity and Responsibility that states psychologists "are aware of their professional and scientific responsibilities to society and to the specific communities in which they work" (p. 3). For example, defendants who successfully malinger insanity or incompetency to stand trial may be returned to the community, giving them the opportunity to further victimize society.[3] In addition to the suffering of victims and families, there are significant monetary costs of crime (Wickramasekara, Wright, Elsey, & Murray, 2015). Using a variety of factors, DeLisi and his colleagues (2010) estimated that the average per case cost of murder was approximately $17 million, for rape $449 thousand, armed robbery $33 thousand, aggravated assault $145 thousand, and burglary $41 thousand (all in 2008 U.S. dollars). Chafetz and Underhill (2013) estimated that malingered disability cost the Social Security Administration (and hence U.S. taxpayers) $20.02 billion in 2011 for adult mental disorder payments. Denning and Shura (2019) estimated the nationwide costs of veterans malingering cognitive deficits due to mild traumatic brain injury to be $136 to $235 million U.S. dollars per year (depending on the classification criteria used).

Moreover, criminal defendants malingering mental illness can lead to protracted litigation, increasing the cost and burden on our legal system (and hence the taxpayer). For example, in a widely covered case, reputed mob boss Vincent Gigante fought a seven-year court battle maintaining that he was incompetent to stand trial, prior to pleading guilty to obstruction of justice in 2003 (Raab, 2005). This protracted dispute was undoubtedly very costly for all involved parties, and likely tied up a great deal of the court's time. Of note, Mr. Gigante reportedly had multiple brain imaging procedures that were read as abnormal, consistent with dementia. However, he later admitted to malingering, making him "...perhaps the only documented case of an Alzheimer dementia diagnosed with a medical certainty who was cured by incarceration" (Simpson & Brodie, 2017, p. 4483).

The Death Penalty

Tom Smith was a 42-year-old inmate who was on trial for first degree murder for the killing of a fellow inmate. This killing was thought to be gang-related and was captured on surveillance video. This was a capital case.

In the course of this litigation Mr. Smith was seen by several defense experts. Proffered diagnoses in the defense expert reports included brain damage, attention deficit/hyperactivity disorder (ADHD), a mood disorder, complex posttraumatic stress disorder (PTSD) with dissociation, intellectual disability, a learning disorder, antisocial personality disorder, and history of a substance abuse disorder.

One of the authors was retained by the prosecution. When interviewed, Mr. Smith reported lifelong debilitating and pervasive emotional distress. He presented as preoccupied with this lifelong distress and frequently returned to this topic during the diagnostic interviews. He described himself as a lifelong social isolate; "like a hermit."

Mr. Smith obtained valid range scores on multiple PVTs. Except for a possible attention-deficit/hyperactivity disorder and a possible specific learning disorder with impairment in mathematics, his neuropsychological test profile did not reveal indications of cognitive impairment.

In contrast, responses on self-report questionnaires with symptom validity scales such as the Minnesota Multiphasic Personality Inventory, 3rd Edition (administered twice), the Personality Assessment Inventory, and the Trauma Symptom Inventory, 2nd Edition (administered twice) were characterized by over-reporting, inconsistent responding, or a failure to follow test instructions. The Psychopathic Personality Inventory-Revised was valid. On this test, Mr. Smith described himself as ignoring rules, not taking responsibility for his behavior, being impulsive and unconcerned about his future, and as a daredevil who is unafraid of danger.

Mr. Smith's results on measures without symptom validity scales were noteworthy for reports of severe psychopathology. He endorsed all the items on the Life Events Checklist-5, except for one that dealt with having caused harm or death to another. On the Clinician-Administered PTSD Scale for DSM-5, Mr. Smith reported significant life-long trauma-related symptomatology, starting "before [he] was born." He endorsed "constant" depersonalization and derealization "most of the time." Two administrations of the Beck Anxiety Inventory produced scores in the ranges of severe and moderate-to-severe anxiety, and both administrations of the Beck Depression Inventory, 2nd Edition resulted in scores in the range of severe depression.

Mr. Smith was generally cooperative with the process of being interviewed, but his presentation was noteworthy for vague responses to factual questions. During the first of five meetings he displayed two episodes of dramatic unresponsiveness (captured on video). He described these as a daily occurrence although he did not exhibit these during the following four meetings, nor were they noted by defense experts. He described unusual psychiatric symptoms, such as experiencing "a big figure" most of his life, which "bit" him on his back.

Mr. Smith had a long history with the criminal justice system. As a result, in addition to the expert reports from the instant offense, documentation from prison health services and probation departments was available. Transcripts of interviews with family members were reviewed. Taken together, these documents did not support Mr. Smith's description of severe, lifelong emotional disturbance and psychiatric symptomatology.

Due to being in prison, all his communications with family and friends were recorded, including communications with a woman he met on a prison pen pal site. These communications likewise did not support Mr. Smith's assertion of debilitating and persisting emotional and psychiatric disturbance. Rather, his presentation when communicating with others was unremarkable. He engaged in normal conversational exchanges. His tone of voice and facial expression (on a video visit) were consistent with the conversational topic; he was in good spirits when appropriate. He provided advice and emotional support to correspondents and was conversant regarding books, movies, and current events.

One of the authors concluded that Mr. Smith was malingering a psychiatric condition based on the test results and marked discrepancies between his presentation and report during our interviews and the available collateral information. It was not concluded that he was malingering cognitive deficits.

Mental health experts for both the defense and prosecution testified at the penalty phase of his trial, which lasted 13 days. The jury sentenced Mr. Smith to death.

Per the Preamble of the Ethics Code, psychologists are advocates,

> ...committed to increasing scientific and professional knowledge of behavior and people's understanding of themselves and others and to the use of such knowledge to improve the condition of individuals, organizations, and society.

The death penalty is among the most, if not the most, ethically and morally laden issue that can confront psychologists. As attributed to an unknown attorney, "death is different," but it should not be "different" in the way that psychologists administer or interpret test results. Psychologists morally opposed to the death penalty may (and perhaps should) advocate against this punishment in public and scientific fora. However, they should not allow any such conviction to influence their opinions when called upon to provide opinions to a factfinder in capital litigation. To do so would be in contradiction of Ethics Code Principle C: Integrity, which states in part:

> Psychologists seek to promote accuracy, honesty, and truthfulness in the science, teaching, and practice of psychology. In these activities psychologists do not steal, cheat, or engage in fraud, subterfuge, or intentional misrepresentation of fact.

Similarly, according to the Specialty Guidelines 1.01: Integrity,

> Forensic practitioners strive for accuracy, honesty, and truthfulness in the science, teaching, and practice of forensic psychology...

And per Guideline 1.02: Impartiality and Fairness,

> When conducting forensic examinations, forensic practitioners strive to be unbiased and impartial, and avoid partisan presentation of unrepresentative, incomplete, or inaccurate evidence that might mislead finders of fact.

Neuropsychologists can be involved in death penalty cases. In the United States, death penalty cases are divided into three phases: (1) the guilt phase, where a jury unanimously determines whether the accused committed the murder beyond a reasonable doubt; (2) the eligibility phase, where a jury unanimously determines whether the murder was committed in a manner that made him eligible for the death penalty; and finally, (3) the penalty phase, where the jury makes a unanimous determination of whether the defendant will be sentenced to life without parole or death.

In addition, the Supreme Court decision in *Atkins v. Virginia* (2002) barred the execution of individuals with intellectual disabilities, making the intellectual status of some defendants an issue that must be decided by the court, frequently with testimony from psychologists or neuropsychologists (Brodsky & Galloway, 2003).

Hagan, Drogin, and Guilmette (2010) opined that the issue of advocacy versus science may be particularly germane for some psychologists who promote "correcting" (e.g., lowering) the IQ scores of capital defendants in Atkins hearings based on the Flynn Effect, the phenomenon of IQ scores shifting over time, even though this is not the standard of practice in non-forensic, clinical settings (Hagan, Drogin, & Guilmette, 2008). They noted,

> The ethical obligation to conduct assessments competently and to interpret outcomes accurately attaches irrespective of the context in which these activities are conducted. Adherence to professional standards should not be parceled out based upon which legal undertakings psychologists deem the most worthy or consequential.
>
> (p. 421)

Apart from Atkins hearings, neuropsychologists are most likely to be involved in the penalty phase of death penalty litigation. Proffered testimony by defense experts can include claims of brain injury or cognitive impairment that are presented as potential mitigators to capital punishment (Cunningham, 2010; DeMatteo, Murrie, Anumba, & Keesler, 2011). These claims may be rebutted by experts retained by the prosecution. The possibility of execution is the *ne plus ultra* of external incentives for defendants, and thus a thorough consideration of possible malingering is required.

The death penalty is controversial and can rightfully invoke strong feelings. According to a Gallup poll published in 2022, 55% of Americans support the death penalty for convicted murderers (Brenan, 2022). Anecdotal reports (e.g., Coleman & Chan, 2020) buttressed by our own observations suggest that psychologists tend to be liberal in their views, and thus may, as a group, be more likely to oppose the death penalty.[4] People are encouraged to possess and advocate for their moral beliefs. However, the testimony provided by mental health experts in these (and lesser-stakes) cases should be driven by science, rather than personal belief or advocacy. This includes a clear-cut duty to investigate the possibility of malingering, even though such a designation could have fatal consequences for the defendant. Melton et al. (2018) wrote, "... mental health professionals should determine before conducting an evaluation whether their beliefs compromise their ability to conduct a valid and objective assessment" (p. 194).

Mr. Smith met the Sherman et al. (2020) criteria for psychiatric malingering. In particular, he displayed compelling inconsistencies pertaining to psychiatric symptoms. Due to advances in technology, there can be multiple sources of information available to document the contemporaneous presentation and functioning of inmates. Many inmates communicate with friends and family via text messages or video visits. Some facilities distribute tablets to inmates, which can document educational endeavors and leisure interests. These communications and activities are typically archived for security reasons (and perhaps abetted by the minimal cost of digital storage). These types of sources were used to document the compelling inconsistencies between Mr. Smith's presentation to one of the authors and his day-to-day functioning.

Inferring Motivation

The determination of malingering requires the examiner to come to a conclusion regarding the examinee's motivation. The ability of mental health professionals to determine a patient's internal state and motivation has been questioned (e.g., see Erickson in Pankratz & Erickson, 1990). However, in a rejoinder in that same article, Pankratz noted that mental health professionals frequently come to conclusions regarding the internal states of patients based upon their observable behavior, writing, "It would not be 'highly speculative' to infer the presence of misery and rumination inside the head of a patient with flat affect, psychomotor retardation, and disdain of previously interesting activities" (p. 387). Similarly, Slick, Sherman, and Iverson (1999) wrote:

> Judgments about internal states are in fact necessary, if not crucial, for many clinical diagnoses. For example, hallucinations-a decidedly nontrivial clinical symptom-are like volition in that they are an internal event or state, the presence or absence of which can only be inferred from behavior.
>
> (p. 548)

Thus, the assignment of many psychological diagnoses typically requires some speculation on the part of the psychologist regarding internal states that are not directly observable. This can be aided by use of standardized self-report instruments (e.g., the Minnesota Multiphasic Personality Inventory-3 [Ben-Porath & Tellegen, 2020]), as well as adherence to a set of reproducible/reliable guidelines (e.g., First, 2024). Similarly, an ethical psychologist may identify the condition of malingering within an appropriate level of certainty if a sufficient assessment is completed and the clinical criteria are met.

Creating Optimal Documentation

Both the Ethics Code and the Specialty Guidelines stress the need for the keeping of detailed records of interactions with examinees. As noted in the Ethics Code, Section 6.01 Documentation of Professional and Scientific Work and Maintenance of Records:

> Psychologists create, and to the extent the records are under their control, maintain, disseminate, store, retain, and dispose of records and data relating to their professional and scientific work in order to (1) facilitate provision of services later by them or by other professionals, (2) allow for replication of research design and analyses, (3) meet institutional requirements, (4) ensure accuracy of billing and payments, and (5) ensure compliance with law.
>
> (p. 8)

More specifically, as recommended in the Specialty Guidelines, Guideline 10.06: Documentation and Compilation of Data Considered:

> Forensic practitioners are encouraged to recognize the importance of documenting all data they consider with enough *detail and quality* to allow for reasonable judicial scrutiny and adequate discovery by all parties.
>
> (p. 16, emphasis added)

The obligation of the forensic neuropsychologist to keep detailed records and data from their assessments for possible "judicial scrutiny and adequate discovery" must be tempered by their ethical duty to maintain test security as stipulated by multiple professional psychological organizations, including the American Psychological Association, the American Educational Research Association, the National Association of School Psychologists, and AACN (Boone et al., 2022). Despite efforts from opposing counsel to gain access to raw test data for purposes of cross examination, the release of psychological and neuropsychological tests to non-psychologists such as lawyers can result in substantial damage to the integrity of the tests themselves, particularly to PVTs and SVTs, to public health and safety, and to the judicial process itself (Boone et al., 2024). Thus, Boone and colleagues (2024) reiterated the critical recommendation stated previously by neuropsychological and psychological organizations to release protected psychological test information only to licensed psychologists. However, neuropsychologists must balance this obligation to protect test security with an awareness of the stakes in serious criminal litigation, where the outcome can literally be life or death, and the resultant need for the factfinder to be presented with all relevant information. More details regarding steps that can be taken to ensure test security are found elsewhere in this text.

The best way to create comprehensive documentation of the interview, but not the testing procedures themselves, of a neuropsychological evaluation is by electronic recording (Siegel & Kinscherff, 2018). This is especially true in criminal cases when documenting whether an examinee's presentation is consistent across other contexts (e.g., in non-evaluation situations). However, recording a diagnostic interview is not without its potential detractors given the strong and unanimous agreement among the major neuropsychological organizations (e.g., National Academy of Neuropsychology, AACN, and American College of Professional Neuropsychology) to prohibit third-party observers or the video/audio recording of neuropsychological testing procedures due to their impact on the cognitive performance of those being observed (Glen et al., 2021). Although not empirically demonstrated to our knowledge, some clinicians may have concerns that videotaping the clinical/diagnostic interview may affect the subject's self-report in a manner consistent with the concerns of observing the testing itself.

Deceit

In a sense, some could perceive that PVTs are deceitful. That is, for many tests to "work," the examinee must be explicitly or implicitly led to believe that an easy task is quite hard, and that the test is a measure of actual cognitive ability, as opposed to performance validity. Thus, the claim could be made that this practice may violate *Principle C: Integrity*, "Psychologists seek to promote accuracy, honesty and truthfulness in the science, teaching, and practice of psychology. In these activities, psychologists do not steal, cheat, or engage in fraud, subterfuge, or intentional misrepresentation of fact." However, the ethical psychologist must provide services that reflect best practices, and the comprehensive assessment of performance and symptom validity are essential in forensic evaluations. In addition, in keeping with the ethical principle of respecting the rights and dignity of those with whom they work, psychologists inform examinees that they are to respond truthfully to questions and to put forth optimal effort on test measures.

However, there is a difference of opinion in the literature as to what form this notification should take. There is a concern that awareness of validity measures may enable some examinees to better evade detection of malingering via PVTs and SVTs (Boone, 2007; Greiffenstein, 2009; Suhr & Gunstad, 2000; Youngjohn, Lees-Haley, & Binder, 1999). Therefore, some authors caution against specific warnings as to the administration of validity measures within a test battery, and instead limit this notification to an admonishment that the examinee should do their best and inform the examiners of any impediments to full effort (Youngjohn et al., 1999).

Gutiérrez and Gur (1998) explored this issue with their university's Biomedical Ethics Center, and were

> told that it may very well be ethical to deceive a patient who is suspected of malingering, but it must be done in a manner that affords the patient the opportunity to deny any deficit and perform well on any given test.
>
> (p. 101)

Other authors write that a more detailed notification is required. Bush et al. (2014) described:

> Psychologists also inform examinees and retaining parties that validity measures will be used, although the specific nature of such measures or the timing of their use is not disclosed. While use of measures that appear to measure mood, personality traits or cognitive abilities but actually measure validity may be considered a type of deception of examinees, such deception is necessary to establish the validity of the assessment results and to accurately inform the trier of fact, and psychologists satisfy ethical responsibilities and the informed consent process through the explanation in general terms that validity measures will be used.
>
> (p. 201)

The informed consent process referred to above by Bush et al. (2014) and also in a sample informed consent document provided in the Official Statement of the National Academy of Neuropsychology Independent and Court-Ordered Forensic Neuropsychological

Examinations, examinees are instructed to give their best effort during testing and that "part of the examination will address the accuracy of your responses, as well as the degree of effort that you exert on the tests" (Bush and NAN Policy and Planning Committee, 2003, p. 9).

This approach is supported by some research, which suggests that a more detailed notification may decrease the frequency of malingering (Horner, Turner, VanKirk, & Denning, 2017; King & Sullivan, 2009; Schenk & Sullivan, 2010).

However, surveys indicate that the majority of neuropsychologists typically do not provide detailed warnings as part of their evaluations. In one survey, 97% of responding neuropsychologists indicated that they often or always encouraged examinees to do their best, whereas 38% indicated that they often or always explicitly warned examinees that testing is sensitive to invalid performance (Martin et al., 2015). The same group of authors polled a smaller sample of neuropsychologists with expertise in neuropsychological validity testing. Similar to the larger group surveyed above, 96% of the experts indicated that they often or always encouraged examinees to do their best. However, only 25% often or always directly warned examinees that testing is sensitive to invalid performance (Schroeder, Martin, & Odland, 2016).

"The Potency of the Malingering Label"

Weiss and Van Dell (2017) describe the "the potency of the malingering label" (p. 339), writing that synonyms "include shirker, slacker, idler, layabout, dead-beat, and gold brick" (p. 340). They raise the possibility that an expert could face liability for categorizing someone as a malingerer.

According to a survey of neuropsychologists, about 90% of respondents rarely or never use the term "malingering" when reporting their findings, even when they suspect exaggeration or malingering to be present (Martin et al., 2015). A survey of a small sample of "experts" in neuropsychological validity testing by the same authors revealed that only about half often or always use the term "malingering" when they suspect exaggeration or malingering to be present (Schroeder et al., 2016). Phrases used instead included reporting that the test data are invalid, that no firm conclusions can be drawn, that test results suggest or indicate exaggeration, or that the test results are inconsistent with the severity of the injury.

The AACN consensus conference on test score labeling recommended that a PVT score be categorized or described as a valid range score, an invalid range score, or an intermediate valid range score (Guilmette et al., 2020), but not as malingering, per se, as this is interpretive, rather than descriptive. In addition, the 2021 AACN consensus conference statement on validity assessment references the explicit recommendation from multiple professional organizations "that examiners incorporate multiple sources of data and information making determinations regarding malingering" (Sweet, Heilbronner et al., 2021, p. 1059).

Sherman et al. (2020) discuss the use of the term "malingering," noting that perhaps an updated model such as they present should use a different descriptor. However, they conclude:

> Currently, malingering has a fairly clear meaning to most practitioners in that it requires the external incentive criterion in particular and cannot be due to other specific conditions. Nevertheless, it is possible that these or future terms will gain traction and be accepted in the field.
>
> (p. 757)

Conclusions

It is imperative that any determination of malingering be based on science as communicated by the evolving literature. This is in keeping with ethical principles and best practices. PVT/SVTs are essential to this determination. Research has demonstrated the insufficiency of relying heavily or exclusively on clinical judgment in determining the validity of an examinee's performance given the significant flaws in using clinical judgment alone when applied to the detection of malingering (Guilmette, 2013).

We believe that, given sufficient evidence, a neuropsychologist can ethically determine and identify the presence of malingering. This determination

> ...most often requires a presentation in the context of an external incentive, pursuit of that external incentive, evidence of noncredible performance and/or feigned or exaggerated symptomatology, and evidence-based informed judgment by the practitioner, who should incorporate multiple pieces of information, including base rate data.
>
> (Sweet, Heibronner et al., 2021, p. 9)

The readers are reminded that regardless of the examinee's presentation, the psychologist is obligated to treat all examinees with respect. Failure to do so would violate *Principle E: Respect for People's Rights and Dignity*, which states in part, "Psychologists respect the dignity and worth of all people..." While there is a natural tendency to resent someone trying to deceive us – regardless of their motivation – the psychologist must maintain the standards of objectivity, professionalism, and ethics dictated by our profession and demanded by our field.

Notes

1 The *Ethics Code* is currently being revised.
2 The *Guidelines* are currently being revised. The APA has approved an extension of the current *Guidelines* through December 31, 2026.
3 A finding of incompetence to stand trial (ITST) is only applicable to the defendant's mental state at the time of adjudication for the instant offense. However, experience suggests that a finding of ITST (rightly or wrongly) can establish a legacy that may prejudice future adjudications. Thus, a class of offenders is created that is to an extent immune from future criminal convictions.
4 Evidence for this can also be seen at the organizational level. For example, in 2016, the APA's *Monitor on Psychology* (a trade magazine) published an article entitled "A matter of life or death," with the lead "Mental health experts play a key role in evaluating the mitigating evidence that informs a defendant's sentence" (Thornewill, Bomysoad, & DeMatteo, 2016). However, the article only describes defense-retained experts; no mention is made of prosecution-retained experts.

References

American Psychological Association. (2013). Specialty guidelines for forensic psychology. *American Psychologist*, *68*(1), 7–19.

American Psychological Association. (2017). *Ethical principles of psychologists and code of conduct*. Washington, DC: American Psychological Association.

American Psychiatric Association. (2022). *Diagnostic and statistical manual of mental disorders*. (5th ed.). Text revision. Washington, DC: Author.

Atkins v. Virginia, 536 U.S. 304 (2002).

Batastini, A. B., & Vitacco, M. J. (2020). *Forensic mental health evaluations in the digital age: A practitioner's guide to using internet-based data*. Cham: Springer.

Bazzell, M. (2023). *OSINT techniques: Resources for uncovering online information* (10th ed.). Los Angeles, CA: Author.

Ben-Porath, Y., & Tellegen, A. (2020). *Minnesota Multiphasic Personality Inventory-3 manual for administration, scoring, and interpretation*. Bloomington, MN: Pearson.

Boone, K. B. (2007). A reconsideration of the Slick et al. (1999) criteria for Malingered Neurocognitive Dysfunction. In K. B. Boone (Ed.), *Assessment of feigned cognitive impairment: A neuropsychological perspective* (pp. 29–49). New York: Guilford.

Boone, K. B., Kaufmann, P. M., Sweet, J. J., Leatherberry, D., Beattey, R. A. Jr., Silva, D., Victor, T. L., Boone, R. P., Spector, J., Hebben, N., Hanks, R. A., & James, J. (2024). Attorney demands for protected psychological test information: Is access necessary for cross examination or does it lead to misinformation? An interorganizational position paper. *The Clinical Neuropsychologist*, *38*(4), 889–906. https://doi.org/10.1080/13854046.2024.2323222

Boone, K. B., Sweet, J. J., Byrd, D. A., Denny, R. L, Hanks, R. A., Kaufmann, P. M., Kirkwood, M. W., Larrabee, G. L., Marcopulos, B. A., Morgan, J. E., Palzer, J. Y., Mindt, M. R., Schroeder, R. W., Sim, A. H., & Suhr, J. A. (2022). Official position of the American Academy of Clinical Neuropsychology on test security. *The Clinical Neuropsychologist*, *36*(3), 523–545. https://doi.org/10.1080/13854046.2021.2022214

Brenan, M. (2022, November 14). Steady 55% of Americans support death penalty for murderers. *Gallup*. https://news.gallup.com/poll/404975/steady-americans-support-death-penalty-murderers.aspx

Brodsky, S. L., & Galloway, V. A. (2003). Ethical and professional demands for forensic mental health professionals in the post-Atkins era. *Ethics & Behavior*, *13*(1), 3–9.

Bush, S. S. and the NAN Policy and Planning Committee. (2003). Independent and Court-Ordered Forensic Neuropsychology Examinations: Official Statement of the National Academy of Neuropsychology Approved by the Board of Directors 10/14/03. https://nanonline.org/docs/PAIC/PDFs/NANIMEpaper.pdf

Bush, S. S., Heilbronner, R., & Ruff, R. M. (2014). Psychological assessment of symptom and performance validity, response bias, and malingering: Official Position of the Association for Scientific Advancement in Psychological Injury and Law. *Psychological Injury and the Law*, *7*, 197–205.

Bush, S. S., Ruff, R. M., Troster, A. I., Barth, J. T., Koffler, S. P., Pliskin, N. H., ... Silver, C. H. (2005). Symptom validity assessment: practice issues and medical necessity NAN policy & planning committee. *Archives of Clinical Neuropsychology*, *20*(4), 419–426. https://doi.org/10.1016/j.acn.2005.02.002

Chafetz, M. D., Bauer, R. M., & Haley, P. S. (2020). The other face of illness-deception: Diagnostic criteria for factitious disorder with proposed standards for clinical practice and research. *The Clinical Neuropsychologist*, *34*(3), 454–476.

Chafetz, M., & Underhill, J. (2013). Estimated costs of malingered disability. *Archives of Clinical Neuropsychology*, *28*(7), 633–639. https://doi.org/10.1093/arclin/act038

Coleman, P. T., & Chan, A. (2020, October 30). Are psychologists too politically close-minded today? And how this might affect our capabilities to heal divides. *Psychology Today*. https://www.psychologytoday.com/us/blog/the-five-percent/202010/are-psychologists-too-politically-close-minded-today

Cunningham, M. D. (2010). *Evaluation for capital sentencing*. New York: Oxford University Press.

DeLisi, M., Kosloski, A., Sween, M., Hachmeister, E., Moore, M., & Drury, A. (2010). Murder by numbers: monetary costs imposed by a sample of homicide offenders. *Journal of Forensic Psychiatry and Psychology*, *21*(4), 501–513.

DeMatteo, D., Murrie, D. C., Anumba, N. M., & Keesler, M. E. (2011). *Forensic mental health assessments in death penalty cases*. New York: Oxford University Press.

Denning, J. H., & Shura, R. D. (2019). Cost of malingering mild traumatic brain injury-related cognitive deficits during compensation and pension evaluations in the veterans benefits administration. *Applied Neuropsychology Adult*, *26*(1), 1–16. https://doi.org/10.1080/23279095.2017.1350684

First, M. B. (2024). *DSM-5-TR handbook of differential diagnosis*. Washington, DC: American Psychiatric Association.

Glen, T., Barisa, M., Ready, R., Peck, E., & Spencer, T. R. (2021). Update on third party observers in neuropsychological evaluation: An interorganizational position paper. *The Clinical Neuropsychologist*, *35*(6), 1107–1116. https://doi.org/10.1080/13854046.2021.1901992

Greiffenstein, M. F. (2009). Clinical myths of forensic neuropsychology. *The Clinical Neuropsychologist*, *23*(2), 286–296. https://doi-org.providence.idm.oclc.org/10.1080/13854040802104873

Guilmette, T. J. (2013). The role of clinical judgment in symptom validity assessment. In D. A. Carone & S. S. Bush (Eds.), *Mild traumatic brain injury: Symptom validity assessment and malingering* (pp. 31–43). New York: Springer.

Guilmette, T. J., Sweet, J. J., Hebben, N., Koltai, D., Mahone, E. M., Spiegler, B. J., … Conference, P. (2020). American Academy of Clinical Neuropsychology consensus conference statement on uniform labeling of performance test scores. *The Clinical Neuropsychologist*, *34*(3), 437–453. https://doi.org/10.1080/13854046.2020.1722244

Gutiérrez, J. M., & Gur, R. C. (1998). Detection of malingering using forced-choice techniques. In C. R. Reynolds (Ed.), *Detection of malingering during head injury litigation*. (pp. 81–104). New York: Plenum Press. https://doi-org.providence.idm.oclc.org/10.1007/978-1-4419-7469-3_3

Hagan, L. D., Drogin, E. Y., & Guilmette, T. J. (2008). Adjusting IQ scores for the Flynn Effect: Consistent with the standard of practice? *Professional Psychology: Research and Practice*, *39*, 619–625.

Hagan, L. D., Drogin, E. Y., & Guilmette, T. J. (2010). Science rather than advocacy when reporting IQ scores. *Professional Psychology: Research and Practice*, *41*, 420–423.

Horner, M. D., Turner, T. H., VanKirk, K. K., & Denning, J. H. (2017). An intervention to decrease the occurrence of invalid data on neuropsychological evaluation. *Archives of Clinical Neuropsychology*, *32*(2), 228–237.

King, J., & Sullivan, K. A. (2009). Deterring malingered psychopathology: The effect of warning simulating malingerers. *Behavioral Sciences & the Law*, *27*(1), 35–49. https://doi-org.providence.idm.oclc.org/10.1002/bsl.839

Knoll 4th, J. L., & Resnick, P. J. (1999). U.S. v. Greer: longer sentences for malingerers. *Journal of the American Academy of Psychiatry and Law*, *27*(4), 621–625. Retrieved from https://www.ncbi.nlm.nih.gov/pubmed/10638789

Larrabee, G. J., Millis, S. R., & Meyers, J. E. (2009). 40 plus or minus 10, a new magical number: reply to Russell. *The Clinical Neuropsychologist*, *23*(5), 841–849. https://doi.org/10.1080/13854040902796735

Martin, P. K., & Schroeder, R. W. (2020). Base rates of invalid test performance across clinical non-forensic contexts and settings. *Archives of Clinical Neuropsychology*, *35*(6), 717–725. https://doi.org/10.1093/arclin/acaa017

Martin, P. K., Schroeder, R. W., & Odland, A. P. (2015). Neuropsychologists' validity testing beliefs and practices: A survey of North American professionals. *The Clinical Neuropsychologist*, *29*(6), 741–776. https://doi.org/10.1080/13854046.2015.1087597

Melton, G. B., Petrila, J., Poythress, N. G., Slobogin, C., Otto, R. K., Mossman, D., & Condie, L. O. (2018). *Psychological evaluations for the courts: A handbook for mental health professionals and lawyers* (4th ed). New York: Guilford Press.

Pankratz, L., & Erickson, R. C. (1990). Two views of malingering. *Clinical Neuropsychologist*, *4*(4), 379–389. https://doi-org.providence.idm.oclc.org/10.1080/13854049008401832

Raab, S. (2005, December 20). Vincent Gigante, mob boss who feigned incompetence to avoid jail dies at 77. *New York Times*, p. A29.

Schenk, K., & Sullivan, K. A. (2010). Do warnings deter rather than produce more sophisticated malingering? *Journal of Clinical and Experimental Neuropsychology*, *32*(7), 752–762. https://doi-org.providence.idm.oclc.org/10.1080/13803390903512678

Schroeder, R. W., Martin, P. K., & Odland, A. P. (2016). Expert beliefs and practices regarding neuropsychological validity testing. *The Clinical Neuropsychologist*, *30*(4), 515–535. https://doi-org.providence.idm.oclc.org/10.1080/13854046.2016.1177118

Sherman, E. M. S., Slick, D. J., & Iverson, G. L. (2020). Multidimensional malingering criteria for neuropsychological assessment: A 20-year update of the malingered neuropsychological dysfunction criteria. *Archives of Clinical Neuropsychology*, *35*(6), 735–764. https://doi.org/10.1093/arclin/acaa019

Siegel, D. M., & Kinscherff, R. (2018). Recording routine forensic mental health evaluations should be a standard of practice in the 21st century. *Behav Sci Law*, *36*(3), 373–389. https://doi.org/10.1002/bsl.2349

Simpson, J. R., & Brodie, J. D. (2017). Neuroimaging, psychiatry, and the law. In B. J. Sadock, V. A. Sadock, & P. Ruiz (Eds.), *Kaplan and Sadock's comprehensive textbook of psychiatry* (10th ed., pp. 4477–4491). Philadelphia: Wolters Kluwer.

Slick, D. J., Sherman, E. M. S., & Iverson, G. L. (1999). Diagnostic criteria for malingered neurocognitive dysfunction: Proposed standards for clinical practice and research. *Clinical Neuropsychologist*, *13*(4), 545–561. https://doi-org.providence.idm.oclc.org/10.1076/1385-4046(199911)13:04;1–Y;FT545

Suhr, J. A., & Gunstad, J. (2000). The effects of coaching on the sensitivity and specificity of malingering measures. *Archives of Clinical Neuropsychology*, *15*(5), 415–424. https://doi-org.providence.idm.oclc.org/10.1016/S0887-6177(99)00033-5

Sweet, J. J., Heilbronner, R. L., Morgan, J. E., Larrabee, G. J., Rohling, M. L., Boone, K. B., ... Conference, P. (2021). American Academy of Clinical Neuropsychology (AACN) 2021 consensus statement on validity assessment: Update of the 2009 AACN consensus conference statement on neuropsychological assessment of effort, response bias, and malingering. *The Clinical Neuropsychologist*, *35*(6), 1053–1106. https://doi.org/10.1080/13854046.2021.1896036

Sweet, J. J., Klipfel, K. M., Nelson, N. W., & Moberg, P. J. (2021). Professional practices, beliefs, and incomes of U.S. neuropsychologists: The AACN, NAN, SCN 2020 practice and "salary survey". *The Clinical Neuropsychologist*, *35*(1), 7–80. https://doi.org/10.1080/13854046.2020.1849803

Thornewill, A., Bomysoad, R., & DeMatteo, D. (2016, July/August). A matter of life or death. Monitor on Psychology. https://www.apa.org/monitor/2016/07-08/jn#:~:text=Mental%20health%20experts%20play%20a,that%20informs%20a%20defendant's%20sentence.&text=Comment%3A,parole%20or%20the%20death%20penalty

Weiss, K. J., & Van Dell, L. (2017). Liability for diagnosing malingering. *Journal of the American Academy of Psychiatry and the Law*, *45*, 339–347.

Wickramasekara, N., Wright, J., Elsey, H., & Murray, A. M. (2015). Cost of crime: A systematic review. *Journal of Criminal Justice*, *43*, 218–228.

Youngjohn, J. R., Lees-Haley, P. R., & Binder, L. M. (1999). Comment: Warning malingerers produces more sophisticated malingering. *Archives of Clinical Neuropsychology*, *14*(6), 511–515. https://doi-org.providence.idm.oclc.org/10.1016/S0887-6177(98)00049-3

41 After the Detection of Invalid Performance

Process and Feedback

Shane S. Bush

Neuropsychological evaluations require that a determination be made regarding the validity of the data that are obtained. The confidence that can be placed in such determinations is dependent upon the nature of the data and the context in which they were obtained. In clinical contexts, a sizable minority of patients (prevalence is approximately 15%) perform at a suboptimal level (Martin & Schroeder, 2020; Roor et al., 2023), and in forensic contexts, the prevalence is even higher, closer to 40% (Bush et al., 2014; Larrabee et al., 2009; Sweet et al., 2021). As a result, neuropsychologists *will* encounter situations in which patients respond or perform in an invalid manner.

Although determining that a patient has dissimulated can, in some cases, be obvious, making such determinations, in other cases, can be quite challenging. Psychological and neuropsychological researchers have generated a considerable amount of information in recent years to assist practitioners in their determinations of symptom and performance validity, although the methods, statistics, and conclusions of some of the research have been questioned recently (Leonhard, 2023a, 2023b). Symptom validity tests and indices (SVTs), free-standing performance validity tests (PVTs), indicators embedded within tests of cognitive ability, and other strategies for determining whether a person being evaluated approached the process in a valid manner have been developed and applied clinically and in forensic contexts. However, agreement on the meaning and use of the results is sometimes lacking among clinicians (Lippa, 2018; Martin et al., 2015; Sharland & Gfeller, 2007). That is, with the exception of extreme cases (and even then sometimes), neuropsychologists may not always agree on the interpretation of the results of validity assessment measures (e.g., valid, invalid, or some point in between – indeterminate). The American Academy of Clinical Neuropsychology proposed using a three-tiered system for labeling validity assessment results: valid range, indeterminate range, and invalid range (Guilmette et al., 2020).

Noncredible and inconsistent responding and performance are cardinal features suggestive of inaccurate information or suboptimal task engagement (Sherman et al., 2020). Patients who respond or perform in a manner that is markedly inconsistent with (i.e., reflecting more pathology than) typical patterns of responding or performance by individuals with similar, or more severe, illness or injury raise suspicion that the results obtained reflect inaccurate information or suboptimal performance. The greater the inconsistency or the more evidence of noncredible responding that exists, the greater the degree of confidence that the examiner can place in conclusions regarding the patient's approach to the tasks. Despite the proliferation of validity assessment research and guidelines for diagnosing malingered neurocognitive dysfunction (e.g., Sherman et al., 2020), limitations in the process persist, and efforts to continue to improve validity assessment are ongoing.

DOI: 10.4324/9781003005063-47

Decisions of whether to use (a) free-standing symptom or performance validity measures, (b) validity indicators embedded within or derived from psychological or neurocognitive measures, and/or (c) a combination of the two approaches remains at the discretion of the examiner. Such decisions should be informed by evidence indicating that the psychometric properties of stand-alone PVTs are typically superior to those of embedded PVTs (Miele et al., 2012; Soble et al., 2022), but also the knowledge that embedded PVTs have alternative benefits such as being easily incorporated within an exam and being more resistant to coaching (Schroeder & Martin, 2022). Regardless of the approach taken, an examiner's subjective opinion alone is often inadequate when making an informed judgment about the validity of a patient's presentation and performance (Dandachi-Fitzgerald et al., 2017; Faust et al., 1988; Guilmette, 2013).

Use of multiple validity assessment measures to aid in the determination of the validity of data obtained during the evaluation is currently standard practice (Bush et al., 2005; Bush et al., 2014; Martin et al., 2015; Sweet et al., 2021), but adequate validity assessment takes on increased importance when (a) the potential for secondary gain increases the incentive for dissimulation or (b) the examiner becomes suspicious of insufficient task engagement or inaccurate or incomplete reporting. The need to assess validity with appropriate quantitative methods applies to patients ranging in age from childhood through older adulthood (Donders & Kirkwood, 2013), and includes those with well-documented neurological impairment (Martin et al., 2020a) and those in various assessment contexts (Bush, 2014; Bush & Bass, 2015; Bush & Graver, 2013; Bush & Morgan, 2012; Bush & Myers, 2013; Carone & Bush, 2018; Kaufman & Bush, 2020, 2021; Schroeder & Martin, 2022).

Despite the general importance of formal validity assessment as part of neuropsychological evaluations, there are some evaluation contexts, such as with persons who have an acquired or degenerative neurological disorder of such severity that they require 24-hour care, in which case the results of psychometric assessment of validity could be misleading, and thus harmful, if traditional cutoff scores are applied (Martin et al., 2020b). In such instances, clinical judgment regarding whether the obtained data accurately reflect the patient's true abilities will become increasingly useful.

In addition to challenges that may be encountered when making determinations about the validity of neuropsychological data, the meaning that is attributed to invalid data may be subject to disagreement among neuropsychologists, in part because there are multiple possible reasons why a patient may produce invalid neuropsychological data (Martin et al., 2020a; Sweet et al., 2021). Survey findings (Martin et al., 2015) described the following possible causes of invalid data as endorsed by respondents, with the order of likelihood varying between clinical (provided here) and forensic contexts: (1) Psychiatric issues (not somatoform), (2) somatoform or conversion disorder, (3) attitude toward testing, (4) physical factors, (5) factitious disorder, (6) malingering, (7) genuine cognitive dysfunction, and (8) stereotype/diagnosis threat.

In addition to the challenges previously described, neuropsychologists vary somewhat in how to describe invalid results in reports and how to conclude the matter with the patient and the referral source or retaining party (Martin et al., 2015). For example, when invalid test performance is evident during an evaluation, should the examiner confront the patient? Should the examiner complete the test battery or discontinue test administration? The potential advantages and disadvantages of each course of action must be considered in advance.

When patients are informed that their results are considered invalid due to suboptimal performance or inaccurate or inconsistent responding, their reactions may range from acknowledgment, with or without explanation, to emotionally charged statements of denial. Reactions from referral sources or retaining parties also may vary considerably depending on the purpose of the evaluation. Although neuropsychologists are not all of the same opinion regarding how to proceed when it is apparent that invalid data have been produced (Lippa, 2018; Martin et al., 2015), it is clear that a plan to address this possibility should be in place prior to beginning the evaluation. The purpose of this chapter is to illustrate the importance of anticipating invalid results and developing ways of handling the situation, whether during the evaluation or, in clinical contexts, during a feedback session.

Case Illustration

Identifying Information

Mr. Z was a 42-year-old married man who, according to his self-report and a consultation report from his neurologist (Dr. H), began experiencing numerous physical, cognitive, and emotional problems following a motor vehicle collision. The collision occurred nine months prior to his neuropsychological intake appointment. Mr. Z was referred for a clinical evaluation by his neurologist to clarify cognitive strengths and weaknesses and emotional adjustment, and to provide rehabilitative and psychotherapeutic services as needed. He underwent the neuropsychological evaluation in an independent practice setting.

Behavioral Observations

Mr. Z presented for his appointment unaccompanied and was a few minutes late, having forgotten the address of the office building. He was appropriately dressed and groomed. He ambulated without gait disturbance or apparent difficulty, and movement of his upper extremities was free of gross impairment. His receptive language was functional for interview questions. His conversational speech was fluent. He was fully oriented. His thoughts were clear and goal-directed. His affect was euthymic. His social pragmatics (greeting, eye contact, etc.) were appropriate.

Informed Consent

The session began with the informed consent process. The purpose and nature of the evaluation were discussed, with Mr. Z indicating understanding and agreement. In order to provide specific information regarding limits to confidentiality, the neuropsychologist inquired about litigation. Mr. Z acknowledged that he was a plaintiff in a personal injury suit related to the collision of nine months before, and he denied additional litigation history. Mr. Z was informed of the potential limits to confidentiality resulting from his litigation status. He was informed that, at a minimum, Dr. H and the automobile insurance company would require copies of the neuropsychological report. In addition, attorneys for both sides would likely require copies of neuropsychological records, and the potential existed that the information could end up, through court transcripts, in the public domain. Mr. Z was also informed that an accurate interpretation of the evaluation results was dependent upon him putting forth his best effort on all tests and responding honestly to questions about himself; he was informed that his effort and truthfulness would be assessed. Following review of all relevant information, the informed consent process concluded with Mr. Z providing his consent to the evaluation.

Clinical Interview

Mr. Z learned after the fact that his collision occurred when he was sitting at a stoplight in his pick-up truck and was rear-ended by an SUV traveling at highway speed. A toolbox flew through the back window of his truck and struck him on the back of his head. His face struck the windshield, resulting in a large laceration. He experienced a loss of consciousness of at least a few minutes. His last memory before the collision was of driving down the road. His first memory following the collision was of thinking "my head's wet. I messed up my face." He reported having continuous memories from that point on. He felt "dazed" and had a severe headache. He was taken by helicopter to the nearest trauma center. He was treated and was discharged home the following day.

He followed up with his primary care physician (PCP) later in the week, and then began chiropractic treatments. Mr. Z reported that he continued to experience headaches and problems with attention, memory, and processing speed. In addition, he reported experiencing weakness on the left side of his body. Five months after his collision, his PCP referred him to Dr. H Dr. H diagnosed Mr. Z with persistent postconcussion syndrome and recommended neuroimaging studies.

> Mr. Z reported that the neuroimaging studies revealed two ACoA aneurysms, which required a right frontal craniotomy for clipping. He further stated that MRIs detected a brain stem tumor, which his doctors considered "inoperable but slow growing." Mr. Z paused as the neuropsychologist finished writing down this information.
>
> Mr. Z then asked, "You don't have to report those things, do you?"
>
> The neuropsychologist replied, "Yes. They are an important part of your medical history."
>
> Mr. Z, "But they're not related to my accident."
>
> Neuropsychologist, "No, but they're probably contributing to your problems with attention and memory and to the other neurological symptoms that you've been experiencing."
>
> Mr. Z, "But my problems started after the accident, way before the aneurysms and the tumor."
>
> Neuropsychologist, "Even though you didn't know about the aneurysms and the tumor, they were probably there. And, even if they didn't contribute to the symptoms that you experienced right after the accident, the fact that you underwent surgery…"
>
> Mr. Z, "After the surgery, everything was the same as it was before the surgery. Nothing got worse."
>
> Neuropsychologist, "In any event, these things are a significant part of your medical history and cannot be left out of my report."
>
> Mr. Z, "Dr. H knows about all of this, and he agreed not to put any of it in his reports. Call him and talk to him about it."

At this point, the neuropsychologist was aware that the case was more complicated than most clinical referrals. Mr. Z appeared to be more concerned about his lawsuit than he was about better understanding and addressing his reported cognitive and emotional problems. Mr. Z was wanting to omit, and possibly misrepresent or fabricate, important information in order to achieve his financial goals, and he was willing to ask others to do the same. This alone was a clear-cut case of Mr. Z wanting to mislead the triers of fact and anyone else who read his neurological and neuropsychological records, for the purpose of secondary gain (i.e., malingering). There was no need to infer his motives from test data.

Although neuropsychological testing had not yet been performed, confidence could not be placed in Mr. Z's willingness to approach testing in a valid manner. The only concern at this point was how to best handle the situation. In addition to concerns about Mr. Z, the possibility existed that taking a higher ethical stance than the referring neurologist had reportedly taken could negatively impact the neuropsychologist's relationship with the neurologist.

> Mr. Z says, "Let's forget I ever said anything about the aneurysms and the surgery and the tumor. I'll come in again, and we can start over."
>
> Neuropsychologist, "I can't do that."
>
> Mr. Z, "Why not? It's just ethics."
>
> Neuropsychologist smiles, "As fate would have it, you happen to be sitting across from someone who takes ethics pretty seriously."
>
> "O.K. Then I don't want you to tell anyone I was ever here. I want to take back what I said about you talking to Dr. H or to other people or sending your report."

Considerations

This was the first time that the neuropsychologist had ever had a patient rescind consent to release neuropsychological information or findings to the referring party. A number of thoughts and possibilities ran through the neuropsychologist's mind, including the following:

1 Should I just tell Mr. Z that I could not help him and send him back to his neurologist?
2 Should I give Mr. Z the names of other local neuropsychologists? If not, could I be accused of abandoning him? If I do give him the names, he will certainly withhold important medical history from them, and I do not have authorization to call and warn them. Some of the lateralizing symptoms are likely to be detected and will be confusing to a neuropsychologist who lacks the complete medical history. Would this approach simply make Mr. Z better at misattributing and malingering symptoms?
3 How am I going to get paid for this session? Automobile insurance regulations require a copy of my notes or reports, and Mr. Z won't authorize me to send them. I can't really chalk up the loss of the fee to "pro bono" since it was not done "for good" (How do you say "lost income by default" in Latin?).
4 What am I going to say to Dr. H when he wants to know my findings?
5 How will Dr. H react when he realizes that I would not engage in the same unethical behavior in which he seems to engage? Can I even trust that what Mr. Z said about Dr. H is true? Knowing Dr. H, it would not surprise me; however, I know that Mr. Z cannot be trusted.

At this point, a neuropsychologist needs to consider professional and ethical responsibilities, with an acute awareness of the need to resolve the dilemma promptly. My thoughts were along the following lines: I have a responsibility to Mr. Z to give him some direction (Ethical Standard A, Beneficence and Nonmaleficence; American Psychological Association [APA], 2017). Despite my personal feelings toward him, I cannot just send him away without offering any suggestions. On the other hand, referring him to another neuropsychologist would be of no clinical value to Mr. Z because, without providing accurate medical history, the conclusions of the neuropsychologist would be inaccurate, and any recommendations provided would be inappropriate. I can share that fact with Mr. Z, and, to the extent that he is concerned about his neuropsychological functioning at all, he may benefit from hearing it. In addition, unnecessary allocation of neuropsychological and financial resources to evaluate Mr. Z would be inconsistent with appropriate use of those resources (APA General Principle D, Justice). Ultimately, I concluded I must refer Mr. Z back to his neurologist, Dr. H, to re-examine his options.

There were additional considerations: I have a responsibility to the referring party, Dr. H, to inform him, at a minimum, that the patient was seen for an initial session, but would not be undergoing neuropsychological testing. Dr. H is going to want to know why. How would I respond to that question? I did not want to tell him that I refused to selectively omit significant aspects of medical history, as, according to Mr. Z, Dr. H apparently had no problem doing so.

Case Resolution

The neuropsychologist determined that he should attempt to preserve Mr. Z's consent to release at least minimal information to Dr. H Therefore, he explained to Mr. Z that Dr. H would want to know the status of the evaluation, including why the evaluation was not performed. Mr. Z responded that *he* would tell Dr. H The neuropsychologist, however, persisted, stating that he preferred to have the ability to discuss the matter with Dr. H, for the potential benefit of Mr. Z. After a relatively lengthy pause, Mr. Z agreed. The neuropsychologist then drafted a modified informed consent form, outlining the parameters as agreed upon by Mr. Z, within which he could discuss the case. Mr. Z signed the new consent form, waited while the original consent form was shredded, and left the office. The neuropsychologist then called Dr. H.

Considerations

Colleagues may disagree about aspects of the way this case was handled, beginning with the decision to inform the patient that his honesty and effort would be assessed. According to the Martin et al. (2015) survey, nearly all neuropsychologists (97%) often or always encourage patients to try their best, whereas only 38% often or always explicitly warn patients that testing is sensitive to invalid performance. The concern is that warning patients about the use of validity assessment measures will only produce more sophisticated malingerers (Youngjohn et al., 1999). Most neuropsychologists (69%) do not require patients to sign a form, which may be part of a consent form, confirming agreement that they will provide their best effort. Thus, whereas most colleagues approach this aspect of the evaluation process differently than the neuropsychologist in this case, a substantial minority of practitioners would have handled this manner of informed consent and warning similarly.

The decision to arrive at a determination about the patient's intent to mislead for secondary gain (malinger), without any psychometric evidence to support such a determination, may be questioned. For example, Millis (2009) stated that the need to use PVTs for making such a determination is "absolute", and the National Academy of Neuropsychology position paper on the topic (Bush et al., 2005) directed that "neuropsychologists can, and must, utilize symptom validity tests (SVTs) and procedures to assist in the determination of the validity of the information and test data obtained" (p. 426). Although clinical judgment alone has been found to be insufficient for making such determinations, and in most situations a combination of approaches is used (Martin et al., 2015), in this case, the patient clearly stated that he wanted to mislead others to support his lawsuit. While PVT failure could have provided objective, converging support that the patient was malingering, it is also possible that he would have demonstrated his true abilities on the tests, producing valid data. Thus, the decision not to administer tests, while supportable, leaves unanswered questions in understanding the patient's presentation. It is noteworthy that when discrepancies exist between clinical impressions and validity assessment results, most neuropsychologists (62%) give preference to validity testing results the vast majority of the time (Martin et al., 2015).

Case Modifications

For purposes of elaboration and illustration, the following sections present alternative ways of attempting to resolve this case example. This discussion is intended to strengthen the reader's knowledge of potential malingering situations and the various pitfalls that may ensue.

Case Modification 1

Suppose that, in the prior scenario, the idealistic outcome did not occur. Suppose that the neuropsychologist, having been taken by surprise and feeling considerable pressure to complete the evaluation, agreed to proceed with the evaluation. Imagine that administration of a commonly used IQ test was begun. During the initial subtests, Mr. Z answered with "I don't know" to numerous items, and considerable prompting for a "guess" resulted in unusual responses. In addition, he at times responded incorrectly to easier items while responding correctly to more difficult items. For these reasons, completion of the IQ test is put on hold while the neuropsychologist administers a PVT: in this case, the TOMM.

Mr. Z then proceeds to achieve the following scores on the TOMM: Trial = 21, Trial 2 = 29, and Retention = 11. At that point, the neuropsychologist stops the evaluation. It is evident that Mr. Z's test performance is invalid. The neuropsychologist then considers how to handle the situation.

Considerations for modification 1. The neuropsychologist considered the following two options and the related issues. First, should he inform Mr. Z that it is clear that Mr. Z is not trying his best, as he agreed to do during the informed consent process? Some colleagues have indicated that once patients are confronted and are informed that they are only doing themselves a disservice, they perform in a valid manner from that point on. However, other colleagues have noted that confronting patients does not result in valid performances; instead, patients perform only marginally better, making the invalidity less obvious as the evaluation progresses. Thus, they do not confront or inform patients when insufficient effort is evident. The Martin et al. (2015) survey found that only a minority of neuropsychologists (23% in clinical contexts; 20% in forensic contexts) often or always directly confront or warn a patient about their effort during testing when exaggeration or malingering is highly suspected or known.

Second, should the neuropsychologist complete the evaluation? Colleagues disagree as to what to do with invalid test performance. Martin et al. (2015) found that, in clinical contexts, neuropsychologists are split fairly evenly on whether to continue the examination with no change in routine (50%) or terminate the examination earlier than planned when exaggeration or malingering is highly suspected or known (41%). In contrast, in forensic contexts, neuropsychologists are much more likely to continue the examination with no change in routine (75%) than to terminate the examination earlier than planned (20%). Some practitioners maintain that completion of the evaluation is important because, although the results of the evaluation will be invalid for the purposes for which the evaluation was initiated, establishing at least a minimum level of neurocognitive ability in some domains could be informative, especially if a subset of results reflect normal functioning, as occurs when patients selectively malinger.

With regard to the above options and issues, the neuropsychologist considered that free-standing PVTs, in addition to validity indicators embedded within neurocognitive ability measures, are used to provide psychometric evidence of the validity of the patient's approach to the evaluation, and thus the test data generated by the patient. The neuropsychologist then considered that the purpose of the evaluation was to provide a clinical diagnosis and recommendations for treatment, not to establish a minimum level of neurocognitive ability based on invalid test results. Thus, there was no need to administer additional cognitive ability tests.

However, the decision to use only one PVT could be questioned. It has been recommended and become standard practice to use multiple PVTs, rather than rely on the results of just one (Bush et al., 2005; Larrabee et al., 2019; Martin et al., 2015; Sherman et al., 2020; Sweet et al., 2021). The rationale underlying the decision to use just one PVT was based on Mr. Z performing below chance on two of the three TOMM trials, with performance on the retention trial falling significantly below chance. Obtaining a score that low can only occur when the examinee knows the correct response and intentionally chooses the incorrect response. It is for that reason that significantly below chance performance on a forced choice test has been referred to as "the smoking gun of intent" (Binder & Chafetz, 2018; Pankratz & Erickson, 1990). Additionally, the atypical performance patterns on the IQ test suggested suboptimal performance (Larrabee, 2003). Because of the strong evidence that Mr. Z was not approaching the evaluation in a valid manner, there was no need for additional testing of performance validity.

The neuropsychologist also considered informing Mr. Z that his suboptimal effort had been detected and that, as such, the test results would be of no clinical (or forensic) value to him unless he began putting forth good effort. However, the neuropsychologist worried that he risked simply making Mr. Z a better malingerer and that, despite improved performance on PVTs and perhaps neurocognitive measures, the test results ultimately may still not reflect Mr. Z's potential. Thus, the neuropsychologist did not believe that he could be confident in the test results if he discussed the matter with Mr. Z and went on to complete the test administration.

Case Resolution for Modification 1

The neuropsychologist informed Mr. Z that it was clear that the test results did not reflect his optimal performance, which was necessary for accurate interpretation of the evaluation results and which he had agreed during the informed consent process to provide. The neuropsychologist also stated that the evaluation would be discontinued and that Dr. H would be informed of the outcome.

Mr. Z acknowledged his attempt to exaggerate his problems, stating that he just wanted the insurance company, his family, and his doctors to know that he really had been injured in the motor vehicle collision and was suffering as a result. With tearful affect, he promised to try his best if he could begin the evaluation again. Although touched by Mr. Z's display of emotion and his apparent genuineness, the neuropsychologist nevertheless maintained the position that Mr. Z could not continue the evaluation. Instead, the neuropsychologist offered to provide Mr. Z with the names of other clinicians in the area who may be willing to conduct the evaluation.

It was at that point that Mr. Z stated that he wanted to withdraw his consent to have information about the session released to anyone. Unsure of how to handle the situation, the neuropsychologist wanted to stall for more time in order to determine an acceptable course of action. The neuropsychologist thought that Mr. Z would only agree to a request for more time if he believed the delay was in his own interest. Thus, the neuropsychologist asked Mr. Z if he would reschedule for the next day so that the neuropsychologist could think things through, with the possibility that the evaluation may be continued. Although the neuropsychologist had no intention of continuing the evaluation and was aware of the ethical responsibility to avoid "subterfuge, or intentional misrepresentation of fact" (APA, 2017; Ethical Principle C, Integrity), he believed that his deception of Mr. Z was justified in order to discover and pursue the most appropriate course of action. Mr. Z agreed to meet the following day but maintained that the neuropsychologist could not release information about the case to anyone.

After Mr. Z left, the neuropsychologist reviewed professional guidelines and consulted with colleagues. Based on the information obtained, he determined that the best course of action would be to attempt to negotiate a modified consent to discuss the matter with the referral source (Dr. H), as had been done in the original scenario. This time, however, Mr. Z was angry about having had to return without the benefit of further testing, and he refused the request. As uncomfortable as the situation was for the neuropsychologist, there were legal and ethical requirements not to disclose information about the session to anyone.[1]

Case Modification 2

Suppose that, in the prior scenario, Mr. Z performed fairly well on the IQ test. No "red flags" were raised to alert the neuropsychologist to the likelihood of dissimulation. Suppose that, consistent with his usual protocol, the neuropsychologist administered the TOMM following completion of the IQ test, and suppose that Mr. Z's scores were 50, 50, and 50. However, following completion of the TOMM, Mr. Z stated, "I always liked that one." The neuropsychologist queried, "What do you mean?" Mr. Z explained,

> A couple years ago I saw an ad in the paper and volunteered for a study over at the university. They taught us how to take these tests and fake like we had a brain injury without getting caught. Who'd have thought I'd actually get a brain injury and need to take these tests for real someday? Pretty ironic, isn't it?

The neuropsychologist was dumbfounded, and his face registered the shock. Mr. Z followed up,

> But don't worry Doc. I wouldn't try to trick *you*. Even if I wanted to, I know that you'd catch me. And besides, I want to get the help that I need. No, Doc, I'm being straight with you; I'm trying my best.

Considerations for Modification 2

The neuropsychologist was aware that malingering research involves a variety of methodologies, which together have improved the ability of neuropsychologists to understand

and detect patient dissimulation. He further understood that one research method involves coaching research participants to malinger. His reading of professional literature (e.g., Powell, Gfeller, Hendricks, & Sharland, 2004) revealed that coaching in the context of malingering research typically takes one of two forms: symptom-coaching or test-coaching. Of the two forms, test-coaching may be particularly problematic for neuropsychology and the public. Test-coached participants are asked to feign cognitive impairment on neuropsychological tests and taught test-taking strategies to help them avoid detection. Mr. Z had apparently been a test-coached research participant.

Confronting the dilemma of what to do with a patient who admits to having been instructed how to malinger neurocognitive deficits (in this case non-maliciously, in contrast to attorney coaching), the neuropsychologist struggled with his options. He first considered that he had no psychometric evidence that Mr. Z was attempting to feign or exaggerate cognitive impairment. However, despite the lack of psychometric evidence, Mr. Z's incentive to dissimulate and his earlier attempt to have the neuropsychologist collude with him (and perhaps Dr. H) to cover up important aspects of his medical history, combined with Mr. Z's acknowledged sophistication with malingering neurocognitive test performance, left the neuropsychologist questioning the value of completing the test administration. If test administration were to be completed, what degree of confidence could be placed in the results? Conversely, should Mr. Z be penalized for having been a neuropsychological research participant? Having never anticipated such an occurrence, the neuropsychologist had no idea what to do. He felt pressured to make a quick decision when Mr. Z stated, "Doc, you O.K.? I'm ready to continue."

Case Resolution for Modification 2

Despite the pressure to proceed, the neuropsychologist knew that he needed more time and input from colleagues. He informed Mr. Z that he had never been in such a situation, was not sure what to do, and would need to consult with a colleague. Mr. Z countered that he had done nothing wrong, did not want to postpone the evaluation, would rescind his consent to release information, and would consider filing an ethics complaint if the evaluation were not completed at that time, as originally agreed. Aware that he was close to responding to the pressure and intimidation tactics in an inappropriately defensive manner, the neuropsychologist suggested that they take a brief break. Following the break, he informed Mr. Z that he wanted to consult with a colleague to ensure that the evaluation was conducted appropriately, for the benefit of Mr. Z. Mr. Z agreed to postpone completion of the evaluation, but he reiterated that if the evaluation were prematurely discontinued, he would follow through with the ethics complaint.

Following the session, the neuropsychologist contacted several respected colleagues to discuss the matter. The colleagues agreed that, although it was unfortunate that the patient had been a test-coached research participant, such participation should not automatically disqualify a person from receiving a complete neuropsychological evaluation. The colleagues emphasized that any reservations regarding performance validity should, as always, be reported. They further suggested that other indicators of performance validity, such as those embedded within or based upon neurocognitive tests, be carefully considered.

The possible need to discuss these issues with the referral source was also considered. The neuropsychologist concluded that because the evaluation was performed for clinical purposes, any limitations of his conclusions could, appropriately, be described in the written report. In contrast, had the neuropsychologist been retained by an attorney to perform a forensic neuropsychological evaluation, it may have been appropriate to contact the retaining attorney to determine if the limitations that would need to be placed on the conclusions would alter the attorney's decision to pursue the evaluation.

The neuropsychologist met Mr. Z for the second session and informed him that it was appropriate to complete the evaluation as originally intended. Test administration was completed, and the neuropsychologist indicated in his written report and in verbal feedback all relevant factors pertaining to his conclusions.

Conclusion and Recommendations

Neuropsychologists have an ethical obligation to provide services that benefit, and do not harm, the recipients of their services in multiple contexts (Bush, 2018). The appropriate selection, use, and interpretation of psychometric ability and performance validity measures are components of the process that leads to beneficial services. The interpretation of neurocognitive and psychological test data requires that a determination first be made regarding the validity of the data. As a result, the assessment of patient characteristics that may threaten the validity of the test results or evaluation conclusions is an essential component of the neuropsychological evaluation. In fact, psychometric assessment of validity, as a component of a medically necessary neuropsychological evaluation, has long been described as "medically necessary" (Bush et al., 2005).

In addition to the *assessment* of symptom and performance validity, implementation of an appropriate course of *action* once invalid responding or performance has been detected is equally vital. Determining what steps to take following the detection of invalid performance is best done in advance. Depending on the evaluation context, neuropsychologists also have an ethical responsibility to provide feedback to patients regarding their performance (Ethical Standard 9.10, Explaining Assessment Results) (APA, 2017). Effective handling of situations after invalid performance has been detected results from effective planning prior to the evaluation and establishing appropriate parameters at the outset of the evaluation. Carone et al. (2013) described a three-phase model for how to approach and provide feedback about invalid test performance in clinical neuropsychological evaluations. The three phases including (1) building rapport and obtaining informed consent, (2) completing the evaluation and initial discussions, and (3) the feedback session.

The initial contact with the patient affords the opportunity to begin establishing rapport, which can reap significant dividends throughout the evaluation and feedback process (Carone et al., 2013). The informed consent process provides neuropsychologists the opportunity to clarify expectations and responsibilities, both for themselves and for patients. Although patient consent indicates agreement with the purposes and procedures of the evaluation, patients in clinical settings are free to rescind their consent, and neuropsychologists should be prepared to negotiate this challenge if it occurs. In contrast to the current case and its modifications, patients in some forensic contexts are not afforded the same rights regarding consent. Neuropsychologists must be aware of the consent requirements for the contexts in which they practice and prepare accordingly in advance.

When completing the evaluation, if there is sufficient evidence to indicate invalid performance, it can be of value to engage the patient in preliminary discussion to determine how willing they are to acknowledge suboptimal or variable performance (Carone et al., 2013). The language used by the clinician can set the tone for the discussion. It is generally helpful to avoid words that have a negative connotation and can trigger defensiveness or anger (e.g., "faking," "lying," "poor effort," "malingering"). Instead, patients may more readily acknowledge that they were "disengaged," "not fully invested," or "did not stay motivated" throughout the evaluation. When such acknowledgment is obtained, the clinician is better positioned to discuss the issue more freely in the feedback session and report and explore reasons for the suboptimal performance.

During the feedback session, the neuropsychologist can begin by explaining their interpretative process; that is, how they compared the patient's test scores to groups of people with similar demographics and both similar and different neurological disorders. It is essential, however, to be aware of test security issues and to not provide information that could lead to successful feigning in the future (Boone et al., 2022). When explaining the patient's specific performance, a "bad news, good news approach" has been found to be helpful (Carone et al., 2013), the bad news being that some test scores were quite low, and the good news being that there is evidence that the patient has the ability to perform much better. Obtaining the patient's perspective on known group comparisons can also help the patient to understand the clinician's perspective. For example, with the present case, the neuropsychologist could ask Mr. Z if he agrees that someone who lost consciousness for a few minutes should perform better than someone who was in a coma for a few days or someone with dementia who must live in a long-term care setting. Having the patient agree to such a general statement helps lay the foundation for the discussion of the patient's very low test scores and the need to consider together explanations other than the mild TBI for the low scores. The feedback session should conclude with any treatment recommendations and the opportunity for the patient to discuss their thoughts and reactions.

Feedback interventions have also been shown to improve cognitive test scores in future evaluations. For example, with a sample of a patient with multiple sclerosis, Suchy et al. (2012) found that a group that received feedback regarding PVT failure performed significantly better on subsequent memory testing. Additionally, in the context of patients with chronic fatigue syndrome who underperformed on neuropsychological testing, Roor et al. (2020) found that a limited feedback intervention resulted in improved performance on measures of processing speed when re-tested. Again, though, it is important to be aware of test security issues and not to provide information that could lead to successful feigning in the future.

Although the provision of feedback is an ethical responsibility in most clinical contexts, the feedback session is a part of the evaluation process that is often neglected or minimized in training; it should not be. Given its importance, feedback should be taught, practiced, and supervised, rather than learned on the job through trial and error (Postal & Armstrong, 2013). Stucky et al. (2022) noted that "Effective supervisors recognize that gaining the competencies necessary to function as an independent clinical neuropsychologist requires intensive and dedicated training over several years in multiple programs (i.e., graduate education, internship, and residency)" (p. 10). As with other competencies, learning to provide effective feedback should take a gradual approach, with trainees first reading about and discussing the topic in didactics, then practicing in supervision, then observing the supervisor, and finally conducting the feedback session with the supervisor present.

The following recommendations are offered to assist the clinician when preparing for, or handling, situations involving invalid or incomplete effort or responding:

1 Plan ahead. Attempt to anticipate where in the informed consent or evaluation process challenges may lay. Determine beforehand how such challenges will be handled. Have a plan for what to do if patient consent is rescinded or if invalid performance is suspected or established.

2 Do not succumb to pressure or threats. Do not allow patients or retaining parties to convince you to do something that you know or suspect is inappropriate. Take your time, being sure to gather adequate information from all relevant sources. Review professional guidelines and jurisdictional laws and consult with colleagues.
3 Openness to input may be valuable during decision-making. Open communication with the patient or retaining party may help clarify misunderstandings and establish a course of action that satisfies the goals of the evaluation. Consultation with colleagues may help clarify ambiguous situations and result in the selection of good courses of action.
4 Inquire about prior exposure to psychological and neuropsychological tests. Such exposure may occur in a variety of contexts or from a variety of sources, including prior evaluations, research participation, the Internet, and attorneys. Consideration of prior exposure to psychological and neuropsychological measures may be important when selecting tests and interpreting test results.
5 When conducting an evaluation subsequent to one in which poor performance on PVTs was obtained, carefully consider whether to use the same PVTs that were used in the previous evaluation. The patient, having previously been exposed to the PVTs, may have exploited that experience between evaluations by researching the measures or by having another party coach them on how to "pass" the tests. Of course, if other psychometrically adequate measures are unavailable, the examiner may have little choice but to use the same measures, documenting any concerns about the validity of the results.
6 When *clear* evidence of invalid responding has been detected, carefully weigh the merits of continuing versus discontinuing the remainder of the planned evaluation. The context and goals of the evaluation are important considerations when determining the course of action. It should be noted that some neuropsychologists routinely complete the entire evaluation in situations in which unequivocal evidence of noncredible performance or frank malingering was identified early in the examination process.

It is noteworthy that other feedback models (e.g., Martin & Schroeder, 2022) are also available, and clinicians should familiarize themselves with the literature on multiple feedback models to ensure that they have multiple options from which they could pull tools and techniques.

Weblinks and Online Materials

American Psychological Association, APA Task Force on Psychological Assessment and Evaluation Guidelines. (2020). *APA guidelines for psychological assessment and evaluation.* Retrieved from https://www.apa.org/about/policy/guidelines-psychological-assessment-evaluation.pdf.

National Academy of Neuropsychology. (2003). *Informed consent in clinical neuropsychology practice.* Retrieved from NANinformedconsent.pdf.

National Academies of Sciences, Engineering, and Medicine. 2015. *Psychological testing in the service of disability determination.* Washington, DC: The National Academies Press. https://doi.org/10.17226/21704. https://nap.nationalacademies.org/read/21704/chapter/1

Note

1 If the neuropsychologist were to be subpoenaed or otherwise legally instructed to disclose to the court information about the session, such requirements may preempt their responsibility to maintain privilege and/or confidentiality. Seeking personal legal counsel and/or explaining the dilemma to the court would be advisable under such circumstances.

References

American Psychological Association (2017). *Ethical principles of psychologists and code of conduct.* Retrieved from www.apa.org/ethics/code.

Binder, L. M., & Chafetz, M. D. (2018). Determination of the smoking gun of intent: Significance testing of forced choice results in social security claimants. *The Clinical Neuropsychologist*, 32, 132–144.

Boone, K. B., Sweet, J. J., Byrd, D. A., Denney, R. L., Hanks, R. A., Kaufmann, P. M., ... & Suhr, J. A. (2022). Official position of the American Academy of Clinical Neuropsychology on test security. *The Clinical Neuropsychologist*, 36(3), 523–545.

Bush, S. S., Heilbronner, R. L., & Ruff, R. M. (2014). Psychological assessment of symptom and performance validity, response bias, and malingering: Official position of the Association for Scientific Advancement in Psychological Injury and Law. *Psychological Injury and Law*, 7, 197–205.

Bush, S., Ruff, R., Tröster, A., Barth, J., Koffler, S., Pliskin, N., Reynolds, C., & Silver, C. (2005). Symptom validity assessment: Practice issues and medical necessity. Official position of the National Academy of Neuropsychology. *Archives of Clinical Neuropsychology*, 20, 419–426.

Bush, S. S. (2013). Ethical considerations in mild traumatic brain injury cases and symptom validity assessment. In D. A. Carone & S. S. Bush (Eds.), *Mild traumatic brain injury: Symptom validity assessment and malingering* (pp. 45–56). New York: Springer Publishing Company.

Bush, S. S. (2014). Assessing symptom and performance validity in veterans. In S. S. Bush (Ed.), *Psychological assessment of veterans* (pp. 433–452). New York: Oxford University Press.

Bush, S. S. (2018). *Ethical decision making in clinical neuropsychology*, 2nd edition. New York: Oxford University Press.

Bush, S. S., & Bass, C. (2015). Assessment of validity with polytrauma veteran populations. *NeuroRehabilitation*, 36, 451–462.

Bush, S. S., & Graver, C. (2013). Symptom validity assessment of military and veteran populations following mild traumatic brain injury. In D. A. Carone & S. S. Bush (Eds.), *Mild traumatic brain injury: Symptom validity assessment and malingering* (pp. 381–397). New York: Springer Publishing Company.

Bush, S. S., & Morgan, J. E. (2012). Improbable neuropsychological presentations: Assessment, diagnosis, and management. In S. S. Bush (Ed.), *Neuropsychological practice with veterans* (pp. 27–43). New York: Springer Publishing Company.

Bush, S. S., & Myers, T. E. (2013). Neuropsychological services following motor vehicle collisions. *Psychological Injury and Law*, 6, 3–20.

Carone, D. A., & Bush, S. S. (2018). *Validity assessment in rehabilitation psychology and settings.* New York: Oxford University Press.

Carone, D. A., Bush, S. S., & Iverson, G. L. (2013). Providing feedback on symptom validity, mental health, and treatment in mild traumatic brain injury. In D. A. Carone & S. S. Bush (Eds.), *Mild traumatic brain injury: Symptom validity assessment and malingering* (pp. 101–118). New York: Springer Publishing Company.

Dandachi-Fitzgerald, B., Merckelbach, H., & Ponds, R. W. H. M. (2017). Neuropsychologists' ability to predict distorted symptom presentation. *Journal of Clinical and Experimental Neuropsychology*, 39, 257–264.

Donders, J., & Kirkwood, M. W. (2013). Symptom validity assessment with special populations. In D. A. Carone & S. S. Bush (Eds.), *Mild traumatic brain injury: Symptom validity assessment and malingering* (pp. 399–410). New York: Springer.

Faust, D., Hart, K., Guilmette, T. J., & Arkes, H. R. (1988). Neuropsychologists' capacity to detect adolescent malingerers. *Professional Psychology: Research and Practice*, 19, 508–515.

Guilmette, T. J. (2013). The role of clinical judgment in symptom validity assessment. In D. A. Carone & S. S Bush (Eds.), *Mild traumatic brain injury: Symptom validity assessment and malingering* (pp. 31–43). New York: Springer.

Guilmette, T. J., Sweet, J. J., Hebben, N., Koltai, D., Mahone, E. M., Spiegler, B. J., Stucky, K., Westerveld, M., & Conference Participants (2020). American Academy of Clinical Neuropsychology

consensus conference statement on uniform labeling of performance test scores, *The Clinical Neuropsychologist*, 34, 437–453.
Kaufman, N. K., & Bush, S. S. (2020). Validity assessment in military psychology. In U. Kumar (Ed.), *The Routledge international handbook of military psychology and mental health* (pp. 211–223). New York: Routledge.
Kaufman, N. K., & Bush, S. S. (2021). Ethical issues in assessing malingering in head injury litigation. In A. M. Horton & C. R. Reynolds (Eds.), *Detection of malingering during head injury litigation*, 3rd Edition (pp. 157–176). Zug, Switzerland: Springer Nature.
Larrabee, G. J. (2003). Detection of malingering using atypical performance patterns on standard neuropsychological tests. *The Clinical Neuropsychologist*, 17(3), 410–425. https://doi.org/10.1076/clin.17.3.410.18089
Larrabee, G. J., Millis, S. R., & Meyers, J. E. (2009). 40 plus or minus 10, a new magical number: Reply to Russell. *The Clinical Neuropsychologist*, 23(5), 841–849. https://doi.org/10.1080/13854040902796735
Larrabee, G. J., Rohling, M. L., & Meyers, J. E. (2019). Use of multiple performance and symptom validity measures: Determining the optimal per test cutoff for determination of invalidity, analysis of skew, and inter-test correlations in valid and invalid performance groups. *The Clinical Neuropsychologist*, 33(8), 1354–1372.
Leonhard, C. (2023a). Review of statistical and methodological issues in the forensic prediction of malingering from validity tests: Part I: Statistical issues. *Neuropsychology Review*, 33(3), 581–603.
Leonhard, C. (2023b). Review of statistical and methodological issues in the forensic prediction of malingering from validity tests: Part II—Methodological issues. *Neuropsychology Review*, 33(3), 604–623.Lippa, S. M. (2018). Performance validity testing in neuropsychology: A clinical guide, critical review, and update on a rapidly evolving literature. *The Clinical Neuropsychologist*, 32, 391–421.
Martin, P. K., Schroeder, R. W., & Odland, A. P. (2015). Neuropsychologists' validity testing beliefs and practices: A survey of North American professionals. *The Clinical Neuropsychologist*, 29, 741–776.
Martin, P. K., & Schroeder, R. W. (2020). Base rates of invalid test performance across clinical non-forensic contexts and settings. *Archives of Clinical Neuropsychology*, 35(6), 717–725. https://doi-org.mu.idm.oclc.org/10.1093/arclin/ acaa0 17
Martin, P. K., & Schroeder, R. W. (2022). A framework for providing clinical feedback when patients invalidate testing. In R. W. Schroeder & P. K. Martin (Eds.), *Validity assessment in clinical neuropsychological practice: Evaluating and managing noncredible performance* (pp. 47–69). New York: Guilford Press.
Martin, P. K., Schroeder, R. W., Olsen, D. H., Maloy, H., Boettcher, A., Ernst, N., & Okut, H. (2020). A systematic review and metaanalysis of the Test of Memory Malingering in adults: Two decades of deception detection. *The Clinical Neuropsychologist*, 34, 88–119.
Martin, P. K., Schroeder, R. W., & Olsen, D. H. (2020). Performance validity in the dementia clinic: Specificity of validity tests when used individually and in aggregate across levels of cognitive impairment severity. *The Clinical Neuropsychologist*, 36, 165–188.
Miele, A. S., Gunner, J. H., Lynch, J. K., & McCaffrey, R. J. (2012). Are embedded validity indices equivalent to free-standing symptom validity tests? *Archives of Clinical Neuropsychology*, 27, 10–22. https://doi.org/10.1093/arclin/acr084
Millis, S. R. (2009). What clinicians really need to know about symptom exaggeration, insufficient effort, and malingering: Statistical and measurement matters. In J. E. Morgan & J. J. Sweet (Eds.), *Neuropsychology of malingering casebook* (pp. 21–37). New York, NY: Psychology Press.
Pankratz, L., & Erickson, R. D. (1990). Two views of malingering. *The Clinical Neuropsychologist*, 4, 379–389.
Postal, K., & Armstrong, K. (2013). *Feedback that sticks*. New York: Oxford University Press.
Powell, M. R., Gfeller, J. D., Hendricks, B. L., & Sharland, M. (2004). Detecting symptom- and test-coached simulators with the Test of Memory Malingering. *Archives of Clinical Neuropsychology*, 19(5), 693–702.

Roor, J. J., Knoop, H., Dandachi-FitzGerald, B., Peters, M. J. V., Bleijenberg, G., & Ponds, R. W. H. M. (2020). Feedback on underperformance in patients with chronic fatigue syndrome: The impact on subsequent neuropsychological test performance. *Applied Neuropsychology: Adult*, 27, 188–196. doi: 10.1080/23279095.2018.1519509

Roor, J. J., Peters, M. J. V., Dandachi-FirzGerald, B., & Pond, R. W. H. M. (published online 2023). Performance validity test failure in the clinical population: A systematic review and meta-analysis of prevalence rates. *Neuropsychology Review*. https://doi.org/10.1007/s11065-023-09582-7

Schroeder, R. W., & Martin, P. K. (Eds.) (2022). *Neuropsychological validity testing in clinical settings: A handbook for non-forensic practice* (pp. 86–103). New York: Guilford Press.

Sharland, M. J., & Gfeller, J. D. (2007). A survey of neuropsychologists' beliefs and practices with respect to the assessment of effort. *Archives of Clinical Neuropsychology*, 22, 213–223.

Sherman, E., Slick, D. J., & Iverson, G. L. (2020). Multidimensional malingering criteria for neuropsychological assessment: A 20-year update of the malingered neuropsychological dysfunction criteria. *Archives of Clinical Neuropsychology*, 35, 735–764.

Soble, J. R., Webber, T. A., & Bailey, K. C. (2022). An overview of common performance validity tests for practicing clinicians. In R. W. Schroeder & P. K. Martin (Eds.), *Validity assessment in clinical neuropsychological practice; evaluating and managing noncredible performance* (pp. 126–149). New York: The Guilford Press.

Stucky, K. J., Bush, S. S., & Heffelfinger, A. K. (2022). A developmental approach to competency-based supervision. In S. D. Bodin, K. J. Stucky, & S. S. Bush (Eds.), *Supervision in neuropsychology: Practical, ethical, and theoretical considerations* (pp. 6–36). New York: Oxford University Press.

Suchy, Y., Chelune, G., Franchow, E. I., & Thorgusen, S. R. (2012). Confronting patients about insufficient effort: The impact on subsequent symptom validity and memory performance. *The Clinical Neuropsychologist*, 26, 1296–1311.

Sweet, J. J., Heilbronner, R. L., Morgan, J. E., Larrabee, G. J., Rohling, M. L., Booner, K. B., Kirkwood, M. W., Schroeder, R. W., Suhr, J. A., and Conference Participants (2021). American Academy of Clinical Neuropsychology (AACN) 2021 consensus statement on validity assessment: Update of the 2009 AACN consensus conference statement on neuropsychological assessment of effort, response bias, and malingering. *The Clinical Neuropsychologist*. 35, 1053–1106.

Youngjohn, J. R., Lees-Haley, P. R., & Binder, L. M. (1999). Comment: Warning malingerers produces more sophisticated malingering. *Archives of Clinical Neuropsychology*, 14, 511–515.

42 Breaking Bad in Neuropsychology

Michael Chafetz, Diana Campos, and Paige Haley

"There are Plaintiff experts. There are Defense experts. And then there are Experts."
From a lawyer's discussion on experts with the first author (MC)

Introduction

In the acclaimed AMC television series *Breaking Bad*, the fictional character, Walter White, was a high school chemistry teacher who had cancer and could not pay his bills. But he had skills. He teamed up with a low-level drug dealer to manufacture high-quality illegal drugs, as befitting his skills. He was only trying to provide for his health and his family's future, and we felt for him. As he got farther along with his nascent drug business, this mild-mannered chemistry teacher eventually developed a drug empire of which he was extremely proud. Along the way, we saw him become more and more unethical until there seemed to be nothing left of his original moral compass.

One might wonder if there are forensic practitioners who share some similarities with Walter White. In the course of conducting forensic practice (whether neuropsychological or otherwise), there are times when we may encounter work product and testimony by opposing experts that appears grossly inconsistent with the findings of peer-reviewed research, seems biased toward a pre-ordained conclusion, and arguably violates ethical guidelines. In this chapter, we will present neuropsychological vignettes to exemplify these problematic behaviors, along with a description of the psychological ethics code standards they may breach. Our goal is to promote and enhance a process of self-examination to prevent one's own work product from being biased and falling below ethical standards.

A Note on the Ethics Code Revision

While the update from the American Psychological Association (APA, 2017) *Ethical Principles for Psychologists and Code of Conduct* (EPPCC) was the main guide used in this chapter for descriptions of ethical breaches, we are mindful of the pending revision by the APA. As of this writing, a proposed revision is out for public comment and debate. As we cannot be certain of the final product, we believe that a crosswalk from the old Code to the *proposed* new Code would be premature. Given that and given that the ethical infractions described in this chapter were conducted under the old Code, we continued to use the existing Code in this chapter.

Guidance on Bias

Goldstein and Morgan (2025) ask us to consider why it is that in forensic practice we occasionally see substandard work from other colleagues or, at a more fundamental level, have

DOI: 10.4324/9781003005063-48

opposite opinions on the same case? One idea is about competence, but another idea has to do with *retainer bias*, a form of confirmatory bias. Goldstein and Morgan (2025) discussed that the tendency to interpret findings in support of the retaining attorney's advocacy about a case may be either intentional (explicit) or unintentional (implicit).

However, it must be considered that the underlying science driving the expression of the findings may actually favor one side or another. For example, the research of Elizabeth Loftus on the malleability and unreliability of eyewitness memory (Loftus, 1997; Loftus & Ketcham, 1991) is not equally attractive to both defense and prosecuting (criminal) attorneys. The fact that criminal defense attorneys found her research useful in impeaching prosecution witnesses was not about retainer bias of the expert per se but about the research findings themselves.

West and Kenney (2011) have defined bias as any "systematic factor that judgments are being attracted toward, besides the truth" (p. 360). Van Gorp and McMullen (1997) wrote about practices that could potentially lead to bias in neuropsychological evaluations. Some of their examples included: (1) an expert agreeing to payment via a lien attached to the final settlement, which creates a contingency in which the final fee is related to the success of the retaining party; (2) the potential retaining attorney attempting to signal, at the time of the initial phone contact, the conclusions expected of the expert; (3) not obtaining adequate relevant records, leading to an inaccurate and perhaps sanitized understanding of the history of the claimant; (4) not taking into account the base-rate of scattered lower scores in persons who are without brain pathology; (5) failure to account for the impact of demographic background on test scores (e.g., low PASAT result in someone with a poor academic record, particularly in math; failure to consider impact of English as a second language on verbal test scores); (6) test-selection to enhance the probability of finding or not finding a particular result (e.g., use of an older performance validity test with a below-chance cutoff); (7) failure to account for comorbid factors on test scores (e.g., drug abuse, premorbid ADHD or learning disability, comorbid medical conditions); (8) allowing retaining counsel to influence the writing of the report through reading of drafts; and (9) revision of the report [perhaps at the request of the retaining attorney] to include or exclude alternative facts (e.g., being asked to omit the conclusion that test results would be most consistent with a degenerative dementia rather than an acquired TBI).

Considering bias, Lees-Haley (1999) asserted that bias is a systematic error and that determining whether our own (or someone else's) work is biased requires knowing the truth. Lees-Haley (1999) illustrated a typical attorney assertion that the expert is biased if their referrals are 100% from the defense or 100% from the plaintiff. If one examines this assertion, it becomes clear that the "50–50" expert might just be giving favorable opinion for whichever side is consulting, in which case, the expert is completely biased. On the other hand, if the "100%" defense-retained expert in civil litigation finds noncredible test performance at the base-rate for the particular population and type of claim, and he or she has cases in which conclusions do not support the retained side, bias is in fact not confirmed. Similarly, if an expert frequently publishes on the development and validation of performance validity tests, this may be less attractive to plaintiff counsel in a personal injury case, who might be averse to careful scrutiny of the validity of their clients' test performance by an acknowledged expert in the field.

Grote et al. (2000) provided examples of potential unethical practices in clinical neuropsychology and discussed the relevant legal and ethical principles involved. They make a distinction between unethical (clear violation of professional norms) versus incompetent (conduct falling below the standards of the profession) practices. The authors discussed ethical violations applicable to a forensic context that included deliberate failure to review significant prior history (e.g., extended loss of consciousness from a previous motor vehicle accident or a previous diagnosis of ADHD), which violates the ethical principle of providing sufficient substantiation for the findings. The authors also argue that ethical principles are violated when the clinician constructs an exam to produce a particular finding, such as by the use of tests that are outdated for the current purpose; failing to take into account test factors that reduce the accuracy of interpretation (e.g., whether race norming is inappropriate for the context or purpose of the exam); and misuse of assessment techniques, for example, by using specific cognitive tests to pinpoint a locus of brain damage in the absence of any evidence of brain damage and without taking into account historical causes for low test scores.

In 1999, Sweet and Moulthrop provided a guide for self-examination of general bias and a separate guide for self-examination of bias in adversarial assessments, which is still relevant today. As advised in these guides, an examiner should ask whether they are deviating in some important way(s) from the general consensus on a topic, the mainstream literature, or from typical clinical decision-making on a similar case. Another issue is whether clinicians form opinions for plaintiff or defense positions prematurely without having garnered enough facts. Do we always reach conclusions favorable to the retaining side? Have we moved from being an expert to being an advocate? Do we routinely provide the same decision rules for defining brain dysfunction no matter which side retains us? The writer of the forensic report might ask him/herself how each statement would be defended (if pressed to do so). Would a panel of expert peers arrive at a consensus regarding each statement that I make? Are the descriptors overly-dramatized? Have facts/evidence been omitted that will detract from my position?

Forensic versus Clinical Exams

The National Academy of Neuropsychology provided an official statement concerning independent and court-ordered neuropsychological examinations (Bush, 2005) in which it was noted that in these types of exams, the examinee is not the *patient* of the examiner. In particular, the forensic examiner's independence is achieved by staying free of the patient's interests so that those interests do not skew the examiner's thinking and reporting. A broader discussion of differences between claimants and patients is also available for reading (e.g., Greenberg & Shuman, 1997, 2007; Strasburger et al., 1997); Schroeder and Chafetz (2021) further revised this discussion for the purposes of comparing disability claimants and neuropsychological patients.

Greenberg and Shuman's (1997, 2007) original goal was to increase the quality of forensic assistance by psychologists. In the update to their work, Schroeder and Chafetz (2021) distinguished between the neuropsychological clinical provider and the forensic disability evaluator (as expert). In the examination that is usually arranged at the request of the defense in civil litigation or the insurance company in a disability case, the examiner's goal is to provide answers to the questions within the legal arena. If the examiner attempts to foster a doctor–patient relationship, this helping relationship can interfere with the accuracy of the findings. The examiner is a consultant who provides information to the retaining party and not to the examinee. By contrast, clinicians who have conducted a purely clinical examination could indeed testify concerning their findings on the neuropsychological conditions of their patients, but this must not be confused with the specialized forensic examination role in addressing legal topics in the case (e.g., cause of the brain injury; whether injury prevents work in their occupation).

The idea is to have clear boundaries and a single role (the examiner) when working with forensic examinees. The dual role (e.g., expert and treating doctor) is sometimes seen, more commonly in the plaintiff's expert, whose reports describe symptoms/deficits that the expert (or a treatment provider in the expert's group) then provides treatment for. However, the Specialty Guidelines for Forensic Psychology (2013) specifically caution that

> Providing forensic and therapeutic psychological services to the same individual or closely related individuals involves multiple relationships that may impair objectivity and/or cause exploitation or other harm. Therefore, when requested or ordered to provide either concurrent or sequential forensic and therapeutic services, forensic practitioners are encouraged to disclose the potential risk and make reasonable efforts to refer the request to another qualified provider.
>
> (Standard 4.02.01).

Ethical Guidelines/Standards Concerning Vignettes

We now describe neuropsychological vignettes involving potential violation of ethical standards, followed by a discussion of the relevant APA Ethical Standards. There are several important ethical guidelines and specialty standards relating to these vignettes, including the APA's EPPCC's General Principles and Standards 2: Competency and 9: Assessment, as well as the *Standards for Educational and Psychological Testing*, and Specialty Guidelines for Forensic Psychology (SGFP) 10: Assessment.

The vignettes will be organized in clusters, each of which represent misuse of a particular realm of neuropsychological testing and/or findings (e.g., validity testing; intellectual disability). Moreover, a vignette may be from a single case or may represent multiple cases from different examiners. When a vignette represents multiple infractions (possibly from multiple cases), this type of vignette will contain similar and/or related ethical infractions.

Please note that these vignettes will refer to performance validity tests (PVTs), symptom validity tests, and to concepts from extant guidelines for malingering (Sherman et al., 2020) that include compelling inconsistencies and marked discrepancies. Named tests include: Test of Memory Malingering (TOMM); Word Memory Test (WMT); Medical Symptom Validity Test; Word Choice Test (WCT); Reliable Digit Span (RDS); and recognition memory tests on the Wechsler Memory Scale-IV (WMS-IV) that include Logical Memory (LM); Verbal Paired Associates (VPA); and Visual Reproduction (VR).

Finally, while the vignettes in this chapter focus on neuropsychological cases, it is important to note that similar infractions can happen in any branch of psychology, medicine, and other fields.

First Vignette Cluster (#1–3): Validity Testing Issues

Vignette #1 (Two Different Neuropsychologists – Multiple Cases): PVTs: Insufficient Number and Quality

A neuropsychologist who assesses TBI cases in civil litigation frequently uses the forced-choice cutoff of < 9 on the 21-Item Test (Iverson et al., 1994). While the claimants rarely if ever fail (i.e., are not positive on) this test at this cutoff level, the findings reported by this neuropsychologist show the claimants "passing" this PVT with about half correct (e.g., 12/21), which is accepted by the neuropsychologist as not providing evidence for malingering. Another neuropsychologist who assesses TBI cases in civil litigation frequently only uses two PVTs and then assesses the cases as not showing malingering when both are "passed."

Concerning Vignette #1: This vignette illustrates two common problems often seen in forensic reports: (1) failure to administer appropriate PVTs and (2) failure to administer an adequate number of PVTs. While it is difficult to decide definitively which psychological tests are obsolete for their purpose (Bush et al., 2018), we note that the 21-item test was developed at a time prior to established multidimensional guidelines for malingering (Slick et al., 1999) and also prior to the development of above-chance cutoffs. This below-chance cutoff had 0% false-positives (Iverson et al., 1994), as it is rare for non-malingerers (even those who are notably impaired) to score below chance even when the below-chance criteria are less restrictive (Binder & Chafetz, 2018). Most malingerers do not score this low on forced-choice tests either (Chafetz, 2008). While it is not possible to read this neuropsychologist's mind, the practical effect of using such an old test with such a rigorous cutoff is to lower the detection of malingering, which is tantamount to a bias in test and cutoff selection. Moreover, there has been little or no research on this test in over 20 years, and it is used by only 2.7% of North American neuropsychologists and 0% of validity assessment experts (Martin et al., 2025).

Regarding the number of PVTs administered, North American neuropsychologists indicate that they administer a median of 6 PVTs in non-geriatric forensic evaluations, and validity assessment experts administer a median of 8 PVTs in these evaluations (Martin et al., 2025). In fact, in the same survey, less than 0.5% of neuropsychologists and 0% of validity assessment experts reported using two or fewer PVTs, indicating that using so few PVTs is a highly atypical practice in a forensic setting. Further, guidelines for the determination of neurocognitive malingering (Sherman et al., 2020) require failure on at least two PVTs, and this will be more challenging to obtain if only two PVTs are administered.

The APA's EPPCC Standard 2.04 (APA, 2017) states "psychologists' work is based upon established scientific and professional knowledge of the discipline." As such, psychologists have an obligation to select assessment methods and make professional opinions that are grounded in up-to-date research evidence. The choice of such an old PVT (21-item test) with an obsolete cutoff as well as the use of too few PVTs fail this standard and appear to tend toward bias in reporting validity in cases in which the neuropsychologist works. In addition, the APA's SGFP Guideline 1.02 regarding Impartiality and Fairness states "when conducting forensic examinations, forensic practitioners strive to be unbiased and impartial, and avoid partisan presentation of unrepresentative, incomplete, or inaccurate evidence that might mislead finders of fact." The decision to use an old validity test or too few validity tests may lead to bias in the case that could call into question the practitioner's impartiality, which invokes Standard 9.08a: "Psychologists do not base their assessment or intervention decisions or recommendations on data or test results that are outdated for the current purpose."

Vignette #2: Misuse of PVT Cutoffs and Dismissal of Test Score Inconsistencies

A civil litigation examinee obtained the following validity scores: TOMM: 32, 43, 50; RDS = 5; 21-Item Test (17/21); WMT: 95%, 100%, 95%; WCT = 27/50; and WMS-IV recognition tests (LM = 22/30; VPA = 36/40; VR = 5/7). Of these, only the WCT was labeled as a Fail, while the RDS was labeled as a "Caution." The examiner also attempted to argue that because TOMM Retention was greater than TOMM Trial 2, the TOMM itself was a pass. This same neuropsychologist has also claimed in other instances that because none of the examinee's PVT scores were below chance, the results of testing were felt to be a valid and reliable representation of current functioning. In the dataset above, the examiner concluded that the test taker failed only one PVT (the WCT), thus failing to meet criteria for malingered neurocognitive dysfunction (Slick et al., 1999).

Concerning Vignette #2: Despite the claims made by the neuropsychologist, the claimant failed the TOMM (both Trial 1 and 2; Martin, Schroeder, Olsen et al., 2020), the WCT (Holdnack et al., 2013), and the RDS (Schroeder et al., 2012), which indicated that three PVTs were failed. This number of PVT failures met standards for the determination of invalid performance (Martin et al., 2025; Sherman et al., 2020). Given the usual specificity standards of PVTs, three positive validity findings have an exceedingly low level of false-positive identification (Chafetz, 2022).

Concerning the claim that because the TOMM Retention trial was higher than Trial 2, the performance on the TOMM was a "pass," we note there is no empirical evidence to support this interpretation. We also note that this interpretation strategy is not standard practice per the test developer. Regarding the "below-chance" requirement, generally speaking, a low proportion of claimants score significantly below chance on forced-choice PVTs (Kim et al., 2010; Binder & Chafetz, 2018). This means that the requirement of significantly below-chance performance for documentation of performance invalidity is a highly ineffective method that results in a high false negative rate, missing a large proportion of individuals who are feigning.

Moreover, the examinee's score on the WCT (27/50) was clearly at binomial chance levels. We keep in mind that chance-level performance is honestly obtained only in individuals who are blind (or blindfolded) and cannot see the visually presented words, or in individuals so cognitively impaired by dementia that they are unable to function on their own and require 24-hour supervision and monitoring. In this context, we also note that above-chance cutoffs are the norm now in PVT development (Boone, 2021), and that there has been over 30 years of evolution in the research on PVTs beyond below-chance cutoffs. Further, the examiner stated there were no compelling inconsistencies seen in the case, but in fact, these were seen across the examinee's test scores. For example, the examinee scored at only the 2nd %ile on a simple test of auditory attention (Digit Span) but obtained a high score (84th %ile) on a test of divided and alternating mental set (Trails B) and an average score (37th %ile) on a problem-solving test that involves careful attention to feedback (Category Test), both of which require solid attention and working memory.

Concerning Vignette #2: While it is impossible to read the minds or intent of these examiners, it would seem clear that the methods employed (e.g., improperly low PVT cutoffs; using unsupported reasoning about the TOMM and RDS; failing to recognize obvious inconsistencies in the data) only serve to not show invalidity in the findings. Practitioners are specifically advised to keep abreast of emerging research on test cutoffs (Sweet et al., 2021; Lippa, 2018), and to understand fully how to use the entire clinical picture to appraise compelling inconsistencies and marked discrepancies (Lippa, 2018; Sherman et al., 2020). A careful review of the relevant records is most important in this regard (Chafetz et al., 2025).

Standard 2.04 ("psychologists' work is based upon established scientific and professional knowledge of the discipline") is also relevant for **Vignette #2**. Clearly, information about established cutoffs for PVTs appears to be lacking in this examiner's report. Moreover, Principle C states: "Psychologists seek to promote accuracy, honesty, and truthfulness in the science, teaching, and practice of psychology. In these activities psychologists do not steal, cheat, or engage in fraud, subterfuge, or intentional misrepresentation of fact." The SGFP Guidelines (APA, 2013) has a similar goal: "Forensic practitioners strive for accuracy, honesty, and truthfulness in the science, teaching, and practice of forensic psychology and they strive to resist partisan pressures to provide services in any ways that might tend to be misleading or inaccurate." Given the misapplication of cutoffs of PVTs, the invention of validity rules for the TOMM that do not exist, the avoidance of significant inconsistencies in the data, and the appraisal of good validity in the findings when the data showed otherwise, there exists the very real possibility of intentional misrepresentation of the data in this case.

Moreover, for **Vignette #2**, Standard 9.02a states: "Psychologists administer, adapt, score, interpret, or use assessment techniques, interviews, tests, or instruments in a manner and for purposes that are appropriate in light of the research on or evidence of the usefulness and proper application of the techniques." To comply with these standards, psychologists are obligated to apply research evidence appropriately to their work. By seemingly avoiding the extant research evidence and thereby creating a false interpretation of the findings, the neuropsychologist in this case appears to be acting in contradiction to the ethical principles and code of conduct of the field.

Vignette #3: Examples of Nonstandard Administration of PVTs

A neuropsychologist examiner stated in one report that the examinee became upset and argumentative when the examiner discussed the examinee's poor performance on a validity test. As test-takers are not to be alerted to concerns about their PVT performance while the tests are being administered, this statement indicated that the test administration was not standard. In particular, no PVT instructions indicate that test-takers are to be questioned or otherwise confronted about how they choose to respond on the tests.

In another case, a neuropsychologist noted in his report that he told the examinee he had been identified as displaying substandard effort on a previous exam (failure on the b-test). On this neuropsychologist's exam two months later, the examinee passed the b-test. If a test taker is alerted to the fact that they failed a specific PVT, it can be assumed that they will not make that same mistake again on the next exam.

In deposition (under oath), a neuropsychologist attempted to explain PVT administration procedures by claiming that some examinees deliberately underperform as a "cry for help" or an attempt to show the neuropsychologist his injuries. The neuropsychologist then advises the examinee that they are not performing to true ability and instructs them to perform to their best ability. If the examinee then fails another PVT administration, the neuropsychologist stops the PVT because it would just yield invalid data and thereby deprive the examiner of a helpful look at real neurological problems.

Concerning Vignette #3: This series of examples reflects the concerning practice of altering PVT administration by either confronting test-takers in real time that they are not performing to true ability, advising them with changed test instructions, or alerting them to previous failures on the same PVTs. All of these practices serve to render the PVTs ineffective. Research on coaching of PVTs shows that when test-takers are alerted or warned about the design or plan of PVTs, the additional knowledge changes their scores by improving them (Brennan et al., 2009), which makes it less likely that examinees will be positive on the validity test. Furthermore, while it is well known that attorneys, who are advocates for their clients' agendas, will coach their clients (Essig et al., 2001), it is a striking thing to contemplate a neuropsychologist providing this information.

Again, Standard 9.02a states: "Psychologists administer, adapt, score, interpret, or use assessment techniques, interviews, tests, or instruments in a manner and for purposes that are appropriate in light of the research on or evidence of the usefulness and proper application of the techniques." The misapplication of PVT administration rules/procedures creates a direct violation of Standard 9.02a, no matter what the reason. If the reason is ignorance on the neuropsychologist's part, then one considers that a violation of Standard 2.04 ("psychologists' work is based upon established scientific and professional knowledge of the discipline") is also relevant. If, instead, the neuropsychologist was deliberately aiding the retaining attorney's agenda, we would consider APA's SGFP Guideline 1.02 regarding Impartiality and Fairness: "when conducting forensic examinations, forensic practitioners strive to be unbiased and impartial, and avoid partisan presentation of unrepresentative, incomplete, or inaccurate evidence that might mislead finders of fact."

Regarding SGFP 10.02, Selection and Use of Assessment Procedures indicates that psychologists administer measures "in the manner and for the purposes that are appropriate in light of the research on or evidence of their usefulness and proper application" (p. 15, APA, 2013). Altering the test taking instructions on a validity assessment to improve the examinee's performance defeats the purpose of the test and what the test is designed to measure/detect.

In general, Principal A (Beneficence and Nonmaleficence) indicates that psychologists should strive to do no harm. In these cases, the obvious avoidance of accurate diagnosis by manipulation of PVTs harms the ability of the trier of fact to get to the truth of the matter.

Vignette #4: Misuse of Records/Findings in the Atkins Death Case

A person who is "intellectually disabled" cannot constitutionally be put to death (*Atkins v. Virginia, 536 U.S. 304, 321 (2002)*). The Defendant has the burden of proving intellectual disability by a preponderance of the evidence. For the determination of intellectual disability (ID), three "prongs" must be satisfied: (1) The person's intellectual functioning must be two standard deviations or more below the mean (*Hall v. Florida, 134 S.Ct. 1986 (2014)*), though one must take into account measurement error; (2) The individual must have significant limitations in adaptive functioning; and (3) The intellectual and adaptive limitations must begin before age 18.

The defense experts gave the opinion that the Defendant suffered from ID. Their opinion was based on a review of records, interviews, and psychological/neuropsychological assessment. They determined a Full-Scale IQ of 71, which they said met the intellectual prong due to the score being within the error range for the two-standard-deviation level. Based on interviews with informants and the use of adaptive function measures, they found that his adaptive skills were two standard deviations or more below average. The defense experts also indicated that the Defendant's problems arose during the developmental period.

However, there are multiple concerns with this case:

1 Government experts found marked discrepancies in Defendant's responses on the same tests, which revealed that the Defendant had more knowledge and better skills than he let on during the defense examination. For example, the Defendant did very well on the Matrix Reasoning subtest (raw score = 18) of the WAIS-IV, even getting some of the hardest items correct, but he did poorly on this test in the Defendant's expert's exam (raw score = 7). These differences were not accounted for by re-test practice experience, as the Defendant had met the ceiling on the first exam before getting the harder items correct (which he had never seen) on the second exam. Moreover, the Defendant answered

questions differently on the Information subtest in the first and second exams; that is, some items he got correct at time 1 he missed on time 2, and vice versa. Given that the Information subtest measures old, over-learned information, it is not plausible that he knew information on one exam that he did not know on another. Such differences in performance on simple test questions over a three-month period have no organic basis, nor are they associated with ID. The defense experts failed to account adequately for these differences in the two examinations, saying that the increase in scores was due to practice effects, when it was clearly not.

2 For adaptive skills, the Defendant's experts used a recently published and sparsely researched instrument: Adaptive Behavior Diagnostic Scale (ABDS; published by WPS). This test has items that purportedly measure "gullibility" and "foolishness," which were believed by defense experts to be integral in the determination of ID. However, this test was norm-referenced on children and young adults from ages 2 to 21, but it was never validated for adults over that age. The Defendant was arrested when she was 22 years old, but at the time of examination, she was 34 years old. Several informants rated her on the ABDS at various target ages: 22, 15, 9, and 8, but no documentation was available as to how the target ages were chosen or the ratings were validated (and age 22 is out of the norm-referenced range). The ratings were low (Extremely Low range) and inconsistent with other sources of information, which appear to have been ignored. Several scores were at the bottom limit (standard score = 40). These ratings were incompatible with the findings on the Vineland Adaptive Behavior Scale-3, which was administered when he was incarcerated. The Vineland findings showed an Adaptive Behavior Composite score of 84. In a video of a police interview, there was clear documentation of the Defendant's awareness of others, memory of specific events from her past, and the financial aspects of her involvement with others (including how to arrange bail from wealthier friends). Also, real-world observations showed no evidence of profound impairment.

3 There was no objective, scientific evidence that the Defendant was ID during the developmental period, as the defense experts had argued. Defense experts relied on his being in Special Education in school as evidence for low functioning, but in fact his placement in Special Education was for being "Emotionally Disturbed" and not for ID.

Concerning Vignette #4

This vignette is about inappropriate application of assessment techniques as well as not taking into account relevant information from records and other assessments.

EPPCC's Standard 9.02 about appropriate and valid use of assessment techniques: To abide by this standard, psychologists should be able to evaluate available data regarding the test's psychometric properties such as validity and reliability. In this case, the Defendant's experts used assessment tools/methods that had questionable psychometric properties and minimal research to support it. To comply with Standard 9.02, psychologists should also use tests that are empirically supported for use with certain populations and purposes. The Defendant's experts used a test that was meant to be used on individuals in a lower age range than the Defendant. By using an assessment instrument that was not appropriate for the Defendant's age, the Defendant's experts violated ethical standards for the use of assessments. In addition, the Defendant's experts were also not in compliance with the *SGFP*, specifically guideline 10.02 Selection and Use of Assessment Procedures and guideline 2.05 Knowledge of the Scientific Foundation for Opinions and Testimony. Guideline 10.02 states: "forensic practitioners use assessment instruments whose validity and reliability have been established for use with members of the population assessed." Guideline 10.02 further states: "when such validity and reliability have not been established, forensic practitioners consider and describe the strength and limitations of their findings," which Defendant's experts did not follow. Guideline 2.05 states "Forensic practitioners seek to provide opinions and testimony that are sufficiently based upon adequate scientific foundation, and reliable, and valid principles and methods that have been applied appropriately to the facts of the case" and this was violated when a tool was used when the Defendant's age range was not applicable to the test.

EPPCC Principle C: Integrity states "psychologists seek to promote accuracy, honesty, and truthfulness in the science, teaching, and practice of psychology." The Defendant's experts did not promote accuracy when suggesting that the Government's experts' findings were compatible with their own. They also misrepresented evidence with regard to the Defendant's difficulties during the developmental period. Although the Defendant did experience difficulties during that time, they were not difficulties typically or necessarily associated with ID. Furthermore, according to the SGFP, guideline 11.01 Accuracy, Fairness, and Avoidance of Deception states "Forensic practitioners make reasonable efforts to ensure that the products of their services, as well as their own public statements and professional reports and testimony, are communicated in ways that promote understanding and avoid deception." The Defendant's experts violated this guideline by misrepresenting their findings and misusing records to present the Defendant as an individual with ID.

Vignette #5: Cutting Corners in a Disability Determination Psychological Exam

In this case, the psychologist stated she frequently performed psychological consultative evaluations for Social Security disability referrals. These exams are short forms of independent medical exams. It is not rare for psychologists to do several of these exams in a day, but this individual frequently did six to ten exams in a day. She said that she had done thousands of evaluations for Social Security disability. These included an interview, mental status examination, WAIS-IV, and report. She testified that she was able to do an entire case, with report, in under an hour. To achieve this remarkable efficiency, this psychologist "cut corners"; further examination of his WAIS-IV raw materials revealed she did not observe basal-ceiling rules and did not query properly. When asked about her administration methods in deposition, the psychologist claimed she had "so much experience" doing these exams that she was able to tell when the claimant would reach the ceiling without having to test further. Further, this psychologist did not administer PVTs, which means that accuracy of test findings could not be verified.

Concerning Vignette #5: This vignette illustrates nonstandard test administration of a well-known test battery, with the apparent goal of shortening the test-administration time. As the Disability Determinations Services pays the psychologist per examination, it appears that the psychologist was simply trying to get more examinations done in a day. This psychologist also failed to validate her examination with performance validity assessment, which is required to demonstrate that test results are in fact accurate and can be relied upon by the trier of fact. Survey results (Martin et al., 2025) show that over 98% of practicing neuropsychologists view validity testing to be mandatory for forensic evaluations. Chafetz et al. (2015) provide guidance for validity assessment within evaluations for Disability Determinations Services.

The most prominent ethical concern in Vignette #5 relates to EPPCC 9.02: Use of Assessments and SGFP 10.02: Selection and Use of Assessment Procedures, which indicates that psychologists administer measures "in the manner and for the purposes that are appropriate in light of the research on or evidence of their usefulness and proper application" (p. 15, SGFP, 2013). Methods, procedures, and instructions for administering measures are signed and developed to maintain the integrity and uniformity of the test. Substituting speed for accuracy by modifying/failing to follow the test's administration instructions to increase the number of evaluations conducted in a day invalidates the tests, as it can result in incorrect scores and lead to inaccurate interpretation. Psychologists also have a responsibility to guard against misuse of our influence (Principal A).

Vignette #6: Test Security Violation

In a civil forensic case, a demand was made by opposing counsel for a neuropsychologist's complete file. The neuropsychologist provided all records that did not contain protected test information to the attorney and sent test materials and records directly to opposing counsel's retained expert. At the deposition of this neuropsychologist, it became clear that the other neuropsychologist had provided test records to the deposing attorney, who then used this material when questioning the neuropsychologist. In particular, the attorney asked whether he should have queried certain vocabulary items and about his scoring of a complex figure.

Concerning Vignette #6: This case involves a significant breach of test security. Test security position papers within the field of neuropsychology indicate that protected test information, including test data sheets that contain protected test questions, answers, and scoring algorithms, are to be exchanged only between licensed psychologist experts (Boone et al., 2022). Attorneys have claimed that they need protected test information to adequately cross-examine neuropsychologist experts, but as carefully discussed in an AACN position paper (Boone et al., 2024), attorneys are not experts in neuropsychological testing and administration. As a result, arguably the questions that they craft will be misleading due to their lack of knowledge, and they will introduce misinformation to the trier of fact. In this case, the expert on the other side should have rescored tests, determined what differences in scoring occurred, and then discussed any significant differences that might have resulted. Minor variations in scores are to be expected with different raters, but if the score differences do not result in changed findings, then the differences are not relevant. The attorney was attempting to impeach the neuropsychologist's scoring, and therefore opinions, in the case, but if the differences in scoring did not result in any change in overall interpretation, then the questions were meant to falsely impugn the conclusions of the neuropsychologist. If there were true anomalies in scoring that resulted in substantial changes in test interpretation, the opposing expert could have helped developed cross-exam questions that exposed the number/type of errors without breaching test security. Moreover, if protected test information is provided to attorneys, that information could be used to coach future test-takers, thereby compromising future use of these tests.

The most prominent EPPCC standard that applies to Vignette #6 is 9.11: Maintaining Test Security. When the neuropsychologist on the other side released the test materials to the attorney, the release failed to protect the integrity and safety of the assessment materials, giving the attorney access to test items and the potential opportunity to coach future clients on how to respond to the test in disingenuous ways. The goal of test security is to prevent exposure of psychometric tests in any venue that could potentially compromise the test's ability to distinguish individual differences in mental functioning or ability (Morel, 2009; Boone et al., 2022). This compromise occurs when attorneys use this information to coach their claimants down the line (Brennan et al., 2009; Essig et al., 2001), helping the claimants avoid performance that damages their case. Even the use of court seals may not be fully protective, as there is no real proof that the attorney has not kept a digital copy or otherwise stored the information for use in coaching down the line.

Self-Examination and Anti-biasing

In taking the Sweet and Moulthrop (1999) anti-biasing guide to heart, a simple practical method for anti-biasing when writing reports is to place an imaginary cross-examining attorney on one's shoulder to watch the writing. The imaginary attorney should challenge the writing in particular spots: "Why did you choose that word?" "Are you sure you have enough evidence for that statement?" "Doesn't the medical evidence point to something different?"

While the attorney-on-the-shoulder method enables anti-biasing during the conduct of an individual case, it is important to keep in mind that anti-biasing starts at the first phone call. There is a dance that some attorneys do with experts no matter which side of the case is being retained. The attorney frequently conveys that they want an independent expert but, at the same time, carefully crafts the statements about the case toward the side they are on; this is normal. Attorneys are on the front line in the adversarial contest and are often looking for every advantage. It is important for one's anti-biasing to understand the dance but not get caught up in it. To do the anti-biasing in the first phone call (whether plaintiff or defense), the same messages are delivered to both sides: (1) what is known about the neuropsychology of the particular case (e.g., TBI); (2) it is the standard to do a full validity examination; (3) the attorney will be the first to know the findings; and (4) the work is done on an expert basis, not within a doctor–patient relationship.[1] It is helpful to emphasize this last principle to attorneys, particularly plaintiff attorneys, for it allows the expert to go into court without the doctor–patient bias. It also allows the expert to present the work product as an independent examination for the plaintiff.

Full understanding of the scientific method allows for balance in the report and testimony. In particular, Popper's (1959) idea is that for any scientific hypothesis to have credence, it must be inherently disprovable. The understanding of how different test findings could potentially falsify one's hypothesis in a report leads to balance and full understanding of the test results.

The potential falsifiability of one's hypotheses leads to impartial discourse in writing and testimony. Weiner and Otto (2014) suggested two techniques to demonstrate impartiality:

> (a) explaining how one sought and considered data from *all* potentially relevant sources, not just those that would be expected to provide information supportive of the retaining attorney's argument; and (b) searching for and referencing (in one's report and/or testimony) data that disconfirm and are inconsistent with one's opinions or that are not helpful to the retaining attorney's argument.

While no one is going to require an expert to dismiss his/her own argument outright (unless proved false), the knowledge of how this could be done but was rejected by the findings or other facts provides balance and depth to the case.

Use of these methods can be asserted in testimony to deflect assertions of bias on the expert's part. As bias is an important part of the attorney's examination of the expert, anti-biasing should be an important part of the expert's writing and testimony.

Summary

Walter White's foray into breaking bad was entirely mercenary: he needed the money! But of course, it was about chemistry, and he prided himself into making the best product that money could buy. He did whatever it took to ensure that his chemical product did very well in the marketplace. On the way to his becoming a drug kingpin, we watched as he began to violate the most tightly bound social mores.

In this chapter, we have been concerned with neuropsychologists who deviate from the standards and norms of the field. We explored that some of these colleagues may be naive or idealistic, others may just be ignorant, while others may be entirely mercenary. Of course, we have no way of reading minds or the actual intent of other professionals, but we do catch a glimmer of inference when their behavior has been pointed out numerous times and they continue with it. We used vignettes to illustrate the behaviors and identified the ethical violations involved in these behaviors. We then explored the issues of bias and anti-biasing methods with self-examination to prevent one's own lapses. Ultimately, the goal is to obtain a work product that honors the science and methods in our field of neuropsychology.

Acknowledgments

We thank those neuropsychologists who provided us with case vignettes that were illustrative of the overall goals and context of this chapter. Care was taken not to identify any of the neuropsychologists seen to be "breaking bad." While the Atkins death case has been fully adjudicated, the presentation here was sanitized and anonymized in order to focus on the facts and principles involved, not the personalities. If any neuropsychologist readers think they are the ones being identified, please be aware that these behaviors are relatively common and that you are not alone in your use of these techniques (and may not be the one in the illustration).

Note

1 It is an entirely different matter when a neuropsychologist who has done a purely clinical examination is later called into court to testify about a legal matter that was not present at the time of the evaluation.

References

American Psychological Association (2013). Specialty guidelines for forensic psychology. *American Psychologist, 68*, 7–19.

American Psychological Association. (2017). Ethical Principles of Psychologists and Code of Conduct (2002, amended effective June 1, 2010, and January 1, 2017). https://www.apa.org/ethics/code/index.html

Binder, L. M., & Chafetz, M. D. (2018). Determination of the smoking gun of intent: Significance testing of forced choice results in social security claimants. *The Clinical Neuropsychologist, 32*, 132–144.

Boone, K. B. (2021). *Assessment of Feigned Cognitive Impairment: A Neuropsychological Perspective* (2nd ed.). New York: The Guilford Press.

Boone, K. B., Kaufmann, P. M., Sweet, J. J., Leatherberry, D., Beattey Jr, R. A., Silva, D., ... & James, J. (2024). Attorney demands for protected psychological test information: Is access necessary for cross examination or does it lead to misinformation? An interorganizational* position paper. *The Clinical Neuropsychologist, 38*(4), 889–906.

Boone, K. B., Sweet, J. J., Byrd, D. A., et al. (2022). Official position of the American Academy of Clinical Neuropsychology on test security. *The Clinical Neuropsychologist, 36*, 523–545. https://doi.org/10.1080/13854046.2021.2022214

Brennan, A. M., Meyer, S., David, E., Pella, R., Hill, B. D., & Gouvier, W. D. (2009). The vulnerability to coaching across measures of effort. *The Clinical Neuropsychologist, 23*, 314–328.

Bush, S. S. (2005). Independent and court-ordered forensic neuropsychological examinations: Official statement of the National Academy of Neuropsychology. *Archives of Clinical Neuropsychology, 20*, 997–1007.

Bush, S. S., Sweet, J. J., Bianchini, K. J., Johnson-Greene, D., Dean, P. M., & Schoenberg, M. R. (2018). Deciding to adopt revised and new psychological and neuropsychological tests: an inter-organizational position paper. *The Clinical Neuropsychologist, 32*, 319–325.

Chafetz, M. D. (eprint:2020; 2022). Deception is different: Negative validity test findings do not provide "evidence" for "good effort." *The Clinical Neuropsychologist, 36*, 1244–1264. https://doi.org/10.1080/13854046.2020.1840633

Chafetz, M. D. (2008). Malingering on the social security disability consultative exam: Predictors and base rates. *The Clinical Neuropsychologist, 22* (3), 529–546.

Chafetz, M. D., Sweet, J. J., Boone, K. B., Cox, D., Hall, V., Kirkwood, M. W., Lafosse, J. M., Merten, T., & Oldenburg, C. (2025, online). Neuropsychological review of records in forensic cases: An AACN best practices paper with international perspectives. *The Clinical Neuropsychologist*. https://doi.org/10.1080/13854046.2025.2461750

Chafetz, M. D., Williams, M. A., Ben-Porath, Y. S., Bianchini, K. J., Boone, K. B., Kirkwood, M. W., Larrabee, G. J., & Ord, J. S. (2015). Official position of the American academy of clinical neuropsychology social security policy on validity testing: Guidance and recommendations for change. *The Clinical Neuropsychologist, 29*, 723–740. https://doi.org/10.1080/13854046.2015.1099738

Essig, S. M., Mittenberg, W., Petersen, R. S., Strauman, S., & Cooper, J. T. (2001). Practices in forensic neuropsychology: Perspectives of neuropsychologists and trial attorneys. *Archives of Clinical Neuropsychology, 16*, 271–291.

Goldstein, D. S., & Morgan, J. E. (2025). Retainer bias: Ethical and practical considerations for the forensic neuropsychologist. *Archives of Clinical Neuropsychology, 40*(2), 174–189..

Greenberg, S. A., & Shuman, D. W. (1997). Irreconcilable conflict between therapeutic and forensic roles. *Professional Psychology: Research and Practice, 28*(1), 50–57.

Greenberg, S. A., & Shuman, D. W. (2007). When worlds collide: Therapeutic and forensic roles. *Professional Psychology: Research and Practice, 38*, 129–132.

Grote, C. L., Lewin, J. L., Sweet, J. J., & van Gorp, W. G. (2000). Courting the Clinician Responses to perceived unethical practices in clinical neuropsychology: Ethical and legal considerations. *The Clinical Neuropsychologist, 14*, 119–134.

Holdnack, J. A., Drozdick, L. Iverson, G. L., & Weiss, L. G. (2013). *WAIS-IV, WMS-IV, and ACS: Advanced Clinical Interpretation*. San Diego, CA: Academic Press.

Iverson, G. L., Franzen, M. D., & McCracken, L. M. (1994). Application of a forced-choice memory procedure designed to detect experimental malingering. *Archives of Clinical Neuropsychology, 9*, 437–450.

Kim, M. S., Boone, K. B., Victor, T., Marion, S. D., Amano, S., Cottingham, M. E., Ziegler, E. A., & Zeller, M. A. (2010). The Warrington recognition memory test for words as a measure of response bias: Total score and response time cutoffs developed on "real world" credible and noncredible subjects. *Archives of Clinical Neuropsychology, 25*, 60–70.

Lees-Haley, P. R. (1999). Comment on Sweet and Moulthrop's debiasing procedures. *Journal of Forensic Neuropsychology, 3*, 43–47.

Lippa, S. M. (2018). Performance validity testing in neuropsychology: A clinical guide, critical review, and update on a rapidly evolving literature. *The Clinical Neuropsychologist, 32*, 391–421.

Loftus, E. F. (1997). Creating false memories. *Scientific American, 277*(3), 70–75.

Loftus, E., & Ketcham, K. (1991). *Witness for the Defense*. New York: St. Martin's Press.

Martin, P. K., Schroeder, R. W., & Odland, A. P. (2025). Neuropsychological validity assessment beliefs and practices: A survey of north American neuropsychologists and validity assessment experts. *Archives of Clinical Neuropsychology*, *40*, 201–223. https://doi.org/10.1093/arclin/acae102.

Martin, P. K., Schroeder, R. W., Olsen, D. H., Maloy, H., Boettcher, A., Ernst, N, & Okut, H. (2020), A systematic review and meta-analysis of the Test of Memory Malingering in adults: Two decades of deception detection. *The Clinical Neuropsychologist, 34*, 88–119.

Morel, K. R. (2009). Test security in medicolegal cases: Proposed guidelines for attorneys utilizing neuropsychology practice. *Archives of Clinical Neuropsychology, 24*, 635–646.

Popper, K. (1959). *The Logic of Scientific Discovery*. New York: Basic Books.

Schroeder, R. W., & Chafetz, M. D. (2021). Validity assessment for clinical patients pursuing Social Security Disability. In R. W. Schroeder & P. K. Martin (Eds.), *Validity Assessment in Clinical Neuropsychological Practice: Evaluating and Managing Noncredible Performance*. New York: The Guilford Press, pp. 378–399.

Schroeder, R. W., Twumasi-Ankrah, P., Baade, L. E., & Marshall, P. S. (2012). Reliable digit span: A systematic review and cross-validation study. *Assessment, 19*, 21–30.

Sherman, E., Slick, D. & Iverson, G. (2020). Multidimensional malingering criteria for neuropsychological assessment: A 20-year update of the malingered neuropsychological dysfunction criteria. *Archives of Clinical Neuropsychology, 35*, 735–764.

Slick, D. J., Sherman, E. M. S., & Iverson, G. L. (1999). Diagnostic criteria for malingered neurocognitive dysfunction: Proposed standards for clinical practice and research. *Clinical Neuropsychologist, 13* (4), 545–561.

Strasburger, L. H., Gutheil, T. G., & Brodsky, A. (1997). On wearing two hats: Role conflict in serving as both psychotherapist and expert witness. *American Journal of Psychiatry, 154*, 448–456.

Sweet, J. J., & Moulthrop, M. A. (1999). Self-examination questions as a means of identifying bias in adversarial assessments. *Journal of Forensic Neuropsychology, 1*, 73–88.

Sweet, J. J., Heilbronner, R. L., Morgan, J. E., Larrabee, G. J., Rohling, M. L., Boone, K. B., Kirkwood, M. W., Schroeder, R. W., Suhr, J. A., and Conference Participants. (2021). American Academy of Clinical Neuropsychology (AACN) consensus statement on validity assessment: Update of the 2009 AACN consensus conference statement on neuropsychological assessment of effort, response bias, and malingering. *The Clinical Neuropsychologist*. https://doi.org/10.1080/13854046.2021.1896036

van Gorp, W. G., & McMullen, W. J. (1997). Potential sources of bias in forensic neuropsychological evaluations. *The Clinical Neuropsychologist, 11*, 180–187.

Weiner, I. B., & Otto, R. K. (2014). *The Handbook of Forensic Psychology* (4th ed.) (I. B. Weiner & R. K. Otto (Eds.)). Hoboken, NJ: John Wiley & Sons, Inc.

West, T. V., & Kenny, D. A. (2011). The truth and bias model of judgment. *Psychological Review, 118*, 357–378. https://doi.org/10.1037/a0022936

43 Admissibility of Expert Opinions Based on Neuropsychological Evidence of Malingering

Paul M. Kaufmann and Kevin W. Greve

All evidence requires scrutiny in litigation, so when expert neuropsychologists apply validity science during evaluations to identify and opine about malingering, their testimony is challenged. That testimony relies, in part, on free-standing tests and embedded validity techniques when formulating expert opinions. Standardized, norm-referenced, and carefully researched symptom and performance validity methodology are primarily the domain of clinical neuropsychology. While other professionals may identify and testify about malingering, neuropsychologists have access to the best scientific methods for quantifying how individuals exaggerate symptoms and feign poor performance. When expert neuropsychologists apply such methods to legal claims, their testimony should be viewed in the historical context of expert opinion evidence. This chapter briefly charts that history and then presents a recent case to show how expert neuropsychologist opinions about malingering can be defended and admitted into evidence.

The law of negligence and medical expert testimony in English jurisprudence has a long and checkered past, but *Slater v Baker and Stapleton* (1767) helped establish "standard of care" as a legal term of art. Standards of care set forth minimal levels of competence for professional practice such that substandard performance constituted malpractice. Further, such standards contributed to the advent of the learned expert who could discern and testify to the competence of others in the same profession. Courts were appropriately skeptical about expert testimony (*Winnans v. N.Y. Erie Railroad Co.*, 1859), well before applied psychology came into existence. An early case (*Frye v United States*, 1923) illustrates this caution when the court unanimously rejected a "systolic blood pressure deception test" (p. 1013). As the science of human behavior and mental states evolved, courts began to consider whether psychologist experts may be of assistance to a jury (*People v. Hawthorne*, 1940). *Jenkins v. United States* (1962) is the first case recognizing clinical psychologist experts, setting forth a two-part test. First, the subject must be related to some occupation, profession, business, or science "as to be beyond the ken of the average layman" (p. 643). Second, the witness must have "such skill, knowledge, or experience in that field" (p. 643) to assist the court in its search for truth. *Jenkins* held that "psychologists may qualify as experts on the question of mental disease or defect under the standards set forth" (p. 647). *Simmons v. Mullins* (1975) extended this holding to neuropsychology, finding that a psychologist was competent to testify "as an expert on organic brain injury" (p. 897).

Previous chapters summarized legal challenges to the admissibility of neuropsychological evidence in criminal proceedings (Kaufmann, 2008) and in civil litigation (Kaufmann, 2012). Kaufmann (2013) detailed admissibility standards as applied to neuropsychological evidence, highlighting cases in which such evidence was wrongfully excluded (*Baxter v. Temple*, 2005)

DOI: 10.4324/9781003005063-49

and wrongfully admitted (*Bennet v. Richmond*, 2012). Appellate litigation has impacted the admissibility of expert neuropsychological opinions; for example, *Baxter v. Temple* (2005) shows how a trial court may exclude the opinions of an expert neuropsychologist, only to be later overruled on appeal (*Baxter v. Temple*, 2008). An Amicus Brief[1] from the American Academy of Clinical Neuropsychology (AACN) played an important role in reversing *Baxter*, showing the need for vigilant advocacy of sound neuropsychological methodology and practice.

This chapter updates key cases and extends previous treatises on the most common admissibility challenges confronting neuropsychologists who provide expert opinions. Use of symptom and performance validity techniques has become a standard within neuropsychology (Heilbronner et al., 2009; Sweet et al., 2021). This chapter describes key legal authority for the admissibility of neuropsychological evidence related to malingering and notes new litigation trends, bearing in mind the following formulation of the specialty practice:

> Clinical neuropsychology is a specialty practice of psychology that uses unique methods and legally protected test materials in conjunction with the brain-behavior knowledge base to evaluate, diagnose, and treat individuals with known or suspected neurological disease and/or injury. Lawyers increasingly seek consultation from neuropsychologist experts on an expanding set of legal issues, in part, because clinical neuropsychologists apply a scientific approach that meets judicial standards for expert testimony.
>
> (Larrabee, 2012)

The Malingering Problem

Malingering is the intentional production of false or exaggerated symptoms, or feigned impairments, with the goal of receiving some benefit or reward. The Social Security Administration debated this disability determination problem at its inception in 1935 In 1996, a retired Social Security Administration (SSA) employee, Herb Borgen, described the early years:

> I did feel there was some potential for fraud and malingering. That sort of stuff is an age-old problem with these kinds of benefits....The issues raised... are the same issues we struggled with in the 1940s and 1950s as we were designing the disability program. We were fully cognizant of these problems, and we simply concluded they could not be resolved, that we would have to live with them. And those same problems are present today, and nobody should be surprised by this.[2]

DSM-5-TR V codes and *ICD-10-CM Z* codes recognize malingering as a "condition that may be a focus of clinical attention," but not a mental illness. Malingering involves deception, rendering true rates difficult to determine and varying across different populations (Ardolf et al., 2007; Chafetz, 2008; Greve, Bianchini et al., 2006; Greve, Ord et al., 2009; Kay & Morris-Jones, 1998; Larrabee, 2003; Larrabee, Millis, & Meyers, 2008; Mittenberg et al., 2002). However, Larrabee, Millis, and Meyers (2009) proposed a "magical number" of 40% +/–10% "representing the average base rate or prevalence of invalid data/probable malingering in settings with external incentive" (p. 843). Given this overall high base rate estimate, it is likely that formal coding for malingering is underutilized, which illustrates physician hesitation to diagnose malingering.

While the failed attempt to use blood pressure to detect deception (*Frye*, 1923) was arguably an early effort to detect malingering, when did psychology first proffer expert opinions on malingering based on psychometric tests? Efforts to detect malingering on personality and intelligence tests began in the late 1930s—a history reviewed by Schretlen (1988). Shortly after the introduction of the Minnesota Multiphasic Personality Inventory (MMPI, 1942), psychologists began to study methods for detecting examinees who exaggerated symptoms. Similar efforts to detect feigned performance were just underway with standardized intelligence tests. At that time, psychologists were only knocking on the courtroom door (*People v. Hawthorne*, 1940) but had not yet been admitted as experts. In *Hawthorne*, after affirming the exclusion of a psychologist's testimony on insanity, the concurring judge wrote,

> There is no magic in particular titles or degrees and, in our age of intense scientific specialization, we might deny ourselves the use of the best knowledge available by a rule that would immutably fix the educational qualifications to a particular degree.
>
> (p. 26)

The first courtroom reference to the MMPI (*Marion v. Gardner*, 1966) and IQ score (*Hobson v. Hansen*, 1967) did not co-occur with the term "malingering" until *United States v. Zovluck* (1977). In *Zovluck*, the defendant was found to be malingering incompetence to avoid going to trial, according to the expert psychologist whose opinion included the defendant's MMPI profile. Soon thereafter, Pankratz and Erickson (1990) described significantly below-chance results on a forced-choice test as "the smoking gun of intent" because a higher (chance-level) score would be obtained if the claimant was blind to the choices and guessed for each item.

In a series of ten professional workshops (2007–2014), Kaufmann highlighted emerging challenges to neuropsychologist expert testimony, warning of attacks on malingering opinions. Briefly, Kaufmann noted legal arguments against the admission of expert opinions on malingering could include that such evidence: (1) is more prejudicial than probative (F.R.E. 403), (2) confuses, rather than assists, the jury (F.R.E. 403), (3) is inadmissible character evidence (F.R.E. 404), (4) is inadmissible hearsay evidence (F.R.E. 802), (5) invades the province of the jury (F.R.E.704), (6) is not generally accepted by the relevant scientific community (*Frye*, 1923), or (7) is based on unreliable tests, yielding merely subjective and speculative opinions (*Daubert*, 1994 and F.R.E. 702). A number of these arguments were subsequently tested in *Howard v. Offshore Liftboats, LLC* (2016) when the plaintiffs filed a motion *in limine* to exclude the testimony of the clinical neuropsychologist retained by the defense.

> Dr. Greve's methodology fails to meet the standards for the admissibility of expert testimony prescribed by Federal Rule of Evidence 702 and the Supreme Court's landmark decision in *Daubert v. Merrell Dow Pharmaceuticals, Inc.* The Plaintiffs also argue that Dr. Greve's opinions with respect to "malingering" are irrelevant, constitute impermissible character evidence, and have a probative value which is substantially outweighed by the danger of unfair prejudice.

The remainder of this chapter presents and analyzes this case and provides instructive commentary from the defense retained neuropsychologist expert and co-author, Kevin W. Greve, PhD, ABPP. Dr. Greve's experience shows how neuropsychologist expert opinions about malingering are defended in pre-trial motion practice to be admitted in federal court trial testimony.

The Case of Howard v. *Offshore Liftboats, LLC* (2016)

Background

There is no dispute that the plaintiffs were injured, by no fault of their own, when a failed personnel-basket transfer occurred during a May 16, 2013, maritime accident. Shortly after boarding, the basket became stuck on a boat railing, causing plaintiffs to be thrown about 15–20 ft in the air before landing on the boat deck. The impact *allegedly* caused plaintiffs to lose consciousness and sustain bodily injuries, including head, brain, back, and unproven brain trauma. The defense hired Dr. Greve, who conducted an independent examination of the brain injury claim of plaintiff A on December 2 and 3, 2014, and of his cousin on June 9, 10, and 15, 2015. Dr. Greve issued reports on both cases on July 16, 2015. This chapter focuses on plaintiff A's brain injury claim. On November 10, 2015, plaintiffs filed their motion *in limine* to restrict the neuropsychologist expert opinions about malingering, arguing the evidence was inadmissible under the federal rules and previous Supreme Court rulings. Those arguments were set aside by the court, finding that Dr. Greve's neuropsychological methodology met *Daubert* requirements of peer review, error rate, and general acceptance by the scientific community. The court also found Dr. Greve's testimony was relevant, and the probative value of his opinions far outweighed the danger of unfair prejudice. Finally, the court held his conclusions about malingering were not inadmissible character evidence and did not invade the province of the jury. After the motion was denied, Dr. Greve testified at trial February 15, 2016, requesting that questions and testimony about the MMPI be sealed to protect test security, consistent with previously suggested legal strategies (Kaufmann, 2005, 2009) and AACN practice guidance (Boone et al., 2022).

Behavioral Observations

Plaintiff A was alert and reasonably oriented, although on Tuesday, December 2, 2014, he stated it was December 3. On Wednesday, December 3, he said it was Tuesday the 12th. He was cooperative and appeared well motivated, with no evidence of disordered thinking or perception. Some pain-related behaviors, e.g., restlessness, grimacing, sighing, and standing up frequently, were noted during the evaluation. There was no dispute that plaintiff A experienced pain after his injury and subsequent surgeries. He was instructed to alert the psychometrist if, at any time, he did not feel able to perform to the best of his ability. He stated that nothing prevented him from doing his best on the evaluation.

Interview

Plaintiff A reviewed what he recalled about the incident. He reported being told he lost consciousness for 30 minutes after falling. The degree and length of altered consciousness was a matter in dispute. Primary presenting complaints were pain in the neck and back, and poor sleep due to pain and nightmares since the incident. He complained about being easily distracted and forgetful, describing an incident in which he forgot about an item on the stove. He reported changes in his speech and handwriting. Plaintiff A spoke out of the side of his mouth and reported his "mouth was slurring." He complained about depression, anxiety, and panic attacks. Concerns included continued dependence on his family and uncertainty about the future.

Record Review

Plaintiff A reported intact memory for almost all events leading up to the impact from his fall. Incident records show that after he fell on the deck, he crawled downstairs. He was carried to the galley, where he was observed to get up to go to the bathroom and to be "cracking jokes." Witness reports suggested that he may have never lost consciousness. Plaintiff A testified about conversations with "the guys on the boat" after the accident. About 3.5 hours after the fall, the boat docked and was met by an ambulance. Earliest Glasgow Coma Scale (GCS) score was 15/15 with no deterioration. Brain CT was negative for acute intracranial injury. Plaintiff A was diagnosed with concussion and back/neck pain and then discharged later the same morning. Five days post-injury, he presented at another hospital, later testifying that he complained of headaches, blurry/double vision, and memory loss. GCS remained 15 and neurological examination was unremarkable. Twenty days post-injury, plaintiff A's pain complaints included his neck, lower back radiating to his left lower extremity, left knee, and both ankles. Some swelling of his right knee was noted, and he was referred to physical therapy and for a neurologic and neuropsychological evaluation.

The July 1, 2013 neurological examination documents primarily self-reported symptoms: (1) vertigo, (2) memory deficits, (3) attention/concentration problems, (4) panic attacks, (5) continuous headaches, (6) flattened left nasolabial folds, (7) occasional difficulty swallowing with slurred speech, (8) loss of balance, and (9) loss of self-esteem, self-deprecating thinking, fear of unemployment, and intermittent crying. Brain MRI was negative. Diagnoses included: (1) traumatic brain injury (TBI) with post-traumatic encephalopathy, (2) post-traumatic stress disorder, (3) affective disorder due to TBI, and (4) traumatic vestibular—cochlear injury. An October 16, 2013, follow-up brain MRI noted an 8 mm "chronic microhemorrhage in the right corona radiata" that was not believed to be "due to trauma necessarily" and was judged to be not clinically significant. Inconsistent with typical recovery patterns, cognitive complaints worsened and on March 12, 2014, the neurologist noted "his clinical progress has actually deteriorated since an evaluation early [sic] evaluation this year" (January 15, 2014). His third MRI on June 3, 2015 showed no incremental change and reported the microhemorrhage could have resulted from trauma, brain inflammation, sustained high blood pressure, stimulant abuse, or cerebral amyloid protein deposits.[3] The cause was unresolved.

Test Results

Neuropsychological Results

Validity indicators showed objective evidence of exaggerated self-reported symptoms and deliberate intention to provide wrong answers on cognitive testing. Plaintiff A performed well below-chance levels on three standalone forced-choice memory tasks, as noted in Table 43.1.

Collectively, his 31% correct 'guessing' performance has a probability of one in one trillion.[4] There is no doubt that Mr. Howard was intentionally providing incorrect responses on these memory tasks.

Likewise, data in Table 43.2 demonstrate a pervasive pattern of under-performance on standardized neuropsychological tests; all embedded performance validity indices were failed.

Findings were consistent with previous neuropsychological evaluations conducted by psychologist A, on July 15, 2013, and a brief neuropsychological screening by psychologist B, on February 9, 2015. Dr. B reported that plaintiff A's "memory scores were significantly

Table 43.1 Free-Standing Performance Validity Tests: The First Column Reports the Number Correct in Each Phase of the Test, Compared With the Number of Trials for Each Phase. Column 2 Shows the Percentage of Wrong Responses. Column 3 Is the Probability of This Outcome if the Examinee Was Guessing. Column 4 Notes How Often This Result is Reported from Individuals with Brain Damage

Test	*(1) Score/Trials*	*(2) (% Wrong)*	*(3) Probability by Guessing**	*(4) Probability in Brain Damage*
Portland Digit Recognition Test (PDRT)				
"Easy"	10/36	72	0.0057	0%
"Hard"	4/36	89	0.00000097	0%
Test total	14/72	81	0.00000008	0%
Test of Memory Malingering (TOMM)				
Trial 1	21/50	58	0.1611	< 5%
Trial 2	19/50	62	0.0595	0%
Retention	10/50	80	0.00001	0%
Test total	50/150	67	0.00003	—
Word Memory Test (WMT)				
Immediate recognition	10/40	75	0.0011	0%
Delayed recognition	8/40	80	0.00009	0%
Consistency	25/40	40	ns	< 10%
Test total	42/120	65	0.0006	—
Grand total	***106/342***	***69***	***<0.000000000001***	—

* Exact binomial calculation (1-tailed probability) using the binomial calculator at http://vassarstats.net/binomialX.html

Table 43.2 Embedded Performance Validity Indicators: All But Four Scores Are Below the Threshold of 10% in Relevant Clinical Samples

Test	*Score*	*Probability*	*Comparison Sample*
Wechsler Adult Intelligence Scale—IV			
Reliable Digit Span	5	0%	Traumatic brain injury (TBI), chronic pain
Digit Span Scaled Score	3	0%	Traumatic brain injury (TBI), chronic pain
Wechsler Memory Scale—IV			
Word Choice	13	≤2%	Overall clinical sample
Logical Memory II Recognition	17	≤10%	Overall clinical sample
Verbal Paired Associates II Recog	12	≤2%	Overall clinical sample
Visual Reproduction II Recognition	0	≤2%	Overall clinical sample
Reliable Digit Span	5	≤10%	Overall clinical sample
Overall combined probability	3/5@2%	0%	Overall clinical sample including TBI
Overall combined probability	5/5@10%	0%	Overall clinical sample including TBI
Neuropsychological Assessment Battery			
Attention Index	52	<4%	Traumatic brain injury
Language Index	58	0%	Traumatic brain injury

(*Continued*)

Table 43.2 (Continued)

Test	*Score*	*Probability*	*Comparison Sample*
Spatial Index	71	<10%	Traumatic brain injury
Executive Functions Index	63	ns	—
Conners' Continuous Performance Test			
Hit Reaction Time Std Err	12.82	ns	—
Omissions	59	0%	Moderate–severe TBI
Wisconsin Card Sorting Test			
Bernard	4.95	2%	Moderate–severe TBI
Suhr	3.16	ns	—
King	1.52	2%	Moderate–severe TBI
Finger Tapping Test			
Combined	59.3	6%	Traumatic brain injury
Dominant	31.9	6%	Traumatic brain injury
Non-dominant	27.4	9%	Full clinical sample

worse which is surprising and unexpected for brain injury recovery, given that there is no evidence of any further brain injuries since 2013." Neither Drs. A nor B specifically identified malingering.

Psychological

Plaintiff A's psychological and emotional functioning were evaluated with the Minnesota Multiphasic Personality Inventory-2 (MMPI-2), the Battery of Health Improvement–2 (BHI–2), Detailed Assessment of Post-Traumatic Stress (DAPS), Modified Somatic Perception Questionnaire (MSPQ), Pain Disability Index (PDI), and Sullivan Pain Questionnaire. Given the neuropsychological findings, the validity of questionnaire responses must be determined. Dr. Greve analyzed under- and over-reporting response accuracy.

Plaintiff A attempted to appear unusually virtuous and to present himself in an overly favorable light on the MMPI-2 L scale (70 T). Six MMPI-2 scales sensitive to over-reporting were examined. MMPI-2 Response Bias raw scores (17, 21, and 20) were extremely elevated and reflective of noncredible memory symptom over-report across three separate administrations conducted by three different psychologists, and consistent with scores likely to be associated with failing neurocognitive performance validity tests. MMPI-2 Symptom Validity Scale FBS yielded T-Scores of 109, 120, and 116, respectively, consistent with marked noncredible over-report of cognitive and/or somatic symptoms. MMPI-2 Hs and Hy scales were also extremely elevated, consistent with a pervasive pattern of extreme over-reporting of physical symptoms.

Interpretation of Test Results

There is no doubt that plaintiff A was malingering and that results were invalid. In fact, there is no reliable evidence that this plaintiff even sustained a brain injury. Further presentation and interpretation of these data would be a useless exercise because it is impossible to determine when plaintiff A may or may not have been cooperating and performing to the best of his ability.

Summary and Conclusions

Test data and questionnaire responses could not be interpreted as valid, reliable, or meaningful reflections of plaintiff A's neuropsychological status or unobservable internal states because of performance and symptom invalidity. Although he did sustain bodily injuries in the fall that affected his ability to return to his previous employment, he had no brain injury, and he was not disabled. Trial testimony showed overwhelming evidence of intentional exaggeration of cognitive deficits, psychological and physical symptoms, and physical disability.

Discussion

After these expert opinions were discovered and challenged at pre-trial deposition, plaintiff counsel filed a motion *in limine* to exclude these opinions about malingering, claiming that the methodology is inadmissible under federal rules and *Daubert*. The second attack was brought under Federal Rules of Evidence 402 and 403. The balance of this chapter analyzes the court's opinion (see Appendix) regarding the admissibility of symptom and performance validity methods and expert opinions about malingering based on those methods.

Validity Techniques and Malingering Opinions Are Admissible under *Daubert* and Rule 702

There is no dispute that forced-choice memory tests to measure performance validity are widely accepted throughout the neuropsychology community (Pankratz & Erickson, 1990; Martin, Schroeder, & Odland, 2025; LaDuke et al., 2018). Indeed, such methods are a standard of neuropsychology practice (Heilbronner et al., 2009; Sweet et al., 2021). There is also no dispute that such standardized tests have been subject to extensive peer review (see summaries of research; Boone, 2021). Dr. Greve's cut-off scores and error rates, as well as the data and statistics used in formulating those scores and error rates, are published in peer-reviewed literature. Dr. Greve authored a number of these publications, a fact that the plaintiff's counsel tried to use against him in their motion *in limine*.

During pre-trial discovery, plaintiff's counsel accused Dr. Greve of destroying his notes on cut-off scores. Plaintiffs attempted to conceal Dr. Greve's testimony and data provided to the court with quotes and article citations that were taken out of context. Plaintiff's counsel was admonished and sanctioned for improper legal arguments based on out-of-state jurisprudence, while ignoring relevant Louisiana cases that allow testimony about malingering. Regarding Dr. Greve's interpretation of the Test of Memory Malingering administered by Dr. A, plaintiffs also alleged that if the cut-off scores recommended by a 20-year-old manual were applied, plaintiff A would have passed the test. However, the manual that plaintiffs relied on did not include the extensive amount of research that had appeared after its publication. In fact, Dr. Greve explained that relying solely on an old manual would effectively halt the progress of validity science and would violate his professional obligation to testify based on current literature; neuropsychologists are in fact specifically instructed to use up-to-date cut-offs ("…it would be inappropriate to rely solely on PVT manuals without attention to newer cut-offs and interpretation strategies based on updated research"; American Academy of Clinical Neuropsychology consensus statement; Sweet et al., 2021).

Dr. Greve provided tables containing the cut-off scores and error rates used in plaintiff A's testing after being challenged in his deposition, referencing published peer-reviewed literature in which the scores and error rates appear. Based on the literature and Dr. Greve's testimony, defense counsel successfully argued that each of these tests have known error rates, cut-offs, and predictive power information in the well-known and accepted scientific literature. Dr. Greve argued that any competent neuropsychologist would be aware of this literature and could easily use it to arrive at the same diagnostic accuracy statistics. Honorable Judge Y found that the methodology was acceptable under *Daubert* and admissible under Rule 702.

Validity Techniques and Malingering Opinions Are Admissible under Rules 402 and 403

After further review, Judge Y ruled that testimony on malingering from Dr. Greve did not invade the province of the jury but would be helpful in making factual determinations with respect to plaintiff A's past, present, and future medical condition. Further, many of plaintiffs' witnesses, including several experts, testified that the plaintiffs were *not* malingering. The court ruled Dr. Greve's proposed malingering testimony was relevant, and his testimony was not impermissible character evidence. The judge noted that Dr. Greve's testimony with respect to malingering is a clinical impression based on the results of various tests. The court found the testimony was pertinent to plaintiff A's medical condition, not whether he has a certain character trait. Finally, the court held that the probative value of such testimony was not outweighed by the danger of unfair prejudice. Judge Y noted that Dr. Greve's testimony did not violate Rules 402, 403, or any other Federal Rule of Evidence. The motion *in limine* was denied and Dr. Greve was allowed to provide testimony without restriction and state his opinion that plaintiff A was malingering.

Validity Techniques and Malingering Opinions Do Not Invade the Province of the Jury

Juries find facts and render justice—they seek the truth, but do not necessarily find it. Dr. Greve testified that plaintiff A exaggerated his symptoms and feigned deficits on scientifically accepted neuropsychological tests. The court found that Dr. Greve did not opine on liability or plaintiff A's general credibility, as that is left to the jury. Consequently, the effort to exclude his testimony as improperly usurping the role of the jury was denied. Dr. Greve was the only expert to identify malingering and other experts disagreed. Juries must weigh all the evidence.

The defense also retained a well-credentialed neuropsychiatrist who did not diagnose malingering but admitted being overly cautious. "I do not like to bring it up. I don't even like to think about diagnosing malingering" (Day 14 Trial Tr. 85–86). While this is a common hesitation among most physicians, this neuropsychiatrist noted his reliance on neuropsychologists being uniquely qualified to offer expert opinions about malingering, testifying,

> "But to be able to say that (plaintiff A) is, you know, faking this symptom or that symptom, I think that's more in Dr. Greve's area because he researches that a lot." (Day 14 Trial Tr. 80). "I don't really study this enough or know the literature enough to be able to say that. Again, I would say that would be something for the neuropsychologists to review."
>
> (Day 14 Trial Tr. 81)

He clearly deferred to the expertise of Dr. Greve, specifically, and neuropsychologists, generally, for identifying malingering. Neuropsychiatrists are not experts on malingering because they are not trained to administer, score, or interpret neuropsychological tests and validity tests.

But neuropsychologists do not all use the same methods, and some may be unaware of recent research and practice standards. Also, practitioners are known to disagree. Dr. B conducted a brief neuropsychological screening. When asked about plaintiff A's word list learning performance, and whether his word recognition was unusual, Dr. B testified "It's sort of unexpected for anybody" (Day 9 Trial Tr. 67). Dr. B noted that plaintiff's deteriorating memory was inconsistent with known patterns of recovery, e.g., recognition memory was worse than recall, and she noted multiple assessment results that were "not valid," even as she testified, "I don't think it was malingering" (Day 9 Trial Tr. 95). Later, Dr. B qualified,[5] "I did not think he was overtly malingering" (Day 9 Trial Tr. 106). Dr. A was asked about Test of Memory Malingering (TOMM) performance that was significantly below chance and whether he would agree such poor performance reflects "someone who is intentionally trying to give the wrong answer?" Dr. A testified, "I would not," explaining that such an opinion "is presumptive, it's speculative, and there could be other reasons" (Day 7 Trial Tr. 55). Dr. Greve used his cut-off scores to show how Dr. A's test results were consistent with malingering.[6] To summarize the neuropsychologist expert opinions about the presence of malingering: Dr. Greve—yes, Dr. B—equivocal, Dr. A—no.[7] Although neuropsychology has made progress in developing validity techniques and incorporating them into practice standards, opinions on proper use and interpretation may vary widely among practitioners, although this should not be the case if all practitioners are appropriately cognizant of peer-reviewed literature in the field.

Medical practice spans millennia, psychiatry for five centuries, clinical psychology only the last 135 years, and neuropsychology, perhaps 80. Law respects and reflects precedent. Even though neuropsychologists have clearly emerged as the preferred brain/mental state/behavior experts, the legal profession historically has shown deference to medical opinions because physicians were the earliest health care providers. Although the neuropsychiatrist clearly testified that identifying malingering was outside his area of expertise, he was asked to put together each "piece of the puzzle" (Day 14, Trial Tr. 58) and make sense of the differing neuropsychologist opinions. Regarding malingering, he testified,

> I thought it needed to be taken into consideration for the reasons that the testing appeared to be at least pretty significantly exaggerated -- Dr. Greve can talk about that – and then his just outright refusal to do any kind of testing, even simple testing was a sign of lack of cooperation. However, the rest of the evaluation, he was pretty cooperative. He answered my questions, so he wasn't universally uncooperative.
>
> (Day 14, Trial Tr. 59)

This testimony may reflect that the neuropsychiatrist doesn't "like to think about diagnosing malingering" and how he prefers clinical judgment. But clinical judgment is prone to bias. Plaintiff A's treating practitioners appeared for the plaintiff and were even more adamant that he was not malingering. When asked whether test results and associated statistical analysis from a single evaluation should substitute for the opinions of practitioner who treated plaintiff A for years, Dr. Greve testified, "yes, when we're talking about detection of malingering, clinical judgment is inadequate" (Day 15, Trial Tr. 175). Expert testimony is weighed by the jury, through their lens of credibility, to render a final judgment—the verdict. The boat operators were liable for injuries arising from transferring the plaintiffs (Offshore Liftboats, LLC) and receiving them (K&K Offshore, LLC). The plaintiffs had no comparative fault. These young men were injured on the job and although not disabled, they were unable to return to the same type of employment due to their injuries. In this case, the jury was charged with the task of restorative justice. Tort law awards compensatory damages to help the plaintiffs return to their original position, that is, where they were before the tort was committed. Plaintiff A's attorney demanded more than U.S. $14 million and the operators of the receiving boat settled on the second day of the trial. Offshore Liftboats completed the trial and awaited the jury determination of comparative negligence and the final verdict.

The Verdict

The jury awarded U.S. $ 3,262,100 to plaintiff A and U.S. $820,000 to his cousin, determining that the operators of the K&K Offshore receiving boat contributed more to comparative negligence (~ 80%), than Offshore Liftboats. Defense counsel for Offshore Liftboats considered this a good outcome and reported that Dr. Greve's testimony played a significant role in moderating the outcome and lowering the award.

Conclusions

This chapter reviews the emergence of neuropsychologist experts and how Federal Rules of Evidence and legal arguments based on *Daubert* are used to challenge symptom and performance validity methodology, and expert opinions on malingering. *Howard v. Offshore Liftboats, LLC* (2016) clearly illustrates how neuropsychologist experts can prepare for and successfully defend against these attacks. Although neuropsychologists have emerged as the preferred brain/mental state/behavior experts in brain injury cases, the challenges to our methodology and opinions will persist. Many neuropsychologists have limited experience in preparing for admissibility challenges. As the disparate opinions of neuropsychologist experts in this case clearly illustrated, neuropsychology has some unique quality control challenges (Kaufmann & Greiffenstein, 2013) in that experts may come to differing conclusions and opinions, particularly if some neuropsychologists have inadequate knowledge and expertise regarding performance validity tests. On a final note, more continuing education is recommended to further the interdisciplinary dialog and understanding among practitioners of law, medicine, and psychology about the proper use of neuropsychological evidence.

Appendix

ORDER AND REASONS issued in *Howard v. Offshore Liftboats, LLC* (2016) by the Honorable U.S. District Court Judge Y on the 11th day of February, 2016.

Discussion

The motion *in limine* is based on two grounds. First, plaintiffs' challenge Dr. Greve's proposed malingering testimony under Federal Rule of Evidence 702 and the principles of *Daubert v. Merrell Dow Pharmaceuticals, Inc.* Second, plaintiffs challenge Dr. Greve's proposed malingering testimony under Federal Rules of Evidence 402 and 403. The court will address the motion with respect to each plaintiff, individually. The court will, as an initial matter, provide some context with respect to the proposed testimony of Dr. Greve, which the plaintiffs challenge. The court will then address, in turn, each ground of the motion *in limine* to exclude that proposed testimony.

Plaintiff C.H.

Pertinent Opinions and Proposed Testimony of Dr. Greve

As stated above, the Defendants retained Dr. Kevin Greve as an expert in the field of neuropsychology. On December 2–3, 2014, Dr. Greve administered a battery of neuropsychological tests to C.H. Those tests included, among others, certain performance validity tests, such as: (1) the Portland Digit Recognition Test; (2) the Test of Memory Malingering; and (3) the Word Memory Test. According to Dr. Greve, these tests are designed to detect whether a person is, or is not, malingering. More specifically, the tests are "standardized and well-research[ed] forced-choice performance validity tests that have been specifically designed to detect attempts to appear more cognitively impaired than is actually the case."

Dr. Greve issued his report with respect to C.H. on July 16, 2015. Based on Calvin's performance on the tests, Dr. Greve opined that his "presentation more than meets the published criteria for a diagnosis of malingering." Dr. Greve further concluded: "Mr. H. meets published criteria for a diagnosis of malingering. There is evidence of intentional exaggeration of cognitive deficits, psychological and physical symptoms, and physical disability." In light of Dr. Greve's opinion that he is malingering, as well as his concerns with respect to the methodology underlying that opinion, C.H. filed this motion *in limine* on November 10, 2015.

Federal Rule of Evidence 702 and Daubert

C.H. does not challenge Dr. Greve's qualifications, in general, or whether he possesses the requisite knowledge to qualify as an expert in the field of neuropsychology. Instead, he attacks the methodology Dr. Greve employed in reaching his conclusion that C.H. is malingering. C. contends, in sum, that Dr. Greve's methodology underlying that conclusion is flawed, and thus unreliable, because he "destroyed key raw data underlying his opinions [and] repeatedly failed to cite specific studies supporting his methodology." Whether Dr. Greve's methodology is flawed—or alternatively, whether his methodology is scientifically valid—goes squarely to the reliability of Dr. Greve's proposed testimony on malingering. As explained above, the Supreme Court in Daubert provided several non-exclusive factors to assist courts in assessing the reliability of expert testimony. The court will now analyze whether Dr. Greve's proposed testimony is reliable, in light of the *Daubert* factors which guide the court's decision.

Peer Review

The Portland Digit Recognition Test, the Test of Memory Malingering, and the Word Memory Test are standardized performance validity tests not created by Dr. Greve. The parties agree the tests and the questions asked pursuant to those tests are widely recognized, accepted, and applied throughout the neuropsychological community. There is no dispute that these standardized tests have been subject to extensive peer review and satisfy the *Daubert* requirements with respect to expert testimony.

Dr. Greve administered these performance validity tests to C.H. In so doing, Dr. Greve used certain cut-off scores and error rates to assess his performance on the tests, vis-à-vis a predetermined control group, to determine whether C. is malingering. Dr. Greve admittedly did not use the scores and error rates that accompany the standardized tests but, instead, used cut-off scores, error rates, and data, which he and his colleagues developed over the course of their careers. Though not developed with the original tests, Dr. Greve's cut-off scores and error rates, as well as the data and statistics used in formulating those scores and error rates, are published in peer-reviewed literature. Dr. Greve testified that his studies, including his cut-off scores and error rates, were published in *The Journal of Clinical and Experimental Neuropsychology* and *The Clinical Neuropsychologist* and were, as a result, subject to extensive review, commentary, and criticism prior to being published. Other experts in the neuropsychological community have attested that the journals in which Dr. Greve's articles are published are peer reviewed. This factor weighs in favor of a finding that Dr. Greve's proposed testimony is reliable under *Daubert*.

The Known or Potential Error Rate

The present motion in limine is based, in large part, on the contention that Dr. Greve destroyed "key raw data" underlying his opinion that C.H. is malingering. C. argues Dr. Greve "destroyed and/or failed to memorialize" the cut-off scores he used to establish the tests' error rates, thereby undermining the reliability of his methodology. Dr. Greve acknowledged in his deposition the importance of determining and identifying cut-off scores and error rates, as that data is vital to assessing a test's methodology. Nevertheless, according to C.H., Dr. Greve failed to memorialize this information with respect to the validity tests administered to him and, for that reason, his methodology is unreliable. C.'s argument is grounded on the fact that this information is not provided or discussed in Dr. Greve's expert report.

The court has reviewed Dr. Greve's original expert report and agrees that the pertinent cut-off scores and error rates are not contained in that report. Dr. Greve was, however, questioned at his deposition about error rates and cut-off scores. Thereafter, Dr. Greve produced validity test tables, which further explained the methodology, cut-off scores, and error rates he employed in the tests administered to plaintiff. The tables reference various articles written by Dr. Greve. Those articles, which are published in peer-reviewed literature, contain the scores and error rates that Dr. Greve employed during his testing of C. As a result, Dr. Greve's cut-off scores and error rates are "easily obtained in the literature" and, for that reason, it is immaterial that the information is not contained in Dr. Greve's original expert report. The Defendants note, because Dr. Greve's cut-off scores and error rates are widely published, "[a]ny neuropsychologist can review the pertinent literature and determine the specificity, error rate, and sensitivity." Dr. Greve provided tables containing the cut-off scores and error rates he used in Calvin's testing after being questioned about that information in his deposition, and those tables reference peer-reviewed literature in which the scores and error rates are published. This *Daubert* factor weighs in favor of a finding that Dr. Greve's proposed testimony is reliable.

Generally Accepted in Scientific Community

In support of the methodology underlying Dr. Greve's opinions that C. is malingering, the Defendants submitted a number of affidavits and declarations from other neuropsychologists "attesting to their own use of Dr. Greve's published peer-reviewed literature."

The following neuropsychologists provided an affidavit or declaration in support of Dr. Greve's methodology: (1) Dr. Robert McCaffrey, of Albany, NY; (2) Dr. Jerry Sweet, of Chicago, IL; (3) Dr. Yossef Ben-Porath, of Copley, OH; (4) Dr. Kyle Boone, of Torrance, CA; (5) Dr. Glenn Larrabee, of Sarasota, FL; (6) Dr. Stuart Anderson, of Haywards Heath, West Sussex, UK; (7) Dr. Michael Chafetz, of New Orleans, LA; (8) Dr. Jacobus Donders, of Grand Rapids, MI; (9) Dr. Manfred Greiffenstein, of Royal Oak, MI; (10) Dr. Robert Heilbronner, of Chicago, IL; (11) Dr. Scott Millis, of Detroit, MI; (12) Dr. Laurence Binder, of Beaverton, OR; (13) Dr. Corwin Boake, of Houston, TX; (14) Dr. Edward Peck, of Richmond, VA; (15) Dr. Alan Moss, of Sutton Coldfield, West Midlands, UK; (16) Dr. Joel Morgan, [*19] of Morris Town, NJ; (17) Dr. Robert Denney, of Springfield, MO; (18) Dr. David Bush, of Palm Beach Gardens, FL; (19) Dr. Elizabeth Glen, of Jacksonville, FL; (20) Dr. Nancy Hebben, of Newton, MA; (21) Dr. David Hartman, of Chicago, IL; (22) Dr. Robin Heinrichs, of Wichita, KS; (23) Dr. Thomas Staats, of Shreveport, LA; and (24) Dr. Kevin Bianchini, of Metairie, LA.

Having considered these affidavits and declarations, the court finds Dr. Greve's methodology is generally accepted in the scientific community. It is apparent that leading neuropsychologists from around the country—and beyond—rely on Dr. Greve's articles and publications, as well as the methodology, which Dr. Greve employs when conducting neuropsychological validity testing. This *Daubert* factor weighs in favor of a finding that Dr. Greve's proposed testimony is reliable.

Federal Rules of Evidence 402 and 403

Alternatively, C.H. argues the court should exclude Dr. Greve's testimony with respect to malingering under Federal Rules of Evidence 402 and 403. C. contends Dr. Greve's proposed malingering testimony (1) invades the province of the jury in making credibility determinations; and (2) is irrelevant, amounts to impermissible character evidence, and has a probative value, which is substantially outweighed by the danger of unfair prejudice.

First, the court acknowledges that several other courts in this district have allowed experts to testify with respect to malingering and whether a certain individual was, or was not, malingering. This court likewise finds that such testimony on malingering from Dr. Greve will not invade the province of the jury but would be helpful in making factual determinations with respect to C.'s past, present, and future medical condition. The court notes, moreover, that many of plaintiffs' witnesses, including several expert witnesses, have testified at trial that R. and C. are not malingering. Second, and for similar reasons, the court finds Dr. Greve's proposed malingering testimony is not irrelevant, and the testimony does not constitute impermissible character evidence. Dr. Greve's testimony with respect to malingering is a clinical impression based on the results of various tests Dr. Greve administered. The testimony is pertinent to C.'s medical condition, not whether he has a certain character trait. Furthermore, the court finds the probative value of such testimony is not outweighed by the danger of unfair prejudice.

For the foregoing reasons, the motion *in limine*, insofar as it pertains to Dr. Greve's proposed testimony with respect to C.H., is DENIED.

Conclusion

For the foregoing reasons, IT IS ORDERED that plaintiffs' motion *in limine* to exclude the proposed testimony of Dr. Kevin Greve be and hereby is DENIED.

Notes

1 https://theaacn.org/wp-content/uploads/2015/10/baxter_v_temple.pdf.
2 *Social Security Administration Oral History* found at https://www.ssa.gov/history/hboral.html.
3 Plaintiff A had *preinjury* head CT scans due to a May 9, 2009, automobile accident and functional MRI and Diffusion Tensor Imaging (DTI) performed in July and October 2015. The reliability of DTI was debated among expert neuroradiologists, but its admissibility was not challenged.
4 As noted in Dr. Greve's report referencing http://vassarstats.net/binomialX.html.
5 The 2021 Update of the 2009 AACN Consensus Conference Statement on Neuropsychological Assessment of Effort, Response Bias, and Malingering practice guidelines allow clinicians to defer on a diagnosis of malingering.
6 The 2021 Update also advises the presence of invalid performance at any point supports a conservative interpretation that other valid-appearing performance may under-represent actual performance capabilities.
7 Defense counsel used Dr. A's *U.S. v. Stanford* (2011) testimony to impeach his malingering opinion.

References

Ardolf, B.R., Denney, R.L., & Houston, C.M. (2007). Base rates of negative response bias and malingered neurocognitive dysfunction among criminal defendants referred for neuropsychological evaluation. *The Clinical Neuropsychologist, 21*(6), 899–916.

Baxter v. Temple, No.01–C–0567 (N.H. Sup. Ct. Aug. 8, 2005) (order granting motion *in limine*).

Baxter v. Temple, 949 A.2d 167 (N.H., 2008).

Bennet v. Richmond, 960 N.E.2nd 782 (Ind., 2012).

Boone, K.B. (Ed.). (2021). *Assessment of feigned cognitive impairment.* New York: Guilford Publications.

Boone, K.B., Sweet, J.J., Byrd, D.A., Denney, R.L., Hanks, R.A., Kaufmann, P.M., Kirkwood, M.W., Larrabee, G.J., Marcopulos, B.A., Morgan, J.E., Paltzer, J.Y., Rivera Mindt, M., Schroeder, R.W., Sim, A.H., & Suhr, J.A. (2022). Official position of the American Academy of Clinical Neuropsychology on test security. *The Clinical Neuropsychologist, 36*(3), 523–545.

Borgen, I.H. (1996). *Social Security Administration Oral History* found at https://www.ssa.gov/history/hboral.html

Brief for Amicus Curiae American Academy of Clinical Neuropsychology, *Baxter v. Temple* (N.H., 2008).

Chafetz, M.D. (2008). Malingering on the social security disability consultative exam: Predictors and base rates. *The Clinical Neuropsychologist, 22*(3), 529–546.

Conners, C.K. (1995). *Conners' continuous performance test computer program: User's manual.* Toronto, ON: Multi-Health Systems.

Daubert v. Merrill Dow Pharm., Inc., 509 U.S. 579 (U.S. 1993).

Diagnostic and Statistical Manual of Mental Disorders, Fifth Edition, Text Revision (2022). Arlington, VA: American Psychiatric Association.

Frye v United States, 509 U.S. 579 (D.C. Cir. 1923).

Greve, K.W., Bianchini, K.J., Black, F.W., Heinly, M.T., Love, J.M., Swift, D.A., & Ciota, M. (2006). The prevalence of cognitive malingering in persons reporting exposure to occupational and environmental substances. *Neurotoxicology, 27*(6), 940–950.

Greve, K.W., Ord, J.S., Bianchini, K.J., & Curtis, K.L. (2009). Prevalence of malingering in patients with chronic pain referred for psychologic evaluation in a medico-legal context. *Archives of Physical Medicine and Rehabilitation, 90*(7), 1117–1126.

Heilbronner, R.L., Sweet, J.J., Morgan, J.E., Larrabee, G.J., Millis, S.R., & Conference Participants (2009). American Academy of Clinical Neuropsychology Consensus Conference on the Neuropsychological Assessment of Effort, Response Bias, and Malingering. *The Clinical Neuropsychologist*, 23, 1093–1129.

Hobson v. Hansen, 269 F. Supp. 401 (D.C. Cir. 1967).

Howard v. Offshore Liftboats, LLC, U.S. Dist. LEXIS 16937 (E.D. La. 2016).

Jenkins v. United States, 307 F.2d 637 (D.C. Cir. 1962).
Kaufmann, P.M. (2005). Protecting the objectivity, fairness, and integrity of neuropsychological evaluations in litigation. A privilege second to none? *The Journal of Legal Medicine*, *26*(1), 95–131.
Kaufmann, P.M. (2007). Competency in forensic consulting: Scope of practice, expert testimony, legal requirements, and ethical dilemmas. *Archives of Clinical Neuropsychology*, *22*(7), 798–799. CE Workshop presented at the 27th Annual Conference of the National Academy of Neuropsychologists, Phoenix, AZ.
Kaufmann, P.M. (2007). Scientific evidence in the courtroom: Legal requirements and ethical dilemmas for the expert neuropsychologist. *Journal of the International Neuropsychological Society*, *13* CE Workshop presented at the 35th annual International Neuropsychological Society (INS) meeting, Portland, OR.
Kaufmann, P.M. (2009). Protecting raw data and psychological tests from wrongful disclosure: A primer on the law and other persuasive strategies. *The Clinical Neuropsychologist*, *23*(7), 1130–1159.
Kaufmann, P.M. (2008). Admissibility of neuropsychological evidence in criminal cases: Competency, insanity, culpability, and mitigation. In: R. Denney & J. Sullivan (Eds.) *Criminal forensic neuropsychology* (pp. 55–90). New York: Guilford Press.
Kaufmann, P.M. (2008). Cases, controversies, and legal authority in neuropsychological practice. *Archives of Clinical Neuropsychology*, *23*(6), 642. CE Workshop presented at the 28th Annual Conference of the National Academy of Neuropsychologists, New York.
Kaufmann, P.M. (2008). Legal requirements and ethical dilemmas for psychologists consulting in court. *The Clinical Neuropsychologist*, 22(3), CE Workshop presented at the 116th annual APA Convention, Boston, MA.
Kaufmann, P.M. (2008). Addressing scientific and legal challenges to neuropsychological testimony. *Journal of the International Neuropsychological Society*, *14* CE Workshop presented at the 36th annual International Neuropsychological Society (INS) meeting, Waikoloa, HI.
Kaufmann, P.M. (2009). Selecting your neuropsychologist expert: What you need to know about neuropsychological records, practice standards, competence, and malingering. *Archives of Clinical Neuropsychology*, *24*(5), 436. Forensic Preconference Workshop presented at the 29th Annual Conference of the National Academy of Neuropsychologists, New Orleans, LA.
Kaufmann, P.M. (2009). Symptom validity science collides with evidence law: The case for SVT admissibility. *Archives of Clinical Neuropsychology*, *24*(5), 440 CE Workshop presented at the 29th Annual Conference of the National Academy of Neuropsychologists, New Orleans, LA.
Kaufmann, P.M. (2009). Neuropsychological practice and forensic consulting: Cases, controversies, and legal authority. *The Clinical Neuropsychologist*, *23*(4), 557 CE Workshop presented at the 7th annual AACN Conference, San Diego, CA.
Kaufmann, P.M. (2010). Enhancing neuropsychology practice with forensic consulting. Common challenges, dilemmas, and solutions. *The Clinical Neuropsychologist*, *24*(4), 548 CE Workshop presented at the 8th annual AACN Conference, Chicago, IL.
Kaufmann, P.M. (2012). Admissibility of expert opinions based on neuropsychological evidence. In: G. Larrabee (Ed.) *Forensic neuropsychology: A scientific approach* (2nd ed., pp. 70–100). New York: Oxford University Press.
Kaufmann, P.M. (2013). Invited contribution: Neuropsychologist experts and neurolaw: Cases, controversies, and admissibility challenges. *Behavioral Science and the Law*, *31*(6), 739–755. Special Issue: Traumatic Brain Injury.
Kaufmann, P.M. (2014). Neuropsychologist experts and neurolaw: Cases, controversies, and new admissibility challenges. *The Clinical Neuropsychologist*, *28*(3), 358 CE Workshop presented at the 12th annual AACN Conference, New York.
Kaufmann, P.M., & Greiffenstein, M.F. (2013). Forensic neuropsychology: Training, scope of practice, and quality control. *National Academy of Neuropsychology Bulletin*, *27*(1), 11–14.
Kay, N.R., & Morris-Jones, H. (1998). Pain clinic management of medicolegal litigants. *Injury*, *29*(4), 305–308.

LaDuke, C., Barr, W., Brodale, D.L., & Rabin, L.A. (2018). Toward generally accepted forensic assessment practices among clinical neuropsychologists: A survey of professional practice and common test use*. *The Clinical Neuropsychologist*, *32*(1), 145–164.

Larrabee, G. (2012). *Forensic neuropsychology: A scientific approach* 2nd ed. New York: Oxford University Press.

Larrabee, G.J. (2003). Detection of malingering using atypical performance patterns on standard neuropsychological tests. *The Clinical Neuropsychologist*, *17*(3), 410–425.

Larrabee, G.J., Millis, S.R., & Meyers, J.E. (2008). Sensitivity to brain dysfunction of the Halstead-Reitan vs an ability-focused neuropsychological battery. *The Clinical Neuropsychologist*, *22*(5), 813–825.

Larrabee, G.J., Millis, S.R., & Meyers, J.E. (2009). 40 plus or minus 10, a new magical number: Reply to Russell. *The Clinical Neuropsychologist*, *23*(5), 841–849.

Marion v. Gardner, 359 F.2d 175 (8th. Cir., 1966).

Martin, P.K., Schroeder, R.W., & Odland, A.P. (2025). Neuropsychological validity assessment beliefs and practices: A survey of North American neuropsychologists and validity assessment experts. *Archives of Clinical Neuropsychology*, *40*(2), 201–223.

Mittenberg, W., Patton, C., Canyock, E.M., & Condit, D.C. (2002). Base rates of malingering and symptom exaggeration. *Journal of Clinical and Experimental Neuropsychology*, *24*(8), 1094–1102.

Pankratz, L., & Erickson, R.D. (1990). Two views of malingering. *Clinical Neuropsychologist*, *4*(4), 379–389.

People v. Hawthorne, 291 N.W. 205 (Mich. 1940).

Schretlen, D.J. (1988). The use of psychological tests to identify malingered symptoms of mental disorders. *Clinical Psychology Review*, *8*, 451–476.

Simmons v. Mullins 331 A.2d 892, (Pa. Super. Ct., 1975).

Slater v Baker and Stapleton, 2 Wilson 359, 95 Eng. Rep. 860 (C.B. 1767).

Sweet, J.J., Heilbronner, R.L., Morgan, J.E., Larrabee, G.J., Rohling, M.L., Boone, K.B., Kirkwood, M.W., Schroeder, R.W., Suhr, J.A., & Conference Participants (2021). American Academy of Clinical Neuropsychology (AACN) 2021 consensus statement on validity assessment: Update of the 2009 AACN consensus conference statement on neuropsychological assessment of effort, response bias, and malingering. *The Clinical Neuropsychologist*, *35*(6), 1053–1106.

United States v. Stanford, 769 F. Supp. 2d (S.D. Tex. 2011).

United States v. Zovluck (1977) 425 F. Supp. 719 (S.D.N.Y. 1977).

Wechsler, D. (2008). *Wechsler Adult Intelligence Scale--Fourth Edition (WAIS-IV)* APA PsycTests.

Wechsler, D. (2009). *WMS-IV: Wechsler memory scale*. Pearson.

Winnans v. N.Y. Erie Railroad Co., 62 U.S. 88, (U.S. 1859).

Subject Index

Note: **Bold** page numbers refer to tables and *italic* page numbers refer to figures.

Author Index

Note: **Bold** page numbers refer to tables; *italic* page numbers refer to figures and page numbers followed by "n" denote endnotes.

For Product Safety Concerns and Information please contact our EU representative GPSR@taylorandfrancis.com Taylor & Francis Verlag GmbH, Kaufingerstraße 24, 80331 München, Germany

Batch number: 10776589

Printed by Printforce, the Netherlands